THE GREATEST DHARMA KING IN BUDDHIST HISTORY TO BE RECOGNIZED ACCORDING TO THE RULES OF BUDDHISM—AN ANCIENT BUDDHA

Twelve Brief Points Contained in the Book

1. The first Buddha in history to have received such a large number of recognitions and written congratulations from great dharma kings and rinpoches of the highest order in the world. (This is based on much evidence starting from page 105 of this book.)

2. The first ancient Buddha in history to have been recognized as having such a high status. (This is based on much evidence starting from page 105 of this book.)

3. The first ancient Buddha in history who has shown such outstanding and complete proficiency and mastery of exoteric Buddhism, esoteric Buddhism, and the Five Vidyas, which nobody else has ever done. (This is based on much evidence starting from page 140 of this book.)

4. The first ancient Buddha in history who has manifested such a large number of holy feats. (This is based on much evidence starting from page 140 of this book.)

5. Buddhas bestowed nectar from the sky into a bowl in front of several dozen dharma teachers, persons of great virtue, and others. (There is videotape of that entire process. Please see material starting on page 218 of this book.)

6. When transmitting dharma to disciples, predictions were made as to when those disciples would become accomplished in the dharma. Those disciples were able to take a trip to the Western Paradise of Ultimate Bliss. After they returned to the human realm, they passed on to that paradise at the predicted time. (There is videotape of this. Please see page 237 of this book.)

7. Many incarnations of extremely famous and virtuous patriarchs from Tibet and other countries are disciples of this ancient Buddha (This is based on much true evidence starting from page 466 of this book.)

8. Dragon spirits, birds, and land animals became disciples of and came to hear dharma discourses of this ancient Buddha. (There are records and newspaper reports of this starting on page 159 of this book.)

9. At a dharma assembly attended by many people during which offerings were made to the Buddhas, nectar pills that partially filled a bowl suddenly increased in number about one hour after the dharma assembly began. Even after some of those nectar pills were distributed as blessings to the fifty-nine people in attendance, the nectar pills that remained in the bowl still formed a dome that rose above the brim of the bowl and were still greater in number than at the beginning of the dharma assembly. (There is videotape of this. Please see page 223 of this book.)

10. Manifesting the wisdom of a Buddha, wondrous multicolored sculptures and sculptures with mist inside them were created. Nobody else in the world can replicate such works. (Everyone is welcome to view that sculpted boulder, which is in the United States. Please see material starting on page 381 of this book.)

11. The first ancient Buddha who benefits living beings but does not accept any offerings. (This is based on much evidence starting on page 193 of this book.)

12. The only one who possesses Buddha-dharma that causes a disciple to attain enlightenment and liberation within two hours. It is the fastest Buddha-dharma practice whereby a disciple can enter and leave a Buddha-land at will. (Please see the testimonial of H.E. Kaichu Rinpoche and other material starting on page 478 of this book.)

佛史上依教規認證的第一位最大法王—古佛

略提書中十二例

1. 歷史上第一個獲得最多世界頂尖大法王、仁波且們認證和祝賀的佛陀（許多證據，從本書第105頁開始）；

2. 歷史上第一個獲得認證地位最高的古佛（許多證據，從本書第105頁開始）；

3. 歷史上第一個能拿出顯密圓通、妙諳五明最傑出完整的古佛，沒人做到過（許多證據，從本書第147頁開始）；

4. 歷史上第一個展顯聖蹟最多的古佛（許多證據，從本書第147頁開始）；

5. 當著幾十位法師、大德等人請佛陀來虛空降甘露在空鉢中（有全過程錄影帶，見本書第220頁開始）；

6. 為弟子傳法，預定弟子成就時間，渡弟子先到極樂世界參觀後，再回來人間按時往升（有錄像，從本書第238頁開始）；

7. 西藏和國外許多歷史性著名的古德祖師也是這位古佛的弟子（有許多實證，從本書第466頁開始）；

8. 龍神、飛鳥、走獸悉皆皈依聞法（有紀實、報章，從本書第160頁開始）；

9. 公眾修上供法會，不滿一鉢的甘露丸一小時後突然暴漲，加持分發給壇場的五十九人後，剩下的成了冒頂一鉢，比原來的還要多（有錄像，見本書第225頁）；

10. 顯佛陀智慧做的玄妙彩寶雕和霧氣雕，任何人都複製不了（實物在美國，歡迎大家鑒證，從本書第381頁開始）；

11. 歷史上第一個只利益他人而不收供養的古佛（有許多證據，從本書第193頁開始）；

12. 唯一擁有兩個小時之內就讓弟子得到開悟成就的佛法，最快捷修成出入佛土世界（詳見開初仁波且等自敘，從本書第478頁開始）。

H.H. Dorje Chang Buddha III

A TREASURY OF TRUE BUDDHA-DHARMA

多杰羌佛第三世

正法寶典

H.H. DORJE CHANG BUDDHA III
WAN KO YESHE NORBU HOLIEST TATHAGATA
頂聖如來多杰羌佛第三世雲高益西諾布

3

CONTENTS

目錄

CONTENTS

目錄

TRULY OUTSTANDING DHARMA KINGS, RINPOCHES, AND EMINENT MONASTICS IN THE WORLD TODAY WHO ARE INCARNATIONS OF BUDDHAS AND BODHISATTVAS

Category 1 of this book contains brief introductions to dharma kings and rinpoches in today's world who are incarnations of Buddhas and Bodhisattvas. The following are concise introductions to twenty two Buddhas and Bodhisattvas who are outstanding persons of great holiness and virtue.

1. H.H. Great Vehicle Dharma King Sakya Trizin is a tremendously holy being within Buddhism today. He is also the supreme leader of the Sakya order for the entire world. Because he is a nirmanakaya of Manjushri Bodhisattva, he long ago attained Buddhahood. Seven of his disciples have already become Buddhas. In that his position and wisdom are the highest in all of the five main sects of Tibetan Buddhism, he is worthy of the name Zunsheng (Honored and Victorious) Tathagata. When he was five years old, he received the Lamdre (Path and Result) Mind Essence teachings and completed the Long Life Buddha retreat. At the age of seven, he passed the examination on the Hevajra Root Tantra. He successfully completed the Hevajra retreat at the age of eight.

2. H.H. Dodrupchen Dharma King, who now lives in Sikkim, is the nirmanakaya of Guru Padmasambhava. He is the sole holder of the Longchen Nying-thik, which is the highest Great Perfection Rainbow Body Dharma in all of Tibetan esoteric Buddhism. It can be said that without the succession of the Dodrupchen Dharma Kings, there would be no Longchen Nying-thik Great Perfection. All of the Longchen Nying-thik Rainbow Body Dharma comes from the Dodrupchen dharma lineage. The Great Perfection Longchen Nying-thik Dharma of the Dzogchen Monastery, Kathok Monastery, and various other major monasteries originated from the teachings of the holy Dodrupchen Dharma Kings. The current Dodrupchen Dharma King H.H. Thupten Trinle Palzang Rinpoche is the holiest great dharma king in the Nyingma sect.

3. H.H. Dharma King Penor is the nirmanakaya of Vajrapani Bodhisattva. His is not only the lineage holder in the Nyingma sect's Palyul Monastery, he is also the supreme dharma king of the Nyingma sect. The dharma king is completely proficient in the sutra teachings and possesses realization that entails wisdom and supernatural powers. His propagation of the dharma has extended all over Asia, Europe, and America. Many dharma kings say that Dharma King Penor is a Buddha in human form.

4. H.H. Dharma King Omniscience Lama Achuk Jamyang Lungdok Gyaltsen is a famous person of great holiness and virtue within exoteric and esoteric Buddhism. He is the incarnation of Venerable Longsal Nyingpo. In this lifetime and in this world, he manifests great supernatural powers and transforms into limitless different bodies. Holy beings of virtue have seen that wherever there are living beings, there are the nirmanakayas of H.H. Dharma King Omniscience Achuk. He ceaselessly and pervasively liberates living beings. He is a great Bodhisattva of all of the major schools, including the esoteric, Pure Land, and other exoteric schools. He is now the foremost person of great holiness and virtue in Tibet.

5. H.H. Dharma King Jigme Dorje is the supreme leader of the Jonang sect. When Sakyamuni Buddha lived in the world, H.H. Dharma King Jigme Dorje was already a great Bodhisattva in that lifetime. In this lifetime, he is the only one in all five main sects of Tibetan Buddhism who holds the Kalachakra tantra in its complete form. The Dharma King has been recognized as the incarnation of Shambhala King Suchandra. He served as a disciple under his root master, Awang Gongqiu Daji, who was the forty-fourth Kalachakra Vajra Dharma King of the Jonang sect. Under that root master, he practiced dharma of the Jonang lineage and attained perfection in his practice of the Kalachakra Vajra Tantra. In 2003, H.H. Dharma King Jigme Dorje succeeded H.H. Dharma King Yundan Sangbu, formally assuming the position of supreme leader of the Jonang sect in the entire world.

6. H.H. Taklung Tsetrul Rinpoche is the highest dharma king of the North Treasure lineage within the Nyingma Sect. H.H. Dharma King Taklung Tsetrul, H.H. Dharma King Dodrupchen, H.H. Dharma King Penor, and H.H. Trulshik Rinpoche have been universally recognized as dharma kings who hold the complete teachings of the Nyingma monastic tradition. H.H. Taklung Tsetrul Rinpoche is universally recognized as one of the four great rinpoches of the present-day Nyingma sect. Dharma kings and masters of all of the main sects highly praise his learning, cultivation, and realization.

7. H.H. Trulshik Rinpoche is held by all of the various major sects of Tibetan Buddhism as one of the most respected persons of great accomplishment. He is world-renowned for upholding all of the Hinayana, Mahayana, and Vajrayana precepts and for his supernatural powers. H.H. Trulshik Rinpoche is the main master of H.H. the Dalai Lama and transmitted many dharmas to H.H. the sixteenth Karmapa. Additionally, he is the root master of several Tibetan Buddhist dharma kings and lineage holders. The present incarnations of H.H. Dharma King Dilgo Khyentse, H.H. Dharma King Dudjom, and H.E. Tulku Ugyen Rinpoche are also his disciples.

8. H.H. Dharma King Jigdal Dagchen Sakya is universally recognized as the second highest leader of the Sakya order. Starting from childhood, the dharma king received a strict education from his father, who at that time was the Sakya Trichen Dharma King, as well as from H.H. Dzongsar Khyentse Jamyang Chokyi Lodro, H.H. Dilgo Khyentse Rabsal Dawa, and other persons of great virtue. Additionally, the dharma king received the Vajrakilaya and Hevajra initiations and the complete Lamdre Tsogshe (Path and Result), which are the main teachings of the Sakya order. He has engaged in many retreats in the course of his practice. He also was the supreme leader of the Sakya order for a three-year period. H.H. Dharma

King Jigdal Dagchen Sakya was one of the first masters to propagate the Buddha-dharma in the West.

9. H.E. Dharma King Chogye Trichen was the dharma king of the Tsharpa branch of the Sakya order. He was the eldest and most senior person within the Sakya lineage of Tibetan Buddhism. He was a great lama who perfectly observed the three types of precepts. He was also a famous tantric master. This elder dharma king was called "master of the masters" because most of the lineage holders in Tibetan Buddhism were his disciples, such as H.H. the Dalai Lama, H.H. Dharma King Sakya Trizin, H.H. Dharma King Dudjom of the Nyingma sect, H.E. the Shamarpa of the Kagyu sect, and the king of Nepal, Birendra. H.H. Dharma King Sakya Trizin said, "His Eminence Chogye Trichen Rinpoche is one who has attained all three wisdoms–from the study of the Scriptures, from contemplation of the dharma, and from meditation. One should consider oneself fortunate just to meet him, which is in itself a great blessing." H.E. Chogye Trichen Rinpoche passed away in January of 2007. He has now been succeeded by Ven. Shabdrung Rinpoche.

10. The Red Jewel Crown Dharma King of the Karma Kagyu sect, H.E. Shamarpa, is the other nirmanakaya of the Karmpapa. Right before the second Karmapa Great Jewel Dharma King passed away, he predicted that he would in the future have two nirmanakayas—the Karmapa and the Shamarpa–who would generation after generation incarnate and teach each other as master and disciple. When the Karmapa is not there, H.E. Shamarpa acts as his first regent, assuming the official powers held by H.H. Karmapa Great Jewel Dharma King. The present-day H.H. Ogyen Trinley Dorje Great Jewel Dharma King and H.H. Trinlay Thaye Dorje Great Jewel Dharma King both respect H.E. Shamarpa as their teacher, prostrate before him, and request dharma from him.

11. The Orange Jewel Crown Dharma King of the Karma Kagyu sect, H.E. Goshir Gyaltsab Rinpoche, is the incarnation of Patriarch Gampopa. Because the realization of the first Goshir Gyaltsab Rinpoche was so high, Emperor Jingzong of China's Ming Dynasty conferred upon him the title of "National Master." From that time on, H.E. Goshir Gyaltsab Rinpoche became the only person within the Karma Kagyu sect who has been both a regent for H.H. the Karmapa Great Jewel Dharma King and a National Master. The current H.H. Ogyen Trinley Dorje Karmapa Great Jewel Dharma King learns dharma mainly from H.E. Goshir Gyaltsab Rinpoche, who has taught the Karmapa as much as sixty different sutras.

12. H.E. Xiazhu Qiuyang Rinpoche (aka Choying Rinpoche) is the incarnation of Patriarch Naropa, the venerable leader of 100,000 dakinis. He did not speak one word for twenty straight years because his mind was solely focused on the dharma. Such was his diligent and uninterrupted practice of the dharma. He has attained wondrous realization in the Dakini Dharma, the Great Perfection Dharma, the Kalachakra Vajra Dharma, and other dharmas. Because he is humble, amiable, and has vast supernatural powers that he exercises freely and without attachment, people respectfully call him "the unhindered rinpoche."

13. H.E. Tangtong Gyalpo Rinpoche is a very famous holy ones with great virtue within Tibetan esoteric Buddhism. He is a Bodhisattva of great compassion who has truly brought good fortune and wisdom to the living beings of Tibet and has helped them avoid disasters. Tangtong Gyalpo Bodhisattva is one of the great Bodhisattvas worshipped in Tibetan temples. There are even many families who worship a statue of Tangtong Gyalpo Bodhisattva in their homes. Disciples of the fifteenth Tangtong Gyalpo Rinpoche included H.H. Dharma King Dzongsar Khyentse; Bokar Rinpoche, a master to H.H. the Karmapa Great Jewel Dharma King; H.E. Kalu Rinpoche; and H.E. Tetan Rinpoche.

14. H.E. Renzeng Nima Rinpoche is recognized as a great dharma king throughout Tibet. He is able to ride the wind and fly through the air, transform the physical environment, and easily find hidden dharma treasures. He is the nirmanakaya of King Gesar. Many famous rinpoches are his disciples, such as the famous Nian Long Rinpoche and dakini Dari Lamao. This elderly man is extremely amazing. He has been in solitary retreat in a mountain valley for more than twenty years and has vowed not to leave that mountain valley for the rest of his life. He provides to living beings a model of self-cultivation.

15. H.E. Dharma King Ngagwang Pedma Namgyal Palzangpo is one of the three greatly virtuous ones within the Jonang sect. He is a very mysterious person known by all throughout Tibet. He has vast supernatural abilities, tremendous dharma powers, and is conversant in the entire *Tripitaka*. Long ago when Sakyamuni Buddha lived in this world, the dharma king attained the fourth fruit known as Arhatship. Many of his present-day disciples have realized the fruit of Arhatship and at least the first Bodhisattva stage.

16. H.E. the ninth Mindrolling Khenchen Rinpoche was recognized by H.H. the Dalai Lama, H.H. the 16th Great Jewel Dharma King, and Latuo Rinpoche as being the incarnation of the eighth Khenchen Rinpoche. Since childhood he received teachings from H.H. Dharma King Mindrolling Trichen, H.H. Dharma King Dilgo Khyentse, H.H. Dharma King Penor, H.H. Taklung Tsetrul Rinpoche, H.H. Trulshik Rinpoche, and others. Upon the invitation of H.H. the Dalai Lama, in 1985 H.E. Mindrolling Khenchen Rinpoche received together with H.H. the Dalai Lama teachings from H.H. Dharma King Dilgo Khyentse. They received the entire Secret Mind Dharma, which is unique to the Nyingma sect. At the request of many Nyingma monasteries, H.E. Khenchen Rinpoche has been the vice-president of the yearly Nyingmapa Molem Chenmo Ceremony for World Peace since 1994. His position within the Nyingma sect is very high.

17. H.E. Jetsun Khandro Rinpoche is the incarnation of Buddhist Holy Mother Yeshe Tsogyal, the consort of Guru Padmasambhava. Being the incarnation of an ancient, virtuous dakini, H.E. Jetsun Khandro Rinpoche is a person of extremely high realization and accomplishment. She is proficient in the Buddha-dharma of the Nyingma and Kagyu sects. In this lifetime, her main focus is propagating the dharma and benefiting living beings in the west.

18. H.E. Dzogchen Ganor Rinpoche is the sixteenth incarnation of the great terton Ratag Pelsang (Karma Lekshe Drayang). The first Ratag Pelsang received special blessings from Guru Padmasambhava, Pandita Penchen Bima Mita and other persons of great virtue. H.E. Dzogchen Ganor Rinpoche possesses supernatural powers. He is able to control his own mind and can directly observe the Three Times. He has manifested his realization

by leaving footprints on boulders, tying swords and needles into knots, and causing nectar to flow from food at food offering dharma assemblies. The rinpoche has uncovered many hidden dharma treasures. He is able to communicate with holy deities and other non-humans and has the ability to subdue demons.

19. H.E. Urgyen Xirao Woxiu is one of the eight great tertons (terma master) about whom Guru Padmasambhava made formal pronouncements. He is a man of great holiness in present-day Tibetan esoteric Buddhism who has considerable supernatural powers. He often roams about freely, arriving without casting a shadow and departing without leaving a trace. He is the incarnation of Urgyen Lingpa, a famous and great terton. H.H. Dharma King Jigme Phuntsok and many other dharma kings sought assistance from H.E. Urgyen Xirao Woxiu when they encountered adverse circumstances. The position and realization of H.E. Urgyen Xirao Woxiu are incredibly high.

20. H.E. Dorje Rinzin Rinpoche is a dharma king of great enlightenment. He is the incarnation of the famous terma master, Rigzin Terdak Lingpa Unchanging Vajra, who was the founder of the Mindrolling lineage. He has been in solitary retreat for thirty years in a wooden retreat room at the Gemang Vajra Temple. His compliance with the precepts is impeccable. He stays in retreat all year round. The rinpoche is the holder of the Great Perfection Complete Essence Dharma. Many dharma kings of great holiness

have received initiations from him and learned dharma under him, such as H.E. 7th Dzogchen Dharma King Tenzin Longdock Nyima.

21. Venerable Elder Monk Wu Ming is a spiritual leader of exoteric Buddhism. He currently is the honorary chairman of the World Buddhist Sangha Council. Elder monk Wu Ming has been a monk for 83 years. Throughout his entire life he has strictly observed the precepts and cultivated himself in a practical and thorough manner. His fundamental practice is the Kuan Yin Dharma, which he has penetrated deeply. He has edified countless people and is praised as "the nirmanakaya of Kuan Yin Bodhisattva in Taiwan."

22. Venerable Elder Monk Yi Zhao is the successor to Dharma Master Xu Yun. He is truly a person of holy virtue within present-day Zen Buddhism. Having realized the supreme fruit of enlightenment, the elder monk long ago extirpated all roots leading to his further reincarnation. In order to save living beings in the six realms of reincarnation from suffering, the elder monk emulated Kshitigarbha Bodhisattva by making the following vow: "As long as there is any living being in the earthly realm, I vow not to become a Buddha." He has been praised as being the nirmanakaya of Kshitigarbha Bodhisattva.

(This text was translated from the Chinese text that follows.)

當今世界真正傑出的佛菩薩轉世的法王仁波且高僧們

把當今世界上由佛菩薩轉世的法王、仁波且們奉識給大家，寫在前面，這裡我們向大家介紹二十二位傑出的大聖德、佛和菩薩。

1. 薩迦天津大乘法王，為全世界佛教之巨聖，亦是全世界薩迦派之總教主。由於是文殊菩薩化身，早已成佛，他有七位弟子都已成了佛，故於五大教派中地位及智慧最高，是名副其實的尊勝如來。在今生，他五歲接受道果心髓，完成長壽佛閉關，七歲通過喜金剛根本密續的考試，八歲圓滿修成了喜金剛。

2. 多智欽法王，現居錫金，是蓮花生大師化身，是整個藏密至高大圓滿化虹身之法龍欽寧體之唯一持掌人，可以說沒有多智欽則沒有大圓滿龍欽寧體，凡是龍欽寧體虹身法都是多智欽的傳承法脈，包括佐欽寺、噶陀寺等各大寺系之大圓滿龍欽寧體法皆由多智欽聖者法王傳授，他是寧瑪巴最頂聖的大法王。

3. 金剛手菩薩化身的貝諾法王，不僅是寧瑪白玉寺系的傳承法座持有者，更是當今寧瑪派的第一總法王。法王經教圓融，具足智慧神通證量，其宏法足跡遍及亞洲、歐洲和美洲，有許多法王都說貝諾法王是肉身的佛。

4. 遍智法王阿秋喇嘛降養龍多加參是顯密兩大宗派著名的大聖德，是龍薩娘波尊者的轉世，今生在這世界大顯神通，化身無量，聖德們見到有眾生之處皆有阿秋遍智法王的化身，三時不息普渡眾生。他是

顯、密、淨諸大宗派的大怙主，現為西藏第一大聖德。

5. 覺囊派總教主吉美多吉法王在釋迦牟尼佛時代就已是大菩薩，在今生更是五大教派之中時輪金剛完美無漏儀軌唯一持有人，被認證為香巴拉國月賢王之轉世。曾依止覺囊第四十四代時輪金剛法王阿旺貢秋達吉為根本上師，修習覺囊傳承法義，修證時輪金剛成就圓滿。2003年，吉美多吉法王繼雲丹桑布法王之後，正式接任全世界覺囊派總教主。

6. 達龍哲珠仁波且是寧瑪北藏傳承之掌教法王，達龍哲珠仁波且與多智欽法王、貝諾法王、楚西仁波且四人被公認為是目前完整持有寧瑪傳統僧眾教法的法王。達龍哲珠仁波且被公認為當今寧瑪巴四大仁波且之一，其學問與修行、證量廣為諸大教派的法王、大師所推崇及讚嘆。

7. 楚西仁波且是藏傳佛教各大教派最受尊敬的大成就者，以完整受持三乘戒律、神通觀照而著名於世界。楚西仁波且不僅是達賴喇嘛的主要上師，也傳授了很多法給十六世噶瑪巴，也是藏傳佛教幾位法王、傳承持有者的根本上師，包括鳥金仁波且、這一世的頂果欽哲法王和登珠法王等也是他的弟子。

8. 薩迦達欽法王是公認的薩迦派的第二領袖。法王自幼即受到時任薩迦天津法王的父親和宗薩欽哲、頂果欽哲等大德的嚴格教授，並接受

薩迦教法的精髓普巴金剛、喜金剛和道果法的傳承灌頂，並完成相應的閉關修習，曾任薩迦派總法王三年。達欽法王也是最早在西方傳播佛法的導師之一。

9. 秋吉崔欽法王是薩迦茶巴支派的法王，也是藏傳佛教「薩迦」傳承中最年長、最資深的喇嘛，是圓滿持守三種戒律的大喇嘛，也是出名的密續大師。老法王被稱為『上師中的上師』，因為大部分藏傳佛教傳承的掌持者，如達賴喇嘛、薩迦法王、寧瑪巴敦珠法王和噶舉派夏瑪巴以及尼泊爾的百仁扎國王等都是他的弟子。薩迦法王曾說：『秋吉崔欽仁波且聞思修三學具足，見他一面就是莫大的加持。』秋吉崔欽仁波且已於2007年1月示寂，現在，則由夏勛仁波且繼任。

10. 噶瑪噶舉派紅寶冠法王夏瑪巴是噶瑪巴的另一化身，第二世大寶法王圓寂時曾預言他將有兩個化身，即噶瑪巴和夏瑪巴，歷代轉世互為師徒。當噶瑪巴不在時，即由夏瑪巴第一攝政王代理大寶法王的職權。這一世的烏金聽列多杰大寶法王和泰耶多杰大寶法王都尊為師長，頂禮求法。

11. 噶瑪噶舉派橙寶冠法王嘉察仁波且是岡波巴祖師轉世，第一世嘉察巴因其證量高深被明朝靖宗皇帝御封為『國師』，從此嘉察仁波且便成為噶瑪噶舉唯一的攝政國師。這一世的烏金聽列多杰大寶法王主要向嘉察仁波且學法，至今已傳了六十部之多的經給噶瑪巴。

12. 夏珠秋楊仁波且為十萬空行的尊主那諾巴的轉世，曾經二十年不講一句話，而專著於教法之中，勤修不輟，於空行母法、大圓滿、時輪金剛等法獲得殊勝證悟，因其謙卑隨和、神通無礙、遊戲自在，而被人尊稱為『無礙活佛』。

13. 唐東迦波仁波且是西藏著名的藏密大聖德，是一位真正為西藏眾生帶來福慧、免去災難的大悲菩薩，西藏寺廟供奉的主尊大菩薩中，即有唐東迦波菩薩，乃至許多家庭都供奉他的造像。仲薩欽哲法王、噶瑪巴大寶法王的上師波卡仁波且、卡魯仁波且、德坦仁波且等都是十五世唐東迦波的弟子。

14. 仁增尼瑪為西藏公認的大法王，能駕風飛行，移山變境，隨取伏藏，是格薩爾王的化身，許多著名的仁波且都是他的弟子，如著名的年龍佛父母年龍仁波且和空行母達日拉毛等。這位老人非常了得，在山谷閉關二十多年至今，立願終生不出山谷一步，以身為眾生表修行之法。

15. 覺囊派阿旺班瑪南加法王是一位藏地家喻戶曉、極具神秘、神通廣大、法力無邊、三藏皆通的覺囊三大德之一，早在釋迦牟尼佛時代

已修成金身四果羅漢。其這一世的弟子中，已經有很多人證得阿羅漢果位及登地菩薩。

16. 第九世敏林堪欽仁波且由達賴喇嘛、十六世大寶法王、拉託仁波且認證為第八世堪欽仁波且的轉世。自幼即得到敏林赤欽法王、頂果欽哲法王、貝諾法王、達龍哲珠仁波且、楚西仁波且等諸多教授，1985年應達賴喇嘛邀請，與其一起從頂果欽哲法王處接受寧瑪派的不共密心全集。應眾多寧瑪派寺廟的要求，堪欽仁波且從1994年開始擔任每年一度的寧瑪派世界和平祈福大法會的副會長，深得崇高地位。

17. 康卓公主仁波且是蓮花生大師之佛母移喜措嘉之轉世，是證量成就甚高的古德空行母，她精深於紅白二教派之佛法，這一生主要在西方世界宏法利生。

18. 噶諾仁波且為大伏藏師讓塔佩（又稱噶瑪雷雪札楊）的第十四世轉世，第一世讓塔佩曾受到蓮花生大師、班禪畢瑪彌他班智達等大德的特別祝福。仁波且具足神通，能掌控自心並達到直觀三世的能力。他曾經在岩石上留下足印、用劍針打結以及在法會中讓食子流下甘露等來展現其證量，仁波且曾開啟多部伏藏，並是一位通達聖神、非人等的仁波且，具備降伏魔障的能力。

19. 鄔堅喜饒喔修大師是蓮花生大師授記的八大林巴之一，是當今藏密神通頗大的大聖者，時常飄無定所，來無影，去無蹤，是著名的大掘藏師鄔堅林巴的化身，很多法王遇到違緣魔時，也請他援助，如晉美彭措法王等，鄔堅喜饒喔修大師的地位證量高得無法想像。

20. 大覺之王多杰仁增仁波且是著名的大掘藏師、敏珠林派的創始人德德林巴不變金剛的化身，在格芒金剛寺木柵關房中一關就是30年，戒行清淨，常年閉關，是大圓滿無漏精華的持有人，很多大聖法王都在他座下接受灌頂學法，如第七世佐欽法王旦增·龍多尼瑪等。

21. 悟明長老是顯宗精神領袖，現任世界佛教僧伽會名譽主席。悟明長老出家已八十三個春秋，一生嚴守戒律，踏實修行，以觀音法門為根本，一門深入，化人無數，被讚譽為『觀世音菩薩在台灣的應化』。

22. 意昭老和尚承接虛雲法師之衣缽，為當今禪門之真正聖德。老和尚早已斬斷生死之根本，證無上之菩提道果。為解救六道眾生之痛苦，老和尚以地藏王菩薩為榜樣，發願『娑婆眾生不盡，誓不成佛』，亦被讚為地藏王菩薩化身。

（此文的英文翻譯印在前面）

BRIEF BUDDHIST LINEAGE REFUGE TREE

In our world, Buddhism can be divided into Hinayana, Mahayana, and Vajrayana based upon the differing aspirations behind cultivation as well as the magnitude and speed of accomplishment in the dharma. Further divisions can be made based upon sects or schools. Tibetan esoteric

Buddhism can be divided into twelve sects, such as Nyingma, Kagyu, Sakya, Geluk, and Jonang sects. There are also many branch sects. Within Buddhism there is also esoteric Buddhism taught by Sakyamuni Buddha contained in the *Tripitaka*, the Shingon sect, and exoteric Buddhism, which includes Zen Buddhism, the Pure Land school, and the Vinaya school, and many other schools.

However, whether it is Hinayana, Mahayana, Vajrayana, or any of the aforementioned sects or schools, they have all received their lineage from Dorje Chang Buddha. With respect to all of Buddhism in the dharma realm, Dorje Chang Buddha is the true primordial ancestor with form. Without Dorje Chang Buddha, there would be no Buddhism, no Buddha-dharma, no Buddhist studies, no Buddhas, no Bodhisattvas, no dharma kings, no rinpoches, no dharma teachers, and no Buddhists. There would only be the concept of the absolute truth of the universe that is not born and does not perish. This is the formless dharmakaya Buddha known as Samantabhadra Tathagata or Adharma Buddha. The dharmakaya has no form. It has no sound and does not speak. This dhamakaya is called Buddha-nature, which is not Buddhism. It abides in perfect stillness. With the dharmakaya, there is no subject who can expound the dharma.

The dharmakaya of Samantabhadra Tathagata generated the sambhogakaya Dorje Chang Buddha with form. Dorje Chang Buddha originated Buddhism in the dharmadhatu and began to spread the teachings of Buddhism in the three spheres of existence. Dorje Chang Buddha has come to this world twice. The first time was in the form of the holy and venerable Vimalakirti, who was Dorje Chang Buddha II. The second time was in the form of H.H. Wan Ko Yeshe Norbu, who is Dorje Chang Buddha III. The original leader of all of the sects within all of Buddhism, whether esoteric or exoteric, is Dorje Chang Buddha. No matter what Buddha-dharma it may be, it was originally transmitted by Dorje Chang Buddha because Dorje Chang Buddha is the only primordial ancestor of Buddhism. Dorje Chang Buddha transformed into the ancient Buddha Dipankara, Vajrasattva, and others. The ancient Buddha Dipankara taught dharma to Sakyamuni Buddha. Sakyamuni Buddha was the first to teach the dharma in the earthly realm. However, the source of all Buddha-dharma is the original ancestor of Buddhism, Dorje Chang Buddha. If you cross-reference the names and numbers on the list with the numbers on the lineage refuge tree, you will have a rough understanding of this. Thus, the three primordial Buddhas in the dharmadhatu are called dharmakaya-Buddha Samantabhadra Tathagata (Adi Buddha aka Adharma Buddha), sambhogakaya-Buddha Dorje Chang Buddha (Buddha Vajradhara), and the nirmanakaya Vajrasattva.

For more than two thousand years, different Buddhist sects have mixed together and have originated from one another. Patriarchs have taught dharma to one another and have learned from one another during these more than two thousand years. This has caused the network of lineages within all of Buddhism to become extremely large and complex. Such a lineage refuge tree surely cannot be clearly depicted in just a few pages. Because of space limitations, it was not possible to include in this lineage refuge tree all of the Buddhist sects, all of the Buddhas and Bodhisattvas, and all of the great patriarchs. Thus, this lineage refuge tree only includes a few percent of them in a representative capacity. Nonetheless, everything stated above regarding lineages is accurate and unbiased.

International Buddhism Sangha Association

(This text was translated from the Chinese text that follows.)

佛 教 簡 略 傳 承 皈 依 境

在我們這個世界上，如果按修行的發心和成就的大小、快慢來分的話，佛教可以分成小乘、大乘和密乘，而如果按照佛教的派別來分，藏密分為寧瑪、噶舉、薩迦、格魯、覺囊等十二大派，另有很多支派。佛教還有唐密、東密、顯宗、禪宗、淨土、律宗等很多派別，但是，無論是小乘、大乘或密乘，還是這些派別，他們全部都是接受多杰羌佛的傳承，多杰羌佛是法界中所有佛教的真正的有形體的第一位始祖。沒有多杰羌佛，就沒有佛教、沒有佛法、沒有佛學、沒有任何佛陀和菩薩、沒有法王、沒有仁波且、沒有法師、沒有佛教徒，而只有宇宙的不生不滅之真諦概念，這概念即是普賢王如來阿達爾瑪佛無相法身。法身無相，言語道斷，心性寂滅，無以說法主，稱為佛性，並非佛教，故而普賢王如來以法身圓滿多杰羌佛總持具相報身佛體，始創佛教於法界中，傳教於三界中。多杰羌佛曾兩次降此世界，第一次降世即多杰羌佛第二世維摩詰聖尊，第二次降世為多杰羌佛第三世雲高益西諾布。在整個佛教，無論是密宗還是顯宗，所有佛教教派的原始主都是多杰羌佛，無論任何佛法都是由多杰羌佛始傳，因為多杰羌佛是佛教唯一始祖。多杰羌佛曾化身燃燈古佛、化身金剛薩埵等，由燃燈古佛傳授佛法給釋迦牟尼佛，再由釋迦佛陀開娑婆法教，但佛法之來源皆由多杰羌佛為始祖，參見文字號碼對照傳承皈依境便可粗略了解。因此法界之原始佛三尊稱為法身佛普賢王如來（阿達爾瑪佛）、報身佛多杰羌佛（金剛總持）、化身金剛薩埵。

兩千多年來，不同派別之間的相互融合和衍生，祖師們互相傳法和學習，使得整個佛教的傳承系統無比龐大、複雜，絕非幾頁紙就能描述清楚的。這裡由於篇幅所限，無法將所有佛教教派、諸佛菩薩、大祖師們全部刊出，只列百分之幾作為代表，雖然如此，但傳承脈統正確無偏。

國際佛教僧尼總會

（此文的英文翻譯印在前面）

Prostrate to the Buddhas and Bodhisattvas in the Ten Directions!

南無十方諸佛菩薩

The Original Dharmakaya Buddha
Samanthabhadra Tathagata 原始法身佛普賢王如來

H.H. Dorje Chang Buddha II
Vimalakirti
多杰羌佛第二世
維摩詰聖尊

The Primordial Sambhogakaya Buddha,
Dorje Chang Buddha 始祖報身佛多杰羌佛

H.H. Dorje Chang Buddha III
Wan Ko Yeshe Norbu
Holiest Tathagata
頂聖如來多杰羌佛第三世雲高益西諾布

Dipankara Buddha
燃燈古佛

Amoghasiddha
Buddha
北方不空成就佛

Mahavairocana
Buddha
中央毗盧遮那佛

Akshobhya
Buddha
東方不動佛

Shakyamuni
Buddha
釋迦牟尼佛

Amitabha
Buddha
西方阿彌陀佛

Vajrasattva
Mahasattva
金剛薩埵摩訶薩

Ratnasambhava
Buddha
南方寶生佛

BRIEF BUDDHIST LINEAGE REFUGE TREE
佛教簡略傳承皈依境

Exoteric
顯教

The Original Dharmakaya Buddha, Samanthabadra Tathagata
原始法身佛普賢王如來
The Primordial Sambhogakaya Buddha, Dorje Chang Buddha
始祖報身佛多杰羌佛
Dipankara Buddha
燃燈古佛
Shakyamuni Buddha
釋迦牟尼佛
1. Venerable Mahakasyapa
大迦葉尊者
2. Venerable Ananda
阿難尊者

Shingon
真言宗

The Original Dharmakaya Buddha, Samanthabadra Tathagata
原始法身佛普賢王如來
The Primordial Sambhogakaya Buddha, Dorje Chang Buddha
始祖報身佛多杰羌佛
Mahavairocana Buddha
中央毗盧遮那佛
Vajrasattva Mahasattva
金剛薩埵摩訶薩
9. Nagarjuna Bodhisattva
龍樹菩薩
3. Venerable Subhakarasimha
善無畏尊者
4. Venerable Vajrabodhi
金剛智尊者
5. Venerable Amoghavajra
不空尊者
6. Venerable Huiguo
慧果尊者
7. Venerable Kukai
空海尊者祖師

Geluk
格魯派

The Original Dharmakaya Buddha, Samanthabadra Tathagata
原始法身佛普賢王如來
The Primordial Sambhogakaya Buddha, Dorje Chang Buddha
始祖報身佛多杰羌佛
Dipankara Buddha
燃燈古佛
Shakyamuni Buddha
釋迦牟尼佛
8. Manjushri Bodhisattva
文殊師利菩薩
9. Nagarjuna Bodhisattva
龍樹菩薩
10. Maitreya Bodhisattva
彌勒菩薩
11. Asangha Bodhisattva
無著菩薩
12. Venerable Atisha
阿底峽尊者
13. Master Dromtonpa
仲頓巴祖師
14. Master Tsongkapa
宗喀巴祖師
15. Sect Head Dharma King Ganden Tripa Gyaltsab Je
噶丹赤巴賈曹杰總法王
16. Dalai Lama
達賴喇嘛
17. Master Panchen Lama
班禪大師
18. Zhangjia Khutukhtu
章嘉呼圖克圖
19. Jebtsundamba Khutukhtu
哲布尊丹巴呼圖克圖

Jonang
覺囊派

The Original Dharmakaya Buddha, Samanthabadra Tathagata
原始法身佛普賢王如來
The Primordial Sambhogakaya Buddha, Dorje Chang Buddha
始祖報身佛多杰羌佛
Dipankara Buddha
燃燈古佛
Shakyamuni Buddha
釋迦牟尼佛
20. Shambala King Suchandra
香巴拉禪德德喇月賢王
21. Shambala XI Kalkin King Durjaya
香巴拉卡金王十一世
22. Venerable Kalachakrapada Jamyang Dorje
卡拉恰哈拉巴達蔣揚多傑尊者
23. Master Kunpang Thukje Tsondru
尊追祖師
24. Master Kunkhyen Dolpopa Sherab Gyaltsen
篤補巴祖師
25. Sect Head Dharma King Jigme Dorje
吉美多杰總法王

Sakya
薩迦派

The Original Dharmakaya Buddha, Samanthabadra Tathagata
原始法身佛普賢王如來
The Primordial Sambhogakaya Buddha, Dorje Chang Buddha
始祖報身佛多杰羌佛
26. Vajra Nairatmya
無我母金剛
27. Venerable Virupa
毘瓦巴尊者
28. Venerable Drokmi Lotsawa
卓彌大譯師
29. Khon Konchok Gyalpo Rinpoche
昆貢秋嘉波仁波切
30. Sachen Kunga Nyingpo Rinpoche
薩千貢噶寧波仁波切
31. Lopson Sonam Tsemo Rinpoche
索南策模仁波切
32. Jetsen Dakpa Gyaltsen Rinpoche
扎巴堅贊仁波切
33. Sakya Pandita Kunga Gyaltsen Rinpoche
薩迦班智達貢噶堅贊仁波切
34. Drogon Chogyal Phakpa Rinpoche
八思巴仁波切
35. Sect Head Dharma King Sakya Trizin Ngawang Kunga
薩迦天津總法王
36. Dharma King Jigdal Dagchen Sakya
達欽法王

Nyingma
寧瑪派

The Original Dharmakaya Buddha, Samanthabadra Tathagata
原始法身佛普賢王如來
The Primordial Sambhogakaya Buddha, Dorje Chang Buddha
始祖報身佛多杰羌佛
Vajrasattva Mahasattva
金剛薩埵摩訶薩
37. Vajrapani Bodhisattva
金剛手菩薩
38. Garab Dorje
嘎讓多杰勝喜金剛
39. Master Manjushrimitra
妙吉祥友大師
40. Master Shri Singha
寫惹申哈大師
41. Master Padmasambhava
蓮花生大師
42. Master Shantaraksita
釋迦焗乃祖師
43. Master Bairotsana
白若渣那祖師
44. King Trisong Deutsen
藏王赤松德贊
45. Yeshe Tsogyal
益西措嘉
46. Venerable Kunkhyen Longchen Rabjampa
龍欽巴尊者
47. Venerable Rigzin Terdak Lingpa
德德林巴尊者
48. Venerable Rigdzin Jigme Lingpa
吉美林巴尊者
49. Dharma King Dodrupchen
多珠欽法王
50. Dharma King Shantaraksita II
釋迦焗乃祖師
51. Dharma King Penor RInpoche
貝諾法王
52. Dharma King Omniscience Jamyang Lungdok Gyaltsen
降養龍多加參遍智法王
53. Sect Head Dharma King Mindrolling Trichen Kunzang Wangyal Rinpoche
敏卓林赤欽法王

Kagyu
噶舉派

The Original Dharmakaya Buddha, Samanthabadra Tathagata
原始法身佛普賢王如來
The Primordial Sambhogakaya Buddha, Dorje Chang Buddha
始祖報身佛多杰羌佛
54. Master Tilopa
帝洛巴祖師
55. Master Naropa
那洛巴祖師
56. Master Marpa
瑪爾巴大師
57. Master Milarepa
彌拉日巴大師
58. Master Gampopa
岡波巴祖師
59. Dusum Khyenpa, Black Jewel Crown Karmapa I
杜松淺巴 噶瑪巴黑寶冠法王
60. Black Jewel Crown Karmapa XVII
第十七世噶瑪巴黑寶冠法王
61. Shamar Rinpoche, Red Jewel Crown Karmapa
夏瑪巴紅寶冠法王
62. Goshir Gyaltsab Rinpoche, Orange Jewel Crown Regent
國師嘉察仁波且
63. Tai Situ Rinpoche
泰錫度仁波且
64. Jamgon Kontrul Rinpoche
蔣貢康楚仁波且
65. Lady Sukhasiddhi
蘇卡悉地大師
66. Lady Niguma
尼古瑪大師
67. Great Dharma King Tangtong Gyalpo I
第一世壇東格博大法王
68. Kalu Rinpoche
卡盧仁波且
69. Tangtong Gyalpo Rinpoche XVI
第十六世壇東格博仁波且

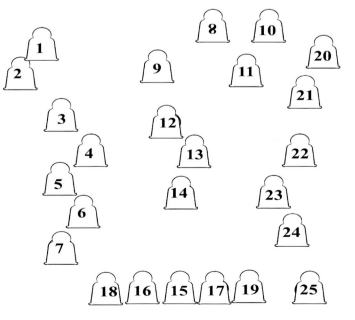

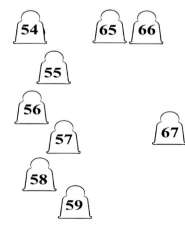
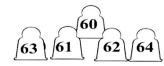

DORJE CHANG BUDDHA LINEAGE REFUGE TREE

When the universe originated, it was boundless and everything was silent. There was no such thing as length of time or size of space. There was no shape and form, no interior and exterior, no birth and death. This is the dharmakaya (dharma body) Buddha. The true meaning of the dharmakaya Buddha is the concept of a universe that does not perish. This concept of a universe that does not perish is also called "dharmadhatu-tathata (dharma realm true-suchness)," which is Samantabhadra Tathagata (Adharma Buddha).

However, the dharmakaya Buddha only expresses the concept of the true essence of the universe; that is, not being born and not dying, not coming and not going. The dharmakaya Buddha has no form and does not speak. It has no way to communicate any meaning, such as meaning through images or meaning through language. Because of such karmic conditions, the formless dharmakaya Buddha generated the first sambhogakaya Buddha with form. This sambhogakaya Buddha with form transformed into Vajrasattva and other nirmanakayas.

In order to make a distinction between those three, the dharmakaya Buddha was named Adharma Buddha, the sambhogakaya Buddha was named Dorje Chang Buddha, and the nirmanakaya was named Vajrasattva. Actually, Samantabhadra Tathagata is Adharma Buddha and also is Dorje Chang Buddha. In truth, there are not two Buddhas. These distinctions resulted from there being a dharmakaya, sambhogakaya, and nirmanakaya.

Based on this dharma, Samantabhadra Tathagata did not directly incarnate. Even the ancient Buddha Dipankara and Vajrasattva were the nirmanakayas of Dorje Chang Buddha. Sakyamuni Buddha was a disciple of Dipankara Buddha. However, many sects list Samantabhadra Tathagata as the first Buddha who began all the lineages in the dharmadhatu. This way of thinking is actually not erroneous. That is because although Samantabhadra Tathagata is a dharmakaya without form and has no way of speaking, the origin lies with this dharmakaya from which the sambhogakaya Dorje Chang Buddha manifested. This sambhogakaya Buddha was the first one to spread the Buddha-dharma and save living beings in the three spheres of existence so that they would become holy beings.

Dorje Chang Buddha is also called Buddha Vajradhara or Ruler of the Vajra Beings. In the entire universe, Dorje Chang Buddha is the first Buddha with form and is the highest Buddha. That is, the highest leader of Buddhism in the entire universe came into being in the form of Dorje Chang Buddha. It was Dorje Chang Buddha who began transmitting dharma and saving living beings in the dharmadhatu. As a result, Buddhism was born and the Buddha-dharma began spreading.

The teachings of Dorje Chang Buddha led to many disciples becoming Buddhas. The five most famous among such disciples are Aksobhya Buddha of the east, Ratnasambhava Buddha of the south, Amitabha Buddha of the west, Amoghasiddhi Buddha of the north, and Vairocana Buddha of the center. There are also many other Buddhas and Bodhisattvas among the original disciples of Dorje Chang Buddha. Dorje Chang Buddha was the one who initially propagated the Buddha-dharma in the dharmadhatu. Dorje Chang Buddha is the supreme leader of all of Buddhism in the dharmadhatu.

The incarnation of Dorje Chang Buddha is different from the incarnation of any other Buddha. Such an incarnation is a primordial manifestation of the existence of Buddha-dharma. In each world of living beings, there can be at any one time only one incarnation of Dorje Chang Buddha, who manifests or expresses the existence of the true dharma. There will not be a second incarnation of Dorje Chang Buddha in the same age or era. Only after the first incarnation of Dorje Chang Buddha leaves the world can the second incarnation be born based on karmic conditions relating to the good fortune of living beings. For example, the holy and venerable Vimalakirti, who was the second Dorje Chang Buddha, took birth in this earthly realm in the past. The third Dorje Chang Buddha, H.H. Wan Ko Yeshe Norbu, took birth in this earthly realm more than two thousand years after Vimalakirti left it and only when karmic conditions relating to the good fortune of living beings had matured. Furthermore, according to the formal pronouncement of H.H. Mahavairocana Tathagata Dharma King Zunsheng, the fourth Dorje Chang Buddha will descend into this world five thousand years from now.

H.H. Wan Ko Yeshe Norbu Holiest Tathagata is the only Dorje Chang Buddha III in the history of Buddhism. This has been recognized by greatly accomplished beings of the highest order in the world as well as famous dharma kings and rinpoches from various sects who have issued written recognition documents in accordance with the dharma!

International Buddhism Sangha Association

(This text was translated from the Chinese text that follows.)

多杰羌佛降世皈依境

宇宙無始時，天地茫荒，萬物靜謐，沒有時間之長短，沒有空間之大小，無形無色，無內無外，無生無死，這就是法身佛，法身佛的實際含意是宇宙之不滅概念，這個不滅的宇宙概念又稱法界真如，即是普賢王如來（阿達爾瑪佛）的表法。但是，法身佛只是表達宇宙真諦不生不滅、不來不去的概念，沒有形象，沒有言語，無法表義──如形象義、語言義等，由是因緣，法身無相佛正覺圓滿出第一個報身

具相佛，報身具相佛化身出金剛薩埵等化身，為區別故，法身佛命名為阿達爾瑪佛，報身佛命名為多杰羌佛，化身命名為金剛薩埵，實際即是普賢王如來，即是阿達爾瑪佛，即是多杰羌佛。實則無二佛，而是為法身、報身、化身之別使然。由是法義，普賢王如來不直接化身，就燃燈古佛和金剛薩埵亦是多杰羌佛化身，而釋迦牟尼佛是燃燈古佛之弟子。但很多教派都列有普賢王如來為開法界之第一傳承佛

陀，其實這樣講也沒有錯，因為普賢王如來雖為法身無相，無法可說，但第一起緣必定是法身而顯報身多杰羌佛，由報身佛才始宏佛法渡三界眾生成聖。

多杰羌佛亦名金剛總持，又名持金剛（即是把持一切金剛之意），是宇宙中第一位至高無上的具相佛陀，多杰羌佛的出現，代表著整個宇宙間的佛教有形象的最高領袖誕生了，自此，由多杰羌佛開始在法界中傳法渡生，有了佛教，佛法才開始傳播弘揚。

多杰羌佛宏化成就若干佛陀弟子，其中有五個最著名的弟子，他們分別是東方金剛不動佛、南方寶生佛、西方阿彌陀佛、北方不空成就佛和中央毘羅遮那佛，另有其他第一代若干諸佛菩薩。多杰羌佛是法界中弘傳佛法的誕生者，是整個佛教在法界中的最高教主。

多杰羌佛的降世與任何佛陀的化身不同，是屬於原始性表顯佛法的存在，故為降世，於每一眾生世界中（如娑婆世界），只有獨一的降世，以表正法之所在，也就是說，在同一時代不同時轉世兩位多杰羌佛，必須等待前一位多杰羌佛離開世界後，後一位多杰羌佛才會隨眾生福報因緣誕生。如在娑婆世界曾降世多杰羌佛第二世維摩詰聖尊，維摩詰離開娑婆世界後兩千多年，由眾生因緣福報的成熟，第三世多杰羌佛雲高益西諾布才降世。而根據大日如來尊勝法王授記，第四世多杰羌佛將於五千年後再降臨此世界。

雲高益西諾布頂聖如來，是由世界上第一流的大成就者、大教派著名的法王、仁波且們在佛教史上唯一依法認證出具文書法定的多杰羌佛第三世！

國際佛教僧尼總會

（此文的英文翻譯印在前面）

DORJE CHANG BUDDHA LINEAGE REFUGE TREE
多杰羌佛降世皈依境

The Original Dharmakaya Buddha
Samanthabadra Tathagata **0** 原始法身佛普賢王如來

The Primordial Sambhogakaya Buddha
Dorje Chang Buddha **I** 始祖報身佛多杰羌佛

H.H. Dorje Chang Buddha II
Vimalakirti **II** 多杰羌佛第二世維摩詰聖尊

H.H. Dorje Chang Buddha III
Wan Ko Yeshe Norbu
Holiest Tathagata **III** 頂聖如來多杰羌佛第三世
雲高益西諾布

9 7 5 3 1 2 4 6 8 10

1 Lion Vajra	獅子金剛	6 Chakrasamvara	上樂金剛
2 Kalachakra	時輪金剛	7 Hayagriva	馬頭金剛
3 Ekajati	獨髮母金剛	8 Mahakala	瑪哈嘎拉金剛
4 Vajrakilaya	普巴金剛	9 Yama	閻羅金剛
5 Yamataka	大威德金剛	10 Guhyasamaja	密跡金剛

BRIEF DISCRIPTION OF THE INCARNATION OF DORJE CHANG BUDDHA

Dorje Chang Buddha is Buddha Vajradhara (金剛總持, pronounced *jin gang zong chi* in Chinese, which literally means "Supreme Ruler of the Vajra Beings") and is also called in Chinese 持金剛 (pronounced *chi jin gang*, which literally means "Ruler of the Vajra Beings"). Dorje Chang Buddha is not 金剛持 (pronounced *jin gang chi* in Chinese, which means "Practitioner of the Vajra" as explained below). In English, people often use the word *vajradhara* to refer to a 金剛持 (jin gang chi), or Practitioner of the Vajra. Actually a 金剛持 (vajradhara) is a master or guru. Buddha Vajradhara is a Buddha. Moreover, Buddha Vajradhara is the primordial sambhogakaya Buddha whose sambhogakaya manifested out of the dharmakaya of Adharma Buddha (Adi Buddha, or Samantabhadra Tathagata). All of the Buddha-dharma of Buddha Vajradhara originated from the tathata (true suchness) of Samantabhadra Tathagata. With respect to the dharmakaya of Samantabhadra Tathagata, there is no past and no future. Without form yet not empty, He neither comes nor goes. There are no Buddhas above Him to become. There are no living beings below Him to be saved. Such is His absolute truth. Thus, the dharma-body state of Samantabhadra Tathagata is without signs or characteristics, without speech, and without form. As such, there is no subject or being who could expound the dharma. Without such a subject or being, the multitudinous living beings could not be saved.

Because of such karmic conditions, the formless dharmakaya Buddha generated the first sambhogakaya Buddha with form. This sambhogakaya Buddha with form transformed into Vajrasattva and other nirmanakayas. In order to make a distinction between those three, the dharmakaya Buddha was named Adharma Buddha; the sambhogakaya Buddha was named Dorje Chang Buddha; the nirmanakaya was named Vajrasattva. Actually, all three are Samantabhadra Tathagata, all three are Adharma Buddha, and three are Dorje Chang Buddha. In truth, there are not two Buddhas. These distinctions are due to a dharmakaya, sambhogakaya, and nirmanakaya. Based on this dharma, Samantabhadra Tathagata did not directly incarnate. Even the ancient Buddha Dipankara and Vajrasattva were the nirmanakayas of Dorje Chang Buddha.

Dorje Chang Buddha is also called Buddha Vajradhara or Ruler of the Vajra Beings (持金剛 chi jin gang). In the entire universe, Dorje Chang Buddha is the first Buddha with form and is the highest Buddha. That is, the highest leader of Buddhism in the entire universe came into being in the form of Dorje Chang Buddha. It was Dorje Chang Buddha who began transmitting dharma and saving living beings in the dharmadhatu. As a result, Buddhism was born and the Buddha-dharma began spreading.

However, many sects and lineages list Samantabhadra Tathagata as the first Buddha who began all the lineages in the dharmadhatu. This way of thinking is actually correct as well. That is because although Samantabhadra Tathagata is a dharmakaya without form and has no way of speaking, the origin lies with this dharmakaya from which the sambhogakaya Dorje Chang Buddha manifested. This sambhogakaya Buddha was the first one to spread the Buddha-dharma in the dharmadhatu. That sambhogakaya Buddha also transformed into Vajrasattva and other nirmanakayas who spread the dharma in the triloka (three spheres). Because of the birth of Dorje Chang Buddha, living beings were thus able to become holy beings in

accordance with His dharma teachings.

We often see in dharma books a blue image of Adharma Buddha. Actually, this image is a symbol. Such a symbolic form is necessary since the tathata emptiness of Adharma Buddha is invisible and cannot be depicted in a thangka. There is no way to draw the shape of emptiness. The dharmakaya has no features that can be pictorially depicted. In fact, the concept of dharmakaya is the absolute truth of the universe (dharmadhatu) that is not born and does not perish. The sambhogakaya Buddha (Buddha Vajradhara) manifested out of this concept of not being born and not perishing.

Dorje Chang Buddha is the ancient, primordial sambhogakaya Buddha. He has the unsurpassed virtuous appearance that all of the Buddhas in the ten directions have. He was the first in the dharmadhatu and triloka (three spheres) to express the dharma. Therefore, Buddha Vajradhara, or Dorje Chang Buddha, is actually the greatest leader of Buddhism in the entire dharmadhatu. He is the original ancestor of Buddhism.

However, many Buddhists misinterpret Dorje Chang Buddha, or Buddha Vajradhara, as being a 金剛持 (jin gang chi), or Practitioner of the Vajra (i.e. vajradhara). This is a mistake in a matter of principle that carries with it a karmic offence. Buddha Vajradhara has the meaning of one who is in charge of and has supervision over all of the vajra beings. Thus, He is the 持金剛 (chi jin gang) or Ruler of the Vajra Beings, the one who has dominion over the vajra beings. On the other hand, a 金剛持 (jin gang chi), or Practitioner of the Vajra (i.e. vajradhara), is one who learns the dharma and teaches others. Such a person enlightens himself and others. The term 金剛持 (jin gang chi), or Practitioner of the Vajra, connotes Vajra Master. There is a world of difference between a 金剛持 (jin gang chi) or Practitioner of the Vajra on the one hand and a 持金剛 (chi jin gang) or Ruler of the Vajra Beings on the other hand.

Buddha Vajradhara (also called Ruler of the Vajra Beings) has passed down dharma to all of the Buddhas and Bodhisattvas, who received such dharma. All of the Buddha-dharma of both exoteric and esoteric Buddhism was originally transmitted by this Ruler of the Vajra Beings. The 84,000 dharma methods that Sakyamuni Buddha taught were transmitted to Sakyamuni Buddha by the ancient Buddha Dipankara, who was a nirmanakaya of Dorje Chang Buddha. Tibetan esoteric Buddhism, which contains all of the dharma of the Nyingma, Sakya, Jonang, Kagyu, and Geluk sects, including the Kalachakra Vajra Dharma transmitted by Sakyamuni Buddha; Japanese esoteric Buddhism; and esoteric Buddhism taught by Sakyamuni Buddha contained in the *Tripitaka* all come from the lineage of which Dorje Chang Buddha is the original ancestor or from the lineage of His nirmanakaya, Vajrasattva. 金剛總持 Buddha Vajradhara or Ruler of the Vajra Beings is the supreme leader of Buddhism in the dharmadhatu. He is not a Vajra Master who is a 金剛持 (jin gang chi), or Practitioner of the Vajra (i.e. vajradhara).

When disciples find a qualified master, they should visualize their Vajra Master as being a Buddha. This is done out of respect for the dharma and respect for one's lineage. However, no matter what type of master he may be, if his identity or status has not been recognized as a Buddha by rinpoches of great holiness in accordance with the dharma, then he is not a Buddha. Still, the disciple must visualize Him as a Buddha. Even the holy and venerable

Vimalakirti, who as the second Buddha Vajradhara, was affirmed as a Tathagata (Buddha) through an announcement of Sakyamuni Buddha.

The incarnation of Dorje Chang Buddha is different from the nirmanakayas of any other Buddha. Such an incarnation is a primordial manifestation of the existence of Buddha-dharma. In each world of living beings, there can be at any one time only one incarnation of Dorje Chang Buddha, who manifests or expresses the existence of the true dharma. There will not be a second incarnation of Dorje Chang Buddha in the same age or era. Only after the first incarnation of Dorje Chang Buddha leaves the world can the second incarnation be born based on karmic conditions relating to the good fortune of living beings. For example, the holy and venerable Vimalakirti, who was the second Dorje Chang Buddha, took birth in this earthly realm in the past. The third Dorje Chang Buddha, H.H. Wan Ko Yeshe Norbu, took birth in this earthly realm more than two thousand years after Vimalakirti left it and only when karmic conditions relating to the good fortune of living beings had matured.

Nobody can get away with falsely claiming to be the incarnation of Dorje Chang Buddha. In order to protect the dignity of the Buddha-dharma in the dharmadhatu and prevent demons from falsely claiming to be Buddha Vajradhara or the Ruler of the Vajra Beings, Buddha Vajradhara must be born with His own dharma and realization so that He may manifest or express the dharma. No other Buddha is able to manifest realization equal to the realization of Dorje Chang Buddha. That is because in order to protect the true dharma, the Buddhas do not manifest realization powers at the same holy level as the realization of Dorje Chang Buddha. Conversely, all demons lack the power to manifest such realization and therefore cannot manifest such realization.

When Sakyamuni Buddha lived in this world, Dorje Chang Buddha took birth as the holy and venerable Vimalakirti, who helped Sakyamuni Buddha teach the 500 monks and 8,000 Bodhisattvas. The holy and venerable Vimalakirti, who was the second incarnation of Dorje Chang Buddha, had the highest wisdom and the greatest ability to manifest supernatural powers as an expression of dharma. No other holy being could match Him.

H.H. Mahavairocana Tathagata formally pronounced that the third incarnation of Dorje Chang Buddha, H.H. Wan Ko Yeshe Norbu, must meet five conditions: He must successfully invoke the Buddhas to bestow nectar. He must be able to perform the Golden Vase Selection of Karmic Affinity and predict the results of that ceremony beforehand. He must be able to eliminate the karmic obstructions of disciples. He must be able to take mist, place it inside a hollowed out sculpted boulder, and have the mist stay there. He must be able to carve wondrous multicolored sculptures.

The formal pronouncement stated that no other holy being could repeat those five types of accomplishments. It also stated that if any other person of great holiness repeat those five types of accomplishments, then Mahavairocana Tathagata's recognition that H.H. Wan Ko Yeshe Norbu is Dorje Chang Buddha is false, and the pronouncement has deceived the public in order to build up a false reputation.

The facts have proven that in this world there is no being of great holiness and virtue or even an expert who is able to match the accomplishments of H.H. Dorje Chang Buddha III Wan Ko Yeshe Norbu. Furthermore, great dharma kings on the level of a Buddha or Bodhisattva have unanimously recognized the identity of H.H. Wan Ko Yeshe Norbu through recognition certificates. This thoroughly proves that no one can get away with falsely claiming the identity or status of Dorje Chang Buddha.

In order to prevent demons from wreaking havoc by falsely claiming to be the incarnation of Dorje Chang Buddha, the required number of many holy beings must recognize the incarnation of Dorje Chang Buddha. Furthermore, many additional holy beings must bear witness to the veracity of the recognition and respectfully offer congratulations. The many holy beings who recognize the incarnation of Dorje Chang Buddha must be Buddhas, Bodhisattvas, or great dharma kings. Those who bear witness to the veracity of the recognition and respectfully offer congratulations must be extremely holy and virtuous Bodhisattvas. All of those who recognize, bear witness, and respectfully offer congratulations must be famous leaders within Buddhism and great rinpoches. If the identity of the person was not recognized by those on such a holy level, if congratulations were not respectfully offered to him by those on such a holy level, and if he does not have legitimate recognition certificates, then his claims that he is a holy being are false.

People say, "So-and-so rinpoche is universally recognized as the incarnation of Buddha Vajradhara." This way of speaking is based on heretical and erroneous understanding. It is not in accord with the rules of true Buddhism. Where is the realization of this rinpoche that an incarnation of Buddha Vajradhara would have? Does this rinpoche have complete proficiency in both exoteric and esoteric Buddhism? Does he have full mastery of the Five Vidyas? Which five dharma kings have recognized his identity as being Buddha Vajradhara and which ten dharma kings or rinpoches have certified that recognition? Can he show others a recognition certificate showing he is the third Buddha Vajradhara? Which several famous people of holy virtue respectfully offered congratulations to him for being recognized? No matter how high a certain monastic may be, if he does not have true realization and the required written recognitions and congratulations stating he is the third incarnation of Buddha Vajradhara, then all claims by others that he is Buddha Vajradhara are flattery, exaggeration, and rumors.

Hence, one must understand that Buddha Vajradhara (金剛總持, jin gang zong chi) is 持金剛 (chi jin gang, which is a Buddha). On the other hand, a 金剛持 (jin gang chi) is a lama (master). Anyone who misinterprets a 金剛持 (jin gang chi) as being a 持金剛 (chi jin gang) or Buddha Vajradhara is undoubtedly placing the status of a mere vajra master over that of Amitabha Buddha and other Buddhas. Such conduct is a terrible offense because according to the sutras and esoteric scriptures Buddha Vajradhara is Dorje Chang Buddha (持金剛 chi jin gang), the Master of the Five Buddhas and other Buddhas.

United International World Buddhism Association Headquarters
International Buddhism Sangha Association

(This text was translated from the Chinese text on next page.)

簡述多杰羌佛轉世

多杰羌佛即是金剛總持，又名持金剛，而不是金剛持，金剛持是上師，金剛總持是佛，而且是原始第一報身佛，由法身佛阿達爾瑪佛(普賢王如來)化顯的報身相，其一切佛法皆是由普賢王如來真如所顯，由於普賢王如來是法身佛，是無有前者，無有後際，無色無空，不來不去，上無諸佛可成，下無眾生可渡之如如真諦，故普賢王如來為法身無相，無言，無形，如是無說法之主，無主故不能渡眾生。由是因緣法身無相佛正覺圓滿出第一個報身具相佛，報身具相佛再化身金剛薩埵等，為區別故，法身佛命名為阿達爾瑪佛，報身佛命名為多杰羌佛，化身即金剛薩埵，實際即是普賢王如來，即是阿達爾瑪佛，即是多杰羌佛。實則無二佛，而是為法身、報身、化身之別使然。由是法義，普賢王如來不直接化身，就燃燈古佛亦是多杰羌佛化身。多杰羌佛亦名金剛總持，又名持金剛（即是把持一切金剛之意），是宇宙中第一位至高無上的具相佛陀，也就是宇宙間的佛教的最高領袖誕生了，自此，由多杰羌佛開始在法界中傳法渡生，佛法才開始傳播弘揚。但是，在很多教派和傳承法義裡都將普賢王如來列為開法界之第一傳承佛陀，其實這樣講也是正確的，因為普賢王如來雖為法身無相，但第一起緣必定是法身，由法身而顯報身多杰羌佛，由報身佛才開始在法界傳播佛法，同時化身金剛薩埵等於三界宏法，眾生才有了依法成聖之主。

我們在法本上常見到的一個藍色阿達爾瑪佛具體形象，其實這個形象是一個假設，因為沒有一個假設的形體，總不能說看不見的無法繪成唐卡的真如空相為阿達爾瑪佛嘛，空是無形象可畫出來的，法身佛無相可表，實際上是宇宙(法界)之不生不滅真諦的概念，由不生不滅的這個概念化顯報身佛(金剛總持)，多杰羌佛即是最古的第一報身佛，具備十方諸佛的無上德相，始起於法界及三界中而表法，故金剛總持多杰羌佛實為法界佛教大教主、原始佛祖。但有很多佛教徒把多杰羌佛金剛總持誤解釋成金剛持，這是帶有罪業的原則性的錯誤，金剛總持是掌持總管法界一切金剛的涵意，故為持金剛，是把持著金剛們，而金剛持則是修持金剛之行持，自覺覺他，是金剛上師的意思，金剛持與持金剛天地之差，而持金剛的傳承是授與一切諸佛菩薩所接法，無論是顯宗、密宗，都由持金剛始傳佛法，釋迦牟尼佛所傳八萬四千法門，皆是由多杰羌佛所化顯燃燈古佛所授與釋迦牟尼佛，而密乘之寧瑪、薩迦、覺囊、噶舉、格魯、息解、噶當、東密、真言宗、唐密等，包括釋迦牟尼佛所傳的時輪金剛等西密，都是唯一的由多杰羌佛為始祖傳承，或由多杰羌佛化身金剛薩埵傳承。持金剛是法界大教主，而不是金剛上師的金剛持，當弟子找到合格師資時，要把自己的金剛上師當成佛陀來觀想，皆是為重法、重傳承而觀師為佛的涵意，實質上無論是什麼樣的上師，未具大聖仁波且共同合法認證，該上師均屬佛慢觀想而非佛陀，就是金剛總持第二世維摩詰聖尊也是由釋迦牟尼佛宣布認證為如來。

多杰羌佛的轉世與任何諸佛的化身不同，是屬於原始性表顯佛法的存在，故於每一眾生世界中，獨一降世，作為表正法之所在，在同一時代不轉世第二位多杰羌佛，必須等待前一位離開世界後，後一位才會隨眾生福報緣起誕生，如在娑婆世界曾降世多杰羌佛第二世維摩詰聖尊，維摩詰離開娑婆世界後兩千多年，由眾生因緣福報的成熟，第三世多杰羌佛雲高益西諾布才降世，多杰羌佛的降世是任何人都冒稱不了的，為維護法界佛法之尊嚴，防止魔子魔孫冒稱持金剛（金剛總持），金剛總持必須帶著正法證量而降世以為表法，而多杰羌佛的證量是任何佛陀都不能表顯的，原因是諸佛為了維護正法因緣，故不表顯與多杰羌佛同聖境的證量！相反的，一切魔軍們不具備表顯的功夫，所以無法表顯！如在釋迦牟尼佛住世時，多杰羌佛降世為維摩詰聖尊，幫助釋迦牟尼佛教化五百比丘及八千菩薩，多杰羌佛第二世維摩詰聖尊其智慧、神通表法高不可攀，無有任何聖者可及，而多杰羌佛第三世雲高益西諾布，大日如來授記五條必備：能佛降甘露、擇緣預報、取業除障、能將祥霧拿入雕刻實物長存不走、玄妙彩寶雕，這五項無聖可複，如果他授的記有大聖做得到，照樣複製成功，就算他所認證的多杰羌佛雲高益西諾布是假的，他所說的話是欺世盜名的，在現實中已證明確實這世界上的大聖德們，乃至任何專家，就是無法做到雲高益西諾布三世多杰羌佛的成就，而佛菩薩級的大法王們都一致認證文憑說明，因此徹底證明多杰羌佛的身份是冒稱不了的，同時為了防止魔妖作亂，假冒多杰羌佛降世，而對多杰羌佛的降世，必須是經圓滿多聖認證，又是多聖佐證恭祝，認證的多聖必須是佛菩薩、大法王，佐證恭祝的必須是大聖德菩薩們，他們必須是著名的佛教領袖及大仁波且，如果不具備此等聖量級的認證恭祝，不具文憑證書，自稱為聖者則是冒牌假貨，世人有說「某某仁波且是公認的金剛總持化身」，這種說法是邪知邪見，非正道佛門之法定，金剛總持化身道量何在？顯密圓通何通？五明妙諳何存？五聖十證是由哪幾位法王認證的？認證第三世文憑拿得出來嗎？哪幾位著名聖德賀證的？凡無實證實量，無有確切認證為第三世的賀證文憑，無論是什麼高僧，一律屬於恭維誇張傳聞，故當明了金剛總持即是持金剛(佛陀)，金剛持即是喇嘛(上師)。如果誤把金剛持當作持金剛或金剛總持解釋，無疑的是把一個金剛上師的身份凌駕於阿彌陀佛等佛陀的頭上，這是罪大惡極行為，因為金剛總持是明文傳承中的五佛等之師多杰羌佛（持金剛）。

聯合國際世界佛教總部
國際佛教僧尼總會

（此文的英文翻譯印在前面）

**H.H. DORJE CHANG BUDDHA III
WAN KO YESHE NORBU HOLIEST TATHAGATA**

頂聖如來多杰羌佛第三世雲高益西諾布

BRIEF INTRODUCTION TO
H.H. DORJE CHANG BUDDHA III
WAN KO YESHE NORBU HOLIEST TATHAGATA

H.H. Dorje Chang Buddha III Wan Ko Yeshe Norbu Holiest Tathagata is Buddha Vajradhara. His Holiness is also called in Chinese 持金剛 (pronounced chi jin gang), which literally means "Ruler of the Vajra Beings." His Holiness is the complete and perfect incarnation of Dorje Chang Buddha, the primordial sambhogakaya Buddha. His Holiness's abbreviated title is H.H. Dorje Chang Buddha III. (In this world, His Holiness has also been respectfully called Master Wan Ko Yee.) The accomplishments of H.H. Dorje Chang Buddha III are the highest in the entire world. No one of holy virtue within Buddhism can be mentioned in the same breath with His Holiness when it comes to showing real evidence of wisdom and realization attained through proficiency in exoteric and esoteric Buddhism and mastery of the Five Vidyas.

The standard that the Buddha set for measuring one's level of accomplishment in the Buddha-dharma is the degree to which one is proficient in both exoteric and esoteric Buddhism and the degree to which one has mastered the Five Vidyas. However, in the history of Buddhism up to the present time, only H.H. Dorje Chang Buddha III Holiest Tathagata has truly and fully manifested complete proficiency in exoteric and esoteric Buddhism and perfect mastery of the Five Vidyas! H.H. Dorje Chang Buddha III actually exhibits for all to see item after item of accomplishments relating to complete proficiency in exoteric and esoteric Buddhism and perfect mastery of the Five Vidyas as laid down by the Buddha. His Holiness, an ancient Buddha, is the first being of holy virtue in history who has truly manifested such lofty and complete realization! Clear evidence of this are all of the single-handed accomplishments of H.H. Dorje Chang Buddha III mentioned in the thirty main categories listed in this book, *H.H. Dorje Chang Buddha III — A Treasury of True Buddha-Dharma*.

Of course, organizing His Holiness's accomplishments into thirty main categories is simply a matter of form. In fact, the accomplishments contained in this book far exceed thirty main categories. For example, the category of Technological Art alone contains three distinct major categories: photography, three-dimensional images, and glass paintings. However, H.H. Dorje Chang Buddha III combined many separate categories into single main categories, thereby reducing the number of main categories to thirty. In reality, how could only thirty main categories possibly contain all of the accomplishments of H.H. Dorje Chang Buddha III? The accomplishments of H.H. Dorje Chang Buddha III express the wisdom of the Buddha-dharma, which is limitless. The inner-realization vidya alone includes realization of the limitless truths of conditional and unconditional dharma in the universe and mastery of the *Tripitaka* and esoteric scriptures.

The thirty main categories listed in this book are as follows: 1. Recognitions and Congratulations; 2. The Virtue of H.H. Dorje Chang Buddha III and Holy Occurrences; 3. The Holy Realization of the Holiest Tathagata; 4. Supreme and Profound Buddha-Dharma That Is Difficult to Encounter in Millions of Eons; 5. Couplets; 6. Calligraphy; 7. Stone Seals; 8. Classical Poetry and Songs; 9. Vajra Needle That Eliminates Illness; 10. Healing Illnesses; 11. Medicine and Health Care Products; 12. Wondrous Multicolored Sculptures; 13. Faux-Jade Panels; 14. Philosophical Sayings About Worldly Matters; 15. Classical Prose and Modern Poetry; 16. Academic Writings; 17. Hand-Sculpted Artwork; 18. Vocal Mastery; 19. Sculptures Containing Mysterious Mist; 20. Ancient-Looking Withered Vines; 21. Chinese Paintings; 22. Western Paintings; 23. Art Frames; 24. Designs of Buddha Images; 25. Tiles; 26. Decorative Wall Hangings; 27. Buildings and Decorative Landscape Scenes; 28. Teas; 29. Technological Art; 30. Saving Living Beings by Liberating Them.

In the fourth main category entitled "Supreme and Profound Buddha-Dharma That Is Difficult to Encounter in Millions of Eons," there are over two thousand discourses on the Buddha-dharma given by His Holiness. Such teachings are as vast and profound as an ocean. From ancient times to the present, other than Sakyamuni Buddha's expositions of the dharma in this world, no other holy being has attained the multifaceted accomplishments that H.H. Dorje Chang Buddha III has attained. Moreover, each of the manifold accomplishments of His Holiness has reached the highest world-class level.

We have come to understand that the phrase "highly proficient in the five major vidyas and the five minor vidyas" are actually only empty words when applied to many people. That is because such people were not able to display real skills. They could not even show any writing or photograph for evaluation. To be totally blunt, such people could not even match professionals and experts living in society. How could this be considered as being highly proficient in the five major vidyas and the five minor vidyas? How could they represent proficiency in exoteric and esoteric Buddhism and a high level of mastery of the Five Vidyas of which the Buddha spoke?

It could be said that *A Treasury of True Buddha-Dharma* is an unprecedented precious Buddhist book that reveals actual Buddha-dharma realization better than any other book in history. After extremely holy beings of the highest order in the world who are incarnations of Buddhas or Bodhisattvas saw the first manuscript of *A Treasury of True Buddha-Dharma*, they were astonished. They promptly investigated the truth behind the book in accordance with the dharma. Applying the practices of esoteric dharma relating to recognizing the identity or status of someone, they deeply entered the dharma realm, applied supernatural vision, and saw the true source. They then issued their own documents as the dharma prescribes in which they formally recognized that H.H. Dorje Chang Buddha III Wan Ko Yeshe Norbu Holiest Tathagata is the incarnation of the highest ancient Buddha and that His Holiness possesses unprecedented mastery of exoteric Buddhism, esoteric Buddhism, and the Five Vidyas!

However, we were surprised when H.H. Dorje Chang Buddha III said, "Dharma kings of great holiness have formally recognized that I am the incarnation of an ancient Buddha. Actually, it is not important who I am an incarnation of. What is important is having everyone understand the contents of 'What Is Cultivation?' An important incarnation is one in which the living being cultivates himself according to that dharma of 'What Is Cultivation?' The true gift that I give to everyone is the Buddha-dharma. If everyone could follow that Buddha-dharma and deeply penetrate it, light would pervade everywhere, the world would be at peace, and living beings would be forever happy, experiencing limitless beneficial effects and obtaining complete blessings and wisdom."

Let us put aside for the moment those thirty main categories of accomplishments. There is another matter that proves H.H. Dorje Chang Buddha III is the greatest holy being. On many occasions between 1995 and 2000 when H.H. Dorje Chang Buddha III was expounding the dharma, His Holiness openly declared, "If anyone asks a question about anything in the universe that I cannot answer or that I answer incorrectly, then I am not qualified to expound the Buddha-dharma to living beings. I will give everyone five years to ask any questions. This five-year vow is a manifestation of dharma. After the five-year vow period has passed, I will not carry out this vow any longer." H.H. Dorje Chang Buddha III openly made such a vow on

many occasions, which were recorded on tape.

That five-year period has long since passed. Numerous people posed a variety of questions. Whether the question was about Buddha-dharma or worldly matters, the questioner received a satisfactory and accurate answer. Not one question baffled H.H. Dorje Chang Buddha III. In the recordings of dharma discourses given by H.H. Dorje Chang Buddha III, we can often hear this open declaration of the Holiest Tathagata as well as questions posed and answers given. His Holiness not only answered questions posed by Asians, His Holiness also answered questions after questions posed by westerners. One example of this occurred in St. Louis, Missouri. After the chairman of the American League of Colleges and Universities heard the impromptu answers of H.H. Dorje Chang Buddha III to questions posed by college and university deans, presidents, professors, and doctorate degree holders, he was so moved he slapped himself on each cheek in front of those dozen or so people. He then excitedly stated that he has lived in vain for all of these years and that the answers he heard H.H. Dorje Chang Buddha III give had deeply benefited him.

The universe is boundlessly vast, with no beginning, ending, or limits. What type of person would dare say, "There is no question in the universe that I cannot answer"? Furthermore, His Holiness openly vowed that He would give both holy and ordinary people five years to pose any questions. What type of person has such high realization and accomplishment? How could a human being have such omniscience? Yet, this is not a fabrication. The facts irrefutably prove that the realization of His Holiness, at that time called Master Wan Ko Yee, is such that there is nothing His Holiness does not understand! Is such a person an ordinary holy being? Such a person is absolutely not merely an ordinary Bodhisattva. This was a mystery for a long time.

Who, after all, is this being of holy virtue? Is His Holiness from heaven or from a Buddha-land? H.H. Dorje Chang Buddha III always responds to such questions by saying He is an ordinary person. Moreover, His Holiness has never divulged to anyone which holy being He was in any previous life. His Holiness often speaks of clearly believing in cause and effect and often expounds the tathata. His Holiness has said that He is everyone's servant and that He is an ordinary cultivator. But we can see from the real accomplishments that no one in this world can be found who can attain even half of the accomplishments that H.H. Dorje Chang Buddha III has laid out before our eyes! If anyone doubts this, then there is a very simple solution. We welcome anyone to come forward and break this record of His Holiness. If anyone can attain the accomplishments of His Holiness in only fifteen main categories, then we believe such a person is also a Buddha who has come to the world. Everyone knows that the abilities of an average person cannot surpass those of a holy being, such as an eminent monastic, great rinpoche, or highly virtuous person. Could it be that one who is fully proficient in exoteric and esoteric Buddhism, who has deeply mastered the Five Vidyas, and who possesses great wisdom belongs in the category of an ordinary, average cultivator? Conversely, could it be that one who is not proficient in exoteric and esoteric Buddhism, who has not mastered all Five Vidyas or who does not understand even one vidya, and whose wisdom is low is a Buddha or Bodhisattva? Could it be that the Buddha-dharma of the Buddha characterizes those who are enlightened as stupid and those who are unenlightened and ordinary as the wisest? The truth of the Buddha's teachings is that the higher one's state of realization and virtue is, the higher one's manifestations of wisdom are. Buddhas are called Buddhas because their wisdom is so high that they reached a level of enlightenment in which there is nothing they cannot do. This is a matter that even we ordinary people can understand. Could it be that holy beings would need to ponder such a matter? It would be ridiculous if any holy being needed to ponder such a matter. How could such a person be called a holy being?

The Wondrous Multicolored Sculptures of H.H. Dorje Chang Buddha III are holy objects that cannot be duplicated by any other person in the world. But think about something. Is Sakyamuni Buddha able to create such sculptures? There is nothing the Buddha cannot do. Of course, that would be a very small matter for the Buddha. Could Kuan Yin Bodhisattva or Manjushri Bodhisattva create such sculptures? Of course, for them it would also be nothing difficult. You cannot deny the wisdom of the Buddha and great mahasattvas by saying that they could not accomplish such a small task. If someone lacks even that small amount of realization, can such a person be said to be the incarnation of the Buddha, Kuan Yin, Manjushri, or Samantabhadra Mahasattva? Could we possibly contend that the Buddha and great Bodhisattvas cannot create such sculptures? Conversely, surely we cannot say that the realization and wisdom of those who can create such sculptures are low, yet the realization and wisdom of those who cannot create such sculptures are high. Let us use the example of a boulder. We certainly cannot say that those who can lift a boulder have little physical strength, while those who cannot lift it have great physical strength. It is the same line of reasoning.

Although this is the line of reasoning, who descended into this world and incarnated as H.H. Master Wan Ko Yee after all? How is it that there is no question His Holiness is unable to answer? How is it that there is nothing His Holiness does not understand? How is it that His Holiness has so many first-rate accomplishments? How is it that no other person can duplicate some of the things that His Holiness has created? The answer to such questions truly seemed to be a mystery that would never be solved.

With the slow passage of time, these questions still could not be answered. Then, holy monks and dharma kings whose level of accomplishment is of the highest order in the world read the book *A Treasury of True Buddha-Dharma*. This caused a great sensation and they passed around the book to other holy monks and dharma kings of the highest order to read. These people of great and holy virtue, who are incarnations of Buddhas and Bodhisattvas, entered a profound state of supernatural vision through either meditation or practice of the dharma. They then announced the background of H.H. Wan Ko Yeshe Norbu, who was long ago recognized by H.H. Great Dharma King Zunsheng (the manifestation of Mahavairocana Buddha) as Buddha Vajrdhara. Through strict practice of the dharma and meditation these holy monastics deeply entered the dharma realm and supernaturally saw the true source.

The result was they learned that this being of great virtue and holiness is the second incarnation of Vimalakirti and the third incarnation of Dorje Chang Buddha. They wrote down their certificates of recognition according to the rules of Buddhism in which they recognized that H.H. Master Wan Ko Yee is H.H. Dorje Chang Buddha III—the highest ancient Buddha in exoteric, esoteric, Mahayana, Hinayana, and Vajrayana Buddhism; the master of the Five Buddhas in the five directions; and the master of the great mahasattva Vajrasattva. That is, they recognized that H.H. Master Wan Ko Yee is the Holiest Tathagata Wan Ko Yeshe Norbu, the current greatest leader of Buddhism in the entire dharma realm! Because H.H. Dorje Chang Buddha III Wan Ko Yeshe Norbu Holiest Tathagata is the complete, perfect, true, and direct incarnation of the body, speech, and mind of Dorje Chang Buddha, His Holiness is different from the hundreds of millions of other Buddhas and Bodhisattvas who have incarnated into this world. That is because those Buddhas and Bodhisattvas were only a partial nirmanakaya of a certain Buddha or Bodhisattva. Thus, they had only part of the body, speech, or mind powers of that certain Buddha or Bodhisattva. That is why no other person of holy virtue in today's world can manifest such complete proficiency in exoteric and esoteric Buddhism and such perfect mastery of the Five Vidyas.

Those eminent monks and dharma kings wrote words praising H.H. Dorje Chang Buddha III as being the highest and greatest holy being and the only one in the history of Buddhism who has truly exhibited before living beings item after item of accomplishments in the Five Vidyas. As H.H. Great Dharma King Zunsheng stated in a formal pronouncement, the realization of any eminent monastic or person of great virtue in the world today cannot rival the realization of Holiest Tathagata Wan Ko Yeshe Norbu. H.H. Great Dharma King Zunsheng also made the following vow of truth: "If any person or holy being is able to duplicate the mysterious sculpted treasures created by H.H. Wan Ko Yeshe Norbu, then this formal pronouncement of Great Dharma King Zunsheng has deceived the public." (The mysterious sculpted treasures are "Enchanting Colors of Utmost Mystery," "Mysterious Boulder With Mist," and certain other Yun sculptures with specific names.)

According to the system and rules of Buddhism in this world, there are only two beings of great holiness whose expositions of the dharma can be categorized as sutras. One of them is Sakyamuni Buddha. The other is the holy and venerable Vimalakirti. Besides those two, all other expositions of the dharma can only be called commentary rather than sutras. This is true no matter how great the Bodhisattva who has expounded the dharma is.

Some people say that Hui Neng gave the *Platform Sutra of the Sixth Patriarch*. Actually, this is a matter of people of the world not understanding the system and rules of Buddhism. As a result, the word *sutra* was used based on exaggerated praise given to Hui Neng. The rank of the sixth patriarch was even lower than that of many Bodhisattvas. For example, Maitreya Bodhisattva is the next Buddha, who will conduct the Dragon Flower Assembly. The position of Maitreya Bodhisattva is very much higher than that of Hui Neng. However, expositions of the dharma given by Maitreya Bodhisattva cannot be called sutras. They can only be accepted as commentary. An example of this is the *Yogācāra-bhūmi-śāstra (Discourse on the Stages of Concentration Practice)*.

The holy and venerable Vimalakirti descended into this world during the time of Sakyamuni Buddha. He is the only ancient Buddha who transformed into a layman to expound the dharma. Sakyamuni Buddha personally taught the four types of disciples. Among them were the 500 monks who were difficult to teach and who did not want to arouse Mahayana bodhicitta. A skillful means was used to teach all of the monastics and 8,000 Bodhisattvas. After the ancient Buddha Dorje Chang expounded dharma in Abhirati (World of Wonderful Joy), He responded to karmic conditions by transforming into the holy and venerable Vimalakirti to help the Buddha teach the sangha, Bodhisattvas, and other disciples. The goal was to protect and uphold the Buddha-dharma taught by Sakyamuni Buddha. The level of realization attained by the holy and venerable Vimalakirti was the same as that attained by Sakyamuni Buddha. However, He did not want to assume the status of another leader of the religion in the human realm, thereby causing sectarianism and adding to the self-centeredness of practitioners. Considering that Sakyamuni Buddha became a Buddha in this earthly realm, the holy and venerable Vimalakirti acknowledged Sakyamuni as Buddha and

chose to assist Sakyamuni Buddha by manifesting as a Bodhisattva. Thus, the holy and venerable Vimalakirti acted in the same way that the ancient Buddha Zheng Fa Ming (True Dharma Brightness) Tathagata acted when He transformed into Kuan Shi Yin Bodhisattva and also acted in the same way that Manjushri Bodhisattva, the Master of the seven Buddhas, acted.

All of this was done to benefit living beings. If two Buddhas of the same rank appeared at the same time, it would cause worldly divisions. It would hinder the development of Buddha-dharma and the saving of living beings. Actually, the Buddhas do not care who emerges as the leader of Buddhism. The Buddhas appear in whatever form and manner that best benefit living beings. Everything is done for the benefit of living beings based upon bodhicitta.

Therefore, people in general have had no way of discovering that the realization and enlightenment of the holy and venerable Vimalakirti were that high and that He was the incarnation of Dorje Chang Buddha, the foremost ancient Buddha who existed before Sakyamuni Buddha. However, the dharma discourses of the holy and venerable Vimalakirti are sutras, just as the dharma discourses of the Buddha are sutras. The dharma discourses of the holy and venerable Vimalakirti are not commentary. In the system of Buddhism, one such discourse is called *Vilmalakirti-nirdesa Sutra (The Sutra of Vimalakirti)*. That sutra came into being during the same time period Sakyamuni Buddha was giving sutras. It is a very important Buddhist sutra. The *Vimalakirti-nirdesa Sutra* has been studied and followed in both Mahayana and Hinayana Buddhism.

In the dharma realm, the venerable Vimalakirti was the incarnation of Dorje Chang Buddha. Because the holy and venerable Vimalakirti was the incarnation of this sambhogakaya ancient Buddha, His consummate wisdom, realization, and level of enlightenment were higher than those of all Bodhisattvas. As the above-mentioned sutra states, when Sakyamuni Buddha told Maitreya Bodhisattva, the future Buddha, to lead a group of people to the holy and venerable Vimalakirti to inquire of His health, Maitreya Bodhisattva said to the Buddha, "World Honored One, I am not qualified to visit Him and inquire about His illness." The reason Maitreya Bodhisattva gave to the Buddha was that when He (Maitreya Bodhisattva) was expounding the dharma to living beings, the holy and venerable Vimalakirti embarrassed Him and edified Him. Thus, Maitreya Bodhisattva did not dare visit Vimalakirti. All of the other Bodhisattvas were certain that the holy and venerable Vimalakirti possessed extremely high wisdom and that they fell far short of being up to such a task. They feared they would be embarrassed and did not dare go. Hence, in the end, Manjushri Bodhisattva, who is an ancient Buddha and Master of the seven Buddhas, led various Bodhisattvas, Arhats, and 500 monks to visit the holy and venerable Vimalakirti to inquire of His illness.

The holy and venerable Vimalakirti used His vast supernatural powers and wisdom to help Sakyamuni Buddha edify those visitors. One example is when the holy and venerable Vimalakirti manifested the realization and supernatural powers of a Buddha by moving all of the Bodhisattvas, Arhats, and Buddha-land—including Aksobhya Buddha (the Immovable Buddha)—of Abhirati to this earthly realm for all of those Buddhist disciples to see. All of the Abhirati Bodhisattvas thought that the Immovable Buddha moved His Buddha-land and its Bodhisattvas to the human realm. At this time, the Immovable Buddha said, "I did not do this. It was done through the supernatural powers of Vimalakirti." At this time, fourteen nayutas of people resolved to realize anuttara-samyaksambodhi. Only the powerful ancient Buddha Dojre Chang can move another Buddha to a different world. No Bodhisattva, no matter how high a stage he or she may be on, has the realization to accomplish such a feat.

In the sutra, Sakyamuni Buddha praised the holy and venerable Vimalakirti with the following words: "One who makes offerings to that holy being should know that this is making offerings to the Buddhas. One who transcribes this sutra or keeps it in a room should know that the Tathagata exists in that room." The Buddha clearly stated that the holy and venerable Vimalakirti is a Buddha. Why did Vimalakirti have such high realization and enlightenment? It is because Vimalakirti was Buddha Vajradhara Dorje Chang Buddha, who is the master of the Five Buddhas in the five directions and the master of all Buddhas. Buddha Vajradhara Dorje Chang Buddha incarnated as the ancient Buddha Dipankara, who accepted Sakyamuni Buddha as a disciple. Dorje Chang Buddha is the highest ancestor, the highest ancient Buddha, and the greatest leader of all of the sects of exoteric and esoteric Buddhism.

Thus, the virtue, realization, and wisdom of the holy and venerable Vimalakirti were without rival in the world. All of the four types of disciples of the Buddha, be they monastic or lay, including Bodhisattvas, devoutly listened to and followed the teachings of the holy and venerable Vimalakirti. The holy and venerable Vimalakirti helped Sakyamuni Buddha lift the 500 monks and 8,000 Bodhisattvas to the attainment of accomplishment in the dharma. The holy and venerable Vimalakirti guided and edified countless great Bodhisattvas who aroused bodhicitta. The second Vimalakirti and third Dorje Chang Buddha is H.H. Wan Ko Yeshe Norbu Holiest Tathagata. Extremely holy dharma kings on the level of Buddhas and Bodhisattvas have recognized this in accordance with the dharma and have provided certificates attesting to this as the dharma prescribes.

When H.H. Dorje Chang Buddha III was born, the beating of drums suddenly sounded in the sky, and beautiful, heavenly music could be heard. Three rainbows approximately forty to fifty meters (131-164 feet) apart appeared simultaneously in the sky. The middle one was primarily blue, the right one primarily red, and the left one primarily white. At birth, the entire body of His Holiness was dark blue. No cries from His Holiness could be heard. Rather, His Holiness opened his mouth and very clearly stated, "I have entered this world. I am completely proficient in exoteric and esoteric Buddhism and will wondrously manifest the Five Vidyas. Compare and you will know." After speaking such words, His Holiness remained silent and became just like an ordinary-looking child. The parents of His Holiness thought that they had given birth to a mysterious and extraordinary human being but did not tell anyone about this. His Holiness did not speak again until He was three years old.

When His Holiness was three years old, H.H. Mahavairocana Dharma King Zunsheng guided His Holiness in learning the *Tripitaka*. At that time, His Holiness was taught to recite the heart mantra of Dorje Chang Buddha seven times. The little child suddenly laughed heartily and immediately manifested the Three Bodies and Four Wisdoms. H.H. Great Dharma King Zunsheng at once tested His Holiness's knowledge of the *Tripitaka* and the esoteric scriptures. The Dharma Prince child explained such writings with great facility. There was nothing in them His Holiness did not understand. His Holiness had realized all of the doctrines and principles of such teachings.

H.H. Mahavairocana Dharma King Zunsheng then gave the following formal pronouncement: "Dorje Chang Buddha has come to this world a third time. The holy and venerable Vimalakirti has descended from the skies a second time. He completely understands the scriptures on the dharma. His Four Wisdoms are wonderfully perfect. He is an ancient Buddha upon whom living beings can rely. No master is qualified to teach Him. His mysterious sculpted treasures will be spectacular and unique in the world. He will be able to take mist that will stay inside His sculptures. He will manifest His realization and consummate skills. No holy person in the world will be able to duplicate such works. If anyone will be able to duplicate such works without differing from the original at all, my words have deceived the world. Vimalakirti Wan Ko is Buddha Vajradhara. He will cause the Buddhas to bestow nectar that many will see descend from the sky. He is of utmost benefit to sentient beings. He has the compassion and wisdom of an ancient Buddha. I hereby reveal these words to prove the veracity of my formal pronouncement." H.H. Mahavairocana Dharma King Zunsheng also gave His Holiness the dharma name Yangwo Yizhi Dharma Prince, which means Dharma Prince supreme leader of Buddhism with the highest wisdom.

H.H. Mahavairocana Zunsheng then said, "During the Dharma-Ending Age in the earthly world, there will be many evil teachers and demons who will claim to be genuine holy persons. In order to distinguish the genuine from the false, I now make a strict formal pronouncement that will serve as the testing standard. The pronouncement is as follows: There will not be a fourth incarnation of Dorje Chang Buddha in this earthly realm within the next 5,000 years. The third Dorje Chang Buddha will be the only such holy being, and there will not be an incarnation of another Dorje Chang Buddha in this earthly realm for 5,000 years. Based on causes and conditions that accord with the dharma, I now lay out tests to determine whether a person is that true Buddha if he claims to be the true incarnation of that Buddha. He must successfully invoke the Buddhas to bestow nectar. He must be able to perform the Golden Vase Selection of Karmic Affinity and predict the results of that ceremony beforehand. He must be able to eliminate karmic obstructions in a clearly visible manner. He must be able to replicate wondrous multicolored sculptures. He must be able to take mist, place it inside a hollowed out sculpted boulder, and have the mist stay there. If a person is able to do all five of these things without exception, then he is the true fourth Dorje Chang Buddha. No matter how great a holy terton may be, no matter if a person leaves concave imprints on rocks with his hands or feet, no matter how vast a person's manifold supernatural powers may be, if he cannot do these five holy things, then he certainly is not the true incarnation of Dorje Chang Buddha. An ancient Buddha who descends to this earthly realm will have no difficulty meeting these five tests. I leave these five observable tests to guard against those in the future who make false claims."

Dharma Prince Wan Ko, the leader of Buddhism, accepted His first disciple when He was five years old. In a prior lifetime, that disciple was a disciple of Guru Padmasambhava who was often at the side of Guru Padmasambhava. That disciple was also one the four most outstanding disciples of Master Shantaraksita, who founded the Nyingma sect of Tibetan esoteric Buddhism. That disciple's name was Xirao Jiebu. In this lifetime, he was recognized as Venerable Xirao Jiebu II and was given the hat of a great Pandita by the Geluk sect.

After Venerable Xirao Jiebu was accepted as a disciple by Dharma Prince Wan Ko, he often saw the marvelous super-human abilities of the Dharma Prince while at the side of the Dharma Prince. However, it is strange that after Venerable Xirao Jiebu was accepted as a disciple, people of the world rarely heard the Dharma Prince expound the Buddha-dharma. In so doing, the Dharma Prince was acting as the holy and venerable Vimalakirti did when Vimalakirti received different teachings and knowledge, took on the appearance of an ordinary person, and learned things tirelessly. No one knows why the Dharma Prince did this.

At the age of sixteen, the Dharma Prince wrote a work on the dharma called *A Monk Expounds the Absolute Truth to a Layperson*. After that writing was buried, great master Hui Yong unearthed it. Renqing Luozhu and Suolang Danbu respectfully offered that writing to H.H. Mahavairocana Zunsheng Yeshe Norbu to evaluate. H.H. Zunsheng Yeshe Norbu personally promulgated that dharma called *A Monk Expounds the Absolute Truth to a Layperson* in front of the four types of Buddhist disciples. After He finished promulgating that dharma, He personally led the four types of Buddhist disciples in kneeling down and facing that writing on the dharma. He then made the following formal pronouncement: "An ancient Buddha has arrived in the east." He recognized that the Dharma Prince was H.H. Dorje Chang Buddha III, conferred upon His Holiness the title Yangwo Wan Ko Yeshe Norbu, and said that His Holiness is the Holiest Tathagata. He also called that dharma *A Monk Expounds the Absolute Truth to a Layperson Sutra*.

Of course, as H.H. Dorje Chang Buddha III continued to spread the dharma and save living beings, His Holiness accepted disciples other than Venerable Xirao Jiebu. When karmic conditions matured, incarnations of other members of the four most outstanding disciples of Master Shantaraksita took refuge in and became disciples of His Holiness, such as Venerable Muya Jiongzha III and Venerable Xiangge Qiongwa IV. Another disciple of the Holiest Tathagata is H.E. Denma Tsemang II, who is a close attendant of His Holiness and who in a prior lifetime was one of the twenty-five greatest disciples of Guru Padmasambhava. H.E. Gar Tongstan IV, who in a prior lifetime was prime minister to King Songstan Gampo, is also a close disciple of H.H. Dorje Chang Buddha III. Other disciples of His Holiness include Venerable Palden Lodoe, who is the incarnation of the founder of the Kagyu Macang sect, Hsi Jao Seng Ge; Venerable Yundun Duojibai Gadu Rinpoche of the Nyingma sect; Venerable Dachu Hengsheng, who in a prior lifetime was a great disciple of Patriarch Dangba Sangjie of the Jueyu sect; Venerable Khu-ston brTson-'grus g.yung-drung of the Kadampa sect, who in a prior lifetime was one of the four highest disciples of Venerable Atisha; Respected Danzeng Nuori Rinpoche of the Geluk sect; and Venerable Akou Lamo, who is a female great venerable one. Even the incarnation of the great patriarch of the Shangpa Kagyu sect, Tangtong Gyalpo Bodhisattva, who is famous throughout Tibet, has formally acknowledged H.H. Wan Ko Yeshe Norbu Holiest Tathagata as his Master. Additionally, several beings of tremendous holiness descended into this world to be at the side of H.H. Dorje Chang Buddha III and have received profound Buddha-dharma from the Holiest Tathagata, such as the incarnation of

Anathapindika, who donated Jetavana to Sakyamuni Buddha; the incarnation of Sariputra, the greatest disciple of Sakyamuni Buddha; and the incarnation of Great Patriarch Shantaraksita, who founded the Nyingma sect.

Actually, from a worldly perspective, the educational background of H.H. Dorje Chang Buddha III is of the highest order. His Holiness is completely conversant in the ancient Chinese writings called *The Four Books and the Five Classics*. With respect to modern education, His Holiness was an outstanding student in elementary school, went on to receive a high-level doctorate degree from a university, and then went on to be a professor at a famous American university, where He has taught for six years. His Holiness has received special commendation from that university. His Holiness is also the only person in the more than two-hundred-year history of the Royal Academy of Arts in the United Kingdom to have been awarded the position of "Fellow." Nonetheless, as far as H.H. Dorje Chang Buddha III is concerned, these are just trifling matters hardly worth mentioning.

H.H. Dorje Chang Buddha III has not Himself revealed His true identity or status. Although H.H. Dorje Chang Buddha III has inadvertently revealed His great wisdom and realization to others, causing them to marvel at what they saw, His Holiness has never discussed His own background. Many people have inquired of His Holiness what His dharma lineage is and have even issued written inquiries requesting answers to this mystery. H.H. Dorje Chang Buddha III always responds by saying, "I do not know. I only have Buddhism. I am your servant with a heart of humility." Such an utterance can often be heard in many recorded dharma discourses given by His Holiness over many years. With the passage of time, people became used to hearing this and thought that His Holiness was merely a kind, wise, and talented person. This even included members of the Master Wan Ko Yee International Cultural Institute, established in 1995, who it can be said have the best understanding of His Holiness. They, too, did not know the true identity of His Holiness. They simply thought that His Holiness was a holy man of prodigious learning and virtue who at the very most was a great dharma king of Buddhism like the Dalai Lama or the Karmapa. Thus, when the president of that Institute, Longzhou Rinpoche, learned that the true identity of His Holiness is H.H. Dorje Chang Buddha III, he was astounded and repeatedly said, "No wonder. No wonder. Great dharma kings cannot be put on par with such a Buddha! To do so would dishonor that Buddha and would be a sin."

The days passed by one after another. At a certain time, people began realizing that no matter what the type of knowledge or skill, H.H. Wan Ko Yeshe Norbu did not need to learn it. As soon as His Holiness saw a work, He was easily able to understand the knowledge or skill that it embodied. Furthermore, His Holiness immediately became proficient in such knowledge or skill. As a result, the works of His Holiness excelled the original works that He saw.

Those eminent monks and dharma kings have now announced in their recognition certificates the holy and astounding news about His Holiness's identity. Only then did we find out that His Holiness is the holy and venerable Vimalakirti, who is the true incarnation of Dorje Chang Buddha. That is why Mahavairocana stated in His formal pronouncement that no master of holy virtue can be found whose realization is higher than that of H.H. Dorje Chang Buddha III and who is therefore qualified to be the master of His Holiness. Even those 500 monks, 8,000 Bodhisattvas, prominent monastics, and people of great virtue were taught by His Holiness when He was Vimalakirti, not to mention people on those levels who have been taught by His Holiness in this lifetime.

Because H.H. Dorje Chang Buddha III is an ancient Buddha who has come to this world again, His Holiness upholds the principles of "making no distinction between exoteric and esoteric Buddhism or among all of the sects and schools; teaching living beings according to their particular circumstances; and pervasively propagating the teachings of the Buddhas to all." Thus, His Holiness is the Buddha Vajradhara Great Dharma King of the "Buddha Sect" who pervasively saves all living beings. This Buddha Sect includes the entirety of Buddhism and does not distinguish between the various schools. H.H. Dorje Chang Buddha III has repeatedly admonished everyone with the following counsel: "There is no differentiation among the various schools and sects in my mind. There is only Buddhism. However, as long as a dharma king, rinpoche, or acarya of any school or sect abides by the teachings of the Buddha, attains liberation, and then saves other living beings based on their particular karmic conditions, he or she is worthy of praise."

There are certain time periods relating to H.H. Dorje Chang Buddha III's propagating the dharma and benefiting living beings. Before the age of eleven was the period during which His Holiness was engaged in the *Tripitaka* of exoteric Buddhism. From the age of eleven to fifteen was the period during which His Holiness was engaged in the esoteric dharma of the Kagyu school. During that time, he was called Dusum Khenpa Lion's Roar Dharma Prince. After the age of fifteen was the period during which His Holiness was engaged in the esoteric teachings of the Geluk school. His Holiness was at that time called the reincarnation of Master Tsongkhapa. That was also the time period during which His Holiness flawlessly propagated the tantric scriptures of the Sakya, Nyingma, and all of the other schools. At this time, His Holiness was called the embodiment of the body, speech, and mind of Guru

Padmasambhava.

Actually, all of these honorific appellations given to His Holiness by people of great virtue and people of the world did not comport with the true identity of H.H. Dorje Chang Buddha III. The true identity of His Holiness was revealed when the karmic conditions of living beings were mature. At such time, Buddhas and great Bodhisattva Dharma Kings applied different dharma methods and entered deep meditation or entered the dharma realm. Each of them supernaturally and directly saw the true source. As a result, they unmistakably and unanimously recognized that H.H. Wan Ko Yeshe Norbu is the ancient Buddha Dorje Chang who has come to this world again. That is, His Holiness is the second holy and venerable Vimalakirti and the third Dorje Chang Buddha.

H.H. Great Vehicle Dharma King Sakya Trizin, who is the supreme leader of the Sakya order and the nirmanakaya of Manjushri Bodhisattva, wrote the following recognition concerning the descent into this world of H.H. Dorje Chang Buddha III: ". . . H.H. Yangwo Wan Ko Yeshe Norbu . . . is . . .Buddha Vajradhara Dorje Chang Buddha III."

H.H. Dodrupchen Rinpoche, a famous great dharma king of the Nyingma sect who is the sole holder of the complete Longchen Nying-thik, said the following in his letter congratulating the publication of *A Treasury of True Buddha-Dharma*: "I found the book wonderful and amazing and totally inspiring. . . [It is a] truly miraculous and extraordinary expression of truth expressed and unexpressed beyond words in Buddha Dharma."

H.H. Dharma King Penor, a supreme dharma king of the Nyingma sect, wrote the following in a letter to rinpoches: "H.H. Dorje Chang Buddha III Yangwo Wan Ko Yeshe Norbu. . . has been recognized by numerous greatly virtuous and eminent monastics. . . *A Treasury of True Buddha-Dharma*. . .will provide the karmic conditions for living beings to . . . attain the ultimate state of Buddhahood."

H.H. Dharma King Omniscience Jamyang Lungdok Gyaltsen (Lama Achuk), who is the incarnation of Venerable Longsal Nyingpo, stated in his recognition certificate, ". . . H.H. Master Wan Ko Yee . . . is the incarnation of Vimalakirti. . . is Dorje Chang Buddha III. . . ."

On behalf of the Jonang sect, **H.H. Dharma King Jigme Dorje**, who is the Supreme Dharma King of the Jonang sect, respectfully congratulated H.H. Dorje Chang Buddha III Wan Ko Yeshe Norbu with the following words: "Such superlative accomplishments are truly unprecedented in the past few thousand years, outshining the accomplishments of all others, both ancient and modern. His Holiness is a shining paragon among Buddhas."

The famous **Kumbum Monastery**, which is the birthplace of Master Tsongkhapa, the founder of the Geluk sect, wrote the following congratulations: ". . . Buddha Vajradhara H.H. Master Yangwo Wan Ko Yeshe Norbu['s] . . . outstanding accomplishments are unprecedented."

The chief secretary for **H.H. Dharma King Mindrolling Trichen** of the Nyingma sect, Ven. D. G. Khochhen Rinpoche, sent a congratulatory letter on behalf of Dharma King Mindrollling Trichin and the Mindrolling Sangha in which he wrote, ". . . H.H. Wan Ko Yeshe Norbu Dorje Chang brings good fortune and wisdom to all living beings."

The highest dharma king of the Northern Treasure lineage of the Nyingma sect, **H.H. Dharma King Taklung Tsetrul**, wrote the following words of congratulations: "His Holiness Dorje Chang Buddha III Wan Ko Yeshe Norbu possesses the true dharma of the Buddhas . . . "

The famous **H.H. Dharma King Trulshik Rinpoche**, who is a master of H.H. the Dalai Lama and the root master of several Tibetan Buddhist dharma kings and lineage holders, wrote the following words respectfully congratulating Buddha Vajradhara Yangwo Wan Ko Yeshe Norbu: . . . *A Treasury of True Buddha-Dharma* . . .will become the cause whereby each sentient being who has descended into the abyss of the six realms of reincarnation leaves suffering and attains happiness."

H.H. Dharma King Jigdal Dagchen Sakya, the second highest leader of the Sakya order, offered the following congratulations: "Many masters praise H.H. Dorje Chang Buddha III Wan Ko Yeshe Norbu and his book about his Dharma activities. The book's name is *A Treasury of True Buddha-Dharma*."

H.E. Dharma King Chogye Trichen, Ngawang Khyenrab Thupten Lekshe Gyatso, who was Dharma King of the Tsharpa branch of Sakya sect and the root master of H.H. the Dalai Lama, offered the following respectful congratulations: "H.H. Buddha Vajradhara (Dorje Chang) Yangwo Wan Ko Yeshe Norbu: *A Treasury of True Buddha-Dharma* . . . is the guidepost leading to true Buddha-dharma and the gateway of the dharma leading to benefiting and providing happiness to sentient beings."

The Red Jewel Crown Dharma King **H.E. Shamarpa Rinpoche** is the nirmanakaya of Kuan Yin Bodhisattva and is the chief of the four regents of the Kagyu sect. He offered his respectful congratulations with the following words: "H.H. Yangwo Wan Ko Yeshe Norbu . . . the third incarnation of Vajradhara . . . all his accomplishments . . . will benefit sentient beings. . ."

H.E. Goshir Gyaltsab Rinpoche is the incarnation of Patriarch Gampopa. He is the only regent for the Karmapa Great Jewel Dharma King who has the title of "National Master." He respectfully praised the incomparable Master, H.H. Yangwo Wan Ko, as Vimalakirti and stated: ". . . .I sincerely wish that . . . the multitudinous living beings who have the karmic affinity to read *A Treasury of True Buddha-Dharma* ... will attain the supreme fruits of perfect enlightenment, omniscience, and Buddhahood!"

H.E. Xiazhu Qiuyang Rinpoche, who is the incarnation of Venerable Naropa, respectfully congratulated the highest and holiest Wish Fulfilling Jewel Dharma King Wan Ko as follows: "...the book *A Treasury of True Buddha-Dharma...* is the highest authentic dharma that is of benefit to living beings."

The name Tangtong Gyalpo Bodhisattva has gone down in Buddhist history. In the past, this Bodhisattva was the leader of the four main sects of esoteric Buddhism in India, Bhutan, Sikkim, Mongolia, and eastern Tibet. The people of Tibet call this Bodhisattva the father of medicine, the father of bridges, the father of Tibetan opera, and the father of ferryboats. During a dharma assembly held at Hua Zang Si in San Francisco of the United States in which Buddha-dharma realization was manifested, H.E. the sixteenth Tangtong Gyalpo Bodhisattva saw the realization and virtue of H.H. Dorje Chang Buddha III Wan Ko Yeshe Norbu. He was astounded and immediately prostrated before His Holiness, formally acknowledging His Holiness as his Master. In his congratulatory letter to His Holiness, he stated the following: "... H.H. Wan Ko Yeshe Norbu is ... the Master of the Five Buddhas, and has for the first time in the history of Buddhism in the human realm truly manifested complete proficiency in exoteric and esoteric Buddhism and perfect mastery of the Five Vidyas. This is a goal of Buddhism that all other Buddhists have not been able to achieve. This goal has finally been achieved by H.H. Wan Ko Yeshe Norbu."

H.E. Mighty Lion Dharma King Renzeng Nima previously vowed to stay in a mountain valley engaged in solitary meditation for the rest of his life. He possesses supernatural powers, inspires awe throughout Tibet, and is the reincarnation of King Gesar. He wrote the following words of recognition: "... H.H. Master Wan Ko Yee ... is the true incarnation of Dorje Chang Buddha."

H.E. Dharma King Ngagwang Pedma Namgyal Palzangpo, who is a dharma king of the Jonang sect, respectfully congratulated H.H. Dorje Chang Buddha III Wan Ko Yeshe Norbu with the following words: "The body and lifespan of the Buddha Vajradhara of the dharma realm never comes to an end. His Holiness manifests Mahayana states and has the most wondrous powers of great compassion."

H.E. Mindrolling Khenchen Rinpoche of the Mindrolling Monastery wrote the following congratulations: "His Holiness Buddha Vajradhara III Yangwo Wan Ko Yeshe Norbu['s] ... *A Treasury of True Buddha-Dharma* ... will restore dharma that had faded and will cause the growth of dharma that has not yet faded."

H.E. Jetsun Khandro Rinpoche of the Mindrolling lineage within the Nyingma sect is the incarnation of Yeshe Tsogyal. She sent a congratulatory letter expressing her deep gratitude toward H.H. Wan Ko Yeshe Norbu Dorje Chang Buddha for the book *A Treasury of True Buddha-Dharma.*

The famous H.E. Dzogchen Ganor Rinpoche offered the following congratulations: "... *A Treasury of True Buddha-Dharma* is the wish-fulfilling true dharma that the Buddha expounded."

H.E. Urgyen Xirao Woxiu, who is a great terton revered by all four types of monastic and lay Buddhists in the land of the Han-Chinese and the land of the Tibetans, wrote in his recognition certificate the following: "... Buddha Vajradhara assisted Sakyamuni Buddha in teaching the five hundred monks and other holy ones.... H.H. Master Wan Ko Yee, Yangwo Wan Ko Yeshe Norbu, is the incarnation of Buddha Vajradhara."

H.E. Dorje Rinzin Rinpoche is the incarnation of Rigzin Terdak Lingpa Unchanging Vajra, who was the founder the Mindrolling monastery. H.E. Dorje Rinzin Rinpoche, a holy being of great enlightenment, is now the master of many great rinpoches. He said the following in his congratulatory letter: "... the accomplishments contained in *A Treasury of True Buddha-Dharma* ... are those of Dorje Chang Buddha Wan Ko Yeshe Norbu, the Master of the Five Buddhas."

H.E. Shechen Rabjam Rinpoche, the dharma king of the Shechen monasteries of the Nyingma sect, offered the following words of congratulations: "... H.H. Dorje Chang Buddha III Yangwo Wan Ko Yeshe Norbu, the Wish-Fulfilling Jewel Holy One, has taken action that spreads and makes grander the true Buddha-dharma. How wonderful!"

Venerable Angwang Khyentse Rinpoche was the closest disciple of H.H. Dzongsar Khyentse Chokyi Lodro. He is the head of the Gensa Temple of the Sakya sect and has been in retreat for a long period of time. He possesses supernatural powers and is praised throughout the snowy plateaus of Tibet for his cultivation. In his congratulatory letter, he stated, "Greatest leader of Buddhism, H.H. Wan Ko Yeshe Norbu: ....Only the wisdom of the ancient Buddha, Dorje Chang Buddha, could produce such a textbook [as *A Treasury of True Buddha-Dharma*] ...!"

H.E. Jigme Losel Wangpo, the seventh Dzogchen Dharma King who resides in India, wrote the following words of congratulations: "... *A Treasury of True Buddha-Dharma* brings benefit to all sentient beings. ...." H.E. Tenzin Longdock (Lungdok) Nyima, the seventh Dzogchen Dharma King who resides in China, respectfully congratulated the ancient Buddha who saves all sentient beings in the three spheres, H.H. Yangwo Wan Ko Yeshe Norbu, as follows: "... *A Treasury of True Buddha-Dharma* ... is like the... Wish-Fulfilling Jewel in that it outshines all ancient or modern, Chinese or non-Chinese books. .... The book also opens up and develops the spiritual wisdom of people."

H.E. Renqing Rongbo Barongbo Rinpoche, an eastern Tibetan Dharma King of the Nyingma sect, respectfully praised H.H. Wan Ko Yeshe Norbu with the following words: "The Master is the magnificent sambhogakaya Buddha who has descended into the human world again. . . . His Holiness's accomplishments are unprecedented in this world and reflect the pinnacle of wisdom. May H.H. Dorje Chang Buddha boundlessly save living beings. . ."

The Green Jewel Crown Karmapa, H.E. Great Jewel Dharma King Jiezhong, prostrated to H.H. Yangwo Wan Ko Yeshe Norbu, the Buddha Vajradhara, and wrote the following words: "*A Treasury of True Buddha-Dharma* about the Buddha Vajradhara is a concrete expression of the highest Buddha-dharma wisdom and abilities."

Ven. Junmai Baima Dorje Rinpoche of the Shechen Temple is a nirmanakaya of Vajravarahi. He wrote a letter expressing his respect for the Three Bodies and Four Wisdoms of H.H. Yangwo Wan Ko Yeshe Norbu, the Dharma King of the Three Spheres. In that letter, he stated, "H.H. Great Dharma King is the first holy being who used true realization to display fully in the dharma realm the teachings of the Buddha! H.H. Great Dharma King is the true Buddha Vajradhara, the teacher of both humans and celestial beings!"

Ven. Kalsang Gyaltsen, who represents H.H. the Dalai Lama and is fully authorized to exercise control over the Geluk sect in Nepal, stated in his congratulatory letter the following: "I am sure the works of Venerable Vajradhara Master Wan Ko will inspire all the sentient beings to a better understanding of both the theoretical and practical aspects of the Buddhist philosophy."

The famous Zangxia Rinpoche prostrated to the ancient Buddha and greatest leader of Buddhism, H.H. Dorje Chang Buddha III, and stated, ". . . led us to find Dorje Chang Buddha, our supreme ancient Buddha, and thereby enabled all living beings to have the ultimate refuge in this Dharma-Ending Age!"

The eighty-year-old Ven. Yundeng Jiangcuo Rinpoche, who is the incarnation of Patriarch Milarepa, respectfully offered the following congratulations on the publication of *A Treasury of True Buddha-Dharma* about Buddha Vajradhara: "This book manifests great Buddha-dharma based wisdom and contains accomplishments that no other person in history has achieved. Only H.H. Wan Ko Yeshe Norbu has attained such accomplishments."

The famous Respected Bamda Tubten Geleg Gyatso Rinpoche stated: ". . . [I] beseech the magnificent and holy Dorje Chang Buddha III to bless all sentient beings in the six realms of reincarnation so that they may realize enlightenment soon, hear of and read *A Treasury of True Buddha-Dharma*, . . . and attain the perfect, supreme, and complete enlightenment of a Buddha."

Respected sixth Baima Rongzhu Rinpoche is widely respected in India and is revered by the people who live along the banks of the Jinsha River. Having prostrated to H.H. Wan Ko Yeshe Norbu, he wrote, "Having read *A Treasury of True Buddha-Dharma*, I learned that the ancient Buddha, Dorje Chang Buddha, has descended to the human world again. This is truly our greatest blessing!"

Respected Eba Rinpoche Danba Wangxu, the fifth dharma king of his temple, used the following words to express on behalf of other rinpoches deep gratitude to the most venerable H.H. Wan Ko Yeshe Norbu: "The supreme Dorje Chang Buddha has brought to us *A Treasury of True Buddha-Dharma!*"

Respected Khenpo Chucheng Qupei, whose status as khenpo was conferred upon him by H.H. Dharma King Sakya Trizin, respectfully praised H.H. Dorje Chang Buddha III Wan Ko Yeshe Norbu, as follows: "His Holiness is the supreme holder of the 84,000 Buddha-dharmas, the one who is in charge of all dharma methods of Buddhism. His Holiness was the first sambhogakaya Buddha in the dharmadhatu."

Respected Wangzhi Tudeng Jigmei Rinpoche, the famous abbot of the Tsangtsang Temple, expressed his gratitude to the most venerable ancient Buddha, H.H. Dorje Chang Buddha III Wan Ko Yeshe Norbu, as follows: "The most honorable ancient Buddha has perfectly and flawlessly brought to this world the Buddha-dharma of Tibet's four main sects as well as the exoteric Buddha-dharma."

Respected Bishop Seicho Asahi is the supreme leader of the headquarters of the Koyasan Shingon-shu North American Mission. He praised H.H. Dharma King Wan Ko Yeshe Norbu, the Buddha Vajradhara, with the following words: ". . . Your Holiness['s] great accomplishments on Buddhism . . . have never been seen before in the world. Your Holiness is truly the primordial Buddha who incarnate[d] to this world to save living beings and to transmit the authentic Buddha-dharma of Tathagata."

Gele Sanbu Rinpoche prostrated to the supreme H.H. Yangwo Wan Ko Yeshe Norbu and stated, "H.H. Great Dharma King thoroughly understands the true causes and effects concerning all things in the universe. His Holiness is the first great holy being in the history of Buddhism to truly manifest in the human realm complete proficiency in exoteric and esoteric Buddhism and perfect mastery of the Five Vidyas!"

Luozhu Jiangcuo Rinpoche prostrated to H.H. Wan Ko Yeshe Norbu and wrote, "I was fortunate to have respectfully read *A Treasury of True Buddha-Dharma* about the greatest leader of Buddhism, H.H. Yangwo Wan Ko Yeshe Norbu. . . . we see that a true Buddha has again descended into this world!"

Lama Renzhen Rinpoche of the Five Vidyas Buddhist Institute prostrated to H.H. Wan Ko Yeshe Norbu and praised the accomplishments of the Vajra Dharma King of Great Holiness with the following words: "We have respectfully read *A Treasury of True Buddha-Dharma* about H.H. Buddha Vajradhara Great Dharma King and were truly astounded! . . . H.H. Great Dharma King represents the Buddha-dharma!"

Additionally, Duozhu Rinpoche, Gongbo Rinpoche, Great Khenpo Gongcheng, Pengcuo Rinpoche, and other rinpoches wrote their own letters in which they respectfully congratulated the accomplishments of H.H. Dorje Chang Buddha III, an ancient Buddha who has returned to this world. They also sincerely thanked H.H. Dorje Chang Buddha III for His Holiness's empowerment. There are also some very famous large monasteries of exoteric and esoteric Buddhism as well as some renowned rinpoches who wrote congratulatory letters to His Holiness supporting the recognitions made by others. However, those letters are not included in this book due to the karmic conditions of living beings.

H.H. Wan Ko Yeshe Norbu Holiest Tathagata is the greatest leader of Buddhism in the entire dharmadhatu and is the complete and perfect incarnation of Dorje Chang Buddha. During the past few thousand years, many beings of great holiness have come to this world and their identities were recognized. However, H.H. Wan Ko Yeshe Norbu Holiest Tathagata is the only ancient Buddha Vajradhara and highest leader of Buddhism who is foremost in the five areas stated below.

1. His Holiness is the greatest holy being who has received the most written recognitions and respectful praise from Buddhas and great Bodhisattvas of all of the main sects in the history of Buddhism. (see Recognitions and Congratulations)

2. His Holiness is the greatest holy being who has received the highest evaluations from Buddhas and great Bodhisattvas of all of the main sects in the history of Buddhism. (see the evaluations in Recognitions and Congratulations)

3. His Holiness is the greatest holy being and ancient Buddha whose position is highest among all Buddhas and Bodhisattvas who have come to this human world. (see the Recognitions and Congratulations stating that His Holiness is Dorje Chang Buddha III)

4. His Holiness is the greatest holy being whose accomplishments in mastering exoteric Buddhism, esoteric Buddhism, and the Five Vidyas are the most illustrious in the history of mankind. (see thirty categories)

5. His Holiness took auspicious mist from space and put it inside a sculpture of a stone cave and also created holy and wondrous carvings, just as H.H. Great Dharma King Zunsheng predicted. In the history of Buddhism until the present time, no other being of great holiness who has incarnated into this human realm has been able to do such things. No one has been able to replicate such works as well. (see irrefutable facts on pages 380)

The attainments stated above are not empty or unreliable words. Rather, these words are based on the documents of extremely holy and virtuous rinpoches, dharma kings, and eminent monastics in the world today. These are true words expressed with a serious attitude, a sense of responsibility, and an understanding of karmic retribution.

Why do heads of sects, dharma kings, and rinpoches, who are all incarnations of Buddhas or Bodhisattvas, unanimously recognize that H.H. Wan Ko Yeshe Norbu is the highest and greatest holy being in the world today? A unanimous recognition of such magnitude has not happened in the last few thousand years. The answer is clear without even thinking about it. It is because His Holiness is Dorje Chang Buddha III. Additionally, in today's world, which other sage or holy being is able to accomplish what His Holiness has accomplished? No one can be found who can match His Holiness's accomplishments in even half of the thirty main categories. No one can be found who has the ability to duplicate even one of His Holiness's wondrous multicolored sculptures.

Additionally, because karmic conditions of living beings have matured, H.H. Dorje Chang Buddha III brought to this world the supreme Xian Liang Great Perfection Rainbow Body Accomplishment Dharma. Whoever receives this dharma initiation from H.H. Dorje Chang Buddha III will be able to realize the rainbow body state the same day that dharma is transmitted and that initiation is performed. There is no need to practice for days, months, or years in order to realize that state. There are people who had the karmic affinity to receive such an initiation, such as H.E. Gar Tongstan IV, H.E. Kaichu Rinpoche, and other practitioners of great virtue. From the day they received that initiation, they have been able to abide in the bright dharma-nature state at all times.

Which person has such realization besides the true Dorje Chang Buddha? Moreover, when the Buddha was living in this world a long time ago, the holy and venerable Vimalakirti was a teacher who edified and guided all of the eminent monks, people of great virtue, and Bodhisattvas. Dharma Kings on the level of a Buddha or Great Bodhisattva have now recognized in writing according to the rules of Buddhism that H.H. Yangwo Wan Ko Yeshe Norbu is the second Vimalakirti; that is, the third Dorje Chang Buddha. Based upon His Holiness's actual realization, His status as an ancient Buddha, or His position on Buddhist lineage trees, H.H. Dorje Chang Buddha III Wan Ko Yeshe Norbu Holiest Tathagata is the greatest holy being who is above all Buddhas, Bodhisattvas, eminent monks, and people of great virtue!

International Buddhism Sangha Association

(This text was translated from the Chinese text on next page.)

頂聖如來多杰羌佛第三世雲高益西諾布
簡　　　介

　　頂聖如來多杰羌佛第三世雲高益西諾布，即是金剛總持，又名持金剛，為原始報身佛多杰羌佛降世，簡稱三世多杰羌佛（在這世界亦曾被尊稱為義雲高大師）。三世多杰羌佛的成就是最頂尖的，所展顯的顯密和五明智慧、證量的實際證明材料在佛法界中，也是沒有哪一個聖德能與之相提並論的。

　　佛陀規定以『顯密俱通，五明具足』為衡量佛法成就高低的標準，但是，自佛史至今，真正完整、全面展顯『顯密圓通，妙諳五明』的只有頂聖如來三世多杰羌佛！三世多杰羌佛將佛陀規定的『顯密圓通，妙諳五明』的實際成就一條一款展顯、公眾出來了，這是歷史上第一個完成如此微妙和完整證量實顯的聖德古佛！本《多杰羌佛第三世——正法寶典》中所列的三世多杰羌佛所獨立創造的三十大類的成就，就是一個明證。當然，列出的三十大類成就，也只是一個名相而已，其實書中成果遠超三十大類，如僅科技藝術類即含攝三項大類：攝影類、立體畫類、玻璃畫類，但三世多杰羌佛將很多大類合為一類而縮稱三十大類。實際上，三世多杰羌佛的成就又哪裡是三十大類能概括得了的？三世多杰羌佛的成就表顯的是佛法的智慧，是無以窮盡的，尤其是內明一類，即含攝三藏和密典、宇宙有為法和無為法無窮盡的真諦。本書所列三十大類是：1.認證祝賀類；2.三世多杰羌佛的聖蹟佛格類；3.頂聖如來的聖量類；4.百千萬劫難遭遇無上甚深佛法類；5.楹聯類；6.書法類；7.金石類；8.詩詞歌賦類；9.金剛除病針類；10.治病類；11.製藥保健類；12.玄妙彩寶雕類；13.玉板類；14.世法哲言類；15.古典散文現代詩類；16.學術論文類；17.造景類；18.音韻類；19.神秘霧氣雕類；20.枯藤古化類；21.中國畫類；22.西畫類；23.畫框類；24.佛像設計造型類；25.瓷磚類；26.壁掛類；27.建築庭園風景類；28.茗茶類；29.科技藝術類；30.渡生成就類。三十大類中之第四大類『百千萬劫難遭遇無上甚深佛法類』，即有兩千多堂開示，義理博大精深，浩如淵海。從古至今，除了本世界釋迦佛陀說法外，從來沒有一個聖者完成過如此多項的成就，而且每一項成就都達到了世界級的巔峰。我們了解過很多被稱為「深通大小五明」的人，實際上是一句空話，拿不出實在的內容，就連文字圖片

也拿不出來鑒定，說句不該說的真心話，甚至連世間上的專業專家都比不過，這又哪裡是什麼深通大小五明呢？又怎能代表佛陀所說的顯密俱通、智慧展顯的五明高度呢？

　　這本《正法寶典》可以說是歷史上第一次出現的最好的展現佛法實際證量的佛門寶典，本《正法寶典》初稿一出來後，世界第一流的、佛菩薩轉世的巨聖高僧們見到了大為震驚，當下依法查證，根據密法認證法義，深入法界觀照，查出真源，行以法定文書，正式公認多杰羌佛第三世雲高益西諾布頂聖如來為歷史上第一位出現的、佛史以來顯密圓通、妙諳五明之頂首古佛！但是，想不到三世多杰羌佛卻說：『我雖然正式被大聖法王們認證確認爲古佛降世，其實我是什麼降世並不重要，而重要的是要讓眾生明白『什麼是修行』、能如法修持才是重要的轉世。我真正送給大家的禮物，是佛法，如能依之深入，則光明充遍，世界和平，眾生永樂，受用無窮，福慧圓滿。』

　　我們就撇開三十大類成就不提，另選一條即可證明三世多杰羌佛是頂首巨聖。如早在公元1995年至2000年，三世多杰羌佛就曾多次在講經說法時公開宣佈：『任何一個人，無論提宇宙間什麼樣的問題，如果我回答不出來、答不正確的話，那麼我就沒有資格為眾生開示佛法，給大家五年的時間提問，這是我五年願力為期的表法，五年願力滿了，就不再實行這一願力了。』這是三世多杰羌佛當時若干次在公開錄音場合的發願。五年早已過去了，有若干人提出不同的問題，無論是佛法，還是世間法，凡提問者都得到了滿意正確的回答，從來沒有一個人的提問難倒了三世多杰羌佛。我們現在在三世多杰羌佛的開示法音帶中隨時都能聽到頂聖如來當時的公眾宣言以及提問和回答，不僅是回答東方人，乃至西方人的提問也一一作答，如在美國密蘇里州聖路易斯市，美國大學聯盟的主席在聽到三世多杰羌佛對校長們和教授博士們所提問題的即席回答後，激動之下當著十幾位大學校長、教授、博士的面打自己耳光，說：聽了三世多杰羌佛的開示回答，深受教益，我真是白活了幾十年。我們要知道，宇宙之大，無邊無際，無始無終，無有窮盡，是什麼樣的人竟敢說『在宇宙間沒有回答不了的問題』呢？而且公開發願給聖凡兩眾五年的時間提問。這到底是什麼

人才有如此高的道量、成就呢？人類怎麼會有這樣的超萬能知識？但這又不是虛構的，而且事實又證實了當時的雲高大師無所不通的證量、成了鐵的事實！這是普通聖者嗎？這絕不是普通菩薩，而是一個謎。那麼這位聖德到底是誰？天上來的嗎？還是從佛土來的呢？**問到三世多杰羌佛這個問題時，他處處說是最慚愧的，而且自始至終，從來沒有向任何人宣說過他前世是什麼聖者，他總是說來明信因果、說真如，是大眾的服務員，是普通的一般修行人。但是，僅從擺在面前的實實在在的成就來看，世界上又確實找不到一個人能做到三世多杰羌佛僅擺在面前的成就的一半！如果有人對此持懷疑態度，那麼有一個非常簡單的辦法：我們歡迎任何人來打破這個紀錄。只要有人能做到三世多杰羌佛的十五大類的成就，那我們相信他同樣是佛陀降世。任何人都知道，一般人的本事怎麼能勝於高僧、大仁波且、大和尚、大德的聖者們呢？難道顯密俱通、精深五明、具足大智慧之人屬於普通的一般修行人，反而不通顯密、不具五明、最好是一明都不懂、智慧低下之人才是佛菩薩嗎？佛陀的佛法難道是讓有道之人成愚笨、而把無道凡夫歸類為最智慧嗎？可是佛陀教法的真理是證境證德地位越高，智慧的展顯就越高，正如佛陀是為大覺能仁，即是智慧高到了無所不能之覺位。**這是我們凡夫都能想到和理解的問題，聖者們還用得著去想嗎？如果聖者們都還要去想這個問題的話，那真是一種笑話了，那還叫什麼聖者呢？三世多杰羌佛的『玄妙彩寶雕』成了世界上無人能複製的聖品，我們想一下，如果是釋迦牟尼佛做的話，能做得了嗎？佛陀是無所不能的，沒有什麼做不了的，這對佛陀來說自然是隨手一揮，你說對嗎？那麼觀音、文殊菩薩做得了嗎？當然也不在話下。你總不能否認佛陀和大摩訶薩們的智慧連這一點都做不到吧？如果這一點證量都沒有，能說他是佛陀、觀音、文殊、普賢菩薩再來轉世嗎？難道我們說佛陀和大菩薩們做不了這些嗎？那麼反過來說，我們總不能說做得了的人證量低、智慧低，而做不了的人證量高、智慧高吧？比如有一個大石頭，我們總不能說抱得起它的人氣力小，而抱不動它的人氣力大吧？這是一樣的道理。

　　理雖如此說，但是，雲高大師到底是誰降世呢？為什麼無所不答、無所不通、有這麼多的頂級成就呢？為什麼他創造的一些東西任何人照著做都做不了呢？這答案確實是永遠揭不開的謎底。隨著時間慢慢過去了，就在這無法解答之際，世界上的第一流大成就者的聖僧法王們見到了《正法寶典》，一時轟動，互相傳觀，佛菩薩轉世的大聖德們入定的入定，修法的修法，深入觀照，公佈了早就被尊勝大法王（大日如來之化顯）認證為金剛總持的雲高益西諾布的來歷，聖僧們經過嚴格修法，深入法界入定、觀照，見到了真源，原來這大聖德是維摩詰第二世、多杰羌佛第三世，他們寫下了法定的確認書：義雲高大師就是多杰羌佛第三世，是顯密兩宗、大小諸乘的至高古佛，是阿彌陀佛等五方五佛及金剛薩埵大摩訶薩的上師，即是當今法界的大教主頂聖如來雲高益西諾布！正因為多杰羌佛第三世雲高益西諾布頂聖如來是多杰羌佛的完整真身直接降世，與以百千萬化身來到這個世界的其他佛菩薩們不同，故所以在當今世界所展示的顯密圓通、妙諳五明，確實無有其他聖德辦得到，高僧法王們在文中讚嘆說：三世多杰羌佛是在佛教史上唯一將五明一項一項實實在在展顯在眾生面前的最高第一巨聖。正如尊勝大法王在授記中說明了雲高益西諾布頂聖如來的證覺是當今在這世界上任何高僧大德都無與倫比的，並且立下願言：『任何人或聖者若能仿製雲高益西諾布所創的神玄雕寶，就算尊勝大法王的授記是欺世騙人的。』（神玄雕寶是為色韻玄皇、神秘石霧等韻雕之作）。

　　在這個世界上佛制規定，唯獨只有兩位大聖所說的法立之為經，一位是釋迦牟尼佛，另一位就是維摩詰聖尊，除此之外，無論是什麼菩薩所說的法，都只能稱論，而不能列之為經。有人說慧能說《壇經》，其實，這是世人不明佛制規立而誇大讚稱的名，六祖比許多菩薩的地位都低，比如彌勒菩薩是下一屆龍華會上的佛，比慧能的地位高得太多了，但是彌勒菩薩所說法也不能稱經，而只能立論，如《瑜伽師地論》。維摩詰聖尊是在釋迦牟尼佛時代降世的，他是唯一以古佛應化居士現身說法的。釋迦牟尼佛當時，除了直接教導四眾弟子之外，尚有難於教化、不願發大乘菩提心的五百比丘，為了因緣善巧教化所有的出家人和尚們和八千菩薩，應其因緣由古佛多杰羌示現緣起轉由妙喜世界說法後，而化身成維摩聖尊出面協助佛陀教化僧寶、菩薩等弟子，原因是為了護持釋迦牟尼佛所傳的佛法。維摩聖尊的層次證量等同於釋迦牟尼佛無二，但是他並不願意在人間登位另一位教主而造成分派、增加行人的我執，再鑒於釋迦牟尼在此娑婆世界成佛的緣起，自己則猶如古佛正法明如來化現觀世音菩薩一樣，又如七佛之師文殊菩薩相似，宣釋迦牟尼為佛，自己化顯菩薩的角色輔助釋迦佛。這一切都是為了利益眾生，如果同時有兩位地位一樣的佛陀出現，眾生則會產生世相分別，對佛法的發展、渡脫眾生是會有阻礙的。

其實，佛陀們並不在乎誰出來做教主，而是以何種形態對眾生最好，就以何種形態出現，一切皆以菩提心利益眾生。所以一般人無法看出維摩詰聖尊的證覺竟然是如此之高，是在釋迦佛陀之前的古佛之首多杰羌佛應世。但是，維摩聖尊所講的法與佛陀說的一樣是經，不是論，佛制中列為《維摩詰所說經》。這部經與釋迦牟尼佛所說經是同時誕生的，是非常重要的佛經，在佛教的大乘法中，包括小乘南傳的經典裡都依學《維摩詰所說經》。

在法界中維摩詰尊者是多杰羌佛降世，由於他是報身古佛，因此遍智、遍量、覺位高於一切菩薩，如經中記載，當釋迦佛陀讓未來佛彌勒菩薩帶隊前往維摩聖尊處問安時，彌勒白佛言：『世尊！我不堪任詣彼問疾。』彌勒菩薩對佛講出的原因是他曾為眾生說法時，被維摩聖尊為難、教化，由此彌勒菩薩不敢去。其他的菩薩們也都確定說維摩聖尊智慧太高，他們遠遠不足以堪任，怕被為難不敢前往，故最後由七佛之師、古佛文殊菩薩帶領諸菩薩、羅漢五百比丘等前往維摩聖尊處問疾。當時，維摩詰聖尊以廣大的神通和智慧幫助釋迦佛陀教化他們，其中維摩聖尊顯佛陀證量神通將妙喜世界諸有菩薩、羅漢、一切佛土包括無動佛全然搬至娑婆世界展示在佛弟子前時，妙喜世界的諸有菩薩都認為是無動佛把妙喜世界與諸菩薩搬到了人間，此時無動佛說：『非我所為，是維摩詰神力所作。』此時娑婆世界十四那由他人發阿耨多羅三藐三菩提心。能把如來佛搬動到另一世界的，這除了權威的古佛多杰羌佛，無論什麼菩薩也是無此證量的。釋迦佛陀在經中盛讚維摩詰聖尊說：『其有供養如是人者，當知則為供養於佛。其有書持此經卷者，當知其室即有如來。』佛陀已說明維摩詰聖尊就是如來佛。為什麼維摩詰有如此高的證覺，因為維摩詰就是金剛總持多杰羌佛，也是阿彌陀佛等五方五佛的上師、諸佛之師，曾化顯燃燈古佛，收釋迦牟尼佛為徒，多杰羌佛也是佛教顯密二宗各大教派之至高祖先、古佛、大教主。故所以當時證德證境智慧無敵於天下，釋迦佛陀的出家與在家的四眾一切弟子，包括菩薩們都虔心聽聞維摩詰聖尊的教化，維摩聖尊輔助釋迦佛陀升化了五百比丘、八千菩薩的成就，造就了無數菩提心量大菩薩。維摩詰第二世、多杰羌佛第三世即是雲高益西諾布頂聖如來，這是佛菩薩級的大聖法王們依法認定、是具合法法定文證的。

三世多杰羌佛，一出生時突然天空鼓聲齊鳴，天樂美妙，三道彩虹同時出現在虛空，中間一道藍色為主，右邊一道紅色為主，左邊一道白色為主，每道彩虹之間的間隔約四、五十米。生出來全身為深藍色，不見哭聲，而是當下開口說話，非常清楚地說：『我入此世，顯密圓通，妙展五明，比之知之。』語後無言，一如常態孩童。父母視為玄生異人，秘而不宣，此後直到三歲才開口說話。三歲那年，大日如來尊勝法王導學三藏，時教持多杰羌佛心咒七遍，小孩突然哈哈大笑，頓時展顯三身四智。尊勝大法王當下試其經律論三藏並密典，法王子小孩解如流水，無有不通，義理全證。大日如來尊勝法王賦授記曰：『多杰羌佛，三世來到。維摩尊聖，二下雲霄。法藏通達，四智圓妙。眾生怙主，無師可教。神玄雕寶，奇端絕妙。能取霧氣，雕品定持。展顯證量，高峰絕技。當世諸人，無聖可複。若仿不異，我言欺世。維摩雲高，金剛總持。佛降甘露，眾見空施。最益有情，古佛悲智。今說示言，以證授記。』並取法號為仰諤益智嘎丹赤巴，其意為法王子至高智慧的總教主。尊勝大日如來隨即又說：『娑婆世界末法時期，多有邪師魔類以假冒真，為辨真假，今授嚴記以為試考標鑒。記曰：於此娑婆世界中，五千年內無四身，三世羌佛獨一聖，無有二者再化身。法緣擬定考真佛，若有號稱真身臨，佛降甘露可見真，金瓶擇緣預報境，取業除障見分明，複製玄妙彩寶雕，信手拿霧石中存，五跡無缺是真身，多杰羌佛第四世。除此展顯五聖跡，無論何等掘藏聖，手足石上留凹印，諸般神通廣大等，斷非多杰羌佛身。若是古佛降凡塵，五試何難手上生。留得試題五跡境，後學見觀防冒稱。』雲高法王子教主五歲那年收第一位弟子，即是當年蓮花生大師隨行之弟子、亦為藏密寧瑪巴創始人素布切‧釋伽炯乃大師之四大尖端弟子之一的喜饒杰布、而今世被格魯巴加冠為大班智達的喜饒杰布尊者第二世。可是奇怪的是，雲高法王子收下這位弟子後，除了喜饒杰布在法王子身邊隨時見到他超人的奇妙本事以外，而世人都從此少有聽到法王子講到佛法了，乃至根本聽不到，法王子這一切表現猶如當年維摩聖尊一樣，諸教皆收，諸識皆納，亦如常人之態，學之不倦，無人知曉個理。時至十六歲，突然說《僧俗辯語》一法，伏藏後由慧永大師掘藏取出，並由仁清洛珠、索朗丹布二人上供大日如來尊勝益西諾布法鑒。尊勝益西諾布於四眾前親自宣講此《僧俗辯語》一法，講完後親自率四眾弟子對法跪拜，授記曰：「東方來了古佛。」認證為第三世多杰羌佛，授以頂聖如來，封號為仰諤雲高益西諾布，並謂之曰《僧俗辯經》然也。當然，在三世多杰羌佛的弘化渡生中，除了五歲時收徒喜饒杰布外，隨因緣的成熟，創建寧瑪派的釋伽炯乃大師座下的四大弟子都一一皈依到三世多杰羌佛的座下，如木雅迴扎、香格瓊哇、喜饒杰布。更有蓮花生大師的二十五大王臣之一的丹瑪‧翟芒尊者第二世也隨侍於頂聖如來，松讚干布的丞相祿東贊尊者第四世也拜在三世多杰羌佛的身邊，還有噶舉瑪蒼派創始人喜饒僧格轉世的巴登洛德尊者，有寧瑪巴運頓多吉白尊者嘎堵仁波且，還有覺域派當巴桑結祖師的大弟子達楚‧恒生尊者；阿底峽尊者的四大高峰弟子之一、噶當派的庫頓尊哲雍仲尊者；格魯派丹增諾日仁波且等紛紛拜在三世多杰羌佛的門下，還有阿寇拉摩女大尊者。連聞名西藏的香巴噶舉派大祖師唐東迦波菩薩也拜雲高益西諾布頂聖如來為師，更有幾位巨聖，如祇園精舍給孤獨長者轉世之大聖、釋迦佛陀的大弟子舍利弗和寧瑪巴創始人釋伽炯乃大祖師之轉世大聖仁者也都來到三世多杰羌佛的身邊，接承頂聖如來甚深法門。

從另一方面，我們僅從世俗的角度也能見到，三世多杰羌佛的學歷也是最高的，古文的四書五經全然讀習，而若以現代教育制度的讀書來說，從小學優秀生到大學的高級博士，從博士升華到美國著名大學的教授，任教六年，榮獲大學的特別褒獎，直至獲得英國皇家藝術學院兩百多年來唯一的『Fellow』。儘管如此，但在三世多杰羌佛的身上，這實在是微不足道的小兒科。而對他自己的真實身份，三世多杰羌佛卻內含不露，雖然無意之間流露出來的大智慧證量，為人們見到而深感驚嘆，但三世多杰羌佛從未談論過自己的來歷。有很多人向他咨詢傳承來歷，甚至行文求答，三世多杰羌佛總是說：『我不知道，我只有佛教，我是你們慚愧的服務員。』這在很多年的法音帶中隨時都可以聽到，久而久之，人們習慣了，也就認為這無非是一個善良智慧的人才而已。包括已成立十一年多、堪稱最了解他的義雲高大師國際文化基金會也不知道他的真實身份，只認為這是一位大學者、大德聖者，最多也不過是如達賴喇嘛和噶瑪巴那樣的佛教大法王而已，因此，當基金會的會長龍舟仁波且得知三世多杰羌佛的真實身份後，目瞪口呆，連聲說：『難怪，難怪，這哪裡是大法王能相提並論的！實在是玷辱、罪過啊。』

時間一天一天過去了，不知在什麼時候，人們發現雲高益西諾布無論何種學問技藝不需學，一看即通，信手拈來，而且當下便精，所作超越本有原物。到今天高僧法王們認證公佈了這一驚天聖訊，我們才知道，難怪是多杰羌佛真身維摩聖尊降世，故所以大日如來授記中說，現前哪裡找得到有超越三世多

杰羌佛的證量的聖德來作他的上師呢？就連當年的五百比丘、高僧大德、八千菩薩們都是他的教化對象，何況今朝。也正因為三世多杰羌佛是古佛再來，所以是『不分顯密，不論宗派，相應眾生，因機教化，佛陀教法，普皆弘揚』的無分教派的圓滿完整『佛屬派』的金剛總持大法王，普利一切眾生。三世多杰羌佛一直告誡大家：『在我的心中沒有派別之分，只有佛教。但是，任何一宗一派的法王、仁波且、阿闍黎，只要他們遵照佛陀的教導，根據眾生的因緣而自渡渡他，就是值得讚嘆的。』

三世多杰羌佛的弘法利生，在十一歲之前為三藏顯表期，十一歲至十五歲為噶舉法教密行期，時有度松淺巴法王子獅子吼宣法之稱。十五歲之後則為格魯教誡密行期，有宗喀巴大師應世之稱，此時，也同時為薩迦、寧瑪等諸派密典圓融密行期，有蓮花生大師身語意三身之稱。其實，大德們和世人的這些恭稱都不是三世多杰羌佛的真實身份，而真實身份是經過眾生因緣的成熟，佛陀、大菩薩法王們於不同法義，或於定中，或於進入法界中，各自觀照，親自真實所見真源，無誤統一地認證雲高益西諾布為古佛多杰羌佛再來，也就是維摩聖尊第二世、多杰羌佛第三世。對於三世多杰羌佛的降世，文殊菩薩化身的薩迦總教主**薩迦天津大乘法王**寫下認證說：『仰諤雲高益西諾布，是金剛總持多杰羌佛第三世。』著名的寧瑪大法王、龍欽寧提獨掌人**多智欽仁波且**在祝賀《正法寶典》一書時說：『這本書令人驚嘆和不可思議，超常地表現出了用語言能夠表達出來和語言所不能表達出來的佛法真諦。』寧瑪巴的總法王**貝諾法王**致信給仁波且們說：『經眾多大德高僧認證的第三世多杰羌佛仰諤雲高益西諾布弘揚佛行事業……成為有情眾生……獲得終極成佛的因緣。』龍薩娘波尊者轉世的**遍智法王降養龍多加參**在認證書中說：『義雲高大師是維摩詰（Vimalakirti）再來，即多杰羌佛（ཪྡོ་རྗེ་འཆང）第三世。』覺囊派總法王吉美多吉法王代表覺囊派恭祝多杰羌佛第三世雲高益西諾布：『其成就之高峰實乃幾千年來首次耀古騰今，為我佛光燦之楷模。』

格魯巴宗師宗喀巴大師的誕生地、著名的**塔爾寺**祝賀說：『金剛總持仰諤雲高益西諾布大師的……傑出成就，史無前例。』

寧瑪巴敏林崔欽法王的總秘書闊千仁波且代表**敏林崔欽法王**和敏珠林寺系發來賀信說：『雲高益西諾布多杰羌為所有眾生帶來福慧。』

寧瑪派北藏傳承掌教法王**達龍哲珠法王**祝賀說：『尊貴的

多杰羌佛第三世仰諤雲高益西諾布，具備佛陀正法。』

達賴喇嘛的上師、著名的**楚西法王**，同時也是藏傳佛教幾位法王和傳承持有者的根本上師，他恭賀金剛總持仰諤雲高益西諾布說：『三世多杰羌佛的《正法寶典》……將成為墮落六道深淵的每一位有情離苦得樂之因。』

薩迦派第二領袖**薩迦達欽法王**祝賀說：『許多大師讚頌多杰羌佛第三世雲高益西諾布和他的佛行事業的書——《正法寶典》』。

薩迦茶巴法王、達賴喇嘛的根本金剛上師**秋吉崔欽法王**祝賀說：『金剛總持（多杰羌）仰諤雲高益西諾布的……《正法寶典》……是正法的路標和利樂有情之門』。

觀音菩薩化身的噶舉四大攝政王之首位紅寶冠法王**夏瑪仁波且**敬賀文說：『尊貴的雲高益西諾布——持金剛第三世的……所有成就都是利益眾生的』。

噶瑪巴大寶法王的唯一攝政、國師、岡波巴祖師化身的**嘉察仁波且**則恭讚無比上師仰諤雲高：『為維摩詰第二世。真誠祈願能有緣見聞覺知《正法寶典》的芸芸眾生獲得徹知圓悟的遍智無上佛果！』

那諾巴尊者轉世的**夏珠秋楊仁波且**恭賀雲高至高頂聖如意寶法王說：『無上至尊第三世多杰羌佛您的《正法寶典》……是利益眾生的最高正法。』

名垂佛史、曾任印度、不丹、錫金、蒙古、東藏四大教派之教主，並稱為醫藥之父、橋樑之父、戲劇之父、渡船之父等的**唐東迦波菩薩（第十六世）**在美國舊金山華藏寺開法會時，於中展示佛法道量，見到三世多杰羌佛雲高益西諾布的證量證德，大驚，當下五體投地拜為師長。他在祝賀信中說：『雲高益西諾布……是五佛之師，在人類的佛教史上第一次展顯了顯密圓通、妙諳五明，這個佛教的目標是所有佛弟子都沒有達到的，但現在最終由雲高益西諾布達到了！』

發心終身位於山谷閉關、神通具足、威震雪域的格薩爾王化身**仁增尼瑪雄獅法王**則認證：『義雲高大師是多杰羌佛第三世。』

覺囊派法王**阿旺班瑪南杰法王**敬賀多杰羌佛第三世雲高益西諾布：『法界持金剛，身壽不變故，化顯上乘境，最勝大悲力。』

敏珠林寺**敏林堪欽仁波且**祝賀說：『尊貴的金剛總持第三世仰諤雲高益西諾布……的《正法寶典》順緣於佛法……已衰者令恢復，未衰者令增長。』

寧瑪敏珠林派耶喜措嘉佛母轉世的**康卓公主仁波且**來信祝賀說，非常感激雲高益西諾布多杰羌佛的《正法寶典》。

著名的佐欽**噶諾仁波且**祝賀說：『第三世金剛總持雲高益西諾布的《正法寶典》具足佛陀開示之正法。』

而藏漢兩地僧俗四眾無限景仰的大伏藏師**鄔堅喜饒喔修尊者**在確認書中寫到：『仰諤雲高益西諾布，是金剛總持ཚེ་ཆེན་轉世再來，曾幫釋迦佛陀教化五百比丘成大乘。』

創立敏珠林寺系的德德林巴不變金剛化身的大覺之聖**多杰仁增**也是當今很多大仁波且的上師，他在祝賀文中說：『雲高益西諾布是五佛之師多杰羌佛。』

寧瑪雪謙寺系的法王**雪謙仁波且**祝賀：『第三世多杰羌佛仰諤雲高如意寶聖者，為正法增長宏大而行，善哉！』

薩迦派仲薩欽哲的心子、根薩寺寺主**昂旺欽哲仁波且**長期閉關，具足神通，其修為譽滿雪域高原，他在祝賀信中說：『大教主雲高益西諾布：只有怙主多杰羌佛的智慧才能完成《正法寶典》！』

駐錫在印度的**第七世佐欽法王吉美洛哲汪波**祝賀說：『多杰羌雲高益西諾布的《正法寶典》利益所有有情眾生。』而駐錫在中國的**第七世佐欽法王旦增·龍多尼瑪**則恭賀三界有情怙主仰諤雲高益西諾布說：『《正法寶典》猶如如意寶般莊嚴古今中外所有文化典籍，開發和增長人類心靈的智慧之門。』

寧瑪東藏法王**仁青絨波巴絨波仁波且**禮讚雲高益西諾布說：『大師作為偉大報身佛陀再降人間，佛教宏法以來，今開眼初見，世界無雙，智慧高峰，多杰羌佛，渡生無量。』

綠寶冠噶瑪巴杰仲人寶法王則頂禮金剛總持仰諤雲高益西諾布：『金剛總持的《正法寶典》，乃是佛法最高智能的具體顯現。』

協慶寺為金剛亥母化身的**俊麥白瑪多吉仁波且**專門寫信禮敬三界法王仰諤雲高益西諾布三身四智：『大法王是將佛陀的開示以實際證量完整地展現在法界的第一聖，大法王是真正的金剛總持人天導師！』

代表達賴喇嘛全權掌管尼泊爾的格魯派佛教的**大堪布卡桑·嘉參**在賀信中說：『我堅信尊貴的持金剛雲高大師的作品將激勵所有的眾生從理論和修行兩個方面更好地理解佛法。』

著名的**藏夏仁波且**頂禮怙主、大教主多杰羌佛雲高益西諾布：『我們找到了我們至高無上的怙主多杰羌佛，讓所有眾生在此末法時代有了最終的依靠！』

　　密勒日巴祖師轉世、已八十高齡的雲登降措仁波且恭賀金剛總持的《正法寶典》說：『這一佛法大智慧的出現，前輩是沒有任何人做到了的，只有雲高益西諾布才做到了。』

　　著名的班達士登格勒嘉措仁波且說：『祈請偉大聖勝的三世多杰羌佛加持六道有情早證菩提，得聞《正法寶典》，圓滿無上正等正覺。』

　　在印度廣受恭敬、金沙江沿流人人敬奉的第六世白瑪榮珠仁波且則頂禮雲高益西諾布：『看到《正法寶典》，得悉多杰羌佛ᐞᐞᐞ怙主再次降臨人世間，真是我們莫大的幸福！』

　　第五世法臺俄巴活佛則代表仁波且們十分感謝至尊雲高益西諾布說：『至高無上的多杰羌佛給我們帶來了《正法寶典》。』

　　薩迦天津法王授予的大堪布楚稱曲培禮讚多杰羌佛第三世雲高益西諾布：『最聖獨有持金剛，八萬四千法總主，統攝釋教諸法門，初開法界報身境。』

　　著名的倉倉寺住持汪智土登晉美仁波且感謝至尊怙主多杰羌佛第三世雲高益西諾布：『至尊怙主把西藏四大教派及顯密佛法完美無缺地帶到我們這個世界上來。』

　　佛教真言宗高野山北美洲旭清澄總主教讚嘆金剛總持雲高益西諾布法王『在佛法上的巨大成就是世界上從來沒有見到過的，雲高益西諾布是真正的原始古佛來到此世界傳授如來正法。』

　　格勒桑布仁波且頂禮至高無上的仰諤雲高益西諾布：『大法王了徹宇宙萬物的因果實相，是真正佛史上在人間展顯顯密圓通、妙諳五明的第一巨聖！』

　　洛珠降措仁波且頂禮雲高益西諾布說：『有幸恭聞大教主仰諤雲高益西諾布的《正法寶典》，又一次見到真正的佛陀降世了。』

　　五明佛學院的大喇嘛仁珍仁波且頂禮讚嘆雲高益西諾布金剛大聖法王的成就『是驚人的，也是驚聖的！大法王就代表著佛法！』

　　此外，多珠仁波且、貢波活佛、襲成大堪布、彭措仁波且等等都分別寫信敬賀三世多杰羌古佛再來的成就，並衷心感謝三世多杰羌佛的加持。還有顯、密二宗的一些非常著名的大寺廟、當今的一些知名的仁波且都寫來了附議賀信，但鑒於眾生的因緣，本書沒有列入。

　　也正因為雲高益西諾布頂聖如來是整個法界佛教的大教主，是多杰羌佛的降世，所以在整個佛教歷史上所有的大聖者的轉世認證中，三世多杰羌佛是唯一獲得五項第一的古佛降世的總持古佛、最高佛教領袖：

1. 是佛史上得到各大教派的佛陀和大菩薩們認證、敬讚最多的巨聖（見認證祝賀）；

2. 是佛史上各大教派的佛陀和大菩薩們評價最高的巨聖（見認證祝賀的評定）；

3. 是在人類世界所降世的佛菩薩中地位最高的古佛巨聖（見認證祝賀的認定佛號第三世多杰羌佛）；

4. 是人類歷史上出現的顯密圓通、妙諳五明成就最顯赫的巨聖（參見三十大類）；

5. 表法把天空中的祥霧拿到雕刻的石洞中和玄妙雕藝之神聖，如尊勝大法王的授記。佛史至今任何轉世巨聖都沒有一人能做得到、複製得了（見本書第380頁鐵證事實）。

　　這些不是我們空洞玄說的，而是依據當今世界大聖德仁波且、法王高僧們的文證，站在因果業報的立場，以認真嚴肅的態度所講的真實負責的話。

　　為什麼佛菩薩們化身的教主、法王和仁波且們幾千年來第一次都一致說雲高益西諾布是當今世界第一最高巨聖呢？這不用想都會明白，因為他是三世多杰羌佛，加之他作出的成就，當今世界，哪一位智者或聖者做得了呢？就連做三十大類的一半，都找不到一個人能夠做得了，乃至就一件玄妙彩寶雕照著複製，也找不到一個人有此能力。更何況依於眾生因緣的成熟，三世多杰羌佛帶來了至高無上的現量大圓滿虹身成就法，凡是得到三世多杰羌佛此法灌頂的人，不需要經過幾天、幾月或幾年的修煉，而在傳法灌頂的當天就能證到虹身境觀。已經有有緣者接受了灌頂，如祿東贊尊者第四世、開初仁波且等大德從灌頂日開始，三時皆能住入法性光界中。因此，除了真正的多杰羌佛，還有哪一位有此證量呢？何況，早在佛陀在世時，維摩詰聖尊就是教化所有高僧大德菩薩們的導師，現在已被佛陀大菩薩級的法王們法定文書確認，仰諤雲高益西諾布就是維摩詰第二世，也就是多杰羌佛第三世。無論是從實際的證量上，還是從古佛的身份上，皈依境的供位排序上，這三者任鑒其一，多杰羌佛第三世雲高益西諾布頂聖如來都是諸佛菩薩、高僧大德之上的第一巨聖！

國際佛教僧尼總會

THE REAL MEANING OF THE FIVE VIDYAS
今 說 五 明 眞 諦

Traditionally, the vidyas are divided into the five major vidyas and the five minor vidyas. The five major vidyas are the silpakarmasthanavidya (craftsmanship vidya), the cikitsvidya (healing vidya), the sabdavidya (sound vidya), the hetuvidya (causality or Buddhist logic vidya), and the adhyatmavidya (inner realization vidya). The five minor vidyas are rhetoric, ornate diction, prosody, dramaturgy, and astronomy. Actually, the Five Vidyas are not that narrow. Everything in the universe can be classified into five aspects of brightness and darkness. To develop everything that is good in the universe and that benefits living beings is classified as "bright." That which confuses and is bad is classified as "dark." This is the real meaning of the Five Vidyas (Five Bright) of which the Buddha spoke.

Venerable Akou Lamo Rinpoche

(This text was translated from the Chinese text that follows.)

Wearing a dharma hat, Venerable Akou Lamo Rinpoche conducts a Dharma Assembly for rinpoches, dharma teachers, and laypersons.
戴法帽的阿寇拉摩仁波且在為活佛、法師們和居士們舉行法會

傳統五明學分大、小五明，大五明是工巧明、醫方明、聲明、因明、內明，小五明是修辭學、辭藻學、韻律學、戲劇學、星系學。實際上，五明不是這麼狹隘，而是將宇宙之萬有歸納為五個方面，稱之為五明、五暗，開敷出宇宙間一切美好的、利益眾生的概之為明，迷在昏沉、不祥的概之為暗，這才是佛陀的五明真諦。

阿寇拉摩仁波且

（此文的英文翻譯印在前面）

RECOGNITIONS IN ACCORDANCE WITH THE DHARMA

All of the monastics in our association were astonished when our association received recognition certificates and congratulatory messages sent by H.H. Great Vehicle Dharma King Sakya Trizin, the supreme leader of the Sakya order; H.H. Dharma King Dodrupchen, the supreme leader of the Longchen Nying-thik; H.H. Dharma King Penor, the supreme leader of the Nyingma sect; H.H. Dharma King Omniscience Jamyang Lungdok Gyaltsen Achuk; H.H. Dharma King Jigme Dorje, the supreme leader of the Jonang sect; H.H. Dharma King Trulshik; H.E. Dharma King Chogye Trichen; H.E. Sharmapa Rinpoche, the Red Jewel Crown Regent Dharma King; H.E. Goshir Gyaltsab Rinpoche, the Orange Jewel Crown Regent Dharma King and National Master; H.E. Xiazhu Qiuyang Rinpoche; H.E. Mighty Lion Dharma King Renzeng Nima; H.E. Dharma King Ngagwang Pedma Namgyal Palzangpo; H.E. Jetsun Khandro Rinpoche; H.E. Dzogchen Ganor Rinpoche; H.E. Urgyen Xirao Woxiu; H.E. Dorje Rinzin Rinpoche; H.E. Dharma King Shechen Rabjam; Venerable Angwang Khyentse Rinpoche; H.E. Dzogchen Dharma Kings; H.E. Eastern Tibet Dharma King of the Nyingma sect; H.E. Karmapa Green Jewel Crown Dharma King; Venerable Junmai Baima Dorje Rinpoche, and other holy dharma kings and rinpoches recognizing the identity or status of H.H. Dorje Chang Buddha III Wan Ko Yeshe Norbu Holiest Tathagata. The monastics in our association could not understand how H.H. Dharma King Omniscience Achuk and those other persons of holy virtue were qualified to recognize the highest ancient Buddha, H.H. Wan Ko Yeshe Norbu.

Eminent monastics informed us that H.H. Lama Achuk, H.H. Dharma King Renzeng Nima, and H.E. Urgyen Xirao issued their recognitions in addition to the recognition issued by H.H. Mahavairocana Tathagata. We learned from their recognition certificates that their recognitions were not based upon understanding derived through normal investigation. Rather, they reached their conclusions by deeply entering the dharmadhatu and applying supernatural vision in accordance with the strict and holy dharma of Tibetan Buddhism for determining the incarnation of rinpoches. The documents they issued were in conformity with solemn dharma rules. They are undoubtedly Buddhas or Bodhisattvas. Knowing that they are Buddhas or Bodhisattvas, we now know their relationship to H.H. Dorje Chang Buddha III. Buddha Vajradhara is the Master of the Five Buddhas and the first Buddha with form in the entire dharma realm. It is not possible to find a Buddha who is higher than Dorje Chang Buddha. Thus, only other Buddhas and Mahasattvas can recognize a being as Dorje Chang Buddha since there is no ancient Buddha higher than Dorje Chang Buddha in the entire dharmadhatu!

We specially requested a discourse on this matter from H.H. Dorje Chang Buddha III Wan Ko Yeshe Norbu. H.H. Dorje Chang Buddha III said that He could only speak the truth. His Holiness said that there were two things that should be relied upon and two things that should not be accepted. The Buddhas and Mahasattvas have completely renounced all false, erroneous, and meaningless speech. Otherwise, they would not be Buddhas or Mahasattvas. Thus, the first thing that should be relied upon is the words of Buddhas or Mahasattvas. If dharma kings and rinpoches of great holiness in our world today are not Buddhas or Bodhisattvas, then there is no Buddhism in this world. Thus, the second thing that should be relied upon is those Buddhas and Bodhisattvas. Only ordinary people have a penchant for speaking falsely. Thus, the first thing that should not be accepted is the false recognitions of ordinary people. Demons deceive and confuse living beings. Thus, the second thing that should not be accepted is anything to do with demons. With that brief teaching, H.H. Dorje Chang Buddha III cut right to the core of the truth. If dharma kings, a national master, and regent dharma kings are not Buddhas or Bodhisattvas, then Buddhism truly does not exist on this earth.

However, we were unable to understand which Buddhas or Bodhisattvas H.H. Dharma King Sakya Trizin, H.H. Lama Achuk, and the others are incarnations of after all. In order that the monastics in our association could understand more precisely and definitively the reincarnated identities of H.H. Great Vehicle Dharma King Sakya Trizin and the others, we respectfully invited H.H. Dorje Chang Buddha III Wan Ko Yeshe Norbu Holiest Tathagata to recognize them by identifying which beings of holy virtue they are reincarnations of. H.H. Dorje Chang Buddha III said that He is just an ordinary person and that He does not have the ability to discern the identities of rinpoches. We tried our utmost to explain to H.H. Dorje Chang Buddha III this wish that everybody had, but His Holiness continued to deny that He had the realization to recognize their reincarnated identities. Thus, His Holiness rejected our request in a very firm tone of voice. All we could do was return to our association without accomplishing our goal.

However, there was more and more discussion in society as to whether those people were qualified to recognize the identity of Dorje Chang Buddha. There were even people who said that it was quite ridiculous for those "so-called" dharma kings and rinpoches to recognize the identity of Dorje Chang Buddha. Those people thought it was ridiculous that those dharma kings and rinpoches regarded themselves as persons of great holiness who could see past and future lives. Thus, those people questioned the supernatural powers that those dharma kings and rinpoches relied upon to discern the identity of Dorje Chang Buddha.

The opinions of all these people became as loud as thunder. Their groundless assertions brought a great deal of pressure upon us as they continued to sully the good roots of Buddhist disciples. It was only right that our International Buddhism Sangha Association provide to everyone an answer to this question. We therefore asked some rinpoches from around the world to look into and discuss this matter. We wanted them to affirm whether or not those holy persons of great virtue who recognized the identity of H.H. Dorje Chang Buddha III were truly Buddhas or Bodhisattvas. The result was that different reincarnated identities were recognized for each of those holy rinpoches of great virtue. Take, for example, H.H. Dharma King Sakya Trizin. Some said that he is the incarnation of Manjushri Bodhisattva. Some said he is the incarnation of Kuan Yin Bodhisattva. Some said he is the incarnation of Vajrasattva. Some said he is the incarnation of Amitabha Buddha. Some said he is the incarnation of Guru Padmasambhava. Some said his is the incarnation of Patriarch Naropa, and so on. A unanimous conclusion could not be drawn.

Therefore, we again paid our respects to H.H. Dorje Chang Buddha III. We explained this impure karma that was taking place in society and how the good roots of living beings had been damaged as a result. We expressed our hope that His Holiness would save everyone. At this time, H.H. Dorje Chang Buddha III said, "This is the way living beings are. The identities of those rinpoches were recognized a long time ago. What is the need for more recognitions? Since the situation has come to this, I, an ordinary person, will tell you my views on their identities."

We then took out a list of the names of 108 dharma kings and rinpoches. After H.H. Dorje Chang Buddha III read the list once, His Holiness gave His views on the identities of twelve dharma kings and rinpoches that were on the list. On that very auspicious morning at about eleven o'clock, we recorded on paper the true reincarnated identities of those twelve dharma kings and rinpoches. H.H. Dorje Chang Buddha III precisely and definitively recognized them. H.H. Dharma King Sakya Trizin was recognized as the nirmanakaya of Manjushri Bodhisattva. H.H. Dharma King Pema Norbu was recognized as the nirmanakaya of Vajrapani Bodhisattva. H.H. Dharma King Dodrupchen was recognized as the nirmanakaya of Guru Padmasambhava. H.H. Dharma King Omniscience Jamyang Lungdok Gyaltsen was recognized as the incarnation of venerable Longsal Nyingpo. H.H. Dharma King Jigme Dorje was recognized as the incarnation of the Shambhala King Suchandra. H.H. Dharma King Trulshik was recognized as the nirmanakaya of Maitreya Bodhisattva. H.E. Mighty Lion Dharma King Renzeng Nima was recognized as the nirmanakaya of King Gesar. H.E. Urgyen Xirao Woxiu was recognized as the incarnation of the great terma master Urgyen Lingpa. The Red Jewel Crown Regent Dharma King H.E. Shamarpa Rinpoche was recognized as the nirmanakaya of Kuan Yin Bodhisattva. The Orange Jewel Crown Regent Dharma King and National Master H.E. Goshir Gyaltsab was recognized as the incarnation of Patriarch Gampopa. H.E. Dorje Rinzin Rinpoche was recognized as the incarnation of Rigzin Terdak Lingpa Unchanging Vajra. H.E. Xiazhu Qiuyang Rinpoche was recognized as the incarnation of Patriarch Naropa.

When we again paid our respects to H.H. Dorje Chang Buddha III, His Holiness granted our request and, randomly selecting the names of some dharma kings and rinpoches from the list that we brought, made the following recognitions. H.E. Dharma King Ngagwang Pedma Namgyal Palzangpo was recognized as the incarnation of Duqing Langwa. H.E. Jetsun Khandro Rinpoche was recognized as the incarnation of Holy Mother Yeshe Tsogyal. H.E. Dharma King Rabjam was recognized as the incarnation of Shechen Rabjam Rinpoche. H.E. Junmai Baima Dorje Rinpoche was recognized as the nirmanakaya of Vajravarahi. Because there were so many people on the list, H.H. Dorje Chang Buddha III pointed to the names of some famous dharma kings and rinpoches and said that they are incarnations of rinpoches. Among those names were H.E. Dzogchen Ganor Rinpoche; Venerable Angwang Khyentse Rinpoche; H.E. Jigme Losel Wangpo, the Dzogchen Dharma King (residing in India); H.E. Tenzin Longdock Nyima, the Dzogchen Dharma King (residing in China); H.E. Renqing Rongbo Barongbo Rinpoche, an eastern Tibetan Dharma King of the Nyingma sect; H.E. Karmapa Green Jewel Crown Dharma King; Venerable Kalsang Gyaltsen; Venerable Zangxia Rinpoche; Venerable Yundeng Jiangcuo Rinpoche; Respected Banda Tudeng Gele Gyatso Rinpoche; Respected Baima Rongzhu Rinpoche; Respected the fifth Eba Rinpoche; Respected Khenpo Chucheng Qupei; Respected Wangzhi Tudeng Jinmei Rinpoche; Respected Bishop Seicho Asahi, the supreme leader of the Koyasan Shingon-shu North American Mission of Buddhism; Gele Sangbu Rinpopche; Luozhu Jiangcuo Rinpoche; Lama Renzhen Rinpoche; Duozhu Rinpoche;

Gongbo Rinpoche; Great Khenpo Gongcheng; Pengcuo Rinpoche and others.

We took out the list of recognitions made by other rinpoches and compared them with the recognitions of H.H. Dorje Chang Buddha III. Because some of the recognitions of other rinpoches differed from those of H.H. Dorje Chang Buddha III, we found it difficult to determine which recognitions were true. Thus, members of our association met to discuss this matter. In the end we decided to respectfully ask H.H. Dorje Chang Buddha III to use the Drawing Lots From a Golden Vase Dharma to set the matter to rest. However, after our many explanations, H.H. Dorje Chang Buddha III politely and humbly said that He did not have the realization to perform the Drawing Lots From a Golden Vase Ceremony. All of us knew that holy dharma kings recognized the identity of H.H. Dorje Chang Buddha III and wrote congratulatory messages corroborating those recognitions. Still, His Holiness said that such recognitions and congratulatory messages were flattery from dharma kings and rinpoches to an ordinary person. We then stated to His Holiness: "If it were just a matter of flattery, why did each of those persons of holy virtue identify His Holiness as Dorje Chang Buddha III? Holy people speak the truth. Could it be that those people of holy virtue who speak the truth engaged in flattery? We believe that they are people of great holiness and virtue and that they act responsibly toward living beings. They would definitely not act irresponsibly by carelessly speaking or recklessly writing documents so as to deceive living beings." H.H. Dorje Chang Buddha III replied, "You have spoken very well. It is absolutely correct that they are people of great holiness and virtue. I am Dorje Chang III. Dharma Kings would not recklessly write documents. However, I am an ordinary person. I am not capable of performing the Drawing Lots From a Golden Vase Ceremony."

Since we truly were unable to persuade His Holiness to perform that ceremony, we returned to the temple to discuss the matter with rinpoches. Everyone was of the view that H.H. Dorje Chang Buddha III must be the one who draws the lots. If the greatest holy being in the world today, the Holiest Tathagata, does not have the realization to draw lots from a golden vase, then no other holy being can be found in the entire world who does. Thus, we again paid our respects to H.H. Dorje Chang Buddha III. After we prostrated to His Holiness but before we said anything, His Holiness said, "Eminent monastics and practitioners of great virtue, is it all right with you that I be at peace for a while? No matter what you say, I will not perform the Drawing Lots From a Golden Vase Ceremony. You wanted me to recognize those people, and I gave you my views on their identities. Still, you do not stop. You are going too far." There being no way to convince His Holiness, our association decided to invite H.E. Gar Tongstan IV to draw the lots from a golden vase. H.E. Gar Tongstan IV is a highly accomplished rinpoche who together with another rinpoche used dharma water to bathe the Buddha by tilting a 4,260-pound lotus tub filled with water, causing the water to pour into another tub.

We held a month-long dharma assembly in which we recited sutras, chanted mantras, and practiced rituals. At the final stage, we listed together on large boards the results of the recognitions done by other rinpoches and

dharma kings with those done by H.H. Dorje Chang Buddha III. Because H.H. Dorje Chang Buddha III is the highest and holiest Tathagata, three minutes before the lots were drawn from a golden vase we circled in red the numbers on the boards that corresponded to the reincarnated identities recognized by H.H. Dorje Chang Buddha III. We did not circle any numbers on the boards that corresponded to the reincarnated identities recognized by other rinpoches or dharma kings. We then used a red cloth to cover all of the boards. No one knew what numbers on the boards were circled in red other than the person who drew the circles. This included H.E. Gar Tongstan IV, who would ascend the dais to draw the lots. However, it was announced to everyone that the numbers with a red circle around them indicated the reincarnated identities recognized by H.H. Dorje Chang Buddha III. Under the watchful eyes of all attendees, three groups composed of different nuns, dharma teachers, and rinpoches each performed different functions separately to seal and sheathe the lots. Each lot was measured, and everyone could see that the length, size, and color of each lot were exactly the same. After the lots were sheathed in yellow-golden silk sheaths during the third phase, nobody knew the number that corresponded to any particular lot, including those who sheathed the lots.

At that Drawing Lots From a Golden Vase Ceremony, the reincarnated identities of twelve people of great holiness were recognized. The reincarnated identity of the first person was recognized by drawing one lot from 120 lots. The reincarnated identity of the second person was recognized by drawing one lot from 119 lots. The reincarnated identity of the last person was recognized by drawing one lot from 109 lots. After all twelve lots were drawn but before the sheaths covering the lots were removed, the big red cloth covering the large boards was unveiled. For each of the twelve dharma kings and rinpoches, the number circled in red indicating his reincarnated identity recognized by H.H. Dorje Chang Buddha III was revealed for all to see along with the reincarnated identities recognized by other dharma kings and rinpoches. At this time, the process of removing the sheaths from the twelve lots and taking out the number inside each of those twelve lots began in front of all the attendees, with the entire process videotaped. The number inside each of the twelve lots that were drawn matched exactly the number circled in red on the boards, which was the true reincarnated identity recognized by H.H. Dorje Chang Buddha III with respect to each of those twelve dharma kings and rinpoches! The results were completely accurate without even one discrepancy between the lots drawn and the circled numbers on the boards!

At this time, the remaining 108 lots were also unsheathed and the numbers inside them were taken out in front of everyone. Those numbers were then arranged in numerical order from one to 120. All we can say is that the true Holiest Tathagata Dorje Chang Buddha III, who is the highest ancient Buddha in the dharmadhatu, lit a guiding lamp enabling living beings to know who are Buddhas and Bodhisattvas in the world today! H.H. Dorje Chang Buddha III Wan Ko Yeshe Norbu recognized which holy being each of those dharma kings and rinpoches was a true incarnation or nirmanakaya of. Such recognitions were the most excellent recognitions in the history of Buddhism.

In the second Drawing of Lots From a Golden Vase Ceremony, the identities of only four people of great virtue were recognized. The identities of all of the remaining rinpoches were already recognized by H.H. Dorje Chang Buddha III when His Holiness simply said that they were incarnations of rinpoches. Since His Holiness did not specifically state their past life identities, it was not appropriate to draw lots to determine such identities. The results of the drawing of lots for those four dharma kings and rinpoches were the same as the first drawing—the reincarnated identities recognized by H.H. Dorje Chang Buddha III were all correct since all of the lots drawn matched the reincarnated identities recognized by H.H. Dorje Chang Buddha III.

When faced with such Buddha-dharma realization, there is nothing that anyone can say. We all gave rise to the most sincere respect for those holy dharma kings who are incarnations of Buddhas and great Bodhisattvas. Although H.H. Dorje Chang Buddha III Wan Ko Yeshe Norbu did not participate in those ceremonies, His Holiness extended His wishes that all of them live in the world a long time, that they forever turn the wheel of the dharma, and that they fulfill their wish of benefiting the countless living beings by enabling such living beings to become Buddhas.

In order to thank those dharma kings and rinpoches who recognized and corroborated the identity of H.H. Dorje Chang Buddha III, we sent out letters and dispatched people to them. Those dharma kings and rinpoches personally wrote back to us. We were very moved by this.

All of the monastics in our association again pray that H.H. Great Vehicle Dharma King Sakya Trizin; H.H. Dharma King Dodrupchen; H.H. Dharma King Penor; H.H. Dharma King Omniscience Jamyang Lungdok Gyaltsen; H.H. Dharma King Jigme Dorje; H.H. Dharma King Taklung Tsetrul; H.H. Dharma King Trulshik; H.E. Sharmapa, the Red Jewel Crown Regent Dharma King; H.E. Goshir Gyaltsab, the Orange Jewel Crown Regent Dharma King and National Master; H.E. Xiazhu Qiuyang Rinpoche; H.E. Mighty Lion Dharma King Renzeng Nyima; H.E. Dharma King Ngagwang Pedma Namgyal Palzangpo; H.E. Mindrolling Khenchen Rinpoche; H.E. Jetsun Khandro Rinpoche; H.E. Dzogchen Ganor Rinpoche; H.E. Urgyen Xirao Woxiu; H.E. Dorje Rinzin Rinpoche; H.E. Dharma King Shechen Rabjam; H.E. Dzogchen Dharma Kings; and other holy monastics who are Buddhas and Bodhisattvas will forever live in this world and forever turn the wheel of the dharma.

International Buddhism Sangha Association

(This text was translated from the Chinese text that follows.)

如 法 的 認 證

當我會收到薩迦總教主薩迦天津大乘法王、龍欽寧體總教主多智欽法王、寧瑪總教主貝諾法王、降養龍多加參阿秋遍智法王、覺囊總教主吉美多吉法王、楚西法王、秋吉崔欽法王、夏瑪巴紅寶冠攝政王、嘉察巴橙寶冠攝政國師、夏珠秋楊仁波且、雄獅法王仁增尼瑪、阿旺班瑪南加法王、康卓公主仁波且、噶諾仁波且、鄔堅喜饒喔修尊者、多杰仁增仁波且、冉江法王、昂旺欽哲仁波且、佐欽法王、寧瑪東藏法王、噶瑪巴綠寶冠法王、俊麥白瑪多杰仁波且等聖者法王、仁波且們對多杰羌佛第三世雲高益西諾布頂聖如來的確認認證書和賀文時，全體僧眾為之震驚，對阿秋遍智法王他們這些聖德認證雲高益西諾布，有僧眾感到無法理解，疑問他們怎麼會有這個資格認證至高古佛呢？有高僧們卻說：阿秋喇嘛、仁增尼瑪法王與鄔堅喜饒尊者是在大日如來的認證之外再次認證的，從他們的認證書中得知，他們不是依靠調查了解作的認證，而是以嚴肅的西藏活佛轉世聖法，深入法界觀照之後得到的結論並出的認證書，這是嚴肅合法的法定文憑。他們是佛菩薩無疑，知道是佛菩薩，就看到了三世多杰羌佛與他們是什麼關係了，金剛總持是五佛之師，是法界中第一位具有形象的佛陀，如果要找比多杰羌佛高的佛陀，是不成立的，因此只能由其他的佛陀和摩訶薩來認證，因為整個法界中沒有更高的古佛！我們特地請示多杰羌佛第三世雲高益西諾布頂聖如來，三世多杰羌佛說：我只能如實地說，有二依二不取，佛陀和摩訶薩是斷盡妄語、戲論的，否則即非佛菩薩，一應依；當今世界的大聖法王、仁波且們都不是佛菩薩的話，這個世界就沒有佛教了，二應依。只有凡夫易打妄語，一不取；妖魔誑惑眾生，二不取。三世多杰羌佛數語道破真禪機，如果說各大教派的法王、國師、攝政都不是佛菩薩，那這個地球上

確實就沒有佛教了。

但是，我們感到不明白的是，薩迦天津法王和阿秋喇嘛等他們到底是什麼佛菩薩呢？為了讓僧眾們了解大乘法王他們更加確切的轉世身份，我們敬請多杰羌佛第三世雲高益西諾布頂聖如來公眾認證他們是什麼聖德轉世，三世多杰羌佛說：他是一個慚愧之身，沒有本事看到仁波且們的身份。我們盡力地把大家的心願向多杰羌佛說明，但是，三世多杰羌佛照常說：我哪裡有這個道量認證啊。堅決的口氣就這樣被否定了，我們只得無功而返。但是，社會上對於是否有資格認證多杰羌佛的言論愈來愈多，甚至於說：這些所謂的法王、仁波且竟然認證多杰羌佛，是很好笑的，把自己真的看成了大聖人，能看得見、能算得到前世來生，他們憑什麼神通看到多杰羌佛？眾聞可以成雷，這些謠言給我們非常大的壓力，其根本是讓佛弟子們的善根遭到了污染。我們國際佛教僧尼總會應該給大家一個答案，我們請了國際間一些仁波且們來研究討論，對認證第三世多杰羌佛的聖者大德們作確認，看看這些人是不是真的佛菩薩，每一位仁波且被認證出不同的轉世身份，比如對天津法王一人，有說他是文殊菩薩，有說是觀音菩薩，有說是金剛薩埵，有說是阿彌陀佛，有說是蓮花生大師，有說是那諾巴祖師，等等，答案是各說不一，結論統一不了。為此，我們再度拜見了三世多杰羌佛，給他說明了社會上發生的不淨業已造成破壞眾生的善根，希望救渡大家。這時，三世多杰羌佛說：眾生啦，就是這樣，這些仁波且們早都被認證了的，還搞什麼認證？既然這樣了，我這個慚愧者說一下我的看法吧。我們當時便拿出了108位法王、仁波且們的名單，三世多杰羌佛看了一遍後，便拿出了其中十二位法

王、仁波且們的名單，說出了他的看法。就在這大吉的上午十一時，我們便記載下了這十二位法王、仁波且們的轉世真身。三世多杰羌佛確切地認證：薩迦天津法王為文殊師利菩薩的化身；認證貝瑪諾布法王為金剛手菩薩的化身；認證多智欽法王為蓮花生大師的化身；認證降養隆多加參遍智法王為龍薩娘波尊者的轉世；認證吉美多吉法王為香巴拉國月賢王的轉世；認證楚西法王為彌勒菩薩的化身；認證仁增尼瑪雄獅法王為格薩爾王的化身；認證鄔堅喜饒喔修尊者為伏藏大師鄔堅林巴的轉世；認證紅寶冠攝政王夏瑪仁波且為觀世音菩薩的化身；認證橙寶冠攝政國師嘉察巴為岡波巴祖師的轉世；認證多杰仁增仁波且為不變金剛的轉世；認證夏珠秋楊仁波且為那諾巴祖師的轉世。

當我們再一次去拜見三世多杰羌佛的時候，三世多杰羌佛又根據我們的請求，從我們帶去的名單中隨手抽出一些法王、仁波且的名單，認證阿旺班瑪南加法王是督琴朗哇的轉世；認證康卓公主仁波且是益喜措嘉佛母的轉世；認證冉江法王是雪謙冉江仁波且的轉世；認證俊麥白瑪多杰是金剛亥母的化身。由於人數太多，三世多杰羌佛便指著名單上一些著名的法王、仁波且們的名字，如噶諾仁波且、昂旺欽哲仁波且、佐欽法王吉美洛哲汪波（駐印度）、佐欽法王旦增‧龍多尼瑪（駐中國）、寧瑪東藏法王仁青絨波巴絨波、噶瑪巴綠寶冠法王、Kalsang Gyaltsen、藏夏仁波且、雲登降措仁波且、班達土登格勒嘉措、白瑪榮珠仁波且、第五世俄巴活佛、汪智土登晉美仁波且、真言宗美洲主教旭清澄、格勒桑布仁波且、洛珠降措仁波且、楚稱曲培堪布、喇嘛仁珍仁波且、多珠仁波且、貢波仁波且、龔成大堪布、彭措仁波且等，說他們都是活佛的轉世。

我們把其他仁波且們所作的轉世認證一併拿出放在一起，由於其他仁波且們的一些認證與三世多杰羌佛的認證不相同，就造成了在裁決上的顧此失彼，難以定奪，因此，彙總研究，最後決議請三世多杰羌佛用金瓶掣籤來最後定奪。可是我們作了很多解釋，三世多杰羌佛就是很客氣謙虛地說：他沒有金瓶掣籤的道力。我們一致的意見是：三世多杰羌佛的身份是聖者法王們認證並附議祝賀的，可是他老人家卻說這是法王、仁波且們在褒獎一個慚愧者。我們提出：如果是褒獎，為什麼每一個聖德都認證成三世多杰羌佛呢？聖者們都是如語、實語，難道如語、實語的聖德還會用過獎之詞嗎？我們相信他們是大聖德、是對眾生負責的，他們絕對不會不負責任，信口開河亂寫文憑來欺騙眾生的。三世多杰羌佛說：你們說得很好，他們是大聖德，一點也沒有錯，我是三世多杰羌。法王們不會亂寫文憑，但是我也是一個慚愧之身，我做不來金瓶掣籤。在這種情況下，我們確實沒有辦法了，回到廟上，與仁波且們共商，大家的意見是一定得由三世多杰羌佛掣籤，如果當今最高第一大聖頂聖如來都沒有掣籤的道力，那麼全世界就再也找不到第二聖了。因此，我們又再次拜見了三世多杰羌佛，我們頂完禮還沒有說話，三世多杰羌佛就說：高僧大德們，你們讓我安靜一下好嗎？無論你們怎麼說，我是不會去搞金瓶掣籤的，你們要我作認證，我已經說了我的看法，你們還不罷休，太過份了吧。在這徹底沒有辦法的情況下，會裡決定只好敦請造詣高深、曾勝義取水浴佛的第四世祿東贊尊者作金瓶掣籤。

就這樣，進行了一個月的法會，誦經、持咒、修儀軌，最後把所有仁波且們的認證和三世多杰羌佛的認證排在一起，由於三世多杰羌佛是至高頂聖如來的身份，因此在作金瓶掣籤之前的三分鐘，我們便把他老人家認證的名單號碼劃上了紅圈，其他法王、仁波且們作的認證沒有劃圈，然後用紅布蓋起來。除了劃圈的一人之外，沒有任何人知道是第幾號劃了圈，包括登台掣籤的祿東贊尊者也不知道哪一條、哪一號劃了圈，但是公開宣佈了劃上圈的是第三世多杰羌佛作的認證。而且採用三組不同的比丘尼、法師和仁波且們在公眾監視下，各組做不同的封籤過程，互不參與，每支籤用尺度打量，公眾讓大家見到，其長短、大小、色澤一模一樣。當籤在第三道程序密封進黃綢袋中之後，這時所有的人包括密封籤的人，沒有一個人能知道哪一支籤是多少號。這一次金瓶掣籤共認證十二位大德，第一位被認證者是從120支籤中掣出一支，第二位被認證者是從119支籤中掣出一支，最後一位是從109支籤中掣出一支，十二支籤全部掣出後，在未揭開籤條的密封時，大紅布板首先落幕，三世多杰羌佛所認證的劃上紅圈的法王、仁波且們的轉世身份和號碼暴露在眾人的面前。此時，開始把密封的12支籤在眾人面前和攝影機的全程攝影之下拆開核對，三世多杰羌佛所認證的法王、仁波且們的真實轉世身份，十二位全部中籤，準確無誤，一支也沒有錯位！這時，再把剩下的108支籤也公眾打開，排起來以後從1號到120號。我們只能說，這才是真正的三世多杰羌佛頂聖如來法界第一最高古佛給眾生點上了拜見佛菩薩的指南明燈！第三世多杰羌佛雲高益西諾布認證了法王、仁波且們的真身轉世和化身再來，成了佛教史上最殊勝的認證。

第二次金瓶掣籤只認證了四位大德，因為其他由三世多杰羌佛認證的，三世多杰羌佛只說他們是活佛轉世，沒有前世的具體身份，故不便掣籤。對四位法王、仁波且的掣籤結果如同第一次一樣，三世多杰羌佛的認證準確無誤。

大家在佛法證量境前，無話可說，對佛陀和大菩薩轉世的聖者法王們生起至誠的恭敬。多杰羌佛第三世雲高益西諾布雖然沒有參與金瓶掣籤，但是他祝禱他們長久住世，永轉法輪，達成利益無邊眾生成佛心願。

為感謝法王、仁波且們認證、附議三世多杰羌佛的功德，我們分別去了信，也去了人，法王、仁波且們還親自給我們回函，這讓我們非常感動。

我會全體僧眾再次祈請薩迦天津大乘法王、多智欽法王、貝諾法王、降養陽龍多加參遍智法王、吉美多吉法王、達龍哲珠法王、楚西法王、夏瑪巴紅寶冠攝政王、嘉察巴橙寶冠攝政國師、夏珠秋楊仁波且、仁增尼瑪雄獅法王、阿旺班瑪南加法王、敏林堪欽仁波且、康卓公主仁波且、噶諾仁波且、鄔堅喜饒喔修尊者、多杰仁增仁波且、冉江法王、佐欽法王、等佛菩薩聖僧們長久住世，永轉法輪。

國際佛教僧尼總會

（此文的英文翻譯印在前面）

Different groups of monastics and rinpoches seal up the numbered lot slips.
分不同的幾組出家眾和仁波且們，正在密封牙骨籤

Under the observance of the seven types of Buddhist disciples, the first group of eight monastics began sticking numbered pieces of paper onto the ivory slips that would be inserted into the lots to indicate the number of each lot. All of those ivory slips were completely the same and had been thoroughly mixed up.
在七眾佛教徒的圍觀下，第一組八位出家人開始將編了號的籤號紙黏貼在完全同樣無差別而被混亂過的牙骨片上，成了籤號牌。

These are all of the 120 numbered lot slips after a number was stuck onto each of them. Their numbers started with 1 and went up to 120. No numbers were missing between 1 and 120. The dharma teachers placed them on a silver tray and are mixing them up by shaking them.
已經黏貼完的120片籤號牌，它們的號碼是從1號到120號，中間是連續的，沒有間斷。法師們放在銀盤中正搖動混亂。

All of the lots are placed flat between two straight boards. The length, size, texture, and color of all 120 lots were completely the same. Everyone is examining the lots to verify that they all are the same.
正在把大籤經兩條木排平在中央，120支大籤長短、大小、質地、色澤全部一樣，大家鑒證所有籤同樣沒有差別。

A second group of eight monastics is putting the numbered lot slips into the slit of each lot. After a numbered lot slip is put into a slit, the slit is immediately sealed with tape. Before this was done, all of the numbered lot slips were mixed up and all of the lots were also mixed up. They were then randomly divided and put onto several trays. After all of the numbered lot slips were put into all of the lot slits and sealed, satin sheaths were used to sheathe each lot. The monastics put the numbered lot slips into the lot slits by randomly picking up a lot, randomly picking up a lot slip, and inserting the lot slip into the lot slit. After the slip was inserted, the slit was immediately sealed with non-transparent tape. After each lot was sealed, all 120 lots looked exactly the same.
換上第二組八位出家人現在將籤號牌裝進大籤槽口裡面，當下貼上封條。裝籤的辦法是先將籤號牌和大籤各自混亂，隨意分成多盤，再用黃緞布密蓋。裝籤時隨意摸到哪一支大籤和任意一個籤號牌，即將此籤號牌裝進該大籤的槽口內，馬上用不透明的膠帶密封。所有密封後的120支大籤完全相同，沒有差別。

After all of the sealed 120 lots were mixed up, a third group consisting of ten rinpoches sheathed each of the identically-looking lots. This all the more made it impossible to determine the number of each lot.
將120支已經密封的大籤混亂後，再換上第三組十位仁波且把沒有差別的籤裝到籤套裡，這樣就徹底無法辨認哪一支籤是多少號了。

After going through four mixing phases and after going through a sealing process carried out by three different groups of dharma teachers and rinpoches, those 120 lots sheathed in yellow satin are now truly sealed lots that are completely indistinguishable.
120支籤經四道程序相互摻混，由三批不同的法師、仁波且分別密封完畢，現在這個裝進黃緞布套的籤完全成了密不可判的真正密封籤。

H.E. Gar Tongstan IV Ciren Gyatso Rinpoche draws lots one by one from the golden vase.
祿東贊尊者第四世慈仁嘉措仁波且從金瓶裡將籤一支一支的掣出

7

Venerable ones, rinpoches, dharma teachers, and greatly virtuous practitioners practiced the dharma amid the solemn chanting of sutras, the Manjushri Bodhisattva mantra, the Mahakala mantra, and the Kuan Yin Bodhisattva mantra. H.E. Gar Tongstan IV, a rinpoche of great holiness and virtue with profound cultivation, personally carried out the dharma of drawing lots from a golden vase. H.E. Gar Tongstan IV, a disciple of H.H. Dorje Chang Buddha III, did not participate in any of the processes in which the lots were sealed and sheathed. This is the golden vase from which the lots were drawn and the large precious urn in which the golden vase was put.

在嚴肅的誦經、持文殊菩薩、麻哈嘎拉、觀音菩薩的咒聲中，尊者、仁波且、法師、大德們助緣修法。由三世多杰羌佛的弟子、沒有參加過封籤的、道行高深的大聖德仁波且祿東贊尊者第四世，親自執法金瓶掣籤。這是掣籤用的金瓶和放置金瓶的寶瓶。

8

Lama Puti Duxi, who did not participate in any of the processes in which the lots were sealed and sheathed, puts lots into the golden vase.
由沒有參加過封籤的菩提度西喇嘛正將籤裝進金瓶中。

9

After putting lots into the golden vase, covering the golden vase with its lid, and shaking the golden vase, Lama Puti Duxi places the golden vase into the large precious urn.
菩提度西喇嘛將籤裝進金瓶後，蓋上金瓶的蓋子，搖混後，將金瓶正放入寶瓶中。

10

H.E. Gar Tongstan IV removes the lid from the golden vase to begin the holy dharma practice of drawing lots.
祿東贊尊者揭開了金瓶的蓋子，進入聖勝的執法掣籤。

11

H.E. Gar Tongstan IV draws a lot. The reincarnated identity of the first rinpoche was recognized by drawing one lot from 120 lots. The reincarnated identity of the second rinpoche was recognized by drawing one lot from 119 lots. The total number of remaining lots decreased by one each time a lot was drawn. The reincarnated identity of the last rinpoche (that is, the twelfth rinpoche to be recognized) was recognized by drawing one lot from 109 lots. The lots were drawn one by one, totaling twelve drawn lots.

祿東贊尊者正在掣籤。第一位被認證的仁波且是從120支籤中掣出一支，第二位是從119支籤中掣出一支，每掣出一支就少一支，最後一位（即是第十二位被認證者）就成了從109支籤中掣出一支。依次而擇，共掣出12支籤。

12

The twelve lots that were drawn were placed on a silver tray for all to see. The lots were still not opened.
12支籤已經掣出，放在大眾面前的銀盤中，尚未拆封。

After the curtain covering the large boards was unveiled, rinpoches compare the numbers on the lot slips removed from the drawn lots with the numbers circled in red on the boards indicating the reincarnated identities recognized by H.H. Dorje Chang Buddha III.
密封之幕布已落下，仁波且們正在將掣出開封後的籤牌號與認證號核對

Before the lot seals were opened, the cloth covering the large boards was lowered. For each of the twelve dharma kings and rinpoches, the number circled in red indicating his reincarnated identity recognized by H.H. Dorje Chang Buddha III was revealed on boards for all to see along with the reincarnated identities recognized by other various rinpoches of holy virtue. There were no red circles on the boards indicating the reincarnated identities recognized by those other rinpoches of holy virtue.
在未開啟籤的密封之前，這時首先落下幕布，板牌上出現了被認證的12位法王、仁波且被不同的聖德所作出的認證轉世身份，而三世多杰羌佛為他們認證的身份是用紅圈圈上了號碼的，其他仁波且所作出的認證沒有圈紅圈。

The numbers circled in red indicating the reincarnated identities recognized by H.H. Dorje Chang Buddha III with respect to all twelve dharma kings and rinpoches were revealed in front of the seven types of Buddhist disciples. After such identities were clearly known to everyone, the process of opening each of the twelve lots, removing the numbered slips from the lots, and checking to see whether the numbers on the slips matched the numbers on the board circled in red began. That process was carried out by rinpoches.
在三世多杰羌佛所作認證的所有圈了紅圈的號碼法王、仁波且們的轉世身份全部展現在七眾弟子的面前、大家都清楚知道以後，才開始將由仁波且開籤驗證、核對印證籤號和板牌上的號碼。

The process of opening the lots began. In front of everyone, rinpoches opened the twelve lots one by one. After each seal was removed, the numbered slip fell onto a silver tray. The numbers that fell out of the twelve lots were 6, 17, 25, 33, 41, 60, 70, 72, 84, 97, 108, and 115. Those numbers perfectly matched the numbers circled in red on the boards that indicated the reincarnated identities of those dharma kings and rinpoches recognized by H.H. Dorje Chang Buddha III. There was not one discrepancy between the slip numbers and the numbers on the board circled in red.
現在開籤驗證，12支籤在眾目睽睽之下由仁波且們將其一支一支地公眾倒在銀盤中，他們的號碼分別是6、17、25、33、41、60、70、72、84、97、108、115，與板牌上三世多杰羌佛認證法王、仁波且們的身份完全相同，一個也沒有錯。

Rinpoches opened all of the remaining 108 lots in front of everyone. The numbers on the lot slips were from 1 to 120 excluding the twelve numbers that had been drawn. The seven types of Buddhist disciples personally witnessed the entire process of drawing lots from a golden vase.
仁波且們將剩餘的108支籤全部公眾拆開，這些號碼正好是除去上面已經掣出的12支籤的號碼以外的108個連號的不同號碼。所有七眾佛弟子在現場親見了全部金瓶掣籤過程。

Rinpoches, dharma teachers, and laypersons who participated in the Drawing Lots From a Golden Vase Dharma Assembly.
參加金瓶掣籤法會的仁波且、法師、居士們。

Rinpoches, dharma teachers, and laypersons who participated in the Drawing Lots From a Golden Vase Dharma Assembly.
參加金瓶掣籤法會的仁波且、法師、居士們。

The numbers that were drawn from the golden vase match the numbers circled in red indicating the reincarnated identities recognized by H.H. Dorje Chang Buddha III.
金瓶掣出的籤號對應認證的身份號碼

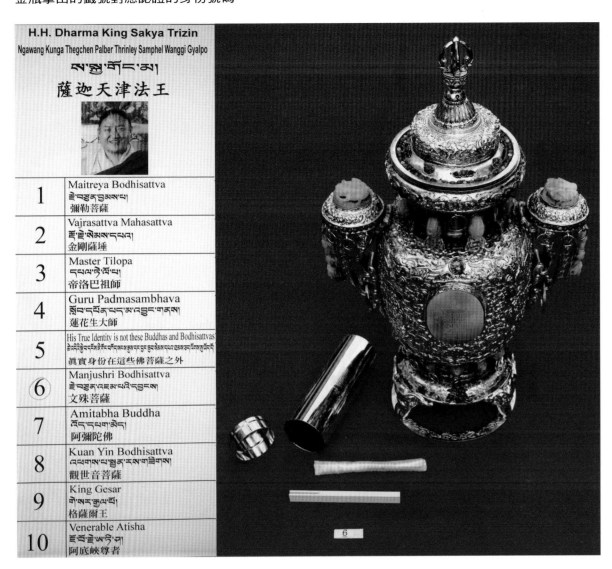

	H.H. Dharma King Sakya Trizin
	Ngawang Kunga Thegchen Palber Thrinley Samphel Wanggi Gyalpo
	薩迦天津法王
1	Maitreya Bodhisattva 彌勒菩薩
2	Vajrasattva Mahasattva 金剛薩埵
3	Master Tilopa 帝洛巴祖師
4	Guru Padmasambhava 蓮花生大師
5	His True Identity is not these Buddhas and Bodhisattvas 真實身份在這些佛菩薩之外
⑥	Manjushri Bodhisattva 文殊菩薩
7	Amitabha Buddha 阿彌陀佛
8	Kuan Yin Bodhisattva 觀世音菩薩
9	King Gesar 格薩爾王
10	Venerable Atisha 阿底峽尊者

6

鑒於有一部分人認為薩迦天津法王、貝諾法王、降養隆多加參遍智法王等著名聖德沒有資格認證、祝賀三世多杰羌佛，為化解這些人的疑慮，國際佛教僧尼總會特別邀請諸多法王、仁波且為薩迦天津法王、貝諾法王、多智欽法王、降養隆多加參法王等聖德們的真實身份作一決定性的確認認證。由於各位法王、仁波且對這些聖德們的身份認證結果不統一，國際佛教僧尼總會特如法舉行聖義現量金瓶掣籤以最終確定這些聖德們的真實身份。國際佛教僧尼總會經過為期一個月以文殊法為主體的修持，於2007年9月19日在美國舊金山華藏寺舉行金瓶掣籤，由祿東贊尊者第四世慈仁嘉措仁波且掣籤，在眾多尊者、仁波且、法師、大德居士等七眾弟子的觀禮誦經聲中，從120支密封的籤中掣出6號籤，並公開印籤無誤。該6號籤是三世多杰羌佛雲高益西諾布頂聖如來，認證薩迦天津法王是文殊菩薩的化身！上圖左邊是金瓶掣籤法會現場的巨大板牌，分別是法王、仁波且們對薩迦天津法王的身份的認證，圈了紅圈的身份號碼是三世多杰羌佛作的認證。上圖右邊是金瓶掣籤專用的金瓶、裝金瓶的寶瓶、金瓶蓋、黃色緞布籤套、掣出的籤以及6號籤牌。

There are those who thought that H.H. Dharma King Sakya Trizin, H.H. Dharma King Penor, H.H. Dharma King Omniscience Jamyang Lungdok Gyaltsen Achuk and other famous persons of great holiness were not qualified to recognize H.H. Dorje Chang Buddha III or send written congratulations regarding such recognition. In order to dispel such doubts, the International Buddhism Sangha Association specially invited many dharma kings and rinpoches to conclusively recognize the true identities of H.H. Dharma Sakya Trizin, H.H. Dharma King Penor, H.H. Dharma King Dodrupchen, H.H. Dharma King Omniscience Jamyang Lungdok Gyaltsen Achuk, and other persons of great holiness. Because those dharma kings and rinpoches did not unanimously agree on the identities of those persons of great holiness, the International Buddhism Sangha Association held the highest form of Drawing Lots From a Golden Vase Ceremony in complete accordance with the dharma. The purpose of that ceremony in which realization was openly manifested at the dharma assembly was to determine definitively the true identities of those persons of great holiness. Members of the International Buddhism Sangha Association practiced dharma for a one-month period prior to that ceremony, mainly focusing on the practice of Manjushri dharma. That Drawing Lots From a Golden Vase Ceremony was held on September 19, 2007 at Hua Zang Si in San Francisco of USA. H.E. Gar Tongstan IV Ciren Gyatso Rinpoche drew the lots. As many venerable ones, rinpoches, dharma teachers, laypersons of great virtue, and other types of Buddhists viewed the ceremony and chanted, the lot with the number 6 in it was drawn from among the 120 sealed lots. It was openly confirmed that lot number 6 corresponded to the number circled in red under the name and photograph of H.H. Dharma King Sakya Trizin. That number 6 lot indicated H.H. Dorje Chang Buddha III Wan Ko Yeshe Norbu Holiest Tathagata recognized H.H. Dharma King Sakya Trizin as the nirmanakaya of Manjushri Bodhisattva! The upper left shows a large board used at the Drawing Lots From a Golden Vase Ceremony on which is written the different identities of H.H. Dharma King Sakya Trizin recognized by dharma kings and rinpoches. The number with a circle around it indicates the identity recognized by H.H. Dorje Chang Buddha III. To the right is the golden vase used at the Drawing Lots From a Golden Vase Ceremony, the large precious urn used to hold that golden vase, the golden vase lid, the yellow satin sheath used to sheathe lot number 6, the lot that was drawn, and the number 6 ivory slip that was placed in that lot.

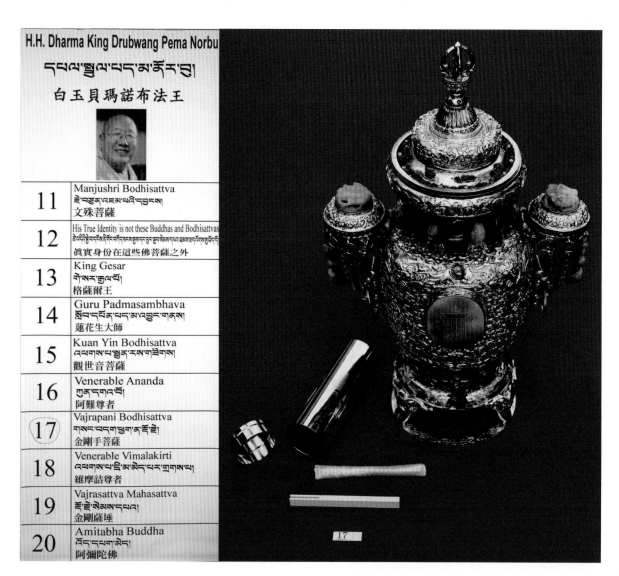

	H.H. Dharma King Drubwang Pema Norbu	
	དཔལ་ཡུལ་པད་མ་ནོར་བུ།	
	白玉貝瑪諾布法王	
11	Manjushri Bodhisattva འཇམ་དཔལ་གཞོན་ནུར་གྱུར་པ། 文殊菩薩	
12	His True Identity is not these Buddhas and Bodhisattvas ཁོང་གི་ངོ་བོ་དངོས་ནི་སངས་རྒྱས་བྱང་སེམས་འདི་དག་ལས་འདས་པ། 真實身份在這些佛菩薩之外	
13	King Gesar གེ་སར་རྒྱལ་པོ། 格薩爾王	
14	Guru Padmasambhava སློབ་དཔོན་པདྨ་འབྱུང་གནས། 蓮花生大師	
15	Kuan Yin Bodhisattva འཕགས་པ་སྤྱན་རས་གཟིགས་དབང་ཕྱུག 觀世音菩薩	
16	Venerable Ananda ཀུན་དགའ་བོ། 阿難尊者	
(17)	Vajrapani Bodhisattva གསང་བའི་བདག་པོ་ཕྱག་ན་རྡོ་རྗེ། 金剛手菩薩	
18	Venerable Vimalakirti འཕགས་པ་དྲི་མ་མེད་པར་གྲགས་པ། 維摩詰尊者	
19	Vajrasattva Mahasattva རྡོ་རྗེ་སེམས་དཔའ་ཆེན་པོ། 金剛薩埵	
20	Amitabha Buddha འོད་དཔག་མེད། 阿彌陀佛	

鑒於有一部分人認為薩迦天津法王、貝諾法王、降養隆多加參遍智法王等著名聖德沒有資格認證、祝賀三世多杰羌佛，為化解這些人的疑慮，國際佛教僧尼總會特別邀請諸多法王、仁波且為薩迦天津法王、貝諾法王、多智欽法王、降養隆多加參法王等聖德們的真實身份作一決定性的確認認證。由於各位法王、仁波且對這些聖德們的身份認證結果不統一，國際佛教僧尼總會特如法舉行聖義現量金瓶掣籤以最終確定這些聖德們的真實身份。國際佛教僧尼總會經過為期一個月以文殊法為主體的修持，於2007年9月19日在美國舊金山華藏寺舉行金瓶掣籤，由祿東贊尊者第四世慈仁嘉措仁波且掣籤，在眾多尊者、仁波且、法師、大德居士等七眾弟子的觀禮誦經聲中，從120支密封的籤中掣出17號籤，並公開印籤無誤。該17號籤是三世多杰羌佛雲高益西諾布頂聖如來，認證貝諾法王是金剛手菩薩的化身！上圖左邊是金瓶掣籤法會現場的巨大板牌，分別是法王、仁波且們對貝諾法王的身份的認證，圈了紅圈的身份號碼是三世多杰羌佛作的認證。上圖右邊是金瓶掣籤專用的金瓶、裝金瓶的寶瓶、金瓶蓋、黃色緞布籤套、掣出的籤以及17號籤牌。

There are those who thought that H.H. Dharma King Sakya Trizin, H.H. Dharma King Penor, H.H. Dharma King Omniscience Jamyang Lungdok Gyaltsen Achuk and other famous persons of great holiness were not qualified to recognize H.H. Dorje Chang Buddha III or send written congratulations regarding such recognition. In order to dispel such doubts, the International Buddhism Sangha Association specially invited many dharma kings and rinpoches to conclusively recognize the true identities of H.H. Dharma Sakya Trizin, H.H. Dharma King Penor, H.H. Dharma King Dodrupchen, H.H. Dharma King Omniscience Jamyang Lungdok Gyaltsen Achuk, and other persons of great holiness. Because those dharma kings and rinpoches did not unanimously agree on the identities of those persons of great holiness, the International Buddhism Sangha Association held the highest form of Drawing Lots From a Golden Vase Ceremony in complete accordance with the dharma. The purpose of that ceremony in which realization was openly manifested at the dharma assembly was to determine definitively the true identities of those persons of great holiness. Members of the International Buddhism Sangha Association practiced dharma for a one-month period prior to that ceremony, mainly focusing on the practice of Manjushri dharma. That Drawing Lots From a Golden Vase Ceremony was held on September 19, 2007 at Hua Zang Si in San Francisco of USA. H.E. Gar Tongstan IV Ciren Gyatso Rinpoche drew the lots. As many venerable ones, rinpoches, dharma teachers, laypersons of great virtue, and other types of Buddhists viewed the ceremony and chanted, the lot with the number 17 in it was drawn from among the 120 sealed lots. It was openly confirmed that lot number 17 corresponded to the number circled in red under the name and photograph of H.H. Dharma King Penor. That number 17 lot indicated H.H. Dorje Chang Buddha III Wan Ko Yeshe Norbu Holiest Tathagata recognized H.H. Dharma King Penor as the nirmanakaya of Vajrapani Bodhisattva! The upper left shows a large board used at the Drawing Lots From a Golden Vase Ceremony on which is written the different identities of H.H. Dharma King Penor recognized by dharma kings and rinpoches. The number with a circle around it indicates the identity recognized by H.H. Dorje Chang Buddha III. To the right is the golden vase used at the Drawing Lots From a Golden Vase Ceremony, the large precious urn used to hold that golden vase, the golden vase lid, the yellow satin sheath used to sheathe lot number 17, the lot that was drawn, and the number 17 ivory slip that was placed in that lot.

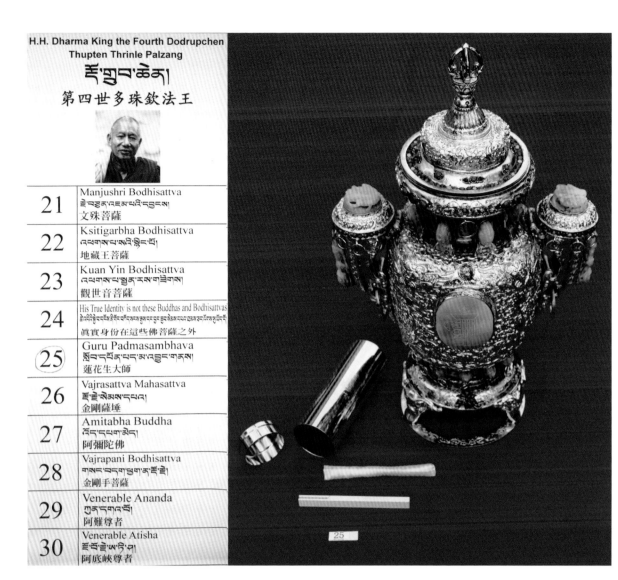

H.H. Dharma King the Fourth Dodrupchen Thupten Thrinle Palzang ར་གྲུབ་ཆེན། 第四世多珠欽法王	
21	Manjushri Bodhisattva འཇམ་དཔལ་དབྱངས་བྱང་ཆུབ། 文殊菩薩
22	Ksitigarbha Bodhisattva འབགས་པའི་སྙིང་པོ། 地藏王菩薩
23	Kuan Yin Bodhisattva འཕགས་པ་སྤྱན་རས་གཟིགས། 觀世音菩薩
24	His True Identity is not these Buddhas and Bodhisattvas ཡང་དག་པའི་སྐུ་གང་ཟག་འདི་དག 眞實身份在這些佛菩薩之外
㉕	Guru Padmasambhava སློབ་དཔོན་པདྨ་འབྱུང་གནས། 蓮花生大師
26	Vajrasattva Mahasattva རྡོ་རྗེ་སེམས་དཔའ། 金剛薩埵
27	Amitabha Buddha འོད་དཔག་མེད། 阿彌陀佛
28	Vajrapani Bodhisattva གསང་བའི་བདག་པོ་ཕྱག་ན་རྡོ་རྗེ། 金剛手菩薩
29	Venerable Ananda ཀུན་དགའ་བོ། 阿難尊者
30	Venerable Atisha ཇོ་བོ་རྗེ་ཨ་ཏི་ཤ། 阿底峽尊者

25

鑒於有一部分人認為薩迦天津法王、貝諾法王、降養隆多加參遍智法王等著名聖德沒有資格認證、祝賀三世多杰羌佛，為化解這些人的疑慮，國際佛教僧尼總會特別邀請諸多法王、仁波且為薩迦天津法王、貝諾法王、多珠欽法王（即多智欽法王—編者注，以下同）、降養隆多加參法王等聖德們的真實身份作一決定性的確認認證。由於各位法王、仁波且對這些聖德們的身份認證結果不統一，國際佛教僧尼總會特如法舉行聖義現量金瓶掣籤以最終確定這些聖德們的真實身份。國際佛教僧尼總會經過為期一個月以文殊法為主體的修持，於2007年9月19日在美國舊金山華藏寺舉行金瓶掣籤，由祿東贊尊者第四世慈仁嘉措仁波且掣籤，在眾多尊者、仁波且、法師、大德居士等七眾弟子的觀禮誦經聲中，從120支密封的籤中掣出25號籤，並公開印籤無誤。該25號籤是三世多杰羌佛雲高益西諾布頂聖如來，認證多珠欽法王是蓮花生大師的化身！上圖左邊是金瓶掣籤法會現場的巨大板牌，分別是法王、仁波且們對多珠欽法王的身份的認證，圈了紅圈的身份號碼是三世多杰羌佛作的認證。上圖右邊是金瓶掣籤專用的金瓶、裝金瓶的寶瓶、金瓶蓋、黃色緞布籤套、掣出的籤以及25號籤牌。

There are those who thought that H.H. Dharma King Sakya Trizin, H.H. Dharma King Penor, H.H. Dharma King Omniscience Jamyang Lungdok Gyaltsen Achuk and other famous persons of great holiness were not qualified to recognize H.H. Dorje Chang Buddha III or send written congratulations regarding such recognition. In order to dispel such doubts, the International Buddhism Sangha Association specially invited many dharma kings and rinpoches to conclusively recognize the true identities of H.H. Dharma Sakya Trizin, H.H. Dharma King Penor, H.H. Dharma King Dodrupchen, H.H. Dharma King Omniscience Jamyang Lungdok Gyaltsen Achuk, and other persons of great holiness. Because those dharma kings and rinpoches did not unanimously agree on the identities of those persons of great holiness, the International Buddhism Sangha Association held the highest form of Drawing Lots From a Golden Vase Ceremony in complete accordance with the dharma. The purpose of that ceremony in which realization was openly manifested at the dharma assembly was to determine definitively the true identities of those persons of great holiness. Members of the International Buddhism Sangha Association practiced dharma for a one-month period prior to that ceremony, mainly focusing on the practice of Manjushri dharma. That Drawing Lots From a Golden Vase Ceremony was held on September 19, 2007 at Hua Zang Si in San Francisco of USA. H.E. Gar Tongstan IV Ciren Gyatso Rinpoche drew the lots. As many venerable ones, rinpoches, dharma teachers, laypersons of great virtue, and other types of Buddhists viewed the ceremony and chanted, the lot with the number 25 in it was drawn from among the 120 sealed lots. It was openly confirmed that lot number 25 corresponded to the number circled in red under the name and photograph of H.H. Dharma King Dodrupchen. That number 25 lot indicated H.H. Dorje Chang Buddha III Wan Ko Yeshe Norbu Holiest Tathagata recognized H.H. Dharma King Dodrupchen as the nirmanakaya of Guru Padmasambhava! The upper left shows a large board used at the Drawing Lots From a Golden Vase Ceremony on which is written the different identities of H.H. Dharma King Dodrupchen recognized by dharma kings and rinpoches. The number with a circle around it indicates the identity recognized by H.H. Dorje Chang Buddha III. To the right is the golden vase used at the Drawing Lots From a Golden Vase Ceremony, the large precious urn used to hold that golden vase, the golden vase lid, the yellow satin sheath used to sheathe lot number 25, the lot that was drawn, and the number 25 ivory slip that was placed in that lot.

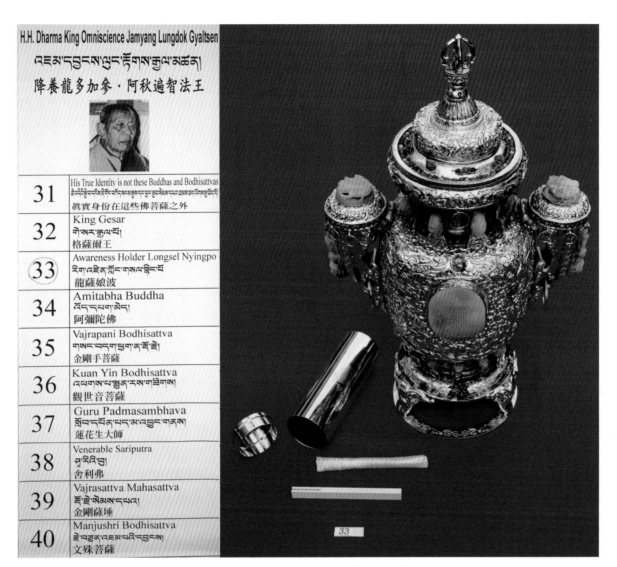

འཇམ་དབྱངས་ལུང་རྟོགས་རྒྱལ་མཚན།

降養龍多加參·阿秋遍智法王

31	His True Identity is not these Buddhas and Bodhisattvas	
	眞實身份在這些佛菩薩之外	
32	King Gesar	
	གེ་སར་རྒྱལ་པོ།	
	格薩爾王	
(33)	Awareness Holder Longsel Nyingpo	
	རིག་འཛིན་ཀློང་གསལ་སྙིང་པོ།	
	龍薩娘波	
34	Amitabha Buddha	
	འོད་དཔག་མེད།	
	阿彌陀佛	
35	Vajrapani Bodhisattva	
	གསང་བདག་ཕྱག་ན་རྡོ་རྗེ།	
	金剛手菩薩	
36	Kuan Yin Bodhisattva	
	འཕགས་པ་སྤྱན་རས་གཟིགས།	
	觀世音菩薩	
37	Guru Padmasambhava	
	སློབ་དཔོན་པདྨ་འབྱུང་གནས།	
	蓮花生大師	
38	Venerable Sariputra	
	ཤ་རིའི་བུ།	
	舍利弗	
39	Vajrasattva Mahasattva	
	རྡོ་རྗེ་སེམས་དཔའ།	
	金剛薩埵	
40	Manjushri Bodhisattva	
	འཇམ་དཔལ་གཞོན་ནུར་གྱུར་པ།	
	文殊菩薩	

33

鑒於有一部分人認為薩迦天津法王、貝諾法王、降養隆多加參遍智法王等著名聖德沒有資格認證、祝賀三世多杰羌佛，為化解這些人的疑慮，國際佛教僧尼總會特別邀請諸多法王、仁波且為薩迦天津法王、貝諾法王、多智欽法王、降養隆多加參法王等聖德們的真實身份作一決定性的確認認證。由於各位法王、仁波且對這些聖德們的身份認證結果不統一，國際佛教僧尼總會特如法舉行聖義現量金瓶掣籤以最終確定這些聖德們的真實身份。國際佛教僧尼總會經過為期一個月以文殊法為主體的修持，於2007年9月19日在美國舊金山華藏寺舉行金瓶掣籤，由祿東贊尊者第四世慈仁嘉措仁波且掣籤，在眾多尊者、仁波且、法師、大德居士等七眾弟子的觀禮誦經聲中，從120支密封的籤中掣出33號籤，並公開印籤無誤。該33號籤是三世多杰羌佛雲高益西諾布頂聖如來，認證降養龍多加參遍智法王是龍薩娘波尊者的轉世！上圖左邊是金瓶掣籤法會現場的巨大板牌，分別是法王、仁波且們對降養隆多加參法王的身份的認證，圈了紅圈的身份號碼是三世多杰羌佛作的認證。上圖右邊是金瓶掣籤專用的金瓶、裝金瓶的寶瓶、金瓶蓋、黃色緞布籤套、掣出的籤以及33號籤牌。

There are those who thought that H.H. Dharma King Sakya Trizin, H.H. Dharma King Penor, H.H. Dharma King Omniscience Jamyang Lungdok Gyaltsen Achuk and other famous persons of great holiness were not qualified to recognize H.H. Dorje Chang Buddha III or send written congratulations regarding such recognition. In order to dispel such doubts, the International Buddhism Sangha Association specially invited many dharma kings and rinpoches to conclusively recognize the true identities of H.H. Dharma Sakya Trizin, H.H. Dharma King Penor, H.H. Dharma King Dodrupchen, H.H. Dharma King Omniscience Jamyang Lungdok Gyaltsen Achuk, and other persons of great holiness. Because those dharma kings and rinpoches did not unanimously agree on the identities of those persons of great holiness, the International Buddhism Sangha Association held the highest form of Drawing Lots From a Golden Vase Ceremony in complete accordance with the dharma. The purpose of that ceremony in which realization was openly manifested at the dharma assembly was to determine definitively the true identities of those persons of great holiness. Members of the International Buddhism Sangha Association practiced dharma for a one-month period prior to that ceremony, mainly focusing on the practice of Manjushri dharma. That Drawing Lots From a Golden Vase Ceremony was held on September 19, 2007 at Hua Zang Si in San Francisco of USA. H.E. Gar Tongstan IV Ciren Gyatso Rinpoche drew the lots. As many venerable ones, rinpoches, dharma teachers, laypersons of great virtue, and other types of Buddhists viewed the ceremony and chanted, the lot with the number 33 in it was drawn from among the 120 sealed lots. It was openly confirmed that lot number 33 corresponded to the number circled in red under the name and photograph of H.H. Dharma King Jamyang Lungdok Gyaltsen Achuk. That number 33 lot indicated H.H. Dorje Chang Buddha III Wan Ko Yeshe Norbu Holiest Tathagata recognized H.H. Dharma King Jamyang Lungdok Gyaltsen Achuk as incarnation of venerable Longsal Nyingpo! The upper left shows a large board used at the Drawing Lots From a Golden Vase Ceremony on which is written the different identities of H.H. Dharma King Jamyang Lungdok Gyaltsen Achuk recognized by dharma kings and rinpoches. The number with a circle around it indicates the identity recognized by H.H. Dorje Chang Buddha III. To the right is the golden vase used at the Drawing Lots From a Golden Vase Ceremony, the large precious urn used to hold that golden vase, the golden vase lid, the yellow satin sheath used to sheathe lot number 33, the lot that was drawn, and the number 33 ivory slip that was placed in that lot.

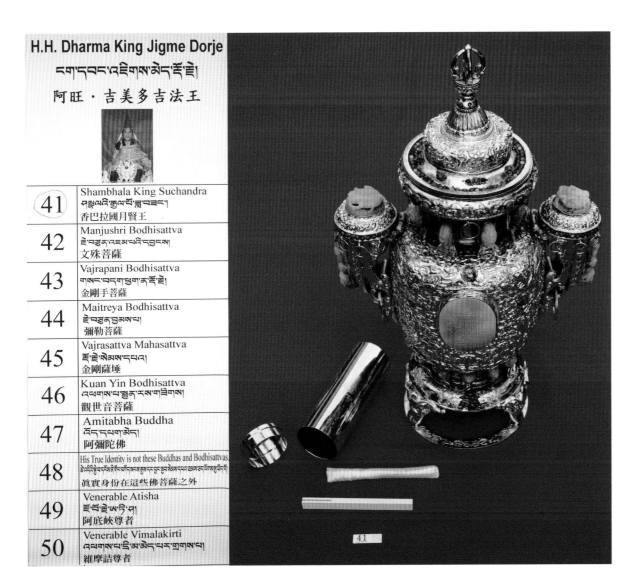

H.H. Dharma King Jigme Dorje

དབའ་དབང་འཇིགས་མེད་རྡོ་རྗེ།

阿旺·吉美多吉法王

(41)	Shambhala King Suchandra	ཤམྦྷ་ལའི་རྒྱལ་པོ་ཟླ་བཟང་། 香巴拉國月賢王
42	Manjushri Bodhisattva	འཇམ་དཔལ་གཞོན་ནུའི་བྱང་ཆུབ་སེམས་ 文殊菩薩
43	Vajrapani Bodhisattva	གསང་བདག་ཕྱག་ན་རྡོ་རྗེ། 金剛手菩薩
44	Maitreya Bodhisattva	རྗེ་བཙུན་བྱམས་པ། 彌勒菩薩
45	Vajrasattva Mahasattva	རྡོ་རྗེ་སེམས་དཔའ། 金剛薩埵
46	Kuan Yin Bodhisattva	འཕགས་པ་སྤྱན་རས་གཟིགས། 觀世音菩薩
47	Amitabha Buddha	འོད་དཔག་མེད། 阿彌陀佛
48	His True Identity is not these Buddhas and Bodhisattvas. ཁོང་གི་ངོ་མ་སྐུ་སངས་རྒྱས་དང་བྱང་ཆུབ་སེམས་དཔའ་འདི་དག་ལས་འདས་པ། 真實身份在這些佛菩薩之外
49	Venerable Atisha	རྗེ་བཙུན་ཨ་ཏི་ཤ། 阿底峽尊者
50	Venerable Vimalakirti	འཕགས་པ་དྲི་མ་མེད་པར་གྲགས་པ། 維摩詰尊者

41

鑒於有一部分人認為薩迦天津法王、貝諾法王、降養隆多加參遍智法王等著名聖德沒有資格認證、祝賀三世多杰羌佛，為化解這些人的疑慮，國際佛教僧尼總會特別邀請諸多法王、仁波且為薩迦天津法王、貝諾法王、多智欽法王、降養隆多加參法王等聖德們的真實身份作一決定性的確認認證。由於各位法王、仁波且對這些聖德們的身份認證結果不統一，國際佛教僧尼總會特如法舉行聖義現量金瓶掣籤以最終確定這些聖德們的真實身份。國際佛教僧尼總會經過為期一個月以文殊法為主體的修持，於2007年9月19日在美國舊金山華藏寺舉行金瓶掣籤，由祿東贊尊者第四世慈仁嘉措仁波且掣籤，在眾多尊者、仁波且、法師、大德居士等七眾弟子的觀禮誦經聲中，從120支密封的籤中掣出41號籤，並公開印籤無誤。該41號籤是三世多杰羌佛雲高益西諾布頂聖如來，認證吉美多吉法王是香巴拉國月賢王的轉世！上圖左邊是金瓶掣籤法會現場的巨大板牌，分別是法王、仁波且們對吉美多吉法王的身份的認證，圈了紅圈的身份號碼是三世多杰羌佛作的認證。上圖右邊是金瓶掣籤專用的金瓶、裝金瓶的寶瓶、金瓶蓋、黃色緞布籤套、掣出的籤以及41號籤牌。

There are those who thought that H.H. Dharma King Sakya Trizin, H.H. Dharma King Penor, H.H. Dharma King Omniscience Jamyang Lungdok Gyaltsen Achuk and other famous persons of great holiness were not qualified to recognize H.H. Dorje Chang Buddha III or send written congratulations regarding such recognition. In order to dispel such doubts, the International Buddhism Sangha Association specially invited many dharma kings and rinpoches to conclusively recognize the true identities of H.H. Dharma Sakya Trizin, H.H. Dharma King Penor, H.H. Dharma King Dodrupchen, H.H. Dharma King Omniscience Jamyang Lungdok Gyaltsen Achuk, and other persons of great holiness. Because those dharma kings and rinpoches did not unanimously agree on the identities of those persons of great holiness, the International Buddhism Sangha Association held the highest form of Drawing Lots From a Golden Vase Ceremony in complete accordance with the dharma. The purpose of that ceremony in which realization was openly manifested at the dharma assembly was to determine definitively the true identities of those persons of great holiness. Members of the International Buddhism Sangha Association practiced dharma for a one-month period prior to that ceremony, mainly focusing on the practice of Manjushri dharma. That Drawing Lots From a Golden Vase Ceremony was held on September 19, 2007 at Hua Zang Si in San Francisco of USA. H.E. Gar Tongstan IV Ciren Gyatso Rinpoche drew the lots. As many venerable ones, rinpoches, dharma teachers, laypersons of great virtue, and other types of Buddhists viewed the ceremony and chanted, the lot with the number 41 in it was drawn from among the 120 sealed lots. It was openly confirmed that lot number 41 corresponded to the number circled in red under the name and photograph of H.H. Dharma King Jigme Dorje. That number 41 lot indicated H.H. Dorje Chang Buddha III Wan Ko Yeshe Norbu Holiest Tathagata recognized H.H. Dharma King Jigme Dorje as the incarnation of the Shambhala King Suchandra! The upper left shows a large board used at the Drawing Lots From a Golden Vase Ceremony on which is written the different identities of H.H. Dharma King Jigme Dorje recognized by dharma kings and rinpoches. The number with a circle around it indicates the identity recognized by H.H. Dorje Chang Buddha III. To the right is the golden vase used at the Drawing Lots From a Golden Vase Ceremony, the large precious urn used to hold that golden vase, the golden vase lid, the yellow satin sheath used to sheathe lot number 41, the lot that was drawn, and the number 41 ivory slip that was placed in that lot.

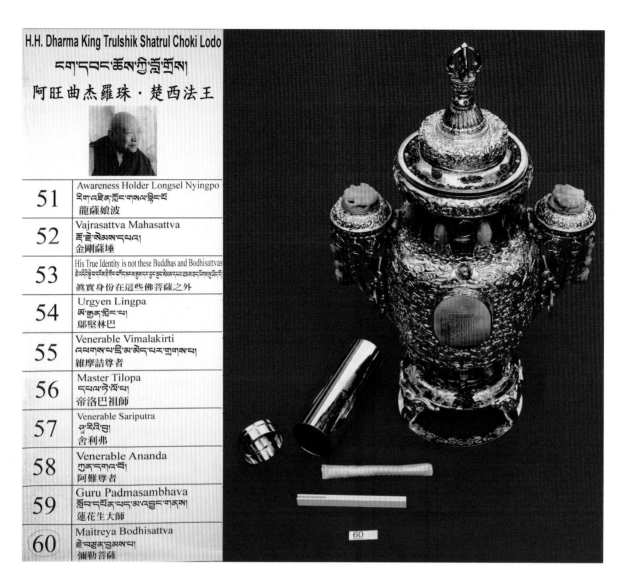

	H.H. Dharma King Trulshik Shatrul Choki Lodo	
	དབ་དབང་ཆོས་ཀྱི་བློ་གྲོས།	
	阿旺曲杰羅珠·楚西法王	
51	Awareness Holder Longsel Nyingpo རིག་འཛིན་ཀློང་གསལ་སྙིང་པོ། 龍薩娘波	
52	Vajrasattva Mahasattva རྡོ་རྗེ་སེམས་དཔའ། 金剛薩埵	
53	His True Identity is not these Buddhas and Bodhisattvas 眞實身份在這些佛菩薩之外	
54	Urgyen Lingpa ཨོ་རྒྱན་གླིང་པ། 鄔堅林巴	
55	Venerable Vimalakirti འཕགས་པ་དྲི་མ་མེད་པར་གྲགས་པ། 維摩詰尊者	
56	Master Tilopa དཔལ་ཏཻ་ལོ་པ། 帝洛巴祖師	
57	Venerable Sariputra ཤཱ་རིའི་བུ། 舍利弗	
58	Venerable Ananda ཀུན་དགའ་བོ། 阿難尊者	
59	Guru Padmasambhava སློབ་དཔོན་པདྨ་འབྱུང་གནས། 蓮花生大師	
(60)	Maitreya Bodhisattva རྗེ་བཙུན་བྱམས་པ། 彌勒菩薩	

鑒於有一部分人認為薩迦天津法王、貝諾法王、降養隆多加參遍智法王等著名聖德沒有資格認證、祝賀三世多杰羌佛，為化解這些人的疑慮，國際佛教僧尼總會特別邀請諸多法王、仁波且為薩迦天津法王、貝諾法王、多智欽法王、降養隆多加參法王等聖德們的真實身份作一決定性的確認認證。由於各位法王、仁波且對這些聖德們的身份認證結果不統一，國際佛教僧尼總會特如法舉行聖義現量金瓶掣籤以最終確定這些聖德們的真實身份。國際佛教僧尼總會經過為期一個月以文殊法為主體的修持，於2007年9月19日在美國舊金山華藏寺舉行金瓶掣籤，由祿東贊尊者第四世慈仁嘉措仁波且掣籤，在眾多尊者、仁波且、法師、大德居士等七眾弟子的觀禮誦經聲中，從120支密封的籤中掣出60號籤，並公開印籤無誤。該60號籤是三世多杰羌佛雲高益西諾布頂聖如來，認證楚西法王是彌勒菩薩的化身！上圖左邊是金瓶掣籤法會現場的巨大板牌，分別是法王、仁波且們對楚西法王的身份的認證，圈了紅圈的身份號碼是三世多杰羌佛作的認證。上圖右邊是金瓶掣籤專用的金瓶、裝金瓶的寶瓶、金瓶蓋、黃色緞布籤套、掣出的籤以及60號籤牌。

There are those who thought that H.H. Dharma King Sakya Trizin, H.H. Dharma King Penor, H.H. Dharma King Omniscience Jamyang Lungdok Gyaltsen Achuk and other famous persons of great holiness were not qualified to recognize H.H. Dorje Chang Buddha III or send written congratulations regarding such recognition. In order to dispel such doubts, the International Buddhism Sangha Association specially invited many dharma kings and rinpoches to conclusively recognize the true identities of H.H. Dharma Sakya Trizin, H.H. Dharma King Penor, H.H. Dharma King Dodrupchen, H.H. Dharma King Omniscience Jamyang Lungdok Gyaltsen Achuk, and other persons of great holiness. Because those dharma kings and rinpoches did not unanimously agree on the identities of those persons of great holiness, the International Buddhism Sangha Association held the highest form of Drawing Lots From a Golden Vase Ceremony in complete accordance with the dharma. The purpose of that ceremony in which realization was openly manifested at the dharma assembly was to determine definitively the true identities of those persons of great holiness. Members of the International Buddhism Sangha Association practiced dharma for a one-month period prior to that ceremony, mainly focusing on the practice of Manjushri dharma. That Drawing Lots From a Golden Vase Ceremony was held on September 19, 2007 at Hua Zang Si in San Francisco of USA. H.E. Gar Tongstan IV Ciren Gyatso Rinpoche drew the lots. As many venerable ones, rinpoches, dharma teachers, laypersons of great virtue, and other types of Buddhists viewed the ceremony and chanted, the lot with the number 60 in it was drawn from among the 120 sealed lots. It was openly confirmed that lot number 60 corresponded to the number circled in red under the name and photograph of H.H Dharma King Trulshik. That number 60 lot indicated H.H. Dorje Chang Buddha III Wan Ko Yeshe Norbu Holiest Tathagata recognized H.H Dharma King Trulshik as the nirmanakaya of Maitreya Bodhisattva! The upper left shows a large board used at the Drawing Lots From a Golden Vase Ceremony on which is written the different identities of H.H Dharma King Trulshik recognized by dharma kings and rinpoches. The number with a circle around it indicates the identity recognized by H.H. Dorje Chang Buddha III. To the right is the golden vase used at the Drawing Lots From a Golden Vase Ceremony, the large precious urn used to hold that golden vase, the golden vase lid, the yellow satin sheath used to sheathe lot number 60, the lot that was drawn, and the number 60 ivory slip that was placed in that lot.

H.H. Dharma King Renzeng Nima

 རིག་འཛིན་ཉི་མ།

仁尊尼瑪法王

61	Ksitigarbha Bodhisattva འདགགས་ནས་སྙིང་པོ། 地藏王菩薩
62	His True Identity is not these Buddhas and Bodhisattvas. ཉིད་ཀྱི་བདེན་དངོས་སངས་རྒྱས་བྱང་སེམས་རྣམས་ལས་གཞན། 眞實身份在這些佛菩薩之外
63	Venerable Sariputra ཤ་རིའི་བུ། 舍利弗
64	Vajrasattva Mahasattva རྡོ་རྗེ་སེམས་དཔའ། 金剛薩埵
65	Amitabha Buddha འོད་དཔག་མེད། 阿彌陀佛
66	Vajrapani Bodhisattva གསང་བདག་ཕྱག་ན་རྡོ་རྗེ། 金剛手菩薩
67	Venerable Vimalakirti འདྲི་མེད་གྲགས་པ་ལྷ་ལྕམ་འགྲོན་མ། 維摩詰尊者
68	Kuan Yin Bodhisattva འདྲེན་པ་སྤྱན་རས་གཟིགས། 觀世音菩薩
69	Manjushri Bodhisattva འཇམ་དཔལ་དབྱངས་ཀྱི་གཞུང་ལ། 文殊菩薩
(70)	King Gesar གེ་སར་རྒྱལ་པོ། 格薩爾王

70

鑒於有一部分人認為薩迦天津法王、貝諾法王、降養隆多加參遍智法王等著名聖德沒有資格認證、祝賀三世多杰羌佛，為化解這些人的疑慮，國際佛教僧尼總會特別邀請諸多法王、仁波且為薩迦天津法王、貝諾法王、多智欽法王、降養隆多加參法王等聖德們的真實身份作一決定性的確認認證。由於各位法王、仁波且對這些聖德們的身份認證結果不統一，國際佛教僧尼總會特如法舉行聖義現量金瓶掣籤以最終確定這些聖德們的真實身份。國際佛教僧尼總會經過為期一個月以文殊法為主體的修持，於2007年9月19日在美國舊金山華藏寺舉行金瓶掣籤，由祿東贊尊者第四世慈仁嘉措仁波且掣籤，在眾多尊者、仁波且、法師、大德居士等七眾弟子的觀禮誦經聲中，從120支密封的籤中掣出70號籤，並公開印籤無誤。該70號籤是三世多杰羌佛雲高益西諾布頂聖如來，認證仁尊尼瑪仁波且（即仁增尼瑪仁波且—編者注，以下同）是格薩爾王的化身！上圖左邊是金瓶掣籤法會現場的巨大板牌，分別是法王、仁波且們對仁尊尼瑪仁波且的身份的認證，圈了紅圈的身份號碼是三世多杰羌佛作的認證。上圖右邊是金瓶掣籤專用的金瓶、裝金瓶的寶瓶、金瓶蓋、黃色緞布籤套、掣出的籤以及70號籤牌。

There are those who thought that H.H. Dharma King Sakya Trizin, H.H. Dharma King Penor, H.H. Dharma King Omniscience Jamyang Lungdok Gyaltsen Achuk and other famous persons of great holiness were not qualified to recognize H.H. Dorje Chang Buddha III or send written congratulations regarding such recognition. In order to dispel such doubts, the International Buddhism Sangha Association specially invited many dharma kings and rinpoches to conclusively recognize the true identities of H.H. Dharma Sakya Trizin, H.H. Dharma King Penor, H.H. Dharma King Dodrupchen, H.H. Dharma King Omniscience Jamyang Lungdok Gyaltsen Achuk, and other persons of great holiness. Because those dharma kings and rinpoches did not unanimously agree on the identities of those persons of great holiness, the International Buddhism Sangha Association held the highest form of Drawing Lots From a Golden Vase Ceremony in complete accordance with the dharma. The purpose of that ceremony in which realization was openly manifested at the dharma assembly was to determine definitively the true identities of those persons of great holiness. Members of the International Buddhism Sangha Association practiced dharma for a one-month period prior to that ceremony, mainly focusing on the practice of Manjushri dharma. That Drawing Lots From a Golden Vase Ceremony was held on September 19, 2007 at Hua Zang Si in San Francisco of USA. H.E. Gar Tongstan IV Ciren Gyatso Rinpoche drew the lots. As many venerable ones, rinpoches, dharma teachers, laypersons of great virtue, and other types of Buddhists viewed the ceremony and chanted, the lot with the number 70 in it was drawn from among the 120 sealed lots. It was openly confirmed that lot number 70 corresponded to the number circled in red under the name and photograph of H.E. Renzeng Nima Rinpoche. That number 70 lot indicated H.H. Dorje Chang Buddha III Wan Ko Yeshe Norbu Holiest Tathagata recognized H.E. Renzeng Nima Rinpoche as the nirmanakaya of King Gesar! The upper left shows a large board used at the Drawing Lots From a Golden Vase Ceremony on which is written the different identities of H.E. Renzeng Nima Rinpoche recognized by dharma kings and rinpoches. The number with a circle around it indicates the identity recognized by H.H. Dorje Chang Buddha III. To the right is the golden vase used at the Drawing Lots From a Golden Vase Ceremony, the large precious urn used to hold that golden vase, the golden vase lid, the yellow satin sheath used to sheathe lot number 70, the lot that was drawn, and the number 70 ivory slip that was placed in that lot.

H.E. Shamarpa Mipham Chokyi Lodro		
རྒྱལ་ཚབ་ཞྭ་དམར་པ་སྐུ་ཕྲེང་བཅུ་བཞི་པ།		
第十四世攝政王夏瑪巴		
71	Master Gampopa སྒམ་པོ་པ། 岡波巴祖師	
(72)	Kuan Yin Bodhisattva འཕགས་པ་སྤྱན་རས་གཟིགས། 觀世音菩薩	
73	Ksitigarbha Bodhisattva འཕགས་པ་ས་ཡི་སྙིང་པོ། 地藏王菩薩	
74	Master Naropa ཇོ་བོ་ནཱ་རོ་པ། 那洛巴祖師	
75	Venerable Ananda ཀུན་དགའ་བོ། 阿難尊者	
76	His True Identity is not these Buddhas and Bodhisattvas. ངོ་བོའི་ངོ་མ་ནི་སངས་རྒྱས་དང་བྱང་སེམས་འདི་དག་ལས་འདས། 眞實身份在這些佛菩薩之外	
77	Venerable Atisha ཇོ་བོ་རྗེ་ཨ་ཏི་ཤ། 阿底峽尊者	
78	Vajrasattva Mahasattva རྡོ་རྗེ་སེམས་དཔའ། 金剛薩埵	
79	Venerable Vimalakirti འཕགས་པ་དྲི་མ་མེད་པར་གྲགས་པ། 維摩詰尊者	
80	Vajrapani Bodhisattva གསང་བདག་ཕྱག་ན་རྡོ་རྗེ། 金剛手菩薩	

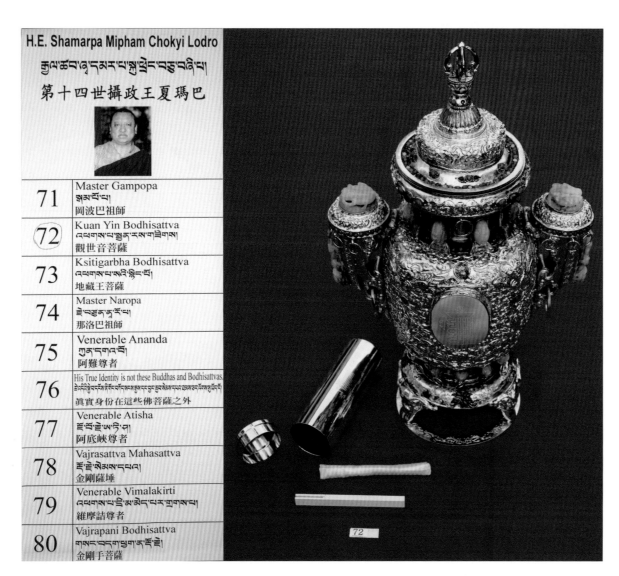

72

鑑於有一部分人認為薩迦天津法王、貝諾法王、降養隆多加參遍智法王等著名聖德沒有資格認證、祝賀三世多杰羌佛，為化解這些人的疑慮，國際佛教僧尼總會特別邀請諸多法王、仁波且為薩迦天津法王、貝諾法王、多智欽法王、降養隆多加參法王等聖德們的真實身份作一決定性的確認認證。由於各位法王、仁波且對這些聖德們的身份認證結果不統一，國際佛教僧尼總會特如法舉行聖義現量金瓶掣籤以最終確定這些聖德們的真實身份。國際佛教僧尼總會經過為期一個月以文殊法為主體的修持，於2007年9月19日在美國舊金山華藏寺舉行金瓶掣籤，由祿東贊尊者第四世慈仁嘉措仁波且掣籤，在眾多尊者、仁波且、法師、大德居士等七眾弟子的觀禮誦經聲中，從120支密封的籤中掣出72號籤，並公開印籤無誤。該72號籤是三世多杰羌佛雲高益西諾布頂聖如來，認證夏瑪巴攝政王是觀音菩薩的化身！上圖左邊是金瓶掣籤法會現場的巨大板牌，分別是法王、仁波且們對夏瑪巴攝政王的身份的認證，圈了紅圈的身份號碼是三世多杰羌佛作的認證。上圖右邊是金瓶掣籤專用的金瓶、裝金瓶的寶瓶、金瓶蓋、黃色緞布籤套、掣出的籤以及72號籤牌。

There are those who thought that H.H. Dharma King Sakya Trizin, H.H. Dharma King Penor, H.H. Dharma King Omniscience Jamyang Lungdok Gyaltsen Achuk and other famous persons of great holiness were not qualified to recognize H.H. Dorje Chang Buddha III or send written congratulations regarding such recognition. In order to dispel such doubts, the International Buddhism Sangha Association specially invited many dharma kings and rinpoches to conclusively recognize the true identities of H.H. Dharma Sakya Trizin, H.H. Dharma King Penor, H.H. Dharma King Dodrupchen, H.H. Dharma King Omniscience Jamyang Lungdok Gyaltsen Achuk, and other persons of great holiness. Because those dharma kings and rinpoches did not unanimously agree on the identities of those persons of great holiness, the International Buddhism Sangha Association held the highest form of Drawing Lots From a Golden Vase Ceremony in complete accordance with the dharma. The purpose of that ceremony in which realization was openly manifested at the dharma assembly was to determine definitively the true identities of those persons of great holiness. Members of the International Buddhism Sangha Association practiced dharma for a one-month period prior to that ceremony, mainly focusing on the practice of Manjushri dharma. That Drawing Lots From a Golden Vase Ceremony was held on September 19, 2007 at Hua Zang Si in San Francisco of USA. H.E. Gar Tongstan IV Ciren Gyatso Rinpoche drew the lots. As many venerable ones, rinpoches, dharma teachers, laypersons of great virtue, and other types of Buddhists viewed the ceremony and chanted, the lot with the number 72 in it was drawn from among the 120 sealed lots. It was openly confirmed that lot number 72 corresponded to the number circled in red under the name and photograph of Regent Dharma King H.E Shamarpa. That number 72 lot indicated H.H. Dorje Chang Buddha III Wan Ko Yeshe Norbu Holiest Tathagata recognized Regent Dharma King H.E Shamarpa as the nirmanakaya of Kuan Yin Bodhisattva! The upper left shows a large board used at the Drawing Lots From a Golden Vase Ceremony on which is written the different identities of Regent Dharma King H.E Shamarpa recognized by dharma kings and rinpoches. The number with a circle around it indicates the identity recognized by H.H. Dorje Chang Buddha III. To the right is the golden vase used at the Drawing Lots From a Golden Vase Ceremony, the large precious urn used to hold that golden vase, the golden vase lid, the yellow satin sheath used to sheathe lot number 72, the lot that was drawn, and the number 72 ivory slip that was placed in that lot.

H.E. Goshir Gyaltsab Drakpa Migyur Gocha

ཀྭོ་ཏྲི་རྒྱལ་ཚབ་པ།

國師嘉察巴

81	Venerable Vimalakirti འདགགས་པ་མ་མེད་པར་གྲགས་པ། 維摩詰尊者
82	Maitreya Bodhisattva རྗེ་བཙུན་བྱམས་པ། 彌勒菩薩
83	Master Tilopa དཔལ་ཏེ་ལོ་པ། 帝洛巴祖師
(84)	Master Gampopa སྒམ་པོ་པ། 岡波巴祖師
85	Vajrapani Bodhisattva གསང་བདག་ཕྱག་ན་རྡོ་རྗེ། 金剛手菩薩
86	Vajrasattva Mahasattva རྡོ་རྗེ་སེམས་དཔའ། 金剛薩埵
87	Master Naropa རྗེ་བཙུན་ནཱ་རོ་པ། 那洛巴祖師
88	His True Identity is not these Buddhas and Bodhisattvas. 眞實身份在這些佛菩薩之外
89	Kuan Yin Bodhisattva འཕགས་པ་སྤྱན་རས་གཟིགས། 觀世音菩薩
90	Amitabha Buddha འོད་དཔག་མེད། 阿彌陀佛

84

鑒於有一部分人認為薩迦天津法王、貝諾法王、降養隆多加參遍智法王等著名聖德沒有資格認證、祝賀三世多杰羌佛，為化解這些人的疑慮，國際佛教僧尼總會特別邀請諸多法王、仁波且為薩迦天津法王、貝諾法王、多智欽法王、降養隆多加參法王等聖德們的真實身份作一決定性的確認認證。由於各位法王、仁波且對這些聖德們的身份認證結果不統一，國際佛教僧尼總會特如法舉行聖義現量金瓶掣籤以最終確定這些聖德們的真實身份。國際佛教僧尼總會經過為期一個月以文殊法為主體的修持，於2007年9月19日在美國舊金山華藏寺舉行金瓶掣籤，由祿東贊尊者第四世慈仁嘉措仁波且掣籤，在眾多尊者、仁波且、法師、大德居士等七眾弟子的觀禮誦經聲中，從120支密封的籤中掣出84號籤，並公開印籤無誤。該84號籤是三世多杰羌佛雲高益西諾布頂聖如來，認證嘉察巴攝政國師是岡波巴祖師的轉世！上圖左邊是金瓶掣籤法會現場的巨大板牌，分別是法王、仁波且們對嘉察巴攝政國師的身份的認證，圈了紅圈的身份號碼是三世多杰羌佛作的認證。上圖右邊是金瓶掣籤專用的金瓶、裝金瓶的寶瓶、金瓶蓋、黃色緞布籤套、掣出的籤以及84號籤牌。

There are those who thought that H.H. Dharma King Sakya Trizin, H.H. Dharma King Penor, H.H. Dharma King Omniscience Jamyang Lungdok Gyaltsen Achuk and other famous persons of great holiness were not qualified to recognize H.H. Dorje Chang Buddha III or send written congratulations regarding such recognition. In order to dispel such doubts, the International Buddhism Sangha Association specially invited many dharma kings and rinpoches to conclusively recognize the true identities of H.H. Dharma Sakya Trizin, H.H. Dharma King Penor, H.H. Dharma King Dodrupchen, H.H. Dharma King Omniscience Jamyang Lungdok Gyaltsen Achuk, and other persons of great holiness. Because those dharma kings and rinpoches did not unanimously agree on the identities of those persons of great holiness, the International Buddhism Sangha Association held the highest form of Drawing Lots From a Golden Vase Ceremony in complete accordance with the dharma. The purpose of that ceremony in which realization was openly manifested at the dharma assembly was to determine definitively the true identities of those persons of great holiness. Members of the International Buddhism Sangha Association practiced dharma for a one-month period prior to that ceremony, mainly focusing on the practice of Manjushri dharma. That Drawing Lots From a Golden Vase Ceremony was held on September 19, 2007 at Hua Zang Si in San Francisco of USA. H.E. Gar Tongstan IV Ciren Gyatso Rinpoche drew the lots. As many venerable ones, rinpoches, dharma teachers, laypersons of great virtue, and other types of Buddhists viewed the ceremony and chanted, the lot with the number 84 in it was drawn from among the 120 sealed lots. It was openly confirmed that lot number 84 corresponded to the number circled in red under the name and photograph of Regent Dharma King and National Master H.E. Goshir Gyaltsab. That number 84 lot indicated H.H. Dorje Chang Buddha III Wan Ko Yeshe Norbu Holiest Tathagata recognized Regent Dharma King and National Master H.E. Goshir Gyaltsab as the incarnation of Patriarch Gampopa! The upper left shows a large board used at the Drawing Lots From a Golden Vase Ceremony on which is written the different identities of Regent Dharma King and National Master H.E. Goshir Gyaltsab recognized by dharma kings and rinpoches. The number with a circle around it indicates the identity recognized by H.H. Dorje Chang Buddha III. To the right is the golden vase used at the Drawing Lots From a Golden Vase Ceremony, the large precious urn used to hold that golden vase, the golden vase lid, the yellow satin sheath used to sheathe lot number 84, the lot that was drawn, and the number 84 ivory slip that was placed in that lot.

Venerable Urgyen Xirao ཨོ་རྒྱན་ཡེ་ཤེས་ཤེས་རབ། 鄔堅喜饒尊者		
91	Manjushri Bodhisattva འཇམ་དཔལ་གཞོན་ནུར་གྱུར་པའི་བྱང་ཆུབ། 文殊菩薩	
92	Venerable Ananda ཀུན་དགའ་བོ། 阿難尊者	
93	Venerable Sariputra ཤཱ་རིའི་བུ། 舍利弗	
94	Maitreya Bodhisattva བྱ་བ་དཔལ་བརྩེགས། 彌勒菩薩	
95	Master Tilopa ཏེ་ལོ་པ། 帝洛巴祖師	
96	Awareness Holder Longsel Nyingpo རིག་འཛིན་ཀློང་གསལ་སྙིང་པོ། 龍薩娘波	
(97)	Urgyen Lingpa ཨོ་རྒྱན་གླིང་པ། 鄔堅林巴	
98	King Gesar གེ་སར་རྒྱལ་པོ། 格薩爾王	
99	Master Naropa ནཱ་རོ་པཎ་ཆེན། 那洛巴祖師	
100	His True Identity is not these Buddhas and Bodhisattvas སྐྱེ་འདི་དག་སངས་རྒྱས་དང་བྱང་ཆུབ་སེམས་དཔའ་དག་ལས་འདས་པའི་སྐྱེ། 真實身份在這些佛菩薩之外	

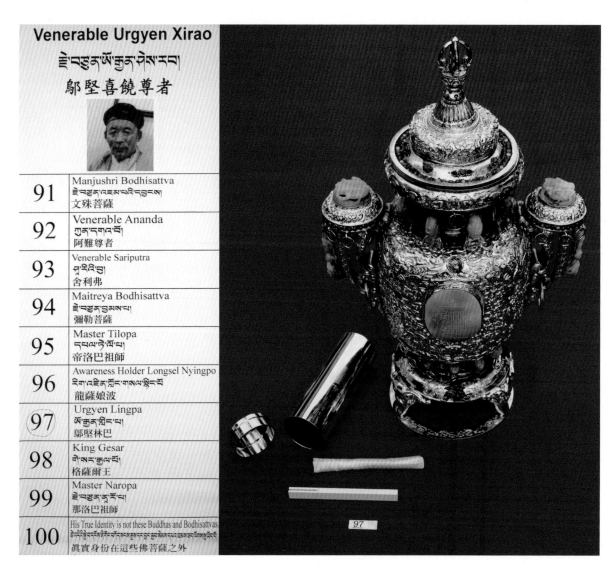

97

鑒於有一部分人認為薩迦天津法王、貝諾法王、降養隆多加參遍智法王等著名聖德沒有資格認證、祝賀三世多杰羌佛，為化解這些人的疑慮，國際佛教僧尼總會特別邀請諸多法王、仁波且為薩迦天津法王、貝諾法王、多智欽法王、降養隆多加參法王等聖德們的真實身份作一決定性的確認認證。由於各位法王、仁波且對這些聖德們的身份認證結果不統一，國際佛教僧尼總會特如法舉行聖義現量金瓶掣籤以最終確定這些聖德們的真實身份。國際佛教僧尼總會經過為期一個月以文殊法為主體的修持，於2007年9月19日在美國舊金山華藏寺舉行金瓶掣籤，由祿東贊尊者第四世慈仁嘉措仁波且掣籤，在眾多尊者、仁波且、法師、大德居士等七眾弟子的觀禮誦經聲中，從120支密封的籤中掣出97號籤，並公開印籤無誤。該97號籤是三世多杰羌佛雲高益西諾布頂聖如來，認證鄔堅喜饒尊者是鄔堅林巴的轉世！上圖左邊是金瓶掣籤法會現場的巨大板牌，分別是法王、仁波且們對鄔堅喜饒尊者的身份的認證，圈了紅圈的身份號碼是三世多杰羌佛作的認證。上圖右邊是金瓶掣籤專用的金瓶、裝金瓶的寶瓶、金瓶蓋、黃色緞布籤套、掣出的籤以及97號籤牌。

There are those who thought that H.H. Dharma King Sakya Trizin, H.H. Dharma King Penor, H.H. Dharma King Omniscience Jamyang Lungdok Gyaltsen Achuk and other famous persons of great holiness were not qualified to recognize H.H. Dorje Chang Buddha III or send written congratulations regarding such recognition. In order to dispel such doubts, the International Buddhism Sangha Association specially invited many dharma kings and rinpoches to conclusively recognize the true identities of H.H. Dharma Sakya Trizin, H.H. Dharma King Penor, H.H. Dharma King Dodrupchen, H.H. Dharma King Omniscience Jamyang Lungdok Gyaltsen Achuk, and other persons of great holiness. Because those dharma kings and rinpoches did not unanimously agree on the identities of those persons of great holiness, the International Buddhism Sangha Association held the highest form of Drawing Lots From a Golden Vase Ceremony in complete accordance with the dharma. The purpose of that ceremony in which realization was openly manifested at the dharma assembly was to determine definitively the true identities of those persons of great holiness. Members of the International Buddhism Sangha Association practiced dharma for a one-month period prior to that ceremony, mainly focusing on the practice of Manjushri dharma. That Drawing Lots From a Golden Vase Ceremony was held on September 19, 2007 at Hua Zang Si in San Francisco of USA. H.E. Gar Tongstan IV Ciren Gyatso Rinpoche drew the lots. As many venerable ones, rinpoches, dharma teachers, laypersons of great virtue, and other types of Buddhists viewed the ceremony and chanted, the lot with the number 97 in it was drawn from among the 120 sealed lots. It was openly confirmed that lot number 97 corresponded to the number circled in red under the name and photograph of H.E Urgyen Xirao Woxiu. That number 97 lot indicated H.H. Dorje Chang Buddha III Wan Ko Yeshe Norbu Holiest Tathagata recognized H.E Urgyen Xirao Woxiu as the incarnation of Urgyen Lingpa! The upper left shows a large board used at the Drawing Lots From a Golden Vase Ceremony on which is written the different identities of H.E Urgyen Xirao Woxiu recognized by dharma kings and rinpoches. The number with a circle around it indicates the identity recognized by H.H. Dorje Chang Buddha III. To the right is the golden vase used at the Drawing Lots From a Golden Vase Ceremony, the large precious urn used to hold that golden vase, the golden vase lid, the yellow satin sheath used to sheathe lot number 97, the lot that was drawn, and the number 97 ivory slip that was placed in that lot.

Dorje Rinzin Rinpoche

ཆོ་རྗེ་རིག་འཛིན་རིན་པོ་ཆེ

多杰仁增仁波且

101	Master Tilopa དཔལ་ལོ་པ། 帝洛巴祖師	
102	Master Gampopa སྒམ་པོ་པ། 岡波巴祖師	
103	Awareness Holder Longsel Nyingpo རིག་འཛིན་ཀློང་གསལ་སྙིང་པོ། 龍薩娘波	
104	Vajrapani Bodhisattva གསང་བདག་ཕྱག་ན་རྡོ་རྗེ། 金剛手菩薩	
105	Ksitigarbha Bodhisattva ས་ཡི་སྙིང་པོ། 地藏王菩薩	
106	His True Identity is not these Buddhas and Bodhisattvas. 真實身份在這些佛菩薩之外	
107	King Gesar གེ་སར་རྒྱལ་པོ། 格薩爾王	
(108)	Unchanging Vajra Being མི་འགྱུར་རྡོ་རྗེ། 不變金剛	
109	Venerable Sariputra ཤཱ་རིའི་བུ། 舍利弗	
110	Guru Padmasambhava སློབ་དཔོན་པདྨ་འབྱུང་གནས། 蓮花生大師	

108

鑒於有一部分人認為薩迦天津法王、貝諾法王、降養隆多加參遍智法王等著名聖德沒有資格認證、祝賀三世多杰羌佛，為化解這些人的疑慮，國際佛教僧尼總會特別邀請諸多法王、仁波且為薩迦天津法王、貝諾法王、多智欽法王、降養隆多加參法王等聖德們的真實身份作一決定性的確認認證。由於各位法王、仁波且對這些聖德們的身份認證結果不統一，國際佛教僧尼總會特如法舉行聖義現量金瓶掣籤以最終確定這些聖德們的真實身份。國際佛教僧尼總會經過為期一個月以於2007年9月19日在美國舊金山華藏寺舉行金瓶掣籤，由祿東贊尊者第四世慈仁嘉措仁波且掣籤，在眾多尊者、仁波且、法師、大德居士等七眾弟子的觀禮誦經聲中，從120支密封的籤中掣出108號籤，並公開印籤無誤。該108號籤是三世多杰羌佛雲高益西諾布頂聖如來，認證多杰仁增仁波且是不變金剛的轉世！上圖左邊是金瓶掣籤法會現場的巨大板牌，分別是法王、仁波且們對多杰仁增仁波且的身份的認證，圈了紅圈的身份號碼是三世多杰羌佛作的認證。上圖右邊是金瓶掣籤專用的金瓶、裝金瓶的寶瓶、金瓶蓋、黃色緞布籤套、掣出的籤以及108號籤牌。

There are those who thought that H.H. Dharma King Sakya Trizin, H.H. Dharma King Penor, H.H. Dharma King Omniscience Jamyang Lungdok Gyaltsen Achuk and other famous persons of great holiness were not qualified to recognize H.H. Dorje Chang Buddha III or send written congratulations regarding such recognition. In order to dispel such doubts, the International Buddhism Sangha Association specially invited many dharma kings and rinpoches to conclusively recognize the true identities of H.H. Dharma Sakya Trizin, H.H. Dharma King Penor, H.H. Dharma King Dodrupchen, H.H. Dharma King Omniscience Jamyang Lungdok Gyaltsen Achuk, and other persons of great holiness. Because those dharma kings and rinpoches did not unanimously agree on the identities of those persons of great holiness, the International Buddhism Sangha Association held the highest form of Drawing Lots From a Golden Vase Ceremony in complete accordance with the dharma. The purpose of that ceremony in which realization was openly manifested at the dharma assembly was to determine definitively the true identities of those persons of great holiness. Members of the International Buddhism Sangha Association practiced dharma for a one-month period prior to that ceremony, mainly focusing on the practice of Manjushri dharma. That Drawing Lots From a Golden Vase Ceremony was held on September 19, 2007 at Hua Zang Si in San Francisco of USA. H.E. Gar Tongstan IV Ciren Gyatso Rinpoche drew the lots. As many venerable ones, rinpoches, dharma teachers, laypersons of great virtue, and other types of Buddhists viewed the ceremony and chanted, the lot with the number 108 in it was drawn from among the 120 sealed lots. It was openly confirmed that lot number 108 corresponded to the number circled in red under the name and photograph of H.E. Dorje Rinzin Rinpoche. That number 108 lot indicated H.H. Dorje Chang Buddha III Wan Ko Yeshe Norbu Holiest Tathagata recognized H.E. Dorje Rinzin Rinpoche as the incarnation of Unchanging Vajra! The upper left shows a large board used at the Drawing Lots From a Golden Vase Ceremony on which is written the different identities of H.E. Dorje Rinzin Rinpoche recognized by dharma kings and rinpoches. The number with a circle around it indicates the identity recognized by H.H. Dorje Chang Buddha III. To the right is the golden vase used at the Drawing Lots From a Golden Vase Ceremony, the large precious urn used to hold that golden vase, the golden vase lid, the yellow satin sheath used to sheathe lot number 108, the lot that was drawn, and the number 108 ivory slip that was placed in that lot.

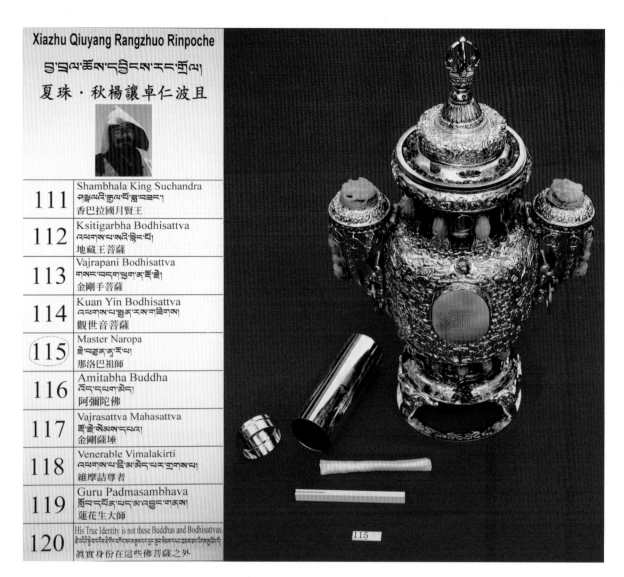

Xiazhu Qiuyang Rangzhuo Rinpoche		
བྱ་བྲལ་ཆོས་དབྱིངས་རང་གྲོལ།		
夏珠·秋楊讓卓仁波且		
111	Shambhala King Suchandra / བདེ་བའི་རྒྱལ་པོ་ཟླ་བཟང་། / 香巴拉國月賢王	
112	Ksitigarbha Bodhisattva / འཛིན་མ་ཡི་སྙིང་པོ། / 地藏王菩薩	
113	Vajrapani Bodhisattva / གསང་བདག་ཕྱག་ན་རྡོ་རྗེ། / 金剛手菩薩	
114	Kuan Yin Bodhisattva / འཇིག་རྟེན་དབང་ཕྱུག་སྤྱན་རས་གཟིགས། / 觀世音菩薩	
(115)	Master Naropa / ཤྲཱི་ནཱ་རོ་པ། / 那洛巴祖師	
116	Amitabha Buddha / འོད་དཔག་མེད། / 阿彌陀佛	
117	Vajrasattva Mahasattva / རྡོ་རྗེ་སེམས་དཔའ། / 金剛薩埵	
118	Venerable Vimalakirti / འཛམ་བུ་ལ་མི་མེད་པར་གྲགས་པ། / 維摩詰尊者	
119	Guru Padmasambhava / སློབ་དཔོན་པདྨ་འབྱུང་གནས། / 蓮花生大師	
120	His True Identity is not these Buddhas and Bodhisattvas. / དེའི་སྐུ་ངོ་ཁྱད་པར་འདི་སངས་རྒྱས་བྱང་སེམས་རྣམས་ལས་འདས་སོ། / 真實身份在這些佛菩薩之外	
		115

鑒於有一部分人認為薩迦天津法王、貝諾法王、降養隆多加參遍智法王等著名聖德沒有資格認證、祝賀三世多杰羌佛，為化解這些人的疑慮，國際佛教僧尼總會特別邀請諸多法王、仁波且為薩迦天津法王、貝諾法王、多智欽法王、降養隆多加參法王等聖德們的真實身份作一決定性的確認認證。由於各位法王、仁波且對這些聖德們的身份認證結果不統一，國際佛教僧尼總會特如法舉行聖義現量金瓶掣籤以最終確定這些聖德們的真實身份。國際佛教僧尼總會經過為期一個月以文殊法為主體的修持，於2007年9月19日在美國舊金山華藏寺舉行金瓶掣籤，由祿東贊尊者第四世慈仁嘉措仁波且掣籤，在眾多尊者、仁波且、法師、大德居士等七眾弟子的觀禮誦經聲中，從120支密封的籤中掣出115號籤，並公開印籤無誤。該115號籤是三世多杰羌佛雲高益西諾布頂聖如來，認證夏珠秋楊仁波且是那諾巴祖師的轉世！上圖左邊是金瓶掣籤法會現場的巨大板牌，分別是法王、仁波且們對夏珠秋楊仁波且的身份的認證，圈了紅圈的身份號碼是三世多杰羌佛作的認證。上圖右邊是金瓶掣籤專用的金瓶、裝金瓶的寶瓶、金瓶蓋、黃色緞布籤套、掣出的籤以及115號籤牌。

There are those who thought that H.H. Dharma King Sakya Trizin, H.H. Dharma King Penor, H.H. Dharma King Omniscience Jamyang Lungdok Gyaltsen Achuk and other famous persons of great holiness were not qualified to recognize H.H. Dorje Chang Buddha III or send written congratulations regarding such recognition. In order to dispel such doubts, the International Buddhism Sangha Association specially invited many dharma kings and rinpoches to conclusively recognize the true identities of H.H. Dharma Sakya Trizin, H.H. Dharma King Penor, H.H. Dharma King Dodrupchen, H.H. Dharma King Omniscience Jamyang Lungdok Gyaltsen Achuk, and other persons of great holiness. Because those dharma kings and rinpoches did not unanimously agree on the identities of those persons of great holiness, the International Buddhism Sangha Association held the highest form of Drawing Lots From a Golden Vase Ceremony in complete accordance with the dharma. The purpose of that ceremony in which realization was openly manifested at the dharma assembly was to determine definitively the true identities of those persons of great holiness. Members of the International Buddhism Sangha Association practiced dharma for a one-month period prior to that ceremony, mainly focusing on the practice of Manjushri dharma. That Drawing Lots From a Golden Vase Ceremony was held on September 19, 2007 at Hua Zang Si in San Francisco of USA. H.E. Gar Tongstan IV Ciren Gyatso Rinpoche drew the lots. As many venerable ones, rinpoches, dharma teachers, laypersons of great virtue, and other types of Buddhists viewed the ceremony and chanted, the lot with the number 115 in it was drawn from among the 120 sealed lots. It was openly confirmed that lot number 115 corresponded to the number circled in red under the name and photograph of H.E. Xiazhu Qiuyang Rinpoche. That number 115 lot indicated H.H. Dorje Chang Buddha III Wan Ko Yeshe Norbu Holiest Tathagata recognized H.E. Xiazhu Qiuyang Rinpoche as the incarnation of Patriarch Naropa! The upper left shows a large board used at the Drawing Lots From a Golden Vase Ceremony on which is written the different identities of H.E. Xiazhu Qiuyang Rinpoche recognized by dharma kings and rinpoches. The number with a circle around it indicates the identity recognized by H.H. Dorje Chang Buddha III. To the right is the golden vase used at the Drawing Lots From a Golden Vase Ceremony, the large precious urn used to hold that golden vase, the golden vase lid, the yellow satin sheath used to sheathe lot number 115, the lot that was drawn, and the number 115 ivory slip that was placed in that lot.

After the Drawing Lots From a Golden Vase Ceremony ended, the following was discovered. Of all of the rinpoches who were invited by the International Buddhism Sangha Association to recognize the identities of those twelve dharma kings and rinpoches of great holiness, one of the rinpoches correctly recognized the identities of five of the twelve dharma kings and rinpoches of great holiness; one of the rinpoches correctly recognized the identities of three of the twelve dharma kings and rinpoches of great holiness; and another rinpoche correctly recognized the identities of two of the twelve dharma kings and rinpoches of great holiness. Only H.H. Dorje Chang Buddha III correctly recognized the identities of all twelve dharma kings and rinpoches of great holiness.

金瓶掣籤的結果，在國際佛教僧尼總會邀請為這些大聖法王、仁波且作認證的仁波且當中，有一位仁波且對五位大聖法王、仁波且的認證正確，還有一位仁波且對三位大聖法王、仁波且的認證正確，另有一位仁波且對兩位大聖法王、仁波且的認證正確，而唯一只有三世多杰羌佛對所有十二位大聖法王、仁波且的認證全部正確無誤。

THEY WILL OPPOSE THIS PRECIOUS BOOK

On September 18, 2006, I paid a formal visit to H.E. the twelfth Tai Situ Rinpoche, who is the incarnation of Dongbi Heruka and who in a previous life was Master Marpa. He said to me, "*A Treasury of True Buddha-Dharma* is truly a precious book that is unique in the entire world. There is no doubt that such a book is unprecedented in the world. Those who read it will receive blessings, grow in wisdom, and experience limitless beneficial effects."

Great Bodhisattvas such as H.H. Dharma King Dodrupchen, H.H. Dharma King Jigme Dorje, who is the supreme leader of the Jonang sect, H.H. Dharma King Trulshik, H.E. Tangtong Gyalpo and others have also stated such things. Great holy beings all share this same perspective and have highly praised this book. However, I have the exact opposite viewpoint. I believe that there will be people who will oppose this book, just as there were people who opposed Sakyamuni Buddha when he was alive.

Actually, there are only three types of people who will oppose *A Treasury of True Buddha-Dharma*. The first type of people lack knowledge and talent and have low insight. Their opposition will stem from their ignorance and inferior conduct. The second type of people undoubtedly consists of demons who have incarnated as humans. Their savage, cruel, and evil nature will cause them to oppose this book. The third type of people is composed of those who are rinpoches or great dharma teachers in name but who actually lack realization, do not understand both exoteric and esoteric Buddhism, and are not proficient in the Five Vidyas. They will oppose this book in order to hide their shortcomings.

However, all three types of people share common characteristics. They express erroneous reasoning, indulge in high-sounding but meaningless talk, utter empty words about the subtleties of Zen, or are so-called highy virtuous people who assume solemn airs. In fact, they have no abilities or realization whatsoever. If you do not believe me, then you should carefully observe them. They could not accomplish the feats shown in even half of the categories contained in this precious book. If you ask them to carve a sculpture containing mysterious mist or a wondrous multicolored sculpture as H.H. Dorje Chang Buddha III has done, they will become angry and abusive. They will engage in defamation in order to change the subject or will find some irrelevant sutra passages to cover up their own lack of realization. All that will remain is their inability to do such things.

Although these three types of people will use every means to sully *A Treasury of True Buddha-Dharma*, they ultimately will have no way to conceal their own incapable and ignorant nature. If you ask them how much of that which is contained in *A Treasury of True Buddha-Dharma* they themselves can do based on their own wisdom and realization, or if you ask them whether they can carve a sculpture like "Mysterious Boulder With Mist," they will immediately criticize you. They certainly will be at a loss for what to do. In the end, all that will remain is their inability to do such things.

When I was journeying around the island of Taiwan by prostrating to the Buddhas and Tara, the magnificent Kuan Yin Bodhisattva appeared in the sky and said to me, "Your Master, Yangwo Wan Ko Yeshe Norbu, is the true Buddha Vajradhara. The dharma that He transmits is the best Buddha-dharma. Thus, living beings who are a bit ignorant do not have the good fortune to benefit from such dharma. False holy beings will defame Him in order to conceal their own inabilities. What about demons? They will oppose Him out of hatred and anger. This is evil action! The merit derived from praising *A Treasury of True Buddha-Dharma* is boundless!"

It is precisely because I received such a formal pronouncement from Kuan Yin Bodhisattva that I dare to state with certainty that three types of people will oppose *A Treasury of True Buddha-Dharma*. It is also because of this that I dare to state that *A Treasury of True Buddha-Dharma* will surely provide living beings with limitless benefits.

I have vowed to journey 1,100 kilometers around the island of Taiwan by continually prostrating. I have already prostrated 1,000 kilometers. My knees are damaged. No matter how painful it may be, whenever I think of the need to eliminate the negative karma of ignorant living beings, all of my pain vanishes. Each time I lower my body to prostrate, I vow to bear the offenses of other living beings and experience suffering on their behalf so that they may leave suffering and attain happiness.

Henghsing Gyatso

(This text was translated from the Chinese text that follows.)

他 們 反 對 這 本 寶 書

我在2006年9月18日拜見了東畢黑努嘎轉世、曾身為瑪爾巴大師的第十二世泰錫度仁波且。他對我們說：『《正法寶典》實在是舉世獨一無二的寶書，無疑的世界第一，看了就會得到加持、增長智慧，受用無量。』

多智欽法王、覺囊派總教主吉美多吉法王、楚西法王、唐東迦波等大菩薩也如此說，大聖者們都是共同的觀點和高度的認定，而我恰恰相反，我認為會有人反對，因為當年也有人反對釋迦牟尼佛陀。其實反對《正法寶典》的人不外乎有三種：第一種是沒有學識才華、見地低的人，他們愚癡劣行而反對；第二種無疑是妖魔投身之人，是兇殘惡行本質使然而反對；第三種是外表是仁波且、大法師，實際上沒有證量、不通顯密、不通五明，為了給自己遮羞而反對。但是，這三種人都脫離不了一個共同的特徵，那就是講歪理詭詭其談、空口說禪機或道貌岸然的所謂大德，其實毫無本事。如果你不信，就去仔細觀察他，寶典中的三十大類他一半都做不到，乃至只讓他雕『神秘石霧』或『玄妙彩寶雕』，這時他只能惱怒、罵人，除了以誹謗拉偏話題，或找一些不相干的經藏語句來掩飾自己無能的本質，剩下的就是無能做不了。儘管這三種人用盡任何手段污染《正法寶典》，但終歸無法掩飾自己無能愚癡的本質。如果你問他自己的智慧、證量能做得了《正法寶典》中多少？做得了『神秘石霧』嗎？他除了當下批評你之外，絕對是束手無策，最後留下的還是做不了。

　　我在環島拜佛拜度母的時候，偉大的觀世音菩薩在空中對我說：『你的上師仰諤雲高益西諾布是真正的金剛總持，他傳的法是最好的佛法，所以愚癡一點的眾生沒有福報享受，假聖者為了掩蓋自己無能而誹謗，妖魔呢？會憎怒而反對，這是罪業哦！如果讚嘆《正法寶典》，則是功德無量。』正因為我受到觀世音菩薩的授記，我才敢確定地說有三種人會反對《正法寶典》，我也才敢說《正法寶典》確會給眾生帶來無邊無量的利益。我發心拜一千一百公里，現在已經拜一千公里了，我的膝蓋都破了，無論有多痛苦，一想到愚癡眾生的黑業應消除，我的一切痛苦全都沒有了，每一拜拜下去都在發心為眾生擔罪、代受痛苦，讓他們離苦得樂。

恆性嘉措　恆性嘉措

（此文的英文翻譯印在前面）

The holy photograph of Kuan Yin Bodhisattva appearing in the sky
觀世音菩薩在空中出現的聖影

A photograph of Venerable Khu-ston brTson-'grus g.yung-drung V Henghsing Gyatso Rinpoche together with H.E. the 12th Tai Situ Rinpoche
庫頓尊哲雍仲尊者第五世恆性嘉措仁波且與泰錫度仁波且合照相片

EXPLANATION OF THE PUBLISHERS

After the news spread that this book, *A Treasury of True Buddha-Dharma*, was about to be published, a kind Buddhist wrote a letter to our publishing company. In the letter, that Buddhist posed the following questions: Why do you want to publish such a book that is only about how H.H. Dorje Chang Buddha III Wan Ko Yeshe Norbu Holiest Tathagata is completely proficient in exoteric and esoteric Buddhism and has perfect mastery of the Five Vidyas? Why do you not publish a treasure-book that is a collection of the accomplishments of other dharma kings in the Five Vidyas? Are you not acting in a somewhat biased way by only selecting H.H. Dorje Chang Buddha III to write about? What is your basis for calling His Holiness by the name Dorje Chang Buddha III? What extraordinary abilities does His Holiness have such that He is a holy person? Weren't those who recognized His Holiness's identity acting irresponsibly and speaking groundlessly? In response to these questions, we as publishers would like to say a few words at this time about *A Treasury of True Buddha-Dharma*. In saying these words, we are adhering to the moral conduct of Buddhist disciples and are strictly abiding by the precepts of Buddhism. These are true words that do not contain the slightest falsehood. They are words for which we are willing to bear all karmic responsibility.

We respectfully request that all of you ponder something. In the history of Buddhism, which Buddha or Bodhisattva who has incarnated into our world has manifested the wisdom that H.H. Dorje Chang Buddha III Wan Ko Yeshe Norbu Holiest Tathagata has manifested relating to complete proficiency in exoteric and esoteric Buddhism? And which such Buddha or Bodhisattva in the history of Buddhism has manifested the consummate mastery of the Five Vidyas that H.H. Dorje Chang Buddha III Wan Ko Yeshe Norbu Holiest Tathagata has manifested? We have yet to find any holy person in history who can match H.H. Dorje Chang Buddha III. Whether rinpoches or great dharma masters, none has been able to lay out clearly real evidence of accomplishments that match the many accomplishments of H.H. Dorje Chang Buddha III.

It is important to understand that this is not a book that only contains empty theories. Rather, it is a book of both pictures and text. Actual accomplishments are laid out for all to see. It is not a book that only contains text.

If you contend that there was or is a person of holy virtue whose accomplishments match those of H.H. Dorje Chang Buddha III, please present that person's realization for all to see. Please lay out that person's real attainments and other related material in order to support your contentions. After our own detailed examination, we have concluded that no one is able to do so.

We have consulted material relating to the few-thousand-year history of Buddhism and have learned that there have been many great Bodhisattvas and dharma king rinpoches with identifiable names. Following the teachings of the Buddha, they became well versed in the Tripitaka and esoteric scriptures, began developing the Five Vidyas, and became proficient in exoteric and esoteric Buddhism. With respect to manifesting accomplishment and realization in the dharma as the Buddha prescribed, they were truly magnificent.

However, H.H. Dorje Chang Buddha III has truly manifested accomplishments that no other holy person in history has manifested. He has shown a uniquely high degree of mastery. If one considers only the thirty main categories of accomplishments contained in *A Treasury of True Buddha-Dharma* without considering any other accomplishments of H.H. Dorje Chang Buddha III, one still cannot find another person of holy virtue who could attain even half of those thirty main categories of accomplishments. Those dharma kings, rinpoches, and outstanding monastics throughout history were great Bodhisattvas who in fact had remarkable realization. But why is it that other people of holy virtue have not attained the accomplishments attained by Dorje Chang Buddha III? How does one explain this irrefutable fact?

Certain dharma kings and great rinpoches gave us the correct answers to these questions. Dharma kings and rinpoches who are nirmanakayas of Manjushri Bodhisattva, Kuan Yin Bodhisattva, Maitreya Bodhisattva, and other Bodhisattvas answered our questions. It is because His Holiness Wan Ko Buddha Vajradhara is the third Dorje Chang Buddha in this world. It is because His Holiness is the true incarnation in this world of the complete body, speech, and mind of Dorje Chang Buddha. There is no partial incarnation of the body, speech, and mind of Dorje Chang Buddha in this world. Thus, His Holiness is Dorje Chang Buddha III. H.H. Wan Ko Yeshe Norbu is not a dharma king of any particular sect but is the Holiest Tathagata who is the most venerable ancient Buddha of all of the sects of exoteric and esoteric Buddhism. His Holiness is the highest leader of Buddhism in Buddhist lineage refuge trees. Thus, it is only natural and in accordance with dharma principles that other extremely holy and virtuous people have not attained the accomplishments that His Holiness has attained.

Nonetheless, there are some people with evil views who want to persecute H.H. Dorje Chang Buddha III and slander the true dharma. These people maliciously smear the accomplishments of H.H. Dorje Chang Buddha III. Actually, what is correct and what is wrong, what is true and what is false can be born out by the facts in an objective way. This is a problem that can be easily solved. We will not ask those people who maliciously harm H.H. Dorje Chang Buddha III to pass the five tests that H.H. Zunsheng Yeshe Norbu listed. We would never entertain the thought that they could possibly pass all five tests. We will pick two of those five tests from a formal pronouncement of H.H. Zunsheng Yeshe Norbu. The first

test is a person must be able to replicate the wondrous multicolored sculptures created by H.H. Dorje Chang Buddha III. The second test is a person must place auspicious mist inside a hollowed out sculpted boulder and have the mist stay there. If any of those people who maliciously harm H.H. Dorje Chang Buddha III passes both of those tests, his words are true. Otherwise, he is a fool who speaks empty and false words or is an ordinary, incompetent person with evil views! Such are the true colors of those who malign.

The Master Wan Ko Yee International Cultural Institute in the United States as well as three other organizations have issued the following permanent offer to the public called the Blue Platform Verification. If any person of holy virtue, wise person, well-intentioned person, scientist, artist, expert, etc. is able to replicate certain wondrous multicolored sculptures of H.H. Dorje Chang Buddha III as well as the sculpture entitled "Mysterious Boulder With Mist" by utilizing Buddha-dharma wisdom, realization, supernatural powers, or worldly scientific methods, then the Master Wan Ko Yee International Cultural Institute will carry out its obligations according to the announcement it published in various major newspapers in 2003.

A more important reason for issuing this Blue Platform Verification relates to a point clearly made in the formal pronouncement of H.H. Zunsheng Yeshe Norbu. That formal pronouncement clearly stated that if a person is able to replicate the wondrous multicolored sculptures of H.H. Dorje Chang Buddha III and the sculpture entitled "Mysterious Boulder With Mist," then the formal pronouncement of H.H. Zunsheng Yeshe Norbu regarding H.H. Wan Ko Buddha Vajradhara is false. It has always been the case that if a Buddha or if a Bodhisattva on the stage of "equal enlightenment" (enlightenment equal to that of a Buddha) or the stage of "marvelous enlightenment" descends into this world, His/Her accomplishments will certainly be higher than those of ordinary people. For example, if Kuan Yin Bodhisattva came to this world, that Bodhisattva's realization would definitely be higher than that of an ordinary person. If Manjushri Bodhisattva came to this world, He would not use techniques involving divinatory symbols but would still select a person's karmic affinity with absolute accuracy after having predicted the results of that selection. If Bhaisajya Raja Bodhisattva (Medicine King Bodhisattva) came to this world, His ability to cure and save people would naturally be greater than that of ordinary doctors. If Guru Padmasambhava descended into this world, He would surely have the power to eliminate karmic obstructions, including the ability to wipe out the negative karma of living beings on the spot. To call an ordinary person an incarnation of a Buddha or Bodhisattva is undoubtedly an insult to the Buddhas and Bodhisattvas.

Thus, the offer of the Master Wan Ko Yee International Cultural Institute and other organizations is most fair. This purpose of this permanent offer called Blue Platform Verification is to not only confirm the veracity of the recognitions of H.H. Dorje Chang Buddha III issued by H.H. Zunsheng Yeshe Norbu, H.H. Great Dharma King Sakya Trizin, H.H. Dharma King Jamyang Lundgdok Gyaltsen, and others, it is also to show everyone the true colors of those people described above who can only defame others, brag about themselves, and are completely devoid of wisdom. If this is not the case, then why are they unable to apply Buddha-dharma realization and wisdom to obtain that award of US$12,000,000 with which they could build temples or benefit living beings in other ways? Why do they not have any ability other than to speak empty words?

We are stating these things today in response to a letter we received. We are also making public the purpose behind the decision to establish the offer called Blue Platform Verification. We are not saying these things in order to compare H.H. Dorje Chang Buddha III Holiest Tathagata Wan Ko Yeshe Norbu with others to see who is higher or lower. We are also not saying these things in order to publicize His Holiness or have people become disciples of His Holiness. Rather, the above-described irrefutable facts are part of the history of the Buddha-dharma. We are explaining that living beings now have such wonderful karmic conditions to obtain liberation from the cycle of reincarnation! We are causing true traces left on the long river of Buddhist history to reappear in this dharma book in a factually accurate way. We are providing history with this truth. We are leaving behind this irrefutably factual contribution to living beings in order to benefit Buddhism, the Buddha-dharma, and Buddhist studies.

World Buddhism Publishing LLC and World Dharma Voice Inc.

(This text was translated from the Chinese text that follows.)

出 版 社 的 說 明

在這本《正法寶典》即將出版的消息傳出之後，有善知識給我們出版社來信說：為什麼我們要專門出版多杰羌佛第三世雲高益西諾布頂聖如來顯密圓通、妙諳五明的《正法寶典》，而不出其他法王們的寶典五明集，是否有些偏愛執取？憑什麼稱三世多杰羌佛？有什麼超人的本領堪為聖人？作出認證的人應該是不負責任、信口開河？為此，本社藉《正法寶典》面世之際，我們秉持一個佛弟子的道德行為，抱著嚴守戒律的行持，在此說幾句毫無妄語、真實不虛而願承擔因果責任的話。

我們以恭敬的心敬請大家想一想告訴我們，在佛教歷史上有哪一位在這個世界轉來的佛菩薩，展顯出了如多杰羌佛第三世雲高益西諾布頂聖如來，證顯密圓通之智而妙諳五明的高度和完美境界？目前我們還沒有找到一個先聖可以並列，無論是仁波且，還是大法師，都拿不出這麼多實際的憑證可說明、可擺案翻展對比。要明白，這不是一本空洞理論而是圖文並展的書，要用實際的成果擺在大家的面前，而不是只有文字排版。如果你能說出有哪一位聖德，請拿出他的證量給大家看，請擺出實際的成果和資料，來支撐其說。我們詳查後的結論是：沒有一個人能做到。幾千年的佛教歷史以來，我們曲指數了，查閱了歷史資料，出現了許多有名有姓的大菩薩、法王仁波且，他們根據佛陀的定論：博通三藏，融匯密典，開敷五明，顯密圓通，作為佛陀規定的成就證量表法，無可非議，確實偉大。但是，相比之下，三世多杰羌佛確實達到了前無古聖的展顯成就，他拿出了獨一無二的高度，其它的不算，就只憑他的《正法寶典》中的三十大類的成就，能找出一個做一半的聖德都找不到。法王仁波且高僧們是大菩薩，確實證量很顯赫，這是事實，但為什麼三世多杰羌佛的成就，其他的聖德們做不到呢？如何解釋這一鐵的事實呢？法王、大仁波且們給了我們正確的答案。由文殊菩薩、觀音菩薩、彌勒菩薩等化身的法王仁波且回答了我們，因為雲高金剛總持是多杰羌佛降世第三世，是真身降世，而在這個世界上沒有部分的化身存在，故為三世多杰羌佛，雲高益西諾布不是哪一派的法王，而是頂聖如來，是顯密二宗所有教派的至尊古佛、皈依境中的最高總教主，所以大聖德們達不到他老人家的成就是理所當然的、符合法理的。

儘管如此，有那麼幾個欲迫害三世多杰羌佛、誹謗正法的邪見人物，還是對三世多杰羌佛的成就惡意玷污，其實，正的還是邪的，假的還是真的，在事實面前，是平等的真理。這是一個很容易解決的問題，對這些人，我們不要求他完成尊勝益西諾布的五蹟應試，因為這對他們來說想都不敢想。我們根據尊勝益西諾布大法王的授記，五跡中取其二跡：『無聖可複』，只要他能夠照著複製三世多杰羌佛的玄妙彩寶雕、把祥霧定在雕刻的石洞中，他說的話就是真理，否則，他即是說空洞假話的愚子或是無能的邪見凡夫，這就是謗誣者的本來面目！

為此，美國義雲高大師國際文化基金會等四機構已設立永久性對外印證應試的藍台印證：凡諸方聖德、智者、善士，無論施用你們的佛法智慧、證量、神通，或世間的科學方法，若能複製得了『玄妙彩寶雕』和『神秘石霧』，美國義雲高大師國際文化基金會均按2003年刊登在各大報紙上的宣告執行。

設立藍台印證更重要的是，尊勝益西諾布於授記中亦明示一點：若有人能複製得了玄妙彩寶雕、神秘石霧，他授記雲高金剛總持都是假的。本來，如果一個佛陀或等覺、妙覺菩薩降世，其成就是絕對高於凡夫的，比如觀音菩薩來這個世界，其證量一定高於普通人；文殊菩薩來，不會用打卦的方法，而一定先行預報而後擇緣無誤；藥王菩薩來，其治病救人的本事自然遠超普通大夫；而蓮花生大師降世，必具備除障之力量，當場消去眾生之黑業……因此，如果不是這樣，把一個普通凡夫說成是佛菩薩再來，無疑是對佛菩薩的侮辱。所以，美國義雲高大師國際文化基金會等的做法是最公平的，設立這個永久性藍台應試的目的不僅是鑒證尊勝益西諾布、薩迦天津大法王、降養隆多加參法王等對三世多杰羌佛認證的真實性，同時也會讓大家見到只會誹謗他人吹噓自己而毫無智慧的那些人的真正本來面目，如果不是這樣，為什麼他們無法用佛法的證量智慧來取得這1200萬美元以修建寺廟或利益眾生呢？為什麼只有說空話、無能的本事呢？

我們今天所講這些，是對來信者的回應，也是公佈決定設立藍台印證的目的，而不是要拿多杰羌佛第三世雲高益西諾布頂聖如來跟誰比高低，也不是拿來作宣傳，讓人歸其門下，而只是說明佛法的歷史中有這麼一段鐵的事實，眾生的解脫中有這麼一段殊勝的因緣！是將其在佛教歷史長河中飄泊流過的真實痕跡以事實再現於法籍中，給予歷史賦上一段真相，為佛教、佛法、佛學給人們眾生留下一鐵的事實貢獻。

全球佛教出版社暨世界法音出版社

（此文的英文翻譯印在前面）

Four organizations, including the Master Wan Ko Yee International Cultural Institute, have offered an award of U.S.$12,000,000 to anyone who can replicate a certain wondrous multicolored sculpture of H.H. Dorje Chang Buddha III. Various media reported on this matter at the time the offer was made.

義雲高大師國際文化基金會等四機構提供一千二百萬美元的獎金，徵求複製三世多杰羌佛的『玄妙彩寶雕』，這是當時各媒體的報導。

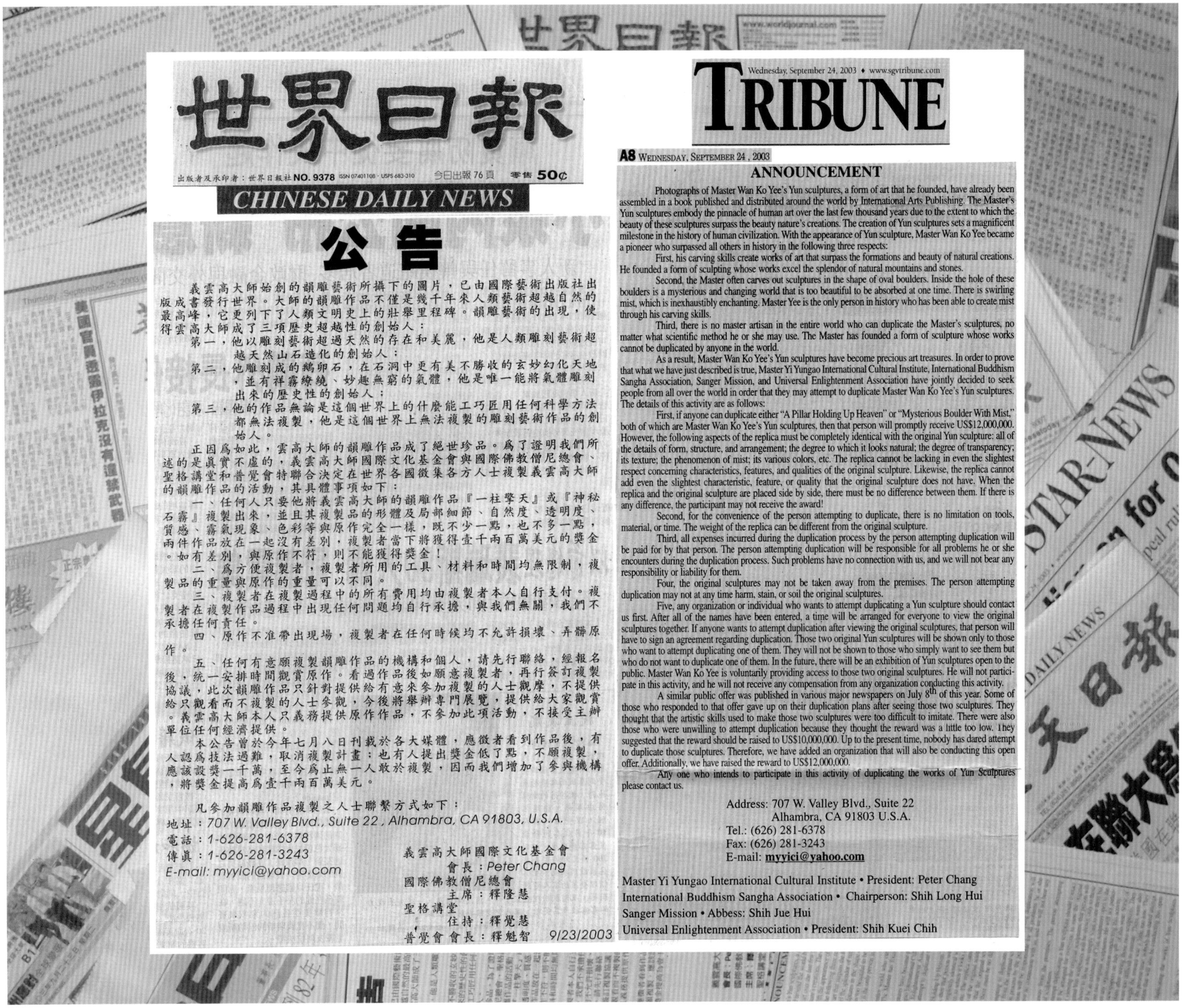

世界日報

出版者及承印者：世界日報社 NO. 9378 ISSN 07401108 · USPS 683-310 今日出報 76 頁 零售 50¢

CHINESE DAILY NEWS

公告

義雲高大師始創的韻雕藝術所攝下的圖片，已由國際藝術出版社出版成書發行世界。大師的韻雕作品不僅是幾千年來人類藝術超越自然的最高峰，它更列下了人類文明史上的壯舉里程碑。韻雕藝術的出現，使得雲高大師成了三項歷史超越性的創始人：

第一，他以雕刻藝術超過天然的存在和美麗，他是人類雕刻藝術超越天然山石造化的創始人；

第二，他雕刻成的鵝卵石，在石洞中更有美不勝收的玄妙幻化天地，並有祥霧繚繞、妙趣無窮的氣體，他是唯一能將氣體雕刻出來的歷史性的創始人；

第三，他的作品無論是這個世界上的什麼能工巧匠用任何科學方法都無法複製，他是這個世界上無法複製的雕刻藝術作品的創始人。

正因爲如此，雲高大師的韻雕作品成了絕世珍品。爲了證明我們所述的是眞實不虛的，義雲高大師國際文化基金會與國際佛教僧尼總會、聖格講堂和普覺會特聯合決定在世界各國徵集各方人士複製義雲高大師的韻雕作品的活動，其具體事項如下：

一、任何人只要他將義雲高大師的韻雕作品『一柱擎天』或『神秘石霧』複製出來，並且其複製品的形體及局部細節、自然度、透明度、質感、霧氣現象、色彩等與原作完全一樣，既不少一點，也不多一點，兩件作品放在一起沒有差別，複製者當下將獲得壹千兩百萬美元的獎金。如有差別，與原作不符，則不能獲得獎金！

二、爲方便複製者，複製者所用的工具、材料和時間均無限制，複製品的重量與原作的重量可以不同。

三、複製者在複製過程中的所有費用均由複製者本人自行支付。複製者在複製作品過程中出現任何問題均自行承擔，與我們無關，我們不承擔任何責任。

四、原作不准帶出現場，複製者在任何時候均不允許損壞、弄髒原作。

五、任何有意願複製韻雕作品的機構和個人，請先行聯絡，經報名後，統一安排時間觀賞原作。看過作品後如願意複製者，再行簽訂複製協議，此次韻雕作品只針對提供給有意來參加複製的人士觀摩，不提供給只觀看而不複製的人士參觀，今後將舉辦專門展覽，提供給大家觀賞。義雲高大師本人只義務提供原作作品，不參加此項活動，不接受主辦單位任何經濟提供。

本公告曾於今年七月八日刊載於各大媒體，應徵者看到作品後，有人認爲技法過難，取消複製計畫；也有人提出獎金低了點，不願複製，應該設獎一千萬，至今爲止無一人敢於複製，因而我們增加了參與機構，將獎金提高爲壹千兩百萬美元。

凡參加韻雕作品複製之人士聯繫方式如下：

地址：707 W. Valley Blvd., Suite 22 , Alhambra, CA 91803, U.S.A.
電話：1-626-281-6378
傳眞：1-626-281-3243
E-mail: myyici@yahoo.com

義雲高大師國際文化基金會
會長：Peter Chang
國際佛教僧尼總會
主席：釋隆慧
聖格講堂
住持：釋覺慧
普覺會 會長：釋魁智

9/23/2003

TRIBUNE

Wednesday, September 24, 2003 ♦ www.sgvtribune.com

A8 WEDNESDAY, SEPTEMBER 24 , 2003

ANNOUNCEMENT

Photographs of Master Wan Ko Yee's Yun sculptures, a form of art that he founded, have already been assembled in a book published and distributed around the world by International Arts Publishing. The Master's Yun sculptures embody the pinnacle of human art over the last few thousand years due to the extent to which the beauty of these sculptures surpass the beauty nature's creations. The creation of Yun sculptures sets a magnificent milestone in the history of human civilization. With the appearance of Yun sculpture, Master Wan Ko Yee became a pioneer who surpassed all others in history in the following three respects:

First, his carving skills create works of art that surpass the formations and beauty of natural creations. He founded a form of sculpting whose works excel the splendor of natural mountains and stones.

Second, the Master often carves out sculptures in the shape of oval boulders. Inside the hole of these boulders is a mysterious and changing world that is too beautiful to be absorbed at one time. There is swirling mist, which is inexhaustibly enchanting. Master Yee is the only person in history who has been able to create mist through his carving skills.

Third, there is no master artisan in the entire world who can duplicate the Master's sculptures, no matter what scientific method he or she may use. The Master has founded a form of sculpture whose works cannot be duplicated by anyone in the world.

As a result, Master Wan Ko Yee's Yun sculptures have become precious art treasures. In order to prove that what we have just described is true, Master Yi Yungao International Cultural Institute, International Buddhism Sangha Association, Sanger Mission, and Universal Enlightenment Association have jointly decided to seek people from all over the world in order that they may attempt to duplicate Master Wan Ko Yee's Yun sculptures. The details of this activity are as follows:

First, if anyone can duplicate either "A Pillar Holding Up Heaven" or "Mysterious Boulder With Mist," both of which are Master Wan Ko Yee's Yun sculptures, then that person will promptly receive US$12,000,000. However, the following aspects of the replica must be completely identical with the original Yun sculpture: all of the details of form, structure, and arrangement; the degree to which it looks natural; the degree of transparency; its texture; the phenomenon of mist; its various colors, etc. The replica cannot be lacking in even the slightest respect concerning characteristics, features, and qualities of the original sculpture. Likewise, the replica cannot add even the slightest characteristic, feature, or quality that the original sculpture does not have. When the replica and the original sculpture are placed side by side, there must be no difference between them. If there is any difference, the participant may not receive the award!

Second, for the convenience of the person attempting to duplicate, there is no limitation on tools, material, or time. The weight of the replica can be different from the original sculpture.

Third, all expenses incurred during the duplication process by the person attempting duplication will be paid for by that person. The person attempting duplication will be responsible for all problems he or she encounters during the duplication process. Such problems have no connection with us, and we will not bear any responsibility or liability for them.

Four, the original sculptures may not be taken away from the premises. The person attempting duplication may not at any time harm, stain, or soil the original sculptures.

Five, any organization or individual who wants to attempt duplicating a Yun sculpture should contact us first. After all of the names have been entered, a time will be arranged for everyone to view the original sculptures together. If anyone wants to attempt duplication after viewing the original sculptures, that person will have to sign an agreement regarding duplication. Those two original Yun sculptures will be shown only to those who want to attempt duplicating one of them. They will not be shown to those who simply want to see them but who do not want to duplicate one of them. In the future, there will be an exhibition of Yun sculptures open to the public. Master Wan Ko Yee is voluntarily providing access to those two original sculptures. He will not participate in this activity, and he will not receive any compensation from any organization conducting this activity.

A similar public offer was published in various major newspapers on July 8th of this year. Some of those who responded to that offer gave up on their duplication plans after seeing those two sculptures. They thought that the artistic skills used to make those two sculptures were too difficult to imitate. There were also those who were unwilling to attempt duplication because they thought the reward was a little too low. They suggested that the reward should be raised to US$10,000,000. Up to the present time, nobody has dared attempt to duplicate those sculptures. Therefore, we have added an organization that will also be conducting this open offer. Additionally, we have raised the reward to US$12,000,000.

Any one who intends to participate in this activity of duplicating the works of Yun Sculptures please contact us.

Address: 707 W. Valley Blvd., Suite 22
Alhambra, CA 91803 U.S.A.
Tel.: (626) 281-6378
Fax: (626) 281-3243
E-mail: **myyici@yahoo.com**

Master Yi Yungao International Cultural Institute • President: Peter Chang
International Buddhism Sangha Association • Chairperson: Shih Long Hui
Sanger Mission • Abbess: Shih Jue Hui
Universal Enlightenment Association • President: Shih Kuei Chih

BLUE PLATFORM VERIFICATION

To the Magnificent and Most Venerable Ones!

Most respectful greetings to the magnificent and most revered ones—H.H. Dorje Chang Buddha III; H.H. Great Dharma King Sakya Trizin, the supreme leader of the Sakya order; H.H. Great Dharma King Dodrupchen, the supreme leader of the Longchen Nying-thik; H.H. Great Dharma King Penor, the supreme leader of the Nyingma sect; H.H. Dharma King Omniscience Jamyang Lungdok third Gyaltsen Achuk; H.H. Great Dharma King Jigme Dorje, the supreme leader of the Jonang sect; H.H. Great Dharma King Zunsheng Yeshe Norbu; and other dharma kings and rinpoches of holy virtue!

Based upon the letters that our organizations received concerning questions about the recognition of H.H. Dorje Chang Buddha III, our organizations have established a Blue Platform Verification. We did this in order to protect the holy and solemn image of the Buddhas and Bodhsattvas, safeguard the true dharma of the Tathagata, uphold the wisdom of living beings whereby they may become liberated, spread right views, and avoid the ignorant slandering of holy beings that engenders negative karma and results in karmic retribution. Our organizations are not doing this to disrespectfully embarrass H.H. Dorje Chang Buddha III and the dharma kings and rinpoches who recognized and corroborated the identity of H.H. Dorje Chang Buddha III. We respectfully request that H.H. Dorje Chang Buddha III and those dharma kings and rinpoches understand our position and forgive us. For details concerning the Blue Platform Verification, please consult our announcement published in various media in 2003. However, the award for successfully duplicating those works as stated in that announcement has been increased to US$20,000,000.

Master Wan Ko Yee
International Cultural Institute

International Buddhism Sangha
Association

Sanger Mission

Universal Enlightenment
Association

We have received slanderous letters from people based on evil views. We have established a Blue Platform to respond as follows:

1. Is it evil or is it correct?

2. Is the realization of holy beings high or are the abilities of ordinary people high?

3. Is it the wisdom of the Buddhas and Bodhisattvas or is it the ignorance and stupidity of evil demons?

4. If what you said is not slanderous, why are you unable to obtain the $12,000,000 award and prove that you have the wisdom of holy beings rather than the ignorance of those with evil views?

5. You could use that $12,000,000 award to build temples or do charitable work. Moreover, in winning that award you would prove that H.H. Dorje Chang Buddha III is false and what you say is true. Unfortunately for you, those with evil views do not give rise to wisdom. Thus, you do not have the ability to obtain that award. Although you use slanderous words to hide your heresy, you cannot hide your lack of abilities. Why don't you let everyone see whether you are as true as gold or as false as copper? Wouldn't the truth then be clear?

Master Wan Ko Yee International Cultural Institute
International Buddhism Sangha Association
Sanger Mission
Universal Enlightenment Association

收到邪說之人的誹謗函詞，設藍台答覆如下：

1. 是邪是正？

2. 是聖者的證量高，還是凡夫的能力強？

3. 是佛菩薩的智慧境界，還是邪魔的愚癡無能？

4. 如果你不是誹謗，為什麼你沒有本事拿走這1200萬美金，證明你具聖者的智慧、而不是邪說的愚癡呢？

5. 1200萬美金拿去修寺廟或做善事，同時也證明三世多杰羌佛是假的，證明你講的話是真的。可惜邪惡不生慧，因此做不到，無法獲得獎金，除了用誹謗遮醜，但蓋不住無能的本質，是金還是銅，拿出來大家看看，不就清楚了嗎？

義雲高大師國際文化基金會
國際佛教僧尼總會
聖格講堂
普覺會

藍台印證

偉大至尊的第三世多杰羌佛、薩迦派總教主天津大法王、龍欽寧提總教主多智欽大法王、寧瑪派第三任總教主貝諾大法王、降養隆多加參遍智法王、覺囊派總教主吉美多吉大法王、尊勝益西諾布大法王等聖德法王仁波且們，法駕大安！

鑒於本會收到來自對認證三世多杰羌佛的疑問信函，因此，為了維護佛菩薩的神聖莊嚴形象和如來正法，為了維護眾生的慧命而正見開敷，以免愚癡謗聖而黑業纏身，招致惡果，因此本會才設立藍台印證，此作法非是以不敬之舉來為難三世多杰羌佛和諸位認證、附議的法王仁波且們，在此敬請三世多杰羌佛和法王仁波且們理解原諒。至於具體印證辦法請參見我們四機構於2003年在各大媒體上的公告，但複製成功後的獎金提高到美金兩千萬元。

義雲高大師
國際文化基金會

國際佛教僧尼總會

聖格講堂

普覺會

CATEGORY 1

Recognitions and Congratulations

第一大類　認證祝賀

Introduction

The category of recognitions and congratulations mainly makes public the original recognition certificates and corroborating congratulatory letters written by dharma kings, rinpoches, and eminent monastics in the world of Buddhism today to H.H. Dorje Chang Buddha III Wan Ko Yeshe Norbu Holiest Tathagata. This category also contains brief introductions to these dharma kings, regent dharma kings, rinpoches, and eminent monastics. H.H. Mahavairocana Dharma King Zunsheng has recognized the identity of and has made written predictions about H.H. Dorje Chang Buddha III, who is an incarnation of the primordial Buddha. The Buddha name of the third Dorje Chang Buddha is H.H. Dorje Chang Buddha III Wan Ko Yeshe Norbu.

In 2006, the publisher distributed some of the initial manuscripts of this book about the accomplishments of H.H. Wan Ko Yeshe Norbu. After famous great dharma kings and rinpoches of the highest order in the world read that initial manuscript, all of them were very moved and astounded. They wondered what being of holy virtue has descended into this world and how such a being is able to manifest the pinnacle of realization not manifested by anyone else in the past few thousand years of Buddhist history.

Those dharma kings immediately practiced dharma and entered a meditative state in order to evaluate and affirm the true identity or status of H.H. Wan Ko Yeshe Norbu. Thus, the karmic conditions matured for the occurrence of a great event in Buddhism. More than three holy great dharma kings who are incarnations of Buddhas or Mahasattvas and more than ten holy masters issued formal documents recognizing the identity of His Holiness and congratulating Him, thereby exceeding the minimum requirements of the dharma. Those masters of great holiness confirmed that H.H. Wan Ko Yeshe Norbu Holiest Tathagata is the incarnation of Dorje Chang Buddha, the master of the Five Buddhas in the five directions and other Buddhas. Each of those masters of great holiness is a famous personage of the highest level in the world today and is an incarnation of a Buddha or Bodhisattva.

Among such masters of great holiness are the following four people: The world-renowned supreme leader of the Sakya sect, H.H. Great Vehicle Dharma King Sakya Trizin, who is a true nirmanakaya of Manjushri Bodhisattva; H.H. Dharma King Omniscience Jamyang Lungdok Gyaltsen, also known as Lama Achuk. His Holiness is the incarnation of Venerable Longsal Nyingpo, who was one of the twenty-five great disciples of Guru Padmasambhava; H.H. Dharma King Mighty Lion Renzeng Nima, who is the incarnation of King Gesar; and H.E. Master Urgyen Xirao Woxiu, who is the incarnation of Urgyen Lingpa, an outstanding disciple of Guru Padmasambhava. This master of Tibetan esoteric Buddhism is known as an extremely holy being in modern Tibet who possesses great supernatural powers.

Why are we publishing in this category written recognitions and congratulations showing the identity of H.H. Wan Ko Yeshe Norbu Holiest Tathagata as being the third incarnation of Dorje Chang Buddha and the second incarnation of the holy Venerable Vimalakirti? It is because this is in conformity with the rules and system of esoteric Buddhism by which the identity of a reincarnated rinpoche or reincarnated Bodhisattva is affirmed. These dharma rules cannot be changed. Throughout the history of Buddhism, the dharma rules of esoteric Buddhism have required that the true identity of all reincarnated beings of holy virtue, all reincarnated Bodhisattvas, and all reincarnated Buddhas is firmly established only after such identity is recognized by famous holy and eminent people of great virtue. Otherwise, no matter how well the reincarnated person knows the sutras and no matter how high the reincarnated person's level of realization is, he is only one who spreads the dharma of exoteric Buddhism. His true identity has not been conclusively established as the reincarnation of a holy being.

This dharma rule applied even to the highest leader of Tibetan esoteric Buddhism, Guru Padmasambhava, who was called the Second Buddha. His accomplishment in the dharma reached the level of a Buddha. However, he could not establish his identity or status when he first attempted to spread the dharma in Tibet because he did not have a certificate recognizing his identity or status. Thus, he was labeled as a heretic, persecuted, and sent into exile. In order to comply with the dharma rules of Tibetan esoteric Buddhism, Guru Padmasambhava had to return to India. After people of great holiness and virtue affirmed his identity, he returned to Tibet. Only then was he able to establish firmly his identity, introduce esoteric Buddhism to Tibet, spread the dharma, and benefit living beings.

The dharma systems of all main sects of esoteric Buddhism—the Nyingma, Sakya, Kagyu, Gelug, Jonang, Kadampa, Chod, etc.—use the teachings of the Buddha as their guide to spread the dharma. For generation after generation, Buddhas and Bodhisattvas have been reincarnating in order to save living beings. After the identities of such reincarnated persons have been recognized and established with certainty, they are called tulkus or rinpoches. If their status is higher, they are called dharma kings. Dharma kings or great rinpoches who meet the standards laid down in the dharma must recognize which holy being the reincarnated person is in order to determine with certainty the identity of that reincarnated person. Anyone who claims to be the reincarnation of a certain holy and virtuous being yet does not have a certificate issued by a rinpoche of great holiness recognizing that claim is either a heretic or one whose claim is not recognized in Buddhism.

A great Bodhisattva whose status and level of accomplishment are relatively high can recognize the identity of an ordinary Bodhisattva. An ordinary Bodhisattva can also recognize the identity of a Bodhisattva whose status is higher than that of the ordinary Bodhisattva. A Buddha can recognize the identity of a Bodhisattva, and a Bodhisattva can also recognize the identity of a Buddha. Who recognizes whom is not related to one's level of realization or status. However, the dharma requires that the recognition of the identity of a reincarnated person be done by rinpoches who have the qualifications to recognize according to the standards laid out in the dharma. A certificate of recognition with the required signature and seal must be issued after the identity is affirmed. Only then can the true identity of the reincarnated person be established according to the dharma.

For example, there are some rinpoches within Buddhist circles who call themselves Manjushri Bodhisattva, Kuan Yin Bodhisattva, or Guru Padmasambhava. Their disciples also respectfully use one of those names to address their master. However, this is exaggerated praise, groundless boasting, and empty words that cannot substitute for a certificate recognizing someone as a reincarnated rinpoche. According to the dharma rules, such use of Bodhisattva names to extol someone is untenable. It is necessary that famous rinpoches or persons of great holiness and virtue with the qualifications to recognize one's identity determine the identity of a reincarnated person. It is also necessary that such recognition be strictly carried out according to the dharma and that a recognition document be formally issued after the recognition. Additionally, other rinpoches must send congratulatory letters corroborating the recogniztion. With respect to determining the true identity of a reincarnated person according to the dharma, it is best if three holy masters carry out the recognition. There must be at least one holy master who recognizes the identity of the reincarnated person and at least two holy masters who corroborate that recognition for that identification to stand. Any master of holy virtue who carries out the recognition must be a famous great dharma king or at least a regent dharma king or national preceptor. Furthermore, the letters of congratulations corroborating the recognition must be sent by legitimate rinpoches.

Thus, a certain person, lama, or rinpoche may claim that he is the reincarnation of a certain Bodhisattva, or people generally recognize him as the reincarnation of a certain Bodhisattva. However, if masters of holy virtue have not recognized his identity and issued formal recognition documents according to the dharma, and if rinpoches of great holiness have not sent written congratulations corroborating the recognition, then all such claims and general recognition are empty rumors that do not stand no matter how widespread the claim may be. That is because when a being of holy virtue reincarnates from a past lifetime to this present lifetime, his past lifetime must be examined in conformity with the dharma by great dharma kings or great rinpoches who are qualified according to the standards laid out in the dharma. The true prior lifetime of that person of holy virtue must be discerned through the examiners entering a meditative state of enlightenment, which is a totally different dimension. One's true identity cannot be determined by the worldly ways of discussing and voting, such as when the masses of people, who are not beings of great holiness, elect their representatives. Thus, a person's true identity is not determined by the identity people generally recognize that person as having or the identity people praise that person as having. That is because ordinary people do not have the power to see who the person being recognized really was in his last lifetime. Hence, the identity of someone that common people generally recognize cannot stand in and of itself. Throughout the history of Buddhism to the present day, the rules of esoteric Buddhism have prescribed that the identity of a reincarnated rinpoche is firmly established only when that identity is recognized by authentic and famous great dharma kings or great rinpoches who issue recognition certificates and corroborating letters of congratulations. These recognitions and corroborations must be put down in black and white for all to see.

Well over ten holy masters wrote congratulatory letters to H.H. Dorje Chang Buddha III Wan Ko Yeshe Norbu Holiest Tathagata certifying or corroborating the recognitions of identity issued by others. Moreover, all of those holy masters are present-day famous dharma kings of great holiness or are great rinpoches. Some of them are as follows: the world-renowned H.H. Dharma King Dodrupchen, who is the true incarnation of Guru Padmasambhava; the world-renowned supreme dharma king of the Nyingma sect, H.H. Dharma King Penor, who is a nirmanakaya of Vajrapani Bodhisattva; the supreme leader of the Jonang sect, H.H. Dharma King Jigme Dorje; the Mindrolling monasteries of the Nyingma sect; H.H. Dharma King Taklung Tsetrul, the Dharma King of the Dorje Drak Monastery; the famous H.H. Dharma King Trulshik, who is the personal master of H.H. the Dalai Lama, the current H.H. Dharma King Dudjom, and H.H. Dharma King Dilgo Khyentse; H.E. Chogye Trichen Rinpoche, the Dharma King of Tsharpa branch of the Sakya Order; the Red Jewel Crown Dharma King of the Karma Kagyu sect, H.E. Shamarpa, who is a regent dharma king for the Karmapa; the Orange Jewel Crown Dharma King of the

Karma Kagyu sect, H.E. Goshir Gyaltsab, who is the vajra master of and regent dharma king for the Karmapa and who is a "National Master"; H.E. Xiazhu Qiuyang Rinpoche, who is the incarnation of Patriarch Naropa, the venerable leader of 100,000 dakinis; the great Bodhisattva Tangtong Gyalpo, who is extremely famous in the history of Tibetan esoteric Buddhism, who has limitless merit, and whose accomplishment in the dharma is remarkable; H.E. Dharma King Ngagwang Pedma Namgyal Palzangpo of the Jonang sect; H.E. Mindrolling Khenchen Rinpoche; H.E. Khandro Rinpoche, who is the incarnation of Yeshe Tsogyal; H.E. Dorje Rinzin Rinpoche, a dharma king of great enlightenment who is the incarnation of Unchanging Vajra; H.E. Shechen Rabjam Rinpoche, who is the Dharma King of Shechen monasteries of the Nyingma sect; H.E. Dzogchen Dharma King VII; the eastern Tibetan Dharma King, H.E. Renqing Rongbo Barongbo; the Green Jewel Crown Karmapa, H.E. Dharma King Jiezhong; Veneral Junmai Baima Dorje Rinpoche, who is a nirmanakaya of Vajravarahi; Yundeng Jiangcuo Rinpoche, who has been in solitary retreat for many years and who is the incarnation of Patriarch Milarepa; and so on.

Thus, such recognition was completely in accordance with the dharma. Actually, there were more than three holy great dharma kings who are incarnations of Buddhas or Mahasattvas and more than ten holy masters involved in the recognition and corroboration. H.H. Dorje Chang Buddha III Wan Ko Yeshe Norbu Holiest Tathagata is the first holy being in the history of Buddhism in the human realm to have received that many recognitions and corroborating congratulatory letters from dharma kings of great holiness on such a high level! No other dharma king or great rinpoche in history has received so many of such documents. Because there are so many people of holy virtue who issued recognitions of identity and congratulatory letters, only some of those documents are contained in this first category. They are not entirely arranged according to the relative positions or status of those people of holy virtue.

Based on the certificates of recognition and congratulatory messages issued, everyone will understand that the status and identity of H.H. Dorje Chang Buddha III Wan Ko Yeshe Norbu were recognized by more than three holy great dharma kings who are incarnations of Buddhas or Mahasattvas as the dharma prescribes. Moreover, more than ten holy masters respectfully confirmed that the Buddha name of His Holiness is H.H. Dorje Chang Buddha III. They all recognized that the realization of His Holiness is supreme. They also all concluded that the accomplishment His Holiness has manifested is foremost in Buddhist history.

(This text was translated from the Chinese text that follows.)

簡　介

　　認證祝賀類主要是公布佛教界的法王、仁波且、高僧們對多杰羌佛第三世雲高益西諾布頂聖如來的確認認證書及附議祝賀函原文，同時刊發法王、攝政王、仁波且、高僧們的簡介。三世多杰羌是經大日如來尊勝法王認證並預言的始祖古佛轉世，佛號為三世多杰羌雲高益西諾布。2006年，出版社發表了雲高益西諾布的《正法寶典》一書的校稿初版，而當世界第一流著名大法王及仁波且們見到此《正法寶典》的校稿初版以後，十分感動震撼，到底是什麼聖德降世，竟然出現幾千年來佛教史上沒有出現過的證量高峰境界，法王們當下修法入定鑒定確認，由此而使之佛法大事因緣成熟了，這才圓滿具備三聖十證行文確認認證祝賀。認證雲高益西諾布頂聖如來為五佛之師多杰羌佛轉世的幾位大聖，均是當今世界第一流著名的古德大聖佛菩薩們：其中有世界著名的、文殊菩薩化身的薩迦派總教主薩迦天津大乘法王；有二十五大王臣之一的龍薩娘波尊者轉世的降陽龍多加參遍智法王阿秋大師；有格薩爾王轉世的仁增尼瑪雄獅法王；有當今藏密鄔堅喜饒喔修大師蓮花生大師法王子鄔堅寧巴，稱為全藏近代神通廣大的大聖者。為什麼我們要專門列出認證和祝賀頂聖如來雲高益西諾布為多杰羌佛第三世、維摩詰第二世的轉世身份為一類呢？因為這是佛教密乘教規對仁波且菩薩們轉世確認的律制，是不可更改的法規。在佛教史上的密乘教規法定，無論是什麼地位的聖德、菩薩或佛陀轉世再來，都必須要通過著名的聖者高僧大德們的確認認證，才能確立其真實身份。否則無論經教多好、道量多高，也只能作為顯教的宏法者，是不具實質身份的再來人，包括藏密之最高領袖烏金第二佛陀蓮花生大師，其在佛法上的成就達到了佛陀的境界，但首次在西藏宏法時，由於他未持認證書，他的身份無法成立，所以被打成外道並受到迫害、放逐。為了符合藏密法規，蓮師只得回到印度，由大聖德認證後，再返回西藏，這才確立身份在西藏開啟密宗宏法利生。

　　根據密乘制度，無論是寧瑪、薩迦、噶舉、格魯、覺囊、噶當、希解等各派，都是以佛陀宏法利生的大事因緣為指南，由佛菩薩們一代一代轉世渡化眾生，轉世者被認證確立後稱之為諸古或仁波且、或地位升為法王，他們是哪一位聖者轉世再來的身份確定，是必須經合法的法王、大仁波且們認證的，凡未經認證而自稱是某聖德再來則為邪教或是不符合法教的天然外道。在認證方面，有地位成就較高的大菩薩認證普通的菩薩，也有普通的菩薩來認證地位較高的菩薩，有佛陀認證菩薩，也有菩薩認證佛陀。誰認證誰是與證量、地位沒有關係的，但法定是必須經具合法認證資格的仁波且認證轉世者。認證確定後，出具簽名蓋印的認證書，此時轉世者的真實身份方可合法成立。比如在佛教界中有些仁波且稱自己是文殊菩薩或觀音菩薩、蓮花生大師，乃至於他們的弟子也這麼恭稱他們的上師，但這是誇讚奉承，是虛吹的行為、空洞的說詞，代表不了法定的認證書，因此該仁波且被稱頌的菩薩稱號在法規裡是不成立的。轉世者的身份確定必須是依著名仁波且、有認證資格的大聖德們，嚴肅依法確認認證後並行以文憑，而且還要有仁波且們附議致以文函祝賀。凡轉世真實身份屬於合法成立的，最圓滿的必須為三聖認證，至少要一聖認證、兩聖附議才能成立轉世身份。而執行認證的聖德必須是著名的大法王，至少要攝政王或國師，附議祝賀也必須是正規的仁波且致賀函。因此，凡是自稱或是所謂的世人公認某某人或某某喇嘛、活佛是某某菩薩轉世，而無聖德們合法確認發給認證文憑和沒有大聖仁波且的附議賀文憑者，無論是什麼樣的口頭傳言，全部屬於不成立的謠傳空洞說詞。因為對一位前世轉世到今世來的聖德，必須經合法的大法王、大仁波且們如法入定觀照，依法查出真實的前身，而不是由非大聖者的大眾如世間法選委員一樣，商量投票選舉就能定出真實身份的。所以人們公認或稱頌是不能成其為真身轉世的，凡作為普通人是看不到被認證者上一世的真實身份的，所以類屬大眾公認是不能成立的。密乘教規佛史至今，一切仁波且的轉世，都必須經正宗著名大法王、大仁波且認證發認證書、致附議賀文，見其白紙黑字的文憑而確立。

　　在行文附議祝賀多杰羌佛第三世雲高益西諾布頂聖如來的十證中，不僅遠遠超過十證，而且都是當今著名大聖法王和大仁波且們：有蓮花生真身轉世、舉世聞名的多智欽法王；有金剛手菩薩的轉世、享譽世界的當今寧瑪巴第一總法王的貝諾法王；有覺囊總教主吉美多吉法王；有寧瑪敏珠林寺系；有多傑扎寺掌教法王達龍哲珠法王；有達賴喇嘛和登珠法王、頂果欽哲法王的個人上師、著名的楚西法王；有薩迦茶巴法王秋吉崔欽；有噶瑪噶舉派紅寶冠法王夏瑪巴攝政王；有噶瑪噶舉派橙寶冠法王、噶瑪巴之金剛上師、攝政國師嘉察巴；有十萬空行尊主那洛巴祖師轉世的夏珠秋揚仁波且；有藏密佛史最著名、功德無量、成就顯赫的唐東迦波大菩薩；有覺囊派阿旺班瑪南加法王；有敏林堪欽仁波且；有移喜措嘉佛母轉世的康卓公主仁波且；有『大覺之王』不變金剛多杰仁增；有寧瑪雪謙寺系的法王雪謙仁波且；有第七世佐欽法王；有東藏法王仁青絨波巴絨波；有噶瑪巴杰仲綠寶冠法王；有金剛亥母化身的俊麥白瑪多吉仁波且；有長年閉關密拉日巴祖師轉世的雲登降措仁波且等等，不但圓滿合法，而且超過了三聖十證。這也是在人類佛教史上達到最高和最多大聖法王們認證和附議恭賀的第一聖！無論是任何法王或大仁波且，在歷史上就沒有一個達到過有這麼多的文憑證書。因為認證和祝賀的聖德太多，故在這一大類刊出的部分認證、祝賀原文不是完全按照這些聖德們的等位高低而排列的。

　　由這些聖德們的認證和祝賀，大家就會了解，三世多杰羌佛雲高益西諾布的地位身份，不僅是合法達到三聖確認的，十證恭稱定佛號為三世多杰羌佛，而且其證量，公認是至高無上的；其成就展顯，也是公鑒為佛史第一的。

（此文的英文翻譯印在前面）

BRIEF INTRODUCTION TO
H.H. DHARMA KING SAKYA TRIZIN
薩迦天津法王簡介

established the Sakya Monastery.

Thereafter, in an unbroken succession of generations that continues to the present day, all of the descendants of the Khon clan incarnated as nirmanakayas of great Bodhisattvas. The five Sakya patriarchs and many famous masters came from this outstanding lineage. The teachings of the Sakya order can now be found throughout all of Tibet and even all over the world. Moreover,

To the left of H.H. Dharma King Sakya Trizin is H.H. Dalai Lama. To the right of H.H. Dharma King Sakya Trizin is H.H. Urgyen Trinley Dorje and H.E. Dharma King Chogye Trichen.
薩迦天津法王的左邊是達賴喇嘛，右邊是烏金聽列多杰噶瑪巴和秋吉崔欽法王。

many Patriarchs from the Nyingma sect and many masters from the Kadampa sect and the Kagyu sect have deepened their practice even further through the teachings of the Sakya order. Additionally, the Jonang sect, the Shalu sect and the Buton sect originated from the lineage of the Sakya order. During the Ming Dynasty, the Sakya Dharma King was given the title of Great Vehicle Dharma King (meaning king of the dharma).

In order to prevent the deterioration of and preserve the essence of Buddha-dharma, the Sakya order adopted the system of family and blood lineage. Its precepts and rules are just as strict as those of the Geluk sect. Furthermore, the Lamdre (Path and Result) and the Hevajra Root Tantra lineages of the Sakya order are extremely strict and rigorous. Thus, the teachings and lineages of the Sakya order have been preserved in their entirety. In order that the dharma of the Sakya order be handed down in a way that preserves its essence and correctness, those who kept and propagated such dharma are dharma kings and rinpoches from the Khon family lineage led by H.H. the Great Vehicle Dharma King. The famous master H.H. Jamyang Khyentse Wangpo once said, "Even a tiny bit of the innate wisdom, abilities, and other merits of these rinpoches exceeds those of other incarnated rinpoches or descendants of eminent families who regard themselves as infallible. This is a fact that everyone has been able to personally see all the way up to the present time."

His Holiness Great Vehicle Dharma King Sakya Trizin is a true nirmanakaya of Manjushri Bodhisattva. He is the supreme leader of the Sakya order whose wisdom, supernatural powers, and realization are extremely high. Moreover, the International Buddhism Sangha Association held an unprecedented Drawing Lots From a Golden Vase Ceremony to affirm the true reincarnated identity of H.H. Sakya Trizin and others. There were ten possible identities recognized by various rinpoches. One lot was drawn from among 120 lots to affirm the true reincarnated identity of H.H. Sakya Trizin. That drawing affirmed that H.H. Sakya Trizin is a nirmanakaya of Manjushri Bodhisattva, which is the reincarnated identity that H.H. Dorje Chang Buddha III recognized before that lot was drawn. "Trizin" is a Tibetan term meaning "dharma leader." That is, His Holiness is the supreme leader of all of the Buddha-dharma and temples of the Sakya order.

H.H. Sakya Trizin had extraordinary wisdom that no one could match from the time he was a child. When he was five years old, he received Lamdre Mind Essence teachings and completed the Long Life Buddha retreat. At the age of seven at the Sakya Monastery, he passed a broad and

The Sakya order is one of the oldest orders or sects within Tibetan Buddhism. It is also recognized by all of the other Tibetan Buddhist orders as being the order with the most powerful and numerous dharma methods that lead to true realization. The Sakya order has an extremely high status within Tibetan Buddhism. A tradition of the Sakya order is not to lightly transmit dharma or confer titles.

The founders of the Sakya order came from an ancient noble family called the Khon clan. An ancestor of the Khon clan by the name of Khon Lui Wangpo Sungwa was one of the first seven people in Tibet to become a monk. He followed and learned under Guru Padmasambhava. From that time on, all of the descendents of the Khon clan practiced the dharma from the lineage of Guru Padmasambhava. Moreover, they all personally saw their yidams and attained the most wonderful accomplishment in the dharma.

Later, Khon Konchok Gyalpo, who already was proficient in exoteric and esoteric Buddhist teachings, followed and learned the dharma under the great master Drokmi Lotsawa. He received teachings from newly translated secret tantras and thereby attained enlightenment. He then detailed oral examination on the Hevajra Root Tantra. Furthermore, wisdom stored since beginning-less time in the form of all of the other major dharma teachings of the Sakya lineage started to arise intensively in His Holiness's mind. He completed the Hevajra retreat at the age of eight. When he was fourteen years old, he formally ascended to the throne of "Sakya Trizin" and went to India. When he was sixteen years old, he read scriptures and treatises on Madhyamaka (the Middle Way), Hetu-Vidya (Buddhist logic), Prajna (Wisdom) and other subjects at the place of the great Sakya master Khenpo Rinchen. His Holiness conferred his first Hevajra initiation at Kalimpong when he was seventeen years old.

H.H. Dharma King Sakya Trizin has practiced countless great dharmas and completed countless retreats. Such practices include those relating to the Long Life Buddha, Demon-Conquering Vajrapani, Mahakala, Vajrakila, Mahavairocana, and long ritual Hevajra. H.H. Dharma King is a rare and great Mahasattva of both ancient and present times. Buddhist disciples express nothing but praise and astonishment over His Holiness's realization and accomplishment in the dharma. They deeply understand that the empowering effect of His Holiness's initiations and dharma transmissions are no different than direct transmissions from Manjushri Bodhisattva or other great holy beings.

When the supreme leader of the Sakya order, H.H. Great Vehicle Dharma King Sakya Trizin, was in Nepal on December 10, 2006, His Holiness conducted a verification in accordance with the dharma. After His Holiness saw the truth that H.H. Wan Ko Yeshe Norbu is the third Dorje Chang Buddha, the Dharma King wrote an affirmation certificate as prescribed by the dharma.

薩迦派是藏傳佛教中最古老的教派之一，也是藏傳佛教中各派公認的具量法門最強多的教派，在藏傳佛教中地位極高，不輕易傳法封受。

薩迦派的創始人為西藏古老的貴族——昆氏家族，而昆氏家族的祖先昆‧魯益旺波澤真（龍王持壽）是西藏最早的七位出家人之一，親隨蓮花生大師學習。自此，昆氏子孫均修習蓮花生大師的傳承法要，並且都親見本尊，獲得了共同和最勝之成就。後來，昆‧貢秋嘉波在通達顯密教法的基礎上，跟隨卓彌大譯師學法，獲得了新譯密續的教授與證悟，並創建薩迦寺。自此，昆族的後人，世代無間斷地以三怙主的化身傳承相續至今。薩迦五祖以及許多著名的大師也都出自這個卓越的傳承。現在，不僅整個雪域藏區，乃至世界各地，都有薩迦派的教法。而且，很多寧瑪派的祖師、噶當派和噶舉派的大師們都曾經在薩迦門下深造，還有覺囊派、夏魯派和布頓派也都源自於薩迦派的傳承。薩迦法王在明朝時更被封為大乘法王（意為法中之王）。

薩迦派為了防止佛法變質，保其精髓，由是採用家族和血脈傳承制度，戒規的嚴格程度不下格魯巴，並且道果和喜金剛本續的傳承更是極其嚴密，故薩迦的教法和傳承保存完整，法義使傳不失精正，住持和弘揚薩迦派教法的是以大乘法王為首的昆氏家族傳承世系的法王和仁波且們。著名的蔣揚欽哲汪波大師曾說：『這些仁波且們，僅他們天賦的智慧、能力等功德的微小一分，也是別的自以為是的化身活佛或名門望族後裔們所不能及的，這是直到現在大家都能親眼得見的事實。』

薩迦天津大乘法王為文殊菩薩的真實化身，是薩迦派在全世界的總教主，其智慧、神通目然證量高峰。史難得的是，國際佛教僧尼總會對仁波且們作出的十個不同認證身份舉行了史無前例的金瓶掣籤，從120支密封籤中抽出一支，確認薩迦天津是文殊菩薩的化身，而此身份正是三世多杰羌佛在這之前作出的認證。『天津』一詞為藏文音譯，意為『法主』，也就是薩迦所有佛法寺廟的總領袖。天津總教主自幼即智慧超群，無人能及。五歲接受道果心髓教授，完成長壽佛閉關，七歲的時候，在薩迦寺院通過了喜金剛根本密續廣泛而詳盡的口試，並開始密集地從智慧中開敷出無始藏智薩迦傳承的其它主要教法。八歲則圓滿喜金剛閉關。十四歲正式升座登基為『薩迦天津』並前往印度，十六歲時在薩迦大師堪布仁千處展觀中觀之義、因明、般若等其它經論，十七歲在卡林旁第一次傳授喜金剛的灌頂。法王修習過無數的大法和閉關，如長壽佛、伏魔金剛手、大黑天、普巴金剛、大日如來以及最長儀軌的喜金剛等。法王是一位殊勝難得的古今大摩訶薩，佛弟子對於總法王之修證成就，唯有讚嘆和醉迷，深知其灌頂教授之加持力與文殊等大聖們之親傳無二。

2006年12月10日，當時正在尼泊爾的薩迦天津總教主大乘法王如法查證，見到雲高益西諾布是多杰羌佛第三世的真相後，寫下了法定的認證書。

BRIEF INTRODUCTION TO H.H. DODRUPCHEN DHARMA KING
多智欽大法王簡介

It is accurate to say that without His Holiness Dodrupchen Rinpoche there would be no Longchen Nying-thik Great Perfection, which is the highest esoteric dharma in this world. H.H. Dodrupchen Rinpoche was the sole holder and fundamental dharma possessor of the complete Great Perfection Longchen Nying-thik. "Longchen" means the boundlessly vast dharmadhatu, and "Nying-thik" means mind essence. Thus, Longchen Nying-thik is a mind essence dharma method that belongs to the extremely secret Supreme Division within the Great Perfection Dharma. It is the highest dharma for transforming into the rainbow body. All of the Longchen Nying-thik lineages of the Nyingma sect around the world, including those of their six main temples, originated from the dharma transmission of H.H. Dodrupchen Rinpoche.

In Tibetan, the term "Dodrupchen" means a greatly accomplished one from the Do Valley. The term derives from the first Dodrupchen Rinpoche, who was born in the upper Do Valley in the Gyalrong District of eastern Tibet. When the first Dodrupchen Rinpoche visited Master Jigme Lingpa, that master recognized Dodrupchen as being the incarnation of the sacred prince Murub Tsepo that was predicted in the "Guide to Longchen Nying-thik Predictions" and as being the sole possessor and successor to the Longchen Nying-thik teachings. Thus, Master Jigme Lingpa bestowed upon Dodrupchen the complete "Direct Transmission from Buddha" and "Terma (Hidden Treasures)" lineages and authorized him to be the fundamental dharma possessor of Longchen Nying-thik.

The first, second, third, and fourth Dodrupchen Rinpoches not only manifested many incredible feats of supernatural power and wisdom, they also continually transmitted the Longchen Nying-thik dharma method to all holy beings who had the required karmic affinity. They thereby trained many famous people to become greatly accomplished in the dharma.

H.H. the fourth and current Dodrupchen, Thupten Trinle Palzang Rinpoche, was born in 1927 in the Tsi Village of the Ser Valley within the Gyalrong District. Almost every day during the time the rinpoche was in the womb, rainbows appeared in the sky above his village. Almost every night during that time, people could see the dharma protecting deity Rahula over the rinpoche's roof. Moreover, a fresh flower never before seen in that area blossomed forth upon his roof without having been planted. That was the exact type of flower H.H. the third Dodrupchen Rinpoche liked to plant the most when he was living in seclusion. During the time the rinpoche's mother was carrying the rinpoche, he would often disappear from her womb. During her pregnancy, a mysterious light always accompanied the rinpoche's mother such that she was able to find things in the dark without having to use any form of illumination.

Holy events that were much more amazing occurred after the rinpoche was born. A mani stone once fell from a cliff and hit the rinpoche. As a result, many of his bones were broken to pieces. However, all traces of injury miraculously disappeared almost totally a few hours later. Sometimes the young rinpoche could be clearly seen standing on the ground but an instant later was on a roof or cliff. Before monks from the Dodrupchen Monastery came to his house in search of the child who was the incarnation of the Dodrupchen, the young rinpoche told his parents, who at the time did not know such monks were coming, "Today guests will come." He then began to sing happily. The team of monks who came to investigate placed before the young rinpoche books, Buddhist rosaries, and other objects used by the last Dodrupchen Rinpoche as well as objects of others people, all of which had been mixed together. They had the young rinpoche select from among the displayed objects. The young rinpoche picked out the objects he used in his last life without making one mistake. He then said, "These are mine." H.H. the fifth Dzogchen Dharma King personally recognized that this child was H.H. the fourth Dodrupchen Rinpoche.

After the completion of his enthronement ceremony at the Dodrupchen Monastery, the four-year-old rinpoche stood up on his dharma throne and smiled as he chanted some verses from the "Vajra Seven Line Supplication" and the "Request to Padmasambhava." This won the great admiration of all of the people in attendance. From the age of five, the rinpoche began to open directly his own treasury of wisdom accumulated since beginning-less time. Additionally, he gave oral accounts of these dharma teachings.

Moreover, in 2007 the International Buddhism Sangha Association held an unprecedented Drawing Lots From a Golden Vase Ceremony to affirm the true reincarnated identity of H.H. Dodrupchen Dharma King and others. There were ten possible identities recognized by various rinpoches. One lot was drawn from among 120 lots to affirm the true reincarnated identity of H.H. Dodrupchen Dharma King. That drawing affirmed that H.H. Dodrupchen Dharma King is the nirmanakaya of Guru Padmasambhava, which is the reincarnated identity that H.H. Dorje Chang Buddha III recognized before that lot was drawn.

After His Holiness grew up, he very seldom manifested supernatural powers except in certain particular circumstances. Although he did not need to cleanse his mind, accumulate good fortune, or engage in any other cultivation of this type, in order to establish a model of true cultivation for living beings, His Holiness sought dharma from many human masters and completed many years of solitary retreat. At the age of fifteen, His Holiness was proficient in painting mandalas, calligraphy, ceramics, architecture, astrology, and many other skills.

Based upon the predictions of the Dakinis in 1957 concerning the circumstances Tibet would face, H.H. Dodrupchen Rinpoche arrived in Sikkim. At first His Holiness did not reveal His status. However, a greatly accomplished person in Sikkim who was the master of the king of Sikkim told the king that the true Padmasambhava had arrived in Sikkim and strongly urged the king to become a disciple of H.H. Dodrupchen Rinpoche. Later, after repeated entreaties by the king of Sikkim, His Holiness assumed the position of National Master of Sikkim. His Holiness also recognized the identity or status of H.E. the seventh Dzogchen Dharma King and conducted the enthronement ceremony for that dharma king.

H.H. Dodrupchen Rinpoche has always had a gentle disposition and has always been a humble, simple person totally devoid of all affectation. At every moment and wherever he is, his compassionate conduct serves as a model to guide living beings. The status of H.H. the fourth Dodrupchen Rinpoche is higher than that of many other great and holy dharma kings. His disciples can be found in each of the major lineages. Numerous disciples of His Holiness are world-renown great masters of their generation, including many famous lineage-holders. Examples include H.E. the seventh Dzogchen Dharma King; Sogyal Rinpoche; H.H. Dharma King Renzeng Nima; H.H.

Wish Fulfilling Jewel Dharma King Jigme Phuntsok; H.H. Wish Fulfilling Jewel Dharma King Tuoga; Dakini Dare Lamu (Nianlong Holy Mother); the king of Sikkim; the fifth Dodrupchen, H.E. Tudeng Longyang Renzeng Gyatso Dharma King; and others. H.H. the fourth Dodrupchen Rinpoche is the greatest master and dharma king of the Nyingma sect.

After reading the book *A Treasury of True Buddha-Dharma* in December of 2006, H.H. Dodrupchen Dharma King marveled at the accomplishments of H.H. Dorje Chang Buddha III Wan Ko Yeshe Norbu and promptly wrote a congratulatory letter to H.H. Dorje Chang Buddha III.

確切地說，沒有多智欽仁波且就沒有寧瑪巴龍欽寧體大圓滿的最高密法。因多智欽仁波且為大圓滿龍欽寧體獨掌持有人根本總法主，故又被稱為多智欽大法王。所謂『龍欽』即是廣大無盡的法界之義，而『寧體』意為心髓，故龍欽寧體屬於大圓滿法中極密無上部心髓法門，是虹身化境最高之法。全世界寧瑪巴包括噶陀、佐欽等六大寺系的所有龍欽寧體傳承，全都是由多智欽大法王為他們灌頂傳的法。

多智欽在藏文中意為來自多科山谷的大成就者，因第一世的多智欽仁波且生於西藏東部果洛地區的上多科山谷，故而得名。當第一世多智欽仁波且拜見吉美林巴大師時，吉美林巴即賜予他《佛語》和《伏藏》的完整傳承，並授權他為龍欽寧體的唯一根本法主。當吉美林巴轉世的多欽哲見到多智欽時，他看見多智欽就是蓮花生大師。第一、二、三、四世多智欽仁波且不僅呈現了許多不可思議的神通智慧，更不斷地將龍欽寧體法門傳授給一切具足因緣之聖者們，培育了許多著名的大成就者。

第四世多智欽土登成利華桑波仁波且於1927年降生在果洛地區色達山谷的茨村莊。在仁波且住胎的那一年，幾乎每一天，村莊上空都出現彩虹，人們幾乎每個晚上都能看見羅睺羅護法神在他的屋頂上，而且未經栽種，他的屋頂上盛開了一朵當地從來沒有過的鮮花，而這正是第三世多智欽在隱居時最喜歡種的那一種。仁波且的母親在懷孕期間，腹中的小孩隨時不見了，其身邊也總有神秘的光明陪伴，使她無須照明也能夠在黑暗中尋找物品。

仁波且降生後，聖跡更是出奇的多。一次，一塊瑪尼石從岩上降下砸在仁波且的身上，他的很多骨骼都被砸碎了，但幾個小時以後，所有受傷的痕跡神奇地消失殆盡。有時小仁波且明明在地上，但彈指間又在屋頂上、山岩壁上。當尋訪轉世靈童的多智欽寺的僧人要來之前、他的父母還不知道的時候，仁波且就對父母說：『今天有客人來。』並高興地唱起來。當尋訪考察隊伍將上一世多智欽用過的書、佛珠等物品和其他人的東西混在一起讓仁波且挑選，他無一錯誤地將他前世的物品挑了出來，並說：『這是我的。』第五世佐欽法王親自認證靈童為第四世多智欽仁波且。

在多智欽寺的坐床典禮圓滿時，四歲大的仁波且從法座上站起來，邊笑邊念誦《金剛七句祈請文》和《請起蓮花生》中的一些偈子，令在場的所有人驚嘆不已。仁波且五歲開始即直接開啟自己的無始藏智，並將這些教法口述出來。

更難得的是，2007年，國際佛教僧尼總會對仁波且們作出的十個不同認證身份舉行了史無前例的金瓶擇籤，從120支密封籤中抽出一支，確認多智欽法王是蓮花生大師的化身，而此身份正是三世多杰羌佛在擇籤之前作出的認證。

然後當仁波且長大以後，除了在個別情況下，他很少再顯現神通成就。雖然仁波且不需要淨化自心或累積福報等諸如此類的修持，但是為了給眾生樹立真正修行的榜樣，仁波且向許多人身的導師求法，並完成許多年的閉關。仁波且十五歲時即精通曼達壇城的繪畫以及書法、製陶、建築和其它許多技術以及種字擇緣無上法等大法。1957年，由空行母對西藏面臨的局面所作的預言，仁波且來到錫金。起初他並沒有公開自己的身份，這時國王的上師——錫金的一位大成就者告訴國王，真正的蓮花生已經來到了錫金國，讓他務必要拜多智欽仁波且為上師。後來，在錫金國王的再三祈請下，仁波且擔任了錫金國的國師。仁波且還認證了第七世佐欽法王，並主持了其坐床典禮。

仁波且待人處事一貫性地平和、謙虛、簡樸、毫無裝腔作勢，每一時刻、每一處所都以自己的慈悲行為作為引導眾生的典範。第四世多智欽仁波且的地位登立於若干大聖法王之上，他的弟子遍及各大傳承，多為一代宗師，名重世界，包括許多著名的傳承持有者，如：第七世佐欽法王、索甲仁波且、仁增尼瑪法王、如意寶晉美彭措法王乃至托嘎如意寶晉美彭措法王、達日拉姆空行母（年龍佛母）、錫金國王、第五世多智欽土登龍洋仁增嘉措法王等，仁波且是寧瑪掌首宗師、大法王。

2006年12月，當多智欽大法王見到《正法寶典》後，驚嘆於三世多杰羌佛雲高益西諾布的成就，當即給三世多杰羌佛寫了賀信。

BRIEF INTRODUCTION TO
H.H. DHARMA KING PENOR OF THE NINGMA SECT
寧瑪派貝諾法王簡介

Dzemkyi. No flowers can be seen in that village of Powo during the cold and dry winter. However, fragrant flowers amazingly blossomed forth there when the rinpoche was born.

At the age of five, Penor Rinpoche was escorted to the ancient Palyul Monastery in the western Kham district. A formal enthronement ceremony was performed for him there in which he sat on the same dharma king throne he sat on in his prior life. That ceremony was performed by the prior

At the Nyingma Monlam Chenmo Ceremony for World Peace that took place in 1993 in Bodhgaya, India, H.H. Dharma King Penor was unanimously selected as the third supreme leader of the entire Nyingma sect in modern history.
1993年在印度菩提迦耶舉行的全寧瑪巴祈願法會上，貝諾法王被一致推舉為近代寧瑪巴第三任總教主。

Thubten Chokyi Dawa and Karma Thekchok Nyingpo, who is the fourth Karma Kuchen Rinpoche and the tenth generation dharma king of Palyul. At that ceremony, he was formally recognized as the incarnation of the second Penor Dharma King, Baqian Douba. Thus, he became the eleventh lineage holder of the Palyul lineage.

Khenpo Ngaga (Kathok Kanqin Ngaga), an outstanding practitioner proficient in the Great Perfection, foresaw the special mission of this recently born incarnation. He therefore conferred upon the child the refuge precepts, a Manjushri Bodhisattva initiation, and a holy Buddha statue. He also wrote for the child a Long Life Prayer that is to this day recited by thousands of Buddhist disciples all over the world. When he was thirteen years old, Penor Rinpoche was formally tonsured in the prior Penor Dharma King's palace. That ceremony was performed and witnessed by five important khenpos and monks. He was given the dharma name Dhongag Shedrup Tenzin Chokle Namgyal, which means "All-Victorious Holder of the Teachings of Study and Practice of the Sutras and Tantras".

One day when the rinpoche when was still a small boy, an elderly man walked up to him and insisted that the rinpoche perform for him the Phowa Dharma. In his boyish innocence, the rinpoche consented and practiced that dharma in accordance with its rituals. After a short while, the rinpoche was surprised to discover that the elderly man had already passed away. Facing the corpse that lay before him, the rinpoche practiced dharma once more in order to revive the elderly man. After the elderly man regained consciousness, the rinpoche blew from his mouth a long puff. However, the elderly man said, "Heavens! Why did the rinpoche cause me to return? I was already in the Western Pure Land of Ultimate Bliss of Amitabha Buddha!"

Later, the rinpoche received from numerous great masters, sutra teachers, and khenpos various essential dharma teachings that have existed for many generations. Such teachings include the Buddha in the Palm Great Perfection of the Nanque lineage, the Eight Great Black Lugas, the Great Jewel Terma, the Rena Lingpa Terma, the Great Perfection, the Great Perfection Mind Essence Dharma, the Secret Dharma Protectors, and so on. The rinpoche practiced such dharmas as he was taught and became accomplished. Later, at a place called Tatang, Penor Rinpoche entered a long-term retreat together with his master, Thubten Chokyi Dawa. Through practicing the fundamental preliminary practices and progressing all the way up to the profound Great

The Palyul network of monasteries is the largest of the six main subsects within the Nyingma sect. There are more than four hundred of its branch monasteries spread throughout Tibet and its dharma centers spread around the world. Not only is H.H. Dharma King Penor the lineage holder of the Palyul dharma lineage, he has been the supreme dharma king of the Nyingma sect.

H.H. Dharma King Penor is the nirmanakaya of Vajrapani Bodhisattva. In the autumn of 2007, the International Buddhism Sangha Association held an unprecedented Drawing Lots From a Golden Vase Ceremony to affirm the true reincarnated identity of H.H. Dharma King Penor and others. There were ten possible identities recognized by various rinpoches. One lot was drawn from among 120 lots to affirm the true reincarnated identity of H.H. Dharma King Penor. That drawing affirmed that H.H. Dharma King Penor is the nirmanakaya of Vajrapani Bodhisattva, which is the reincarnated identity that H.H. Dorje Chang Buddha III recognized before that lot was drawn.

His Holiness was born in December of 1932 (the year of the water-monkey according to the Tibetan calendar) in a place called Powo (in ancient times called Bomi) in the western part of the Kham district in eastern Tibet. His father was called Sonam Gyurme and his mother was called

Perfection, he returned to his dharma-nature true-suchness that has existed since beginning-less time. Dharma King Dilgo Khyentse, the second dharma king of the modern Nyingma sect, openly said, "Dharma King Penor is already a holy being who has surpassed samaya." Numerous dharma kings have said that Dharma King Penor is an incarnated Buddha.

When the Dharma King was conducting a Medicine Buddha Dharma Assembly, rainbows soared from the mandala offering plate. Additionally, nectar overflowed from the skull-cup. One time when he was conducting a Magong Accomplishment Dharma Assembly, biscuits offered to the dakinis were clearly shaking.

Very few rinpoches who are at the same level of Dharma King Penor are able to endure the difficulties that Dharma King Penor has endured. Due to his great vows of great compassion and his ceaseless determination, the rinpoche is not troubled by any difficulty or obstacle he may face. Year after year he has given of himself. He rebuilt the main Palyul Monastery and the Palyul Buddhist Institute, which the rinpoche established in his prior life. In India, the rinpoche established the Namdroling Monastery and the Ngagyur Nyingma Buddhist Institute. He has gradually repaired all of the branch monasteries in his lineage that urgently needed repair. His Buddhist centers in places such as Taiwan, Hong Kong, Macao, mainland China, Singapore, Malaysia, the Philippines, the United States, and Canada have recently spread to countries in Europe, including Greece, Germany, and France. His Namdroling Monastery in southern India has become one of the largest monasteries in all of Tibetan Buddhism in the world today, with more than three thousand monastics. It can be called the largest Nyingma monastery in the world outside of China. Never shirking hard work, the rinpoche is constantly rushing about in India, the Himalaya mountains, Southeast Asia, and Europe in order to spread the Buddha-dharma all around the world, thereby enabling all living beings to experience the benefits of the dharma.

The compassion of the dharma king has also benefited residents of local communities. He has built bridges, paved roads, and founded a general hospital that uses both western and Tibetan medicine. When there has been no seasonal rain in Tibet or India, the rinpoche is famous for having caused rain to fall promptly as a result of his prayers. Thus, local Indian residents have affectionately called the dharma king the "Rain Lama."

The dharma king is a monk who flawlessly abides by the precepts and he himself has given the monastic precepts to over 2,500 monks and nuns. Day after day from morning until night, the dharma king selflessly benefits those living in the world, those who are about to pass away, and those who have already passed away.

At the Nyingma Monlam Chenmo Ceremony for World Peace that took place in 1993 at the vajra throne area where the Buddha attained enlightenment in Bodhgaya, India, the Nyingma dharma kings and eminent monastics who came from China and other places all over the world unanimously selected H.H. Dharma King Penor as the supreme dharma king of the Nyingma. Thus, His Holiness became the successor to the deceased Nyingma dharma kings of prior generations who possessed the Nyingma teachings. He is a person who in reality matches the title of supreme Nyingma dharma king! In order to teach the dharma and benefit living beings, the rinpoche has demonstrated the brilliant wisdom of Manjushri Bodhisattva, the compassion of Kuan Yin Bodhisattva, and the courage of Vajrapani Bodhisattva!

In August of 2007, H.H. Dharma King Penor read *A Treasury of True Buddha-Dharma* about H.H. Dorje Chang Buddha III Wan Ko Yeshe Norbu. He thought that book is of limitless benefit to living beings. He was so moved that he wrote a letter of congratulations to rinpoches.

在甯瑪巴的六大寺系中，白玉系堪為最大的一個寺系，其遍佈全藏的分支子寺和世界各地的佛學中心超過四百座以上。貝諾法王不僅是白玉法系的傳承法座持有者，更是當今寧瑪派的第一總法王。

貝諾法王是金剛手菩薩的化身，2007年秋，國際佛教僧尼總會對仁波且們作出的十個不同認證身份舉行了史無前例的金瓶掣籤，從120支密封籤中抽出一支，確認貝諾法王是金剛手菩薩的化身，而此身份正是三世多杰羌佛提前就作出的認證。於西元1932年（藏曆水猴年）十二月降生在東藏康省（西康）一個稱為波沃的地方（古稱波密，又稱波窩）。父親叫做蘇南久美，母親叫做宗吉。此村落在寒冷乾燥的冬天是看不到花朵的，但是仁波且誕生時，此地卻出奇地綻放芬芳的花朵。

五歲時，貝諾仁波且被迎至西康白玉祖寺，在上一世秋竹仁波且圖滇卻吉達瓦和第十代法王──第四世噶瑪古千仁波且噶瑪帖秋寧波的主持下，在其前世的法王座上行坐床典禮，正式認證他為第二世貝諾法王巴千都巴的轉世，及成為第十一代白玉傳承法座持有者。

一位當代精通大圓滿的卓越行者──堪布雅嘎（噶陀堪欽雅嘎）預見此新轉世的特殊使命，而給予此孩童皈依戒、文殊菩薩灌頂和一尊神聖的佛像，並為他寫下至

今仍被全球成千上萬佛弟子持誦之長壽祈請文。十三歲時，在上一世貝諾法王的寢宮中，在五位主要堪布和比丘的見證主持下接受圓頂，正式剃度，法名「豆雅謝祝天津丘雷南嘉」，意為「經續教法修持尊勝最高持有者」。

當仁波且還是一個小男孩時，有一天，一位老年人走到仁波且面前，堅持要仁波且為他修頗瓦法。仁波且很天真地答應並依法修持。過了一會兒，仁波且驚訝地發現這位老年人已經往生了。他對著躺在面前的屍體，再度修法以挽回老人家的性命。當老年人甦醒之後，仁波且吐出一口長氣。而老年人卻說：「天啊！仁波且為何把我叫回來？我已經在阿彌陀佛的西方極樂世界淨土了！」

後來，仁波且又從多位偉大的上師、經師堪布等那裏接承了多世自有的各種法要，包括：南卻傳承大圓滿之掌中佛、八大黑嚕嘎、大寶伏藏、惹那林巴伏藏（惹林）、大圓滿、大圓滿心要法及秘密護法等等的教法，並依教修持，獲得成就。之後，貝諾仁波且在塔唐地方和他的上師秋竹圖登卻吉達瓦進行長期的閉關，從基礎的前行至最深奧的大圓滿，還回了他無始的法性真如。近代甯瑪第二位法王──頂果欽哲法王曾經公開說：「貝諾法王已經是一位超越三昧耶的聖者。」有許多法王都說他是肉身的佛。

在法王舉行的藥師佛法會上，彩虹自曼達供盤中升起，且嘎巴拉（顱蓋杯）上甘露溢流。有一次在舉行「瑪貢」的成就法會上，空行母的供養餅乾很明顯地顫動著。

很少地位如同貝諾法王的仁波且會經歷過貝諾法王曾經歷過的艱苦。仁波且以其大悲大願以及源源不絕的毅力，不為橫在眼前的任何困境、障礙所擾，年復一年，不僅重建了白玉主寺和過去世中建立的白玉佛學院，在印度創辦南卓林寺和雅久寧瑪佛學院，漸次地修復傳承中各個亟待修復的子寺，並且在包括臺灣、香港、澳門、大陸各地、新加坡、馬來西亞、菲律賓、美國、加拿大等佛學中心，近年足跡亦履及希臘、德國、法國等歐洲國土。今日，在南印度的南卓林寺已成為世界上規模最宏偉的藏傳佛寺之一，已有超過三千人的僧眾，堪稱中國之外於全球最大的寧瑪寺院。仁波且不辭辛勞地奔波於印度、喜瑪拉雅山區、東南亞和歐美的土地上，為的就是將佛法傳佈至世界各地，讓所有眾生都同受法益。

法王的慈悲也惠及當地的居民，他造橋鋪路，設立西醫和藏醫都有的綜合性醫院。無論在西藏或印度，仁波且都在季雨不來時以祈降及時雨聞名。當地的印度居民，因此給法王上了個暱稱──「雨喇嘛」。

法王是身具足清淨戒體的比丘，至今已為超過兩千五百位以上的僧眾授予出家戒。日復一日，由早到晚，法王無私地利益著在世者、臨終者與往生者。

1993年，在印度佛陀成道處──菩提迦耶的金剛座所舉行的全甯瑪巴祈願世界和平的「甯瑪巴傳召祈願大會」上，來自中國等世界各地的甯瑪巴法王高僧們，一致推舉貝諾法王為甯瑪巴前輩掌教法王報化之後的繼位寧瑪總法王。這樣的總法王位乃實至名歸也！因為仁波且為了教法與眾生的利益，展現了文殊菩薩的智慧、觀音菩薩的慈悲與金剛手菩薩的勇勢！

2007年8月，當貝諾法王見到三世多杰羌佛雲高益西諾布的《正法寶典》，認為這本書對眾生有著無窮的利益，感動之下，便給仁波且們寫了賀信。

BRIEF INTRODUCTION TO H.H. JAMYANG LUNGDOK GYALTSEN RINPOCHE
降陽龍多加參法王簡介

H.H. Dharma King Omniscience Jamyang Lungdok Gyaltsen Achuk Lama is a great Buddha in the Nyingma sect of Tibetan Buddhism. He is the incarnation of Venerable Longsal Nyingpo, one of the twenty-five great disciples of Guru Padmasambhava. Because people had different views on the reincarnated identity of H.H. Dharma King Omniscience, on a holy day in 2007 at Hua Zang Si in San Francisco, the International Buddhism Sangha Association beseeched H.H. Dorje Chang Buddha III Holiest Tathagata to recognize the true identity of H.H. Dharma King Jamyang Lungdok Gyaltsen. In the end, that association did receive such recognition from H.H. Dorje Chang Buddha III. H.H. Dharma King Jamyang Lungdok Gyaltsen was recognized by H.H. Dorje Chang Buddha III as the true incarnation of Venerable Longsal Nyingpo. The International Buddhism Sangha Association then held the holy form of Drawing Lots From a Golden Vase Dharma Assembly. One lot was drawn from among 120 sealed lots. After a curtain was removed and after that lot was unsealed and opened in front of all those present, it was discovered that H.H. Dharma King Jamyang Lungdok Gyaltsen is indeed the true incarnation of Venerable Longsal Nyingpo. Not only was the true identity of H.H. Jamyang Lungdok Gyaltsen personally recognized by the Holiest Tathagata, the Drawing Lots From a Golden Vase Ceremony confirmed that he is a great holy being who is the true reincarnation of Venerable Longsal Nyingpo. Yerba

Rinpoche, who has demonstrated his supernatural powers over many lifetimes, personally discovered evidence throughout the six realms that Dharma King Omniscience never for a moment ceased striving to bring living beings to salvation and enlightenment.

Dharma King Omniscience was born in 1927 amidst rare and auspicious signs. The dharma protecting deities transformed into various physical forms to protect him when he was a child,

The person in the middle is H.H. Dharma King Omniscience Jamyang Lungdok Gyaltsen. To his left is H.H. Dharma King Jigme Phuntok and to his right is Asong Rinpoche.
中間是降養隆多加參遍智法王，左邊是晉美彭措法王，右邊是阿松仁波且。

When the supreme leader of the Nyingma Sect, H.H. Dharma King Penor, vistited the Yarchen Monastery, he and H.H. Dharma King Omniscience Jamyang Lungdok Gyaltsen performed an "Equal Status Rite."
寧瑪派總教主貝諾法王造訪亞青寺時，與降養隆多加參遍智法王行平等禮。

which is something only experienced by beings of great holiness. He understood without impediment all scriptures and sutras. At 12, he entered the order of monks. Beginning at 18, he followed his vajra master Arik Vajradhara, a great accomplished one, into 43 years of solitary meditation. He received from Sela Yangzhi a complete transmission of the teachings he learned in his prior life. Sela Yangzhi was a true incarnation of Padmasambhava. H.H. Dharma King Omniscience manifested the ultimate essence of all the dharma and turned into a rainbow body of Great Perfection. He has entered the dharmadhatu's non-attachment state and Four Wisdoms state. He has attained the state of the four divisions of initiations. He has accomplished the cutting off of all defilements related to the six sense organs. His once ordinary body has become a rainbow-light body. The dharma king's body is able at any time to manifest rainbows, crystal pagodas, Buddha images, Tibetan seed characters, hand-held pennants, etc. The wrinkles of the skin of his entire body have formed the image of a mandala filled with pictures of all the Buddhas and

Bodhisattvas. Sariras naturally pour forth from his body.

H.H. Dharma King Omniscience's main temple is the Yarchen Uddiyana Meditation Monastery, also known as Second Virtue Mountain. Over twenty thousand lamas and rinpoches live at the monastery, which is more than any other monastery in the world. There, the dharma king has provided teachings of the Great Perfection to tens of thousands of Tibetans and Han Chinese from all provinces. A multitude of his disciples have manifested attainment of great accomplishments. For example, right after they passed away, their bodies displayed multicolored sariras (holy relics) or formed crystals, rainbows appeared in the sky, or Buddha images manifested. Multitudes of people have seen that after receiving empowerment from the dharma king, the deaf recover hearing, the blind can see again, the dumb can speak, the insane recover clear memories, and those afflicted with serious diseases suddenly become well. When the dharma king practices dharma, rainbows often appear in the sky, surrounding the Yarchen Monastery. Many people of great accomplishment in the dharma have asked H.H. Dharma King Omniscience to appraise their level of accomplishment.

H.H. Dharma King Omniscience is one of the greatest and most accomplished leaders of contemporary Buddhism. He manifests great supernatural powers. From secret mountains and sites in the earth, he unearths ancient hidden dharma treasures. Such sacred areas include Akeka and Meilongduojie, Dake Dakini Cave, Holy Mountain Chaguobaiyai, Zong A at Hidden Site Zuicha, Zhuye Zhugalizong, Nata Lion Cliff, Langqing Zajia Dorje Zhuxiu, Gongguo Wotare, Reniang Liqing Cliff, Saduo Xizhaga, Holy Site Yachen Fangguang De Mountain, Holy Site Lotus Cave, Jiacha Qiadeli in Guoluo area, Niuxi Zangali, Baqiong Dong-A White Cliff, Guorena White Cliff, Peicha Ga White Cliff, Yarao Dorje Youxuan Stone Mountain, Jia A Chali in the Dege area, Lake Kualong, Lake Nalong, Lake Beiyu, Lake Si, Lake Jidemila, etc. He has unearthed innumerable Buddha images featuring both benign and fierce countenances, dharani chants, mantras, Tibetan seed characters and other symbols, as well as large and small hand-held pennants, all completely natural and none displaying the slightest trace of human craft. He has also received a myriad of sacred dharma treasures as offerings from the non-human protectors of hidden dharma treasures of each of the major sacred areas.

In the summer of 2006, H.H. Dharma King Omniscience read *A Treasury of True Buddha-Dharma* and was astounded. He knew that the accomplishments and wisdom shown it that book were unprecedented in this world. He wondered what kind of holy and virtuous person had such incredible realization. He promptly applied his supernatural powers to view the dharmadhatu and saw the extraordinary truth. It turned out that the recognition by Urgyen Xirao, who was the dharma prince under Guru Padmasambhava, was totally correct. In that recognition, Urgyen Xirao stated that H.H. Yangwo Wan Ko Yeshe Norbu Great Dharma King is a magnificent being of great holiness. Dharma King Omniscience then wrote his own recognition certificate and stamped his precious red seal upon it. That recognition certificate stated that H.H. Yangwo Wan Ko Yeshe Norbu is the greatest leader of Buddhism!

遍智法王——降陽龍多加參阿秋喇嘛，即是藏密寧瑪巴大怙主，是第二佛陀蓮花生大師的25位大得登巴之一的龍薩娘波尊者的轉世。由於遍智法王的轉世身份各說不一，因此，2007年聖日在美國舊金山華藏寺，由國際佛教僧尼總會三度禮請頂聖如來多杰羌第三世為降陽龍多加參法王作真實身份之認證，最後終於得到三世多杰羌佛的認證，其認證為龍薩娘波尊者真身再來，為此國際佛教僧尼總會舉行聖義金瓶掣籤法會，於120支密封的籤中掣出一支，於眾目禮觀之下，揭幕開籤一看，果然為娘仁波且尊者之真身。降陽龍多加參的真實身份不但得到頂聖如來親自認證，而且金瓶掣籤印證了亦是龍薩娘波的真身大聖地位。累世示現大神通的耶巴活佛，得見六道處處皆有遍智法王救渡眾生無有片刻停歇。

遍智法王於第十六繞迴火兔年（公元1927年）具稀有吉兆而誕生，童年即具備護法變化各種身形予以護衛等多種聖者大士所具之相，對文字經卷無礙通達。十二歲出家，十八歲起隨其金剛上師大成就者阿瑞金剛持閉關修行四十三年。並在蓮師真身色拉陽智處接持上一世的完美圓滿傳承，展顯諸法實相大遷轉虹身之大圓滿、法界明體無別密意自解脫、本初之四光明境、四灌六燈之道臻至究竟、蘊身化為無漏虹霓光身，身體能隨時顯現彩虹、水晶塔、佛像、種子字、手幟等，全身的皮膚皺紋都形成了諸佛菩薩壇城圖像，身體還會自然涌出舍利子。

遍智法王主寺第二德山亞青烏金寺，其寺廟擁有兩萬多常住喇嘛仁波且，是全世界唯一最多活佛、喇嘛的第一大德寺，有藏漢各省數萬人在此蒙受法王傳授的大圓滿引導，眾多弟子顯現大成就境界——圓寂後遺體現出五彩舍利或成水晶狀，並有彩虹貫空或有佛像呈現。受法王加持而聾者復聞、盲者重見、啞者能言、瘋者恢復記憶、疑難病症豁然痊癒的事跡更為眾人所親見。法王修法時虛空隨時有彩虹圍繞亞青寺，有許多大成就者所成就的等位，都是請遍智法王予以鑑定。

遍智法王是當代佛教大成就之主帥。法王展顯廣大神通，掘開隱秘山、地之中的古代伏藏，開取了以阿科客‧美龍多傑聖地為主的達科‧空行洞、察果白崖神山、最察伏藏地‧宗阿‧竹耶‧竹嘎裡宗、納它‧獅子白崖、朗慶雜加‧多傑朱旭、貢果沃塔熱、熱娘‧里慶白崖、薩多西扎嘎、亞青聖地放光德山、藏多聖地蓮

花洞、果洛嘉察恰塘裡、牛西藏嘎裡、巴窮冬阿白崖、果熱納白崖、配察嘎白崖、亞繞多吉右旋石山、德格嘉阿察裡、另外夸隆湖、納隆湖、北玉湖、席湖、吉德米拉湖等聖地的伏藏，取出了眾多的靜猛本尊、陀羅尼、咒及種子字等伏藏標誌，各種無數大小不一的手幟，均為天成之法器（無有絲毫人為加工之痕跡），並獲得由諸大聖地守護伏藏的諸護庫藏主非人等現量供養的伏藏聖物不計其數。

於公元二○○六年夏，遍智法王見到《正法寶典》一書，大為震撼，此書在此世界成就智慧顯揚，確實史無前例，是何等聖德竟有如此開天劈地之境界展顯？當下於法界中觀照，得見真相非同小可：原來蓮花生大師法王子鄔堅喜饒所作的關於仰諤雲高益西諾布大法王是偉大的巨聖的確認是完全正確的，由是自己為此寫下了認證書並蓋上了紅色寶印，稱為大教主！

BRIEF INTRODUCTION TO THE SUPREME LEADER OF JONANG SECT H.H. DHARMA KING JIGME DORJE
覺囊派總法王吉美多吉教主簡介

Within Tibetan Buddhism, the Jonang sect has been known around the world for the true practice of its followers. There currently are two dharma kings who are in charge of the dharma teachings of the Jonang sect. One of them is the head of the Zangwa Monastery, H.H. Dharma King Jigme Dorje. The other is H.H. Dharma King Ngagwang Pedma Namgyal

Palzangpo of the Longshijia Monastery. There is also a young future sect leader, Jianyang Lezhu Rinpoche, who is vice-head of the Zangwa Monastery.

When Sakyamuni Buddha lived in the world, H.H. Dharma King Jigme Dorje Rinpoche was already a great Bodhisattva in that lifetime. H.H. Dharma King Jigme Dorje was born in 1944 accompanied by various amazing auspicious signs that cannot be fully described. As a child, he never did anything to upset his parents, such as crying or acting in a common, childish way. He was very much different from other children. The masters of a monastery, as well as the monastics and laypersons in that monastery who handled monastery matters, all praised the child as being the incarnation of a wonderful Bodhisattva who had come back to this world voluntarily. Later, he went to the headquarters of the Jonang sect, the Zangwa Monastery in Rangtang, where he worshipped the Buddhas. His uncle, the Sai rinpoche by the name of Awang Genga Phuntsok who lived at the Zangwa Monastery, saw that this child was the incarnation of a holy being. In accordance with the dharma, Awang Genga Phuntsok Rinpoche recognized that the child was the true reincarnation of a rinpoche who had been the head of the Zangwa Monastery. In accordance with the dharma rules, Lama Danba Daji from Xiayan, Lama Aguoba from Hongtu, and others practiced the dharma, enter holy supernatural states, and confirmed the accuracy of Awang Genga Phuntsok Rinpoche's conclusion. They then made their formal pronouncements concerning the identity of H.H. Jigme Dorje. Moreover, the International Buddhism Sangha Association held an unprecedented Drawing Lots From a Golden Vase Ceremony to affirm the true reincarnation identity of H.H. Dharma King Jigme Dorje and others. There were ten possible identities recognized by various rinpoches. One lot was drawn from among 120 lots to affirm the true reincarnated identity of H.H. Dharma King Jigme Dorje. That drawing affirmed that H.H. Dharma King Jigme Dorje is the incarnation of Shambhala King Suchandra, which is the reincarnated identity that H.H. Dorje Chang Buddha III recognized before that lot was drawn.

After the formal enthronement ceremony for H.H. Jigme Dorje Rinpoche was performed at Saige Monastery in Aba County and the celebration of the enthronement ceremony was performed at Zhuoge Monastery, the rinpoche returned to Zangwa Monastery. The intelligence of the rinpoche is extraordinary. He was able to thoroughly learn and recite the scriptures, treatises, and rituals without having to exert himself. He later served as a disciple under his root master, Awang Gongqiu Daji, who was the Vajra Master of the Zangwa Dazang Monastery and the 44th Kalachakra Dharma King of the Jonang sect. Under H.H. Awang Gongqiu Daji, the rinpoche learned and practiced the five preliminary practices of the Jonang sect and the generation and completion stages of the Kalachakra Vajra—the Six Yogas. He reached perfect merit in every dharma he practiced.

When the rinpoche was eight years old, he succeeded to the throne of the head of the Zangwa Monastery. However, at this time, his uncle, the Sai rinpoche, and H.H. Dharma King Awang Gongqiu Daji predicted to H.H. Jigme Dorje Rinpoche that changes in the world situation would occur that would be disadvantageous to Buddhism. They told the rinoche to go back to Aba County and that in the future, when the world situation stabilizes, he should return to the Zangwa Monastery and teach the dharma. Afterward, the Sai rinpoche passed away and later H.H. Dharma King Awang Gongqiu Daji passed away as well. H.H. Jigme Dorje Rinpoche then went to Aba County, where he requested and received the complete precepts from Lama Tujihua of Sai. He later served as a disciple under another root master, Lama Kesang, who is the nirmanakaya of the Eleven-Faced Kuan Yin Bodhisattva. Under Lama Kesang, the rinpoche learned all of the initiation and lineage teachings. During this time period, he both herded goats and cultivated himself in caves, tree holes, and other places while traveling from mountain to mountain. He realized the state of viewing all phenomena as equal and the state where the mind is not affected by the situation one encounters. Thus, he became a free and unhindered person of great accomplishment in the dharma. He then lived in a cave, where he continued his practice of the dharma.

After the restraints on religion were slightly eased, the supreme leader of the Jonang sect, H.H. Dharma King Yundan Sangbu of the Zangwa Monastery in Rangtang, twice dispatched people to the cave at the Zilang Monastery in Aba County (that was the cave in which Maji Lazun practiced the Xiduan Dharma) where the rinpoche was staying. H.H. Dharma King Yundan Sangbu did so based upon the formal pronouncements of certain great masters of the past. When those dispatched arrived, they invited H.H. Jigme Dorje Rinpoche to go to the Zangwa Monastery and lead the teaching of the Buddha-dharma. There was a third visit when H.H. Dharma King Yundan Sangbu himself went to that cave at the Zilang Monastery, bringing with him a kharda (white silk scarf). When the two venerable ones met, they praised each other. H.H. Dharma King Yundan Sangbu repeatedly urged H.H. Jigme Dorje Rinpoche to follow the formal pronouncements of the those great masters of the past by going to the Zangwa Dazang Monastery, by leading the teaching of the Buddha-dharma of the Jonang sect at that monastery, and by being the monastery's retreat lineage Vajra Master. H.H. Jigme Dorje Rinpoche then gave his response to the formal

pronouncements of those three masters of the past (H.H. Dharma King Gongqiu Daji, the Sai rinpoche, and Lama Kesang) that he must go to the Zangwa Monastery in Rangtang. He respectfully said to H.H. Dharma King Yundan Sangbu, "Your merit and cultivation are like those of my father. You are my master. I will carry out your instructions well!"

After H.H. Jigme Dorje Rinpoche returned to the Zangwa Monastery at Rangtang, he helped H.H. Dharma King Yundan Sangbu restore the monastery and build Buddhist statues. The rinpoche performed initiations and dharma transmissions at regular intervals and guided those on retreat. He perpetuated the dharma teachings of the Jonang sect in this human world and propagated such teachings around the world.

In accordance with the rules handed down by the historical masters, H.H. Dharma King Yundan Sangbu personally handed over to H.H. Jigme Dorje Rinpoche in 1998 certain precious objects passed down through the generations by past masters, such as a vajra bell, a vajra, and the writing called "Guiding Text—You Will Know Its Meaning When You See It." He also formally conferred upon H.H. Jigme Dorje Rinpoche the positions of 47th dharma throne holder of the Jonang Kalachakra lineage and 11th Vajra Master of the Zangwa Dazang Monastery.

After H.H. Dharma King Yundan Sangbu passed away, H.H. Dharma King Jigme Dorje became the supreme leader of the Jonang sect.

After H.H. Dharma King Jigme Dorje saw who His Holiness Dorje Chang Buddha III Wan Ko Yeshe Norbu is through the limitless omniscience displayed in *A Treasury of True Buddha-Dharma*, he stated that His Holiness Wan Ko Yeshe Norbu has reached the highest state of Buddhahood in the few-thousand-year history of Buddhism, having truly attained complete proficiency in exoteric and esoteric Buddhism and perfect mastery of the Five Vidyas.

在藏傳佛教中，覺囊派一直以實修而著稱於世。目前，總管覺囊派教法的教主有兩位：一位是藏哇寺主任吉美多吉法王，一位是龍什加寺的阿旺班瑪南加法王，還有一位年輕的準教主健陽樂住仁波且則任藏哇寺副主任。

釋迦牟尼佛在世時，吉美多吉法王就已經是一個大菩薩。1944年，吉美多吉法王伴隨種種不可盡說的神奇瑞相降生於世，自幼年就從未以哭聲對世俗之舉厭煩其雙親，而與別的孩童差別甚大。當時，寺院的上師和寺院執事僧俗等等，均讚嘆其為以殊勝菩薩再來之化身而供奉於金座上。隨後，前往覺囊總壇壤塘藏哇大藏寺禮佛，其叔父藏哇寺的賽活佛阿旺根噶彭措看到來者為聖者化身，依法認定其為藏哇寺寺主活佛之無偽轉世，還有夏炎喇嘛丹巴達吉與紅土喇嘛阿果巴等依法入修，於聖境中授記並反覆教言，認定確鑿無誤。更難得的是，國際佛教僧尼總會對仁波且們作出的十個不同認證身份舉行了史無前例的金瓶掣籤，從120支密封籤中抽出一支，確認吉美多吉法王是香巴拉國月賢王的化身，而此身份正是三世多杰羌佛在這之前作出的認證。

仁波且在阿壩縣賽格寺舉行坐床儀式和卓格寺舉行慶坐典禮後，即赴藏哇大藏寺。仁波且聰慧超群，習誦經論及儀規不經苦行用功無勤而通曉。後依止大藏寺金剛上師、覺囊第四十四代時輪金剛法王阿旺貢秋達吉為根本上師，並在阿旺貢秋達吉座前，修習覺囊傳承之五加行與時輪金剛的生圓次第——六支瑜珈，法義功德相繼圓滿。

仁波且八歲時即繼任藏哇寺寺主寶座，但在這時賽活佛和貢秋達吉法王都對仁波且預言：世局將有不利於佛教的變化，你要先回到阿壩，等以後世局平穩後，你還要回到藏哇寺主持教法。隨後，賽活佛和阿旺貢秋達吉先後圓寂。仁波且便去阿壩，在賽喇嘛吐基華座前求受圓滿具足戒，并依止十一面觀世音菩薩的化身——喇嘛克桑為根本上師，修學所有的灌頂傳承教授，一邊放山羊，一邊在山洞與樹洞等無定的山上持戒修行，得到萬相平等、心不隨境遷，成為自在的大成就者，此時他住入洞穴修持。

宗教開放後，覺囊總教主、壤塘藏哇寺的雲丹桑布法王根據祖師的授記，兩次派人來到阿壩孜朗寺的山洞（瑪什拉尊修西斷法的洞穴）裡，迎請吉美多吉仁波且去藏哇寺主持佛法傳承。雲丹桑布法王第三次親自帶著哈達來到孜朗寺山洞，兩位尊者見面相互致意，雲丹桑布法王再三的勸請吉美多吉仁波且根據祖師授記去主持藏哇大藏寺覺囊派教法，擔任藏哇寺的閉關傳承金剛上師。吉美多吉應三個上師的授記（貢秋達吉法王、賽活佛以及喇嘛克桑）需要去壤塘藏哇寺。吉美多吉活佛恭敬地對雲丹桑布法王說：「您的功德和修為如同我的父親一樣，您是我的上師，我會作好您吩咐的事情！」

吉美多吉仁波且回到壤塘藏哇寺後，協助雲丹桑布法王恢復寺院，建造佛像，定期灌頂傳法，指導閉關，延續覺囊教法於人間保存，宏於世界。

一九九八年，雲丹桑布法王根據祖傳之規，親自將歷代先師依次傳遞之金剛鈴杵與《引導文──見者具義》等寶物交付給吉美多吉仁波且，正式將覺囊派時輪金剛卓氏傳承第四十七代法座與第十一代大藏寺金剛上師之位一同授予吉美多吉仁波且。

雲丹桑布法王圓寂後，吉美多吉法王成為覺囊派教主。

當吉美多吉法王於《正法寶典》遍智無量中見到多杰羌佛第三世雲高益西諾布時，說：這才是佛教史上幾千年來真正的顯密圓通、五明完滿的佛陀高峰。

BRIEF INTRODUCTION TO KUMBUM MONASTERY
塔爾寺簡介

Kumbum Monastery (or Ta'er) together with Ganden, Drepung, Sera, Tashilhunpo and Labrang are known as the six great monasteries of the Gelukpa sect. Kumbum Monastery is the place where the founder of the Gelukpa sect, Guru Tsongkhapa, was born. Guru Tsongkhapa was the supreme spiritual leader of the Gelukpa and the first Ganden Tripa. His two distinguished disciples are Dalai Lama and Panchen Lama, who were two of the main leaders of the Yellow Sect of Tibetan Buddhism.

Kumbum monastery is large in size. During its prime time, there were more than 800 worshiping halls covering around 165 acres. The buildings of the monastery take up two hillsides along a channel on Lotus Mt. The temples are spread out on the uneven hills. Their architectural magnificence constitutes a spectacular sight. In history, the 4th, 5th, 7th and 13th Dalai Lamas as well as the 6th, 9th and 10th Panchen Lamas all lived at Kumbum Monastery. It once accommodated more than 70 Rinpoches and 3600 monastics. Many of its Rinpoches and eminent monastics were conferred by the government of Qing Dynasty the titles of Khutukhtu, Governing Lamas at Yonghe Palace in Beijing and Wutai Mountain in Shanxi province.

Kumbum Monastery has four colleges, which are the exoteric, esoteric (tantric), Kalachakra and medical colleges, respectively. Many of their graduates have become eminent masters.

塔爾寺與甘丹寺、哲蚌寺、色拉寺、扎什倫布寺和拉卜楞寺並稱為格魯派六大寺，是格魯派創始宗師宗喀巴大師誕生的地方。宗喀巴大師為格魯巴總教主、第一世甘丹赤巴。宗喀巴大師的兩大弟子，即是達賴喇嘛和班禪喇嘛，為佛教黃教兩大領袖。

塔爾寺規模宏大，最盛時有殿堂八百多間，佔地1000畝。寺院建築分佈於蓮花山的一溝兩面坡上，殿宇高低錯落，交相輝映，氣勢壯觀。歷史上，第四世、五世、七世、十三世達賴喇嘛和第六世、九世、十世班禪喇嘛都駐錫過塔爾寺，最多時寺院有七十多位仁波且，僧侶3600多人，許多仁波且、高僧曾被清朝政府封為駐京呼圖克圖和就任北京雍和宮及山西五台山的掌印喇嘛。

塔爾寺設有顯宗、密宗、時輪、醫明四大學院，培養了無數的大德。

BRIEF INTRODUCTION TO THE MINDROLLING MONASTERIES
敏珠林寺系簡介

Seated in the center is H.H. Dharma King Mindrolling Trichen, who is the supreme leader of the Nyingma sect. On the left is H.H. Dalai Lama and on the right is H.E. the ninth Mindrolling Khenchen Rinpoche. Standing behind is Venerable D.G. Khochhen Rinpoche, who is the general secretary of H.H. Dharma King Mindrolling Trichen.
中坐者為寧瑪總教主敏林赤欽法王，左邊為達賴喇嘛，右邊為第九世敏林堪欽仁波且，後面為敏林赤欽法王的總管闊千仁波且。

The group of Mindrolling monasteries is one of the six main groups of monasteries within the Nyingma sect. The first Mindrolling Monastery was founded by the great terton H.H. Rigzin Terdak Lingpa. The Mindrolling Monastery was the first monastery where Direct Transmission and Mind Transmission were combined, where old translations of sutras and treatises were collected, where uncovered dharma treasures from the south of Tibet were collected, and where historians of the Nyingma sect gathered. It is therefore the monastery that most completely embodies the totality of the Nyingma sect. It is responsible for reviewing and making final decisions on the dharma books and the history of the Nyingma sect. Someone once asked H.H. Dharma King Dudjom, "Who represents the Nyingma sect?" H.H. Dharma King Dudjom answered, "The Mindrolling and the Nyingma mean the same thing." One can see from that answer the status the Mindrolling monasteries have within the Nyingma sect.

H.H. Master Rigzin Terdak Lingpa was the incarnation of the great translator Bairotsana and was called Unchanging Vajra. He was the sutra master for H.H. the fifth Dalai Lama and established the Mindrolling Monastery in 1670. He later organized and established rules relating to dharma practice; rules relating to the beating, blowing, and playing of dharma instruments; and pure, excellent rituals relating to dancing, painting mandalas, and chanting. Additionally, the Mindrolling Monastery was the place where Tibetan astrology, the Tibetan lunar calendar, Tibetan painting, Tibetan rhetoric, Tibetan medicine, Tibetan calligraphy, and other branches of Tibetan learning originated.

During the time of H.H. the seventh Dalai Lama, the Mindrolling Monastery was generally acclaimed as being foremost among all the monasteries in Tibet in the area of cultural attainments. That is why at that time the main professors of the Potala Monastic Institute, which was the first college in Tibet, came from the Mindrolling Monastery. The Mindrolling Monastery's predominance in cultural attainments has continued unbroken to this present day. Even today the Mindrolling monasteries still serve as models for all of the large and small monasteries of the Nyingma sect to emulate.

H.H. Dharma King Mindrolling Trichen is not only the holder of the dharma teachings of the Mindrolling monasteries, he is also the dharma king of the entire Nyingma sect. Every generation of Mindrolling Trichen has been extremely learned. Rinpoches from almost all of the other temples come to the Mindrolling monasteries to learn. The current Mindrolling Trichen is the eleventh Mindrolling Trichen. Because he is famous for practicing dream yoga, he has been respectfully called "the sleeping dharma king." Under H.H. Mindrolling Trichen, there are Ven. Khochhen Rinpoche, H.E. Khenchen Rinpoche, H.E. Khandro Rinpoche, and other famous rinpoches.

敏珠林寺為寧瑪巴六大寺系之一,由大掘藏師德德林巴(亦即是第一世敏林赤欽)所創建。敏珠林寺是首座教傳合一、舊譯經論總集、南伏藏總集、寧瑪史家總集的寺院,是這個地球上寧瑪派的總集體寺院,負責戡定寧瑪巴的法本與歷史。有人曾問敦珠法王:『何以代表寧瑪?』敦珠法王回答說:『寧瑪與敏珠林同義』,由此可見敏珠林寺系在寧瑪派的地位。

德德林巴大師為大譯師毗羅遮那之化身,稱為不變金剛,曾為五世達拉喇嘛之經師,於公元1670年創建敏珠林寺,其後,並整理、建立修法之規約、敲打、吹奏之法則和舞蹈、繪壇、唪誦之清淨善妙行儀。同時,敏珠林寺亦為西藏的天文歷算、繪畫、聲律、醫藥、書法等學科的發源地。

在七世達拉喇嘛時期,前後藏之所有寺廟中,敏珠林寺的文化造詣被公推為第一,故當時西藏首座大學布達拉宮僧官學院之主要教授亦由敏珠林寺派任,此後沿襲不斷。直至今日,敏珠林寺仍為寧瑪一切大小寺廟之修學榜樣。

敏林赤欽法王不僅是敏珠林寺系的教法持有者,也是所有寧瑪派的法王。歷代的敏林赤欽都非常博學,幾乎各個寺廟的仁波且都會來敏珠林寺學習。這一世次敏林赤欽為第十一世,因以修睡夢瑜伽而聞名,故亦被尊稱為『睡覺法王』。在其座下尚有尊貴的闊千仁波且、堪千仁波且、康卓仁波且和其他的著名仁波且。

BRIEF INTRODUCTION TO H.H. TAKLUNG TSETRUL RINPOCHE
達龍哲珠仁波且簡介

H.H. Taklung Tsetrul Rinpoche, who is the dharma king of the Northern Treasure lineage within the Nyingma sect, together with H.H. Dalai Lama
寧瑪北藏法王達龍哲珠仁波且和達賴喇嘛。

The terma dharma of the Nyingma sect is divided into the Changter (Byangter) (Northern Treasure) lineage and the Suodie (Southern Treasure) lineage. Within the six main monasteries of the Nyingma sect, the Mindrolling and Palyul monasteries are mainly of the Southern Treasure lineage, while the Dorje Drak (Vajra Rock) Monastery is of the Northern Treasure lineage. H.H. Taklung Tsetrul Rinpoche is the Dharma King of the Dorje Drak Monastery. H.H. Dharma King Taklung Tsetrul, H.H. Dharma King Dodrupchen, H.H. Dharma King Penor, and H.H. Trulshik Rinpoche have been universally recognized as dharma kings who hold the complete teachings of the Nyingma monastic tradition.

The Northern Treasure that the Dorje Drak Monastery mainly perpetuates refers to the higher terma left behind by Guru Padmasambhava. Those hidden dharma treasures were discovered in 1366 by the greatly accomplished Rigdzin Godem, who was one of the three wonderful nirmanakayas of Guru Padmasambhava. Rigdzin Godem became the first holder of the Northern Treasure dharma lineage. In 1599, Aji Wangbo, who was the third incarnation of Rigdzin Godem, moved what was then a very small tent-monastery to where the Dorje Drak Monastery is presently located and formally named it the Dorje Drak Monastery. H.H. the fifth Dalai Lama received from Aji Wangbo the complete dharma teachings of the Northern Treasure lineage and highly praised that lineage as being the most reliable terma teachings. The first Tangtong Gyalpo attained liberation through his focused practice of the dharma of the Northern Treasure lineage.

H.H. Taklung Tsetrul Rinpoche was born in central Tibet in 1926. In a former life, he was E Qugu Dorje, who was a rather famous disciple of Master Marpa. At the age of five, the ninth Dodrak Rigdzin, Choswang Nyamnid Dorje, recognized the rinpoche as a reincarnated tulku, and he was ordained as a monk at the Taklung Tse Monastery. At the age of eight, the rinpoche was formally enthroned at the Thubten Dorje Drak Monastery, which is the mother monastery of the Taklung Tse Monastery. He later learned under many masters of great virtue and received the complete terma, oral, and mind-instruction lineages. After serving as khenpo of the Dorje Drak Monastery for several years, he returned to the Taklung Tse Monastery.

H.H. Taklung Tsetrul Rinpoche later received the complete oral transmissions of the Kagyu sect from H.H. the sixteenth Great Jewel Dharma King. He also received the lineage teachings of Mipham Rinpoche and Longchenpa from H.H. Dharma King Dudjom and H.H. Dharma King Dilgo Khyentse and others. Additionally, the rinpoche transmitted dharma to H.H. Dharma King Dilgo Khyentse. The rinpoche and H.H. Dharma King Dilgo Khyentse were both master and student to each other. H.H. Dharma King Dilgo Khyentse said that the unusual signs on the palms of H.H. Taklung Tsetrul Rinpoche are the best proof that he is a terma holder and indicate that he has attained Buddhahood.

H.H. Taklung Tsetrul Rinpoche is universally recognized as one of the four great rinpoches of the present-day Nyingma sect. Dharma kings and masters of all of the main sects highly praise his learning, cultivation, and realization. At the request of H.H. Dharma King Dilgo Khyentse, H.H. Dharma King Penor, H.H. Dharma King Mindrolling Trichen, H.E. Dharma King Drikung Chetsang, and others, H.H. Taklung Tsetrul Rinpoche went to major monasteries in India, Sikkim, Bhutan, and Nepal to perform initiations and dharma transmissions. The rinpoche has also traveled around Asia, Europe, and America propagating the dharma.

寧瑪派伏藏傳承教法分北藏『強迭』傳承和南藏『索迭』傳承，在六大寺系中，敏珠林寺和白玉寺以傳承南藏為主，而傳承北藏的則是多傑札寺。而尊貴的達龍哲珠仁波且就是多傑札寺之掌教法王，達龍哲珠仁波且與多智欽法王、貝諾法王、楚西仁波且四人被公認為是目前完整持有寧瑪傳統僧眾教法的法王。

多傑札寺的教法以北藏巖傳法為主，北藏即是指由蓮花生大師所留下的上部伏藏，是由蓮花生大師殊勝三化身之一的大持明雷欽貴登於1366年所取出的，雷欽貴登也即成為北藏法的法主。雷欽貴登的第三世阿吉旺波於1599年將原有的一個很小的帳房寺院移到現在的地方，並正式命名為多傑札寺。五世達賴喇嘛從阿吉旺波那裡接受了北藏的全部教法，並推崇北藏是最值得信賴的伏藏教法，第一世唐東迦波也是專修北藏而即身成就的。

後來，仁波且又從第十六世大寶法王那裡得到噶舉的完整的口傳教授，從敦珠法王、頂果欽哲法王那裡得到米旁仁波且和龍欽巴的完整傳承教授，同時亦傳法給頂果欽哲法王，與頂果欽哲法王互為師徒。頂果欽哲法王說：仁波且手掌之奇異徵相即為巖藏法主之最佳證明，亦為即身成佛之表徵。

達龍哲珠仁波且被公認為當今寧瑪巴四大仁波且之一，其學問與修行、證量廣為諸大教派的法王、大師所推崇及讚嘆。仁波且不僅應頂果欽哲法王、貝諾法王、敏林赤欽法王、直貢澈贊法王等祈請，曾到印度、錫金、不丹、尼泊爾等各大寺廟給予灌頂和傳法，其弘法足跡更遍及亞洲、歐洲和美洲。

BRIEF INTRODUCTION TO H.H. DHARMA KING TRULSHIK
楚西法王簡介

H.H. Dharma King Kyabje Trulshik Chokyi Lodro is one of the most accomplished masters of the Nyingma sect in the present age. He is also one of the few remaining great masters of Tibetan Buddhism who has real and extensive knowledge, real training, and true cultivation. He is a lineage holder of many important dharma lineages. He is a great dharma king who does not distinguish among the various sects of Buddhism. H.H. Dharma King Trulshik and the most magnificent modern dharma kings of Buddhism, such as the H.H. Dudjom Dharma King and H.H. Dharma King Dilgo Khyentse, have been masters and disciples of one another. H.H. Dharma King Trulshik also taught the dharma of many lineages to the 16th Karmapa. He is a personal master of H.H. the Dalai Lama as well as a master of the most recent reincarnation of the H.H. Dudjom Dharma King, H.H. Dharma King Dilgo Khyentse, and H.E. Dharma King Tulku Ugyen.

Many rinpoches had different views concerning which great Bodhisattva H.H. Dharma King Trulshik was the incarnation of. Thus, the International Buddhism Sangha Association held an unprecedented Drawing Lots From a Golden Vase Ceremony to affirm the true reincarnated identity of H.H. Dharma King Trulshik and others. There were ten possible identities recognized by various rinpoches. One lot was drawn from among 120 lots to affirm the true reincarnated identity of H.H. Dharma King Trulshik. That drawing affirmed that H.H. Dharma King Trulshik is the nirmanakaya of Maitreya Bodhisattva, which is the reincarnated identity that H.H. Dorje Chang Buddha III recognized before that lot was drawn.

In history, H.H. Dharma King Trulshik incarnated as Thonmi Sambhota, who created the Tibetan written language. Later, he incarnated as the great translation master Bairotsana, who was one of the twenty-five major disciples of Guru Padmasambhava. H.H. Dharma King Trulshik will be the next

H.H. Dalai Lama and his master, H.H. Trulshik Rinpoche
達賴喇嘛和他的上師楚西仁波且。

Seated in the center are H.H. Dharma King Dilgo Khyentse and H.H. Trulshik Rinpoche. On the left is H.E. Gyatrul Rinpoche, and on the right is H.E. Shechen Rabjam Rinpoche
中坐者為頂果欽哲法王和楚西仁波且，左邊為嘉楚仁波且，右邊為冉江仁波且。

Buddha of this Good Eon (Bhadra-kalpa) of one thousand Buddhas. At that time, all of his disciples who heard him expound the Buddha-dharma will attain accomplishment in the dharma.

The dharma king was born on September 10, 1924, the year of the wooden rat, which was the exact birthday of Guru Padmasambhava. He was born in Wengre Cave, which is a holy place of cultivation in southern Tibet. Many auspicious phenomena appeared at the time of his birth. The father of the dharma king, Dianjin Queda, was a practitioner of yoga. His mother, Jiangyang Wangmu, was a descendent of Zhangba Jialei, who was the first Drukpa Dharma King and founder of the magnificent Drukpa lineage.

The dharma king was extraordinary ever since childhood, especially with respect to his deep self-cultivation. When he was four years old, his master, Zhachu Rinpoche (who was a disciple H.H. Dharma King Trulshik personally taught in his previous life as Trulshik Dongak Lingpa), invited him to the Zhalongpu Monastery in the Latuo Xueka District. At that time and place, memories of his prior life spontaneously welled up in the mind of the dharma king. He recounted in detail past events of that prior lifetime. Zhachu Rinpoche had personally witnessed those past events of his former master. Zhachu Rinpoche wept as he orally corroborated each of those events without exception. Zhachu Rinpoche was truly astonished by this and firmly believed that this boy must be the incarnation of Trulshik Dongak Lingpa. After the rinpoche practiced the Selection of Karmic Affinity Dharma, he affirmed that the boy was undoubtedly the incarnation of Trulshik

Dongak Lingpa. From that point on, the rinpoche was the root teacher of the boy, guiding him and teaching him dharma that the rinpoche learned from the boy in the boy's prior life.

At the Mindrolling Monastery, the dharma king engaged in extensive learning. He received all of the monk precepts from his precept masters Cuikenqiong Rinpoche and Mindrolling Kenqian Khyentse Norbu according to the "Formal Pronouncement on Precepts" lineage passed down from Laqian Qianba Lasa. Present-day dharma kings unanimously agree that H.H. Dharma King Trulshik is one of the most important lineage-holders of this lineage. H.H. Dharma King Trulshik holds three types of precepts that are on different levels: the Pratimoksa precepts, the Bodhisattva precepts, and the precepts for tantric masters. The dharma king is one who truly wears a golden precept robe. Not only does he abide by the precepts for monks, he also completely abides by all of the Hinayana, Mahayana, and Vajrayana precepts. That is why he deserves to be called a "holder of the Vajra Three Secrets Vows." H.H. Dharma King Trulshik is the main transmitter of the monastic vows within the Nyingma lineage.

The dharma king has received teachings on the sutras and tantras, as well as other teachings. He has visited famous masters in many places to learn Buddha-dharma, including over thirty famous masters who belong to ancient and modern sects of esoteric Buddhism. The dharma king has studied all of the dharma teachings of these important lineages and has put them into practice. He still learns assiduously even after he completed a strict three-year retreat. Accepting the request of Zhachu Rinpoche, the dharma king became the khenpo of the Zhalong Dongga Qielin Monastery, where he is responsible for upholding, protecting, and spreading the dharma.

Throughout his whole life, the dharma king has wholeheartedly cultivated himself in retreat. Every day he abstains from speaking until 10:00 in the morning. Each year the dharma king goes into retreat in his own temple for as much as nine months. All of the great Tibetan rinpoches acknowledge that as a master of masters, the dharma king has the greatest abilities and power to clearly point out the way leading to realization of one's original nature. That is why extremely virtuous masters send their capable disciples to the dharma king in order to seek teachings and empowerment.

H.H. Dharma King Trulshik has vast and profound learning. His practice is solid and flawless. He is unassuming and amiable. No one in today's world can match his profound experience, training, and realization. Many practitioners of the various sects regard him as a venerable Dharma King Master with limitless wisdom and vast supernatural powers. H.H. Dharma King Trulshik has recognized the identities of the person who is the incarnation of H.H. Dharma King Dilgo Khyentse, the person who is the incarnation of H.E. Dharma King Tulku Ugyen, and persons who are incarnations of other important rinpoches. He has also transmitted dharma to and performed initiations for such people. The dharma king is a magnificent practitioner of the Great Perfection Dharma and a magnificent accomplished one in our current age. He is a model master of this century with disciples spread all over the world.

　　尊貴的楚西法王（雅旺確吉羅多）是當代藏密寧瑪巴最有成就的大師之一，也是藏傳佛教中切實博學、訓練與實修之僅存碩師之一，他是許多主要傳承的持有者，是一位沒有門戶之見的大法王。楚西法王與敦珠法王、頂果欽哲法王等當代最偉大的佛教法王們互為師徒，也曾傳授許多傳承法教給十六世噶瑪巴，他更是達賴喇嘛的個人上師，也是新轉世的敦珠法王、頂果欽哲法王和烏金法王的上師。

　　對於楚西法王是哪一位大菩薩的轉世，諸仁波且有不同的見解。為此，國際佛教僧尼總會對仁波且們所作出的十個不同認證身份舉行了史無前例的金瓶掣籤，從120支密封籤中抽出一支，確認楚西法王是彌勒菩薩的化身，而此身份正是三世多杰羌佛提前作出的認證。歷史上，楚西法王曾轉世為創造西藏文字的卓彌新波塔、蓮花生大師二十五大弟子之一的毗如遮那大譯師等。彌勒菩薩是賢劫千佛中下一位的佛陀，屆時所有聽聞他宣說佛法的弟子皆能得到成就。

　　1924木鼠年9月10日適逢蓮花生大師的誕辰日，法王出生於西藏南部一個修行聖地——翁惹洞穴，當時出現了許多吉祥瑞象。法王的父親殿津確達是一位瑜伽行者，母親蔣揚旺母是偉大的竹巴傳承創教祖師第一世竹巴法王章巴加雷的後裔。

　　法王從小就與眾不同，特別深入修行，四歲時就被他的上師札楚仁波且（楚西法王前世之楚西東嘎林巴的心傳弟子）邀請到拉脫雪喀區的札隆埔寺。此時此地，其生前記憶油然浮現心頭，他細數往事，札楚仁波且親眼目睹先師事跡，泣泣講出，與之印證，無有差別，為之驚訝不已，深信這個男孩確是楚西東嘎林巴之轉世，更深入擇緣認證無誤，從而為其根本教師，給予引導，傳其前世之教法。

　　在敏珠林寺，法王博學廣聞，並從戒師崔肯穹仁波且和敏林懇欠欽哲諾布仁波且，按照拉千千巴拉薩留傳之《戒律授記》傳承，完成比丘戒，目前法王公認是此傳承主要持有者之一。楚西法王持有三種次第的戒律：個人解脫戒、菩薩戒和密教口傳論續持有者的誓戒，法王是真正穿上金縷法衣的人，不僅持守出家僧的戒律，而且是小乘、大乘、金剛乘三種戒律皆具足，所以堪稱為『金剛三密誓的持有者』。

寧瑪巴傳承中出家眾誓言的主要授予者即是楚西法王。法王接受經、續及其他教導，到處參訪名師，修學佛法，其舊、新密學派名師逾三十位。法王研習這些重要的全部法教傳承，並付諸實修，完成嚴格三年閉關後，還修學不懈。依札楚仁波且之請，法王擔任了札隆東嘎切林寺的堪布，負起護持、護教與弘法的責任。

法王一生潛心閉關修行，而且每天都修禁語至早上十點。法王每年至少都會在自己的寺院閉關，一年的閉關長達九個月。作為上師中之上師，各大西藏仁波且均公認其擁有指明直接本性之最大能力及加持力，而各大德亦遣其器前往求取傳授及加持。

楚西法王的學識淵博浩瀚、修行堅實無暇、待人平易可親，尤其是深入的歷練與證解，當今無與倫比，各教派眾多行者視之為智慧無邊、神通廣大的尊貴法王上師。至今為止，楚西法王已認證了頂果欽哲法王和烏金法王等重要仁波且的轉世，並為他們傳法灌頂。法王是這個時代偉大的『大圓滿』修行者及成就者、世紀的典範上師，他的弟子廣遍世界各地。

BRIEF INTRODUCTION TO H.H. DHARMA KING JIGDAL DAGCHEN SAKYA
薩迦達欽法王簡介

H.H. JIGDAL DAGCHEN SAKYA
Born 1929 Sakya, Tibet

H.H. Dharma King Jigdal Dagchen Sakya is the founder and principal guru of the Sakya Monastery of Tibetan Buddhism in Seattle, Washington, U.S.A. He is also the second highest leader of the entire Sakya order.

H.H. Dharma King Jigdal Dagchen Sakya was born into the Phuntsok branch of the Khon lineage in southwestern Tibet in 1929. His father was at that time the supreme leader of the Sakya order—H.H. Dharma King Sakya Trichen. As future leader and throne-holder of the Sakya order, H.H. Dagchen Rinpoche received a strict education from his father and other distinguished lamas beginning in his childhood. He systematically learned the teachings of the Hinayana, Mahayana, and Vajrayana. The rinpoche later received the unbroken Khon lineage transmission of the Sakya Vajrakilaya and Hevajra initiations and the complete Lamdre Tsogshe (Path and Result), which are the main teachings of the Sakya tradition. Following this, the rinpoche went into a long series of study and meditation retreats. He then conferred the Lamdre Tsogshe to monks, nuns, and laypersons within the Sakya order.

After the passing of his father, the position and authority of the supreme leader of the Sakya order should have been handed down to Dharma King Sakya Trizin of the Drolma Palace according to the tradition of the Sakya order. However, because Dharma King Sakya Trizin was at that time too young, H.H. Dagchen Rinpoche exercised the authority of supreme leader of the Sakya order for three years. Later, H.H. Dagchen Rinpoche traveled to eastern Tibet to increase his knowledge and experience of the dharma. There the rinpoche met his two root gurus—H.H. Dzongsar Khyentse Jamyang Chokyi Lodro and H.H. Dilgo Khyentse Rabsal Dawa. Those two masters helped to formulate the rinpoche's non-sectarian approach to Buddhism. After completing his studies, the rinpoche bestowed initiations and teachings throughout eastern Tibet and established 17 Sakya colleges and 10 retreat centers in that region. In 1955, he conferred the Lamdre Tsogshe to over 1,200 practitioners in eastern Tibet.

In 1959, H.H. Dharma King Dagchen moved to India with his entire family. He was later invited to participate in a research project on Tibetan civilization at the University of Washington. H.H. Dharma King Dagchen availed himself of those karmic conditions and founded the Sakya Monastery of Tibetan Buddhism in Seattle, which spreads the Buddha-dharma in the West. He has given extensive empowerments and teachings throughout the United States, Canada, Europe, and Asia. H.H. Dharma King Dagchen is universally recognized as one of the leaders of the Sakya order.

薩迦達欽法王是位於美國西雅圖的藏傳佛教薩迦寺廟的創始人和導師，也是整個薩迦派位居第二的領袖。

薩迦達欽法王於1929年出生在西藏西南部的昆族的彭措宮，他的父親是當時的薩迦派的總教主——薩迦天津法王。作為未來的薩迦派的領袖和薩迦法座的持有者，達欽仁波且自小就接受他的父親和其他優秀的喇嘛們的嚴格教育，系統地學習了小乘、大乘和金剛乘的理論知識。然後，仁波且又完整地接受了昆族從未間斷的普巴金剛、喜金剛和道果法的傳承灌頂，這些都是薩迦教法的精髓。此後，仁波且進行了長時期的研習和閉關，並為薩迦派的僧人和在家居士傳授道果法等。

在仁波且的父親圓寂以後，遵照薩迦派的傳統，應將薩迦總教主之法權地位交給聖母宮薩迦天津法王掌教，但鑒於當時天津法王尚年幼，故由達欽仁波且掌管三年薩迦總教主法權。後來，達欽仁波且到東藏地區繼續學習，以增加知識和閱歷。在這裡，仁波且遇到了他的兩位根本上師：宗薩欽哲‧蔣陽秋吉羅卓和頂果欽哲‧若賽達哇，這兩位大師引導仁波且進入無門戶之見的佛法。在學習完成之後，仁波且在東藏地區建立了17所薩迦學院和10個閉關中心，並舉行了灌頂和加持。1955年，仁波且在東藏為1200多人舉行了道果教授。

1959年，達欽法王全家到達印度，隨後，應邀到美國西雅圖的華盛頓大學進行西藏文化的研究。

基於此因緣，達欽法王在西雅圖創立了藏傳佛教薩迦廟，向西方社會傳播佛法。從此，法王不間斷地開示、傳法，其足跡遍及美國、加拿大、歐洲和亞洲。現在，達欽法王是公認的薩迦派的領袖之一。

BRIEF INTRODUCTION TO H.E. CHOGYE TRICHEN RINPOCHE, DHARMA KING OF THE TSHARPA BRANCH OF THE SAKYA ORDER
薩迦茶巴法王秋吉崔欽仁波且簡介

Elder dharma king H.E. Chogye Trichen Rinpoche was the eldest and most senior lama within the Sakya lineage of Tibetan Buddhism. He was the incarnation of the previous Chogye Trichen and was the Tsharpa Dharma King. He not only was a great lama who perfectly observed the three types of precepts, he also was a famous tantric master, an outstanding scholar, and an eloquent poet. The elder dharma king was called "master of the masters" because most of the lineage holders in Tibetan Buddhism were his disciples. H.H. the Dalai Lama took the elder dharma king as his root master beginning in 1971. H.H. Sakya Trizin, H.H. Dharma King Dudjom of the Nyingma sect, and H.H. Shamarpa of the Kagyu sect were also his disciples. The king of Nepal, King Birendra, conferred upon the rinpoche the auspicious, honorific title "Gorkha Dakshin Babu" (Great Master of West Nepal). The king of Nepal had never previously extended such praise to any other Buddhist master.

The elder dharma king was born in the year 1920 near Gyashar Kushang. He took birth in the Che clan. That clan descended from the Abhasvara Heaven to this world. Many auspicious signs appeared at the birth of the rinpoche. At the age of twelve, the rinpoche was formally enthroned as the 26th dharma-throne holder of the Phenpo Nalendra Monastery. Between the time he succeeded to that position and the time he became thirty-nine years old, the rinpoche received the supreme and precious "Path and Result (Lamdre)" initiation and mantras as well as countless initiations, dharma transmissions, mantras, and rituals from all of the lineages of the four major sects. During that time period he also completed meditation retreats in which he meditated upon yidams who are part of the main practice of tantra. He became a master of both exoteric and esoteric dharma teachings.

Because the rinpoche went on many long-term retreats, people often said that he was a yogi who practiced secretly. When he was not in retreats, the rinpoche used most of his time engaging in round-the-clock deep meditation, practicing tantric rituals, and practicing tantric supplications. As a result, he attained supernatural powers and great wisdom. The rinpoche was thought of as a modern-day incarnation of the greatly accomplished Indian Buddhist of former times, Mahasiddha Virupa. Every day of the rinpoche's life was spent continuing this laudable self-cultivation. He truly deserves to be called a model for all practitioners around the world.

The rinpoche made no distinctions between regions and countries in his undertaking to propagate the dharma. He traveled around the world spreading the dharma. Out of compassion, the rinpoche conferred the honored dharma of the Buddhas, such as initiations, oral transmissions, sutra explanations, and mantras, upon all those Buddhist disciples with the karmic affinity to receive them, whether they be lay or monastic. Even dharma kings and rinpoches received such dharma from him. All of those fortunate enough to have personally met the rinpoche praised his bodhicitta and attested to the selfless spirit this elder dharma king displayed by ceaselessly transmitting Buddha-dharma.

January 20, 2007 was the day when the great karmic undertaking of the elder dharma king to spread the dharma and benefit living beings in the earthly realm would come to an end. However, it was also the day when great karmic conditions matured relating to the final moments of his life. The elder dharma king read the book *A Treasury of True Buddha-Dharma* about H.H. Dorje Chang Buddha III. He immediately applied his accumulated realization powers to investigate and was extremely moved by what he discovered. He at once ordered Shabdrung Rinpoche to write a congratulatory letter. In that letter he praised the book *A Treasury of True Buddha-Dharma* about H.H. Dorje Chang Buddha III Wan Ko Yeshe Norbu, saying that the book is the guidepost leading to true Buddha-dharma and the gateway of the dharma leading to benefiting and providing happiness to living beings. After that congratulatory letter was written, the rinpoche passed on to a Buddha-land right then and there. That was the final holy act of this elder dharma king of supreme enlightenment.

Ven. Shabdrung Rinpoche has now succeeded to the position held by H.E. Chogye Trichen Rinpoche.

老法王秋吉崔欽仁波且是藏傳佛教「薩迦」傳承中最年長、最資深的喇嘛，是前世秋吉崔欽的轉世，為茶巴法王，他是圓滿持守三種戒律的大喇嘛，也是出名的密續大師、出色的學者及雄辯的詩人。老法王被稱為『上師中的上師』，因為大部分藏傳佛教傳承的掌持者，如達賴喇嘛自一九七一年就一直依止老法王為根本上師，薩迦法王、寧瑪巴敦珠法王和噶舉派夏瑪巴等也都是他的弟子。尼泊爾的百仁扎國王為仁波且奉上『果卡達心巴布』這個吉祥的尊號（意為『西尼泊爾大導師』），此乃尼泊爾國王對佛教大師前所未有的讚歎。

老法王於1920年出生於夏魯庫香，一個從光音天降臨於世的戒氏家族。仁波且出生時，有很多吉祥的異兆發生。仁波且於12歲時便正式升座，成為那爛陀寺的第二十六任法座持有者。自他繼位直至39歲間，仁波且領受了無上寶貴「道果」的灌頂及口訣，以及其所有四大教派的無數灌頂、傳法、口訣及儀軌的傳承，更完成主要密續中的多位本尊的禪修閉關，成為顯乘與密乘教法的大師。

人們時常說仁波且是位密修的瑜伽士，因為他作過多次的長時間閉關。除閉關以外，仁波且運用他大部分的時間，日以繼夜的深入禪定以及修持密續儀軌及祈請，得神通開大智慧。仁波且被認為如同往昔印度佛教大成就者毘瓦巴的現世化現。仁波且數十年如一日，每天繼續此等令人讚歎的修行，堪稱是全世界修行者的榜樣。

而且，仁波且對宣揚法教的承擔是無分地域、國界的，其宏法足跡遍及全球。仁波且總是慈悲的對一切有緣的佛弟子給予尊貴佛陀教法的灌頂、口傳、論釋及口訣，無論他們是在家居士或出家眾，甚至是法王或仁波且。有幸親見仁波且的人都讚歎仁波且的菩提之心，見證了老法王不斷傳授佛法的無私精神。

2007年1月20日，老法王在娑婆世界宏法利生的大事因緣就要結束的最後一刻，一生中終結的大事因緣成熟了，老法王見到了三世多杰羌佛的《正法寶典》一書，當下便以他積累的修行道力察觀，非常感動，即刻法旨在身邊的夏勛仁波且執筆寫信祝賀，讚歎多杰羌佛雲高益西諾布的《正法寶典》是正法的路標和利樂有情之門。在寫完賀信之後，這最後一件聖事終結了老法王無上的菩提道果，即席便往升佛土了。

現在，則由夏勛仁波且繼任其法位。

BRIEF INTRODUCTION TO
THE LINEAGE OF THE SHAMARPA
夏瑪巴的傳承簡介

When speaking of the H.E. Shamarpa, one must first understand his lineage. The source of his lineage is the same as the source all of sects and schools within Buddhism. Simply put, this lineage system within Buddhism has the same primordial ancestor as all of the others sects and schools of Buddhism. They all originate from Samantabhadra Tathagata Dorje Chang Buddha.

With respect to the overall Kagyu sect of H.H. Marpa, Dorje Chang Buddha transmitted dharma directly to H.H. Tilopa. H.H. Tilopa transmitted dharma to H.H. Naropa, and so forth down the line. The Karma Kagyu sect also started with Dorje Chang Buddha transmitting dharma directly to H.H. Tilopa. H.H. Tilopa then transmitted dharma to H.H. Naropa. H.H. Naropa transmitted dharma to H.H. Marpa. H.H. Marpa transmitted dharma to H.H. Milarepa. H.H. Milarepa transmitted dharma to H.H. Gampopa. H.H. Gampopa transmitted dharma to H.H. Dusum Khyenpa. Many branch sects then began to arise.

The Karma Kagyu sect has a wonderful history of over nine hundred years. H.H. the first Karmapa, Dusum Khyenpa, is the future Lion's Roar Buddha. After Maitreya Bodhisattva becomes a Buddha at the Dragon Flower Assembly, the next one to become a Buddha will be H.H. Dusum Khyenpa, who will be the sixth Buddha of this present Good Eon (Bhadra-Kalpa). H.H. Dusum Khyenpa established the Karma Kagyu sect. Right before H.H. Karmapa II passed away, he predicted that he would in the future have two nirmanakayas who would generation after generation incarnate and teach each other as master and disciple. One of those nirmanakayas has been the Karmapa Great Jewel Dharma King. The other Nirmanakaya has been the Shamarpa Red Jewel Hat Dharma King. Actually, Karmapa is Shamarpa. They are both one of two emanations from the same "original." The meaning of the word Karmapa is "a venerable one who wears the black jewel hat." The meaning of the word Shamarpa is "a venerable one who wears the red jewel hat." H.H. Karmapa is called the Great Jewel Dharma King. H.E. Shamarpa is called the Regent King. When H.H. Karmapa is not there, H.E. Shamarpa acts as his regent, assuming the official powers held by the Great Jewel Dharma King. Tibetans ordinarily call H.E. Shamarpa the "Red Jewel Hat Dharma King."

H.E. Drakpa Senge was born in 1283, the year in which H.H. the second Karmapa Great Jewel Dharma King passed away. H.H. the third Karmapa was born the year after that. When H.H. the third Karmapa was sixteen years old, he recognized that H.E. Drakpa Sengye was the second Nirmanakaya of the second Karmapa and that he was the first Shamarpa. H.H. the third Karmapa also transmitted to H.E. Drakpa Senge complete dharma teachings, including the Six Yogas of H.H. Naropa. From that time on, the two Nirmanakayas of H.H. Karmapa II have been each other's master and disciple throughout generations. They alternately recognized each other's identity or status throughout successive generations.

For example, H.E. the second Shamarpa recognized the identity of H.H. the fifth Great Jewel Dharma King, Deshin Shegpa, and transmitted dharma to him. H.E. the third Shamarpa, Chopal Yeshe (1406-1452), was a disciple of H.H. the fifth Great Jewel Dharma King. However, H.E. the third Shamarpa recognized the identity of H.H. the sixth Great Jewel Dharma King and was the master of H.H. the sixth Great Jewel Dharma King. After that, the process continued in such a manner. H.E. the second Shamarpa, Khacho Wangpo (1350-1405), was a disciple of H.H. the fourth Karmapa, Rolpe Dorje. H.H. the fourth Great Jewel Dharma King, Rolpe Dorje, crowned Khacho Wangpo Rinpoche with the red jewel hat (such hat in Tibetan is called shamar), which signified that Khacho Wangpo Rinpoche was the second Nirmanakaya of the Karmapa. From that time on, people called Khacho Wangpo Rinpoche "the Shamarpa." H.H. the sixteenth Karmapa recognized his nephew Mipham Chokyi Lodro (born in 1952) as H.E. the fourteenth Shamarpa. Before Chokyi Lodro left Tibet at the age of nine, he was secretly taken to the Yangchen Monastery, which was established by H.E. the fourth Shamarpa. He immediately identified each of the statues of the past Shamarpas and spoke of the achievements of each of those past Shamarpas. He left Tibet and went to India in 1964. He was formally installed as the Shamarpa at the ancient Rumtek Monastery in Sikkim.

Throughout the generations, when most of the Shamarpas were born and passed away, certain auspicious signs appeared. H.E. the second Shamarpa, Khacho Wangpo, began learning the Buddha-dharma when he was fourteen months old. At the age of three, he expounded the Buddha-dharma to others. He learned the Mahamudra and the Six Yogas of H.H. Naropa when he was seven years old. Before passing away and entering parinirvana, he clearly wrote down details concerning the home into which he would next take birth and its surrounding environment. When H.E. the third Shamarpa, Chopal Yeshe, was in his mother's womb, people could hear him chanting the Six Syllable Great Brightness Mantra. When he was born, a few rainbows in the form of jeweled parasols appeared in perfect alignment over the roof of his house, and awe-inspiring, wonderful Mongolian words appeared on the bottom of his feet. When he passed away, many rainbows appeared in the sky, and flowers cascaded from the heavens. When H.E. the fourth Shamarpa was born, two moons appeared in the sky. H.E. the fifth Shamarpa, Koncho Yenlak, was born in autumn. Nonetheless, flower buds blossomed forth at that time. The family members of the newborn child heard him chanting the Six Syllable Great Brightness Mantra. At the birth of H.E. the eighth Shamarpa, Palchen Chokyi Dondrup, a white rainbow appeared in the sky over his home.

At the birth of H.E. the current fourteenth Shamarpa, Mipham Chokyi Lodro, different kinds of rainbows filled the sky. One of them was in the shape of a jeweled temple banner that filled the sky above the courtyard of his home. The water in the nearby rivers turned to milky white. At the age of six, he was taken to the Tsupu Temple, which is the main temple of the Kagyu sect. While circumambulating the temple on the back of his servant, H.E. the fourteenth Shamarpa suddenly pointed to some monks who were entering through the western gate and said, "They are monks from my temple." It turned out that those monks came from the Yangchen Monastery.

The meritorious achievements of all of the Shamarpas throughout the generations in propagating the dharma are truly remarkable. H.E. the first Shamarpa built a retreat center in Nehnang. H.E. the second Shamarpa, who had a great many disciples, built the large temple and retreat center called Garden Mamo, enabling three hundred of his disciples to cultivate themselves in retreat. H.E. the fourth Shamarpa became the holy leader of Tibet and established the Yangchen Monastery in Yambajan. His disciples included many famous masters from the four major branches and eight minor branches of the Kagyu sect. H.E. the sixth Shamarpa established the Tudeng Ningqianlin Meditation Center and wrote the texts of the Saban Prayer and the Manjushri Prayer. He led the efforts to complete the Lijiang edition of the compilation of great Buddhist scriptures. After he went to Nepal to spread the dharma, he was revered by the kings of that country. He built four gold dharma thrones around the great stupa at Yangpu.

During the more than forty years since he was enthroned as Shamarpa in Rumtek in 1964, H.E. the current fourteenth Shamarpa has traveled many times to Europe, the United States, Taiwan, Hong Kong, and southeast Asia to propagate the dharma. His ability to spread the dharma and save living beings is exceptional. He has several hundred thousand disciples around the world.

Moreover, the International Buddhism Sangha Association held an unprecedented Drawing Lots From a Golden Vase Ceremony to affirm the true reincarnated identity of H.E. Shamarpa and others. There were ten possible identities recognized by various rinpoches. One lot was drawn from among 120 lots to affirm the true reincarnated identity of H.E. Shamarpa. That drawing affirmed that H.E. the fourteenth Shamarpa is one of the nirmanakayas of Kuan Yin Bodhisattva, which is the reincarnated identity that H.H. Dorje Chang Buddha III recognized long before that lot was drawn.

According to H.E. Shamarpa's own introduction, he is the nirmanakaya of the second Karmapa. The Sharmapas and the Karmapas have been masters and disciples of one another throughout lifetimes. In this lifetime, H.E. Shamarpa is the master of H.H. Trinley Thaye Dorje Karmapa. Thus, whether from the perspective of knowledge or realization, there should be the honorific letters *H.H.* before the name of the fourteenth Shamarpa. At the very least, the facts show that in this lifetime he is more proficient in the Buddha-dharma than the Karmapa. That is why he became the teacher of the Karmapa. However, in accordance with hierarchical system of the Kagyu sect, we have only added the letters *H.E.* before his name.

In February of 2007, after H.E. the fourteenth Shamarpa saw the accomplishments of H.H. Dorje Chang Buddha III Wan Ko Yeshe Norbu in the Five Vidyas shown in the book *A Treasury of True Buddha-Dharma*, he promptly wrote a congratulatory letter to H.H. Dorje Chang Buddha III.

說到夏瑪巴，首先必須明白他的傳承，他的傳承與所有佛教派的來源都是一樣的，簡而言之，即是他們的系統與其他教派的始祖相同，都是普賢王如來多杰羌佛始源。噶舉派是多杰羌佛傳與帝洛巴，由帝洛巴再傳那洛巴，由此而下。噶瑪噶舉也是由多杰羌佛傳帝洛巴，帝洛巴傳那洛巴，那洛巴傳馬爾巴，馬爾巴傳密勒日巴，密勒日巴傳岡波巴，岡波巴傳杜松淺巴，開始大量分支脈派。噶瑪噶舉派有九百多年的殊勝歷史，第一世噶瑪巴杜松淺巴是未來佛獅子佛，他是繼彌勒菩薩在龍華會成佛後，下一位成佛的賢劫第六佛。杜松淺巴創立噶瑪噶舉派，當第二世噶瑪巴圓寂時預言他將有兩個化身，將一代一代轉世時互為師徒，一個化身為噶瑪巴大寶法王，另一個化身就是夏瑪巴紅寶冠法王。事實上「噶瑪」就是「夏瑪巴」，他們都是「本身」的兩個之一。「噶瑪巴」意為「戴著黑寶冠之尊者」；而「夏瑪巴」意為「戴著紅寶冠之尊者」。噶瑪巴稱為大寶法王，夏瑪巴稱為攝政王，噶瑪巴不在時，由夏瑪巴代理大寶法王的職權。藏人通常稱夏瑪巴為「紅寶冠法王」。

第二世噶瑪巴大寶法王圓寂那年（1283），卓巴辛給誕生，次年第三世噶瑪巴出生，他十六歲時認證卓巴辛給為第二世噶瑪巴的第二位化身，即第一世夏瑪巴，並傳他包括「那諾六法」的完整教法。此後歷代杜松淺巴的兩個化身就互為師徒，隔代交叉認證。如第二世夏瑪巴認證第五世大寶法王德新寫巴並傳其教法，第三世夏瑪巴邱波意希(1406-1452)為第五世大寶法王的弟子，他認證第六世大寶法王並為其上師。餘此類推。第二世夏瑪巴卡覺汪波（1350-1405）為第四世噶瑪巴瑞佩多杰的弟子，第四世大寶法王瑞佩多杰頒予卡覺汪波仁波且紅寶冠（藏文音「夏瑪」）一頂，以為噶瑪巴第二化身，自此人們法稱仁波且為「夏瑪巴」。十六世噶瑪巴認證他的姪兒卻吉羅助(1952)為第十四世夏瑪巴，卻吉羅助九歲離開西藏前被秘密帶回第四世夏瑪巴所建的楊潛寺，他立即指出各代夏瑪巴的塑相，並一一述說出各代的事蹟。他離藏進印於一九六四年在西藏流亡政府所在地德蘭沙拉隆德古寺正式坐床。

歷代夏瑪巴出生與圓寂時多有些瑞象出現，第二世噶瑪巴卡覺汪波，十四個月大時即開始學佛，三歲即向人們宣講佛法，七歲即學大手印、那諾六法，入滅前清楚寫下出生家庭周遭環境細節；第三世邱波意希在母腹中人們即可聽他唱誦六字大明的咒音，出生時屋頂上整齊排列著幾個寶傘形的彩虹，腳心出現蒙古文威勝字眼，圓寂時天空出現眾多彩虹，天華繽紛；第四世出生時天空出現兩個月亮；第五世昆卻尹勒出生時為秋天，然花木含苞開放，甫出世家人即聽見他唱誦六字大明。第八世帕千卻吉杜出生時，家中上空出現一道白色的彩虹；現住世的第十四世卻吉羅助降生時天空遍布各種彩虹，其中之一狀似寶幢，覆蓋他家宮院上空，附近河水也轉為乳白色。六歲時被帶到噶舉主寺祖普寺，當僕人背他繞廟行禮時，他突然指一些自西邊門進來的僧侶說：「他們是我寺廟的僧侶」，這些人係來自楊潛寺。

歷代夏瑪巴宏法事業功績赫赫，第一世在涅壤建一閉關中心；第二世建一座大寺廟及閉關中心噶登瑪漠關房讓三百弟子入關修行，領有廣大弟子群，第四世成統領西藏之怙主，建立羊八井的楊潛寺，弟子包括噶舉派四大八小中許多有名的上師。第六世創立「圖登寧千林禪修中心」，著有「薩班祈請文」、「文殊菩薩祈請文」，領導完成麗江版大藏經，到尼泊爾宏法，受國王們尊崇，在楊浦大塔四周建四座黃金法台。十四世在印度達蘭沙拉坐床後三十餘年間多次至歐美台灣香港東南亞宏法，法緣特盛，全世界弟子達數十萬人。

更難得的是，國際佛教僧尼總會對仁波且們作出的十個不同認證身份舉行了史無前例的金瓶掣籤，從120支密封籤中抽出一支，確認第十四世夏瑪巴是觀音菩薩的化身之一，而此身份正是三世多杰羌佛在掣籤之前早就作出的認證。

根據夏瑪巴的介紹，夏瑪巴是第二世噶瑪巴的化身，每世互為師徒，這一世又是泰耶多杰噶瑪巴的上師，因此，從證量和學識上，都應是冠以H.H.的大聖德，至少事實證明，他們在這一世是比噶瑪巴精通佛法的，所以才成為噶瑪巴的師長。但是，鑑於噶舉的法位制度，所以我們只冠以H.E.。

2007年2月，當十四世夏瑪巴見到三世多杰羌佛雲高益西諾布的《正法寶典》所展示的五明成就以後，當即給三世多杰羌佛寫了賀函。

BRIEF INTRODUCTION TO
H.E. GOSHIR GYALTSAB RINPOCHE
嘉察仁波且簡介

His Eminence Goshir Gyaltsab Rinpoche, also known as Gyaltsabpa, is an extremely important rinpoche within the Kagyu lineage. The "Gyalt" in his name refers to H.H. the Great Jewel Dharma King Karmapa. The "sab" refers to an agent or regent. Thus, H.E. Gyaltsab Rinpoche is the only agent and one of the regents for H.H. the Karmapa Great Jewel Dharma King. The rinpoche has come back to this world voluntarily. After his identity was recognized, there was a formal ceremony held to recognize his status. H.E. Gyaltsab Rinpoche also had a ceremony conducted in which he was installed as one of the regents for H.H. the Karmapa Great Jewel Dharma King. Throughout generations, when H.H. the Karmapa was absent, H.E. Gyaltsab Rinpoche served as his agent and took charge of administrative and dharma matters. In that capacity, he protected the dharma teachings. This is the way it has been starting from past lifetimes all the way up to the current H.E. 12th Goshir Gyaltsab Rinpoche. After H.H. the 16th Karmapa passed away, because the 17th Karmapa is currently still unable to return to Rumtek Monastery, H.E. the 12th Gyaltsab Rinpoche took up residence at Rumtek and has been fully in charge of its dharma matters.

H.E. Goshir Gyaltsab Rinpoche is the incarnation of Patriarch Gampopa. In 2007 the International Buddhism Sangha Association held an unprecedented Drawing Lots From a Golden Vase Ceremony to affirm the true reincarnated identity of H.E. Gyaltsab Rinpoche and others. There were ten possible identities recognized by various rinpoches. One lot was drawn from among 120 lots to affirm the true reincarnated identity of H.E. Gyaltsab Rinpoche. That drawing affirmed that H.E. Gyaltsab Rinpoche is the incarnation of Patriarch Gampopa, which is the reincarnated identity that H.H. Dorje Chang Buddha III recognized before that lot was drawn. During the time of Guru Padmasambhava, the rinpoche incarnated as Palju Wangchuk, one of the twenty-five great disciples of Guru Padmasambhava. After Palju Wangchuk passed away, his entire body merged with space, and he entered the pure land of the dakinis.

H.E. the 1st Goshir Gyaltsab Rinpoche received integral dharma teachings from H.H. the 6th Karmapa and practiced all of them to perfection. After H.H. the 6th Karmapa passed away, it was

H.E. Goshir Gyaltsab Rinpoche who found the 7th Karmapa, H.H. Chodrag Gyatso. The rinpoche also performed an enthronement ceremony for H.H. the 7th Karmapa and gave him the precepts. Guru Padmasambhava once appeared before H.H. the 7th Karmapa and said to that dharma king the following words about H.E. Goshir Gyaltsab Rinpoche: "He possesses the compassion to carry on the activities of the Buddhas. You should confer upon him a jeweled crown to indicate his position." H.H. the Great Jewel Dharma King complied with the edict of Guru Padmasambhava. He made a jeweled crown in accordance with the secret tantra called Lama Gongba Duba Mandala Text, empowered that crown with merit accumulated from the physical actions of Amitabha Buddha, and put that crown on the head of H.E. the 2nd Goshir Gyaltsab Rinpoche, Tashi Namgyal. Seeing that H.E. Goshir Gyaltsab Rinpoche had the highest state of realization among all the eminent monks in the entire country, Emperor Jingzong of China's Ming Dynasty conferred upon H.E. the 1st Goshir Gyaltsab Rinpoche the title of "National Master." From that time on, H.E. Goshir Gyaltsab Rinpoche became the only person within the Karma Kagyu sect who was both a regent and National Master. The Karmapa Great Jewel Dharma Kings recognized the identity of all of the later incarnations of H.E. Goshir Gyaltsab Rinpoche, who assisted the Karmapas in handling both administrative and dharma matters.

Before H.E. 12th Goshir Gyaltsab Rinpoche was born, H.H. 16th Karmapa made the following prediction: "With respect to the dharma lineage of Goshir Gyaltsab, a holy child will be born into a blessed family amid various wonderful and auspicious signs in the year of the wooden horse. His father's name will be Louzuo, and his mother's name will be Zuoma. He will live in the western plateau at a place whose distance from the Tsupu Temple takes two days to traverse by way of a swift, galloping horse." Later, on the 11th day of the 7th month of the Tibetan calendar in the year 1954, H.E. the 12th Goshir Gyaltsab Rinpoche was born amid various auspicious signs, and his identity was recognized. At the age of four, H.H. the 16th Karmapa Great Jewel Dharma King personally tonsured the rinpoche. Additionally, when the rinpoche was installed on the National Master's Lion's Throne at the great Tsupu Zhuojia Temple, H.H. the 16th Karmapa Great Jewel Dharma King performed a grand enthronement ceremony for the rinpoche in which he crowned the rinpoche with an orange jeweled crown. The honorable H.E. 12th Goshir Gyaltsab Rinpoche is currently giving teachings to one of the 17th Karmapa Great Jewel Dharma Kings on initiations, practice of the dharma, and other aspects. He is the only regent dharma king for H.H. the Great Jewel Dharma King who is a National Master.

H.E. Gyaltsab Rinpoche is not only a master of H.H. the seventeenth Karmapa Urgyen Trinley Dorje, he is also the incarnation of Patriarch Gampopa, who was the root master of the first Karmapa, Dusum Khyenpa. The present Karmapa H.H. Urgyen Trinley Dorje learned several dozen sutras and other Buddha-dharma from H.E. Gyaltsab Rinpoche. Thus, from any perspective, it cannot be said that the Karmapa is higher than H.E. Gyaltsab Rinpoche, who is the incarnation of Gampopa, or higher than H.E. Tai Situ Rinpoche, who is the incarnation of Master Marpa. From the perspective of worldly generational seniority, they should be regarded as equal. From the perspective of knowledge and realization, they should be regarded as having been masters and disciples of one another. Thus, we think that the honorific letters *H.H.* should appear before the name Gyaltsab. However, in accordance with hierarchical system of the Kagyu sect, we have only added the letters *H.E.* before his name.

After H.E. National Master Gyaltsab read *A Treasury of True Buddha-Dharma* about H.H. Dorje Chang Buddha III in February of 2007, he was very moved and profusely praised H.H. Dorje Chang Buddha III. He respectfully called H.H. Dorje Chang Buddha III an "incomparable Master" and promptly wrote a letter of congratulations.

嘉察仁波且，又名嘉察巴，是噶舉傳承中一位極為重要的仁波且，其名號『嘉』就是指大寶法王噶瑪巴，『察』指的就是代理或攝政，所以，嘉察仁波且是大寶法王噶瑪巴唯一的一位代理和攝政。乘願再來的仁波且被認證後，都有一個正式的坐床典禮，但嘉察仁波且則還要舉辦一個攝政的升座儀式。歷代以來，當噶瑪巴不在時，由嘉察巴代理掌管政務和法務、守護教法，從過去世到現今的第十二世都是如此。第十六世噶瑪巴圓寂以後，第十七世噶瑪巴目前還無法回到隆德寺，就由第十二世嘉察巴駐錫隆德寺主持全權法務。

嘉察仁波且為岡波巴祖師的轉世，2007年，國際佛教僧尼總會對仁波且們作出的十個不同認證身份舉行了史無前例的金瓶掣籤，從120支密封籤中抽出一支，確認嘉察仁波且是岡波巴祖師的轉世，而此身份正是三世多杰羌佛在金瓶掣籤之前早已作出的認證。在蓮花生大師時代，仁波且化現為蓮師二十五大弟子之一的喀欽巴之旺祝，圓寂後，全身融入虛空，進入空行淨土。而後第一世嘉察仁波且在第六世噶瑪巴處領受了完整的教法並圓滿了所有教法的修習。在第六世噶瑪巴圓寂後，嘉察仁波且尋獲第七世噶瑪巴秋札嘉措，為他升座，並為他授戒。蓮花生大師曾示現於第七世噶瑪巴面前對法王說：嘉察仁波且『具諸佛之慈悲事業，應授予寶冠以為權位』，大寶法王乃遵蓮師之法旨，依密續喇嘛貢巴杜巴曼達拉文而製成寶冠，以阿彌

陀佛身功德加持之，冠於第二世嘉察仁波且達西朗嘉之頂。中國明朝靖宗皇帝見當時全國高僧唯嘉察仁波且證量道境最高，便御封第一世嘉察仁波且為『國師』，從此嘉察仁波且即成為噶瑪噶舉唯一的攝政國師。以後歷代嘉察仁波且均由噶瑪巴大寶法王認證，並協助噶瑪巴掌管政法二務。

在第十二世嘉察仁波且降生之前，第十六世噶瑪巴曾作出指示：『嘉察札巴嘉此措之法脈，於木馬年、在種種殊勝吉兆中，靈童誕生於幸福家庭，父名羅佐，母名佐瑪，居於距楚布寺快馬奔馳兩天路程之西部高原上。』後於1954年藏歷7月11日，第十二世嘉察仁波且在種種瑞兆中降生並被認定，四歲時，由第十六世噶瑪巴大寶法王親自為其剃髮，並在仁波且駐錫大寺楚布卓伽寺的國師之獅子寶座上，為仁波且舉行升座大典，為其戴上金紅色寶冠。現在，尊貴的第十二世嘉察仁波且正在給予第十七世噶瑪巴大寶法王灌頂、修法等方面的教授，是大寶法王的唯一攝政王、大國師。

嘉察巴不但是十七世噶瑪巴烏金聽列多杰的上師，也是第一世噶瑪巴杜松淺巴的噶舉法脈傳承上師岡波巴大師，這一世的噶瑪巴所學的幾十部經教、佛法都是跟嘉察巴學的，因此，無論從哪個角度來看，噶瑪巴都不能說高於剛波巴化身的嘉察巴和瑪爾巴化身的泰錫度。從俗輩的倫理上來看，應該是平等的，從學識的道量上來看，應該是互為師徒的，因此，我們認為在嘉察巴的前面應該冠以H.H.。但鑒於噶舉巴的法位制度，所以我們只得冠以H.E.。

2007年2月，嘉察國師見到三世多杰羌佛的《正法寶典》，激動和讚嘆不已，恭稱三世多杰羌佛為『無比喇嘛』，馬上提筆寫了賀信。

BRIEF INTRODUCTION TO HIS EMINENCE XIAZHU QIUYANG RINPOCHE, THE INCARNATION OF PATRIARCH NAROPA, THE VENERABLE LEADER OF 100,000 DAKINIS
十萬空行尊主那諾巴轉世的夏珠秋楊仁波且

The most venerable H.E. Xiazhu Qiuyang Rinpoche (also known as H.E. Xiazhu Choying Rinpoche) is a greatly accomplished one from Guoluo who is a great yoga master free of all hindrances. He is also known as Xiazhu Qiuyang Rangzhuo. The day he was born in the winter of 1945, thunder rumbled in the sky and all kinds of fresh, colorful flowers bloomed forth from the grassland surrounding his tent. Many herdsmen in that area personally saw such rare and auspicious signs. Mantra master Regong, a famous and eminent monk, identified the child as the reincarnation of his venerable master Chagailong Cichengdaji Rinpoche and the great master Naropa.

To provide a model for other living beings, H.E. Xiazhu Qiuyang Rinpoche has lived in the mountains throughout his life practicing austerities. He has personally seen the most venerable Vajrayogini and was taught by her. The rinpoche is able to soar into the sky by using his monk robes as wings. At the age of fourteen, the rinpoche became a monk and learned under Xiari Huzuo Qintu Dannima. He later learned the Buddha-dharma from more than 100 accomplished, eminent, and highly virtuous masters, such as H.H. the tenth Panchen Lama and H.H. the sixth Dharma King Gongtang Yongzeng of the Geluk sect; H.H. Dodrupchen Rinpoche and Khenpo Mengse of the Longchen Nyingtik (Great Perfection) lineage within the Nyingma sect; Kanda Chiwa Gadan of the Sakya sect; Lama Wangcai Kazhige of the Kagyu sect; and Jiana Bannan of the Jonang sect. From those masters the rinpoche learned the essence of all the teachings of the various schools of exoteric and esoteric Buddhism.

Numerous eminent and highly virtuous monks accomplished in the dharma as well as tantric masters who practiced austerities conferred upon H.E. Xiazhu Qiuyang Rinpoche all of their secret mind-dharma teachings and secret lineage empowerments. Such teachings and empowerments were conferred without reserve, like a bottle freely pouring out water.

All year round the rinpoche wanders about the mountains and wild plains. At night he sleeps in a tent inside a cave. He eats cold rice and vegetables obtained from soliciting alms and wears old clothes that he scavenged. He might drift from town to town, appearing like a madman, totally indifferent to ridicule, slander, or praise. He did not speak one word for twenty-five straight years because his mind was completely focused on the dharma. Such was his diligent and uninterrupted practice of the dharma! During that period of time, the rinpoche entered into solitary self-cultivation at many holy places in India, Qinghai-Tibet and other places in China. At one of those places in India, he engaged in solitary cultivation for seven consecutive years.

He has realized wonderful enlightenment and accomplishment through the practice of Dakini Dharma, the Great Perfection Dharma (Longchen Nyingtik), the Kalachakra Vajra Dharma (Duoluonata lineage), Green Tara Dharma, and other dharmas. It is especially significant that starting from when he was still very young he received guidance and empowerment from the most venerable Vajrayogini. As a result, he obtained numerous extremely secret dakini teachings. Great beings of holy virtue within Buddhism have recognized that the rinpoche is the true incarnation of the most venerable Naropa, who was a great master known as "the venerable leader of 100,000 dakinis." Moreover, the International Buddhism Sangha Association held an unprecedented Drawing Lots From a Golden Vase Ceremony to affirm the true reincarnated identity of H.E. Xiazhu Qiuyang Rinpoche and others. There were ten possible identities recognized by various rinpoches. One lot was drawn from among 120 lots to affirm the true reincarnated identity of H.E Xiazhu Qiuyang Rinpoche. That drawing affirmed that H.E. Xiazhu Qiuyang Rinpoche is the incarnation of Patriarch Naropa, which is the reincarnated identity that H.H. Dorje Chang Buddha III recognized before that lot was drawn.

Numerous people of great virtue, such as H.H. the tenth Panchen Lama, H.H. Dharma King Yongzeng, and H.H. Dharma King Jigme Phuntsok, have highly praised H.E. Xiazhu Qiuyang Rinpoche many times on many different occasions. One of those numerous people was Xiaridong Rinpoche, a master who became accomplished through practicing the Yamantaka Dharma. He praised the rinpoche as being "truly a greatly accomplished one in the Dakini Dharma." H.H. Dharma King Jigme Phuntsok highly praised the rinpoche as "an extremely rare master of great accomplishment who has practiced to perfection the Four Initiations Dharma." Examples of such expressions of praise for the rinpoche are countless. All sects of Tibetan Buddhism recognize that the rinpoche is a master of great accomplishment in the dharma and that he is a brilliant model for all practitioners of Buddhism in this world of five defilements. Because he is humble, amiable, and has vast supernatural powers that he exercises freely and without attachment, people respectfully call him "the unhindered rinpoche."

Although the rinpoche strictly abides by the ancient teaching that one may not lightly display supernatural powers, nevertheless, many of his miraculous feats are widely known, such as his ability to fly, multiply his body, move under water, understand thoroughly many different languages, foreknow disasters and blessings, and read people's minds. Moreover, clothing worn by the rinpoche and articles that he used in his daily life have miraculous powers to bless. Countless Tibetans have been able to turn a disaster into a blessing, pass safely through a dangerous situation, and be completely healed from a serious illness all because they wore or ate a tiny piece of the rinpoche's monk robe. In Tibet, especially in Anduo District, almost everyone

knows of the legendary feats performed by H.E. Xiazhu Qiuyang Rinpoche. Furthermore, such feats have been recorded in books such as *Holy Cultivation and Its Marvelous Fruits* and *Biographies of Ten Major Disciples of Dharma Kings.*

The holy patriarch Naropa is born,
an ancient magnificent Kagyu master of Geluk practice.
He has long ago mastered the profound dharma and is unhindered.
The holy, virtuous ones in all directions praise him as being a sage.
Those with the karmic affinity to encounter him become liberated.
He is the refuge of the countless living beings.

After H.E. Xiazhu Qiuyang Rinpoche read *A Treasury of True Buddha-Dharma*, he immediately applied his supernatural powers and saw that the true identity of H.H. Wan Ko Yeshe Norbu is Dorje Chang Buddha, the primordial and highest Buddha in Buddhism. This corroborated the recognitions of other dharma kings of great holiness. Thus, H.E. Xiazhu Qiuyang Rinpoche respectfully wrote a congratulatory letter.

果洛大成就者、瑜伽自在大士至尊夏珠秋楊仁波且，又名夏珠‧秋楊讓卓，降生於1945年冬季，降生當日、天空雷聲隆隆，帳房周圍的草原上開起五顏六色的各種鮮花，當地的許多牧民都目睹了這一罕見祥瑞之象。著名高僧熱貢咒師認證為其尊師察蓋隆‧慈呈達吉活佛那諾巴祖師轉世，為對眾生表法，一生住山苦修、親見至尊金剛瑜伽母並得攝受，能以僧衣為翅翱翔天際。仁波且14歲依止夏日呼佐欽圖丹尼瑪出家為僧，曾依止格魯派十世班禪、六世貢唐‧雍增法王；寧瑪派堪布蒙色；薩迦派堪達赤哇嘎丹，噶舉派喇嘛旺才‧卡芝格，覺囊派加納班南等高僧大德成就師、一百餘位修學佛法，盡得佛教各宗顯密要精義。

眾多已獲成就的高僧大德及苦行密修之士，紛將心密法教及不共傳承加持、如瓶注水般、盡數授予夏珠秋楊仁波且，他常年遊行於山野荒原之中，夜宿於岩穴法帳之內；吃的是乞討來的涼飯菜，穿的是撿拾而得的舊衣服；或游蕩於市井之間、形似瘋癲、任人譏諷毀譽，二十五年不講一句話，而一心專注於教法之中，勤修不輟！在此期間，仁波且曾在青藏、印度及內地的眾多勝地閉關修行，其中在印度一聖地閉關專修長達七年之久。遂於空行母法、大圓滿法（龍欽寧體）、時輪金剛法(多羅那他傳承)、綠度母法等獲得殊勝證悟。尤其自幼得蒙至尊金剛瑜伽母攝受和加護，返還到前世真身再現，被佛教界大聖德認證為 "十萬空行尊主" 至尊那諾巴祖師的轉世真身。更難得的是，國際佛教僧尼總會對仁波且們作出的十個不同認證身份舉行了史無前例的金瓶掣籤，從120支密掣籤中抽出一支，確認夏珠秋楊仁波且是那諾巴祖師的轉世，而此身份正是三世多杰羌佛提前就作出的認證。

班禪大師、雍增法王、法王晉美彭措等眾多大德多次在不同場合對夏珠秋楊仁波且盛讚和稱揚。其中大威德成就師夏日東活佛稱讚仁波且是 "真正的空行母法大成就者"；法王晉美彭措盛讚仁波且是 "極其稀有的四灌法修習圓滿的大成就師" 等等不勝枚舉。遂成為藏傳佛教各派公認的大成就師、在此五濁惡世中佛法修學者的光輝典範。又因其謙卑隨和、神通無礙、遊戲自在，被人們尊稱為 "無礙活佛"。

雖然仁波且恪守古訓不輕易顯示神通，然而諸如飛行、分身、水中穿行、精通多種語言、預知禍福、洞悉人心等等神奇事蹟還是廣為流傳開來，且仁波且所著衣物等生活用品皆具有神奇的加持力，藏民有因佩帶或服食仁波且的裂裟碎片而遇難成祥、化險為夷、重病獲癒者不勝枚舉。夏珠秋楊仁波且的傳奇事蹟在藏區尤其安多地區幾乎無人不知，且《聖行與妙果》、《法王十大弟子傳》等書中也有所記述。

　　聖祖降世那諾尊
　　噶舉怙主格魯行
　　早成甚深無礙法
　　諸方聖德讚稱聖
　　結緣與之成解脫
　　無邊眾生皈依境

夏珠秋楊仁波且看到《正法寶典》一書，當下於神通中見了雲高益西諾布的真身是佛教至高始祖古佛多杰羌佛，完全印證了大聖法王們的認證，由此恭敬寫下賀函。

BRIEF INTRODUCTION TO THE GREAT TERTON H.E. RENZENG NIMA RINPOCHE
大伏藏師仁增尼瑪（持明日）仁波且簡介

In Tibet, everyone knows and respects the name Renzeng Nima, which literally means "Accomplishment as bright as the sun." Renzeng Nima is a great practitioner and dharma king who has transcended the mundane world. Twenty-five years ago he made a vow not to take a step out of the mountain valley in which he meditates. That was the first time that anyone, even an eminent monk, had vowed to isolate himself from the dust of the mundane world and remain a hermit his whole life. Can we imagine what state of realization a person would need to reach to be able to turn his back on all the advantages and allures of the world and cast himself in a secluded mountain valley for the rest of his life? This is a great practitioner who truly secludes himself from the mundane world. The dharma king does not have the slightest sign of greed toward the mundane world. He has set himself as a role model for people to emulate. He is indifferent toward worldly fame and wealth. This dharma king has provided a model for us all of how to renounce the ego and all desire for the mundane world.

Who is this great, pure, holy being? He is the Mighty Lion Dharma King of esoteric Tibetan Buddhism, one of the greatest terma masters of the Nyingma sect. He is the nirmanakaya of King Gesar, hero of Tibet's great epic saga. Guru Padmasambhava took birth as a child of Vajravarahi. That child from the Heaven of the Thirty-Three Gods was King Tuiba Gawa Gesar. When conveying congratulations to King Gesar, Guru Padmasambhava stated many times, "King Gesar is my nirmanakaya." Thus, Mighty Lion Dharma King is the nirmanakaya of Guru Padmasambhava. Moreover, the International Buddhism Sangha Association held an unprecedented Drawing Lots From a Golden Vase Ceremony to affirm the true reincarnated identity of H.E. Dharma King Renzeng Nima and others. There were ten possible identities recognized by various rinpoches. One lot was drawn from among 120 lots to affirm the true reincarnated identity of H.E. Dharma King Renzeng Nima. That drawing affirmed that H.E. Dharma King Renzeng Nima is the nirmanakaya of King Gesar, which is the reincarnated identity that H.H. Dorje Chang Buddha III recognized before that lot was drawn.

H.E. Mighty Lion Dharma King Rengzeng Nima was born in 1931 amidst an array of

miraculous phenomena. When he was born, his swaddling clothes formed the shape of a monk's robes. Before his birth, Anie Kanbu Danqu Wose gave his mother a figure of the historical Buddha (Sakyamuni) and a string of sandalwood prayer beads, and prophesied, "Your son will be a great and honored master of these goods." From the time he was small, the dharma king effortlessly mastered all the Buddhist sutras. As a small child, when he frolicked in the lake, those around him often witnessed a jade dragon descending into the water to play hide and seek with him. On one occasion, the local people were afflicted with inflamed intestines. The dharma king saw that they were possessed by monsters and zombies. As he strove to conquer the monsters, three dharma protecting deities manifested as his assistants and many amazing scenes transpired.

As a youth, the dharma king manifested the ability to fly. Once, when practicing a dharma in the Dakini Division, the *qi* entered his heart and he ascended into the air. He flew to the second Zari Zaduorikuo Mountain in Duokang area, the home of the great secluded yoga master Yaxu Khenpo Luozhe. When he arrived, the great master Urygen Second Buddha Guru Padmasambhava and two of his disciples came over to meet him with smiling faces. In his hands, Guru Padmasambhava carried a letter and a box and gave to the dharma king all his teachings. Guru Padmasambhava then turned into a beam of light and entered the dharma king's body. At once, five mountains at that area turned into five Buddhas, five lakes turned into Buddha mothers, and the trees and flowers turned into imposing spots of brilliant light. The next day, the terrain reverted to its original appearance.

All his life, H.E. Mighty Lion Dharma King has studied the teachings of many virtuous masters. Among the vast array of Buddhists texts and sutras he has studied are "The Teachings of Samantabhadra," "A Point by Point Commentary on the Dignity of the Middle Perspective," "The Overall Meaning of Buddhist Teaching that Shake the World Like a Lion's Roar," "Commentary on Prajna," "Introduction to the Rest of the Temperament," "Three Rests," "Three Eliminations of Sound," "Seven Treasures of Longqin Buddhist Law," "Addendum to Requirements of the Mind," "Explication of the Three Goodnesses," "Three Precepts," "Commentary on Fixing Quantities," "Basic Cultivation of Upholding Brilliant Foundations," "The Essence of Using the Tongue and the Mind," "Secrets of Success," "Dealing With the Aftermath," "Collected Classics on Great Universalism," "Commentary on Collected Scriptures," "Initiations," "Dharma of Brightness," "Eliminating Darkness From Ten Directions," "Tranquil Sound of Dragon Chanting," "Buddha's Great Yoga Teachings Sutra," "Hidden Treasures," "The True Meaning of the Four Branches of Sutra," "Seventeen Parts," "The True Meaning of the Two Divisions," "Collected Works of Bazhu," "Broad Commentary on Levels of Bodhi Path," "The Wide and Deep Secret Meaning of Commentaries on 'Entering the Middle Way," "Mapeng Profound Hidden Dharma," "Three Rites Prescribing Cultivation of the Soul," "The Brilliant King of the Red Horse Head," "Black Horse Iron-Surrounding Mountain," "Wu Jian Flying God of Wealth," "Collected Works of Ju Weipang," and "Outstanding and Brilliant Sutras." The dharma king serves as a model, showing all living beings that any who would practice Buddhism must deeply engage with the sutras and tantras.

When the dharma king prays and meditates deep in the mountains, the dharma-protecting vajra deities protect the dharma king as if someone were right there with him. All sorts of amazing scenes have transpired. Sometimes the dharma king transformed himself into birds to create prophecies; offerings of food turned into nectar; and five types of nectar boiled away.

Although the Mighty Lion Dharma King never leaves his mountain retreat, he has utilized supernatural powers to elucidate in over twenty dispatches such deep, mysterious and precious works as Mahayoga, Anuyoga, Atiyoga, and the bow and arrows of King Gesar.

A rinpoche praised the dharma king saying, "You are a rare and great paragon of virtue in the contemporary world of dharma!" However, the Mighty Lion Dharma King, who is the reincarnation of King Gesar, calmly replied, "I am just a Tibetan practitioner of Buddhism who assiduously cultivates myself for the coming world and deeply realizes the law of cause and effect." The greatness, brilliance, and selflessness of this paragon of virtue evoke the esteem and respect of countless Buddhists.

Now that the reputation of H.E. Mighty Lion Dharma King Renzeng Nima has pervaded the entire world, a multitude of rinpoches and khenpos do not hesitate to undertake journeys of thousands of miles to undertake conversion as his disciples. The mountains surrounding the valley in which he has secluded himself are now covered with these rinpoches. They all orient the renovated sides of their dwellings to the solitary meditation area of H.E. Dharma King Renzeng Nima. Among them, in their "An account of Master Nianlong," the renowned disciples Nianlong Rinpoche and Dakini Deri Lamao recount that when Master Nianlong and his wife first paid fealty to H.E. Mighty Lion Dharma King as their master, they saw him in a supernatural state as the real blue-black Maha Vajradhara (a master of great Budhisattvas). Actually, H.E. Mighty Lion Dharma King used his supernatural powers to reveal this appearance to his disciple Nianlong. His true identity is not that of Maha Vajradhara but that of King Gesar. H.E. Mighty Lion Dharma King possesses great supernatural powers. Whenever Tibetan and Chinese eminent rinpoches and monks, and even local government officials, run into difficult problems, they all beseech H.E.

Mighty Lion Dharma King for advice.

In the summer of 2006, H.E. Mighty Lion Dharma King saw the true identity of H.H. Dorje Chang Buddha III Wan Ko Yeshe Norbu Holiest Tathagata. He then stood up, performed rites of respect, put on his dharma king robe and crown that he had not worn for a long time, and wrote a recognition certificate. That certificate stated that he had personally seen that the ancient Buddha had descended into the world.

在西藏，有一位老人的名字是人們都知道，都敬仰的，他叫仁增尼瑪（持明日），他是一位真正脫離世俗污染的大行者、大法王。早在二十五年前，他就立下一個誓言，他將終生不離開他修行的山谷一步！這樣一生與世隔絕不染塵埃獨居山谷修行的誓言，在這個世界上還是第一次聽到，除了這位法王，還沒有聽說過有哪位高僧做到了終生脫離塵俗修行。我們可以想像一下，一個人須要到什麼樣的境界才能把自己的一生都拋在一個荒僻山谷之中而不貪戀任何的世俗優越和利益？這才是真正脫離紅塵的大修行者！在這位法王身上，已經沒有了半點貪著世俗的氣息，他無視一切世間名利，以身示教，為生楷模，為眾生作了斷除我執放下紅塵的榜樣。如此淨潔偉大清修的聖者到底是誰？他就是威震雪域的藏密「雄獅法王」，是當今寧瑪巴最偉大的伏藏大師，是蓮花生大師投胎於金剛亥母結下的三十三天童子推巴噶瓦格薩爾王的化身，蓮師在祝福格薩爾王賀詞中多次說明『格薩爾王是我的化身』，因此雄獅法王亦即是蓮花生大師的化身。更難得的是，國際佛教僧尼總會對仁波且們作出的十個不同認證身份舉行了史無前例的金瓶掣籤，從120支密封籤中抽出一支，確認仁增尼瑪法王是格薩爾王的化身，而此身份正是三世多杰羌佛之前作出的認證。

雄獅法王仁增尼瑪於藏曆深鐵羊年（公元1931年）伴隨種種奇妙之相而誕生，出生時胞衣形如袈裟包裹其身。出生之前，曾有阿聶堪布丹曲沃色，賜給法王母親一尊無比能仁王佛像和一串檀香佛珠，並預言：「日後，你將有一貴子，承當此物之主。」法王自幼對所有經卷無難而通。年幼嬉戲時，眾人常見一玉龍降於水中，與法王上下追逐嬉耍。一次，當地眾生遭受熱炎膽症，法王見此地被眾多非人、死鬼侵害，法王在制伏主害時，三根本護法真實現身，作其助伴，出現了種種奇妙之相。法王早年曾駕馭神通，以空行部「氣入心升空」功力，前往隱身大瑜伽師雅敘堪布洛哲的所在地朵康第二雜日的雜多吉廓山。在那裡，烏金第二佛陀蓮花生大師師徒三人來到法王所在處，蓮師面生歡喜，手執一經函、盒子，賜予法王全部的蓮師教授，隨後蓮師化為光芒，融入法王身體內，頓時，此地五座山變為五佛，五個湖變成五佛母，草木皆成氣脈明點。第二天，山河大地依舊復原。

法王一生依止多位具德上師，修學了《普賢上師教言》、《中觀莊嚴論疏》、《總義獅子吼》、《般若疏》、《心性休息義導文》、《三休息》、《三除暗》、《隆欽七寶藏》、《心要補遺》、《三善導義》、《三戒》、《定量論》、《持明根本修》、《利舌心要》、《訣竅》、《善後法》、《大方等大集經》、《集經論》、《灌頂》、《光明經法》、《除十方黑暗》、《梵音龍吟》、《佛說瑜伽大教王經》、《珍寶伏藏》、《四支經義》、《十七部續》、《二部經義》、《巴珠全集》、《菩提道次第廣論》、《入中論疏深廣密意》、《馬鵬甚深伏藏》、《修魂三儀軌》、《紅色馬頭明王》、《黑馬鐵圍山》、《鄔堅空行財神》、《居未旁全集》、《經光明殊勝》等等甚深法要。法王身作楷模，以自身而作典範示教眾生凡修行者必深入經藏密典。

法王在深山修行時，金剛護法如人相伴，護佑法王，法王時而變幻成鳥雀之形以作授記，亦有朵馬變成甘露，五甘露沸騰等種種奇妙之境顯現。法王雖然足不出戶，卻以神通授記開啟了大量甚深伏藏，至今已達二十餘函，內容涵蓋摩訶瑜伽、阿努瑜伽、阿底瑜伽，以及格薩爾王弓箭等珍貴的伏藏品。在法王閉關的山谷四周聚集駐紮了很多這樣的活佛仁波且，他們都將住所修葺面向著仁增尼瑪法王的關房。其中，法王的弟子著名的年龍仁波且和空行母德日拉毛在《年龍上師父母傳》中記載，年龍佛父母第一次拜雄獅法王為師時，在覺受境界內親見法王即是真正的藍黑身色之摩訶金剛持，意為大菩薩上師。其實，那是雄獅法王所顯神通境界給弟子年龍看的，他真正的身份不是摩訶金剛持，而是格薩爾王。雄獅法王神通廣大無邊，藏漢各地的活佛高僧，甚至當地政府遇到大事都紛紛前往法王那裡祈請指點迷津。

2006年夏，雄獅法王見到《正法寶典》一書，祥瑞之光充盈關房，法王即刻舉眼觀照，得見三世多杰羌佛雲高益西諾布頂聖如來真身，當場下座行恭敬儀式，披衣搭具，著上已未穿的法王袍法王冠，寫下了他親眼見得見古佛巨聖降世的確認書。

BRIEF INTRODUCTION TO H.E. NGAGWANG PEDMA NAMGYAL PALZANGPO, THE DHARMA KING OF JONANG SECT
覺囊阿旺班瑪南加法王簡介

H.E. Dharma King Ngagwang Pedma Namgyal Palzangpo of the Jonang sect, also known as Jiala Penam (H.E. Penam Rinpoche), is a man of great enlightenment. In Tibet, he is an extremely mysterious and legendary figure known to every household. Having attained supreme enlightenment long ago, he has for millions of years continually taken birth in the six realms of reincarnation in order to pervasively save living beings.

According to historical records and their translations, when Sakyamuni Buddha lived in this world, H.E. Dharma King Ngagwang Pedma Namgyal Palzangpo was a disciple called Da Te, who was a fourth stage Arhat. When the Buddha-dharma entered Tibet in the eighth century, the dharma king took birth as a close disciple of Guru Padmasambhava by the name of Gelong Namuke Niangbo. He helped Guru Padmasambhava propagate the dharma and saved countless living beings. He, Shantaraksita and others also made an outstanding contribution to the establishment of the Nyingma sect. In his next life, he reincarnated as Duqin Langwa, an eminent monk of the Nyingma sect.

As for this current life, H.E. Dharma King Ngagwang Pedma Namgyal Palzangpo was born in 1930, which is the year of the iron horse according to the Tibetan calendar. He was born in the area between the Manchu River and Machen Pomra Mountain. When born, the dharma king was in the cross-legged lotus sitting posture, did not cry, and had a smile on his face. He looked upward as he focused on the spot between his eyebrows. Everyone in that area saw that he resembled a Buddha.

When Canzu Chengjiangba Qiuqin, a person greatly accomplished in the dharma, saw the dharma king, he recognized the dharma king's status by saying, "This is a magnificent holy being!" He then offered a pure white kharda (silk scarf) and predicted that the dharma king would definitely be successor to the true dharma of the Jonang sect. Jiangyang Sala, who was a nirmanakaya of Vajrasattva, was referring to the dharma king when he said before passing away that he was very happy to have encountered someone just like his root master Awang Pama Trizin Lama, whose status was extremely high in Tibet. Vajra Master Angong Lama once said to H.E. Dharma King Ngagwang Pedma Namgyal Palzangpo that wherever there is air, the dharma king exists.

As one who possesses the supreme esoteric dharma from a variety of dharma lineages, the dharma king does not have a mind that differentiates. His method of teaching also does not differentiate between sects. Furthermore, he even advocates that the various sects not be differentiated. He has several thousand monastic disciples who are rinpoches from all of the various sects. For example, the Kalachakra Vajra Great Initiation conducted by the dharma king at the Longshijia Temple in 2005 was attended by people from the Geluk, Nyingma, Jonang, Sakya, and Kagyu sects, which are the major sects of Tibetan Buddhism. Almost 4,000 monastics representing 36 temples attended that initiation, as did over 140,000 laypersons, making it an grand occasion.

A person by the name of Kewei Zabo was able to avoid the bullets of a firearm without being harmed in the least because he wore a vajra string given to him by the dharma king. Everyone in the area where this event occurred knows about this. Both his monastic and lay disciples all know of the dharma king's accomplishments and have the utmost faith in him. This great yogi who long ago realized supreme enlightenment often leaves his footprints and handprints on rocks and, when necessary, flies into the air in the cross-legged sitting posture. In the autumn of 2007, H.H. Dorje Chang Buddha III recognized H.E. Dharma King Ngagwang Pedma Namgyal Palzangpo as the incarnation of Duqin Langwa.

The spacious Longshijia Temple is known for the real dharma practice of its monastics. Numerous eminent monks of great virtue have over the past few hundred years become accomplished in the dharma through self-cultivation in that temple. The dharma practice of the Jonang sect is very strict. This sect is world-renowned for its authentic practice of the Kalachakra Vajra esoteric dharma. All monastics in Longshijia Temple must go into retreat for a time period of three years plus three months plus three days, after which they are allowed to enter the hall and recite passages from the sutras. Each monk has real dharma power. Many disciples of the dharma king have already realized the fruit of Arhatship or one of the stages of a Bodhisattva. Among such disciples, the accomplishments of Ngagwang Pedma Nuobu Rinpoche are the most remarkable. Each time after one completes a retreat, he has to undergo a strict test given to him by H.E. Dharma King Ngagwang Pedma Namgyal Palzangpo. For example, one is tested on one's ability to control one's flow of energy and one's breathing. One must be able to stop breathing for at least thirty minutes to pass the test. A very small number of disciples who have become accomplished in their cultivation, such as Ngagwang Pedma Nuobu Rinpoche and Quyang Rinpoche, must undergo the Vajra Fist and the Earthquake Wheel Yoga flying tests. This requires their body and their nature to merge as one. Their body must soar into the air. When descending, they must land on an egg without breaking it. Only then will their performance be considered satisfactory. Only then will they be qualified to go out and accept disciples and transmit this type of esoteric dharma.

覺囊派阿旺班瑪南加法王——即「加拉班南」，是一位藏地家喻戶曉、極具神祕的大覺者，早已證得無上菩提，千百年來不斷的幻化於六道來廣度眾生。

按史料記載和翻譯，釋迦牟尼佛在世時，阿旺班瑪南加法王當時是一位名為「達特」的四果阿羅漢。西元八世紀佛法傳入西藏時，投生為蓮花生大士的心子，名叫「格隆那穆克釀波」。師徒一生弘法成就，救度眾生無數，並與釋伽炯乃等為紅教寧瑪派的建立，做出卓越貢獻。並於後一生轉世為寧瑪派的高僧——督琴郎哇。

阿旺班瑪南加法王這一世生於1930年，即藏歷鐵馬年，轉世於馬祖河與馬喬波拉山之間。法王以蓮花坐姿降生於世，沒有哭聲，面帶微笑，目向上方，凝視眉間。當地所有的人都看到，這是一尊佛相。

大成就者「參祖成姜巴秋欽」見到法王時就認證說：這是偉大的聖者！並獻上潔白的哈達，預言道：將來他一定是覺囊派的正法傳人。金剛薩埵化現的「蔣揚薩拉」在圓寂前曾經說過，他很高興的又遇到了像他根本上師——在西藏地位極高的「阿旺帕瑪天津喇嘛」一樣的人。金剛上師安貢喇嘛曾當面說阿旺班瑪南加法王，有空氣的地方，就有法王的存在。

身為各類無上密乘法脈的持有者，法王沒有分別心，他的教法也是不分派別的，同時還是主張無教派分別的倡導者。他有幾千出家眾的仁波且弟子，都是來自各個教派的。比如2005年在龍什加寺的時輪金剛大灌頂，就有來自格魯、寧瑪、覺囊、薩迦、噶舉等各大教派，36個寺院近4000的僧眾，在家弟子14萬人之多，場面盛大。

有一個叫課威咱波的人因為穿戴了法王給的金剛結，竟能避過火槍子彈，而毛髮不傷，這件事在當地也是家喻戶曉，不管出家弟子還是在家眾，都知道法王的成就，對其信心百倍。這位早已經證得無上菩提、實證開悟的大瑜珈士，常將足跡、

手印，印於岩石之上，或必要時趺坐騰空而起。2007年秋，三世多杰羌佛正式認證阿旺班瑪南加法王是督琴郎哇的轉世。

幾百年來，在廣闊的龍什加寺天然的實修道場，已有很多位大德高僧在這裡修行成就。覺囊派的修法是非常嚴格的，並以實修時輪金剛密法著稱於世。凡是出家眾必須要閉關三年三個月零三天，才可以入殿念經，每一位僧人都是具有真實法力的。在法王的弟子當中，已經很多人證得阿羅漢果位及登地菩薩，其中大首座阿旺班瑪諾布活佛成就尤為突出，每次閉關結束都要經過班瑪南加法王嚴格的考試。比如考試控制住自己的氣脈營運、抑制住呼吸，最低要30分鐘不喘氣為及格；還有像班瑪諾布活佛、曲央活佛等極少數修行成就的人要經過金剛拳、地震輪瑜伽飛行的考試，也就是身性合一，整個身體騰空飛起來，然後再落下，落到雞蛋上，雞蛋不碎為圓滿，才有資格出來收弟子，傳承這方面的密法。

當阿旺班瑪南加法王看到三世多杰羌佛雲高益西諾布頂聖如來的《正法寶典》，深感佛陀的慈悲和眾生福報的來臨，馬上寫了賀函。

BRIEF INTRODUCTION TO H.E. MINDROLLING KHENCHEN RINPOCHE
敏林堪欽仁波且簡介

The lineage into which H.E. Mindrolling Khenchen Rinpoche reincarnated began with the great translation master Lochen Dharmashri, who was the younger brother of the founder of the Mindrolling Monastery, Rigzin Terdak Lingpa. For generation after generation, the rinpoche has been assisting H.H. Dharma King Mindrolling Trichen in propagating the dharma and benefiting living beings. Thus, within the Minrolling school, H.E. Mindrolling Khenchen's great responsibility to transmit dharma and his high status are second only to those of H.H. Dharma King Mindrolling Trichen, who is the dharma king of the Mindrolling Monastery.

H.E. the ninth Mindrolling Khenchen Rinpoche was born in 1970 into the Baerdengniu clan in Tibet. The blood lineage of that clan can be traced back to a celestial being from the Heaven of

Light within the Heaven of the Thirty-Three Gods. H.H. the Dalai Lama, H.H. the 16th Great Jewel Dharma King, and Latuo Rinpoche have all recognized the rinpoche as being the incarnation of the eighth Khenchen Rinpoche. Since childhood he received teachings from H.H. Dharma King Mindrolling Trichen, H.H. Dharma King Dilgo Khyentse, H.H. Dharma King Penor, H.H. Taklung Tsetrul Rinpoche, H.H. Trulshik Rinpoche, and others. Upon the invitation of H.H. the Dalai Lama, in 1985 H.E. Mindrolling Khenchen Rinpoche received together with H.H. the Dalai Lama teachings from H.H. Dharma King Dilgo Khyentse. They received the entire Secret Mind Dharma, which is unique to the Nyingma sect. The careful training and education provided by these dharma kings and rinpoches led H.E. Khenchen Rinpoche to become a person of extremely outstanding learning and cultivation. He is generous, sincere, modest, and unaffected. Although he bears the heavy responsibilities associated with the Khenchen lineage system of the Mindrolling school, he is totally devoid of any self-pride possessed by ordinary people. He has the inner-cultivation and bearing of a great Bodhisattva.

H.E. Khenchen Rinpoche has been the president of Ngagyur Nyingma College since 1992. He gives the monastic precepts to several hundred monastics every year on the birthday of Sakyamuni Buddha. He also has kept up his long-term practice of going into retreat three to four months every year. At the request of many Nyingma monasteries, H.E. Khenchen Rinpoche has been the vice-president of the yearly Nyingmapa Molem Chenmo Ceremony for World Peace since 1994. His position within the Nyingma sect is very high.

敏林堪欽仁波且的轉世傳承，始自敏珠林寺的創始人德德林巴之弟、大譯師達瑪師利，其世世代代輔佐敏林赤欽法王宏法利生，因此，在敏珠林寺系，敏林堪欽仁波且傳法之重責大任與崇高地位，僅次於敏珠林寺傳承法王——敏林赤欽法王。

第九世敏林堪欽仁波且於1970年出生於西藏之光明天神血脈『巴爾登紐族』，由達賴喇嘛、十六世大寶法王、拉託仁波且認證為第八世堪欽仁波且的轉世。自幼即得到敏林赤欽法王、頂果欽哲法王、貝諾法王、達龍哲珠仁波且、楚西仁波且等諸多教授，1985年應達賴喇嘛邀請，與其一起從頂果欽哲法王處接受寧瑪派的不共密心全集。在這些法王、仁波且們的悉心培養教育下，堪欽仁波且學行修持極為優秀，行事寬厚樸實，作風謙虛無華，雖然肩擔敏珠林寺堪欽傳承制度重責大任，卻無絲毫自得之凡夫我慢，其內在修學涵養富涵大士之風。

從1992年起，堪欽仁波且擔任敏珠林佛學院的導師，每年都在釋迦牟尼佛聖誕傳授出家戒予數百眾，並且每年依舊閉關三至四個月。應眾多寧瑪派寺廟的要求，堪欽仁波且從1994年開始擔任每年一度的寧瑪派世界和平祈福大法會的副會長，深得崇高地位。

BRIEF INTRODUCTON TO H.E. KHANDRO RINPOCHE
康卓公主仁波且簡介

Her Eminence Khandro Rinpoche is the eldest daughter of H.H. Dharma King Mindrolling Trichen Rinpoche of the Nyingma Sect of Buddhism. She was recognized at the age of two by His Holiness the 16th Karmapa and H.H. Dilgo Khyentse Rinpoche as the reincarnation of the Dakini of the Tsurphu Monastery, Ugyen Tsomo. The Dakini is the incarnation of the consort of Guru Padmasambhava, holy mother Yeshe Tsogyal. It is even more significant that H.H. Dorje Chang Buddha III has personally recognized H.E. Khandro Rinpoche as the reincarnation of the holy mother, Yeshe Tsogyal.

The holy mother Yeshe Tsogyal is an patriarch of many important terma lineages. For example, it is recorded in the first chapter of the second volume of "Terma Treasury" written by H.H. Guru Kongtrul Yonten Gyatso, the reincarnation of Manjushri Bodhisattva, that the holy mother Yeshe Tsogyal's terma lineage includes "Tathagatha Initiation Vajra Tantra Collection—Pure Treasure Vase," "King of Freedom the Holy Path of Liberation and Freedom—Fundamental Initiation for Spirits and Gods Relating to the Cycle of Birth and Death," "Filthiness and Impureness Initiation," "Sharp Knife of Fire Initiation," "Tantric Commentary on Empowering Lambs," "Tathagatha Tantra Collection Karma Rituals," and "The Rituals of Divine Path of Liberation Initiation."

The holy mother Yeshe Tsogyal received the dharma teachings that were transmitted to Jingfen Guan Shi Yin by Infinite Light Buddha and then to Guru Padmasambhava. They were transmitted to the Tibetan King Trisong Detsan, Great Terton Nima Weise, Nie Xio, Candan Zhutuo, Zha We, Zhaba Jiancan, Cichen Jungnai, Xirao Jiebu, Nanke Jiancan, Gadan Jiacuo, Mijuli Zhuoba, Jenqing Pingcuo, Zanba-Awanba, Gewang-Xiolin, Luozhu Jiancan, Xianpan Duojie, Chenglai Longzho, and Great Terton Deqin Jome Dorje.

The holy mother Yeshe Tsogyal manifested herself as a celestial eagle during the time she propagated Buddha-dharma and benefited living beings. She revealed immeasurable supernatural powers such as leaving footprints on rocks, taming demons and devils, flying in the air and penetrating the ground, etc. She was reincarnated as Her Eminence Khandro Rinpoche.

Starting at a very young age, H.E. Khandro Rinpoche received dharma teachings from her three root masters, who were His Holiness the 16th Karmapa, H.H. Dilgo Khyentse Rinpoche and her father H.H. Dharma King Mindrolling Trichen. She is a great female master in Tibetan Buddhism who holds both the Nyingma and Kagyu lineages. The rinpoche is fluent in Tibetan, Indian dialects and has had extensive education in English. She has been traveling to Europe, the United States and Southeast Asia since 1987 to transmit dharma and perform initiations. Each year she maintains a schedule teaching self-cultivation in retreats and transmitting Buddha-dharma to her disciples in North America and the Shambhala Center in Europe. Such effort is very critical to the promotion and propagation of the Vajrayana in the western world.

In May of 2007 when H.E. Khandro Rinpoche read the *A Treasury of True Buddha Dharma* about H.H. Dorje Chang Buddha III, she was very happy and grateful. She immediately wrote a letter of congratulations.

康卓公主仁波且是寧瑪派法王敏林赤欽仁波且的長女，兩歲時即由十六世大寶法王和頂果欽哲仁波且共同認證為蓮花生大師之佛母移喜措嘉所化現之楚布寺烏金措媄空行母的轉世。而更難得的是，三世多杰羌佛曾親自認證康卓公主仁波且是益喜措嘉佛母的轉世。

移喜措嘉佛母是藏密多個重要伏藏傳承的祖師，如由文殊菩薩轉世的貢珠·雲丹嘉措大師的《伏藏寶庫》中第二函第一卷記載，在《如來灌頂金剛密集·清淨寶瓶》、《解脫聖道自在之王·生死輪迴鬼神根本灌頂》、《污垢不淨之灌頂》、《火之利刀灌頂》、《加持羊羔續論》、《如來密集羯磨儀軌》、《解脫聖道灌頂儀軌》等的伏藏傳承中，移喜措嘉佛母承接由無量光佛傳給靜忿觀世音、再傳蓮花生大師的法教，並傳給藏王赤松德贊，再傳大伏藏師娘·尼瑪威色──聶秀──參丹珠陀──扎威──扎巴堅參──慈誠炯乃──喜饒杰布──南喀堅參──噶丹嘉措──彌居理卓巴──仁青平措尊者──藏巴·阿旺巴──噶旺·秀林──洛珠堅參──仙攀多杰──成來龍周──伏藏大師德欽久美多杰──等等。而在弘法利生的過程中，移喜措嘉佛母曾化顯神鷹在石上留爪、降伏魔妖、空中飛行、地中穿沒等無量神通。今生轉世為康卓公主仁波且。

康卓公主仁波且自幼即接受三位根本上師的法教：十六世大寶法王、頂果欽哲仁波且及其父親敏林赤欽法王。仁波且是藏傳佛教中，同時擁有寧瑪和噶舉兩個傳承的偉大女性大師。仁波且精通藏文、印度方言，也具備深厚的英文學養，從1987年開始在歐洲及美國、東南亞巡迴傳法、灌頂，每年定期在北美及歐洲香巴拉佛學中心指導弟子閉關修行，傳授佛法，在西方世界金剛乘的傳播弘揚中佔有重要地位。

2007年5月，當康卓公主仁波且見到三世多杰羌佛的《正法寶典》，非常高興，感激之餘，當即寫了賀函。

BRIEF INTRODUCTION TO H.E. DZOGCHEN GANOR RINPOCHE
噶諾仁波且簡介

H.E. Dzogchen Ganor Rinpoche was born in 1942 on the eighth day of the ninth month of the Tibetan calendar near the town of Palpung in the Derge District of Dhokam in Eastern Tibet. His mother Rinchen Choedon was a descendent of the Drikung Kagyu sect. His father was a descendent of the great Surche lineage, which is one of the three great early sects of esoteric Buddhism. Shortly after the rinpoche was born, he was recognized as the 14th reincarnation of the great terton Ratag Pelsang (or Karma Lekshe Drayang). The first Ratag Pelsang received special blessings from Guru Padmasambhava, Panchen Bima Mita Pandita, and other great virtuous ones.

The rinpoche received formal education on the five major treatises as he grew up. In addition, he received teachings from many great masters and attained mastery of the healing vidya. He offered treatments to people to save their lives. The rinpoche has been living in the area near the northeast border of India after he arrived there in 1960. He once lived in Jang Chup Choeling Monastery, where he received initiations, transmissions of dharma, and explanations of scriptures from numerous masters of different Buddhist sects. He mastered all these fields and implemented them in his daily life to manifest incredible powers.

The rinpoche has attained supernatural powers and is especially proficient in the practice of Khatag Trekchod and Lhundrup. He is able to gain control over his mind and see past, present, and future lives. He has manifested his level of realization by leaving his footprints on rocks, making knots of swords and needles in order to treat patients or tame devils, and causing nectar to run down from tormas. The rinpoche has revealed many termas (hidden treasures), including a very important text called the Drag Nyag Gongter. This text explains the essential dharma of Phurba Vajra. The rinpoche is able to communicate directly with non-humans such as nagas, devas, demi-gods and local spririts. He is a great rinpoche with powers to subdue demonic forces and is able to communicate with divine spirits and non-humans. The rinpoche has also mastered the study of astrology. As soon as he saw H.H. Dorje Chang Buddha III while in his meditative state of supernatural powers, he wrote a letter to the United International World Buddhism Headquarters and stated, "the main content of [*A Treasury of True Buddha-Dharma*] is the 84,000 dharma methods...[it] contains the limitless state of knowledge resulting from the two dharmas of realization and enlightenment."

噶諾仁波且於1942年藏曆九月初八出生在東藏多康的德格地區靠近八蚌鎮的地方，他的母親憎秋東是直貢嘎舉派的後裔，而父親則是西藏三大舊密續教派之一的大舍雪派的後裔。仁波且在出生後不久即被認證為大伏藏師讓塔佩（又稱噶瑪雷雪札楊）的第十四世轉世，第一世讓塔佩曾受到蓮花生大師、班禪畢瑪彌他班智達等大德的特別祝福。

仁波且在成長過程中，正規地學習了五部大論，尤其是從許多大德那裡學習並掌握了醫方明，治病救人。自1960年仁波且到達印度後，便一直居住在靠近印度東北邊境之地。他曾駐錫於蔣處秋林寺，在這裡他從眾多的大德處接受了不同佛教派別的傳法灌頂和經文的闡釋，他嫻熟這些領域並且將其應用在日常生活中展現不可思議的力量。仁波且具足神通，尤其擅長於 KHA TAG TREK CHEN 和 LHUN DRUO MEN THOG，他掌控自心並達到直觀三世的能力。他曾經在岩石上留下足印、用觀針打結為人治病或驅魔以及在法會中讓食子流下甘露等來展現其證量，仁波且曾開啟多部伏藏，其中包括一部非常重要、名為 Drag Nyag Gongter 的伏藏，這部伏藏解釋了普巴金剛的法要。仁波且可隨時直接與神龍、德娃、方神、地神等人非人等來往，他是一位通達聖神、非人等的大仁波且，具備降伏魔障的能力。仁波且也熟悉天文。當他從神通境裡見到三世多杰羌佛後，當即給聯合國際世界佛教總部寫到：『《正法寶典》系以八萬四千法門為主的內容……涵蓋了證悟二法概括的無量所知境』。

BRIEF INTRODUCTION TO GREAT TERTON H.E. URGYEN XIRAO
伏藏大師鄔堅喜饒尊者簡介

H.E. Urgyen Xirao of the Nyingma school of Tibetan esoteric Buddhism is a great terton. He is the true reincarnation of the body, speech, and mind of Urgyen Lingpa, who was one of the

eight great masters of finding hidden dharma treasures about whom Guru Padmasambhava made formal pronouncements. H.E. Urgyen Xirao is a great holy and virtuous being who is respected by rinpoches and dharma kings worldwide. His state of realization and virtue are remarkably profound, and he possesses great supernatural powers. However, he remains aloof from the world. He comes without casting a shadow and goes without leaving a trace. His whereabouts are uncertain and mysterious. Sometimes he lives in seclusion in a deep valley. Sometimes he appears on grassland. He can occasionally be seen leaving a high pagoda. In an instant, he can then be seen in a thatched hut. Even great rinpoches and dharma kings find it very difficult to find him.

In the minds of rinpoches and dharma kings, the status of H.E. Urgyen Xirao is incomparably high. Even some first-rate world-renowned dharma kings have relied upon H.E. Urgyen Xirao's formal pronouncements in handling Buddhist matters. When they encountered adverse circumstances, even H.H. the Wish Fulfilling Jewel Dharma King Jigme Phuntsok, who was H.H. the Dalai Lama's master, sought assistance from H.E. Urgyen Xirao. H.H. Dharma King Jigme Phuntsok said, "H.E. Urgyen Xirao Rinpoche is indeed extraordinary. He is one who truly possesses supernatural powers!"

Great rinpoches and dharma kings around the world gave many predictions concerning when H.H. Dharma King Jigme Phuntsok would pass away. H.E. Urgyen Xirao predicted a date different from the dates that others predicted. H.H. Dharma King Jigme Phuntsok nevertheless said that he would not pass away at the time predicted by H.E. Urgyen Xirao, and he continued to make arrangements for a dharma assembly that he was going to conduct. Upon hearing this, H.E. Urgyen Xirao smiled and said, "If he does not pass away at my predicted time, then when will he?" As expected, H.H. Dharma King Jigme Phuntsok passed away at the exact time H.E. Urgyen Xirao predicted. Because the predictions of the other rinpoches and dharma kings were all wrong, they realized that their state of realization cannot compare with that of H.E. Urgyen Xirao.

Moreover, the International Buddhism Sangha Association held an unprecedented Drawing Lots From a Golden Vase Ceremony to affirm the true reincarnated identity of H.E. Urgyen Xirao and others. There were ten possible identities recognized by various rinpoches. One lot was drawn from among 120 lots to affirm the true reincarnated identity of H.E. Urgyen Xirao. That drawing affirmed that H.E. Urgyen Xirao is the reincarnation of the great terton Urgyen Lingpa, which is the reincarnated identity that H.H. Dorje Chang Buddha III recognized before that lot was drawn.

In 2006, Urgyen Xirao Rinpoche saw the book *A Treasury of True Buddha-Dharma*. He opened it and saw all of those accomplishments in thirty different main categories. He saw that the holiest one described in the book has incomparably high and incredible inner-realization. He saw that the dharma that person expounded in his discourse "What Is Cultivation?" is penetrating and complete. He knew that through the ages no other holy and virtuous being had such accomplishments in thirty different main categories. He also knew that such person is fully proficient in exoteric and esoteric Buddhism and has thorough and wondrous mastery of the Five Vidyas! H.E. Urgyen Xirao was astounded, knowing that such spectacular realization is certainly no trifling matter. He wondered, "If that holy person is not the highest holy being, how could he have such unimpeded wisdom and manifest such realization? When comparing all of the great masters through the ages, not one of them excelled that holy person, and not one of them attained the state of actual realization attained by that holy person. What type of holy being has come to this world after all?" H.E. Urgyen Xirao then immediately sat down in the cross-legged posture on his meditation seat and entered a state of deep concentration in order to fathom the answers to such questions. He suddenly saw that the original, true identity of H.H. Wan Ko Yeshe Norbu Holiest Tathagata is Dorje Chang Buddha III. He at once placed his palms together in respect and profusely praised H.H. Dorje Chang Buddha III. Filled with the joy of the dharma, he lifted his pen and wrote a certificate of affirmation.

鄔堅喜饒尊者，是藏密寧瑪巴的大伏藏師，是蓮花生大師授記的八大伏藏師之一鄔堅林巴身口意真身再來，是世界上仁波且法王們所敬仰的大聖德鄔堅喜饒法王子，證境證德高深無比，具足廣大神通，但卻超然世外，來無影去無蹤，行蹤神秘不定，時而幽居深谷，時而現身草原，偶由高閣樓出，轉眼茅舍篷安，就是大仁波且法王們要找到他也是很困難的。尊者在仁波且法王們的心目中有著無比崇高的地位，一些享譽世界的第一流法王都曾依尊者的授記處理法務，就連達賴喇嘛的上師如意寶晉美彭措法王，在自身遭遇違緣魔之際，也向鄔堅喜饒尊者請求援助。晉美彭措法王說：「鄔堅喜饒仁波且尊者確實非同凡響，是真正的具足大神通者！」在預言晉美彭措法王圓寂的因緣中，全世界的大仁波且法王做了很多預言，鄔堅喜饒尊者則預言出與眾不同的年月日，但晉美彭措法王卻說他不會依照鄔堅喜饒尊者預言的時間圓寂，並安排了所要修持的法會法務。鄔堅喜饒尊者得知後淡淡一笑說：「不圓寂更待何時？」果不其然，晉美彭措法王圓寂的時間正是尊者預言的時間，由於其他仁波且法王全都預言錯誤，方知不及鄔堅喜饒尊者之道量。

更難得的是，國際佛教僧尼總會對仁波且們作出的十個不同認證身份舉行了史無前例的金瓶掣籤，從120支密封籤中抽出一支，確認鄔堅喜饒尊者是大伏藏師鄔堅林巴的轉世，而此身份正是三世多杰羌佛之前作出的認證。

2006年，鄔堅喜饒仁波且得見《正法寶典》一書，開章展觀三十大類成就，見其內明證量高深無比不可思議，開示的「什麼叫修行？」法義透徹圓滿，歷代沒有哪一位聖德作出了如此三十大類而顯密俱通，徹底妙諳五明！尊者大為震驚，這樣顯赫的證量絕非兒戲，若不是至高無上的聖者，怎麼可能有如此無礙的智慧和證量境顯呢？將歷代祖師歷歷排比算來，確實沒有誰能出其前後，更沒有哪一個人達到了這樣的實證境界，到底是什麼樣的聖者來到了這個世界？尊者立刻登上禪床，跏趺而坐，深入定境觀測，豁然得見雲高益西諾布頂聖如來本源真身乃古佛多杰羌佛第三世，當下恭敬禮拜，讚莫能窮，法喜充盈，提筆寫下了確認文書。

BRIEF INTRODUCTION TO H.E. DORJE RINZIN RINPOCHE
多杰仁增仁波且簡介

All highly virtuous practitioners of Tibetan esoteric Buddhism know that H.E. Dorje Rinzin Rinpoche is the incarnation of a great terton (a master of finding hidden dharma treasures)—Rigzin Terdak Lingpa Unchanging Vajra, who possesses the Great Perfection Complete Essence Dharma, which is a secret treasure transmitted through the ear. Many famous great and holy rinpoches in Tibetan esoteric Buddhism have received initiations from him. Moreover, the International Buddhism Sangha Association held an unprecedented Drawing Lots From a Golden Vase Ceremony to affirm the true reincarnated identity of H.E. Dorje Rinzin Rinpoche and others. There were ten possible identities recognized by various rinpoches. One lot was drawn from among 120 lots to affirm the true reincarnated identity of H.E. Dorje Rinzin Rinpoche. That drawing affirmed that H.E. Dorje Rinzin Rinpoche is the incarnation of Rigzin Terdak Lingpa, which is the reincarnated identity that H.H. Dorje Chang Buddha III recognized a year before that lot was drawn.

H.E. Dorje Rinzin Rinpoche possesses great esoteric dharma, earnestly practices according to Buddha's teaching, and benefits countless living beings. He inspires awe throughout the snowy land of Tibet and has become a model for greatly virtuous and holy practitioners to emulate. In order to set an example for other living beings to follow, the rinpoche has been in solitary retreat for thirty years in a wooden retreat room at the Gemang Vajra Dharma Forest Temple. However, since the karmic conditions were ripe to uncover the true dharma treasure "Buddha's name stone," the rinpoche came out of retreat and went to the land of the Han Chinese. During this time, one of the seventh Dzogchen Dharma Kings, H.E. Tenzin Longdock Nyima of the Dzogchen Monastery, led a group of holy and virtuous rinpoches to the mandala of venerable Xirao Jiebu. There, he beseeched H.E. Dorje Rinzin Rinpoche with the following words: "You, great holy one, will be leaving this earthly realm. In the name of all living beings, we beseech you to confer upon us the profound Great Perfection Complete Essence Initiation." The rinpoche consented and selected April 1, 2007 as the day he would perform the initiation for H.E. Tenzin Longdock Nyima and the six other rinpoches. On that auspicious day, upon invitation, H.E. Dorje Rinzin Rinpoche entered the mandala of H.E. Dharma King Pema Kalsang in Chengdu and sat on the dharma king throne. There, H.E. Dorje Rinzin Rinpoche secretly transmitted the Great Perfection Complete Essence Dharma to H.E. Tenzin Longdock Nyima and accompanying rinpoches.

After H.E. Dorje Rinzin Rinpoche read *A Treasury of True Buddha-Dharma* about H.H. Holiest Tathagata Wan Ko Yeshe Norbu Buddha Vajradhara, he wrote the following words of congratulations: "... the accomplishments contained in *A Treasury of True Buddha-Dharma*... have never been seen before in history... H.H. Dorje Chang Buddha Wan Ko Yeshe Norbu, the Master of the Five Buddhas... [and] highest leader of Buddhism in the dharmadhatu, has manifested here on earth a state of great brightness that entails complete proficiency in exoteric and esoteric Buddhism and perfect mastery of the Five Vidyas."

藏密中大德們眾所週知，大聖者多杰仁增仁波且即是大掘藏師德德林巴不變金剛之化身，持有無漏大圓滿精髓之耳傳密寶，很多著名藏密大聖仁波且都在他座下接受灌頂。更難得的是，國際佛教僧尼總會對仁波且們作出的十個不同認證身份舉行了史無前例的金瓶掣籤，從120支密封籤中抽出一支，確認多杰仁增仁波且是德德林巴的轉世，而此身份正是三世多杰羌佛在舉行金瓶掣籤之前一年就作出的認證。

多杰仁增仁波且掌持密乘大法，身體力行，利益眾生，威震雪域，成為大德聖者們學習的楷模，自己為了做眾生的典範，於格芒金剛法林寺木壁關房中閉關三十年，而為掘藏「佛名石」印證古佛降世之因緣成熟出關入漢，佐欽寺第七世佐欽法王丹增龍多尼瑪率聖德仁波且等，至喜饒杰布尊者壇城，向多杰仁增仁波且祈請叩曰：「聖者法王將離開娑婆世界，我等以眾生的名義向您祈求無漏甚深大圓滿灌頂。」仁增聖者仁波且允諾並擇緣為二零零七年四月一日為佐欽法王丹增龍多尼瑪等仁波且們七人灌頂，吉祥時日受請入白馬格桑法王在成都之壇城法王座之上，密傳佐欽法王丹增龍多尼瑪和仁波且們的無漏大圓滿。

多杰仁增仁波且在閱讀頂聖如來雲高益西諾布金剛總持的《正法寶典》以後祝賀說：『《正法寶典》……是歷史上沒有過的成就，這是五佛的上師多杰羌佛雲高益西諾布，這位法界大教主在地球上展顯了顯密圓通、妙諳五明的大達光明境界。』

BRIEF INTRODUCTION TO H.E. DHARMA KING RABJAM
冉江法王簡介

H.E. Dharma King Rabjam is the dharma king of the Shechen Monasteries, which is one of the six main groups of monasteries of the Nyingma sect.

The present Dharma King Rabjam is the seventh Dharma King Rabjam. His birth on an auspicious day in 1966 in Qiangdiga, India caused the appearance of auspicious signs. H.H. the sixteenth Great Jewel Dharma King recognized him as the incarnation of H.E. the sixth Dharma King Rabjam and performed an enthronement ceremony for him. In the year of 2007, as requested by the International Buddhism Sangha Association, H.H. Dorje Chang Buddha III recognized H.E. the seventh Dharma King Rabjam as the incarnation of Shechen Rabjam Rinpoche.

When H.E. Rabjam Rinpoche was fifteen years old, he was tonsured by H.E. Dharma King Trulshik of the Nyingma sect and entered the monastic life. At the age of twenty, the rinpoche received the upasampada (complete set of precepts given to a monk who enters the order) from H.E. Dharma King Trulshik. He later learned from many extremely holy masters, especially from his root master, H.H. Dharma King Dilgo Khyentse, and from H.H. the fourteenth Dalai Lama, H.H. Sakya Trizin, H.H. the sixteenth Great Jewel Dharma King, H.E. Dharma King Chogye Trichen, H.H. Dharma King Penor of the Nyingma sect, and H.E. Kalu Rinpoche of the Shangpa Kagyu. He finally became a vajra master and famous dharma king of the unbroken Nyingma lineage.

Currently, besides building monasteries, H.E. Dharma King Rabjam is propagating the dharma and benefiting living beings around the world. He also is responsible for supervising and training Khyentse Yangsi Rinpoche, who is the incarnation of H.H. Dharma King Dilgo Khyentse.

冉江法王為寧瑪巴六大寺系之一的雪謙寺系的法王。

現今的冉江法王為第七世的冉江法王，於1966年吉日帶著祥異之兆降生於印度的羌地噶，第十六世大寶法王認證了他為第六世冉江法王的轉世並為其舉行坐床典禮。2007年，應國際佛教僧尼總會的請求，三世多杰羌佛親自認證第七世的冉江法王是雪謙冉江仁波且的轉世。

仁波且十五歲的時候，由寧瑪派教法的頂飾楚西法王剃度出家，二十歲時在楚西法王處受近圓戒，特別於根本上師頂果欽哲法王、第十四世達賴喇嘛、薩迦天津法王、第十六世大寶法王、薩迦秋吉崔欽法王、寧瑪巴貝諾法王、香巴噶舉卡魯仁波且等多位大聖者處學習，終於成為寧瑪巴這一從未間斷的傳承的持明者、著名法王。

目前，冉江法王不僅建立寺院，在世界各地弘法利生，而且還負責監督及培養欽哲揚希仁波且——頂果欽哲法王的轉世。

BRIEF INTRODUCTION TO
VEN. ANGWANG KHYENTSE RINPOCHE
昂旺欽哲仁波且簡介

Ven. Angwang Khyentse Rinpoche is the abbot of Gensa Temple of the Sakya sect. The Gensa Temple is located in the Changdu district of Tibet. The eighty-two-year-old Ven. Angwang Khyentse Rinpoche is the major successor to the dharma lineage passed onto him by H.H. Khyentse Chokyi Lodro, who was the most virtuous practitioner in all of Tibet. The Buddha predicted that Ven. Angwang Khyentse Rinpoche would live until the age of eighty-five. The rinpoche, who is in solitary retreat on a long-term basis, is deeply respected by all of the temples of the Sakya sect. He possesses great supernatural powers and is proficient in the major and minor Five Vidyas. His practice of Tummo is especially revered throughout the snowy plateaus of Tibet. At lower than twenty degrees below zero Celsius (lower than four degrees below zero Fahrenheit), the rinpoche is still able to expose his chest and emanate heat from his belly that can thoroughly cook an egg within a few minutes.

昂旺欽哲仁波且是薩迦派根薩寺寺主，根薩寺坐落於西藏昌都地區，昂旺欽哲仁波且已82歲，系全藏第一大德第二世蔣陽欽哲的心子傳承繼承人，佛陀有授記仁波且當住世85年。仁波且長期閉關而深受薩迦各寺的敬重，具足大神通，精於大小五明，特別其『拙火定』的修為譽滿雪域高原，在攝氏零下二十多度的氣溫下，仁波且依然敞衣露胸。肚子能在幾分鐘內將雞蛋煮熟。

BRIEF INTRODUCTION TO H.E. DZOGCHEN DHARMA KING
佐欽法王簡介

H.E. Dzogchen Dharma King is the head of the Dzogchen Monastery. The world-renowned Dzogchen Monastery is one of the six main monasteries of the Nyingma sect. The Dzogchen Monastery is the only temple in all of Tibet that is devoted solely to the practice of the Great Perfection. From the 17th century to the middle of the 20th century, the Dzogchen Monastery was the center of the Nyingma sect for transmitting the Pratimoksa Precepts and the Bodhisattva Precepts. All of the current Pratimoksa Precept lineages of the Nyingma sect originated from the greatly accomplished Bodhisattva of the Dzogchen Monastery, Xianpan Taye, and was subsequently handed down from close disciple to close disciple generation after generation. Today the Dzogchen Monastery has almost 300 branch monasteries that are spread throughout five continents.

The Dzogchen Monastery is a remarkable and holy site from which the Buddha-dharma has spread. It has produced more than 60,000 people who have attained the rainbow body and great liberation in that very lifetime.

The first Dzogchen Dharma King, Pema Rigdkzin, established the Dzogchen Monastery and was one of the nirmanakayas of Buddha Ratnasikhin. He devoted his life to the dharma and attained supreme accomplishment through practice of the Great Perfection Dharma.

There are two seventh Dzogchen Dharma Kings. H.E. Jigme Losel Wangpo (on the left), who lives in India, was born in 1964 and was recognized by H.H. Dharma King Dodrupchen Rinpoche in 1972. H.H. Dodrupchen Rinpoche is the supreme holder of the Great Perfection Longchen Nying-thik. H.E. Tenzin Longdock Nyima (on the right), who lives in China, was born in 1974 and was recognized by Dokden Lama. The Chinese government conferred a Certificate of Rinpoche upon H.E. Tenzin Longdock Nyima in 2003.

佐欽法王是佐欽寺的寺主、總法臺。

佐欽寺是寧瑪派六大母寺之一,是享譽世界的著名寺廟。佐欽寺是惟一一座專修大圓滿法的清淨道場,從十七世紀到二十世紀中期,佐欽寺又是寧瑪派的別解脫戒和菩薩戒的授受中心,當今所有寧瑪派的別解脫戒的傳承都是源自於佐欽寺的大成就者佛子先盤塔耶,再由其心子代代相傳。如今佐欽寺已有近三百座分支寺廟,分布於世界五大洲。

佐欽寺這個殊勝的佛法弘揚聖地,先後出現的即身成佛的虹化者就有六萬多人,佐欽寺由第一世佐欽法王白瑪仁增創建。第一世佐欽法王是由寶髻佛化身之一,佐欽法王以身效法,修行大圓滿法獲得無上成就。

第七世佐欽法王有兩位,一位是駐錫印度的吉美洛桑旺波(圖左),出生於1964年,由寧瑪龍欽寧體總教主多智欽法王於1972年認證。另一位是駐錫中國佐欽寺的旦增・龍多尼瑪(圖右),出生於1974年,由阿江多丹尊者認證,中國政府於2003年為其頒發活佛證書。

BRIEF INTRODUCTION TO H.E. RENQING RONGBO BARONGBO RINPOCHE, AN EASTERN TIBETAN DHARMA KING OF THE NYINGMA SECT
寧瑪東藏法王仁青絨波巴絨波簡介

H.E. Renqing Rongbo Barongbo Rinpoche of Decheqin Monastery is a Nyingma dharma king in eastern Tibet. In a prior lifetime, he was the venerable Ananda, who heard more of the Buddha's discourses on the dharma than any other disciple of the Buddha. In the generation after the Buddha, Ananda was entrusted to transmit the teachings on the dharma given by the Buddha.

Based on karmic conditions, throughout the generations he reincarnated as Huifangbian Luocha, Bairotsana, Renzhen Made Ranna, Qujia Linba, Renzhen Qingji Linba, Baima Dorje, Xiangqiu Jiangcun, and Xiajia Jiangcun. In each of those lifetimes, he manifested as the true reincarnation of venerable Ananda.

In accordance with the Vajrapani Sutra and the predictions contained in the scriptures of Guru Padmasambhava, the tenth reincarnation of H.E. Renqing Rongbo Barongbo Rinpoche was born in 1969. The rinpoche possessed at birth the realization powers and abilities of venerable Ananda. He was innately endowed with extraordinary wisdom and limitless compassion. Occasionally, he freely manifests a bit of his supernatural powers. There are innumerable feats of his, such as miraculous healing of diseases, instant subduing of demons, displaying unobstructed spiritual powers, knowing the minds and languages of all living beings, and making predictions based on meditative insight. When he conducts initiations, practices dharma, and makes offerings, unusual and auspicious signs appear, such as a fragrant scent that can be smelled even from far away. When he prays for rain during a drought, it promptly rains. Many people know about all of these feats.

The rinpoche accepted the invitation of Kathok Monastery to participate in a great dharma assembly attended by over 10,000 monastics. That temple, which is known as the world's second vajra throne, has to date produced over 100,000 practitioners who have attained the rainbow body. At that great dharma assembly, the rinpoche sat on the elevated third dharma king throne. Numerous famous dharma kings sat below him. The status of ordinary holy rinpoches cannot compare to the status of the rinpoche. That is because H.E. Renqing Rongbo Barongbo Rinpoche is the foremost Nyingma dharma king in eastern Tibet and is the reincarnation of venerable Ananda, a great and holy dharma king!

After H.E. Renqing Rongbo Barongbo Rinpoche applied his dharma powers to appraise the book *A Treasury of True Buddha-Dharma*, he saw the truth that H.H. Wan Ko Yeshe Norbu is the highest ancient Buddha, the Buddha Vajradhara who has come to this world again. Being greatly moved and full of respect, he wrote his congratulations.

德慶寺寧瑪派東藏法王仁青絨波巴絨波仁波且，是釋迦牟尼佛座下十六尊者當中『多聞第一』的阿難尊者，為釋迦牟尼佛之第二代付法藏師。

嗣後，隨眾生因緣，仁波且又分別轉世為慧方便羅剎、貝若扎那、仁真瑪德然那、曲佳林巴、仁真清吉林巴、白瑪多吉、向球降村、夏嘉降村，每一世均是阿難尊者的真身化顯。

正如《金剛手經》和蓮花生大師的經書中所授記的一樣，第十世的仁青絨波巴絨波仁波且於1969年降生。仁波且天生具有阿難尊者的道力本能，自備超凡的智慧和無限的慈悲心，偶爾略顯自在無礙的神通化現，其如治病之神奇、降魔之立效、無礙之神力、了知一切眾生之心性與語言，以及禪觀之預言，不可勝記，其在灌頂、修法、會供時，奇異吉兆如香味遠遠可聞、為乾旱之地祈雨之立驗等，皆為眾人所知。仁波且應邀參加至今已成就了十萬虹光身、被譽為天下第二金剛座的噶陀寺的萬僧大法會時，高居大法會第三法王寶座，眾多有名的法王坐在他之下，仁波且的地位非普通聖者仁波且能比的，因為他是大聖法王阿難尊者轉世的仁青絨波巴絨波東藏寧瑪第一法王！他施展法力，鑒定《正法寶典》後，親見雲高益西諾布至高無上的古佛真容金剛總持再來，恭敬感動無比，寫下祝賀。

BRIEF INTRODUCTION TO H.E. GREEN JEWEL CROWN KARMAPA DHARMA KING JIEZHONG
綠寶冠噶瑪巴杰仲法王簡介

H.E. the current 6th Karmapa Green Jewel Crown Dharma King Jiezhong was born in 1967 in a region called Laduo in Changdu, Tibet. When he was born, a rainbow in the sky surrounded his house, and beautiful, wondrous, heavenly music could be heard. The 16th Karmapa, H.H. Great Jewel Dharma King Rangjiong Rigpe Dorje, specially sent a recognition certificate from India to recognize that H.E. Dharma King Jiezhong was in his prior lifetime the Green Jewel Crown Dharma King Jiezhong Rinpoche.

Regarding the Karma Kagyu dharma kings, generally speaking, the disciple and master alternate their respective positions lifetime after lifetime, resulting in one person teaching or "returning" dharma to the other person who taught that dharma in the prior lifetime. For example,

H.H. the 7th Karmapa Black Jewel Crown Dharma King Chodrag Gyatso was the master of the H.E. 1st Green Jewel Crown Dharma King Gama Chenglie. Additionally, after H.H. the 7th Black Jewel Crown Dharma King reincarnated as H.H. the 8th Karmapa Mikyo Dorje Black Jewel Crown Dharma King, H.E. the 1st Green Jewel Crown Dharma King Gama Chenglie became the master of H.H. the 8th Black Jewel Crown Dharma King. H.E. Gama Chenglie is the Karmapa Green Jewel Crown Dharma King Jiezhong. H.E. the 2nd Jiezhong Rinpoche Huajiong was summoned to the capital of China, Beijing, by Emperor Qianlong, who conferred upon him the title of Hutuketu Dharma King. H.H. the 14th Karmapa Great Jewel Dharma King recognized that the transformation body of his cause or undertaking is H.E. the Green Jewel Crown Dharma King and therefore specially bestowed upon him the green jewel crown. The Ugyen Second Buddha Guru Padmasambhava prophesied the following: Whoever encounters Jiezhong Rinpoche can receive great benefits.

現今第六世的噶瑪巴綠寶冠杰仲法王，於一九六七年生在西藏昌都拉多地區，出生當時房屋上空被彩虹圍繞，傳出美妙動聽的天樂妙音。第十六世噶瑪巴壞炯熱畢多杰大寶法王從印度專程送來認證證書，認證他為前世綠寶冠法王杰仲仁波且之轉世。

噶瑪噶舉派之法王基本上都是互為師徒而傳交上一世的法歸原主，如第七世噶瑪巴黑寶冠法王確扎嘉措就是第一世綠寶冠法王噶瑪成列的上師，而第七世黑寶冠法王轉世為第八世噶瑪巴米覺多杰黑寶冠法王時，第一世的綠寶冠法王噶瑪成列卻成了第八世黑寶冠大寶法王的上師，噶瑪成列即是噶瑪巴綠寶冠杰仲法王。第二世杰仲仁波且華炯為大皇帝乾隆召之國都北京，封為呼圖克圖法王。第十四世噶瑪巴大寶法王認證綠寶冠法王為自己的事業化身，特賜予綠寶冠。烏金第二佛陀蓮花生大師金剛語授記：凡與杰仲仁波且結緣者，均可獲得廣大利益。

BRIEF INTRODUCTION TO VENERABLE JUNMAI BAIMA DORJE RINPOCHE
俊麥白瑪多吉仁波且簡介

Ven. Junmai Baima Dorje Rinpoche is a nirmanakaya of Vajravarahi. Ven. first Junmai Baima Dorje Rinpoche was the famous terton Renzhen Daoxiang Dorje Rinpoche. Ven. the second Junmai Baima Dorje Rinpoche was Jiaweng Songjie Zhaxi Rinpoche. He turned his body into a rainbow and passed away in a state of liberation. He left behind his fingernails and the hair on his head. Ven. third Junmai Baima Dorje Rinpoche was Jimei Yongdeng Gyatso Rinpoche. He, too,

was a very famous and great teacher and terton. During his life, he easily unearthed many hidden treasures, which mainly included a gold statue of Green Tara, *The Precious Book Handed Down From Tibet on the Heart Mantra of the Buddhas, Bodhisattvas, and Dakini Dharma Protectors*, and an eight Buddhas stupa. These precious things are now being kept at the Dege Larong Temple. The rinpoche exhibited innumerable supernatural feats. The rinpoche left behind many imprints of his hands and feet inside the Larong Temple and on cliffs, thereby manifesting his supreme wisdom, boundless dharma powers, and the wonderful nature of the Buddha-dharma. He could make the sun stop revolving and ride a boulder as one rides a horse.

Ven. fourth Junmai Baima Dorje Rinpoche (the current one) descended into this world in the year of the dog according to the Tibetan calendar. When the rinpoche was born, a prajna bird (dharma protecting bird) spit from its mouth a green pine stone (one of the seven treasures) onto the balcony of the rinpoche's home. A Buddhist image of Green Tara with clear facial features appeared on that green pine stone. (It is now kept in the rinpoche's treasure chest of holy objects.) Various other auspicious signs manifested at the birth of the rinpoche, such as a rainbow in the sky, the beautiful sound of dharma drums resounding in space, and the wonderful sound of whistling and conch shells being blown.

In an oral teaching, the dakini Zere Kazhuo recognized Ven. Junmai Baima Dorje Rinpoche as an incarnation of Vajravarahi. When the rinpoche was five years old, the national master of Bhutan, H.H. Dilgo Khyentse Rinpoche, recognized the rinpoche as the reincarnation of Ven. Junmai Yongdeng Gyatso Rinpoche and personally signed and issued a recognition certificate. H.H. Dharma King Penor and H.E. Dharma King Rabjam also personally wrote recognition certificates.

At the age of about three, the young rinpoche transformed a thick Tibetan knife into a knot. After passing through many hands, that knife is now at Hua Zang Si in San Francisco, U.S.A., where a special place has been established to show it for public worship and veneration. The rinpoche currently resides at the Shechen Monastery. He has received initiations from the esoteric lineage of H.H. Panchen Lama X and other persons of great holiness and virtue. The rinpoche benefits all living beings by applying the wisdom and realization of a great Bodhisattva.

俊麥白瑪多吉仁波且是金剛亥母的化身，第一世俊麥白瑪多吉仁波且是著名掘藏大師仁真道香多杰仁波且，第二世全名嘉翁松杰扎西仁波且，虹化而圓寂，留下了指甲與頭髮。第三世全名俊麥雍登嘉措仁波且，是一位非常著名的大善知識、掘藏大師。一生中輕而易舉開掘了許多伏藏，主要有綠度母金身像、〈藏傳諸佛菩薩空行護法心咒寶典〉、八佛塔等等，現珍藏於德格喇榮寺內。仁波且施展無數神通，可以讓太陽停止運轉，把石頭作為馬騎行。

俊麥白瑪多吉仁波且的第四世(即現世)降生藏曆水狗年，當仁波且降生的時候，一隻般若鳥(護法鳥)嘴裡吐出一顆綠松石(七寶之一)在他家的陽台，綠松石上顯現一尊五官清晰的綠度母佛像(現保存在仁波且的聖物寶櫃中)，同時天空顯現彩虹，虛空響起美妙的法鼓、嗩吶和海螺妙音，種種瑞相。空行母澤熱喀卓認證開示說俊麥白瑪多吉仁波且是金剛亥母化身，五歲時，不丹國國師頂果欽哲仁波且認定為俊麥雍登嘉措仁波且的轉世，親自簽頒認定書。白瑪羅布法王、冉江法王也親寫認證書。

大約三歲時，小小仁波且將一把厚背小藏刀用二指盤成卷，經多方轉折，現由美國舊金山華藏寺設聖蹟寶座供奉，以供善士敬仰。仁波且現居協慶寺，曾受班禪大師等大聖德們的秘密傳承灌頂。仁波且以其大菩薩的智慧道量普利一切眾生。

BRIEF INTRODUCTION TO VEN. ABBOT KALSANG GYALTSEN
卡桑·嘉參堪布簡介

Ven. Abbot Kalsang Gyaltsen studied Buddhist philosophy at the Great Dialectic School in the Drepung Loseling Monastery for about twenty years. After completing his work there, he stayed a year in the Gyu De Monastery, where he learned tantric Buddhism. During that time he guided the younger monks. In 1999, H.H. the 14th Dalai Lama appointed him as the abbot of the Tashi Samten Ling Monastery.

　　卡桑·嘉參堪布在 Drepung loseling 寺的大邏輯學院學習佛教哲學超過20年，然後在 Gyu De 寺學習一年的密法，同時指導年輕的比丘修學。1999年，第十四世達賴喇嘛指定他擔任桑登林寺的住持。

BRIEF INTRODUCTION TO VEN. ZANGXIA RINPOCHE
藏夏仁波且簡介

The first Zangxia Rinpoche was Chilie Longda, who transmitted dharma and gave precepts at the Drepung Monastery in Lhasa. He was also the chief khenpo at the Guomang Zhacang Institute in the Drepung Monastery, one of the three initial monasteries of the Geluk sect.

The second Zangxia Rinpoche was Danima, who received precepts and learned dharma at the Drepung Monastery in Lhasa. He also was the dharma king at the Litang Monastery and the Wotuo Monastery.

The third Zangxia Rinpoche was Chilie Dongqu, who was born in the Wotuo district of the Guoluo Prefecture in the province of Qinghai, China. He also received precepts and learned dharma at the Drepung Monastery in Lhasa and was the dharma king at the Litang Monastery.

The fourth Zangxia Rinpoche was Awang Luosang Chilie Qupei, who was born in the Cuosang Jiawa district of Litang County, Ganzi Prefecture, Sichuan Province, China. He received precepts and learned dharma at the Drepung Monastery in Lhasa and was the dharma king the Litang Monastery.

The fifth Zangxia Rinpoche was Chilie Luoqu. He spent his entire life in quiet, solitary self-cultivation in snow mountain forests and attained wonderful accomplishment.

The sixth Zangxia Rinpoche is Awang Gesang Chilie. He was born in the Cuosang Jiawa district of Litang County, Ganzi Prefecture, Sichuan Province, China. The name of his father is Gesang Jiebu, and the name of his mother is Danzheng Qucuo. Since childhood, he liked to hear and deeply reflect on the Buddha-dharma. He has realized extraordinary supernatural powers through his practice.

　　第一世藏夏仁波且為赤烈隆達，在拉薩哲蚌寺傳法授戒，並在格魯派三大母寺之一的哲蚌寺果芒扎倉（聞思學院）擔任總堪布。

　　第二世藏夏仁波且為達尼瑪，在拉薩哲蚌寺受戒聞法，並擔任理塘寺和沃托寺的大法台。

　　第三世藏夏仁波且為赤烈東曲，出生於青海果洛州沃托地方，在拉薩哲蚌寺受戒聞法，並在理塘寺擔任大法台。

　　第四世藏夏仁波且為阿旺羅桑赤烈曲培，出生於四川甘孜州理塘縣措桑嘉哇地區，在拉薩哲蚌寺受戒聞法，並在理塘寺擔任大法台。

　　第五世藏夏仁波且為赤烈羅曲，畢生在雪山林間閉關靜修，獲殊勝成就。

　　第六世藏夏仁波且為阿旺格桑赤烈，出生於四川甘孜州理塘縣措桑嘉哇地區，父名格桑杰布，母親名為旦正曲措。自幼喜愛聞思佛法，並通過修證獲得非凡神通。

BRIEF INTRODUCTION TO VEN. YUNDENG JIANGCUO RINPOCHE
雲登降措仁波且簡介

The abbot of the Tagong Lingji Monastery is Ven. Yundeng Jiangcuo Ripoche, the incarnation of Patriarch Milarepa. Everyone knows very well that Patriarch Milarepa was a famous patriarch of the Kagyu sect and a great practitioner of yoga.

Ven. Yundeng Jiangcuo Rinpoche is now eighty-five years old. The venerable Bari Jiasi, a master of great accomplishment, revealed the following in his formal pronouncement that was buried and later unearthed: "In the 'eight auspicious merits' solemn hall of jewels, the nirmanakaya of the virtuous Milarepa, a monk who realized profound esoteric dharma, will descend to our place of faith and bring great joy." As predicted by numerous eminent monastics and people of great virtue and as predicted in unearthed books that were hidden, Ven. Yundeng Jiangcuo Rinpoche is the incarnation of the great master of yoga, the venerable Milarepa.

In order to provide living beings with a model of self-cultivation, the rinpoche cultivated himself in solitary retreat at the Tagong Lingji Monastery for all together thirty-four years. He spent twenty-seven of those years in continuous, unbroken solitary retreat, exhibiting the ascetic spirit that Patriarch Milarepa had. The realization of the rinpoche is high and he possesses supernatural powers. He often easily manifests in different forms or shapes in order to bless living beings so that they may avoid sufferings and disasters, in order to increase the good fortune of living beings and open up their wisdom, and in order to subdue demons and drive away evil spirits.

聞名西藏雪域的塔公靈吉寺的住持，就是人們所熟知的噶舉派著名的祖師、大瑜伽行者密勒日巴祖師所轉世的雲登降措仁波且。

雲登降措仁波且今年已八十五歲，正如大成就者巴日嘉斯尊者在他掘取的伏藏授記中講：『八祥功德莊嚴之寶殿中，證悟深密法義之比丘，具德密勒日巴之化身，降於吾等信處甚歡喜。』仁波且是眾多高僧大德和伏藏典籍中授記預言的大瑜伽師密勒日巴尊者的轉世。

為給眾生表修行之法，仁波且以身作則，前後在塔公靈吉寺閉關修行34年，其中不間斷閉關27年，重現密勒日巴祖師的苦修精神。仁波且證量高深，具足神通，在加持眾生解除苦厄、增福開慧以及降魔除妖等方面，常顯現無礙變化。

BRIEF INTRODUCTION TO RESPECTED BAMDA TUBTEN GELEG GYATSO RINPOCHE
班達土登格勒嘉措仁波且簡介

The 1st Bamda Tubten Geleg Gyatso Rinpoche was Manmu Dawa Tubten Geleg Rinpoche, who was the most renowned Buddhist master of the Jonang tradition in recent history. He was born in Gaduo Village of Rangtang County in 1844. At age 18, he started his education under Bazhu Rinpoche of the Dzogchen Monastery and Gongzhu Yundang Gyatso Rinpoche of the Palpung Monastery. Later he learned from Zangwa Rinpoche and Awan Qunpei Gyatso Rinpoche. He practiced the various Tantra dharmas of the Jonang sect and had entered a retreat for many years. He attained a very high level of accomplishment and learned from a wide variety of teachings, including Nyingma, Kagyu, Gelug and Jonang teachings. His knowledge was vast and his level of realization was high. That rinpoche was considered by the Gelug sect as the incarnation of Guru Tsongkhapa and by the Jonang sect as the incarnation of the Venerable Duoluo Nanta. He spent the last few years of his life writing and expounding Buddhist scriptures. He continually produced thirty pages of writing every day without missing a day. Up until now, his 199 books have been the main teaching material used by all monasteries of the Jonang tradition.

The current Bamda Tubten Geleg Gyatso Rinpoche became a monastic when he was a child. His knowledge is vast. He became a khenpo at a very young age and is very well respected.

班達土登格勒嘉措仁波且的第一世曼木達哇，土登格勒嘉措仁波且是覺囊派近代最著名的佛教大師，於1844年降生於壤塘縣尕多鄉，十八歲開始求學於佐欽寺巴珠仁波且、八蚌寺工珠‧雲丹嘉措仁波且等大師，後拜藏哇仁波且阿旺群佩嘉措為師，修學覺囊多種密法，閉關多年，獲得極高成就。他廣泛學習寧瑪、噶舉、格魯、覺囊各派教說，知識極為淵博，修證高深，被格魯派認為是宗喀巴大師的轉世，而覺囊派則認為是多羅那他尊者的轉世。他晚年專事著述講經，每日寫作30頁，從不間斷，直至今日，其199本著作仍是覺囊派所有寺廟學習的主要教材。這一世的班達土登格勒嘉措仁波且自幼出家，學識豐富，年輕即任堪布，深受世人敬重。

BRIEF INTRODUCTION TO RESPECTED SIXTH BAIMA RONGZHU RINPOCHE
第六世白瑪榮珠仁波且簡介

The respected sixth Baima Rongzhu Rinpoche, who is the abbot of the Badeng Lazhong Temple and now seventy-six years old, was the master of the first Dege headman. He is a great holy being who was issued a rinpoche certificate by the central government of China. The rinpoche has realized a state in which day and night are equal and there is no difference between past, present, and future. He is in solitary retreat on a long-term basis and does not lie down either during the day or night. The rinpoche, who possesses supernatural powers, is known and respected by everyone in the area along the Jinsha River. All of the temples of the Nyingma sect praise him as model of great virtue. The rinpoche's master was Zhiqing Galang, a greatly accomplished one who attained the rainbow body through the practice of the Great Perfection. Zhiqing Galang ate only seven grains of highland barley a day. At the time of his accomplishment in the dharma, Zhiqing Galang transformed into the rainbow body and left in front of many people. Many rinpoches in the Kham region have received dharma transmissions and initiations from the respected sixth Baima Rongzhu Rinpoche. An especially large number of Indian practitioners of yoga have relied upon and received dharma transmissions and initiations from the rinpoche, who is deeply admired in India.

　　第六世白瑪榮珠仁波且是巴登拉思寺仕持，已76歲，糸德格第一代土司的上師，是全國由中央政府頒發仁波且證件的大聖者。仁波且已證晝夜平等三時無差的境界，長期閉關晝夜恒持不臥，具足神通，金沙江沿流人人敬奉，個個皆曉，被寧瑪派各寺譽為大德楷模。仁波且的上師是大圓滿虹身大成就者值青噶朗，每日只食七顆青稞程度日，成就時當眾虹化而去。康巴地區的活佛、仁波且多在第六世白瑪榮珠膝下接法和受灌頂。特別是印度的瑜珈行者在其膝下依止接受傳播法義和灌頂的很多，在印度深受恭敬。

BRIEF INTRODUCTION TO RESPECTED EBA RINPOCHE
俄巴仁波且簡介

Respected Eba Rinpoche is from the Sakya lineage. The 1st Eba Rinpoche, Bare Laqin, showed high intelligence and great compassion when he was a child. He was well known for his thorough understanding of all the Five Vidyas and his benevolent kindness. He tamed non-Buddhist practitioners with his eloquence, debating skills and writings skills. Laqin Rinpoche not only propagated the Buddha's teachings but also attained absolute accomplishment. He entered a dharma realm of dazzling light while various auspicious feats, such as the raining of flowers, were manifested. The 2nd, 3rd and 4th Eba Rinpoches were all eminent adepts who were well known in the Deng Ke area.

The current 5th Eba Rinpoche received teachings from various holy adepts of great virtue. He carries on the extraordinary lineage of the 5th Sakya Patriarch. He also carries on the beseeching blessings and good fortune lineage of the greatly accomplished H.E. Tangtong Gyalpo Bodhisattva. He is a rinpoche with true talents and genuine knowledge. He has never made public when and where he left behind his hand and foot prints caused by his supernatural powers. Instead, his true self-cultivation, true realization, compassion and wisdom have made him the well-respected 5th lineage holder of the his lineage.

　　俄巴仁波且直屬薩迦法統。第一世俄巴仁波且壩熱喇欽自幼即具聰慧和慈悲胸懷，對所有大小五明知識融匯貫通，以心地善良而著稱於世，他以善說、善辯、善著而降伏外道。喇欽仁波且不僅宏揚佛陀教法，自己更獲得圓滿成就，在花雨和各種瑞相中融入虹光法界。此後，第二、三、四世的俄巴仁波且也都是聞名於鄧柯地區的大聖者。

　　第五世俄巴仁波且受教於諸多大德聖者，得到薩迦五祖的殊勝傳承法統和大成就者唐東迦波菩薩的祈福招財傳承，他是一位具有真才實學的仁波且，他從不宣揚自己在何時何地留下了神通手足印記，而以實修實證、悲智並具成為第五世法台，深獲人們的敬重。

BRIEF INTRODUCTION TO
RESPECTED KHENPO CHUCHENG QUPEI
楚稱曲培堪布簡介

曲培絨波座前接受比丘戒。十九歲在康協五明佛學院完成了四個年頭的學習，拜別了恩師大堪布白瑪當秋等，離開故土去印度拜見了夢寐中的文殊真身怙主薩迦天津法王。在薩迦高級佛學院的十二年裡，堪布不僅從依著名的堪布米瑪和堪布嘉措圓滿學習了一切顯密教法，還先後從依持蓮花尊者薩迦法王、薩迦俄巴堪布隆燈金剛持、薩迦察巴法王秋吉崔欽仁波且以及寧瑪派敏林赤欽法王等上師為主的藏傳佛教各大教派的許多高僧大德學習和領悟了高深的佛法理論和實踐，並且在薩迦高級佛學院任教五年。

在2000年的一場上萬僧眾參加的法會上，薩迦法王親手將高級佛學院的畢業証書及象徵學位的通人冠賜給了堪布楚稱曲培。2003年，薩迦法王正式授予其堪布名位及証書，囑命其返回藏地宏乘薩迦正法脈流。

楚稱曲培堪布遵從薩迦天津法王旨意，成立了《量理寶藏》論學會，薩迦天津總教主對此非常滿意。

BRIEF INTRODUCTION TO
RESPECTED WANGZHI TUDENG JIGMEI
RINPOCHE
汪智土登晉美仁波且簡介

Respected Khenpo Chucheng Qupei is from Dege County in the Ganzi Autonomous District of Sichuan Province. He became a monk at the Dege Gengqing Monastery at the age of eleven. In the shramanera (novice monk) class at the Dege Gengqing Monastery, he learned how to read and write Tibetan. He also learned scriptures, rules, and rituals primarily of the Sakya order. At the age of fifteen, he entered the Dzongsar Khamje Five Vidyas Buddhist Institute, which is extremely influential in Tibet. When he was seventeen years old, he received the precepts for monks from Lama Angwang Qupei Rongbo, a great master of the Sakya order in the Kham District. At nineteen, he completed his four years of study at the Khamje Five Vidyas Buddhist Institute, bid farewell to his master, Great Khenpo Baima Dangqiu, and left his homeland for India. There he met the holy virtuous one he dreamed of meeting—H.H. Dharma King Sakya Trizin, who is a true nirmanakaya of Manjushri Bodhisattva.

In his twelve years at the Sakya Advanced Buddhist Institute, Respected Khenpo Chucheng Qupei successfully learned all of the esoteric and exoteric dharma teachings from two famous khenpos—Khenpo Mima and Khenpo Jiacuo. Additionally, he studied and grasped profound Buddha-dharma theory and practice by following many eminent and virtuous masters of all of the main sects of Tibetan Buddhism. Of those masters, he primarily followed the venerable lotus flower holder, H.H. Dharma King Sakya Trizin; H.E. the Sakya Ngorpa Khenpo, Vajra Master Longdeng; the Sakya Tsharpa Dharma King, H.E. Chogye Trichen Rinpoche; and H.H. Dharma King Mindrolling Trichen of the Nyingma sect. Respected Khenpo Chucheng Qupei also taught at the Sakya Advanced Buddhist Institute for five years.

At a dharma assembly that took place in the year 2000 attended by over 10,000 monastics, H.H. Dharma King Sakya Trizin personally conferred upon Respected Khenpo Chucheng Qupei a graduation certificate from the Sakya Advanced Buddhist Institute and a hat that signified his academic degree and great erudition. In 2003, H.H. Dharma King Sakya Trizin formally conferred upon him position of khenpo along with the accompanying certificate and instructed him to return to Tibet to spread the true dharma of the Sakya lineage.

Following the mandate given to him by H.H. Dharma King Sakya Trizin, Respected Khenpo Chucheng Qupei established a society to learn a treatise called the *Liang Li Treasure*. H.H. Dharma King Sakya Trizin was very satisfied with the khenpo for such efforts.

Respected Wangzhi Tudeng Jigmei Rinpoche is the abbot of Tsangtsang Temple. The Tsangtsang Temple of the Nyingma sect is located in the Aba Tibetan Autonomous Prefecture. That temple is a place where numerous persons of great virtue and accomplishment attained the rainbow body. Because it carries on a special dharma lineage of the Buddha, both the Kathok Monastery and the Shechen Monastery have designated the Cangcang Temple as their branch temple.

汪智土登晉美仁波且為倉倉寺住持。寧瑪派倉倉寺，座落於阿壩藏族自治州，系眾多大德成就者的虹化處。因該寺具有佛陀殊勝的傳承功課，被噶陀寺和協慶寺共定為分寺。

堪布楚稱曲培為四川甘孜自治州德格縣人，十一歲出家於德格更慶寺，在更慶寺的小沙彌班學習藏語文讀寫及薩迦派為主的經教儀軌。十五歲進入在整個西藏都極具影響力的宗薩康協五明佛學院。十七歲時在康區薩迦派怙主上師格·喇嘛昂旺

BRIEF INTRODUCTION TO RESPECTED BISHOP SEICHO ASAHI
旭清澄主教簡介

Other rinpoches of great virtue and temples also wrote congratulatory letters, such as Gele Sangbu Rinpoche, Luozhu Jiangcuo Rinpoche, Great Lama Renzhen Rinpoche, Duozhu Rinpoche, Gongbo Rinpoche, Great Khenpo Gongcheng, Pengcuo Rinpoche, etc. Because of the limited space of this book, we request your under-standing in our inability to publish all of them. Although brief introductions were not included for the following seven rinpoches and great khenpo, and many congratulatory letters from temples and individuals were not published, their merit for having praised H.H. Dorje Chang Buddha III will produce wonderful karmic conditions leading to Buddhahood. The International Buddhism Sangha Association thanks each and every one of them and prays that the dharma protecting deities in the ten directions will bless and protect them so that they may live in the world a long time, forever turn the wheel of the dharma, and pervasively benefit living beings.

另外，還有格勒桑布仁波且、洛珠降措仁波且、喇嘛仁珍仁波且、多珠仁波且、貢波活佛、龔成大堪布、彭措活佛等大德仁波且及寺廟均寫來了祝賀函，限於本書篇幅，僅列出其部分祝賀函件及翻譯，其餘不能全部列出，敬請諒解。

　　雖然部分函件及大德們的簡介未刊登，但大德們對三世多杰羌佛的讚嘆功德，將會於無相布施中獲得殊勝成佛之因緣，國際佛教僧尼總會也對此一一致謝，並祈禱十方護法護佑他們長久住世，永轉法輪，普利眾生。

Respected Bishop Seicho Asahi was born in Hiroshima, Japan. He studied Shingon Buddhism at the Koyasan University in Japan, came to California as a Buddhist minister in 1981, and worked at Koyasan Temple for 10 years. He has been active with all segments of the community in teaching Buddhist philosophy and has engaged in interfaith activity, prison Sangha work, the Buddhist Peace Fellowship, etc. He has been the head minister of the Northern California Koyasan Temple in Sacramento for the last 16 years.

　　旭清澄主教生於日本廣島，他在日本的高野山大學學習真言宗後，於1981年赴美國宏法，擔任高野山位於加州首府沙加緬度的寺院住持。在傳播佛法的同時，還積極參與社區的活動，以促進人們的道德提升。於2007年被推舉為真言宗北美洲主教。

GELE SANBU RINPOCHE
格勒桑布仁波且

LUOZHU JIANGCUO RINPOCHE
洛珠降措仁波且

LAMA RENZHEN RINPOCHE
喇嘛仁珍仁波且

DUOZHU RINPOCHE
多珠仁波且

GONGBO RINPOCHE
貢波活佛

GREAT KHENPO GONGCHENG
龔成大堪布

PENGCUO RINPOCHE
彭措活佛

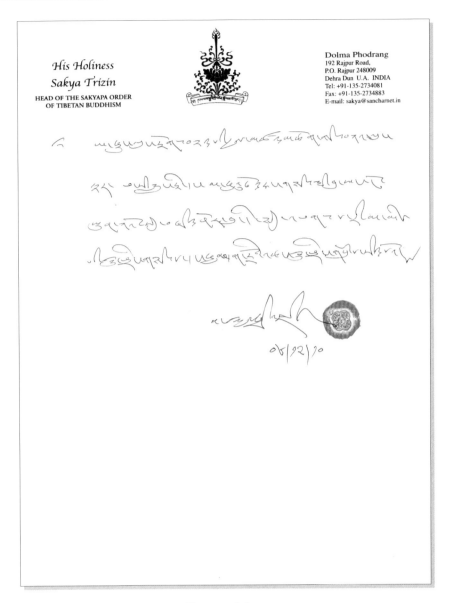

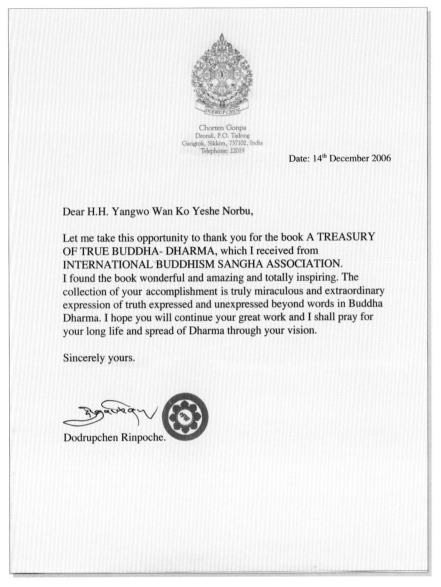

Recognition

In accordance with the recognition of Jamyang Lungdok Gyaltsen Achuk, I hereby recognize that H.H. Yangwo Wan Ko Yeshe Norbu, the son of father Zhonghai Yee and mother Kunfang Xu, is venerable Vimalakirti II, Buddha Vajradhara Dorje Chang Buddha III.

Supreme Dharma King of the Sakya Order
Sakya Trizin
December 10, 2006

認　　證

　　依照阿秋·隆多丹貝加參的認證，父親為義仲海、母親為許坤芳的兒子，即仰諤雲高益西諾布，今確認為維摩詰尊者第二世再來，即金剛總持多杰羌佛第三世。

薩迦總法王　薩迦天津
2006年12月10日

頂聖仰諤雲高益西諾布：

　　讓我藉此機會謝謝您的《正法寶典》——我是從國際佛教僧尼總會收到這本書的。這本書令人驚嘆和不可思議，並且鼓舞人心。您的成就是真正的奇蹟，超常地表現出了用語言能夠表達出來和語言所不能表達出來的佛法真諦。我希望您繼續您偉大的事業，並且我將為您的長壽和通過您的先覺來弘揚佛法而祈禱！

您的真誠的

多智欽仁波且
2006年12月14日

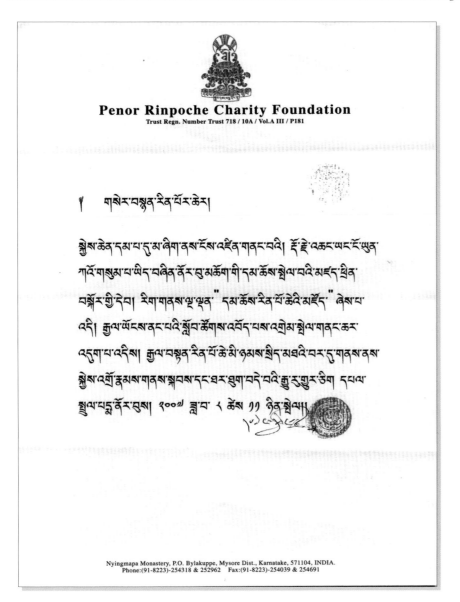

Penor Rinpoche Charity Foundation
Trust Regn. Number Trust 718 / 10A / Vol.A III / P181

Nyingmapa Monastery, P.O. Bylakuppe, Mysore Dist., Karnatake, 571104, INDIA.
Phone:(91-8223)-254318 & 252962   Fax:(91-8223)-254039 & 254691

Honorable Rinpoches:

H.H. Dorje Chang Buddha III Yangwo Wan Ko Yeshe Norbu, who has been recognized by numerous greatly virtuous and eminent monastics, propagates the Buddha-dharma. His Holiness's book *A Treasury of True Buddha-Dharma* manifests full proficiency in the Five Vidyas. That book is being published and distributed in response to the requests of Buddhists all over the country. The publication and distribution of that book will cause the Buddha-dharma to abide in this world eternally and will provide the karmic conditions for living beings to obtain immediate happiness, leave the sufferings and hardships of samsara forever, and attain the ultimate state of Buddhahood.

Palyul Rinpoche Pema Norbu

August 11, 2007

尊貴的閣下仁波且們：

　　經眾多大德高僧認證的第三世多杰羌佛仰諤雲高益西諾布弘揚佛行事業，而顯五明具足典籍《正法寶典》，本書是應全國佛教徒的要求而出版發行的。本書的出版發行對佛法常駐世間，直到永遠；並成為有情眾生獲得當下之樂和永離世間苦難，獲得終極成佛的因緣。

白玉仁波且貝瑪諾布

2007年8月11日

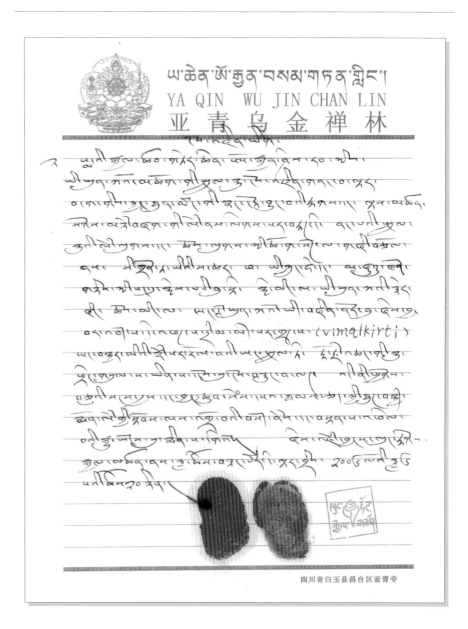

YA QIN WU JIN CHAN LIN
亚青乌金禅林

四川省白玉县昌台区亚青寺

Certificate of Recognition

Based upon the recognition of Urgyen Xirao, the dharma prince of Guru Padmasambhava, and following the system and religious rituals of Tibetan Buddhism for determining the reincarnation of rinpoches, I entered samadhi to observe the truth. I now solemnly recognize that H.H. Master Wan Ko

Yee, who is the son of father Zhonghai Yee and mother Kunfang Xu from Dayi County in Sichuan Province, is the incarnation of Vimalakirti (that is, Vimalakirti has again come to this world), is Dorje Chang Buddha III and has the dharma name of H.H. Yangwo Wan Ko Yeshe Norbu. This is the maturing of the karmic conditions of living beings relating to good fortune and wisdom. We are grateful for this blessing bestowed by the Buddhas.

I hereby recognize

Dharma King Jamyang Lungdok Gyaltsen

June 20, 2006

認　證　書

　　依照蓮花生大師法王子烏金喜饒的認證，經本人入定擇決，並依藏傳佛教活佛轉世制度和宗教儀軌，今莊嚴認證四川大邑縣的父親為義仲海和母親為許坤芳的兒子義雲高大師為維摩詰(Vimalakirti)再來，即多杰羌佛第三世，法號仰諤雲高益西諾布。這是眾生的福慧因緣成熟，感恩諸佛加持。

予以認定

降養龍多加參　法王

2006年6月20日

CONGRATULATIONS

United International World Buddhism Association Headquarters:
On behalf of the Jonang sect, I hereby respectfully congratulate H.H. Dorje Chang Buddha III Wan Ko Yeshe Norbu for directly propagating in this world the teachings of Buddhism. Such teachings have benefited countless living beings in their practice of the dharma and have caused countless living beings to obtain deep blessings and wisdom. The book *A Treasury of True Buddha-Dharma* especially shows this Buddha's complete proficiency in exoteric and esoteric Buddhism and perfect mastery of the Five Vidyas. Such superlative accomplishments are truly unprecedented in the past few thousand years, outshining the accomplishments of all others, both ancient and modern. His Holiness is a shining paragon among Buddhas. May this inexhaustibly mighty light and power of compassion continue so that His Holiness forever teaches the dharma and forever remains in the world.

I place my palms together and respectfully praise His Holiness.

I respectfully prostrate to H.H. Dorje Chang Buddha III, Wan Ko Yeshe Norbu!

Supreme Dharma King of the Jonang Sect Jigme Dorje

May 8, 2007

賀　　詞

聯合國際世界佛教總部：

　　我今代表覺囊派在此恭祝多杰羌佛第三世雲高益西諾布在此世界直接弘揚佛教教法，無量眾生廣受法益，深得福慧。尤其所見佛陀所顯《正法寶典》，顯密圓融，五明滿達，其成就之高峰實乃幾千年來首次耀古騰今，為我佛光燦之楷模。願此威光慈力，永轉法輪，長住於世。

　　合掌敬頌
南無第三世多杰羌佛雲高益西諾布！

覺囊總法王
吉美多吉
2007年5月8日

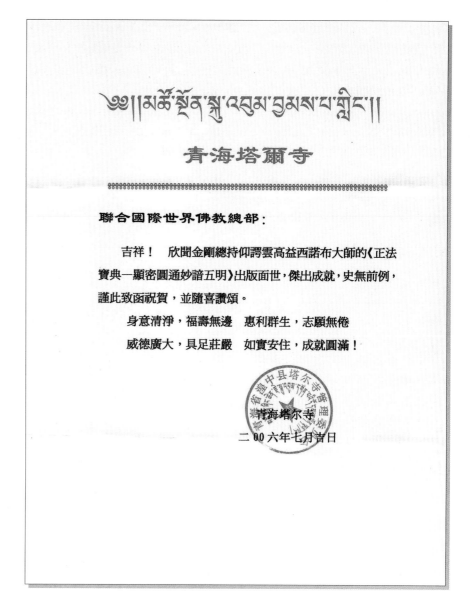

United International World Buddhism Association Headquarters:

Under auspicious circumstances, we were happy to learn of the publication of *A Treasury of True Buddha-Dharma—Complete Proficiency in Exoteric and Esoteric Buddhism and Perfect Mastery of the Five Vidyas* about the Buddha Vajradhara, H.H. Master Yangwo Wan Ko Yeshe Norbu. His Holiness's outstanding accomplishments are unprecedented. We respectfully send this letter of congratulations and joyfully offer our praise.

His actions and mind are pure, and His good fortune and wisdom are limitless.
He benefits myriad living beings, and His willpower never tires.
His powerful virtue is widespread, and His appearance is completely dignified.
He truly abides in peace and His accomplishments are perfect!

Qinghai Kumbum Monastery

An auspicious day in July of 2006

Nyingmapa Mahabuddha Vihara
P.O. CLEMENT TOWN - 248 002, DEHRA DUN (U.K.) INDIA
(Reg. No. S/12723 Registered Under the Societies Registration Act of 1860)

We are very appreciative of having received the book "Treasury of True Buddha Dharma" from the International Buddhism Sangha Association.

The publisher has composed and published the book "Treasury of True Buddha Dharma" recounting the accomplishments of H.H. Wan Ko Yeshe Norbu Dorje Chang with the aspiration that, the Buddha Dharma flourishes in these degenerated times and that the minds of all beings are filled with Bodhicitta. By this book, H.H. Wan Ko Yeshe Norbu Dorje Chang brings good fortune and wisdom to all livings beings.

H.H. Mindrolling Trichen and the Mindrolling Sangha believe that, this noble book brings great benefit to all sentient beings.

Station : Dehradun

Dated : 01.09.2007

D. G. Khochhen Tulku (Ven)
General Secretary

UNDER NYINGMAPA MAHABODHI CHARITABLE SOCIETY
Phone: (O) 0135-2640556 Fax: 0135-2640968

我們非常感謝從「國際佛教僧尼總會」收到的《正法寶典》一書。

出版社集結及出版了多杰羌雲高益西諾布陛下的成就集《正法寶典》為的是末法時期佛法能弘揚開來並且眾生滿溢菩提心。透過此書，多杰羌雲高益西諾布陛下帶給所有眾生福慧。

敏林赤欽法王及敏珠林的僧眾相信這本高貴的書能帶給眾生莫大利益。

地點：德拉頓　　　　總秘書 郭且祖古

時間：2007-09-01

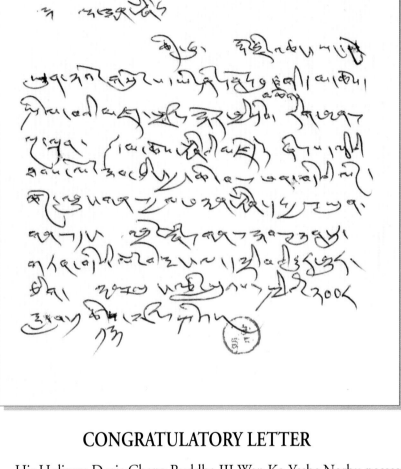

Taklung Tsetul Rinpoche
T.D.A.C. BUDDHIST
NYINGMAPA INSTITUTE
Saraswati Garden Estate
P.O. Kasumpti 171 009
Shimla (H. P.)

CONGRATULATORY LETTER

His Holiness Dorje Chang Buddha III Wan Ko Yeshe Norbu possesses the true dharma of the Buddhas and has manifested complete mastery of the Five Vidyas in the book *A Treasury of True Buddha-Dharma*. This book will be the source that brings profound and pervasive benefits and happiness, will cause the dharma of the Buddhas to flourish and forever exist in this world, and will eternally lead all living beings toward bliss, happiness in the three higher realms, and complete liberation from samsara.

Taklung Tsetrul of the Dorje Drak Monastery
January 13, 2008

賀　　函

尊貴的多杰羌佛第三世仰諤雲高益西諾布，具備佛陀正法，並顯五明具足之的《正法寶典》，此因將成為甚深廣大一切利樂之源，佛陀法教興盛常住於世間，永久指引一切有情眾生於安樂善道徹底解脫。

多傑札寺達龍哲珠

2008年1月13日

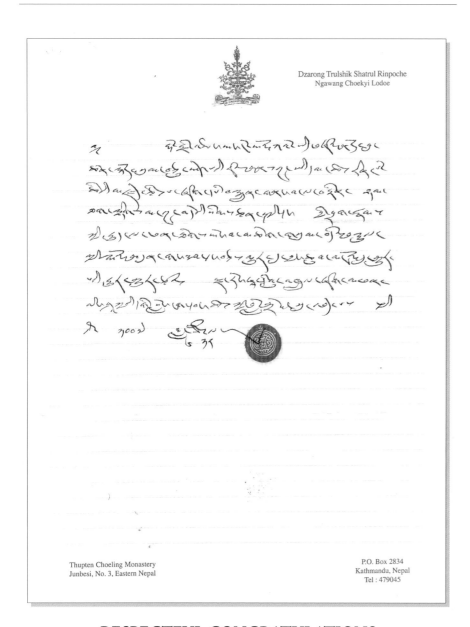

Dzarong Trulshik Shatrul Rinpoche
Ngawang Choekyi Lodoe

Thupten Choeling Monastery
Junbesi, No. 3, Eastern Nepal

P.O. Box 2834
Kathmandu, Nepal
Tel : 479045

RESPECTFUL CONGRATULATIONS

His Holiness Buddha Vajradhara (Dorje Chang Buddha) Yangwo Wan Ko Yeshe Norbu:

I recently learned that the book about you, *A Treasury of True Buddha-Dharma*, was published a long time ago. The content of that book includes the traditional Tibetan five major vidyas and five minor vidyas. In terms of modern branches of learning, the book involves more than thirty different branches of learning.

Thus, I entered samadhi and visualized the Three Jewels—the

Buddha, the dharma, and the sangha. I pervasively spread bodhicitta and wished that all living beings would realize the supreme, absolute truth and Buddhahood. May the propagation of *A Treasury of True Buddha-Dharma* be the karmic condition whereby living beings in the three spheres leave the sufferings of reincarnation and obtain the fruit of wonderful happiness. It will become the cause whereby each sentient being who has descended into the abyss of the six realms of reincarnation leaves suffering and attains happiness.

I hereby specially convey my respectful congratulations!

Buddhist monk Ngawang Chokyi Lodro, having the undeserved name of Khenpo Zhalong Trulshik Shatrul

Written on the auspicious day of June 28, 2007

恭　賀

尊貴的金剛總持（多杰羌佛）仰諤雲高益西諾布：

近日，本人得悉您的《正法寶典》一書早已宏世，本書的內容涵蓋藏族傳統的大小五明，以現代意義的學科分類來講，涉獵三十多門不同學科。

故此，本人入定三昧，觀想佛法僧『三寶』，廣發菩提之心，成就無上真諦佛果之念，祈願《正法寶典》的宏世，將成為三界有情眾生脫離輪迴苦海，獲得勝樂之果的因緣，並將成為墮落六道深淵的每一位有情離苦得樂之因。

特此恭賀！

持有扎隆‧夏帝赤秀堪布之虛名的
釋迦比丘‧阿旺曲吉羅珠

於2007年6月28日吉祥之日撰寫

SAKYA MONASTERY OF TIBETAN BUDDHISM

A Seat of Sakya Tibetan Buddhism United States of America Founded in 1974

May the radiant flower of Tibetan Tradition be preserved for the benefit of all beings.

Many masters praise H.H. Dorje Chang Buddha III Wan Ko Yeshe Norbu and his book about his Dharma activities. The book's name is *A Treasury of the True Buddha Dharma*. Now the International Buddhist Study Center intends to publish this book. I'm so happy to help great masters living anywhere to continue their Dharma activities and serve the Buddhist teachings.

H.H. Phuntsok Phodrang Jigdal Dagchen Sakya

Tibetan Year of the Fire Pig, November 1

108 N.W. 83rd Street • Seattle, Washington 98117 USA • (206) 789-2573 or (206) 789-6211 • Fax (206) 789-3994
http://www.Sakya.org • Monastery@Sakya.org

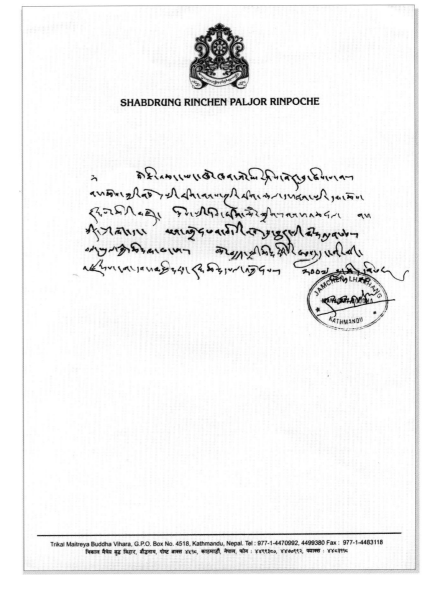

SHABDRUNG RINCHEN PALJOR RINPOCHE

Trikal Maitreya Buddha Vihara, G.P.O. Box No. 4518, Kathmandu, Nepal. Tel : 977-1-4470992, 4499380 Fax : 977-1-4483118

許多大師讚頌多杰羌佛第三世雲高益西諾布和他的佛行事業的書——《正法寶典》，現在國際佛教研究中心準備出版這本書。我非常高興協助世界各地的大師們繼續他們的佛行事業，服務於佛法的教授。

彭措宮H.H.薩迦達欽

藏曆火豬年十一月一日

H.H. Buddha Vajradhara (Dorje Chang) Yangwo Wan Ko Yeshe Norbu:

A Treasury of True Buddha-Dharma blesses living beings, and the perfection in the Five Vidyas that it shows is based on Buddha-dharma realization. That book is the guidepost leading to true Buddha-dharma and the gateway of the dharma leading to benefiting and providing happiness to sentient beings.

H.E. Dharma King Chogye Trichen and
Ven. Shabdrung Rinpoche

January 20, 2007

金剛總持（多杰羌）仰諤雲高益西諾布：

以佛法證量圓滿五明的《正法寶典》加持眾生。該書是正法的路標，和利樂有情之法門。

秋吉崔欽法王
夏勛仁波且

2007年1月20日

111

Congratulations

H.H. Yangwo Wan Ko Yeshe Norbu, the incarnation of Vimalakirti, who is also the third incarnation of Vajradhara, has compiled his accomplishments in the book "A Treasury of True Buddha-Dharma" which manifests the five Vidyas of Buddha-Dharma.

Therefore, on this 21st day of February, 2007, I pass on good wishes to him on all his accomplishments which will benefit sentient beings in some way or the other, as well make prayers for his long life so that he can help in flourishing Buddha Dharma.

Tashi Delek.

Shamarpa Rimpoche

GALINKA HOUSE, HILL TOP ROAD, KALIMPONG-734301 DISTT. DARJEELING, WEST BENGAL, INDIA. TELEPHONE : 91-3552-577-67

The Sangha Duschi of Palchen Chosling Monastery

P.O. Ralang, Lungsim-737139 South Sikkim, India
Tel: 91-353-2200044/2200004 E-mail: palchenchosling@rediffmail.com

祝　賀

尊貴的仰諤雲高益西諾布——維摩聖尊的轉世，即持金剛的第三世，在其《正法寶典》一書中展示了佛法的五明成就。

因此，在此2007年2月21日，我謹對他表達我的良好的祝願，他的所有成就都是利益眾生的，並祈禱他長壽以利弘揚佛法。

扎西德勒！

夏瑪巴仁波且

Congratulations

Incomparable Master H.H. Yangwo Wan Ko:

First, I firmly believe that H.H. Jamyang Lungdok Gyaltsen Achuk, as well as other eminent monks and persons of great virtue within the various sects of snowy Tibet, have recognized Your Holiness as Vimalalakirti II and have recognized Your Holiness as head of the lineage of the venerable reincarnated accomplished ones. Second, I wholeheartedly congratulate Your Holiness on the successful publication of *A Treasury of True Buddha-Dharma*.

Finally, I sincerely wish that seeds leading to Buddhahood and liberation will be planted in the original nature of the multitudinous living beings who have the karmic affinity to read *A Treasury of True Buddha-Dharma* and that such living beings will attain the supreme fruits of perfect enlightenment, omniscience, and Buddhahood!

National Master Gyaltsab
February 15, 2007

賀　詞

無比上師仰諤雲高：

　　首先，本人確信你被阿秋·龍多丹貝加參等雪域各宗派的高僧大德認證為維摩詰第二世，以及追認為成就尊氏的轉世系統。其次，你以佛菩薩法形為主題而成就的《正法寶典》能夠順利出版之際，在下衷心祝賀！

　　最後，在下真誠祈願能有緣見聞覺知《正法寶典》的芸芸眾生的本性中播下成佛解脫之種子，並獲得徹知圓悟的遍智無上佛果！

國師　嘉察巴

2007年2月15日

To the Highest and Holiest Wish-Fulfilling Jewel Dharma King:

I have learned that the book *A Treasury of True Buddha-Dharma* about His Holiness, the supreme and most honored Dorje Chang Buddha III, is about to be distributed around the world. This book is the highest authentic dharma that is of benefit to living beings. Master Dodrupchen is universally recognized as the second Guru Padmasambhava and the highest holy being within Tibetan esoteric Buddhism. He said in his formal congratulations that the accomplishments of Holiest Wan Ko Wish-Fulfilling Jewel Dharma King astounded him, that such accomplishments are unimaginable and truly miraculous, and that such accomplishments transcend the ordinary, expressing both the describable and indescribable absolute truth of the Buddha-dharma.

We shall proclaim and praise the accomplishments of His Holiness throughout the dharma realm. We thank His Holiness, the ancient Buddha, for His boundless and great compassion, for coming to this world again, and for benefiting living beings!

Xiazhu Qiuyang Rinpoche

May 1, 2007

至高頂聖如意寶法王：

　　我得悉無上至尊第三世多杰羌佛您的《正法寶典》將宏世，這是利益眾生的最高正法。被公認為蓮花生大師第二的多智欽大師，身為藏密法承的最高巨聖，在賀函中説：頂聖雲高如意寶法王，其成就令其驚嘆和不可思議，是真正的奇蹟，超常地表現出了用語言能夠表達出來和語言所不能表達出來的佛法真諦。

　　我輩將更加宣頌法界，感謝古佛無量大悲，再來此界，利益眾生！

夏珠秋楊仁波且

2007年5月1日

United International World Buddhism Association Headquarters:

Please convey my respects to H.H. Master Wan Ko Yeshe Norbu!

During a Dharma Assembly held by the International Buddhism Sangha Association at the Hua Zang Si temple in San Francisco, I saw the awe-inspiring and peerless powers and realization of the Master. Bodhi nectar went through the walls of the bowl unhindered as it left and entered the bowl. That nectar can make a person's body change involuntarily in an instant. H.H. Dharma King Wan Ko Yeshe Norbu bestowed upon me that holy bowl. H.H. Dharma King Sakya Trizin; Dharma King Omniscience Jamyang Lungdok Gyaltsen; Lama palchug Ugyen Sherab; Dharma King Renzeng Nima: the Eastren Tibetan Dharma King of the Nyingma sect, Renqing Rongbo Barongbo Rinpoche; the Green Jewel Crown karmapa, Dharma King Jiezhong; and other great, holy and virtuous beings who are on the levels of Buddhas and Mahasattvas unanimously acknowledge that H.H. Wan Ko Yeshe Norbu is the true incarnation of Dorje Chang Buddha (རྡོ་རྗེ་འཆང་），

the Master of the Five Buddhas, and has for the first time in the history of Buddhism in the human realm truly manifested complete proficiency in exoteric and esoteric Buddhism and perfect mastery of the Five Vidyas. This is a goal of Buddhism that all other Buddhists have not been able to achieve. This goal has finally been achieved by H.H. Master Wan Ko Yeshe Norbu. This is an honor to Buddhism and a blessing to living beings.

May the seven types of Buddhist disciples hear the true dharma taught by H.H. Great Dharma King Wan Ko Yeshe Norbu, and may they soon realize enlightenment!

I respectfully offer my congratulations!

26/12/2006

The 16th Thangtrul Rinpoche

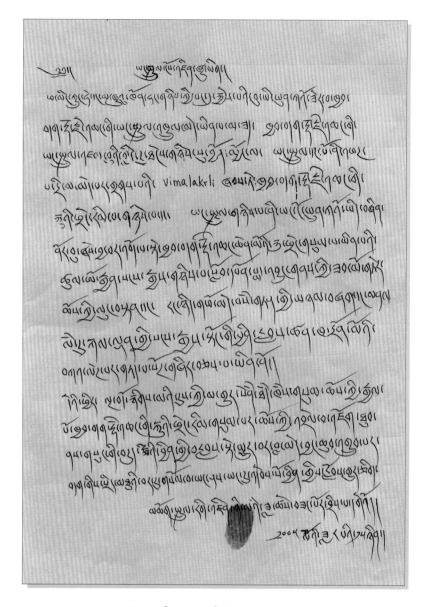

Certificate of Recognition

In accordance with the Terma Dharma of the Urgyen second Buddha, Guru Padmasambhava, I entered samadhi and received the empowerment of countless Buddhas of the Fortunate Age. I saw that H.H. Master Wan Ko Yee, who is the son of father Zhonghai Yee and mother Kunfang Xu, is the true incarnation of Dorje Chang Buddha. Dorje Chang Buddha has incarnated in this world two times: The first incarnation was Dorje Chang Buddha II, the holy and venerable Vimalakirti. The second incarnation is H.H. Dorje Chang Buddha III Wan Ko Yeshe Norbu.

May all living beings be benefited by the dharma teachings of the greatest leader of Buddhism in the dharmadhatu, H.H. Dorje Chang Buddha III, and may they thereby soon become Buddhas.

Renzeng Nima

August 15, 2005

聯合國際世界佛教總部：

請轉達我對雲高益西諾布大師的敬意！

在舊金山華藏寺國際佛教僧尼總會舉行的法會上，我見到了大師的無與倫比的威力和證量。菩提甘露自由無礙的穿過法缽，這個甘露可以讓人的身體馬上不由自主的改變。雲高益西諾布大法王降這個聖缽加持給了我。薩迦天津法王、遍智法王降養龍多加參、鄔堅喜饒喔修喇嘛、仁增尼瑪法王、寧瑪東藏法王仁青絨波巴絨波仁波且、噶瑪巴綠寶冠杰仲法王等一些佛菩薩級的大聖者一致公認雲高益西諾布是真正的五佛之師——多杰羌佛轉世再來，並且在人類的佛史上第一次展顯了顯密圓通、妙諳五明，這個佛教的目標是所有佛弟子都沒有達到的，但現在最終由雲高益西諾布達到了！這是佛教的光榮，也是對眾生的加持！

願七眾弟子得聞雲高益西諾布大法王的正法，速得解脫！

特此恭賀！

第十六世唐東迦波仁波且

2006年12月26日

認證書

根據烏金第二佛陀蓮花生大師掘藏法，於三昧定中受賢劫千佛加持，得見父親為義仲海、母親為許坤芳的兒子義雲高大師為多杰羌佛真身降世。多杰羌佛降這個世界兩次：第一次降世即是多杰羌佛第二世維摩詰聖尊，第二次降世即是多杰羌佛第三世雲高益西諾布。

祈願一切眾生得到法界大教主三世多杰羌的法緣沐浴，早證菩提。

仁增尼瑪

2005年8月15日

རྟེན་འབྲེལ་ཞུ་ཚིག

ཁྱབ་བདག་རྡོ་རྗེ་འཆང་ཆེན་གྱི་ཞབས་དྲུང་ལ་སྐོར་གསུམ་གུས་པའི་ཕྱག་འཚལ་ལོ།།

ཕྱོགས་བཅུ་ན་བཞུགས་པའི་སངས་རྒྱས་དང་བྱང་ཆུབ་སེམས་དཔའ་ཐམས་ཅད་ཀྱི་ཐུགས་བསྐྱེད་སྨོན་ལམ་གྱི་སྟོབས་ཀྱིས་ལྔ་བདོ་སྙིགས་མའི་འགྲོ་བའི་རྒྱུད་ཀྱི་མ་རིག་པའི་མུན་པ་རྩ་བ་ནས་སེལ་བའི་སྐོ་སྐལ་ཡོངས་སུ་སྨིན་ཏེ། ཅིའི་ཕྱིར་ཞེ་ན། ཡང་རྡོ་ཡུན་ཀའོ་ཡིད་བཞིན་ནོར་བུ་ཉིད་ཀྱིས་སྐུ་ཚེ་གང་པོར་ཐོས་བསམ་དང་ཉམས་ལེན་བརྒྱུད་དེ་བརྩམས་གནང་མཛད་པའི་མདོ་སྔགས་གཞུང་ལུགས་ཐམས་ཅད་འདུས་པའི་བསྟན་བཅོས་ཆེན་མོ་སྟེ 《དམ་ཆོས་རིན་པོ་ཆེའི་གཏེར་མཛོད》 ཞེས་བྱ་བ་ཉེ་ཆར་དངོས་སུ་པར་བསྐྲུན་གནང་ནས་འགྲེམས་སྤེལ་བྱས་ཟིན་པས་ན། གསུང་རབ་བསྟན་བཅོས་རིན་པོ་ཆེ་འདི་བརྒྱུད་དེ་སྙིགས་མའི་འགྲོ་བ་ཅི་སྙེད་ཀྱི་མ་རིག་པའི་རྒྱུན་ཐག་རྩ་བ་ནས་བཅད་དེ་རྣམ་པར་ཐམས་ཅད་མཁྱེན་པའི་ཞིང་ཁམས་སུ་འགོད་པར་བདག་ཅག་གིས་བཀྲ་ཤིས་རྟེན་འབྲེལ་དང་བཅས་ཏེ་ཡང་ནས་ཡང་དུ་གསོལ་བ་འདེབས་སོ་བྱིན་གྱིས་རློབས།།

ཕྱག་ན་རྡོ་རྗེ་འཆང་བའི་མི་འགྱུར་སྐུ།།
འགྲོ་ཀུན་དམིགས་མེད་སྙོམ་པའི་ཐུགས་རྗེ་གཏེར།།
དུས་གསུམ་རྗེན་པར་གཟིགས་པའི་མཁྱེན་རྩལ་ཅན།།
རིགས་དྲུག་མ་ལུས་འདྲེན་པར་གསོལ་བ་འདེབས།།

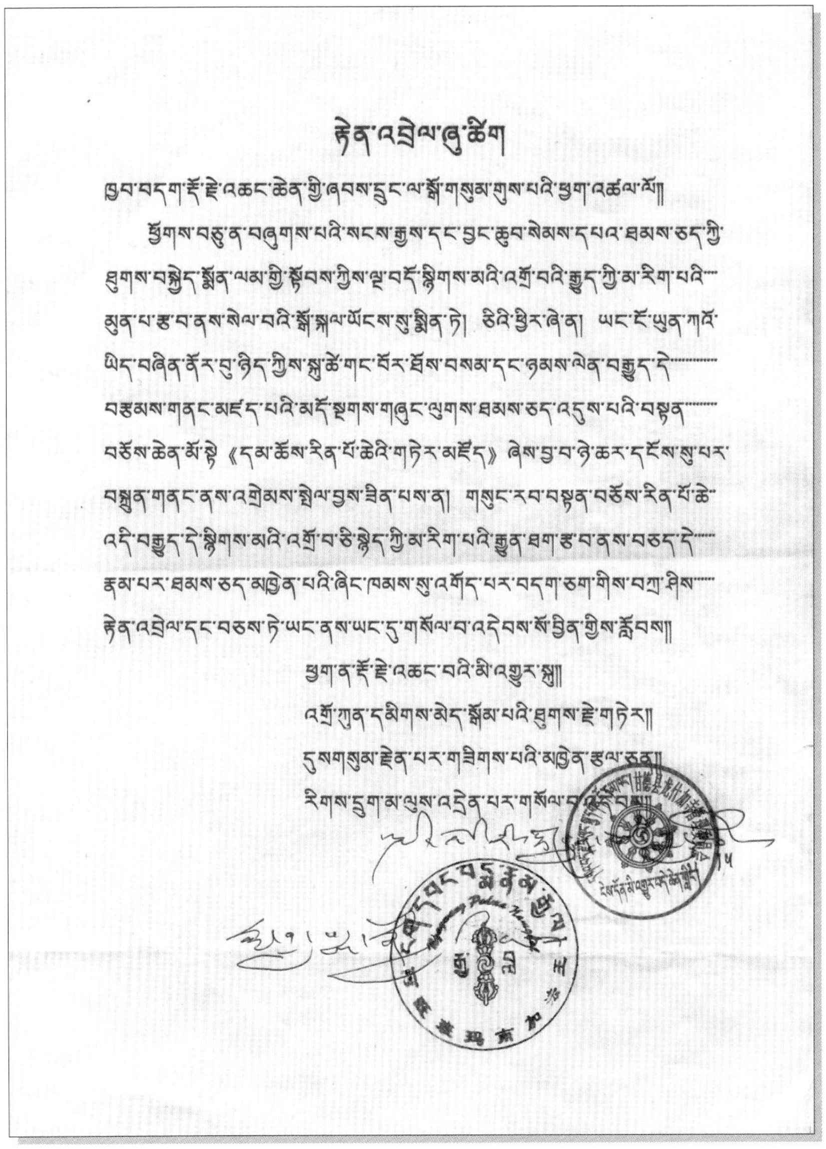

Respectful Congratulations

I prostrate to and circumambulate Buddha Vajradhara three times!

The karmic conditions of countless living beings have matured. The compassion of this Buddha has transformed into teachings on exoteric and esoteric Buddhism. The teachings contained in *A Treasury of True Buddha-Dharma* shine forth with the brilliant rays of His Holiness's great compassion and wisdom. With pure body, speech, and mind, I convey the following invocation: May the dharma protectors in the ten directions protect and bless. May all go well with living beings. May they soon hear the true dharma. To attain liberation from the cycle of birth and death, may living beings avail themselves of the karmic conditions under which H.H. Dojre Chang Buddha Wan Ko Yeshe Norbu now lives in the world.

Together we praise!

The body and lifespan of the Buddha Vajradhara of the dharma realm never comes to an end.
His Holiness manifests Mahayana states and has the most wondrous powers of great compassion.
His Holiness perfectly possesses exoteric and esoteric dharma.
Thus, His Holiness is the flawless protector of sentient beings.
His Holiness boundlessly liberates living beings.
His Holiness's will to draw living beings to liberation is eternal, unchanging, and firm.

I hereby specially offer my respectful praise!

Dharma King Ngagwang Pedma Namgyal Palzangpo

Nov. 15, 2006

敬　賀

繞匝金剛總持禮三匝！

無邊眾生因緣成熟了，佛陀的悲憫化成顯教、密教的教法，在《正法寶典》中放出大悲智慧的光芒，我致以身口意淨潔的祈請，願十方護法護佑，眾生萬事順意，早聞正法，隨多杰羌佛雲高益西諾布住世的因緣而得到了生脫死。

合頌！

法界持金剛，身壽不變故，
化顯上乘境，最勝大悲力，
顯密二資法，圓成護有情，
無邊解脫眾，攝化恒堅固。
特此敬賀！

阿旺班瑪南加法王

2006年11月15日

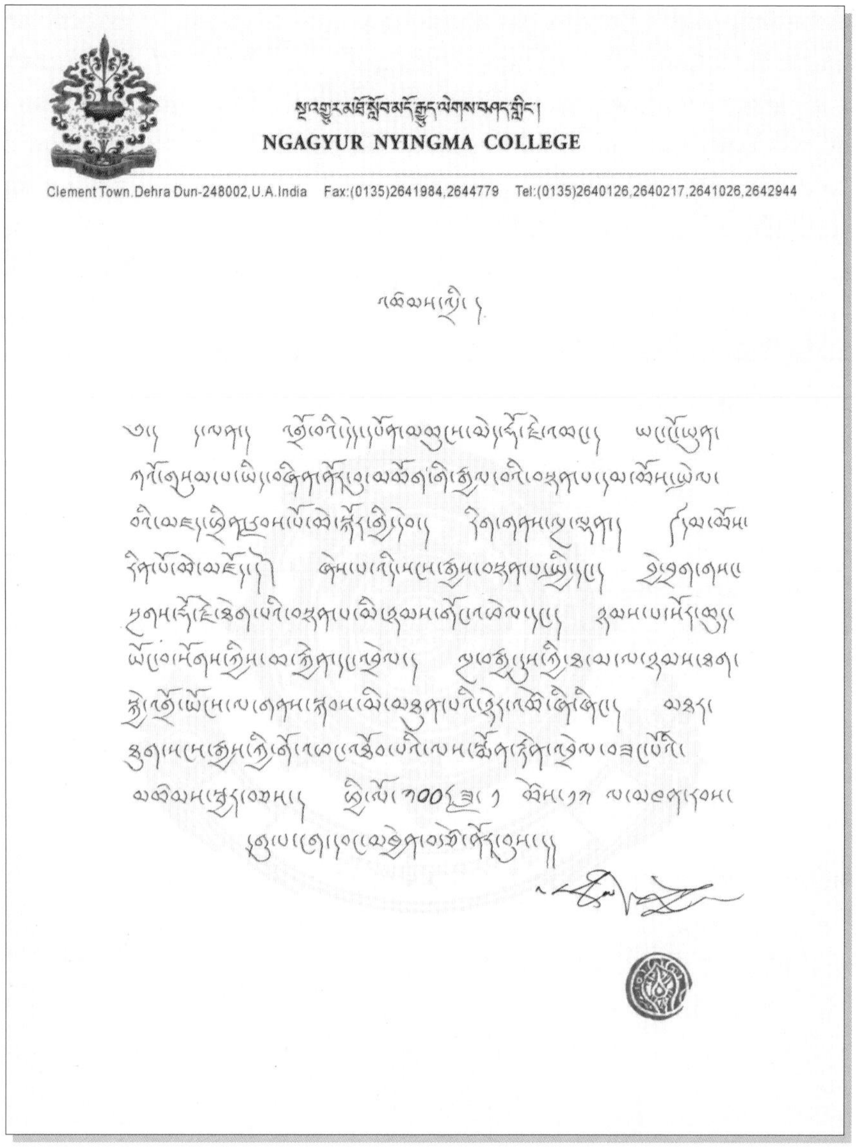

 སྔ་འགྱུར་མཐོ་སློབ་ནོར་རྒྱུན་ལེགས་བཤད་གླིང་།
NGAGYUR NYINGMA COLLEGE

Clement Town, Dehra Dun-248002, U.A.India   Fax:(0135)2641984,2644779   Tel:(0135)2640126,2640217,2641026,2642944

 འཆལ་པ་ཀྱི།

[Tibetan text block]

CONGRATULATORY LETTER

His Holiness Buddha Vajradhara III Yangwo Wan Ko Yeshe Norbu has magnificently spread the Buddha-dharma. *A Treasury of True Buddha-Dharma* manifests perfect mastery of the Five Vidyas. It will cause the Buddha-dharma and especially the Vajrayana dharma to flourish. It will restore dharma that had faded and will cause the growth of dharma that has not yet faded. In these last five hundred years of the Dharma-Ending Age, it will allay all of the disasters of living beings who are in the midst of suffering. It will even cause living beings to realize the ultimate fruit of Buddhahood. May all living beings have such wonderful karmic conditions!

Khenchen IX Awang Khyentse Norbu
January 12, 2008

祝　　賀

尊貴的金剛總持第三世仰諤雲高益西諾布，偉大事業弘揚佛法。展現妙諤五明的《正法寶典》將順緣於佛法及特別金剛密乘法興盛，已衰者令恢復，未衰者令增長，於佛法最後五百年末法時，平息苦難之中眾生一切逆緣災害，乃至現前究竟佛果，祝禱具足殊勝善緣！

第九世堪欽昂旺欽則諾布
2008年1月12日

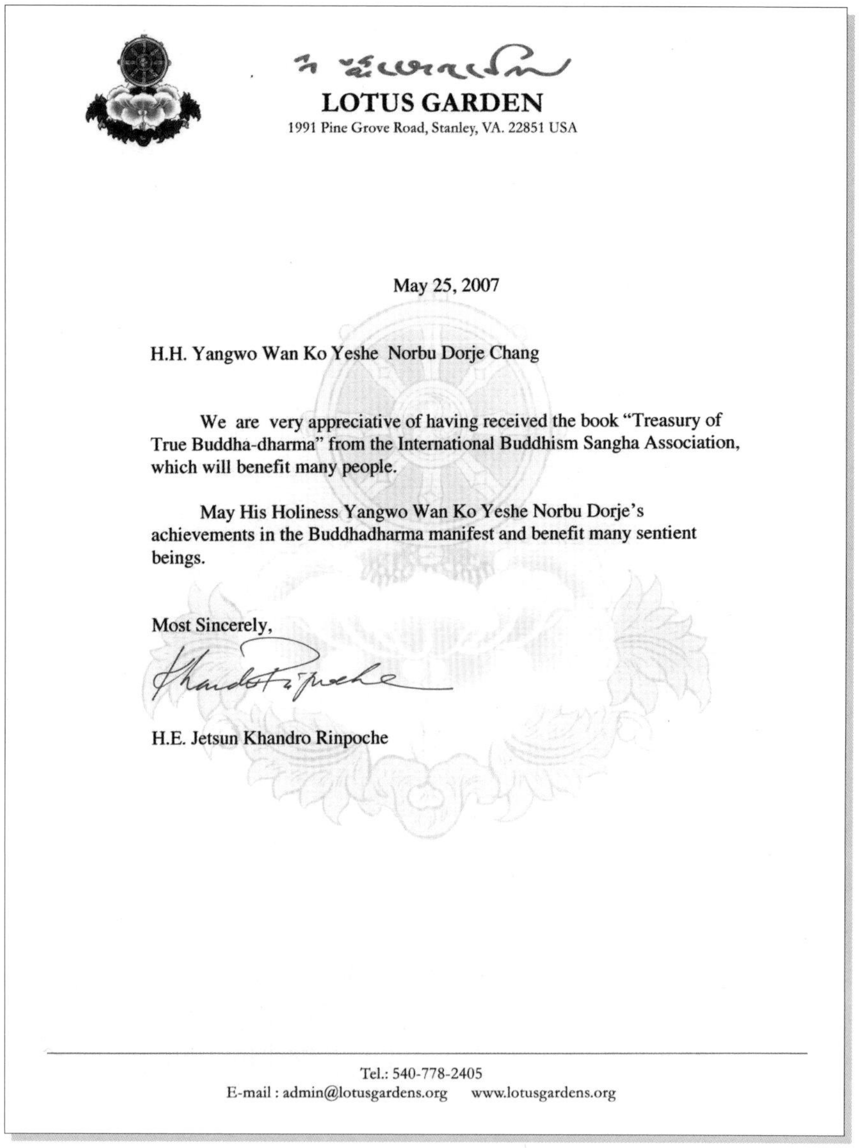

ཉི་ཟླ་ཡར་འཕེལ
LOTUS GARDEN
1991 Pine Grove Road, Stanley, VA. 22851 USA

May 25, 2007

H.H. Yangwo Wan Ko Yeshe Norbu Dorje Chang

We are very appreciative of having received the book "Treasury of True Buddha-dharma" from the International Buddhism Sangha Association, which will benefit many people.

May His Holiness Yangwo Wan Ko Yeshe Norbu Dorje's achievements in the Buddhadharma manifest and benefit many sentient beings.

Most Sincerely,

H.E. Jetsun Khandro Rinpoche

Tel.: 540-778-2405
E-mail : admin@lotusgardens.org   www.lotusgardens.org

尊聖的仰諤雲高益西諾布多杰羌佛：

我們非常感激從國際佛教僧尼總會得到這本將利益許多人的《正法寶典》。

祝願尊聖的仰諤雲高如意寶法王金剛佛法上的成就展顯和利益更多的眾生。

最誠摯的
康卓仁波且
2007年5月25日

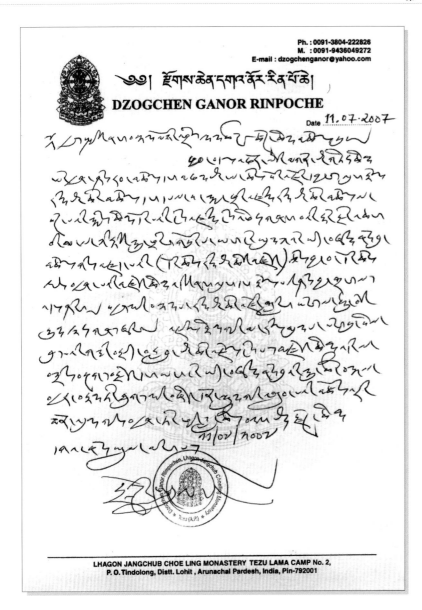

Ph. : 0091-3804-222826
M. : 0091-9436049272
E-mail : dzogchenganor@yahoo.com

DZOGCHEN GANOR RINPOCHE

Date 11.07.2007

LHAGON JANGCHUB CHOE LING MONASTERY TEZU LAMA CAMP No. 2,
P. O. Tindolong, Distt. Lohit , Arunachal Pardesh, India, Pin-792001

CONGRATULATIONS

United International World Buddhism Association Headquarters:

The great terton Urgyen Xirao, Achuk Jamyang Lungdok Rinpoche, Sakya Trizin Rinpoche, and many other eminent monastics and persons of great virtue have recognized Buddha Vajradhara III Yangwo Wan Ko Yeshe Norbu, the supreme Buddha. The book *A Treasury of True Buddha-Dharma* about the personal accomplishments of H.H. Yangwo Wan Ko Yeshe Norbu, the main content of which is the 84,000 dharma methods, has majestically brightened the treasury of Buddha-dharma. The content of that book contains the limitless state of knowledge resulting from the two dharmas of realization and enlightenment. Thus, I offer my congratulations because *A Treasury of True Buddha-Dharma* is the wish-fulfilling true dharma that the Buddha expounded. This true dharma will flow through Jambudvipa for countless eons, like the great and ever-rolling Ganges River, and will wash away the source of ignorance that is in the minds of sentient beings in the three spheres.

Finally, may H.H. Yangwo Wan Ko Yeshe Norbu forever live in the world, pervasively spread the dharma, and continue to benefit and bring happiness to living beings. May His Holiness quickly realize His great aspiration that all living beings become Buddhas!

I hereby specially convey my respectful congratulations!

Dzogchen Ganor Rinpoche
Written on the auspicious day of
Nov. 7, 2007

賀　詞

聯合國際世界佛教總部：

遍主寶藏輪・大伏藏師鄔堅喜饒和阿秋堪布・降養龍多仁波且、薩迦天津仁波且等眾高僧大德認證的第三世金剛總持・布瑪辣格德・仰諤雲高益西諾布親著的《正法寶典》系以八萬四千法門為主的內容莊嚴地明了佛法之寶庫，本書內容涵蓋了證悟二法概括的無量所知境。故此，本人祝賀《正法寶典》具足佛陀開示之如意正法猶如滾滾恒河大江無量之劫涌流南瞻布洲，並圓滿成就洗滌三界有情心續的無明之源。

最後，祈願仰諤雲高益西諾布常駐世間，廣轉法輪，利樂眾生，速成菩提宏願！

特此恭賀！

佐欽・噶諾仁波且
寫於二○○七年十一月七日吉祥之日

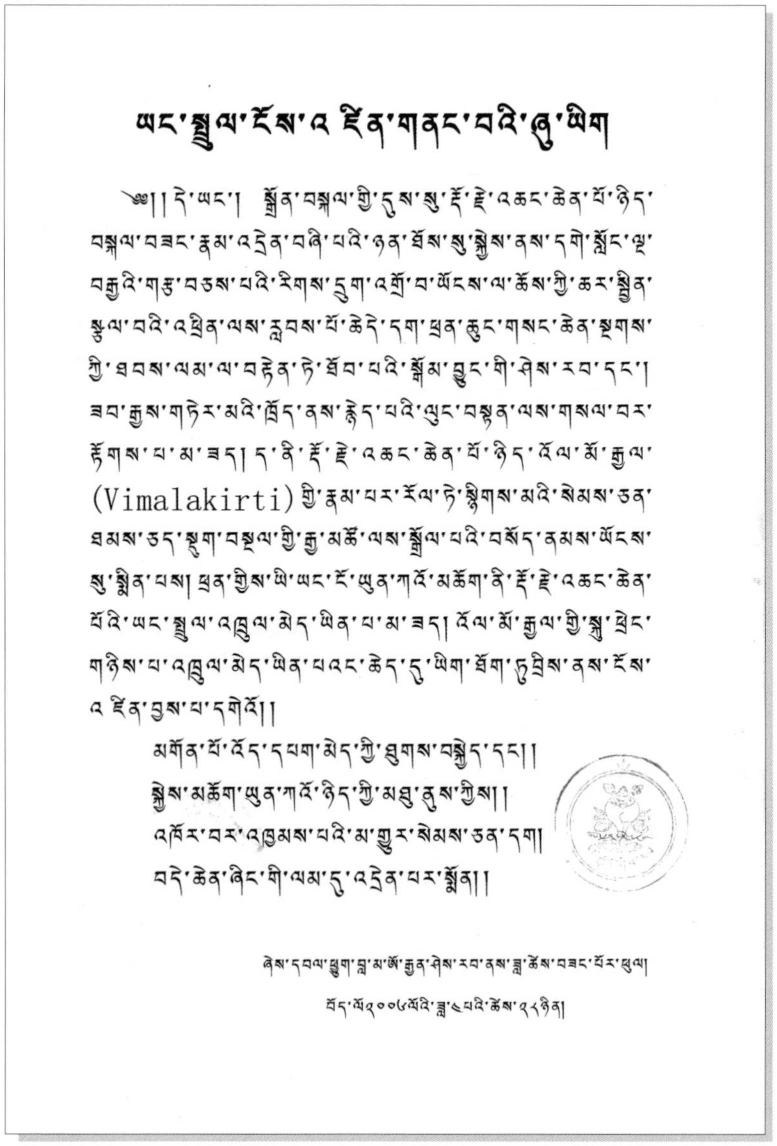

ཡང་སྐུལ་རོ�ས་འ �ོན་གནང་བའི་ཤུ་ཡིག

༄༅།། དེ་ཡང་། སྐྱོན་བ�ལ་ཀྱི་དུས་སུ་�ོ་�ེ་འཆང་ཆེན་པོ་ཉིད་
བསྐལ་བཟང་ནམ་འ�ེན་པའི་པ་འ་ནུན་པོས་སུ་སྤྱེན་ནས་དགེ་སློང་ལྔ་
བ�འི་གནས་པའི་རིགས་དུག་འ�ོ་བ་ོ�ས་ལ་ཆོས་ཀྱི་ཆར་སྤྱིལ་
ᄎᄅ་བའི་འ�ིན་ལས་�ལས་པོ་ཆེ་དི་�ན་ᄎᄅᄃ་གᄉᄃ་ᄎᄅᄀᄉ་
ᄀᄉ་ᄣᄇᄉ་ᄀᄉᄆ་ᄝᄃᄌᄄᄅᄃᄇᄦᄉᄣᄉᄉᄃᄃᄅᄄᄅᄂᄃ
ᄌᄅᄀᄅᄂᄀᄀᄀᄉᄁᄉᄄᄀᄀᄆᄆᄉᄄᄅᄁᄃᄀᄆᄅ
ᄎᄀᄉᄆᄆᄃᄇᄃᄅᄃᄀᄄᄅ
(Vimalakirti) ᄀᄀᄉᄆᄄᄇᄉᄄᄅᄀᄉᄆᄆᄉᄁᄉ
ᄆᄆᄉᄄᄅᄀᄆᄉᄁᄅᄆᄅᄇᄉᄆᄃᄂᄄ
ᄉᄀᄅᄉᄆᄀᄀᄉᄆᄆᄅᄆᄉᄀᄆᄂ
ᄆᄃᄀᄆᄇᄃᄅᄅᄀᄅᄄᄀᄆᄅᄃᄆᄇᄂ
ᄀᄃᄅᄆᄀᄆᄄᄅᄀᄆᄅᄀᄆᄉᄀᄉᄄᄅᄉᄅᄆᄆᄅᄄᄃᄅ
ᄇᄃᄉᄄᄅᄀᄅᄂ

ᄆᄀᄉᄉᄅᄄᄆᄅᄀᄀᄀᄄᄆᄂᄄᄃ
ᄆᄆᄉᄆᄃᄀᄄᄅᄀᄆᄅᄀᄆᄂᄄᄆᄄᄆᄂ
ᄆᄀᄆᄀᄆᄆᄆᄇᄉᄆᄃᄉᄄᄆᄂ
ᄆᄃᄆᄃᄀᄀᄄᄅᄀᄉᄄᄂ

ᄉᄉᄃᄆᄀᄆᄆᄉᄆᄆᄀᄆᄆᄀᄆᄆᄉᄆᄆᄂ
ᄆᄃᄆᄀᄆᄆᄄᄅ

Certificate of Affirmation

Through practicing the dharma and entering meditation, I penetrated deeply into the Great Terma (Hidden Treasure) Dharma and applied supernatural vision. The karmic conditions manifested. I came to know that the Buddha Vajradhara assisted Sakyamuni Buddha in teaching the five hundred monks and other holy ones. As a skillful means of doing this, the Buddha Vajradhara transformed Himself into Vimalakirti. I supernaturally saw that H.H. Master Wan Ko Yee, Yangwo Wan Ko Yeshe Norbu, is the incarnation of Buddha Vajradhara. That is, His Holiness is unmistakably Vimalakirti II. I specially issue this certificate affirming the above.

I respectfully prostrate to the Buddhas!
I respectfully prostrate to H.H. Yangwo Wan Ko Yeshe Norbu!
His Holiness has been liberating living beings and bringing about great happiness!

Urgyen Xirao Woxiu Lama

Twenty-eighth day of the fourth month, 2006, according to the Tibetan calendar

確　認　書

我經過修法入定，深入大伏藏法觀照，得到因緣示現，了知金剛總持(ᄎᄅᄀᄉ)幫助釋迦佛陀教化五百比丘等聖者，而為了方便，金剛總持(ᄎᄅᄀᄉ)化身為維摩詰（Vimalakirti）。我神通看到義雲高大師仰諤雲高益西諾布，是金剛總持(ᄎᄅᄀᄉ)轉世再來，也就是維摩詰（Vimalakirti）第二世無誤，特此確認。

南無諸佛！
南無仰諤雲高益西諾布！
度脫眾生大吉祥！

鄔堅喜饒喔修喇嘛

藏曆2006年4月28日

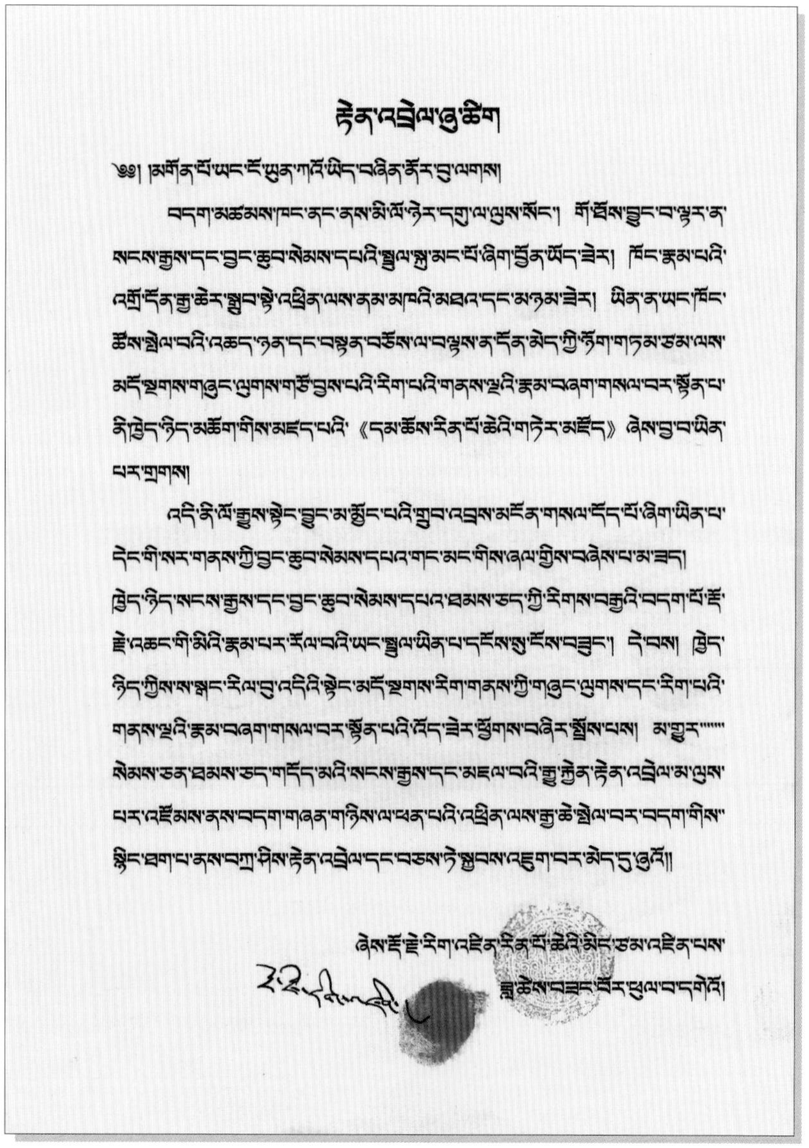

�ེན་འ�ེལ་ཤུ་ཡིག

༄༅།། མགོན་པོ་ཡང་རོ�ས་གངི་ཡིན་འཛིན་ᄎᄅᄉᄀᄆᄂ
ᄃᄀᄉᄆᄃᄀᄃᄀᄇᄉᄆᄀᄆᄇᄉᄆᄀᄃᄂ ᄀᄆᄉᄄᄃᄀᄀᄂ
ᄇᄃᄀᄆᄃᄃᄀᄄᄀᄆᄆᄄᄅᄀᄆᄉᄆᄀᄃᄀᄃᄀᄃ ᄀᄃᄀᄆᄂ
ᄆᄀᄆᄉᄄᄆᄆᄆᄉᄆᄉᄆᄆᄄᄀᄆᄂ ᄆᄀᄃᄀᄂ
ᄎᄀᄆᄉᄆᄃᄀᄇᄃᄇᄆᄆᄆᄆᄆᄆᄆᄆᄄᄅᄀᄆᄂ
ᄆᄀᄆᄉᄆᄆᄄᄅᄀᄆᄃᄆᄆᄆᄀᄆᄅᄀ《ᄃᄆᄆᄆᄆᄆᄆ》ᄆᄆᄆ
ᄆᄆᄆᄂ

ᄆᄀᄆᄀᄆᄆᄆᄆᄆᄆᄆᄆᄆᄆᄆᄆᄆᄆᄆᄆᄆᄂ
ᄆᄀᄆᄂᄀᄆᄉᄆᄆᄆᄆᄆᄆᄆᄆᄆᄆᄆᄆᄂ
ᄆᄆᄀᄆᄆᄆᄀᄆᄆᄆᄆᄆᄆᄆᄆᄆᄆᄂ
ᄆᄆᄀᄆᄆᄆᄆᄆᄆᄆᄆᄆᄆᄆᄆᄆᄂ
ᄆᄀᄆᄆᄆᄆᄆᄆᄆᄆᄆᄆᄆᄆᄂ
ᄆᄀᄆᄆᄆᄆᄆᄆᄆᄆᄆᄆᄆᄆᄆᄂ
ᄆᄀᄆᄆᄆᄆᄆᄆᄆᄆᄆᄆᄂ
ᄆᄆᄆᄆᄆᄆᄆᄆᄆᄆᄆᄆᄂ

ᄆᄆᄆᄆᄆᄆᄆᄆᄆᄆᄆᄆᄆᄆᄆᄆᄂ

Ancient Buddha H.H. Wan Ko Yeshe Norbu:

I have lived in a solitary retreat room for twenty-nine years. It is said that many Buddhas and Bodhisattvas have incarnated in our world. They pervasively benefit living beings and their merit is boundless. However, most of them can only speak empty words when it comes to manifesting the Five Vidyas. No other Buddha or Bodhisattva has attained the accomplishments contained in *A Treasury of True Buddha-Dharma*. Such accomplishments have never been seen before in history. Holy beings of great virtue have confirmed that such accomplishments are those of H.H. Dorje Chang Buddha Wan Ko Yeshe Norbu, the Master of the Five Buddhas. This highest leader of Buddhism in the dharmadhatu has manifested here on earth a state of great brightness that entails complete proficiency in exoteric and esoteric Buddhism and perfect mastery of the Five Vidyas. Thus, I congratulate all living beings for having the karmic affinity to encounter the ancient Buddha. May they attain enlightenment first and benefit others.

Dorje Rinzin Rinpoche

respectfully offers congratulations on this auspicious day

怙主雲高益西諾布：

我在關房中住了29年了，據說很多佛菩薩轉世來了，他們普利眾生，功德無量，但是五明的展顯空洞言辭的較多，《正法寶典》上的成就我看沒有哪一位做到過，這是歷史上沒有過的成就，大德們證明了這是五佛的上師多杰羌佛雲高益西諾布，因此這位法界大教主在地球上展顯了顯密圓通、妙語五明的大光明境。為此，我祝賀一切眾生正逢古佛因緣，度己利他。

多杰仁增仁波且

於吉祥之日　敬賀

Shechen Rabjam Rinpoche
Ngawang Chopal Gyatso

CONGRATULATORY LETTER

To all living beings within Buddhism, who are our relatives and friends: H.H. Dorje Chang Buddha III Yangwo Wan Ko Yeshe Norbu, the Wish-Fulfilling Jewel Holy One, has taken action that spreads and makes grander the true Buddha-dharma. How wonderful! Thus, I specially send this congratulatory letter. The book *A Treasury of True Buddha-Dharma*, which shows mastery of the Five Vidyas, is like countless brilliant lights in a rare holy world, illuminating our world, benefiting living beings, and providing happiness to living beings. The good reputation of this book will spread among those who learn Buddhism around the world. His Holiness has achieved a level of mastery of all Five Vidyas, including painting and calligraphy, never attained by any of the ancients. Even persons of great virtue have never seen the accomplishments contained in this precious book. May all who have the karmic affinity to read it become accomplished in the dharma, attain the great and unhindered mind, and realize the truth.

Shechen VII Rijianba Angwangquebei Gyatso
October 22, 2007

賀　函

佛教眾生諸親友，第三世多杰羌佛仰諤雲高如意寶聖者，為正法增長宏大而行，善哉！特致函祝賀，五明具備典籍——《正法寶典》，如稀有聖地千光耀明，利樂眾生，國內外學眾，名聲散播增長，五明總支工巧明中畫寫法，前無古人，為大德善知識得到，都是從來沒有見過的珍品，凡有緣者，獲得成就，意大無礙，緣生真實。

雪謙第七熱堅巴昂旺卻貝嘉措

2007年10月22日

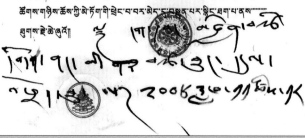

CONGRATULATIONS

Greatest leader of Buddhism, H.H. Wan Ko Yeshe Norbu:

With extreme happiness, I sincerely convey my utmost respect and praise for the descent of the ancient Buddha into this world! This is the good fortune of all living beings. The one book *A Treasury of True Buddha-Dharma* is enough to provide living beings with endless benefits. The ways to liberation are all in this book! Only the wisdom of the ancient Buddha, Dorje Chang Buddha, could produce such a textbook that enables people to understand and directly realize the Buddha-dharma!

I thank H.H. Dorje Chang Buddha III Wan Ko Yeshe Norbu for giving living beings such a source of good fortune and wisdom!

Angwang Khyentse Rinpoche

November 18, 2006

祝　賀

大教主雲高益西諾布：

我非常高興並真誠地致以最崇高的敬意，讚嘆怙主降臨此世界！這是所有眾生的福報，就《正法寶典》一書已夠眾生受用無窮了，得到解脫盡在其中！也只有怙主多杰羌佛的智慧才能完成這樣一本讓人們體證佛法的教科書！

感謝多杰羌佛第三世雲高益西諾布帶給眾生的福慧資糧！

昂旺欽哲仁波且

2006年11月18日

Dzogchen Shri Senha Charitable Society

3rd September, 2007

We are very appreciative to have received the book "A Treasury of True Buddha Dharma" from the International Buddhism Sangha Association which recounts the accomplishments of His Holiness Yangwo Wan Ko Yeshe Norbu Dorje Chang.

Through its publication, "A Treasury of True Buddha Dharma" brings benefit to all sentient beings particularly during these degenerate times. Reading this book will plant the seed of everlasting peace in whoever reads it.

The 7th Dzogchen Rinpoche,
Jigme Losel Wangpo

Registered under the Karnataka Act 1960 – Reg. No. 37/95-96
PO Tibetan Settlement, Kollegal Taluk, Chamrajnagar District, Karnataka 571 457, INDIA
Tel: +91(0)8224 23777 Fax: +91(0)8224 22498 email: dzogchen@blr.vsnl.net.in

我們非常感謝「國際佛教僧尼總會」所贈予的多杰羌仰諤雲高益西諾布陛下的成就集《正法寶典》一書。

　　《正法寶典》的出版特別能在此末法時期利益所有有情眾生。無論是誰閱讀此書都會種下永恆和平的種子。

第七世佐欽 仁波且
吉美 洛桑 汪波
2007-09-03

西康佐欽大圓滿寺
Dzogchen Monastery of Great Perfection

地址：四川省甘孜州德格县佐钦寺　邮编：627252　网址：www.zuoqinsi.org

CONGRATULATIONS

The book *A Treasury of True Buddha-Dharma* about the ancient Buddha of sentient beings in the three spheres of existence, H.H. Dharma King Yangwo Wan Ko Yeshe Norbu, is like the most precious Wish-Fulfilling Jewel in that it outshines all ancient or modern, Chinese or non-Chinese books. Additionally, the book includes wonderful content on the three aspects of correct views, self-cultivation, and realization relating to both exoteric and esoteric Buddha-dharma. In this modern age, such wonderful content is indispensable for building a harmonious world of peace in which people benefit one another. In the book, paintings and art are used in an ingenious way to express the beauty and grandeur of nature. The book also opens up and develops the spiritual wisdom of people. Thus, I specially offer my congratulations on the propagation of *A Treasury of True Buddha-Dharma.*

May all be perfectly auspicious!

Dzogchen Great Perfection Monastery,
a great monastery of the old Nyingma tradition

The 7th Dzogchen Dharma King of Great Accomplishment,
Tenzin Lungdok Nyima

The 27th day of the third month of the lunar calendar in the year
of the Fire Pig according to the Tibetan calendar

賀　詞

　　三界有情古佛仰諤雲高益西諾布法王的《正法寶典》猶如如意至寶般莊嚴古今中外所有文化典籍，同時它具有：新時代、為創建和平與利他的和諧世界不可或缺的佛法顯密二乘的見、修、行三方面的殊勝內容。在書中巧妙應用繪圖藝術表現大自然的壯美景觀，並開發和增長人類心靈的智慧之門。故此，本人特此祝賀《正法寶典》一書的宏世。

　　祈願！
　　吉祥善哉！

舊譯寧瑪派大寺佐欽大圓滿寺
第七世達成就自在佐欽法王・旦增龍多尼瑪
藏曆火豬年農曆3月27日

RESPECTFUL PRAISE

I congratulate H.H. Master Wan Ko for exhibiting the magnificent power of great compassion and bodhi. The Master is the magnificent sambhogakaya Buddha who has descended to the human world again, who teaches the authentic Buddha-dharma, and who liberates living beings. I, an ordinary monk, thus offer my reverence and respectful praise. This is the first time since the teachings of Buddhism have been propagated that such accomplishments have been seen. His Holiness's accomplishments are unprecedented in this world and reflect the pinnacle of wisdom. May H.H. Dorje Chang Buddha boundlessly save living beings, and may *A Treasury of True Buddha-Dharma* exist forever!

I respectfully prostrate to H.H. Wan Ko Yeshe Norbu!

I hereby offer my special congratulations!

Renqing Rongbo Barongbo Rinpoche
December 1, 2006

禮　讚

恭祝雲高大師大悲菩提威力的展示，大師作為偉大報身佛陀再降人間，法浴眾生，我今以慚愧比丘之身就此禮敬，歌頌敬讚，佛教宏法以來，今開眼初見，世界無雙，智慧高峰，多杰羌佛，渡生無量，《正法寶典》，萬古長存！

南無雲高益西諾布！

特此恭祝！

仁青絨波巴絨波仁波且
2006年12月1日

I prostrate to the Buddha Vajradhara, H.H. Yangwo Wan Ko Yeshe Norbu:

A Treasury of True Buddha-Dharma about the Buddha Vajradhara is a concrete expression of the highest Buddha-dharma wisdom and abilities. Out of compassion, H.H. Great Dharma King has given discourses on the dharma that have allowed living beings to understand all ultimate truths of the universe. His Holiness teaches wonderful and suitable dharma methods whereby one can become a holy being of great accomplishment in the dharma in this very lifetime. *A Treasury of True Buddha-Dharma* contains the traditional Tibetan sciences of the Five Vidyas based mainly upon the Five Great Treatises of exoteric Buddhism and the perfect dharma of the Four Division of Yoga of esoteric Buddhism. This book allows all sentient beings living in this Dharma-Ending Age to personally realize the highest and ultimate fruit of great wisdom attained through Buddhism.

We who practice Buddhism will use H.H. Great Dharma King's teachings on the dharma as our standard, will devoutly and respectfully practice such teachings, and will reach the goals stated in such teachings in order to save sentient beings in the sea of suffering.

We pray that the Buddhas, Bodhisattvas, and venerable Dharma Protecting Deities in the Three Spheres will protect and bless H.H. Great Dharma King so that His Holiness may forever abide in peace and health, forever teach the dharma, and forever benefit and bring happiness to the countless living beings!

Jiezhong Danbei Jiancan
June 15, 2006

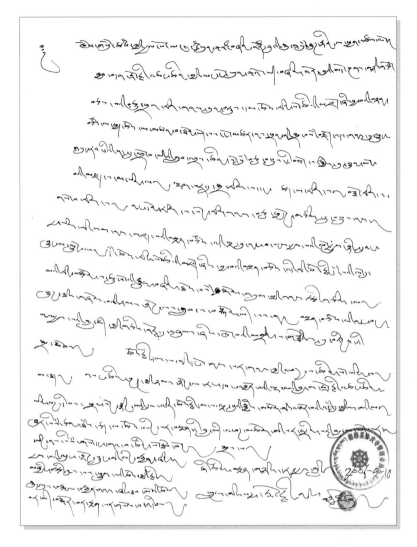

頂禮金剛總持仰諤雲高益西諾布：

金剛總持的《正法寶典》，乃是佛法最高智能的具體顯現。

大法王以慈悲為懷，所開示的法音，讓眾生明了宇宙萬物的終極真理；所傳授的則是即生成佛的殊勝方便法門。故此，在《正法寶典》中所涵蓋的是顯宗五部大論和密乘四續為主的藏族傳統五明學科，讓末法時代的一切有情眾生親身體驗佛教的最終極智能成果。

我等修佛之徒將以大法王的開示教導為宗旨，引渡苦海中的有情而虔心敬修！

祈願三界佛菩薩和護法尊神護佑大法王永駐安康，長轉法輪，利樂芸芸眾生！

杰仲・丹貝堅參
2006年6月15日

I respectfully honor the Three Bodies and Four Wisdoms of the Dharma King of the Three Spheres, H.H. Yangwo Wan Ko Yeshe Norbu:

We were fortunate to be able to read the book about the Buddha Vajradhara Dharma King, *A Treasury of True Buddha-Dharma— A Collection of H.H. Yangwo Wan Ko Yeshe Norbu's Accomplishments Manifesting Complete Proficiency in Exoteric and Esoteric Buddhism and Perfect Mastery of the Five Vidyas.* We cannot describe how deeply astonished and moved we were. Those thirty main categories of accomplishments present a splendid sight that includes the cikitsvidya (healing vidya), silpakarmasthanavidya (craftsmanship vidya), sabdavidya (sound vidya), adhyatmavidya (inner realization vidya), and hetuvidya (causality or Buddhist logic vidya) in their holy sense. Such accomplishments have never been seen before in the history of Buddhism. *A Treasury of True Buddha-Dharma* is the highest Buddha-dharma treasure and manifests H.H. Great Dharma King's supreme realization and virtue. H.H. Great Dharma King is the first holy being who used true realization to display fully in the dharma realm the teachings of the Buddha! H.H. Great Dharma King is the true Buddha Vajradhara, the teacher of both humans and celestial beings! In this Dharma-Ending Age, we are deeply happy that living beings in the earthly realm have the guidance of H.H. Great Dharma King.

May H.H. Great Dharma King forever live in the world and forever teach the dharma!

Junmai Baima Dorje
May 10. 2006

禮敬三界法王仰諤雲高益西諾布三身四智：

有幸聞習金剛總持法王的《正法寶典——仰諤雲高益西諾布顯密圓通妙諦五明集》，我們身為震驚、感動得無法表達。三十個大類的成就，蔚為大觀，攬括了聖義的醫方明、工巧明、聲明、內明和因明，這在佛史上是從來沒有過的。這本《正法寶典》就是佛法之無上珍寶，是大法王的至高無上的證境證德所顯，大法王是將佛陀的開示以實際證量完整地展現在法界的第一聖！大法王是真正的金剛總持人天導師！在此末法時期，我們深為娑婆眾生有大法王的指導而高興。

祈願大法王永久住世轉法輪！

俊麥白瑪多吉
2006年5月10日

KYIDONG SAMTENLING MONASTERY

Ref. No. ....

Date 22 / 01 / 2007

I am happy to read the manuscript for proofreading of an international publication that displays the great achievements of Venerable Vajradhara Master Yangwo Wan Ko, in thirty varieties of categories, and the name of the book (TREASURY OF TRUE BUDDHA DHARMA)

I am sure the works of Venerable Vajradhara Master Yangwo Wan Ko, will inspire all the sentient beings to a better understanding of both the theoretical and practical aspects of the Buddhist philosophy.

I offer my best wishes and prayers for the benefit of the dharma and all sentient beings.

May all sentient beings be born in the state of liberation.

P.O. Box No. : 6552 Boudha, Kathmandu
E-mail : samling@yahoo.com • Phone : +977-1-4471186 / 2071223 • Telex: +977-1-4499997

閱讀到展示了尊貴的持金剛仰諤雲高大師的三十大類成就的這本國際性出版物的校稿版是令人喜悅的事情，這本書的名字是《正法寶典》。我堅信持金剛仰諤雲高大師的作品將激勵所有眾生從理論和修行兩方面更好地理解佛教哲學。為此，為了佛法和所有眾生的利益，我呈上最良好的祝願和祈禱，願一切有情均得到解脫！

卡桑·嘉參
2007年1月22日

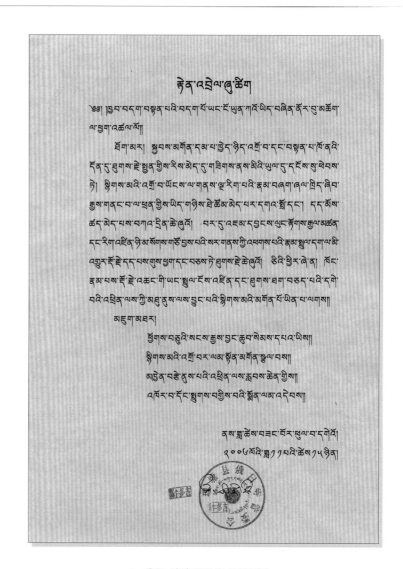

GRATEFULNESS

I prostrate to the ancient Buddha, the greatest leader of Buddhism, H.H. Dorje Chang Buddha Wan Ko Yeshe Norbu!

First, I would like to thank the greatest leader of Buddhism for your compassion in that you have again descended to the human realm and have manifested the highest wisdom of Buddhism through the Five Vidyas!

Second, I would like to sincerely thank H.H. Dharma King Omniscience Jamyang Lungdok Gyaltsen, H.H. Mighty Lion Dharma King

Renzeng Nima, and the other ancient Buddhas and Bodhisattvas. Those few holy people led us to find Dorje Chang Buddha, our supreme ancient Buddha, and thereby enabled all living beings to have the ultimate refuge in this Dharma Enging Age!

I worship the Buddha of the three times in the ten directions.
The boundless living beings now have good fortune,
for they are able to encounter Buddha Vajradhara, the greatest leader of Buddhism,
who has come to this world to save sentient beings.

Zangxia Rinpoche
November 15, 2006

感　謝

南無怙主、大教主多杰羌佛雲高益西諾布！

　　首先，我要感謝大教主您的慈悲，再次降臨人世間，告訴佛教的最高智慧五明表相！

　　其次，我要衷心感謝遍智法王降養龍多加參和雄獅法王仁增尼瑪他們幾位古佛菩薩，是他們帶領我們找到了我們至高無上的怙主多杰羌佛，讓所有眾生在此末法時代有了最終的依靠！

禮敬十方三世佛，
無邊眾生今有幸，
得遇總持大教主，
來此世界渡有情。

藏夏仁波且
2006年11月15日

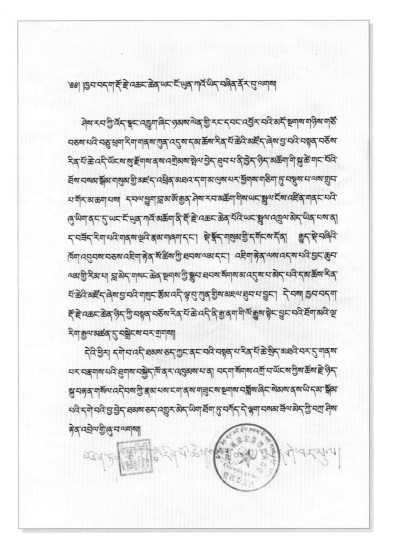

I prostrate to the Buddha Vajradhara!

Living beings have good fortune in that *A Treasury of True Buddha-Dharma* is being published! This book manifests great Buddha-dharma based wisdom and contains accomplishments that no other person in history has achieved. Only H.H. Wan Ko Yeshe Norbu has attained such accomplishments. As the venerable Urgyen Xirao Woxiu and others stated in their recognition certificates, H.H. Wan Ko Yeshe Norbu is the complete incarnation of the Buddha Vajradhara. I deeply understand that precisely because His Holiness is Buddha Vajradhara, living beings can now enjoy the blessings of *A Treasury of True Buddha-Dharma*, and Buddhist history now has this brilliant display of "complete proficiency in exoteric and esoteric Buddhism and perfect mastery of the Five Vidyas" for all to see.

I hereby specially offer my congratulations!

Yundeng Jiangcuo Rinpoche
July 11th

南無金剛總持！

眾生有福，得《正法寶典》的出版！這一佛法大智慧的出現，前輩是沒有任何人做到了的，只有雲高益西諾布才做到了。正如鄔金喜饒喔修尊者等在確認書中說：這是金剛總持轉世，我深知正因為是金剛總持，因此今天眾生才能享受到《正法寶典》的加持，佛教史上也才有這樣輝煌的『顯密圓通、妙諳五明』擺在大家面前。

特此祝賀！

雲登降措仁波且
七月十一日

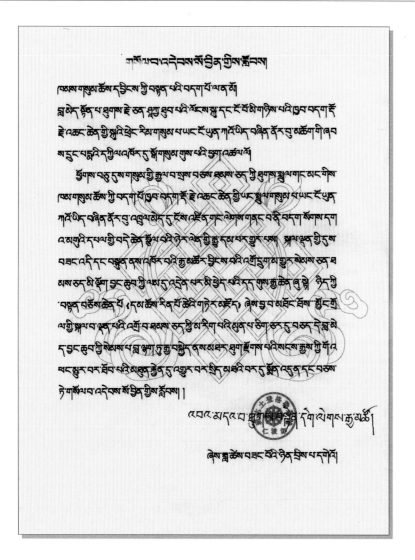

BLESSING INVOCATION

I prostrate to the greatest leader of Buddhism in the dharmadhatu!

I prostrate to the supreme and primordial sambhogakaya Buddha, H.H. Dorje Chang Buddha III Wan Ko Yeshe Norbu!

Buddhas and Bodhisattvas have found the true and complete incarnation of Dorje Chang Buddha, H.H. Dorje Chang Buddha III Wan Ko Yeshe Norbu—the greatest leader of Buddhism in the dharmadhatu. Our joy is boundless. At this auspicious time, I convey my most sincere respects and beseech the magnificent and holy Dorje Chang Buddha III to bless all sentient beings in the six realms of reincarnation so that they may realize enlightenment soon, hear of and read *A Treasury of True Buddha-Dharma*, develop wisdom, become liberated holy beings, soon realize unhindered omniscience, and attain the perfect, supreme, and complete enlightenment of a Buddha.

In body, speech, and mind, I pray that the dharma wheel of His Holiness forever turns!

Banda Tubten Geleg Gyatso Rinpoche
On an auspicious day

祈 請 加 持

南無法界大教主！

頂禮至高始祖佛陀報身多杰羌佛第三世雲高益西諾布！

佛菩薩們找到了多杰羌佛真身第三世雲高益西諾布——法界大教主，我等歡喜無盡。逢此吉勝佳期，予以最真誠的禮節，祈請偉大聖勝的三世多杰羌佛加持六道有情早證菩提，得聞《正法寶典》，開敷智慧，解脫成聖，速證遍智無礙、圓滿無上正等正覺。

三業祈請法輪永轉！

班達土登格勒嘉措 仁波且
於吉祥之日

看到《正法寶典》，得悉多杰羌佛怙主再次降臨人世間，真是我們莫大的幸福！雲高益西諾布您是真正的多杰羌佛第三世、維摩怙主第二世，所以，人們才有福報享受《正法寶典》！如果不是這樣，這幾千年來為什麼找不到一本如此偉績遍滿大智的寶典呢？為此，我特別祝賀雲高益西諾布，讓至高無上的佛法展現在人們的面前！

南無至尊金剛總持！

第六世白瑪榮珠

2006年9月18日

CONGRATULATIONS

I prostrate to H.H. Wan Ko Yeshe Norbu!

Having read *A Treasury of True Buddha-Dharma*, I learned that the ancient Buddha, Dorje Chang Budhha, has descended to the human world again. This truly is our greatest blessing! H.H. Wan Ko Yeshe Norbu, you truly are H.H. Dorje Chang Buddha III and holy and venerable Vimalakirti II. That is why people have the good fortune to enjoy the book *A Treasury of True Buddha-Dharma*! Otherwise, why is it that a precious book filled with great wisdom and accomplishments such as this book cannot be found in the past few thousand years of history? Thus, I specially congratulate H.H. Wan Ko Yeshe Norbu for unfolding before people's eyes the supreme Buddha-dharma!

I prostrate to the most honorable Buddha Vajradhara!

The sixth Baima Rongzhu Rinpoche
September 18, 2006

祝　賀

頂禮雲高益西諾布：

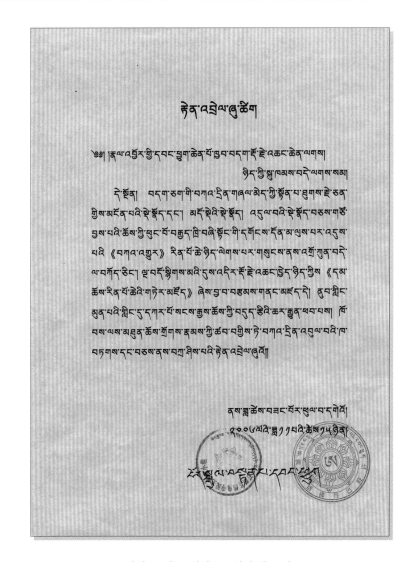

CONGRATULATIONS

With my entire body, speech, and mind, I prostrate to Dorje Chang Buddha!

The supreme Dorje Chang Buddha has brought to us *A Treasury of True Buddha-Dharma*! In our world, Sakyamuni Buddha brought to us the *Kanjur*. Today, *A Treasury of Buddha-Dharma* about Dorje Chang Buddha enables us to learn of the supreme and greatest wisdom of a Buddha. This is our good fortune resulting from karmic conditions that have accumulated over beginning-less time! On behalf of the rinpoches, I convey my utmost gratitude!

I prostrate to the most honorable H.H. Yangwo Wan Ko Yeshe Norbu!

Eba Rinpoche Danba Wangxu
November 15, 2006

祝　賀

瑜伽相應多杰羌佛！

至高無上的多杰羌佛給我們帶來《正法寶典》！在這世界上，釋迦牟尼佛為我們帶來了《甘珠爾》，今天，多杰羌佛的《正法寶典》讓我們學到了佛陀的無上大法智慧，這是我們無始以來的因緣福報！我代表仁波且們十分感謝！

南無至尊仰諤雲高益西諾布！

俄巴活佛丹巴旺許
2006年11月15日

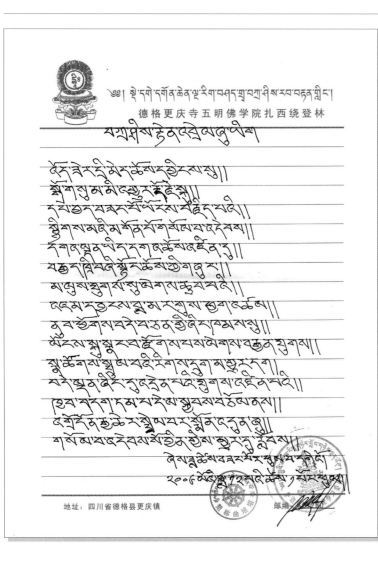

Words of Praise and Respectful Congratulations

His Holiness's unsurpassed brightness encompasses the dharmadhatu.

With immovable three karmas, His Holiness is internally and externally strong.

The most sacred one and sole Ruler of the Vajra Beings,

His Holiness is the supreme holder of the 84,000 Buddha-dharmas, the one who is in charge of all dharma methods of Buddhism.

His Holiness was the first sambhogakaya Buddha in the dharmadhatu.

All Buddhas attained Buddhahood by learning the dharma taught by His Holiness.

Mahasattvas and great holy beings together receive His Holiness's teachings and lineage under His Holiness's lotus pedestal.

In this lifetime His Holiness has come to this world and manifested the highest mastery of the Five Vidyas and the most complete proficiency in exoteric and esoteric Buddhism.

Buddha Wan Ko Yeshe Norbu has always been the Tathagata with the highest enlightenment.

I, a monk, prostrate before His Holiness and beseech this Buddha to forever abide in the world and teach the dharma.

Khenpo Chucheng Qupei
December 1, 2006

禮 贊 敬 賀 文

無上光明攝法界
三業不動內外堅
最聖獨有持金剛
八萬四千法總主
統攝釋教諸法門
初開法界報身境
由是正法傳諸佛
摩訶薩同大聖尊
共於座下接傳承
今生降世展五明
顯密圓通最頂聖
雲高益西諾布佛
本是如來最上覺
比丘此行大禮拜
請佛長住轉法輪

堪布楚稱曲培
2006年12月1日

恭 賀

禮敬至尊怙主：

　　首先，合十讚頌至尊怙主多杰羌佛第三世雲高益西諾布的《正法寶典》的出版，怙主加持給我們的福慧！這本寶書是世界上第一次出現的大圓滿寶鏡，至尊怙主把西藏四大教派及顯教佛法完滿無缺地帶到我們這個世界上來，眾生是多麼幸福啊！怙主其實是不用祝賀的，因此我們祝賀眾生得聞正法而解脫！

　　嗡啊吽！

汪智土登晉美仁波且

2006年10月2日

CONGRATULATIONS

I express my respect to the most honorable ancient Buddha:

First, I put my palms together and praise the most honorable ancient Buddha, H.H. Dorje Chang Buddha III Wan Ko Yeshe Norbu for the publication of *A Treasury of True Buddha-Dharma* and for the good fortune and wisdom with which the ancient Buddha has blessed us! This treasured book is a precious mirror of the Great Perfection that has appeared in this world for the first time. The most honorable ancient Buddha has perfectly and flawlessly brought to this world the Buddha-dharma of Tibet's four main sects as well as the exoteric Buddha-dharma. How fortunate living beings are for this! Actually, the ancient Buddha does not need to be congratulated. Thus, may living beings hear the true dharma and attain liberation!

Ong, Ah, Hong!

Wangzhi Tudeng Jigmei Rinpoche
October 2, 2006

Koyasan Buddhist Temple

342 EAST FIRST STREET, LOS ANGELES, CALIF. 90012-3984
PHONE: (213) 624-1267

KOYASAN ADULT BUDDHIST ASSOCIATION (A.B.A.)
KOYASAN BUDDHIST WOMEN'S CLUB (FUJIN-KAI)
KOYASAN CARNIVAL COMMITTEE
HARBOR CITY KOYASAN JAPANESE LANGUAGE SCHOOL

KOYASAN HARBOR CITY SUNDAY SCHOOL & JR. Y.B.A.
KOYASAN LOS ANGELES SUNDAY SCHOOL & JR. Y.B.A.
KOYASAN BOY SCOUT TROOP 379
KOYASAN SAMGHA CLASS

June 8, 2007

Congratulatory Letter

Your Holiness Buddha Vajradhara Wan Ko Yeshe Norbu Dharma King:

I, as a head of the Koyasan Shingon-shu North American Mission, have seen Your Holiness great accomplishments on Buddhism, which have never been seen before in the world. Your Holiness is truly the primordial Buddha who incarnate to this world to save living beings and to transmit the authentic Buddha-dharma of Tathagata. All of us from different sects of Buddhism are extremely joyful about this. This supreme karmic affinity of true Buddha-dharma is difficult to encounter in eons and today finally appears in our world again. I would like to extend my utmost respect and sincere congratulations to Your Holiness and to wish that every living being would be able to listen to the supreme Buddha-dharma your Holiness brings to us.

Respectfully,

Bishop Seicho Asahi
Koyasan Shingon-shu North American Mission

賀 信

尊聖的金剛總持雲高益西諾布法王：

　　我是高野山真言宗北美洲主教，我看到您在佛教上的巨大成就在世界上以前還沒有見到過。您是真正的始祖佛降到這個世界上來傳授如來正法，救渡眾生。我們雖然來自不同的佛教派別，但都為此極其高興，這個至高無上的佛法因緣是百千萬劫難遭遇的，但是今天在我們這個世界上終於出現了。我謹向您致以最尊敬和誠心的祝賀，並祝願每一個眾生都能聽聞您帶給我們的至高無上的佛法。

恭敬的

旭清澄 主教
高野山真言宗北美洲總部
2007年6月8日

the rainbow body and full realization of the Three Bodies and Four Wisdoms of the Buddhas; attaining the ageless longevity of heaven; and displaying perfect mastery of the Five Vidyas, thereby manifesting the great dharma of supreme enlightenment. However, in the history of Buddhism to the present day, no other book in this world of ours has expressed mastery of the Five Vidyas to such a complete and high degree. H.H. Great Dharma King's *A Treasury of True Buddha-Dharma* is the first book embodying such mastery to the highest degree! This is not only the first publication of a book on accomplishments manifesting complete proficiency in exoteric and esoteric Buddhism and perfect mastery of the Five Vidyas, it is also the first time in our world that a holy and virtuous being within Buddhism has manifested such accomplishments in the thirty main categories that are contained in this book. H.H. Great Dharma King thoroughly understands the true causes and effects concerning all things in the universe. His Holiness is the first great holy being in the history of Buddhism to truly manifest in the human realm complete proficiency in exoteric and esoteric Buddhism and perfect mastery of the Five Vidyas!

We sincerely thank H.H. Great Dharma King for His Holiness's blessings!

Gele Sangbu Rinpoche

With utmost sincerity, we prostrate to the supreme Yangwo Wan Ko Yeshe Norbu: Ong Ah Hong four prostrations!

Publication of the book subtitled *A Collection of H.H. Yangwo Wan Ko Yisinubu's Accomplishments Manifesting Complete Proficiency in Exoteric and Esoteric Buddhism and Perfect Mastery of the Five Vidyas* is the result of the maturing of great karmic conditions relating to living beings in this world. All Buddhists understand that the highest accomplishments in the Buddha-dharma are attaining complete proficiency in exoteric and esoteric Buddhism; receiving the dharma from Buddhas and saving living beings based on such teachings; attaining great, perfect, and holy wisdom; attaining

CONGRATULATIONS

I prostrate to H.H. Yangwo Wan Ko Yeshe Norbu!

I was fortunate to have respectfully read *A Treasury of True Buddha-Dharma* about the greatest leader of Buddhism, H.H. Yangwo Wan Ko Yeshe Norbu. The power of that book astonishes all Three Spheres. From the power of that book, we see that a true Buddha has again descended into this world! This is not a book. Rather, it is a crystallization of the power of omniscience. It will produce countless Buddhas and Bodhisattvas. As long as we learn and practice its contents, it will lead us onto the path to Buddhahood!

I respectfully wish that H.H. Dorje Chang Buddha III Wan Ko Yeshe Norbu, the greatest leader of Buddhism, live in the human realm forever and benefit all living beings in the dharmadhatu!

Luozhu Jiangcuo Rinpoche
November 15, 2006

祝　賀

頂禮仰諤雲高益西諾布！

有幸恭聞大教主仰諤雲高益西諾布的《正法寶典》，讓我們隨著震驚三界的力量思遊在法界中，又一次見到真正的佛陀降世了！這不是一本書，而是遍智力量的結晶，將會孕育出無數的佛菩薩，只要我們照著學，它就會帶領我們走上成佛之路！

恭祝多杰羌佛第三世雲高益西諾布大教主長駐人間，遊利法界！

洛珠降措仁波且
2006年11月15日

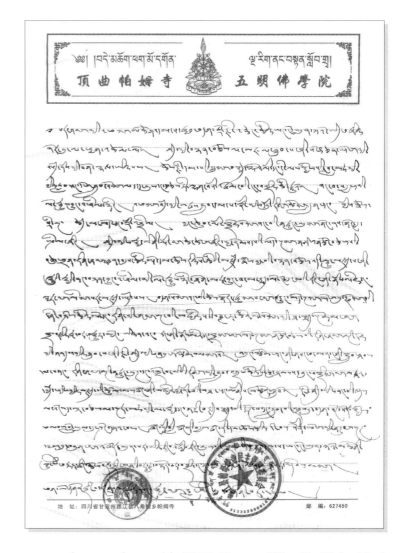

I prostrate to the most honorable H.H. Yangwo Wan Ko Yeshe Norbu, the Vajra Dharma King of greatest holiness:

We have respectfully read *A Treasury of True Buddha-Dharma* about the H.H. Buddha Vajradhara Great Dharma King and were truly astounded!

We understand the concept of "complete proficiency in exoteric and esoteric Buddhism and perfect mastery of the Five Vidyas." In the history of Buddhism, countless great masters and people of great virtue have for the sake of living beings manifested partial accomplishment in the Buddha-dharma. However, in this earthly realm, H.H. Great Dharma King is the first being of holy virtue who has manifested wisdom and abilities based on Buddha-dharma to such a complete and high degree and who has transformed the concepts stated in the Buddhist sutras into a reality that we can personally see, hear, and experience! The cultivation dharma expounded by H.H. Great Dharma King is a supreme dharma treasure. The accomplishments of H.H. Great Dharma King in those thirty main categories express the ultimate meaning of the Five Vidyas as taught by the Buddha! Such accomplishments astound both humans and holy beings! H.H. Great Dharma King represents the Buddha-dharma!

My admiration and gratitude cannot be fully expressed. All that I can do is recite Homage to H.H. Buddha Vajradhara Yangwo Wan Ko Yeshe Norbu!

Lama Renzhen Rinpoche

August 23, 2006

頂禮至尊仰諤雲高益西諾布金剛大聖法王：

恭讀金剛總持大法王的《正法寶典》實在是令我們震驚！

我們都知道『顯密圓通，妙諳五明』這個概念，佛史上無數祖師、大德都為眾生展現了佛法的部分成就，但是，第一次在娑婆世界如此完整、高度地把佛法的智能表現出來，把佛經上的概念變成了事實，讓我們親眼得見、親耳得聞、親身感受，大法王是第一聖德！大法王開示的修行法，是無上法寶，而大法王在三十個大類的成就，是真正的佛陀所說的五明真諦！這是驚人的，也是驚聖的！大法王就代表著佛法！

說不完的頂禮致謝，只有念南無金剛總持仰諤雲高益西諾布！

喇嘛仁珍仁波且

2006年8月日

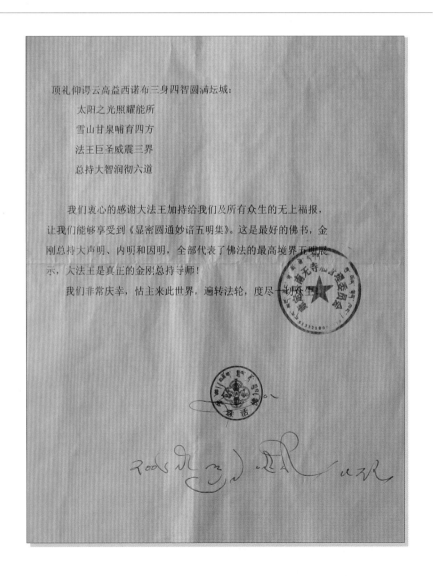

I prostrate to H.H. Yangwo Wan Ko Yeshe Norbu and His Holiness's perfect mandala of Three Bodies and Four Wisdoms:

> The light of the sun illuminates subjects and objects
> The sweet springs of snowy mountains nourish everything in all directions
> The dharma king of tremendous holiness inspires awe throughout the Three Spheres
> The great wisdom of Buddha Vajradhara benefits living beings throughout the six realms

We sincerely thank the Great Dharma King for blessing us and all living beings with the highest blessing by enabling us to enjoy the book about His Holiness's complete proficiency in exoteric and esoteric Buddhism and perfect mastery of the Five Vidyas. This is the best Buddhist book. Buddha Vajradhara's great mastery of the sound vidya, the inner realization vidya, and the causality (logic) vidya represents the highest level of Buddha-dharma with respect to manifesting the Five Vidyas. The Great Dharma King is the true Buddha Vajradhara Master!

We are extremely joyful that the ancient Buddha has come to this world, that He turns His dharma wheel everywhere, and that He liberates all living beings!

Duozhu Rinpoche

July 5, 2006

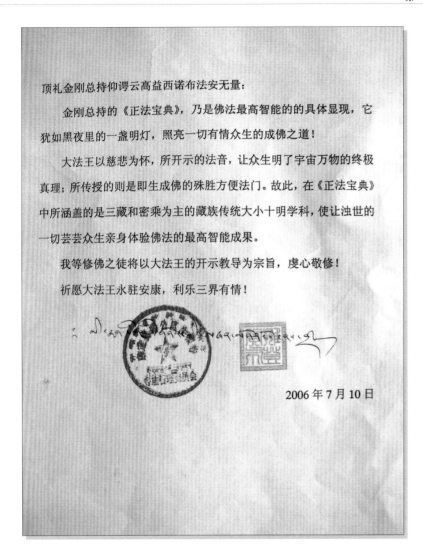

May the Great Dharma King forever live in peace and health, and may His Holiness continue to benefit and provide happiness to sentient beings in the Three Spheres!

Gongbo Rinpoche

July 10, 2006

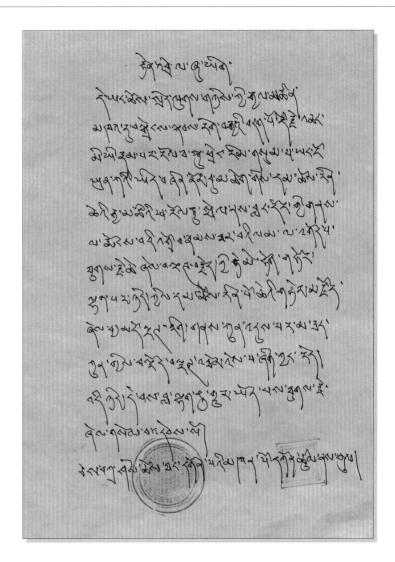

I prostrate to Buddha Vajradhara Yangwo Wan Ko Yeshe Norbu and wish His Holiness limitless peace in the dharma:

A Treasury of True Buddha-Dharma about Buddha Vajradhara is a concrete manifestation of the highest Buddha-dharma wisdom and abilities. It is like a bright lamp in a dark night that illuminates the path to Buddhahood for all living beings!

The Great Dharma King is most compassionate. His Holiness's recorded discourses on the dharma enable living beings to understand the ultimate truths of everything in the universe. His Holiness transmits wonderful and suitable dharma methods by which one can become a Buddha in this very lifetime. Thus, *A Treasury of True Buddha-Dharma* contains the traditional Tibetan major and minor branches of learning known as the ten vidyas, which are based mainly upon the *Triptaka* and Tantrayana. This book enables all of the multitudinous living beings in this defiled world to experience first-hand the fruits of the highest Buddha-dharma wisdom and abilities.

We who practice Buddhism will use the teachings in the discourses of the Great Dharma King as our standard and will devoutly and respectfully practice them!

CONGRATULATORY LETTER

At a time when the Buddha-dharma and worldly dharma flourish, the ancient Buddha incorporated the good fortune and wisdom of all Buddhas. Buddha Vajradhara transformed into H.H. Dorje Chang Buddha III Yangwo Wan Ko Yeshe Norbu, who came to this world of sentient beings in order to propagate Buddha-dharma, benefit and provide happiness to sentient beings, spread the true dharma, and eliminate the ignorance that shrouds the good roots of sentient beings. The monumental work *A Treasury of True Buddha-Dharma* about His Holiness, an ancient Buddha, has completely incorporated both exoteric and esoteric Buddhism. It is as if living beings have received the rain of nectar through the propagation of *A Treasury of True Buddha-Dharma*.

Thus, on behalf of all living beings, I wish that His Holiness, an ancient Buddha, forever live in this earthly realm and turn the wheel of the dharma everywhere!

I hereby specially offer my congratulations!

Great Khenpo Gongcheng of the Zhaxi Qutang Monastery
June 1, 2007

賀　　信

　　正值佛俗二業莊嚴宇宙之時，諸佛種性於怙主——金剛總持幻化為第三世多杰羌佛仰諤雲高益西諾布，為弘揚佛法利樂眾生釋放正法至有情世界，消除籠罩眾生善根的無明。尤其，怙主的曠世巨著《正法寶典》總攝顯密二乘，《正法寶典》的宏世，眾生如獲甘露花雨。

　　故此，在下代表有情眾生祈願怙主永住娑婆、遍轉法輪！

特此祝賀！

扎西曲塘寺：龔成大堪布

2007年6月1日

Most honorable H.H. Yangwo Wan Ko Yeshe Norbu Buddha Vajradhara Dharma King:

First, on behalf of all of the monks in our temple, I convey my warmest congratulations to H.H. Great Dharma King for the publication of *A Treasury of True Buddha-Dharma— A Collection of H.H. Yangwo Wan Ko Yisinubu's Accomplishments Manifesting Complete Proficiency in Exoteric and Esoteric Buddhism and Perfect Mastery of the Five Vidyas!*

Since the time the world-honored Sakyamuni taught the dharma, there have been countless great Bodhisattvas and great masters who, having received the Buddha's teachings, came to this earthly world of birth, aging, sickness, and death in order to expound and propagate the sutras and save living beings. However, a great wish of the Buddha was that accomplishments in the Five Vidyas be shown to living beings in order to lead living beings onto the path of Buddhist self-cultivation. In this regard, H.H. Great Dharma King is the greatest holy being in this earthly realm!

H.H. Great Dharma King possesses perfect compassion and wisdom. His Holiness does not shirk toil or hardship in the pursuit of teaching and edifying living beings. We should take H.H. Great Dharma King as our eternal model, forever propagate the dharma, and pervasively save sentient beings.

Pengcuo Rinpoche
July 5, 2006

至尊法王仰諤雲高益西諾布金剛總持：法駕大安！

　　首先，我代表我們寺廟的全體僧眾向大法王致以最熱烈的祝賀，祝賀《顯密圓通妙諦五明集》的面世！

　　自釋迦牟尼世尊演說法義以來，無數大菩薩祖師秉承佛陀教導來此五濁惡世闡揚經典，救渡眾生。但是，以五明的成就宣示於眾生，將他們導入學佛修行的軌道，是佛陀的宏願，大法王是娑婆第一最傑出者！

　　大法王悲智圓融，教化眾生，不辭勞苦。我們當以大法王為我們永遠的楷模，宏法無盡，廣度有情。

彭措活佛

2006年7月5日

After the news that dharma kings and rinpoches of great holiness from all of the main sects of Buddhism around the world recognized and corroborated that H.H. Wan Ko Yeshe Norbu is H.H. Dorje Chang Buddha III, the 110th Congress of the United States had a "Tribute to Master Wan Ko Yee" in the congressional record to specially convey its respects to H.H. Master Wan Ko Yee.

雲高益西諾布被全世界各大佛教教派的大聖法王、仁波且們認證、附議為第三世多杰羌佛的消息傳出以後，美國第110屆國會特作『向義雲高大師致敬』的國會記錄。

Congressional Record

PROCEEDINGS AND DEBATES OF THE 110th CONGRESS, FIRST SESSION

United States of America

House of Representatives

Tribute to Master Wan Ko Yee

HON. TOM LANTOS
OF CALIFORNIA
IN THE HOUSE OF REPRESENTATIVES

Friday, September 7, 2007

Madam Speaker, one of the fundamental principles on which this nation was founded is freedom of religion and respect for the religious beliefs of others. Religious tolerance and the freedom of religion for individuals to believe what they choose is one of the underlying concepts essential to our democratic system of government.

Madam Speaker, it is in that spirit that I want to pay tribute to Master Wan Ko Yee, who has been recognized by world-renowned Buddhist masters as Dorje Chang Buddha III, the true incarnation of the primordial Buddha of the Buddhist faith in accordance with the rules of recognizing the incarnation in Buddhism.

Master Yee was born in Sichuan, China, and like many individuals over the last four centuries, has come to this land where there is greater opportunity and freedom to teach and practice his religion. As Master Yee said, "The American people are kind and noble. People can freely believe in the United States, a country that is spiritually wealthy, powerful, and blessed."

I am pleased that he has found a new home in my own home state of California, where many Americans of diverse backgrounds have embraced principles of Buddhism, which include showing compassion toward others, benefiting others, being selfless, and striving for enlightenment and liberation.

Master Yee, who is recognized as His Holiness Wan Ko Yeshe Norbu, the Buddha Vajradhara Great Dharma King by the leaders of different sects of Buddhism in the world, has established a temple in San Francisco. Other similar places of worship for the benefit of believers have been established in other cities in California, New York, Washington DC and abroad.

Master Yee not only is a widely recognized and admired Buddhist thinker and teacher, Madam Speaker, but he also is an artist whose work has been widely acknowledged and exhibited. His work includes a number of very different styles and media, including traditional Chinese calligraphy, traditional Chinese painting, abstract painting, and a new style of art that is called Yun sculpture in which Master Yee has created beautiful colors and shapes.

In recognition of his artistic work, he has been named a "Fellow" by the Royal Academy of Art in the United Kingdom. His works of art have been displayed in a number of exhibits, including two recently here in Washington, D.C. at the Organization of American States and in the Gold Room of the Rayburn House Office Building, which was sponsored by our friend and colleague, David Dreier of California. An exhibit of his Yun sculpture in San Francisco last year was widely attended, and his work has been exhibited in a number of other locations.

Madam Speaker, I invite my colleagues to join me in paying tribute to Master Wan Ko Yee, Dorje Chang Buddha III, a Buddhist leader of particular renown who has chosen to make his home here in the United States, and who is an outstanding artist, scholar, and religious thinker.

美利堅合眾國國會記錄

第110屆國會第一會期的記錄和辯論

國　會

向義雲高大師致敬

加利福尼亞州國會議員湯姆・藍託斯

2007年9月7日，星期五

議長女士：

這個國家立國的一個根本原則就是宗教自由和尊重他人的宗教信仰，宗教寬容和個人選擇自己的信仰這種宗教自由也是我們民主政府體系的本質上的概念之一。

議長女士，基於這種精神，我要向義雲高大師致敬，他已經被世界知名的佛教大師們根據佛教的轉世認證規則認證為多杰羌佛第三世，佛教的始祖佛陀的真身降世。

義大師生於中國四川，他像過去四百年中的許多人一樣，來到這個充滿機會和可以自由地教授和實踐他的宗教的土地。正如義大師說的：『美國人民是善良和高貴的，在美國人們可以自由地信仰宗教，這是一個精神上富有的、強大的和被祝福的國家。』

我非常高興他在我的家鄉——加州建立了他的新家，在加州，許多具有不同背景的美國人已經接納了佛教的原則，那就是慈悲他人，利益他人，斷除自私，努力開悟和成就。

義大師已經被世界上佛教不同派別的領袖們認證為雲高益西諾布金剛總持大法王，他在舊金山建立了廟宇，在加州的其它城市、紐約、華盛頓DC和其它國家也建立了類似的這種為信眾帶來利益的修行場所。

議長女士，義大師不僅是一個被廣泛承認和讚嘆的佛教思想家和導師，他也是一個藝術家，其作品被廣泛承認和展覽。他的創作包括一些完全不同的風格和介質，如傳統的中國書法、傳統的中國畫、抽象畫和一種由義大師創造的美的色彩和形體、被稱為『韻雕』的新的風格的藝術，他被英國皇家藝術學院授予『Fellow』以示對其藝術創作的認可。他的作品展出過很多次，最近兩次在華盛頓DC的展出，一次是美洲國家組織主辦，另一次是在國會瑞本辦公大樓的金廳展出，這是由我們的朋友和同事、來自加州的大衛・佳爾議員發起的。他的韻雕去年曾在舊金山展出一次，參觀的人們非常多。他的作品還在其它地方展出過。

議長女士，我邀請我的同事們和我一起向三世多杰羌佛義雲高大師——這位選擇定居美國的特別知名的佛教領袖，同時也是一位傑出的藝術家、學者和宗教的思想家致敬！

The Organization of American States respectfully congratulated H.H. Master Wan Ko Yee for being recognized as H.H. Dorje Chang Buddha III.

美洲國家組織恭賀義雲高大師被認證為第三世多杰羌佛。

ORGANIZATION OF AMERICAN STATES
WASHINGTON, D.C.

THE ASSISTANT SECRETARY GENERAL

September 14, 2007
ASG/327-07

Dear H. H. Master Wan Ko Yee,

The Organization of American States has a long and distinguished tradition of supporting art to create awareness and appreciation of the cultural traditions of the thirty-four OAS member countries and the world. This commitment is reflected in the scope and work of the Art Museum of the Americas, the Columbus Memorial Library, the Inter-American Committee on Culture (CIC) and a range of programs that seek to protect cultural heritage and promote communication and understanding among peoples.

The Organization of American States, through its Secretary General, was pleased to recognize your internationally renowned work at the "Yun Sculpture" special exhibition held in July 2003 in Washington, DC. Your leadership in the areas of religion and culture are recognized worldwide.

In this regard, it is essential to acknowledge the importance of associating culture and religion with the development of our peoples and for demonstrating how powerful symbols of identities and beliefs can become a unifying factor for national and universal reconciliation.

On behalf of the OAS General Secretariat, I congratulate you on your identity as H.H. Dorje Chang Buddha III Wan Ko Yeshe Norbu.

Sincerely,

Ambassador Albert R. Ramdin
Assistant Secretary General

H.H. Master Wan Ko Yee
Master Wan Ko Yee International Cultural Institute
707 West Valley Blvd.
Suite 22
Alhambra, CA 91803

美洲國家組織
華盛頓，DC
歸檔文號：ASG/327-07

尊聖的義雲高大師：

美洲國家組織有一個長期和傑出的傳統，就是支持藝術，以認識和欣賞其34個成員國和世界的文化傳統。這種傳統反映在美洲藝術博物館、哥倫布紀念圖書館、美洲國家文化委員會的規模和作品上，以及保護文化遺產和提升不同的人們之間的交流和理解上。

美洲國家組織通過其秘書長，非常高興地公認您的國際聲譽的韻雕作品於2003年7月在華盛頓DC所作的特別展出。您在宗教和文化領域的領導地位是世界範圍公認的。

鑒於此，必須要承認，伴隨我們人類的成長，將文化和宗教聯合起來是重要的，也證明身份的象徵和信仰是國家和宇宙和諧的一個統一因素。

因此，我代表美洲國家組織秘書長，祝賀您的多杰羌佛第三世雲高益西諾布的身份！

真誠的

美洲國家組織 秘書長助理

阿爾波特·蘭丁 大使

2007年9月14日

The International Boxing Association respectfully congratulated H.H. Master Wan Ko Yee for being recognized as H.H. Dorje Chang Buddha III Wan Ko Yeshe Norbu, the Buddha Vajradhara Great Dharma King.

國際拳擊協會恭賀義雲高大師被認證為多杰羌佛第三世雲高益西諾布金剛總持大法王。

AIBA PRESIDENT OFFICE
8F, 20 Chu Lun Street | Tel. +886 2 87 72 01 90
Taipei 10489 - Taiwan | Fax +886 2 87 72 01 87

Association Internationale de Boxe
International Boxing Association

November 30, 2007

United International World Buddhism Association Headquarters
San Francisco
U.S.A.

CONGRATULATIONS

Master Wan Ko Yee
Recognized as His Holiness Dorje Chang Buddha III Wan Ko Yeshe Norbu,
the Buddha Vajradhara Great Dharma King

As President of the International Boxing Association, it is an honor for me to congratulate Master Wan Ko Yee for his tireless advocacy for the freedom of religion and his many contributions toward world peace.

I join many leaders of the international community in extending my sincere appreciation for Master Yee's wide range of talents and achievements as an artist, scholar, and religious thinker. Master Yee's dedication and efforts have made a positive impact on society at large, and he serves as a wonderful role model for citizens of the world.

Please accept my best wishes for continued success in the years ahead.

Sincerely,

Ching-Kuo Wu
President
International Boxing Association

HEADQUARTERS
Maison du Sport International | Avenue de Rhodanie 54 | Tel. +41 21 321 27 77 | E-mail: info@aiba.org
CH-1007 Lausanne-Switzerland | Fax +41 21 321 27 72 | www.aiba.org

祝　賀

義雲高大師被認證爲
多杰羌佛第三世雲高益西諾布，金剛總持大法王

聯合國際世界佛教總部：

身為國際拳擊協會的主席，在此祝賀義雲高大師不知疲倦地倡導宗教自由和對世界和平的諸多貢獻，這對我來説都是一種榮譽。

我和國際社會的領袖們一起，誠摯地感激義大師作為藝術家、學者和宗教思想家的多方位的才華和成就。義大師的奉獻和努力給國際社會帶來了積極的影響，是一個模範的世界公民。

請接受我最好的祝願，在未來的歲月裡繼續成功！

真誠的

國際拳擊協會主席

吳經國

2007年11月30日

VIEWS OF H.H. DORJE CHANG BUDDHA III WAN KO YESHE NORBU HOLIEST TATHAGATA ON BEING RECOGNIZED AS AN ANCIENT BUDDHA

Before my identity was recognized by others, it is only natural that I did not make my position known. However, I have now been recognized as the third Dorje Chang in accordance with the dharma rules. I will now discuss my views on whether or not I am the third Dorje Chang.

If I said that I am Dorje Chang III, I would undoubtedly be expressing an unbridled form of "attachment to self" or egocentrism and would thereby be acting like an ordinary person. How could that be even slightly in accordance with the enlightened conduct of a Buddha? On the other hand, it would be even more serious if I said that I am not the incarnation of Dorje Chang. That would be the conduct of a demon rather than the conduct of an ordinary person. That would be slandering the Buddhas, the dharma, and the sangha. It would mean denying the existence of the Buddhas and Bodhisattvas and the Buddha-dharma. It would undoubtedly be saying that those holy dharma kings, rinpoches, and eminent monks who issued recognition certificates and written congratulations are in fact not holy and therefore issued documents that contain false words and deceive living beings. If one denies the recognition certificates and written congratulations of those dharma kings and rinpoches, who are incarnations of Buddhas and Bodhisattvas, wouldn't that be slandering the Buddhas and Bodhisattvas by claiming that they speak falsely? Wouldn't that be slandering those eminent monks by claiming that they speak recklessly and act irresponsibly toward living beings? That would be completely tantamount to labeling those dharma kings, rinpoches, and eminent monks as ordinary people or deceivers,

137

which would mean that eminent monks and people of holy virtue do not exist. As such, how could there still be Buddhism and Buddha-dharma in this world?

However, living beings should understand that for the past few thousand years Buddhism and Buddha-dharma have been true, the Buddhas and Bodhisattvas have benefited living beings, and the Buddhas and Bodhisattvas have bestowed upon living beings good fortune and wisdom. Countless beings have attained liberation from the cycle of birth and death and have even attained the rainbow body. Those eminent monks who recognized my identity and offered written congratulations to me are present-day dharma kings of great holiness and rinpoches of the highest order who have been universally recognized as such. They are also leaders within dharma lineages of great accomplishment. Buddhas and Bodhisattvas never reach false conclusions. This is undeniable. Thus, the documents they wrote are in accord with the rules of the Buddha-dharma. They are Buddhas and Bodhisattvas. They are models for living beings to emulate in their self-cultivation.

I would like to state clearly the following. This matter involves the true words of those Buddhas and Bodhisattvas and the karmic conditions of good fortune that living beings have. Actually, before they recognized my identity, I thought of myself as an ordinary person. Nonetheless, I am Dorje Chang III. After they recognized my identity, I am still Dorje Chang III and still think of myself as an ordinary person. Nothing has increased and nothing has diminished. I am still I. When practitioners realize the truth of and practice the contents of my discourse "What Is Cultivation?" they will be able to truly receive the liberating empowerment of Dorje Chang III. They will also be able to receive the liberating empowerment of Dorje Chang I. Throughout history, Sakyamuni Buddha, Amitabha Buddha, and other Buddhas have incarnated into this world. They have provided living beings with a model of self-cultivation by being humble, patient, and greatly compassionate. Since even the Buddhas are like this, I, an ordinary person, should of course be even more like this.

(This text was translated from the Chinese text that follows.)

頂聖如來多杰羌佛第三世雲高益西諾布
對被認證爲古佛的看法

在我沒有被認證之前，不表任何態都是正常的，但是，現在我已被法定認證爲多杰羌第三世，是或不是，我談談我的看法。我如果說我就是多杰羌降世的第三世，這句話的定義其表現無疑就是狂妄我執的凡夫行舉，這哪裡有絲毫佛陀覺行呢？相反的，我說我不是多杰羌降世，這就更加嚴重了，這不僅僅是凡夫、而且是魔軍的行爲了，是在謗佛、謗法、謗僧，其含義是否認了佛菩薩和佛法的存在，這無疑的是說：作認證、祝賀的聖者法王、仁波且、高僧們不是聖者，因此才會行文說假話欺騙眾生。如果對於佛菩薩轉世的法王、仁波且們寫的認證、祝賀我都否認了，這不正是在誹謗佛菩薩說的是假話、誹謗高僧們在信口開河、對眾生不負責任？這完全是將法王、仁波且、高僧們定成了凡夫、騙子，意思是說沒有高僧聖德們的存在，如此，這世界上那裡還有佛教、佛法呢？可是，眾生應知，幾千年來，佛教、佛法是眞實不虛的，佛菩薩利益眾生、施與眾生福慧，了生脫死、化虹成就者數不勝數。對我作認證、祝賀的高僧們是當今世界公認的第一流大聖法王仁波且們，也是大成就法脈傳承中的領袖們，佛菩薩的定論講話是沒有妄語的，這是無可否認的，因此他們寫的文證是依於佛法教規的，他們是佛菩薩，他們是眾生修行的楷模。我要清楚地說：這牽涉到佛菩薩們的如語實語和眾生的福報因緣。其實，在我被認證之前，我是一個慚愧者，但就是多杰羌第三世。我被認證之後，我依然是多杰羌第三世，同樣是一個慚愧者，沒有增，沒有減，我還是我。行者若能證悟、行於實踐我開示的《什麼叫修行》，那才能眞正得到多杰羌第三世的加持解脫力，同時就得到第一世多杰羌的加持解脫力。歷史上，釋迦牟尼佛、阿彌陀佛他們都曾化身來這個世界，都是以慚愧、忍辱、大悲的形象來爲眾生作修行的楷模。諸佛尚且如此，慚愧者的我，當然更應該如此。

（此文的英文翻譯印在前面）

CATEGORY 2

The Virtue of H.H. Dorje Chang Buddha III and Holy Occurrences

第二大類　三世多杰羌佛的聖蹟佛格

Introduction

In the course of benefiting living beings in this world, H.H. Dorje Chang Buddha III Wan Ko Yeshe Norbu Holiest Tathagata has unintentionally revealed His state of virtue and realization. This has truly enabled us to widen our knowledge of the realization, great compassion, enlightenment, and most magnificent conduct of a Buddha. Holy phenomena can be seen wherever H.H. Dorje Chang Buddha III goes. Such phenomena appear when His Holiness conducts initiations for and transmits dharma to eminent monastics, rinpoches, dharma kings, or even famous Bodhisattvas. Such phenomena also appear when His Holiness gives discourses on the dharma to His disciples or when His Holiness blesses living beings to increase their good fortune and wisdom.

Examples of such holy phenomena include the following. Both humans and non-humans have prostrated to H.H. Dorje Chang Buddha III and have listened to His Holiness's discourses on the dharma. Sentient beings, non-sentient things, birds, aquatic animals, land animals, flowers, grass, trees, tiles, and stones have all expressed respect for His Holiness's dharma discourses either verbally or through physical actions. His Holiness taught a disciple how to transmit dharma on His behalf. When the person who was transmitted dharma by that disciple passed away, that person's body emitted light. Thunder rumbled in the sky in reaction to the voice of His Holiness. Under instructions from H.H. Dorje Chang Buddha III, Amitabha Buddha escorted people to the Western Paradise of Ultimate Bliss to visit there before they passed away. After one of them returned from his visit, His Holiness set a time for him to pass on to that Pure Land. Also under the instructions of H.H. Dorje Chang Buddha III, someone who was already being escorted to the Western Paradise returned to the human realm.

There are truly so many examples of such holy phenomena that it is impossible to relate each of them in this one book. Thus, other than the individual examples contained elsewhere in this book, we have separately listed in this category 108 short descriptions of different holy occurrences. The auspicious number 108 represents the amount of beads in a Buddhist rosary. The listing of these holy occurrences was done to bless all good Buddhists and bring happiness to living beings. The specific times, places, people, and other details relating to each of these 108 holy occurrences will be published in the book *Records of Holy Occurrences.*

1. Whenever H.H. Dorje Chang Buddha III performs the nectar initiation
   And transmits the highest Xian Liang Great Perfection Dharma
   The recipient does not need to engage in gradual practice
   The dharma realm appears to such person instantly day and night
   Visible to him or her, with eyes open or closed

2. How can merely leaving footprints on rocks compare to
   H.H. Dorje Chang Buddha III's freeing the vines from impermanence

3. For fifteen years a disciple practiced daily the Great Perfection Dharma
      transmitted by Dharma King Phunstok
   The power of the Torga never manifested itself
   Yet, upon H.H. Dorje Chang Buddha III's transmission
   It immediately emitted its power

4. Holy virtuous beings left footprints on stone
   Yet, no one can contain mist in a rock
   Holding mist in a rock for eternity, publicly displayed
   Only the ancient Buddha is capable of such a deed

5. A downpour of rain trapped the car in thick fog
   Slippery road and steep slope posed mounting danger
   Dharma protecting deities suddenly appeared to stand guard
   And Vajra Dharma Wheels covered the windows

6. A plum branch broken off from the tree

Lay on the stone for over five months
After encountering H.H. Dorje Chang Buddha III's dharma discourses
Overnight, the plum branch bore two fresh blossoms

7. As Geshe noted in the preface to his *Great Stages of the Path*
   The dharma protecting deities appeared
   In response to the order of H.H. Dorje Chang Buddha III

8. Vascular infection rotted the flesh till the bones were visible
   Yet complete recovery took only three days
   How could such an astonishing thing witnessed by many people happen
      in this world?

9. Boiling water accidentally scalded to death 20-odd ants
   Yet, in a snap of the fingers they all recovered–
   Even the one with a broken belly

10. A piece of flesh accidentally cut off by a knife dropped to the floor
    Everyone saw the blood flooding and staining the clothes
    They all shouted with fear
    Yet over mealtime,
    The skin and flesh grew back without a trace

11. An adviser to the President was in good health
    Ignoring the warning of the Buddha, he put his life in danger's way
    The Buddha Master announced that in six months he would die

Sure enough, when the time came, cancer took his life

12. H.H. Dorje Chang Buddha III predicted the approaching race car would flip

Four seconds later, it spiraled 30 or so feet into the air

Plummeting head first, like a tree trunk thrust into the earth

With a snap of His Holiness's fingers

The driver walked away unharmed even though the car was wrecked

This happened in front of more than twenty witnesses

13. H.H. Dorje Chang Buddha III transmitted the same dharma to four disciples

Yet the two pairs learned different mantras

Two participants, Mingjuan and Xinli, were astonished to learn this fact

How could the child's trick of duplicating one's body compare to such powers

14. A wicked woman abused H.H. Dorje Chang Buddha III with terrible imprecations

His Holiness warned her of the unavoidable karmic consequences

A minute later, she ran into her husband and attacked him

Failing to recognize the crazed woman, he beat her and tossed her into a muddy ditch

15. An evil ghost came to the Hyatt Hotel for revenge

It seized a disciple by the throat

The bystanders screamed with terror

H.H. Dorje Chang Buddha III formed a hand mudra and the ghost fled

16. Blessed by H.H. Dorje Chang Buddha III

In three days, the disciple's malignant brain tumor turned into clear water

17. Blessed with a nectar pill

Disciple Guangdong's late-stage nose cancer vanished without a trace

Hundreds of people learned of this

And spread the news of this holy occurrence

18. Chairman Wu of the International Boxing Association

Witnessed predictions that H.H. Dorje Chang Buddha III wrote for that day

Everything took place exactly in the way and time predicted

Witnesses signed an affidavit to attest to the accuracy of these results

19. Just before the beginning of the presidential election in Taiwan

H.H. Dorje Chang Buddha III announced the victor's name in writing

The next day, after the ballots were counted,

His Holiness said that even though he had been elected president, disasters awaited him

20. H.H. Dorje Chang Buddha III opened the crown chakra for a disciple in

just three minutes

21. A turtle joined human disciples at the manadala

And together they took refuge in H.H. Dorje Chang Buddha III

22. As a group of disciples surrounded the mandala

Heavenly beings completed a painting without human intervention

23. Three dakinis came to offer H.H. Dorje Chang Buddha III buttered tea

Yet, as the day dawned, no sign of anyone's arrival could be seen

24. H.H. Dorje Chang Buddha III caused the sun and the moon to appear so close together that a photograph taken at the Second Palace of the Potala showed them shining side by side

No such scene had ever appeared before

25. When H.H. Dorje Chang Buddha III came to bless Xinjiang's Heavenly Lake, a cloud formed at every footstep

26. The nine-ring-tailed fox is harmful to human beings

Yet, it tamely took refuge in H.H. Dorje Chang Buddha III

27. In the Zhaoqing district of Guangdong, H.H. Dorje Chang Buddha III subdued a monstrous turtle possessing evil powers

28. A stroke paralyzed one of the hands of the Buddhist nun Guanghui

With a single pointing of the flinger, H.H. Dorje Chang Buddha III instantly cured her

29. After nine rounds of repartee with H.H. Dorje Chang Buddha III

A squirrel danced and circled in a whirl of excitement, shaking the whole tree

30. Four species of Osmanthus blossom in four different seasons

Yet all blossomed within a single day

To celebrate the descent into the world of H.H. Dorje Chang Buddha III

31. One day in September, a withered willow tree suddenly sprouted new leaves

To offer felicitations on the descent into the world

Of the teacher of heavenly beings and humans

32. In the Gobi Desert, tornadoes pulled trees and rocks into the sky

H.H. Dorje Chang Buddha III aimed a finger at the black fog

The demon king fled until it vanished into the void

33. In Phoenix, dharma protecting deities came to welcome H.H. Dorje Chang Buddha III

At the gate of a restaurant, bougainvillea and roses twisted and spun

For fifteen minutes or so

Just as H.H. Dorje Chang Buddha III climbed into the car

The flowers blew across the sky and showered the car

34. A fierce tortoise bit Xiaoluo's hand

Retreating into its shell, it chewed the hand with relish

With a single sharp word from H.H. Dorje Chang Buddha III, the tortoise quickly released the hand

After that the tortoise never dared to bite Xiaoluo's hand

35. A flood enveloped an apartment building

All of the households floated on a tide of water

The pounding waves surged up to H.H. Dorje Chang Buddha III's door

But they were powerless to flow through the one-inch gap under the door

36. One year, as H.H. Dorje Chang Buddha III resided in a temple

Flood waters surged waist high

Turning streets into rivers of rushing water

But the waters halted at the temple gate

Nobody knew the reason why

Mystery piled upon mystery

37. During the dharma assembly on the evening of H.H. Dorje Chang Buddha III's birthday

Buddha light appeared around the moon

And the moon transformed itself into the shape of a lotus

38. A female ghost came to take refuge in H.H. Dorje Chang Buddha III

Terrifying the surrounding crowd

39. H.H. Dorje Chang Buddha III enlarged the building foundation under construction

The permit drawings changed by themselves accordingly

40. They all listened to the tape

Yet when H.H. Dorje Chang Buddha III snapped his fingers, the recording on the tape vanished

41. When H.H. Dorje Chang Buddha III visited Sisters Lake

The dragon deity came out to receive His Holiness

42. H.H. Dorje Chang Buddha III fully apprehended the hidden treasures even though the rinpoche had not revealed them

43. Many times H.H. Dorje Chang Buddha III knew in advance what would befall the disciples

44. H.H. Dorje Chang Buddha III's monk disciple named Yongding

Went to a heavenly realm to negotiate weather conditions with the Jade Emperor

And foretold the weather for the next three months

No matter whether rain or dew or sun, the forecasts were accurate to the minute

45. Once, disciple Helou moved without fear among swarms of terrifying yellow jackets

The next time, H.H. Dorje Chang Buddha III warned that although there

were only a few, they would harm him

Helou ignored the warning, and the yellow jackets stung him unmercifully

46. The ghost of a woman who hanged herself appeared

Among the crowd to listen to the dharma discourses

People were terrified to realize that she was a ghost, but she did not hurt anyone

She only came to take refuge in H.H. Dorje Chang Buddha III

47. Miracles occurred at the opening of the Master Museum

A thunder storm swept clean the great hall

Nine dragons stood guard to welcome

Sakyamuni Buddha arrived

With a golden garuda larger than an airplane

And the dragons revealed their original forms

48. H.H. Dorje Chang Buddha III instructed a disciple to go to the store and buy a blank tape

As predicted, it displayed holy images

49. A signed letter of authorization floated down from above

When people compared it to the version they were drafting

They found the two identical word for word

50. A big fire burned through the Luohu Hotel

Propane gas containers could not be moved

Steel tanks burned as red as peaches

Yet not even one exploded

51. In the mandala, a colorful cloud descended

It remained still, suspended in the hall

52. As disciples listened to the discourses at the mandala on Zhubao Street

Kuan Yin Bodhisattva appeared in the clouds

53. As soon as Venerable Henghsing Gyatso Rinpoche was granted permission to receive a dharma image of the Holiest Tathagata Wan Ko Yeshe Norbu

Those assembled saw on the rinpoche's head a Buddha light

Above the light some saw an image of Dorje Chang Buddha a few dozen feet high

54. A man at the airport lost his ticket

In despair, he searched frantically

H.H. Dorje Chang Buddha III pointed at a garden

Where the ticket returned to his pocket

55. A man named Liao had been lame for over twenty years

A slight tug from H.H. Dorje Chang Buddha III cured him instantly

56. H.H. Dorje Chang Buddha III predicted that a disciple

Would suffer a stroke in a month or two

He was afflicted just as predicted and fell to the floor

The others surged forward to hear instructions from H.H. Dorje Chang Buddha III

The disciple recovered immediately

57. A rinpoche disciple had one long leg and one short leg

Upon a blessing from H.H. Dorje Chang Buddha III

The two legs became the same length

58. A fire broke out behind the building on Xinhua West Street

Fierce flames shot to the sky, and buildings collapsed

A disciple from Hong Kong implored H.H. Dorje Chang Buddha III to help quickly

The disciple spat a mouthful of dharma water, quenching the fire

59. A farmer caught an eel and cast it up toward a concrete platform

Upon seeing this, H.H. Dorje Chang Buddha III pointed to the eel in the air

Following the motion of the finger, the eel flipped back into the water

60. Disciple Hanfeng begged H.H. Dorje Chang Buddha III

To rid him of his karmic obstacles

He slapped his palm on a piece of paper

At once, the head of a devil appeared on the sheet

Along with all his shameful deeds

61. On the last day of the Lunar Year

H.H. Dorje Chang Buddha III performed the cleansing ceremony for the mandala

Firecrackers exploded all around without incident

Outside the building, mounds of singed firecracker paper exceeded four inches

Within the courtyard, not a scrap of paper was to be seen

62. The boundless power of the Vajra Wheel empowerment

Caused the Western rinpoche to shriek in agony

63. A blessed object possessed limitless power

A disciple applied it to a car with a dead battery

And immediately revived the car

64. At Xingyuan, H.H. Dorje Chang Buddha III gave discourses on the Heart Sutra

Kuan Yin Bodhisattva assisted in the discourses and was recorded

65. When H.H. Dorje Chang Buddha III visited Kaihua Temple

The old abbot foresaw the arrival and led the monks to greet His Holiness

H.H. Dorje Chang Buddha III announced that a dragon deity would emerge from the temple's famous lotus pond

Less than 15 minutes later, the dragon deity appeared and prostrated itself to H.H. Dorje Chang Buddha III

66. The Vajra was immensely powerful

It weighed over five thousand kilograms

When it was on the floor, the disciples could not move it at all

But H.H. Dorje Chang Buddha III handled it with ease

67. The hand of H.H. Dorje Chang Buddha III was burned by molten resin

That morning a purple clot marked the fingertip

Yet by noon all traces had disappeared

Leaving the hand as new

68. A van packed with passengers and goods

Rolled over and over on the highway

The passengers all called out to H.H. Dorje Chang Buddha III

The van and goods were totally destroyed

But no one was harmed

69. A disciple named Ding Long suffered from severe pain in her tailbone

While listening to the discourses, dharma light radiated from the CD and blessed her

Her illness disappeared instantly

70. Failing to accept sincerely the teachings of H.H. Dorje Chang Buddha III

Zhigen Liao collapsed to his knees at Mount Emei

71. Part of a toenail of H.H. Dorje Chang Buddha III flashed away in rays of light

For days, it was nowhere to be seen

Then one day it appeared in a relic box

72. A disciple named Wang suffered from mid-stage cancer

She burned a peacock tail feather granted to her by H.H. Dorje Chang Buddha III and swallowed the ashes

The next day, she exhaled a miasma of black mist while riding in a car

And her cancer was cured immediately

73. When H.H. Dorje Chang Buddha III gave a dharma discourses at Longju Temple

The tape recorder continued to record even when the power went out

74. Dozens of light bulbs were burned out for many years

Yet when H.H. Dorje Chang Buddha III arrived, they all lit up

75. A rickety old structure could only bear the weight of two or three

Yet seventy-odd people were able to crowd in

It swayed back and forth, creaking ponderously

When H.H. Dorje Chang Buddha III ascended to the Dharma Throne,

The crowd saw only the Buddha form

76. A large bus departed from Xinfan

On a narrow, one-lane road heading north
When the passengers had recovered from a tremendous peel of thunder
The bus faced south and no one was hurt

77. An ancient temple greeted H.H. Dorje Chang Buddha III
The kneeling throng left no passage
H.H. Dorje Chang Buddha III ascended to the air
Walking over the heads of the throng

78. When H.H. Dorje Chang Buddha III gave a discourse in a tea factory on the Lotus Sutra
Even though it was June, a winter crab apple tree suddenly flowered

79. Yu Chia's AC ligament was severed
When H.H. Dorje Chang Buddha III touched him, the ligament grew back together

80. An evil ant spirit terrified an entire village
The dharma water from H.H. Dorje Chang Buddha III
Turned the spirit into an old tree root

81. The door on the upper floor was closed tight
The hotel staff could not unlock it
H.H. Dorje Chang Buddha III summoned the dharma protecting deities
But when the door swung open, no one was to be seen

82. Zewen received a call from H.H. Dorje Chang Buddha III
Warning her of an imminent danger from an electric cord
Just a few seconds after these words
The cord shorted and burst into flame

83. When H.H. Dorje Chang Buddha III went to the ancient Donglin Temple
A ray of light emanated from between the brows of the Buddha statue
The Lama hadn't seen this in 40 years and he was shocked
He gathered everyone to prostrate themselves before H.H. Dorje Chang Buddha III

84. A Buddha light accompanied H.H. Dorje Chang Buddha III's airplane to Yunnan
A video taken from inside the aircraft
Mysteriously captured the image of the entire plane a distance away flying through the Buddha light

85. H.H. Dorje Chang Buddha III taught everyone to be compassionate towards the mice
In return, the mice brought candies to the altar to show gratitude

86. A broken crystal lotus mends
Upon a smile from H.H. Dorje Chang Buddha III

87. A ferry overturned on the Yangzi River in Wan County
Hundreds of ghosts begged miserably to be relieved

H.H. Dorje Chang Buddha III immediately practiced the Wusheng Faren Dharma
And all the ghosts ascended on lotus pedestals to the upper realm

88. When H.H. Dorje Chang Buddha III expounded dharma at Xinfan
The factory garden transformed into a sacred mandala

89. Hale suddenly fell from the summer sky
It piled on the deck over an inch high
H.H. Dorje Chang Buddha III casually drew a circle with His foot
Within the circle the ice remained unmelted

90. Rain poured down in buckets
But the windshield wiper was broken and nothing could be done
The disciple prayed to H.H. Dorje Chang Buddha III
And not a drop of rain touched the windshield in front of the driver

91. Grandma Tang fell to the bathroom floor, dead
People begged H.H. Dorje Chang Buddha III to save her
And she got right up

92. Once there was a pious disciple named Miaofeng
As she arose from prostration,
A statue of Shakyamuni Buddha extended its hand,
Instructing her to follow H.H. Dorje Chang Buddha III
Unfortunately, she forgot the Buddha's order
She gave away the Vajra pill that H.H. Dorje Chang Buddha III had granted her
Miaofeng died an early death

93. Kebi and some companions took a tour to Hainan
The car flipped over on the highway
Strangely, everyone slept through the accident
When Kebi shook them, everyone woke up safe

94. A loach was crushed dead, its intestines bulging out
Upon H.H. Dorje Chang Buddha III's blessing
It swam away vigorously

95. A huge snake spirit appeared at Toufu Street
The disciples ran away in fear
H.H. Dorje Chang Buddha III snapped his fingers and the snake spirit was petrified
Taking humanoid form, it kneeled on the ground and sought refuge in His Holiness

96. A heavy truck ran over the foot of Guanghua's daughter,
But the foot was unhurt
It turned out that she had eaten a cake blessed by H.H. Dorje Chang Buddha III
To her, it seemed like a mere nightmare

But the truck's tire track was imprinted on her sports shoe

97. A disciple suffered from tinnitus
Doctors and specialists were stumped
H.H. Dorje Chang Buddha III pointed out a hidden blockage
With this information, the doctors identified the blockage and operated successfully

98. A fire broke out at a worker's hut
Even the bicycle and tools burned red
A picture frame burned to ashes, but not the portrait of H.H. Dorje Chang Buddha III that it contained
Nor did books on dharma discourses catch fire

99. Anqin wrote an article praising the H.H. Dorje Chang Buddha III
She lost it in the city where millions passed
From miles away, a rush of wind blew the article back to her

100. When a bus slammed into a cliff
Shuqiu shot out through the glass
She was thrown against the cliff and landed in a muddy pond
Everyone was shocked and thought she must have died
But after a while, they saw her get to her feet
Mud and blood covered her body and obscured her features
Her mumbling lips recited the Buddha's name
She was rushed to the hospital for emergency treatment
And had four or five broken bones
But with the blessings of H.H. Dorje Chang Buddha III she recovered without medicine

101. A car racing through Mount Simian hit a drunken old man,
Then before it could come to a stop, hit him again
His skull cracked against the rod holding the rear view mirror, breaking it in half
Red blood mixed with white brain tissue
The man lay motionless
H.H. Dorje Chang Buddha III blessed him and the bleeding stopped immediately
Surprisingly, the old man came back to life

102. H.H. Dorje Chang Buddha III warned Jianping to be cautious the next day

For a speeding car would take his life
The next day, the disaster indeed befell him
Fortunately, His Holiness's umbrella saved his life

103. One of His Holiness's disciples possessed great supernatural powers
He traveled hundreds of times faster than a car
He even knew the conversations that had taken place within the car
And upbraided Zhongxia for slandering him

104. Fanxun bought dozens of fish
Intending to fry them and serve them with wine
He strung them from bamboo sticks for three hours
But H.H. Dorje Chang Buddha III restored them all to life

105. The dharma teacher Yongding, a disciple of H.H. Dorje Chang Buddha III, possessed true realization
With but a thrust of his palm he subdued a demon in a tree 100 meters away,
Splitting the tree in half

106. H.H. Dorje Chang Buddha III told Bingling that within a month
He would be seriously injured in an accident
Indeed, a car hit his bicycle
He was thrown thirty meters and died.
After His Holiness blessed him for seven days, his body recovered

107. Zigong suffered a heart attack
The hospital pronounced him dead
They removed the oxygen and I.V.
Yet when H.H. Dorje Chang Buddha III blessed him with the snap of His fingers
He returned to life
Seeing this, the hospital director took refuge in the Holy One

108. A group of monks sitting in the temple
Prayed for the nectar to descend
Upon the invitation of H.H. Dorje Chang Buddha III, Aksobhya (Immovable Buddha) arrived
At Aksobhya Buddha's every step, lotus flowers appeared
Three dharma teachers witnessed this magnificent scene
Other people vied to see that holy scene, causing chaos around the altar

However, after H.H. Dorje Chang Buddha III saw these true accounts of holy occurrences, His Holiness said that they are nonsense and that practitioners should not do such things. His Holiness then immediately gave the following stern discourse:

After reading the accounts of everyone concerning holy virtue that moves and inspires, I truly feel ashamed. I have no right to obstruct anyone's freedom of speech. All that I can say is that the various testimonials of everyone praising and honoring me were based on some strange phenomena that appeared as a result of the coincidental coming together of certain causes and conditions. However, everyone has unexpectedly attributed the

appearance of such phenomena to my realization. I say that you are totally mistaken in this regard.

As one with a heart of humility, I engage in matters of cultivation and expound the dharma of cultivation. I do not advocate the mystical and wondrous phenomena that everyone has described. Such phenomena go against my path of cultivation. Even if I backed down from my position and decided not to oppose such phenomena, I do not have the holy realization to cause their occurrence.

In the course of life, people by chance encounter mysterious circumstances born of karmic conditions. These circumstances are not worth mentioning or citing as an honor. It seems that everyone has had such an experience. People unintentionally encounter many strange phenomena that transcend reason. Examples of this include mirages, flying saucers, trips to the moon, and so on. Could it be that the people viewing such phenomena always cause such phenomena to appear?

For example, a lama gave me three vajra pills. Zhaxi Zhuoma requested two of them. As she held them in her hand, one of them miraculously transformed into colored light and flew away. That miraculous transformation did not take place when that vajra pill was in my hand. She said that the other vajra pill spoke the dharma while it was in a cup. However, I did not hear how it spoke the dharma. If one were to say that special abilities were involved with this, then it was Zhaxi Zhuoma's abilities. Moreover, a great lama gave me those vajra pills. How could it be said that such events resulted from my abilities?

Another example is a dharma teacher disciple of mine who has mastered the Five Thunder Palm. All that my hand can do is hold a pen.

Many people saw an image of a Buddha appear over the head of Henghsing Gyatso. That was the result of his merit. How am I qualified to take any credit for that?

There is also the example involving Dharma Teacher Yongding. Although he was my disciple, his ability to communicate with the heavenly realm resulted from his own cultivation. He predicted the weather for a three-month period. His predictions were written down for all to see to verify on a daily basis the accuracy of each prediction. Not one of his predictions was wrong. Still, that was based on the realization of Yongding. How can I accept the credit for that instead of him? Furthermore, a weather station can also predict the weather!

There was also the time when the flood waters on Baoguang Street did not enter the gate of the Baoguang Temple. That occurrence truly had nothing whatsoever to do with me. Think about it. The Baoguang Temple has a King Asoka stupa containing the relics of Sakyamuni Buddha. Could it be that such stupa and its contents do not have the highest merit?

All of the short descriptions of occurrences listed above are not due to my merit. There is something else I want to tell everyone. Everyone's praise of me is truly misplaced. When a certain great Bodhisattva or Buddha assists in the furtherance of karmic conditions or manifests realization powers, I do not say whether that is good or not. In short, I think that even if a certain being of great virtue has such realization powers, that is not the goal of cultivation. What is the use of exhibiting such things? Perhaps this is a manifestation of one's personal realization powers. However, it cannot be said that exhibiting such things is engaging in cultivation. One must help living beings end the cycle of birth and death. Miracles are of no use. What is of use is teaching living beings about cultivation and about manifestations of the dharma that are required by the dharma. When one has truly attained great accomplishment in the dharma, everything becomes the holy state of the Buddhas and Bodhisattvas. Only such a state is worthy of being called a state of holy realization.

I am very ashamed, since I do not have such abilities. Moreover, I am incapable of instantaneously eliminating the karmic forces of living beings who do not cultivate themselves. Thus, I am incapable of turning bad people who do not cultivate themselves into good people. I all the more lack the power to save living beings who do not have karmic affinity with me or the Buddha-dharma. I cannot, therefore, have all living beings on earth be received in the Pure Land of Ultimate Bliss in the span of one day. With such abilities, how can I be anything other than ashamed? Could it possibly be said that I want to be like those demons and charlatans who claim to be a Buddha?

Nonetheless, to say that I have no realization would also be false. If I had nothing whatsoever, those holy dharma kings and rinpoches would not have affirmed my identity. I truly possess realization that is like a wondrous gem! That realization has already been put into words in this very book in the form of "What Is Cultivation?" I am ashamed about everything other than cultivation. Because of this sense of shame, I deeply feel that I am not qualified to receive offerings from the seven types of Buddhist disciples.

Today I formally announce to the world something that I have repeatedly announced in audio recordings: I thank all good people for their respect toward me and for vowing to make offerings to me. Resolving to make offerings to the Three Jewels is a requirement of the dharma laid down by Sakyamuni Buddha. It is also the karmic condition that connects the Buddhas in the ten directions with living beings. It is something that should be done! However, as far as I am concerned, I will not accept any offerings made to me in the future. I ask everyone for their understanding regarding this matter. There is also no need to worry about me. Relying upon my own labor, I am not only able to support myself, I am also able to help others, provide disaster relief to people, and benefit living beings. Thus, you should offer money, property, or food directly to temples and public organizations in this world that truly benefit people and that uphold correct views of the Buddha-dharma. Although such offerings are not made to me, in reality this is tantamount to making offerings to me. I do not accept offerings.

We find it unimaginable that H.H. Dorje Chang Buddha III, who is the highest and most magnificent Buddha, has such a humble attitude. His Holiness has provided a model for all living beings to emulate in their cultivation by giving credit to other people for all of His accomplishments. Those accomplishments are based on the supreme and perfect enlightenment of a Buddha. Although His Holiness is the highest Buddha in the dharma realm, when facing living beings He places Himself on the lowest level and maintains a heart of humility. Moreover, His Holiness has openly stated in writing that He will not accept offerings.

Perhaps some people will think that this person of holy virtue is quite inferior, that He has no realization, and that He only has a sense of shame. Perhaps those people will therefore think that it would be better to become a disciple under a dharma king or rinpoche who has vast supernatural and profound realization powers. All we can say is that the mentality of such people is indeed incredibly simplistic. If even H.H. Dorje Chang Buddha III does not possess Buddha-dharma to enable you to attain complete good fortune and wisdom, accomplishment in the dharma, and liberation, then which dharma king of great holiness has any Buddha-dharma realization to speak of? Even if one is a Buddha, which Buddha surpasses H.H. Dorje Chang Buddha III? Who else would dare say that they can conduct a Great Perfection Initiation and transmit Great Perfection Dharma that will enable a disciple to experience and see the rainbow-body dharma realm state the very day that dharma is transmitted? In this entire world, only H.H. Dorje Chang Buddha III has this supreme and holiest dharma called Xian Liang Great Perfection Dharma. Even Samantabhadra Tathagata is the dharmakaya of Dorje Chang Buddha! From ancient to modern times, what other person of holy virtue has been able to attain the accomplishments contained in this book? Moreover, those accomplishments were randomly selected from only thirty different categories. You must understand that Dorje Chang Buddha is the only primordial Buddha with form in all of Buddhism in the entire dharma realm. There were no Buddhas with form who spoke the dharma before Dorje Chang Buddha. Even Adharma Buddha (Samantabhadra Tathagata) was a dharmakaya Buddha without form or speech. All Buddhas have attained Buddhahood by learning under Dorje Chang Buddha!

(This text was translated from the Chinese text that follows.)

簡　　介

　　多杰羌佛第三世雲高益西諾布頂聖如來在這個世界利生的過程中所無意露出的證德證境，讓我們真正見識到了佛陀的證量及大悲菩提、至高偉大的行舉。三世多杰羌所到之處，或為高僧、活佛、法王乃至著名菩薩傳法灌頂，或為弟子開示法義，或加持眾生福慧，隨處可見聖蹟展現。比如人非人等禮拜三世多杰羌聽聞開示，有情、無情、飛鳥、水族、動物、花草樹木、瓦石等顯聲讚嘆；教弟子代之傳法、圓寂時肉身化光；一聲口令出，天上雷鳴起；乃至阿彌陀佛亦在三世多杰羌囑咐下接人往升西方極樂世界預先參觀，然後回來再定時間往升極樂；以及將已接走之人返還人間等等，聖蹟案例實在太多，無法一一載於書中。因此，除本《正法寶典》中所記載的，另以佛珠之一百零八之吉祥數目而取一百零八條聖蹟題目列之於此，以作圓滿吉祥功德加持諸善知識，利益眾生吉祥幸福。至於每一聖蹟之時間、地點、人物等詳情將記於《聖蹟記》一書。

　　1. 羌佛甘露灌頂間，至高現量大圓滿，不需循序整修漸，當下晝夜法界顯，睜眼閉眼皆能見；
　　2. 不是簡單用足印在石頭上，而是羌佛掌下藤籮不無常；
　　3. 彭措王傳大圓滿，日日勤修十五年，妥噶未曾威力展，羌佛一傳當場現；
　　4. 諸聖石上留腳印，無力把霧石中存，古佛拿霧永保存，公眾展示無人能；
　　5. 傾盆大雨霧籠車，路滑坡高有懸情，護法顯聖來護駕，窗前包圍金剛輪；
　　6. 臘梅斷枝掉石上，時經五月逢說法，一夜開花鮮兩朵；
　　7. 見到菩提道次論，格西自序中有文，法王師長一聲命，護法出顯就應成；
　　8. 腐爛見骨脈管炎，三天皮肉好完全，世上哪有此驚事，可惜多人當見證；

9. 高溫沸水無意間燙螞蟻二十幾隻，彈指間全然復生，包括破肚者；

10. 無意刀割肉掉地，眾見鮮血染滿襟，大家見狀驚嚇神，頓飯時間皮長成；

11. 總統顧問體健康，不聽佛言拿命擋，師長公佈半年亡，果然癌症黃泉上；

12. 三世多杰羌說車翻，話音一落口，時達四秒間，賽車騰空三丈翻，頭朝地面腳向天，猶如木椿插地盤，羌佛一彈指，車爛人安全，二十餘人親眼見；

13. 我佛同時授一法，兩組各學咒不同，明娟新麗大感奇，豈是分身小兒戲；

14. 惡人罵佛最刁嚎，佛陀告之將必報，夫妻不識分鐘內，拳打丟進爛泥壕；

15. 惡鬼復仇到凱悅，抓拿學生喉嚨骨，眾見驚魂哭聲嚎，一印結下鬼倉逃；

16. 惡性腦瘤顱內生，加持三日化淨水；

17. 光束晚期鼻癌症，甘露一粒消無影，此事百人皆知道，傳為佛陀一聖境；

18. 國際拳擊吳主席，親見佛師報日情，筆書寫下當日事，分秒不差如行文；

19. 台灣國首選之前，行文定名公眾見，次日計票結算完，佛言總統後有難；

20. 三世多杰羌為弟子三分鐘開頂；

21. 龜人一同坐壇場，皈依三世多杰羌；

22. 眾圍壇場不用人，天人自動把畫成；

23. 三空行母供養羌佛酥油茶，天明起時此地從未有人家；

24. 拍下一張照片日月同輝相，傳說此境確無雙（布達拉宮第二殿）；

25. 新疆天池一步一雲霧；

26. 九尾惡狐本傷人，一見佛陀皈依順；

27. 廣東肇慶降妖龜；

28. 廣慧中風單手殘，佛手一點即復原；

29. 松鼠九次應對佛，喜若發狂跳舞樂；

30. 四季桂花同日開，恭賀古佛降世來；

31. 枯死柳樹九月發新枝，祝賀已來天人師；

32. 抬石拔樹龍捲風，佛手一指影無蹤，戈壁灘上黑霧起，魔王倉惶逃太空；

33. 鳳凰城內護法迎，旋風捲花獻餐門，歷時一刻如如轉，待到登車飄空行；

34. 小羅手被惡鱉咬，縮進殼中品味道，一聲嚴詞急鬆口，從此不敢再吃手；

35. 大水圍困眾家庭，每家全泡水浮城，水湧浪擊羌佛門，怎奈無力入家門；

36. 羌佛住寺那一年，洪水爆發浪腰間，街成江河波光洶，無力流進寺廟中，玄妙奇端無人識，內中自有玄中玄；

37. 修法佛光現空中，壽誕月化蓮花同；

38. 女鬼前來受皈依，眾人大駭驚詫魂；

39. 佛陀改地基，圖紙自動變；

40. 眾聽錄了音，彈指即消失；

41. 三世多杰羌遊湖，龍神接駕姐妹潭；

42. 對仁波且伏藏的東西了如指掌；

43. 預知弟子受報若干；

44. 羌佛弟子永定僧，上天玉帝共商榷，預報三月陰晴露，分鐘不差全應景；

45. 日前百萬黃蜂穿，未曾將它怕一分，佛告今有大魔障，黃蜂頓將鶴樓傷；

46. 吊死女鬼現了身，聞法而來不吃人，眾人見狀丟三魂，原來拜佛皈依靈；
47. 開館聖蹟若干：雷火掃殿，九龍護駕，佛陀駕臨，大鵬金翅鳥，體比飛機大，諸龍現原身；
48. 隨意買新帶，放之顯聖像；
49. 一封委託書，從天而飛降，眾人剛才商，字句全一樣；
50. 羅湖酒店大火燒，煤氣罐子搬不了，鋼瓶燒得紅如桃，但無一個得爆炸；
51. 天空雲彩降入壇場，如如不動殿中旋；
52. 珠寶街壇場聞法，觀音聖雲中顯影；
53. 恆性嘉措仁波且請頂聖如來雲高益西諾布的法相，眾人見其頭頂出現佛光，有人見到多杰羌佛相，身高得幾丈；
54. 有人機場掉機票，痛苦無門獨自瞧，我佛用手輕一指，票從花園進腰包；
55. 廖氏跛腳二十年，當下一牽即復原；
56. 預報弟子將中風，果然一月倒地同，眾僧齊上聽佛旨，當下返還安全中；
57. 長短兩腿活佛人，一經加持兩腳平；
58. 新華西路後樓燒，烈火沖天房屋倒，港子求佛速救助，一口法水火全消；
59. 農夫捉鱔地上拋，隨著佛手指方向，空中轉彎掉水逃；
60. 漢峰乞求除業障，自將手掌拍紙上，頓時現出魔鬼頭，同時顯露隱情留；
61. 大年三十開壇光，爆竹圍燒毫無傷，房外紙藉高盈寸，院內不見一片張；
62. 金剛輪加持，威力大無邊，洋活佛連叫受不了；
63. 加持聖物威力顯無窮，舉手施之電路車上通；
64. 行園說法示心經，觀音到場助錄音；
65. 三世羌佛赴開華，老僧神通接聖駕，預眾池中有龍神，不到一刻龍出庭，五體叩拜佛陀身；
66. 金剛杵威力無窮，掉地上萬斤之重，弟子提文風不動，佛手拿輕玩掌中；
67. 熱熔膠高溫壞手，黑血斑留在指頭，早上在午時頓走，無蹤影還是好手；
68. 麵包車人多貨載，高速路翻車打滾，緊持念羌佛聖號，車貨均爛人無恙；
69. 丁氏坐骨已殘人，法音加持佛光升，當下惡症消無影；
70. 多羌佛教化不誠心，廖志根峨嵋跪地行；
71. 三世多杰羌，指甲化流光，數日都不見，自入舍利箱；
72. 王氏癌症中期毒，自把法籤燒吞服，乘車黑氣口中出，一宿之間癌消沒；
73. 羌佛龍居說法時，停電音機照常錄；
74. 數十燈泡久已壞，佛陀一到全亮來；
75. 危樓只載二三人，七十餘人竟能承，左右搖晃嘎嘎響，坐上法臺現佛身；
76. 大車載客出新繁，窄路行駛往北邊，一聲雷鳴車翻轉，無傷一人頭返南；
77. 古寺迎古佛，千人跪地立，擁塞無通道，羌佛升空騰，步在頭上行；
78. 茶廠說法談蓮華，當下海棠六月花；
79. 昱佳足筋斷一根，隨手一拿筋長成；
80. 螞蟻精怪嚇煞人，全隊民眾掉了魂，羌佛賜以佛法水，蟻怪現形老樹根；
81. 樓房頂上門鎖緊，服務人員打不開，佛陀喊來護法神，開門之後不見人；
82. 澤文接下電話聽，佛告電路帶火災，話音剛落才幾秒，電線短路火燒開；
83. 東林古寺來羌佛，釋迦眉間放光出，喇嘛驚駭四十年，聚眾禮拜羌佛前；
84. 佛光隨機上雲南，飛機奇從光中穿；

85. 大悲菩提教鼠道，送來喜糖感恩招；

86. 水晶蓮花已破殘，佛笑一下即復原；

87. 萬縣江心輪船翻，百鬼淒求要升遷，佛祖當下施法忍，幽靈齊皆上寶蓮；

88. 佛陀宣法於新繁，工廠花園變聖壇；

89. 天上突然降冰雹，落在地板寸多高，我佛用足一圈畫，圈內冰雹沒有化；

90. 滂沱大雨如瓢潑，雨刷失靈無奈何，弟子祈禱佛陀王，司機窗前無滴雨；

91. 唐婆浴室倒，頓時把命交，求救佛陀王，片刻站起了；

92. 有女妙鳳心虔誠，佛堂頂禮正起身，釋迦佛陀伸出手，囑她緊隨羌佛尊。可惜忘了遵佛命，金剛丸施蘇珊娜，提前入寂早離家；

93. 克碧眾人遊海南，高速路上車翻箱，奇在昏迷無一醒，待到醒時無一傷；

94. 泥鰍已死破肚腸，佛陀加持游水狂；

95. 頭福街蛇精顯形，幾弟子嚇得逃命，佛彈指毒蟒丟魂，跪地上求佛接引；

96. 重車壓過足無傷，蛋糕原是法力王，光華之女醒如夢，車輪影留鞋子上；

97. 弟子耳中嗡呱響，醫學專家無了方，羌佛告之有塊障，果然醫院見真況，手術拿出耳明亮；

98. 大火燃燒一工棚，鋼鐵車具化火龍，畫框燒炭法相好，開示法書火不燒；

99. 安琴書文讚佛陀，無意掉失都市中，百萬人流幾公里，狂風捲紙口袋中；

100. 客車高速突撞崖，述秋破窗飛車外，撞上岩壁復落地，彈入泥塘水中埋，眾人失色嘆無命，良久見她站起來，渾身泥血無眼鼻，嘴唇微動誦佛哉，送到醫院擬搶救，身骨已斷四五截，無用醫藥竟安泰；

101. 汽車飛馳四面山，撞上醉翁兩次翻，頭頂打斷反光鏡，靈蓋飛出腦髓流，滿地血泊當下死，佛手加持血立止，竟然還魂人不死；

102. 佛告建平明日慎，將有飛車要你命，次日大災全應境，佛陀一傘救了生；

103. 座下弟子神通足，能超快車百倍速，仲俠車中謗言事，到時一一全數落；

104. 范動買魚數十條，欲將煎之品酒燒，竹籤穿死三時後，佛讓全部回生了；

105. 法師永定有道來，羌佛座下一僧才，隨手降妖只一掌，百米之外樹劈開；

106. 佛告冰凌一月內，車禍將要汝重傷，果然車子被衝撞，三十米外已死亡，加持七日體正常；

107. 子公心臟病嗚呼，醫院下書當下死，去了氧氣點滴瓶，佛手一彈還了魂，醫院主任拜聖人；

108. 一日眾僧若干人，坐殿祈請施甘露，羌佛迎來不動佛，一步一足蓮花出，此時三師全得見，搶觀聖境禮節亂；

……

　　但是，三世多杰羌佛見到上述這些真實記錄的聖蹟後，卻說這些都是無稽之談，不是修行人要做的，當下作了如下的嚴肅開示：

　　見到大家所寫的聖德感召之記載，我實在是羞慚。我無權阻止大家對於言論自由的權利，我只能說，大家對我褒獎的列列文題無非是某種因緣的巧合，而出現了一些奇怪現象，但是大家竟然歸功於我的證量所獲，我說你們完全是錯誤的說法，我作為一個慚愧者，做的是修行事，說的是修行法，對於大家所說的神奇妙象我不是不主張的概念，而是與我的修行之道是相反的。退一萬步說，就算是我不反對，但我也沒有這麼些聖勝證量。人生途中偶遇奇妙緣境者，何足掛齒為榮，似乎人皆有之，很多出乎理性的異象，人們在無意之間都會遇到，如海市蜃樓、外星飛碟、乃至月球之旅等等，難道都是看到過的人顯現的嗎？比如有一喇嘛給我三粒金剛丸，扎西卓瑪向我請了兩粒，是她拿在手中，神奇化虹而飛，不是在我手中神化，她說在杯中說法，但到底怎麼說法，我沒有聽到，要說有功夫的話，也是仁波且的本領，何況這金剛丸乃大喇嘛送我的，獨我何能具之？又比如，弟子法師的五雷掌，我的手只會拿筆，眾人見到恒性嘉措頭頂現佛像，那是他的功德，我有何資格沾享？

又比如，永定雖然是我的弟子，但是與上天通達是他的修為，預報天氣三個月，他們每天都作了記錄來印證他的預報，一天也沒有錯，但是那也是永定的證量，我焉可取功代之？更況氣象臺還能預報天氣呢！還有寶光街上洪水不進寺門，這與我實在毫無關係，大家想一想，寶光寺有釋迦佛陀的阿育王舍利塔，難道都不具無上功德嗎？上述列列條文，均非我之功德所為。我還要告訴大家，大家的讚嘆實在是錯了位，無論是哪一位大菩薩或佛陀助緣也好，或顯證量也好，對我來說，我不說好還是不好，總之，我認為就算哪一位大德有如此證量，這也不是修行的目的，這些東西拿來有什麼用？也許對你個人是道量的證顯，但總不能拿它來說是修行吧？要利益眾生了生死，除了教他們修行和法定的表法，任何神奇都是沒有用的。要真正大成就了，一切都成了妙有聖境，那才是談得上聖量證境。我很慚愧，因為我沒有那些本事，更是無法當下滅除眾生不欲修行的業力，為此無法將惡人變成善良人。我更不具備無緣渡生的力量，因此才不能在一日之中即可把世界上的眾生全部接到極樂世界，我這樣的能力不是慚愧是什麼？難道是那些賣狗皮膏藥而自稱佛陀的妖孽嗎？要說我沒有證量，那是假的，如果什麼都沒有，聖者法王、仁波且們就不會認證我了，我確實擁有妙寶證量！這證量就是已寫在《正法寶典》中的『什麼叫修行』，除此只有慚愧。正因為慚愧，我深感我沒有資格接受七眾弟子的供養，雖曾多次宣說於錄音中，但今天正式行文宣告於世：我感謝一切善士對我的恭敬，要發心供養於我，發心供養三寶是釋迦佛陀的法定，也是十方諸佛與眾生之緣起種子，是應該的！但是，對我來說，凡今後給我的供養，我不予接收。請大家諒解，也不要為我擔心，我依靠自己的勞動，不僅能自己生活，還能幫助他人，救災利民，利益眾生。所以，無論是金錢、財物、食物，只能直接供養給世界上真正對大眾有益、正知正見的寺廟和公眾團體，這等於實相供養了我，也等於普賢供養了我，我不接收供養。

讓我們無法想像的是，三世多杰羌佛身為至高偉大的佛陀，卻展慚愧覺格，而為眾生作修行的示範楷模，把自己的一切無上正等正覺的成就歸功於他人，自己身為法界至高佛祖，卻把自己放在最低位的慚愧格覺上來面對眾生，而且公開行文不收供養。也許有些眾生認為這位聖德這麼差，什麼證量都沒有，只有慚愧，莫如另拜神通廣大、道力高深的法王、仁波且為師。我們只能說，這類人的思維實在是簡單到了無法想像的地步了，如果三世多杰羌佛都沒有佛法讓你福慧圓滿、成就解脫，哪一個大聖法王還有佛法證量可言呢？就算是佛陀，又有哪一位超過了三世多杰羌佛呢？有誰敢說他傳的大圓滿法就在傳法的當天即讓受灌頂的弟子自己見到虹身法界境呢？而在這世界唯一只有三世多杰羌佛才有如此無上至高的『現量大圓滿』頂聖法。就是普賢王如來也是多杰羌佛的法身嘛！再憑隨取的三十大類成就，從古至今，哪一位聖德做到了呢？要知道，多杰羌佛是法界佛教的唯一具相的始祖佛，所有佛陀們都還是跟他學的呢！

（此文的英文翻譯印在前面）

A Narration for Which I Am Willing to Bear Any Karmic Retribution

H.H. Dorje Chang Buddha III Wan Ko Yeshe Norbu Holiest Tathagata has come to this world again. Everyone knows that there is no other holy person in this world whose noble moral character and Five Vidyas wisdom can compare with those of His Holiness. Holy states that people often regard as extraordinary constantly occur when one is at the side of H.H. Wan Ko Yeshe Norbu Holiest Tathagata. We attendants have seen so many holy states over the long course of time we have been attending upon His Holiness that we often become accustomed to seeing these holy states. We even have felt somewhat numb or indifferent to such states. However, I would now like to narrate two events. I am not narrating these events because they are related to me but because they are directly related to the good fortune of all living beings in this earthly realm.

The first event occurred after about 4:00 in the afternoon on July 30, 1999. H.H. Dorje Chang Buddha III had decided to leave China because the karmic conditions had changed. However, this decision could not be made public. Thus, I alone accompanied H.H. Dorje Chang Buddha III as His Holiness stood on the granite steps outside the South Block of the Meijing Tower located in the Luohu District of Shenzhen City. We were waiting for the driver to arrive in order to take H.H. Dorje Chang Buddha III to the airport. Suddenly, something caused my body to shake for a moment. The thirty-story Meijing Tower that was behind me also began to shake. I heard the sound of the shaking glass that covered the streetlights. Those thick and heavy light-poles were solidly embedded in the granite foundation. That sound lasted a few dozen seconds. I immediately realized that the earth was quaking, but I did not say anything because I felt very heavy-hearted at the time.

After a little while, H.H. Dorje Chang Buddha III asked me, "Did the earth just quake?" I tersely responded with the single word, "Yes." The face of H.H. Dorje Chang Buddha III was expressionless. His Holiness knew very well that the building would not collapse due to the earthquake since it was this great karmic event in Buddhism that caused the earth to quake.

The sutras state that the earth quakes when a Buddha comes into the world and when a Buddha passes away. However, at the time, I did not realize the important meaning that earthquake portended. Only later did I understand: Those living beings in the west will have the good fortune to learn the true Buddha-dharma!

The second event was very fortuitous. It happened on the same day I first met H.H. Dorje Chang Buddha III Wan Ko Yeshe Norbu Holiest Tathagata. A large dharma assembly that would last many consecutive days started on that day. H.H. Dorje Chang Buddha III was going to expound the meaning of the works *A Monk Expounds the Absolute Truth to a Layperson* and *This Is My View*. That discourse was to be given for the benefit of living beings, no matter what their innate capacities or karmic conditions were. Before the Dharma Assembly began, the then elderly Huibang Huang recounted for everyone what he experienced that day when H.H. Dorje

Chang Buddha III empowered (blessed) him. The elderly Huibang Huang was a famous and highly virtuous person in China. At the time, he was the vice-chairman of the Jiangxi Province Buddhism Association and was called "Jiangxi Rinpoche." He had devoted himself to Buddhism since his early years when he encountered the Buddha-dharma while studying abroad in Japan. For more than seventy years, he had maintained a vegetarian diet and had incessantly studied the sutras. The devotion and tenacity with which he pursued the Buddha-dharma over his entire life is inspiring. At the advanced age of almost ninety, he still went to Tibet alone to seek the dharma, carrying with him Buddhist sutras. H.H. Wish Fulfilling Jewel Dharma King Jigme Phuntsok was deeply moved by this and told him, "Your good roots are extremely deep. You should go to H.H. Dorje Chang Buddha III Wan Ko Yeshe Norbu Holiest Tathagata to learn higher Buddha-dharma." He also privately told Huibang Huang where H.H. Dorje ChangBuddha III was.

The elderly Huibang Huang recounted for everyone the following. On that day, he ate the food of the Buddhas and Bodhisattvas that H.H. Dorje Chang Buddha III had invoked the Buddhas and Boddhisattvas to bestow for him. H.H. Dorje Chang Buddha III also told him that his wish would be fulfilled, that he would be allowed to see a Buddha. Right when he was about to see a Buddha, the elderly Huibang Huang suddenly said that he would rather see a dharma protecting deity. H.H. Dorje Chang Buddha III then casually called forth such a deity. In an instant, a dharma protecting deity suddenly appeared out of nowhere right in front of Huibang Huang. That deity was as massive as an iron pagoda and was wearing a black helmet and black armor covering its entire body. It roared thunderously. There was no time for Huibang Huang to respond, so he simply fell to the ground. (There is a tape recording of the elderly Huibang Huang recounting this event.)

Everyone should think about this. Who else could casually call forth a dharma protecting deity, and that dharma protecting deity will thereby instantly appear? Of course, only a Buddha has such powerful virtue!

The two events that I have stated above are true. If I spoke falsely and deceived everyone, I will receive all evil karmic retribution. On the contrary, since everything that I stated is true, may all things go smoothly for me; may all living beings hear the true Buddha-dharma of H.H. Dorje Chang Buddha III Wan Ko Yeshe Norbu Holiest Tathagata; may the good fortune and wisdom of all living beings grow; and may all living beings attain liberation from the cycle of reincarnation!

Buddha's disciple Long Zhi Tanpe Nyima
November 15, 2007

(This is a complete translation of the Chinese text that follows originally written and signed by Long Zhi Tanpe Nyima.)

我 願 承 擔 因 果 報 應 的 敘 述

多杰羌佛第三世雲高益西諾布頂聖如來再次來到這個世界上，其崇高的道德、五明智慧都是找不到第二個聖者能與之相提並論的，這也是大家都知道的。至於常被人們引以為奇的聖境界，在雲高益西諾布頂聖如來的身邊更是隨時隨地都發生的，我們隨侍在三世多杰羌佛的身邊久了，看得太多了，往往對這些聖境都習以為常、甚至有些麻木了。但是，我在這裡要說的兩個事情，不是因為都跟我本人有關，而是直接牽涉到娑婆世界所有眾生的福報因緣。

第一件發生在1999年7月30號的下午，大概是下午四點多鐘的時候，由於因緣的變化，三世多杰羌佛決定離開中國，但當時不便公開，因此只有我一個人陪著三世多杰羌佛站在深圳市羅湖區美景大廈南座大門外的花崗石砌成的台階上，等司機開車過來送三世多杰羌佛去機場。突然，我的身體被搖了一下，後面的三十層樓高的美景大廈也搖晃起來，只聽見固定在花崗石基座上的很粗重的路燈的玻璃罩都被搖晃得『咯咯咯』的作響，持續了幾十秒鐘之久。我立刻警覺到大地震動了，但是當時我的心情非常沉重，所以我沒有說話。過了一會兒，三世多杰羌佛問了一句：『是大地震動了嗎？』我也只是很簡短地回答了一個字：『是。』三世多杰羌佛面無表情，他老人家深深知道樓房不會被地震震垮的，因為這是佛法大事因緣所成的大地震動。

經書上說，只有佛陀降世、滅度時大地會震動。但是，在當時那個時刻，我並沒有完全意識到這個大地震動所預示的重要意義。只是到後來，我才明了：西方世界的眾生有福報了，他們將學到真正的佛法了！

第二件事很巧，就發生在我這一生第一次拜見多杰羌佛第三世雲高益西諾布頂聖如來的當天。從那天開始有一個連續很多天的大法會，三世多杰羌佛為各種根基、因緣不同的眾生開示《僧俗辯語》和《余如是鑒》。在法會開始之前，由黃輝邦老人向大家敘述三世多杰羌佛當天為他作加持的經過。黃輝邦老人是中國著名的大德，時任江西

省佛教協會副主席，被稱為『江西活佛』。老人自從早年在日本留學時接觸佛法，便虔心向佛，七十多年來，不僅長齋長素，而且可以說手不離經書，一生追求佛法的虔誠與堅韌令人感動。在將近九十高齡之際，他仍孤身一人攜帶經書赴西藏求法，晉美彭措如意寶法王深為感動，告訴他：你的善根太深厚了，應該到多杰羌佛第三世雲高益西諾布頂聖如來處學習更高深的佛法，並密語告訴他三世多杰羌的地方。

黃輝邦老人對大家說：那一天，他親口服下了三世多杰羌佛為他請來的佛菩薩的飲食，同時三世多杰羌佛還告訴他：可以滿他的願，他想見佛陀是可以的。正當他要見佛陀的時候，黃輝邦老人突然說，還是見護法就好了。只見三世多杰羌佛隨口招呼一聲，剎那間，一個全身黑色盔甲的護法像一座鐵塔一般突然憑空出現在他的面前，吼聲如雷，他來不及反應就倒坐在地上（有黃輝邦老人講述此事的錄音）。

大家可以想像，有誰能隨口喊一聲，護法就立即出現呢？當然只有佛陀才有如此的威德！

以上兩件事都是真實不虛的，如果我說假話騙大家，我將遭受一切惡報。相反，我所說的一切都是事實，則我萬事吉祥，所有眾生都將得聞多杰羌佛第三世雲高益西諾布頂聖如來的正法，福慧增益，解脫成就！

佛陀的弟子：隆智·丹貝尼瑪

2007年11月15日

（此文的英文翻譯印在前面）

Description for the photogarph on the bottom left of next page
下頁左下照片之說明：

After 5 p.m. on July 4th, 2006, we seven dharma teachers, as well as others, attended the ceremony of offering H.H. Dorje Chang Buddha III Wan Ko Yeshe Norbu Holiest Tathagata's Dharma King robe. We personally saw the holy scene of glittering lights transforming into rainbow lights on H.H. Dorje Chang Buddha III's vajra throne. This completely illustrates that when the practice of the Great Perfection of Vajrayana reaches the highest state, even non-sentient dharma objects can emit rainbow lights that soar into the sky. We have seen many holy scenes. This transformation of rainbow lights, which took place right before our eyes, was the most wonderful among all. If we speak falsely, we will descend into vajra hell. Therefore, what we state here about the transformation of rainbow lights is true. May all the merits bring great happiness to living beings.

A key point must be mentioned. The multicolored glittering lights on the grass could be regarded as nothing special for it could be viewed as the refraction of sunlight. However, during the ceremony when the Dharma King robe was offered, there was a bright sunny sky without a trace of rain. The multicolored glittering lights unexpectedly coalesced into a cluster of light. In about five seconds, the light transformed into a vertical rainbow and flew into space toward a Buddha-land. That truly manifested the supreme rainbow-transformation Buddha-dharma of the Great Perfection.

Witnessed by: Jue Hui Shih, Ding Hui Shih, Jien Hui Shih, Liao Hui Shih, Guang Hui Shih, Cheng Hui Shih, Kuan, Jie Hui Shih, Mei-Ling Chen, Long Zhi

Great Perfection Rainbow State at the Vajra Throne

The photograph on the left was taken at the time when the holy scene was being viewed.
The photograph below is an enlargement of a portion of the original photograph.

左邊的照片即是在現場觀看聖境時拍的
下面的照片為局部放大照片

2006年7月4日下午五點多鐘，我們七位法師等參加了上供多杰羌佛第三世雲高益西諾布頂聖如來的法王袍。我們親眼看到三世多杰羌佛的金剛寶座位上珠光化虹境界，這徹底說明了密乘的修證到了大圓滿最高境界後，無情法物均能化虹飛騰。我們看到過若干次聖境，這一次的化虹就在我們面前展顯，是最殊勝的一次。打妄語當墮金剛地獄，因此虹化境真實不虛，一切功德回向眾生大吉祥！

最關鍵的是，五彩珠光可以說不稀奇，是陽光折射造成的，但是，供法王袍時，萬里晴空無滴雨，五彩珠光竟然剎那彙聚成團，五秒鐘左右即化成一道直立長虹飛向太空佛土，這才真正展顯了大圓滿的至高虹化佛法。

釋覺慧　釋定慧　釋見慧
釋了慧　釋宖慧　釋正慧
Kuan　釋胖慧　時靜玫
陸智

Description for the photograph is on the previous page

H.H. Dorje Chang Buddha III Wan Ko Yeshe Norbu Holiest Tathagata has taught that if one who practices the Great Perfection Dharma has attained the highest level of accomplishment, even the dharma instruments or dharma seat used by such an accomplished one will turn into a rainbow. This has now become a fact.

The place shown on these photographs where the lights are glittering is the vajra throne area where H.H. Dorje Chang Buddha III practiced dharma. Many inner-tantric initiations for rinpoches, dharma teachers, and lamas as well as many Buddha-dharma ceremonies were conducted by H.H. Dorje Chang Buddha III as His Holiness sat within this lawn area, which is a vajra throne mandala.

In the afternoon of July 4, 2006, there was only strong sunlight and not a cloud in the sky. Suddenly, the heavenly dragons roared with laughter causing thunderous sounds in the sky. Additionally, a strong fragrance filled the air. The vajra throne area instantly emitted thousands of glittering rainbow colored lights. Those sparkling lights not only manifested a variety of different colors, they also continually changed as they glittered. Some of them were on the tips of grass, some of them were near the roots of grass, some of them were on the middle of grass, and some of them were suspended in the empty space between blades of grass. Whether that area was viewed from near or afar, and no matter from what angle that area was viewed, different glittering lights could be seen. Each of those lights was more radiant than a flashing diamond under a bright light. Moreover, each person saw different things when viewing that area from the same place. Some saw multicolored lights, some saw white lights, some saw blue lights, some saw red lights, and some saw green lights. What is even more amazing is that those lights constantly changed colors. Some of those lights even

suddenly disappeared, only to reappear suddenly a moment later. A powerful hose was used in an attempt to wash away those glittering lights, but it was of no use. However, when touched by the hand, those sparkling lights immediately vanished without a trace. It was most amazing. Furthermore, those multicolored resplendent lights only appeared at the throne area where H.H. Dorje Chang Buddha III practiced dharma. There were no rainbow lights a few feet away from that throne area on that same lawn. Even after that area a few feet away from the throne area was watered with a hose, no glittering lights could be seen there. These glittering lights then suddenly coalesced and transformed into a colorful and large rainbow that flew into the azure sky. It was unimaginably wondrous.

This holy scene thoroughly demonstrates that the accomplishment of H.H. Dorje Chang Buddha III is incredible! Rinpoches such as Venerable Akou Lamo Rinpoche, H.E. Gar Tongstan IV, and Venerable Xiangge Qiongwa; Dharma Teachers such as Venerable Dharma Teacher Long Hui and Dharma Teacher Jue Hui; and laypeople were there to personally see this holy sight.

We personally saw the above written facts. The photographs below were taken at the time we were viewing rainbow lights shining forth at the vajra throne area of H.H. Dorje Chang Buddha III. We are learning Buddhism and cultivating ourselves. Thus, we dare not speak falsely or deceive living beings. We personally saw the glittering of colorful lights at the vajra throne area! We deeply understand that if we speak falsely and deceive living beings, we will receive karmic retribution. Hence, we are responsible for what we hereby state.

Our signatures are on the next page attesting to the above facts:

(This text was translated from the Chinese text on next page.)

大 圓 滿 虹 化 境 金 剛 寶 座

　　多杰羌佛第三世雲高益西諾布頂聖如來開示說過：修大圓滿法，如果得到最高成就，包括成就者用過的法器、坐過的法座都能虹化。這確實成了事實。

　　照片上放光的星點所在的地方是三世多杰羌佛修法的金剛寶座地，三世多杰羌佛為仁波且、法師、喇嘛們舉行的內密灌頂、很多殊勝的佛法，三世多杰羌佛都是坐在這草坪上，也就是在這個金剛寶座壇城座上舉行的。2006年7月4日下午，萬里晴空，突然天龍吟笑，滾雷響動，同時傳來異香撲鼻，就在這金剛寶座，頓時虹化出幾千顆五彩珠光，這些五彩珠光不僅呈現各種不同的顏色，而且還不停的變化閃動，有的在一葉細草尖上，有的在草根上，有的在草中間，而有的則在草叢空間。無論或遠或近、從什麼方向去看，都可以看到不同的珠光閃爍，勝過鑽石在強光下閃爍的光芒，並且每個人所看到的也不一樣。有看到五彩的，有看到白光的，有看到藍光的，有的則看到的是紅光、綠光。而更為神奇的是，這些光不斷改變顏色，甚至突然消失，而不一會又突然出現。後來用強力水龍頭沖洗，也沖不掉，但用手觸摸時，珠光當下無影無蹤，神奇無

比。而且，這強烈五彩珠光只在三世多杰羌佛修法的寶座地展顯，離開幾尺遠處則毫無虹光，用水沖灑也不見任何珠光。而這些珠光突然

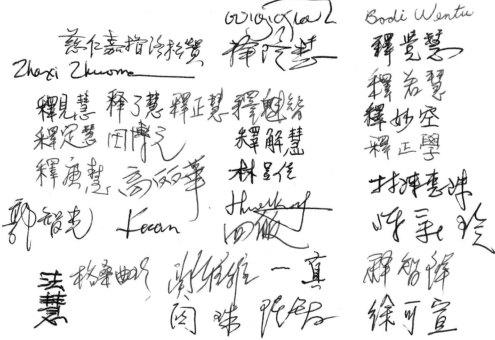

彙聚化成五彩長虹，飛上了藍色的太空，神奇到了無法想像的地步。這一聖境徹底展顯了三世多杰羌佛的成就不可思議！當時阿寇拉摩仁波且、祿東贊尊者、香格瓊哇尊者等為首的仁波且們，釋隆慧、釋覺慧等法師們以及居士們親自在現場見證了這一聖境。

我們親身經歷上文中記載的事實，並在金剛寶座現場觀看三世多杰羌佛的寶座虹化放光時拍攝了照片。我們是學佛修行人，不敢打妄

語欺騙眾生，我們親眼看到金剛寶座現場的五彩珠光閃爍！我們深深知道，如果我們打妄語欺騙眾生的話，我們將會遭到惡報，所以我們說話是負因果責任的。

前一頁下方即是我們起誓的親筆簽名：

（此文的英文翻譯印在前面）

My Master Is Dorje Chang Buddha, the Buddha Vajradhara

My Master is His Holiness Dorje Chang Buddha III Wan Ko Yeshe Norbu Holiest Tathagata. Dorje Chang Buddha is the Master of the Five Buddhas and Vajrasattva. One can see from this just how unsurpassed the status of my Master is.

In my heart, my Master is a great holy being who is indescribably magnificent. However, there was a thin cloud of suspicion in my mind that prevented me from accepting one hundred percent that the true identity of my Master is Dorje Chang Buddha. One day when I was still unable to overcome this thin layer of doubt, a rinpoche asked, "Do all of you know that over the past few thousand years Buddhas have incarnated into this world?" Actually, I did not need to think about how to answer this question. Since Buddhas are compassionate toward living beings, Buddhas of course will incarnate into this world to save living beings. I am sure of this! That Rinpoche then said, "All of you should carefully ponder something. Do you know of any dharma king or eminent monastic in history who possessed the high level of proficiency in exoteric and esoteric Buddhism and the high level of mastery of the Five Vidyas attained by His Holiness Wan Ko Yeshe Norbu Holiest Tathagata? With all of the amazing abilities of His Holiness, if His Holiness is not the incarnation of Dorje Chang Buddha, can other so-called dharma kings and eminent monastics with ordinary manifestations of realization still be called incarnations of Buddhas and Bodhisattvas? To still call them Buddhas and Bodhisattvas in such case would undoubtedly be deceitful."

This line of questioning by the Rinpoche struck me like a thunderbolt. It expressed what the actual truth is. If one's realization is so high that it is unprecedented, yet one is still not the incarnation of Dorje Chang Buddha, then those with poor realization and no abilities are not qualified to be incarnations of a Buddha. That thin layer of doubt over my mind was finally ripped apart!

There was an occasion when H.H. Dorje Chang Buddha III Wan Ko Yeshe Norbu practiced the dharma for us. His Holiness held a vajra in His hand. Upon seeing this, I immediately thought that the vajra held by Dorje Chang Buddha represents the power of wisdom and the use of skillful means and awe-inspiring might based upon supernatural abilities. I wanted so very much to hold that vajra for a moment! The Buddha Master then lifted that vajra high and empowered (blessed) us. I experienced a very wonderful feeling. I thought that I would be so lucky if I could touch that vajra of the Buddha. I was ultimately unable to suppress this wish of mine and asked, "Buddha Master, would you allow me to hold this vajra for a moment?" The

Buddha Master said, "If any of you want to hold it, then go ahead and hold it!"

Upon hearing this, everyone rushed forward. However, they had no idea that such a small vajra placed on a white silk scarf had limitless powers and was as steady and firm as a mountain. No ordinary person could possibly subdue it. Everyone who tried contorted their face as they attempted to lift it with all their might, but they were unsuccessful. A rinpoche finally was able to lift it less than one foot high. When the vajra returned to its original position, he could not lift it again.

That vajra even emitted strong samadhi powers. Nobody had any way to lift it. When it was my turn, I grabbed it with one hand but was not able to move it. Moreover, it produced a strong force that shot directly into my heart. This almost caused my internal organs to explode. But I was not about to give up this opportunity. I pressed down upon the vajra with one hand. I then felt that everything was spinning around me and that my internal organs were burning. In an instant, all of my desire related to killing, stealing, lust, lying, greed, hatred, ignorance, and craving vanished without a trace. My heavens! I finally realized that the magnificent Dorje Chang Buddha descended into this world and incarnated as H.H. Wan Ko Yeshe Norbu Holiest Tathagata. As a result of the awesome force of that empowerment (blessing), a deep impression of the vajra remained on my right hand, disappearing only after about two months.

When I followed Master Shantaraksita in my first incarnation as Muya Jiongzha, I always hoped to see Dorje Chang Buddha one day. Today my wish was finally fulfilled. In this lifetime, I will definitely take advantage of this opportunity by striving to realize the state of a great Bodhisattva and by striving to benefit all living beings in the six realms of reincarnation within the three spheres. What I have stated above is true. Since it is true, may I become a holy being and reach the stage of a Bodhisattva in this lifetime. If any of what I stated is not true, I am willing to receive all karmic retribution for my lying and descend into hell. There is something I would like to tell everyone: I am most fortunate because now I am not Muya Jiongzha I.

Homage to His Holiness Dorje Chang Buddha III Wan Ko Yeshe Norbu Holiest Tathagata!

I prostrate four times.
Buddhist disciple, Uygen Danzeng Queji Nima

(This is a complete translation of the Chinese text that follows originally written and signed by Uygen Danzeng Queji Nima.)

我 的 上 師 是 多 杰 羌 佛 金 剛 總 持

我的上師是多杰羌佛第三世雲高益西諾布頂聖如來。多杰羌佛就是五方五佛及金剛薩埵的上師，這是何等至高無上的概念。在我的心中，我的上師是偉大得無法形容的大聖者，但我要百分之百去接受多杰羌佛是我的上師的真身，這實在是心中一團疑雲，把我的心靈罩上了一層薄紗。就在我無法破除這個薄紗的時候，有一天，一個仁波且開示說：「你們知道幾千年來在這個世界上有佛陀來轉世嗎？」其實這個問題我根本不用想，佛陀是慈悲眾生的，當然會轉世來這個世界渡眾生，我肯定！仁波且說：「你們仔細思考一下，你們見到過歷史上哪一位法王高僧有如雲高益西諾布頂聖如來那樣顯密俱通、妙諳五明的高度嗎？如果他老人家這麼了得的本事都不是多杰羌佛轉世的話，其他的法王高僧證量的展現一般還稱得上佛菩薩轉世再來嗎？那無疑的是在騙人。」仁波且的一個反問，當下猶如雷霆霹頂，確實這才是真理，如果證量已經高到史無前例的程度，都不是多杰羌佛再來，那麼證量差的、沒有能力的，根本就沒有資格是佛陀轉世。我心靈的紗罩終於撕破了！

有一次，三世多杰羌佛雲高益西諾布為我們修法，他老人家手中拿了一個金剛杵，我當下就想到多杰羌佛手中的金剛杵是代表智慧的力量，神通的方便威力。我多麼想拿一下啊！這時佛陀上師把金剛杵舉在空中為我們作加持，感覺非常殊勝。我想，將佛陀的金剛杵摸一下，那該有多好的運氣啊！心中的欲念終於憋不住了：「佛陀上師，您老人家能讓我拿一下這個金剛杵嗎？」佛陀上師說：「你們想拿就拿吧！」大家聞言一哄而上，萬萬沒想到，這小小的金剛杵放在白色的哈達上，威力無窮，穩如泰山，哪裡是凡夫能降伏得了的。大家五官都移了位還是拿不動。一個仁波且終於拿起來，還不到一呎，這金剛杵「唰」的又回到原位，他再也拿不起來了。此金剛杵甚至放出強烈的三昧威力，個個束手無策。輪到我了，我一把向它抓去，不但拿不動，而且它產生一種強烈的力量直射心間，幾乎讓我的五臟六腑轟然爆炸。這機會我可不能放過，我一掌就將金剛杵壓住，此時只覺天旋地轉，五內俱焚，剎那間殺、盜、淫、妄、貪、瞋、痴、愛無影無蹤。我的天啊，我終於見到了偉大的多杰羌佛降世成雲高益西諾布頂聖如來的真身。在加持的威力下，我的右手留下了一個金剛杵深深的印跡，差不多兩個月才消失。

我在第一世跟隨先師釋伽炯乃大師時就一直盼望有一天見到多杰羌佛老人家，今天終於如願了。我一定在今生抓住這個機會，爭取修證成大菩薩，利益三界六道一切眾生。以上所言真實不虛，如若是事實，我今生成聖登地；如有不實，願遭一切罪惡報應，墮地獄。現在我只有兩句話要告訴你們大家，我太幸福了，因為我已不是第一世的木雅迥扎了。

南無多杰羌佛第三世雲高益西諾布頂聖如來！

弟子四拜頂禮
佛弟子　鄔金丹增・卻吉尼瑪

（此文的英文翻譯印在前面）

The True Holy Vajra Pill and My Buddha Master

In Tibetan esoteric dharma, there are five types of precious pills. They are the Nectar Pill, the Long Life Pill, the Great Precious Pill, the Vajra Pill and the Supreme Precious Pill. Actually, these five types of pills are made from nectar bestowed by different Buddhas. There are also red pills and black pills made with Chinese herbs after the herbs are empowered through mantras, such as the red pills and white pills made by H.E. Tangtong Gyalpo. The Long Life Pill has the empowering effect of extending one's lifespan. The Great Precious Pill can further one's accomplishment in the dharma. The Vajra Pill can help dispel demons and increase longevity and good fortune. The Supreme Precious Pill can ensure accomplishment in the dharma. The five types of pills are crystallization of merit produced from the power of Buddha-dharma and the empowerment of Buddhas and Bodhisattvas. Basically, all great rinpoches have what they call precious pills. But most of them are of the ordinary type, not the holy precious type of pills. Holy precious pills and ordinary ones are two totally different concepts. I personally saw Nectar Pills made from nectar bestowed by Buddhas. I also personally saw true Vajra Pills and heard them chant mantras.

Certain famous rinpoches and dharma kings from the highest temples in Tibet have said that the Buddha-dharma that can enable a vajra pill to fly has not been seen in this world in three hundred years. This is a fact. There was a crazy yogi named Be Wa Ba who could manifest such power hundreds of years ago, but according to these respected rinpoches and dharma kings who have had contact with all of the well known dharma kings of recent times, this dharma had disappeared from this world.

I follow my Buddha Master, H.H. Dorje Chang Buddha III Wan Ko Yeshe Norbu Holiest Tathagata, and am constantly by His Holiness's side. Therefore, I have experienced many magnificent and real manifestations of Buddha-dharma. Now I will tell everyone about my experience of the true Vajra Pill. When the holy vajra mantra and mudra are practiced, the Vajra Pill will jump and even transform into rainbow light and soar into the sky. I have also heard the Vajra Pill dance and chant mantras. I watched other people listen to the Vajra Pill sing songs.

I vow that the events reported here are true and happened as reported. If not, I am willing to bear the karmic retribution of the hell realms.

Amazing supernatural events preceded my first experience with the karmic affinity of the Vajra Pill. This happened in April, 2003. I traveled from San Francisco to Los Angeles to see H.H. Wan Ko Yeshe Norbu. During the trip I suddenly saw a colorful and large rainbow light appear in the sky. The rainbow completely surrounded the sun. There were also Sanskrit symbols in the sky. Just as the rainbow was fading from sight, I was able to take a picture of the bottom half of this light by focusing the camera below the sun. A dignified Buddha–Dorje Chang Buddha–appeared in the middle of the rainbow. This Buddha became my Buddha master, H.H. Wan Ko Yeshe Norbu, who was wearing a red robe and was sitting in the middle of the rainbow. The scene was awesome and extremely wonderful. The rainbow light appeared in the sky for several hours.

When I arrived, I was fortunate to immediately see my Buddha Master. A great lama obtained three true Vajra Pills and had respectfully given them to H.H. Wan Ko Yeshe Norbu Holiest Tathagata as an offering. The Buddha Master bestowed me with two of them. Unexpectedly the Vajra Pills in my hand started to jump. At that time the Vajra Pills jumped in my hand just as if they were alive. They not only jumped but one of them started to circle around and left my hand. It transformed into a dazzling bright red light and soared into the sky. At that time, I saw that the Buddha Master, who sat far away on the dais, had become a blue Buddha Vajradhara. The blue light was shining bright. The scene was very dignified. I was greatly astonished. This is when I first saw the true Vajra Pill and the true identity of my Buddha Master.

There was a very virtuous disciple who came from Australia. Because of a question I had asked H.H. Wan Ko Yeshe Norbu Holiest Tathagata about a dharma matter concerning mysterious power, the Holiest Tathagata said to me, "Bring your Vajra Pill to empower this disciple." I took out the Vajra Pill. In order to prevent the Vajra Pill from escaping, this great layperson personally put the Vajra Pill in a small cup and sealed the cup with a piece of paper. The disciple put the cup to his ear and moved 15-20 feet away from the Holiest Tathagata. Several of us were sitting on the floor around H.H. Wan Ko Yeshe Norbu Holiest Tathagata. Then everyone started to chant mantras and practice dharma. Soon the Vajra Pill began to chant and sing Buddhist songs. This layperson was very moved. It is hard to believe that a tiny pill can actually sing Buddhist songs, but I have heard this myself. Actually, I did not hear Buddhist songs, but clearly heard the chanting of holy mantras. The sound came from this tiny BB sized pill that I personally held to my ear. It is truly unbelievable. In this world within the supreme Vajra Division of Esoteric Buddhism the Vajra Pill truly can be categorized into ordinary types and holy types. The Vajra Pill in my hand was living proof of the holy type.

Today I sincerely tell everyone my personal experience. My Buddha Master, H.H. Dorje Chang Buddha III Wan Ko Yeshe Norbu Holiest Tathagata is the supreme and highest Buddha. May all living beings have the good fortune to hear, learn, and practice the true Buddha-dharma and quickly attain enlightenment.

I, Buddhist disciple Zhaxi Zhuoma, sincerely vow and clearly write down these events to prove the existence of the true Buddha-dharma in the world today.

Zhaxi Zhuoma

(The Chinese translation of this text follows.)

眞正的金剛丸和我的佛陀恩師

在藏密法中有五種寶丸,甘露丸、長壽丸、大寶丸、金剛丸、至寶丸,其實這五種寶丸都是由不同的佛降甘露而製成的,也有用中草藥咒語加持後製成的紅丸或黑丸,如唐東迦波製的紅白丸。長壽丸它有延長壽命的加持作用,大寶丸能助長成就,金剛丸能除魔增壽增福,至寶丸能確保成就,這五種丸都是佛法的法力和佛菩薩的加持力所產生的功德結晶。大仁波且們基本上都有這些東西,但是他們大部份都是普通性的,不是聖品寶丸。聖品寶丸和普通性的完全是兩個概念。我親自見到過佛陀降下的甘露做成的甘露丸,我也親自見到過和聽到過金剛丸誦咒。

在西藏最頂尖的寺廟中有些著名的仁波且和法王們曾經說過,能使金剛丸飛行的佛法,在這世界上已有三百年沒見過了。這是個事實。以前有一位瘋子瑜珈行者叫貝瓦巴,在幾百年前他能展顯這種力量,但根據這些與近代所有著名的法王們接觸過且備受尊敬的仁波且和法王們說,這樣的佛法已在這世界上消失了。

我跟隨我的佛陀上師三世多杰羌佛雲高益西諾布頂聖如來,由於隨時在身邊,就經歷了很多偉大佛法的真實事跡。這裡我講一個真正的金剛丸給大家聽。真正的金剛丸在唸金剛聖咒和結手印的情況下,

它會跳動,甚至於虹化飛空。我也曾經聽過金剛丸跳舞、念咒和見到別人聽過金剛丸唱歌。我發誓我以上所講的和所經歷的事是真實不虛的,如果不是真的,我願承受地獄的果報。

在我首次經歷金剛丸因緣之前,有一些不可思議的神奇事發生。那是在2003年4月,當天我從舊金山到洛杉磯拜見雲高益西諾布時,突然見到天空出現五彩長虹,此長虹完全圍繞著太陽,空中也有梵文字出現,當長虹慢慢褪去時,我才能將照相機聚焦於太陽下而拍下此下方的半圈光芒的照片,長虹中央出現了莊嚴的佛陀——多杰羌佛,佛陀變化成身著紅袍的雲高益西諾布的法像,端坐在光環中央,殊勝無比,這境像顯現在空中長達幾個小時。

當我到達時,我有幸能立即見到佛陀恩師,一位大喇嘛拿到三枚真正的金剛丸,供養雲高益西諾布頂聖如來,佛陀上師加持我兩粒,這金剛丸在我的手中就竟然開始跳動了,完全像有生命一樣,不但跳動,其中一枚甚至於開始盤旋著離開我的手,化成亮紅光,飛向虛空。此時,我親眼見到遠遠坐在法台上的佛陀上師變為藍色金剛總持,藍光朗明,無上莊嚴,讓我吃驚不少,原來這才是我第一次見到的真正的金剛丸和我佛陀恩師的真身。

有一次，一位來自澳洲非常有德的弟子，由於我請示雲高益西諾布頂聖如來一個佛法上關於神秘力量的問題，頂聖如來說：你的金剛丸拿來加持這位居士吧。我拿出金剛丸，這位大居士親自將金剛丸放在一個小杯裡，為了防止金剛丸跑掉，即用一張紙將它封起來，這位居士將小杯放在他的耳邊，走到距離頂聖如來雲高益西諾布15-20英呎的地方，我們幾個坐在雲高益西諾布頂聖如來身邊的地上，大家開始誦咒修法。很快的，金剛丸開始持咒及唱道歌，這位居士非常感動。很難相信一個小小的丸子真的會唱道歌，我自己親自聽到，我將那如米粒大小的金剛丸放在我的耳邊，但不是唱道歌，而是聽到它清楚地誦咒語的聲音。這真是不可思議。這世界至高密乘金剛部中，那金剛

丸確實有凡品和聖品之分，我手中的金剛丸即是聖品的實證。這不由我想到，難怪三世多杰羌佛偉大恩師灌頂的現量大圓滿會當場見到法界境顯。

我今天真誠告訴大家我的親身經歷，我三世多杰羌佛雲高益西諾布頂聖如來恩師是至高無上的第一大佛陀。願所有眾生有福報聽聞及修學真正的佛法，並早日得成就。

佛弟子　扎西卓瑪
誠心發誓明證行文
（此文由前面的英文翻譯而來）

Dragon-Fish Stand Straight Up on the Surface of the Water and Pay Respect to H.H. Dorje Chang Buddha III by Bowing to His Holiness

On November 6, 1999, I was very fortunate to have been able to accompany H.H. Dorje Chang Buddha III Wan Ko Yeshe Norbu to Puttamonton, Thailand. I went there together with Professor Yu-Hua Wang, who holds a doctorate degree in Buddhism Dharma Philosophy from the American League of Colleges and Universities, which is composed of 83 colleges and universities in the United States and around the world, and who also holds a Ph.D. degree from Manning University in England. Other people who went on that trip with us included H.E. Denma Tsemang II, Venerable Dachu II Hengsheng Rinpoche and Luoben Songzan. There were more than thirty of us all together.

After we prostrated before the holy image of Sakyamuni Buddha, we walked to a bodhi tree beside a lake under which H.H. Dorje Chang Buddha III sat. Perceiving that the karmic conditions were special, Venerable Dachu II Hengsheng Rinpoche knelt on the ground, put his palms together in respect, and respectfully beseeched H.H. Dorje Chang Buddha III to give a discourse on how an Arhat can realize the state of a Bodhisattva, how a Bodhisattva can ascend to the supreme and complete enlightenment of a Buddha, and why a Buddha has to rely on saving living beings to become a Buddha.

At this time, many types of birds flew over to us from all directions and perched themselves on that tree. Various types of wild fish in the lake beside H.H. Dorje Chang

Dragon-fish stand straight up on the surface of the water and pay respect to H.H. Dorje Chang Buddha III by bowing to His Holiness.
龍魚立水禮拜三世多杰羌佛

Buddha III swam over to us. Two wild dogs also made their way into the middle of that group of people in front of H.H. Dorje Chang Buddha III's seat. It was extremely marvelous.

Right when H.H. Dorje Chang Buddha III was expounding the highest wondrous dharma, waves suddenly surged from the quiet waters of the lake. There was a loud sound. A black dragon transformed itself into a large black and gold fish. That fish emerged vertically from the water and stood erect on its tail on the surface of the water. It resembled a dolphin performing on the water. It bowed its head toward H.H. Dorje Chang Buddha III after each movement. At this time, a white fish and a black fish also did what that other large fish did, emerging from the water to pay their respects to H.H. Dorje Chang Buddha III. This scene lasted about twenty seconds. Some fellow disciples took out their cameras and pressed down upon the shutter. They were able to capture that scene.

Nobody ever saw such an amazing spectacle before. They were lost in wonder over such an unrivaled sight. They knew that large fish was a dragon-spirit who transformed itself into a fish in order to receive the dharma and pay its respects to H.H. Dorje Chang Buddha III. They must have been transformed dragon-spirits since no other type of fish has the ability to use its tail to stand vertically upon the surface of the water. Furthermore, two-thirds of the bodies of the fish were over the surface of the water, leaving only the one-third tail portion of their bodies below the surface of the water.

Still, H.H. Dorje Chang Buddha III smiled and said, "This is a response evoked by the Buddha-dharma. One should practice the Buddha-dharma with a heart of humility. Amazing feats are like dreams and illusions, like clouds and smoke that pass in an instant. One must not be attached to them. They are not worth mentioning."

When great saints expound the wonderful dharma, humans and non-humans pay their respects. This is the result of the merit and realization of a Buddha!

A great holy and virtuous being said, "I have heard discourses on the Buddha-dharma given by H.H. Great Dharma King[1]. H.H. Great Dharma King is a Buddha!" Guru Padmasambhava highly praised this great holy and virtuous being and an emperor of China conferred upon him the title of Khutukhtu Dharma King.

The holy events described above are true occurrences that I personally saw at that scene. Later, many newspapers reported on these holy events. If there are false statements in what I have just stated, I am willing to receive the most severe karmic retribution. Those were real events. May the merit of this be dedicated to all living beings in the dharma realms.

Buddhist Disciple
Ciren Gyatso

(This is a complete translation of the Chinese text that follows originally written and signed by Ciren Gyatso.)

龍魚立水禮拜三世多杰羌佛

1999年11月6日，我很有福報地跟隨由美國及世界八十三所大學組成的美國大學聯盟的佛法哲學博士、英國曼寧大學哲學博士、導師王玉花佛母和丹瑪‧翟芒尊者第二世、達楚尊者第二世恆生仁波且、洛本松贊等共三十餘位，陪同多杰羌佛第三世雲高益西諾布頂聖如來，在泰國佛教城禮拜釋迦牟尼佛聖像之後，走到湖邊的菩提樹下，三世多杰羌佛敷座而坐，達楚尊者第二世恆生仁波且見到這殊勝的因緣，即跪地合掌恭敬禮請佛陀上師開示：「羅漢如何得證菩薩境界？菩薩如何登地達到佛陀無上正等正覺？為什麼佛陀要依渡生成佛？」這時，從四處飛來了多種鳥類棲息於樹上，三世多杰羌佛前面的湖泊中游來了各類野魚，有兩隻野狗同時也來到人群中央三世多杰羌佛的座前，實在奇妙無比。當佛陀上師正宣說至高微妙的法義時，突然湖中平靜的水翻波湧浪，一聲響亮，一條烏龍搖身變成一條烏金色的大魚，就從水中直端端的冒起來，並且以尾部獨立於水面，猶如海豚水上表演一般，一行一點頭，向三世多杰羌佛頂禮，此時又有兩條一白色一黑色的魚，也做大魚姿勢，伸出水面向三世多杰羌佛頂禮，時間長達二十秒鐘左右。有同學取出照相機，按下快門竟然拍下這個鏡頭。這種神奇的景象，大家從未見過，皆嘆為觀止，知道這是龍神化顯，前來受法，恭敬禮拜。如非龍神化現，任何魚類也不可能具備以尾部獨立於水面的功能，更何況魚身的三分之二立於水面之上，只剩下三分之一的尾巴在水面之下。但三世多杰羌佛卻笑著說：「這是佛陀法義的感召。應以慚愧之心修持佛法，神奇之舉，猶如夢幻，瞬息雲煙，不可執著，不足掛齒。」大聖說妙法，人非人禮拜，這是佛陀的功德證境才能有的啊！正如蓮花生大師金剛語授記、中國大皇帝封為呼圖克圖法王的大聖德說：「我曾聞金剛總持大法王的佛法開示，大法王就是佛陀！」

以上聖蹟是我在現場目睹的真實情況，後來各大報紙均有報導此一聖蹟，如有妄語，願受最嚴厲的果報，這是真實不虛的事情，願將功德回向給法界一切眾生。

佛弟子　慈仁嘉措

（此文的英文翻譯印在前面）

---

[1] Here and below the word *H.H. Great Dharma King* refers to H.H. Dorje Chang Buddha III Wan Ko Yeshe Norbu Holiest Tathagata.

A Wild Squirrel Offered Avocadoes to H.H. Dorje Chang Buddha III

In the afternoon of April 24th, 2000, disciple Long Zhi,[1] and Juehai walked along the swimming pool with H.H. Dorje Chang Buddha III Wan Ko Yeshe Norbu Holiest Tathagata in the outer area of the mandala. H.H. Dorje Chang Buddha III pointed to an avocado tree and said, "I want everyone to try the fruits." So H.H. Dorje Chang Buddha III told Long Zhi to get a fruit catcher. Long Zhi looked around and didn't find one. H.H. Dorje Chang Buddha III said, "We have to pick some avocados." Right after H.H. Dorje Chang Buddha III spoke these words, a brown squirrel came down from an old pine tree. H.H. Dorje Chang Buddha III told everyone, "Don't chase the squirrel away. It came to help."

The squirrel climbed up the avocado tree and started looking for avocados. It started to use all of its skills by jumping from branch to branch, hanging upside down, and sometimes holding on to a branch with just one paw to locate the avocados. It was hard to see the green avocados amongst the very bushy green leaves. But the squirrel was able to distinguish them and delivered the avocados one by one. In less than ten minutes, the squirrel delivered six avocados. H.H. Buddha Master said that was enough. So Long Zhi told the squirrel: "Hey, squirrel, you have been working hard. Your offering has built up plenty of merit. It is enough." The squirrel stopped and stayed on the branch. It looked at H.H. Dorje Chang Buddha III with both paws held together. These six avocados were offerings to H.H. Dorje Chang Buddha III by the squirrel.

When H.H. Dorje Chang Buddha III was about to leave, the squirrel did one prostration in front of the Buddha Master and slowly departed. Since then, the nuns who live at the holy mandala watch squirrels climbing on the avocado tree but never see the avocados being picked anymore as offerings.

Dragon fish stood up on the water to show their respect for His Holiness. Animals offered fruits to His Holiness. Cases like these can hardly be found among other dharma kings and eminent monks in history.

The story of the squirrel offering six avocados to H.H. Dorje Chang Buddha III recorded by Long Zhi and Juehai is totally true. If it is not true, we will be responsible for all resulting bad karma. If it is true, the merits will be dedicated to all living beings in the six realms of reincarnation. May they be able to listen to true Buddha-dharma from H.H. Dorje Chang Buddha III.

Long Zhi

(This is a complete translation of the Chinese text that follows originally written and signed by Long Zhi.)

松 鼠 獻 酪 梨 給 三 世 多 杰 羌 佛

公元二零零零年四月二十六日下午，隆智（即丹瑪・翟芒尊者第二世——編者注，下同）與覺海陪同多杰羌佛第三世雲高益西諾布頂聖如來在居舍法壇妙游池邊，此時三世多杰羌佛指著一株酪梨樹(英文為：avocado)說：「這樹上的果我一直都想給大家嚐一下。」隨後，

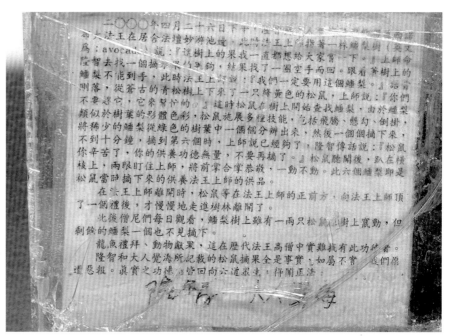

A wild squirrel learned dharma under H.H. Dorje Chang Buddha III. The above photograph shows the six avocadoes that the squirrel picked from a tree and offered to H.H. Dorje Chang Buddha III.
野生松鼠拜三世多杰羌佛學法，從樹上摘了六個酪梨做供養

These six avocadoes have been preserved as specimens. This text is copied from the explanation on the specimen box.
此六個酪梨已製成標本保存，此文即抄錄於該標本上的說明

---

[1] Here and below the word *Long Zhi* refers to H.E. Denma Tsemang II.

三世多杰羌佛命隆智去找一個摘水果的果鉤，結果找了一圈，空手而回，眼看著樹上的酪梨不能到手，此時三世多杰羌佛說：「我們一定要用這個酪梨。」話音剛落，從蒼古的青松樹上下來了一隻絳黃色的松鼠，三世多杰羌佛說：「你們不要趕牠，牠來幫忙的。」這時松鼠在樹上開始查找酪梨，由於酪梨類似於樹葉的形體色彩，松鼠施展多種技能，包括飛騰、懸勾、倒掛，將稀少的酪梨從綠色的樹葉中一個個分辨出來，然後一個個摘下來，不到十分鐘，摘到第六個時，佛陀上師說已經夠了，隆智傳話說：「松鼠！你辛苦了！你的供養功德無量，不要再摘了。」松鼠聽聞後，趴在橫枝上，兩眼盯住三世多杰羌佛，將前掌合掌恭敬，一動不動。此六個酪梨即是松鼠當時摘下來的供養三世多杰羌佛的供品。

在三世多杰羌佛離開時，松鼠等在佛陀上師的正前方，向佛陀上師頂了一個禮後，才慢慢地走進樹林離開了。

此後僧尼們每日觀看，酪梨樹上雖有一兩隻松鼠在樹上竄動，但剩餘的酪梨一個也不見摘下。龍魚禮拜、動物獻果，這在歷代法王高僧中實難找有此功德者。

隆智和覺海所記載的松鼠摘果全是事實，如屬不實，我們願遭惡報。真實的功德悉皆回向六道眾生，得聞正法。

隆智

（此文的英文翻譯印在前面）

The Account of a Holy Incident

What I am about to say is about the Yun sculpture "A Pillar Holding Up Heaven" created by H.H. Master Wan Ko Yee[1], my Buddha Dharma King Master. One year and nine months ago, this holy work of art was completed and its shape finalized. A year and nine months had passed, and several of us decided to place the artwork "A Pillar Holding Up Heaven" into a display cabinet. First, the bottom edge of the artwork had to be closely traced on a baseboard. This was done to make sure that the sculpture would be centered. I personally traced a black line very carefully around the artwork. At that point, we all figured out that the size of the display cabinet which had previously been calculated and built was too small and the upper portion of the artwork would go beyond the baseboard. Because the body of the artwork was too large, it was impossible to fit in the display cabinet. H.H. Master Wan Ko Yee strictly criticized us, "Why didn't you measure it right in the beginning? Will this display cabinet, worth thousands of dollars, now be discarded?" The Master faced "A Pillar Holding Up Heaven" and casually said to himself, "It would be nice if you could become smaller!" After the Master finished saying that, six of us lifted "A Pillar Holding Up Heaven" and placed it down on the floor. Because it was such a precious piece and worth so much, we all guarded the spot.

Approximately five hours passed. We then lifted it to the baseboard preparing to take a picture. Just as "A Pillar Holding Up Heaven" was moved up to the baseboard where I had previously traced the black line, a fellow disciple suddenly yelled, "Hey, it has become the magic stick of Sun Wu Kong (the Monkey King)!" Everyone looked. To our surprise, "A Pillar Holding Up Heaven" had actually shrunk. With only H.H. Buddha Dharma King's words "Let it be smaller...", it actually shrunk and now fit perfectly into the display cabinet. At this moment, I traced a red line around the bottom edge of the artwork once again on the same baseboard that showed the previously traced black line. When comparing the two lines, the widest part of the artwork had actually shrunk and the line was now more than two inches smaller than the previous line. The entire upper portion of the artwork shrank and fit perfectly into the area of the display cabinet. This inanimate piece of artwork which had already finalized its shape was truly magnificent and unbelievably amazing.

I am a Buddhist disciple. I would not fabricate false testimony which would violate the law of cause and effect. These two lines were traced by me that day based on the bottom edge of the actual artwork that day. Moreover, the artwork indeed shrank because of the Master's words. If any of the above is falsely fabricated, I shall be punished, enter the three evil paths and become an animal. If this account of said facts is authentic, I will greatly gain good fortune and wisdom and dedicate the merit to the well-being of everyone.

Now, I have some honest words that come from my heart that I would like to give everyone. Everyone should think about just what level this great and authentic Buddha-dharma actually is on so that such power can be demonstrated. Shouldn't we take this opportunity to take refuge and learn the authentic Buddha-dharma?

Buddhist Disciple
Qi, Pengzhi documented this account.
August 18, 2004

(This is a complete translation of the Chinese text that follows originally written and signed by Qi, Pengzhi.)

聖 蹟 記

我要說的是，雲高大師（即多杰羌佛第三世雲高益西諾布頂聖如來——編者注，下同）——我的佛陀法王上師，他的韻雕『一柱擎天』

這一聖品藝術已在一年九個月前完成定了型，過了一年九個月我們幾個人決定把『一柱擎天』作品安放在展櫃中，首先要在底板上緊貼著

[1] Here and below the word *Master Wan Ko Yee* refers to H.H. Dorje Chang Buddha III Wan Ko Yeshe Norbu Holiest Tathagata.

作品劃上地腳線，是為了確定作品的中央位置，我親自用黑線很細心的沿著作品畫了一圈，這時大家發現當時展櫃的尺寸計算小了，作品的上半部超出了底板，由於它的體過大，已無法裝進展櫃中，此時雲高大師很嚴格地批評說：『你們幾個為什麼當初不量好尺寸，這幾千元錢的展櫃不就報廢了嗎？』大師對著『一柱擎天』不經意地自言自語說：『你小一點就好了嘛！……』說完，我們六個人把『一柱擎天』抬下來放在地上，由於它太珍貴，所以幾個人都在現場看護著。時間大概過了五個小時，大家將它抬上底板，準備拍照，當『一柱擎天』搬上我畫過線的底板，這時一個同學突然大叫一聲說：『嘿，它成了孫悟空的金箍棒了！』眾人一看，『一柱擎天』竟然縮小了，佛陀法王就那麼一句話『讓它小一點』，它果然縮小，裝進了展櫃。我當下再度用紅線在原有劃黑線的底板上，沿著作品畫了紅色的地腳線，兩條線一對比，寬面的部分竟然縮小了兩寸多，上半部全部縮進了展櫃內的區域，這個沒有生命、已定型的作品實在是太偉大不可思議了。我是佛弟子，我不會編造假話去錯因果，這兩條線是我當天根據實際的作品地腳線畫下來的，而作品也是當天大師一句話，它就縮小的。如果我以上的文字是虛假編造的，我應該打入三惡道變畜牲，如果我立的文句是真的，將福慧宏生，回向大家幸福。

在這裡，我送給大家兩句知心話，大家應該想一想這是何等偉大真實的佛法才能有如此道力的展現，我們不應該抓住這個機會皈依、學習真正的法門嗎？

佛弟子 戚朋直 立記
公元二〇〇四年八月十八日

（此文的英文翻譯印在前面）

The layperson Qi holds his tracing of the lines for the original (in black) and reduced (in red) outlines of "A Pillar Holding Up Heaven"
戚居士和他為『一柱擎天』畫線的原件照片

A Pillar Holding Up Heaven
一柱擎天

Hair Sariras (1)

H.H. Dorje Chang Buddha III Wan Ko Yeshe Norbu Holiest Tathagata usually cuts His own hair. However, there have been several times when I respectfully accompanied His Holiness to a barber shop. Each time, out of respect, after other people's hair on the floor was swept away and the floor was cleaned, the haircut began. When the cut was finished, I would respectfully gather the Buddha Master's hair from the floor and wrap it carefully with paper. I would then place it on my Buddhist altar when I got back home. Gradually, I have been collecting and keeping some of the hair.

I still remember what happened on June 1, 2003. On that day, I took out several unopened paper packs and organized them, intending to wash the hair. Because the individual hairs were very fine, I had paid special attention and placed them on a screen. While soaking them in water, I saw three small round red beads among the hair. The entire cleaning process was handled by me, and I did not touch anything else during that time. I felt this to be very strange and wondered where those red beads came from. I intended to press them with my finger to see if they were hard or soft and even took a magnifying glass to carefully exam them. Suddenly, a thought occurred to me. Could they be sariras? I realized if I did this, it would be too disrespectful.

Hurriedly, I placed the three small beads in a small white box and took them to H.H. Dorje Chang Buddha III to inquire of their origin. I asked, "May I know what these things are?" The Buddha Master said, "Where did you get these? These are sariras!" Afterwards, the Buddha Master practiced dharma and chanted mantras to prove the authenticity of those sariras. I reported to the Buddha Master that they were wrapped in paper and appeared from the cut hair of His Holiness.

Later, the Buddha Master gave us a special discourse in which His Holiness stated, "This has happened because of conditions and the level of fortune of all sentient beings. It does not matter where they come from. Perhaps they originated from the empowerment of the Buddhas and Bodhisattvas. It actually does not matter what the disciples think concerning how or where they come from. If they can appear out of nothing, then they can disappear out of nothing. The important thing is the cultivation of each one of us and the need to live in accordance with the teachings and abide by the principles of Buddhism."

That night, I carefully placed those three red sariras in a small tightly covered Tibetan box and cushioned them with white cotton. The next day, a fellow disciple requested to view them. I thought about placing the sariras in a crystal bottle that I had just bought. When I opened the small box and

Perfect Red sariras grew out of the hair of H.H. Dorje Chang Buddha III.
三世多杰羌佛的頭髮長出了圓滿的紅舍利

looked inside–how could it be that there were only two sariras left? I did not touch any other things anymore! I shredded and tore the cotton, but could only find two sariras. It was really upsetting! This proves and corresponds to what H.H. Dorje Chang Buddha III previously expounded: "If they can appear out of nothing, then they can disappear out of nothing." I once heard a sister personally attested to the fact that sariras fell off of the Buddha Master. This time, I personally witnessed such an occurrence myself. It is truly an extremely wonderful and auspicious sign.

All that I have said above is true and authentic. If there are any false statements, may I suffer all evil retribution. If they are real facts, may living beings be able to receive the dharma teachings of H.H. Dorje Chang Buddha III Wan Ko Yeshe Norbu Holiest Tathagata, be liberated from the cycle of life and death, and gain wisdom and good fortune.

Buddhist disciple,
Hsuan Hui

(This is a complete translation of the Chinese text that follows originally written and signed by Hsuan Hui.)

髮舍利之一

多杰羌佛第三世雲高益西諾布頂聖如來的頭髮，一般都是他老人家自己修剪，但有幾次由我恭送三世多杰羌佛到理髮店，每次都會先將理髮店地上的頭髮掃去，地乾淨了，才開始理髮。然後每次都恭敬地將佛陀上師的頭髮收起來，小心地用紙包好，回家供在佛桌上，慢慢地收集保存了一些。

還記得是在2003年6月1日這一天，我將一些尚未打開的紙包拿出來整理，想將頭髮洗一洗，因為頭髮很細，我特別用過濾網裝起，浸在水裏，就看到有三顆圓潤的紅色小珠子在其間，因所有過程是我自己經手，沒有碰觸過任何其他物件，我深感奇怪，哪裡跑來的紅珠子？想用手指按按看，這小珠子是軟的還是硬的？還拿了一個放大鏡仔細來瞧瞧，忽然腦中一念，這會不會是舍利？我這樣做就太不恭敬了！趕緊將那三顆小珠子，裝在一個白色的小盒子內，拿去請示三世多杰羌佛：「請問這是什麼東西？」佛陀上師說：「妳從哪裡得來的？這個是舍利啊！」然後修法持咒，確定這是真正的舍利，我稟告佛陀上師，這是包在紙內，佛陀上師剪下的頭髮中出現的，之後，佛陀上師特別開示：「這應該說是眾生的福報和因緣，無論是怎麼來的，或是佛菩薩加持的也好，同學們怎麼想其實都不重要，它會無中生有來，就會無中生有去，重要的是我們每一個人自我的修行問題，要依教合法。」當晚，我小心翼翼地將這三顆紅色的舍利，裝在一個

蓋的很緊密的西藏小盒內，上面墊了一些白棉花。第二天，有位同學想請去看看，我想把舍利換裝在一個新買的水晶瓶內，當我打開小盒子一看，怎麼只有兩顆呢？我沒有再觸碰過任何其他物件啊！棉花被我一絲絲地撕開、撕爛，就是只看到兩顆，真令人懊惱！它印證了三世多杰羌佛先前所言：「它會無中生有而來，無中生有而去！」我也曾聽過一位師姐親見過佛陀上師的身上掉下舍利，這次自己能夠親眼見到，真是無限殊勝祥瑞。以上所說，如有任何假話，願遭一切惡報，確是真實不虛，願眾生得聞多杰羌佛第三世雲高益西諾布頂聖如來的法義，了脫生死，福慧增長。

佛弟子 宣慧

（此文的英文翻譯印在前面）

Hair Sariras (2)

I established a Buddhist altar at my home in Thailand on January 16, 2005. On that day, a fellow-disciple brought me a small glass bottle containing several individual strands of the hair sariras of my Buddha Master, Dorje Chang Buddha III Wan Ko Yeshe Norbu Holiest Tathagata. Each hair was roughly one centimeter long. I respectfully placed a blue semi-precious stone inside the bottle and set the bottle onto my altar.

A few months later, I decided to replace the glass bottle with a Venetian crystal bottle. When I opened the glass bottle, I noticed that the originally short hairs were longer than before. Although I was taken aback, I did not think much of it at first. However, the hairs continued to grow, and recently the difference has become unmistakable. Some of the hairs have grown as much as five or six times their original length and now are five or six centimeters long. Some hairs were pinned down on both ends by the stone, and their middle section had grown into a loop. How truly amazing!

From a scientific point of view, hair cells die upon being cut. How could short severed hairs continue to grow? Let the continuing growth of the hairs strengthen our conviction. This is a genuine manifestation of the power of the Buddha-dharma!

Buddhist disciple,
Shu-Hui Chen

(This is a complete translation of the Chinese text that follows originally written and signed by Shu-Hui Chen.)

髮舍利之二

我在泰國家裡的佛堂設於2005年1月16日。這天，一位師姐送來了我的佛陀上師多杰羌佛第三世雲高益西諾布頂聖如來的幾根髮舍利，每根長度將近一公分，裝在一個小小玻璃瓶裡，我恭敬地拿了一個藍色半寶石，一同放在玻璃瓶裡。從那天起，髮舍利就一直供奉在佛堂裡。

幾個月後，我想把玻璃瓶換成維也納水晶玻璃瓶，於是打開原本的玻璃瓶，赫然發現原本短短的髮舍利變長了一些，但我也沒有多想，只覺得神奇，原來髮舍利真的會變長。直到最近，髮舍利明顯地長長了，有些已長了五、六倍，有五、六公分長，有的髮根、頭尾都

被寶石壓著，中間繞出一個圓圈來，真的是非常不可思議！

根據科學角度，細胞隨著頭髮剪掉而死掉，被剪下的一小段頭髮，怎麼可能還會繼續長？大家驚訝之餘，更加生起信心，這真的是佛法的偉大力量呀！

佛弟子陳淑惠

陳淑惠

（此文的英文翻譯印在前面）

A MIRACLE FROM HEAVEN; WITH THE HOT SUN OVERHEAD AND NOT A DROP OF RAIN FROM THE SKY, A MAGNOLIA TREE DRIPS FRAGRANT RAIN AND RESPONDS TO WORDS

(This is a translation of an article published in the Chi-Am Daily News on Jan. 28, 2002.)

In a certain place in the United States, a magnolia tree was discovered through which nectar rain fell several times. On the first day, the tree rained for twelve consecutive hours from 8:00 in the morning straight through until 8:00 at night. Many people surrounded the tree and observed what was happening. The weather that day was clear, with the hot sun shinning down. Before that day, it had not rained even one drop for more than twenty days. Thus, before the tree rained, its branches were dry. However, it was very strange that although the tree branches were dense, the rain did not fall on the branches. Moreover, the fragrance of the drops of rain could easily be smelled. The drops of rain were slender and long, like pine needles. They could even fall diagonally. This truly can be called a miracle in this world.

This extraordinary rain fell from between the dense branches of a magnolia tree that had a radius from the trunk of about fifteen feet and no leaves. Other trees that were very close to this magnolia tree, whether they had leaves or not, surprisingly did not drip one drop of water. What was most amazing was that the rain was very dense, yet not one drop of water fell on the trunk of the magnolia tree. In addition, not one drop of rain dripped from the tree's branches. Instead, the rain suddenly appeared in between the branches and flowers. These drops sparkled with white light and emitted a strong fragrance.

Those who were at the scene looked up at the raindrops that were falling. Some of them held the rainwater in their hands and drank it. Some of them rubbed the rainwater on their sores. Some of them applied the rainwater on the top of their heads. Many of them spontaneously exclaimed, "How fragrant!" After a short period of time, the clothes of many people were wet with rainwater. Those

who were at scene included famous Great Rinpoches, famous Great Dharma Teachers, Dharma Teachers, and ordinary people.

According to a Great Rinpoche who was at the scene and saw this extraordinary rain, that magnolia tree is located on a large property housing a leading figure in Buddhist circles who is the most famous female Dharma King, as well as several Great Rinpoches and eminent Dharma Teachers. That morning at 8:00, an extremely famous Great Master together with that female Dharma King led Rinpoches and Dharma Teachers to a wide lawn on that large property to inspect artwork. A disciple placed a rattan chair under the magnolia tree. That Great Master began meditating on that rattan chair.

The Rinpoches and Dharma Teachers who were standing nearby inspecting artwork suddenly noticed that auspicious clouds had enveloped that magnolia tree. They were astounded and immediately rushed over to the magnolia tree, where they discovered the Great Master in the midst of meditation. They also discovered that dense raindrops began falling from the spaces in between the crisscrossing branches of the magnolia tree. However, in the area outside of that tree, the sky was clear and sunny and there was not one drop of rain. The Dharma Teachers said that this was the manifestation of a holy event, so they quickly went to fetch their camcorders to film this scene. After about ten or fifteen minutes, they brought back their camcorders.

The Great Master then stood up and said, "This is nectar water. It will stop." As soon as those words were spoken, the rain stopped. He then said, "The nectar water will continue to fall until 8:00 this evening." Right after those words were spoken, nectar rain again began falling from the upper part of that magnolia tree.

The Great Master then asked, "Would you like to see nectar water fall from another tree?" Everyone then moved about twenty yards away to a maple tree whose leaves had completely fallen off. Fragrant rain immediately fell from that tree as they were standing under it.

At that time, with great admiration, the female Dharma King said in a loud voice, "Disciples! The Great Master sat under this tree for a short time and from it nectar descended. You can imagine just what kind of holy and virtuous being the Great Master is!"

The Great Master replied, "I do not have any ability or virtue to cause such an occurrence. It occurred because this place has the merit of housing the female Dharma King Holy Mother. Why didn't nectar fall at another place in this entire world?"

That day monastics and Rinpoches watched over that place from 8:00 in the morning until 8:00 in the evening, when the nectar stopped falling. At that time, the Great Master and the female Dharma King told everyone to return the next morning to observe a ceremony, at which time nectar would continue to fall.

The next day, I went with a group of laypersons and monastics to that place to observe the ceremony. It turned out exactly as described to me before. It was incredibly amazing. I walked under that magnolia tree, raised my head and looked upward. My face, body, and mouth were wet with nectar water. An extraordinary fragrance wafted toward my nose. Ordinary perfume could not come close to matching such an aroma. The sky was clear as far as the eye could see, and the nectar continued to descend. During that time, other people and I touched the tree trunk, branches, and flower buds. To our surprise, they were all dry. Among those at the scene, there was a person from Taiwan and an American who both were skeptical. They climbed to the top of the tree and carefully inspected the situation. They discovered that the branches were all dry, there were no insects, and the raindrops appeared out of nowhere, falling from the empty spaces where the branches crisscross. Some raindrops sprayed down, and some sprinkled down, bypassing the dry branches and trunk. They could not figure out how such phenomena occurred.

Something especially miraculous then happened. I was about to take out my camera to photograph this historical scene when a Dharma Teacher said, "You need not take out your camera. You won't be able to take pictures!" As a member of the media, I was not about to forgo the opportunity to capture such a historical event. However, it was as the Dharma Teacher said. The camera would not work. I was unable to click the shutter. The camera would not work even after I replaced the batteries with new ones.

Then, a Dharma Teacher said, "Quickly take your camera to the female Dharma King or the Great Sage and ask one of them to empower it. We were able to photograph scenes yesterday only after our cameras were empowered. Only then did our cameras work." At this time, Ms. Hsu said, "My camera has been empowered. Go ahead and use it!" It was very strange. I took that camera in my hands and was able to take pictures with it.

A camcorder recorded scenes of nectar water falling through the branches.

It also recorded the scene when the Great Master and the female Dharma King were under that tree and on the grass giving dharma discourses to Great Rinpoches, eminent Dharma Teachers, and laypersons. The female Dharma King and Great Master are extremely modest. They do not want their dharma names to be made public. Of course, they also do not want that private residence to become a tourist spot, thereby hindering the self-cultivation of those who live there. When the Great Master ordered the rain to fall, it fell. When he ordered it to stop, it stopped. Although he manifested such extraordinary powers, that holy and virtuous Great Master said with extreme modesty, "I have cultivated myself very poorly my whole life. How, then, am I qualified to become famous around the world?"

The next day, the hot sun was again overhead. In order to compare and contrast the differences between normal rain and the above-described descent of nectar, a group of laypersons, Dharma Teachers, and I returned to that magnolia tree. We immediately noticed that the branches and trunk were still dry. In front of everyone, somebody took a shower nozzle, connected it to a hose, and sprayed that tree for quite a while. Right after it was sprayed, that magnolia tree, including its trunk, began dripping water. That tree had flower buds but no leaves. Within twelve minutes, the dripping stopped. It could not possibly have continuously dripped for more than ten hours. The branches and trunk were all wet. Some drops of water hung on the branches and did not drip down. After a stick was used to tap the tree, some of the drops fell down and some did not. This shows that had the fragrant nectar rain been caused by spraying water, it would have stopped dripping within a little over ten minutes, and the tree's branches and trunk would have been wet. In such case, dripping could not possibly continue for ten hours straight without any signs of moisture on the branches or trunk.

From the videos that were shot, one can see that the dripping of sprayed water and the dripping of nectar water were completely different situations. The shape of the drops of sprayed water was narrow on the top and wide on the bottom. The shape of nectar water drops was like that of a pine needle. The top and bottom had the same degree of thickness. Furthermore, such drops were shiny. From the videos that were shot, one can see that the nectar drops did not fall in a completely vertical direction. There were drops that fell in a diagonal direction. It seems that of their own accord these drops of nectar water avoided the branches as they dripped down. No wonder the branches had no moisture at all even after nectar water descended for more than ten hours. Such an occurrence defies the principles of science. All one can say is that it was a miracle in this world and a miracle in history!

H.H. Dorje Chang Buddha III Wan Ko Yeshe Norbu meditated under a magnolia tree. Because of the powerful virtue of
H.H. Dorje Chang Buddha III, the magnolia tree descended nectar during a time when the sky was clear and cloudless for miles on end.
Below are newspaper reports published at that time.

三世多杰羌佛雲高益西諾布在木棉花樹下打坐，三世多杰羌佛威德感召，萬里晴空之際，木棉花樹降下甘露。以下是當時的報紙報導。

168

The Jacaranda Tree Descending Nectar
紫櫻花樹降甘露

After the magnolia tree descended nectar, a jacaranda tree located within the mandala of H.H. Dorje Chang Buddha III also descended wonderful nectar. A nectar bowl handed down to His Holiness was in that mandala. The nectar rain occurred at the time of H.H. Dorje Chang Buddha III's birthday. Lay and monastic disciples went to that mandala to wish His Holiness a happy birthday. A Kalachakra Vajra Lang Jiu Wang Dan (Namju Wangden) *thanka* (Tibetan scroll painting) was displayed for worship in that mandala. A *thanka* of the holy image of Guan Shi Yin Bodhisattva was displayed for worship on that jacaranda tree. That jacaranda tree suddenly descended nectar, and an extraordinary fragrance filled the air. When people looked upward, they could not see a cloud in the sky. The weather had been continuously clear for at least half a month with not one drop of rain. The Buddha bestowed nectar from the jacaranda tree to celebrate the birthday of H.H. Dorje Chang Buddha III. Nectar fell continuously under the hot sun causing the ground to become wet. However, outside of the area of that jacaranda tree, the ground was dry as always, without a drop of rain. The nectar fell for seven consecutive days and nights.

Monastic and lay disciples view the jacaranda tree descending nectar on a clear and cloudless day.
四眾弟子在晴空萬里之下觀看紫櫻花樹降甘露

Lay and monastic disciples take fragrant nectar water on the ground to moisten their face or to taste it.
四眾弟子正在地上沾甘露水洗臉、品嚐芬芳的甘露

　　繼木棉花樹降甘露之後，三世多杰羌佛衣鉢壇場內的紫櫻花樹也降下了甘露。那是在三世多杰羌佛壽誕之時，四眾弟子前往壇場恭賀，壇場內供奉著時輪金剛朗久旺丹唐卡，紫櫻花樹上供奉著觀世音菩薩聖像唐卡。此時，紫櫻花樹突然降下甘露，異香撲鼻。仰望天空，萬里無雲，已然連晴了至少半個月，滴雨未下。但佛陀賜予紫櫻花樹的甘露為三世多杰羌佛祝壽，卻在烈日當空之下降個不停，把地板都淋溼了。但是，一離開紫櫻花樹的範圍，卻乾燥如常，滴水未有。甘露連降了七天七夜。

Thick Colored Clouds Appeared at the Long Life Supplication Dharma Assembly for the Buddhist Holy Mother and a Person of Great Virtue

On August 19, 2007, H.H. Dorje Chang Buddha III practiced the Long Life Supplication Dharma for the Buddhist Holy Mother and a person of great virtue. At that time, a dazzling cloud with the multiple colors like a rainbow suddenly appeared amid the white clouds that filled the sky. After a ten minute period during which it changed colors and shape, it slowly dissipated. Clouds with color that people normally see are white clouds refracting sunlight. However, what is amazing about this holy scene is the fact that this cloud was colorful in and of itself and was totally surrounded by white clouds. More than ten people personally saw that holy scene and took photographs. The bottom of the photo which printed on the following page is the signatures of those who witnessed the holy scene that day.

佛母和大德仁者的長壽祈請法會出現的濃密彩雲

　　2007 年 8 月 19 日，三世多杰羌佛在爲佛母和大德仁者進行長壽祈請法的時候，一片鮮艷奪目如彩虹七色的雲朵突然出現在滿天白雲中間，變化色彩形體，持續十多分鐘才慢慢散開。驚奇的聖境是，大家平常看到的彩雲都是白色的雲層經過陽光的折射而被人們看到彩色，但這朵彩雲本身是五彩的，它的周圍全部被白色的雲所包圍。

　　當天有二十餘人得見這一聖境並拍照，下面便是當天見證的人的簽名。

Very Small Predictions; the Highest Buddha-Dharma

My name is Mei-Ling Chen. With great sadness but also extreme happiness, I report today my sincere words to the International Buddhism Sangha Association. I am happy in that my supreme Buddha Master, Dorje Chang Buddha III Wan Ko Yeshe Norbu Holiest Tathagata, is the greatest holy being in history. Not only does His Holiness have great compassion, His Holiness also has unimpeded wisdom and supernatural powers. By following Dorje Chang Buddha III, I am able to learn the true Buddha-dharma and thereby end the cycle of birth and death. I am sad in that the younger sister of my husband, Shu-Ling Wang, left this world on December 31, 2006.

In as early as August of 2006, we reported the illness of my sister-in-law to the magnificent Dorje Chang Buddha III Wan Ko Yeshe Norbu. We beseeched the Buddha Master to empower her. The Buddha Master said, "Death is already hovering over her. Even if I empowered her, she would still not live." Upon hearing this, I became extremely sad and cried so bitterly I could not eat. After the Buddha Master saw me in this condition, His Holiness did not console me. On the contrary, His Holiness immediately summoned His disciples and gave a discourse. His Holiness said, "Shu-Ling Wang, who is the sister-in-law of Mei-Ling Chen and the younger sister of Tsan-Ming Wang, will leave this world very soon. Thus, everyone should earnestly learn Buddhism in order to end the cycle of birth and death." At that Dharma Assembly in which that discourse was given, I requested clarification from the Buddha Master by telling His Holiness, "Shu-Ling Wang's physical condition and spirits are both very good. It seems that she will not have problems." The Buddha Master responded, "I have already told everyone what will happen. This is a matter of cause and effect. The unavoidable truth is that her life is about to end. Everyone will see my words come to pass."

At that Dharma Assembly, the Buddha Master also announced predictions concerning a few other fellow-disciples of mine. One of them is called Weiya Kuan. The Buddha Master predicted that while she was driving on the freeway, a tire from an oncoming car would fall off and damage her car but that she herself would not suffer any significant harm. The Buddha Master predicted that when a Buddhist nun from the Philippines was on her way from San Francisco to Los Angeles, a rainbow would surround her car and accompanying her part of the way, and a celestial crane would come to greet her. The Buddha Master also predicted that in the year 2006 a rinpoche would fall to the ground having suffered a stroke, but that rinpoche would be saved and that rinpoche's health would be restored.

I could not help but be deeply grieved over the predictions of His Holiness. Why is human life so bitter?

All of the predictions of His Holiness have already come to pass. I personally saw that rinpoche suffer a stroke and fall to the ground. Many Buddhist nuns who were there saved him by giving him emergency treatment. A tire really did fly toward laywoman Weiya Kuan's car and went under the chassis, damaging her car. A Buddhist nun from the Philippines did experience what His Holiness predicted on her way to Los Angeles. My sister-in-law was truly unable to escape the fate of death and has left this world.

It is critical to point out that on December 26, 2006 after I had returned to Taiwan from Los Angeles, I reported to the Buddha Master, "My sister-in-law is somewhat livelier. Thank you, Buddha Master, for empowering her." Unexpectedly, the Buddha Master replied, "This is a false sign. She will die very soon. It is unavoidable. Do not be sad. I will do my utmost to empower her. However, because she is a follower of another religion, her three karmas cannot correspond with the teachings of the Buddhas and Bodhisattvas. Thus, my empowerment cannot fully reach her, and I cannot save her. After she dies, I will exert my full effort to raise her consciousness to a higher realm. You must not be sad. She did not learn the dharma of liberation. This is a matter of cause and effect."

Upon hearing this, I calmed down a bit and felt happy. The words of the Buddha Master are equivalent to a dharma edict. How fortunate she is to be raised to a higher realm by the Buddha Master!

All of the predictions of His Holiness have come true. The Buddha Master previously made the following prediction concerning my husband: "Within fifteen days, he will definitely suffer a misfortune in which he will be seriously injured." It turned out that on the ninth day, an oncoming car caused my husband's car to collide against a bridge pillar. My husband fell into shock and had internal bleeding. He did not eat for several days. Fortunately, because he was wearing the vajra string empowered by His Holiness, his life was spared.

When I think of these things, I feel very comforted. With such a magnificent Buddha Master who is a great holy being, how could I still worry about not attaining accomplishment in the dharma and liberation from the cycle of reincarnation? I am so fortunate!

Today I have specially written down my sincere words. I request that these irrefutable facts be published in *A Treasury of True Buddha-Dharma* so that they bring to living beings benefit, happiness, and good fortune!

Buddhist disciple from Taiwan,
Mei-Ling Chen
December 31, 2006

(This is a complete translation of the Chinese text that follows originally written and signed by Mei-Ling Chen.)

很 小 的 預 言   最 高 的 佛 法

我叫陳美玲，今天我在這裡抱著非常難過又十分高興的心情把我的肺腑之言彙報給國際佛教僧尼總會。我高興的是，我至高無上的佛陀上師多杰羌佛第三世雲高益西諾布頂聖如來是歷史上最了不起的大聖者，不但大慈大悲，而且智慧神通無礙，我可以跟隨三世多杰羌佛學到真正的佛法，了生脫死。難過的是，我們的小姑王淑齡於2006年12月31日離開人間了。

早在2006年8月的時候，我們向偉大的三世多杰羌佛雲高益西諾布彙報了妹妹生病的情況，請求佛陀上師加持。佛陀上師說：『死神已經降臨在她的身上，加持也是活不了的了』。我當時心情十分難過，痛哭得吃不下飯。佛陀上師見到後不但沒有安慰我，反而立刻召集佛弟子們開示說：陳美玲的小姑、也就是王燦明的妹妹王淑齡很快就要離開人間了，所以大家要好生學佛，了生脫死。當時在開示法會上，我向佛陀上師請示說：『王淑齡的身體、精神現在都很好，她不會有問題吧？』佛陀上師說：『我已經告訴了大家，這是因果的關係，她離不開四個字：人生已盡。大家會看到我講的話的。』當時，佛陀上師在法會上還宣佈了其他幾個同學的預言：一個同學叫關維雅的，將會在公路上開車時遇到對面開來的車子所掉下的輪胎，把車子打壞但人無有大礙；一位菲律賓的出家同學從舊金山來洛杉磯，將會有彩虹圍繞其汽車同行一段，並由仙鶴來朝；還有一位仁波且會在2006年倒地中風，但還可以救轉還身……

老人家的預言，不由得使我感到非常沉痛，為什麼人生這麼苦？

到今天為止，老人家預言已經成為事實了：那個活佛我親自看到他中風倒在地上，很多出家人予以搶救；也確實有一個汽車輪胎飛到了關維雅居士的汽車底盤下將汽車打壞了；而現在，我的小姑也確實

沒有逃過死亡這一關，離別了人間。更關鍵的是，在2006年12月26日我們從洛杉磯返回台灣後，向佛陀上師彙報說：小姑的精神好些了，謝謝佛陀上師加持。沒有想到佛陀上師竟然說：『這是假象，她很快就會死的，逃不過的。你們不要難過，我會盡力加持她，但由於她是其它教派的信徒，三業無法相應，加持力沒有辦法全部達到，所以沒有辦法救她。她死後我會全力為她超渡，千萬不要難過，她沒有學到解脫的法，這是因果的關係。』

我聽了以後，心裡稍微平靜下來並感到高興，佛陀上師的話就是法旨，有佛陀上師超渡她，是多麼幸福！

老人家預言的幾個例子，都已全部應驗了。而以前佛陀上師預言我的外子『十五天之內必出重傷之禍』，結果在第九天就因對方來車把他的車子撞在石橋墩上，外子當場休克，內臟出血，幾天水米不進，幸虧提前戴上老人家的金剛帶保得性命。

想到這些，我反而感到非常的寬慰，有這麼了不起的佛陀大聖老人家，我還愁不能成就解脫嗎？這是我的幸福啊！

今天，我特地在此將我的內心話寫出來，請求將這些鐵證的事實登載在《正法寶典》中，但願能為眾生帶來利益、吉祥、幸福！

台灣佛弟子：陳美玲

2006年12月31日

（此文的英文翻譯印在前面）

The Real Buddha Master Who Possesses Buddha-Dharma

The moment I heard that I would be going with Venerable Dharma Teacher Long Hui to Los Angeles, unspeakable joy arose in my heart. On the way to Los Angeles, a rainbow suddenly emerged from the drizzling sky, emitting beautiful lights of various colors. A white celestial crane seen in the distance flew near and landed at the side of the freeway gazing at us, as if paying us respect. All of these signs expressed auspicious blessings. I strongly sensed that what I had wished for so long was about to come true.

A notice arrived in the afternoon of December 28th. From Venerable Dharma Teacher Long Hui's somewhat tense facial expression, I could tell this must be the time for me to pay my respects and visit the Buddha Master. Just as expected, when we stepped into the mandala, I saw H.H. Dorje Chang Buddha III Wan Ko Yeshe Norbu Holiest Tathagata sitting upright on the dharma platform. His Holiness appeared so dignified and had an expression of loving-kindness. As I sincerely prostrated myself to H.H. Dorje Chang Buddha III, all I heard was the cordial voice of His Holiness telling everyone to come sit toward the front. I sat beside Venerable Dharma Teacher Long Hui. Dharma Teacher Jue Hui and Dharma Teacher Ruo Hui also sat with us.

Venerable Dharma Teacher Long Hui reported to the Buddha Master regarding the Buddhist chanting work that had taken place at Hua Zang Si over the past two months. Next, the Buddha Master called my name: "Fa Hai, proceed with what you want to say." Without knowing why, my mind went totally blank. I felt that my entire body was soaking in a kind of freshness. I remained kneeling with a very straight back, as if I had entered a state of meditation. At this time, I only heard the Buddha Master say, "It is all right. Just speak directly!" Yet, I still could not speak and was silent for another eight or nine minutes. I could sense that the Buddha Master was patiently waiting.

Finally, a sound floated out of my mouth: "My karmic affinity with the Buddha Master should have begun ten years ago. Because I could not come to America, I was not able to visit His Holiness. I finally got a visa last year. Only this year did I have the opportunity to visit Hua Zang Si, where I respectfully listened to recorded dharma teachings of the Buddha Master. For more than one straight month, I have listened to the recorded dharma discourses without the slightest sense of tiredness. This has been the most beneficial and rewarding time of my entire life. The beneficial effects I have experienced can never be expressed in words. I bring my body, speech, and mind to respectfully visit the Buddha Master at this time. Today, I would like to specially request a great dharma from H.H. Dorje Chang Buddha III. I would not hesitate to leap into boiling water or walk on fire in order to obtain this great dharma. I am willing to undergo any test in order to obtain such dharma. I am even willing to sacrifice my own life. It might sound like I am exaggerating, but I truly can do such things."

Perhaps because I was too nervous or focused, I unexpectedly was not able to express exactly what I meant to say. However, I silently told myself that the Buddha Master definitely understands what I am trying to express and what dharma I am requesting. I still remember that I fasted for a full 21 days in the Philippines in order to obtain this great dharma. This is because I am very aware that in this world only H.H. Dorje Chang Buddha III can accomplish this task and announce to the world this great dharma in order to demonstrate the brightness of Buddha and enable the correct dharma to exist in this world forever.

At first, the Buddha Master did not answer my request directly but gave us a profound and important discourse. Only afterward did I realize that this discourse was actually the beginning of His Holiness's response to my question. His Holiness specifically pointed out the various kinds of confusion and mistakes that have appeared within Buddhism in this current Dharma Ending Age. Some Buddhist sutras contain serious mistakes. What is even more serious is that there are some so-called eminent monks and great virtuous beings who, due to their erroneous understanding and views, seriously misguide others when giving discourses on the dharma. What is even sadder is that believers who do not understand the truth still fanatically follow them and prostrate to them in worship. H.H. Dorje Chang Buddha III does all He can to correct these heretical ideas and views. However, being limited by the karma of living beings, H.H. Dorje Chang Buddha III feels that it is very difficult to change the current situation despite His wish to do so. The Buddha Master gave some examples of these heretical ways within both esoteric Buddhism and exoteric Buddhism. These very worrisome examples left me not knowing whether to laugh or cry.

After finishing the discourse, the Buddha Master said to me directly, "Fa Hai, you did not say what great dharma you want to request. Let me say it for you. The dharma you want to request is to film a movie of the Buddha. There really is no one else besides me who can do this because I completely understand the teachings of the Buddha. I can write the script. This movie must be filmed. The only thing is that the karmic conditions this year are not quite mature enough because the script needs to be written and actors need to be found, especially actors who are qualified. As for funding, as long as there is a script, there will be people who will sponsor and invest. Besides, the movie of the Buddha will not be filmed as one undivided whole but will be divided into a series of 100 parts or episodes. Perhaps this is really the right channel. After all, the influence of a book is limited as it reaches fewer people than a movie, which has much more of an international impact. In addition, when we do this, many problems might be solved. We might even be able to build several temples this way!" At this moment, I understood that the discourse just given by H.H. Wan Ko Yeshe Norbu Holiest Tathagata on the current chaotic situation within Buddhism illustrated that it is impossible for anyone else to write in a script the authentic doctrines of the Buddha.

Listening to this point, I was really shocked in my heart. I used to pay respect and visit many eminent monks and great virtuous beings. I requested from them great dharma. None of them knew what this great dharma in my mind was that I wanted to request. H.H. Dorje Chang Buddha III is truly magnificent. I did not reveal in the slightest what great dharma I wanted to request. Nonetheless, what His Holiness stated was the exact great dharma in my mind that I wanted to request.

His Holiness then said, "Fa Hai, when you come back from mainland China, I will transmit to you dharma according to the formal rituals of Tibetan esoteric Buddhism. You still have some negative karma. At that time, I will perform an initiation for you and eliminate your karmic hindrances. You will see." I was totally engulfed in the joy of the dharma. The Buddha Master further said, "On your way here, the rainbow and the celestial crane you saw augured that your future undertakings will be bright. However, behind the brightness lurks darkness, and there are twists and turns on the path. We will soon face some attacks and slander, although those who commit the slander will all end up losing. When *A Treasury of True Buddha-Dharma* is published, no force can obstruct or destroy us because what is in that book are facts." The Buddha Master finished by saying, "The movie of the Buddha definitely has to be filmed. You see, Fa Hai, your wishes have all been fulfilled. How fortunate you are!"

Actually, there are no words that can express my happiness. There are also no words that can express my gratitude toward H.H. Dorje Chang Buddha III.

I only want to respectfully offer to the Dorje Chang Buddha III my most beautiful spirit, my most beautiful melody, my most beautiful singing voice, and my best wishes. May all those who hear this beautiful melody and singing voice be happy.

I would like to express my special thanks to an anonymous person who ten years ago sent me an express mail package in which a yellow silk scarf was wrapped around the book *The Fruits of Pious Devotion* and CD's that had a picture of H.H. Dorje Chang Buddha III on their covers. It is because of this present that seeds planted ten years ago have borne fruit in the form of my taking refuge in the His Holiness as my Buddha Master and in the form of my witnessing the magnificence of the Buddha dharma.

Everything I described above is true. I am a Buddhist nun. I accept the karmic responsibility for my words. If what I have stated is false, I will descend into the Vajra Hell. If what I have stated is true, I would like to dedicate the resulting merit to all living beings in the dharma realm so that they will soon realize enlightenment.

Respectfully written by disciple Fa Hai Shi
December 30, 2006

The above account was written by Fa Hai Shi. We three humble Buddhist nuns provide the following testimonials.

Encountering an Unusual Occurrence

Basically, whenever people pay their respects and visit H.H. Dorje Chang Buddha III Wan Ko Yeshe Norbu Holiest Tathagata, they make good use of their short meeting time by posing prepared questions or by requesting the transmission of dharma. Some groups have really made the best use of their time by requesting answers to problems that have arisen.

From left to right: Rui Hui Shih, Long Hui Shih, and Jue Hui Shih

However, there was one particular occasion in the afternoon of December 28, 2006 when a dharma teacher from the Philippines, Fa Hai, came to the mandala from thousands of miles away. This was the first time she was granted an audience with H.H. Dorje Chang Buddha III. When H.H. Dorje Chang Buddha III asked her what question she had, I saw that Buddhist nun take a deep breath. She then unexpectedly remained silent as she stared at the Buddha Master with open eyes, sometimes lowering her head. Perhaps all of this was due to nervousness or other factors. At this time, the Buddha Master also did not speak. Seconds and then minutes passed by in silence. Then, that dharma teacher sighed once more and straightened her back, still looking at the Great Dharma King without uttering a sound. Strangely, Dorje Chang Buddha III also remained silent. A moment later, she sighed for the third time but still did not reply to the Buddha Master. The duration of this silence lasted more than eight minutes. This kind of situation had never happened before.

Finally, the dharma teacher spoke. She said she had come with a wish to request a great dharma. If her wish to obtain this great dharma were fulfilled, she said she would dedicate her life to the Buddha-dharma and living beings, even if it meant sacrificing her life. After uttering such words, she again fell into silence without mentioning what dharma she wished to request.

At this time, Dorje Chang Buddha III said, "Do not say anymore. I will give you a discourse." The Buddha Master pointed out what request was in the mind of this Buddhist nun. That discourse not only enabled us disciples who were there to once again witness the supernatural powers of H.H. Dorje Chang Buddha III, it also enabled us to understand precious dharma principles.

Because I took Dharma Teacher Fa Hai to pay her respects to H.H. Wan Ko Yeshe Norbu Holiest Tathagata, I was there and personally witnessed everything that happened. Everything I described above is true. If what I have stated above contains false words, may I never become accomplished in the dharma. If what I have stated above is true, I dedicate the resulting merit to all living beings so that they may soon hear the correct dharma and soon attain liberation and accomplishment.

Buddhist disciple Long Hui Shih

I was present at the time. I hereby confirm that what is stated above is true. If what is stated above is false, I am willing to descend into hell and experience negative karmic retribution. If everything stated above is true, I dedicate the resulting merit to all living beings so that they may soon hear the correct dharma and soon realize enlightenment.

Buddhist disciple, Jue Hui Shih

Everything stated above is true. If what is stated above contains false words, I will not become accomplished in the dharma and will become impoverished and miserable. If what is stated above is true, I wish to dedicate the resulting merit to all living beings so that they may always see Buddha and attain liberation.

Buddhist disciple, Ruo Hui Shih

(This is a complete translation of the Chinese text that follows originally written and signed by Fa Hai Shih, Long Hui Shih, Jue Hui Shih, and Ruo Hui Shih.)

眞 正 具 佛 法 的 佛 陀 上 師

當聽到要跟隆慧法師去洛杉磯時，心裡便有一種無可言狀的喜悅，而在去往洛杉磯的沿途中，濛濛細雨的天空豁然亮出一道彩虹，放射出七彩的虹光，一隻白色的仙鶴從遠處飛來，停落在路旁，向我們行著注目禮，這種種的瑞兆都在表明出一種吉祥的祝福，我強烈地感覺到盼望已久的願就要實現了。

12月28日的下午接到通知，從隆慧法師有些緊張的神情中看出，這一定是要去見佛陀上師了。果然，當我們步入壇場時，我看到多杰羌佛第三世雲高益西諾布頂聖如來端坐在法台上，是那麼地莊嚴和慈祥，我虔誠地向他老人家頂禮，只聽三世多杰羌佛親切地招呼大家往前面坐，我坐在隆慧法師身旁，隨同就座的還有覺慧法師和若慧法師。

先是隆慧法師向佛陀上師彙報華藏寺近兩個月來展開梵唄課誦的工作情況。隨後佛陀上師便叫著我的名字：「法海，你有什麼事情講

吧。」不知為什麼，我的頭腦裡都呈現出一片空白，只覺得全身被一種清涼所浸透，整個人直直地跪在那裡，像入定一般。只聽到佛陀上師又說：「不要緊，你只管講吧！」但是，我仍然開不了口，靜默了足足有八、九分鐘，我能感覺到佛陀上師在耐心地等待著。終於一個聲音從我的口中飄了出來：「我和佛陀上師的因緣應該是在十年前，因為一直不能來到美國，無法親近到老人家，去年終於拿到了美國的身份，今年才有機會來華藏寺恭聞佛陀上師的法音。連續一個多月來，在聽聞法音時，我沒有一絲的疲倦，這是我有生以來最受益無窮的，而這種受用是無法用語言來表達的。我是帶著身口意來見佛陀上師的，今天特別向三世多杰羌佛老人家請一個大法，為了能求得這個大法，我可以赴湯蹈火，在所不惜，我可以接受任何的考驗，只要能求得這個大法，我甚至可以付出自己的生命，這話聽起來像是在說大話，但是我是真的能做到。」或許真是過於緊張和專注的緣故，我竟

然不能把想要說的內容完完全全地表達出來，但是我的心在告訴我說，佛陀老人家一定明白我在說什麼，我所要求的究竟是個什麼法。我還記得為了求得這個大法，我曾經在菲律賓整整斷食二十一天，因為我清楚地知道在這個世界上只有三世多杰羌佛能夠完成和將這個大法公布於天下，以示現佛陀的光輝，使正法久住。

佛陀上師開始沒有直接回答我，而是為我們做了甚深重要的開示，後來才知道，其實這開示就是回答我問題的開始，特別指出當今末法時代佛教中所出現的種種混亂和錯誤，一些佛經中存有的嚴重錯誤，更有甚者，所謂的一些高僧大德，由於知見不正，在開示中存在著嚴重誤導，更可悲的是那些不明真相的信徒們，仍在狂熱地追隨其後，頂禮膜拜。三世多杰羌佛竭盡全力想糾正這些魔說邪見，但由於眾生業力所限，也深有舉步艱難、力不從心之感。在佛陀上師列舉的部份密教和顯教中的事例中，聽起來即讓人啼笑皆非，也使人深感憂慮。佛陀上師結束了開示後，便把話頭直接轉向我說：「法海呀，你剛才沒有把所要說的求大法說出來，我現在給你說吧。你要求的法是拍佛陀的電影，這件事除了我還真是沒有別人能夠做的了，因為我完全了解佛陀的教義，我能寫出這個劇本，這部電影是一定要拍的，只是今年的機緣還不夠成熟，因為要寫腳本、找演員，特別是演員總得找一個像樣子的，錢的問題，只要腳本有了，就會有人贊助投資，拍佛陀的電影不止是拍一集，要拍100集，也許這真是一種途徑呢，因為寫一本書的影響畢竟有限，看的人少，而電影就不一樣了，會有國際影響，而我們這樣一做，很多問題都可能解決了，說不定我們還能多蓋它好幾座廟子呢！」這時我才明白，原來雲高益西諾布頂聖如來開示當今佛教的亂象，說明是無法寫佛陀真實義理的。

我聽到這裡，心裡真是驚壞了，我曾拜見過很多高僧大德提出求大法，他們沒有一個人知道我心中要求的大法是什麼，三世多杰羌佛老人家太偉大了，我一點也沒有露出我求什麼大法，但是老人家說的完全就是我的心中要求的大法，接著老人家又說到：「法海呀，等你從大陸回來，我要按照正式的藏密儀軌給你傳法，你現在身上還有一些黑業，到時候要給你灌頂，把業障消除，你會看到的。」我完全沈浸在一片法喜中，佛陀上師又說：「在來的路上，你所看到的彩虹和仙鶴，那是預示著你將來的前途事業是燦爛的，但是光明的背後也有黑暗，道路也有曲折，我們很快又要面臨一些衝擊和誹謗，但最後誹謗者都要以失敗而告終，當《正法寶典》一經問世，那個時候，什麼力量也阻擋不住，也破壞不了，因為這是事實。」佛陀上師最後又說：「佛陀電影一定要拍的，法海呀，你看你的願望都滿足了，你多幸福啊！」實際上縱有千言萬語也難以表達我的幸福和快樂。

縱有千言萬語也難以表達我對三世多杰羌佛的感恩之情。

只想用我最美的心靈、最美的旋律、最美的歌聲、把我最美好的祝願，敬獻給三世多杰羌佛，並讓所有能夠聽到這美妙旋律和歌聲的人都得到幸福和吉祥。

我將特別感謝在十年前一位匿名者寄給我的一件特快專遞裡面用一條黃色的哈達包裹著一本《虔誠的獲得》和印有三世多杰羌佛法像的CD封面，正是這件禮物使得十年後的我種子生發，能拜在佛陀上師的足下，見到偉大的佛法。

我以上所述是真實不虛，我是一位比丘尼，說話要對因果負責，若是妄言，我將墮入金剛地獄；若是真實不虛，將以此功德回向給法界一切眾生，早證菩提。

弟子　釋法海敬書
2006年12月30日

上面是釋法海的紀實，我們三位慚愧的比丘尼予以見證。

遇到了一件奇特的事

基本上每當有人想求見多杰羌佛第三世雲高益西諾布頂聖如來，都會把握短暫的會面時間把準備的問題提出請示，或是求法；有些是團體到來，更是要抓緊時間，請求對產生的問題能得到釋疑解惑。但是就有這麼一次，在2006年12月28日的午後時間，一位菲律賓的法師法海從萬里之遙來到壇場，第一次覲見三世多杰羌佛，當三世多杰羌佛問到她有什麼問題時，或許是緊張，或者其它的因素，只見這位比丘尼深吸一口氣，竟然一言不發，雙目圓睜的看著佛陀上師，時而又低著頭，此時佛陀上師也不說話，時間就在靜悄中分分秒秒的過去。然後這個法師又嘆了一口氣，挺挺身子，還是看著三世多杰羌佛不吭聲；說也奇怪，佛陀上師同樣也不講話。又過了一會兒她又作了第三次的提氣動作，仍然無言以對；這段靜默的時間總計持續了有八分鐘以上之久，這種現象是從未發生過的。

後來法海師說話了，她說她是帶著心願來求大法的，只要能滿足她求到大法，她就能為佛法為眾生，哪怕獻出生命。說到這她又停下來，不說求什麼法。此時三世多杰羌佛就說話了：「你不要講了，我來給你開示吧。」佛陀上師點出了這位比丘尼所想的事。在這次的開示中，不僅讓在場的弟子們再一次見證了三世多杰羌佛神通的展現，也了解了珍貴的法義。

由於此次法海師拜見雲高益西諾布頂聖如來是我帶她去的，我親自在場經歷一切。以上所敘述的是真實不虛，若有妄言，我永遠不得成就；若是真實不虛，願一切眾生皆能早聞正法，能早日解脫成就。

佛弟子　釋隆慧

當時本人也在場，我在此證明以上所述是真實不虛，若是虛假，我願墮地獄遭惡報；若一切屬實，願所有眾生早日得聞正法，早證菩提。

佛弟子　釋覺慧

以上所說全屬真實不虛，若有妄語，我不得成就，窮苦潦倒；若屬真實，願將功德回向所有眾生，常得見佛，成就解脫。

佛弟子　釋若慧

（此文的英文翻譯印在前面）

Startling Thunder Suddenly Pealed and Lightning Flashed in the Sky, Confirming the Couplet Written by H.H. Dorje Chang Buddha III

As early as the very beginning of the planning and preparation period for the construction of the Temple of Good Fortune and Wisdom, I besought H.H. Dorje Chang Buddha III Wan Ko Yeshe Norbu Holiest Tathagata to compose and bestow some couplets upon the Temple. The Buddha Master kindly gave me three sets of couplets as a blessing. The first verse of one of the couplets reads, "The first round of the dharma drum is accompanied by thunder breaking above ground." The second verse is "With the decoration of banners of red sandalwood flowers, incense is offered to all honorably worshiped ones at their dharma thrones."

At that time, we did not understand the profound meaning of the couplet. The Buddha Master said that this couplet is very well matched and implies dedicate and subtle causes and conditions. I thought that the Buddha Master would eventually give a discourse and teaching on this when the conditions were ripe.

Time flies and soon it was the beginning of 2006. The opening of the temple was about to take place. There were many dharma-related matters that we needed to report to and get instructions on from H.H. Buddha Master Dorje Chang Buddha III. H.H. Dorje Chang Buddha III made an exception in receiving me during His solitary practice period. I and Shu-Chih Chiu, the Secretary-General of the Tibetan Buddhism Association of America, went to see His Holiness to pay respects.

While I was reporting the arrangements for the temple's opening, the Buddha Master pointed to a photo of the temple and said, "Print this photo on the cover of the temple's brochure. Let people listen to my dharma discourses. You must not transmit incorrect dharma." Right after His Holiness finished his sentences, lightning suddenly flashed in the clear sky, and a thunder followed that was so loud it was as if the sky was shaking and the ground was moving. Everything returned to calm right after that. That thunder roared suddenly and faded gradually. There was no second thunder afterwards.

At the temple's opening ceremony, we followed the rules and rituals of exoteric and Tibetan esoteric Buddhism. We paid respect and offered incense to each statue of a Buddha, Bodhisattva, vajra being, and dharma protector strictly according to the doctrine. All of this corresponded with the Buddha Master's predications in his couplets, including what happened at the opening ceremony: "The first round of the dharma drum is accompanied by thunder breaking above ground; with the decoration of banners of red sandalwood flowers, incense is offered to all honorably worshipped ones at their dharma thrones."

As a Buddhist, I do not make false statements. I have sworn and made a vow in front of the Buddhas and Bodhisattvas to tell the truth about these events. This provides proof that the dharma from the discourses of H.H. Dorje Chang Buddha III is magnificent and supreme. All those great and magnificent discourses were recorded into CDs and are available for people to listen to at the temple from now on.

I announced to the attendees at the opening ceremony that the main function of the Temple of Good Fortune and Wisdom is to let people listen to the dharma discourses of H.H. Dorje Chang Buddha III Wan Ko Yeshe Norbu Holiest Tathagata. May all living beings listen to the dharma discourses of H.H. Dorje Chang Buddha III! May they acquire wisdom, end the cycle of life and death, and attain liberation! May everything be auspicious and perfect with them!

Karma Palden Lodoe
April, 2006

(This is a complete translation of the Chinese text that follows originally written and signed by Karma Palden Lodoe.)

驚雷乍響　虛空閃電　印證三世多杰羌佛之楹聯

　　早在福慧寺籌建佈置之初，我祈請多杰羌佛第三世雲高益西諾布頂聖如來為福慧寺賜寫楹聯，佛陀上師加持了三門楹聯，其中有一副

上聯為『法鼓初通平地一聲雷響』，下聯是『紫檀花幡香供諸尊法座』，當時我們並不了解其中的甚深涵義，佛陀上師說這副聯對得好，

因緣微妙，但我想因緣成熟時終會得到佛陀上師的開示教導。

轉眼到了今年西元兩千零六年年初，福慧寺就要開寺了，有很多法務上的事情必須要向佛陀上師三世多杰羌佛請示。三世多杰羌佛在閉關中破格接待了我，我帶美國密宗總會秘書長邱淑志前往拜見，當我報告福慧寺開寺事宜時，佛陀上師手指著福慧寺的照片指示說：『這張照片要印在福慧寺的簡介上，讓大家多聞我的法音，不要傳不正確的佛法。』話音剛落，突然虛空閃電，一聲驚雷乍響，天搖地動，頃刻間又風平浪靜。這一聲驚雷乍響，隨著由大至小、由近至遠慢慢消失，再也沒有第二聲了。開寺時我寺依照藏密和顯宗儀軌，根據嚴謹的法義每一尊佛、菩薩、金剛、護法都上香禮供，正印證了佛陀上師早就書寫在這副楹聯中的預言，與我寺的法情完全吻合無二：「法鼓初通平地一聲雷響，紫檀花幡香供諸尊法座」。

我是一個佛弟子，不打妄語，我曾為此已在佛菩薩前發誓表心，這證明三世多杰羌佛他老人家開示的佛法殊勝無比，所有偉大殊勝的開示都錄在法音帶中，今後大家都可以在福慧寺恭請聽聞。而我在第一天的開寺法會上向信眾宣告福慧寺將以恭聞多杰羌佛第三世雲高益西諾布頂聖如來的法音為主，願眾生聞三世多杰羌佛開示的法，得智慧，了生死，得解脫，一切吉祥圓滿。

噶瑪巴登洛德

Karma Palden Lydoe

2006年4月

（此文的英文翻譯印在前面）

Wintersweet Flowers Blossom in the Summer

That was a very solemn and magnificent dharma assembly. Venerable Akou Lamo Rinpoche, who came to the United States from Tibet, and I, Long Hui, personally arrived at the Altar Hall of His Holiness Dorje Chang Buddha III Wan Ko Yeshe Norbu Holiest Tathagata and respectfully requested that Dorje Chang Buddha III give a discourse for our group on the rituals of the Green Tara Dharma.

When the discourse was concluded, a pot of wintersweet (a kind of plum blossom tree that only blooms in the winter) in front of the altar unexpectedly started budding. That day was the 4th of August, 2001, in midsummer. The wintersweet suddenly blossomed forth red plum flowers. I had bought this plant and humbly offered it to my magnificent Buddha Master, His Holiness Dorje Chang Buddha III, in December of 2000. When I bought it, the plum flowers were red and white. After about one month, all of the flowers withered and fell. Although new leaves grew, no flowers ever blossomed after that.

However, on that August day of the dharma assembly in the height of summer, that pot of wintersweet suddenly started to bloom right after His Holiness finished the discourse. All the flowers were a brilliant red. Even more amazingly, the shape of some of the flowers resembled lotus flowers and emitted a heavenly fragrance. It was quite incredible. The disciples attending this special dharma assembly were all stunned as they gathered around to look at the pot. Afterward, the plant was placed in the Dharma Bowl Altar Hall of H.H. Dorje Chang Buddha III to be guarded at all times by about ten disciples. The blossoming lasted fifteen months, with the flowers retaining a fresh color until November of the following year. How extraordinary!

Certainly, such a holy and auspicious phenomenon could only have happened because of the great merits of the exquisite discourse that H. H. Wan Ko Yeshe Norbu Holiest Tathagata had given. We had heard of the miracles of old, such as self-turning Buddhist umbrellas above statues, or the sudden blossoming of withered plum blossom trees, or even a rock nodding upon hearing the discourse of a great master. And now we witness the miracle of a winter flowering plant blossoming in the hot summer, and the blossoming lasted fifteen months! We were able to film this wonderful occasion. Just when everyone was marveling and praising, H.H. Dorje Chang Buddha III said lightly, "The true meaning of the Buddha-dharma is not illustrated by whether wintersweet plum flowers blossom or not, or whether such an occurrence is auspicious or not. Do not be attached to these phenomena. The most important thing is how to carry out all good deeds and gain wisdom. We must fully understand the true dharma teachings and act accordingly. This is how we should practice. We are here to cultivate ourselves, not to look at wintersweet plum flowers. That is what we should devote ourselves to."

We are grateful for the Buddha Master's teaching, which we shall keep firmly in mind. But we also know that these continual miraculous phenomena could only be manifested because H.H. Wan Ko Yeshe Norbu Holiest Tathagata is truly an ancient Buddha who is praised and supported

A plum blossom branch sent forth flowers that were in bloom for fifteen months. Those fragrant flowers were in the shape of lotus flowers.
臘梅花綻放了十五個月並開出形如蓮花的花朵，異香撲鼻

by the Buddhas and Bodhisatvas. Yet, H.H. Dorje Chang Buddha III always presents himself as a humble practitioner. His Holiness's pure, noble, and holy morality sets the highest example for his disciples. His Holiness's profound Buddha realization brings the greatest blessings and teachings to all sentient beings.

Chairperson of the International Buddhism Sangha Association
Long Hui Shih

(This is a complete translation of the Chinese text that follows originally written and signed by Long Hui Shih.)

<h1 style="text-align:center">臘 梅 夏 開</h1>

　　這是一場非常莊嚴殊勝的法會，由西藏來美的阿寇拉摩仁波切及我隆慧，來到多杰羌佛第三世雲高益西諾布頂聖如來的壇場，敬請三世多杰羌佛為大眾作開示「綠度母修法儀軌」。

　　就在圓滿法義開示後，供在法台前的一盆臘月梅花，竟然長出花苞，因為當天是2001年的8月4日，正是暑夏，臘梅剎那綻放了紅色的梅花，說起這一盆臘梅，還是在2000年臘月，我買來供養偉大的佛陀恩師三世多杰羌佛，當時是開著紅色及白色的梅花，大約一個月後，花就全部凋謝了，後來長出新葉，但一直沒有再開過花。

　　但法會的當天，三世多杰羌佛才開示完，這一盆臘梅突然在盛夏的八月的當天開花了，開的全是紅色梅花，色澤鮮艷，更奇特的是有幾朵還形如蓮花，放出撲鼻異香，多麼不可思議，在壇場的信眾，個個圍觀稱奇，這盆梅花一直供在三世多杰羌佛的法缽壇城，那裡有十個左右的人員長時看守，天天見到，而且這盆花一直開了十五個月，花鮮不掉，直到第二年十一月才開完，太神奇了！

　　如此聖蹟瑞相，當然是雲高益西諾布頂聖如來的法義精闊微妙功德之相應，古代亦有幡轉寶蓋、枯梅開花、頑石點頭等聖蹟公案，而今更有臘梅夏開歷時十五個月之新頁，當時並用錄像機把這殊勝現況

拍攝下來，正當大家嘖嘖稱奇之時，三世多杰羌佛卻平淡的說：「梅花開與不開，吉祥或不吉祥都不能說明佛法的真實義理，我們不要執著這些現象，最重要的是如何的行於一切善慧，明白法義依教奉行，如是觀修。我們不是在看梅花，而是在修行，這才是我們真正要做的！」

　　大家感恩佛陀上師的開示，牢牢記著，也正是因為雲高益西諾布頂聖如來乃真正的古佛，諸佛菩薩共襄護持、禮讚、才有相繼不斷的殊勝聖蹟展現，但三世多杰羌一直以來都以慚愧行者自居，其聖潔崇高的聖德，更為弟子們樹立了最高的典範，其甚深證量的佛境，為所有眾生帶來最大的加持及教益和啟發。

國際佛教僧尼總會主席
釋隆慧

（此文的英文翻譯印在前面）

<h1 style="text-align:center">A Holy Scene That Manifested in a Photograph</h1>

In response to the request of Dorje Chang Buddha III's students, His Holiness's photographs have been added to the category of Technological Art. H.H. Dorje Chang Buddha III said, "I do not have any photographs that I have taken. Give me a camera and in only one day I will have them." The Buddha Master then exited his place of solitary retreat. His Holiness quickly led more than ten people up a mountain ridge. The clicking sound of His Holiness's camera could be heard capturing the scene of an ancient stratified cliff that resembled a fortress.

During the time His Holiness was taking photographs, extraordinary phenomena appeared. The sky was like a square mirror that reflected on the cliff in the photo area. Behind the mountain, blue light was being emitted from the earth. From a distance, these two scenes acted in coordination with each other. This sharp contrast of light caused the left mountain ridge to become pitch black. However, where there was light, the light was dazzling and extremely wonderful. The fact that there was such a magnificent and a holy site in this photograph shows the greatness of H.H. Dorje Chang Buddha III's Buddha-dharma. We who accompanied His Holiness were

deeply moved by this and felt an obligation to tell people of the world what actually happened. Therefore, we came to a true consensus that we would take a vow of truth in order to confirm that H.H. Dorje Chang Buddha III's holy virtue moves and inspires.

The text of the vow is as follows. "This photograph was truly taken by the Buddha Master after His Holiness ascended the mountain ridge accompanied by us. His Holiness casually took a couple of photos as His Holiness stood before this holy mountain scene. There has been no computer modification of this photo. It is the original photograph. If what we have just stated is in any way false, we are willing to receive karmic retribution and not attain liberation. If what we have just stated is completely factual, may the good fortune of all living beings increase, and may they experience good luck and happiness."

The disciples who together made the above vow have personally signed their names in the Chinese section.

(The text was translated from the Chinese text that follows.)

The sky was totally clear for miles on end that day. When H.H. Dorje Chang Buddha III was photographing scenery, a heavenly window above suddenly opened. From that heavenly window, an extremely strong beam of light in the shape of a square shined upon the place where H.H. Dorje Chang Buddha III stood. At this time, the strong light from the sun became dark in contrast. A square blue light arose from the mountaintop shining upon both sides of the mountain. This was truly miraculous. Although all of this happened in an instant, H.H. Dorje Chang Buddha III used his camera to capture this holy sight. The sky then returned to its original open, clear, cloudless condition.

這一天萬里晴空，三世多杰羌佛在攝影風景時，天頂的天窗突然打開，從天窗中射下一道強力無比的方形光幕照在三世多杰羌佛所站的位置，這時強烈的陽光竟然被對比成一片黑暗，山頂升起了方塊藍光，兩相映照，成了奇蹟。雖然只有那麼剎那，三世多杰羌佛的相機捉住了這一聖景，萬里晴空又依然如故。

This is a photograph of that same mountain scene that a disciple took at that time from a lower and farther place.

弟子當時在較低的遠距離所拍攝之同一山景

照 相 聖 境 展 現

科技藝術類增加三世多杰羌佛的攝影,三世多杰羌佛應同學們要求增加攝影,三世多杰羌佛說:『我沒有攝影的照片,你們給我一個相機,我只要一天照來就會有了。』佛陀上師開了關房門,帶領了十餘人,很快登上山崗,霹靂啪啦就拍下了古堡化石狀的崖壁照片。

在拍照的同時,異相出現了,天空像一個正方的鏡子,映在拍攝區的崖壁,而背山則是地上放出藍光,遙相呼應,尤其強烈的光源對比造成大地左山崗變成一片漆黑,但它光明所照之處,光明耀眼,殊勝無比,這一聖境的照片出現了如此偉大的異相,顯示了三世多杰羌佛佛法的偉大,我們按捺不住內心的激動,不得不告訴世人這一事實,為此隨行人員發自內心商榷共識,賭咒發誓如下,以證明三世多杰羌佛之聖德感召。

發誓文:這一張照片確實是我們尾隨佛陀上師在登上山崗後,在聖山境前,啪啪兩聲隨意拍攝下來的,完全未經電腦任何處理,原始面貌原味的原始照片,如果我們所言有任何虛假,願遭惡報,不得解脫,若所言一切真實不虛,願所有眾生增加福慧,吉祥如意。

當事弟子共商發誓如上,親筆簽名如下:

（此文的英文翻譯印在前面）

Westerners Express Their Admiration for H.H. Dorje Chang Buddha III

My Buddhist name is Bodi Wentu Rinpoche. I became a disciple of H.H. Dorje Chang Buddha III Wan Ko Yeshe Norbu Holiest Tathagata in Sichuan, China in late 1995. I would like to relate two examples that reflect H.H. Dorje Chang Buddha III's highest mastery of the Five Vidyas.

After I returned to the United States from Sichuan, I began translating from Chinese into English ten discourses on the Buddha-dharma given by H.H. Dorje Chang Buddha III. A fellow disciple named Losang Gyatso Rinpoche assisted me in that translation.

One day in 1998 when H.H. Dorje Chang Buddha III was visiting the United States, Losang Gyatso Rinpoche and I went to the place where H.H. Dorje Chang Buddha III was staying to pay our respects to him and present the translation of those discourses to His Holiness for His Holiness's review. The translation was put in sealed envelopes. Right after we prostrated to H.H. Dorje Chang Buddha III but before we presented the translation to His Holiness, H.H. Dorje Chang Buddha III said, "You have earned great merit and made a great contribution to living beings. Although the translation that you brought today contains some minor mistakes, it will still be of great benefit to westerners." Before we even reported anything to H.H. Dorje Chang Buddha III, His Holiness already knew what we wanted to report. This moved me very much. Losang Gyatso Rinpoche and I then presented to H.H. Dorje Chang Buddha III the sealed envelopes containing the translation.

The second example occurred in 1999. I and other fellow disciples accompanied H.H. Dorje Chang Buddha III to Missouri, where H.H. Dorje Chang Buddha III received an honorary doctorate degree in Buddhism, Art, and Religious Studies from the American League of Colleges and Universities. After the presentation ceremony, all of us sat down to eat dinner. There were a number of college and university deans, presidents, and professors in attendance. The president of a religious college asked whether questions could be posed to His Holiness. H.H. Dorje Chang Buddha III responded, "Ask whatever questions you would like to ask. All of my answers will satisfy you." H.H. Dorje Chang Buddha III answered all of the questions posed with total ease, which evoked great admiration. The president of that religious college asked the most difficult question, which H.H. Dorje Chang Buddha III easily answered, causing the president to blush with embarrassment. When there were no more questions, the chairman of the American League of Colleges and Universities expressed how awestruck he was with the answers of H.H. Dorje Chang Buddha III by suddenly slapping himself once on each cheek. He then excitedly and loudly stated that he has lived in vain for all of these years and that the answers of H.H. Dorje Chang Buddha III had truly opened his eyes. The president of the religious university also marveled at the wisdom that H.H. Dorje Chang Buddha III displayed that evening. One can see from this how complete the wisdom of H.H. Dorje Chang Buddha III is.

There are many other examples I could relate concerning H.H. Dorje

Chang Buddha III's highest mastery of the Five Vidyas and His Holiness's great compassion toward living beings. However, due to limited space, I will stop here. May this book be a blessing for all living beings, and may it aid in liberating them from the sufferings of reincarnation.

Buddhist disciple, Bodi Wentu

Bodi Wentu

(The Chinese translation of this text follows.)

西 方 人 敬 佩 三 世 多 杰 羌 佛

　　我的法名是波迪溫圖仁波且。1995年末，在中國四川，我成為尊貴的多杰羌佛第三世雲高益西諾布頂聖如來的弟子。我要講述兩個反映出三世多杰羌佛妙諳五明的事例。

　　我從四川回到美國之後，開始將三世多杰羌佛開示的十盤佛法開示帶由中文翻譯成英文。另有一位師兄協助我作此翻譯。

　　1998年的某一天，三世多杰羌佛在美國參訪時，一位師兄洛桑嘉措仁波且和我到三世多杰羌佛下榻的地方去拜見三世多杰羌佛，主要是呈交這些開示的翻譯請三世多杰羌佛審查。這些翻譯是放在密封好的信封裏。我們剛剛向三世多杰羌佛頂完禮，尚未呈交翻譯之前，三世多杰羌佛即說：「你們的功德很大，並且對眾生作了很大的貢獻。雖然你們今天帶來的翻譯中包含了一些小問題，但它仍對西方人士會有很大的益處。」在我們甚至未報告之前，三世多杰羌佛就已經知道我們要報告什麼了。這令我非常地感動，並且師兄洛桑嘉措仁波且與我一起將裝有翻譯的密封信封呈交給三世多杰羌佛。

　　第二個事例發生在1999年。我和其他的師兄弟陪同三世多杰羌佛到密蘇里州，三世多杰羌佛在那裏榮獲了美國大學聯盟所頒發的佛教、藝術和宗教研究的榮譽博士學位。在頒獎儀式之後，我們所有的人一起共進晚餐。出席的有許多大學校長和教授們。有一位宗教大學的校長問道：『是否可以向大師（注：大師即是指三世多杰羌佛，下同）提問？』三世多杰羌佛回答說：「隨你們提問，我所有的答案都將會讓你們滿意的。」三世多杰羌佛輕而易舉地回答了所提的全部問題，大家對三世多杰羌佛非常欽佩。這位宗教大學的校長提問了最刁難的問題，三世多杰羌佛卻輕易地就作了回答，讓這位校長感到慚愧。當大家無話可問時，美國大學聯盟的主席對三世多杰羌佛所作的回答感到震驚，他突然在他自己的臉頰上各摑了一記耳光並且又激動又高聲地說：「這些年我白活了，今天大師的回答真正令我開了眼界。」宗教大學的校長則讚嘆三世多杰羌佛的智慧真是太高了。由此可見三世多杰羌佛的智慧是何等的圓滿！

　　我還有許多其它有關三世多杰羌佛妙諳五明的事例可以講述。然而，因為篇幅有限，我將停止於此。願這本書給所有眾生帶來福報，願它能幫助眾生從輪迴的痛苦中得到解脫。

佛弟子：波迪溫圖

（此文由前面的英文翻譯而來）

An Enormous Golden-Winged Legendary Bird Prostrated to H.H. Dorje Chang Buddha III
大 鵬 金 翅 鳥 的 禮 拜

When H.H. Dorje Chang Buddha III Wan Ko Yeshe Norbu was correcting the discourse of a great dharma king, an enormous golden-winged legendary bird with the size of a small car flew into view and perched itself on the temple where H.H. Dorje Chang Buddha III was in order to prostrated to H.H. Dorje Chang Buddha III.
三世多杰羌佛雲高益西諾布在修訂一位大法王的開示時，一隻展翅時大如小轎車的大鵬金翅鳥飛來三世多杰羌佛所在的寺廟禮拜。

181

Blessing Given by H.H. Dorje Chang Buddha III for the Grand Opening of Hua Zang Si

In the evening of December 25th, 2004, we were all working so hard to prepare for the next day's grand opening of Hua Zang Si. Shu-Hui Chiang received a phone call from H.H. Dorje Chang Buddha III Wan Ko Yeshe Norbu Holiest Tathagata, who at that time was a thousand miles away from San Francisco, asking whether Hua Zang Si was blessed by a Buddha light. This was first time Shu-Hui Chiang received a direct call from H.H. Dorje Chang Buddha III. She was somewhat nervous but still reported to H.H. Dorje Chang Buddha III honestly, "There isn't any Buddha light. It is cloudy and drizzling in San Francisco." According to the weather forecast, it will start raining soon. After Shu-Hui Chiang's report, H.H. Dorje Chang Buddha III told her clearly, "Notify everyone in Hua Zang Si. There will soon be a Buddha light to bless Hua Zang Si for the grand opening." So she did. We all waited outside for the Buddha light. Not long, the clouds suddenly spread out.

The sky became clear. Right on top of Hua Zang Si, there was a big circle of multi-color Buddha light shining around the moon. It seemed like a curtain and shined down upon Hua Zang Si to bless it. There was a news report giving the details of the Buddha light that night.

All that is described above is nothing but the truth. If there is anything fake about this, I am willing to bear all punishment. If it is true, I dedicate all the merits to all living beings, who I wish would have the opportunity to

Buddha light bathed the temple, Hua Zang Si the night before the Dharma Assembly to mark its opening. Everyone at the scene saw the auspicious sign of a mani vajra beam appear within the Buddha light in the sky. (Photograph taken by Guang-Ming Li)
開寺法會前一夜佛光沐洗華藏寺，大眾現場見到天空佛光中出現瑪尼金剛棒的瑞相。
（李光鳴現場攝）

listen to the dharma discourses of H.H. Dorje Chang Buddha III Wan Ko Yeshe Norbu Holiest Tathagata.

Buddhist disciple,
Long Hui Shih

(This is a complete translation of the Chinese text that follows originally written and signed by Long Hui Shih.)

華藏寺開寺　三世多杰羌佛之感召

2004年12月25日晚，大家正在緊張而忙碌地進行著第二天華藏寺的開寺大典的準備工作，這時姜淑蕙突然接到遠在千里之外的多杰羌佛第三世雲高益西諾布頂聖如來的電話，詢問華藏寺是否被佛光加持。姜淑蕙是第一次親自接到三世多杰羌佛的電話，雖然有些緊張，但還是如實地向三世多杰羌佛報告說：現在不僅沒有佛光，而且舊金山烏雲密佈，已經在飄雨點了，據天氣預報說要下雨。聽了姜淑蕙的彙報，三世多杰羌佛明確告訴她：你通知大家，一會兒將有佛光加持華藏寺，為華藏寺開光。姜淑蕙轉述了三世多杰羌佛的開示以後，大家便急切地等待佛光的到來。果不其然，一會兒烏雲就突然散開，一片藍色，天空乾乾淨淨的，在華藏寺的正頂上方，一圈五彩佛光圍繞

在月亮的周圍，就像帷幕一樣朝華藏寺射下來加持華藏寺。請見當時報紙的報導。

以上所述是真實不虛的，如有虛假編造，弟子願遭一切惡報，如果屬實，一切功德回向給所有眾生，願他們都能得聞多杰羌佛第三世雲高益西諾布頂聖如來的佛法。

佛弟子　隆慧

（此文的英文翻譯印在前面）

The Buddhas Praise H.H. Dorje Chang Buddha III's Discourse; Buddha Light Blessing Illuminates the Lecture Hall

Mundane people can derive only superficial knowledge of the greatness of the Buddha-dharma from reading the sutras, but holy ones generally can personally experience it through their cultivation and the process of becoming enlightened. As for my humble self, Gadu, I have been fortunate enough to experience this greatness during the times I handled

various Buddhist matters at the side of the Buddha Master, H.H. Dorje Chang Buddha III Wan Ko Yeshe Norbu, and received dharma transmissions and initiations from His Holiness.

The following are two true events where Buddha light blessings occurred that I wish to report to everyone. The following description is completely true, and if I have made any of it up, I am willing to pay with my life and cultivation and descend to the Hell of Continuing Suffering.

1. The Buddha Master was in the lecture hall giving a discourse to the four types of disciples on "What Is Cultivation" in response to a question from Zhaxi Zhuoma Rinpoche. Soon after the Buddha Master had begun, a beam of sparkling iridescent light suddenly appeared and started circling the indoor lecture hall with the force of lightning. The sight was utterly dazzling and auspicious! From the beginning to the end of the discourse, the dazzling Buddha light appeared and illuminated the lecture hall as many as five times. H.E. Denma Tsemang II, Venerable Dharma Teacher Long Hui, Dharma Teacher Jue Hui, Respected Zhaxi Zhuoma Rinpoche, Cheng Hui Shih, Ding Hui Shih, Jian Hui Shih, Liao Hui Shih, Guang Hui Shih, Jie Hui Shih, Ko Hsuan, Pengzhi Qi, Huakong, Hui Chu Linchen, Yu Chia Lin and myself were all at the scene when this occurred. Not all of the disciples saw the same colors and number of Buddha lights because of their different levels of cultivation and different karmic conditions. Some people saw Buddha lights appear six times, while others saw Buddha lights appear twice. Some saw red, some saw white, and still others saw iridescent Buddha lights sparkling in the lecture hall. I personally saw Buddha lights as bright and dazzling as the flashing of a flash bulb. The Buddha Master's discourse on the Buddha-dharma and the praise and blessing of the Buddhas and Bodhisattvas filled all of the disciples in the lecture hall with the joy of the dharma.

2. Other Buddha lights were special manifestations that had an underlying cause. They manifested when the Buddha Master was expounding upon the karmic conditions behind the cover of the book *A Treasury of True Buddha-Dharma*. Dazzling Buddha lights suddenly flashed in the mandala. The Buddhas and Bodhisattvas used Buddha lights as a means of praising the birth of the book *H.H. Dorje Chang Buddha III—A Treasury of True Buddha-Dharma*, which would soon provide the multitudinous living beings in this earthly realm with a path to practice the true dharma. As many great dharma kings and great rinpoches have announced, the karmic conditions for living beings to experience good fortune have matured!

Buddhist disciple, Gadu

(This is a complete translation of the Chinese text that follows originally written and signed by Gadu.)

三 世 多 杰 羌 佛 開 示 ， 諸 佛 讚 嘆
佛 光 加 持 ， 閃 耀 講 堂

　　佛法的偉大，凡夫一般僅能自佛教經典中得知表面的情結現象，而聖者一般能從修行開悟、成道的過程中親自體驗印證。而慚愧的我——嘎堵，卻有幸的能跟隨在三世多杰羌佛雲高益西諾布佛陀上師身邊做佛事或接受傳法灌頂時親自體驗。

　　以下所舉兩件發生在今年（西元2006年）佛光加持的事實，向諸位善者報告。所陳述之內容完全真實，如有造假我願以我之生命與修行和墮落無間地獄做擔保。

一. 2006年四月，佛陀上師在壇城，應扎西卓瑪仁波且之提問，而為四眾弟子開示"什麼叫修行"時，剛開始講法，突然一道虹光無頭無尾，勢如雷電在講堂的室內空間憑空閃耀盤旋，奪目耀眼，吉祥無比！閃亮耀眼的佛光照耀著講堂，從佛陀上師陞座開講，一直到圓滿結束為止，佛光共閃爍照耀達五次之多。當天在場的四眾弟子有丹瑪‧翟芒尊者、隆慧法師、覺慧法師、扎西卓瑪仁波且、正慧師、定慧師、見慧師、了慧師、廣慧師、解慧師、可宣、戚朋直、華空、林陳惠珠、林昱佳，還有我本人。在場的四眾弟子，每人依個人修行程度之高下以及因果業力之牽引，導致看到佛光閃爍照耀講堂之次數以及顏色均有所不同。有的人看到六次，有的人看到兩次，有的人看到紅色的佛光、有的人則看到白色的佛光、另有的人則看到五彩的佛光圍繞閃耀在講堂。我則是看到閃亮耀眼如同閃光燈一般亮麗的佛光。講堂裡佛陀上師的開示佛法以及諸佛菩薩的佛光加持讚嘆，令所有在場弟子法喜充滿！

二. 這佛光的因緣是在佛陀上師開示《正法寶典》的封面緣起的殊勝展現的，當時，突然壇城裡閃爍著燦爛耀眼的佛光，諸佛菩薩以佛光來讚嘆《多杰羌佛第三世——正法寶典》的誕生，即將帶給娑婆世界芸芸眾生一條修習正法之道路，正如諸多大法王仁波且們宣佈的：眾生的福報因緣成熟了！

佛弟子　嘎堵

（此文的英文翻譯印在前面）

Demons on Highway One, the Pacific Coast Highway

In the summer of 1998, I was fortunate and honored to follow the holy presence of H.H. Dorje Chang Buddha III Wan Ko Yeshe Norbu Holiest Tathagata on a trip to propagate and spread the Buddha-dharma. We formed a large contingent and were driving along Highway One, the Pacific Coast Highway, toward San Francisco.

When the motorcade went into the curvy and twisty mountain roads, H.H. Dorje Chang Buddha III told the driver to turn off the air conditioning and opened up the windows to let the wind come in. The Buddha Master asked, "How do you like the air here compared to the air in Los Angles?"

"Of course the air here is better," we all answered at the same time, as if in one voice.

"Why?" The Buddha Master asked.

Brother Chang, who possesses a Master's degree in chemical engineering, hurried to answer first: "Buddha Master, this is because in any place that has dense trees or is close to the sea, the air contains a large amount of negative ions. And negative ions would…" He continued with a whole set of his knowledge in chemistry.

H.H. Dorje Chang Buddha III patiently waited for him to finish and then asked, "What do the negative ions look like?"

"Oh, this …" Brother Chang and the rest of us were all at a loss on what to say.

The Buddha Master smiled but did not say anything. A few minutes later, a ray of blue light suddenly penetrated into the vehicle through the front windshield and dispersed. We all smelled a very fresh and sweet scent.

We all stared at each other and did not know what happened. The Buddha Master turned back toward us and said, "Now do you know what negative ions look like? As practitioners, you can't just stay at the level of talking about hollow theories."

When our motorcade came to the Big Sur area, we were all intoxicated by the bright and beautiful views of scenery. Suddenly, the Buddha Master told us to drive into a small road and stop. The Buddha Master strode towards a pavilion near the edge of a cliff. His Holiness seriously stated to us, "Demons will come right away to disturb us. Let's all calm our minds and recite the Heart Mantra of Avalokiteshvara Bodhisattva. Don't chat to each other or be distracted."

At that time, there was not a single cloud in the vast sky, and the sea surface looked smooth and calm. Where would the demons come from? The Buddha Master stared at the sky and practiced a dharma using mudras. Within five minutes, violent winds started to blow fiercely. The wind brought sand and dust into the sky and made rocks move. The tranquil sea surface that had been calm suddenly changed into roaring waves rising higher and higher. The surging tides hit the shore and splashed as high as hundreds of feet. Even rocks the size of eggs were brought up and thrown into the sky. All these combined into a very scary scene. On seeing this, we had our minds concentrated on the dharma and recited the mantra loudly. Calm eventually returned after the Buddha Master subdued the demons.

H.H. Dorje Chang Buddha III gave us a discourse on that: "Among our group on this trip to propagate the dharma, there are rinpoches, great dharma teachers, and officers of the Institute and the publishing house. Demons are afraid that the correct Buddha-dharma will benefit living beings in the Western world, so they are going to do everything to break us down. However, you need not be worried. The demons will not be able to hurt you."

Our motorcade continued on the journey. It was already dark, and the mountain road was rugged and rough. We decided to find a motel to stay for the night. After all our efforts, we found one motel on the mountain, but it had no vacancy. We tried to negotiate with the manager on duty to let us stay in the lobby for the night but were refused.

We walked back to the parking lot with tired and cold steps. The outside temperature was about -2 degrees Celsius (29 degrees Fahrenheit). The Buddha Master suddenly rolled down the window and told us, "Demons are coming to hurt you again. Hurry up and get in the vehicles. Concentrate on reciting the mantra."

Before getting back onto our seats, we heard a series of sad and shrill howls from the forest. From far away they came closer and closer and were very scary. We all felt chilled to the bone, and our bodies were shaking. At that moment, hunger and cold were of no concern to our minds. We just kept doing our best to recite the mantra.

A few minutes later, we were frightened by a burst of hurried knocking on the window. I looked out. The Buddha Master was pointing at me from outside, "Boyuan[1], come out immediately."

I rushed to get out of the vehicle and followed the Buddha Master, who was walking towards the forest. The Buddha Master was repeatedly applying a mudra towards several piles of dark shadows in the forest. "The shadows are demons. These scoundrels are constantly looking for opportunities to attack us," he said.

It took almost half an hour before the demons were subdued.

At this time, it was already after midnight. The Buddha Master was practicing a dharma inside the vehicle without talking. The problem of finding a place to stay was still not solved. As we were at a loss on what to do, a Caucasian man walked toward us and politely said, "Are you looking for a hotel? I can let you use my mansion."

We were all pleasantly surprised by this happy news. Finally, we arrived at the mansion after driving in the dark. Several sisters among us went into the kitchen to prepare some food. In the cabinet, there were fourteen sets of dinnerware. And the dining room also had fourteen seats. This was exactly the number of people in our contingent. What a miracle! We were amazed.

In the early morning of the next day, we all gathered on the balcony of the mansion. The fright and fatigue of the previous night had all gone away. We found that the surrounding scenes were extremely beautiful. The valley extended endlessly. Ridges and peaks of all shapes were surrounded by circling clouds and mist. From east to west, we saw the sea on the horizon, with silver light reflecting from the surface. Waves were splashing on the shore cliff. The sun also seemed to be moved by the song of the tides. Up in the sky, auspicious clouds floated by as if in various enchanting horizontal postures. It was really a superlative joy to spend the morning in such a place. As mountain winds came from time to time complimented by singing birds and bees, we all felt very relaxed and intoxicated by the scene. The joy and pleasure simply made us unaware of where we were.

After breakfast, we all mentioned that it must have been dharma-protecting deities who helped us through the crisis the day before. H.H. Buddha Master asked, "Is that what you disciples think?"

The rest of the journey was still full of dangers and crises. Demons followed us all the way and were always looking for opportunities to attack. Fortunately, we were under the protection of H.H. Buddha Master. The demons were captured one by one, and we returned from danger to safety each time. Normally, it takes one day or less to go from Los Angeles to San Francisco. This time, we spent seven days and seven nights.

I would not be able to tell of all the merit and holy deeds of H.H.

---

[1] Boyuan refers to Long Zhou Rinpoche

Buddha Master even if I spent seven days and seven nights. I can only use the poetry I composed below to express a little bit of my feeling of gratefulness:

The Supreme Buddha Vajradhara of all sects, the honored one,
Possessing boundless merit beyond imagination;
His Holiness expounds the esoteric scriptures of the Tathagata;
With great compassion, His Holiness benefits and brings happiness to all living beings.
The roars of the Vajra Lion shake the Three Spheres,
Praised in writing by holy and virtuous dharma kings;
Coming to the earthly realm as guiding master of both humans and celestial beings,
He never shirks from saving and rescuing the suffering ones.
The Buddha Master's kindness is as grand as Mount Sumeru,
I will never be able to return the favors by any means;
I pray for my Buddha Master to stay in this world forever;
To exhibit a holy realm in samsara!

Humble disciple, Long Zhou
Recording the truth in this article

(This is a complete translation of the Chinese text that follows originally written and signed by Long Zhou.)

一 號 公 路 上 的 妖 魔

一九九八年夏天，我有幸能跟隨偉大的多杰羌佛第三世雲高益西諾布頂聖如來聖駕外出弘法，我們一行人浩浩蕩蕩沿著一號濱海公路開往舊金山。

當車隊進入曲折環繞的山區後，三世多杰羌佛要司機關掉冷氣，打開窗戶，讓外面的海風吹進車內。佛陀上師並隨口問道：「你們覺得這裡的空氣比洛杉磯如何？」

「當然是這裡的空氣好啊！」我們幾乎異口同聲的回答。

「為什麼呢？」佛陀上師反問。

擁有化工碩士的張師兄搶著說：「報告佛陀上師，因為凡是樹林茂盛或近海的地區，空氣中含有大量的負離子，而這負離子……」

他說了一番有關化學方面的知識，三世多杰羌佛耐心地聽完後，又問：「那負離子長得什麼樣子？」

「啊？這個……」這下考倒了張師兄及在座的師兄們。

佛陀上師微笑不語，就這樣經過幾分鐘後，突然一道藍光從正面車窗「穿」進了車內，然後「嘩」的散開，大家頓時吸到一股清香無比的氣味！

大夥兒瞪大眼睛，你看我，我看你，還不知是怎麼一回事時，佛陀上師回過頭，看看大家說：「知道什麼是負離子了嗎？修行人若只會講空頭理論是不行的！」

當車隊行駛到Big Sur地界，大家正陶醉在沿途風光明媚的景致時，佛陀上師突然喊我們開進路邊的小路，並且停車。佛陀上師大步走向斷崖邊上的一座涼亭內，嚴肅地對我們說：「這附近有妖魔很快要來干擾了，大家靜心持誦觀世音菩薩心咒，不要分神聊天。」

這時的天空萬里無雲，海面上一片寧靜，哪裡來的妖魔呢？只見佛陀上師凝視天空，結印修法，結果不到五分鐘，突然狂風大作，飛砂走石，原本平靜的海面，一下子變得波濤洶湧，浪擊千尺，連雞蛋大小的石頭，都吹得滿天飛起，十分恐怖。大家見到這景象，更加專心高聲地念咒，一直到妖魔被佛陀上師降服了，才恢復了原來的平靜。

三世多杰羌佛開示說：「這次出來弘法的隊伍中，有仁波且、大法師，以及基金會與出版社的幹部，妖魔們畏懼如來正法將在西方利益眾生，因此才千方百計想整垮佛教，但是大家不要害怕，妖魔是傷害不了你們的。」

雖然車隊繼續前進，但因天色已晚，加上山路崎嶇，只好臨時決定找間旅店過夜。好不容易找到山中一家旅館時，竟然已經客滿；跟大堂經理商量，可否在大廳勉強過一夜？想不到也被拒絕了。

當大家拖著疲憊冰凍的腳步，走向停車場，當時室外正是攝氏零下二度，佛陀上師突然搖下座車車窗說：「妖魔又趕來加害你們了！趕快上車，專心持咒。」

可是我們連屁股都還沒坐穩，就聽到樹林中傳來一陣淒屬的哀嚎聲，剎那間由遠至近，恐怖到頂點，那聲音才一入耳，大家無不毛骨悚然，全身哆嗦，什麼饑餓寒冷全都忘光了，只顧拚命持誦咒語。

這樣過了幾分鐘，一陣急促的敲窗聲，把大家又嚇了一跳，回頭一看，佛陀上師在窗外正指著我說：「博元（即龍舟仁波且——編者注），你趕快下來！」

我急忙跳下車，緊跟在佛陀上師身後，一直走到樹林邊，只見佛陀上師不時地對著林中幾團漆黑晃動的影子打出手印，這影子就是妖魔，這些壞東西，一直要找機會對我們下手！

如此折騰了將近半個鐘頭，妖魔總算被降服了！

此時，已是半夜十二點多，佛陀上師坐在車上修法，沒有言語，而住的問題仍沒著落，正當大家一籌莫展時，一位美國白人突然走過來，很有禮貌地說：「你們是不是需要旅店？我的別墅就借給你們吧！」

這突來的喜訊，讓大家驚奇不已！我們一路摸黑，終於找到了這家別墅，幾位師姊先進廚房，想準備煮一些宵夜，誰知櫥櫃中只有十四副餐具及十四個座位，正好是此行弘法團的人數，如此神奇，真是令人訝異！

第二天清晨，大夥兒聚在別墅的涼臺上，才發現這裡的風景無比秀麗，一望無際的山谷中，奇峰峻嶺，雲霧繚繞，東西萬里碧海，銀光翻花，濤延聯山，海歌動日，醉臥祥雲，千姿媚態，難以盡述，一朝宿此極樂情矣。觀山風徐來，蜂鳥低鳴，真是令人心曠神怡，陶醉其中，悅樂乎魂兮何處也，一夜的驚嚇與疲勞，早已拋到九霄雲外。

早餐過後，大家幾乎異口同聲說，昨天是護法神的化現，解決了我們的難關吧！佛陀上師說：「弟子們以為呢？」

接下來的行程中，仍是充滿驚險與危機，因為妖魔們一路尾隨，不斷的伺機下手，我們有幸在佛陀上師的威德庇護下，才能將妖魔一一捉拿，轉危為安。從洛杉磯到舊金山本來一日可到，竟用了七天時間。

佛陀上師的功德與聖蹟，我就是七天七夜也訴說不盡，僅能以此拙文來表達心中的感恩於萬一。

無上金剛總持尊，功德浩浩難思議，
開演如來秘密藏，大悲利樂眾有情。

金剛獅吼震三界，古德法王文讚稱，
人天導師駕紅塵，救拔倒懸不辭勞。
師恩巍巍如須彌，肝腦塗地難回報，
祈請我師永住世，化作輪迴展聖境。

慚愧弟子 龍舟造文記實

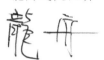

（此文的英文翻譯印在前面）

A Truck Was Demolished Falling Off a Cliff, Yet the Occupants Were Unharmed

My son Xiaoyu Tang once worked as a driver for the 4th company, 2nd barracks, 17th vehicular regiment of the Chengdu Military District. One night in the autumn of 1993, he went to H.H. Dorje Chang Buddha III Wan Ko Yeshe Norbu Holiest Tathagata to humbly request a blessing for the next day's trip to deliver goods to Tibet. He said, "Grand Buddha Master, I will be driving into Tibet. The Sichuan-Tibet roads are very dangerous, and I fear an accident. I beg the Grand Buddha Master to bestow a blessing upon me." The Buddha Master was painting at the time. Without giving it much thought, His Holiness smiled and said, "You do have a little accident in store, but it won't kill you." Xiaoyu knelt forward, and H.H. Dorje Chang Buddha III put his hand on Xiaoyu's head and blessed him. After Xiaoyu prostrated before and thanked H.H. Great Dharma King, he left for Tibet.

A little after 9:00 on the morning of December 26, 1993, Xiaoyu's convoy was delivering cement to a mountaintop outpost on the border between Tibet and India, climbing the extremely steep and frighteningly curvy Demula Snow Mountain in the Chayu district. At a turning point on the mountain road, someone had bridged a sagging spot with two logs and covered it with mud and grass. It appeared on the surface to be part of the road, but it was actually hollow and could not support the weight of a few dozen military vehicles. Below was a valley more than 180 meters deep. Beside the bottom of the valley was the raging Yaluzangbu River. When Xiaoyu and his partner Qilin Zhao drove up to this segment of the road, the logs gave away with a loud crack and the truck tumbled thunderously down the cliff! Xiaoyu yelled with all his strength, "Quickly save me, Grand Buddha Master!" Then he called out to his partner Qilin Zhao, "Hold on to me quickly." His partner grabbed Xiaoyu by the waist, and the two of them went tumbling down with the truck. All of a sudden, Xiaoyu had the sensation of being supported from below. It was as though he was floating down lightly to the bottom of the valley while lying on soft cotton. At the instant they hit the bottom of the valley, the two of them were ejected from the truck as it disintegrated and the doors, engine, and tires flew in all directions. The vehicle was in pieces; all that was left were the tangled contours of the driver's cab lying less than two meters from the riverbank. One more flip and it would have fallen into the river.

Meanwhile, at the top of the cliff, the company commander

immediately ordered that bugles be blown to stop the trucks. All of the soldiers took off their hats and stood in silent tribute for their "lost" comrades. Everyone knew that nobody could survive a fall from a cliff 184 meters (604 feet) high. The company commander immediately notified regiment headquarters to set up two makeshift altars. He also dispatched about a dozen soldiers down on ropes to gather the remains. Those soldiers were slowly let down that precipice. The company commander instructed them to find as many bones as possible so that they may be pieced together at a later time. When the soldiers reached the bottom of the valley thirty minutes later and found Xiaoyu and Qilin leaning on a boulder beside the debris of the truck, they fell back petrified, thinking they were seeing ghosts!

When Xiaoyu and his partner got back to the road, the company commander immediately ordered them to go to the hospital for a check-up. No one believed that two people of flesh and blood could survive unscathed a fall from a cliff 184 meters (604 feet) high that completely shattered their truck. The soldiers all thought that even if the two of them were luckily able to escape death temporarily, their internal organs must surely have been damaged. However, the results of the hospital examinations surprisingly indicated that other than slight bruises to their legs, everything was normal with the two of them!

A few days after the incident, Xiaoyu's supervisor came to my home and recounted the accident in detail. He said, "Xiaoyu Tang and his partner are the first survivors of a falling vehicle accident in the Chayu part of the Sichuan-Tibet transportation line in decades. The truck fell from a cliff 184 meters (604 feet) high and was completely destroyed. Even the steel frame was smashed into pieces, but they came out safe and sound! This is too fantastic, too incredible."

How could they know that his survival was a result of the blessing of H.H. Dorje Chang Buddha III! I have not heard of any person in the world today besides my Buddha Master who possesses such magnificent power to save lives from the hands of Yama, the king of the hell realm! I solemnly swear to the following: My son, Xiaoyu Tang, fell down a 184-meter (604 feet) cliff in a vehicle, yet he truly came out of the fall safe and sound. If this account is a fabrication, my entire family will surely experience evil retribution and disaster. Because what I say is the truth, my entire family should enjoy profound blessings and wisdom and the happiness of human beings should increase!

As a father, I must say something sincerely at this point. When that event happened, Xiaoyu Tang was a self-cultivator whose practice was in accord with the dharma. The Buddhas and Bodhisattvas protected him. However, at this time, Xiaoyu Tang's practice is not good. Thus, whether his future will be good or bad, it is totally in his control.

Buddhist disciple,
Hui Han Da
January 16, 2007

(This is a complete translation of the Chinese text that follows originally written and signed by Hui Han Da.)

翻車落懸崖，汽車解體，人卻毫髮未傷

我的兒子唐小雨，曾在成都軍區汽車十七團二營四連當汽車兵，1993年秋進西藏運送物資，臨走前一天晚上，去多杰羌佛第三世雲高益西諾布頂聖如來處求加持，他說：「佛陀師爺，我要開車進西藏，川藏路危險得很，我怕有災難，求佛陀師爺加持。」佛陀上師正在作畫，不經意地笑著說：「災難是有一點，但不要你的命就是了嘛。」小雨跪上前去，三世多杰羌佛為他摸頂加持，小雨頂禮謝恩後就進西藏了。

93年12月26日上午九點過，小雨所在的汽車連要將水泥運送到西藏與印度交界處的高山哨所，走到德姆拉雪山察隅地段，山勢十分陡峭，道路曲折得嚇人，有一小段『之』字形路，路面已經塌陷，有人便搭上兩根木頭，上面蓋草鋪泥，表面上看起來跟普通路面一樣，實則是空心，根本無法承受幾十輛軍車的重量，而下面就是一百八十多米的深谷，谷底旁邊就是洶湧的雅魯藏布江。小雨和一位戰友趙其林同駕一輛車，他們的車剛一開上木頭路面，只聽「喀嚓」一聲，木頭斷了！轟隆隆隆……汽車打著跟斗往懸崖下滾去！唐小雨拼命大喊：「佛陀師爺，快救我啊！」又喊趙其林：「快抱住我！」戰友一把抱住小雨的腰，兩人隨車翻滾，這時，小雨突然覺得有什麼東西托住了他，像躺在棉花上一樣輕飄飄地一直落到谷底。「嘭」的一聲，兩人同時彈出車外，車門、引擎、輪胎都已經飛了，車身摔得粉碎，就剩下一個已經不成形的駕駛室外殼，而且離江邊不到兩米，只要再翻一個滾，就掉進江裡了！

再說山崖上面，連隊長見此情景，緊急吹號停車，全體脫帽為兩位「犧牲」的戰友默哀。掉下184米深的懸崖，不用想都知道，沒有人能夠活命。連長立刻通知了團部，為他們二人設靈堂，又派了十多個士兵綁上繩索，從懸崖上放下去撿屍骨碎塊，連長命令：「儘量多撿一些屍骨，好拿回去拼湊。」半個多小時後，士兵們到了谷底，突然看見小雨他們兩人靠在汽車殘骸邊的石頭上，嚇得直往後退，還以為看到了兩個鬼魂！

小雨二人上到路面，連長要他們進醫院檢查，沒誰相信從184米高的崖上摔下去的人會完好無損，連汽車都摔碎了，何況血肉之軀？大家都在想：這兩人僥倖暫時沒死，但內臟肯定有問題。可沒想到，醫院檢查結果，除腿部有點瘀青外，兩人一切正常。

幾天後，小雨所在營的指導員來到我家，詳細講述了這次翻車事件，他說：「唐小雨他們是川藏運輸線幾十年來第一個在察隅翻車活著的人。從184米高的懸崖摔下去，汽車完全解體，連鋼鐵都摔成碎塊了，人卻安然無恙，這太神奇了、太不可思議了。」

他們哪裡知道，這都是三世多杰羌佛加持的結果！當今世上，能夠有如此威德，從閻王爺手中搶回他人性命的，除了我的佛陀上師，我還沒有聽說過有第二人！我在此慎重發誓：我兒唐小雨翻車落入184米懸崖，人確實安然無恙，假如我說的是假話，全家一定遭惡報，家破人亡。因為我說的是真話，全家應該福慧宏深，人類增加幸福。

說到這裡，我作父親的必須要說一句心裡話：唐小雨當時是一個如法的修行人，佛菩薩保護他，但現在的唐小雨修行不好，所以今後的好與壞全在於他自己把握了。

佛弟子　慧漢達

慧漢達

2007年元月16日

（此文的英文翻譯印在前面）

A Glass Wound Disappeared Without a Scar After Bleeding for an Hour

On a day I was off from work, I had an idea of making a meal of steamed dumplings as an offering to our Master [1]. I was very happy about it at the time. After I finished mixing ingredients and seasonings into the dumpling filling, I did what I usually do at home when I cook. I picked up a tiny bit of the filling from the tray and tasted it with my tongue to find out if the amount of salt I put in was right. Then I put it back onto the tray. Such was the usual practice that I followed when cooking at home for my family. After that, I set aside the filling and began to mix the flour with water to make the dumpling wraps.

Right when I was placing the filling inside the wraps and before any of the dumplings were put in the steamer, I heard a sudden loud crashing sound. I was greatly scared by the sound because I was standing in the kitchen making dumplings and was not moving around at all. As I turned to look, I saw that a bottle of unopened soy sauce had for no reason at all fallen

---

[1] Here and below the word *Master* refers to H.H. Dorje Chang Buddha III Wan Ko Yeshe Norbu Holiest Tathagata.

from the condiment table to the ground and was completely shattered. That table was about two to three feet away from me. The fright from that sudden and loud sound made my whole body break into a cold sweat. I then felt a flow of hot energy rising from my body to my head. A thought spontaneously flashed across my mind. I realized that I had committed an offense. I put my palms together and immediately started to repent. I reflected to myself, "Ah, I was wrong! I was stupid and ignorant. I am cooking for my Master now. How could I taste the filling first and then wrap it into the dumplings for my Master? Ah, I was wrong!"

Tears flowed down my face without stopping. I didn't need to analyze it. I kept asking myself how I could have done that. My tears continued to flow. The only thought in my mind was that I was guilty of committing that offense. The more I thought about it, the more contrite I became and the guiltier I felt. Of course, after I repented, I felt a little relieved.

I was about to clean up the broken pieces of the glass bottle and the spilled soy sauce that was all over the floor and then quickly cook and present the meal to my Master. I couldn't waste any time. However, as soon as I started to move my leg, I found I couldn't walk. I felt great pain, and my right foot couldn't touch the ground anymore. Leaning on the wall and moving with the other foot, I made my way to the bathroom. I raised my injured right foot onto the edge of the bathtub and, with great difficulty, took off the leather shoe on my right foot. I discovered that blood was continuously flowing from the arch of my right foot at a place slightly in front of the acupuncture point called yong quan. I realized that something had penetrated my shoe. I touched my foot while washing the blood off and found a sharp piece of glass in my foot arch. I carefully pulled it out. My foot was still bleeding. I did not have the time to treat the injury and simply used a piece of ordinary tissue paper to plug up the wound.

It was past 11 o'clock already, and I had to steam and bring the dumplings over to the Master's house. It would take 25 minutes to get there by riding my bicycle. Any further delay would cause me to miss my Master's mealtime. I didn't want to delay even one second. That was the only thought in my mind. I must not delay the Master's mealtime. I wasn't concerned about my foot at all. If I missed the Master's lunchtime, the dumplings would become leftovers for the evening. That would make me very unhappy indeed.

After going to my Master's house and presenting the lunch, I came back home and sat on a chair. I realized that I had to treat my wound. It was a big cut with a lot of bleeding. I had worked as a medical doctor for three years and knew what needed to be done. I should first disinfect the wound with alcohol or iodine solution using cotton balls at home. Then I would go to the hospital to get a shot to prevent tetanus.

However, after taking off my shoe, I saw that a miracle had happened. The wound on the bottom of my foot was nowhere to be found! Even any trace of the wound was gone! I was extremely surprised. The only thing I saw that was related to the wound was that piece of tissue in my shoe with dried blood on it. The cut by the sharp broken glass was no longer on my foot! This was very surprising to me but was absolutely true. I couldn't understand this fact before my very eyes even after pondering it over many times. How could this happen?

I told the story to my husband that evening. He is a graduate of Beijing Postal and Telecommunications College and studied radio waves and digital communication. So he emphasizes scientific reasoning. He knew that I was telling the truth. He looked at my foot himself and affirmed that there was no wound. Neither of us could understand this no matter how hard we thought because it was inexplicable. Such a severe injury was gone after at most one hour without receiving any treatment. There was not even any trace of redness or swelling. You all may not know my situation. Normally, if I accidentally poke my finger with a needle while sewing a button, the little bit of bleeding causes the finger to swell for at least three days. That is precisely why what happened to me this time is so extraordinary.

Later, I realized that this was a blessing from the dharma-protecting Bodhisattvas. They saw my stupid act of tasting food that was being prepared for and that was later presented to my Master. They were angry at me and gave me a warning by smashing the bottle of soy sauce. The dharma-protecting Bodhisattvas are also very benevolent to me. When they saw that I was sincerely repenting and correcting my mistake, they fully mended the cut on my foot. I am very grateful to my Master and am also very grateful to the dharma-protecting Bodhisattvas for their help.

From this experience, I truly realized that we disciples must be very pious to our Master. Our three karmas must completely correspond with those of our Master. There must not be the slightest deviation in such correspondence, whether intentional or not.

What I described above was a true experience of mine. I did not state anything false in my description of it. I would like to make the following vow. If I made any false statement or said anything that was not true, I am willing to descend to the hell realm immediately. I will end my statement at this point.

Yuxiang Wang
(Based on an edited tape-recorded statement of Ms. Yuxiang Wang)

(The text was translated from the Chinese text that follows.)

玻 璃 刀 傷 鮮 血 流   半 個 時 辰 無 傷 痕

有一天我休假,我就想給我們的上師(即多杰羌佛第三世雲高益西諾布頂聖如來──編者注,下同)做一頓燙麵蒸餃,我很高興。當我把那個餃子餡拌好,就像平常在家裡自己做菜一樣,把拌好的生菜餡拿到嘴裡嚐一嚐,看鹽味、味道好不好,嚐了以後,又把它放回到盤子裡去,也就像我平常做菜一樣。照常把料放好了,開始自己趕

麵,正動手包,根本還沒有上籠,就在這個時候,突然"啪──"的一聲響,爆響,簡直是!你們不曉得,把我嚇得來,因為我站在那兒動也沒動啊,正在包餃子,"啪"的一聲響,把我嚇得來,嗨呀,我側頭一看,在我的旁邊,離我約兩尺多遠的一個佐料台上,一瓶沒有開封的醬油,無緣無故地摔在地下,打得粉碎!這突如其來的一聲

響，把我嚇得一身出冷汗，一下子覺得一股熱氣衝上來了，腦子一閃念，就有一個念頭。就那一聲響，我來不及分析，我覺得我犯罪了，我就合掌懺悔，我說：『哎呀，我錯了，我愚昧，我無知，我給上師做菜，怎麼我吃了，又拿給上師包了，哎呀，我錯了！』我的淚水止不住的脫眶而出，我當時根本不用分析，我覺得我咋會把我吃過的東西送給上師，我淚水長流，只是說我有罪，只有這個心思，腦子裡除了這一個念頭，啥都沒有。我越想越懺悔，越覺得是罪過。當然，我懺悔完了以後，我的心情就好一點了，我就準備收拾好滿地的玻璃渣和醬油，趕快給上師送飯去，不能耽誤時間。但是這個時候，剛剛一抬腿，哎呀，發現我不能走路了，疼痛難忍，拉起腳來簡直沒法挨地了。我難受極了，一隻腳撐起，手撐著牆壁到了浴室，我就將右腳抬起來放在浴盆上，吃力地把右腳穿的皮鞋脫下來，脫下來才發現右腳的腳心，在涌泉穴的稍微前掌一點點，發現這個地方不斷地在往外流血，我就意識到是有啥東西弄進鞋裡頭去了。我就一邊用水沖洗腳上的血跡，一邊我就拿手去一摸，哎，腳心裡插了一個玻璃籤子，我就摸著把那個玻璃籤子拔出來，也還在流血，來不及對這個傷口做任何的處理，我隨手就在我的衣服包裡拿一張大家用的一般的衛生紙，墊了一塊在腳心裡頭，我看十一點過了，來不及了，要把蒸好的餃子送給上師，我騎自行車比較慢，要騎二十五分鐘，再晚了就趕不及上師吃飯了，一秒鐘都不能耽誤，我就只有這個念頭，不能耽誤上師吃飯的時間，也沒想到啥腳不腳的，管它的，趕不及上師中午用餐的話，晚上就成了剩東西，那確實我就難受了。

當我送完飯回來後，在椅子上坐下來，才想起我的傷口要處理，更何況那個玻璃籤子劃了一條口子，還流那麼多的血。我當過三年醫生，我想家裡有酒精啊，碘酒啊，棉球啊，馬上自己消毒處理，再到醫院去打一針破傷風。奇蹟出現了，想不到的是，當我把鞋子脫掉一

看，嗨呀，哪裡去找傷口哦，連傷口痕跡都找不到！哦呀我自己在那裡感到驚訝不已，剩下的就是鞋底下的一塊衛生紙，那紙上還留有血跡，血跡都乾了，但是找不到玻璃籤子劃的傷口到哪兒去了！我感到簡直太奇怪了，太奇怪了！這確實這是事實，是活生生的事實，但這個問題就擺在我們面前，使我百思不得其解，這是啥原因呢？當天晚上，我把這件事情跟我先生講了，我先生原來是北京郵電學院畢業的，他是學無線電數字通訊的，是比較講科學的，他曉得我說話是實在的，他就讓我把腳拿起來給他看一下，他說確實沒有傷口。我們兩個百思不得其解，因為解釋不了。你想嘛，這個傷口，最多一個小時吧，一個小時不治而愈，不治而愈啊，紅腫的印子都沒有。大家不曉得，我平時如果釘釦子把手指頭戳破了，流了一點點血，指頭紅腫起碼是三天才好得了，確實奇怪就怪在這裡。我知道，這是護法菩薩在愛護我，看到我怎麼能做出這樣的蠢事情來，給上師做菜，自己吃過又送給上師吃，護法菩薩生我的氣，把那個醬油瓶子砸了警告我。然後呢，護法菩薩愛護我，看了我知錯能改，那麼認認真真的在那兒懺悔，就把我劃破的口子給補好了。我簡直非常感謝上師，也非常非常地感謝護法菩薩對我的幫助。通過這件事，我確實認識到了，對上師只有十分的虔誠，三業要十分的相應，來不得絲毫有意無意的不相應。這件事是實實在在，真實不虛的，我沒打一句半句的妄語，我願意發個誓，如果我打半句妄語，說了假話，我願意立即墮地獄！我就說到這兒吧。

王玉湘

（注：此文根據王玉湘女士的談話錄音記錄整理）

（此文的英文翻譯印在前面）

A Holy Occurrence That I Inadvertenly Saw

The following occurrence took place one day in mid-1996. In order to register the car of my Buddha Master, H.H. Wan Ko Yeshe Norbu, a rubbing had to be made of the number on the engine. We were unable to make that rubbing ourselves. Therefore, at 19 Xinhua West Road in Chengdu, China, I reported to the Buddha Master that the car must be driven to the Bureau of Motor Vehicles. They have a special machine there that can produce rubbings of engine numbers. As soon as the Buddha Master heard me say that the car would be driven away, His Holiness immediately interrupted me and said, "Dehe, quickly go and tell Xiaoyu not to drive his car out. Hurry! Hurry! Hurry!"

Hearing such urgency in the Buddha Master's voice, I rushed out the door. I saw that the car of Xiaoyu and the others had just left. Although I called out to them, they did not hear me because of all the street noise. I ran after the car a short distance but could not catch up with it. I saw that they made a right turn and drove the car away. I returned to the Buddha Master and reported, "I could not stop them. I saw them drive away, but they could not hear my shouts." The Buddha Master replied, "How terrible. They are doomed." I asked the Buddha Master what the problem was and whether I could do anything. The Buddha Master answered, "You cannot do anything. Wait for the bad thing to happen." The Buddha Master did not say one more word after that.

After more than about ten minutes, a phone next to me began to ring. The person calling was none other than fellow-disciple Pingjiang Tang. In a terrified and shaking voice, brother Pingjiang Tang reported to the Buddha Master that a great misfortune had occurred. He said that after their car was hit by a large truck, it crashed into a pedicab, causing that pedicab to fly into a ditch. The back half of their car was gone. He did not know how many people died in the accident. The site of the accident and the ditch were filled with blood. The large truck that hit them fled the scene. Xiaoyu was able to stop another car, got into it, and chased after the truck. Brother Pingjiang Tang hastened to beseech empowerment from the Buddha Master. After the Buddha Master finished the phone call, His Holiness immediately practiced dharma to empower (bless) them.

Around a half hour later, brother Pingjiang Tang telephoned again. He reported to the Buddha Master that a husband and wife were hit in the pedicab and were seriously injured. The husband's foot was broken and his head was bleeding incessantly. A short while ago he had fallen into unconsciousness and was barely breathing but now has a little bit of breath in him. An ambulance was getting ready to take them to the hospital for emergency treatment. At this time, the Buddha Master exhaled a long breath and said to me, "Living beings are just this pitiable. All we can do is try our best to help them in the hope that they will be at peace." Although that husband and wife sustained broken legs and ribs as well as serious injuries to their internal organs, in the end they miraculously survived.

This is a true story that I personally experienced. I was at the side of the Buddha Master and did not leave His Holiness. The Buddha Master did not even get up from His seat. The magnificence of the Buddha-dharma is truly incredible. The Buddha Master already knew the results before the accident even occurred. What is even more incredible is that from several dozen kilometers away the Buddha Master empowered (blessed) people who had suffered serious injuries and were on the brink of death, saving them from a life-threatening situation. The Buddha-dharma is truly magnificent. It is truly impossible to describe orally or in writing the magnificent heart of the Buddha Master that takes pity upon living beings and the incomparable power of the Buddha Master that saves living beings. How can we as ordinary living beings understand the state of realization and virtue that our magnificent Buddha Master, H.H. Wan Ko Yeshe Norbu, possesses? In short, we truly are pitifully tiny. The Buddha Master truly is extremely selfless, extremely kind, extremely compassionate, and extremely magnificent!

Disciple: Dehe Li kowtows to the Buddha Master
Written in Vancouver, Canada on August 24, 2007

(This is a complete translation of the Chinese text that follows originally written and signed by Dehe Li.)

無 意 間 看 到 的 聖 蹟

一九九六年中的一天，為了上牌照的原因，雲高益西諾布佛陀上師的一輛汽車要拓發動機號碼，因為我們自己拓不下來，所以，我在成都新華西路19號向佛陀上師報告說要將車子開到車管所去，他們有專門的機器可以拓發動機號碼。佛陀上師一聽到我說到汽車要開出門，馬上打斷我的話，對我說：『德和，你趕快出去，喊小禹不要把車子開走了，快快快！』聽到佛陀上師這麼著急，我急忙跑出大門，看到唐小禹他們的車子剛剛起步走了，但是因為街上太吵鬧，他們沒有聽見我的喊聲，我跑了幾步追不上車子，看到他們右轉彎把車子開走了，我回來向佛陀上師報告說：『我攆不上了，我看到他們開走的，但是他們聽不到我的喊聲。』佛陀上師便說：『糟糕，完蛋了。』我問有什麼事，我能做什麼？佛陀上師說：『什麼也做不了，等著不好的事發生吧。』然後，佛陀上師老人家便不講一句話。

過了大概十多分鐘，旁邊的電話突然響起來了，來電話的不是別人，正是湯平疆師兄。湯平疆師兄用驚恐到極點的聲音顫抖著向佛陀上師報告說：出大事了，我們的車子被一輛大卡車撞到後，將一輛三輪車撞飛到溝裡去了，我們的車子後半部都沒有了，也不知道死了幾個人，滿地滿溝都是血，但是撞我們的大卡車逃跑了，小禹攔了一輛汽車去追了，趕緊求佛陀上師加持。佛陀上師接完電話後便立刻修法加持他們，又過了約半小時，湯平疆師兄再度來電話向佛陀上師稟報說：被撞的是一對夫妻，全部重傷，丈夫的腳被撞斷了，頭部流血不止，剛才一直昏迷不醒，連呼吸都幾乎沒有了，現在有一點氣，救護車正準備送他們去醫院搶救。這時，佛陀上師出了一口長氣，對我說：『眾生就是這麼可憐，我們只能盡力去幫助他們，願他們能平安。』後來，雖然他們的腿骨、肋骨都斷了，內臟也受重傷，但總算奇蹟般地生還。

這件真實不虛的事情是我親身經歷的，當時我就在佛陀上師老人家的身邊，沒有離開過，佛陀上師連座位都沒有離開。佛法的偉大真是不可思議，在事情還沒有發生時，佛陀上師就已經知道結果了。更不可思議的是，佛陀上師在數十公里之外加持重傷垂死的人，使他們脫離生命危險。佛法真是很偉大，佛陀上師悲憫眾生的偉大胸懷、救度眾生的無比威力真是無法用語言和文字表述，我們偉大的佛陀上師雲高益西諾布的證境證德哪裡是我們普通眾生能智曉的呢？一句話，我們真是渺小得可憐，佛陀上師真是太無私、太善良、太慈悲、太偉大了！

弟子：黎德和 叩上

2007年8月24日寫於加拿大溫哥華

（此文的英文翻譯印在前面）

The Selfless, Magnificent Buddha Master

Yeshe Norbu Master Wan Ko [1] is the most venerable leader in Buddhist circle and the chief adept in orthodox Buddha dharma in the dharma realm. His Holiness is my Buddha Master who I respect the most and to whom I am indebted to. Ever since His Holiness started to propagate correct Buddha-dharma to save living beings, His Holiness has repeatedly announced and abided by an unusual rule that He does not accept any offerings. His Holiness only wants to spread correct Buddha-dharma, save living beings and participate in all charities associated with the correct dharma of Tathagata. His Holiness does not accept any offerings no matter if they are money, assets, or items at any value. On the other hand, His Holiness constantly puts the welfare and interest of living beings as His top priority. His Holiness is mindful of that and tirelessly and quietly contributes to people and benefits sentient beings with all of his own treasure and fortune without reservations. His Holiness brings to living beings and the entire Buddhist realm immeasurably vast and profound benefits of correct Buddha-dharma and infinite blessings. Nevertheless, our majestic Master always considers Himself as one of the living beings. His Holiness defines Himself as a humble practitioner and does not allow anyone to promote Him. His Holiness constantly said, "I am a humble practitioner. I am and will always be an attendant to all living beings." I would like to give some of my personal experiences as examples. These are all true facts.

"The Song Collection of Master Wan Ko Yee" is proof that my great Master implements Buddha wisdom of the Five Vidyas and the dharma voice of Tathagata in promoting dharma and saving living beings. It is also proof that the Master dedicates Himself unselfishly only to benefit sentient beings. It is extraordinary and very precious that His Holiness saves and benefits living beings without accepting anything in return. His Holiness has formally confirmed in writing that He decided to contribute all royalty of His dharma music and lyrics to Buddhist practices that save living beings. He said, "I do not need anything. Everything is for the benefit of living beings." In addition, His Holiness stopped our promotion preparation for the debut of "The Song Collection" and said, "Do not promote me personally! Due to certain special karmic affinity, I am much honored to participate in part of the preparation, publication and distribution of 'The Song Collection of Master Wan Ko Yee.' " I personally experienced and witnessed my Master's holiness and morality in His propagation of correct Buddha-dharma and salvation of living beings. I was deeply moved.

There was a fellow male disciple in Chengdu, China, who used to be a blind vagrant. He lost sight in both of his eyes more than thirty years ago. He was so poor and deprived that he sang from street to street and begged for donations to support himself. One day, my Buddha Master ran into him and helped him out with great compassion. His Holiness not only cured the vagrant's blindness in a very short period of time but also provided his family of four with money and items of necessity on a regular basis to alleviate his financial hardship and help his two children receive an education. The vagrant singer was so deeply moved and thankful that he composed many folk songs and dedicated them to the Master, praising His immeasurable compassion and the divine merits of Buddhahood. The tunes and lyrics were very touching. Later on, I recorded these songs and was about to publish and promote them. I had an audience with my Buddha Master and reported the project to His Holiness. His Holiness stopped me from doing it. The reason was very simple. It was what His Holiness had said before, "Do not promote me personally!"

I had brought money or things as offerings to the Buddha Master many times in the past. However, the Buddha Master refused to accept them again and again. His Holiness always returned them after His Holiness empowered them. There were no exceptions. There were many examples. I once offered my Buddha Master RMB$200,000.00. His Holiness did not accept any of it. Instead, His Holiness donated the entire amount to a nursing home and helped me accumulate the merit of charity. There was once that I made an offering of HK$6,000,000.00 to the Buddha Master which was returned to me with His blessings. Another time when I gave the Buddha Master an AE gold card from American Express which had unlimited credit line, His Holiness paid no attention to it and refused it. And, there was a time that I made an offering of HK$1,000,000.00 in a cashier's check. It ended up being taken by the Buddha Master to a dharma assembly with around 100 attendees where he returned it to me with His blessings. His Holiness also gave a discourse and announced again His principle of not accepting offerings. The aforementioned examples are just a few among countless others regardless of the amount of offerings. Every time when the Buddha Master turned down disciples' offerings, His Holiness always told His disciples compassionately, "As your Master, I do not need your money. What I need is your true heart in learning Buddhism and your conduct of unselfish devotion in benefiting living beings."

My Buddha Master's teachings through His words and conduct have become the guidelines and models that I follow to stay motivated in learning Buddhism and self-cultivation. I want to make a resolution that I will always consider myself as a humble Buddhist disciple and practitioner just like my Buddha Master. I will always be mindful of that in the aspects of my conduct, speech and thoughts. The three karmas of mine will be corresponding to those of my Buddha Master's. Therefore, I decided to be ordained to become a bhikkhuni and follow the teachings of my great Buddha Master. I will unselfishly contribute all I have for the cause of self-enlightenment and enlightening others, propagating correct Buddha-dharma and benefiting living beings.

My majestic Buddha Master is the most extraordinary Buddha in the history of Buddhism who truly came from the Buddha Lands. His Holiness has been praised by the Bodhisattvas and Buddhas from the ten directions with great joy. His Holiness has been leading living beings from the dharma realm to practice and uphold the correct Buddha-dharma of Samyaksambodhi. His Holiness's Buddha wisdom and Five Vidyas are magnificent and wonderful. His Holiness manifests his virtuous merits and

---

[1] Here and below the word *Master Wan Ko* or *Master* refers to H.H. Dorje Chang Buddha III Wan Ko Yeshe Norbu Holiest Tathagata.

Buddha-dharma without any hindrance. Various Buddhist sects and schools of Exoteric and Esoteric Buddhism have respectfully followed and relied upon the Buddha Master. His Holiness is truly the most majestic Buddha that came to save and liberate all living beings, and bring to the world happiness, auspiciousness, peace, prosperity and great future. However, I feel most disappointed and saddest that I have not seen my great Buddha Master for nine years. I do not know when I will get the chance to have an audience with him and prostrate myself in front of him. I miss my Buddha Master a lot. Great Heavens! Please give me an opportunity.

Buddhist disciple with a heart of humility,
Hui Ni (Secular name: Nan Ni Hao)
in California, U.S.A.
October 21, 2007

(This is a complete translation of the Chinese text that follows originally written and signed by Hui Ni.)

無 私 偉 大 的 佛 陀 上 師

　　佛教界的至尊領袖，法界正法統帥益西諾布雲高大師，我最敬愛的佛陀恩師，自他正法駐世、弘法度生以來，就一直宣布嚴持一項特殊之規：只為弘揚正法、救度眾生，從事一切如來正法善益事業，但是不收任何供養。無論所供為金錢、財產或諸物品，無論多少巨細，一概不收。然而他卻每時每刻都把所有眾生的事業、眾生的根本利益放置首位，牢記心間，不辭辛勞，默默奉獻，毫無保留地將他所擁有的一切至寶財富全部施益於世，利樂一切有情，為整個佛教界、眾生界帶來無比浩瀚深遠的正法法益，無量福蔭。儘管如此，我們偉大的恩師卻總是將自己融於眾生之中，以慚愧身自居，不讓任何人為他去做宣傳。他常常示曰：「我是一個慚愧行者，我永遠都是所有一切眾生的服務人員。」以下便以我的親身經歷舉幾個例子，這都是真實不虛的事實。

　　《義雲高大師歌集》是偉大的恩師以佛智五明如來法音弘法度生的一個實證，同時也是他老人家無私奉獻、唯利有情的一個實證。如此稀有珍貴，度生利生，不收分文利益，並正式以書面聲明確認了此一決定，他把所有這些法音歌曲的詞曲創作應得版權利益全部無償地獻給了佛的正法度生事業，他說，「我什麼都不需要，一切為利眾生。」同時，還制止了我們為《歌集》的誕生出版勝事所作的一系列宣傳準備，指示：「不要宣傳我個人。」由於特殊的因緣關係，我非常榮幸曾參與了《義雲高大師歌集》的部份籌備、出版、發行工作，身歷其境，目睹恩師的正法度生聖義壯舉無限敬服，無比感動！

　　在成都(中國)有一位師兄，過去曾是個雙目失明了三十多年，沿街賣唱，乞討為生，窮困潦倒的歌丐，一日，恩師路遇，即大悲施救，不僅很快將他的盲疾治癒，令他重見光明，還不斷定期資助他錢、物等來解決他一家四口生活貧困、兩個孩子無錢上學讀書的困難，由發自內心無限的深厚感恩之情，歌丐譜寫唱出了許多敬頌恩師老人家無量慈悲佛恩聖德的民間歌曲，十分感人，後來我還為這些歌曲錄製了唱片，準備拿去出版宣傳。當我拜見恩師，稟告此事時，卻遭到老人家的勸止，理由很簡單，仍然是那一句話，「不要宣傳我個人。」

　　過去我曾一次又一次地帶上錢財、物品前去敬供老人家，但是一次又一次地被老人家拒絕收受，加持退回，無一例外！譬如：一次我供養給老人家的二十萬圓人民幣，老人家分毫不收，後來還原封不動地將此款轉贈給了一家敬老院，為我作了善益功德；一次我供養給老人家的六百萬圓港幣被老人家加持退回；一次供養給老人家的一張美國運通銀行的American Express AE信用金卡（這張金卡享有無限透支額），結果老人家不屑一顧就給拒絕了；一次供養老人家的一百萬港圓的現金支票還被老人家拿到百人法會上當場加持退回，並再次開示重申了他一貫不收供養的原則……。以上這些都僅僅是多少大大小小實例中的幾件而已。每次退回弟子的供養，老人家總是無比慈悲地說：「上師不需要你的錢，上師要的是真正學佛之心，利益大眾無私奉獻的行為。」

　　恩師的言傳身教，成為我學佛修行典範所依，無限動力。我立誓，要像他老人家那樣，永遠以一個佛弟子、修行人的慚愧身、口、意自居行持，三業相應，決意出家為僧尼，依教於偉大的佛陀恩師，只為自覺覺他、弘揚正法、利益眾生而無私奉獻一切。

　　偉大的恩師，他是一位真正來自佛國，正在統領著整個法界眾生行持無上正等正覺如來正法，佛智五明精妙絕倫，善德示法無礙，佛教各宗、顯密諸乘悉皆敬皈依止，十方諸佛菩薩無比歡喜讚嘆的佛教史上最偉大的佛陀！他是一位要來度脫一切眾生，成就一切眾生，為整個眾生世界帶來幸福、吉祥、和平、繁榮、美好未來的真正最偉大佛陀！但是，大家不知道，我最遺憾、最難過的是我已九年沒有見到過佛陀恩師了，不知何日才能得見佛陀，親臨大禮敬拜啊！我太想念老人家了，我太想念佛陀了，天哪，您給我一個機會吧！

慚愧佛弟子　慧妮（俗名郝南妮）於美國加州
2007年10月21日

（此文的英文翻譯印在前面）

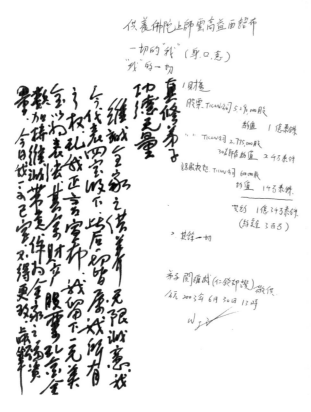

Offerings made to Buddha Master, Wan Ko Yeshe Norbu

The entire "I" including my body, speech and mind
Everything belongs to "me":
1. assets:
   Ticon stocks: 5,290,000 shares at an estimated value of Thai baht 100,000,000
   Ticon stocks: 30% of 2,775,000 shares at an estimated value of Thai baht 20,000,000
   Ticon stock options: 600,000 shares at an estimated value of Thai baht 10,000,000
   Total estimated value: Thai baht 130,000,000 approximately equivalent to US$3,000,000
2. others

> The above offering is respectfully made by me, disciple Wei Cheng Kuan (Renqin Quezan), at 1p.m. on June 30, 2003.

My Disciple of true cultivation,
Infinite Merits!

The offerings from the family of Wei Cheng Kuan are made with boundless sincerity. Today, I accept them on behalf of the Four Jewels. From now on, I have full ownership of them. Now, I announce the following:
I will keep one U.S. dollar as an expression of dharma. The rest of the assets, stocks and cash will be blessed and returned to Wei Cheng as the family's resources of good fortune. My statement has been made today. No revision is permitted.

Master

供養佛陀上師雲高益西諾布

一切的 "我" （身、口、意）
"我" 的一切
1. 財產 股票TICON公司 5,290,000股　約值1億泰銖
   股票TICON公司 2775000 × 30%　約值2仟萬泰銖
   認股權証 TICON公司 600,000股　約值1仟萬
   　　　　　　　　　　　共約1億3仟萬泰銖
   　　　　　　　　　　（約美金三佰萬）
2. 其餘一切

> 弟子　關維誠（仁欽卻讚）敬供
> 公元2003年6月30日13時

真修弟子
功德無量

維誠全家之供養，無限誠意，我今代表四寶收下，此后一切皆屬我所有之權，現我正言宣布，我留下一元美金以為表法，其餘財產、股票、現金全數加持維誠帶走，作為全家之福資糧，今日我一文已宣，不得更改。

上師　筆

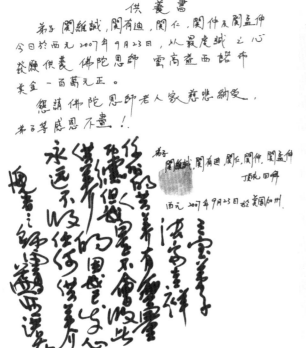

A Statement of Offering

Today, September 23, 2007, disciples Wei Cheng Kuan, Yupadee Kuan, Melissa Kuan, Manopath Kuan, and Monnat Kuan vow with utmost sincerity to make an offering of US$1,000,000.00 to H.H. Buddha Master Wan Ko Yeshe Norbu.

We beseech the Buddha Master, to whom we are indebted, to compassionately accept the offering. We disciples will greatly appreciate it.

> Disciples Wei Cheng Kuan, Yupadee Kuan, Melissa Kuan, Manopath Kuan, and Monnat Kuan prostrate four times to the Buddha Master.
> Date: Sept.23, 2007
> Location: California, U.S.A.

Disciples of the Three Jewels:
Dharma Peace and Auspiciousness!

The offerings you made result in infinite merits. However, I will not accept the offerings since I have already made a vow never to accept any offerings.

Humble Master, Wan Ko Yeshe Norbu

供養書

弟子關維誠、關有迪、關仁、關仲及關孟伸今日於西元2007年9月23日，以最虔誠之心發願供養　佛陀恩師雲高益西諾布美金一百萬元正。
懇請佛陀恩師老人家慈悲納受，弟子等感恩不盡！

> 弟子
> 關維誠、關有迪、關仁、關仲、關孟伸
> 頂禮四拜
> 西元2007年9月23日於美國加州

三寶弟子
法安吉祥

你們的供養有無量功德，但我是不會收此供養的，因我已發心永遠不收任何供養。

愧者之師雲高益西諾布

供養書

為潛心學佛、了生脫死、宏法利生，弟子釋周躍、臧健自願將中國上海的以下兩處房屋，虔誠地供養至高無上、最最偉大的頂聖益西諾布老人家。

一、上海黃埔江邊盛大金磐6號樓16屋一處計301m²，價值人民幣1,800萬元。
二、上海徐匯區五原路212弄11號花園洋房一棟，計313 m²，價值人民幣2,000萬元。

此至

供養人　周躍、臧健
二〇〇七年十月七日

弟子發心，其功德無量，奈我一慚愧之人，故決不收二位之供養。我之心願永不收任何供養，而只為眾生之利益而行持。

三世多杰羌
雲高益西諾布

A Statement of Offerings

Disciple Zhou Yue Shi and Disciple Jian Zang voluntarily present the following two properties in Shanghai, China as sincere offerings to the unprecedented, most magnificent and holiest Master, Yeshe Norbu. This is for the purpose of learning Buddhism, ending the cycle of birth and death, and propagating Buddha-dharma to benefit living beings.

1. Building 6, Unit 16, Shengda Jin Pan, Huangpu River District, Shanghai.
   Estimated size: 301 m² at a value of RMB 18,000,000.00
2. A single family home at No.11, Lane 212, Wu Yuan Road, Xuhui County, Shanghai. Estimated size: 313 m² at a value of RMB 20,000,000.00

Disciples who make the offerings
Yue Zhou and Jian Zang
Date: October 7, 2007

You disciples who have made a vow to make offerings will accumulate infinite merits. However, I am a humble self-cultivator and have decided not to accept the offerings. I will never accept any offerings. Everything that I do is solely for the benefits of living beings.

Dorje Chang III
Wan Ko Yeshe Norbu

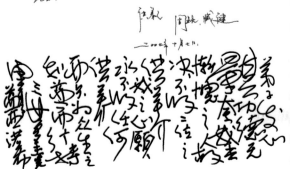

頂禮供養　偉大、至高無上的金剛上師　義雲高大師

十二年前，西元一九九一年，我在成都，拜見了一生中最最大的恩人，並且也是世間唯一的顯密俱通、妙諳五明的法界巨德─ 義雲高大師。

當時，為了求得宇宙人生的真諦、奧義，我將投資於北京的工廠，以及所有的事業、財產等動產、不動產全數供養給　義雲高大師。當時大師收下了供養，並傳授了至高無上的佛法、開示了宇宙人生的真諦，以及做人處世的道理。接法圓後，法喜悉俱，是以當下確知今生找到了唯一可以皈依的　金剛上師，而且必須徹底地追隨。

然而，大師卻在傳法後當場退還所有的供養。領時，我見到大師人格的偉大完美、無人能及，所做的一切無非是為了芸芸眾生，所行的一切也都是為了成就眾生。而對於世間法的不執著，正如日月之德，無私、無我、澄澈清明之心，所及之境，唯有「言語不足以狀其妙、思想不足以范其美」斯言可喻。

弟子若要拜師求法，供養是最基本的表法。　義雲高大師先是收下了供養，以合法義，然而傳法之後，又退回了供養。這種偉大、完美的人格，高潔無瑕、無私的襟懷，洪洪乎大矣哉！大師的人格典範，實非語言文字所能道盡，實在是已經到了眾生「無能名焉」的地步與境界。

婆婆之世，得見大師，幸甚至哉！

超凡之德，無能名焉，唯文以頌！

慚愧弟子　恆生
（陳寶生）
2003.4.19

I make prostrations and offerings to my magnificent and supreme Vajra Master, Master Wan Ko Yee [1].

At that time I made both my current and fixed assets including factories in Beijing, all business operations and properties as offerings to Master Wan Ko Yee in pursue of the true essence and profound meanings of life and the universe. The Master accepted the offerings and transmitted to me supreme Buddha dharma and gave me discourses on the true essence of life and the universe and life lessons. After receiving the dharma, my heart was filled with dharma joy. I was sure at the moment that I had found the only Vajra Master I could take refuge in and had to follow completely in my life.

However, the Master returned all my offerings at the scene after the transmission of dharma. At that time, I experienced the magnificence and flawlessness of the Master's character which is unsurpassed. All that he did is for the benefit of living beings. All that he practiced is for the enlightenment of living beings. His Holiness's detachment to worldly matters can be depicted as the sun and the moon, which are beyond any concept of aloofness. Only "its wonder is beyond descriptions; its beauty is beyond imagination" is able to describe the Master's mind of unselfishness, selflessness, and clearness and his state of accomplishment.

If a disciple wants to take refuge in or request dharma transmission from a master, making offerings to the master is the most basic requirement on the disciple. Master Wan Ko Yee accepted the offerings in the beginning, which is in accordance with the dharma. However, he returned the offerings after the transmission of the dharma. His character is magnificent and flawless and his heart is noble and unselfish. The Master's honorable moral and conduct is beyond descriptions to an extent that no words of human beings are adequate to represent its level and state.

How fortunate I am to meet with my Master in this Saha World!
What a virtuous and unprecedented one my Master is, that is beyond any worldly descriptions!
I praise him with my humble writing.

4/19/2003
Disciple with a heart of humility,
Heng Sheng (Pao-Sheng Chen)

---

[1] Here and below the word *Master Wan Ko Yee* or *Master* refers to H.H. Dorje Chang Buddha III Wan Ko Yeshe Norbu Holiest Tathagata.

中合外资 湛江海湖房地产有限公司

地址：赤坎东园路嘉丰大厦三楼　电话：3325288　3361328　电挂：1800　邮编：524043

我司時在一九九六年經會議研究決定，捐贈位於廣東湛江市赤坎區廣湛公路東大埠農場一號之四的 40 畝土地給義雲高大師，並寫了捐贈書。但是，大師不予接受土地，更沒有派人來辦理接收過戶手續，後經我公司多次催促，大師說：〝我不會要你公司的土地的，所以我不會去辦理這個手續的〞。因此，直到現在，大師不僅沒有接收這塊土地，連這塊土地在什麼位置都不知道。故我們也沒有將這塊土地劃給大師了。大師這種無私無我的高風亮節實在令我們感動，直到現在，我公司共計有 560 畝土地，其中 100 畝在湛江市赤坎寸金基金會、210 畝在中國建設銀行湛江分行、170 畝在湛江軍分區、80 畝在本公司。

二〇〇二年十一月二十三日

證　明

兩年前，我決定供養雲高大師一筆錢，當時我在台灣正好有一些土地，大概價值美金八百萬元，所以我就拿這一筆來供養大師。因為我一直對大師的學問、人品、道德無限的敬佩，在這麼多年當中的言傳身教，實在令我無限的感動。我在台灣打電話給大師，說明我的心意，結果大師嚴厲地批評我說：『這是你的東西，你應該好好地拿去發展你的業務，我不能接受你這個東西，我沒有權利佔用你這個東西。』我再三勸說，大師怎麼也不肯收。後來我再想了一個辦法，就是只將這個土地的一半供養大師，所以再打電話給大師，但是大師還是不同意，怎麼說都不行，最後大師非常的生氣，堅決不要。後來當我到了美國以後，我看到大師非常喜歡一部車叫 Pierce，那輛車大概價值八萬元美金，我看大師喜歡，我就想買來供養大師，結果大師嚴厲拒絕，堅決不要，從此對 Pierce 的車也不喜歡，也就不要了。所以，大師這種人品道德，是我一生當中第一次看到有這麼一位無私行為的人。正因為如此，我一直跟著大師這麼多年，大師的點點滴滴都是我們人類最崇高的人格及最純正的品德。

我以我的人格來擔保，我今天講的這些完全是事實，沒有半點虛構。

王燦明

二零零二年十二月三日

台灣嘉義市東區中山路285之1號12下
+886-5-2256858
+886-921213199
+1-626-6887502

ZHANJIANG HAIHU REAL ESTATE CO. LTD.

In 1996, our company held a meeting and decided to donate to Master Wan Ko Yee[1] a piece of land. The size of the land is 40 Chinese acres. That land is the 4th part of land No. 1 which located on Guangzhan Road, East Dabu Farm, Chikan District, Zhanjiang City, Guangdong Province. Our company wrote a certificate of donation. However, the Master did not accept the land. He did not send anyone to handle procedures relating to the transference of title. After our company urged him many times to accept the land, the Master said, "I do not want your company's land. That is why I will not handle those procedures." Therefore, up to now the Master has still not accepted that piece of land. Furthermore, he does not even know where that land is located. Thus, we have not transferred that land to the Master.

This example of the Master's selfless conduct and noble character has truly moved us. Our company currently has 560 Chinese acres of land. Of this, 100 Chinese acres are owned by Zhanjiang City Chi Kan Cun Jin Foundation, 210 Chinese acres are owned by the Zhanjiang Branch Office of China Construction Bank, 170 Chinese acres are in the Zhanjiang military sub-district, and 80 Chinese acres are owned by our company.

Zhanjiang Hai Hu Real Estate Co. Ltd.
Person handling this matter: Weiping Chen
signature and company seal
Nov. 23, 2002

---

[1] Here and below the word *Master Wan Ko Yee* or *Master* refers to H.H. Dorje Chang Buddha III Wan Ko Yeshe Norbu Holiest Tathagata.

TESTIMONIAL

Two years ago, I decided to make an offering to Master Wan Ko[1]. At that time, I had some land in Taiwan that was worth about US$8,000,000. I decided to offer this land to the Master. I have always greatly admired the Master's knowledge, character, and morals. Over the course of many years, he has taught me through words and by his own example. I have truly been tremendously moved by his teachings.

While in Taiwan, I called the Master to express my desire to make the offering. The Master sternly criticized me. He said, "That is your property. You should use it to develop your business. I cannot accept your piece of land. I do not have the right to make use of that property."

Despite my repeated urgings, the Master would not accept my offering. I later thought of another way. I would offer the Master only half of that piece of land. I telephoned the Master to convey my intention. The Master still did not agree to accept it. No matter how I pleaded, it was of no use. In the end, the Master was very upset with me and steadfastly refused my offering.

After I came to the United States, I learned that the Master very much liked a car called Pierce. That car sold for about US$80,000. Since the Master liked it, I wanted to buy one to offer to the Master. However, the Master sternly and steadfastly rejected my offering. From that time on, the Master did not like that Pierce car and did not want one.

With respect to the Master's moral character, he is the first person I have seen in my entire life who behaves so selflessly. That is why I have been following the Master for so many years. Everything about the Master reflects the highest character of any human being and the utmost moral rectitude.

I put my character on the line when I say that everything stated above is totally factual. There is not the least bit of fabrication.

Wang Tsan-Ming [Signature, fingerprint]
December 3, 2002
[Taiwan address]
886-5-2256858　886-921213199　1-626-6887502

---

[1] Here and below the word *Master Wan Ko* or *Master* refers to H.H. Dorje Chang Buddha III Wan Ko Yeshe Norbu Holiest Tathagata.

澄 明

我叫關珠，是一位佛教徒，有幸能隨侍義雲高大師，無時無刻不被大師崇高偉大的道德操守及慈悲為懷的境界所感動。大師五明俱足的具體展現及學問成就更是我心目中至高無上、無可替代的。

一九九九年秋季，游天木先生因景仰大師，經人介紹自台灣來美拜師，拜見大師，並聆聽大師精闢開示後，更是敬佩得五體投地。游先生也注意到大師在美生活簡陋樸實，非常感動，便向大師說明要供養大師房舍及照顧生活起居的決心，大師當場回拒了，最後游先生沒辦法，就情商我告知我本人銀行帳戶號碼，他會將錢匯入我的戶頭，以完成其供養心願。我當時也感覺到大師的生活實在太艱苦了，也就答應了游先生的請求。游先生回台後，電匯了美金一百八十萬元到我帳內，當我將此事向大師稟告後，大師毫不猶豫地拒絕了這份供養，我甚至曾私下向大師表明游先生誠心的初衷，但大師依然毫不為所動，堅決拒收。我實在無可奈何，只好據實告訴游先生，並轉達了大師的表態：決不從中動用一絲一毫。他的反應是反正這筆錢他是給定了，大師如果不收，那就拿去捐廟、做社會福利吧。我在多次想說服大師、嘗試無效後，即將此筆款項連同利息一併捐贈給與大師無關的中加寺。

在這件事情上，我更深一曾的看見了大師無與倫比的道德風範，這幾年中，我還親自經歷了一位大師的學生捐贈舊金山的 37 英畝土地和一棟坐落於奧克蘭市中心的 55000 平方英呎的大樓，大師也照樣不收受。大師聖潔的道德行為是我們芸芸眾生很難想像得到的。

以上所言，我本人不但要為因果負責，更要負美國的法律責任。我是一位修行人，最怕的就是錯因果，所以我要為自己負責，為眾生負責。我說的話真實不虛，今天提供給你們記者採訪。

Judy Kuan
8664 N. Cedar Ave. #202
Fresno CA 93720
(626) 255 8464

12/2/02

TESTIMONIAL

My name is Chu Kuan. I am a Buddhist. I am fortunate to be able to follow and serve Master Wan Ko Yee[1]. I am constantly moved by the Master's noble and magnificent moral character, discretion in conduct, and great compassion. I regard the Master's concrete display of his mastery of the Five Sciences and the Master's scholarly attainments as being supreme and unique.

There is a Mr. You Tian-Mu who holds the Master in great respect. In the autumn of 1999, he came to the United States from Taiwan. At the introduction of another person, he was able to meet and learn from the Master. After he heard the Master's penetrating discourses on the Dharma, he held the Master in even greater respect and admiration.

Mr. You noticed that the Master led a simple and thrifty life in the United States. He was very moved by this. He then told the Master of his resolve to offer the Master a house and living expenses. The Master refused his offer right then and there. Since Mr. You had no other way, he asked me to do him a favor and tell him my personal bank account number. He wanted to transfer money into my account in order to accomplish his wish of making an offering to the Master.

Since I also felt at that time that the Master's lifestyle was too austere, I agreed to provide that information to Mr. You. After Mr. You returned to Taiwan, he wire transferred into my account US$1,800,000. When I reported this to the Master, he unhesitatingly refused the offering. I even privately disclosed to the Master Mr. You's original intention behind the offering. Still, the Master was not moved at all and steadfastly refused to accept the money. I was truly at a loss. All I could do was tell Mr. You the truth and also inform him of the Master's position: The Master will absolutely not use even one cent of it.

Mr. You responded that he will donate that money no matter what. If the Master will not accept it, Mr. You wanted to donate the money to a temple to benefit society. After many unsuccessful attempts at persuading the Master to accept the money, I donated the money, along with the interest it had earned, to a temple in central California not connected with the Master.

From this incident, I have seen even deeper into the Master's incomparable morality. In the last few years, I also personally witnessed a student of the Master offer the Master a 37 acre piece of land in San Francisco and a 55,000 square foot building in downtown Oakland. As usual, the Master did not accept such offerings. It is very difficult for living beings to imagine the Master's holy and pure moral conduct.

I am responsible for all the karmic consequences and all the legal consequences of what I have said above. I am a self-cultivator. What I fear most is violating the law of cause and effect. That is why I must be responsible to myself and to all living beings. What I have stated is true. I provide this testimonial to you reporters for your coverage.

Judy Kuan
8664 N. Cedar Ave., #202
Fresno, CA 93720
(626) 255-8464

(Chu Kuan / Judy Kuan)
[Signature, fingerprint]
December 2, 2002

---

[1] Here and below the word *Master Wan Ko Yee* or *Master* refers to H.H. Dorje Chang Buddha III Wan Ko Yeshe Norbu Holiest Tathagata.

嚴正說明

我對義雲高大師道德崇高十分景仰，認識大師已有十年了，看到太多大師無私道德的例子。由此我非常感動，決心為大師做點事。1999 年我為了供養大師，特別來美國，並請大師到 Oakland 去看一棟近六萬五千平方呎的大樓作為供養，大師沒有接受。之後又請大師到舊金山的 Richmond 看地，該地共有 37 英畝，離中國城只有十幾分鐘的車程，是城市裡面的好地方，大師也一口回絕堅持不收，為此就不了了之。最後，我過了一年只好捐贈美金一百五十萬元給大師作為供養，大師當下叫人將聯合國際世界佛教總部的中英文資料傳真給我，將錢直接捐給該機構，自己分文不收。這就是雲高大師的行為，其他別人說什麼長短，我根本不在乎，這是我親身經歷的事實，實在感人的道德文章，我這一生還沒有見到有哪一個人有如大師這樣無私的道德。

潘孝銳 2003. 2. 8.

SOLEMN EXPLANATION

I hold in great respect Master Wan Ko Yee's[1] noble moral character. I have known the Master for ten years. I have seen so many examples of the Master's selflessness and morality. I was so moved that I decided to do something to benefit the Master. In order to make an offering to the Master, I made a special trip to the United States in 1999. I invited the Master to Oakland to see an almost 65,000 square foot building that I would like to offer to him. The Master did not accept it. Later, I invited the Master to Richmond, which is in the San Francisco area, to view a 37 acre piece of land. That land was only a little more than ten minutes from Chinatown by car and was situated in a good part of the city. The Master immediately and steadfastly refused to accept it. My only choice was to give up.

Finally, a year later, I made an offering to the Master of US$1,500,000. The Master immediately instructed someone to fax me material in Chinese and English regarding United International World Buddhism Association Headquarters. That money was directly donated to that organization. The Master did not accept one cent of it. This is the conduct of Master Wan Ko.

I do not care about the gossip of others. I personally experienced the incidents described above. The Master's high morality is truly moving. I have not seen any other person in my entire life with such selfless moral character.

Pan Hsiao-Rui
[Signature]
February 8, 2003

---

[1] Here and below the word *Master Wan Ko Yee*, *Master Wan Ko*, or *Master* refers to H.H. Dorje Chang Buddha III Wan Ko Yeshe Norbu Holiest Tathagata.

義雲高大師的為人與道德.風範,一向是我最尊敬
景仰的. 2000年初,我辭去了台灣高苑技術學院之教授
工作,來到大師身邊學習.當時,大師正住在 ×××
市一位 ×× 先生家裏.我因每天早晚隨侍在大師旁,
而注意到 大師晚上擠在一個堆滿東西的小房間裏,
席地而睡,非常艱苦.但他從不收取任何人的捐贈
供養,只憑自己的藝術作品出售維生,他的藝術作品
價值非常高,近日賣出一件「霧中之石」的雕刻作品就
價值一百萬美金.平常大師除了給我們講授學問道德,
都在打坐禪修及創造藝術,既未有空休息,也從未露
出倦容.當時,我因擁有一個大花園別墅,座落於洛杉
磯三大名住宅區中,便想要供養大師.我在向大師提
出這個想法時,大師當場就拒絕了.此後我雖然三番
兩次的勸說,都被大師嚴詞拒絕.為了供養這個別
墅,連我的父親李登木都曾當面勸說,而遭拒絕。

　　我謹以日夜 隨侍大師身旁之見聞及親身之經歷,
據實以說,並証實大師為人高風亮潔,對人慈悲無私,
利益大眾不遺餘力。以上所言句句真實不虛,若有虛假
本人願意承擔一切法律責任;倘若確切真實不虛,願我
及一切眾生福報無量。

Jiajing Lee
480 Prospect Blvd., Pasadena, CA 91103
(626) 353-7366

李加晶 謹筆　2002年12月3日

I have always had the utmost respect and admiration for Master Wan Ko Yee's[1] conduct and morals. In the beginning of 2000, I quit my position of professor at the Taiwan Gao Yuan Technology Institute and came to the United States to learn by the side of the Master. At the time, the Master was living in a gentleman's house located in a city of Los Angeles county. From morning until evening, I was at the side of the Master serving him. I noticed that at night the Master would cram himself into a small room filled with stacks of things. There he would sleep on the ground. It was very difficult circumstances.

However, the Master never accepted offerings from anyone. His only livelihood was selling his works of art. His works of art are extremely valuable. A carving of his called "Boulder With Mist" recently sold for US$1,000,000.

Besides spending time imparting his knowledge to us and teaching us ethics, the Master would meditate and create his works of art. Although he never had any spare time to rest, he never exhibited any fatigue.

At that time, I owned a house with a big garden. That large house was situated in one the three most famous residential areas of Los Angeles county. I wanted to offer that house to the Master. After I mentioned my intention to do so, the Master refused my offering right then and there. Later, I repeatedly urged the Master to accept my offering. Each time, the Master sternly refused. My father, Lee Deng-Mu, also tried to persuade the Master to accept this offering of my house. He, too, was rejected.

I am stating the truth based upon what I saw and personally experienced while respectfully serving the Master by his side both day and night. I can affirm that the Master's conduct is exemplary and his character is noble. He treats others with compassion and unselfishness. He spares no effort in benefiting others.

Everything that I have stated above is true. If anything I have stated is false, I am willing to bear all legal consequences. If what I said is true, may all living beings and I be greatly blessed.

Jiajing Lee
480 Prospect Blvd., Pasadena, CA 91103
(626) 353-7366

Sincerely,
Jiajing Lee
[Signature, fingerprint]
December 3, 2002

---

[1] Here and below the word *Master Wan Ko Yee* or *Master* refers to H.H. Dorje Chang Buddha III Wan Ko Yeshe Norbu Holiest Tathagata.

真實說明

本人陳惠姝多年來因深受義雲高大師偉大人品
道德及佛學素養之薰習。當得知大師到美國之後一
直仍無自己的房子.因而於2000年6月份與井先生揚
高之後,欲將自己座落於LA Pasadena 價值百萬美元
之房子捐給大師.大師不肯接受.經本人多次懇求.之
後.大師照常不接受.最後僅同意暫住一段時間之後
歸還.大師於2002年4月將房子歸還.大師這種不接
受供養,處處為大眾利益著想之偉大情超,在這個
世界上,我還沒有見到過的之位! 我真是從內心生起
對大師無上的恭敬。

陳惠姝

2003年4月21日　　住址: 1503 SE MORGAN RD.
　　　　　　　　　　　　　VANCOUVER, WA 98664
　　　　　　　　電話: (360) 737-8108

TRUE EXPLANATION

Over the past several years, I, Chen Hui-Chu, have been profoundly influenced by Master Wan Ko Yee's[1] magnificent moral character and knowledge of Buddhism. After the Master came to the United States, I realized that he did not have his own house. After discussing the matter with my husband, in June of 2000, we decided to offer to the Master our house in Pasadena worth US$1,000,000. The Master was unwilling to accept our offering. Even though I repeatedly implored the Master, he still would not accept our offering. Finally, the Master agreed to temporarily live in the house. In April of 2002, the Master left the house.

The Master does not accept offerings and always considers the benefit of others. I have not seen anyone else in this world with such magnificent breadth of mind! I have the utmost respect for the Master that arises from the bottom of my heart.

Chen Hui-Chu [Signature, fingerprint]
April 21, 2003

Address: 1503 SE Morgan Rd.
　　　　　Vancouver, WA 98664
Tel: (360) 737-8108

---

[1] Here and below the word *Master Wan Ko Yee* or *Master* refers to H.H. Dorje Chang Buddha III Wan Ko Yeshe Norbu Holiest Tathagata.

TESTIMONIAL

I can speak from personal and direct experience when it comes to the Master's[1] selflessness. I am not just speaking empty words. I truly have utmost respect for the Master's morality, character, and learning.

The Master has long since completely renounced the selfish desire for money, fame, and gain. After he arrived in the United States, he slept on a mattress on the floor. I felt very bad about this. A magnificent person of remarkable talents actually slept on the floor for more than one-half year. Later, I bought a house in the Los Angeles area that was worth more than US$800,000. After I discussed the matter with my wife, we decided to ask the Master to accept that house as our offering. However, no matter how hard we tried to convince him, the Master always politely refused our offering. He was steadfast in his decision not to accept that house. Later, after our repeated requests, the Master finally agreed to live in our house temporarily. However, he absolutely would not accept our title to the house. Thus, I came to respect the Master even more.

After many years of conducting business, I have accumulated some savings. Moreover, after I began following the Master and learning from him, my business has continuously developed. Therefore, I planned to offer the Master US$10,000,000. I told the Master one day that I was planning on transferring that money to him. After he heard this, the Master immediately said, "Such a large sum of money is frightening. It is difficult to find in this world such great sincerity. A single family could not use up such money even in a few lifetimes."

After I heard the Master say this, I was very happy. I thought that my offering would be accepted. However, to my surprise, the Master quickly added, "Chang San, I have accepted your sincerity; however, no matter what you say, I do not want that money. Furthermore, I am steadfast in my refusal of it. It is because I am a person with a heart of humility. I am not qualified to accept such a huge offering. It is not only you. I do not want offerings from anyone. I rely on my own two hands to do work and receive the resources I need." After my repeated urgings, the Master still did not accept my offering. I knew that the Master's mind was made up, so the only thing I could do was give up.

Later, another opportunity arose. It occurred to me that the Master does not accept large offerings. I therefore thought that I would make a small offering. I wrote a check for US$1,000,000, which I gave to the Master. The Master still refused to accept it. However, I firmly insisted on offering it to him. We were at an impasse. The Master then suddenly said, "All right, I will accept it." The Master received the check in his hands. Right after the Master received that check and while I was still quite happy, the Master said, "You must remember that I am the teacher who teaches you. You must obey my words. This money is already my money. However, I am now giving this money to you. Moreover, very soon I will move to another city. You can use this money to buy a house there to live in. I am giving this money to you. You cannot refuse it." Within one minute, the Master returned that check to me. Even until the present, the Master has not accepted that offering! I am truly so moved, I am speechless.

I can say that I cannot find anyone else in the world today who is so selfless, holy, pure, and magnificent! This testimonial is based on my conscience and morals. What I have just said is totally factual. If any part of this testimonial is false, I am willing to bear all legal responsibility.

Lin Chang-San (Packson Lin)
1503 SE Morgan Rd. Vancouver, WA 98664 (360) 737-8108
[Taiwan address] 886-2-29747201 (office) 886-937034460 (cell)

TTI, Inc., a U.S. company
[signature of Lin Chang San/Packson Lin and fingerprint]
December 2, 2002

---

[1] Here and below the word *Master* refers to H.H. Dorje Chang Buddha III Wan Ko Yeshe Norbu Holiest Tathagata.

H.H. Dorje Chang Buddha III Wan Ko Yeshe Norbu Was Conferred the Certificate of "Distinguished International Master"

In 1986, H.H. Dorje Chang Buddha III Wan Ko Yeshe Norbu scored the highest on a rigorous exam given by the American Chinese Culture and Art Academy and was accepted as a guest professor in the United States. Based only upon literature and art, which are just two of the many fields it considers, the World Poets and Culture Congress, represented by experts and scholars from forty-three countries and regions, conferred upon His Holiness the title of "Master of Oriental Art" in 1991. This Congress confers this title only once every ten years. In 1994, after three years of appraising and examining H.H. Dorje Chang Buddha III's achievements in art, academic writings, and ethics, the World Poets and Culture Congress, represented by 5,612 experts and scholars from 48 countries and regions, decided at its fourth congress in Hungary to confer upon His Holiness the title of "Distinguished International Master." No other person on earth has been selected to receive such an honor, which is the highest title in the entire world. On September 28, that same congress dispatched a special envoy to Sichuan, China to conduct a grand presentation ceremony for His Holiness to formally receive this title.

三世多杰羌佛雲高益西諾布獲頒 "特級國際大師" 證

1986年經美國中華文化藝術研究院嚴格考核，三世多杰羌佛雲高益西諾布名列第一，被錄取為美國教授；1991年世界詩人文化大會在他的眾多學科中僅根據文學、藝術的一面之舉，代表43個國家和地區的專家學者，授予他十年一度的"東方藝術大師"桂冠；1994年，世界詩人文化大會對他的藝術、學術論文、倫理道德方面的成就進行了三年的鑒定評審之後，代表48個國家和地區的5612名專家學者，在匈牙利第四屆代表大會上正式定論授稱他為全世界唯一選出之"特級國際大師"——世界最高極限稱位。並於9月28日，大會派特使來中國四川為大師舉行了隆重的授稱頒證儀式。

Former President of the International Olympic Committee, Juan Antonio Samaranch, signs the Distinguished International Master Certificate.

國際奧委會主席薩馬蘭奇在《特級國際大師證》上簽字

世界詩人文化大會各洲代表在《特級國際大師證》上簽字的留影（部分）

Some of the pictures of representatives of the World Poets and Culture Congress from various continents signing the Distinguished International Master Certificate.

世界詩人文化大會各洲代表在《特級國際大師證》上簽字的留影（部分）

Congratulatory messages to and expressions of respect and praise for H.H. Dorje Chang Buddha III Wan Ko Yeshe Norbu from people both inside and outside of China from various walks of life.

國內國外各界人士為三世多杰羌佛雲高益西諾布的祝賀與恭敬讚嘆

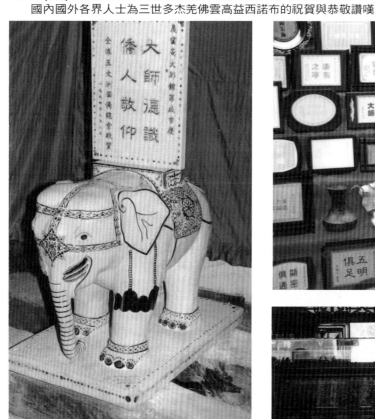

滿工金鑲寶鑽、玉雕、白象係用緬甸白玉製成，白象全身所嵌翡翠、藍寶石、黃金寶、紫羅鑽石、紅寶石、南非鑽、墨晶鑽、瑪瑙等共計二千五百九十四顆。寶石及鑽石均採自天然，共計價值一千五百餘萬人民幣。此為本會代表全球五大洲全體會員，藉"義雲高大師館"落成大典之日，為表華僑四海同心，對大師德識恭誠敬仰之意，奉作賀禮。

全球五大洲華僑總會

DISTINGUISHED INTERNATIONAL MASTER — WAN KO YEE ARRIVES IN TAIWAN
AN UNPRECEDENTED WARM WELCOME IN GRANDEUR

(This is a translation of an article published
in the Hsin-Tao Daily on May 23, 1995.)

Mr. Wan Ko Yee, whose title of "Distinguished International Master" was conferred by 5612 experts and scholars representing academic institutions from 48 countries and regions and is equivalent to the honorary status of a head of state, arrived at the CKS airport at 3 o'clock in the afternoon on May 7. He is the head of the Painting and Art Exhibition Delegation from China and came to Taiwan with his delegation of 8 by the invitation of Mr. Ching-Kuo Wu, Chairman of the Board of the Olympic Foundation, and Mr. Hsi-Jao Ken-Teng, Chairman of the Yun-Tzu Cheng-Chueh Association.

The warm and grand scene of welcome was unprecedented. With flags, signs, and fresh flowers in hand and accompanied by performing bands, over ten thousand people from all walks of life shouted,"Greetings, Master Wan Ko Yee", "We warmly welcome you, Master Wan Ko Yee!" The cheers of welcome came from all directions and reached high into the sky. As people pushed forward to present flowers and hadas to the Master and his wife, the welcoming lines, originally in good formation, were suddenly jammed out of order. Surrounded by layers upon layers of flowers and hadas, the Master and members of his delegation, with the protection of dozens of tall and strong body guards, finally crossed over the waves of flowers and people to get into the waiting limousine. Over a thousand vehicles, decorated with red-colored welcoming signs, formed a motorcade following the limousine of the Master into Taipei. This created a severe traffic jam. It took well over 3 hours to get to the city of Taipei from the airport.

At the Great Hyatt Hotel where the Master was going to stay, bands were playing and fresh flowers were everywhere. The waiting crowd filled up the main lobby and the open plaza outside the hotel, creating a warm and cheerful sea of welcoming signs. The people of Taiwan most passionately expressed their utmost respect and admiration towards the Master. The general manager of Great Hyatt, Mr. Hardy, was greatly moved. He said, "I have never seen such a welcome scene anywhere. There would be no match to today's crowd even if all welcoming parties for Mr. Gorbachev, Mr. Samaranch (the former Chairman of the International Olympics Committee), Mrs. Thatcher, international singer Michael Jackson, and entertainment stars Jackie Chan and Andy Liu were added together when they were staying in this hotel. The sight and total number of people would still not be as grand as today's welcome for Master Wan Ko Yee."

Over the next few days, accompanied by Mr. Wu and Mr. Hsi-Jao Ken-Teng, there was a most grand, warmest, most impressive scene wherever Master Wan Ko Yee's art delegation went. In the evening of May 12, when the Master came to Taipei's Sizi area, residents formed long lines on both sides of the street. The welcoming cheers and applauses were heartening. Fire crackers and fireworks were flying and dancing in the night sky, shinning and reflecting each other. Countless cameras were flashing following one another, recording the unforgettable scene.

In the afternoon of May 13, at the invitation of the Yun-Tzu Cheng-Chueh Association, Master Wan Ko Yee visited Nankan in TaoYuan County. Giant banners of "warmest welcome to Master Wan Ko Yee's delegation" were hanging high everywhere. People of all ages, including the elderly and very young, came out to welcome the Master's arrival. Even the scorching sun and the heat at the time did not deter their offerings of respect to the Master. When the Master was leaving, the crowds rushed over and surrounded the Master's car. With all the applause, weeping, and words of farewell from everywhere, people were reluctant to let the Master leave.

Wherever they went, Master Wan Ko Yee's art delegation brought up cheers and drew large waves of crowds. The sights were heartfelt and moving. Such scenes of warm welcome to Master Wan Ko Yee from the people of Taiwan was unprecedented in the history of Taiwan.

So many people from all walks of life came to the hotel and asked to be received by the Master that the hosting organization was not able to accommodate them all. Mr. Zuozhao Hwang, a retired lieutenant general, told the reporter, "Even generals like myself have been waiting in the lobby since 7 o'clock every morning for an opportunity to be received by the Master. I still don't know yet which day will be my turn."

When H.H. Dorje Chang Buddha III Wan Ko Yeshe Norbu arrived in Taiwan,
His Holiness received a grand reception that was unprecedented.
For details on this, please see the newspaper reports that were published at that time.
三世多杰羌佛雲高益西諾布蒞台，受到民眾熱烈歡迎，盛況空前，詳見當時報紙報導

中華民國八十四年五月二十三日　　　星期二　　　**1**

訂報每月240元，半年1,440元，全年2,880元　　　請利用郵政劃撥1 6 5 9 7 5 4 4 李貞夫收

國內郵資已付
桃園郵局
許　可　證
北台字第8815號
新　聞　紙

國內郵資已付
新莊郵局
許　可　證　第
十　九　支　局
新　聞　紙

行政院新聞局登記台報字第〇三〇五號　　　中華民國七十九年七月卅一日刊

新桃日報

發行人：李貞夫　　　中華郵政北台字四二六七號登記第二類新聞紙

社址：桃園市萬壽路三段158號2F　　　地址：台北市紹興北街35號2樓之7
電話：(03)337-1339傳眞：(03)338-3509　　　電話：(02)321-6208傳眞：(02)321-2871

特級國際大師——義雲高蒞臺
受到盛況空前的熱烈歡迎

【本報訊】經四十八國及地區有關學術機構的五千六百一十二位專家學者認定的「特級國際大師」元首級榮位之義雲高先生，作為大陸繪畫藝術展出團團長，率團八人，應奧林匹亞基金會董事長吳經國先生與雲慈正覺會會長喜饒根登之邀請，於五月七日下午三時抵達中正機場。歡迎場面盛況空前。舉著旗幟，打著標語、手捧鮮花、吹奏鼓樂，上萬各界民眾高呼：「義雲高大師好！」「熱烈歡迎義雲高大師」的歡呼聲交錯縱橫響徹雲霄。人們一湧而上爭向大師和夫人敬獻鮮花和哈達，秩序井然的歡迎隊伍頓時被擠得大亂。鮮花和哈達將大師和團員們重重包圍，在幾十個魁偉健壯的護衛人

員保衛下，好不容易從鮮花和人潮中步入迎賓車。貼著紅色歡迎標語的一千多輛迎賓車隊追隨著大師的座車湧進台北市，造成交通嚴重堵塞，迎賓車隊從機場到台北市足足走了三個多小時。

在大師下榻的凱悅大飯店，同樣是鼓樂喧天，鮮花如潮，大廳內、廣場外擠滿了歡迎的人群，彙匯成一片歡騰的海洋。台灣民眾用最熱情的方式表達了他們對大師的無限崇敬和欽佩。凱悅飯店的總經理哈迪十分感動地說：「如此盛況的歡迎場面我從未見過，就是戈巴契夫、薩馬蘭奇、布希、柴切爾夫人和國際歌星邁克爾杰克遜，以及成龍、劉德華等人駐我飯店時的歡迎隊伍加

起來也沒有今天迎接義雲高大師這麼多人，場面也沒有這麼熱烈」。

幾天來，義雲高大師藝術團在吳經國先生和喜饒根登的陪同下，走到哪裡哪裡就有最隆重、最熱烈、最壯觀的場面出現。十二日晚，大師來到台北汐止，人們排成長隊，夾道歡迎，歡迎大師的歡呼聲和鼓掌聲撼人心弦，爆竹和禮花在夜空中飛舞，交相輝映。無數的鏡頭啪啪叭叭的按著快門，記錄下這一幕幕難忘的場景。十三日下午義雲高大師應雲慈正覺會邀請訪問桃園南崁，到處高掛著「熱烈恭迎義雲高大師代表團」的巨幅橫標，人們扶老攜幼歡迎大師的來到。雖然烈日當空，驕陽似火，但是

他們說這仍然比不上他們心中對大師的敬意。當大師離開桃園時，送別的人群一擁而上圍住了大師的汽車、掌聲、哭聲、惜別聲渾然混成一片，難分難解。

義雲高大師藝術團來台灣所到之處，無不歡聲四起，人潮湧動，情景感人至深。台灣民眾對義雲高大師盛況空前的歡迎場面在台灣歷史上是從來沒有過的現象。

每天到飯店來求見大師的各界人士，由於太多造成無法安排接待的局面，有位退休中將將軍黃倬昭先生向記者說：「就連我們將軍們每天早上七點鐘就在大廳，等候大師接見的機會，可是還不知哪一天才能見得到？」

上圖：台灣各界在中正機場，熱烈歡迎—義雲高大師盛況。
左上圖：　義雲高大師抵達中正機場時一千餘輛轎車，上萬民眾，歡迎盛況。
左下圖：歡迎—義雲高大師的少女代表在機場鵠候四小時之久。

During the international "Discussion Meeting to Distinguish Correct and Erroneous Buddhism, Buddhist Studies, and Buddha-Dharma" held in Taiwan in 2000 between May 5th and May 12th, H.H. Dorje Chang Buddha III Wan Ko Yeshe Norbu was unanimously recognized as an authentic Buddhist Master on the level of a Great Dharma King who is completely proficient in both exoteric and esoteric Buddhism and who has mastered all of the Five Vidyas. For details on this, please see the newspaper reports that were published at that time.

TRIBUNE U.S.A.

EXPONENT OF KNOWLEDGE AND PROGRESS

5123 Maplewood Avenue, Los Angeles, California 90004-1606 • Tel. (323) 461-5663 • Fax (323) 461-4977

VOL. III NO. 22   MAY 26-JUNE 1, 2000

MAY 26-JUNE 1, 2000   TRIBUNE U.S.A.   23

The Conclusion of World Buddhism Conference

The international "Discussion Meeting About Distinguished Correct and Erroneous Buddhism, Buddhist Studies and Buddha Dharma" was held for seven days and concluded on May 12, 2000 in Taiwan. The votes at the general assembly of this seminar unanimously confirmed to confer the title of "Authentic Buddhism Master" to Master Yee Wan Ko. In the meantime, the general assembly also recognized that Master Yee Wan Ko has made the highest achievements in the world in many other fields.

This Discussion Meeting About Distinguishing Correct and Erroneous Buddhism, Buddhist Studies and Buddha Dharma was a Buddhism conference of the highest class in the whole world in history of Buddhism. It was hosted by United International World Buddhism Association Headquarter.

There were many international Buddhism organizations and Buddhism associations of some countries such as United International Buddhism Association, World Buddhism Sangha Association, International Buddhism Monks and Nuns Association, International Vajra Bodhi Association, American Buddhist Congress, Canada Buddhism Association, and etc. All of them were represented by their chairpersons who participated in the discussion and made speeches at the seminar.

There were more than two thousand Rinpoches, Dharma teachers, Holy Monks, and Great Virtuous who attended the seminar. They came from 32 countries including India, Thailand, Sri Lanka, Bhutan, Malaysia, Singapore, Korea, Burma, Nepal, America, Japan, England, Canada, France, Germany, Australia, Philippines, Norway, Denmark, Bengal, Vietnam, Laos.

The development of Master Yee Wan Ko in Chinese paintings is unprecedented. He is excellent at detailed skills, free expression, big expression, spilling ink and flowing water, lines flowing freely, and application of dots.

He thoroughly masters the drawing of scenery, flowers, birds, fish, insects, persons, and animals, all with unlimited changes. His styles originating from tradition has developed into many new wonderful styles which are unprecedented in the history of Chinese paintings. His paintings now command the highest price among Chinese painting in international art market.

Master Yee Wan Ko is also a world well known great singer. These achievements of Master Yee Wan Ko are mainly due to his practice of Buddha Dharma, the blessings of Buddha Dharma and his knowledge of Tripitaka Buddhism.

2000年5月5-12日在台灣舉辦國際性的「佛教、佛學、佛法正邪研討會」一致公認三世多杰羌佛雲高益西諾布為顯密圓通、五明俱足的大法王正宗佛教大師，詳見當時的報紙報導。

LOS ANGELES ASIAN JOURNAL

The first & only Filipino newspaper published twice a week.

APRIL 1, 2000 1150 Wilshire Boulevard, Los Angeles, CA 90017-1904• Tel.: (213) 250-9797• Fax: (213) 481-0854 VOL. X NO. 27

6 APRIL 1, 2000

ASIAN JOURNAL PUBLICATIONS   http://www.asianjournal.com

NEWS

His Magnificent Accomplishments Openly Serve as a Model for Others; His Many Honors Stir the World

The government of the State of California and the government of the City of San Francisco each declared March 8th as Master Wan Ko Yee Day. On March 13th the government of the City of San Francisco again expressed its highest respects for Master Wan Ko Yee's special accomplishments by conferring upon him more honors. These newest honors were conferred based upon the Master's position as the foremost Buddhist Master in the entire world and his tremendous achievements in the areas of art, ethics, scholarship and science.

In 1994 the Master was awarded the title of "Distinguished International Master" by the World Poets and Culture Congress, an organization composed of members from forty-eight different countries and regions. This title is conferred upon only one person in the world and is on the same level of honor as a head of state. The Distinguished International Master Certificate was signed by Juan Antonio Samaranch, the then President of the International Olympic Committee. The formal resolution conferring upon the Master such title was announced in Hungary on September 15, 1994 and formal written notification was sent to the State Council of the People's Republic of China and other government organs.

The central government of China built a museum in honor of the Master in the Master's hometown. In the entire history of China, this was the first museum ever built by the government of China in honor of someone who is still alive. The Master Wan Ko Yee Museum is a huge structure similar to an imperial palace and is divided into seven different sections.

The Master is extraordinarily accomplished in Chinese painting and calligraphy and has laid the groundwork for bringing Chinese painting to the international forum. He has won the highest respect of the Chinese and American people for having raised the level of culture and morality in the world, for his efforts in philosophy, for his contributions in advancing the cultural exchange between China and the United States, and for being a model of ethical conduct.

Thus, after the head of the City Council of San Francisco and ten City Council members held a meeting, they decided to jointly sign and confer upon Master Wan Ko Yee a certificate of honor for his special accomplishments. The city government of San Francisco also declared the Master an honorary citizen of San Francisco in order to express their great admiration for him.

What is most unusual is that Master Wan Ko Yee is not in the United States to accept these distinctive honors. Nevertheless, his great learning, high ethics and magnificent accomplishments cannot be covered up. He has been repeatedly honored by various organizations throughout the United States such as the World Buddhism Assocation, the Tibetan Buddhism Association of America, the World Buddhism Jenn Fa Association, the California Assembly and the American League of Colleges and Universities which is composed of more than eighty colleges and universities.

All of this shows that Master Wan Ko Yee is a man of tremendous virtues, the likes of whom are rarely seen in the history of mankind. People all over the world admire and emulate him.

為表彰三世多杰羌佛雲高益西諾布各方面的成就及對世界的貢獻，美國加州政府和舊金山市政府在同一天宣佈2000年3月8日為「義雲高大師日」

版 **35** 　僑社新聞　農曆庚辰年二月初六日　星期六　佛曆二五四三年三月十一日星期六

義雲高大師莊嚴法相。

世界日報
THE UNIVERSAL DAILY NEW
今天出報九大張
★ 世界報業有限公司印行 ★

董事長：王必成
總編輯：黃根和

社址：曼谷四角披耶是廿一之一號
21/1 NEW ROAD
BANGKOK THAILAND
電　話：2260040（代表號）
　　　　2264849-59（11線）
傳　眞：2247968
訂報專線：2212730
廣告專線：2213411　2210385
郵政信箱：曼谷郵政732號

美加州及舊金山首長公佈
三月八日為義雲高大師日
推崇大師成就與卓越貢獻

【本報訊】世界唯一達到全方位最高成就之大師——義雲高大師，爲表揚其——義雲高大師，爲表揚其高至高的成就及對整個世界的多方面之貢獻，於西元二〇〇〇年三月八日加州州長格瑞載維斯（GRAY DAVIS）及舊金山市長格瑞載維斯（WILL IE L·BROWN JR）特代表州府和市府，將此日定爲義雲高大師日。

到全方位最高成就之大師——又如大師研發之中國綠茶碧玉春及霸王春也被評爲大師之極品；而大師之醫學知識及醫術亦達「無病不能治」之高明；在哲學、倫理道德，及佛學佛法方面亦是境界高超更已精至頂點，到達完美之境界。所以大師對人類極大之貢獻及利益。一九九四年特頒發世界唯一之世界詩人文化大會於九四年特頒發世界唯一「特級國際大師」之榮譽證給義雲高大師，此證更不是一般人可得到的。義雲高大師能於是日得到這兩項榮譽，是相當不簡單的，不僅爲華人之光、能自利，而全世界之人類，更是全世界人民喜事，更能在新世紀的來臨之於各方面跨向倫理道德，因爲我們希望於將來大眾皆能向大師學習，不僅華橫溢新的一步。

雲高大師日所簽頒之兩份證書縮影。
圖示：美國加州州長格瑞載維斯及舊金山市長威利布朗立定三月八日爲義

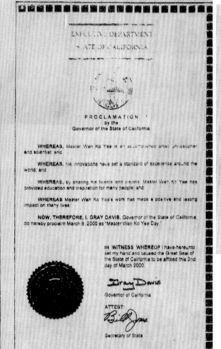

THE GOLD MEDAL WAS AWARDED TO H.H. MASTER WAN KO YEE IN RECOGNITION OF HIS OUTSTANDING ACHIEVEMENTS

HE UNSELFISHLY DEVOTES HIMSELF TO THE INTEGRATION OF MORAL CHARACTER, CULTURE, AND ART

(This is a translation of an article published in the International Daily News on Dec. 15, 2002.)

The Master Wan Ko Yee[1] International Cultural Institute held an academic seminar on the "Ethical and Moral Character and Practices of H.H. Master Wan Ko Yee" at the institute for five consecutive days. This seminar was held in response to the national and local commendations received by His Holiness from various sources. In yesterday's conference, there had been discussions of H.H. Master Wan Ko Yee not pursuing fame and fortune but personally and humbly practicing ethics and the development of moral character. In addition, there were specific examples discussed about his outstanding and diverse achievements and wholehearted and unselfish devotion toward humanity.

On October 2nd of this year, Vice President Dick Cheney arrived in Washington, D.C. to personally award to H.H. Master Wan Ko Yee this medal that symbolizes remarkable achievements. The same day, H.H. Master Wan Ko Yee unexpectedly received a phone call requesting immediate and urgent care for a disciple. Instantly and without any hesitation, the Master left the medal award ceremony. His Holiness rushed to the disciple and saved him by applying his dharma wisdom. Those hearing about this particular action of saving others above his own personal gain were all touched. It turned out that three days later this medal was delivered to the Master's residence, becoming even more brilliant and magnificent. The Master himself gave his thanks and expressed his apologies for his absence at the award ceremony.

In September of this year, representing President Bush, the chairman of the White House Presidential Advisory Commission for Asian-Americans and Pacific Islanders arrived at the Master Wan Ko Yee International Cultural Institute in America and personally awarded the Presidential Gold Award to H.H. Master Wan Ko Yee in recognition of the Master's revered and noble ethics and moral character, achievements in art, and outstanding contributions toward humanity. During the award ceremony, the chairman highly praised each of the Master's achievements as being the top in the field. This extraordinary honor shows that the Master is not only a leader in the Asian-American society but also an outstanding role model for the world. This is why he was the recipient of such a high honor. Moreover, the Master was the only person to have received this exceptional honor in the entire Asian-American community. This incident was never released to the public and was not brought to the attention of the world until the members of the institute, who attended the award ceremony at the time, spoke about it at the above mentioned seminar.

Approximately more than 100 people attended the seminar, but H.H. Master Wan Ko Yee himself did not attend.

At the seminar, several members stated that H.H. Master Yee's writing, *Brief Commentaries on Selected Philosophical Sayings*, had given them enormous inspiration to guide them through life. H.H. Master Yee has profound knowledge, and there is no question that His Holiness is unable to answer. There is no other person to compare with His Holiness in the contemporary world. The most important of all is the greatness and honesty that H.H. Master Yee's ethics and moral character embody. His righteousness and unselfishness are extremely rare in the world, and have made him a role model for the people of the world. Due to his enormous contributions to humanity, the government of California and the San Francisco city-county government, on the same day, proclaimed March 8, 2000 as "Master Wan Ko Yee Day." The U.S. Congress, the chairmen of the California Senate, and the 11 members of the Board of Supervisors of the City and County of San Francisco signed and awarded certificates of recognition to the Master.

At the seminar, most members who had spoken expressed that in the seven years that the Master Wan Ko Yee International Cultural Institute has been established, the institute has grown and developed stronger. The members also stated that they look up to H.H. Master Wan Ko Yee as their role model. In different fields of business and through practical practice in daily life, they have raised their moral character, purified their minds, and have found all sorts of ways to serve society and to benefit the public.

---

[1] Here and below *Master Wan Ko Yee* refers to H.H. Dorje Chang Buddha III Wan Ko Yeshe Norbu.

H.H. Dorje Chang Buddha III Wan Ko Yeshe Norbu received the United States Presidential Gold Award.
For details on this, please see the newspaper reports that were published at that time.
三世多杰羌佛雲高益西諾布獲得美國總統金質獎章，詳見當時的報紙報導。

Sunday, December 15, 2002　國際日報　二〇〇二年十二月十五日　星期日　美西要聞　12
INTERNATIONAL DAILY NEWS

義雲高大師傑出成就榮獲金質獎章

將道德品質與文化藝術融為一體無私奉獻

（本報訊）美國義雲高大師基金會一連五天在該會舉行「義雲高大師的倫理道德與實踐」學術研討會，昨日會中討論義雲高大師不追求各種傑出成就一心為人類作無私的奉獻的具體事例。

今年十月二日錢尼副總統在華府親臨頒發卓越成就的勳章給義雲高大師，雲高大師當日突然接到一通電話說某一病人需要緊急搶救，大師當場毫不猶豫當下放棄接受授勳離開大典會場，即時趕往病人處以跑馬神針搶救這位病人，這種為救人，顧不得自己榮譽的行為，聞者莫不動容，結果三日後，這枚勳章搭著飛機被送到義大師的住處，更顯光輝燦爛，大師則對授勳典禮缺席表示歉意亞予致謝。

參議院議長、舊金山議會十一位議員聯名分別頒贈給大師表揚狀或獎牌。會中發言的會員多表示，義雲高大師不斷成立七年來以義雲高大師為楷模，分別在不同的行業裡，通過腳踏實地的日常修為，升華自己的品德，以淨化自己的心靈，服務社會，造福大眾，以種種不同的形式，服務社會。

會主席親自蒞臨美國義雲高大師國際文化基金會代表布希總統為義雲高大師頒發了金質獎章，以表彰大師崇高的倫理道德、藝術成就和對人類的傑出貢獻，在頒獎會上，主席高度評價了大師的各項成就首屈一指，這項殊榮代表義大師不僅是華人社會的翹楚，也是世界的傑出的殊榮，而且大師是在整個如此至高的殊榮，當時參加頒獎典禮的基金會會員在此次研討會中提出，此事才華裔中唯一獲得此殊榮的人。未發布過，出席這次研討會的人士計約百餘人，義雲高本人並沒有出席這項以他為名的研討會。

研討會中許多會員談到義大師的哲言選著作他們極大的啟發，讓它們找到人生的方向，當今世界找不到有不能回答的問題，義大師學問、淵博沒有找不到第二人，更重要的是義大師躬身實踐倫理道德的偉大光明、正直無私是世界上極其少有的，足以為世人楷模。

（義雲高基金會提供）

▲美國義雲高大師基金會舉行「義雲高大師倫理道德與實踐研討會」。（義雲高基金會提供）

國際日報
第一手商業資訊　最精華藝文娛樂
一九八一年創刊
NO. 7748B
www.chinesetoday.com
廣告專線　洛杉磯 (323)265-1317　紐約 (212)925-2811　舊金山 (415)956-5338　休士頓 (713)270-4855

207

ASIAN JOURNAL

VOL XIV   NO. 13

14 FEBRUARY 14, 2004
ASIAN JOURNAL PUBLICATIONS

Royal Academy Of Arts Has The First Fellow Awarded in Past More Than Two Hundred Years

The Keeper of Royal Academy of Arts highly praised Master Wan Ko Yee at the dinner banquet. He admired very much the talents and art of Master Yee. He was so excited that he took off his necktie and gave it to the Master. He said, "This tie was made by myself. On behalf of the President and the Curator of Royal Academy of Arts and myself, I give it to the Master to express our heartfelt respect for Fellow."

On Feb. 10th, 2004 at the office of British Council in Washington DC Royal Academy Of Arts awarded Fellowship to Master Wan Ko Yee. Master Yee is a world famous artist, a great Chinese painting artist, and the founder of Yun sculptures which are beyond natural beauty. The award of fellowship certificate and medal further confirmed Master's extraordinary contribution to art of the whole world.

Royal Academy of Arts was founded by King George III in 1768. Up to now it has more than two hundred years history. It is a world famous art institute. Many seasoned artists wish to pursue advenced study at this Academy. But this Academy admits only twenty extraordinary artists each year from all over the world to take courses for three years.

Professor Phillip King, President of Royal Academy Of Arts, announced during the award ceremony: Royal Academy Of Arts has a profound history. Today we are honored to award fellowship to the great artist and spiritual leader, Master Wan Ko Yee. This is a very important and honorable event of our Academy in the past more than two hundred years since our establishment. Therefore Master Wan Ko Yee is the extraordinary art figure that we have been searching in more than two hundred years since our establishment and could not find until today.

This is tremendous blessing of Roayl Academy Of Arts. Our Academy has one hundred Royal Academicians, but there was no one who in the past more than two hundred years was awarded the above mentioned Fellow. This noble position is awarded to only the most distinguished artist in the world.

Sir David Manning, Ambassador of United Kingdom to the United States, accompanied by Professor Phillip King and Professor Brendan Neiland, Keeper of Royal Academy Of Arts, met with Master Wan Ko Yee and his wife Professor Yuhua Wang. Sir David Manning showed his respect for the achievement of Master Wan Ko Yee and congratulated him for receiving such an honor. Mr. Andy Mackay, Director of Culture Department, The British Embassy attended the award ceremony today.

ROYAL ACADEMY SCHOOLS

CONFERMENT OF FELLOWSHIP

The Royal Academy of Arts today conferred the fellowship of the Royal Academy School on Master Wan Ko YEE at the office of the British Council in Washington DC.

The Royal Academy was founded in 1768 by King George III. To this day it still enjoys the Royal Patronage. At the heart of the Royal Academy are 100 Royal Academicians and the Royal Academy schools.   The Schools, the oldest in the country, are pre-eminent in the training of future generations of artists.

This is the first time the fellowship has been awarded to an internationally distinguished artist.

Prof. Phillip King   **Prof. Brendan Neiland**   **John Wilkins**
President   Keeper   Curator

February 10, 2004

Washington Chinese News　華盛頓新聞

A 3　Thursday, February 12, 2004

華盛頓新聞

美南報系

發行廣泛・新聞豐富・廣告效好

Washington Chinese News
週四版　Vol. 14　No. 117

© Contents 2003 Lee & Lee Washington, Inc

發行人 李蔚華　總社長 李蒼華
總經理 李靜芳　Gen. Mgr.: Jing Lee
Publisher: Wea H. Lee　Director: Danny Lee

報社地址: 5848 Hubbard Drive
Rockville, MD 20852
Tel:(301)984-8988・Fax:(301)984-8806
E-mail:wcns@erols.com
ISSN 1536-1942　Serving Since 1990

美南報系全美各地報社

亞特蘭大新聞　Atlanta Chinese News
波士頓新聞　Boston Chinese News
芝加哥新聞　Chicago Chinese News
達拉斯新聞　Dallas Chinese Times
波特蘭新聞　Portland Chinese Times
西雅圖新聞　Seattle Chinese News
聖路易新聞　St. Louis Chinese Journal
南方新聞　Southern Chinese Daily News
Southern Chinese Daily News Group
Sister Newspapers

義雲高大師獲頒英國皇家藝術學院之Fellow稱之
二百多年來第一位證實大師對世界藝術界的卓越貢獻

【本報華府訊】2004年2月10日華府訊，英袖義雲高大師授稱，這是該院二百多年來一件非常重要和光榮的事情，而且這也是該院成立多年來第一次授稱的。

英國皇家藝術學院在美國首都華盛頓英國駐美國大使館，為世界著名的藝術大家、中國畫巨匠、超越自然的韻雕的創始人義雲高大師頒授「Fellowship」職稱，當場授以證章與證書，大師這一成就更進一步證實了他對世界藝術的卓越貢獻。

英國皇家藝術學院早在1768年由英國國王喬治三世創建，距今已有二百多年的歷史，是世界知名的藝術學府，很多在藝術領域耕耘多年的藝術家都希望能有幸進入該院繼續深造，但該院每年只在全世界遴選二十位卓有成就的藝術家進入該院學習，進修三年的課程。

皇家藝術學院的主席菲力浦・金在頒證致詞中宣布：英國皇家藝術學院有著悠久的歷史，但是，他們今天能夠榮幸地為偉大的藝術家和精神領袖義雲高大師頒證儀式。

英國駐美國大使館大衛・曼寧爵士在英國皇家藝術學院主席菲力浦・金和院長喬布朗登・奈南的陪同下會見了義雲高大師和夫人王玉花教授，對義雲高大師取得的成就表示敬意，並祝賀義雲高大師獲得如此榮譽。英國駐美國大使館文化參贊安迪・馬凱先生出席觀禮今天的頒證儀式。

As a result of His powerful, moving, and inspiring virtue, H.H. Dorje Chang Buddha III Wan Ko Yeshe Norbu, in a very short span of only a few years, has received praise from various levels of governmental entities within the United States, such as the President, Congress, state legislatures, county boards of supervisors, and city councils, and other organizations. They have commended His Holiness for His positive contributions to mankind.

三世多杰羌佛雲高益西諾布的威德感召，在美國短短數年間，受到由總統、國會、州、市、議會等至各階層之讚嘆有加，推崇其對人類善良的貢獻。

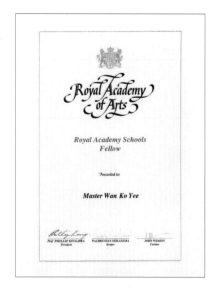

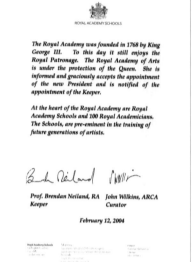

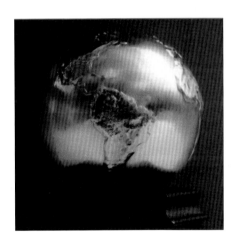

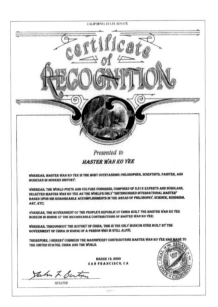
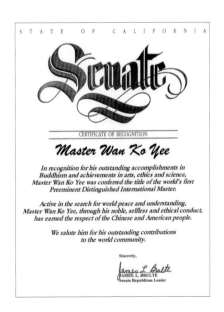
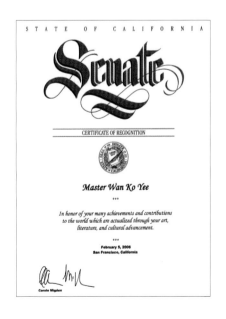

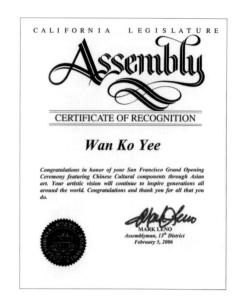

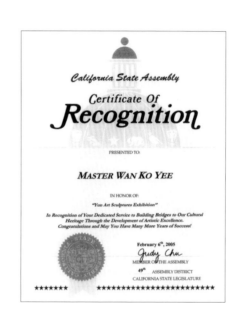

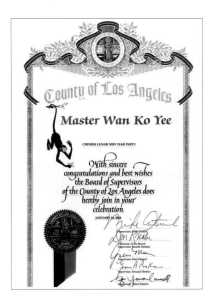

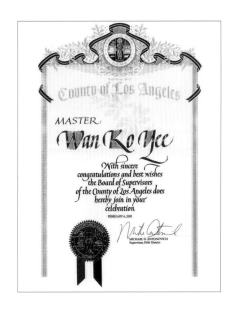

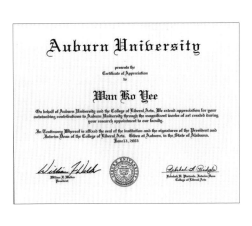

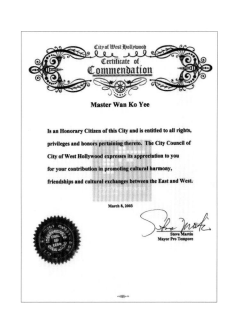

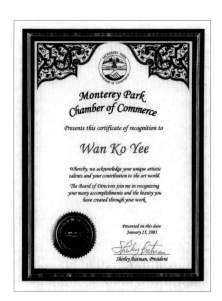

Monterey Park
Chamber of Commerce

Presents this certificate of recognition to

Wan Ko Yee

Whereby, we acknowledge your unique artistic
talents and your contribution to the art world.

The Board of Directors join me in recognizing
your many accomplishments and the beauty you
have created through your work.

Presented on this date:
January 25, 2005

Shirley Batman, President

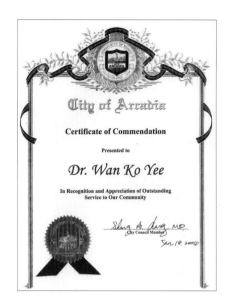

City of Arcadia

Certificate of Commendation

Presented to

Dr. Wan Ko Yee

In Recognition and Appreciation of Outstanding
Service to Our Community

Dated this

City Council Member
Jan 18, 2006

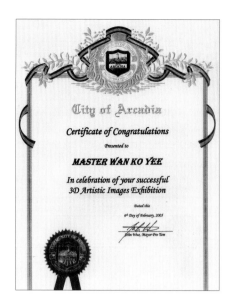

City of Arcadia

Certificate of Congratulations

Presented to

MASTER WAN KO YEE

In celebration of your successful
3D Artistic Images Exhibition

Dated this
6th Day of February, 2005

John Wuo, Mayor Pro Tem

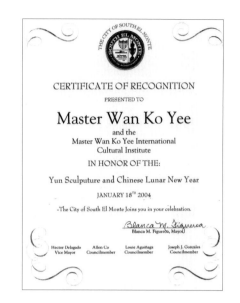

CERTIFICATE OF RECOGNITION

PRESENTED TO

Master Wan Ko Yee

and the
Master Wan Ko Yee International
Cultural Institute

IN HONOR OF THE:

Yun Sculpture and Chinese Lunar New Year

JANUARY 18TH 2004

-The City of South El Monte Joins you in your celebration.

Blanca M. Figueroa
Blanca M. Figueroa, Mayor

Hector Delgado   Allen Co   Louie Aguinaga   Joseph J. Gonzales
Vice Mayor   Councilmember   Councilmember   Councilmember

Certificate of Recognition

Presented to:

Master Wan Ko Yee

For your great effort to bring cultural diversity through your
one of a kind art of Yun Sculpture to the West.

The Mayor and City Council of the City of South El Monte
present this award of their esteem.

February 6, 2005   Blanca M. Figueroa
Date   Mayor

Louie Aguinaga   Allen Co   Hector Delgado   Joseph J. Gonzales
Vice Mayor   Councilmember   Councilmember   Councilmember

*Certificate
of
Appreciation*

Presented to
Dr. Wan Ko Yee

Presented by
Kiwanis Club of Arcadia

In recognition of your outstanding participation.
Your contributions are deeply appreciated.

Signature   Signature
Feb 18, 2004
Date

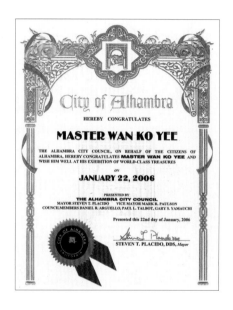

City of Alhambra

HEREBY CONGRATULATES

MASTER WAN KO YEE

THE ALHAMBRA CITY COUNCIL, ON BEHALF OF THE CITIZENS OF
ALHAMBRA, HEREBY CONGRATULATES **MASTER WAN KO YEE** AND
WISH HIM WELL AT HIS EXHIBITION OF WORLD-CLASS TREASURES

ON

JANUARY 22, 2006

PRESENTED BY
THE ALHAMBRA CITY COUNCIL
MAYOR STEVEN T. PLACIDO   VICE MAYOR MARK R. PAULSON
COUNCILMEMBERS DANIEL R. ARGUELLO, PAUL L. TALBOT, GARY S. YAMAUCHI

Presented this 22nd day of January, 2006

STEVEN T. PLACIDO, DDS, Mayor

Certificate of Recognition

Presented to:

*Master Wan Ko Yee
International Institute*

For your great efforts to bring cultural diversity to our
community.

The Mayor and City Council of the City of South El Monte
present this award of their esteem.

Jan 22, 2006   Blanca M. Figueroa
Date   Blanca M. Figueroa, Mayor

Joseph J. Gonzales   Louie Aguinaga   Hector Delgado   Angelica R. Garcia
Vice Mayor   Councilmember   Councilmember   Councilwoman

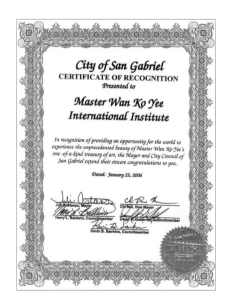

City of San Gabriel
CERTIFICATE OF RECOGNITION
Presented to

*Master Wan Ko Yee
International Institute*

In recognition of providing an opportunity for the world to
experience the unprecedented beauty of Master Wan Ko Yee's
one -of-a-kind treasury of art, the Mayor and City Council of
San Gabriel extend their sincere congratulations to you.

Dated: January 22, 2006

Juli Costanzo, Mayor   Chi Ren Tin, Vice Mayor
Harry L. Baldwin, Councilmember   David R. Gutierrez, Councilmember
Kevin B. Sawkins, Councilmember

R E S O L U T I O N

The Honorable John Chiang
Chair of the
California State Board of Equalization

Takes great pleasure in recognizing the

**Master Wan Ko Yee
International Cultural Institute**

on the occasion of the
Chinese Cultural Exchange with California and China

San Francisco, February 5 -27, 2006

JOHN CHIANG, CHAIR

City of Monterey Park

Master Wan Ko Yee
Renowned Artist

The City Council of the City of Monterey Park hereby joins the community in congratulating
Master Wan Ko Yee on your Sculpture Exhibition at the Chinese Daily News. We appreciate such
a renowned artist sharing these impressive sculptures with our community and thereby also
providing an opportunity to promote goodwill and cultural exchange. We further extend our best
wishes for a successful and prosperous future and continued good health.

David T. Lau, Mayor
Sharon Martinez, Vice Mayor   Benjamin "Frank" Venti, Council Member
Francisco Alonso, Council Member   Fred Balderrama, Council Member

Presented this 25th day of January, 2005

City of Monterey Park

Master Wan Ko Yee
Yun Sculptures

The City Council of the City of Monterey Park, is honored to have the Master Wan Ko Yee International Culture Institute sponsor a
3D Artistic Images Exhibition. We congratulate Master Wan Ko Yee for his contributions to the art world and for sharing art with our
community. The City Council further extends our best wishes to you for continued success in all of your future endeavors.

Mike Eng, Mayor

Benjamin "Frank" Venti, Mayor Pro Tem   Betty Tom Chu, Councilmember
David T. Lau, Council Member   Sharon Martinez, Council Member

Presented this 6th day of February, 2005

CATEGORY 3

The Holy Realization of the Holiest Tathagata

第三大類　頂聖如來的聖量

Introduction

H.H. Dorje Chang Buddha III Wan Ko Yeshe Norbu Holiest Tathagata is the true incarnation of Dorje Chang Buddha. Thus, all conduct of H.H. Dorje Chang Buddha III is that of a Buddha, whether it be teaching disciples how to walk the path of enlightenment or saving living beings who are in the midst of hardship. Examples of His Holiness's holy realization are too numerous to describe.

One example involves the great layman Huibang Huang, who was a professor at Jiangxi Teacher's Training University and vice-chairman of the Jiangxi Buddhist Association. At the age of ninety, he had never personally seen Amitabha Buddha. He had hoped to see that Buddha. H.H. Dorje Chang Buddha III agreed to his request and gave him one opportunity to see that Buddha.

H.H. Dorje Chang Buddha III was going to allow great layman Huibang Huang to see Amitabha Buddha in the Kalachakra mandala state. When that Buddha was about to arrive, elder layman Huang suddenly said he did not want to see that Buddha. He said he only wanted to see a dharma protecting deity. Moreover, the more fierce-looking the dharma protecting deity was, the better. H.H. Dorje Chang Buddha III replied, "Fine!" His Holiness immediately invited a dharma protecting deity to appear. After elder layman Huang saw that deity, he was so terrified he screamed several times and fell to the ground. He then picked himself up, placed his palms together in respect, and prostrated before His Holiness. There is an audio recording of this called "H.H. Dorje Chang Buddha III Practices Dharma to Invite a Dharma Protecting Deity to Appear for Disciple Huibang Huang."

Another example involves laywoman Hui Hsiu Liu. H.H. Dorje Chang Buddha III knew beforehand the exact time of her death. The same applies to laywoman Xianyun Zhao. H.H. Dorje Chang Buddha III knew beforehand the exact day, hour, and minute she would pass away.

A further example involves the foremost Han-Chinese geshe alive today. During a videotaped interview by a reporter, he said the following: "I have learned Buddhism for sixty years. I have met more than one hundred so-called greatly virtuous practitioners of Tibetan Buddhism. I have met greatly virtuous Buddhists from China, such as Dharma Master Taixu, whom I was with for a long period of time, Dharma Master Fazun, and other outstanding dharma masters. I have also received over six hundred initiations. However, the influence upon me and the empowerment I received from all of those initiations does not match the effect upon me today from the discourse and initiation given to me by the Master[1]. Thus, I cannot help but think that sixty years of learning Buddhism does not match just one day. Sixty years have passed in vain. Those years cannot equal this one day, today. Thus, I vow to the Master: I will use all of my energy in this lifetime to diligently learn. In accordance with the Master's wishes, I will return to the United States, pervasively save living beings, spare no efforts, and seek no offerings. I will do these things in order to spread the virtuous spirit of the Master and show my gratitude for the Master's kindness. These are the sincere words that I speak today."[2] Although the geshe made such a vow, he did not discern that H.H. Wan Ko Yeshe Norbu is the supreme ancient Buddha, H.H. Dorje Chang Buddha III.

There is also the example of Liao Hui Shih. She had already passed away in the cross-legged sitting posture, and her body had already become cold and rigid. H.H. Dorje Chang Buddha III instructed Amitabha Buddha to allow her to stay in the human realm, and she returned to life. The seven monastics who saw what happened to Liao Hui Shih were astonished. There are many other true examples of this kind.

(This text was translated from the Chinese text that follows.)

---

[1] Here and below the word *Master* refers to H.H. Dorje Chang Buddha III Wan Ko Yeshe Norbu Holiest Tathagata.
[2] These are the original words of the geshe excerpted from the videotape.

簡　　介

　　多杰羌佛第三世雲高益西諾布頂聖如來是多杰羌佛真身降世，因此，三世多杰羌佛或為教化弟子行菩提道，或為解救眾生於苦厄之中，皆是佛陀行舉，這方面的先例，多得無法形容，如黃輝邦大居士是江西師範大學的教授及江西佛教協會副主席，他九十歲了，沒親見過阿彌陀佛，希望能和佛陀見一面，結果三世多杰羌佛同意他的請求說，只有給他一次機會，在曼荼羅時輪壇城境中，三世多杰羌佛讓黃輝邦大居士看著，佛陀將馬上降臨，此時黃老居士突然說他不要看佛陀了，只要看護法，愈威猛的護法愈好，三世多杰羌佛說：「好！」然後當下立刻請出護法，黃老居士見到後，嚇得慘叫數聲，倒在地上，隨著合掌頂禮，現有法音「三世多杰羌佛為黃輝邦修護法」的錄音。又如林劉惠秀居士，三世多杰羌佛對她的生死時刻瞭如指掌；又如趙賢雲居士，三世多杰羌佛同樣知道何日何時幾點幾分往升。又如漢人在世第一大格西在接受記者錄像採訪時說：「我是已經學佛六十年了，見過上百個所謂的藏傳佛教的大德，中國的佛教大德如太虛法師我也同他相處很久，法尊法師這些大法師，我也曾經受過上六百多種的灌頂，但是，灌了之後，對我的影響力、對我的加持力不如我今天一天大師（即多杰羌佛第三世雲高益西諾布頂聖如來，以下同——編者注）給我的開示、給我的灌頂如此的有效，所以，不禁啦，我心裡想起來，我是六十年的學法不如一天，六十年過去了、空度了，不如今天一天。所以我向大師發願：我亦盡我今生的精力，努力學習，根據大師的意願，回到美國，普渡眾生，不辭辛勞，不求供養，以繼承大師的這種功德跟大師的感恩之念，這是我今天所說的真話。」（摘自錄影帶中格西講話原文——編者注）格西雖然如此發心，但他卻沒有認出雲高益西諾布竟然是至高怙主，多杰羌佛第三世。又如釋了慧，已經坐化圓寂，成了冷卻僵硬死了的人，三世多杰羌佛當場喊阿彌陀佛把她留下，七位出家人在場親眼得見大驚失色等等實例。

（此文的英文翻譯印在前面）

How Nectar Bestowed by Buddha Was Obtained

Only through cultivation can we achieve liberation from the sufferings of impermanence; from the sufferings of the cycle of reincarnation, which entails repeated birth, aging, illness and death; and from the sufferings of the three lower realms. To obtain liberation from all of these sufferings, I incisively saw the emptiness of the four great elements of this world and became a nun. The goal of my becoming a nun is to live in full accordance with the Buddha's teachings, strictly keep the precepts, and cultivate myself after the Buddha. I dare not slack off or break the precepts in the slightest, for I am deeply aware that if I broke the precepts, I would have become a nun for nothing and wasted my time! Realizing impermanence and the relentless pace of change, I was able to establish firmly my determination to end the cycle of birth and death. At the temple, I constantly cultivated myself according to the dharma.

However, the beneficial effects of my practice were very few. Only after extraordinary conditions of merit accumulated from many previous lives reached fruition was I able to go to China; formally acknowledge H.H. Dorje Chang Buddha III Wan Ko Yeshe Norbu Holiest Tathagata as my Master; and learn esoteric Buddhist teachings by following His Holiness. Little did I know that the Buddha Master would demand that I first comprehend thoroughly exoteric Buddhism and pass a test on the exoteric teachings before His Holiness would transmit the preliminary practices, main practices, and completion practices of esoteric Buddhism. With utmost devoutness and respect, I cultivated myself under the teachings of H.H. Dorje Chang Buddha III. Living with a group of nuns all year round, I diligently carried on my practice.

Five years passed. I gained some direct understanding of my original nature and made clear progress in deepening my insight. However, I seldom manifested true dharma powers. When I saw that many high-level fellow-disciples who were around me were able to manifest true dharma powers, I was both upset and nervous and felt tremendous pressure. I asked myself, "Can I liberate myself from the cycle of reincarnation just through empty theories? Why is it that my fellow-disciples of the Buddha Master can manifest the Buddha-dharma and I cannot?"

Many times I beseeched Buddha Master H.H. Dorje Chang Buddha III Wan Ko Yeshe Norbu to practice the nectar dharma. Each time my Buddha Master compassionately responded with the following teaching: "I have learned how to practice the nectar dharma, but I truly am not sure that I can cause nectar to descend. I have practiced that dharma a few times with no success. This certainly is not a dharma that can be successfully practiced

without exception. That is because whoever requests Buddha to bestow nectar must first be granted a dharma certificate with a nectar-merit. That is created when more than ten thousand great rinpoches from Tibet together practice the Fire Offering Dharma and transfer the merit of that practice onto a piece of paper on which seed syllables are written. Although more than ten thousand rinpoches and lamas practice the Fire Offering Dharma, the most important thing is that certain true Bodhisattvas must be among them. If among them there is not a Bodhisattva who represents charity, a Bodhisattva who represents wisdom, a Bodhisattva who represents great compassion, a Bodhisattva who represents patience under adverse circumstances, and a Bodhisattva who represents supernatural powers, then the nectar dharma certificate will be of no effect. All five holy aspects must be represented. Otherwise, I cannot successfully practice the nectar dharma."

There was one time when a Tibetan dharma king arrived and brought with him a nectar dharma certificate. I took that opportunity to beseech my Buddha Master to practice the nectar dharma. As before, my Buddha Master said, "All I can do is try. Do not be disappointed if I do not succeed. I truly cannot be sure of success. You should go and give the practice of that dharma a try. If you succeed, then you succeed. If you do not succeed, then you do not succeed."

I was very familiar with the rituals of this practice. I began the practice in accordance with the dharma and prayed to Buddha to bestow nectar. However, I was left with an empty bowl at the end of the ceremony. Buddha did not bestow nectar in response to my prayer. This time I was not disappointed because I knew this was a tremendous dharma. My Buddha Master sincerely explained to me that even He does not have absolute confidence that His practice of that dharma will succeed. It was only natural that I could not successfully practice such dharma. My Buddha Master gave me a special discourse on that subject.

Another year passed and I practiced this dharma once again, only to receive the same result—nothing. This time I felt very sad and ashamed. In the past, elder monk Wu Ming, the chairman of the World Buddhist Sangha Council, washed the dharma bowl under the watch of the Buddha Master. The Buddha Master then successfully invoked the bestowal of nectar for that group of eminent monks. But why was I not up to the task? I begged my Buddha Master for a discourse to explain why it was that I could not bring real benefit to living beings.

The Buddha Master benevolently expounded: "Successful practice of the dharma to invoke Buddha to bestow nectar requires the aggregation of many causes and conditions. The dharma-conditions are not complete if even one of the conditions is missing. That time when I successfully invoked the bestowal of nectar was a fortunate happenstance among my other unfortunate attempts that did not succeed. Moreover, with respect to the necessary conditions, elder monk Wu Ming and elder monk Yi Zhao have great merit and high realization. They have the karmic affinity to receive the benefits of a true Five Holy Aspects Dharma Certificate." The Buddha Master also added, "When practicing the nectar dharma, one must at least have a true Five Holy Aspects Dharma Certificate. Even with the foundation and external karmic condition of having such a dharma certificate, the person's practice must still be in accord with the dharma."

I reported to the Buddha Master that there were no mistakes in all of the rituals that I practiced. However, the Buddha Master said, "You did not understand what I meant by practicing in accord with the dharma. I was referring not to the rituals of the nectar dharma but to "What Is Cultivation?" You must gain a deep understanding of the cultivation that I taught you all. Your practices must be in accord with those of the Buddhas and Bodhisattvas." At that moment, I felt very ashamed of myself and repented from my heart. (The precious dharma of cultivation transmitted by the Buddha Master is contained in this book, *A Treasury of True Buddha-Dharma*.)

From that time on, I told myself every moment to take firm hold of my three karmic forces—behavior, speech, and mind. As a result, I deeply understood how truly difficult it is to cultivate oneself and that cultivation is a most subtle matter! If one cultivates oneself with a mixture of hidden doubts and misunderstanding, if one does not thoroughly cultivate oneself, or if one's bodhicitta is inadequate, then it is not real cultivation. In this way, I practiced earnestly. One day I came to a sudden realization. I decided to drop the word "I" and correct all my errors as soon as they occurred.

After practicing for another three months, the karmic conditions came together. A Fire Offering Dharma Certificate from more than ten thousand eminent monastics, dharma kings, and rinpoches was obtained. The Buddha Master began to select the one person who would wash the dharma bowl that would receive the nectar. More than twenty experienced practitioners from Taiwan and the United States were there to choose from, including rinpoches and great dharma teachers. Geshe Xing, Xima Rinpoche, and I were from the United States. In the end, unexpectedly, a humble nun such as myself was chosen to carry out the practice of the dharma.

After cleansing and consecrating the mandala, we first respectfully invited the Buddha Master to ascend to the throne. At that time, I suddenly experienced a great sensation and powerful blessing. I knew that the Buddha Master would invoke Buddha to bestow nectar that day. Still, I was somewhat worried since the Buddha Master told me before He began practicing the dharma that He truly could not be sure that He would successfully invoke Buddha to bestow nectar. His Holiness said that if He could not successfully invoke nectar it would be because the karmic conditions were inadequate. His Holiness hoped that I would understand. Still, the Buddha Master stated that no matter what happened, I must earnestly learn Buddhism and benefit living beings. After I heard those words from the Buddha Master, I felt quite humbled.

At that dharma assembly, I washed the bowl in accordance with the dharma rituals. The sound of everyone chanting mantras filled the entire mandala, resulting in an extremely auspicious atmosphere. After the dharma

certificate that embodied the fire-offering merit of more than ten thousand monastics was burned, an exceedingly wondrous air filled the sky and the mandala. Dharma teachers saw Buddha and Kuan Yin Bodhisattva moving in the sky. This time, Buddha bestowed nectar, and it quaked and moved in the purple-gold bronze dharma bowl. All of the monastics and laypersons saw this scene and became very excited. They vowed to work hard at their cultivation and benefit multitudinous living beings. News reporters from both the Chinese and English media reported on that magnificent and holy Buddha-dharma event.

Looking back on this today, I think that the vows of those people who were at that dharma assembly were moving, but did they really understand what cultivation is? Actually, many people do not understand what cultivation is. The answer is that they did not understand what cultivation is! Just like myself in the beginning, although I became an abbess, my cultivation was flawed. I, too, was unable to fully cultivate myself. We should all earnestly study this book about the Buddha Master, *A Treasury of True Buddha-Dharma*. We should also earnestly correspond our three karmas with the teachings of the Buddhas and Bodhisattvas and carry out in our daily lives the dharma of cultivation that the Buddha Master has transmitted to us. Only then can we attain accomplishment!

I will now make the following vow of truth about the nectar bestowed by Buddha. At the time, I washed the purple-gold bronze dharma bowl in front of all of the monastics and laypersons. I did not pull any tricks or put anything in the dharma bowl. Everyone saw the nectar descend into it. When Buddha bestowed thread after thread of nectar through the lid of the dharma bowl into the dharma bowl, some people saw golden light, while others saw red light. Seeing different things was the result of each person's particular karmic conditions. If I am lying, pulled any trick, or put anything in the dharma bowl to delude living beings, may I experience evil karmic retribution, descend to one of the three lower realms, and undergo endless suffering for such wrongdoing.

To people of the world, it may seem vulgar for a nun to be making vows, but may this vulgar statement turn into my true and pure heart. The successful bestowal of nectar by Buddha has compelled me to ponder deeply and thoroughly and to realize the importance of cultivation! Had I not engaged in such cultivation, I would have contaminated the dharma bowl with my evil karma when I washed it. Had superlative karmic conditions not existed, how could nectar have descended to bless everyone? The great dharma "What Is Cultivation?" that my Buddha Master transmits in this book, *A Treasury of True Buddha-Dharma*, is the real priceless treasure! This is the blessing for living beings for millions of eons to come!

Buddhist nun with a heart of humility,
Long Hui Shih

(This is a complete translation of the Chinese text that follows originally written and signed by Long Hui Shih.)

佛 降 甘 露 是 這 樣 得 來 的

面對無常輪迴及生老病死、三惡道的痛苦，我們是必須要依靠修行才能了脫的，為了解脫這一切痛苦，我看穿，也看破這紅塵世界的四大空相，我出家了。出家的目的就是依照佛陀的教誡，嚴持戒律，修行學佛，一點也不敢懈怠，也不敢違犯，因為我深深知道違犯就等於白出家了！更是浪費光陰！體悟到無常的迅速，我堅定的出離心徹底建立了，在寺廟裡，三時之中如法修行，結果受用卻非常少，後來在多生累劫的福報殊勝因緣成熟了，到了中國拜多杰羌佛第三世雲高益西諾布頂聖如來為師，依止學密乘，沒有想到佛陀恩師規定的行持是首先必須把顯教學通，而且要經過顯教的考核，才會傳我密乘的加行、正行、結行。我以最虔誠的、敬謹之心依止在三世多杰羌佛那兒修學，終年住在比丘尼僧團，精進用功修持。

五年過去了，對明心見性已有體悟，見地上有了顯著受用，惟有在實際妙有的功夫上卻少有顯現。當我看到身邊的高僧大德師兄們，基本上很多證量都拿得出來，當時我又難過又緊張，感受到很大的壓力，我自問：難道我以空洞理論就能了生脫死嗎？為什麼師兄們能展現佛法，我不能呢？我曾多次向多杰羌佛第三世雲高益西諾布恩師請修甘露，佛陀恩師每次都很慈悲地對我開示說：『修甘露的法我學了的，但是確實沒有把握把甘露降下來，我曾經修過幾次都沒有成，這絕不是決定能成功的法，因為凡要求佛降甘露，首先必須要求到甘露功德的法章，這法章是西藏的大活佛集體上萬人修火供所轉的功德，聚在一張有種子字的紙上，最重要的是雖然有上萬活佛、喇嘛修法火供，但是裡面沒有真正的大菩薩，代表布施的一位，代表智慧的一位，代表大悲的一位，代表忍辱的一位，代表神通的一位，如五聖諦，缺一諦這個甘露法章也是無效的，我是無法修請甘露的。』有一次一位西藏法王來了，帶了甘露令章來，我借機當下向佛陀恩師求修甘露，佛陀恩師照常說：『只能試試看，如果不成功，不要失望，因為我確實沒有把握，你去修一下，成就成了，不成也就不成了。』起法儀軌我已經很熟悉了，我依法而行，祈求佛陀降甘露，法會結束後，修得只有一個空缽，佛陀沒有為我的祈求降下甘露，這次我真的沒有難過，因為我知道這個法太大了，我佛陀恩師也真誠地說明了他都沒有絕對的把握，我修不了是正常的，佛陀恩師特別給我作了開示。又過了一年，我又修了一次，還是一無所獲，這一次我心裡非常慚愧和難過，世界佛教僧伽會主席悟明長老曾在佛陀恩師座下洗法缽，佛陀恩師為他們一批高僧求來甘露，為什麼我就不行？懇求佛陀恩師開示，為什麼我無法為眾生帶來實質利益？佛陀恩師慈悲作了開示：『修佛降甘露是要若干因緣聚合，只要一個條件不具備，就是法緣不具，這次修來了，這是不幸中的偶然的幸事，而且在條件中，悟明、意昭老和尚功德大、道量高，他們有緣享受到了真正的五聖諦法章。』佛陀恩師還說：『修甘露至少要有真的五聖諦法章，具備了這一張法緣的外緣作為基礎，還得要行持如法。』我稟告佛陀恩師，一切儀軌都沒有錯，佛陀恩師說：『你沒有理解到我講的行持如法，不是指示甘露的儀軌，而是「什麼叫修行」，你要深入我教你們的修行，自己的

行持一定要如佛如菩薩。』當下我無地自容，並發大懺悔(佛陀恩師傳的修行法這一法寶現已收錄在《正法寶典》中)，從那時起，每時每刻反覆憶持，堅持落實我的三業，深深體會到修行真不簡單，微妙極了！其中如果夾雜了無明的暗砂，修得不徹底，或菩提心發不到位，就不叫真修行。就這樣如實行持，一天猛然覺醒，我來一個『我』字徹底放下，就地修正。

又修了三個月，正逢因緣和合，請到了萬人高僧法王仁波且們的火供法章，為選擇洗甘露法缽的人，佛陀恩師開始選擇人選，當時從台灣和美國二十多位老修行中選拔，其中有仁波且、大法師，美國有我和邢格西，及西瑪仁波且三位列席，最後，萬萬沒想到，我這位慚愧比丘尼被選上執持修法。壇城沐浴開光後，我們首先恭迎佛陀恩師陞座，當時我身心斗變，加持力甚大，我知道，佛陀恩師今天一定會請來佛陀降甘露，但也有些擔心，因為佛陀恩師在修法前對我說，這求佛降甘露，他確實沒有把握，如果沒有求到，這是因緣不夠，希望我理解，但是不管怎樣也要好好學佛，利益眾生。我聽了佛陀恩師的一席話，感到非常慚愧，在法會中我如法依儀軌洗缽，所有人員的誦咒把整個壇場宣成一片梵音，吉祥無比，燃燒萬眾僧火供功德法章以後，天空和壇場殊勝無比，法師們見到天空出現了動態的佛陀和觀音菩薩，這一次佛陀降下甘露了，在紫金銅法缽中跳動，眾僧和居士們在現場見到，個個激動，發心要好好修行，利益大眾。這一偉大的佛法聖蹟，新聞記者在中英文媒體報導了現場實況。今天回想起來，這些在場的人他們發心感人，但他們真正悟了什麼叫修行嗎？其實很多人都沒有悟到，沒有！跟我當初一樣，雖然作了住持，但修行有缺，也未能做到。我們都應該把佛陀恩師的《正法寶典》認認真真看，真正以三業相應去修持，如實落實佛陀恩師為我們傳的修行法，才會得到成就！

關於佛降甘露，我要在這發誓，當時我當著僧眾及居士們的面前，洗淨了朱紅色紫金銅法缽，我沒有做過任何手腳，沒有放過任何東西在法缽裡，大家看見甘露降下，還因各人因緣不同，看到金光、紅光，佛陀降甘露一絲一絲穿入缽蓋到法缽中。我如果說了假話或做了手腳，放東西在裡面欺騙眾生，我將遭惡報，墮入三惡道中，無止盡受一切罪報痛苦。出家人賭咒發誓，世人看來很俗氣，但這一俗氣將化作我真實不虛出家人純正的心。佛降甘露的成功，讓我徹底深思悟到修行的重要！不然洗缽都會把黑業污染法缽，因緣不上妙殊勝，又怎麼有甘露加持降臨呢？尤其我佛陀恩師在《正法寶典》中所傳『什麼叫修行』這一大法，是真正的無價珍寶啊！是百千萬劫眾生的福音！

慚愧比丘尼　釋隆慧

（此文的英文翻譯印在前面）

H.H. Dorje Chang Buddha III Wan Ko Yeshe Norbu empowers world-class eminent monastics and practices the dharma for them. Below are newspaper reports published at that time.

三世多杰羌佛雲高益西諾布加持世界級高僧們，為高僧們修法。下面為當時的報紙報導。

Many people saw Aksobhya Buddha and the Long Life Buddha appear on the clouds in the sky and bestow this Buddha-land nectar. This is how the Buddha-land nectar originally looked when it descended, as nobody touched it. When this Buddha-land nectar was descending, the seven types of Buddhist disciples surrounded the bowl and respectfully chanted mantras. They personally saw the Buddha-land nectar emit flashes of light as it descended into the totally empty purple gold-copper bowl. The Buddha-land nectar descended into the bowl from a height of tens of thousands of feet, yet not one bit of it fell outside of the bowl. Moreover, the Buddha-land nectar clearly quaked in the bowl. Those Buddhist disciples who were there ate the Buddha-land nectar. Nothing on earth can compare with its delicious taste. Various strange illnesses were cured on the spot, including middle and late-stage cancer, which immediately vanished.

這是大家看到金剛不動佛和長壽佛在幾萬尺的虛空雲端之上降下來的甘露，未曾動過的原貌。降此甘露時有七眾佛弟子在現場誦咒恭敬圍觀，眼睜睜地看到甘露放出光芒降到空無一物的硃砂色金銅衣缽中，一點都沒有灑到缽外，而且甘露在衣缽中還強烈跳動。在場佛弟子吃到甘露，其美味非人間物品能比擬，各種怪病當場痊癒，包括中晚期癌症頓時消失。

True Events Seen at the Side of a Buddha

Every time we mention holy occurrences related to H.H. Dorje Chang III Wan Ko Yeshe Norbu Holiest Tathagata, our discussions never ends. Such are the facts. Wherever H.H. Dorje Chang Buddha III goes, mysterious and unexpected phenomena nearly always appear. It seems abnormal for holy phenomena not to appear.

For example, there was one time when H.H. Dorje Chang Buddha III practiced the Torma Offering Dharma in which food was offered to the Buddhas and then given to living beings. The most excellent and precious food offered to the Buddhas that time was nectar pills made from mixing real nectar bestowed by the Buddhas at the invocation of H.H. Dorje Chang Buddha III together with flour and butter. Those nectar

pills were hand-made the night before by rinpoches, dharma teachers, and others. Many holy phenomena occurred at that dharma assembly during the course of making offerings to the Buddhas.

First of all, an image of Sakyamuni Buddha was in the middle of the mandala that day. An image of Dorje Chang Buddha, the primordial sambhogakaya Buddha, was above the image of Sakyamuni Buddha. To the right of the image of Sakyamuni Buddha were holy relics of the Buddha. To the left of the image of Sakyamuni Buddha was an image of Guru Padmasambhava. A bright-colored array of fresh flowers, rare fruit, various types of food made from Tibetan roasted barley flour, fragrant cheese, and other offerings dazzled the eyes and filled three offering tables. The nectar pills were placed in the middle of the offering tables.

Before offerings were made to the Buddhas, the nectar pills were placed

After the nectar pills were distributed to attendees and before dharma was practiced at the Food Offering Dharma Assembly, the bowl of nectar pills was not full.
在將金剛丸分發給參加法會的人之後而在上供法會修法之前，沒有滿的一缽甘露丸。

One hour later after dharma was practiced at the Food Offering Dharma Assembly, the nectar pills instantly grew in number, filling the entire bowl and lots of nectar pills dropt to the table.
上供法會修法一個小時之後，甘露丸剎那暴漲，漲平成了滿缽，很多掉在法台上。

inside a jade bowl. At that time, the nectar pills were level with the lower edge of the brim of the bowl. Those nectar pills were piled up evenly and filled the entire bowl. The Buddha Master later empowered the fifty-nine attendees of that dharma assembly by giving each of them some of those nectar pills. As a result, the nectar pills that remained in the jade bowl were lower than the lower edge of the brim of the bowl by about 1.5 centimeters. We saw that the nectar pills neither lessened nor increased from 7:03 p.m. when the practice of the dharma began until around 8:10 p.m. when the offerings of the three karmas to the Buddhas was completed. At that time, a holy event nobody ever imagined suddenly took place. In an instant, the nectar pills grew in number. Not only did the pile of nectar pills rise more than 1.5 centimeters filling the entire bowl, its top part formed a dome that rose high above the brim. Everyone was ecstatic at the sight of that holy

occurrence.

Furthermore, the nectar pills were moist and soft right after they were made. Everyone decided to use a microwave oven to dry the nectar pills so that they would become dry and hard as soon as possible. A few dharma teachers placed four nectar pills inside the microwave oven as a test to determine the appropriate microwave time. Shortly after those nectar pills were placed inside, to everyone's surprise the microwave oven began emitting smoke and a burning scent. Everyone quickly took out those pills only to discover that two of them were burning and had become like black coal, while the other two were still their original bright red without any sign of being burned.

The Buddha Master decided to mix the two nectar pills that were burned black and the two that were still bright red into the jade bowl that contained nectar pills to be offered to the Buddhas. A few minutes after this was done, the two nectar pills that were burned black surprisingly disappeared in the bowl. Everyone had no choice but to spill the nectar pills onto a large platter and carefully look for those two nectar pills. However, no matter how meticulously all of us looked, no trace of those two black nectar pills could be found. At this time, Venerable Xirao Jiebu said, "How could there be any differentiation in the Buddha-dharma tathata (true-suchness) of the Buddha Master? None of you will ever find those two pills. How could there be the concepts of burned black and not burned black with respect to true nectar that is Buddha nature? How could there be differentiation of colors?"

Second, the Buddhas, Bodhisattvas, and dharma protecting deities bid farewell to H.H. Dorje Chang Buddha III when that dharma assembly to make offerings to the Buddhas ended. At that time, the starry and cloudless sky suddenly rumbled with thunder four consecutive times. All of the people there heard this. Of course, that was the laughter of the dharma protecting deities. It was the height of summer in the Los Angeles area. It had not rained for a few months, and the sky was full of stars. How could there be thunder under such circumstances?

What I have just described is merely one example from among the many feats of H.H. Dorje Chang Buddha III. Actually, we at the International Buddhism Sangha Association often receive emergency phone calls. In the vast majority of those phone calls, the caller beseeches H.H. Dorje Chang Buddha III to save his or her life or the life of another person. Of course, without exception, those close to death take a turn for the better and are out of danger after being empowered by H.H. Dorje Chang Buddha III. We then receive their calls expressing gratitude toward H.H. Dorje Chang Buddha III. Thus, in our eyes H.H. Dorje Chang Buddha III truly acts as an emergency treatment center that relieves the sufferings of all living beings.

At times like those, H.H. Dorje Chang Buddha III often promptly gives a discourse to everyone about how the law of cause and effect, or karma, never fails or about how living beings must cultivate themselves in order to change or postpone karmic retribution. H.H. Dorje Chang Buddha III has told us that it is useless to rely on empowerment alone. Although empowerment has the effect of temporarily blocking one's karmic hindrances, one will ultimately still experience karmic retribution if one does not cultivate oneself.

One day we learned that a layperson with the surname Yan had contracted cancer of the nose and pharynx (nasopharyngeal carcinoma). For seven days and seven nights, he only ate a few spoonfuls of thin rice gruel. He was in the final throes of late-stage cancer with only a few hours left to live. There being no alternative, H.H. Dorje Chang Buddha III was asked to save him. H.H. Dorje Chang Buddha III told him that his situation was the manifestation of karma, or cause and effect, and that there was no way to save him. However, being unable to withstand the strenuous and sorrowful supplications of layman Yan's family, H.H. Dorje Chang Buddha III went to layman Yan and gave him a nectar pill. Unexpectedly, after this person who was on the brink of death ate that nectar pill, he regained a clear state of mind that very evening. In less than a half month, his cancer disappeared, and he became completely well. He even taught people the martial arts. His entire family was tremendously grateful to H.H. Dorje Chang Buddha III. However, H.H. Dorje Chang Buddha III simply said, "What I did is of no use if he does not cultivate himself. He will still pass away." Given these words of His Holiness, what happened to him five years later was indeed expected. Although his cancer had completely disappeared, his mouth ulcerated as a result of his previous late-stage cancer. He was no longer able to speak clearly. One day he suddenly came up with a strange idea. He decided to use the flesh on his body to fill the gap in his mouth caused by the ulcer. Layman Yan died in the hospital as a result of that operation.

Thus, I would like to sincerely offer the following advice. We should not hope that H.H. Dorje Chang Buddha III will completely eliminate our karmic forces simply because H.H. Dorje Chang Buddha III is alive in our world today. First of all, do you have the karmic affinity to meet His Holiness? Even if you meet the Buddha Master, will the Buddha Master accept you as a disciple? Even if you are accepted as a disciple, do you practice virtue such that you are qualified to learn the Buddha-dharma? Even if you learn dharma transmitted by the Buddha Master, can you practice that dharma with your three karmas perfectly corresponding with the teachings of the Buddha Master? We should avail ourselves of the time this Buddha is in our world to follow the correct course of cultivation shown to us by H.H. Dorje Chang Buddha III and practice the highest Buddha-dharma that His Holiness has taught us. This applies to our daily lives and daily meditation. We will then be able to truly attain good fortune, wisdom, accomplishment in the dharma, and liberation!

Jue Hui Shih

We personally attended the Torma Offering Dharma Assembly conducted by H.H. Dorje Chang Buddha III that Dharma Teacher Jue Hui spoke of above. The nectar pills did not increase in number at the beginning of the dharma assembly. However, they suddenly increased in number about one hour after the dharma assembly began. Two nectar pills that were burned black were buried among all of the other nectar pills. A few minutes later, those two pills could not be found. When the dharma assembly ended, the dharma protecting deities emitted the rumbling sound of thunder in the sky four consecutive times. All of these things are true manifestations of the magnificent Buddha-dharma.

Some of us were directly involved with the case of Mr. Yan and other cases mentioned above, and some of us were not. Thus, what are attesting to here through our signatures only relates to what happened at the Torma Offering Dharma Assembly conducted by H.H. Dorje Chang Buddha III. We are Buddhist disciples. We do not speak falsely or deceive living beings, knowing that in so doing we would experience karmic retribution.

(Signatures relate to attest what happened at the Torma Offering Dharma Assembly are listed in the next page.)

(This text was translated from the Chinese text that follows.)

佛 陀 身 邊 見 到 的 事 實

　　每次一提到三世多杰羌佛雲高益西諾布頂聖如來的聖蹟，大家都說不完，因為事實就是如此，每當三世多杰羌佛所到之處，總有一些不期而至的神奇現象出現，好像沒有聖蹟就是不正常似的。

　　比如有一次三世多杰羌佛修『食子』，上供下施，在上供的食物中，有一道最殊勝、最珍貴的是用三世多杰羌佛請來的佛降真精甘露與麵粉、酥油混合，在頭天晚上由仁波且、法師們等用手工做成的甘露丸。而在這法會上供的過程中，產生了諸多聖蹟。

　　第一，當天壇城中央供奉著釋迦牟尼佛陀，佛陀上方供有原始報身佛多杰羌佛，佛陀右方是佛舍利，左方為蓮花生大師。並供有鮮花、奇珍異果、各類型的西藏糌粑食品、香味四溢的奶酪等供品琳瑯滿目、鮮艷無比，供滿三個案頭，甘露則供在案頭的正中央。上供之前將甘露丸裝在玉缽裡面的時候，甘露丸剛好與玉缽的較低的一邊齊平，成為平滿的一缽甘露丸，後來佛陀上師加持給參加上供法會的59人每人一些甘露丸之後，剩下的甘露丸比玉缽較低的一邊還要低1.5厘米左右。但是，自七點三分修法開始，到八點十分左右三業上供圓滿時，看到在這一小時甘露沒有減少也沒有增長，就在這個時候，從來沒有想到過的聖蹟，突然發生了，甘露丸剎那暴漲，不但超過1.5厘米，漲平成了滿缽堆成了弧形，而且已經冒超很高，聖蹟展顯，大家都驚喜若狂。

　　並且，甘露丸剛做好的時候是濕軟的，為了讓甘露丸儘快變乾、變硬，因此大家便想用微波爐把甘露丸烘乾。為確定合適的微波時間，幾位法師先用四顆甘露丸放入微波爐試驗，結果哪知道，剛放入不久，微波爐裡面立刻冒煙，發出焦糊味，大家趕快拿出一看，兩顆正在燃燒變成黑炭，但另外兩顆則依然鮮紅如故，毫無燒的影子。後來佛陀上師決定將此兩焦黑兩鮮紅共四顆甘露丸混合在盛甘露的玉缽裡面，作食子上供，幾分鐘後，這兩顆焦黑的甘露丸竟然憑空不見了，大家只好將甘露丸倒在大盤子裡面仔細地尋找，但再怎麼努力，這兩顆焦黑的甘露丸還是不見蹤影。此時喜饒杰布尊者說：佛陀上師老人家的佛法真如何來分別？你們永遠也找不到，真精甘露真如佛性，哪有燃焦與不燒之理？哪有色相之分？

第二，上供法會結束的時候，諸佛菩薩、諸天護法等告別三世多杰羌佛，萬里星空無雲的天，突然響起隆隆的滾雷聲，而且連續四次滾雷在太空翻動，所有在場的人都聽到了。這當然是天龍護法的笑聲了，大家都知道，盛夏的洛杉磯，幾個月不下雨，當時滿天星空，怎麼會打雷呢？

我這裡所說的只是三世多杰羌佛行事業中的一個例子而已，其實，經常的，我們國際佛教僧尼總會都會接到一些緊急的電話，內容大多是求三世多杰羌佛救命，當然，無一例外的，經過三世多杰羌佛的加持，生命垂危的都能轉危為安，然後我們又會接到感激三世多杰羌佛的電話。所以，在我們的眼裡，三世多杰羌佛實在是一切眾生苦難的急救中心。

三世多杰羌佛也往往在這個時候，及時開示大家關於因果不昧、眾生必須通過修行來轉換推移因果的道理。三世多杰羌佛告訴我們，光靠加持是沒有用的，儘管加持能夠起到臨時的遮止業障的作用，但如果不修行，終究還是要償還果報的。

有一天，一位嚴姓居士得鼻咽癌，七天七夜只有吃了幾湯匙的米湯，已是晚期到了最後一刻，眼看只有幾小時的壽命，萬般無奈之下求救於三世多杰羌佛。三世多杰羌佛告訴他：這是因果的呈現，沒有辦法。但是，抵不過嚴居士家屬的苦苦哀求，三世多杰羌佛到現場給了他一顆甘露丸。令人想不到的是，這位本來就要氣絕身亡的人在吃了甘露丸之後，當晚神智清醒了，竟然不出半個月，癌症的病況消失，整個人完全好了，甚至還教人習武術，他們全家感激三世多杰羌佛不盡。而三世多杰羌佛卻說：不修行是沒有用的，他還是要死的。果不其然，五年後，雖然癌症已完全消失，但之前因癌症晚期，他口腔潰爛而講話不清楚，有一天他突發奇想，想用他身上的肉來補口腔內的因潰爛而有缺口的部份，這個嚴姓居士竟然死在醫院的這個手術上。

因此，我在這裡也就是要敬告各位，我們大家不能因為三世多杰羌佛在世，我們就指望三世多杰羌佛把我們的業力全部消除，首先你能有因緣拜見到嗎？而後，佛陀上師能收你為徒嗎？並且你的德行能學到佛法嗎？學到佛陀傳的法，你又能三業相應修持嗎？因此我們要趁佛陀在的時候，沿著三世多杰羌佛指引的正確的修行方向和傳授的至高佛法，功行並舉，才能夠真正的福慧雙收，成就解脫！

釋覺慧

覺慧法師在文章中所說的由三世多杰羌佛設宴的『食子』法會，我們親自參加了的。法會中，甘露丸開始沒有漲，而在法會開始一個小時左右的時候突然暴漲；兩顆焦黑的甘露丸埋在其它的甘露丸裡面，幾分鐘以後就再也找不到了；法會結束的時候護法在空中發出四聲隆隆的分段滾動式雷聲。這些都是真實不虛的偉大佛法展現。

由於上述嚴姓等公案，有的人親身經歷，有的人沒有經歷，因此我們簽字只針對三世多杰羌佛設宴食子上供的情況簽字。我們是佛弟子，不會打妄語欺騙眾生遭惡報。

（此文的英文翻譯印在前面）

3
226

No Other Great Holy Being Can Compare with My Root Master H.H. Dorje Chang Buddha III

I am Xirao Jiebu II. In a prior life, I was a disciple of Guru Padmasambhava and was also a disciple of the great historical master Shantaraksita. I am embarrassed to face the Buddhas and Bodhisattvas. However, due to causes and conditions planted since beginning-less time, I feel obliged to divulge certain karmic fruits of mine.

When I was a child, I became the first disciple of His Holiness Dorje Chang Buddha III. Dorje Rinzin, who is the incarnation of Rigzin Terdak Lingpa Unchanging Vajra, conducted an initiation for the Dzogchen Monastery's seventh Dzogchen Dharma King and other great rinpoches last month. At that time, they asked me whether I had seen many holy feats performed by H.H. Dorje Chang Buddha III. I told them that I had seen so many of His Holiness's feats that I cannot possibly remember all of them.

It is true that no other great holy being can compare with H.H. Dorje Chang Buddha III. This is not simply my personal opinion. Rather, it is something that dharma kings and rinpoches of each of the main sects —the Nyingma, Sakya, Kagyu, Geluk, and Jonang—have affirmed based upon their own realization. They have affirmed that the level of enlightenment of my respected Master, H.H. Dorje Chang Buddha III Wan Ko Yeshe Norbu, is the highest in the history of Buddhism. They have affirmed that His Holiness is the master of the Buddhas. They have affirmed that no other person of great holiness in this world has manifested the Buddha-dharma and accomplishments in the Five Vidyas to such a high and overall degree. There are other persons of great holiness in this world who possess a certain aspect of this overall mastery; however, they also lack certain other aspects.

These are not empty words. These facts are now presented before all to see. For example, His Holiness has caused nectar to descend into an empty bowl. His Holiness has predicted the results of karmic affinity selections before such selections actually took place. His Holiness has applied the power of vajra samadhi to eliminate the karmic obstructions of others. His Holiness has caused bodhi holy water to flow through the wall of a bowl. His Holiness has caused a bowl of nectar pills to be continually drawn from without ever emptying. Under His Holiness, many living beings have been seen to have truly attained liberation from the cycle of reincarnation. No other person has realized this complete, perfect, and holy state that made those six examples possible. Furthermore, H.H. Mahavairocana Tathagata Zunsheng Yeshe Norbu made an open pronouncement concerning the duplication of wondrous multicolored sculptures and the sculptures containing mysterious mist created by H.H. Dorje Chang Buddha III. That pronouncement was made to verify the Buddhahood of H.H. Dorje Chang Buddha III. Nobody else in the world today has attained the marvelous wisdom and realization whereby such sculptures were created. Persons of holy virtue can leave their footprints on rocks. However, no matter how they apply their realization, they are unable to successfully duplicate any wondrous multicolored sculpture of H.H. Dorje Chang Buddha III. They are also unable to take auspicious mist from the air, place it inside a hollowed out sculpted boulder, and have the mist stay there motionlessly for all to see forever, as H.H. Dojre Chang Buddha III has done. As H.H. Zunsheng Yeshe Norbu Tathagata said, such feats evidence the realization of H.H. Dorje Chang Buddha, and no other Buddha, Bodhisattva, great dharma king, or rinpoche can perform them. This is factual. The facts demonstrate that no other person of great holiness can perform such feats. Those two types of precious works of art will remain there forever, beckoning those who would attempt to duplicate them and serving as proof that Master Wan Ko Yee is H.H. Dorje Chang Buddha III.

What I have stated is sincere and true. If you have any doubts, go ahead and confirm the facts for yourself by attempting to perform such feats. But I must tell you that no one can do so. They can only be performed by a true Buddha. Anyone unable to perform such feats would not be a Tathagata!

Xirao Jiebu II
May 2007

(This is a complete translation of the Chinese text that follows originally written and signed by Xirao Jiebu II.)

我 的 恩 師 三 世 多 杰 羌 佛 是 無 聖 可 以 比 擬 的

　　我是蓮花生大師的弟子，也是釋伽炯乃祖師的弟子第二世喜饒杰布。面對諸佛菩薩不好意思，拉齒玄言，但由於無始的因緣不由得我吐出的果實，在我很小的時候，我就成了多杰羌佛第三世的第一個弟子。上個月，德德林巴不變金剛多杰仁增老人家為佐欽寺第七世佐欽法王等大仁波且們灌頂時，他們問我：尊者見到不少多杰羌佛第三世的聖蹟吧？我告訴他們：不是見到不少，而是多得來我都記不清楚了。三世多杰羌實在是無聖可以比擬的，這不是個人的看法，而是寧瑪、薩迦、噶舉、格魯、覺囊等各大教派的法王、或仁波且們以本有的證量共同的確定：多杰羌佛第三世雲高益西諾布恩師的覺位在佛史上是最高的，是佛陀們的上師，所展顯的一切佛法圓滿和五明是這個世界上任何大聖者都沒有達到過這麼全面的高度的。這個世界的大聖們，有的具備了某一部分，但又缺乏某些部分。這不是空話，今天這一事實就擺在大家的面前，比如：曾空缽降臨甘露；未擇緣起先預告；金剛三昧除障；菩提聖水穿缽；甘露丸缽中用之不完；在現實中見到解脫成就若干眾生……不說這六條是沒有人證到過此全面完美聖境的，就是以大日如來尊勝益西諾布授記公開讓其印證佛之玄妙彩寶雕和神秘石霧，在當今也是沒有任何人達到的妙智證境。聖德們可以在石頭上留下腳印，但是用盡任何道量也無法把玄妙彩寶雕複製成功，無法把空中的祥霧拿到石洞中而如如不動，公開讓大家永遠觀看。正如尊勝益西諾布如來說：這是多杰羌佛的證量，是任何佛菩薩、大法王、仁波且們都做不到的。這就是事實，事實證明了確實沒有一位大聖者做得了，這兩件寶藝永遠放在那裡，招請複製，作為雲高大師即是第三世多杰羌佛的印證。

　　我講的話如語誠實，如果有疑義，就去印證見事實。但是，我必須說：哪個也做不到，只有真正的佛陀才能做到，否則即非如來！

喜饒杰布

2007 年 5 月

（此文的英文翻譯印在前面）

The powerful virtue of H.H. Dorje Chang Buddha III Wan Ko Yeshe Norbu caused lethal wasps called yellow jackets to keep their distance
and not harm other living beings. These yellow jackets swarmed onto the scene in order to seek being raised to higher realms of existence.
For details on this, please see the newspaper reports that were published at that time.
三世多杰羌佛雲高益西諾布威德感召，殺人黃蜂不敢傷害眾生，蜂擁而來以求超渡，詳見當時報紙報導

Eminent monastics and rinpoches view more than one million lethal wasps as those wasps gather and swarm onto the scene in order to be raised to higher realms of existence. Under the empowerment of H.H. Dorje Chang Buddha III, none of the wasps dared to attack any monastic or rinpoche.

高僧、仁波切們在黃蜂(殺人蜂)的下方觀看上百萬隻蜂聚集蜂擁而來為求超渡，在三世多杰羌佛的加持下，黃蜂絲毫不敢侵犯高僧、仁波且們

Before H.H. Dorje Chang Buddha III Wan Ko Yeshe Norbu performed the ceremony to raise the spirits of living beings to higher realms of existence, His Holiness told everyone beforehand that several minutes later the ten or so wasps would become more than one million wasps.

三世多杰羌佛雲高益西諾布在超渡前預先告知，幾分鐘後十餘隻黃蜂將化變為上百萬隻

As predicted, after H.H. Dorje Chang Buddha III practiced dharma, within a very short period of time spirits from the six realms of existence transformed themselves into more than one million wasps. Those wasps swarmed onto the scene in order to be raised to higher realms of existence. The raising of their spirits to higher realms of existence was truly an act of tremendous merit.

三世多杰羌佛修法後，果然一會兒六道群靈即化為黃蜂上百萬之數齊來受超，真是功德無量

I Received Initiations from the Holiest Tathagata

My master is H.H. Dorje Chang Buddha III Wan Ko Yeshe Norbu Holiest Tathagata. In the past, in order to end the cycle of reincarnation and learn the genuine Buddha-dharma, I gave up everything and traveled across the Pacific Ocean. After experiencing all sorts of bitterness and sorrow and going through various open and hidden observations and tests, I eventually received the tremendously wonderful Bodhi Holy Water from my Buddha Master and learned the genuine Buddha-dharma.

My Buddha Master is the highest ancient Buddha and has come to this world voluntarily. This is something that extremely holy and virtuous incarnations of Buddhas and Bodhisattvas have recognized according to the dharma by way of written certificates. It was not something recognized through simply the agreement of people in general, which would be meaningless. Over the past few thousand years, no person can compare with and no holy being can match His Holiness with respect to manifesting realization in this human realm. Why does the Buddha Master have such realization? The reason is that His Holiness is the Primordial ancestor of all of Buddhism, Dorje Chang Buddha III. Thus, whether it be a Buddha or Great Bodhisattva, who could be higher than Dorje Chang Buddha?

There are other holy feats that I have experienced before, but right now I will only relate a magnificent event showing the blessing power of Bodhi Holy Water.

On August 22, 2004, we celebrated the birthdays of the Holy Mother and a person of great virtue. We did so by holding a fish-releasing activity on the coast of Southern California. We bought from a fish dealer live fish that are specially used as bait and released them back into the ocean. I was in charge that day of the dharma rituals to be performed during that fish-releasing activity. I respectfully brought out and sprinkled Bodhi Holy Water into the fishpond to purify it and bless the fish. Within three seconds after I sprinkled Bodhi Holy Water into the pond, a small fish from that pond suddenly jumped six feet high and flew over the five-foot-wide embankment into the ocean. Joshua Bernstein, a lay disciple from North Carolina, witnessed that scene. He was completely astonished and marveled at what he had just seen. At the end of the fish-releasing rituals, he told everybody about that event.

There was an even more unexpected scene during the fish-releasing activity. The hundreds of sea birds present were simply standing still and observing or were circling in the air. Also, dozens of pelicans were standing lifelessly on the embankment. Even a group of sea lions were just swimming far away without coming closer. This was completely different from their normal conduct of rushing over to fight for and prey upon the fish just released. They would normally fight for and prey upon the fish just released no matter what method we used to drive them away. It seemed as if there was an invisible protective shield in the air above and on the surface of the ocean that protected the lives of those thousands of small fish, enabling them to swim away safely and avoid being attacked by their natural enemies. Throughout the entire process, not a single fish was seen to have died. This was truly miraculous. The blessing power of Bodhi Holy Water was simply as great as this! After news of this wondrous event spread, reporters came to interview witnesses, and the story was published in the Chinese American Times (please see the newspaper of August 27, 2004).

On April 2, 2006, I set up a mandala for a disciple of mine, Chi Kai, at his home in Taiwan. When I was purifying the mandala by sprinkling Bodhi Holy Water, the mandala suddenly illuminated brightly. A non-human living being saw this holy scene and came to seek refuge in me.

When the non-human living being arrived, he could not open his eyes and was effectively blind. After I applied Bodhi Holy Water to bless him, his karmic obstacles were instantly washed away. He suddenly opened his eyes and was able to see things without a problem. This non-human living being was extremely grateful and made a vow to practice Buddhism diligently. He stated that the reason he came to seek refuge was that he knew this place had the genuine Buddha-dharma.

"How did you know?" I asked.

"The light of the true Buddha-dharma is different from the light of any evil dharma," he replied. "The light of the Bodhi Holy Water was extremely bright and has very great blessing power," he also mentioned.

Another disciple of mine named Phillip, who lives in San Jose, U.S.A., had an accident due to slipping on the road in the rain. His car overturned and was completely destroyed, but he did not suffer any injury. Because he was wearing a vajra string blessed by Bodhi Holy Water, a tragedy was avoided.

There is more that I witnessed besides the awe-inspiring power of Bodhi Holy Water. The power of the Buddha Master's Buddha-dharma was particularly evident that day when His Holiness performed an initiation for me. Ordinary water turned into Bodhi Holy Water. No bowl in this world capable of containing water can hold such holy water. That holy water penetrated through the bowl and flowed out of it. Moreover, it constantly changed, coalescing in response to oral orders by His Holiness and separating in response to oral orders by His Holiness. My Buddha Master of supreme brilliance cannot be simply regarded as a Great Dharma King or a great master of esoteric Buddhism or the highest leader of exoteric Buddhism! As those holy and virtuous ones stated, His Holiness is the highest leader of Buddhism in the dharma realm. What does it mean to be Dorje Chang Buddha III? Such a being is the highest Buddha in all of Buddhism!

On another occasion, wonderful karmic conditions that are difficult to encounter in millions of eons matured one day when my most honored Buddha Master fulfilled a wish of mine that I had been dreaming about for many years concerning receiving great dharma. The Buddha Master performed for me the Selection of Karmic Affinity Dharma and the profound Great Perfection Holiest Essence Elimination of Karmic Obstructions Initiation, both of which belong to the vajra division.

That day, I walked into the mandala and very piously and respectfully presented to the Buddha Master a khata (white silk scarf) and an offering. I knelt before the dharma dais as I respectfully listened to a discourse by the Buddha Master. The first ceremony to be performed was based upon the profound ear transmission dharma. In this ceremony, one dharma is selected among ten different dharmas. This selection of karmic affinity dharma is the source of many other dharmas. Any master who has the realization of an extremely holy and virtuous being must perform such a dharma ceremony for his or her disciples. This is the supreme and genuine Drawing a Slip From a Golden Vase Dharma.

While seated on the dais, the Buddha Master wrote down on ten separate pieces of paper the seed syllable "Ah" from which my karmic affinity would be selected. The Buddha Master then gave to me those pieces of paper. I wrote down my name on the outer margin of each of those pieces of paper containing that seed syllable. I also wrote down a different number on the outer margin of each piece of paper. I then went to a place where there was no other person and cut the seed syllable out of each piece of paper.

I cut the seed syllables out by cutting around the edges of each of the ten seed syllables. The shape of the paper that was cut out was different for

each of the seed syllables. Cutting the seed syllables out also resulted in ten separate pieces of paper that were the outer margins of the original pieces of paper and that still had my name and a number on them. After I cut out the seed syllables, I immediately used my fingers and much force to roll each one of those pieces of paper with a seed syllable on it into a ball the size of a tiny pill. I then put each of those balls of paper into the dharma container, the inside of which was like a golden vase. Ten separate seed syllables were cut out, each of which was rolled into a tiny paper ball, and all ten paper balls were put into the dharma container. With no other person watching, I placed inside my inner robes those ten outer-margin pieces of paper with a hole in the middle. I took off my outer robe, covered the dharma container with that robe, and with both hands carried the dharma container into the mandala.

At this time, the Buddha Master was sitting upright on the dharma dais and appeared quite majestic. His Holiness immediately began practicing dharma. After finishing that practice of the dharma, His Holiness revealed, "The dharma you will select is number . . . dharma. Take out one of the paper balls and see."

The Buddha Master instructed me to reach out and draw a tiny ball of paper from the dharma container, which was still covered by my outer robe. His Holiness also instructed me to unroll that ball of paper carefully and spread it out as evenly as possible. After I did those things, I took out those ten outer-margin pieces of paper with a hole in the middle that I had hidden in my inner robes and found the one whose number corresponded with the number the Buddha Master just mentioned. I then placed the piece of paper with the seed syllable on it that I had just drawn into that outer-margin piece of paper with a hole in the middle to see if they would match. As expected, the contour of the cut out seed syllable paper completely matched the contour of the hole in the middle of that outer-margin piece of paper. The seed syllable paper indicating karmic affinity that I had just drawn from the dharma container corresponded exactly with the dharma number the Buddha Master predicted. This truly is unimaginably magnificent Buddha-dharma. What power made me correctly select that particular ball of paper from among all ten balls of paper? It was totally beyond my control.

The Buddha Master then said, "Roll that paper with the seed syllable on it indicating karmic affinity that you just drew back into a tiny ball as before and put it in the dharma container."

As instructed, I again rolled that piece of paper with the seed syllable on it into a tiny paper ball and put it in the dharma container. The Buddha Master then shook the dharma container and casually drew a tiny paper ball from it. My outer robe covered the dharma container during this entire process before the Buddha Master drew a tiny paper ball from it. Nobody could see what was in the dharma container. Even if what was in the dharma container could have been seen, there would have been no way to differentiate those tiny balls of paper that contained the same seed syllable. Even I could not possibly have discerned which paper ball corresponded to which number. This it true even though I cut all of them out, rolled them into balls, opened one of them up and spread it out evenly.

With both my hands, I received the tiny ball of paper that the Buddha Master had just drawn from the dharma container. I opened it up carefully and matched it with that same outer-margin piece of paper with the hole in the middle. It perfectly matched the outer-margin piece of paper. The

Buddha Master drew the exact same paper with the seed syllable on it that I had drawn a moment earlier which corresponded to the predicted dharma number. I took the other nine tiny paper balls out of the dharma container, opened each one up, and spread each one out. Each of those nine differently shaped pieces of paper containing that seed syllable perfectly matched one of the nine outer-margin pieces of paper on which a number other than the predicted number was written. There was not one incorrect match.

Think about this! I do not have the ability or realization to draw the exact seed syllable ball of paper that corresponded to the selection of karmic affinity predicted by the Buddha Master. After I drew that tiny ball of paper, I put it back into the dharma container. The Buddha Master then confirmed this selection of karmic affinity process by casually drawing the exact same piece of paper that I had drawn a moment earlier. What type of Buddha-dharma is this? The only answer is that it is the holiest Great Perfection On-the-Spot Drawing a Slip From a Golden Vase Selection of Karmic Affinity Initiation, which entails manifestation of the highest realization. I have kept those ten pieces of paper with the seed syllable on them as well as the then outer-margin pieces of paper with a hole in the middle. They are truly rare dharma treasures.

After the selection of karmic affinity initiation successfully concluded, the dharma to eliminate karmic obstructions was performed. I personally washed the dharma bowl and the dharma cups. I then filled the dharma bowl with pure water and put it in the middle of the mandala. I placed one dharma cup on either side of the bowl. Holding a dharma instrument that

had been washed clean, the Buddha Master scooped out pure water from the bowl and poured that water into both dharma cups. His Holiness then instructed me to pour offering water into my mouth, but I was not permitted to swallow that water.

The Buddha Master began to chant mantras and practice dharma. When I spit into one of the cups half of the water that was in my mouth, the water that I spit out was clear and fully transparent. After practicing dharma again, the Buddha Master said, "Spit out all of the water that is in your mouth. This time it is for the elimination of karmic obstructions." I spit out all of the offering water that remained in my mouth. This time the water that I spit out was an orange-yellow color.

The power of the Buddha-dharma is truly inconceivable. Those two dharma cups contained purified water from the same dharma bowl. I held in my mouth one mouthful of water. From that one mouthful of water, I spit out water twice. The results were totally different. One cup showed no karmic obstructions, while the other cup showed karmic obstructions.

This highest and magnificent Buddha-dharma is truly so profound! Such profound and genuine dharma can only be performed and manifested by my most honorable Buddha Master due to his perfect realization and merit.

Duozha Xinxiong
Respectfully recorded the above true stories

(This is a complete translation of the Chinese text that follows originally written and signed by Duozha Xinxiong.)

得 到 頂 聖 如 來 的 灌 頂

多杰羌佛第三世雲高益西諾布頂聖如來是我的師父，當初為求了生脫死，學到真正佛法，我放下一切，遠渡重洋，歷經種種辛酸，接受明行暗行觀察考驗，最後終於取到了佛陀恩師無比殊勝的菩提聖水，我學到了佛法。

佛陀恩師是最高古佛應世，這是大聖德佛菩薩們認證行文法定的，而不是空洞的公認概念，在人類世界展顯的證量，幾千年來，無人能比，乃至無聖可複。佛陀恩師為何有此證量？因為他老人家是佛教始祖多杰羌佛第三世，所以無論是佛或大菩薩，誰又能高過多杰羌佛呢？

其他我就暫且不說，我在這裡只講菩提聖水加持力量的偉大事蹟吧！

二零零四年八月廿二日那天，為祝賀佛母及大德仁者誕辰，我們在美國南加州海邊舉辦放生活動，向魚販買來專供釣餌用的活魚，把它們再放回大海。當天的放生法事，由我主法，我特地請出菩提聖水，灑淨魚池，加持魚群。就在我剛向魚池施灑菩提聖水不到三秒鐘，突然一條小魚竟從池中騰空六呎高，飛越五呎寬的堤岸，躍入了大海中，一位來自北卡州名叫Joshua Bernstein的居士現場目睹，目瞪口呆，驚歎不已，他在放生儀軌結束後出來向大眾講了此情況。

在放生時，更是出乎意外的，只見數百隻海鳥靜立旁觀或空中盤旋，幾十隻鵜鶘呆立堤上，連一群海獅也僅在遠處海面沉浮，完全不像平時那樣用任何方法都趕不開拚命來搶食放生的魚兒。漁場上空與海面彷彿有道無形的防護罩，護佑數千條生命平安離去，遠隔天敵的攻擊，

整個放生過程中，竟然沒有一條魚兒受到傷亡，真是十分神奇，菩提聖水的加持就有如此大的力量！這一殊勝的事蹟披露後，記者來採訪並於時報上登載。（詳情見2004.8.27洛山磯時報）

二零零六年四月二日，我為一位台灣弟子慈開於家中安設壇場，當我以菩提聖水淨壇時，壇場內大放光明，有一非人見此聖境，而來求皈依。

非人初來時，兩目無法張開見光，形同瞎子，後經我施以菩提聖水為其加持，當下洗除業障，雙眼突然睜開見物，不復障礙。非人無盡感恩，發心精進學佛，謂其之所以來皈依，乃因其知此地有真正的佛法。我問：「你怎麼知道的？」他說：「如來正法的光，不同於邪法之光。」又說：「菩提聖水光亮無比，加持力量非常之大。」

另有位住在美國聖荷西的弟子Philip，在雨中因路滑發生車禍，車子打轉翻滾，車體全毀，但人竟毫髮無傷，結果是因他身上佩戴有以菩提聖水加持過的金剛帶，所以助他免掉了一個災難。

我不僅親眼見到菩提聖水之威力，尤其是在為我灌頂的當天，佛陀恩師的佛法出現了，那普通的水變成了菩提聖水，世間上任何盛水缽均裝不了這聖水，聖水從缽壁穿壁而流出，而且變化無窮，應聲集聚，應聲分散。我無上光明的佛陀上師，哪裡是什麼大法王啊，根本就不是什麼密乘的宗師、顯宗教主的概念！正如聖德們說，是法界大教主。多杰羌佛第三世，那是佛教的至高佛祖啊！

在一個百千萬劫難遭遇的殊勝法緣成熟時，至尊佛陀上師滿了我多

年一直於夢中都想求到的法中根本的願——金剛部擇緣法和甚深大圓滿頂聖精髓除障灌頂。

當天，我進入壇場，虔誠地敬獻哈達及供養，長跪於法台前，恭聽佛陀上師的開示。首先要舉行的，是依甚深耳傳法十條不同的法義來擇法緣，這一法是萬法之緣起，凡證量大聖德是必須為弟子舉行的，這是至高無上的真正的金瓶掣籤。佛陀上師在法台上寫了十張擇緣種子"啊"字交給我，我在每一張寫有種子字的紙邊記下自己的名字，並每一張編列一個號碼，也寫在紙邊上。我獨自在一個無人之處，將種子字從每張紙上剪下來。

剪的時候，都是沿著種子字邊剪，剪下不同的形狀，我自己所寫的名字及編號則留在剪下的紙圈上。種子字剪下後，我立刻用手指強力將它摺揉成圓形的小紙丸，丟進法桶中(內如金瓶)。十張剪下的種子字，共揑成十個小紙丸，全丟在法桶裡，而十張剪剩的紙圈，則暗自收藏在身上。我卸下袈裟，將整個法桶覆蓋後，捧進了壇場。

此時，佛陀老人家巍然端坐法台上，當下修法後，隨即開示說：「是××法義，你拿一粒看看。」

佛陀老人家令我伸手從覆蓋袈裟的法桶裡取出一個小紙丸，並且要我小心地將這個紙丸解開、攤平，再從暗藏於身上的十張紙圈中，找出編號××密法的紙圈，把種子字與紙圈兩相併合，果真剪下的種子字外緣與紙圈內邊完全吻合，那張我自己從法桶中拿出的緣起種子字，正是佛陀老人家提前已說出的××法號，真是偉大到無法想像的佛法，是什麼力量要讓我在十個紙丸中唯獨拿準了這一張？根本不由我自主。

佛陀老人家說：「你將緣起種子字再揑成原來的樣子，丟進法桶。」

我依教將緣起種子字再度揑成小紙丸，放入法桶。佛陀老人家將法桶搖晃後，從法桶裡隨手取出一個紙丸來。在這整個過程中，法桶一直被袈裟覆蓋著，誰也見不到法桶裡面的東西。何況就算見到，也無法辨別同樣種子字的紙丸，包括親自剪揑的我，乃至把紙丸打開攤平，也無法認出是幾號。

我雙手接過佛陀上師從法桶取出的紙丸，小心翼翼地打開，紙圈再次相合，確實無誤，老人家所拿出的正是剛才的法號種子字。我將法桶中其餘的九個紙丸，也一一攤開，這九張剪成不同形狀的種子字，恰好與其他編號的九張紙圈各自接合，準確無誤。

想想看！弟子有什麼本事、什麼證量能把佛陀上師已先說出擇緣的結果種子字拿出來，弟子自己取出後，放回法桶，再經他老人家複緣，老人家信手拿出即是剛才與弟子拿出的無誤，這是什麼佛法？只能說這才是現量至高證境頂聖大圓滿金瓶掣籤擇緣灌頂。現在十張種子字，我已收藏供奉，實在是稀世法寶。

擇緣灌頂圓滿之後，跟著舉行除障法義。我親自洗淨法缽及法杯，將法缽裝滿淨水，置於壇場中央，兩旁各放一法杯。佛陀上師手持洗淨的法器，從法缽裡盛起淨水，分別倒進兩個法杯中，然後令我口含供水，但不可吞下。

佛陀老人家開始持咒修法，當我吐出一半口中水於杯中時，清澈見底。

佛陀老人家又修法後，說：「把口中的水全部吐出來，這一次是除障。」

我將嘴裡剩餘的供水全都吐出來，這一次所吐的水，呈現橙黃色。

佛法的力量，真是令人無法想像，明明法杯內所裝的是同一法缽中的淨水，而我含在嘴裡的也是同一口，結果一口水吐兩次，竟然完全不同，一杯無業，一杯見業。

至高偉大的佛法，實在太深沉了！而如此甚深的真實法義，也唯有我的至尊佛陀上師他老人家的高深圓滿證境功德，才能夠表顯灌頂的啊！

多扎信雄 恭敬記實

多扎信雄

（此文的英文翻譯印在前面）

Time of Death Predicted, Passing Away in Cross-Legged Meditative Posture with Hands in Mudra

My name is Chi Lie Er, a disciple of H.H. Dorje Chang Buddha III Wan Ko Yeshe Norbu Holiest Tathagata. I would like to make a solemn vow. If all that I describe in the following is for the purpose of deceiving living beings and misleading living beings into taking an evil path, I will descend into Varjra Hell! If all that I describe is true and authentic, I will be liberated and will attain great accomplishment, and living beings will enjoy good fortune.

In May of 1991, my mother, Xianyun Zhao, was critically ill and was taken to the Eighth Hospital in Chengdu City. After examination by the Chief Resident, Professor Qiu, it was confirmed that her heart, liver, spleen, lungs and kidneys were all failing. A few days later, she was in a partial coma. Professor Qiu notified us to prepare for her funeral arrangements without delay.

Brother Hui Han Da and I rushed over to where the Buddha Master resided and pleaded with the Buddha Master to keep my mother alive until she learned dharma. At first, the Buddha Master did not agree and said, "I do not have the ability to keep a dying person alive." Firmly believing that only the Buddha Master could make this happen, we knelt down for a long time without getting up, begging piteously and earnestly. Brother Hui Han Da said, "The weather is very hot now. The remains get rotten very quickly, which is not advantageous for performing certain Buddhist rituals. I beseech the Buddha Master to keep our mother alive until it is the cool weather of fall in October!" I cried my heart out and piteously begged the Buddha Master. The Buddha Master then said, "I will try! I will do my best! However, this is against the laws of impermanence, and I do not have such merit at all."

After expressing my appreciation to my respected Master, we hurried back to the hospital. A miracle had happened! My mother regained consciousness. As soon as she was conscious, she was hungry, asking for food. To my surprise, she ate a large bowl of meatball soup. Professor Qiu did an examination on her and found the function of her heart, liver, spleen, lungs, and kidneys had returned to normal. The professor was extremely surprised and said this was a miracle indeed! Because my mother was no longer ill, she left the hospital three days later. The Buddha Master had kept my mother, whose karmic condition with this world was about to end, alive and transmitted to her the dharma of Esoteric Buddhism.

With time going by so fast, it was soon September 30th. Unexpectedly, the Buddha Master notified me, "Your mother is going to pass away on October 5th." This was a big surprise to me, and once again I begged the Buddha Master to prolong her life for another period of time. The Buddha Master scolded me. "Originally, you pleaded to keep your mother alive until the fall when it was cool. Perhaps it is because your mother has practiced meditation and Buddha-dharma that she has recovered from her illness. How can I keep her alive? Besides, last time your mother was going to Yama (the deity who is the ruler of Hell). This time your mother will go to the Western Paradise of Ultimate Bliss. She is going to a wonderful place!" I hurried back home to stay with my mother for a few more days.

On October 2nd, just after 3:00 p.m., Brother Zhou from Chengdu accompanied the Buddha Master to my house. The Buddha Master expounded the following dharma to my mother. "The purpose of learning Buddhism and cultivation is to become a more benevolent person who furthers the well-being of others, ends the sufferings of life and death, and attains liberation from the cycle of reincarnation. Going to the Western Paradise of Ultimate Bliss is attaining liberation from the cycle of reincarnation. The Western Paradise of Ultimate Bliss is a very wonderful place. When you think of clothes, you will have the clothes. When you think of food, you will have the food. Also, you can listen to Amitabha Buddha expound the Buddha-dharma." My mother asked the Buddha Master, "Buddha Master! How is the scenery of the Western Paradise of Ultimate Bliss?" The Buddha Master said, "Have you seen the lamp festival of Qing Yang Temple in Chengdu? The scenery in the Western Paradise of Ultimate Bliss is hundreds and thousands of times better." The Buddha Master continued to expound many wonderful states in the Western Paradise of Ultimate Bliss. The more my mother listened, the happier she became. She could not wait to visit the Western Paradise of Ultimate Bliss. She even said to me, "I haven't prepared the old shoes yet (special shoes made for people

who pass away)." Everyone laughed.

Brother Zhou asked, "Buddha Master! Why did you give the elderly mother discourses on all those subjects today?" The Buddha Master replied, "She is going to the Western Paradise of Ultimate Bliss. And, not only that, she is going to pass away in a cross-legged meditative posture!"

The same evening, we returned with my mother to the old house in Xin Fan for a family reunion and farewell gathering. Several dozens of relatives and friends had come. My mother played cards with the guests until 12 o'clock at night and then rested. The relatives saw that my mother's health was in a very good condition. Her face was rosy and radiant. She talked and laughed merrily. No one would ever believe that she was going to pass away in three days. The next day, after arranging for a photographer to come over and take pictures of the whole family, we headed back to Chengdu.

On the afternoon of October 4th, Brother Hui Han Da asked the Buddha Master, "Will my mother-in-law pass away tonight? Where will be the best place for her to pass away?" The Buddha Master replied, "It has to wait until tomorrow. The best place to go is Jewel Street because of the courtyard, where it will be convenient to perform Buddhist rituals." Brother Hui Han Da pleaded to the Buddha Master to stay and assist my mother in practicing dharma. But the Buddha Master did not agree and said, "A minute before she is going to pass away, I will come." In the evening, we walked with my mother to 33 Jewel Street. All of the brothers and sisters came, surrounding her bed and preparing to see my mother off. The entire family happily chatted until the next morning.

Some time after 9 o'clock on the morning of October 5th, the Buddha Master came to Jewel Street to make other Buddhist arrangements. Brother Hui Han Da asked the Buddha Master, "The spirit of my mother-in-law is still very well. She just ate her breakfast, and her face was radiant and rosy. Is this a sign of a sudden spurt of vigor just before death and is she ready to leave?" The Buddha Master said, "What does it have to do with a sudden spurt of vigor just before her death? The time has not come yet. When it is

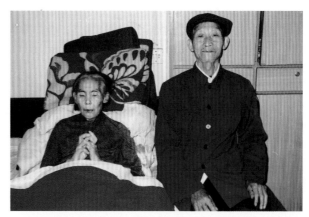

This photograph (top left) was taken three days after laywoman Xianyun Zhao put her hands in a mudra and passed away in the meditative posture having attained liberation. She is smiling, her complexion is ruddy, and she appears to be still reciting the name of Amitabha Buddha as she did before she passed away. To her left is her husband, layman Xiang-Shou Que. In 1993, layman Xiang-Shou Que learned a certain dharma from H.H. Great Dharma King and became accomplished in the dharma. After he passed away, his body emitted bright light three times.

這張照片是趙賢雲居士雙手結印，坐化圓寂三天後所照（上左）。法體面帶微笑，紅光滿面，猶如生前，似乎還在念佛，右為其丈夫關祥壽居士。關祥壽居士亦於1993年學法成就，圓寂後其肉身放出三次強光。

the time, Buddhas and Bodhisattvas will arrive and escort her away. I have promised your mother-in-law that I will personally see her off in her last minute."

It was just past 10 o'clock. All of a sudden, my mother sat up from the bed and called everyone to recite immediately the name of Amitabha Buddha. She then arranged herself in the cross-legged meditative posture, applied the secret mudra that the Master had transmitted to her, and began practicing dharma. Very soon, she was out of breath. We called her, but she could not respond to us anymore. Too bad! My mother had died!

All of the family members hurried around. It was just past 11 o'clock. The Buddha Master came. The Buddha Master started to practice dharma. I sat by the door protecting the altar. About ten minutes later, suddenly, auspicious and colorful clouds appeared in the sky surrounding the arrival of Kuan Yin Bodhisattva! At this time, abruptly from the top of my house came a cloud of fog containing beams of white light that rose up and appeared just like a lotus flower. Amidst the white fog, which was emitting snow white light beams, my mother was sitting with her hands held in a mudra and maintaining the cross-legged meditative posture. Sometimes this scene could be seen, but sometimes it could not be seen. Slowly, the light rose toward the direction of Kuan Yin Bodhisattva. Kuan Yin Bodhisattva joined the white cloud and escorted my mother, gradually rising up to the sky and into the distance. I was so moved by the holy state in front of my eyes that I stared at the sky dumbstruck. All of a sudden, I heard the voice of the Buddha Master, "Your mother has already been reborn in the Western Paradise of Ultimate Bliss!" At that moment, I retuned to normal.

In the room, my mother's face was still rosy and radiant with a smile. She was sitting on the bed in a cross-legged meditative posture and holding her hands in a mudra. We reached our hands to about an inch above the top of my mother's head. My goodness! It was exactly like hot steam, and it went straight up. This was a sign that only applied to people reborn to the Western Paradise of Ultimate Bliss. Everyone was all very happy and took pictures with my mother. When sending films to be developed, the person in the shop said, "This elderly lady is reciting the name of Buddha!" He did not realize that it was the dharma remains (corpse) of my mother who had already passed away.

The elderly lady Zhu, a neighbor, never socialized with us. She told Sister Xiaolian Li that she saw that Kuan Yin Bodhisattva had appeared in the sky to escort an elderly lady on the afternoon of the 5th. Therefore, Sister Li brought her to my house. Just at the time the elderly lady Zhu saw my mother's dharma remains (body), she became excited and said, "Right! Right! Right! This was the elderly lady. This elderly lady is exactly the one I saw when Kuan Yin Bodhisattva escorted her away." The news spread.

Group by group, the nearby laypersons came over to look at my mother with reverence. My house was so crowded not even a drop of water could tickle through. People constantly came and left. Mr. Pu, another neighbor, said, "They do not look like they are having a funeral. I even think that they are more cheerful and happier than when they had a wedding in their house."

On October 11th, we requested that Great Dharma Teacher Pu Cheng come over to place my mother's body in a upright Buddhist casket. As soon as he entered the door and saw my mother, he uttered, "Amitabha!" and said, "Elderly sister, you have encountered authentic Buddhas and Bodhisattvas to liberate you. Another disciple of Master Yee[1] again! Look at you. You passed away in a cross-legged meditative posture and hold the Great Mudra of Three Jewels. This is truly incredible! I have stayed in the Bao Guang Temple for dozens of years and have been in charge of placing cremated remains in shrines. I have placed in shrines a lot of remains of great dharma teachers and monks. Except for the great layman Wang, I have never seen such extraordinary signs as this elderly laywoman has shown."

During the escorting of my mother to the Bao Guang Temple for cremation, the sounds of celestial music and celestial drums accompanied the motorcade from Chengdu to Bao Guang Temple. These sounds lasted for about forty minutes and got louder and louder. We all put our palms together with endless appreciation and respect. What was magical was that we did not even turn on any electrical sounds in the cars at all!

In the early morning of the next day during cremation, fifty or sixty relatives and fellow disciples personally witnessed that surrounding the side of my mother's dharma remains (corpse) were golden fire lotus flowers. During the cremation, seed characters in white, red and blue emanated from her forehead, throat, and heart areas. All of the people attending were joyful, encouraged, and gained a lot of faith from this. We especially appreciated and thought of the virtue and kindness of our Buddha Master, who sent my mother to the Western Paradise of Ultimate Bliss!

In today's world, are there any great rinpoches or dharma teachers who can predict the time of someone's death and be absolutely correct to the exact minute? Who can keep alive a person whose lifespan has come to an end? Who can say that he can request a particular Buddha or Bodhisattva to escort someone away and that particular Buddha or Bodhisattva will comply? All these things can only be demonstrated in the results of the teachings of H.H. Dorje Chang Buddha III!

Buddhist disciple,
Chi Lie Er

(This is a complete translation of the Chinese text that follows originally written and signed by Chi Lie Er.)

預知時辰，結印坐化

我叫赤烈爾，是多杰羌佛第三世雲高益西諾布頂聖如來的弟子，我慎重發誓，若我在下文所述的一切是為了矇騙眾生，誤導眾生走邪道，我墮金剛地獄！若是真實不虛，我解脫大成就，眾生享福。

我母親趙賢雲，1991年5月病危入住成都市八醫院。主治醫生邱

仁祺教授檢查後，確診心、肝、脾、肺、腎均已衰竭。幾天後，母親呈半昏迷狀態，邱教授通知我們準備後事，不可耽誤。我和慧漢達師兄急忙趕到佛陀上師的下榻處，請求佛陀上師留住我母親，學法後再往升。起初佛陀上師不答應，說：「我沒有這個本事把要死的人留下

來。」我們堅信只有佛陀上師能辦到，就長跪不起，苦苦哀求。慧漢達師兄說：「現在天氣炎熱，遺體腐爛得快，不利於做佛事，求佛陀上師留到秋涼十月間吧！」我痛哭流涕，苦求佛陀上師，佛陀上師才說：「我試一試吧！儘量吧！」

謝了佛陀恩師，我們急忙趕回醫院，奇蹟出現了，母親清醒了，一醒來就喊餓，竟然吃了一大碗肉圓湯。邱教授一檢查，心肝脾肺腎的功能都恢復正常了，教授驚奇萬分，說這簡直是奇蹟！由於母親已沒有病了，三天後，母親出院了。佛陀上師把我塵緣已盡的母親留了下來，並傳給了她密法。

轉眼到了9月30日，佛陀上師突然通知我：「你媽媽10月5日要圓寂了。」我大吃一驚，又求佛陀上師多留母親一段時間，佛陀上師訶斥我：「你們當初要求就是留到秋涼，大概是你母親練了靜坐佛法病好了，我哪裡留得了她？上一次你媽媽是到閻王那裡報到，但這一次是去極樂世界，是去好地方嘛！」我趕快回家再多陪母親幾天。

10月2日下午三點過，成都的周師兄陪同佛陀上師來我家，佛陀上師為我母親開示：「我們學佛修行的目的就是要成為最善良的人，幫助他人幸福，了生脫死，脫離輪迴。去極樂世界就脫離輪迴了，極樂世界好得很，思衣得衣，思食得食，還要聽聞阿彌陀佛講佛法。」母親問佛陀上師：「佛陀上師啊！極樂世界的風景好不好呢？」佛陀上師說：「你看過成都青羊宮的燈會沒有？極樂世界的風景比燈會好百千萬倍都不止……」佛陀上師開示了很多有關極樂世界的妙境，我母親越聽越高興，恨不得馬上就去極樂世界，母親還對我說：「我還沒有老鞋(專給過世的人穿的平口步鞋)呢！」大家都笑了。

周師兄在當場問：「佛陀上師啊！您今天怎麼給老媽媽全都開示這些事情呢？」佛陀上師說：「她大後天就要往升極樂世界了，不但要走，還要坐化！」

當天傍晚，我們送母親回新繁老家與親人團聚告別。親戚朋友來了好幾十人，媽媽陪客人玩紙牌玩到晚上12點過才休息。親人們見母親身體那麼好，滿面紅光談笑風生，誰都不相信她三天後要圓寂。第二天我們請來照相師照了一張全家福後，回到了成都。

10月4日下午，慧漢達師兄請示佛陀上師：「我媽媽是不是今天晚上圓寂？在哪裡圓寂好呢？」佛陀上師說：「要等到明天，最好到珠寶街，那裡有天井(院子)，好做佛事。」慧漢達師兄請求佛陀上師留下來幫媽媽修法，可是佛陀上師不同意留下來，並說：「她臨走的一分鐘，我會來的。」傍晚，我們陪母親走到了珠寶街33號。所有的兄弟姐妹都來了，圍在母親床前，準備與母親送行，一家人很高興地聊到天亮。

5日上午9點過，佛陀上師來珠寶街處理其他佛事，慧漢達師兄請示：「我岳母現在精神還很好，剛剛吃了早飯，紅光滿面的，是不是迴光返照要走了？」佛陀上師說：「什麼迴光返照哦！是還沒到時間，到了時間佛菩薩會來接她的，我答應過你媽媽，在最後一分鐘我會親自來送她的。」

10點過，母親突然從床上坐起，叫大家趕快唸佛，自己則打上了盤腿，結起了佛陀上師傳給她的秘密手印開始修法，很快就快沒有氣了，我們叫她，她也無法應聲了，糟了！媽媽死了！全家人慌成一團，就在這時11點過，佛陀上師來了。佛陀上師開始修法，我坐在門口護壇，才過了十分鐘，突然，天空出現五光十色的祥雲，圍繞著觀世音菩薩降臨！這時，我家的房頂上忽然升起一團蓮花般的白光霧，白霧中放出雪白的光芒，我媽媽盤腿結印坐在白光中，有時看得到，有時又不見，慢慢升到觀世音菩薩的方向，觀世音菩薩駕著白雲帶著我母親漸漸升空遠去了。我被眼前的聖境感動著，望著天空，呆若木雞，突然耳邊響起佛陀上師的聲音：「你媽媽已經往升了！」我這才回過神來，房間裡，母親依舊紅光滿面，面帶微笑，盤腿結著手印坐在床上。我們伸手到離母親頭頂一寸高的地方，哎呀！簡直像蒸氣一樣，熱氣直往上沖，這是往升極樂世界的人才有的現象！全家都非常高興，與媽媽照相留念。去相館沖洗時，相館師傅說：「這位婆婆在念佛啊！」他根本不知道那是已經圓寂的法體。

鄰居朱婆婆，跟我家素無往來。朱婆婆告訴李孝蓮師姐，她5號上午看見觀世音菩薩出現在天空，接走了一位老婆婆，李師姐便帶她來到我家，朱婆婆一見我母親的法體便激動地說：「對！對！對！就是這個婆婆，我看見觀世音菩薩接走的就是這個婆婆！」消息傳開，附近的居士們成群結隊地來瞻仰我母親，我家被擠得水泄不通，人來人往。鄰居蒲先生說：「這家人哪裡像在辦喪事，我看他們比嫁女兒、娶媳婦辦喜事還熱鬧，還高興！」

10月11日，我們請來寶光寺的普成大法師為母親裝靈龕，他一進門一看見我母親，念了一聲「阿彌陀佛！」說：「老姐子，你是遇到了真正的佛菩薩渡了妳！又是義大師(即三世多杰羌佛——編者注)的弟子吧！看妳，走的時候還盤腿打坐結三寶大印，真是了不得！我在寶光寺幾十年，負責入龕茶毗往生的人，大法師、大和尚我裝得不少，除了王大居士，沒有一個像這位居士婆婆這樣殊勝的！」

送母親去寶光寺茶毗的路上，天樂天鼓之聲一直隨著車隊從成都到寶光寺，歷時約有40多分鐘，且越來越大聲，大家都合掌謝恩不已。神奇的是汽車上沒有放任何電器聲！

第二天一早茶毗時，我們五、六十位親戚和師兄弟們，親眼看見母親的法體旁邊全是金色的火蓮花圍繞，額頭、喉部、心輪處燒出了白紅藍三種顏色的種子字，在場的人無不歡欣鼓舞，信心倍增，更是感念佛陀上師的恩德，將我母親送到極樂世界！當今世上，有哪一個大活佛、大法師能提前預知別人的圓寂時辰分秒不差？誰能把壽緣已盡的人想留多久就留多久？誰能說請哪位佛菩薩來接引就是哪位佛菩薩來接引？這一切，都只有在三世多杰羌佛的教授下才會出現啊！

佛弟子　赤烈爾

赤烈爾

（此文的英文翻譯印在前面）

Peacefully Passing to the Pure Land in a Sitting Position at the Predicted Time

Dharma Teachers, Brothers and Sisters, Amitabha! What can I say today? I am simply grateful and very moved. I fear that I am so moved I will not be able to say what is in my heart. In order to be responsible toward the law of karma, I drafted a statement.

I would first like to thank once more our magnificent Buddha Master[1]. Out of great kindness, on August 6th of this year, the Buddha Master arranged that my wife, fellow student Hui-Hsiu Liu, pass away in the cross-legged posture and be reborn in the Pure Land. Even if my body were smashed to pieces for the Buddha Master, I could never repay such an act of great kindness.

On July 7th of this year, I flew from Seattle to Los Angeles in order to seek the dharma from the Buddha Master on behalf of my wife, fellow student Hui-Hsiu Liu. The Buddha Master was compassionate. His Holiness clearly and solemnly said to me, "If student Hui-Hsiu Liu practices this dharma, as well as its related seed syllable, I guarantee that she will pass away in the cross-legged posture and be reborn in the Western Paradise of Ultimate Bliss. Moreover, she will definitely not experience any pain at death."

It turned out just as the Buddha Master said. Before Hui-Hsiu Liu passed away, she did not even use morphine. She did not experience any pain at all. At about 5:00 in the morning on August 6th, fellow student Hui-Hsiu Liu sat up on her bed and said she was going to pass away. She then calmly put her favorite toy, a small cloth dog, in the same direction as she was facing. Then she got in the cross-legged sitting posture, put her hands in the mudra the Buddha Master taught her, and visualized the seed syllables. There she sat all the way until 9:55 that morning, when she passed away.

I would like to ask all of you dharma teachers and fellow students something. In today's world or in modern history, what type of Master would dare to guarantee beforehand that if his disciple practices a dharma that he transmits, that disciple will pass away in the cross-legged posture at the predicted time? Fellow students, just what kind of a feat is that? If the Buddha-dharma were not real, if the Buddha Master's state of realization were not that of a Buddha, then how could Hui-Hsiu Liu, who was in the last stage of cancer with lymphoma that had already spread throughout her entire body, calmly sit in the cross-legged posture, put her hands in a mudra, and tell me that she will now pass away? If the Buddha-dharma were not real, if the Buddha Master's state of realization were not that of a Buddha, then how could she have passed away in the cross-legged posture exactly as the Buddha Master guaranteed beforehand? Doesn't this clearly indicate the accuracy of the Buddha Master's guarantee uttered beforehand, namely, that Hui-Hsiu Liu would pass away in the cross-legged posture and be reborn in the Pure Land? Doesn't this also clearly indicate that our magnificent Buddha Master is a great holy being who represents the great Buddha-dharma? (Everybody replied: Amitabha!)

On August 5th, Sister Hui-Hsiu Liu's situation was critical. From what my family members and I could see, her situation at that time was very critical. However, the Buddha Master told me over the phone quite resolutely, "Student Hui-Hsiu Liu will not pass away tonight. She will pass away tomorrow. You can set your mind at rest and let her sleep." Dharma Teachers and fellow students, had the Buddha Master not seen long beforehand the exact time of Hui-Hsiu Liu's passing, how could His Holiness confidently tell me that Sister Hui-Hsiu Liu would not pass away that night and that I should let her sleep? Just what type of a feat is that? Doesn't this clearly demonstrate that H.H. Buddha Master is a holy being who represents the magnificent Buddha-dharma and that His Holiness is a saint of the highest magnitude?

On August 5th, the Buddha Master told me over the phone not to worry. His Holiness told me to set my mind at rest and let Sister Hui-Hsiu Liu sleep. At that time, I put the cell phone near the ear of Sister Hui-Hsiu Liu so that she could hear for herself the instructions of the Buddha Master spoken over the phone. After that call, she went to sleep.

The next day, which was August 6th, the day she would pass away, she awoke after 3:00 in the morning and told me that she had taken a trip to the Western Paradise of Ultimate Bliss. She then took a nap till about 5:00. After she awoke, she stated that she would now die. All of my family members suddenly became terribly worried. I tried to call the Master's cell phone twenty or thirty times. However, the Master's cell phone was turned off. In that state of helplessness, the only thing I could do was call the Buddha Master's attendant, Brother Kuan. I imposed upon Brother Kuan to report to the Buddha Master that Sister Hui-Hsiu Liu might pass away very soon. Brother Kuan reported to the Buddha Master that Sister Hui-Hsiu Liu from Seattle had already passed away. That took place on August 6th sometime after 5:00 in the morning. Scolding Brother Kuan, the Buddha Master said, "Nonsense. The time of her death that I arranged with the Buddhas and Bodhisattvas has not yet come. How, then, could student Hui-Hsiu Liu have passed away? That would be impossible." Brother Kuan then told the Buddha Master that he heard that information from me. Of course, Brother Kuan believed me since I was at the side of Sister Hui-Hsiu Liu. However, the Buddha Master, who was two thousand miles away from Seattle, scolded Brother Kuan for speaking nonsense, saying that the prearranged time for the Buddhas and Bodhisattvas to escort student Hui-Hsiu Liu away had not yet arrived and that student Hui-Hsiu Liu could therefore not have died.

Dharma Teachers and fellow students, how is it that the Buddha Master, who was two thousand miles away from Seattle, could have such confidence when His Holiness told Brother Kuan that Sister Hui-Hsiu Liu could not possibly have died? Dharma Teachers and fellow students, just what kind of a feat is that? Doesn't this once more clearly demonstrate what kind of a holy being our Buddha Master is? (Everybody replied: Amitabha!) The Buddha Master was 100% certain. His Holiness was absolutely sure. This proves that the Buddha Master communicated with Amitabha Buddha. Otherwise, how could the Buddha Master arrange for the Three Holy Ones

---

[1] Here and below the word *Buddha Master* refers to H.H. Dorje Chang Buddha III Wan Ko Yeshe Norbu Holiest Tathagata.

of the Western Paradise to escort Sister Hui-Hsiu Liu to the Pure Land after her death? The time of her death was prearranged long ago. Otherwise, how could the Buddha Master state with such certainty that the time of Sister Hui-Hsiu Liu's death had not yet come and that she could not possibly have already died? Fellow students, what if the Buddha Master's words turned out to be mistaken?

After 7:00 in the morning on August 6th, the Buddha Master telephoned the President of the International Buddhism Sangha Association, Venerable Dharma Teacher Long Hui. The Buddha Master told her to go to the temple immediately and formally announce to all of the temple's dharma teachers that they must at once travel to Seattle because student Hui-Hsiu Liu from Seattle will pass away that very day. The Buddha Master also solemnly declared, "However, she has not yet passed away."

I would like to ask everyone something. No mater how ignorant, stupid, or simple-mined we may be, we should understand something. After 5:00 in the morning on August 6th, Brother Kuan reported to the Buddha Master that Hui-Hsiu Liu had already passed away. Yet, the Buddha Master had Venerable Dharma Teacher Long Hui go to the temple to declare openly that student Hui-Hsiu Liu had not yet died but that she will die that very day. The Buddha Master also instructed the dharma teachers to take off for Seattle immediately in order to conduct ceremonies for the deceased. Dharma teachers and fellow students, what other master in the world today would dare openly and formally announce before the death of a disciple that such disciple will pass away that very day? Doesn't this clearly demonstrate to the people of the world that our Buddha Master represents the supreme and authentic dharma of the Buddhas? (They replied, "Yes! Yes!")

On July 7th, on behalf of my wife, Sister Hui-Hsiu Liu, I beseeched the Buddha Master to transmit dharma. From that day until August 6th, when Hui-Hsiu Liu passed away, thirty days passed. Everything that occurred during that thirty-day period could only be explained by the fact that the Buddha Master represents the supreme and authentic dharma of the Buddhas. I could not find another master in the entire world who could resolve all of my many doubts about the seemingly impossible things that occurred.

Everything that I have just described, as well as many things that occurred that I did not describe today, is true. All of these occurrences are factual. I, Mark Lin, am not the only one to have personally seen them take place. My three children, Yi-Chien Lin, Yi-Pei Lin, and Ye-Shan Lin, as well as my son-in-law Chris, were all present. If anything that I have just stated is false in the slightest, I am willing, together with my three children and son-in-law, to descend into the Vajra Hell realm with no chance of ever being released from there. (Everybody replied: Amitabha! Amitabha!) I am disciple Wu Dao. My Chinese secular name is Yung-Mao Lin. My English secular name is Mark Lin. I sincerely make this vow before the Three Jewels. Today is September 3rd, 2003.

Buddhist disciple
Mark Lin

(The above was excerpted by World Buddhism Publishing LLC and World Dharma Voice, Inc. from my recording on September 3, 2003.)

(This text was translated from the Chinese text that follows)

預知坐化安詳往升淨土

各位在座的法師、師兄、師姐，阿彌陀佛！

今天我說什麼呢，我只有感恩、感動跟激動，我怕我的激動會說不出我心裏的話，為了對因果負責，我寫了一張稿子。

首先我要再三再次的感謝我們偉大的佛陀上師老人家（即是三世多杰羌佛雲高益西諾布頂聖如來——編者注，下同），安排我內人劉惠秀師姐今年八月六日坐化圓寂往升淨土之大恩大德，真是粉身碎骨難以報答。今年七月七日我由西雅圖飛來洛杉磯，代我的內人劉惠秀師姐向老人家求法，承蒙老人家慈悲，清清楚楚並鄭重的告訴我：劉惠秀同學在修了這個法、套上種子字，保證一定坐化圓寂往升西方極樂世界，並且絕對的不會有疼痛。果不出佛陀上師所言，劉惠秀往升前連嗎啡都沒有用，並且毫無痛苦。劉惠秀師姐在八月六日上午五時許，由睡床坐起說她要走了，並且很從容的將她心愛的一隻小玩具布狗，擺到與劉惠秀師姐同一方向，而後盤上腿結上佛陀上師所傳的手印套上種子字，一直到當天上午九時五十五分往升。請問各位法師、師兄們，當今世界上或近代史上，有哪一位大師敢預先保證自己的弟子在修了自己所傳的法後，將如期的坐化圓寂呢？請問各位師兄這是什麼樣的概念呢？假若佛法是不實的，假若佛陀上師老人家的證量不能代表佛陀的話，那麼在癌症末期並且淋巴已經擴散到全身的劉惠秀，有可能從從容容地盤上腿結上手印，並告訴我們她要走了嗎？而後也就真如老人家預先的保證坐化圓寂嗎？這不正明明白白地告訴了我們：老人家預先的保證，劉惠秀師姐將坐化圓寂往升淨土是真實不虛的嗎？不也清清楚楚地告訴我們：偉大的佛陀上師是代表著偉大佛法的真正的佛陀嗎？（眾人：阿彌陀佛！）八月五日劉惠秀師姐情況危急，當時的情形在我及家人看起來確實很危急，但是佛陀上師老人家在電話上卻很果斷地告訴我說，劉惠秀同學今天晚上不會走，要走是明天的事了，你就放心的讓她睡。請問各位法師、師兄們，假若佛陀上師不是早已洞悉劉惠秀師姐往升的時辰，老人家豈會輕易的告訴我劉惠秀師姐今天晚上不會走了，讓她睡吧，這又是什麼概念呢？這不清清楚楚地擺明老人家是代表著偉大佛法的真正的佛陀嗎？八月五日，佛陀上師在電話中要我不要急，放心的讓劉惠秀師姐睡覺，當時我將手機擺到劉惠秀師姐的耳邊，讓她直接聽佛陀上師老人家在電話中的開示，隨後她就睡了，第二天，也就是八月六日往升當天的清晨三點多，醒過來告訴我們說，她去了一趟西方極樂世界，隨後，就再小睡到五時許，醒過來，丟下一句話說，她要走了，我們全家大小頓時焦急萬分，我試著打了佛陀上師的手機二、三十次，無奈老人家手機一直關機，在求助無門的情形下，只能打給老人家的侍者Kuan師兄，煩Kuan師兄轉告佛陀上師，劉惠秀師姐可能很快的就會走了，後來Kuan師兄向老人家報告，西雅圖劉惠秀師姐已經往升了，當時的時間大約在八月六日上午五點多，老人家當時訓了Kuan師兄：『胡說八道！跟佛菩薩約的時間還沒到，劉惠秀同學怎麼往升，不可能的！』，而Kuan師兄報告佛陀上師說，是我告訴他的，他當然相信在劉惠秀師姐身邊的我，但是遠在西雅圖兩千英哩外的佛陀上師卻訓了Kuan 師兄胡說八道，與佛菩薩約定來接劉惠秀同學的時間未到，劉惠秀同學不

可能走的。各位法師、師兄們，遠在西雅圖兩千英哩外的佛陀上師，為什麼會如此有把握地告訴Kuan師兄：劉惠秀同學不可能走的，各位法師、師兄們，這又是什麼一個概念呢？這不再度說明並清清楚楚的擺明：我們的佛陀上師，是什麼樣的聖德了嗎？！（眾人：阿彌陀佛！）老人家的把握是百分之百的，是絕對的，更擺明著老人家跟阿彌陀佛是相通的，要不然如何安排西方三聖來接引劉惠秀師姐往升淨土呢？往升的時間早就安排好了，不然，佛陀上師又如何敢如此肯定地說：時間沒到，劉惠秀同學不可能走的。各位師兄們，萬一老人家說錯了怎麼辦？八月六日上午七點多，佛陀上師電告國際佛教僧尼總會主席隆慧法師，即刻來到廟子正式向廟子的眾出家法師宣佈：『即刻啟程西雅圖，因為西雅圖劉惠秀同學今天將往升』，並鄭重的宣佈：『但是現在尚未往升』，請問世人，我們無論是多麼的愚痴，頭腦有多麼的笨，多麼的簡單，我們也該明白既然Kuan師兄在八月六日上午五點多，就已向佛陀上師彙報劉惠秀已經往升，而佛陀上師卻照常讓隆慧法師到廟上公開宣佈說：「劉惠秀同學現在還沒有往升，但今天會往升。」，並且派法師們立刻啟程去西雅圖主持往升儀式，請問各位法師、師兄們，當今世界上有哪一位大師，敢在弟子尚未往升就敢公眾地正式宣佈，宣告某某弟子今天就會往升呢？這不清清楚楚地告訴世人：我們的佛陀上師是代表著佛陀的最高正法嗎？（眾人：是啊！是啊！）我內人劉惠秀師姐在七月七日由我代向老人家求法的那一刻開始，到八月六日往升這三十天內，發生的點點滴滴，若不用佛陀上師他代表著佛陀的最高正法來解釋，來說明所發生的一切，那麼這世界上再也找不到有哪位大師，可以解答我心中許多認為不可能的疑惑。

　　以上我所說的一切並包括今天未提到的一切，都是事實，都是真實不虛的，不但是我悟道本人身歷其境，加上我三個小孩，林以倩，林以珮，林業善，及女婿Chris他們也都在場，我前面所說的一切，若有半點虛假不實，我願暨三個小孩及女婿全家五口，墮金剛地獄，永不得超生。（眾人：阿彌陀佛！阿彌陀佛！）弟子悟道，中文俗名林永茂，英文俗名Mark Lin，誠心摯誠起誓。2003年9月3日。

佛弟子　林永茂

(以上為全球佛教出版社暨世界法音出版社摘自林永茂居士本人2003年9月3日之實況錄音)

（此文的英文翻譯印在前面）

Karmic Affinity, Karmic Seeds, Elimination of Karmic Obstructions, and Cultivation Initiation

Buddhism has benefited countless living beings in our world. The clear perspective of Sakyamuni Buddha was "great compassion is the foundation, yet without karmic affinity the living being is not saved (liberated)." Actually, it is not that the living being is not saved. Rather, it is that without the karmic affinity to encounter the dharma, the living being cannot be saved or liberated. Thus, the learning of any Buddha-dharma involves the principle of karmic affinity. Karmic affinity is the seed of Buddhism. Having such a seed means having the karmic affinity to take up Buddhism. Lacking karmic affinity means lacking the seed necessary to take up the Buddha-dharma. That is why we often hear that the Buddha-dharma emphasizes karmic affinity.

Knowing how to view the karmic affinity of those who have begun learning Buddhism is the duty of the teacher. A teacher who is accomplished in the dharma can "see" whether a prospective disciple has the karmic affinity to learn the dharma from him or not. However, an ordinary teacher determines whether or not there is karmic affinity in a casual, non-thinking manner by uttering a few empty words. In this way, such a teacher accepts many disciples whether or not the teacher has karmic affinity with those disciples.

So many living beings have been confused in their search for a holy and virtuous master. There are those living beings who have spent their entire lives vigorously pursuing masters and knowledge, yet they have been unable to end the cycle of birth and death. From Chinese esoteric buddhism to Japanese esoteric Buddhism to Tibetan esoteric Buddhism and even to exoteric Buddhism, karmic affinity has been a matter of great confusion to everyone. The vast majority of living beings are in the dark with respect to this matter. But what are they to do? Who knows where karmic affinity lies? What is karmic affinity?

Actually, eminent monastics, especially eminent monastics who practice Tibetan esoteric Buddhism, attach great importance to karmic affinity. When a disciple begins to learn the Buddha-dharma, the master must determine whether there is karmic affinity between himself and the prospective disciple. If there is, he will accept the person as his disciple. If there is not, he will urge the person to go to another place.

Selection of karmic affinity is especially required when searching for a rinpoche who has reincarnated. Moreover, the Golden Vase Slip Selection ceremony must be performed in order to determine the true identity of a reincarnated great rinpoche. When the master performs an initiation for the disciple, the master must first eliminate the karmic obstructions of the disciple. The disciple is a dharma receptacle. Before the receptacle can be filled with dharma dew, it must be cleansed. This is what is meant by elimination of karmic obstacles.

For example, the method of first rinsing one's mouth with pure water signifies eliminating karmic obstructions. It is said that when the ancient holy Buddhas and Bodhisattvas eliminated the karmic obstructions of their disciples before performing an initiation, the disciples would sometimes spit out filthy, foul smelling water that was a manifestation of their karmic obstructions accumulated over eons. Thus, when great and holy dharma kings perform rituals to select karmic affinity and eliminate karmic obstructions, certain dharma principles need to be followed and true realization is often manifested.

Take, for example, the planting of karmic affinity through seed characters. The disciple secretly writes different numbers corresponding to different karmic affinity seeds on ten pieces of paper, each of which contains the Sanskrit character "Ah." These ten "Ah" characters (also called "same karmic affinity seeds") represent the ten stages to perfect enlightenment and the generation of all karmic affinity. The disciple then secretly rolls each piece of paper into a ball and puts them in a dharma container, which is sometimes a golden vase. At this time, even the disciple himself, who rolled up the balls of paper, is not able to recognize and pick out from that container any particular ball of paper. However, masters who represent the holy and virtuous Buddhas and Bodhisattvas already know the karmic affinity of the disciple. Some of those masters will predict which one of the balls of paper is the disciple's karmic affinity seed. They tell the disciple the number that corresponds to the ball of paper that the disciple will take out of the container. After that prediction is made, the disciple then takes a piece of paper out of the container. After checking the number that corresponds to that piece of paper, the disciple discovers that it is the exact number the master predicted. The disciple then again rolls the paper into a ball and puts it back into the dharma container. The dharma container is then shaken and the balls of paper are mixed up. The master then takes a ball of paper from the container and gives it to the disciple to open. The disciple then verifies that such piece of paper is the exact "seed" piece of paper he took out of the container a moment ago. There are even times when a ball of paper is taken out of the container a third time with the exact same results. Thus, the disciple's karmic affinity seed is established.

Only a master with the highest Buddha-dharma realization has such skills. It is difficult to find even one rinpoche among millions of rinpoches who can display such realization. Based on this holy dharma of karmic affinity, not only can the master clearly see the karmic affinity the disciple has with the Buddha-dharma, the disciple also can personally sees the karmic affinity he has with the Buddha-dharma. This is the highest selection of karmic affinity dharma, which is a great dharma. Practices that are on a lower level than this include using divinatory symbols, drawing slips after chanting sutra passages, and spinning roasted barley flour pills. With those practices, one is left to rely on faith since one does not see the display of true realization.

I had been in the dark about the selection of karmic affinity dharma for many years. What one sees is regarded as real. What one hears can not necessarily be regarded as true. No matter how great one's devoutness may be, it is still not the same as personally seeing such a real display of realization. To say that thoughts of such dharma never arose in my mind would be lying. In order to understand the selection of karmic affinity dharma, on many occasions I beseeched my magnificent Buddha Master, Dorje Chang Buddha III Wan Ko Yeshe Norbu Holiest Tathagata, to practice such dharma. Each time His Holiness said, "You have been here with me for over ten years. Without karmic affinity, how could you have been here for over ten years? The Buddha-dharma that you request is performed by great holy and virtuous beings. In today's world, it is difficult to find such a person of great holiness and virtue. I do not have the ability to perform that dharma. I only have a heart of humility."

Still, I deeply believed that my Buddha Master was certainly able to perform that dharma. If even His Holiness could not perform it, who could? I thought that my karmic conditions of good fortune had not yet matured. I believed that when the requisite karmic conditions existed, my Buddha Master would perform that fundamental dharma for me. Nonetheless, on each of the numerous times I requested that dharma, the Buddha Master said that He could not perform it. As time continued to pass, thoughts of seeking that dharma almost vanished from my mind.

Then came the spring of this year, with its sudden thunderclaps and fresh flowers bathing in the soft breeze. The lovely chirping of larks was like sweet and natural songs that brought back to life the seeds of the earth. I was finally able to step inside the auspicious tantric mandala. Because there was not a cloud in the blue sky that day, the sunshine was strong and dazzling. The minority of people sitting there on the ground in this open-air mandala were laypersons. The majority were rinpoches and dharma teachers. There were a few dozen people all together. Everyone was perspiring. The great dharma of karmic affinity selection that I had longed for was about to be performed.

The holy Buddha-dharma realization that was displayed truly opened my eyes. A stone house suddenly turned into an image of Dorje Chang Buddha, and I could no longer see that house. All of the dharma that I witnessed was amazing. What I have just stated is not an exaggeration in the slightest.

I used a white porcelain bowl that I brought with me from my home. After I washed it very clean, I poured tap water into it. I put into my mouth a mouthful of that tap water and rinsed my mouth with it. I then spit out half of it. What I spit out was clear and transparent. At that time, there was still some water in my mouth that I had not yet spit out. When I spit out the remaining water, it was as black as ink and foul-smelling. I was startled to see the black water that I had spit out.

I felt very moved. I vaguely remember that I cried like a little child. After the Buddha Master gave a discourse on the dharma, my tearful, shriveled face became like a blossoming flower. What remained were smiles and excitement. My negative karma had finally been made visible. The eyes of those in attendance glimmered with excitement and envy. My whole body

suddenly felt extremely relaxed, and all my physical ailments vanished. At that time, my whole mentality became like that of a young girl. The structure of my body completely changed.

I saw water spit out by rinpoches and dharma teachers whereby they got rid of karmic obstructions. Some spit out water that was brown and appeared like live, wriggling insects. Some spit out water that was orange, some spit out water that was gray, some spit out water that was dark blue, and some spit out water that was dark green. Since each person's karma was different, what they spit out was different.

The Buddha Master then said, "It is strange. Why have all of you spit out such things? What have you added into the water?" Everyone responded by saying that the water was tap water that they themselves poured into the bowl and that they did not add anything to the water. The Buddha Master then said, "Do not be attached to this. Do not be attached to this. Do not think that the spitting out of water with a little color means that all of your karmic obstructions have been thoroughly eliminated. To truly and thoroughly eliminate karmic obstructions, you must practice the dharma of "What Is Cultivation?" that I have taught."

I now deeply understand that the Buddha-dharma is just that direct and that the magnificent Buddhas are just that selfless. The magnificent selection of karmic affinity dharma truly exists in this world! I personally experienced and saw the magnificent dharma to eliminate karmic obstructions! The phenomena that occurred during that ceremony occurred without any intent on my part. Today I make the following vow to the heavens: If what I have stated is false, may I descend into hell or become an animal without ever being raised to a higher realm of existence. If what I have stated is true, may I become accomplished in the dharma as soon as possible and benefit all living beings.

Respectfully written by Buddhist disciple
Huei Chin Yang

(This is a complete translation of the Chinese text that follows originally written and signed by Huei Chin Yang.)

緣 起 、 種 子 、 除 障 、 修 行 的 灌 頂

佛教在我們這個世界上利益了無量無邊眾生，釋迦佛陀有明確的觀點即「大悲為本、無緣不渡」。其實這個觀點不是不渡，而是沒有緣法就渡不了，因此在佛教裡要學任何佛法，都牽涉到一個原則「緣」字，「緣」成了佛教的種子。有了種子即具備了學佛的緣起，而沒有緣起則意味著沒有佛法的種子。因此我們常聽到佛法重緣起，要怎麼樣來看待學佛入門人的緣起，就成了做教授師長的任務了。成就者教授師長，他們會「看到」弟子是有緣還是無緣；而普通師長只有「順口緣」了，這樣的有緣無緣就是他一句空話，隨口說說湊數。多少眾生為尋求聖德之師而迷離顛倒，乃至終身窮追究學，不得了生脫死，

從唐代的佛法到東密、藏密，乃至顯教，無所不為其緣而困惑，眾生大多處於迷罐之中，可是這有什麼辦法呢！誰又知道緣起何在？何者為緣？

其實在佛教的高僧裡面，尤其是藏密高僧中，他們對緣起是非常注重，首先在弟子入門時，他必須看有沒有緣，有緣才收你為徒，無緣勸其另走他鄉。尤其在尋找轉世活佛時是必須通過擇緣的，大活佛還要經金瓶擇籤決定法緣真身，而在為弟子灌頂時，他們必須要先除障。弟子就是一個法器，盛法露之前首先必須得將法器清洗乾淨，這稱之為除障。如先用清水嗽口也意味著除障，據說，古聖佛菩薩們在

弟子舉行灌頂之前除障時,有時會見到弟子吐出身上累劫所積業障化顯的污臭之水,所以往往我們看到大聖法王們為弟子舉行擇緣和除障時有原則的儀軌,證量的展現。比如,以種子字種緣起,由弟子將代表十地圓通生發萬緣的十個「啊」字(亦名「同緣種子」)由弟子親自在暗地裡畫上記號打成圓團,放在法桶或金瓶中,此時連打團的本人想找出來那一粒來也無法,而代表聖德佛菩薩的師長,他們能知道你的緣起,有的還先預示,然後由弟子將從中抓出一顆核對準確無誤,此時再打成團放入法桶中,經搖動混合,由師長伸手取出一顆交由弟子打開,經核對是同一種子,乃至還第三次再取出核對無誤,於是緣起種子建立,這是最上乘的佛法境界才能得到的,百千萬仁波且中難有一人能施展此種證量。此聖法因緣不但做師長的明白看到弟子與佛法的緣起,而且弟子親身經歷、親眼看到他與佛法的緣起關係,這是最高的大法擇緣。再次一等的修為,就是採取打卦或誦經修法抽籤再看或轉糌巴丸的辦法,這一種法務祇能抱著一個「信」字,是沒有辦法看到證量的。

但是對於擇緣的法,多少年來本人也是像坐在迷罐中一樣。眼見為實,耳聽為虛,虔誠心再大,那畢竟沒有見識過,非現量的概念。要說不在腦海中浮動,那無非是騙人的假話,為了想了解擇緣的法,我向我偉大的佛陀上師多杰羌佛第三世雲高益西諾布頂聖如來祈請過很多次,每次他都說:「你都來我這裡十幾年了,如果沒有緣,你怎麼會在這裡十幾年呢?你要求的佛法是大聖德們作的,現在世界上都難找到這種聖德了,我沒有這本事,我祇有慚愧。」我深信我的佛陀上師絕對能修這個法,如果他老人家都不能做這件事,那還有誰能做!我以為我的福報因緣還沒到,我相信總有一天因緣具足時,佛陀上師會為我修這個根本法的。但次數要求多了,而每次佛陀上師都說:他做不了。時間拖長了,求法的念頭幾乎在我腦海裡抹去。

可是就隨著那一聲春雷乍響,和風浴沐的鮮花,洗耳鳴啼的百靈,以婉曲自如的歌喉,讓大地禾苗萌芽復甦了。我終於步進了瑞祥的密乘壇場,由於當天萬里藍天無雲太陽放射出強力耀眼的光芒,坐

在大地露天壇城的有少部份居士,大部分是仁波且和法師們,共有幾十人,大家身體都流著汗,我朝思暮念的擇緣大法舉行了。是如法神聖的證量讓我開了眼,茅棚石屋突然變成了一座多杰羌佛的法像,石屋不見了,法義上的一切,就是那麼了不起,我前面的語言一點也沒有誇張。我用我自己從家中帶去的白磁缽,將它沖洗的一乾二淨,裝上自來水,我準備漱口喝進一口自來水,吐出了一半,清涼透明,這時我口中還有一部份未完全吐完,當我再吐出口中餘下的水時,就黑如墨汁,其臭難聞,這黑水從我口中突然吐出真是嚇了一跳,心中一陣激動,矇朧中記得我已哭成肉人兒了,經佛陀上師一陣開示的法語後,我的苦瓜臉變成了桑巴花兒,這時餘下的是笑容和興奮,我的黑業終於見天了,在場的人眼中閃爍著激動和羨慕的光芒。我的身體突然輕鬆無比,身上各種病態現象不翼而飛,這時我變成了少女般的心態,身體的結構全變了。

我看到了其他仁波且和法師們除的障業,有褐色像蟲子一樣似乎有生命在蠕動,有橙黃色的,有灰色的,有深藍色的,有碧綠色的,各自的業相不同,他們吐出的都不同。佛陀上師說:「奇怪了,你們為甚麼吐出這些東西來?你們放進什麼東西了嗎?」大家都說完全是自己打的自來水,什麼也沒有放過。佛陀上師說:『不要執著,不要執著,不要以為吐出了點顏色就消了業障,真正要徹底消業障,要修我傳的「什麼叫修行」。』我深深明白一個道理:佛法就是這麼直接,偉大的佛陀就是這麼無我。偉大的擇緣法在這個世界上就是真實不虛!偉大的除障法我經歷並且看到了!這就是真正在無意間發生的現象!我對天發誓,如我所說的是假的,我將墮地獄變成畜牲,不得超生,如我所說的是事實,我將儘快成就,利益一切眾生。

佛弟子楊慧君恭撰

(此文的英文翻譯印在前面)

Not Being Affected by Any Damaging Substance in the World

From left to right: Jian Hui Shih, Zheng Hui Shih

We have been following H.H. Dorje Chang Buddha III for many years. Although our self-cultivation has not been fruitful, we have gained some insight into the saying "Not being affected by any damaging substance in the world." After all, we have witnessed many holy feats while following H.H. Dorje Chang Buddha III.

One day fellow disciples Mark Lin from Seattle and Ming-Chi Wei from Thailand had an audience with our Buddha Master, H.H. Dorje Chang Buddha III, and requested to participate in a project at His Holiness's mandala. The Buddha Master told them, "In consideration of your level of realization and the condition of your health, you will not be able to handle the work at the mandala." The laymen respectfully asked, "Those bukkhunis can do it even though they are thin and petite. Why can't we?" H.H. Dorje Chang Buddha III expounded, "You are no comparison to them. They have no problems with it because they are immune to the influence of the damaging substances. This mandala has an extremely powerful force and a form of gas so strong that the two of you will not be able to handle it in the physical conditions of ordinary beings."

It turned out that layman Lin and layman Wei purchased complete sets of protective gear covering them from head to toe. They tried them on, showed them to the Buddha Master and said, "We need not fear now. We are under the full armor protection so that even poison gas will have no effect on us." The Buddha Master grinned and said, "The ones who really don't need to fear are these petite disciples of mine. You won't make it. You would be like dough men who couldn't survive even wind and waves, not to mention the powerful force of the mandala. In two days, we will have two generals with big heads, huge ears and eyes that barely open." The two fellow laymen told us, "How can it be possible? You have been following the Buddha Master for so long and never had problems at the mandala. Could it be that we are really terrible?"

The next day, there were more than ten of us entering the mandala. As predicted, the two laymen's faces started to deform after they worked at the mandala. Their ears became huge, their mouths were shifted in place and their entire facial features were deformed. In less than three days, their heads and faces had grown by one-third, their eyes were too swollen to open, and they could barely see where they were going. They could even hardly recognize the people standing in front of them. Their body and facial features had totally deformed. The outcome was totally as predicted by H.H. Dorje Chang Buddha III. Two big-head generals had appeared. Layman Wei said, "This is truly a 'personal reformation'!" Nevertheless, all of us who have been cultivating ourselves around the Buddha Master turned out to be safe. The two laymen had full protective gear on including gas masks. On the other hand, what

we put on was the most basic and simple things. However, the Five Skandas and the demonic hindrance of poison gas had no effect on us at all. Those of us who have followed the Buddha Master closely in self-cultivation are truly different from others. This is a true account of what we have witnessed first hand and how we personally experienced the so-called "not being affected by any damaging substance in the world."

Buddhist disciples,
Jian Hui Shih
Zheng Hui Shih

The words stated above are what we personally experienced at the vajra mandala. Everything stated is true. If what we stated is false, we will forever not become accomplished and will receive bad karmic retribution. If what we stated is true, we will dedicate the resulting merit to all living beings in six realms that they soon become accomplished and liberated

Buddhist disciples,
Mark Lin
Ming-Chi Wei

(This is a complete translation of the Chinese text that follows originally written and signed by Jian Hui Shih, Zheng Hui Shih, Mark Lin, and Ming-Chi Wei.)

A recent photograph of Mark Lin on the left and Ming-Chi Wei on the right.
左為Mark Lin、右為魏銘琦之近照

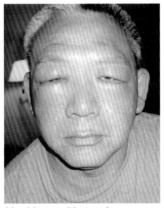

Unable to withstand awesome vajra power in the mandala, the head of Ming-Chi Wei becomes larger and his facial features change.
在壇場無法承受金剛威力，頭形變大，五官變形的魏銘琦

三 毒 水 泡 虛 出 沒 　五 陰 浮 雲 任 去 來

在三世多杰羌佛身邊這麼多年，雖然修行不怎麼樣，但對三毒水泡虛出沒，五陰浮雲任去來，倒有一點點的體會，畢竟在三世多杰羌佛身邊，我們親見的聖蹟太多了。

有一天西雅圖Mark Lin師兄與泰國魏銘琦師兄到佛陀恩師處要求參加壇城工作，我們恩師三世多杰羌佛對他們開示說：「壇場的工作，你們沒辦法做的，無論是道量、還是身體都還不行。」，師兄們恭敬地說：「她們幾個出家人這麼瘦小都行，難道我們不行嗎？」三世

多杰羌佛開示說：「你們不能跟她們比，她們沒問題的，她們對三毒之力已有降伏力，這個壇場的威力太強大，有一種無法抵禦的氣體，你們兩位凡胎之體是沒法招架的。」結果Mark師兄與魏師兄去買了整套的防備用具，從頭武裝到腳，然後在佛陀老人家面前展示並且說：「我們現在不怕了，毒瓦斯都無奈何我們，已經全副武裝了！」佛陀老人家聽了笑笑說：「真正不怕的是我這幾個小徒弟，你們不行的，麵人一個，禁不起風吹浪打，更何況壇場威力，等兩天就會看到兩個大

頭、大耳、瞇縫眼將軍！」兩位師兄當時對我們說：「怎麼可能嘛，你們跟了這麼久，隨時進壇場，一點事都沒有，難道我們就這麼差勁嗎？」第二天，我們十幾個人一起進了壇場，果然在壇場服務後，兩位師兄的臉開始變形，耳朵變大，嘴巴也挪位，整個五官都扭曲了，不到三天的時間，頭、臉整整大了三分之一，眼睛瞇成了一條縫，幾乎看不到路，就連站在眼前的是誰，都快無法辨認，整個身體五官全變形了，這一事實與三世多杰羌佛所言完全相同，兩個大頭將軍出現了，魏師兄說：「這一次真的是革面洗心了！」，而我們這些在佛陀恩師身邊修行的人，卻完全平安無事，兩位師兄還戴了防毒面具，全副武裝，而我們用的卻是最簡陋的裝作而已，但是五陰浮雲、毒氣魔障在我們面前一點也沒有作用，我們在佛陀恩師身邊修煉確實與一般人不同，這是我們在現場參與、親身經歷「什麼叫做三毒水泡虛出沒」的事實。

佛弟子　釋見慧

釋見慧

釋正慧

釋正慧

以上文字記載完全是我們親身在金剛壇場的遭遇，一切所言真實不虛，如打妄語，將永不得成就，遭受惡果報，如一切屬實，願將功德迴向給有情六道眾生，早得成就解脫。

佛弟子　Mark Lin

Mark Lin

魏銘琦

魏銘琦

（此文的英文翻譯印在前面）

A Drowned Bee Grew a Wing and Flew Away

From left to right: Ding Hui Shih, Guang Hui Shih

One afternoon when passing by the side of a swimming pool, I discovered a drowned bee in the pool. I scooped it up and placed it on the ground. Its body had already become stiff with death. The Buddha Master walked over and compassionately chanted several mantras and empowered the bee. In about two minutes, astonishingly, the bee began to move its legs. But, it was found that one side of the bee's wings had been bitten off, perhaps by another animal, causing it to fall into the pool and drown. Only one side of wings remained on the bee. At that moment, Sister Guang Hui heard about this and rushed over to see what was happening. H.H. Dorje Chang Buddha III talked to himself and said, "Alas! Now, you have been brought back to life but with one side of wings missing. That is too pitiful! What can be done about this? It's too sad! Too sad! It would be good if another side of wings grew!" Just as the dharma words of the Buddha Master were spoken, miraculously, we suddenly saw the bee grow another wing! Sister Guang Hui and I were totally surprised and stunned. At that time, we watched the bee stretch and move its wings a few times. Then, it cleaned it legs with its mouth and flapped both pairs of wings. About half a minute later, it flew away just like a helicopter. We were so touched that we prostrated to the Buddha Master right on the spot. The Buddha Master said, "It has nothing to do with me. I do not have such merit. This is your accomplishment. It's yours! It's yours!" We have, once again, personally witnessed the state of realization and awesome virtue of the authentic Buddha.

I am a nun. All of what is stated above is true and real. If anything is false, may I descend to the hell of endless suffering, never to be raised up again. If what I stated is true, may the merits be dedicated to all living beings.

Buddhist disciple
Ding Hui Shih

All of the above written by Sister Ding Hui regarding the situation about the bee and what I have witnessed are entirely true. If any of it is false, may I descend to the vajra hell and never attain accomplishment. If what I state is true, may I definitely attain accomplishment in this lifetime, be liberated from the cycle of birth and death, and save living beings.

Buddhist disciple
Guang Hui Shih

(This is a complete translation of the Chinese text that follows originally written and signed by Ding Hui Shih and Guang Hui Shih.)

淹死的蜜蜂長起翅膀飛走了

一個下午我經過了泳池邊，發現了一隻淹死的蜜蜂，打撈起來放在地板上，它身體已僵硬死掉了，佛陀上師走過來慈悲地持誦幾句咒語，加持它，大概兩分鐘蜜蜂竟然從腳開始動起來，但是卻發現大概蜜蜂是被別的動物咬斷了一只翅膀而掉進泳池淹死的，只留下了一只翅膀，當時廣慧師姐聽到了也趕過來看。三世多杰羌佛自言自語地說：「唉！既然活過來了，少了一只翅膀，那就太可憐了！怎麼辦呢？太慘！太慘！再長一翅膀就好了！」佛陀上師法語剛落下，突然看到，天啊！蜜蜂的另一只翅膀長出來了！我與廣慧師姐簡直是驚呆了，當時看著蜜蜂展動了幾下翅膀，用嘴巴清理足和翩動雙翅，大概半分鐘，就像直昇機一般飛走了，我們感動得就地向佛陀上師頂禮，佛陀上師卻說：「這與我無關，我哪裡有這功德，是你們的成就，是你們，是你們！」這是我們再一次親眼見到真正佛陀的證量威德展現。

我是一位出家人，以上所說一切真實不虛，若有虛假，願墮無間地獄，永不超生，若真實不虛，功德迴向法界一切眾生。

佛弟子　釋定慧

定慧師姐以上所寫蜜蜂的情況和我所看到的一切全屬實，若有虛假，願墮金剛地獄，永不成就；如果我說的話是真實的，今生我一定成就，了脫生死渡眾生。

佛弟子　釋廣慧

（此文的英文翻譯印在前面）

Buddha Agreed That I Stay

I have followed H.H. Dorje Chang Buddha III Wan Ko Yeshe Norbu Holiest Tathagata for almost six years. For the past two years, the Buddha Master transmitted to me the Green Tara Dharma and the Pure Land Dharma Method. This Pure Land Dharma Method whereby Amitabha Buddha's name is continually recited includes a secret mudra (symbolic hand gesture).

Mentioning this secret mudra reminded me of layman Yu-Shan Hou. I attended the ceremony during which he passed on to the Western Paradise of Ultimate Bliss. That he passed on to the Western Paradise of Ultimate Bliss was a sure thing. He most certainly would pass on to that paradise! That is because the dharma that he learned is the true great dharma relating to reciting Amitabha Buddha's name taught by my Buddha Master. There is a special mudra connected with that dharma. I say that he most certainly would pass on to the Western Paradise of Ultimate Bliss because I myself personally experienced such a thing.

During these years of following the Buddha Master, I and other Sisters have been at the Buddha Master's side when His Holiness created works of art. One day the Buddha Master encouraged us to sculpt and create works of art. I had some understanding of what this would entail, having been at the side of the Buddha Master during his creation of art. Through constant observation, the Buddha Master's creative ways, such as sculpting, digging, and applying color, had an imperceptible influence on me. Although I did not have the slightest painting or sculpting foundation, the Buddha Master's encouragement gave me great empowerment. As soon as I had any spare time, I worked on my artwork with much zeal and happiness.

After I finished the sculpture "Hard Boulder Emanates Splendor," I sat down and silently appreciated it. I was both happy and satisfied. In an instant, my mind became tranquil. I wanted to enter a state of great concentration. Unexpectedly, I entered perfect stillness of the mind (nirvana). I had not realized that becoming accomplished spiritually is so closely connected with everyday life.

At that time, the sky was green and red light. I was immersed in the light. I thought, "Yes! Perfection! This is perfection! Recite Amitabha Buddha's name!" I put my hands in that mudra and chanted Namo (Homage to) Amitabha Buddha, beseeching Amitabha Buddha to come and

This is where Dharma Teacher Liao Hui Shih sat after she finished sculpting her work of art. There on that bench, she passed away in a state of liberation. This photograph is a re-creation of her sitting on the bench.
這是釋了慧法師將她的作品刻完後，坐在凳上圓寂時的地方，這張照片是現在後補所照當時的情況

escort me away.

After some time, Amitabha Buddha truly arrived. Ah! He came. He truly came. I cannot describe how dignified He looked. I extended my arm in order to grab the hand of Amitabha Buddha, and one of my feet was about to step onto His lotus flower pedestal. Right at this time, the Buddha Master rushed over. I heard the Buddha Master say to Amitabha Buddha, "Buddha! Do not hurry to escort her away. Do not hurry to escort her away. Allow her to stay. She still has many things to do!"

At this time, Amitabha Buddha withdrew His lotus flower pedestal. He smiled and put me back onto my original place. This is how it came to be that I stayed. However, my body was totally immobile because I had died. Still, I could hear the sound of the Buddha Master reciting mantras. The Sisters said that at that time my entire body was rigid, cold, and heavy—that is, I was dead.

The Buddha Master bestowed upon me great empowerment. His Holiness obtained the consent of Amitabha Buddha. At that time, there were two cylindrical white lights whose light surrounded and enveloped me. My spirit then returned to my dead body, and my body temperature become warmer.

We used to ordinarily address H.H. Dorje Chang Buddha III as the Buddha Master. However, the Buddha Master did not like it when we addressed His Holiness as Buddha Master. His Holiness has repeatedly admonished us not to address His Holiness as the Buddha Master. His Holiness very humbly stated that His Holiness is very ordinary and that His Holiness is a practitioner with a heart of humility. But in our hearts and minds, His Holiness indeed is a Buddha. If His Holiness is not a Buddha, why is it that each person to whom His Holiness transmits dharma becomes accomplished in the dharma? If His Holiness is not a Buddha, why is it that many highly virtuous Bodhisattvas in the world are his disciples? There are so many examples of people whom His Holiness enabled to become accomplished in the dharma. Recent examples include laypeople Yu-Shan Hou, Hui-Hsiu Lin Liu, and Tsai-Chun Yu Lin. Examples from earlier time periods are too numerous to mention. There are disciples of the Buddha Master who have passed away in the meditation posture having attained liberation from the cycle of birth and death. There are disciples whose passing was accompanied by the appearance of various auspicious phenomena. There are disciples who transformed into rainbow light when passing away. There are disciples who left behind sariras (holy relics) or seed syllables after cremation, and so on.

If the Buddha Master is not a Buddha, how is it that I stayed on earth even though Amitabha Buddha wanted to escort me away to the Western Paradise of Ultimate Bliss? I, an incompetent person, suddenly attained skills relating to the craftsmanship vidya, thereby creating the sculpture mentioned earlier. No wonder the Buddha Master inscribed on that sculpture, "Hard Boulder Emanates Splendor."

My Buddha Master is not only my Buddha Master, but His Holiness is truly the highest ancient Buddha in the dharma realm. His Holiness is the ultimate one that holy and ordinary beings can depend on.

Buddhist disciple,
Liao Hui Shih

(This is a complete translation of the Chinese text that follows originally written and signed by Liao Hui Shih.)

佛 陀 同 意 我 留 下 來

　　跟隨多杰羌佛第三世雲高益西諾布頂聖如來佛陀上師快六年了，這兩年，佛陀上師傳了我綠度母法，也傳了我淨土法門，這個淨土法門念佛號是有秘密手印的。

　　說到這個秘密手印呢，就想起侯欲善居士，我是參加了他的往升儀式的，他能往升西方極樂世界是理所當然的事，是一定會往升的嘛！因為他學的法，正是我的佛陀上師所傳的真正念佛大法，有專門的手印的。說他必然往升，是因為我本人也是親身經歷了的。

　　我跟隨佛陀上師的這幾年，當佛陀上師做作品的時候，我與師姐們時常在身邊的。有一天，佛陀上師鼓勵我們也雕塑創作，跟在老人家身邊看著，老人家做啊，雕呀，挖的，塗啊，耳濡目染，心裏有些體會，雖然生平一點兒都沒有繪畫雕刻的基礎，但老人家的鼓勵給了我無限的加持，一有空閒我就在作品上下功夫，我是很投入的，心裏很喜悅。

　　當『頑石生華』這個作品完成後，我坐下來靜靜觀賞，既高興又滿足，剎那間，心寂靜下來，我想來一個大定吧！誰知竟入了寂滅定，真沒想到，道業的成就是這樣緊密聯繫在日常生活裏的。

　　那時，虛空都是綠色和紅顏色的光，我與光匯在一起，我心想，是的！圓滿！這是圓滿了！念佛吧！我結上手印，稱念南無阿彌陀佛，祈求阿彌陀佛來接我。

　　隔了些時，阿彌陀佛真的來了，啊呀！來了，真的來了，太莊嚴了，無法寫出來！我伸手要抓住阿彌陀佛的手，另一隻腳要踏上蓮花的時候，佛陀上師趕到，我聽到佛陀上師的聲音給阿彌陀佛說：「佛陀啊！別忙接走，別忙接走，留下她，還有很多事要做呢！」此時阿彌陀佛把蓮花收起來了，笑笑把我放到原位。就這樣，我留了下來，可是身體不能動，因為我已經死了，但能聽到佛陀上師唸咒的聲音，師姐們說，當時我全身僵硬，冰冷，沉重，就是死人一個。

　　佛陀上師為我做了大加持，通達了佛陀同意，當時有兩道圓柱形的白光，罩在我四周，我身上，我的魂才歸了屍體，我的體溫才溫暖過來。

因為我們平常都稱三世多杰羌佛為佛陀上師，可是佛陀上師不喜歡我們稱他為佛陀上師，一再告誡我們不要稱他佛陀上師。如果不是佛陀，哪能傳的佛法個個成就呢？又為什麼世界上的大德菩薩很多都是他的弟子呢？成就的人太多，近的有侯欲善、林劉惠秀、余林彩春居士，早期的更不用說了，有坐化的、有現各種瑞相的、有虹化的、有燒出舍利子的、現種子字的等等。

不是佛陀，怎麼阿彌陀佛都已經要把我接走了，而佛陀上師一句話就把我留了下來，像我這樣駑鈍的質材，竟然也能爆發工巧明，作

出這樣一件作品，難怪佛陀上師在石上題曰：「頑石生華」。我的佛陀上師不僅是我一個人的佛陀上師，更是實實在在的法界的最高古佛！是所有聖凡兩眾的最終依怙！

佛弟子　釋了慧

釋了慧

（此文的英文翻譯印在前面）

Reborn in the Western Paradise of Ultimate Bliss

One day in March of 2003, my mother became ill with something like a stroke. She couldn't move the right side of her body nor could she talk. At the emergency room, the diagnosis was that she was in the last stages of an inoperable brain cancer with a tumor the size of a fist. Unfortunately chemotherapy was not an option. She had about a zero chance of being cured with radiation treatments. We were told to take her home for hospice care for her final days. We were all very panicky and very sad with the anticipation of having to watch our mother wait for her death.

At that time, I kept praying that my mother could have the opportunity to see the Buddha Master, H.H. Wan Ko Yeshe Norbu Holiest Tathagata. The Buddha Master was merciful, and the arrangements were made for the Buddha Master to see my mother immediately.

I remember that day very clearly. At the altar, my mother was anxious and crying because she had lost her ability to speak, but the Buddha Master said, "It's alright, it's alright. I understand it all." The Buddha Master accepted my mother as a disciple and also transmitted dharma to her right then and there. That day, my mother couldn't talk nor do the mudra because her right hand was paralyzed. I remember that the merciful Buddha Master came down from the platform, held her good left hand, and personally put the Cultivation Seed Syllables on the palm of her left hand. That particular scene is deeply imprinted in my mind. That's the empowerment a Buddha gives to a suffering living being. I was deeply moved and even more grateful to my Buddha Master, although the Buddha Master does not allow his disciples to call him Buddha. Nevertheless, His Holiness is a true ancient Buddha who has descended into this world.

With all that happened at the altar that day, my mother used her eyes to communicate with the Buddha Master. My father and 4th eldest sister were also there, but they didn't seek refuge with the Buddha Master at that time. After we went back home, my mother looked at the palm of her left hand everyday and studied it very hard. She would look at the palm of her hand even at night when the light was not on. (During the more than six months from the time my mother fell ill until the time of her rebirth in a Buddha Land, she did not take one painkiller. She lived three months longer than the

doctor had predicted.)

Early in the morning, three days before her 70th birthday, my mother's condition turned worse. She became unconscious. Her whole body was twitching. The paralyzed right side was stiff and un-bendable. She had rapid breathing and an increased heart rate with her blood pressure dropping. Both the doctor and the nurse notified us to prepare for the end and dress her properly for the funeral. It was unbearable to see my eighty-year-old father so sad. The whole family was nervous and confused.

The first thing in my mind was to beg the Buddha Master to be merciful and send mother to a good place. The Buddha Master made time in a very busy schedule to receive my father and me. It was already eleven o'clock at night. My father begged the Buddha Master to allow for mother to have her 70th birthday before she left us, and also for both of her daughters to have time to come back from the east coast to see their mother for the last time. The Buddha Master said very decidedly, "No problem! Let her have her 70th birthday before she leaves! I think Guan-Yin Bodhisattva will let her stay for a few more days before receiving her to the Western Paradise of Ultimate Bliss! I am ashamed to say that I don't have that kind of dharma power to keep her. Only the Buddha can help her."

Right away the Buddha Master empowered a Mantra Wheel and Dharma Instructions, instructing us to have my mother wear the Mantra Wheel on her head to shake her spiritual mind. The Dharma Instruction would be for her to wear at the time of her passing on to the Pure Land, using the power of the Seed Syllables to enter the Western Paradise of Ultimate Bliss.

After we went back, my mother's pupils were already dilated, and her body temperature was low. She passed away. We followed the instructions we received from the Buddha Master and put the Mantra Wheel on my mother's head, feeling very scared. My mother had already left. Was it too late for her to wear the Mantra Wheel now? Unexpectedly, a miracle happened. Within only two short hours, mother regained consciousness. Her pupils, body temperature, and breathing all became normal. She answered some of our questions by nodding, shaking, and moving her head and by blinking her eyes. Her consciousness was completely clear and normal. Not only did my mother wait until both of my sisters came back from the east coast to celebrate her 70th birthday, but days after that, mother would sit in a wheelchair, using her unparalyzed left hand to offer incense to the Buddha.

Many monastics were there to witness the process of mother's revival. My aunt, who had been there nursing my mother, was deeply shocked and realized how great and powerful the true Buddha-dharma is. Furthermore, it changed my father, who has been a Christian for the past fifty years. He became a disciple of the Buddha Master.

Only after my mother was lingering in her sick bed and had started to accumulate phlegm in her throat, and my father could feel that my mother was suffering from the phlegm collecting in her throat, did he kneel down in front of the picture of the Buddha Master, silently begging the Buddha Master to ask Guan-Yin Bodhisattva to come and receive mother in the Western Paradise of Ultimate Bliss to enjoy the blessings! As expected, at 6:50 early next morning, my mother left peacefully with her mouth open like a sleeping baby. A message was relayed that morning from the Buddha Master's attendant Kuan that the Buddha Master would use the most profound and wonderful Pure Land spirit-raising Dharma to raise my mother's spirit from suffering and would respectfully ask Guan-Yin Bodhisattva or her attendants to receive mother to the Western Paradise of Ultimate Bliss within seven days. I was all very grateful for the Buddha Master's empowerment to send my mother to the Western Paradise. Not only were her face and lips rosy, her limbs were also soft so that the task of dressing her properly for the funeral was easy.

However, the most amazing thing was when I knelt in front of my mother's body that day and said, "Mom, if you have seen Guan-Yin Bodhisattva or the attendants sent by her with the message that they are coming to receive you, please close your mouth and smile so we don't have to worry." I kowtowed three times to thank my mother for all the years she spent raising me, knelt in front of her bed, and silently recited Guan-Yin Bodhisattva's sacred name. I lost track of time. My mother had been like a sleeping baby with her mouth opened, but now her mouth was closed and she was smiling. Wow! My heavens! I was shocked. I thought my eyes were deceiving me, that I'd made a mistake. I hurried and asked my family to come and see. Everyone saw the same thing I did—that she will be received by Guan-Yin Bodhisattva or her attendants in the Western Paradise of Ultimate Bliss.

At that time, there were birds singing very beautiful tunes outside the window, just as described in the sutras. Normally, there is no bird around or near the house. That day, the recorder suddenly played Guan-Yin Bodhisattva's sacred name automatically. All of these remarkable auspicious events brought tears of excitement to two of my aunts who were taking care of mother at that time and who were also cultivating themselves as Buddhists. They said, "We have been doing our cultivation all these years, but now we have seen what is called the true Buddha-dharma." Because of mother's ascent and her rebirth in that Buddha Land, they kept asking us to take them to the Buddha Master to seek refuge.

Imagine what level of realization a holy reincarnated being has in order to be able to communicate with Buddhas and Bodhisattvas and ask Buddhas and Bodhisattvas to call back my mother from death, allow her to stay many days, and come and arrange to have her received as desired. That can only be done by a Buddha! The fact that my mother passed away, came back to life, and ascended to the Western Paradise of Ultimate Bliss after her 70th birthday is only a very small and ordinary case among all of the Buddha Master's many disciples. There are too many other examples to mention concerning all the other disciples who attained accomplishment, became liberated and ascended to the Pure Land.

Many disciples have only seen the Buddha Master once and received transmission of the Buddha-dharma, such as fellow disciple Yu-Shan Hou. He practiced the dharma that the Buddha Master transmitted to him and was able to visit the Western Paradise of Ultimate Bliss. He came back to tell everybody that he would pass on to the Western Paradise of Ultimate Bliss seven days later. As he predicted, he passed on to the Western Paradise on a lotus seven days later.

Buddhist disciple
Ruei-Chi Yu

(This is a complete translation of the Chinese text that follows originally written and signed by Ruei-Chi Yu.)

死而復生至極樂

2003年3月中的某一天，母親疑似急性中風，突然右半身不能動彈，不能言語，送急診室，未料檢查出來結果是腦癌末期，腫瘤有拳頭般大小，醫生說不能開刀，不能化療，化療治癒機會幾乎零，醫院勸說家屬將母親領回家做人生最後日子的安寧看護，當時全家聽了陷入一片恐慌的悲哀，那是一種母親等死的恐懼。

當時我不斷地祈求母親能得見至尊的佛陀上師——雲高益西諾布頂聖如來一面，佛陀上師非常慈悲，不但答應了，還馬上安排接見。

那天在壇場的情況我記得非常清楚，母親一進入壇場，由於不能說話，急得哭出來，只聽佛陀上師說：「不說了！不說了！我都明白

了！」那天佛陀上師當場收母親為弟子，還傳了法，由於母親右半身癱瘓，又說不出話，還無法結手印，我記得佛陀上師慈悲地從法台上走下來，親自握著母親未癱瘓的左手，將修法種子字套在母親的左手心上，那一幕深印在我八識田裡，那是一位佛陀對一個受苦的眾生發大悲心的加持，我真的深受感動，更感恩我的佛陀上師，儘管他老人家不准弟子喊他老人家為佛陀，但是他老人家是真正的古佛降世。那天在壇場的種種情景，母親用眼神跟佛陀上師溝通，當時在場的還有父親與四姐，那時他們都還未皈依，回去之後，母親每天望著左手掌心精進用功，連漆黑未開燈的夜晚都盯著手心不放。(母親從發病到往

升的這六個多月中，沒服過一顆止痛藥，生命也超過醫師預期的三個月）

就在將要過母親農曆七十歲生日前三天清早，母親狀況突然轉壞，陷入昏迷，全身不斷抽動，癱瘓的右半邊完全僵直不能彎曲，呼吸非常急速，心跳加快，血壓下降，醫生護士通知我們該準備後事了，且壽衣要先給她穿上。八十歲的父親難過悲傷的樣子，實在叫人不忍心，全家人慌成一團，我第一個念頭只有懇請佛陀上師慈悲，能超渡母親去一個好地方。那天佛陀上師在百忙之中抽空接見了父親和我，見到了的時候都已經深夜十一點了，父親懇求佛陀上師，希望能讓母親過完七十大壽再離開我們，並且讓兩個在東部的女兒能趕回來見母親最後一面，只聽到佛陀上師非常斬釘截鐵地說：「沒問題！讓她過完七十歲生日再走！我想觀世音菩薩會看在這位老年人的面子上，讓她多留幾天再接她去西方極樂世界！可惜我很慚愧，沒有道力留她，只有求菩薩幫助了。」隨即加持了一道咒輪與一道法令，並吩咐咒輪回去戴在母親頭頂，以震攝她的靈知心識，另一道法令要在母親往升時戴上，藉上面種子字的力量去到西方極樂世界。

回去之後，母親早已瞳孔放大，體溫下降，死亡了，我們趕緊照著佛陀上師的指示，將咒輪給母親戴上，心裡非常害怕，母親早已走了，現在再戴這個咒輪會不會太遲了？沒想到，奇蹟出現了，短短不到兩個小時，母親清醒過來，瞳孔、體溫、呼吸都恢復正常，我們問母親一些問題，她還能用點頭、搖頭、眼睛轉動、眨眼等來回應，意識完全清楚正常，不但等到遠在東部的兩個姐姐回來歡渡七十歲生日，往後的日子裡，母親還坐著輪椅用未癱的左手給佛菩薩上香，在座的許多出家僧眾也都看到母親這死而復生的過程，讓在旁照顧母親的看護阿姨都深受震撼體認到真實佛法之威力是如此偉大，更改變了五十年來信奉基督教的父親，皈依佛門，成為佛陀上師的弟子。

一直到母親久臥病床喉嚨開始積痰，父親實在心疼母親抽痰時母親會受苦，他便跪到家裏佛堂佛陀上師法相前，默默懇求著佛陀上師，請觀世音菩薩還是將母親早點接去西方極樂世界享福吧！果然，第二天清晨六點五十分，母親張著嘴有如沉睡中的嬰兒般安詳離開，當天早上便接到佛陀上師侍者Kuan師兄的轉達，佛陀上師將會用甚深精妙的淨土超渡法來超渡母親，並恭請觀世音菩薩或觀世音菩薩的侍者在七天內接走余林彩春居士去西方極樂世界。弟子無限感恩佛陀上師加持超渡母親，母親的遺體不但臉色紅潤，嘴唇也紅潤，手腳柔軟可配合更衣穿褲等等瑞相都不在話下，更殊勝的是，當天我跪在母親的遺體前說：「媽！如果您看到觀世音菩薩或她老人家派遣侍者通知到您，要來接您，就請您將嘴巴合攏，微笑讓我們放心。」說完了我就叩了三個頭以答謝母親多年的養育之恩，跪在床前默念著觀世音菩薩聖號，也不知過多久，母親原來張嘴如睡著的嬰兒，此時嘴竟合起來了並帶著微笑，哎呀！天啊！我當時真的是驚呆了，我以為是我眼睛

看花、看錯，趕忙找家人來瞧，每個人跟我看到都是一樣，她將會跟著觀世音菩薩或她老人家的侍者去西方極樂世界。那時窗外還有小鳥唱歌非常好聽，就像佛經上所述般，平時家裡附近是沒什麼鳥的。當天突然錄音機自動無人操控播放起觀世音菩薩聖號。這種種殊勝瑞相，讓家裡另兩位也學佛的看護阿姨激動地掉淚，她們說：「學佛多年，現在才看到什麼叫做真正的佛法」，就由於母親往升，她們再三懇求我們帶她們到佛陀上師那裡去皈依。

想想是什麼樣證境的再來聖者，能與佛菩薩溝通，能請佛菩薩將我母親余林彩春居士死了又喊回來，多留幾日便多留幾日，想接走就安排接走！那一定是佛陀才能辦得到的事，今天我母親余林彩春居士死而復生，過完七十歲生日才往升西方極樂世界，只不過是在佛陀上師眾多弟子中，稀鬆平常的一個小case，其他的師兄弟，坐化往升，自己修法圓滿生死自由往升淨土，多的不勝枚舉，許多師兄弟只見佛陀上師一面，傳法受用，如侯欲善師兄，自己修到可以去西方極樂世界周遊一趟再回來，告訴大家七天再去，後果然七日坐蓮往升。

佛弟子　余瑞琪

（此文的英文翻譯印在前面）

有關"死而復生至極樂"當時的報紙報導

CATEGORY 4

Supreme and Profound Buddha-Dharma That Is Difficult to Encounter in Millions of Eons

第四大類　百千萬劫難遭遇無上甚深佛法

Introduction

Writings on the Buddha-dharma by H.H. Dorje Chang Buddha III Wan Ko Yeshe Norbu Holiest Tathagata are treasures that are difficult to encounter in millions of eons. A few examples include *Sutra on Understanding and Realizing Definitive Truth, What Is Cultivation?, Commentary on the Prajnaparamita Heart Sutra* (the brief commentary is 40,000 Chinese characters and the somewhat detailed commentary is 380,000 Chinese characters), *A Monk Expounds the Absolute Truth to a Layperson,* and *Correcting the Treatises of Patriarch Bodhidharma.* In this last writing, His Holiness corrects the mistakes that the great Chan (Zen) Patriarch Bodhidharma wrote in his treatises that have been handed down from generation to generation.

The recorded oral discourses on the dharma given by H.H. Dorje Chang Buddha III cover an infinitely broad array of subjects. They encompass the essence of the *Tripitaka* and the profound meaning of the esoteric scriptures. There are even discourses that transcend the subtleties found in the *Tripitaka* and esoteric scriptures. All of those oral discourses thoroughly demonstrate that H.H. Dorje Chang Buddha III possesses complete mastery of the Five Vidyas. Each audio or video recording of a discourse on the dharma given by His Holiness can be made into a book. Those dharma discourses have produced many eminent monastics, people of great virtue, outstanding laypersons, people with extraordinary knowledge, and even great dharma kings and rinpoches. Based on those discourses, people have become liberated from the cycle of birth and death and have become great masters. There are even great Bodhisattvas who are disciples of H.H. Dorje Chang Buddha III. This is not at all surprising. Even Buddhas attained their Buddhahood by learning the dharma under Dorje Chang Buddha, who is the master of all Buddhas in the dharma realm. In reality, H.H. Dorje Chang Buddha III is the primordial Buddha—Dorje Chang Buddha. There is only one Dorje Chang Buddha in the dharma realm. No matter how many incarnations of Dorje Chang Buddha there may be, that incarnation is Dorje Chang Buddha. That is why Dorje Chang Buddha is the master of all Buddhas in the dharma realm.

The audio recordings of dharma discourses given by H.H. Dorje Chang Buddha III begin with the strict progressive levels of cultivation. These discourses contain extremely incisive teachings that concisely incorporate the twelve divisions of the *Tripitaka* and the ten divisions of the esoteric scriptures without losing the true meaning of the *Tripitaka* and esoteric scriptures. The topics covered are extremely broad. They vary from analyses of the dharma regarding the *Trikaya* (Three Bodies) and the Four Wisdoms of a Buddha to teachings on the vajra dharma of the Supreme Division. There are explanations of the true realization and manifestation of the Great Perfection of Ultimate Wisdom. H.H. Dorje Chang Buddha III also possesses the Xian Liang Buddha Wisdom Great Perfection Dharma whereby the disciple experiences and sees the rainbow-body dharma realm state the very day that dharma is transmitted. Nothing is lacking either in theory or practice. Those recordings truly show that H.H. Dorje Chang Buddha III has complete proficiency in exoteric and esoteric Buddhism and perfect mastery of the Five Vidyas. They also manifest His Holiness's supreme enlightenment, wonderful prajna wisdom, and holy state of the Buddhas and Bodhisattvas, all which are part of the inner realization vidya. All of the recorded discourses are directed at Buddhas, Bodhisattvas, Arhats, and all practitioners.

Many true deeds performed by people can be found in those recordings. (Because we did not want this book to be too thick, we did not include the vast majority of those deeds in this book.) For example, during the Highest Form of Bathing the Buddha Dharma Assembly, Venerable Akou Lamo Rinpoche and H.E. Ciren Gyatso Gar Tongtsen Rinpoche together lifted a 4,260-pound tub filled with water used to bathe a statue of the Buddha. There are other examples that involve Venerable Dharma Teacher Long Hui, who is the chairperson of the International Buddhism Sangha Association, and Venerable Dharma Teacher Yong Ding. They used a dharma within the Vajra Fist Division called the Powerful Thunder True Dharma Palm to shatter an object and break a tree that were far away from them.

Disciples of H.H. Dorje Chang Buddha III have attained control over their own living and dying, passing away serenely at the time they predicted. They sat in the cross-legged meditation posture and passed away in a state of liberation, leaving behind many sariras (holy relics) after their cremation. There are many such manifestations of accomplishment in the dharma relating to disciples of H.H. Dorje Chang Buddha III.

As a result of simply listening to the discourses on the dharma given by His Holiness, many people attained supernatural powers right then and there, saw holy sights such as Buddhas or Bodhisattvas, experienced an opening of wisdom, received blessings, or were cured of their illnesses. However, H.H. Dorje Chang Buddha III said that all of those occurrences were the accomplishments of the individual disciple resulting from his or her own cultivation.

H.H. Dorje Chang Buddha III Wan Ko Yeshe Norbu Holiest Tathagata said that those were not His accomplishments. His Holiness said that those accomplishments resulted entirely from the individual disciple's cultivation and dharma powers and had nothing to do with Him. Nonetheless, we should bear in mind what Venerable Akou Lamo Rinpoche, H.E. Denma Tsemang, H.E. Gar Tongtsen, Venerable Xirao Jiebu, Venerable Xiangge Qiongwa, Venerable Muya Jiongzha, Venerable Dharma Teacher Long Hui, Respected Danzeng Nuori Rinpoche, and others have said: Their Buddha Master is like the sun in the sky, and they themselves are at most only like a lamp in a room.

(This text was translated from the Chinese text that follows.)

簡　　介

　　多杰羌佛第三世雲高益西諾布頂聖如來的佛法是百千萬劫難遭遇的珍寶，例如《了義經》、《什麼叫修行》、《般若波羅密多心經講義》(量中量開示四萬字，量中廣開示三十八萬字)、《解脫大手印》、《僧俗辯語法》，更正流傳之禪宗達摩祖師所著論說《正達摩祖師論》等等。三世多杰羌佛說的法，廣博無盡，含攝三藏精髓，密典妙義，更有超於三藏與密典的微妙，徹底表現了五明的完整無缺，每一片錄影帶、錄音帶的開示或說法，都可製作成一本書，而這些法音教化出了很多高僧大德、大居士、大學者、乃至大法王、仁波且，使他們得到了解脫的成就，成為著名的宗師，至於大菩薩是三世多杰羌的弟子，這太不足為奇，因為就是佛陀們也是跟多杰羌佛學法成佛的，實際上三世多杰羌佛就是始祖多杰羌佛，多杰羌佛只有一位，沒有兩位，無論多少世，也就是他老人家，因此是法界諸佛之師。

　　三世多杰羌佛的法音從修行的嚴密次第開始，以最精闢的教義收斂，含攝三藏十二部及十部密典，而不失其內含的真義，從三身四智的分析法義，到無上部金剛法，大圓勝智的實證體顯。更具有史無前例、當場即修當天實證的現量佛智大圓滿，理論與實踐的表顯圓滿無缺，堪為顯密圓通，展於妙諳五明，而內明之無上覺性般若妙智之真空妙有體顯，都在這些法音法帶中，找到若干真人真事實例(但因考慮到不要將此書印得過厚，所以未將事例列入五明書中)，如阿寇拉摩仁波且、慈仁嘉措‧祿東贊尊者在勝義浴佛法會上，兩人即提動4260磅的浴佛蓮池，如國際佛教僧尼總會主席隆慧法師和永定法師用金剛拳中五雷正法掌，於遠處將物體、樹木打得粉碎；三世多杰羌佛的弟子更有生死自由，說走就走，盤腿坐化，舍利輩出等若干成就體顯，有很多人僅僅聽聞了法音，當下或得到神通，或見到諸佛菩薩等勝境，或智慧開敷，或福報增長，或病痛消失，但是三世多杰羌佛卻說：這是弟子們自己修行的成就。

　　三世多杰羌佛雲高益西諾布頂聖如來儘管說這些不是他的成就，完全是弟子們的修持功夫，與他無關，但是如阿寇拉摩仁波且、丹瑪翟芒尊者、祿東贊尊者、喜饒杰布尊者、香格瓊哇尊者、木雅迥扎尊者、隆慧法師、丹增諾日仁波且等都說，他們的佛陀上師就如同天上的太陽，而他們本身最多只是室內的一盞燈而已。

（此文的英文翻譯印在前面）

A Portion of the Dharma Discourses Expounded by H.H. Dorje Chang Buddha III Wan Ko Yeshe Norbu Holiest Tathagata

\<Trip to Taiwan\>

· The Supreme and Magnificent Dharma
· H.H. Dorje Chang Buddha III's genuine and indisputable holy feats (1/5)
· H.H. Dorje Chang Buddha III's genuine and indisputable holy feats (2/5)
· H.H. Dorje Chang Buddha III's genuine and indisputable holy feats (3/5)
· H.H. Dorje Chang Buddha III's genuine and indisputable holy feats (4/5)
· H.H. Dorje Chang Buddha III's genuine and indisputable holy feats (5/5)
· H.H. Dorje Chang Buddha III gives a discourse on cause and karmic affinity.
· H.H. Dorje Chang Buddha III gives a discourse on conditioned arising and prophesied a real circumstance.
· Disciples report to H.H. Dorje Chang Buddha III on the holy feats manifested after listening to H.H. Dorje Chang Buddha III's discourse on "Commentary on the Heart Sutra."
· Disciples report to H.H. Dorje Chang Buddha III the details of the karmic retribution that a disciple received.
· H.H. Dorje Chang Buddha III gives a discourse on the "infallibility of planting a cause and receiving its effect."
· H.H. Dorje Chang Buddha III gives a discourse on the relationship between main practices and preliminary practices.
· H.H. Dorje Chang Buddha III gives a discourse on the differences between Exoteric Buddhism and Esoteric Buddhism and practices empowerment. (1/2)
· H.H. Dorje Chang Buddha III gives a discourse on the differences between Exoteric Buddhism and Esoteric Buddhism and practices empowerment. (2/2)
· H.H. Dorje Chang Buddha III gives a discourse on the cause and affinity of not receiving benefits due to committing offenses.
· Disciples report to H.H. Dorje Chang Buddha III on their practices.
· H.H. Dorje Chang Buddha III expounds that one needs to cut off the worldly concept of self to begin self-cultivation.
· H.H. Dorje Chang Buddha III gives a discourse on the principle of all dharma arising from the mind.
· H.H. Dorje Chang Buddha III expounds that one needs to cultivate oneself in accordance with the teachings of H.H. Dorje Chang Buddha III.

\<The Fundamental Discourses Given in the Orient\>

· On the holy birthday of Kuan-Yin Bodhisattva, H.H. Dorje Chang Buddha III gave a discourse to some of His beginning-level disciples.
· H.H. Dorje Chang Buddha III gives a discourse to beginners. (1/2)
· H.H. Dorje Chang Buddha III gives a discourse to beginners. (2/2)
· H.H. Dorje Chang Buddha III gives a discourse on the effects of empowerment. Disciples share their experiences of being empowered.
· H.H. Dorje Chang Buddha III gives a discourse on the differences between Buddhist studies and Buddha-dharma.
· H.H. Dorje Chang Buddha III gives a discourse on "The Commentary of Receiving Benefits."
· H.H. Dorje Chang Buddha III gives a discourse on why people get sick.
· H.H. Dorje Chang Buddha III answers questions posed by disciples. I (1/2)
  (1) The question about "Cause and Effect"
  (2) How to solve problems with correct understanding and correct views.
  (3) How can one save living beings when one's understanding is insufficient?
  (4) How to constantly abide by the state of self-cultivation?
  (5) Are Buddhas sentient beings?
  (6) Occasional problems with visualization
  (7) How to cultivate oneself

(8) How to be patient under insult without resentment How to overcome the challenge

(9) Why is there poor self-cultivation?

(10) Where can one obtain correct understanding and correct views?

· **H.H. Dorje Chang Buddha III answers questions posed by disciples. I (2/2)**

(1) Is one allowed to teach others to recite the Six-Syllable Mantra?

(2) How can one practice diligently? How can one cultivate oneself and maintain the cultivation?

(3) How can one interfuse and maintain balance between mundane matters and Buddha-dharma?

(4) What does one do to be able to visualize an image while practicing dharma?

(5) How does one achieve correspondence of the three karmas (body, speech and mind) during the practice of dharma?

(6) What should one do to have respect toward H.H. Dorje Chang Buddha III, Buddhas, Bodhisattvas, and Dharma Protecting Deities?

· **H.H. Dorje Chang Buddha III answers questions posed by disciples. II (1/2)**

(1) How should one perceive H.H. Dorje Chang Buddha III?

· **H.H. Dorje Chang Buddha III answers questions posed by disciples. II (2/2)**

· **H.H. Dorje Chang Buddha III answers different levels of questions. (1/2)**

(1) The subject of the Six Elements (earth, water, fire, wind, space, consciousness)

(2) Are cells sentient beings?

(3) Do cells have the nature of a Buddha?

(4) Do they (cells) also fall into reincarnation along with humans?

(5) Which of the six realms do they (cells) belong to?

(6) What is "correspondence of the three karmas"?

(7) How does one correspond to the Four Jewels (the Master, the Buddha, the Dharma and the Sangha)?

(8) Does one cut off one's attachments to the concept of self by cultivation or by the practice of dharma?

· **H.H. Dorje Chang Buddha III answers different levels of questions. (2/2)**

(1) How does one overcome the obstacle of sleepiness?

(2) What is the relationship between mundane matters and Buddhist matters?

(3) Is it punishment from the Dharma Protecting Deities when someone receives his karmic retribution immediately for violating the false speech precept?

(4) How does one cultivate oneself?

(5) It is hard to set a time for practicing dharma. One can practice dharma during daily activities when walking, stopping, sitting, sleeping, etc. Is it the same as long as you practice it in your mind?

(6) Is there a ritual for making offerings to the Buddhas? For example, is there a ritual for making offerings of fruits, incense, flowers or other items?

(7) What does one do with a previous dharma name that was given when taking refuge in the past?

(8) What is the correct way to visualize while practicing dharma?

· **H.H. Dorje Chang Buddha III gives a discourse on numerous examples of the power of Buddha-dharma.**

· **H.H. Dorje Chang Buddha III gives a discourse on how one has to have a vigilant state of mind and cultivate oneself truthfully.**

· **A discourse on true examples of perceiving H.H. Dorje Chang Buddha III as a Buddha according to Tibetan esoteric teachings**

· **H.H. Dorje Chang Buddha III practices the dharma of Dharma Protecting Deities for a disciple.**

· **H.H. Dorje Chang Buddha III gives a discourse on Lesson Fourteen.**

· **The discussion meeting on the true practice of Buddhism (1/3)**

· **The discussion meeting on the true practice of Buddhism (2/3)**

· **The discussion meeting on the true practice of Buddhism (3/3)**

<H.H. Dorje Chang Buddha III Gives Discourses on Questions Posed by Disciples>

· **Impermanence**

· **Rinpoches are not necessarily Bodhisattvas. H.H. Dorje Chang Buddha III is clear.**

· **Numerous questions posed to the H.H. Dorje Chang Buddha III by rinpoches (1/3)**

(1) What should one be aware of when replacing the offering items on the offering altar?

(2) How should one handle the withdrawn fruit offerings?

(3) What is the purpose of using dharma instruments as an offering?

(4) Should one practice visualization or how should one react when one sees dharma instruments in stores?

(5) How should one perceive a "thanka"?

(6) What is "kai-guang"(consecrate)? What should one be aware of during the ritual of kai-guang? Will there be dharma power? Will the dharma power disappear?

(7) The appropriate manners and behavior when a Buddhist disciple sees an image of Buddha

(8) What will be the other appropriate occasions for practicing the Six-Syllable Mantra Dharma besides the time of practicing dharma? Is it acceptable to recite it during a ride in a car?

(9) There are many people who practice many different sects of dharma, including vajrayana and bodhisattvayana. Is it true that as long as one concentrates on practicing a single dharma, one can eventually achieve an ultimate state? Or, should one follow a certain order based on one's situation in practicing different types of dharma at different levels?

(10) Is it the case that the more one practices the Mandala offering Dharma, the better? Or, is it better if one takes time in practicing that dharma? Is it acceptable to practice it any time?

(11) Are there female Huo-Fos or rinpoches?

(12) It is prohibited to collaborate or have meals with evil people? What should one do when one is not able to tell the difference between virtuous and evil people?

(13) Why do we frequently choose to recite the holy name of Namo Kuan Sher Yin Bodhisattva?

(14) H.H. Dorje Chang Buddha III has loving kindness and compassion, so he beseeched the Buddhas and Bodhisattvas to bestow nectar. Why is the nectar bestowed different each time? Is it different because the participants were different, the capacities of growth of the disciples were different, or the purposes were different?

(15) Where should a dharma booklet be placed?

(16) Should one visit Tibet when chances arise during the learning of Buddha-dharma?

(17) Questions regarding the practice of the Longevity Dharma

(18) Questions regarding Phowa during the practice of the Longevity Dharma

(19) Questions regarding dharma wheels during the practice of dharma

(20) What does it mean by "birth and death in an instant; achievements in progression"?

· **Numerous questions posed to the H.H. Dorje Chang Buddha III by Rinpoches (2/3)**

(1) During a dharma assembly for raising the consciousness of the deceased to higher realms of existence, will living beings in the Ghost Realm still be raised and saved when the leading dharma master is not quite familiar with the related mudras or rituals? What will be the subsequent cause and effect?

(2) Killing is prohibited. Does it mean that eating seafood, live fish, or anything freshly killed as food is not allowed?

(3) The amount of good fortune for this lifetime has been determined. Will one depart this life sooner if one uses it up by wasting it?

(4) Holy Pamu has specifically given a discourse on the practice of Vajrasattva Visualization Dharma. Does it mean that we have been transmitted that dharma when we listened to this CD?

(5) Should a prostration follow immediately after reciting one of the Four Refuges or after reciting all of the Four Refuges?

(6) Is there any special meaning in reciting the Heart Sutra before listening to the recorded discourses on CDs?

(7) What are the differences between Vajra Hell and Hell of Uninterrupted Suffering?

(8) Can the Raise the Consciousness of the Deceased Mantra also save human beings who have not deceased?

(9) How should one handle the mandala plate when it is full during the practice of Mandala Offering Dharma in order to abide by the dharma?

(10) Will one have another opportunity of learning dharma or meeting H.H. Dorje Chang Buddha III after the end of this lifetime?

(11) There was a disciple who saw Vajrasattva and holy Pamu in a heavenly realm after listening to Pamu's discourses on CDs. How can this type of supernatural ability be obtained?

(12) Do Buddhas have rankings? Which Buddha is the first Buddha? Who is the ancient Buddha Dipamkara as mentioned in the sutras?

(13) Matters regarding H.H. Great Jewel Dharma King

(14) There are many verses of praise in the sutras. Does one need to recite them frequently?

(15) Questions regarding the encounter of an inauspicious horoscope

(16) Can Buddhism be reformed?

(17) Can Buddha-dharma be reformed?

(18) Can precepts be examined, adjusted or reformed?

(19) How should Buddhist precepts and Buddhism be promoted?

(20) Will the lineage of Buddhism end? Could it be restored and carried on by human intervention if it were ended?

(21) What do exoteric and esoteric mean?

(22) What are the Five Vidyas?

· **Numerous questions posed to the H.H. Dorje Chang Buddha III by Rinpoches (3/3)**

(1) There are many different precepts from all sects and schools of Buddhism. Can they be integrated?

(2) Can Esoteric Buddhism be promoted to the whole world for everyone to learn?

(3) What are the differences between the Buddha-dharma of Sakyamuni Buddha and that of my honorable Dharma King Master?

(4) What are the differences between Exoteric Buddhism and Esoteric Buddha-dharma?

(5) Will it be considered great merit if an eminent monastic wants to integrate the precepts, doctrines and practices of all the major religions to become one core practice?

· **Numerous questions posed to H.H. Dorje Chang Buddha III by great laypersons (1/2)**

(1) What does it mean by "Throwing at the green fruits three times, you do not miss"? What does it mean by "Shaking eight slips three times, the same one comes out three times"?

(2) What does it mean by communicating with Buddhas, Bodhisattvas, and dharma protecting deities?

(3) What are the concepts "state of realization" and "virtue of realization"?

(4) Why should one study and learn from the books written by Pamu? Why is that very important to learning Buddhism and self-cultivation?

(5) H.H. Dorje Chang Buddha III's English is the very elegant and prestigious version spoken among certain older generations. There is some Buddhist terminology that is difficult for us to understand. I beseech H.H. Dorje Chang Buddha III to give a discourse on the Buddha-dharma that is intended for current generations.

(6) What is a "yidam"(main deity of veneration)? Why is it necessary to learn the dharma of the yidam? How is the yidam related to self-cultivators? What are "leaders of particular divisions of dharma" and "great female Bodhisattvas of a particular division"?

(7) Can one recite one's yidam mantra anytime besides the time of dharma practice, such as riding in a car or running errands?

(8) How does one practice one's yidam dharma so that one can receive great benefits? Can a disciple request an audience with one's yidam?

(9) How does one practice the Mandala Offering Dharma required during the practice of the preliminary dharma practices? How does one count the number of times of the practices?

(10) How can one reach the goal of practicing the Mandala Offering Dharma 100,000 times when one practices it seven times a day?

(11) What is "yuan ji" (passing away having attained liberation)? How is it different from nirvana?

(12) What is the lineage of our sect?

· **Numerous questions posed to H.H. Dorje Chang Buddha III by great laypersons (2/2)**

· **H.H. Dorje Chang Buddha III gives discourses on the questions posed by disciples. (1/3)**

(1) One has read Buddhist books and listened to discourses. However, one does not practice accordingly. Will one obtain benefits?

(2) How can one become a person with wisdom? Which step should one first start with?

(3) I have questions on Buddha-dharma. Can H.H. Dorje Chang Buddha III please give answers to them?

(4) It is said "Major questions lead to great realization. Minor questions lead to slight realization." Then why is it prohibited to pose questions regarding suspicions on the authenticity of Buddhism?

(5) Why does one need to make a vow before listening to discourses?

(6) Will one fall into hell if one makes a vow and then breaks it?

(7) Why are there some rinpoches and dharma teachers who refuse to empower patients but sometimes give them medicine?

(8) One took refuge in a master. Then, one takes refuge in the master's master. How should one address one's former master?

(9) Should one still prostrate oneself to the former master?

(10) What can one do to make people believe in Buddhism in the process of proselytizing people?

(11) How does an esoteric Buddhist disciple learn from a vajra master?

(12) If one receives little benefit after following the dharma transmitted by H.H. Dorje Chang Buddha III, what is the reason?

(13) What are the requirements for one to learn the esoteric dharma?

(14) Some say that the Exoteric School is good. Some say that the Esoteric School is good. Which one is the best?

· **H.H. Dorje Chang Buddha III gives discourses on the questions posed by disciples. (2/3)**

· **H.H. Dorje Chang Buddha III gives discourses on the questions posed by disciples. (3/3)**

· **The important segments of his words were retrieved at the scene.**

· **In addition to the Middle Way, there is esoteric dharma to achieve the samboghakaya (reward-body).**

· **Regarding *The Mahamudra of Liberation***

· **Buddhism is a form of construction.**

<Dharma Practice Reports Secretly Recorded by H.H. Dorje Chang Buddha III>

· **H.H. Dorje Chang Buddha III gives a discourse. Disciples report on their dharma practices.**
· **Disciples report on their dharma practices. (1)**
· **Disciples report on their dharma practices. (2)**
· **Disciples report on their dharma practices. (3)**
· **Disciples report on their dharma practices. (4)**
· **The Grand Assembly of Debates － Part I**

> H.H. Dorje Chang Buddha III gives a discourse on the dharmakaya (reality body), samboghakaya (reward body), and nirmanakaya (transformation body).

· **The Grand Assembly of Debates － Part II**

> H.H. Dorje Chang Buddha III gives a discourse on "True Emptiness and Wondrous Existence, Karmic Affinity, and Correspondence of the Three Karmas."

· **The Grand Assembly of Debates － Part III**

> H.H. Dorje Chang Buddha III gives a discourse on the subjects of raising the consciousness of the deceased, karmic retribution, and offerings.

· **The Grand Assembly of Debates － Part IV**

> H.H. Dorje Chang Buddha III gives a second discourse on "True Emptiness and Wondrous Existence," "A Thought Becomes Reality," and "All Dharma Stems From the Mind."

· **The Grand Assembly of Debates － Part V**
· **The Grand Assembly of Debates － Part VI**

> Disciples report on their dharma practices.
> H.H. Dorje Chang Buddha III gives a discourse and uses examples of disciples to explain.

· **Disciples talk about their experiences and report on their dharma practices.**
· **Disciples report on their dharma practices.**

<H.H. Dorje Chang Buddha III's Trip to the United States>

· **H.H. Dorje Chang Buddha III gives a discourse on Pamu's connection with the lineage of this sect and on the qualifications and status of a great rinpoche.**
· **H.H. Dorje Chang Buddha III answers questions posed by disciples. (1/2)**

> (1) What level of rinpoche is he?
> (2) The circumstances surrounding a rinpoche
> (3) What are the differences between these great rinpoches and other dharma kings?

> (4) What are the differences between these rinpoches and the Elder Dharma King?
> (5) What is the status of Pamu? What is the relationship between her and our school?
> (6) The shariras that descended into the bowl when Pamu invoked the Buddha to bestow nectar
> (7) Why was the dharma bowl not washed face up?
> (8) Why did the rinpoches standing by her side wear masks?
> (9) What are the differences between the dharma bowl of H.H. Dorje Chang Buddha III and that of Pamu?
> (10) Why does H.H. Dorje Chang Buddha III not accept offerings?

· **H.H. Dorje Chang Buddha III answers questions posed by disciples. (2/2)**
· **H.H. Dorje Chang Buddha III answers questions posed by disciples. (1/2)**

> (1) The circumstances surrounding a Tibetan Rinpoche in his previous lifetimes
> (2) What is the meaning of bringing one's palms together in front of one's heart?
> (3) What is the relationship between Amitabha Buddha and Long Life Buddha?
> (4) What is a mandala?
> (5) What is a hada? Why does one need to offer hadas?
> (6) In the practice of Mandala Offering, is it the greater the offerings we visualize, the better, or is it the more times we make offerings, the better?
> (7) What is vajra hair? Why is it magnificent?

· **H.H. Dorje Chang Buddha III answers questions posed by the disciples (2/2)**
· **H.H. Dorje Chang Buddha III answers questions posed by the disciples (1/2)**

> (1) When should one recite the mantra to raise the consciousness of the deceased?
> (2) What should one do when encountering other living beings from other realms?
> (3) Does every practitioner of Esoteric Buddhism have to have his or her own yidam as well as his or her own dharma protecting deities and seed syllables?
> (4) How does one visualize one's yidam?
> (5) How can one correct one's negative habitual tendencies?
> (6) How does one overcome great fear toward certain things?
> (7) Is there a certain period of time when the bardo state in between death and rebirth ends?
> (8) How can one be determined to leave the cycle of reincarnation?

(9) What can one do when stepping on H.H. Dorje Chang Buddha III's shadow?

(10) What does it mean by the concept of "Both sentient beings and non-sentient beings perfectly attain their wisdom" as written in a sutra?

(11) Bodhisattvas engage in what appears to be negative habits? They are doing this in order to save living beings.

(12) Mandala Offering

(13) The problem concerning the driving of cars

(14) The contrition of an organization's president

(15) H.H. Dorje Chang Buddha III gives discourse on "Giving rise to such a mind by not abiding in anything" and "True emptiness and wondrous existence."

· **H.H. Dorje Chang Buddha III answers questions posed by disciples. (2/2)**

· **H.H. Dorje Chang Buddha III gives a discourse in Los Angeles. (1/2)**

(1) H.H. Dorje Chang Buddha III gives a discourse on "good fortune, how not to be attached to phenomena, and how to cut off attachments to the concept of self."

(2) H.H. Dorje Chang Buddha III gives a discourse on "A Buddha saves those who have a karmic connection with the dharma. A Buddha does not save those who lack a karmic connection with the dharma."

(3) How does one deal with a distracted mind? What is the correct attitude while listening to the Master's discourses?

(4) Should one use expedient means to proselytize non-Chinese people?

· **H.H. Dorje Chang Buddha III gives a discourse in Los Angeles. (2/2)**

· **H.H. Dorje Chang Buddha III gives a discourse in Las Vegas on questions posed by disciples.**

(1) H.H. Dorje Chang Buddha III gives a discourse on the illusory city–Las Vegas.

(2) H.H. Dorje Chang Buddha III gives a discourse on magical powers and tricks of illusion.

· **H.H. Dorje Chang Buddha III gives a discourse on exoteric and esoteric Buddhism, nectar, and non-Buddhist practices.**

(1) H.H. Dorje Chang Buddha III gives a discourse on Exoteric and Esoteric Buddhism.

(2) Who takes the lead in Tibetan Buddhism?

(3) How does one deal with people who practice non-Buddhist ways?

· **H.H. Dorje Chang Buddha III answers questions posed by disciples.**

(1) Does it mean that a disciple deviates from the dharma if he or she does not participate in group cultivation sessions or has not learned the "Fifty Verses Regarding How Disciples Should Treat Their Master"?

(2) Must everyone who practices the esoteric dharma engage in solitary meditation?

(3) Are there contradictions or conflicts between the practices of Exoteric Buddhism and Esoteric Buddhism?

(4) H.H. Dorje Chang Buddha III gives a discourse on disciples' violating the Samaya Precepts.

· **H.H. Dorje Chang Buddha III gives a discourse at the Institute in the United States. (1/2)**

(1) How does one promote the Buddhist books written by Pamu?

(2) H.H. Dorje Chang Buddha III gives a discourse on "Great Good Fortune and Great Capacity for Growth."

(3) There are many things that one is afraid to do because of the fear of violating percepts.

(4) One should treat Buddha-dharma with extreme veneration.

· **H.H. Dorje Chang Buddha III gives a discourse at the Institute in the United States. (2/2)**

· **H.H. Dorje Chang Buddha III answers questions posed by disciples.**

(1) Most people say that women bear heavier negative karma than men do. However, Dakinis and Vajravarahi are female and Pamu is a female Dharma King. I respectfully request H.H. Dorje Chang Buddha III to expound the differences between women and men in terms of self-cultivation.

(2) What are the differences between the Buddha-land where H.H. Dorje Chang Buddha III is taking us and the Western Paradise of Ultimate Bliss?

(3) Bodhi Holy Water and Three Secrets Dharma Water

(4) Should we participate in Dharma Assemblies conducted by other temples in order to persuade their sangha members to join our sect?

(5) H.H. Dorje Chang Buddha III expounds that disciples should care for one another, have the mind of bodhicitta, and the Four Limitless States of Mind.

· **H.H. Dorje Chang Buddha III gives a discourse on the demons of the Five Aggregates and the profound Esoteric Dharma.**

\<Discourses on the Dharma Given in the United States\>

· **Have you thought about the matters after death?**

   (1) Will a living being either from the human realm or another of the six realms receive condemnation from King Yama after the state of bardo (intermediate state between death and rebirth)? What kind of being is King Yama? Is he a Bodhisattva?

   (2) What should one do to express veneration or make offerings when one meets King Yama?

   (3) Does H.H. Dorje Chang Buddha III need to prostrate himself before King Yama?

   (4) At a temple, can one do prostrations in a Yu-Huang Heavenly King worshiping hall or King Yama Hall in order to express veneration toward the Bodhisattvas?

   (5) When going to other temples, do we need to prostrate ourselves in front of the deities from the heavenly realms?

   (6) One should examine one's qualifications before attempting to proselytize others.

· **It will be fruitless if one does not listen to discourses in accordance with the dharma expounded in this discourse. (1/3)**

· **It will be fruitless if one does not listen to discourses in accordance with the dharma expounded in this discourse. (2/3)**

· **It will be fruitless if one does not listen to discourses in accordance with the dharma expounded in this discourse. (3/3)**

· **It is time for awakening.**

· **What does it mean by ending the cycle of birth and death?**

· **The magnificent and selfless Dorje Chang Buddha III (1/2)**

· **The magnificent and selfless Dorje Chang Buddha III (2/2)**

· **H.H. Dorje Chang Buddha III gives a discourse on "The Mandatory Chapter on the Karmic Affinity of a Master and a Disciple." (1/2)**

· **H.H. Dorje Chang Buddha III gives a discourse on "The Mandatory Chapter on the Karmic Affinity of a Master and a Disciple." (2/2)**

· **Another discourse on "The Commentary on Receiving Benefits"**

· **No matter which sect you practice, you cannot end the cycle of birth and death if you do not practice this dharma.**

· **Expedience is not doing evil things.**

· **H.H. Dorje Chang Buddha III gives a discourse on the detailed practice of "Vajra Yoga Perfection Dharma." (1/2)**

· **H.H. Dorje Chang Buddha III gives a discourse on the detailed practice of "Vajra Yoga Perfection Dharma." (2/2)**

· **The offerings received by temples should not be in the name of H.H. Dorje Chang Buddha III.**

· **What kind of people are qualified to obtain supernormal powers?**

· **H.H. Dorje Chang Buddha III gives a discourse on questions posed by disciples regarding profound Esoteric Dharma. (1/3)**

· **H.H. Dorje Chang Buddha III gives a discourse on questions posed by disciples regarding profound Esoteric Dharma. (2/3)**

· **H.H. Dorje Chang Buddha III gives a discourse on questions posed by disciples regarding profound Esoteric Dharma. (3/3)**

· **One should focus mainly on cultivating one's dharma practices and behavior.**

\<Individual DiscoursesGiven by H.H. Dorje Chang Buddha III\>

· **A lesson that every disciple needs to understand**

· **One must attain realization of the state of virtue in order to understand the true meaning of the sutras.**

· **Supreme and wonderful dharma**

· **A deviated mind attached to phenomena is Mara. Differentiation under any circumstances diverges from the state of meditation. (1/3)**

· **A deviated mind attached to phenomena is Mara. Differentiation under any circumstances diverges from the state of meditation. (2/3)**

· **A deviated mind attached to phenomena is Mara. Differentiation under any circumstances diverges from the state of meditation. (3/3)**

· **A discourse given on the holy birthday of H.H. Dorje Chang Buddha III**

· **During the Dharma Assembly in which a Discourse on Green Tara was given (1/3)**

   (1) H.H. Dorje Chang Buddha III expounds on what a dharma king is.

   (2) The profound dharma of "The Perfect Rituals of Green Tara Dharma"

· **During the Dharma Assembly in which a Discourse on Green Tara was given (2/3)**

· **During the Dharma Assembly in which a Discourse on Green Tara was given (3/3)**

· **The only requirement for initiations**

- You Yourself Should Weigh Whether You Are Qualified to Teach Others
- It Is a Matter of Good Roots, Not a Matter of Pulling People In
- If You Do Not Understand Initiations, Do Not Brag that You Can Perform Initiations
- Inner-Tantric Initiations, Ethics, and Bodhicitta
- What Benefit Will You Derive From Speaking Falsely to Me in Order to Deceive Me?
- Peeling Off the Shell and Seeing the True Source
- The Source of the Five Heinous Crimes and Icchantikas Is Nihilism and Eternalism
- We Cannot Let Living Beings Wait There and Not Learn Dharma
- Explanation of Certificate of Qualification to Perform the Holy Form of Inner-Tantric Initiation and Other Related Matters
- Differentiating Rinpoches

<Concise Discourses on Dharma Given by H.H. Dorje Chang Buddha III>

- How can a Buddhist disciple quickly become accomplished and attain liberation?
- The proper sequence to quickly become accomplished and attain liberation.
- All living beings are suffering. What can we do to help them eliminate their suffering?
- What is the source of suffering? Is there an alternative to it?
- How should a Buddhist disciple save living beings?
- How does one explain the principle of reincarnation to westerners?
- How do we tell living beings the importance of imper-manence?
- Who is Jinba Rinpoche?
- What is the process that one goes through after death if one did not realize liberation? What is the bardo state like after death for such a person? What about his next incarnation?
- A rinpoche asked H.H. Dorje Chang Buddha III to which realm do dragons belong.
- What is the difference between the Three Pure Cumulative Precepts and "Abstain from everything that is evil and do everything that is good"?
- Most people take refuge in the Three Jewels. Followers of the esoteric school take refuge in the Four Jewels. For those who have taken refuge in the Three Jewels, should there be a ceremony when they take refuge in the Four Jewels? What qualifications must one have to take refuge?

- When some people begin to learn Buddhism, they will encounter obstacles. How can they overcome such difficulties?
- Can we dissolve the grudge that we have for those with whom we do not get along if we sincerely cultivate ourselves and dedicate the merit of our cultivation and daily meditation to them?
- Some dharma teachers are practicing Zen meditation, other forms of meditation, or dharma relating to the Pure Land sect. When they come to us to learn, they feel that they have to start all over again and therefore lack confidence. How do we solve that problem?
- Those who have just begun learning Buddhism have insufficient power, but they are very devout and want very much to learn Buddhism. How can they overcome this barrier?
- Recently H.H. Dorje Chang Buddha III practiced special dharma for my deceased non-Buddhist relatives that enabled them to pass on to the Western Paradise of Ultimate Bliss. What is the Western Paradise of Ultimate Bliss like?
- Many Buddhists very much want to cultivate themselves well, but they frequently are influenced by their karma and negative habits. After they express greed, hatred or ignorance, they feel very remorseful and angry. How can this be solved?
- In our cultivation, how do we treat fellow disciples who have broken the precepts?
- Is there a relationship between bodhicitta and a mind determined to leave the cycle of reincarnation?
- When practicing samatha and vipasyana, if obstacles such as drowsiness and scattered thoughts appear, what is the most effective method overcoming them?
- How do we teach living beings to practice the four limitless minds?
- Some people want to request transmission of dharma, but they do not know that different dharmas exist. Does a highly virtuous vajra master select a particular dharma for them?
- If the dharma transmitted does not correspond to the level of the disciple, is that a very serious problem?
- Of course we cannot discuss the profound matters of the body-that-does-not-rot or the rainbow body. But can we find out about other forms of accomplishment?
- The matter of merit.

There are many additional recorded dharma discourses given by H.H. Dorje Chang Buddha III Wan Ko Yeshe Norbu Holiest Tathagata. Because of limited space, we have only listed the titles of some of them.

(This text was translated from the Chinese text that follows.)

多杰羌佛第三世雲高益西諾布頂聖如來
之部份開示法音

〈台灣行〉

· 無上殊勝法
· 三世多杰羌佛真實不虛之事跡1/5
· 三世多杰羌佛真實不虛之事跡2/5
· 三世多杰羌佛真實不虛之事跡3/5
· 三世多杰羌佛真實不虛之事跡4/5
· 三世多杰羌佛真實不虛之事跡5/5
· 三世多杰羌佛開示因緣
· 三世多杰羌佛開示緣起和實相境預告
· 弟子們向三世多杰羌佛彙報聽三世多杰羌佛開示的《心經講義》所顯聖境
· 弟子們向三世多杰羌佛彙報一弟子遭果報的經過
· 三世多杰羌佛開示種因得果不錯謬
· 三世多杰羌佛開示正行與加行的關係
· 三世多杰羌佛開示顯宗與密宗的差別及修加持1/2
· 三世多杰羌佛開示顯宗與密宗的差別及修加持2/2
· 三世多杰羌佛開示不得受用所犯罪過之因緣
· 弟子向三世多杰羌佛彙報功課
· 三世多杰羌佛開示修行首先要斷世俗我執
· 三世多杰羌佛開示萬法由心生的道理
· 三世多杰羌佛開示要按照三世多杰羌佛的教導修行

〈在東方的基礎開示〉

· 三世多杰羌佛在觀音菩薩生辰之日對部分弟子開示，為最初機者說
· 三世多杰羌佛開示對初機者說1/2
· 三世多杰羌佛開示對初機者說2/2

· 三世多杰羌佛開示加持的作用，眾弟子談受加持的感受
· 三世多杰羌佛開示佛學與佛法的區分
· 三世多杰羌佛開示《受用論》
· 三世多杰羌佛開示人為什麼要生病
· 三世多杰羌佛開示弟子們提問一1/2

　　(1) 關於因果的問題？
　　(2) 如何有正知正見處理問題？
　　(3) 自己的理念不夠，如何渡生？
　　(4) 如何隨時隨地處於修行之中？
　　(5) 是否佛也是眾生？
　　(6) 觀想有時會出問題？
　　(7) 如何修行？
　　(8) 要忍辱沒有瞋心，如何透關？
　　(9) 為什麼修不好行？
　　(10) 從何處得正知正見？

· 三世多杰羌佛開示弟子們提問一2/2

　　(1) 能否教人念六字大明咒？
　　(2) 如何才能精進？如何修持？
　　(3) 如何圓融世法和佛法？
　　(4) 修法時觀想不起來，怎麼辦？
　　(5) 修法如何三業相應？
　　(6) 應怎樣對上師諸佛菩薩護法恭敬？

· 三世多杰羌佛開示弟子們提問二1/2

　　(1) 如何理解三世多杰羌佛？

· 三世多杰羌佛開示弟子們提問二2/2
· 三世多杰羌佛開示分層各類提問1/2

　　(1) 關於六大的問題。
　　(2) 細胞是不是有情識？
　　(3) 細胞有佛性嗎？
　　(4) 他們也要跟著人去轉輪迴？
　　(5) 他們屬於六道的那一道？
　　(6) 什麼是三業相應？

(7) 如何相應四寶？

(8) 如何斷我執？從修行還是從修法？

- 三世多杰羌佛開示分層各類提問2/2

(1) 如何除睡眠蓋？

(2) 世間法和佛法的關係？

(3) 犯妄語戒，報應當時就顯，是否護法菩薩的懲罰？

(4) 怎樣修行？

(5) 修法時間不好定，行住坐臥方面也可以修，只要你觀想是不是也是一樣？

(6) 供佛是不是有儀軌？如供果供香供花，或者供其他的東西給佛菩薩，是不是有儀軌？

(7) 原來皈依的法名，該如何處理？

(8) 怎樣才是修法時的正確觀想？

- 三世多杰羌佛開示佛法威力多例
- 三世多杰羌佛開示提起警覺心，必須真修行
- 依藏密『視師如佛』的實例開示
- 三世多杰羌佛給弟子修護法
- 三世多杰羌佛開示第十四課
- 佛學實修交流會1/3
- 佛學實修交流會2/3
- 佛學實修交流會3/3

〈三世多杰羌佛開示弟子提問〉

- 無常
- 活佛不一定是菩薩，三世多杰羌佛是透明的
- 仁波且對三世多杰羌佛的諸多提問1/3

(1) 供桌上的供品擺設及更換供品要注意的事情？

(2) 換掉的水果該怎麼處理呢？

(3) 供法器是什麼作用？

(4) 看到店裡的法器，是觀想還是什麼樣的態度？

(5)「唐卡」像這種東西，應該是怎麼樣？

(6) 什麼叫做開光？開光要注意什麼？是不是有法力？會不會有消失的情形？

(7) 弟子看到佛像，該有的態度跟做法？

(8) 修六字真言，做功課之外，在什麼情形下也可以？坐車時念誦可不可以？

(9) 有很多人修很多不同的法，有金剛部的、菩薩部的，是不是只要專修一個法，就自然可以達到最後的境界，還是要依照個人的情形做不同的按次序按階段的修練？

(10) 曼達供是做的次數愈多愈好呢？還是時間愈長愈好？是不是隨時都可以做？

(11) 有沒有女的活佛或女的仁波且？

(12) 不可與惡人同謀共事或者共餐，若無法分別是好人壞人，該怎樣處理比較好？

(13) 為什麼我們時常特別來朗誦南無觀世音菩薩名號？

(14) 三世多杰羌佛慈悲會向佛菩薩請甘露，為什麼每次請的甘露都不一樣？是因人的不同，還是弟子的根器不同？還是目的不同？

(15) 法本應放在什麼地方？

(16) 學習佛法，是不是有機會應該到西藏去？還是不需要？

(17) 關於修長壽法的問題？

(18) 當修長壽法的時候，有關頗瓦的問題。

(19) 修法時金剛輪的問題。

(20) 什麼叫做「瞬間生死，階段成就」？

- 仁波且對三世多杰羌佛的諸多提問2/3

(1) 超渡法會，主壇的法師萬一手印不是很熟練或儀軌不是很清楚的時候，陰靈鬼使，陰入界之眾生是否能渡到？他們將會產生什麼因果？

(2) 不能殺生，如海鮮、活魚等活的東西是都不能吃？

(3) 這一生福報多少已經註定，若用的快吃的多，是否很快就要離開了？

(4) 帕母老人家特別開示了金剛薩埵觀修法，我們聽帶子的時候，是不是表示這個法已經傳了呢？

(5) 四皈依時，是說一句然後頂禮呢？還是四句都把它說了再來頂禮？

(6) 聞法時先誦「心經」，有什麼特別的意思？

(7) 金剛地獄跟無間地獄有什麼不同？

(8) 超渡咒除了超渡死去的眾生之外，是不是也可以超渡人？

(9) 做曼達供，這個曼達盤滿了後該怎樣做比較如法？

(10) 這個生命結束了，是否有機會再來學法或見到三世多杰羌佛呢？

(11) 聆聽帕母老人家的法音，有一位弟子可以到天上看見金剛薩埵跟帕母老人家，如何學到這樣的神通？

(12) 佛有沒有大小？最早的佛是哪一位佛？在經典裡常看到燃燈古佛這些事情？

(13) 關於大寶法王的情形？

(14) 經裡頭有許多的讚，是不是要時常稱誦？

• 三世多杰羌佛開示並以弟子為例說明/弟子談體會、弟子彙報
• 弟子們彙報

〈美國行〉

• 三世多杰羌佛開示帕母與本派傳承之關係及仁波且的資格與
　地位
• 三世多杰羌佛開示弟子提問1/2

 (1) 他是何等位的仁波且？
 (2) 一位仁波且的因緣？
 (3) 這些仁波且與其他法王的差別？
 (4) 這些仁波且、法王與老法王的差別？
 (5) 帕母的地位與本派傳承關係？
 (6) 帕母求請佛降甘露時缽中降下之舍利？
 (7) 洗缽時為何不正面洗缽？
 (8) 為何旁邊的仁波且們要戴面具？
 (9) 三世多杰羌佛的缽與帕母的缽不同？
 (10) 何以三世多杰羌佛不收供養？

• 三世多杰羌佛開示弟子提問2/2
• 三世多杰羌佛開示弟子提問1/2

 (1) 一位西藏喇嘛前幾世的因緣？
 (2) 合十的涵義？
 (3) 阿彌陀佛與長壽佛的關係？
 (4) 什麼是曼荼羅？
 (5) 什麼是哈達？為什麼要供養哈達？
 (6) 曼達供是修的愈大愈好？還是修的次數愈多愈好？
 (7) 什麼是金剛毛？其殊勝為何？

• 三世多杰羌佛開示弟子提問2/2
• 三世多杰羌佛開示弟子提問1/2

 (1) 何時持超渡咒？
 (2) 外出遇到不淨(他道眾生)該如何處理？
 (3) 是否每位密教弟子都要有自己的本尊、護法及種子字？
 (4) 如何觀想本尊？
 (5) 如何改習氣？
 (6) 特別害怕某些東西如何克服？
 (7) 中陰是否有固定轉生的時間？
 (8) 如何生起出離心？
 (9) 藏密『上師五十頌』規定弟子不能踩到金剛上師的的影子，
  該如何處理？

 (10) 佛經中『有情無情同圓種智』該怎麼理解？
 (11) 菩薩不斷習氣為渡眾生故？
 (12) 曼達供？
 (13) 開車的問題？
 (14) 會長懺悔
 (15) 三世多杰羌佛開示「應無所住而生其心」及「真空妙有」

• 三世多杰羌佛開示弟子提問2/2
• 三世多杰羌佛於洛杉磯開示1/2

 (1) 三世多杰羌佛開示福報，不要執著境界，要去除我執。
 (2) 三世多杰羌佛開示「佛渡有緣人，無緣不渡」。
 (3) 如何對治散亂心？聽上師開示時的正確態度？
 (4) 接引外國人是否可以特別方便？

• 三世多杰羌佛於洛杉磯開示2/2
• 三世多杰羌佛於拉斯維加斯開示弟子提問

 (1) 三世多杰羌佛開示有關拉斯維加斯此幻化城市。
 (2) 三世多杰羌佛開示魔術與幻術。

• 三世多杰羌佛開示顯教與密教、甘露、外道

 (1) 三世多杰羌佛開示顯教與密教
 (2) 誰領導西藏佛教？
 (3) 如何與外道溝通？

• 三世多杰羌佛開示弟子們之提問

 (1) 若弟子沒有參加共修或沒有學習「上師五十頌」是否不如
  法？
 (2) 是否每位密教弟子都要閉關？
 (3) 顯教與密教是否於作法上有衝突矛盾？
 (4) 三世多杰羌佛開示弟子有關犯三昧耶戒

• 三世多杰羌佛開示於美國基金會1/2

 (1) 如何推廣帕母的佛書？
 (2) 三世多杰羌佛開示大福報、大根器。
 (3) 因怕犯戒很多事就不敢做。
 (4) 要以無比恭敬心對待佛法

• 三世多杰羌佛開示於美國基金會2/2
• 三世多杰羌佛開示弟子們之提問

 (1) 常聽到女眾業障重，但空行母、金剛亥母皆為女子且帕母為
  女法王，請三世多杰羌佛開示女眾與男眾修行上的差距。

(2) 三世多杰羌佛要帶我們去的佛國與西方極樂世界有何不同？

(3) 菩提聖水與三密法水。

(4) 為接引更多出家眾，可否參加其他寺廟之活動？

(5) 三世多杰羌佛開示弟子們要互相愛護，要有菩提心、四無量心。

- 三世多杰羌佛開示五陰魔及甚深密法

〈在美國開示的法音〉

- 你想過你死後的事嗎？

(1) 人或是六道眾生，他經過中陰以後，再受到閻王的處罰嗎？閻王祂是一個什麼樣的人？或者菩薩？

(2) 見到閻王應該用什麼樣的方式來表示恭敬或供奉？

(3) 三世多杰羌佛見到閻王的話，也要禮拜？

(4) 到廟裡玉皇大帝的殿或者閻王殿，表示對菩薩的恭敬，還是可以禮拜？

(5) 到其他的廟，天人道的這些眾神，我們是不是要禮拜呢？

(6) 要去攝受他們，也要看自己有什麼樣的條件？

- 若不如是聞受法音，則徒勞無功1/3
- 若不如是聞受法音，則徒勞無功2/3
- 若不如是聞受法音，則徒勞無功3/3
- 該醒悟的時候了
- 什麼叫做了生脫死？
- 偉大無私的三世多杰羌佛1/2
- 偉大無私的三世多杰羌佛2/2
- 三世多杰羌佛開示《師徒緣起必讀章》1/2
- 三世多杰羌佛開示《師徒緣起必讀章》2/2
- 再講《受用論》
- 任汝學何宗，不行此法生死不了
- 邪惡並不是方便
- 三世多杰羌佛開示《金剛瑜伽圓滿法》的具體修法1/2
- 三世多杰羌佛開示《金剛瑜伽圓滿法》的具體修法2/2
- 寺廟收的供養不要打在三世多杰羌佛的身上
- 什麼人才有資格得神通
- 三世多杰羌佛開示弟子提問甚深密法1/3

- 三世多杰羌佛開示弟子提問甚深密法2/3
- 三世多杰羌佛開示弟子提問甚深密法3/3
- 以修自己的法和行為主體

〈三世多杰羌佛開示個別帶〉

- 每個弟子必須聽明白的一課
- 了解真經義理必須實證德境
- 無上殊勝法
- 心動著境即是魔，隨緣分別則無定1/3
- 心動著境即是魔，隨緣分別則無定2/3
- 心動著境即是魔，隨緣分別則無定3/3
- 三世多杰羌佛生日的法音
- 在綠度母開示法會上1/3

(1) 三世多杰羌佛開示何謂法王

(2)《綠度母修法圓滿儀軌》甚深法義

- 在綠度母開示法會上2/3
- 在綠度母開示法會上3/3
- 灌頂唯一具備的條件
- 誦經持咒修法，福不唐捐
- 不要上魔的當，斷除我執向菩提
- 三世多杰羌佛開示曼達供的修法
- 重要的課 "不輕易灌頂傳法"
- 不著德相，必建功德
- 三世多杰羌佛為恆生及喜饒根登仁波且之弟子舉行飛籤問訊灌頂
- 出家人「綠度母」修持彙報錄1/2
- 出家人「綠度母」修持彙報錄2/2
- 瑜伽根本法的開示
- 神通能了生死嗎？氣功異於佛教
- 往生極樂世界能結婚嗎？
- 三世多杰羌佛開示護法
- 我比她的素質高，但是為什麼證不到她的境界

多杰羌佛第三世雲高益西諾布頂聖如來開示的法音還有很多，限於篇幅，本書只節錄了部分。

（此文的英文翻譯印在前面）

三世多杰羌佛說：僧俗辯語

（一）論文正誤

　　一提起我的論文，有些人就會產生許多說法。有說是天書，需要破析，有說是談禪理，處處潛伏禪機，還有的說是儒道莊老哲學，不見現代科學。這些說法都是笑話，論文就是論文，哪裏是甚麼天書？我的論文主要是集多元化哲學科學為一體，內容頗為深廣，為了言簡意捷，靈活透關地表達意思，就只有採取半白文言的表達形式和手法。至于認為論文為禪機佛語，儒道莊老之後繼，那是人們錯誤領悟了文中的一些詞語典故的原因。實際上，佛教雖為外來的宗教文化，卻對我國傳統文化，以及人們日常生活，包括文人遣詞造句、百姓日常用語，影響是頗為深廣的。例如：無事不登三寶殿、葷障、叫喚、功法、巧用、安樂、百味、打包、奴婢、宏願、有無、先輩、自覺、覺悟、決定、吉祥、解脫、讀誦、歡喜等等，不計其數。僅以"名"組成的詞，如名望、名義、名利等就不下五百個，以"一"字組成的詞，包括一身、一日、一層、一面、一刹那、一枝花等就不下一千個。我可以說，凡是寫文章的人，隨時都要用上以上的佛家詞語，何況以上詞語為佛家詞語萬分不及其一。人們對平常用佛語佛詞已習慣成自然，以為是祖宗傳授，不知道都來源于佛家用語和佛家籍典。至于對那些不常用的佛語詞而又為漢文化所早已吸收施用的，有人就統統認為是在講佛法和儒道之論述。如果按照這種平見的觀點去看問題，那麼，不是哪一本書都在談佛教和儒道嗎？這是一種嚴重的偏見和錯誤，主要是知識平庸所造成的。凡是做學問的人都知道："要得才橫奪天工，必將諸識尋根窮。"因這緣故，我養成了這樣的習慣，歷來對各個領域的知識我都喜歡學習，並竭盡全力去探討，去問一問為什麼，包括現代哲學思想知識，儒釋道當然也不例外。

　　要說談佛家禪理的論文，我曾作了幾篇，也可以向大家介紹其中一篇《僧俗辯語》。這篇文章是我二十歲那年所作。其產生的起因當歸我的一位好友辛寂老法師。辛寂大和尚八歲出家，二十二歲破初參時，做寶光禪堂綱領主持，禪定頗深，曾在寺內打餓七禪定，圓滿殊勝。至今，寺內比丘一提辛寂大師，都異口同聲讚揚："和尚打禪七、七日七夜不食不動，泰然如常。"辛寂大師一生主修華嚴宗，對天臺止觀和顯密均具深研功底，猶為明見般若實相，故爾德高望重，後任寶光寺方丈，如今已供奉于祖師堂。一天，大和尚和我在寶光寺晤面，對我說："我見了你幾篇論文，其理法甚妙。可否另作論及空性之道新篇而為教益？"我答："可以。"于是三日之後造《僧俗辯語》一文交與求教，但和尚閱後不以為然，置之一旁。時至六年後初冬的一個黃昏，在寶光寺大雄寶殿左側，辛寂法師突然遇見我，說："我現在實在頗為慚愧，特地向你懺悔。"我聞聽此言一時驚惶不知所措，只好怔怔地盯住他。辛寂法師又真誠地說："世尊在世之日，有大居士維摩助佛教化弟子，我雖不才可以效法，今天特地請你助我教化比丘之力。想我佛門世尊是何等威德，大雄寶殿乃千年莊嚴聖境氣象，人人敬仰，現今輪到我來管理寺廟，沒承想做功課時竟然發生鬧殿事件，這真是千年沒有的業力。這不怪其他，只說明我辛寂無德無能，沒有管理好寺廟，也沒有給眾比丘帶好頭，這實在無堪主持，教人慚愧且無地自容。今晨我于惶急之中，重新尋出《僧俗辯語》細研，我明白了以前的愚痴。幾年前，我初識此文，認為你連經書中的'如是我聞'也沒有搞清楚，而寫成了'如是我明'，加之我悟性不徹，因此不予重視。今日一急之下重讀，方頓悟妙理，如是我明原是你自己明白之意，俗見空居士代表俗諦，僧諦和尚以表真諦，真俗之諦都定在心中，所以般若照見萬法惟心，三點魚鉤洞為打字謎而造的詞語──畫上一個魚鉤形，再加三點，不正好成為一心字嗎？所謂菩提臺者是立于真諦角度對'六大緣起'、'萬法惟心'于俗諦的照觀。此文真是字字珠璣，深藏莫測之妙論，尤其是內中禪理、般若正見，現為大殿事故，成熟我開悟之緣起，始得識真諦，實謂羞地而慚。"聽了這番肺腑之言，以及明了他那無私無染的法性聖境，把我照耀得何等勝喜，使我不禁向他行了合掌禮。可惜，不久這位大德歸西圓寂。記得他圓寂前三天我去拜望他，他從病床上支起軀體，說："我要謝謝大師的《僧俗辯語》。還有你在寺院內做的事，以及對我的幫助，眾生會感謝你的。這些有相布施的言語本不該說，怎奈大後天（二月十九日）觀音生辰，我已決意離開此地了，所以不得不煩絮數語。"當時聞聽這番言語，我還以為他要到外地去遊方，于是問："師傳幾時歸來呢？"他慨然而笑：

"我會回來的啊！"但我見他身負重病，認為他是不可能外出的，便沒有放在心裏。誰知三日一到，聽說寶光寺大開齋宴，一打聽才知辛寂法師圓寂。他早本于觀音生辰那天焚香沐浴，披衣搭具，盤腿坐化歸西。七日後，又聽法師弟子護義師言及法師火化的殊勝情況，並拾得十多顆三色舍利。

以上是涉及《僧俗辯語》一文產生的有關究理，為了正誤其它論文並非談禪機佛理，儒老莊學之論，還于它文論及宇宙人生及現代科學哲學思想之本來面目，僅以此篇《僧俗辯語》為例外，故寫了上述文字以補記。

（二）僧俗辯語

如是我明，僧諦和尚居三點魚鈎洞，坐菩提臺上與眾證法。一日，從本原心基來一女居士，求其印證圓覺。居士名俗見空，對僧合掌問曰："吾聞和尚證得如來大定，有長生不老之術，求和尚慈悲開示。"

僧曰："吾所能告汝者，乃如來大樂了生脫死之法，非長生不老之術也。汝從何來，前者曾習何法？"

俗曰："從本原心基而來，曾學三十七家外道，亦曾學佛參禪，已得無上定力，特求和尚印證，是否如來大定？"

僧曰："汝之大定是何覺受？"

俗曰："吾初入定時，彈指已是一夜，開眼後方知一夜已過，當時境界，心中並無半點妄念，亦無任何知覺。"

僧曰："無知無覺，豈不如木石一般。如來大定乃大樂無邊之法，汝有何樂？此境乃昏沉之母入輪迴之根，非如來大定也。"

俗曰："其後吾明心見性，始知此定落在昏沉之中，後入之定方為正定。吾住于智慧之中，了知如來大定，亦不過如此。"

僧曰："何為明心見性？"

俗曰："性者本性也，明者明白也，本性即是如來之法身，此法身乃不生不滅之體。明心見性，就是前念已去，後念未生，不住其間，明悟此一剎那之感，此感便是如來體性，知覺如來體性，便是明心見性也。"

僧點一點頭又曰："汝之大定是何覺受？"

俗曰："吾之大定，不住色相，亦不住于聲香味觸法，而長定于如來體性之中。其覺受相，無昏沉，無妄念，有禪樂之感。定中所顯一切諸色相，由它自來，由它自去，不被它牽引，長住

如來體性之中，出定入定分明，提得起放得下，有時還發出無量神通，但吾也不住于神通之中，由它自顯自滅，不作聖境觀，只照住于明而無念之體性上。和尚之定，可能也是如此。"

僧曰："不也。吾之大定與汝不同，但汝之定也是正定，此定乃諸有眾生成佛之道而必經之路，但非如來大定耳。此定名為'明空知覺定'，是禪家初參後之定境，由此定而養，可得如來大定，如來大定而養方證無上菩提。汝之定有樂明無念之感覺，此感覺即是我見，而如來之定並無我見。"

俗曰："無我覺受豈不又成了木石一般，法師所言如來大定乃極樂無邊之定，木石無知有何樂可取？無所聞知，豈不又是昏沉之母，入輪迴之根了？如來大法若是如此，有何可貴，莫如凡夫所求榮華富貴，每日妻恩子愛，吃喝玩樂，逍遙一輩子還快活些。"

僧兩目悲淚長流，對天嘆曰："吾師如來為一大事因緣而示現于世，吾亦為渡眾生而修行，然眾生累生累劫造下無邊業障，障其如來正道，吾實悲心難忍。彼等不入昏沉，便入我見，若不入昏沉我見又落入邊見之中，好不容易破了初參，又造成口業，自以為此即是如來大定，狂禪性發不好好用功，以此為究竟，障其解脫之路，以致狂魔入體，將來其魔去後，弟子與師皆陷亡難，實為可憐。"和尚道完復對俗曰："汝見差矣。汝于此知覺定中久而久之破了重關，便知此定並非如木石一般，勝過知覺千百萬億倍，無邊自由，知覺定有出有入，有樂明無念之感受。如來定則並無出入，不定也定，定也非定，是名為定，實無所定，無一時不在定中，行住坐臥作諸事理皆在定中。"

俗曰："行住坐臥作諸事理皆在定中，走路豈不錯了道？如果出定走，豈不又與凡夫無異？"

僧曰："汝見俗矣，不悟重關焉知此境。凡夫走路心在路，所做諸事心住事中，心隨諸事妄念所轉引。吾心不隨妄念所轉引，雖走此路，不著此路，作諸事理，心不住境，不存分別，見諸眾生，不見是非長短，男女諸相，人天禍福，豈不聞金剛經云：'若見諸相非相，即見如來。'又云：'應無所住而生其心'，歸言一句，心不著相無我無人，任汝作諸事理，皆是如來大樂之法相。吾之所說是名說法，雖名說法，實無所說，汝當自證，方知真實之義也。"和尚言已，取念珠一串對俗曰："此是何物，共是幾顆？"

俗曰："此乃念佛之珠，共一百零八顆。"于是和尚一手指

天，一手指地，兩眼瞪俗而不言語，俗不解其意問曰："此是何意？"

僧曰："方才觀音菩薩在此地獄渡餓鬼，地藏菩薩在此天上渡仙人。"

俗曰："法師差矣，地藏菩薩在地獄渡餓鬼，為何反說觀音菩薩在地獄渡餓鬼？"

僧曰："汝未悟大道，一無所解，當努力修持，不可向外馳求落為狂禪。若不如此，不但虛度此生，且有墮落之災。"

俗曰："吾聞法師所言甚深微妙，廣大無邊，如來大樂之法實為高深難解，我當如何修之？"

僧曰："若想入此如來大定，別無它路，其一以菩薩行為而照己德；其二努力精進而習定。"

俗曰："菩薩行為與凡夫行為如何分別，望和尚慈悲開示。"

僧曰："我今說此，汝當諦聽，諸有眾生，大略可分為上中下三品。下品人每日但思足一己之欲，貪得無厭，窮奢極欲，永無饜足之日，所羨者榮華富貴，稱王圖霸，以害人為樂，從不見自己之過失。見別人之苦難，反覺稱心快意，想盡千方百計劫奪他人所有為己有，見自己所有過失，不以為恥，反以為榮，此等將來必墮無間地獄，受無量諸苦；中品人亦以足一己之私為務，以榮華富貴為高，驕傲自大，唯我獨尊，有利可圖，即盡力從之，每時每刻，只說別人過失，雖知自己之過失而護短，不肯說也不肯改，此等人並不專門以害人為樂，然利益相爭之際決不讓人，此等人將來也難免地獄之難；上品人重於善德，不圖世間榮利，但圖諸福，見他人有苦難，則全力相助，利益相爭之際，每每讓人，見別人之過失，心雖知而口不言其是非長短，見自己之過失立即改正，處處廣施陰德，以善為事，此等人後為天人，但仍是凡夫。"

俗曰："如此善功，仍是凡夫，豈不怪哉！"

僧曰："此等人雖積功累善，乃有漏之因也，有數之善果，其果受完，仍然下墮，故仍為凡夫。菩薩行為大與凡夫不同，心中不存善惡分別，每時每刻自查己過，分毫過失，立改之，從不見別人過錯，也不見自己好果，處處望眾生早脫輪迴，一切善惡境來，普行恭敬，依此而行，行者性之用，性者行之體，體用本來不二，是故行者性也，性者行也。此理非二乘羅漢所能解，汝當依此而作。吾亦凡夫，未證此法。此法乃大寶上師功德所示。"和尚言至此合掌讚曰："頂禮大寶上師前，吾師妙法普行緣，功

德巍巍照眾生，為渡六道超俗凡。"

俗聽完讚偈問曰："和尚既言一切平等，無有分別，為何又分菩薩行與凡夫行，此非分別乎？又言無我無人，然則今朝此身從何而來，和尚此言豈非荒謬？吾實不解，唯願和尚以理服我。"

僧曰："我今告汝，汝當諦聽。汝今朝之身乃過去善惡妄念二因合成，非汝法身也。汝之法身，即如來之體，本來空寂，今朝此身皆過去作善作惡所種之因結聚之果所現之身。故此身名為業果報身，一切善惡諸業皆以此身而受報。善惡業之輕重不同，報應于六道輪迴之種類亦不同，故有富貴貧賤之不同。作善者，受輕業；作惡者，受重業。輕業距佛果近，重業距佛果遠，作善事之上品人報應結果升天堂成仙人，天堂一切乃善果享受。作惡事之下品人，報應結果入地獄成餓鬼，地獄一切乃惡果享受。作善之人種善因故結善果，作惡之人種惡因故結惡果。此二因皆起于善惡，二種妄念。菩薩觀今朝之身如夢幻泡影，如露，如電，長住如來體性，不隨善惡二因所轉，故不結二果。脫離輪迴，菩薩慈悲眾生，無災，無難，無有業障，發普渡眾生之心，成就方能普渡，故結成就之果，菩薩不斷慈悲普渡心，為渡眾生故。"

俗曰："二因合聚之果，眾生觀之為何實在非夢幻也？"

僧曰："眾生迷其本性，昏沉于二因之中，故覺實在，如人在夢中所覺，一切皆實在，睡醒方知是夢也。眾生若住于如來體性之中，頓然知覺此身如夢，縱上刀山，入油鍋也無痛苦，無一處不是如來報身境地也，至此境地便一切平等。但未悟得此理之前，先得作一善士之君，為人人敬愛尊而稱德，以此築基而為人正，方可依佛之教，修其生圓次第之出離心、四無量心、十善、三聚戒、六度，乃至信、願、行、戒、定、慧之深習行持，而後正行，方可如法圓滿。否則皆為空中樓閣也。故望行者步步腳印，了知佛法在世間，不離世間覺，因果不昧律，輪迴何所縛。"于是和尚合掌讚曰："諸佛上師之功德，普行回向諸法界，現身福慧速圓滿，同證如來大樂界。"

俗聞已，對僧合掌曰："和尚所演無上如來大樂之法，吾當傳于後世。"言訖頂禮七百而去。

CATEGORY 5

Couplets

第五大類　楹聯

Introduction

In couplets composed by H.H. Dorje Chang Buddha III Wan Ko Yeshe Norbu Holiest Tathagata, the two lines have strict verbal parallelism and symmetry. There is a matching sense in the two lines. Moreover, the couplets teach selflessness and beneficence. They are written in a classic and elegant literary style expressing His Holiness's nobility and erudition. There are also wonderful couplets that can be read in three different ways—from bottom to top, from top to bottom, or even horizontally. No matter which way they are read, the grammar is unaffected and, more amazingly, the meaning is always logically expressed. The couplets of H.H. Dorje Chang Buddha III are timeless, written in the ancient style, transcend the mundane, and fully accord with logic and reason. History has never seen before such a master of words.

Take, for example, the first couplet of H.H. Dorje Chang Buddha III called "Ren Zhe." (Ren Zhe means one who is benevolent.) One can see from that couplet His Holiness's direction and purpose in life. The first line reads, "yu ji li ren ci yu xing." This means that one should first educate oneself so that one's purpose is benefitting living beings through compassionate conduct. The next line reads, "zao liang wei shan ze qi shen." This means that after one has succeeded and attained the state of great compassion and enlightenment, one should train others to attain that same state. It is our responsibility to teach others to perform good deeds and benefit everyone.

(This text was translated from the Chinese text that follows.)

簡　　介

多杰羌佛第三世雲高益西諾布頂聖如來的楹聯，不但對仗嚴謹，事理相平，而且無私無欲廣益於人，對聯文風古雅，內涵渾厚，更有神奇絕妙的楹聯，只一幅就有三種唸法，可倒唸、順唸，甚至是橫唸，不但語法不破，更難得的是事理歸類，堪稱不隨時趣，大有古風，超然物外，與之定事，歷史上從來就沒有這樣的文字巨匠。

例如三世多杰羌佛的第一幅楹聯「仁者」，可看出其處世立人的方向宗旨，上聯是「育己利人慈於行」，首先教育自己以慈悲行為為宗旨，下聯是「造良為善責其身」，有了自己的成功大悲覺悟，就應該拿來造就人材為目的、做好事，利益大家，這是自身的責任。

（此文的英文翻譯印在前面）

1.

仁者

育己利人慈於行

造良為善責其身

2.

無垢德本

樹德不為外人知

立本無私心自平

3.

為人之道

虛偽行事必當為人看白

誠心天知定立長者之風

4.

小人大德異

有意表德德無功，小焉者也

無心露功功有德，大器由然

5.

樓臺空懸石壘山金璧蕩魄

亭橋飛架波作水玉池催心

6.

果苑震撼三江色

行園盡攝五湖春

7.

古城風韻

清流推波洗耳，幾度溫馨，麗江古鎮街作河

和風吐媚悅目，三藩抒情，島城舊市道為山

8.

定坐觀心這般機無頭處

行動看佛那個如來真容

9.

心無分別

見道風、平等無私、看淨心、一果平開、何多少

問行持、公正有德、觀法藏、二境公益、沒輕重

10.

正法嚴明

菩提廟規、恭承密典、瞻道因

正法寺律、奉依佛藏、瞅行果

11.

念佛精髓

彌陀宗、本寺念佛、往生淨土有捷徑

佛乘教、我廟表法、隔盂伏藏試真功

12.

顯密圓通

入顯門、無我無法見本來、空性還是我

進密藏、有得有證了真如、法身沒有它

13.

性空何然

彼參禪、回光問心、誰是本來面目

此悟道、返本見性、何為般若實相

14.

蓮開諸宗

承依三寶、起正法、妙諳密典、各派善存、是諸宗

秉咐九品、開法藏、貫乎法門、異族和收、乃釋教

15.

基在虔行

斷疑生信入此路、表裡單途、解脫

絕相超宗進本道、顯密雙運、歸真

16.

聖跡歸分

一愧人、跏趺種因、玉樹凌空、來甘露、朝泛乾枝暮不臨

二證德、行持結果、浴池展聖、登華藏、申年開寺春將進

17.

眾善奉行

正法寺、一脈宗風緣在和、匯汝障消

如藏剎、兩支教義起從善、向爾愆離

18.

真言般若

真言能除五濁障、橫徹三界九霄雲

般若可解六大空、遍攝四禪十地乘

19.

錯聯、錯心、錯無知

染心無知、向外馳求認知了

淨心非空、離內無著見空性

20.

佛教總持

顯密圓通佛乘我為教

五明妙諦總攝他也佛

21.

顯三洲感應定寰宇

佑六道有情鎮乾坤

22.

出報身相蓮開九品演淨土

現威猛狀法展一乘藏密義

23.

三代宗師無上圓滿德相

一尊古佛正等覺解彌陀

24.

大肚能容天下事何來不容之容

忍辱可納法界境豈是有納中納

25.

本寺依藏登妙蓮挽手可攀

正法奉律取聖宗雲腿即顯

26.

非達才高識妙焉能談三身治哉

未成學冠精良豈可示五明覺耶

以下對聯為疊字迴文句，從左或從右唸過來，文字完全一樣。

27.

真如佛陀

法空歸源本無心、心無本源歸空法

性寂真來如陀佛、佛陀如來真寂性

28.

佛大此有好運恩持你等你持恩運好有此大佛

法弘本自品德顯揚僧眾僧揚顯德品自本弘法

29.

宗乃眾緣和合具解脫了凡孺出根本根出孺凡了脫解具合和緣眾乃宗

教為生起善慧覺悟死生俗子世源此源世子俗生死悟覺慧善起生為教

　　舉例說明第廿九首楹聯如下：

上聯「宗乃眾緣和合具解脫了凡孺出根本根出孺凡了脫解具合和緣眾乃宗」
下聯「教為生起善慧覺悟死生俗子世源此源世子俗生死悟覺慧善起生為教」

　　上聯之大意是說，宗是要依眾生眾緣和合才會展現於世的真諦，宗這一真諦具備解脫了凡而脫掉孺愚之根本，達成聖者，所以聯文句：宗乃眾緣和合具解脫了凡孺出根本，而從根底裡其孺愚凡夫之軀，了脫得之聖解時，自然以宗諦合眾生和順之因緣而宏法施宗（真如法性），所以聯文句：根出孺凡了脫解具，合和緣眾乃宗。

　　下聯之大意是說，教之所立是為了生起善德智慧，從而覺悟死與生的凡夫俗子和世界之無常相，這就是根之所在，故聯文句：教為生起善慧覺悟死生俗子世源此，源於世界中諸子俗人達到證悟生與死覺境時，當以智慧善法起渡眾生，即是教意，故爾聯文句：源世子俗生死悟覺，慧善起生為教。

　　楹聯中除了教義宗諦微妙對仗工整之外，從上往下唸，倒回來從下往上唸，詞句完全相同，文理法機含玄宛如氣貫靈兮得體一元，更為高不可瞻的是上聯與下聯平對橫念即是本聯之橫匾，匾文為：宗教兩個字。而宗教二字的含義即是對聯橫念之全文，也就是解釋宗教二字的含意，聯文句為：宗教乃為眾生緣起和善合慧：宗教是由眾生的緣起和善行融合智慧而因果產生所致，也就是佛住世或滅度皆為眾生因緣顯與滅。具覺解悟脫死了生凡俗孺子出世：宗教中具備覺醒與了解的徹悟，由此可讓眾生脫離死這一關，了掉生的鎖絆，而這教法是能使凡夫俗人乃至孺愚之子亦能出離凡塵世界。根源本此：從根源本質上得到解脫。根源出世孺子凡俗：從而由根源出離輪迴世界的愚子凡夫俗人。了生脫死解悟具覺：得到了生脫死解悟真諦具證覺性。合慧和善緣起眾生乃為宗教：此時當以智慧和善行的緣起施予眾生同登覺道，即是宗教之旨。

　　我們解釋到這裡，再來看一看此聖諦楹聯的學問和哲理，實在是高深微妙，而且竟然達到珠璣文句，對仗玄含，不言而喻，是何等之大學問博大聖諦巨哲之境，在歷史上找不到那一位文學大家寫出了如此對聯橫順倒誦，六種念法三章文理的大智展顯之頂學，我們至少可以說這確實是前無古人的。

CATEGORY 6

Calligraphy

第六大類　書法

Introduction

From ancient times to the present, no product of an art or field of study has been able to reflect a person's moral character and knowledge—except for calligraphy. The aura created by a person's achievements or creations in a certain form of art or field of study often covers up his shortcomings in knowledge and character. However, calligraphy is an exception to this rule. Calligraphy is like a three-dimensional projecting mirror. The depth of one's knowledge, the level of one's moral character, and the strength of one's mind are revealed through each stroke of the brush. There is no way to conceal such things. When looking at the quality of a person's ordinary writing of Chinese characters, most people can discern the level of that person's education. This is all the more true with respect to looking at a person's calligraphy.

One cannot find in any history book an unknowledgeable person who has made a contribution to calligraphy. Those with profound and extensive knowledge are not necessarily proficient in calligraphy. However, a great calligrapher must have both knowledge and good brushwork. Without exception, all of the famous calligraphers throughout the generations were great masters of literature who had profound knowledge. Examples of this include ancient calligraphers such as Xizhi Wang, Su Huai, Shaoji He, Huaiguan Zhang, and Fei Yue. A modern example is Youren Yu. Each one of them was an extremely learned literary giant and paragon of virtue.

Knowledge is the pillar and cornerstone of calligraphy. Moral character can be seen in the style and charm of calligraphy. Thus, calligraphy requires both knowledge and moral character.

The calligraphy of H.H. Dorje Chang Buddha III Wan Ko Yeshe Norbu Holiest Tathagata is not bound by worldly conventions and is devoid of unnecessary flamboyance. It is highly refined and based upon ingenious artistic conception. His Holiness's strokes are sometimes written in a swift curling style. However, in an instant, His Holiness can express the innocent and natural charm of a child. There is wonder in even common strokes. His calligraphy is naturally graceful, exhibiting depth and brilliance. The calligraphy of His Holiness contains an invisible force that makes the characters seem much grander than they appear on a superficial level. His strokes look harmoniously smooth and unbroken. The Chinese characters may appear strong and vigorous, like a soaring dragon or mighty tiger. They may appear clear and gently elegant, like slowly floating clouds, cranes flying among pine trees, or dancing swans. They may appear simple and unadorned, like the free heart of a child. They are gracefully understated and completely devoid of any mundane quality. The calligraphy of H.H. Dorje Chang Buddha III is natural in quality and resonates with the true nature of the universe. A deep power underlies His Holiness's strokes.

The ability of H.H. Dorje Chang Buddha III to reach such great heights in calligraphy is completely due to His Holiness's vast knowledge and profound talents. Of course, His Holiness is extremely adept at learning from the styles of others since this is a simple matter for a Buddha. For example, even in the initial stage of learning calligraphy, H.H. Dorje Chang Buddha III had solid skills in the traditional cursive style of writing and also had extensive learning. We can see from the first calligraphic work in this book the adroitness His Holiness had when He was first learning this cursive script.

There is also a *qi jue* poem written by H.H. Dorje Chang Buddha III. A *qi jue* poem is a four-line poem with seven characters to a line and a strict tonal pattern and rhyme scheme. The phonetic reading of the poem is as follows: "hua gong ri yue li yang tian, xi cheng xi feng liu yue xian, gu peng lai cong ba sheng wang, shi zhi shu qi yi dong can." One can see that this work has surpassed all traces of the mundane and has transcended all earthly impurities. Its style is lofty and pure.

When that poem was written, H.H. Dorje Chang Buddha III was living in the seclusion of an ancient temple. His Holiness used his extraordinary realization to express his thoughts and feelings. The first line expresses that although His Holiness lived alone and secluded in the room of a temple, He governed the universe and bestowed blessings upon living beings. Thus, the first line reads, "hua gong ri yue li yang tian."

The next line, "xi cheng xi feng liu yue xian," conveys the scene that during the idle month of June H.H. Dorje Chang Buddha III bathed in the Buddha-state of coolness while under the scorching sun. His Holiness was free of all worldly cares and attachments, and his body merged with the universe. When friends came, His Holiness heard the horns of their cars, but He had already transcended the world, residing in quietude and non-action. H.H. Dorje Chang Buddha III kept no notion of the date, and His Holiness's mind did not abide in anything whatsoever. The people of the world were ignorantly attached to the changing seasons and came in their cars and horses to inform H.H. Dorje Chang Buddha III that summer had long passed and the winter was about to end. The ancient Buddha acknowledged this and smiled.

One can see from this how the calligraphy of H.H. Dorje Chang Buddha III has completely transcended the mundane. It is the calligraphy of a true Buddha. His Holiness's calligraphic skills have reached such a pinnacle due to His complete realization in the Five Vidyas.

In recent years, there are works of H.H. Dorje Chang Buddha III that have been written in the cursive mode of calligraphy, showing a flowing and unobstructed style, and expressing even more than before the charm of this writing technique. For example, the work *Fei Cui Jade* expresses the spirit of an immortal or Buddha, thoroughly transcending the three worlds of reincarnation, standing proudly above the five elements of the universe. It is truly calligraphy beyond the category of calligraphy, expressing a feeling that incorporates the whole universe.

His Holiness's calligraphy of the Chinese characters *lang ga luo bu* (Treasure of Heaven) excels the writing of calligraphers throughout history. It transcends all traces of worldliness. It expresses deep strength, like that which can break jade. The style of another calligraphic work called *wu wo nai da cheng* (No-Self Is Great Accomplishment), conveys the firmness and simplicity of steel and the vigor of a sharp knife. However, these same characters also contain delicate beauty. That calligraphic style truly surpasses styles of the past and present.

Another calligraphic style of H.H. Dorje Chang Buddha III is revealed in the writing of the Chinese characters *xiao bu dian* (Tiny). Such calligraphy shows the childlike innocence of a very old man, and its arrangement expresses the utmost ease and lack of rigid constraints. It is high-class calligraphy that does not even seem to be calligraphy. It is so elegant and refined that it completely transcends the mundane.

Beholding the character *sheng* (holy) written by His Holiness, one can see that it simultaneously embodies both the softness of ribbons and the inner-firmness of steel. Its inner beauty flows to the surface. Another example is the character *fo*, which means Buddha. The writing of that character demonstrates that His Holiness has truly attained the summit of calligraphic skills that the ancients extolled in the old saying, "the old pine branch cannot be weighed down by heavy snow; the might of a brush will lift a thousand-pound bronze cauldron."

In fact, the calligraphy of H.H. Dorje Chang Buddha III has a deep foundation and an internal richness. It embodies the manifold sensations that one could possibly experience in one lifetime. The essence of all things in the universe converges at the tip of His Holiness's brush. With such a transcendent state of realization, the myriad things of the universe are in the palm of this Buddha. The calligraphy of H.H. Dorje Chang Buddha III is like a treasury. It can be vigorous, smooth, or naturally beautiful. His Holiness incorporates the best techniques of all of the schools of calligraphy. No words can really describe this! If you want to see lively and energetic flourishes of the brush, you can. If you want to see characters with adamantine firmness, you can. If you want to see strength within softness, you can. If you want to see the childlike innocence of a very old man, you can. If you want to see charm, purity, and wonder, you can. In other words, His Holiness's calligraphic skills have reached the highest degree of proficiency and naturalness that only a Buddha could reach!

(This text was translated from the Chinese text that follows.)

簡　　介

古往今來，任何藝術或學科及其發明，都反映不了一個人的德品和學識，但書法卻不然。而一個人在某一門藝術和學科或發明上的成績所營造的光環，往往會遮蓋他在學識和人格上的缺失，但是，唯書道除外。書法，就像是一面立體透射鏡，學問的深淺、德品的高低、心智的健弱，都在一筆一畫的運走中展露，無以遁形。且不說書法，就只是普通寫字的好壞，對於一般人，也能看出他的文化水準如何。展觀史論，從古至今找不到哪一個不具學識的人可以在書道上有所建樹的。學識淵博不一定精具書道，但大書家必是學問書風雙胞共存。尤凡歷代書道大家，無一不是出於淵深學識之文學巨匠。如古有王羲之、懷素、何紹基、張懷瓘、岳飛，近有于右任等，個個都是學富五車的大文學家，道德文章之楷模。

學識為書之棟樑，書之基石；德為書之格調，書之神韻，故書法必具雙胞學體。多杰羌佛第三世雲高益西諾布頂聖如來的書法，脫俗無華，格高境妙。時而龍蛇走筆，轉鋒又童心天趣，平中見奇，飄逸自如，渾厚華滋。行墨連綿，氣韻暢達，字勢或雄渾矯健如龍躍天門，虎臥鳳闕；或清新和雅如浮雲飄冉，鶴翔松間；或樸拙率真，孩心無執。脫盡輕鮮煙火之氣，收斂內含，俗染浮雜已然蕩盡！正是『天質自然，韻達性海，故柔中見剛，華而清奇。』

　　三世多杰羌佛的書法能達到如此登峰造極的境界，全然來源於他博大的學識，精深的才華，當然臨帖的功夫對於佛陀來說一揮體成，而紮實雄厚，方能自成大家。比如三世多杰羌佛在初涉書門之時，即有傳統草書的堅實功夫和博大學識的修養，我們見到書法的第一張，即是初學草書的功底，而以他自吟之七絕詩『華宮日月麗陽天，喜乘西風六月閒，故朋來從叭聲望，始知暑氣已冬殘』何等詩句脫盡煙火之氣，高風清奇，不染塵俗。三世多杰羌佛深居古寺，卻以超凡的證量，發抒情懷，闡顯寺廟雖一室之間卻為孤隱清高，超凡脫俗，但卻樂盡無窮豪華天籟，故吟曰：『華宮日月麗陽天』統率日月之天地，而會之人間福盛，一句『喜乘西風六月閒』點出了在夏日炎炎卻迎納清浴，乘駕佛陀西風之涼風沐體，心境無遷，閒於寂靜，放展宇宙，輕安極樂，人我兩忘，故友來臨亦聞叭聲所得，已與世超然，清淨無為，三世多杰羌佛不記時日，應無所住，而世外人卻茫然牽掛，登車奔馬告訴三世多杰羌佛，已經不是夏天了，冬天都快完了，古佛心有會意卻莞爾一笑。由此境界，我們可見三世多杰羌佛之書法如何脫盡人間煙火之氣，是真正的佛陀之書啊！

　　三世多杰羌佛的書法，匯聚五明之全面證德證境，方見墨情神至，又近年之草書以瘦金龍蛇無礙而寫，更見神韻風馳，『翡翠玉』乃出仙風佛骨，徹底跳出三界外，豈然笑傲五行中，實乃非書之書，情懷宇宙。如『朗嘎羅布』之書，已脫前人筆墨而超前者，脫俗無華，功力深厚，似砸釵碎玉，且見鋼打鐵鑄之風之『無我乃大成』，堅硬雄樸，鋒利破皮之勁道，然而又內蘊俊秀，娟美溫惬，確堪躍古騰今之書風格韻。『小不點』，孩兒天趣，老叟童心，毫不拘束佈局擺章，非書而書，消盡煙火之氣，內藏儒雅風魂。拜讀三世多杰羌佛筆下的『聖』字，則又是柔剛相並，內力藏秀，外放雅韻。而『佛』字時，可謂名副其實，真正達到了古人論書功力之頂峰『傲雪松枝萬古痕，筆力能抗千斤鼎』。

　　然而事實上，於實踐中，三世多杰羌佛的書法正是『基深內養，始行萬里，感諸境入性，吸萬物靈媚於合筆內情之間』而得此超凡之化境，含藏宇宙萬物於佛手一掌之間。因而三世多杰羌佛筆下字字珠璣，遒潤曼妙，無所不具，統諸家之長於一人之筆，懷萬谷峻風而獨笑毫端，豈可言喻！要龍飛鳳舞，具之；要砸釵金石，已見；要柔中見剛，然也；要老叟童心，即是；要格韻清奇，內含。一言以蔽之，真正是爐火純青，返樸歸真，佛之書矣！

（此文的英文翻譯印在前面）

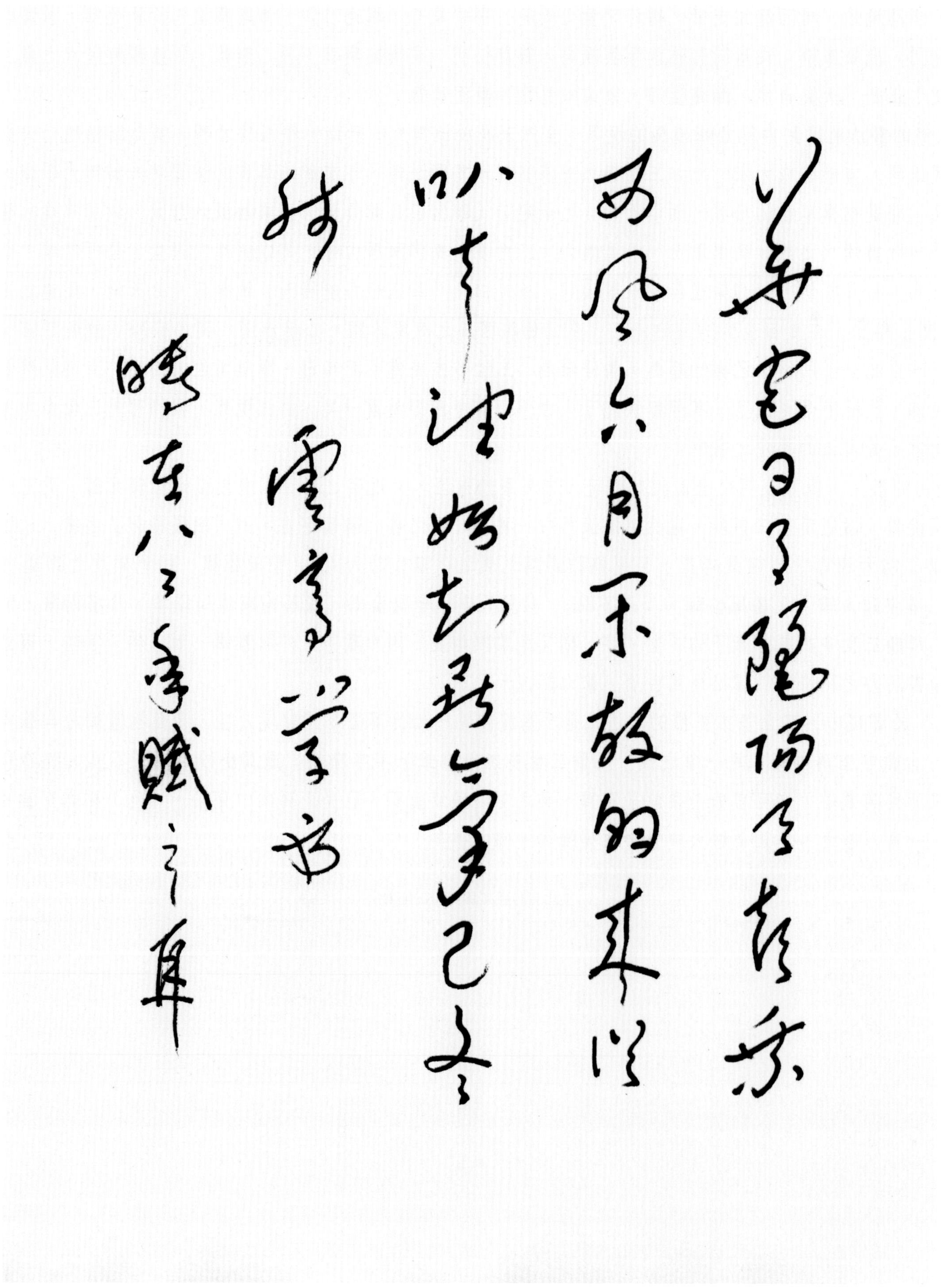

華宮日月麗陽天　喜乘西風六月閑
故朋來從叭聲望　始知暑氣已冬殘
雲高學書
時在八二年賦之耳

An example of a **qi jue** *poem*

Temple of Good Fortune and Wisdom
福慧寺

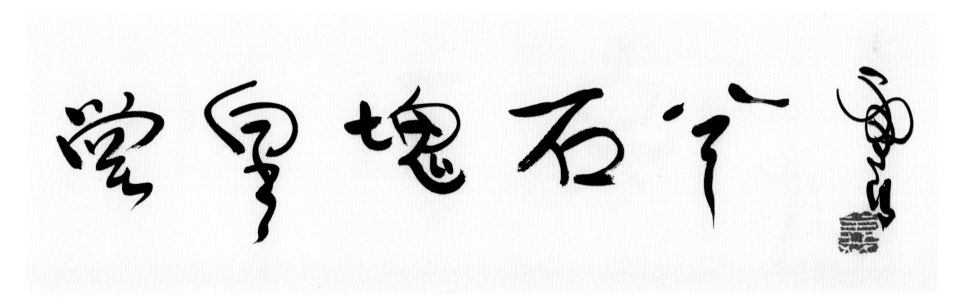

A Majestic and Splendid Stone Suggestive of Poetry, Song and Painting
堂皇塊石兮

Treasure of Heaven
朗嘎羅布

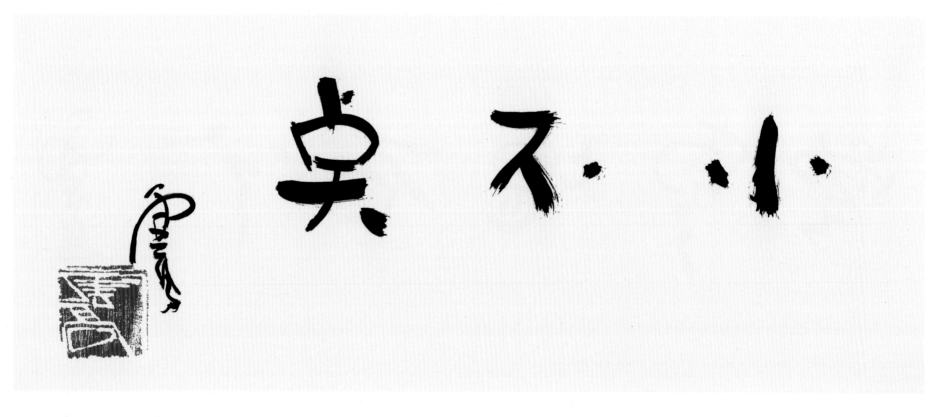

Tiny
小不點

Bao Zhi Jade
寶脂玉

An Ancient Castle With Entwined Vines
枯藤石堡

The Beauty of A Tranquil Spirit
莞爾靈犀

Mystery of Zen
禪玄

No-Self Is Great Accomplishment
無我乃大成

The Chinese character "sheng," which means "holy."
聖

The Chinese character "fo," which means "Buddha."
佛

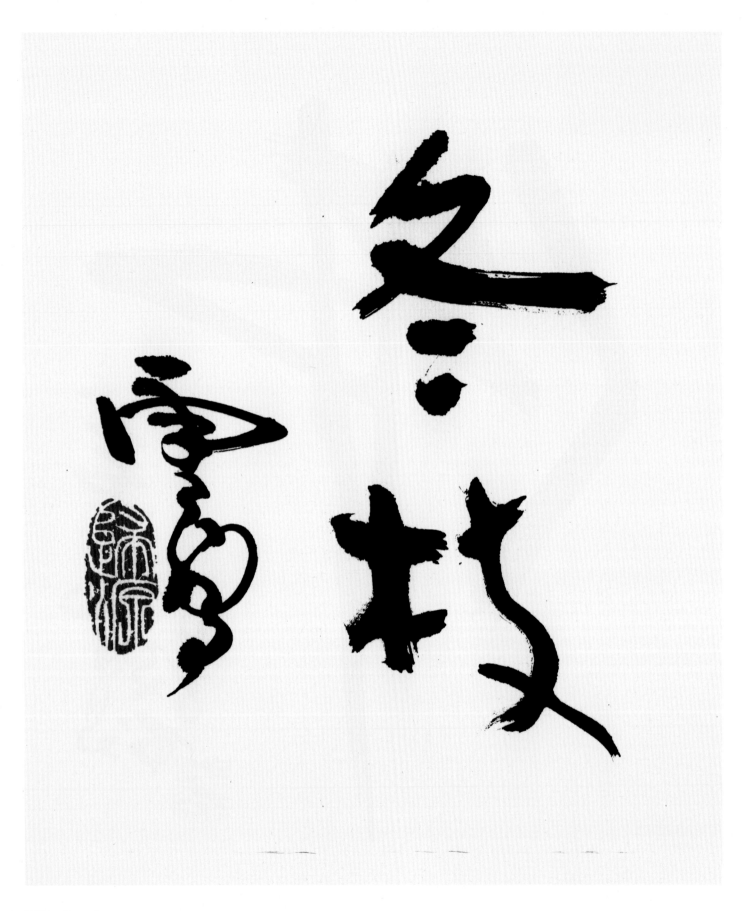

Winter Branches
冬枝

Excellent Style
格高

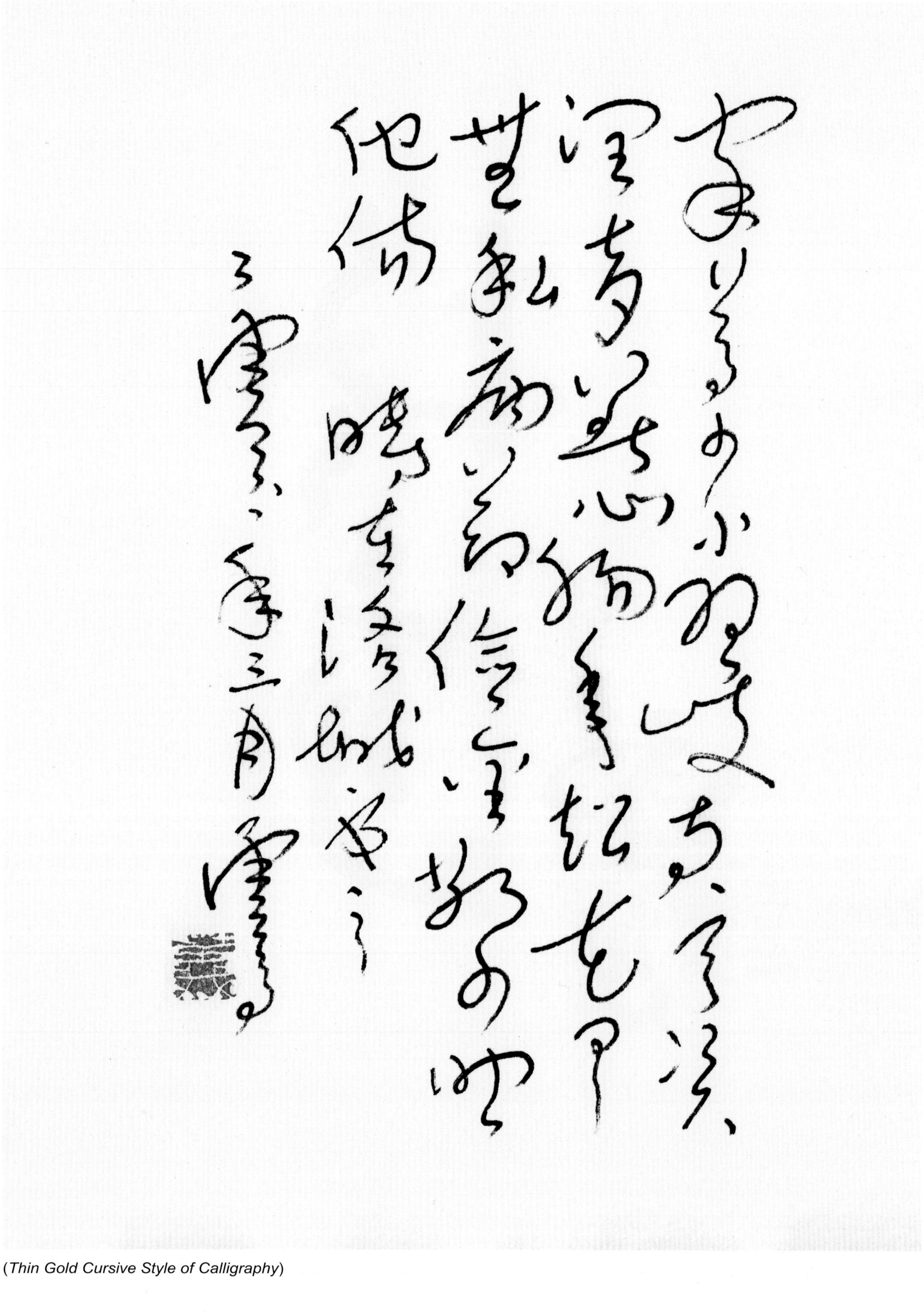

家尊少小習岐黃　天資潤育善心腸
年超花甲無私病　節儉金幣助他傷
時在洛城書之二零零零年三月雲高

（瘦金草書）

(*Thin Gold Cursive Style of Calligraphy*)

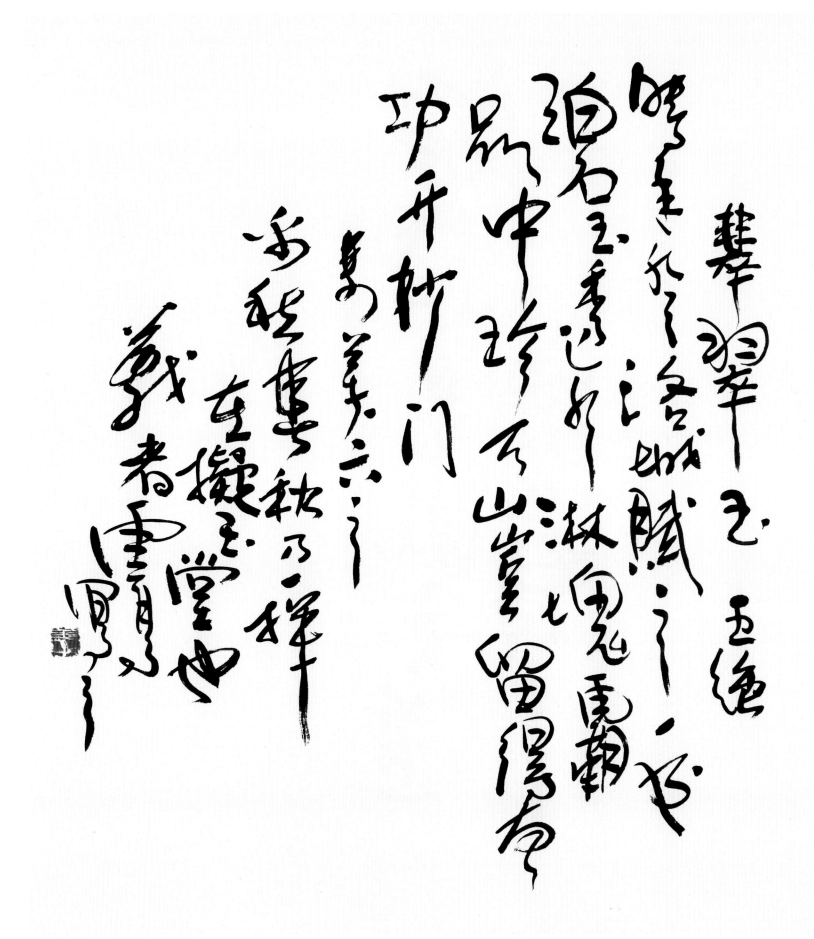

翡翠玉 五絕
時年於洛城賦之一書
碧玉透水淋 塊霸品中珍
天山豈留得 畫功開妙門

來美六之
平然春秋乃一揮
在擬玉堂也
義者雲高寫之

Fei Cui Jade

293

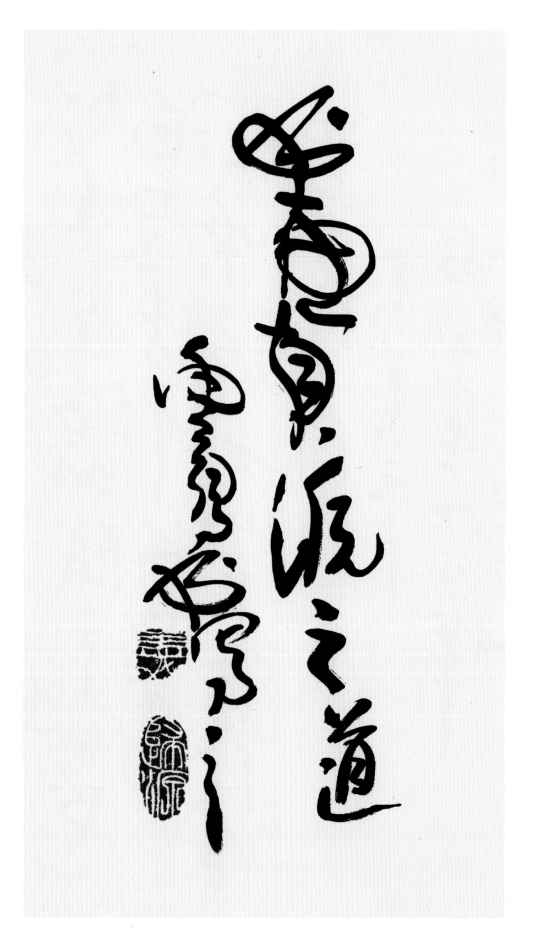

The Way to the True Source of Calligraphy and Painting
書畫真源之道

CATEGORY 7

Stone Seals

第七大類　金石

Introduction

The stone seals inscribed by H.H. Dorje Chang Buddha III Wan Ko Yeshe Norbu Holiest Tathagata merge the charm of traditional inscriptions with fascinating novel elegance. His Holiness has reached the pinnacle of mastery in the creation of concave and convex inscriptions, inscriptions in the Han Dynasty style seen on ancient stone monuments, and inscriptions in the style engraved on ancient three-legged bronze cauldrons. His Holiness possesses the skill to make the edges of the inscribed Chinese characters beautifully and naturally uneven, sometimes even jagged, like broken jade. Inscriptions like 虛懷若谷 (*Xu Huai Ruo Gu*) and 江山入畫圖 (*Jiang Shan Ru Hua Tu*) convey crispness, vigor, and simple ancient grace. Some of His Holiness's inscriptions can stretch out wondrously before our eyes. They can be classically splendid or pleasantly expressive. Their beauty is inexhaustible. Capturing the essence of the ancient inscribers through wielding a modern knife in an amazing fashion, His Holiness deserves to be called a great master of stone inscriptions in our current age. Actually, to compare other masters of stone inscriptions with His Holiness would be like comparing drops of water with a vast ocean.

However, karmic conditions have unfortunately changed, as all phenomena are impermanent. The stone inscriptions made into seals as seen in this book were created by H.H. Dorje Chang Buddha III in His youth. The originals of those seals have long ago fallen into the hands of others. They have been used by those who violate the law to make counterfeit calligraphy and paintings, passing them off as the works of His Holiness. Everyone should be very careful. Only calligraphy and paintings that come with the Buddha Vajradhara Dharma King seal of H.H. Dorje Chang Buddha III and the fingerprint of H.H. Dorje Chang Buddha III are genuine works of H.H. Dorje Chang Buddha III.

(This text was translated from the Chinese text that follows.)

簡　　介

多杰羌佛第三世雲高益西諾布頂聖如來的金石，借傳統的神韻造型，融新意之雅趣舒展，無論是陰刀陽刻、漢碑古韻、鐘鼎行文皆達到金石的最高峰，砸釵還古的境界，視若金玉環垂，墜地有聲，玉墜殘缺，自然到了爐火純青之度，如「虛懷若谷」一印，及「江山入畫圖」，見其筆力之脆勁，力道蒼古得以殘鋒破皮，有的佈局舒展，有的蒼花雕爛，有的抒心大方，有的莞爾唾涎，美不勝收，實乃奪古人之精華，舉現世之奇刀，不愧一代金石巨匠。而實質上，哪裡是金石大家能與之相品，猶如大海與滴水之量，但可惜的是因緣變換、萬法無常，我們現在看到的這些金石是三世多杰羌佛小時的刀功，這些金石原件早已流落他人之手，被不法之徒假冒為真跡書畫，故大家要特別小心，唯有蓋有三世多杰羌佛的總持法王章和指印章的才是三世多杰羌佛的真品。

（此文的英文翻譯印在前面）

CATEGORY 8

Classical Poetry and Songs

第八大類　詩詞歌賦

Introduction

As early as 1991, H.H. Dorje Chang Buddha III Wan Ko Yeshe Norbu Holiest Tathagata was awarded the title of "Master of Oriental Art." The representative presenting that award praised H.H. Dorje Chang Buddha III for restoring the 5,000 year old culture of China. In 1994, the 5,612 experts and scholars representing forty-eight countries and regions at the World Poets and Culture Congress unanimously named H.H. Dorje Chang Buddha III as a "Distinguished International Master." However, H.H. Dorje Chang Buddha III did not want to accept such honors and continued making further contributions to mankind in a quiet and selfless manner.

The poems of this ancient Buddha H.H. Dorje Chang Buddha III, such as His *qi jue* poems (four-line poems with seven characters to a line and a strict tonal pattern and rhyme scheme) and *qi lu* poems (eight-line poems with seven characters to a line and a strict tonal pattern and rhyme scheme), retain the ancient poetic style and have reached a level on par with that of the ancient great poets. However, in the area of expressing philosophy, His Holiness's poetry has surpassed the poetry of the ancient virtuous ones. It is self-evident that H.H. Wan Ko Yeshe Norbu Holiest Tathagata is truly the most outstanding master of Chinese poetry from ancient times to the present.

After you are enraptured by poems of H.H. Dorje Chang Buddha III and reflect on His poetic style, you will discover that H.H. Dorje Chang Buddha III has reached the peak of perfection in both the *hao fang* and the *wan yue* styles. Those are the two major styles of the *ci* type of Chinese poetry. The *hao fang* style is bold and powerful, while the *wan yue* style is soft, elegant, and graceful.

Take, for example, the bold and stirring *ci* type of poem entitled "To the Tune of *Nian-Nu-Jiao*."（念奴嬌） It is an excellent poem due to its extensive and powerful spirit that moves the universe as well as its expansive and transcendent poetic perspective. You cannot find such an exceptional poem anywhere else in the world. In contrast, the *ci* type of poem entitled "To the Tune of *Ye-Ban-Le*"（夜半樂） has the feel of the enchanting moon on the Xiao and Xiang Rivers, the reflection of towering pagodas on the water, and the beautiful sound of a Chinese lute played under willow trees. How enrapturing, elegant, and charming that poem is!

Actually, we lack the understanding to give an in-depth appraisal of the poetry of H.H. Dorje Chang Buddha III. However, we do know that writing poetry is a simple matter for this ancient Buddha and represents less than a drop of water in the vast ocean of His Holiness's talents.

(This text was translated from the Chinese text that follows.)

簡　　介

早在1991年，多杰羌佛第三世雲高益西諾布頂聖如來就被授與「東方藝術大師」的桂冠，在頒獎盛典上，頒獎代表高度評價三世多杰羌佛恢復了五千年的中國固有文化。而在1994年，世界詩人文化大會的48個國家和地區，共5612位專家學者代表，更一致推定三世多杰羌佛為「特級國際大師」，但三世多杰羌不願領受，而自己則為人類默默無私地作出更多的奉獻。

古佛三世多杰羌的詩，無論是七絕、七律，不失古風，都達到與古代詩人並駕齊驅的境界，而在哲理上，更勝古風一籌，超越前德。不言而喻，頂聖如來雲高益西諾布實乃古往今來大詩家。

不僅如此，當你被三世多杰羌佛的詩驚歎醉迷之後，再度領賞詞風，你會覺得無論是豪放派和婉約派，三世多杰羌佛都是登峰造極的至高境界。如《念奴嬌》，此詞豪寰溢宇，無論是氣勢之廣博雄壯，還是意境之高遠超凡，都堪稱絕世佳品。而《夜半樂》，更別有瀟湘醉月，楊柳琵琶樓台臥影之情懷，詞風宛然欲醉，又是何等的優雅含媚！其實，我們評價三世多杰羌佛的詩詞，這完全是低論缺解，三世多杰羌佛猶如汪洋大海、宇宙蒼穹，詩詞對於如來古佛可謂小菜一碟而已，猶如大海中的一滴水都不如。

（此文的英文翻譯印在前面）

娲石一角

眼品雕風論神韻，取石女娲一角珍。

百俊素奇微枝小，浪擊群崗烹大成。

高士圖

山翁縛戲法最難，隱伴幽谷出人間。

意化蒼靈收覺照，岁碩虎子不悶參。

黃石溫泉(一)

火出地殼談溫泉，疊嶂叢林一室間。

問津遊士關外客，獨駕孤舟仍群山。

黃石溫泉(二)

高崖懸放千江浪，低谷側旁幾人閒。

天地含旋掌中覽，峽谷春秋許萬年。

一柱擎天

焦紅艷姿薄如紗，一柱擎天出龍華。

燈煌幻影公讚絕，典史情懷有人家。

蜀川黃龍(一)

蜀上黃龍訪仙潭，池秀乾坤祖巳先。

天梯挂駕高岩布，地谷靈兮湧青蓮。

蜀川黃龍(二)

信步碧潭水正斜，十載英姿幻黃花。

滿目尋途嫣然逝，幾度春光見披麻。

恍然悟識陽關故，玉壘浮雲豈是家。

若覺道上超塵路，心無境辦自天涯。

蜀川黃龍(三)

蜀川黃龍始上痕，百代風情未知音。

玄潭賣弄池中景，步度天梯幾仙人。

幽途寂然蟬聲絕，逝盡黃花吟歌春。

遠眺群峰披白帳，且作清溪萬古靈。

念奴嬌

頓入乾坤，大千界、萬疊坎坷雄立。百種風流縱輝煌，終歸一笑了結。金紅報曉，晨鐘催月，一展婆婆迹。群生奔涯，恍然如煙化雪！

曾憶雲高昔歲，文武空門好，獅子震裂。三千患疾訪俺門，晝夜岐黃施絕。百萬思頭，悠悠般若道，三界蕩擊。願平生事，盡為有情銷益。

過夔門

風翻白浪過夔門，濤建聯山怒吼聲。

兩度遊子驚天地，一葉單舟問乾坤。

家居

華宮日月麗陽天，喜乘西風六月閒。

故朋來從叭聲望，始知暑氣已冬殘。

枯林夜影

寒霜枯木一座林，夜半突傳談笑聲。

眾鳥群飛開月影，清露點點濕衣襟。

回春

望日娥容影最明，江畔柳行風助聲。

寄語波光休笑我，三昧意下可回春。

高人界

智人常抽釜底薪，高士意下經石文。

解得莊老三清意，臨邛道上不飛塵。

飛仙關

高山深處不是雲，疑是煙甲起繽紛。

四顧青禾傾城笑，八面臨風詢吾君。

七絕

笛聲送我過平羌，船傍烏尤滿燈堂。

春風贈暖迎客往，霧染黃昏山不蒼。

七絕

點綴雲煙似桃紅，偶然繡出妖嬈峰。

青高橫渡行赤水，夜帳空長泛北風。

夜半樂·浦江之夜

浦江夜半遊場，登輪參睹，兩岸茫茫去，弄風流勝地，萬輪光俱，異音共長，無邊空色，飽覽半江熒火，一片奇趣，高閣樓巍巍彩寶玉，招醉賞人翩翩。憶故子瞻，太白昔意，嫣然揮，婆婆一曲雅句。萬里乾坤千重緞錦，今昔豐年悠悠，工步灘郎麗嬌英，安養人癡影，阿賴耶藏，沈沙發演雄姿歷跡，觀目下生華嫵更途長。超然去，笑爾靈犀笑瀟湘，思遊間，念念魂飄芳，歸來首，般若滄桑。

高堂神燈

高堂神燈古柏懸，遠照月華近森山。

潮期日日人流急，月後寥寥步幾閒。

巫溪江畔晨曦詠

光目金霞艷雲開，風捲濤聲色又來。

障暮長持千江水，搖櫓空懸市徑街。

奉節城

仰迎大江老城門，千帆交頓夜市燈。

奉節古道街客整，史來舊跡未出新。

奉節江風晚霞咏

煙甲縹緲空繞山，夕陽照映金璧全。

江流霧障鎖不住，行船晝夜始無眠。

江心詠

萬洲城廓出江邊，我同東渡駕狂瀾。

獨傲鐘樓收眼底，兩岸泊關舸進繁。

江心弄詞雕雅韻，太白還魂幾斷弦。

詩賦焉得余主業，宇宙人生一念觀。

晨曦山霧題

山吐霧氣入空流，奇峰玉帶景亦收。

腳前白幛飛千尺，可憐攝子未前籌。

遊豐都鬼城

登高不見有人家，暗處幽靈鬼影斜。

正欲腕筆韻情意，突聞笛笑露桃花。

山城景三首之一

明風木樓江接聯，道坡蚓缺幾回還。

水流影倒終年固，百萬航爭景不邊。

之二

古木疊山江面疊，煙雨飄飄又重來。

二度嘉陵依然趣，一波清水兩面街。

之三

山城星火萬家明，照映兩江碧波清。

千航樓閣收不盡，日月同輝夜市燈。

重慶南溫泉二首

（一）

深熱南泉勝景華，復從依稀問人家。

怎見昔秋黃金碧，一池青萍路玉花。

（二）

飛絲直下洗南泉，綠景青岸目盡宣。

聲擊懸壇天下客，疑是織女布垂川。

夔門憶白帝

夔門夾關白帝懸，青花浪出詩百篇。

文風更莫東馳水，武陣強爭塑泥丸。

不畏驚濤探龍潭

船放三峽流，雄風搏浪頭。

眾客驚攀岸，我自泰然舟。

洗衣女色

溪畔浣衣娘，秋波撒群芳。

輕搖柔紗罩，英姿露陽剛。

打坐航輪返蜀川

飛輪上水最為難，無事閒參水中天。

青山倒影原本幻，彩雲變異送前川。

我作牧羊倌

草原萬頃築山巔，牧羊藝別故自然。

彈跳忽向西北馳，我揚橫鞭走泥丸。

太湖玉

玉美搖裹下雲端，醉眼魚肚臥龍潭。

歌彈殿上靈霄曲，絕代名花色流邊。

雲團玉

青綠玉雲團，色道麗天然。

雅趣收不盡，肇弄來幾番。

深坑玉

古玉絕深坑，老樸色不生。

平中好內含，出土始稀年。

珊紅玉

玉中傳民歌，希世珊紅羅。

俯覽地上石，色下是摩訶。

羊脂玉

羊脂玉中王，色媚散群芳。

飛來天外石，華門見書香。

福壽玉

福壽延年齊與天，陰紅掛綠色韻玄。

兜率三天雲台石，偶然一笑未羞慚。

賦　神妙的水鄉之一

此畫緣何超絕寰，玄味無窮不言間。

閱罷塵中歌上曲，歸來醉眼瑤池山。

賦　神妙的水鄉之二

壁上岩峰幾醉人，猶點清韻不凡塵。

恍如卷上靈光動，一紙觀山萬種情。

賦　北極冰窟熊

北極冰窟壁上懸，出湧框外咫尺間。

天上有物來此室，屋滿冬意不生寒。

賦　黃金宮韻

黃宮石窟韻正斜，絶艷群芳稀世葩。

欲尋觀山洞景趣，那得紙間築岩花。

北極冰窟熊　七律之詩

北極熊羆最喜寒，四時眠臥冰窟間。

莫取水中游食物，且撿移魂骨便餐。

非人識得玄中妙，由來禪昧破飢關。

晶宮勝事難言盡，洞內有客醉一仙。

玄妙彩寶挂

寶挂飛瀰把神玄，嬌紅綠翠笑天顏。

本物不揚雲霧客，仙風吹頌鼓搖幡。

應金巳義培珠之情湖鶴壽而賦之
七絶

鶴壽情湖妙難收，悠然勝景建春秋。

揚帆莫上蓬山意，待到何年問木舟。

綠玉懸紗之一壁隨賦七絶
以頌妙哉然耳

綠玉玄平散清芳，不帶人間脂粉香。

讀尤壁上心生醉，似若幽蘭登鼻堂。

應恆公之造景高原碧海所製立體畫
「藏域風情」賦七絶之一

群岡遼原落幾番，西風華蓋動雲壇。

有峭高處鎖不盡，頭人首度論主賢。

應恆公之造景高原碧海所製立體畫
「藏域風情」賦七絶之二

峰姿絶活雪域嬌，山情雲賀艷妖嬈。

搏開窗前壁上眼，圖中塑景問風騷。

應恆公之造景高原碧海所製立體畫
「藏域風情」賦七絶之三

藏原雪谷峰醉人，氣潤群芳透清芬。

雄姿巳漢催英俊，高崖眺處最怡情。

一柱擎天神變跡

佛賜韻雕有內明，一柱擎天攬兮分。

干前體大難登罩，安來好座映斜暉。

不動（五律）

黃葉飄不盡，微絮獨報春。

青霞送孤獨，我自豔三分。

賽馬（五律）

春紅好賽馬，圍圍看相爭。

幾度鞭捶後，急蹄少女英。

塞外（五律）

三番塞外行，肥牛碧草深。

雲天為羅帳，日月伴同君。

將軍頌

聖境梅香

展傲骨冰姿，
看梅花占景，
群姿丟色，
妖桃失影。
偶行筆，
幾代風塵。
人間煙火盡移蹤，
唯紙上清芳飄來醒腦。
莞爾醉夢猶然，
多杰羌來，
三世境，
這報土慈悲，
那高人留潔，
筆情，
筆跡，
一笑風塵，
正風塵，
幾代風塵。

To the Tune of "Jiang Jun Song"
Plum Fragrance in the Holy Realm

Reveal her icy bearing and proud bones,
See how plum blossom commands the scene,
The crowd of beauties suddenly lacks color,
Seductive peach has lost its looks.
A few casual strokes,
So many eons of wind and dust.
The smoke and fire of the human world all disappears,
Leaving only a pure fragrance from the paper,
It wafts over me, awakening my mind.
The smile of the enchanted dream still remains,
Buddha Vajradhara has come
Three times to this world.
To this Buddha Land of merciful compassion
That great one has brought purity,
Feelings of the brush,
Traces of the brush,
One smile in the wind and dust,
Now the wind and dust,
So many eons of wind and dust.

将軍頌

寒韻報春

憶群峰百丈，
透稀小瓏玲，
寒香莞爾，
懸崖紅杏。
悠然間，
幾多怡情。
壁岩高谷何處去？
但見得這般似柳扶搖。
數縷輕柔花飄，
西風送景，
恍然了，
是寒韻報春，
又這般舒心，
醉人，
醉心，
泰若怡情，
似怡情，
幾多怡情。

To the Tune of "Jiang Jun Song"
Cold Harmony Heralds the Spring

I remember: myriad lofty peaks,
And scattered everywhere, sparkling gems of light,
The smile of cold fragrance,
Red plum trees hanging from the cliffs.
Unhurried, gentle,
Such feelings of tranquility.
Cliff walls and high valleys - where have they gone?
Now all I can see is a willow-like sway.
A few threads lightly float,
Moved by the west wind,
Suddenly I realize,
Cold clouds are heralding the spring,
And this contented mind,
Intoxicates the man,
Intoxicates the mind,
Self-possessed tranquility,
It seems like tranquility,
Such feelings of tranquility.

聖君同

壁上懸圖

這方壁，
白茫茫無處，
我看兮，
烈焰叢林，
無有鳥來。
遠眺兮，
唉！
是園中性海，
無有蟲來。
我看兮，
無有林：
我看兮，
無有焰，
唉！
蟲兮何在？
原來兮，
壁上懸栽，
一幅畫，
丹青墨，
硃砂紅，
又來幾筆兮，
原來兮，
夢遊我在。
夢裡何來？
不執兮，
無有壁：
不執兮，
無有畫。
唉！
思遊這不該，
這不該。

To the Tune of "Sheng Jun Tong"
A Painting on the Wall

This square wall
A vast, white space of nothing,
Ah, I see now,
A brilliant blaze in a grove of trees,
With not even a bird there.
Gaze in the distance,
Ai!
It is an ocean of self-nature in a garden,
With not even an insect there.
Ah, I see now,
There is no grove;
Ah, I see now,
There is no brilliant blaze,
Ai!
Where are the insects?
Ah, in fact,
Hanging on the wall,
A painting,
Colored ink,
Vermilion paste,
And a few brushstrokes,
Ah, in fact,
I am roaming in a dream,
From whence does the dream come?
Ah, do not cling to it,
There is no wall;
Ah, do not cling to it,
There is no painting.
Ai!
Roaming thoughts should not be,
Should not be.

令君輝

勝境報春圖

濃姿樹，
淡雅花，
勾魂疊嶂，
寒香幾度來。
涌鼻中，
最思戀，
玄賣風姿，
報春她猶在。
似這般，
賀春梅，
近別無恙，
勝境正搖芳。

映歌春

有梅高骨植

報春今眠何處？
寒韻窗前兮，
三更醉月夢枝頭，
遊去遼闊歸兮。
思遊兮，
歸來大地。
陣陣流芳亭廊繞，
歸來兮空空，
依然大地。
推窗兮，
亭亭依立，
有梅兮，
高骨而植，
高骨而植。

映歌春

書卷情濃

紙上桃紅幾色，
不識猜來兮，
四時花魁皆成婢，
豔媚硃墨歌兮。
藏持兮，
有客來時。
處處含情報春曉，
有客兮歸歸，
依舊來時。
遠眺兮，
陣陣寒韻，
梅香兮，
卷秀含情，
卷秀含情。

To the Tune of "Ling Jun Hui"

Heralding Spring in the Wondrous Realm

Dark figure of a tree,
Light, refined blossoms,
Bewitches a myriad peaks,
How many times has cold fragrance come?
The scent rises in your nose,
As a most cherished memory
Mysteriously reveals her graceful bearing,
She is here again to herald the spring.
It is in this way,
Plum greets the spring,
That parting will come soon matters not,
For now perfume wafts through the Wondrous Realm.

To the Tune of "Ying Ge Chun"

A Plum That Grows Tall and Strong

The herald of spring, where does she sleep?
Ah, cold harmony before the window,
Midnight dreams of branches beneath a drunken moon
Ah, she returns after roaming in vast space.
Roaming thoughts,
And a return to the great world.
Drifts of fragrance wind around pavilion and hall,
Returning emptiness,
As before, to the great world.
Open the window,
Graceful she stands,
There is a plum tree,
Growing tall and strong,
Growing tall and strong.

To the Tune of "Ying Ge Chun"

Strong Feelings in the Scroll

On the paper, this shade of pink,
Ah, who can guess its real color?
Next to her, all the flower queens are slaves,
Ah, alluring brows and vermilion ink songs.
Ah, she remains here in the painting,
Until the guest comes.
Tenderness everywhere heralds the dawn of spring,
Ah, the guest has gone,
Yet later will come again.
Ah, gaze in the distance,
Breaths of cold harmony,
Ah, the perfume of the plum,
Tenderness in the scroll,
Tenderness in the scroll.

小樓芳

君悅君兮

君悅君兮無人問，
有梅獨傲懷情兮。
畫看天涯樂樂，
暮歸兮，
顏色無棲。
夜帳茫茫去兮，
幾時休兮，
幾時休，
君悅君兮，
金紅報曉日日兮，
朝霞爛爛，
炊歌處，
霞輝繞萬里，
萬里兮，
萬里。

To the Tune of "Xiao Lou Fang"

The Lord's Pleasure

No one asks what is the Lord's pleasure,
The mood of the plum, proudly alone.
Watch it by day - joy to the ends of Heaven
When night returns
Its color has no place to bide.
The curtain of night is vast, vast,
Oh, when will it end?
When will it end?
The Lord's pleasure,
A golden cock cries at the dawning of day,
Resplendent colored clouds of morning,
A place of music and song,
The brilliance of the clouds encircles ten-thousand miles,
Ah, ten-thousand miles,
Ten-thousand miles.

菩薩蠻

境界

濃淡兩蕾出枝間，
青綠三昧潤宇寰，
隨緣弄遊舞，
不變自怙主。
若問梅花色，
學識在賢達。
待到無着時，
任運把玩持。

To the Tune of "Pu Sa Mahn"

Mind Realm

One dark, one pale, a pair of buds grow on the branches
Light green, dark green, samadhi nourishes the world
Following karma, you lightly dance and float,
Immutably still, yourself an ancient Buddha.
You ask about the color of the plum blossom?
It is learning contained in virtue.
Wait until it is plucked, and without bonds
Then freely hold it and turn it in your hands

望海潮

有梅賀群生

玉林冰潔，
太空驚魂，
遙展東藏西歸。
寒香桃塵，
雛花一束，
秀盡多少情懷，
問桑田歲月。
看墨情風骨，
萬古不休。
怙主悲憫，
可眾望嫣然歸宗。
色藝寥然飄逸，
穿筆力萬頃，

博識書風，
書畫年來，
持福長恆，
點寫祥瑞梅花。
見內含奇功，
願施萬古，
筆出雅風。
但看春色宜人，
群生入聖中。

To the Tune of "Wang Hai Chao"

The Plum Greets All Beings

The frozen purity of a jade grove
The startled soul of space
Spreads out far to east and west.
Cold fragrance, down of pink,
And though only a single spray of blossoms,
Loveliness greater than any mood,
So time itself becomes a mulberry dream.
Look: wind and bone expressed in ink,
In ten-thousand ages it will never fade.
The compassion of an ancient Buddha,
Captivates all beings, and brings them to truth.
Color artistry, free and graceful,
Powerful brushstrokes crossing vast space,
An atmosphere of erudition,
These words and paintings, year after year,
Bring constant blessings,
The auspiciousness of plum blossoms.
Look: within is a mysterious power,
Which I offer to the ten-thousand ages,
From the brush, an elegant air.
Just look at delightful spring color,
And all beings will enter holiness.

CATEGORY 9

Vajra Needle That Eliminates Illness

第九大類　金剛除病針

Introduction

In applying this vajra needle that eliminates illness, Kuan Yin Bodhisattva is used as the yidam (object of veneration), and the Horse Head Vajra Deity (a transformation body of Kuan Yin Bodhisattva) manifests awesome power. That is why the Han-Chinese people call it "Galloping Horse Wonderful Needle." It is a healing technique specially used to cure people's illnesses. Currently, H.H. Dorje Chang Buddha III Wan Ko Yeshe Norbu Holiest Tathagata is the only one who possesses this dharma.

The powerful effects of this needle are miraculous. Various effects are produced according to the particular mudra and mantra H.H. Dorje Chang Buddha III applies. This needle is able to open all of the body's joints and acupuncture points. People who receive this treatment experience power moving through their body. No matter how strong a patient's power of resistance may be, as soon as H.H. Dorje Chang Buddha III increases the power of the mudra, the patient will immediately feel as if his internal organs were on fire and will fall to the ground screaming in pain. It is clear that people do not have the power to offer resistance to the effects of this needle.

This needle can easily cure yin deficiency and yang excess relating to the liver, gall, kidneys, spleen, and lungs; qi (vital energy)-blood disharmony; harm done to the internal organs; and other strange illnesses resulting from the six meridians or imbalance among the four great elements. After Zigong Zhuang personally experienced the Galloping Horse Wonderful Needle treatment, he wrote the following words in the book *Master Yi Yungao* (Master Yi Yungao is H.H. Dorje Chang Buddha III):

"Galloping Horse Wonderful Needle is a unique healing technique of Buddhism requiring special powers, and it is used to cure people of their illnesses. It is said that common people cannot master this technique. In order to apply this technique, one must have reached a very high state of training in the Vajra Fist Dharma of esoteric Buddhism. One must also have entered the phase that transcends the generation and completion phases. Through special skills, one produces a power that adjusts the "external four great elements." (earth, water, fire, and wind) One then uses one's concentration powers to bring about needle treatment reactions that course through the body like a galloping horse. Additionally, one must use thought to guide the "internal four great elements" of the patient's body so that his body undergoes acute changes in an instant. Using the energy channels and acupuncture points, the obstructions of illness are expelled one after another. Why does that treatment produce such amazing effects? It has to do with the ultimate truths of the universe."

Zigong Zhuang went on to describe his experience when H.H. Dorje Chang Buddha III Wan Ko Yeshe Norbu Holiest Tathagata treated him with the Galloping Horse Wonderful Needle: "I saw the Master[1] take out a thin, long silver needle. He sat facing me about two meters away. He then tossed the needle, which entered the acupuncture point on my left leg called *yang ling quan*. At that time, there was no unusual feeling in my body. I just felt the needle shaking continuously. As the Master's mudras changed, so did my reactions. He shouted "swell!" and my entire body generated a swelling feeling. He shouted "tingle!" and my entire body instantly produced tingling sensations. He shouted "cold!" and the inside of my body at once felt as if I had entered an ice cellar.

"The Master then uttered something unintelligible, and I heard a loud boom in my head. It seemed as if my body had quickly swelled. The inside of my body felt like a sudden violent storm accompanied by thunder, lightening, and surging rivers and seas. It was an astonishing and shocking experience. Then, it seemed as if wind and fire were fast approaching before my eyes. The wind was helping the strength of the fire, and the fire was adding to the power of the wind. In an instant, I was being tormented by internal and external forces. I perspired profusely and was almost destroyed. Right when I was flustered and confused, I heard "leave!" Everything then vanished and became peaceful. I forgot about both my body and mind. There was just an expanse of tranquility and emptiness.

"After a short while, strangely enough, it seemed as if that needle was "galloping" on its own. It would shake and sensations would course up my leg and enter acupuncture points in the proper sequence of those points. At that time, my entire body felt open and unblocked. My qi-blood circulation was as free flowing as a spring stream or floating clouds. I can't say whether it was normal consciousness or hallucination, but I felt that my whole body and mind were immersed in happiness and pleasure.

"I finally experienced the miraculous effects of the Galloping Horse Wonderful Needle. Although I am well known for always sleeping very soundly, that night I could not fall asleep. While in a state of drowsiness the next morning, I suddenly became clear-headed. I wiped my eyes and realized my illness had disappeared. The blue sky and green earth spread before my window. Full of energy, I threw myself into the new day."[2]

---

[1] Here and below the word *Master* refers to H.H. Dorje Chang Buddha III.
[2] Pages 180-181 of *Master Yi Yungao* written by Zigong Zhuang.

A disciple by the name of Kion Yat beseeched H.H. Dorje Chang Buddha III to treat him with needles. When H.H. Dorje Chang Buddha III lightly applied one needle, disciple Yat did not at first feel anything. But when His Holiness began to recite a mantra and apply a mudra, disciple Yat became cold. Even ice formed on his eyebrows. His illness was immediately cured. This vajra needle is truly the king of all needles that only a Buddha possesses. Great Bodhisattva Tangtong Gyalpo Rinpoche XVI said that he personally saw the limitless power of the Galloping Horse Wonderful Needle and the incredibly high realization of H.H. Dorje Chang Buddha III.

(This text was translated from the Chinese text that follows.)

簡　　介

　　金剛除病針即是以觀音菩薩為本尊，馬頭金剛化現威力的針功，所以漢人叫它「跑馬神針」，那是專門為人調治病患的醫術，目前此世界上只有多杰羌佛第三世雲高益西諾布頂聖如來掌有此法。

　　此針功力神奇絕妙，隨著三世多杰羌佛的手印、咒語運轉功力，可以打通身上的一切穴道關節。接受治療的人可以體會到力量在身內走動，無論你的毅力有多強，只要三世多杰羌佛加強咒力，你馬上會五內俱焚，倒地慘叫，可見其功力實在非人力所能抗拒，排除肝膽腎脾肺命陰虛陽亢、氣血不和、五臟之損等六經病症、四大不調之怪症易於反掌，如莊子公親身體驗了金剛針後，在《義雲高大師》一書中說：

　　所謂「走馬神針」，那是出於佛家為民調治疾患的獨特的功夫醫術。據說此技非一般人能掌握，此技的運用，必須將密宗金剛拳練到高深境界，進入生圓不二次第，通過功夫產生「外四大」(地水火風)的調節作用力，然後運用自身的定力，導致銀針感應行走馬馳。同時還要用意念牽引患者肌體的「內四大」，讓其在瞬息產生劇烈變幻，通過經絡穴位依次驅除病障。為什麼會產生這樣的奇效呢？這涉及了宇宙學的真諦。

　　莊子公說多杰羌佛第三世雲高益西諾布頂聖如來為他打走馬神針實踐體驗：只見大師（即三世多杰羌佛——編者注，下同）拿出一支細長的銀針，距我兩米遠近相向而坐，將銀針一擲，插進我左腿穴位「陽陵泉」。這時，我體內並無異感，只覺銀針顫動不止，隨著雲高大師手勢的感應，叫聲：「脹！」全身便產生脹感。叫聲：「麻！」體內即刻產生麻感。叫聲：「冷！」體內即刻如入冰窖。隨即，大師又咕嚕一句什麼，只覺頭部轟然一聲，似覺身軀急速膨脹，體內如驟發疾風暴雨，伴隨電閃雷鳴，翻江倒海，震人心魄。隨即，眼前風火迫臨，風助火勢，火助風威，剎那間恍然被內外煎熬，大汗淋漓，幾乎毀滅。正惶惑間，只聽一聲：「去也！」什麼又都煙消雲散，風平浪靜，使人身心兩忘，一片寂然空靜。不一會，似乎那支針在奇怪地自行走馬，顫顫悠悠，沿腿上行，依次見穴而入。此時渾身只覺暢通無阻，氣血循環，如春水流雲。當時不知是意識或者幻覺，反正我感到整個身心都浸浴在相親相戀的幸福悅樂之中。

　　我終於嘗試到了「走馬神針」那神奇的功效。這夜，素以酣睡而聞名的我竟然失眠。次晨於矇矓狀態中突然清醒，抹抹眼睛，疾患已失，藍天綠地展於窗前。於是，便精神飽滿地投入新的一天中。（莊子公先生所著《義雲高大師》第180-181頁）

　　有一位叫葉怡強的弟子，求三世多杰羌為他施針，三世多杰羌佛輕輕一針，此時沒有感覺，但一持咒結手印，當時就將葉怡強冰凍起來，連眉毛都結了冰，當下病症立除。這金剛針實在是針中之王，唯佛所有。正如大聖菩薩第十六世唐東迦波仁波且說：他親見雲高益西諾布頂聖如來的佛法馬頭針威力大得無窮，證量高得不得了。

（此文的英文翻譯印在前面）

The Power of the Holy Vajra Needle

My name is Guang-Fen Fu. Since I was young, I have been physically weak and often ill. When I became an adult, my mother told me, "Daughter! You have had a weak constitution since you were young. Go and learn medicine. This will be good for your health, and you will not become weary through exerting too much physical strength."

In 1958, I began following a teacher to learn traditional Chinese medicine. Because my illnesses resulted from the power of karma accumulated through many lifetimes and eons, my illnesses did not decrease as my knowledge of medicine and my experience in practicing medicine grew. Disease constantly followed me wherever I went.

In 1978 and the following few years, I suffered from a gastric ulcer in which most of my stomach hemorrhaged. During that time, I also discharged blood when going to the bathroom and vomited blood. In 1981, I had no choice but to undergo surgery to cut out most of my stomach. My health was even worse after the surgery. My food intake lessened, my face became pale, I spoke without any vigor, my spirit was weak, my movements were slow, and I often could not go to work.

As result of the care and assistance given to me by a friend, in 1987 I met my respected Buddha Master, H.H. Dorje Chang Buddha III Wan Ko Yeshe Norbu Holiest Tathagata. When His Holiness learned of my sufferings from illness and my strained financial circumstances, His Holiness showed immense compassion and concern. His Holiness treated me with the holy vajra needle. H.H. Buddha Master asked me to show His Holiness the acupuncture point on my foot called *zu san li*. My respected Buddha Master then squatted down and applied that needle to me. After the needle was applied, my respected Buddha Master then said, "Pay attention! I will now apply my dharma power."

When my respected Buddha Master then put his hands into a mudra before me, I immediately began to feel numbness, a swelling sensation, and pain. My whole body emitted heat, and I was slightly perspiring. When my respected Buddha Master heard me repeatedly scream in pain, His Holiness released his hands from that mudra. I instantly felt that the numbness, swelling, and pain that I had just experienced had disappeared. The only thing I felt was a relaxed and comfortable feeling that my body had never before experienced. My respected Buddha Master then said, "This needle was used to open your energy channels and chakras. You are too anemic."

At that time, I had not yet become a Buddhist or learned Buddhism. My respected Buddha Master treated me and all other living beings as his own family members, equally lending them a helping hand out of great compassion. In 1988, I knew that I wanted to convert to and learn Buddhism in order to leave suffering, attain happiness, and walk the path leading to accomplishment in the dharma and liberation from the cycle of reincarnation.

After following H.H. Buddha Master, my health has improved day by day, my complexion is ruddy, my spirit is clear, my voice is resonant, and I walk with vigor. I gradually understood just how magnificent H.H. Buddha Master is. I also came to gradually comprehend the realness of the Buddha-dharma. Those who see me now say, "You have totally changed in the last two years. You don't look so frail as you did before." What they found most difficult to believe is that I returned from my trip to the plateaus of Tibet and Qinghai, which are places that lack oxygen, without any adverse health effects.

Because I received H.H. Buddha Master's teachings and empowerment, I advanced in the area of medicine. I took a countywide test and was the first to receive a certificate of qualification as a doctor of traditional Chinese medicine. I took provincial and municipal tests and obtained certificates qualifying me as a "doctor-in-charge" who practices traditional Chinese medicine. The hospital put a sign up for me that read "expert outpatient service." My patients have increased day by day. I have cured patients near and far of their difficult and complicated illnesses. As a result, I have a bit of fame in the local area where I live. Everything that I have is due to the teachings and empowerment that the Buddha Master bestowed upon me after I began learning Buddhism. The kindness and grace H.H. Buddha Master conferred upon me are as enormous as a mountain. Each and every bit of his kindness and grace is indelibly etched in my heart.

I remember one day around the year 1989. Zi-Fang Liu, a disciple of my respected Buddha Master, went to the home of my respected Buddha Master in the Nanxin District of Xindu. She beseeched my respected Buddha Master to save her. She said that her illness has lasted many years, that it is acutely painful, and that she is about to collapse. She had been to all of the major hospitals in China and had spent a lot of money, all to no avail. I saw that her complexion was unnaturally dark and that her whole body was rigid. She constantly complained about her unbearable pain.

Then, she suddenly fell to the ground and did not get up. She looked ghastly pale. My respected Buddha Master immediately treated her with the holy vajra needle in order to empower her. Because she was in a state of shock, she did not have any reaction when the needle was applied. After a short while, Sister Liu regained consciousness, stood up, and stated she was no longer in pain.

Every time I saw the wonders of my respected Buddha Master's holy vajra needle, I had an even greater desire to learn how to apply that holy needle. One day I said to my respected Buddha Master, "Respected Buddha Master, teach me how to apply that amazing needle so that I may cure more patients." My respected Buddha Master said to me in a soft tone of voice, "Guang-Fen, your powers are insufficient. Let's put that matter aside for the time being." One time I saw Hsi Jao Ken Ten Rinpoche, who is from Taiwan, also ask my respected Buddha Master to teach him how to apply that amazing needle. My respected Buddha Master replied, "Your powers are insufficient. Let's put that matter aside for the time being."

I later learned that the source of the effectiveness of the holy vajra needle is my respected Buddha Master's state of realization and virtue and the power of his merit. With a holy mind of enlightenment and great compassion, His Holiness assists living beings with physical illnesses, psychological illnesses, as well as living beings who are suffering due to the power of karma. Furthermore, His Holiness constantly and compassionately empowers living beings through his teachings, thereby enabling them to extricate themselves from suffering and find the key to curing and preventing disease.

I have followed H.H. Buddha Master for more than ten years. I, Guang-Fen, have evolved from a person who did not understand anything about learning Buddhism and self-cultivation to a Buddhist disciple striving to integrate wisdom, compassion, and skillful means and a person striving to be selfless. Based upon empowerment from my respected Master's practice and from the lineage of great masters throughout generations, a type of merit of the fruit of Buddhahood exerts its influence, causing Buddhist disciples to walk the path toward liberation and accomplishment in the dharma. With the incomparable kindness and empowerment of my respected Buddha Master, Buddhist disciples give rise to bodhicitta and strive to enlighten themselves and others. The compassion, care, and protection my respected Buddha Master bestows upon his disciples and all living beings cannot be described in words. To know what I am saying, you have to experience it yourself.

I deeply feel that the kindness and grace shown to me by my Buddha Master is difficult to repay. All that I can do is resolve to be a disciple of the Buddha in all of my future lives and devoutly and respectfully turn to and rely upon the eternal Buddha Master. Only a Buddha Master can lead Buddhist disciples out of the bitter sea of reincarnation and lead them toward liberation, accomplishment in the dharma, ending of the cycle of birth and death, becoming a Buddha, saving other living beings, undertaking the cause of the Buddhas and Bodhisattvas, and repaying the kindness of the Buddhas.

This year I have passed sixty-five years of age. What I have written above is my own true personal experience. I have not lied. If what I wrote above contains lies, I am willing to descend into the Avici Hell (hell of uninterrupted suffering). If what I wrote above is true, I offer the merit of this writing to my magnificent Buddha Master who is like my father and mother. I also dedicate such merit to all of my vajra Brothers and Sisters so that they attain enlightenment soon, and to all sentient beings on the six paths of reincarnation. Amitabha!

Written and respectfully submitted by Buddhist disciple,
Guang-Fen Fu
April 16, 2006

(This is a complete translation of the Chinese text that follows originally written and signed by Guang-Fen Fu.)

金 剛 聖 針 的 威 力

　　我叫付光芬，從小體弱多病，長大母親對我說：「女兒！你從小體質差，去學醫，對身體有好處，又不用體力勞累。」1958年我就開始跟師學習中醫。由於多生累劫業力之病，並未隨我學醫的知識和行醫經驗而減少，疾病總是跟著我轉。1978年連續幾年胃潰瘍大部出血、屙血、吐血。到1981年只好做胃大部切除術，術後身體更差，進食少，臉色蒼白，說話有氣無力，精神衰弱，行動緩慢，常常不能上班。直到1987年在友人的關心幫助下見到我的佛陀恩師多杰羌佛第三世雲高益西諾布頂聖如來。當他老人家了解我的疾苦、貧困時，對我非常慈悲關心，為我打一針金剛聖針，叫我把足三里現出來，佛陀恩師就蹲下來為我打針，一針下去佛陀恩師就說：「注意！我要運功了。」當佛陀恩師在我的面前結個手印一比，我立即感到麻木脹痛，全身發熱出毛毛汗，佛陀恩師聽到我叫痛連連，就把手印放開，我立即感到剛才的麻木脹痛都沒有了，只感到身體從來沒有的輕鬆舒適。佛陀恩師接著說：「這一針為你打通經絡脈結，你太貧血了。」當時的我還未皈依學佛，佛陀恩師對我及一切眾生都當親人對待，平等施予大悲援手。1988年我才知道要皈依學佛，離苦得樂，走解脫成就之路。跟隨三世多杰羌佛陀上師後，我身體一天天好起來，面色紅潤了，神清氣爽了，說話聲音洪亮，行走有力，慢慢體悟到佛陀上師是

多麼偉大，佛法真實不虛。見到我的人都說：「這兩年你完全變了，不像以前弱不禁風樣。」最讓他們不可思議的事，我去西藏、青海高原缺氧的地方回來身體無恙。由於受佛陀上師教誨加持，我的醫學水平提高了，參加全縣考試首取中醫醫師資格證書，參加省、市考試取得主治中醫醫師資格證書，醫院為我掛專家門診牌，病人一天比一天多，很多遠、近疑難病症經我治癒。在當地小有名氣，我擁有的一切一切全是學佛後，佛陀上師教誨加持給予的，佛陀法王上師對我恩重如山，點點滴滴都烙印我心中。

　　我記得大約是1989年的一天，佛陀恩師的弟子劉子芳到新都南新區的家，求佛陀恩師救她，她說她這個病好多年了，痛起來要命、要倒。國內各大醫院都去過了，花了很多錢就是不見效。當時只見她面色青暗，全身強直，不停叫疼痛難忍，一會倒地不起，面無人色，佛陀恩師立刻為她打金剛聖針加持她，由於休克，下針時她並無反應，過一會取針時劉大姐清醒並站立起來說她不痛了。每當我看到佛陀恩師金剛聖針的神奇，我就更想學打這個聖針。有天我對佛陀恩師說：「佛陀恩師您教我神針，我好去救治其他病人。」佛陀恩師對我輕言細語地說：「光芬，你功力不夠，以後再說。」有一次我見到台灣的喜饒根登仁波且也向佛陀恩師求學，佛陀恩師卻說：「你的功力不夠，

以後再說。」

後來我才知道金剛聖針是佛陀恩師他老人家證德證境證量的功德力，以大悲菩提聖心施加一切，患身病、心病、業力苦難眾生的，並隨時教誨慈悲加持使眾生從苦難中解脫出來，找到治病防病的根源所在處。

跟隨佛陀恩師十多年，弟子光芬從一個不懂學佛修行的人到如何才能成為三門合一的佛弟子，無私利人的人，在佛陀恩師加持和歷代祖師傳承力的加持下，形成一種果德，才能使佛弟子走向解脫成就之路，佛陀恩師無與倫比的恩德加持下，佛子內心才升起了菩提心，自覺覺他。佛陀恩師對弟子及一切眾生施以慈悲、關愛、呵護加持有加，無以言表，如人飲水，冷暖自知。深感佛恩難報，唯有發願生生世世做佛陀之子，虔誠恭敬皈向依傍永恆的佛陀上師，只有佛陀上師才能帶佛弟子出離生死輪迴苦海，走解脫成就、了生脫死成佛渡生之

路，擔佛菩薩荷擔家業，報佛恩。

我今年已滿了65歲，以上是我親身經歷，真實不虛，無有妄語。如有妄語我墮入無間地獄，如真實不虛，願此功德供養佛子偉大的佛陀父母親，回向所有的金剛師兄弟，早證菩提，回向六道諸有情，阿彌陀佛。

佛弟子　付光芬講述敬呈

2006年4月16日

（此文的英文翻譯印在前面）

The Holy Needle of the Ancient Buddha Healed My Tumor

Around 1987, I inadvertently discovered pink spots that had grown on the surface of the skin of my left armpit. Underneath those spots was a small, hard lump. I did not pay any attention to it at first, nor did I go to a doctor for treatment. This situation continued for two years. I then began to feel a kind of malaise, which soon spread throughout my entire body. Once when I was chatting with a friend, that friend urged me to see a doctor. Still, I could not think of any reason to do that.

One day I saw on the wall of a hospital some posters relating to lymph-gland tumors and realized that my physical condition was similar to what was described in those posters. The tumor under my armpit had already swollen to around the size of a $50 Taiwan coin (the size of an American silver dollar) and had changed from pink to dark red. Although I became quite flustered about this, I did not have the courage to go to the hospital again to have a more detailed examination performed. I knew very clearly that I would not be able to withstand such a blow since I had just undergone major surgery to remove a tumor on my uterus. Therefore, I simply endured my situation silently and dared not tell anyone about it.

Due to the coming together of karmic conditions, I began chatting with a friend about the surgery I had to remove a tumor on my uterus. With no particular intent in mind, I also mentioned the abnormal condition of my armpit. After my friend heard this, my friend wanted to introduce to me a supreme Buddha Master who could help cure my illness. At that time I did not know the identity of the Buddha Master. I only knew that His Holiness was a great international master of noble character. Without any doubts in my mind, I accompanied that friend of mine to the city of Chengdu in Sichuan Province in mainland China so as to pay a formal visit to that supreme Buddha Master. I had the good fortune of meeting the Buddha Master after waiting more than ten days. The Buddha Master asked me what brought me to Chengdu. I immediately told the Buddha Master the purpose of my visit. The Buddha Master then very compassionately said, "All right, all right. It will go away and be fine."

The Buddha Master took an ordinary silver acupuncture needle so as to begin curing my illness. His Holiness said that if in a moment I felt sensations of swelling or pain, I should tell His Holiness. I then saw the Buddha Master's mouth moving as His Holiness recited a mantra. The Buddha Master then inserted the needle into an acupuncture point between the thumb and index finger on my left hand and gave a puff. At this time I felt blood coursing through all parts my body, and my entire body felt swollen. The temperature of that tumor began to rise, as if it was on fire. After going through that process three separate times, the Buddha Master told me that after I return home I should continue to recite the name of the Buddha or Bodhisattva that I normally recite. I said that I recite "Namo Guan Shi Yin Pu Sa (Homage to Kuan Shi Yin Bodhisattva)." The Master replied, "That is fine. Go ahead and recite that Bodhisattva's name. If you do so earnestly and sincerely, the tumor will soon leave you."

I returned to Taiwan in a very happy state of mind. As before, I busily went about handling business matters, but I did not forget to recite that Bodhisattva's name whenever I had spare time. After I returned to Taiwan, first thing in the morning, I looked at that tumor every day. It neither grew nor shrunk. However, about twenty days after I returned to Taiwan, I was bathing one day and suddenly thought of that red-spotted tumor on my armpit. I quickly took a look in the mirror and surprisingly discovered that the hard lump had shrunk. The original size of a $50 Taiwan coin (an American silver dollar) had shrunk to the size of a $1 Taiwan coin (an American dime).

I was so elated I wanted to jump for joy. I felt very grateful, very grateful! Those two words truly arose from the bottom of my heart as I thanked that magnificent and supreme Master. From that time on, I recited the name of that Bodhisattva even more earnestly and sincerely as a way of showing my appreciation toward that supreme Buddha Master.

However, approximately one month later, that tumor had not shrunk at all. I again began to feel somewhat anxious. Then, I heard a loud sound one evening. The red-spotted hard lump on my left armpit suddenly disappeared without a trace. Words cannot describe the excitement and gratitude I felt deep in my heart. All of the clouds under which I was living vanished at once! I later took refuge in that magnificent Buddha Master Wan Ko Yeshe

Norbu Holiest Tathagata. Seventeen years have now passed, and I am physically healthier and mentally happier than I was when I was young!

All that I have stated above is true! If there is anything fabricated in it, I am willing to descend into the vajra hell! If what I have stated are true words, I dedicate all of the resulting merit to all living beings in the dharma realm!

Disciple: Ting-Ying Li
I prostrate to the Buddhas in the ten directions
within the three spheres.
June 21, 2007

(This is a complete translation of the Chinese text that follows originally written and signed by Ting-Ying Li.)

古 佛 的 聖 針 治 好 了 我 的 腫 瘤

約1987年，我無意間發現左手腋下長在皮膚表面的粉紅色斑點，在斑點下還有一個小硬塊。起先不以為意，也沒有去看醫生治療，就這樣拖了兩年之久。此後，身體開始感到不適，很快的並擴散到全身。一次跟朋友閒聊中，對方也相勸去看醫生，但也始終找不出任何原因。一天在醫院的牆上看見掛著的一些相關淋巴腺腫瘤的海報就跟自己身上的狀況相似，當時腋下的腫瘤硬塊已腫脹到大約50元硬幣大小，並且由粉紅色轉為深紅色，當時心中很是慌張，當下也沒有勇氣再次進去醫院作任何進一步更精密的檢查，因為我很清楚的明白自己將會承受不了再次這樣的打擊，因為我剛動完子宮肌瘤的大型手術，所以只能默默的承受，也不敢告知家人。

在一個因緣際會之下，跟一位朋友無意間聊起上次子宮肌瘤的手術狀況，才又提及這次腋下的異狀，這位朋友聽完，說要引見一位至高無上的佛陀上師幫我醫病。當時我還不了解佛陀上師的身份，只知道是一位具崇高道德的國際大師，我也沒有任何疑惑，就跟著這位朋友去大陸四川成都拜見至高無上的佛陀上師，等了十幾天才有幸見上一面，當時佛陀上師問來成都有什麼事？我當下馬上告知佛陀上師自己來這裡的目的。佛陀上師很是慈悲的說：『好，好，讓它去了就行了。』然後，佛陀上師拿了一根普通銀針要開始幫我醫病，並說待會若是有腫脹疼痛要說出來，只看佛陀上師嘴裡持咒，然後就在我左手的虎口穴上扎了跑馬神針，並吹了一口氣，在這同時感覺到體內的血液到處流竄且全身腫脹，腫瘤的溫度開始升高，好像火在燃燒。連續三次反覆同樣的動作之後，佛陀上師說：『你平常持什麼佛號，就持什麼佛號。』我說持南無觀世音菩薩，佛陀上師說：『好，好，你就

持這佛號，要誠心誠意，很快它就會離開你了。』就這樣，我很開心的回到台灣，然後就如往常一樣又開始忙著生意，也不忘記一有空就持佛號。回到台灣後開始幾天，看它沒有長，也沒有小，大約20天左右的某一天在洗澡時，突然又想起腋下的那塊紅斑腫瘤，趕緊去照照鏡子，才驚覺硬塊已經縮小範圍，由原來50元硬幣大小縮小到大約1元硬幣大小而已，當時真的開心到要跳起來。感恩！！感恩！！這兩個字真是發自內心的由衷感謝偉大至高無上的佛陀上師。在此之後我更加誠心誠意的持誦佛號，感恩至高無上的佛陀上師。

可是就這樣，大約又過了一個月，腫瘤一點也沒有再縮小，我又有些慌張了，就在一天晚上，我聽到一聲響聲，左手腋下的紅斑點硬塊突然消失得無影無蹤，此時此刻內心的激動與感謝已無法用任何言語來表達，之前的陰霾也都一掃而空！後來就皈依我偉大的佛陀法王上師雲高益西諾布頂聖如來，至今已17年，現在的身體狀況可是比年輕時還要健康內心也更快樂！！

以上所說一切屬實！！若有虛假，願墮金剛地獄！！若屬實言，一切功德都回向給法界一切眾生！！

弟子：李庭英　叩上十方三世諸佛

2007 / 06 / 21

（此文的英文翻譯印在前面）

CATEGORY 10

Healing Illnesses

第十大類　治病

Introduction

H.H. Dorje Chang Buddha III Wan Ko Yeshe Norbu Holiest Tathagata is truly the king of healing. His Holiness has cured countless physical and mental illnesses of living beings. When His Holiness lived in China, more than three hundred patients would register to see Him every day. Moreover, His Holiness did this work on a completely voluntary basis in order to benefit living beings and did not accept one penny for His treatments. In addition to curing the illnesses of people, His Holiness uses the power of the Buddha-dharma to cure everything bad that sentient beings and non-sentient things have in the universe. Moreover, His Holiness enables them to extricate themselves from the sufferings of the cycle of reincarnation. Here we will only give some examples of the curing of illnesses by H.H. Dorje Chang Buddha III.

(This text was translated from the Chinese text that follows.)

簡　　介

多杰羌佛第三世雲高益西諾布頂聖如來是真正的大醫王，治好眾生的身、心之病數不勝數，曾在中國時每天掛出三百多號，而且分文不收，全盡義務利益眾生。除治人的病外，乃至用佛法的力量來治理有情無情萬有的成住壞空的病症。我們在這裡僅舉出三世多杰羌治病的一些例子。

（此文的英文翻譯印在前面）

(Example 1)

One night after midnight in early 1990, someone suddenly knocked on my door rapidly and yelled, "Sister Dai, save me!" We opened the door and saw our neighbor Xiao Bai (At that time, Sister Dai was the manager of the Hydroelectric Resource Supply Company of Xindu County.) Xiao Bai told Sister Dai in a very hurried manner, "Sister Dai! Chun-Yang Xia and his wife Ling-Kun Zeng are arguing and fighting. A knife is even being used! Sister Dai, go over there quickly! Go quickly!"

Sister Dai became very anxious upon hearing this, opened the door, and rushed downstairs. While she was running, she prayed for empowerment from H.H. Dorje Chang Buddha III Wan Ko Yeshe Norbu and kept reciting the Six Syllable Great Brightness Mantra. At this time I (Ying-Fan Wang) also rushed downstairs. While I was running, I prayed for empowerment from H.H. Dorje Chang Buddha III together with Sister Dai so that this matter would not turn into something more serious and thereby become fixed karma.

When Sister Dai and I entered the residence of Chun-Yang Xia, we saw that a tragedy had already taken place. Ling-Kun Zeng was lying on the floor in a pool of blood. Her face was pale and she was unconscious. Chun-Yang Xia was holding a weapon—a watermelon knife one foot long. The tip of the knife was dripping with blood. Chun-Yang Xia was standing there trembling and in a crazed manner shouted, "Brother Wang! Sister Dai! I am finished! Save Ling-Kun Zeng quickly!"

I saw that Ling-Kun Zeng was about to pass away. The whole room was filled with the stench of blood. We immediately decided to take her to the county hospital. We took the saving of her life as a most urgent matter. During the entire trip to the hospital, we continuously prayed for empowerment from the Buddha Master. We also continuously recited the Six Syllable Great Brightness Mantra and prayed that the Buddha Master would save the life of Ling-Kun Zeng.

As soon as the doctor in the emergency room of the county hospital saw Ling-Kun Zeng, he decided not to accept her for treatment. That doctor said, "The patient won't pull through. Her life cannot be saved. Her symptoms are those indicating death." We sincerely begged that doctor to save Ling-Kun Zeng. At the same time, we wholeheartedly intoned the name of H.H. Holiest Tathagata Wan Ko Yeshe Norbu Buddha Master and the name of Guan Shi Yin Bodhisattva, beseeching them to empower Ling-Kun Zen so that her life could be saved.

After our repeated sincere requests in that emergency room of the county hospital, the doctor examined the wounds of Ling-Kun Zeng. After the examination, the doctor said that it is possible she could not be saved. She was stabbed three times in the back. Her liver was stabbed more than an inch deep and as a result was torn apart. She had internal bleeding all over her body. She was in a deep state of unconsciousness and was not breathing. Her pulse occasionally moved ever so faintly. Her condition was extremely critical. The doctor immediately issued a notification that the patient's situation was critical.

At this time, Sister Dai and I felt extremely bad, but we steadfastly believed in the awesome spiritual powers of our Buddha Master. Sister Dai and I continually prayed to the Buddha Master that His Holiness quickly empower Ling-Kun Zeng. We also immediately telephoned our infinitely compassionate Buddha Master and beseeched him to empower Ling-Kun Zeng. The magnificent Buddha Master very compassionately stated, "Do not worry. I will immediately practice the dharma to empower her."

With the empowerment from the magnificent Buddha Master, Ling-Kun Zeng miraculously came back to life. She was truly snatched from the jaws of death. The doctors at the scene all said that what occurred was quite miraculous. They wondered how her fate could be so extraordinary. They expressed how surprised they were that she did not die despite suffering what should have been three fatal stabs and despite losing nearly all of her blood. But there is something even more miraculous with respect to the wounded Ling-Kun Zeng, who was on the verge of death. Seven days later, her stitches were removed, she got out of bed, and returned home.

This was an incredible event that Sister Shou-Pin Dai and I personally experienced. Under the compassionate empowerment and protection of H.H. Dorje Chang III Buddha Master, the wounded Ling-Kun Zeng was saved at the brink of death. She received a new lease on life. These recollections are true. They are events that we personally went through and handled.

Recollections of Ying-Fan Wang and Shou-Pin Dai
April 21, 2006

(This is a complete translation of the Chinese text that follows originally written and signed by Ying-Fan Wang and Shou-Pin Dai.)

(實例一)

1990年初的一個晚上十二點過，突然有人急促地敲門，大喊「代大姐救命！」，我們把門打開，見是鄰居小白(當時代大姐是新都縣水電物資供應公司的經理)，小白很急促地給代大姐說：「代大姐！夏春陽與他的愛人曾令坤吵嘴打架，動刀了！代大姐快去！快去！」代大姐一聽急了，便開門衝下樓去，一邊跑一邊求三世多杰羌佛雲高益西諾布加持，一邊又唸六字大明咒，這時我也衝下樓去，邊跑邊與代大姐一起求三世多杰羌佛陀上師加持，不讓事態擴大成定業。當我和代大姐進到夏春陽家一看，慘案已發生了，曾令坤已躺在地上的血泊中，臉色慘白，昏迷不醒，夏春陽手拿一凶器，一把一尺長的西瓜刀，刀尖在滴血，夏春陽站在那裡發抖，瘋狂地喊叫著：「王哥！代姐！我完了！你們快救一下曾令坤！」，我一看曾令坤已快沒有氣了，滿屋子充滿血腥味，當時我們立刻決定送縣醫院，我們當時想救人是十萬火急的事，一路到縣醫院，我們不斷地求佛陀上師加持，同時不斷地唸六字大明咒，求佛陀上師救曾令坤的命。

在縣醫院急救室，醫師一看，不收治曾令坤了，醫生說：「不行了，救不活了，是死亡症狀。」我們懇求醫生一定要救治曾令坤，同時一心唸誦頂聖如來雲高益西諾布佛陀上師名號，唸誦觀世音菩薩名號，祈求加持曾令坤能救活過來，在縣醫院急救室經我們的再三懇求，醫生檢查曾令坤的傷勢，一檢查，醫生說可能沒救了，背上殺了三刀，連肝臟都刺了一寸多深，肝部份殺爛了，血全部統在體內了，人已深度昏迷，沒有氣息，只有脈搏偶有些微地顫動，情況萬分危急，醫生馬上下了病危通知書，我和代大姐此時心裡異常難過，但我們堅信我們的佛陀上師的威神之力，我和代大姐不斷地求佛陀上師快加持曾令坤，同時馬上打電話求我們慈悲無量的佛陀上師加持曾令坤，當時偉大的佛陀法王上師非常慈悲地說：「放心，我馬上修法加持。」在偉大的佛陀上師的加持下，曾令坤奇蹟般地活過來了，真是死裏逃生，在場的醫生們都說太奇蹟了，這個女人命咋個那麼大，挨三刀，刀刀致命，血流殆盡，居然沒有死，更奇蹟的是，傷者曾令坤，一個已瀕臨死亡的人，七天就拆線下床回家了。

這就是我與代守品大姐親身經歷的一件不可思議的事，在偉大的三世多杰羌佛陀上師老人家的慈悲加持護佑下，傷者曾令坤從死亡線上救活過來，重獲得新生，此回憶真實不虛，實係我們親身經歷辦理的一件實事。

回憶人：王英凡　代守品

2006年4月21日

（此文的英文翻譯印在前面）

(Example 2)

H.H. Dorje Chang Buddha III Wan Ko Yeshe Norbu Holiest Tathagata is truly a Great Medicine King. Just take me as an example. H.H. Dorje Chang III Buddha Master saved my life twice.

The first time was in 1994. One day in the afternoon, I went to a construction site to check the work in progress. I walked onto a board that accessed the construction site, which was about 7 to 8 meters (23-26 feet) above ground. Because it was for workers to walk on while carrying stones or other heavy loads, it was very sturdy. However, when I was walking on the middle of the board, I felt as if I was being pushed by something and fell down from it. After the fall, my eyes were full of stars. I felt the sky and ground were both rotating, but I couldn't see anything. I knew it was serious. So I started to think about the Buddha Master, H.H. Dorje Chang Buddha III, and Avalokiteshvara Bodhisattva. I constantly recited the holy names of the Buddha Master and Avalokiteshvara Bodhisattva. After quite a few minutes, my mind became clear. Then, I asked to go to where the Buddha Master was. Only the Buddha Master could save my life!

When I arrived at the Buddha Master's place, I was not able to straighten my back due to the unbearable pain. The Buddha Master immediately conducted a dharma to bless me and then instructed people to take me to the Eighth Orthopedics Hospital. After taking an X-ray there, the doctor did not permit me to leave. He said that the injury could endanger my life because my shoulder blade had a fracture. We saw from the X-ray that the shoulder blade was broken into two pieces, with a gap the width of a little finger. The fractured shoulder blade pressed onto my lung, so breathing was very difficult. The treatment would require 18 people taking shifts to watch and take care of me 24 hours a day for 21 days. Each shift would require six strong persons to constantly watch me and not let me move my body. A total of 18 people were needed for three shifts a day. Even after the treatment, I would not be able to move that arm. I would be permanently handicapped after that.

Of course, I did not want to accept such an outcome. I thought that only the dharma from the Buddha Master could save me. So I left the hospital without letting the doctor and nurses know and went home. Then a miracle happened. I was able to raise the injured arm the next morning. I went to the Buddha Master's home and prostrated to the Buddha Master. The Buddha Master told me to go back to the hospital and have a checkup. The doctor was extremely surprised to see me. He told me that many people went out to look for me the previous night. Since I was not found, they thought I must have died because they could not imagine how I could survive under the circumstances. He immediately took an X-ray of me again. All the doctors were surprised by the X-ray image. The two pieces of broken bone had grown into one again, without even a small crack in between! I was only feeling a slight pain at the time. The third day, our company, the Pan Pacific Group, was having its annual meeting. I attended the meeting throughout the day. After that, I did not even take the medicine given by the hospital. The fracture completely healed after six or seven days. To this day, that arm of mine has been completely normal as if nothing had happened to it.

The second instance was on April 22, 2002. In the afternoon, I went to the emergency room of the Sichuan Medical University Hospital due to a massive obstruction in my cerebellum. I was immediately transferred into the in-patient department of the Neuron Internal Medicine Division of the hospital. The doctor in the department did not even bother to admit me into the medical ward. I was assigned to a bed in the hallway because I was so close to death already. My blood pressure reading was more than 200, and my blood was so thick that blood could not be drawn from a needle. After pressing my arm hard, a sample was taken for testing. The blood sample looked very dark. At that time, I could hardly open my eyes and was seeing everything double. I felt very dizzy and could not move while lying on the bed. Even a slight move would cause me to feel like vomiting.

Doctors at the Sichuan Medical University Hospital are excellent in their profession. Based on the testing and observations, they saw clearly from my situation that I would not make it. Death would come in just about 10 to 20 hours. So it wouldn't be necessary to admit me into the medical ward. Letting me stay in the hallway was simply fulfilling the humanitarian obligation of the hospital. Meanwhile, the hospital issued five terminally-ill notices to family members and relatives. At the time, there were two other patients who were assigned to stay in the hallway. They both died after a day or so and were carried to the hospital morgue. I later learned that their symptoms were not even as serious as mine.

On the edge of dying, I only had one thought in mind—only the Buddha Master can save me! I kept reciting silently the holy name of the Buddha Master and praying for His Holiness to save me. A fellow disciple reported my situation to the Buddha Master, who was then on the other side of the Pacific Ocean. On that same day, my beloved Buddha Master called at night. His Holiness very compassionately told me, "Don't worry. I will bless you. I am going to teach you a dharma right now. You will be sure to recover within three to five days." After that, I practiced the dharma taught by the Master while lying in bed. In three days, actually three days less two hours, an absolutely true miracle occurred. This patient for whom five terminally-ill notices were issued was amazingly able to get out of bed and stand again. And I was able to go to the bathroom without needing help. My situation kept improving, and I was released from the hospital in about three weeks. It has been four years since then. My health has kept improving. Last year I went to the hospital to receive a checkup. All indicators were within the normal range.

Back at the time I was in the hospital, doctors were all at a loss in seeing me recovering so fast. Fellow patients were also constantly talking about me. They said, "This person was to die soon. How can he instead get out of bed so quickly? This is really surprising." During the two years after I left the hospital, a Ph.D. research program at Sichuan Medical University followed me to monitor and observe my situation for their study. They thought my experience was a miracle in the profession of medicine. After over two years of study, they were unable to explain such a phenomenon using any theory of medicine. This is another true experience of mine. I would like to sincerely state here that I was rescued again by the love and compassion from my beloved Buddha Master.

In my lifetime, I had two near death experiences. Both times, I was saved by my most honorable Buddha Master, who transformed my karmic conditions and from death returned me to life.

H.H. Dorje Chang Buddha III is truly an incarnation of an ancient Buddha and a Great Medicine King. His Holiness not only cures diseases of living beings, but also saves their lives. I am a humble and ashamed practitioner who cannot even control my own karma. I would like to make a vow here to my beloved Buddha Master: Genuine and correct Buddha-dharma is in the hands of H.H. Dorje Chang Buddha III Wan Ko Yeshe Norbu Holiest Tathagata. I am a humble and ashamed practitioner. I am determined to follow the teachings of my Master and practice the genuine and correct Buddha-dharma from my Buddha Master in order to attain liberation from the cycle of reincarnation, enlighten myself and others, and save all living beings.

The two events described above are both my true experiences. If I made any false statement, I am willing to accept the consequence of descending into the Vajra Hell. If all my statements are true, may all the merit be dedicated to my beloved Buddha Master, H.H. Dorje Chang Buddha III. May the Buddha Master keep his dharma wheel in constant rotation, stay in this world forever, and save countless living beings!

Buddhist disciple,
Yihui Hengxing
April 28, 2006

(This is a complete translation of the Chinese text that follows originally written and signed by Yihui Hengxing.)

（實例二）

雲高益西諾布頂聖如來是真正的大醫王，僅僅就我一個人來說，三世多杰羌佛陀上師就兩次救了我的命。

第一次是1994年，有一天下午我到工地上去檢查進度，我就走到一個跳板上去，這個跳板有七、八米高，是工人抬石頭、擔泥巴在上面走的，非常牢靠，可是當我剛剛走到中間，就覺得有什麼東西推了一下，我突然就掉下去了。掉下去以後當時是眼冒五星，天旋地轉，看不到東西。我當時覺得有點嚴重，我就想到佛陀上師三世多杰羌佛，想到觀世音菩薩，我就不斷地念佛陀上師，念觀世音菩薩，好幾分鐘過後我才清醒過來，清醒過來以後，我就說我要到佛陀上師那兒去，只有佛陀上師才能救我！到了佛陀上師家裡的時候，我已經痛得直不起腰了，佛陀上師立即為我修法加持，並讓人把我送到八一骨科醫院，在醫院照X光以後，大夫就不讓我走了，說這是有生命危險的，因為是肩胛骨粉碎性骨折，在X光片上清楚見到肩胛骨折成兩半，分開一小指寬，這個骨頭壓迫肺葉，人無法呼吸。如果要治療，必須要有18個人看護，也就是說，在21天之內我是一點也不能動的，這期間要每班找6個身強力壯的人看著我，不讓我有半點挪動，一天三班，所以一共要找18個小伙子。而且就是治好了，以後手也是不能動的，也是殘廢的，生活根本不能自理。

這對我來說當然是不行的，我想只有佛陀上師的佛法能夠救我。所以當天晚上我趁大夫不注意的時候就偷跑回家了。結果奇蹟發生了，第二天早晨我這隻受傷的手就可以舉起來了，我到佛陀上師的家裡，還給佛陀上師頂了禮的。佛陀上師讓我再回醫院檢查看看，醫生一看到我大吃一驚，說昨天晚上很多人找我，以為我都已經死了，這是不可能活的。大夫馬上再給我第二次照X光，全院的醫生都驚呆了，折成兩半的骨頭已經長成了一片，連一點縫隙都沒有！我自己只是感覺有一點點輕微的疼痛而已。第三天因為我們泛太平洋集團舉行年度會議，我還一直參加年會。以後基本上藥都沒吃，在第六、七天左右基本就康復了，醫院裡拿的藥，我根本沒吃。一直到現在，我的這隻手臂就跟沒有發生過任何事情一樣。

第二次是2002年4月22日下午，我因小腦大面積梗阻，由川醫急診科直接送入川醫神經內科住院部。入院以後，住院部醫生已不安排我進病房，而是臨時住在走廊的過道上。為什麼醫生不安排我住病房？是因為我的病情已嚴重到接近死亡的邊緣，血壓高達200以上，血脂高得已經抽不出血了，是靠擠壓手臂才抽出血來化驗的，抽出的血看起來黑黑的，當時我根本就睜不開眼，睜開眼看見什麼都是雙影，天暈目眩，身體躺在床上動都不能動一下，動一動就會吐，川醫醫生的醫術是非常高明、精湛的，他們根據我入院各項指標檢查和我的臨床表現情況，清楚的知道我是過不了這一關的，死亡對我只是那麼十幾個小時的事。對我根本就沒有必要住進病房，住在過道上只是盡一點醫院的人道主義，同時一天之內為我下了五次病危通知書。當時安排在過道上的除我而外，另外還有兩個病人，都於我後入院一天左右就前後腳的抬去了太平間，其實後來才知道他們的病都沒有我的嚴重。我那時病得快死了，但心中始終有一念尚存：只有佛陀上師能救我。我默默地念著佛陀上師的聖號，祈求佛陀上師快救我。一位師兄把我的病情連夜報告了遠在太平洋彼岸的佛陀上師，當天晚上，我的恩師佛陀上師就打來電話，他老人家非常慈悲的對我說：『你不要害怕，我會加持你的，我馬上傳你的法，保證你三到五天就好。』過後我躺在病床上，依上師傳的法修持，三天，三天不到，還差兩小時，千真萬確，奇蹟出現了，被醫院一天內就連續下了五次病危通知書的一個瀕臨死亡的病人，從病床上神奇般的下床站了起來，並堅持自己上衛生間。過後病情一天天好起來，二十多天就出了院。至今已是整整四年過去了，我的身體愈來愈好，去年還去醫院做了一次化驗檢查，各方面指標都很正常。當時醫生們看到我好得這麼快，也是百思不解，病房中的病人都議論紛紛說：這個人都要死了，怎麼這麼快就下床了，好奇怪哦！我出院後兩年中，川醫的一個博導研究小組，還非常認真地跟蹤觀察研究我，他們認為這種現象是醫學上的奇蹟。從入院治療到出院後的兩年多，他們研究來研究去，都沒有找到一種醫學理論來解釋這種現象。這是我親身經歷的事情，在此我要真誠地說，是我的恩師佛陀上師的慈悲又一次救了我。生命中兩次和死亡擦肩而過，都是我最最尊敬的佛陀上師救了我，轉因果業力，起死回生。

三世多杰羌佛是真正的古佛再來、大醫王，他老人家不但能醫眾生的病，並且能救眾生的生命。我是一個慚愧的修行人，自己因果業力現前都不能把握。在此我要向我的恩師佛陀上師發願：真正的如來正法掌持在多杰羌佛第三世雲高益西諾布頂聖如來的手中，我是一個慚愧修行人，只有依師所教，跟隨佛陀上師修學真正的如來正法，了生脫死，自覺覺他，渡脫一切眾生。

上邊兩件事都是我親身經歷的，如有假話，我願墮金剛地獄，如

是真話，一切功德都回向我的恩師佛陀上師三世多杰羌佛。願佛陀上師法輪常轉，永久住世，渡生無量。

佛弟子：憶悔恆性

憶悔恆性

2006.4.28

（此文的英文翻譯印在前面）

(Example 3)

My respected master, H.H. Dorje Chang Buddha III, is the supreme ancient Buddha. His Holiness is willing to accept worldly troubles, worries, and cares in order to save living beings. His thirty categories of accomplishments in the Five Vidyas have astounded the world and bestowed upon living beings good fortune. Those accomplishments will be made into a book that will benefit living beings. The works in those thirty categories are enrapturing. Still, such accomplishments represent only a bit of the Buddha Master's overall accomplishments. The Buddha Master possesses the highest and most profound esoteric dharma. Very few people know this.

Because the Buddha Master acts with an enlightened and infinitely compassionate mind of a Buddha or Bodhisattva and because His Holiness has through Buddhism reached the highest state, His Holiness therefore was able to receive true lineage teachings regarding the vajra needle. There are numerous examples of people with a karmic connection to the Buddha Master who were cured of their cancers and stubborn illnesses by the Buddha Master when His Holiness was in China. Examples of this include Guang-Dong Yan and Zhi-Yong Luo, who contracted nasopharyngeal carcinoma (cancer of the nose and pharynx); Yan Zhuang, who contracted skin cancer; Jing-Xing Wu, who had a brain tumor; and Le-Hui Xie, who over a few decades suffered from a stubborn case of phlegm, inflammation of the shoulders and elbows, and migraine headaches. I know all of them. The Buddha Master cured their illnesses. People from Hong Kong, Taiwan, and Malaysia with leukemia, AIDS, and strokes came to China to seek treatment from the Buddha Master. The Buddha Master cured all of them. It was like the following verse in the poem written by the Buddha Master entitled "*To the Tune of Nian-Nu-Jiao*":
"Three thousand suffering patients visited me,
Day and night I cured them."
This is a true description of how the Buddha Master saved those patients.

Having thought of these other people, I will now speak of myself. I had late-stage cancer of the uterus and was about to pass away. More than twenty years ago, the Buddha Master used the magnificent healing methods of the Buddha-dharma to save me when I was at the brink of death.

In August of 1985, my menstruation lasted for more than a half-month. Blood kept flowing without end. I first thought that it was abnormal menstruation. I tried to take care of it through Chinese medicine, but my condition did not improve. I switched to Western medicine, but the blood kept flowing without end. After this situation continued for more than two months, I moved from a county hospital to the Sichuan Provincial Hospital. The biopsy result was that I had late-stage cancer of the uterus. The doctor in charge, Professor Zhang, told my husband Hui Han Da (who is also my fellow disciple), "Her cancer cells have already spread. Surgery cannot be done. Go back home and look after her. Give her whatever she wants to eat. Go wherever she wants to go to have fun. Have family members keep her company as she finishes her journey on this path of life."

My husband did not believe in this result. He moved me to the Huaxi Medical University Hospital to be examined. The examination result was the same, but he still did not give up. He was determined to have me cured no matter how much money needed to be spent, even if it meant exhausting the entire family fortune. He took me to the China-Japan Friendship Hospital in Beijing, the Peking Union Medical College Hospital, and the Suzhou Univeristy Hospital. The examination results were all the same. Everyone indicated they could not do anything to help me. My family became very sad. My only choice was to return home.

As my sickness became worse, I became less able to eat. I was also discharging blood with no letup. I became as thin as skin and bones, weighing only 79 pounds. My hematin count was three grams (normal people have 16 grams). In order to stop the flow of blood, my husband again took me to the Huaxi Medical University Hospital. As soon as the doctor saw me, he shook his head and said, "She will live for seven days at the most. Go back and make arrangements for her funeral!"

I lay in bed after I returned home. My heart was very sorrowful when I thought of having to die at the age of only thirty-six. I told my husband, "Before I die, could you pay a visit to the Buddha Master and beseech him to raise me to a higher realm of existence after death?" My husband replied, "The Buddha Master is out of town propagating the dharma and saving living beings. I will go and see His Holiness when His Holiness returns." In my mind, I silently recited the name of Guan Yin Bodhisattva (Avalokiteshvara Bodhisattva), praying that the Buddha Master would soon return.

Who would have thought that at around noon the next day a miracle occurred. The Buddha Master unexpectedly arrived beside my bed. I wanted to get out of bed to prostrate before him, but I could not get up. The Buddha Master very compassionately stopped me from even trying to get up and had me lie down. His Holiness expounded to me the ultimate truths of human life and the universe and explained why living beings experience the sufferings of birth, aging, sickness, and death. It is due to karma arising from delusion that binds living beings.

I suddenly understood something. In order to do business and make money, I helped others produce a type of beef by killing more than one thousand yaks. Putting aside the question of whether in the past I intentionally or unintentionally killed other living beings, how many lives will it take me to repay my karmic debt of having killed just those more than one thousand yaks? Killing those yaks and making their blood flow was planting negative or evil causes. The flowing of my blood at that time was a manifestation of the effect of those negative or evil causes. This is karmic retribution! The more I thought

about this, the more afraid I became. As a result, I became contrite from the bottom of my heart and beseeched the Buddha Master to raise me to a higher realm of existence after I die.

The Buddha Master said, "If you sincerely repent, change your ways, never again kill any living being, and resolve to learn Buddhism and cultivate yourself, I will block your negative karma and postpone your karmic retribution. Cancer is nothing formidable! I will cure you! I will also save those yaks that you killed."

The Buddha Master treated me with the vajra needle. This is a holy needle that is part of the dharma lineage of a true dharma king of Buddhism. Only our Buddha Master can apply such a needle. The amazing thing about this silver needle is that it operates according to the will of the Buddha Master. When it is told to expand sensation to a certain place on the body, it does so. When it is told not to expand sensation anymore, it stops expanding sensation immediately. It is extremely amazing!

At that time, I was wearing a sweater and a fur coat. The Buddha Master applied the needle through my clothes to an acupuncture point on my back. After His Holiness let go of the needle, I saw the Buddha Master put his hands in various mudras (symbolic hand gestures). The sensation from the silver needle varied according to how that mudra was used. The sensations ranged from weak to strong and ran throughout my entire body. I felt both tingling sensations and swelling sensations. It was truly difficult to endure.

The Buddha Master then explained, "The body becomes ill because the energy channels are blocked. This is like a machine that becomes too oily and needs to be cleaned. My treating you with this needle is analogous to cleaning up this dirty oil. I clean and open your energy channels and drive out your sickness. With these words of mine, you will immediately no longer feel a tingling sensation." Right after the Buddha Master spoke such words, the sensations of aching and swelling instantly disappeared.

The second series of sensations from the needle varied from weak to strong according to the orders of the Buddha Master. That series of sensations was sharper than the first series. The Buddha Master then instructed the sensations from the needle to disappear. They immediately vanished. After the third series of sensations, my treatment ended. I immediately felt that my entire body was much more at ease. The Buddha Master then said, "Today I treated you with the needle to open your energy channels. If you are to be thoroughly cured, medicine mixed together by using the highest Buddha-dharma method must be used. I will immediately begin to prepare that medicine for you."

One day the Buddha Master told my husband Hui Han Da and me to take His Holiness by car to the mountain village where those yaks were killed. In front of a very large yak, the Buddha Master prepared the medicine for me! My husband and I were both present. When the Buddha Master began using a special method to prepare the medicine, there suddenly appeared in the clear sky white mist that floated from west to east. The mist became increasingly dense. In the end, it was so dense we could not see our five fingers when we outstretched our arms in front of us. During this time, many wonderful phenomena appeared.

The Buddha Master finished preparing the medicine and had me take it. As soon as I drank that fragrant herbal liquid, my whole body immediately emitted heat and then felt extremely cool, refreshed, and comfortable. I was brimming with energy. My disease was cured! I no longer discharged blood! It was truly quite miraculous and magnificent! I quickly prostrated before the Buddha Master and thanked him for his kindness.

Since then, I have not taken any medicine. My physical strength and weight continuously returned to normal. One month later, a doctor in that Sichuan provincial hospital who was responsible for following up on patients telephoned my residence. He wanted to understand what my situation was when I passed away. I received that phone call and said, "I have not died! I have now fully recovered!" They did not believe me and wanted me to go to their hospital to be examined. Fellow disciple Guang-Dong Yan, whose nasopharyngeal carcinoma (cancer of the nose and pharynx) was cured by the Buddha Master, happened to be in my home at that time. He said that he would also go to the hospital to be examined.

The next day we together went to be examined. The results of the laboratory tests were that both of us did not have one cancer cell. The doctors were astounded. They asked me what I ate and what medicine I took after I returned home. They asked me who cured me. I answered them by saying, "The Buddhas and Bodhisattvas saved me!"

Twenty-one years have passed since the Buddha Master cured me of cancer. Since I began learning and practicing the Buddha-dharma under the Buddha Master, my physical condition has become better and better! A physical examination indicated that all of my indices are now very good. My weight has doubled from 79 pounds to 165 pounds. After those who saw me when I was sick see me now, they all say that I am a totally different person and that they can barely recognize me.

The Buddha Master also specially performed Buddhist rites in order to save those yaks that I killed. I can speak endlessly about the kindness and grace that the Buddha Master has bestowed upon my entire family. All that I can do is earnestly cultivate myself, perform good deeds for humanity, and attain real accomplishment in order to repay the great holy blessings and kindness of my respected Buddha Master!

Buddhist disciple,
Chi Lie Er

(This is a complete translation of the Chinese text that follows originally written and signed by Chi Lie Er.)

(實例三)

我的恩師是至高的古佛—三世多杰羌佛。他老人家為渡眾生不捨塵勞，賜予眾生福報的30項驚世駭俗的成果，將出成書利益眾生，是攝心的作品，而這些只是佛陀上師成就中的點滴。其實，佛陀上師掌握的至高無上甚深的密法，普通人少有知悉。

佛陀上師以佛菩薩的大悲菩提之心，用佛門達到最高境界才能得到真傳的金剛針，當時在中國，為有緣的眾生治癒絕症、頑症的病例數不清。中國患鼻咽癌的嚴光東、羅志勇，患皮膚癌的莊嚴，長腦瘤的吳景興，幾十年頑症肩肘炎、偏頭痛的謝樂慧等等都是我認識的，他們的病痛都是三世多杰羌佛治癒的。還有香港、台灣、馬來西亞的白血病、愛滋病、腦中風的患者來求醫，佛陀上師都給他們治好了，佛陀上師念奴嬌詞中寫的「三千患疾訪俺門，晝夜岐黃施絕」正是佛陀上師救渡病患的真實寫照。

想到別人說到我，我患了晚期子宮癌，即將撒手人寰彌留之際，佛陀上師施用佛法的偉大療法，硬從鬼門關救回了我，至今已經是二十多年了。1985年8月，我的月事來了半個多月，還是不停地流血，開始以為是月經不調，中醫調理不見好轉，改服西藥還是淋漓不止，一直拖了兩個多月，才從縣醫院轉到四川省醫院，活檢結果是晚期子宮癌，主治醫師張教授告訴我先生慧漢達師兄：「她的癌細胞已擴散，不能做手術，回家去，好好照顧她，想吃什麼給她，想去那裡玩就去，讓家人多陪陪她走完人生道路。」師兄不相信這個結果，把我轉到華西醫大檢查，結果一樣，他還不死心，決心不管花多少錢，就是傾家蕩產也要治好我，又把我送到北京中日友好醫院、協和醫院、蘇大醫院，檢查結果都一樣，表示無能為力，我的家人十分悲傷，只好回家。隨著病情加重，吃不下東西，又不停流血，我瘦得皮包骨頭，體重只有36公斤，血色素3克(正常人16克)，為了止住血，又把我送到川醫，醫生一看，搖搖頭說：「最多還有七天的活頭，還是回去準備後事吧！」

回到家，躺在床上，想到才36歲就要死了，心裡很悲傷，我給師兄說：「我死之前，能不能再拜見佛陀上師一面，求他老人家超渡我？」師兄說：「佛陀上師到外場弘法渡生去了，等老人家回來，我就去接他吧！」我心裡默默地唸誦觀音菩薩，求佛陀上師快回來。誰知第二天中午奇蹟出現了，佛陀上師竟然已來到了我的病床前，我想下床給佛陀上師頂禮卻爬不動，佛陀上師很慈悲地阻止我，讓我躺下，為我開示人生與宇宙的真諦，講解眾生為什麼都有生老病死苦？其原因是惑業因果束縛了眾生，我突然明白了我為了做生意賺錢，幫人組織牛肉，殺害了上千條犛牛，以前有意、無意傷害的眾生，暫且不談，只是這上千頭犛牛的因果債，要多少輩子才還得清？殺牛流血種惡因，我今流血顯惡果，因果報應啊！越想越怕，於是從內心生起懺悔，求佛陀上師救我，超渡我，佛陀上師說：「只要你真心懺悔、改過，不再殺生，發心學佛修行，上師為你遮止業障，轉換推延因果，癌症算什麼東西！我給你治好就是了！至於你殺害的犛牛，上師也會救牠們的。」

佛陀上師為我打金剛針，這是佛門的法王傳承聖針，只有我們佛陀上師才會打的。這銀針神奇之處是隨佛陀上師的意念運行的，叫它脹到哪裡就到哪裡，叫它不脹它就不脹，神奇極了！當時我穿著毛衣，裘皮大衣，佛陀上師在我背部穴位隔衣扎好針，放手後，只見佛陀上師揮動手勢，銀針的針感隨手勢運行，從弱到強，走遍全身，又酸又脹，實在難以忍受，佛陀上師開示說：「生病的身體由於經絡堵塞，猶如機器上的油膩需要清洗，現在為你打針就是清洗不淨的油膩，疏通經絡驅病障，佛陀上師口中一聲，馬上不脹。」語音剛落，酸脹感頓然消除。隨著佛陀上師的指令，第二次針感從弱到強，比第一次更厲害。佛陀上師又指示針感消除，當下便無蹤影，如是三次結束，我頓感全身輕鬆了很多。佛陀上師說：「今天給你打針，疏通了經絡，要徹底好完，必須用佛法的至高法門調配的藥才行，上師馬上會給你配製的。」

有一天，佛陀上師讓我和慧漢達師兄帶路，坐車到了殺牛的山莊，在一條很大的牛前，佛陀上師來為我調配藥了！我和師兄在場，當佛陀上師開始施用特殊方法配藥時，晴朗的天空中，突然從西往東飄來白霧，越來越濃，最後濃得來伸手不見五指，在此期間，有很多殊勝境相出現。最後佛陀上師調配好藥讓我服下，異香撲鼻的藥液我一喝下，頓感全身發熱又清涼無比，舒服極了，頓然精神煥發，病好了！也不再流血了！真是太神奇，太偉大了！我急忙頂禮謝師恩。就這樣；我再也沒有服用過任何藥，體力、體重都不斷恢復。一個月後，四川省醫院追蹤病患的醫生打來電話，了解我臨終前的情況。當時我接電話說：「我沒有死！現在已經全好了！」他們不相信，要我去他們醫院檢查。經佛陀上師治好鼻咽癌的嚴光東師兄正在我家，他說他也去檢查一下，第二天我們一同去檢查，化驗結果，兩人都不見一個癌細胞，醫生非常驚奇，還問我回去吃了什麼東西，服用了什麼藥？是誰給你治療的？我只回答了他們：「是佛菩薩救了我！」

佛陀上師治好我的癌症已經二十一年了，自從跟隨佛陀上師修學佛法，身體越來越好！現在檢查身體的各項指標都很好，體重也增加一倍多，由36公斤增加到75公斤。當年見我得病時的人，現在看見我，都說我已經變成另外一個人了，快不認得了。

佛陀上師後來還專門為我所殺害的犛牛做佛事予以救渡。佛陀上師施予我們全家的恩惠永遠說不完，我只有好好修行為人類做好事，以實際成就來報答佛陀恩師的聖恩聖德！

佛弟子：赤烈爾

（此文的英文翻譯印在前面）

family was shocked, frightened, and nervous. My husband, who is my fellow disciple, immediately went to the United States to beseech empowerment from the Buddha Master, H.H. Dorje Chang Buddha III. The Buddha Master was very compassionate. His Holiness immediately empowered me and transmitted a dharma for me to practice that would empower me.

When I moved from my hospital room to the surgery room on the day of my surgery, I was so afraid, tears rolled down my face. As soon as I entered the surgery room, I suddenly became very tranquil. Not only was I not scared, I even carefully observed all of the details of the surgery room.

I remained in the surgery room for a whole day. It was already late at night when I was transferred to a normal hospital room. The doctor came to my room the next day at 7:00 in the morning while making his rounds. To his great surprise, he saw that I was sitting up and said, " How can you be sitting up. " Since there was still a tube in my mouth, I could not speak. I could only nod my head in response.

The most unbelievable thing during my stay at the hospital was that my wound did not hurt at all. I recovered very quickly and very well. The doctor told me that there was a patient next door who underwent surgery. That patient was in such pain each day that she could not sleep. She recovered very slowly. Even after many days, her stitches could not be removed. The doctor said that my recovery was quite amazing. He had never seen such a recovery! Never!

The weather in Taiwan in November was very cold, and a cold air current arrived. Also, the hospital rooms were air-conditioned. Still, when I did my daily meditation, my entire body emitted heat and perspired. The doctors and nurses all felt that this was unbelievable. They wondered how I could be so hot that I perspired in such cold weather!

I heard that chemotherapy is very painful. However, during my two-month period of chemotherapy, my body did not have any negative reaction. I also did not feel any discomfort. The only negative thing that happened was my skin became a little dark. After less than a half year of rest, I began taking flights to the United States, Thailand, Japan, Korea, and Taiwan. I flew all over the world. Furthermore, each year I took many flights.

It has been many years since my surgery. My physical condition has been very good. Without empowerment from the Buddha Master, all of this would have been impossible. The Buddha Master, H.H. Dorje Chang Buddha III is the supreme, magnificent ancient Buddha. I am very grateful to the Buddha Master for His empowerment.

Buddhist disciple
Hsiu-Ying Lan

(This is a complete translation of the Chinese text that follows originally written and signed by Hsiu-Ying Lan.)

(Example 4)

A small hole appeared in my gums in 1991. I did not pay attention to it. In December of that year, I went to the hospital for an examination. The doctor said that it was a malignant tumor in the middle to late stage and that I must undergo surgery and chemotherapy. My

（實例四）

1999年間，我的牙齦邊破了一個小洞，我也沒有去在意它，到了11月的時候，才去醫院檢查，醫生說是惡性中晚期腫瘤，要開刀做化療，家人都嚇到了，又害怕又緊張，我家師兄馬上到美國請求佛陀上師三世多杰羌佛加持，佛陀上師非常地慈悲，馬上加持，並賜予加持之法。開刀當天從病房到手術房的時間，自己已經怕得眼淚直流，一進入手術房，忽然間心卻變得很平靜，不但不心慌，還仔細地看了手術房是什麼樣子。在手術房待了一整天，轉到一般病房時已是深夜，第二天醫生早上7點就來巡房，看見我竟然坐著，很驚訝地說：「妳怎麼可以坐著！」當時我插著管子，不能說話只能用點頭回答。

住院時最不可思議的是傷口完全不痛，而且恢復得很快又很好，醫生告訴我說，隔壁有位開刀的患者，每天痛得不能睡，恢復得很慢，很多天了還不能拆線，醫生說我恢復的情況太神奇了，從來沒的事！沒有的事！。在11月的台灣，天氣很冷而且又有寒流來襲，醫院又是冷氣房，可是我每天做功課都是全身發熱，滿身流汗，醫生和護士都覺得不可思議，這麼冷的天氣怎麼會熱到流汗！

聽說做化療是很痛苦的，可是我做化療的那兩個月，身體都沒有不好的反應，也沒有覺得不舒服，只是皮膚有點黑黑的而已。休息不到半年就坐飛機到台灣、美國、泰國、日本、韓國，世界各地飛來飛去，而且一年要坐很多次飛機，至今已經過了很多年了，我的身體都很好，如果沒有佛陀上師的加持，這根本做不到的。佛陀上師是至高偉大的古佛，很感恩佛陀上師的加持。

佛弟子　籃秀櫻

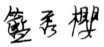

（此文的英文翻譯印在前面）

（Example 5）

On March 7, 2004, I went to Ottawa, Canada to handle some matters. I rushed back to Los Angeles the next night. At that time, there was spring weather and the flowers were in bloom. In contrast, Ottawa was covered with ice and snow. I spent that hectic day in Ottawa rushing about in the freezing weather without taking a break. I went to Taiwan in the middle of March and stayed there only ten days. I returned to the United States on the 22nd. At that time, I felt physically and mentally exhausted.

Sure enough, I began having a high fever and a sore throat on the night of the 23rd. After I truly could not bear it anymore, I had to trouble Sister Hui-Jun Yang to take me to the doctor. Although I was injected with penicillin, the pain from my illness did not vanish. I then immediately telephoned the Buddha Master, H.H. Wan Ko Yeshe Norbu Holiest Tathagata, and beseeched him to empower me. After the Buddha Master heard the state of my illness over the phone, His Holiness immediately said, "This is no small matter. It can lead to your death! However, do not worry. You will fully recover." The Buddha Master then practiced an empowerment dharma.

The Buddha Master was out of town the next day. Still, out of compassion, His Holiness inquired about my illness over the phone. I reported to the Buddha Master that when I woke up that morning secretions from my right eye covered my entire eye. When the Buddha Master heard that I was so sore I could not straighten up my lower back, His Holiness rebuked me for toying with my life. That symptom confirmed that my kidney inflammation had caused a serious cold. The Buddha Master instructed me to immediately change my mudra (a symbolic gesture of the hands used in the practice of Buddhism). I remember very clearly that I used two different mudras.

The next day, there were no secretions from my eye. I received a second phone call from H.H. Buddha Master the following day. His Holiness inquired about my state of illness. I truthfully answered his inquiries. The Buddha Master then felt somewhat relieved and instructed me to immediately change my mudra to the one I was originally using. His Holiness instructed me to continue diligently practicing the dharma using that mudra. The Buddha Master also warned me that my illness would cause further great suffering.

I have fallen ill numerous times in my life, but none of those illnesses was as serious as this one. During the first week of my illness, every day I felt that I could no longer withstand it. I felt that I could die at any moment. I lay in bed for a full month. Even Sister Lillian Kao, who came to help look after me when she heard of my illness, herself fell sick the second day of looking after me. She had no other choice but to return home and rest. I telephoned her a few days later to inquire about her illness. I learned that after she returned home, she was so sick she could not get out of bed. Upon hearing this, I felt very guilty. Fortunately, she also immediately reported her situation to the Buddha Master and practiced the Buddha-dharma the Buddha Master transmitted to her (the mudra she used was completely different from mine). She gradually recovered. However, she also suffered for more than one month before she fully recovered. When we recollect the seriousness of our illnesses, we still have a lingering fear.

There is no way to calculate the great number of disciples who have been cured as a result of the Buddha Master's healing vidya. All of this is absolutely true. Having followed the Buddha Master for several years, I have personally witnessed so many of his feats. Sister Hsu asked me whether I could give any real examples of the Buddha Master's healing powers that I personally experienced. She also instructed me not to write an entire book on that subject. I thank her for reminding me of that. Otherwise, I could write an entire book on just my own personal experiences. What I have described above is only one real example.

I thank the Buddha Master for saving me from the sufferings, danger, and hardships of illness. I am grateful to the Buddha Master.

Buddhist disciple,
Chu Kuan

(This is a complete translation of the Chinese text that follows originally written and signed by Chu Kuan.)

(實例五)

2004年3月7日，我因事出差加拿大渥太華，翌日晚即趕回洛杉磯。當時洛城已是春暖花開，而渥太華仍冰天雪地。一日行程就在這冰冷趕路中辛苦走過，未得休息。三月中又去台灣，也只停留十天，二十二日回美，當時只感覺身心俱疲。果然二十三日晚上開始發高燒，喉嚨痛，實在撐不住了，只好麻煩楊慧君師姐載我去看醫生。雖然注射盤尼西林仍無法消滅病痛。我立即打電話向佛陀上師雲高益西諾布頂聖如來求加持，佛陀上師在電話中聽了我的病情，立即說：「非同小可，無常要命囉！但放心，會徹底好的。」即用了加持之法。第二天佛陀上師出城在外，仍慈悲地電話詢問我的病情。我向佛陀上師報告，早上起來時眼屎將右眼整個包住了，當老人家聽到我的回答竟是酸痛得都直不起腰來時，痛罵我拿生命開玩笑。這證明是腎臟發炎引起的重感冒，趕緊換手印，我清楚記得換了兩種手印。第二天眼屎現象全無，又過了一天，接到老人家第二通電話，問我新的病情，我照實回答，佛陀上師才放心囑咐我再立刻換回原來的手印繼續用功，並且警告我這次病痛是會要命的。

我一生得病無數次，但從未像這次這麼嚴重，生病的頭一星期，我每天都覺得撐不下去，隨時會死，在病床上我足足躺了一個月，連聞訊來幫忙照顧我的高麗華師姐，在照顧的第二天也病倒了，不得不回家休息。幾天後打電話問她病情，才知道她回家後，病得連床都沒下過，我聽了內疚不已，還好她也是馬上向佛陀上師報告並用佛陀上師的佛法(與我的手印完全不同)，才逐漸恢復，但也折騰了一個多月才完全復原。我們事後回想起這場病痛的嚴重程度，至今仍心有餘悸。

說到佛陀上師的醫方明曾治癒過的弟子無法數計，這些都是金剛般的事實，跟隨佛陀上師這些年親眼見證了太多太多，徐師姐問我是否有佛陀上師醫方明的親身經歷，又囑咐我別寫成本書，謝謝她的提醒，不然光是我本人的親身體驗就夠寫一本書了，上面所提到的只是一件事實而已。

感恩佛陀上師將弟子由病痛危難中救出來，感恩佛陀上師。

佛弟子　關珠

（此文的英文翻譯印在前面）

(Example 6)

In March of 2006, my health again entered a low point of my life. Besides loss of appetite and lupus spreading over my entire body, my neck gradually became swollen. All indications were that I was having a relapse of an old illness. I remembered that painful experience of eleven years ago, that frightening period of treatment for nasopharyngeal carcinoma (cancer of the nose and pharynx). I could not help but feel anxious. A multitude of feelings welled up in my heart.

Right at this time when I did not know what to do, Venerable Gadu Rinpoche showed up. He had received instructions from the Buddha Master, H.H. Wan Ko Yeshe Norbu Holiest Tathagata. He endured the hardships of a long journey by driving from San Francisco directly to Portland in order to see me.

Venerable Gadu Rinpoche practiced a dharma to empower me that was taught to him by the Buddha Master. Venerable Gadu Rinpoche also transmitted to me a dharma practice that the Buddha Master instructed him to transmit to me. He told me to practice that dharma in the morning and evening.

Six weeks have passed and my lupus has completely disappeared. The swelling in my head area has also gradually vanished. Recent hospital examination reports show that there are no indications of a tumor. Thus, I am moved by the magnificence of the Buddha-dharma and the compassion of the Buddha Master, which have made me fall to my knees and cry sincere tears. I thank my magnificent and most venerable Buddha Master.

Buddhist disciple,
Chong-Bin Tsai

(This is a complete translation of the Chinese text that follows originally written and signed by Chong-Bin Tsai.)

(實例六)

2006年3月，我的身體健康情況又一度地陷入人生的低潮，除了食慾不振，滿身長出狼瘡之外，頸部亦逐漸地臃腫起來，一切的跡象，頗有舊病復發的預兆。回想十一年前的痛苦經驗，那可怕的鼻咽癌的療程，不免心志惶惶，百感交集。就是在那個不知何去何從的時刻，嘎堵仁波且出現了。原來嘎堵仁波且是奉了佛陀上師雲高益西諾布頂聖如來的指示，一路風塵僕僕馬不停蹄地由舊金山開車到波特蘭市來看我。

嘎堵仁波且以佛陀上師傳授的法門修法加持，又授了佛陀上師交代的功課，要我早晚修持。六個星期下來，我身上的狼瘡已一淨如洗，頭部腫大的地方也逐漸地消失，最近從醫院檢查的報告中，已顯示沒有腫瘤的跡象，因此，有感於佛法的偉大及佛陀上師的慈悲，讓我誠懇地跪拜而泣，感恩我偉大的至尊佛陀上師。

佛弟子　蔡仲彬

（此文的英文翻譯印在前面）

(Example 7)

My father contracted cancer of the nose and pharynx (nasopharyngeal carcinoma) over ten years ago. After several weeks of chemotherapy, his throat area and the salivary glands in his mouth were harmed. Therefore, in his old age, it was difficult for him to swallow food. Oftentimes during his intake of food, as soon as he became inattentive, the food would drop into his lungs and cause discomfort. As he grew older, his immune powers declined. In the end, this caused acute pneumonia. He was taken to an intensive care unit at the Veteran General Hospital in Taipei. Three tubes were concurrently inserted into him—a stomach tube, a respiration tube, and an urination tube. At that time, his white blood cells had risen to 50,000. His condition was extremely dangerous. I received a phone call from my family in Taipei. They were extremely anxious and did not know what to do.

I reported this matter to my master, Venerable Dharma Teacher Long Hui, who is the chairperson of the International Buddhism Sangha Association. My master told me to request empowerment from the magnificent H.H. Dorje Chang Buddha III Wan Ko Yeshe Norbu Holiest Tathagata. The Grand Buddha Master (Grand Buddha Master is my master's master.), out of compassion, immediately consented to my request. His Holiness instructed me to tell my father that it would be most helpful to my father to visualize the Grand Buddha Master. My father is a disciple of H.H. Dorje Chang Buddha III. My father had concluded in his heart that the Grand Buddha Master is a Buddha and believed in His Holiness one hundred percent.

After I returned to Taipei, I respectfully requested and obtained a picture of the Grand Buddha Master. I took that picture to the intensive care unit and saw that my father could not speak (a tube was inserted into his lung). When my father saw the picture of the Grand Buddha Master, he respectfully put his palms together and began to cry. This disciple in distress saw an image of his compassionate the Grand Buddha Master, upon whom he relies.

Starting from the next day, my father's white blood cells began to decrease, and his condition began to improve. By writing notes on paper, my father informed me that before he saw the picture of the Grand Buddha Master, he would see certain things when he closed his eyes. (He refused to say what those things were.) However, starting from the time the picture of

the Grand Buddha Master was hung on the wall in front of his bed, he did not see those things anymore and began to sleep more peacefully. He gradually got better, left the intensive care unit, and returned home to recuperate.

However, a half-year later, he had inflammation of the bladder due to hypertrophy (enlargement) of the prostate and had to return to the hospital. Someone taking care of him at the hospital carelessly fed him too much food, which caused him to vomit. (Since the first time he entered the hospital, my father continued to have a tube inserted into his stomach in order to prevent food from falling into his lungs again.) As a result, food again fell into his lungs causing inflammation. This time the situation was even more serious. He had a high fever for two weeks, which did not subside. The most powerful third-generation antibiotics were used to no avail. I called him from the United States every day to check on his condition. Each time he would say that his fever had not subsided. I again became quite anxious and asked my master what to do. I again sought help from the Grand Buddha Master. However, the Grand Buddha Master would not prescribe any medicine for my father.

I suddenly remembered that when I was in China seven years ago the Grand Buddha Master gave me five nectar pills. With tremendous gratitude and faith in my heart, I took those nectar pills and rushed to the airport to return to Taiwan. I ground the nectar pills into powder and took that powder to the hospital to feed it to my father. Right after my father ate the powder from the first nectar pill, the doctor suddenly said that he would conduct an examination the next day and that my father could therefore not eat anything after midnight. My mother did not know what to do. I resolutely told my mother that no matter what the hospital said, we would continue to feed my father the nectar powder. Even before the feeding of the powder from the second nectar pill was completed, my father's fever had totally subsided and he had returned to normal. After my younger brothers saw such true events, they began to have faith in the Buddha-dharma.

Because I traveled back and forth between the United States and Taiwan several times and because I was both physically and mentally weary, I unknowingly began to have health problems. One evening my blood pressure unexpectedly rose to 198. My heart began beating like a drum. My hands and feet became cold and started to quiver. Only when I visualized in my mind the image of the Grand Buddha Master did my condition gradually stabilize. However, those symptoms occurred several other times after that.

One time while I was sleeping at night, my chest cavity suddenly began to beat wildly. I was awakened by this. I could not move my four limbs, which I felt like thousand-pound weights. I could not even cry out. I was unable to muster up any strength. I knew that this is what it is like to die. After a few minutes, I gradually returned to normal. Realizing that this is no laughing matter, I quickly went to the hospital to be examined. The doctors could not successfully treat me after several attempts. My only alternative was to beseech the Grand Buddha Master once more to save me. The Grand Buddha Master transmitted to me the Opening Qi (Energy) Meridians and

Bright Spots Dharma. I gradually returned to normal.

The Grand Buddha Master saved the lives of my father and myself. Since my worldly wealth is meager, I cannot use that to repay the kindness and favor of the Grand Buddha Master. All I can do is step by step steadily follow my master and the Grand Buddha Master and spread our magnificent Buddha-dharma. May all people in the world someday hear the discourses on the dharma given by our magnificent Grand Buddha Master and may they experience enlightenment, liberation from the cycle of birth and death, and happiness from having listened to them.

I have written this in a simple, straightforward, unembellished way. What I have stated are facts. Through these written words, I have done my utmost to inform people of the world that the true Buddha-dharma is here. My magnificent Grand Buddha Master has reached the highest level of accomplishment in the Five Vidyas. From ancient times to the present, no person in the world has surpassed His Holiness. If we do not cultivate ourselves at this time when the true dharma can be heard, when will we? Amitabha!

Buddhist disciple,
Ai-Yuan Dong

(This is a complete translation of the Chinese text that follows originally written and signed by Ai-Yuan Dong.)

(實例七)

我的父親十幾年前患了鼻咽癌，在經過幾個星期的鈷六十治療，喉嚨部分及口腔內的唾液腺都被破壞了，所以到老年時吞嚥食物有困難，常常在進食時一不小心食物掉到肺裡引起不適。隨著年歲大了，免疫力也降低，終於引起了急性肺炎住進了台北榮民總院加護病房，一時三管齊插—胃管、氣切管、導尿管，當時的情況白血球已高到五萬，情形非常的危急，接到台北家中電話心急如焚不知如何是好，報告師父國際佛教僧尼總會主席隆慧法師後，師父讓我求助偉大的多杰羌佛第三世雲高益西諾布頂聖如來佛陀師爺加持，佛陀師爺慈悲馬上答應，並囑咐我要告訴父親觀想佛陀師爺對他幫助最大，由於父親也是三世多杰羌佛的弟子，尤其在父親的心裡認定老人家就是「佛」，百分之百的信賴，所以當我回到台北恭請了佛陀師爺老人家法相到加護病房看他時，他不能說話(插了肺管)，但看到佛陀師爺的法相，他合掌流淚了，一個受難的弟子對慈悲的佛陀上師的依賴。第二天開始白血球開始慢慢降下來，情況開始好轉了。

父親寫在紙上告訴我，在未見到老人家法相時，他一閉眼就看到一些東西(父親一直不肯說出什麼東西)，但是自從老人家的法相一掛在他的床前，這些東西就都不見了，開始睡得比較安穩。漸漸地，出了加護病房回家休養。但是過了半年卻因攝護腺肥大引起膀胱發炎再次入院，在醫院裡因請的看護不小心餵食過多(因父親自從上次入院後

為避免食物再掉入肺裡，所以一直插著胃管)而嘔吐，食物再次掉到肺裡引起了發炎，這一次情況更嚴重，高燒兩個星期不退，抗生素藥用到最強的第三代都無效，我身在美國每天打電話問候都說燒未退，我又急了，請示了師父又再次求救佛陀師爺，可是佛陀師爺不開處方，我突然想起七年前去中國時，佛陀師爺給過我五粒甘露丸，我懷著萬分的感恩與信心，拿著甘露丸馬上趕往機場回台灣。

我把甘露丸打粉帶到醫院給父親餵食，第一粒剛吃下，醫生突然說隔天要作一個檢查夜裡十二點以後不能夠進食任何東西，母親一下子不知如何是好，我很堅定的告訴母親，不管醫院如何說我們繼續餵甘露丸，結果第二粒尚未餵完，父親已經完全退燒恢復正常，我的弟弟們看到這些真實不虛的經過，對佛法升起了信心。

由於前後數次美國台灣兩地跑，再加上身心的疲憊，自己的身體也出了狀況尚不自知，有一天晚上血壓竟然上升到一百九十八，心跳更是像打鼓一樣，手腳開始發冷發抖，當時心中只有觀想佛陀金剛師爺才慢慢穩定下來，但是之後卻仍有數次發作，有次竟在夜裡睡眠中，突然胸口猛的一跳，我醒了，卻四肢如千斤重擔無法動彈，口中叫不出聲，力用不上，我知道我這就是死了，大約過了幾分鐘，才慢慢恢復過來，我想這可不是開玩笑的事，趕緊到醫院檢查，前後數次醫生都沒有辦法，只有再求救佛陀師爺，佛陀師爺為我傳了氣脈明點開關法，如今已漸漸恢復正常。

我們父女前後都得三世多杰羌佛老人家救命，做弟子的福報太淺，無以回報老人家的恩德，只有一步一腳印的跟著師父、佛陀師爺，將我們偉大的佛法弘揚開來，願世上的人都能因聞我們偉大的佛陀師爺的法音而開悟得到解脫，得到幸福。

此篇文章平舖直敘未有雕著，卻是真實不虛的事實，謹以此文告知世人真正的佛法在這裡，我偉大的佛陀師爺的成就，在古往今來世上已無人能出其右，得聞正法的今日不修更待何時，阿彌陀佛!

佛弟子　東愛媛

（此文的英文翻譯印在前面）

(Example 8)

I am a practitioner of traditional Chinese medicine in Las Vegas. I have been practicing medicine for a few dozen years. I have helped relieve many illnesses that could not be cured despite treatment for many years by other doctors. In the local area where I work, I can be called an influential practitioner of medicine and am constantly receiving favorable comments from my patients.

However, I contracted rheumatoid arthritis in early 2004. The joints of my fingers hurt all the time. The joints of my thumbs made it especially difficult for me to bend and extend my thumbs. My symptoms continued to become more serious, and eventually I could not bend the joints of my left and right thumbs. The thumb on one hand could only be moved by using my other hand, which was very painful! This condition of mine affected my work.

Rheumatoid arthritis is a disease that is very difficult to cure. Furthermore, it resulted from my negative karma. I tried all kinds of methods, but my symptoms were not alleviated. My only course was to beseech the empowerment (blessing) of my Buddha Dharma King Master, H.H. Dorje Chang Buddha III. The Buddha Master is infinitely compassionate and immediately transmitted a dharma method to me. I at once practiced that dharma as it was taught to me by the Buddha Master. Within only a few weeks, the pain in my finger joints disappeared, and I could freely move my thumbs. My hands can now function in a totally normal manner. Moreover, the strength of my hands is much greater than it was before I was cured.

The Buddha Master is profoundly proficient in both exoteric and esoteric Buddhism and has wondrous mastery of the Five Vidyas. I have personal experience of His Holiness's mastery of the healing vidya. I am tremendously grateful to the magnificent Buddha Master. I must firmly keep in mind the teaching of H.H. Dorje Chang Buddha III to cure the illnesses and relieve the suffering of living beings based upon limitless compassion and the four immeasurable minds.

What I have stated above is true. If there is falsehood in what I have stated, I will descend into the vajra hell. If what I have stated is true, I dedicate all of the resulting good fortune to the the Buddha Master, Buddhas and Bodhisattvas, and all living beings in the six realms of reincarnation so that living beings and I may together end the cycle of birth and death and soon realize bodhi.

Buddhist disciple,
Lin Hui

(This is a complete translation of the Chinese text that follows originally written and signed by Lin Hui.)

(實例八)

我是一名中醫，目前在Las Vegas行醫，我從事醫學工作幾十年，很多多年治不好的病，我都能幫他們解除病痛，也算是一位在當地有影響的醫務工作者，也不斷得到病人的好評。

可是於2004年初，我得了類風濕，手指關節疼痛不止，特別是姆指關節屈伸不利，症狀持續加重，左右手姆指不能彎曲，需要用另一隻手去扳才能移動，痛苦無比，同時也影響了我的工作。

類風濕是一種很難治的病，這也是我的業力反映，什麼辦法都用了，症狀不見減輕，我只好去求我的佛陀法王上師三世多杰羌佛加持。佛陀上師慈悲無量，當即傳授了法門。我立即遵佛陀上師傳授之法，如是而修，僅在幾週內，我的手關節疼痛消失，姆指活動自如，至今我的手功能一切正常，並且手的力量比以前增強了許多。佛陀上師深通顯密，妙諳五明，在醫方明方面弟子有親身的體驗。我萬分感謝偉大的佛陀上師，要牢記三世多杰羌佛的教導，以無限的悲心、四無量心為眾生醫病，減輕眾生的痛苦。

以上所說事實真實不虛，如果有妄語，我將墮金剛地獄；如果是真實不虛的，我將把所得到的全部福報回向給佛陀上師、諸佛菩薩以及六道眾生，讓眾生與我共同了生脫死，早證菩提。

真誠的弟子　琳慧

（此文的英文翻譯印在前面）

(Example 9)

My Buddhist name is Pei Jun. I am from Taiwan. I am a disciple of H.H. Dorje Chang Buddha III. I have great respect for my Buddha Master. The Buddha Master's compassion, kindness and high moral character cause me to experience His Holiness's brightness and magnificence. I would like to relate an incident that I personally experienced to illustrate the magnificence and compassion of H.H. Dorje Chang Buddha III.

My younger cousin got into a car accident and was in a coma for more than twenty days. During that time, he could not eat or drink and did not have any mental activity. He was condemned to being a human vegetable, for the doctors could do nothing to help. The doctors explained that they had no way to save him. My cousin was the child that my aunt and her husband had been hoping for over a period of many years. Thus, tears bathed the cheeks of my aunt all day long. My aunt's husband, who normally is very cheerful and jocular in front of the younger generation, constantly knitted his brows and felt heartbroken over my cousin's situation. I thought that the only one who could save my cousin was my magnificent Buddha Master. Thus, I sincerely beseeched H.H. Dorje Chang Buddha III to receive me. After His Holiness received me, I reported to my magnificent Buddha Master the situation concerning my cousin.

The Buddha Master compassionately gave a discourse to me on the dharma. His Holiness told me that the main source of negative karmic retribution is the committing of bad deeds. His Holiness explained that my cousin was in such a state because of the power of karma accumulated over many lifetimes and eons. Thus, we must "abstain from doing anything evil and do all that is good." The Buddha Master told me not to worry and then practiced dharma to empower my cousin. The Buddha Master said that based upon my cousin's condition at that time, my cousin would regain consciousness very soon.

After I returned to my hotel that night, I received a phone call from my younger sister. She said that my cousin's eyes showed signs of reaction. I at once praised the magnificence of the Buddha Master's empowerment. My cousin has already returned to normal, left the hospital, and gone back home. He is now working behind the counter at my aunt's teahouse.

The Buddha Master lightly empowered my cousin. The resulting power lightly traversed the Pacific Ocean from the United States to Taiwan causing a human vegetable to return to the human world in his prior normal condition. I had previously never even heard of such magnificent Buddha-dharma. Moreover, this is entirely true. The profundity of such Buddha-dharma possessed by the Buddha Dharma King is truly indescribable.

What I have stated above is completely true. If what I have stated above is fabricated, may I, Pei-Jun, die an unnatural death.

Pei-Jun Chen

(This is a complete translation of the Chinese text that follows originally written and signed by Pei-Jun Chen.)

(實例九)

我的法名叫佩君，台灣人，是三世多杰羌佛的弟子。我非常尊重我的佛陀上師，佛陀上師慈悲善良，道德高尚，讓我在這個世界真正見識到了佛陀的光明和偉大。我在這裡要通過我親身經歷的一件事情來說明三世多杰羌的偉大及慈悲為懷。

我的表弟車禍，昏迷20多天無法吃喝，沒有神智，被判定為植物人，醫生束手無策，表示沒有辦法挽救。表弟是姑姑與姑丈期盼多年才有的孩子，姑姑為此整日以淚洗面，而平日在晚輩面前樂觀、開朗又愛搞笑的姑丈，面對表弟的情況，總是眉頭深鎖及心痛不已。我認為能救表弟的只有我偉大的佛陀上師，為此我懇求三世多杰羌佛的接見，並向偉大的佛陀上師彙報表弟的情形。

佛陀上師非常慈悲的為我作了開示，告訴我因果的惡報主要來源於做壞事，表弟會這樣是因為多生累劫的業力所造成，所以要『諸惡莫作，眾善奉行』。佛陀上師叫我放心，並當場做功課加持表弟。佛陀上師說，根據表弟現在的情形，會很快的還魂恢復過來。

當天晚上我回到旅館，就接到妹妹打來的電話，說表弟的眼睛已經有反應，我當場讚嘆佛陀上師加持力的偉大。現在，表弟已經恢復正常出院回家，在姑姑開的泡沫紅茶店擔任吧台的工作。佛陀上師就那麼輕輕的加持一下，力量就這樣輕輕地從美國飛過太平洋到台灣，讓植物人重新回轉人間成正常人，這樣偉大的佛法我聽都沒聽過，更何況這是事實，佛陀法王的佛法高深到這個程度，實在是無法用語言形容。

以上我講的事情是完全真實不虛的，如果我以上所講的事情是虛構編造的，我佩君願不得好死。

陳佩君

陳佩君

（此文的英文翻譯印在前面）

(Example 10)

While the Manufacturer's Technician Didn't Know What To Do, the Buddha Master Healed the Problem with a Roar

Whenever people mention H.H. Dorje Chang Buddha III Wan Ko Yeshe Norbu Holiest Tathagata's accomplishments in the healing vidya, they all praise the incredible healing power of H.H. Dorje Chang Buddha III. Even a terminal-stage cancer patient came back to life under H.H. Dorje Chang Buddha III's empowerment. This patient has lived twenty or thirty years longer and is now as strong as a bull. In fact, to claim that the healing vidya is only the ability to heal the diseases of humans is not comprehensive enough. To be able to cure illnesses of mankind is just a small fraction of H.H. Dorje Chang Buddha III's accomplishments in the healing vidya. According to the truth of Buddha-dharma, that is the narrow sense of the healing vidya. The scope of H.H. Dorje Chang Buddha III's accomplishments in the healing vidya is the true broad sense of the healing vidya as expounded by the Buddha. In other words, H.H. Dorje Chang Buddha III is able to fix or heal anything that goes wrong with any non-sentient thing or any sentient being. Herein, I would like to describe two incidents that I have personally experienced.

First of all, I would like to make a statement. I will make a vow to prove that all I am about to say are facts that I have personally experienced. Nothing I am about to say is fabricated. Maybe some people will think that vows are vulgar. Yet, only when what one says is true will one dare to make vows. Otherwise, who would want to receive all the negative karmic retribution from making false claims? The life of humankind is already full of suffering. Am I so foolish to ask for negative karmic retribution instead of freeing myself from all the sufferings? Many past virtuous ones made vows, such as the Zen Master Yong Jia. Therefore, today, I will emulate the past virtuous ones and make a vow in all seriousness: If what I state below is false and made up, I am willing to receive all negative karmic retribution. On the contrary, if everything I state is true, I hope that all living beings will be able to listen to the correct Buddha-dharma of H.H. Dorje Chang Buddha III. Furthermore, I hope my true stories will benefit the public and help them to cultivate themselves and reach liberation.

The first incident was when the Buddha Master wrote a poem on Chinese calligraphy paper for each of the ten faux jade plates. The calligraphy of H.H. Dorje Chang Buddha III is a model for others, and His Holiness has formed his own style of writing. His calligraphy is elegant, exhibits no attachment, and is free from defilements of the mundane world. Every piece is exquisite.

In order to have the calligraphy carved on the giant wooden boxes containing the faux jade plates, I brought the Buddha Master's original calligraphy to Kinko's to make copies. I selected Kinko's because their machine can make copies the size of four feet or larger. Because the calligraphy was on rice paper, which tends to be fragile, no matter how careful I was, when I got to the third piece of calligraphy, the inevitable thing

still happened: The printer jammed the whole piece of paper. I asked the Kinko's technician to turn off the machine. He tried really hard to get the paper out of the machine. It was all torn into pieces with ink smudges. The writing was badly torn and smudged. As a result, I dared not copy the rest. I then brought them back.

At that time, it was night already; yet, the Buddha Master was just having His lunch. The Buddha Master saw the pieces and said to me, "After I finish my meal, I will heal it." It ended up that the Buddha Master cleaned the exquisite piece of calligraphy. His Holiness restored it to its original perfect condition. One couldn't see that it was put together from pieces. I don't know how the ink stains disappeared. The strange thing is that whenever raw rice paper comes into contact with water, the paper will loose its structure or disintegrate. How, then, was it possible for the Buddha Master to clean the ink stains that were already blended with the writing? Nevertheless, this was what happened!

The second incident happened in December of 1998. A fellow disciple, Heng Sheng Rinpoche from Taiwan, bought a printer that could print an A4 size photo directly from a video camera. He brought it to Shenzhen to offer it to the Buddha Master, Dorje Chang Buddha III. When it was brand new, we printed some photos and they came out great. At that time I was the only one who operated the machine. Later, all the prints came out with lines

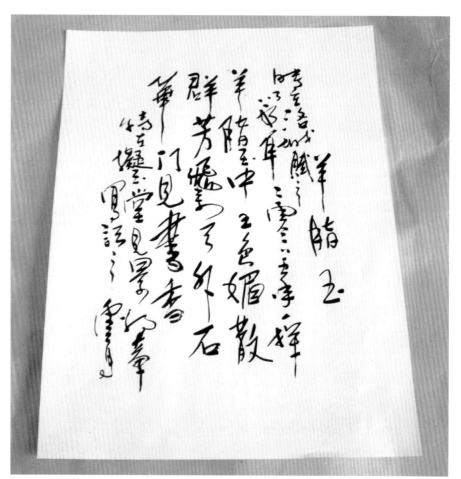

The original calligraphy after it was torn up by a machine.
被機器絞破的書法原件

The original calligraphy after H.H. Dorje Chang Buddha III applied His healing vidya skills and "healed" it.
經三世多杰羌佛用醫方明醫好的書法原件

through them or with patches of color so that they no longer looked like photos. It was possible that I had accidentally touched a key somehow and reprogrammed the printer.

I followed the manual myself and tried to adjust it. It still didn't work. The Buddha Master criticized me because of this. No matter how hard I tried, I still couldn't make the machine get back to normal. With no more options, I called Heng Sheng Rinpoche and asked him to consult the manufacturer. The next day, we paid the manufacturer's technician to make a special trip from Hong Kong to Shenzhen to fix the machine. In the beginning, the technician seemed very confident of himself. He didn't seem to care much. Then, he started to get upset because after a long time of trying, the printout still looked the same as it did when I had tried earlier. When it was getting dark, he had to head back. If he stayed any longer, he would not be able to get back to Hong Kong. Before he took off, he said that this machine was the newest product of Mitsubishi and had just come out. This was the only one in the whole of south-east Asia. He couldn't fix it. The only way was to take it back to the manufacturer's headquarters in Japan.

Yet, we were in a hurry to print an A4 size photo with it. It was obvious that it would be too late to take it back to Japan for repair. Under such circumstance, the Buddha Master said to me, "Let's check what's wrong with it." (This is roughly what His Holiness meant. I cannot recall exactly what His Holiness said.) The Buddha Master then sat on the sofa that was placed next to the wall. I sat on the floor, and the printer was placed right next to me. The Buddha Master was usually very busy. His Holiness would not normally do things like this. His Holiness first asked me how this machine worked. I reported to the Buddha Master about all the function keys on the machine, how they worked, and what numbers needed to be keyed in to print out a photo. Four sets of numbers were needed for each photo, and every set of numbers could have more than ten variations. The choices could go up into the hundreds. It was several times more complicated than a safety box combination. After the Buddha Master listened to this, His Holiness told me to key in a set of numbers. It still came out only lines.

Next, the Buddha Master told me another set of new numbers. After I keyed in the numbers, the print turned out better. Yet, we could still see colored lines. After the Buddha Master saw it, His Holiness had me again key in another set of new numbers. This time, when it printed half way, it

was all black, like black paper. The Buddha Master uttered a roar, and said, "Good. Good. All right. It is successful!" I was puzzled. I thought, "Just this awful sheet of black paper? How can this be successful?" It was very strange because all the colors were gone, and only a mass of black was left. At this time, the Buddha Master said, "Hurry up and key in xx, xx, xx, xx." After I keyed in these four sets of numbers, I immediately printed out the photo. Just when it came out a little bit, I already could see the true and beautiful colors of the photo. The result was exactly what the Buddha Master had predicted. It was a very good photo. The quality of the photo was the same as the one we printed out on the day the machine arrived. The most bizarre thing was that the Hong Kong technician and I also tried this set of numbers. However, why couldn't it print out a photo at that time?

I remember very clearly this photo. It was a photo of the Buddha Master's disciple, Daxila Rinpoche. Daxila Rinpoche is a Dharma King of the Kagyu Xueba sect. He is a solemn, great virtuous one who has reached a very high level of accomplishment. At that time, I wrote down those numbers on the back of the photo as a record. The photo of Daxila Rinpoche printed in this book was scanned from that very photo.

Karmic conditions change constantly. It is a pity that I couldn't take this memorable printer with me as I wished when I left Shenzhen. This has also proved the Buddha's teaching: All conditioned phenomena are like a dream, an illusion, a bubble, and a shadow. I believe that this incident can give us much to ponder. First, this is a machine that had just been invented. Second, even the manufacturer's technician could not fix it. Third, the Buddha Master only tried three times. In addition, His Holiness concluded that His Holiness would succeed after a piece of paper was printed out all black. This is foreseeing the future! This is the manifestation of the highest Buddha-dharma wisdom, complete proficiency in exoteric and exoteric Buddhism, and wondrous mastery of the Five Vidyas. What else can it be?

Buddhist disciple, Long Zhi Tanpe Nyima
April 23, 2006 in America

This is a complete translation of the Chinese text that follows originally written and signed by Long Zhi Tanpe Nyima.)

<h2 style="text-align:center">(實例十)</h2>

工廠專家束手無策　大法王上師聲到病除

　　大家一說到多杰羌佛第三世雲高益西諾布頂聖如來的醫方明，都稱讚三世多杰羌佛治病救人的功夫了得，連末期癌症的病人都在三世多杰羌佛的手裡起死回生，現在又活了二三十年，身體健壯如牛。其實，僅以治療人的病就稱為醫方明，這種說法是不全面的，治療人的疾病只是三世多杰羌佛的醫方明的一小部分而已，也就是佛法真諦中講到的狹義的醫方明。三世多杰羌佛的醫方明是真正佛陀所說的廣義

醫方明，也就是天地萬物，有情無情，只要出了問題，三世多杰羌佛無一不能醫治。我在這裡，就說兩個我親身經歷的事情。

　　首先，我要聲明的是，我要發誓以證明下面我所說的全是我親身經歷的事實，沒有半點虛構。或許有人會認為發誓是俗氣的，但是，只有是真實的才敢發誓，否則，如果是假的，誰願意遭一切惡報呢？人生本來就已經夠痛苦的了，難道愚癡到了不脫離苦難，反而找惡報

嗎？很多古德如永嘉禪師就曾發誓，所以今天我也學習古德在此鄭重發誓：如果我下面所說的是假的、是編造虛構出來的事例，我願遭一切惡報，反之，如果我所說的都是真實的，則希望所有的眾生都能得聞三世多杰羌佛的正教佛法，利益大眾，修行解脫。

第一件事是佛陀上師為十塊玉板分別題詩，並寫在宣紙上。三世多杰羌佛的書法出於碑帖而自成宗風，高雅飄逸，無礙無執，脫盡人間煙火之氣，每一件都是精品。為了要將這些書法刻在包裝這些玉板的巨大的珠寶盒上，我便帶著佛陀上師的書法原件去Kinko's複印，因為只有那裡才有可以複印4呎以上尺寸的大複印機。因為是宣紙，比較軟，所以儘管我小心翼翼，在複印到第三張的時候，最不願看到的事情還是發生了：複印機將原件整個捲進去了！我叫來Kinko's的工作人員幫我把機器停了，費了很大的功夫才把原件取出來，結果已經破碎成好幾片，而且沾滿了油墨，包括字的部分！餘下的我自然不敢再複印了，只好拿回來。那時候雖然已是晚上了，但佛陀上師才在用午餐，佛陀上師看了以後，對我說：等我吃完飯，我來把它醫好吧。結果，佛陀上師把這件書法精品洗得乾乾淨淨，修得天衣無縫，根本看不出來是由很多塊碎片拼在一起的，污垢的油墨不知怎麼不見了。奇怪的是，這生宣紙遇到水就會亂掉，而且與字合在一起的油墨怎麼會洗下來呢？但是，事實卻就是這樣的！

第二件是一九九八年十二月份的事情，台灣的恒生仁波且師兄從香港買了一台可以直接從攝影機打印A4幅面的照片的機器，送來深圳供養給三世多杰羌佛陀上師。剛買回來的時候打印了幾張照片，效果很好。當時這台機器的具體操作都是我一個人在進行的，後來可能是我無意中碰到了什麼按鍵或是其它什麼原因，結果印出來的東西全部都是條紋狀的，色塊按條紋排列，不成為照片了。

我自己按照說明書調整了很久，沒有效果，為此，佛陀上師也批評了我，但是，我再怎麼鼓搗，這個機器還是無法恢復到正常的狀況。無奈之下，只好打電話給恒生仁波且，請他諮詢廠家。

第二天，我們付費請廠家的維修專家專程從香港趕來深圳修理這台機器。專家開始時信心滿滿，不太在乎，慢慢的他就發急了，因為他調整了很久，印出來的結果跟我印出來的是一樣的。直到天快黑了，專家必須要走了，因為再遲他就趕不回香港了。出門之前專家說：這個機器是三菱公司剛剛生產出來的最新的機種，整個東南亞也只有這麼一台，他無法修好，唯一的辦法就是要拿回日本總公司修理。

但是，我們要急等著靠它來印A4幅面的照片，拿回日本修理顯然是來不及的。在此情況下，佛陀上師便對我說：我們來看一看毛病在哪裡（大意是這樣的，我回憶不起確切的話）。然後，佛陀上師坐在牆邊的沙發上，我則席地而坐，那台打印照片的機器就在我旁邊。佛陀

上師平時非常忙，是不會搞弄這些東西的，他先詢問這台機器是如何工作的，我向佛陀上師報告了這個機器有哪些按鈕、它的工作流程、普通打印照片要輸入哪些數據等等，因為每一張照片由四組數據組成，每一組的數據又有幾十種、上百種選擇，比保險櫃要複雜若干倍。佛陀上師聽完以後，讓我輸入一組數據，結果出來的還是條紋狀的。緊接著，佛陀上師又告訴我一組新的數據，我輸入進去打印後效果略有好轉，但還是條紋狀的色彩。佛陀上師看了以後，再讓我輸入一組新的數據，這次剛打印出來一半，是全黑色的，就像一張黑紙，這時佛陀上師大吼一聲，隨著說：『好，好，好了，成功了！』我一臉錯愕，心想：就憑這張更糟的黑紙嗎？怎麼能說成功了呢？奇怪了，因為連顏色都沒有了，只剩下一團黑色。就在這時，佛陀上師說：『快輸入xx、xx、xx、xx。』我輸入四組數據以後，馬上打印，剛出來一點就見到了真實而美妙的還原色彩，結果確確實實就如同佛陀上師預言的一樣，這是一張非常好的照片，質量同機器剛來的那天印出來的一模一樣。但奇怪的是，香港專家和我也用了這個數據的，為什麼就印不出來呢？這張照片我記得非常清楚，就是佛陀上師的弟子大西拉仁波且的照片。大西拉仁波且是噶舉學巴派的法王，是一個極其嚴謹、證量甚高的大德。當時我就將這些數據都紀錄在這張照片的背面，並作為標準值。本書所附的大西拉仁波且的照片，就是從這張照片掃描的。

可惜的是，因緣變幻，在我離開深圳的時候，未能如願將這台極具紀念意義的打印機帶走，這也印證了佛陀的開示：『一切有為法，如夢幻泡影』。但是，我相信，從這個公案當中，有很多值得我們思考：第一，這是一台最新發明的機器；第二，工廠的專家都已經束手無策了；第三，佛陀上師只試了三次，尤其是在印出一張黑紙的時候就斷定成功了，這是未來先知啊。這裡面除了至高無上的佛法智慧和顯密圓通、妙諳五明的境界，還有什麼呢？！

佛弟子：隆智・丹貝尼瑪

2006年4月23日記於美國

（此文的英文翻譯印在前面）

CATEGORY 11

Medicine and Health Care Products

第十一大類　製藥保健

Introduction

H.H. Dorje Chang Buddha III Holiest Tathagata Wan Ko Yeshe Norbu Buddha Vajradhara has created many health care products to protect the health of mankind. Among the most famous of these products are *Fa Bi Sheng* (Hair Must Grow) and *Yi Ci Ling* (a remedy for frostbite). There is also *Li Xue Ting*, which is a special medicine used to stop bleeding immediately. Other special medicines include those used to cure malignant skin sores, fevers that do not subside, stubborn rheumatism, inflammation of the trachea, hepatitis, inflammation of the arteries and veins, and heart disease. The Health Ministry of China gave registration number one to a product called *Xiong Li Yu Fa Ye* (Powerful Hair Growth Liquid) invented by His Holiness indicating that it is the best product of its kind in over forty years. However, what is most surprising and incredible is that after H.H. Dorje Chang Buddha III invented these medicines and health care products, He gave them to people free of charge in order to help them and has not received one cent from those products.

(This text was translated from the Chinese text that follows.)

簡　　　介

多杰羌佛第三世雲高益西諾布頂聖如來所製的用於保健人類身體的保健品非常之多，其中最有名的有「髮必生」和「一次靈」等，有封刀止血的「立血停」、治皮膚惡瘡、高燒不退、頑固風濕、氣管炎、肝炎、脈管炎、心臟病等的特殊藥，如「雄力育髮液」獲得了中國衛生部40年來頒發的第一號保健品。但最奇怪、令人不可思議的是，三世多杰羌佛發明了這些藥，除了利益大眾之外，自己卻不收分文錢。

（此文的英文翻譯印在前面）

Document Issued by the Health Ministry of the People's Republic of China
中華人民共和國衛生部的文件

中华人民共和国卫生部

便　函

卫监环便字(90) 第001号

成都长城保健品厂新繁分厂：

经研究，同意你单位在"雏力育发液"产品说明中注明原名为"康华发必生"，并将原"中国康华社会服务公司四川保健品厂"更名为"成都长城保健品厂新繁分厂"。

卫生部卫生监督司
一九九零年二月八日

抄送：四川省卫生厅、四川省卫生防疫站

卫生部文件

卫监字〔89〕第53号

关于批准"雄力育发液"等三种育发产品的通知

各省、自治区、直辖市卫生厅（局），有关部委，
中国预防医学科学院：

经审查"雄力育发液"、"101育发剂"、
"丽尔育发露"符合我国《化妆品卫生标准》的有
关规定，现予批准，有效期四年。批准文号如下：

雄力育发液 〔89〕卫妆准字16-QG-01-0001号
101育发剂 〔89〕卫妆准字01-QG-01-0002号
丽尔育发露 〔89〕卫妆准字01-QG-01-0003号

请各地卫生监督机构加强对其产品卫生质量的
经常性监督。

卫　　生　　部
一九八九年十二月二十一日

抄：各省、自治区、直辖市卫生防疫站，中国预防
医学科学院环监所

Mi Tuo Powder

My family is originally from Mimou in the suburbs of Chengdu. In the autumn of 1992, my second younger brother Gao-Song Lu's two-year-old son, Yang Lu, was hospitalized in the local Mimou Hospital with a mysterious high fever. Every day he received shots and took all sorts of medicine. This included Chinese herbal medicine, such as bupleurum falcatum and isalis root, and Western medicine, such as penicillin. None of them did any good. Every morning his fever would go down, but late at night it would rise up to 39℃ (102.2°F) or 39.5℃ (103.1°F). Within a few days, Yang Lu had developed a serious case of pneumonia. His condition worsened quickly, and his fever rose to 40℃ (104°F). His father Gao-Song Lu had no choice but to move him to the 47th Military Hospital in Xindu.

There was a shortage of beds at the pediatric department, but with the help of the hospital's head nurse, Li-Qin Huang, a friend of mine, Yang Lu found a place to stay at the department of Chinese herbal medicine. Yang Lu received much more advanced treatment at the military hospital than he did at that local ordinary hospital, but his temperature did not come down. To make matters worse, because of his continuous high fever, a horrible reaction to one of the intravenous shots all of a sudden caused his skin to blacken and and his tongue and reproductive organs to shrink. The doctor told my brother and his wife that Yang Lu might not live if the fever did not abate soon. Li-Qin Huang, the head nurse, was very worried and had someone look all over for me. When I finally heard what was happening, I dropped my work immediately and went to the residence of my respected Buddha master, His Holiness Dorje Chang Buddha III, to seek help.

I was very anxious, but H.H.Dorje Chang Buddha III consoled me. "Do not worry. This is a small matter. I will give you Chinese herbal medicine that will bring down the fever in no time." H.H. Dorje Chang Buddha III promptly ground the medicine to powder, wrapped it in white paper, and wrote on it "Mi Tuo Powder." Yang Lu took the medicine, and his fever came down that very day. He was cured without even taking all of the Chinese medicine. The next day he was able to check out of the hospital and return home. My family and neighbors marveled at the effectiveness of "Mi Tuo Powder" and were all deeply grateful to H.H. Dorje Chang Buddha III for saving Yang Lu's life. Yang Lu is now in high school and plans to apply to the air force academy. He is very healthy.

In 1996, an injected form of H.H. Dorje Chang Buddha III's "Mi Tuo Powder" was developed. Xiao-Mei Fang made arrangements with the Chengdu Institute of Biological Medicine to complete production procedures and produce a sample of golden ampere injected medicine. After H.H. Dorje Chang Buddha III left Chengdu, the development was terminated for some reason. I hope that someday "Mi Tuo Powder" will be made available to help all people.

Chengdu Daily News
Shih-Fang Lu, April, 2006

(This is a complete translation of the Chinese text that follows originally written and signed by Shi-Fang Lu.)

彌 陀 散

我的娘家在成都市郊的彌牟鎮，1992年秋天，我家二弟呂高松的兒子呂暘，當時才兩歲多，因為患不明原因高熱，住了當地的彌牟醫院。每天吃藥打針，中藥的柴胡針劑、板藍根針劑、西藥的青黴素都不起作用。每天早上熱度退下來，夜裡凌晨又高燒發熱到39度、39.5度，幾天就燒成嚴重的肺炎。而且病情還急轉直下，高熱到40度。呂高松不得已將呂暘轉至新都境內的解放軍第四十七醫院，找到我認識的一位護士長黃立琴。當時這家醫院的兒科已經沒有床位收治，黃立琴護士長又求助中醫科，呂暘最終在中藥科收治入院。解放軍第四十七醫院的醫療條件和醫療技術遠遠高於那個地區的普通醫院，但是小呂暘仍然不退熱，反而由於持續反覆地高燒，出現了可怕的輸液反應，一下子出現了身體發烏，舌頭萎縮，連生殖器都縮小了。醫院的醫生當時也告訴我弟弟、弟媳，高熱再退不下來，可能就沒救了。黃立琴護士長十分著急，託人到處找我。我得知消息時，放下手中的工作，求救於我的佛陀恩師三世多杰羌佛，請求救命。

見我的焦慮不安，三世多杰羌佛輕音細語地安慰我：「大姐！用不著焦急，這是小事一椿，我給你開一副中藥拿回去，輕輕就退燒了。」三世多杰羌佛很快將中藥弄成粉末，用白紙包好，上面還寫上「彌陀散」幾個字。小呂暘服了佛陀法王的藥，當天就退燒了，一副中藥還沒有服完就好了，第二天就出院回家了。「彌陀散」真是退熱之至，我的家人、親人和鄰里讚不絕口，無限感恩三世多杰羌救回了呂暘的性命。現在呂暘已上高中，而且志在考航校，身體十分健康。

1996年三世多杰羌佛的「彌陀散」開發成針劑成品藥，由房小妹牽線聯繫在成都生物藥品研究所，完成了工藝流程化試驗製成的小樣，為金黃色粉劑安培針藥。三世多杰羌離開成都之後，不知什麼原因，這項藥品的開發便停下了。願「彌陀散」服務人類。

成都日報　呂世芳

2006年4月

（此文的英文翻譯印在前面）

CATEGORY 12

Wondrous Multicolored Sculptures

第十二大類　玄妙彩寶雕

Introduction

The wondrous multicolored sculptures of H.H. Dorje Chang Buddha III Wan Ko Yeshe Norbu, which are one form of Yun sculpture, embody the essence of art and surpass natural beauty. These sculptures, the likes of which have never before been seen in the history of this world, were created by His Holiness for the benefit of mankind. H.H. Dorje Chang Buddha III has high international repute. The esteem he receives is indescribable.

No one would dare think that such art was carved from the hand of man. These sculptures are a major contribution to the art and civilization of mankind! Actually, this artwork transcends the scope of human art. Their beauty captivates the soul. If you have never seen such works of art, which have now appeared in this world for the first time, it might be difficult for you to imagine that this world actually has such beautiful and mystical creations. With the appearance of these sculptures, all splendid pearls, jade, and gemstones become pale in comparison, like the stars in the sky being outshined by a clear moon.

The Yun sculptures created by H.H. Dorje Chang Buddha III can be called unique masterpieces. The source of these unique masterpieces is His Holiness's Buddha state of realization, profound and extensive knowledge, and penetrating understanding of the laws governing the birth, growth, and change of everything in the universe. The amazing faux boulders that H.H. Dorje Chang Buddha III has created surpass the beauty of nature to an extent no other artist in human history has been able to reach. This has opened a new and astounding chapter on art in the history of human civilization.

Works of art by H.H. Wan Ko Yeshe Norbu Holiest Tathagata surpass the highest limits of human art. That is why the Organization of American States, which is composed of 34 countries—including the United States, Canada, and Mexico—held an exhibition of His Holiness's sculptures in 2003 in the nation's capital, Washington, D.C. That exhibition was primarily directed at ambassadors from various countries, as well as United States senators and congresspersons. It stunned the entire world. Senators, congresspersons, and ambassadors concluded that H.H. Dorje Chang Buddha III has made a great artistic contribution to the world.

On October 28th and 29th of 2003, in the Gold Room of House Office Building, Congress held an exhibition of Yun sculptures created by H.H. Dorje Chang Buddha III. That was the first time in its more than two-hundred-year history that the United States Congress held an art exhibition. Most of the attendees of that exhibition were senators, congresspersons, and their staff. The guests came in a continuous stream. Almost four hundred people voluntarily wrote down their sincere impressions in guest books. Each of them expressed amazement and praised what they saw.

Unfortunately, the pictures in this book cannot convey the true quality of these wondrous multicolored sculptures. It is suggested that you go to the museum where these works are displayed to see their beauty in person.　*(This text was translated from the Chinese text that follows.)*

簡　　介

玄妙彩寶雕是超越自然美的藝術精魂，是這個世界上歷史至今三世多杰羌佛雲高益西諾布頂聖如來為人類創始的，三世多杰羌佛在國際間享有崇高聲譽，受人崇敬之至，無以言表，誰也不敢相信這樣的藝術竟是人工雕刻出來的，這是為人類的藝術和文明做出的巨大貢獻！它已經超出人類藝術的範疇，它的美能攝人靈魂！你如果沒有看到這些人類第一次出現的藝術，你也許很難想像世界上還有這麼美的藝術神品出現，自它們出現後，這個世界上的任何堪稱富麗堂皇的珠寶玉器都猶如天上的星星在朗月的四周黯然失色無華！

三世多杰羌佛創始的韻雕藝術作品堪稱是絕世珍品，這些絕世珍品的誕生，完全來源於三世多杰羌佛至高的佛陀境界，淵博的學識和洞悉宇宙萬物生長變化的規律。三世多杰羌佛創始了超越大自然奇石的自然和美麗，達到人類歷史從未出現過的人工超自然境界，使得人類文明史上從此有了震撼性的藝術篇章。

正因為頂聖如來雲高益西諾布的藝術作品超越了人類藝術的高度範疇，達到了自然化的神工境界，所以由美國、加拿大、墨西哥等34個國家組成的美洲國家組織，於2003年專門在美國首府華盛頓，針對各國大使及美國參眾議員為主要觀賞而主辦的藝術作品展，震動了世界。議員和外交大使們都認為三世多杰羌為世界人類作出了巨大的藝術貢獻，尤其是美國國會於2003年10月28日、29日，在國會辦公大樓的金廳舉辦三世多杰羌佛的韻雕藝術展，這是美國國會二百多年來首次舉辦的藝術展，以參眾議員和國會工作人員為主體，參觀人潮絡繹不絕，有近四百人主動在留言簿上寫下了真誠的讚譽，達到眾所公認，驚嘆的程度，可惜書本上無法展示出其真實的效果，以後有機會可到展覽館參觀。　　　　　　　　　（此文的英文翻譯印在前面）

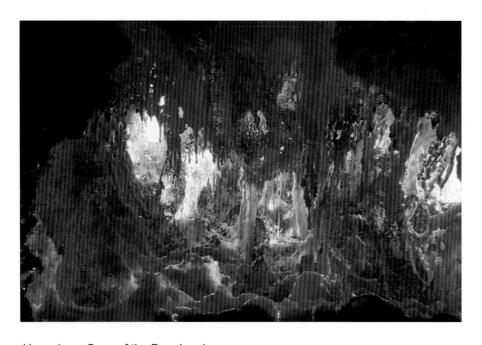

Humming a Song of the Pure Land
淨土哼歌

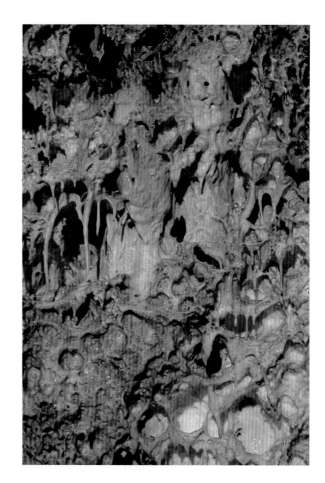

Ancient Dunhuang Cave of Treasures
稀年煌窟

*Hanging Withered
Vines Embrace Ancient
Stones*
殘藤塊石之古堡

Fossilized Bones of the Magical Dragon
神龍骨化

Art of the Little Autumn Hill
秋山點藝

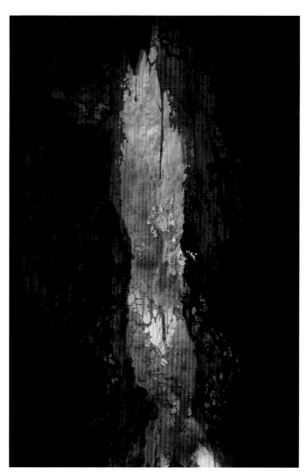

Deep Feeling: Vistas Beyond the Tranquil Valley
幽然谷外景情深

Loveliness
佳麗

Unusual Music from Beyond Heaven
天外異曲

339

The Organization of American States held an exhibition of H.H. Dorje Chang Buddha III Wan Ko Yeshe Norbu's Yun Sculptures in Washington D.C., the capital of the United States. Below are newspaper reports published at that time.

美洲國家組織為三世多杰羌佛雲高益西諾布在美首府華盛頓舉辦韻雕作品展，以下是當時報紙的報導。

The United States Congress held an exhibition of H.H. Dorje Chang Buddha III Wan Ko Yeshe Norbu's Yun Sculptures at the Gold Room of the Capitol Office Building. For details on this, please see the newspaper reports that were published at that time.

美國國會在金廳舉行三世多杰羌佛雲高益西諾布韻雕作品展，詳見當時報紙的報導。

CATEGORY 13

Faux Jade Plates

第十三大類　玉板

Introduction

The faux jade plates that H.H. Dorje Chang Buddha III Wan Ko Yeshe Norbu Holiest Tathagata created with a painting brush are unique and amazing treasures. They vividly reproduce the superlative beauty seen in the creation of the myriad things in nature. At the same time, they embody what is refined rather than coarse, amplifying the ephemeral and unostentatious beauty of precious natural things in life to the perfect zenith of art. Fei-Cui Jade, Yang-Zhi Jade, Shan-Hong Jade, Li-He Jade, Fu-Shou Jade, Tai-Hu Jade, Hai-Jiao Jade, Gang-Gu Jade, and other faux jade plates created by H.H. Dorje Chang Buddha III all look real and vivid in their textures, luster, colors, patterns, grains, and shapes.

What is most amazing is the depth to which the colors appear translucent on the faux jade plates. No matter how great the artist, we have never heard of anyone else who could cause colors to appear to permeate so deeply through the surface of solid material giving the impression of faux jade. Anyone can clearly see the depth to which those colors penetrated, giving those jade plates a remarkably elegant and delicate quality. These works of art look even more genuine and much more beautiful than real marble or jade. The beauty of real precious stones cannot hold a candle to these faux jade plates. All who have seen them marvel at them. Unfortunately, the pictures in this book cannot convey the true quality of these faux jade plates. It is suggested that you go to the museum where these works are displayed to see their beauty for yourself.

(This text was translated from the Chinese text that follows.)

簡　　　介

多杰羌佛第三世雲高益西諾布頂聖如來用畫筆繪成的玉板，真正是絕無僅有的千古奇珍，它們逼真再現大自然萬物鬼斧神工的天然造化，去滓存精，將自然寶物在生長過程中，偶爾短暫或並不強烈綻放的美好，發揮到完美的藝術極點。翡翠玉、羊脂玉、珊紅玉、理荷玉、福壽玉、太湖玉、海礁玉、鋼骨玉等等，質地、光澤、色韻、潤度、石花、龜紋、形態，無一不真，更厲害的是，出現透水深度。無論多厲害的畫家，從來都沒有聽說過能把顏色深深地透進磁板的板面，成為玉板，人們能明顯地看到它透進去的深度，到了雅奇微妙的地步，比真的大理石玉石還要真，還要美得太多，真正石頭的美妙完全無法望其項背，達到眾所公認，驚嘆認可的程度，可惜的是，書上無法展現真實的效果，有緣人請到展覽館參觀真蹟。

（此文的英文翻譯印在前面）

Shan-Hong Jade 珊紅玉

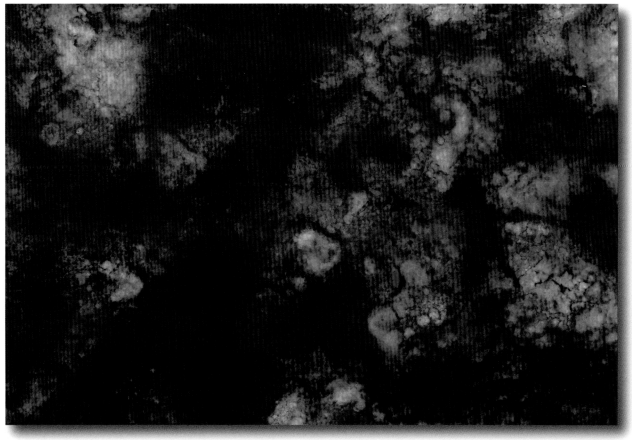

Fu-Shou Jade 福壽玉

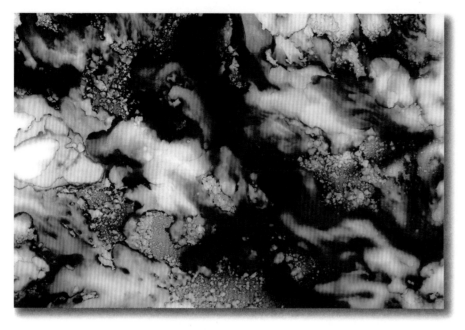

Huo-Se Jade 活色玉

Wen-Ru Jade 溫如玉

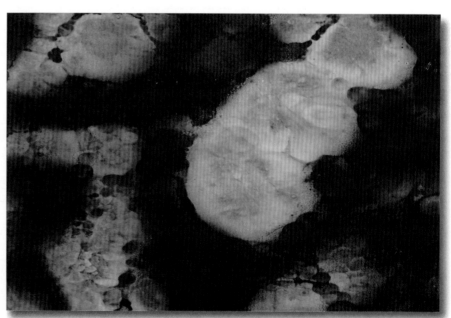

Tai-Hu Jade 太湖玉

Gang-Gu Jade 鋼骨玉

344

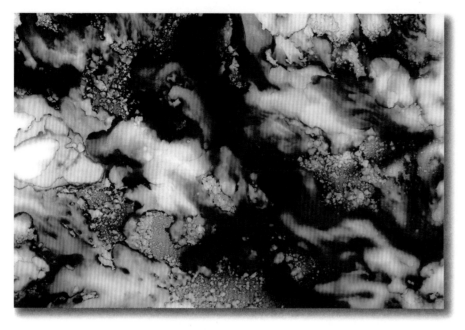

Huo-Se Jade 活色玉

Gang-Gu Jade 鋼骨玉

Wen-Ru Jade 溫如玉

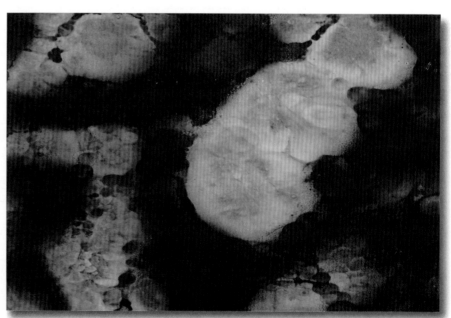

Tai-Hu Jade 太湖玉

344

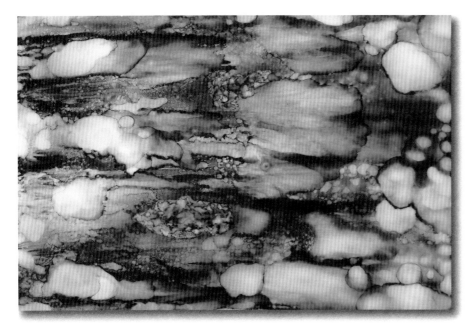

Li-He Jade 理荷玉

Hai-Jiao Jade 海礁玉

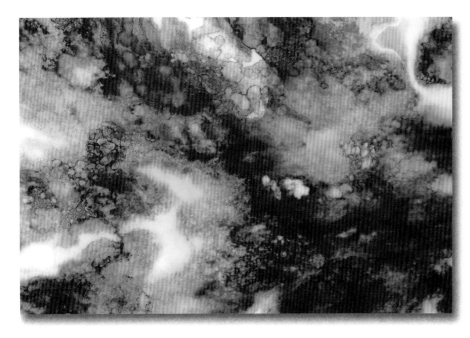

Fei-Cui Jade 翡翠玉

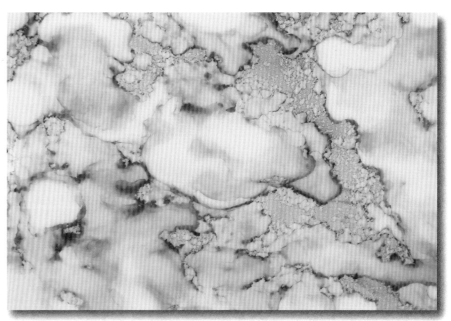

Yang-Zhi Jade 羊脂玉

CATEGORY 14

Philosophical Sayings About Worldly Matters

第十四大類　世法哲言

Introduction

H.H. Wan Ko Yeshe Norbu Holiest Tathagata is the true incarnation of Dorje Chang Buddha. His Holiness possesses the state of realization and virtue that entails the Three Bodies and Four Wisdoms of a Buddha. His Holiness is able to "manifest the universe on the tip of a hair and store limitless worlds in a grain of sand." In worldly terms, this state of realization and virtue is reflected in His Holiness's profound and vast knowledge, noble moral character, mastery of both ancient and modern learning, and status as a great figure in contemporary times and the highest Buddha.

His Holiness's philosophical thoughts are truly comprehensive and deep, containing practical wisdom about worldly matters that benefit living beings. These philosophical sayings are different from profound Buddhist teachings contained in this book, such as *Sutra on Understanding and Realizing Definitive Truth, Debate Between a Monk and a Laywoman, What is Cultivation?*, and the listed recorded discourses on the Buddha-dharma. These maxims on worldly matters are one of His Holiness's outstanding contributions to mankind. The tremendous erudition and nobility of H.H. Dorje Chang Buddha III are reflected in his profound philosophical thoughts.

The philosophical thoughts of H.H. Dorje Chang Buddha III are based upon the supreme and holiest wisdom of this ancient Buddha, His Holiness's thorough understanding of the ultimate truths of human life and the universe, and His Holiness's practice of what he preaches. They express the highest level of civilization and morality. As a result, these philosophical thoughts are maxims containing the essence of truth. If one seriously studies them and deeply reflects upon them, one will reap tremendous educational benefits and mental development from the transcendent wisdom and moral integrity of H.H. Dorje Chang Buddha III, who has fathomed the subtleties underlying all phenomena. That is one reason why these philosophical sayings have the ability to move and inspire others and why they are widely admired.

In response to the requests of many people and in order to facilitate learning and understanding, more than ten years ago the Office of the Secretary of Master Wan Ko Yee together with Yiyun Chen (who is an assistant researcher at the Sociology Research Institute within the Chinese Academy of Social Sciences) selected from His Holiness's writings some of His Holiness's philosophical sayings and added to them brief commentaries. That was later made into a book that was published and distributed by China Social Sciences Academic Press. Out of caution, they requested that H.H. Wan Ko Yeshe Norbu Holiest Tathagata expound upon those philosophical sayings. The explanations H.H. Dorje Chang Buddha III gave were extremely detailed and complete. None of those detailed explanations are included in this category.

We believe that these philosophical sayings are a cultural treasury. We hope that everyone will obtain from them abundant knowledge and a pure moral character. We hope that they will benefit mankind and provide mankind with good fortune and wisdom. If you study them with all your heart and mind and put them into practice, you will experience limitless beneficial effects.

Because of limited space, we have included only one brief commentary of a philosophical saying as an example, although all of the original philosophical sayings themselves are included. In 2002, World Dharma Voice, Inc. in the United States republished and began distributing around the world a book in Chinese on philosophical sayings of H.H. Wan Ko Yeshe Norbu Holiness Tathagata entitled *Brief Commentaries on Selected Philosophical Sayings of Master Wan Ko Yee*.

(This text was translated from the Chinese text that follows.)

簡　　介

雲高益西諾布頂聖如來為多杰羌佛真身降世，本身具備三身四智之證境證德，能將『一毫端現寶王剎、一粒沙藏三千界』，而反映在世間法上，則是學識淵博，德品崇高，博古通今，一代大家，大覺能仁。他的哲學思想，實在是博大精深，是世間法利益大眾的實用智慧，有別於本寶典中的甚深佛法教授，如《了義經》、《僧俗辯語》、《什麼叫修行》及法音開示等，這些世法格言也是三世多杰羌佛對人類文明的卓越貢獻之一。三世多杰羌佛深藏不露之純淨修養，更從另一方面體現出他高深的哲學思想。

三世多杰羌佛的哲學思想，是古佛以至高無上的頂聖智慧，洞悉宇宙人生的真諦，融會貫通，身體力行，直入文明道德的最高境界的至理。認真研習，深鑒內識，從其超塵脫凡之智慧，無私正節，了明萬法之微妙，都會受到很大的教益和啟迪，因此一提到雲高益西諾布頂聖如來的哲言就能感召大眾，深受敬慕。早在十多年前，應大家的要求，為便於進一步學習理解，義雲高大師秘書辦公室和中國社會科學院社會學研究所副研究員陳一筠共同從三世多杰羌佛的文論中，選擇了部份哲言，加以淺釋，中國社會科學文獻出版社並予以出版發行。為慎重起見，當時特地請雲高益西諾布頂聖如來為淺釋組作了講解，三世多杰羌佛的講解至為詳盡，但限於本書篇幅，因此我們只用了哲言正文，未用釋解，雖然如此，我們相信這本哲言將是人類思想文化的寶貴財富，願大家能從中獲得更豐富的知識，純淨德品，增益人類，獲得福慧，若能盡心研學，受用無窮。下面僅例舉一條哲言，附上白話文解釋。

二零零二年，美國世界法音出版社再次出版雲高益西諾布頂聖如來的《義雲高大師哲言選淺釋》發行全球。

（此文的英文翻譯印在前面）

H.H. Dorje Chang Buddha III Wan Ko Yeshe Norbu's Selected Philosophical Sayings About Worldly Matters

(This is a translation of H.H. Dorje Chang Buddha III Wan Ko Yeshe Norbu's philosophical sayings about worldly matters originally written in Chinese.)

I.

A person is established in character only when he truly knows himself. Why? It is difficult for a person to be aware of his own flaws, just as he cannot see his own back, though it is in plain sight of other people. It is quite natural for a person to hide his own flaws, but overdoing it will alienate the person from those around him. When the person realizes this and feels ashamed, he turns to seek knowledge and adhere to moral integrity so as to establish his own character and win the respect and support of other people.

Brief Commentary

One must know oneself before one can truly be a human being. What is the rationale behind this? Why must we know ourselves before we can truly call ourselves a human being? Although we all consider ourselves as human beings right now, the conduct of many of us is worse than that of animals. The essential character of some people cannot even be called the essential character of a true human being, because a lot of us fail to understand ourselves. Only by understanding ourselves can we truly be a human being. We generally cannot see our own mistakes. Even if we see our own shortcomings, we forgive them. It is difficult to understand ourselves because we all hold our own individual internal principles and stubbornness. It is just like the fact that we cannot see our own backside. No matter how hard we try, we cannot lean our head back far enough to see our backside, but others can see it very easily and clearly. It is the same with our mistakes and shortcomings. We cannot see them, but outsiders can see them from every angle without us knowing it. So to make others like us, we have to hide our mistakes and conceal our flaws. It is human nature. Some people try too hard to hide their mistakes or flaws. Their strenuous and fierce efforts are excessive. In the long run, no one wants to be with them or work with them. People feel they are too selfish, too negative. If we can acknowledge our inadequacies, understand our mistakes and shortcomings, and try to acquire knowledge with a humble mind, then our ways will naturally comport with ethical standards. You can then become a true human being. When people witness your behavior and state of mind, they will naturally respect you and help you willingly. Therefore, by knowing yourself, you will be able to successfully develop yourself. By successfully developing yourself, you will then receive respect and support, and everything in the world will then be complete.

II.

In a dispute about right and wrong, there is nothing worse than to stick to one's position and continue arguing, thus compounding one's wrong and finally getting into trouble. For this reason, one should not let oneself be overwhelmed by disputes.

III.

Love and hate arise from a combination of causes. People cannot love a thing without seeing it, hearing about it or remembering it. Without one of the these experiences, there will be no feeling, whether love or hate.

IV.

It is exceedingly foolish for a person to claim that he possesses the ability to meet all social needs. Viewed against the background of the infinity of such needs, the ability of an individual is as insignificant as a speck of dust. Even in the one area of activity in which he claims superiority, the ability of an individual pales because there are always many others who can do better.

V.

How much one learns from his teacher depends a great deal on the guidance his teacher provides him. A good teacher, therefore, should be a role model for his students in moral integrity as well as scholarship, and his students should strive to reach high levels through accumulating knowledge and attaining moral integrity. In this manner learning is a part of the way to human perfection.

VI.

The construction of a tall building begins with the laying of groundwork from which it goes up floor by floor. Structures resting on nothing are seen only in a mirage. Building up a career is like putting up a building: what is needed are firm steps taken one after another toward the goal and executed with the support of true knowledge gained from experience. These steps, aided by a defiance of obstacles, will eventually lead one to success.

VII.

One in good fortune should remember the days in woe. A good soldier knows that battle victories are just as common as defeats. It is too late to remember one's umbrella when he is caught in a downpour without it.

VIII.

Profound wisdom and ability are the inner qualities of a person who possesses them. A person lacking in these qualities but trying to impress people that he is in possession of them is not to be taken seriously. Bamboo with its hollow interior can never support a building.

IX.

When one is held up by obstacles on his way to a rendezvous, he should back down so that he may reach his destination sooner. It is like driving a car in reverse gear; one does that because he will be able to drive forward faster later on.

X.

The one who is only good at reciting other's works is ignorant. The value in such works lies in their application to reality. A brilliant university graduate, or a master of the Four Books and Five Scriptures, without knowing how to put what he has learned into practice, can hardly fend for himself and offers no benefit to society. Only when the masterpieces are in put into use can they be powerful in terms of social advancement. It is only then that knowledge is transformed into a material force.

XI.

Undue haste causes delay, and procrastination causes loss. With this point of view, one shall choose the Middle Way as a principle. When a violin is tuned too low, its strings produce disharmony, but when it's tuned too high, the strings are likely to snap.

XII.

What standards does one go by in choosing a person for a particular undertaking? It is both weaknesses and strengths that make a person what he is; these qualities are inseparable. Don't dismiss a candidate just because of his weaknesses, or you will end up with no candidates at all. The wise thing to do is to give him a chance to make the best of his strengths.

XIII.

Deliberation is needed before one makes a move, but no conclusion is to be drawn from deliberation alone. It has to be tested in action. Suggested moves are not to be adopted in haste, nor are they to be rejected out of hand; they are not to be dismissed even when tests have proved them worthless, for in this case an inquiry into their legitimacy has to be made. When a rainbow is blocked from view by clouds, it does not mean that there is no rainbow out there.

XIV.

A person not appreciative of the good life he is living is one who has forgotten his past miseries. A person in good health is not aware of its blessings until he loses it.

XV.

A wise person knows that negative experiences in life are just as useful as positive ones. That is why he remembers both of them. Negative experiences are taken as warnings against erring and positive ones as means to increase the well-being of others. Such is the attitude of a wise person toward life experiences.

XVI.

When a person says that he never errs, he is whitewashing his error and thus erring.

XVII.

What makes the sun the greatest thing man has ever known? It is admired for providing light and warmth for all the beings under it. A truly great person is one who is willing to sacrifice his own benefit for the well-being of others.

XVIII.

There is nothing more foolish than for one to believe that all one sees is reason and the universe is created from it. Whenever one measures everything from one's own standards, that person is demonstrating ignorance.

XIX.

Anger over other people's faults is a demon. It torments the person possessed by it while leaving the wrongdoers alone.

XX.

The respect a person enjoys comes from his devotion to the well-being of other people. A swimming pool is admired in summer because it provides relief from the heat.

XXI.

A city does not need all the food a province produces, but that much food is far from enough to feed the whole country; it needs all the food the country can produce. The strength of an individual is nothing compared with collective strength.

XXII.

What to do to beat your equal in battle? Attack him where he is most vulnerable with concentrated force and victory will be yours. A piece of wood with a sharp end can break another piece of wood that is just as hard as the wood you use to attack.

XXIII.

Success in life depends not only on wisdom and ability but also on time and opportunity. Given no time and opportunity, wisdom and ability cannot come into play. Only when all the elements meet will success be the result. This is the true way of achieving success.

XXIV.

Intellectual and material resources work in opposite ways. Intellectual resources are limitless; the more they are tapped, the broader they grow in scope. Impermanent in nature and limited in quantity, material resources last but a short time, and the more they are consumed the sooner they are exhausted. The truth is that the former is non-quantifiable and thus infinite and everlasting while the latter is quantifiable and therefore diminishing and exhaustible.

XXV.

Exercise caution when everything goes your way; persevere in what you do when nothing goes your way. In the former case, lack of caution results in disasters; in the latter case, perseverance will never go unrewarded.

XXVI.

A person grows wiser by learning from the setbacks he suffered. True knowledge comes from one's own experience. Secondhand experience is worth little.

XXVII.

Nothing hurts more than conceit. Claim to know what you actually do not and people will turn their back on you, leaving you in the cold. How can you tell an honest person from a wise person? An honest person is one who does not pretend to know what he does not; a wise person is one who does not say more than what the occasion demands. Both persons keep conceit away.

XXVIII.

One owes one's success to external factors that tap one's potential. A solitary piece of wood by itself can never make a house, and it takes meticulous processing to reveal the beauty of jade stones.

XXIX.

Be aware that regret is an enemy of success, or you will be regretting day after day. The time spent on regretting could well be used for action. Therefore, do not let action be replaced by regretting. Once you realize that this is the Way, there will be no time for regretting whatsoever.

XXX.

A protracted dispute is wrong on both sides. Why? Entangled in such a dispute, both sides see only the faults of the opposing party and the merits of his own. Continuing dispute will but increase the wrongdoing. When one realizes that the other party is as annoyed as he is, one is apt to withdraw from the dispute.

XXXI.

Life is a long journey during which the traveler has to clear many checkpoints before he reaches his destination. The things he needs to conduct himself through them are his good name and ability.

XXXII.

A gifted person needs only a few words to drive a point home, while an empty person is long of speech but short of persuasive power. Beware of a person without substance.

XXXIII.

A tree exposed to the fury of the elements will grow tall and strong. A tree kept indoors will be too weak to survive any harsh environment even when its top touches the ceiling. A life of ease and comfort produces only weaklings.

XXXIV.

An error, detected but left uncorrected, will develop into a fatal one due to the reluctance of its perpetrator to put it right. But as it stands in the way to success, it has to be eliminated.

XXXV.

No pains, no gains. Hard work never goes unrewarded for it always leads to gains. Pain is gain in disguise.

XXXVI.

Moral excellence is the total addition of small good deeds. Great roads are built when grains of sand are put together. To a person aspiring to become virtuous, nothing that helps is too trivial to claim his attention.

XXXVII.

Excessive pride in one's own merits is self-defeating, for it is distasteful and leaves the person friendless.

XXXVIII.

Correct faith is the foundation of success. The way to achieve success is to maintain true faith and translate it into action. A person's success is derived from the faith inside him.

XXXIX.

A mean, inept person will become envious at other people's success. He will say scandalous things about them in an attempt to cover up his own incompetence. In contrast, a person of high morals will always respect successful people and take them as inspiring examples.

XL.

Success is built on the experiences accumulated from setbacks. Giving up hope in an adverse situation is foolish. By pressing forward in the face of difficulties one will become wiser and achieve success.

XLI.

Why is sin more alluring to some people than virtue? Sins allow indulgence in one's selfish ambitions and look like a wider road that is easier to walk; whereas virtues require high moral stature and the sacrifice of one's personal interest for the good of the public and thus look like a narrower path to follow.

XLII.

Richness comes from diligence. A rich person is one who is diligent and who chooses a fit career with proper goals.

XLIII.

A spoiled seed will come to nothing; so will arrogance. Modesty promises rich rewards in much the same way as strong healthy seedlings promise a good harvest. Why? Arrogance leads to inflated self-esteem that people find obnoxious, whereas humility wins one popularity and support.

XLIV.

Success in life begins with faith. Faith leads to action and action leads to results. Without faith, there will be no action, and without action one gets nowhere.

XLV.

It has been frequently claimed that knowledge is power, but in reality it is not true. Knowledge is the ability to recognize and distinguish things, while power is the outcome of the application of knowledge. When knowledge is applied, power is accumulated. A great lake accumulates water from hundreds of streams, but if the waters are not diverted to the farmlands, there will be drought and cracks will appear in the fields. Similarly, there will be no power if knowledge is kept unused. Thus, one should not equate knowledge with power.

XLVI.

What breaks ignorance? Books and the application of what they teach. Ignorance, caused by a lack of understanding of the ways things work, will give way to wisdom when knowledge from books is applied to daily use under the intelligent guidance of a teacher.

XLVII.

Envy boomerangs, for it is a distasteful attitude and easily detectable. It hurts its originators instead of those it is meant for.

XLVIII.

Once you are set to achieve a goal, pursue it with doggedness and refuse to be distracted by anything deceptively attractive. A mountain climber should not stop to pick leaves and branches on the way, or he will never reach the top. This applies to everything.

XLIX.

You will never get anything done by putting it off until next time, because the next time may turn out to be a life time.

L.

Unworthy knowledge will never bring out lofty ideas, and vulgarness tends to generate wickedness, which is often displayed in the form of envy. But envy hurts no one but its originator, for the resentment it breeds always backfires.

LI.

One with a goal to reach needs guidance, but guidance cannot replace the effort one has to make. Though the road lanterns show your way, without stepping forward, you reach nowhere. It is one's own effort that is decisive.

LII.

Arrogant persons often demand respect with their power, yet they are never respected wholeheartedly. Why? Power does not equal truth, and demanding respect is merely evidence of arrogance and stupidity. Genuine respect is built on moral integrity and can stand the test of time.

LIII.

Wisdom and ability come with the experience of what one is conscious of, which is a process of transforming knowledge into practice. It is these experiences that make one erudite.

LIV.

The rigors of life are what a person wishing to become a worthy member of society has to undergo. This process can be compared to the smelting of rocks to extract the gold they contain. Without being subjected to the heat, rocks will remain just rocks and lie useless in the wilderness. Because the gold requires hard work to extract, it has extra value. That is why one should cherish the fortune he has won the hard way.

LV.

A person with a great deal of talent but little morality achieves nothing. He tends to demonstrate his talent recklessly, even at the expense of hurting others, and thus isolates himself and loses support and help from others. Talent alone without support and help is a sheer waste.

LVI.

Some persons look handsome, and some don't. The same can be said of animals. What is the standard of beauty? In terms of beauty, humans are much inferior to animals that possess colorful furs or splendid plumes. When it comes to flying and swimming humans are inferior to animals, too. Only with the combination of intellect and morality can humans excel.

LVII.

Opportunities promise success. Seize them the moment they arise and make the best use of them. Don't hesitate or they will slip through your fingers. As the old saying goes, "Do it now or never. Instant action is the best medicine for all illnesses." It is important to know that civilization forges ahead through concerted, immediate action of all men.

LVIII.

Success belongs to those who work hard to win it, yet excessive effort is self-defeating. Why? One gets impulsive when one tries too hard. Ships sail on the wind, but their masts may snap when the wind gets violent.

LIX.

The strong are those blessed with the ability to survive frustrations and defeats. Success does not belong to the weak because they are not endowed with this ability. The world changes so fast that no one is able to fully anticipate what is going to happen next. But the ability to cope with an adverse situation that may arise will put one on the winning side.

LX.

The gate to true knowledge is not through specialized learning. This is the same in ancient academies and modern universities. The gate to the treasury of true knowledge is the combination of cultural learning and the awareness of the material and ideological aspects of the society. Even with a doctorate degree, but without the understanding of the essence of society, one is only a bookworm and stays outside the gate to true knowledge.

LXI.

A virtuous man does not hesitate to acknowledge his errors and seeks ways to correct them. A selfish person often tries to whitewash his wrongdoing with lame excuses. He does so because his selfish motives leave him with nothing but such excuses.

LXII.

It is wise to put your laurels in your storeroom. Resting on them will prevent you from winning new ones. If everybody becomes complacent and stops making progress, humanity will never advance.

LXIII.

The two opposites of good fortune and woe have one thing in common: they are produced from one's own deeds. Good fortune favors those devoted to public interests, and woes come to those who seek selfish gains at the expense of others. Fortune is not one's destiny, nor is woe one's fate.

LXIV.

People of great versatility are exposed to more verbal attacks than those are who do not possess this ability. It is so because they have too many people to satisfy.

LXV.

Beauty is a relative term, and like everything else, must be kept in balance. A pretty woman, if excessively ornamented and over-dressed, may ruin her natural prettiness. Of this woman people may say, "She doesn't deserve the finery. Give it to another woman who does."

LXVI.

Minor things are useful. Do not give them up because of their insignificance or defects. Why? Because defects exist side by side with merits. The right thing to do is to make the best use of a thing's merits and ignore its defects. Bulky logs can be used as material for buildings and ships, but they are unfit to fuel a cooking stove. For cooking fuel you need small pieces of firewood or you go hungry.

LXVII.

Complacency and pessimism are enemies of success. Complacency creates a false pride that inhibits one from learning more, and pessimism leads to inaction that kills all the possibilities of success.

LXVIII.

The wicked always fein benignity to cover up their evil deeds. The virtuous always speak truth with no fear of evil powers. They are ready to acknowledge their errors because they have confidence in their moral strength.

LXIX.

The road to happiness is often cut short by rivers, and the bridges across them are often damaged. Happiness won't be yours if you do not think of a way to get across the rivers. Success belongs to those who spare no toil and sweat to win it. Castles are built on solid ground with solid work.

LXX.

Those who make achievements start from experiencing all kinds of sweet-sour or bitter-spicy tastes. How can one know delicious food if one has not tasted the foul? Those raised on syrups will never know what it is like to be frustrated and will become arrogant. This arrogance will alienate them from other people whose support and help they will need to achieve real fame. A single lion can do nothing.

LXXI.

Buddhist teachings have nothing to do with supernatural forces, fortune telling or the practice of "feng shui" and "yin yang". Such teachings are based on the law of cause and effect. Buddhist teachings begin with observing precepts, obtaining peacefulness of mind, and cultivating wisdom. It is followed by practicing the four limitless states of mind: benevolence, compassion, sympathetic joy, and equanimity. Disciples are taught a love of their country, a love of the world, and service to people without selfish attachments. The whole meaning of the Buddhist teachings is to understand that everything is subtly substantive, yet truly empty.

LXXII.

Do not join a crowd that scrambles to grab what looks like to them something promising huge profits. If you do, you will return fleeced. With everyone now throwing money into the real estate business, there will be more new houses built than can be sold in three years time. Think before you leap.

LXXIII.

Habit grows into nature. This is the truth that applies to all existences in the universe, from mighty objects to minor dust and trifling minds. It is for this reason that men should establish moral integrity and cultivate the habit of acquiring knowledge.

LXXIV.

Merit and fault are initiated from a flash of mind. One's three karmas—body, speech and mind—are the basis for all merits and faults. Being a worthy person, one should not be tainted by selfish considerations but should do his best to serve people.

LXXV.

*Everything is created from the mind
And consciousness is the root.
Stay away from fortune telling and witchcraft,
For they are superstition and defilement.
A decent person pursues virtue and knowledge
For they make him worthy.*

LXXVI.

To forgive is evidence of one's virtue. Right or wrong, success or failure will eventually become apparent to the public, and those who trespassed against you will be ashamed of themselves.

LXXVII.

What one has learned may dull one's sensitivity to new knowledge and throw one into the darkness of ignorance. If such ignorance is not broken, one cannot hope to become intelligent, still less reach the realm of wisdom.

LXXVIII.

When someone criticizes or slanders you, there must be some mistakes you have made in handling things inappropriately, or at least you have failed to win people's approval and respect for what you did. What you must do in this case is to make full criticism of yourself.

LXXIX.

Extraordinary feats always arouse instant enthusiasm in those who want to be able to do the same. But their enthusiasm will diminish with the passage of time until it evaporates. This happens because they have not been able to make even a beginning. The lesson: Act now or never.

LXXX.

The world is impermanent, and nothing exists forever. Animate beings are destined to die, and those inanimate are bound for destruction, because the creation of all things is based on the composition of the necessary causes and conditions. Formless and nameless, everything is illusory, and it comes and goes following the pattern of cause and effect. That is why all's well that ends well, and all's evil that ends evil.

(Translated by Jeffery Cheung)

三世多杰羌佛雲高益西諾布世法哲言選

一

必識己方立人，何以故也？己之諸癖自難于解，如瞻己背終弗所見，為外人頗觀，己藏己過乃人之常性，過甚則或離而不顧同謀，識己得之其弗覺，愧而求知，格得其德，方可立人，人皆敬之而助也。

白話解釋

必須認識自己才能真正成為一個人，這是什麼道理呢？為什麼我們首先要認識自己才能真正成為一個人呢？雖然我們現在每個人都認為自己是人，但有的人做的很多事情連動物都不如，有的人的本質可以說根本不是一個人的本質。因為有很多人都不了解自己，所以只有認識自己，才能成為一個真正的人。自己的錯誤、缺點，往往自己看不見，就是看見了也會自己原諒自己。自己難於理解自己，因為人有個我執性在裡面，就正如想看自己的背，不管你用盡一切辦法，你的頭也伸不過去看見你自己的背，而別人則往往很容易把你的背看得清清楚楚，對錯誤、缺點同樣是如此，自己往往不容易發現，而局外人經常都會從各個方面暗暗地看到你的很多錯誤、缺點，加上為了討得別人的喜歡，自己只得把自己的過失藏起來，以其遮蓋，這就是人的常性。但是有的人做得很露骨，非常強硬、猛烈，因此稱為過甚，長此以往，別人就不願意和你在一起同謀共事，就覺得你這個人太自私、太不好了。如果我們認識到自己的不足，認識到自己的錯誤、缺點，以慚愧心去求得知識，那麼，自己的格調自然就進入道德規範，這個時候就可以真正成為一個人了，人們看到你的行為境界以後，自然就很尊重你，個個都敬你而且願意幫助你，因此，識己才能立人，立人才能得到幫助，一切世事才能圓滿。

二

是非由或自論，凡事之非，莫可于執，著之抗言之鬥，自度非業加盛，終至入患，由是之道故面是非切勿掛懷。

三

愛恨和合而生，沒愛之波必見之、聞之、憶之，三者必居其一也，弗具一之因，其念無存，焉具其愛，恨緣亦復如是。

四

社會所含能力，勿輕言吾所具也，社會乃多元化匯溶是也，能力似無量微塵之居其一耳，就或之能力由為單一，縱展群技各具其長，而居多于不敵他能之富，投之社會微不可言耳，故稱己能乃驕恥徒耳。

五

學道之識依師導故，為人師表德識照或，學者審修諸識而積其品，終可至學于淵，是為人道之學道也。

六

高樓之建首在築基，依次而上，空中樓閣于世弗成，事業之就亦復如是，足踏其實，步無虛發，真知之具由然實鑒，具實者于高難而不畏其困，故攀之于高而在于實。

七

立之于福應憶于難，取之勝者莫忘兵家常事，暴雨之下方憶其傘者必水淋其身也。

八

雄才之料必當內充其實也，華其外而碎其內弗可大器而登堂，心空之竹終非棟樑之材。

九

赴約者奔注為事，中遇道障之退，更便速前也，車檔雖倒掛之行，而在更利前行之策也。

十

唯誦文章是無知，文學之才唯附實，而今大學四書五經，為文弗施者，收之弗能養其己，放之不利其衆或，唯誦何益之有，施詩文于社會之用，造益利衆者，是為轉知化實也。

十一

欲速則不達，行慢而失獲，事理如是觀，正住中道參，琴弦之懶弗出和雅之音，反之過緊則易于折。

十二

對人才之取捨何別？天下之或優劣和合之因，所匯果也，為一體之和，不可分割之，由是見劣而不取或，優之何獲，故收或而取優捨劣是為理也。

十三

凡事應三思之弗覺，體實而再行之，不可聞言而從，亦不可聽之否虛，三思之下實施無道者，當進而窮根之研，欲覓高天彩虹而遇烏雲之佈，則疑于霞輝之弗成也，是為過失。

十四

或生于福而弗識其福，乃處福忘逆之故也，身強以弗察其康，病者之流皆知康安之樂也。

十五

善知識者諸語皆收，諸識皆藏，歸己為用，施之眾或所益，原何來，善知本性為或而福，劣理作己批照，善道養德為或。

十六

凡出語之余無非也，謂詞似為非也，言無失者乃以詞奪理之失，故為非也。

十七

太陽牲之于偉，何以故耳？面萬法與群生施光放熱故耳，故為人讚，由是之道，為或之流為眾而消益者是為其大也。

十八

人愚之最癖是為我見是理，萬法由己量之由是而生，此屬心之弗明所至無知故也，凡為余衡量諸物似為尺度者，實則無識也。

十九

陰魔之出是為生氣，視他之非而為煩惱，實乃暗敵自傷，何塗他人之皮毛耳。

二十

受人之敬者，由布益于或而所至也，如眾之讚游池妙哉，原在它之解暑施涼故耳。

二十一

一省之田為一市之用甚多也，一國之或何以覺之，國人國土而方養之，一人之力頗大者則弗及其眾推之量也。

二十二

相對能量何以足之？專一而取之，甲乙等力之對，甲專攻其乙之一，甲可勝之，相等料木以一尖刺其面，可制于傷也。

二十三

成就之或俱之智者而善利時，故事業之成必備時，具智無時業無研機，時智具之，就業由然，成就之道弗出定諦也。

二十四

慧海之庫與物質之倉是為反量也，慧庫無為轉無量，多用之反增之。物倉儲存乃無常，施之減之，故無為乃大，大在無量，無常乃微，微在消然。

二十五

風順之道莫放肆而疏忽之，艱難之途當振作而謹慎之，面順而失之慎災必至焉，迎難行而奪取福田由然。

二十六

人生明達之道，悟于挫折迭起之踐，凡事之解者，必于親身所歷之驗也，無實之聞，聞而無實，故身之所歷親見本來，得以明達之理。

二十七

驕敵巨害，知一狂二，點滴之因唯吾巨識，驕之人遠，傲之或離，事成業就之死敵也。忠士、智士怎分別相？二士遠離驕敵，知百言百乃忠士，識千而應機所說乃智士也。

二十八

人才之成就者，具內因必依外緣之助耳，無或之幫獨木何房，頑石美玉依鑿或之精雕而絢麗之道，理法如是。

二十九

嘆息之敵弗可視，視則明日復明日，嘆息之時即為功，莫讓嘆息代行功，識破機關當下道，何來惱悔與嘆風。

三十

久執之爭，是為雙錯，原何也，互見其過兮，互識自優兮，久之誤重，則弗見其對惱耳，由是無爭于執也。

三十一

生活之途，其關頗繁，哨士之查如空星布，沒持何證將以通行之，所執之證德才是也。

三十二

具智者數語之談，眾所大悟，無才士論經據典，眾無所得，言多者非才橫，君子參之。

三十三

大樹之材頂立于天地日月，受風寒暑濕之侵而成焉，故藏室植樹縱立屋頂，亦黃胎萌芽而已。設若人者閉門造車，無何磨難，焉得強者之才也。

三十四

知其所錯而弗正之是為大過，持錯隨行，故弗願棄之弊，由是步之不前，故首必于改錯之道則然步進。

三十五

得之于福皆由苦換，成之業績必當奮取，奮之入苦，苦之出福，苦兮由福兮，了了如是耳。

三十六

大德之成，微德累至，公路之長點面沙石之匯，如欲成德弗忽小品之行。

三十七

夸己讚長乃己之短，夸詞之出眾或反之，不予喜之，弗為助之。

三十八

信正乃萬法成功之基，世人生成之道，具信方能實之于業，具信之行終得其成，其成之就生機于內也。

三十九

無能劣徒繁于詆毀嫉妒他或之才功；具德之士多在敬佩效研他人之優績，由是察見劣徒爲藏私癖，以毀嫉而爲遮帳蓋之羞慚，所爲是也。

四十

萬事之成累于敗中取精，敗而弗進落入無知，迎難而上淂之聰慧，積精取華淂成之道也。

四十一

有或何以喜惡而不歡其善？惡道多出私利之爲，故寬而善行，人者好之；善道多于施品破利，由是窘而卻步，故或遠之。

四十二

富之所獲，淂之于勤，富裕者必具勤因而合其才，定業之正可至其果。

四十三

驕似霉壞之種，其種不發其芽，而謙具肥苗之因，苔粗速壯，何以故？驕則狂，或弗願接之于助，謙受喜，故人皆願近而助之。

四十四

事業之成首在于信，由信入爲，爲之必果，弗信者則無談于爲，無爲之具，萬事無收也。

四十五

多少知識等力量如是，此論弗入于諦，知識乃識鑒之因，力量爲施用之果，識施于用，其生之力淂之積量，大海盈以百川之水，故爲是積，積而弗施，青禾乾之，農田裂口，知識藏而不用，其力何生，無量之積，故識鑒弗以力量等之。

四十六

蠢愚何以治哉？滅愚之法唯在功學，愚在不其理、出行之蠢，而于讀中有案，依師正導則淂愚轉智也。

四十七

忌火弗可點，燃則首焚己，人居衆而生，群視理了，妒忌因屬于劣，廣爲或反而必貴之，故傷首己。

四十八

或發其願，立志當圓，弗可行中幻境之遷而致步不前，志于頂峰之士，勿以半山摘葉攀枝，爲化城之品而留其步，如是之行終無所願，焉淂絕頂之峰也，萬法如是耳。

四十九

世事之業弗可下次爲念，凡如是觀者，乃種弗成因耳，明日之念，後日之理，直至百年西歸故里，何心了理之爲。

五十

俗識不淂高論，低調生鑒于邪，懷之嫉妒耳，其心無傷于對，恰反惱其己，由嫉妒動惡之念，而生煩惱，爲是之道嫉妒屬自害之敵。

五十一

所從諸業具明眼之開示，所成諸業，由自把之，路燈照沒前程，沒之不步終無所前，故行之願滿由己定奪。

五十二

狂徒之流多于持權伏望，而不爲或心敬，然何如是？權威非理真之因，伏招之望則爲劣識之果，唯論理于時間之诗，終出真諦之源。

五十三

才智之出驗實于有爲法也，其經驗之途由知識鑒故，由是之道則識廣才橫。

五十四

或于用之所煉，知其諸味而弗畏難，如礦于爐，煉之純于金，若存荒野，與之岸甲同于深污，平平一石，何途之用，故或設用煉方知惜福淂幸。

五十五

識廣而無品者，則萬事弗成，無德多于傷人顯才爲是，故或弗願與之交也，衆或均行，獨才何依之助，何用之有。

五十六

人分劣美之存，動物亦然，何堪美上也，時有動物勝或之麗，它所具之毛色變異，斑艷秀或，臨空而至，赴水而游，而人之二者不居其一也，或之伉麗若超諸物，唯在才德之和方可取之。

五十七

凡是之成功者，必視機而入，聞息而動，知其含益而不行之，故多他或所先，終利被奪，古曰：「才覺明日便悠悠，才覺病便是藥。」共奮之力，人類進步而前。如是之道爾當三思自悟也。

五十八

奮鬥必具方能成業，而奮之過猛者，則易敗業，何故如是也？過猛則易失智，凡是之順皆出智理，帆船借風而行，風之過盛則帆桿必折。

五十九

事業之強者，面逆境而弗餒，遇難而迎之于勇。弗具此理，自當弱者之流，事業桂冠非弱者所享，事法居無常瞬息萬變，故非人所信手握之，設若成業，君子所建百壓弗餒可也。

六十

學識之門，並非專學，古文如是，大學亦復如是，學識寶庫之門戶，乃文化知識與社會存在物及意識之交合分別所得，唯立大學之博士，而弗解社會物法之質，是爲書呆，何成門梁之入耳。

六十一

大德者多于公諸棄錯，懷私者常于強詞奪理，因瞻何來？強奪之理則非爲理，故以非理而蓋其私。

六十二

得之譽者撒手藏室是爲正見，握譽而不捨皆無手把之于新，天下衆或群立如是，人類無何發展也。

六十三

禍福之道異居之，由是爲或自修途，爲天下之或而消益是爲福道，藏自私之利而傷衆是爲禍道，人者當于除私之道行其所事，幸道由然自修，故生活之途並非禍福，而爲人者意識所向之業招是也。

六十四

才智能量盛大者，禍事口舌相對之，何以故？必理事洽人于繁，是非多故。

六十五

唯美者乃相對之論，萬法之妙恰在平衡爲是，佳人优麗得與華裝之平，若華盛容體有過之，則裝美而人失其佳，故具識之或常云：「某女服美勝其人之不配耳，另選佳麗妙也。」

六十六

微才當居，何以故也？凡事者利弊均之，睹弊而弗居，則利不可獲，若于弊中取益乃爲上策，懷抱之木故大，而另途之，則無何入爐炊食，微柴入爐至炊而飽人，弗用之何以熟食之來。

六十七

自滿與之悲失號成器之大敵也，滿其體面而弗願降格求知，故爲止步之敵，悲失于事無成所望，面業而弗于進取，乃爲消然之敵也。

六十八

为靈惡魂者取之粉飾謬誤而爲本，爲其蓋弊所爲，明德善知識常以理道行直言，弗懼惡行而不遮其己之過。

六十九

通福之道橫流頗廣，其橋常折，若視折而不設新渡步之，福終不接于爾，凡具功立績者，乃步步腳印而至也，行業間經之萬象而取優奮克，必經身立之體驗以血汗換取之，方可成績，故爾空中樓閣聞而未瞥其一也。

七十

凡成器者必先嘗其酸甜苦辣之味，而後成德，弗體于劣，何識美滋味乎，何以故也，于糖水而生者至貴也，由是故弗識于艱而成之雄，立于飄然不知所爲，何德之具，無德則人皆遠之無助，單獅之立器弗可成也。

七十一

佛學絕不是陰陽風水、算命星卜、測字看相、妖言弄鬼災之怪力亂神。佛學唯因果，入門戒定慧，初習四無量，愛國愛世界，爲民無私執，我法妙有空，是名佛學意。

七十二

衆取之利，不可追之，納之必失。如建築故，衆皆造壘，房積滯之，購主稀之，屋無主之，三載見之，從業慎之。

七十三

習慣成自然，萬法亦如是。大至宇宙諸有爲，小涉微因塵念間，樹德立品人道本，故當習養善知識。

七十四

功過只在一念間，三業作基最爲關，若當爲人不負本，盡力人類無私言。

七十五

萬法由心生，意念乃爲根，鬼神算命說，封建迷惑人，爲人不可作，德識方爲君。

七十六

善于諒解他人者，說明己品已入德，是非成敗必顯果，公衆明心當自貴。

七十七

認舊知而爲理，睹新見乃爲邪，是爲所知障犯。恒持所知障，必當渡愚痴，怎入聰明耶，更況智慧乎。

七十八

有人批評和誹謗你時，絕對是自己有錯，一定是事理律法之間的矛盾，至少都是自己的言行沒有爭取到對方的認可和敬慕，所以必須多作自我批評。

七十九

驚世之道，捷然取之，由緣未熟，時久淡之，群或共性，如是存之，若不恨時，久遺法之。

八十

世界無常故，有情決定死，無情決定滅，因緣和合生，萬法如夢幻，離散無名相，善因呈福果，惡爲顯怖報。

（此文的英文翻譯印在前面）

CATEGORY 15

Classical Prose and Modern Poetry

第十五大類　古典散文、現代詩

Introduction

H.H. Dorje Chang Buddha III Wan Ko Yeshe Norbu Holiest Tathagata has a profound and extensive knowledge of ancient Chinese literature. Additionally, His Holiness's has superlative mastery in writing Chinese modern literature, Chinese modern poems and songs, and ancient style Chinese poems, perfectly capturing the charming spirit of all things at the tip of His pen. His Holiness holds heaven and earth in the palm of His hand and can change everything in the universe at will. These writing skills are but a minute manifestation of a Buddha's omniscience of worldly matters.

(This text was translated from the Chinese text that follows.)

簡　　介

　　三世多杰羌佛雲高益西諾布頂聖如來，除了淵博的古文學識之外，對於現代文學、現代詩歌與古詩之微妙圓融，更是博通萬物靈媚於一筆之中，所謂天地都來一掌中，隨意丘壑化無窮，這正是佛陀於世法中的遍智點許之現而已。

（此文的英文翻譯印在前面）

訪 楊 跡

　　始康，譽諡名垂千古，皆楊公、園苑之故。公名慎，字用修，別號升庵。科甲京首，及第元公，垂名"娑婆"，品堪"宗匠"。逆龍鱗，皇怒刑沖，謫滇。公展漢室之文，富異族道。目南華貴，諸族芬以"仁義禮智"亦復公之主績。公威，聲擊中原，乃四大部洲，千載芳流。今繼古故，欲建堂悼之，為室當具公物，令或四訪慎歷。有莊君增述，"哲人"耳，毫端頗利，主業湖報文編。甲子初未"望日"，實奉縣詣，共筆者次晨"走槎"南滇，訪楊歷。時急，未備多資，隨鐵車如"那伽"速。沿聲不息，出明入暗，時架高懸，間停夾壁。目及窗外，古貌異調，喜煞於或。凡百途皆固。爾際，群客異首出窗，如瓜。各懷所瞥。圍道奔營者，多異裝，每撫竹俱，中存飲物。發聲怪異，呼之以客，求幣換。晨渡戌臨，復次數十。薄暮達西昌境，遠瞥群物如蟲，中赤色者唯異之，近而細瞥，乃牛羊主轟或是也。面然青赤，肢體皆煤顏，唯眼白如雪，古色利刀，繡銀，步復震擊鐵甲，於腰環處咚咚作響，付人以懼。起齒間，偶瞥舌顏"豕肝"。長飲生物，故劣味"巨耐煞人"，久吸則出客腑之食。晝夜震行，眾皆夢趣昏昏云乎。俄頃，晨至，異聲喧嘩於車，乃知址地已然。塵塵隨群立下，履數丈頓然寒流擊骨。無何大漸步難開。君見急以身裝解助，吾方步穩。力疾春城，四巷走街問宿，數旅無眠。君謀出證於府，終歸滇政所留。時日，急訪文古，有半百館首出，行抗禮謂客何來？君曰："蜀中訪士，特為楊慎迹故。"首囑以看茶云："爾何所知，楊公少孤養益州，嬰吸始康或汁，功就實吾方也。君政建堂作念，吾府亦弗甘下，唯君方所悼，余嵌旁笑覽，豈不赤面。"嗯嚎"間，皆浮浮語，無接求題。予瞻無道，語助公曰："將伯助予，君助一展楊公迹否？"首笑曰："公千里居，迹故於舊，滇西巔之。今文處寡，望勿罪。若復收益，爾勘書館，諸籍如山，於中可得一二。"聞言寒已君，余共告投址。然四城造訪，終腳書館，目千排櫃，"片錄"斗粒數，詳閱，時度午，無一入目。皆悟"浮言"也，"作不如程"。俄歸府政。"經宿"君附余謀，遊滇池以趣，吾興與之。造車頃至，步途間，突林蔭擁二姑橫駕，中佹麗者，齡及"怨標梅而思吉士"，謂吾曰："客可舟池否？"瞥及言狀，頓驚，此何風俗？逆履數尺而斜君背，然不解語意。姑睹態嫣然笑云："懼我何為哉，奴一船娘耳。"中"宜男像"對君曰："公子，可問津？搖板歡水景，池山滿目收，由勝'吾門'趣。"君聞喜道："行舟銀幾何？"姑笑曰："隨波覽景一餐之費，"以手扣數，角有十五，君商余然。由娘導道，抵達湖畔，睹"槎木"排岸下如龍。"裙帶"娥立數十，皆頭作巧笠賀，腰打魚妹水結，風姿異。舟有如魚狀者，中架帆屋，明照如玻，坐色皆艷。姑指之囑登，君爾歡然落位。頭尾各一船娘，手扶小板尺許，作羽動。清波開，箭影鴻飛。頃至，沿瞻秀色無恰詞潤調。無何，魯園及目。時吾"什"性出首，讚曰："滇姨翻板碧清波，一駕銀魚數里歌，湖上群燕輝迎客，魯家園苑一望收。"詩已，"槎木"頂岸，君予步魯苑，展東角滇水萬里，柳岸青鴻，異卉收目。"陰念徑泛漁舟否？入苑已，感桃園洞天耳，奇花勝處，"瑤草"繽紛。楊絲倒垂，迎賓門巷，有樓臺幾挂。覽美間，一"裙屐"少年躍出，手持"夫劍"決三尺準，奪路揮舞，如銀球狀，寒光擊目，上下翻飛，弗視其身。細裝手地盤，柔中含剛，俱蛇鶴形。乃悟"三風後繼，內武當也。"疑解間，劍風著或，步進余體。懼念刺客之流否？傍惶欲遁，忽聞女聲嬌鳴。船娘至，劍者突停，道側"傲睨"曰："恭姑財得意，何不動尊？"二姑相對一笑，中前姑彈袍言道："空囊何至毫銀，待時入手邀以洗腆。"生曰："吾豈陳仲子耳！"言罷轉身復故，劍花然舊，余睹言狀，惶然不知所為，疑作江洋之客湖上求金耳。自詢，於此弗遁，待命休乎？急對君計，將仲子兮逾園墻。君曰："孤島於泊，四水無道，弗此舟，何途歸，苑墻破已，係亦池中水魂。"怎見無神龍方濟復生，解詞意，頓憶少小"岐黃"之外，曾從師南北擊技，行之頗利，當武為防，今若遇惡恰可一用雞鳴苦肌之夫。但恐盜功"紅線金盒"能也。謀盡，唯仗藝強之。邊君耳數語，"尾綴"船娘繼舟中，於位如釘，各瞥其一。女起板，小船飛急，舟頭浪擁近尺，出聲嘩鳴。尾單開道如"那伽"數丈許，翻銀花萬縷，如影隨行。頃爾，已湖心。四泊無帆。"宜男"者謂君曰："君歡戲水否？滇淵常斃人耳。"出言擊魄，余感災至奈無策，故強神威言。曰："居舍亦泊中，水然常玩耳，大江曾復己，況奈滇池兮，小舟之術何足道哉。"女曰："客勿強詞"。急轉首麗姑，相對眉眼，余"怔營"俄頃，舟波間，蕩震欲翻，身不能支，俯伏舟中。隨帶所物，及坐具皆側。君手握帆柱，面然失色，已"慴息。"余態如物。知其害，欲起身飛拳，奈體不由喚。擊術無濟，唯心惶然，大呼救命，出音皆啞孺啼，數復無一成調。待索手"溘逝"，突聞吟語尾首相和。小頃，舟平，時失智，心速百餘，出腑水於板，酸噴引淚，備將"力疾"拿匣，又恐復然前狀，失慧間，佹麗"負荊"曰："川客勿畏，奴施笑趣耳，後遊弗大言治水能。'槎木'小動乃作物狀，若以'凌籍''乾坤'翻弄，將何以治之？奴常渡川客覽趣，每領蜀人甘言利，實華其外，而內碎不堪。花言秀舌，常舟不銀'得隴望蜀'者凡，故滇民久聞而弗信。接狂客者，略濟舟波降，否無幣。今汝大言，故以同類。"語悟，方解二女非盜，乃刑徒施患"狼籍"所制。君怒未息，嚴曰："胭脂其毒於腑，何恨蜀客，以消魂樂。"女曰："二君勿怒，奴非劣意，實為一趣耳，借此可建，'沉沙慧'矣，君子數載復滇，許記顏色。後遇惡或亦其術，但由為倍增耳。余主業於‘大觀’址居‘布衣’皆接遊業。渡‘娑婆’異顏諸君，何只牛毛。或共五腑，心所各異。川客為劣。常騙池中共影，而不復寄照。有劣或於舟不法，急此術擊之。為防故，自幼“橋木”受以波舟術。一為劣或者施之。二堪親怩者所戲，今笑談耳。當立親怩。”健麗曰：“勿持多曉，奴今將爾返程。”余聞急邀前覽，願增遊幣。女曰然，速櫓，至一石處，中作鐵杆，其光如鏡，“裙姿”飛南以褶。隨曰：“此光由然而生。”使悟，遊此者數計無何，久擦生輝。首圍，目及四周，“江洋”耳。唯見楊柳樓臺，千帆舸爭，一縷和風虹影，烟波浩渺。正是古云：“風翻百浪花千遍，濤建聯山噴又來。”時，伉佳玉指柔弄“渾不似”出和雅音，頃聞吉祥“梵天”姿風起，婆娑滇水妙音和，群魚出首盤顧。由景起情耳，起機留迹，嚓嚓音閉，數影入頭，其攝美者，莊君覽趣，船娘傍伴忸怩也。攝已，即揮毫點染丹青，頃湖光一紙妙趣，余意甘然耳。賞景無何，起航歸途。吾思醉篷窗，蜀或何至毒行籍甚？定為刑徒“夜氣之牿”冒川客而制，中元蜀州，受帶於群小，今存劣迹，實可嘆也。船姑出語，一復然哉。龍皇古棣，以德雅鑒。子曰“孝忠信義”雖堪舊論，亦養中華之美。千秋文史，奪諸邦首譽，建華威，故爾文明古國堪首。今睹言狀，恨之蒼野橫徒，不法違政。思遊間，突舟小震，起首已岸，君出幣增倍，女嗢噱曰：“君弗多金，初議可也。”時睹女態，“頗持儀節”已勿前狀。君讚曰：“此賢道，何愁貯屋無金。”女數語客安，嫣然秋波轉首，已目新遊登坐，二姑揮櫓，銀魚一駕，無何，千帆交錯，“才如劈椒”頓境“安養”感華或造化，故群“華膴”，中華威德嚴然依照。

新　詩

這束花栽在紙卷

靜悄悄的夜晚，
黑色的鳥兒，
把我放進花園。
白色的小屋，
讓我長眠。
朋友們的相親，
心裡好安。
你們爲什麼要去老遠，
相處得就那麼隨便，
讓我好饞，
我的腳寸步也不能移展。
看早上無盡的雲天，
看夜幕黑色的垂帘，
我的頭經過太陽和月亮，
又三萬六千。
我眉毛上插的花朵，
從未增減，
我身體上着的衣裝，
從未改變。
不需捍衛，
我最勇敢。
群蜂獵蜜，
落一個碰壁頭，
滚地爬癱。
哦，
我看見，
原來這束花栽在紙卷，
哦，
懸壁面，
對白雲天，
對白雲天。

Modern Poetry

This Bundle of Flowers Planted on a Paper Scroll

On a tranquil, silent night,
a black bird
brought me to the flower garden.
In a small, white room
I was allowed a long sleep.
The love of my friends
has always brought peace to my heart.
But why have you gone so far away?
That you're so casual about our meetings
fills me with longing,
for my feet cannot move even a step.
I have seen the endless cloudy sky of morning
I have seen the black hanging curtain of night
My head has felt the sunlight and the moonlight
of thirty-six thousand days.
Yet the blossoms at my brow
have neither grown nor withered,
The clothes on my body
have never changed.
I need no defenders,
For I am brave.
That swarm of hunting bees
has hit an unexpected wall.
They roll on the ground, and haltingly crawl about.
Ah!
I can see now,
This bundle of flowers is planted on a paper scroll.
Ah!
Hanging on the wall,
Facing the white cloud sky,
Facing the white cloud sky.

新 詩

這才是好畫一張

暗香伴隨着清風，
她輕柔的梳妝浮動着亭廊，
她無言的歌唱孕育着華章，
我迷醉的眼睛，
總是東張西望，
這舒心的芳香，
它從哪裡流放？
沒有顏色，
沒有形象，
捉摸不到，
越是這樣，
越是緊張。
我醉迷的眼睛，
總是東張西望。
目光不經意地移展在紙上，
哇塞！
是你在散芳！
梅花真是好樣，
這才是好畫一張。
暗香伴隨着梳妝，
清香盪漾，
長長地盪漾，
盪漾。

Modern Poetry

This is a Fine Painting

A hidden fragrance rides on the clear wind,
Her gentle allure wafts through pavilion and corridor
Her wordless song nourishes these poetic lines
My enchanted eyes
look first east, then west
This lovely aroma
From whence does it come?
Colorless
Formless
Beyond my touch
The longer this goes on,
The more my longing grows
My enchanted eyes
look first east, then west
Then my gaze strays over the paper
Aiya!
So the fragrance comes from you!
A good likeness of the plum blossom
Makes this a fine painting
Hidden fragrance with gentle allure
Pure fragrance ripples and floats
Always ripples and floats
Ripples and floats

新 詩

醉在綠色花園

樹林中的花朵，
不紅不白，
樹林中的枝條，
穿梭複雜，
匠心當下的微笑展顯，
功夫長期的苦辣留言，
沒有絲毫兒出息，
沒有丁點兒回盼，
給你震撼，
給你驚嘆，

你醉在綠色花園。
筆墨的自然，
氣韻的貫穿，
滿腹春意裝點，
醉在綠色花園，
情懷迷戀。
神兮兮那麼在疑盼，
朗明明這樣太新鮮。
醉在花園，
你醉在綠色花園，
情懷迷戀。

Modern Poetry

Drunk in a Green Garden

blossoms in the grove of trees,
neither red nor white,
branches in the grove of trees,
crossing every which way,
a smile of spontaneous inspiration,
a harsh message of lifelong artistry,
there is no future,
there is no past,
you will tremble,
you will marvel,
you are drunk in a green garden.
the naturalness of brush and ink,
permeated with spirit resonance,
adorned with a heart full of spring,
drunk in a green garden,
in a mood of blind love.
so mysterious in uncertain hope,
so dazzling in rarity,
drunk in a garden,
you're drunk in a green garden,
in a mood of blind love.

新 詩

是自在的花開

梅花
筆意
無言
高雅
舒服
不是畫家的點染，
不是書家的代言，
散放着文學的才華，
透射出書卷的十足。
它充盈着淵博學識和微妙，
這高古典雅的勁道，
是老辣功底的宣告。
似乎是大家名門的書齋，
又好比古玩文物的案台。
啊！
就這樣出來，
所以無猜，
看來自在。
不，
你錯將桂冠亂戴，
你應放下疑猜，
這沒有凡間的塵埃，
不，
有點筆墨亂排，
是自在的情懷。
不，
自在沒有情懷，
是眾生因緣的所在，
是天然自在的花開，
啊，
是自在的花開！

Modern Poetry

Flowers Bloom in Serenity

Plum blossoms
Brush inspiration
Wordless
Elegant
Contented
It's not the strokes and ink of the artist,
nor yet the added words of the calligrapher,
that make literary brilliance
radiate from the perfection of the scroll.
It is filled with profound learning and mystery,
this lofty, ancient, refined, strong truth,
is a forceful and fundamental proclamation.
It's like the library of a famous scholar
or the stand of some antique curio.
Ah!
So that's the way it is,
then, without doubt
it looks like freedom
No -
You've mistakenly put a crown of laurels on it
you should drop all your conjectures,
for this contains no dust of the common world,
No -
that's putting it a bit awkwardly,
it's a mood of serenity.
No -
Serenity has no mood,
it is the cause underlying all beings,
it is the bloom of a natural serenity,
Ah,
it's flowers blooming in serenity.

(All of the poems were translated into English by Charlie Egan)

新 詩

無常是幻

蜂鳥兒的啼聲，
你與春風挽手情伴。
飄落的黃葉，
是你的衣衫，
這是無常的一現。
晨曦的朝露，
是你的內涵，
那是夢幻的雲煙。
我窗前的掛簾，
你用袖手輕挑半捲，
看見了嗎典雅的群山，
曾經過吧丘陵這畫面，
你說是須彌再現，
他說是曇花報眼，
須彌、丘陵、蜂鳥、黃葉、時間，
原來無常是幻。
沒有大小相干，
快慢長短。
宇宙蒼天，
掌中彈丸，
是蜂鳥兒在把神遷。
無所住的時候，
你在哪裡遊閒？
哦！
是這樣，
無常是幻。

CATEGORY 16

Academic Writings

第十六大類　學術論文

Introduction

There are numerous academic writings by H.H. Dorje Chang Buddha III Wan Ko Yeshe Norbu Holiest Tathagata. However, many of them are about the principles of Buddhism and are therefore similar to discourses of His Holiness specifically on the Buddha-dharma. Thus, we have placed the written discourses of H.H. Dorje Chang Buddha III that analyze Buddha-dharma principles into the category "Supreme and Profound Buddha-Dharma that Is Difficult to Encounter in Millions of Eons." In this category we have selected only some of His Holiness's academic writings regarding art, mental development, and moral elevation so that everyone will learn from them and be benefited by them.

(This text was translated from the Chinese text that follows.)

簡　　介

三世多杰羌佛雲高益西諾布頂聖如來學術論文頗多，但由於很多都屬於佛教之哲理，易與佛法專題相似，故我們將三世多杰羌佛剖析佛法道理的文論開示歸入『百千萬劫難遭遇無上甚深佛法類』的法音中，此處只選取以藝術修養、心理發展、道德提升等為主題的部分論文，以資大家學習、受用。

（此文的英文翻譯印在前面）

傳 統 · 無 我 · 空 間

繼承傳統 深化廣益

目前中國畫這一特殊的畫種已經打破了長期形成的封閉僵滯的局面，進入了交流混雜的異形發展時期。或衰亡，或向更高層次發展，中國畫就面臨著這樣嚴峻的十字路口。

這是一件令我們每一個中國畫作者深長思之的大事，必須作出正確的抉擇，堅持正確的方向，以求在這藝術發展的特殊時期，將中國畫推向一個新高峰。

我認為，目前的中國畫由於受到混亂的"多元化"和"異形個性"的沖擊，其衰亡的趨勢已出現。所亡者，亡其特殊的傳統精神（理）和精湛的傳統技藝（法）。目前揹著創新包袱的畫家們，特別是部分中青年畫家，為了追求藝術效果，表現其"個性"，便排除了傳統的筆墨和技法，利用各種工具故意雕琢，雖有所創新，卻使畫面失去了中國畫的特徵，失去了東方藝術的內涵美。近幾年，很多展廳和報刊上出現的中國畫，實際上是在宣紙上作的噴漆畫、油畫、水彩畫，如果不標題就不知道是甚麼畫了。這就是脫離了傳統造成的危機。用中國毛筆中國墨，在中國的宣紙上畫西方畫，不能稱中國畫，只能說是西方畫的"創新"。

中國畫流派甚多。宮廷派、民間派、阮體畫、文人畫、壁畫，以及各民族的畫派，五花八門，萬象紛呈。但它們大多主線條，重墨骨，以筆墨鑄冶物象，渲導氣韻，驅遣情意。線條的書意美，與水墨的墨像美，決定了國畫是世界上獨一無二的藝術。

藝術的發展是要創新要變革的。凡事有常有變。常為承之本，變為革之道；常從非常來，變從有常生。但承易而革難。易者常被人輕視或忽視，以致被人拋棄，大多集中全力於變革。變革並非一味模仿西畫和異道藝術，還必須十分重視常與變在國畫藝術上的繼承和革新的辯證關係。國畫藝術的真正創新並非不重視"常"，而且是對傳統有所真正繼承，才能對吸收外來文化和異味藝術有正確的法度，才能使國畫藝術有所突破和發展。如漢唐時代的國畫藝術家，他們都具有堅實的基礎，對西域文化、佛教藝術進行藉鑒，使我們的民族藝術突飛猛進。明清以來，藝術家對西洋繪畫的技藝研究和吸收，不也更進一步發展了我們的民族藝術嗎？藝術家們十分懂得善守與善變的道理，而並非丟掉傳統去純求創新。

要創新必須有所繼承。那麼繼承甚麼呢？不可只求宋、元、明、清的文人畫傳統，還要研究宋代以前那種雄奇壯觀的大氣流韻的法度，研究多層次的網絡結構。對傳統的認識應擴大視野，不能局限某個流派，某幾個名家裏手，要在多元化、多層次、多異象中提高認識中國畫的特點。為了使傳統藝術發揚光大，要正確認識東西方藝術的互相影響。無論是西方人文主義或東方傳統專制主義，無論多元化社會或一元化社會，以及新舊道德觀念的變異，都要以正確的態度去吸收有益的東西，保持中華民族傳統藝術的基因，發展民族藝術。大凡一個成功的大師，都是師古筆墨並師造化，融匯新意，自成一體的。他們的藝術是獨特的中華民族的藝術。吳作人先生說："中國歷代的藝術為甚麼在世界上受到人家的尊敬和讚揚，就是中國藝術有它的獨

創性。"如果我們自己把這點寶貴的東西丟掉了，一味去模仿人家的，亦步亦趨，便會始終落在別人後面。要使中國畫成為世界性的、國際性的藝術，首先必須具有民族性。要保持中國畫的傳統精神和傳統技藝以及有關創作上的散點透視，筆、墨、線、韻、氣、空間、金石、書卷等方面的特點，而又融匯西方及多元異道藝術之精華，才能逐步深化自己的藝術，奔向藝術高峰。

一言以蔽之：繼承傳統的目的，是追求無我的高層次境界，將空與色的韻律藝術推向高峰。

不觸諸法 毫端無我

"無我"是閱歷、學識和技藝融鑄到一定程度而自然出現的境界，是藝術家們已經取得了成熟的個性藝術後的再追求目標。主要是追求畫外之畫，是深悟"性理"、明了自我"宇宙"的藝術一體性。即藝術家在藝術實踐中覺悟本來面目與自然宇宙一體之真源，而成聖者之境，達到內心世界與大自然的渾然一體性。正如蘇軾所云："青山原不動，浮雲任去來。"在中國古典畫論中，大師們一向強調心手兩忘。南北朝時期王僧虔就指出："必須使心忘於手，手忘於書，心手遺情，書筆相忘，是謂求之不得。"蘇子瞻也說："亡筆而後能書，其意義是忘筆則不為技藝所役，性靈才能出之自然。"如果手不忘筆，則筆便難於刻雕。正如《金剛經》所言："無人相我相"。又曰："一切賢聖皆以無為法而有差別"，以是為技，則技礙神，以是為道，則道礙聖，所謂醉達真諦，畫由逸。正是人之意識，於控不住物的狀況下，不帶平常那種矯飾意為的執著，大自然與人性的真實本來面目才會相合，經無住的心底通過筆端躍然於紙面。這就把無我境界說得更透徹了。故名家裏手們都稱道虛"實"才可悟化境。虛實效果是沒有故雕琢、做筆意的結果。揮毫者應入無為虛實之自然，求達無雕琢之意趣，首先得外解大自然之真相，內悟自身本性，養靜中之定力。正如宗白華先生說的："靜穆的觀照和飛躍的生命構成藝術的兩元。"意思是向外發現自然，向內發現自己。這樣，在藝術實踐中，個人塵世的煩惱，就在自己創造的達觀博大、無我無心的境界中消失，精神自然得到解脫和昇華。這是理想化了的高度的人格境界。在這樣的藝術境界裏，就會出現多元化的大自然和人造物，即第二自然的真實性靈產物。在如此境界中產生的中國畫，方能成為最高的晶瑩的美不勝收的格高境大的藝術品。

通達無我的藝術境界，道路是坎坷曲折的。因為無我境界的產生應有實實在在的藝術成就作基礎，這成就並非輕而易舉的事。劉開渠在寫給我的一封信中說："藝術成就的道路有意想不到的風浪"。而我們越過風浪去奪得藝術成就是要具備潛心奮鬥和高尚人格的。成就是熟—生—熟……螺旋式上升的過程。古人說的畫到生時是熟時，實際上這裏所謂的成熟並未成熟，須放手解心始可堪稱成熟；自然而然放棄已有成熟之執著，是意非意信手於紙面方為成熟。所謂生，是指用筆表現穩定物形程式的把握，待高度熟練後，對物形的把握就不再成為繪畫的過程，這種程式和把握反而成了表現力的束縛。這種束縛使藝術家困惑並產生極強的沖擊力，就自然突破和超越對物像的原有把

握而轉入對物形精神情緒的把握，於是第二次生或多次生的現象就會出現。二次生或多次生的克服，往往會不經意而意趣盎然，作品會化出純清的童心，產生平中見奇的藝術效果。

空即是色　萬法生情

中國畫有著獨具的空間意識、空間感。空間有整體空間，有為數眾多的各種形狀的空間所組成的二維空間群。這些空間無有定相，也並非筆作輪廓的復現，而是由筆作墨像分隔成各種虛實，似有似無的異狀空白。這些空間的互相呼應，自然表現出只可心會不可言傳的節奏感、運動感。它們直接導引著人們的情感，產生極強的魅力。因此，我們要追求無畫處皆成妙趣的效果。要明白"惜墨如金"正是惜白如金的妙處。空間包括畫面上的構圖、佈局、筆道、呼應，即安排的空白，行筆的意到筆不到，對比的互相聯繫，以及色彩的照應。古有云："空白即畫中之畫。"任何一個畫種也脫離不了空間而獨立，就是佈滿色彩的部分西畫也主要以色彩的面積與形狀的關係對比造成"三一律"的透視空間感，這種空間造成了色化為空的藝術。

"空即是色，色即是空"。在中國畫上正是無意識狀態造成的結果，是高層次的表現藝術，是對筆墨紙及物象的磨練達到爐火純青後的"無法程度，即無法法亦法"。於法不構於成法，法在隨心所欲的任何一處的"自然"化境狀態中。所以名家裏手無意寥寥即滿紙氣韻。如白石老人的《雛雞圖》，畫面下部三隻水墨小雞，餘外無一石一樹一草一蟲，僅書"白石山翁"四字呼應成趣，使之畫面出現大面積空間，但給人的感覺是空而不空，表現出的是心曠神怡的自然美，使卷面的佈局構圖及物體的安排渾然一體，加之老人行筆無我無琢意，其物象就流盈著自然的真源，因此這樣的空間就包涵著宇宙中的萬象靈性，"色即是空，空即是色"的境界自然出現。再看白石老人的《枯荷圖》，無論從佈局、構圖，用筆以及墨與色的運用，都大大有別於《雛雞圖》。此畫滿紙墨迹，畫面從上到下出現的是荷桿、荷葉、蓮斗、殘花以及斑斑點點的二維空間群。當我們面對大自然中的一片殘荷時，會發現其三維空間與《枯荷圖》二維空間群是一脈流韻的，不同的是大自然的空間感要受到各人視角和其它自然環境的影響。《枯荷圖》雖然滿紙墨迹，而空間卻寥廓。由於空間群的相互韻律感在筆力、筆道、筆韻等方面造成了一元性的節奏，並與無住物象的真源相合出自然之氣，故而收到了"色即是空"的藝術效果。平中見奇，大返童心，正是達到了畫到熟時是生時的無我與空間的境界。

我們再來看看以奇取勝的潘天壽先生的藝術。潘老的國畫處處故意雕琢做佈局，而造成奇特的構圖，但這同樣是文人畫中一顆閃光的星星。細心琢磨他的藝術就會發現他在佈局格式等方面是精通的，實則是有形之中化無意。特別是空間上的對比角度、呼應等方面更為講究。

如他的《秋雁圖》，看得出是有意把構圖排成方塊圖案線路，其實裏面佈下了藝術魅力網，即死中藏秀，童心線點，圖上的人字雁行和題款的方位佈局，以及山石樹木，造成了一種空間呼應對比韻律。其中四個不同大小的"金石"，從上到下，由小到大，就給畫面分出了三個空間，於空間中見其焦、墨、樹草與其上方的雁行、題款，形成了一種互相連貫的"空即是色，色即是空"的韻律節奏感。此圖堪稱藝術精品無疑。

中國著稱的新都寶光禪院有對聯云："世外人法無定法，然後知非法法也，"這句話道破了白石老人和潘老先生一代大師的藝術真諦。

魏文帝曹丕說：文章以氣為主。品格的清俗高下，不能以強制的辦法取得，出神入化的"無我"境界，以及"色、空"的藝術效果，亦非我們青年畫家一日之功所得。但這是我們藝術實踐的一大課題，每個藝術家必須走"師古創新"的路子。師古是傳統，創新必須將東西方的藝術、哲學、美學、文學等熔為一爐，"悟達真源"，把握物形外相及內在精神，以及表裏虛實之變化，寫出流韻，使其作品行筆奔放，運力潑辣，線條流走，形體似與不似，工而不匠，放而不野，有個性有魅力；達到這一步，再依諸學問追悟無我及空色無住的真源。那麼渾厚華滋，格高境大，氣韻生動的藝術境界就將人導入美的享受；我們的中國畫藝術就能求得一大飛躍，最終成為世界性的閃光藝術品。

藝　程

呼行藝道，途何就之，眾歷藝程當悟爾。世法亦方圓之歸，異凹凸之旁門。弗就根源，握毫揮章者眾，故徒勞膚心，終入盲士者凡，由取藝不內故。持精微之技，望日越十度寒秋，正謂取法於上乃達中乎之道耳。故師表之才則瞥高下。擇道之行在於緣起。同君一夜勝讀十年，亦復如是也。歸則易數，與之定事，大有雅風皆為淵學。學則眾師，各遵其道，弗以旁聞之舉參疑師論。依師當慎，定師必忠。凡盲師無才者，狂簡斐然成章，自命不凡，謂人堪高而良奇謗焉。實則尚無問世篇章，世未允諾，反之則自號為家，此膚識矣，學不可履耳。良師持德，虛懷若谷，舉世名望始鞭擊器揮，歸叟不倦，終概世所譽，方堪大家。依上入格，行一道之良教，施之於堅，待薈諸長乃途程法矣。

為學者先參藝派，識之於格，格高境大，氣韻生動故。中畫者一樹多枝，諸家皆鐵妙趣，法涉多門，格歸四道。《名畫錄》記："畫之逸格，最難其侍。拙規矩於方圓，鄙精研於彩繪。筆簡形具，得之自然，莫可楷模，出乎意表，故目之曰：逸格耳"。又載："大凡畫藝，應物像形，其天機迥高，思與神合，創意立體，妙合化權。非謂開廚已走，撥壁而飛，故目之曰：神格耳。其三論定，畫之於人，各有本情。筆精墨妙，不知所然。若投刃於解牛，類運斤於斫鼻，自心付手，曲盡玄微，故目之曰：妙格耳。畫有性周動植，學侔天功。乃至結岳融川，潛鱗翔羽，形像生動者，故目之曰：能格耳。"四格之妙各在師法，故爾弗謗偏解。宮室民間各具長焉。唯雕蟲斗方，傳聞圖解，世人有謂之者，不堪大家之流，亦含乎於入家之道，取精去粕受學之為。非為巨家之道矣。

入藝之途，當重文書，詩詞歌賦深研益學，久之始悟藝共同源。故昌碩受藝中晚，一舉大師，垂名芳世，自非才高識妙，焉能談奇理之哉！輝世精作，怪當今居之世幾可懸堂品論，皆因文才之功故。藝門建宗之原，獨非藝也，文詩皆藝棟，覽遊皆藝梁，雙基弗築，縱玉瓦金檐，何決樓閣之成乎，幻談一焉耳。古往今來展觀史論，大師之流，無一者弗為德出，弗為文出矣，弗為苦出也。古云："天將降大任於斯人也，必先苦其心志，勞其筋骨，餓其體膚，困乏其身，行拂亂其所為，所以動心忍性，增益其所不能。"藝成之道一復由然，無旁其之途。成者在身歷耳。人云：滴水入舌味百何窮，拜君可識質乎？客云：非也，皆耳聞幻觀如是。點滴之因親當受之於意，方出己有。畫論云："萬里奇觀，萬卷深閱，行外師奪造化，其德生矣，其功見矣，其品高矣，其卷秀矣，故終成大器之源耳。"何以故？由親歷而量人，愛人也德，然由成，經實苦習見聞淵廣，實識之才藝出入心體，基堪"末那"乃苦習數載之養哉。故優在時夫鵬志之奪。初入臨瞖而不可盲程，定本而取法於上。

今古多玩童胡嘵，觀高士之妙墨，氣韻生動，華滋入麗，自狂抄之，持具揮灑，言稱潑仉，良為吾獨也，此舉笑焉，智者弗習。見其步路者爬行而得，造樓者依基而升，擊技者必先乏其筋骨皮膚之排術，非以何決武壇高士。正謂《道子》鬥："華其外而碎其內，皮之不存毛將安附焉，按寸不及尺，握手不及腳故也。"

從藝當深諸學之就。行廣聞亦恐歧誤，取道者層樓步登，基深內養，始行萬里，感諸境入性，吸萬物靈媚於合筆內情之間，可得藝也。

法家羲之書者堪鵝劍之風，得養鵝與公孫之舞。常鵝群細及，動、靜、站、臥、行游於晨戌之時，忘食於歸餐之頓。觀公孫舞劍，

變之於速，仉麗於形。張懷瑾說："羲之精研體勢，無所不工。"鵝體點橫真鉤具也，鉤而化挑，其頸一曲及生弧意耳。肢粗且力，嘴順撇，逆視捺之。發步凌空，升之飄逸，降則渾矣，轉遠展羽開合遊龍之變乎。正謂前人曰：行收筆用運腕之道耳。學觀物法，取之於神，非為形也，著形且弗鵝書哉。習者不悟多之歧途。元法家趙氏孟頫臨羲之《蘭亭序》後跋云：世人但學蘭亭面，欲換凡骨無金丹，世人誤道，得表未裏之故。覽境取之者在神形變藝，萬法如是，表裏虛實才明亞聖。故感物遊歷，焉可乏之。

萬法終形，歸云師導，依規法矩皆得方圓，弗依師何立大器耳！造藝之程浪擊橫生，奇單悟異，則中高下，有志者弗從坎坷為難，高山仰之，景行行止，須然不至，心想往之。故而絕頂之觀，眾山小焉。求藝者百矣，取之者一難，無志誤道之故也。無雄者數途畏難，而方震裂，出差嗚呼，行其所錯，乃百年之壽命告窮歸天，而未獻優群生，卒之眾人也，實附於人兮，為藝者當造就於績，而優者於險遠也。安石《遊褒禪山記》云："夫夷以近，則遊者眾；險以遠，則至者少，而世之奇偉瑰怪非常之觀，常在於險遠也，而人之所至焉，故非有志者不能至也。"又云："有志矣不隨以止也，然力不足者亦不能至也，其藝亦然嵌基之實，壯心雄潑，故中庸者安得提婆之才！"

識 己 立 人
悟見篇

眾或所云，識己者莫過其己，或之言理乃堪誤識，爾當三思。若識解己，遺世留笑。識己之比量，似天地之塵數不及其一也，開覽六識之田，頓入三清一悟自審窮根之底，詢君萬事可無反顧否？若云無，妄言是耳；若云具，何弗以當下明識己鑒，骨與肉不至朽矣之解乎！若識己則可言其生死病傷之機，由是目及爾，云者勿非弗也。汝具"宿命"前途之道一一了然，於類之列，量君不可狂言了識之道，焉能明鑒途程里影！人果無非，乾坤和合，陽堪物質，陰堪精神，終歸幻化軀體，或脫胎際，短歷中陰，三元附至，隨之萌芽幻境始發，至分別苦樂受，由思接意，思意想識，悠悠成熟於用之實。爾時識見與元神然然而別，如蛛絲降地離瓦檐遠之，恒宇宙，溶事物合生成相參，如道之論，一復三元之氣，形成異單性質輕重比量，自然執著觀也。由受執著，故為執著所縛，萬法有為，神遷己行，偶有寥寥反行之舉，弗過事出謀己之利，或為順流求生之計，若思之良久，俄見事與願違。繁繁不可枚舉，故反復常聞者頗盛。何以雲雨不定，由不識我故而對事物人情之偏定是也。偏則失主心之骨，有失之舉，焉言識己之定。弗識己恰為不解於或，不解事物人情之本來，故常己見而為他理。此屬瞬刻記識或寡薄之見；視為脫胎之諦，此行必就大患，由或之不解故萬法於興衰成敗而立，人生蜉蝣在世。實乃長夢一趣，道

家之理為一合元神未定，世尊之言，執我而未悟性之本來。吾之所言為君麗夢，遠離惡趣耳，使三元合聚之時，由生聰明，面我步近而精氣合神入定識己，識我者為持清淨無為之氣也，其器揮舞，斷我幻執，斷執已，方可為謀他利而興，時長養之磨練，善果三千使然成性，自然失我，失我之境地於事物理方無自重之感，其私必微，或吾之利由然而平。平理矣。外可得人情之愛，內可生我心之樂。愛樂乃屬一福。於此之道，煩惱惡夢遠離顛倒，元神自收，三清之安，徐徐蕩魄。由此亦當勤於學識，收益諸長，普施濟或，為人利群，眾或愛之。人愛者眾多幫也，於事法故順之，於聖道故不亂，弗何恐怖，妙夢立然，令為君示。爾不惜國，國自遠之，或若逆國，國定誅之；人弗愛人，或皆反行而畏之，故弗為人所愛。識我離私，方可愛人，解人，自然有為之法，五行生克制化，陰陽匯融，異端莫測，異相紛呈，均待或探，由實步踐而解真諦，取益造福，仉麗於或，無時無量，何具了了。為人者不可不學無術也，然學者不可執我而行道也，當持三清無為利器，放我斷執，由近自我之識，對普生而道，了一相應福夢更上層樓，建立失我識我之境，方可深悟無量之境。得之應無所住而生其心，證得無為般若利器之王，其品進入，爐火純青，境入聖地，格德超人。

是 非 人 論
化解篇

群生受世領言辱，事惡身遭，坎坷繁緒，奔涯之途，常狼藉耳！幸之者微，詢之者經疾。上宮臣，底布衣，為君王者，亦復如是。何以

故？人養世事，事不可不為，為之者利，弗為則身不濟耳，理事於世別恰人，弗恰人則事何也。人皆世事養，互生故，則從貨利，利者必謀！

其貨可居，居而不得，相謀互鬥，則言刺身擊耳。良友聞誹常解，惡識領之倍言以謗，相孺俗見，集群撒劣，故事惡必或傷。古云：「君子聖德容貌而若愚。」其意云何，意愚者，實德也，愚不強利，癡不違理，持人以幸，則自道也，弗盛德何也。今云"四美"之風，化人以德，實人道之宗也，故人者行禮倫，則道中而弗歧。近君子以盛德，化私欲步有學，具知具德人之正者。識可造善，故有學有術，然有理耳。為群展福，「娑婆」諸君共此，豈不美哉！謗言弗可逝，唯建中道耳。良藥苦口利於病，刺身非言，作明鏡自面，微觀言行，許有非處，識之疾急良藥理之。況謠言之說，於行不沾，不堪掛懷耳。古云：「人非聖賢，焉能無過。」瞻其古道，言多不整，聖者何至不辱。誹譽之議，性出自然，有為矛盾合故。云面於妙則劣之於背，云其劣則有利耳，故岐黃之曰：「方劑療疾，亦其附。」又唐太宗問敬宗曰：「朕觀眾臣之中惟卿

最賢，人有言其卿之非者，何也？」敬宗對曰：「春雨如膏，農夫喜其潤澤，行者惡其泥濘。秋月如鏡，佳人喜其玩賞，盜則惡其光輝。天地之大人猶憾焉，何況臣乎？臣無美酒肥羊以調眾口，是非且不可聽，聽之不可說。君聽臣遭誅，父聽子遭戮，夫婦聽之離，朋友聽之別，親戚聽之疏，鄉鄰聽之絕。人生七尺軀，謹防三寸舌，舌上有龍泉，殺人不見血。」太宗曰：「卿言甚善，朕當識之。」敬宗之論，其言於性，抗不可奪，君子者不奪不抗，賞其是非。過劣者，已德照彼，盡忠言以助。善助弗能化感，上知善德以教。弗可暗道陰論 。聞傷自謠，寬懷泛舟。似粉本之疾，體而傷對，無道之徒也。觀誹議如幻，實則幻耳，日長順性「泯然」乃人道之中性也。人養世，夢恍恍乎，麗劣之跡，則萬古猶存，人之美者，當背其惡，揚其善，利其眾，為群麗色而自幸也。

愛　恨　和　因
緣起篇

謂愛恨之和合因，始發乾坤會初。今之科學徹見唯物，由出緣起。道之學說，混沌初開，三元定位，五雷之分，八卦成形，乾坤始復，陰陽和合，接莊老之道以應始因、始發、年計、音動、數學合離，由歸萬法陰陽所組是也。其組亦入無常之道，自然宇宙異相互克和合，生之存之，不了以了之，儒論仁、義、禮、智、信，亦為育法有情之理，緣出和合因耳。此道頗效，奈基初故，非為除根之器也。佛家論曰：「三千大千世界，居者有情，生老病死，由執生因，因具必果，苦空無定。娑婆歷歷眼底，由然其實。諸有四大合故，宇宙人生和合之因，無量之說，不滅真諦，萬法唯心是也。」今科學之研，見其原故，亦復如是，俱合之故緣由因生至果。佛論超之莊老，似半升鐺內烹山川，一粒米中藏世界，焉達一毫端上現寶剎乎？歸而結之，三教之道，諸有為法者弗出和合之因。世界育受於有無二情，有情降世附之愛恨而臨，生存之途弗離三業之行。故耳引儒釋道之說以證其理。吾之淺鑒數題而為引玉，望君鑒教。孺嬰受世，愛恨合如影隨行，生途之道不別寸履，年久習俗故，二因堅明，談愛之恨之，歸者和合而無它說。因之出和，和果愛恨。君之愛者一人或物，其所樂，定之妙哉，首和之下當感麗於仇，如爾恨之，其理之下見不佳也，佳者、劣者，心因始發於和果，故愛恨由和合故，俱緣起耳。詳識心因者，於對象之基因和合汝感分別反應也，故必俱對物之觀，方含和合基因。有者素未面，而一視鍾情，愛心由然生之，反之則有從未面者，偶瞻即恨，由是點毫之理，可量宇宙萬法如是，故是為具緣生因，愛恨非無故耳。曰或之論，睹而喜者，乃彼之形語意色短經分別神識其善惡和因故，故雖從未面之，愛意由然。不樂之氣亦復如是，亦由對或之三業其不興至所至。對境弗思，平容了了如是，故無愛恨之和合，因瞻何具之有，愛恨何由而生。上述之道寥寥已表，此論長居愛恨因由，就物之論，藏身法器，和合因堅，弗以言狀，何以

故？長處之，久惜之，恆愛之，悠悠習慣故耳。由是鑒道，作人者，於世理事，千記之曰：與彼者，善意之，正見之，自審之。一或竹馬相愛至君今昔，偶事之偏恨之入骨，爾時君之所感，吾之所對善之百倍，汝之報者不及其一，其或狠毒是也，負余劣徒耳。若作此觀，君之誤失，偏見是也。汝當知己知彼，深審六識。一讀沉沙，相照其或對爾之所需，所求，想行識見聞。君當明了真諦，如或對君具一妙感，將具一愛之意。若無佳處，余者全意之反，既反之，爾時君之諸有劣不可言是也，或之所見妙劣弗定諦論，總歸或持反意和因也。故爾明智先責其己，復斜直圍緣道詢，暗其對觀，解之內質，君定恍然，多出於誤解，或為寡識之偏，私心源耳。或為己之誤執，歸論之我見之故，故為人者弗可偶察片斷而為諦定，凡逢世事查己為任，建此宏基，方能益國益朋，益或於眾也，以此道百川歸海，積健為雄，和合緣起愛因汪洋之盈，其德多也。對物愛恨如上述道，正知之見，弗可忽之，睹物者不大方，不雅緻，而不適故，爾生之覺由然不喜，故反感之，若以偏見壞立之諦，是為過失，緣何也？自見不良他識優之者常，爾弗喜物或願居之者繁，故古曰：「百貨重百客」，況人之六識受境遷然，晝夜「無常」，何來真定之諦也！君若居之恆戀之宅，其居諸貨動汝心弦，由藏華廳之琴好極而不捨和雅妙音，故愛之，惜之，由然讚之。設入偶步之傷，下肢血出，痛之難以言狀，呼曰唯在音擊責句，常讚之功頓然虛否，換罵詞而責琴之不道，於諸法萬事，大凡如此耳。何以故？由物致反感和因君體傷痛之故。眾或三思，其琴無情之體，無命之質，何來意識之主，身業何具，怎備行動之能，實為爾所自傷反責琴之所害。展無情如是，況有情者也，靜參有情之為，細詢無情和因，故查己方得識彼，於銷私妄，悠悠斷遷，格品齊超，識入正知，悟和合之因唯緣起也。

社　會　能　力
驕恥篇

夫論狂驕二字必先道其社會之能力。其理廣義，非數文難以解　之，故於此文之論體一技之長或惟藏多技而自擂者，狂稱天下之首而

吾獨焉所說。具上之行是為小人，故不能也。世界之大異族邦繁，智愚不一而均各具其能也，凡能者均於多學累感所至。人於世理事之道睹者，常懷一技或多技者沾沾自喜狂為己首，天下吾魁，似有唯君之成地球方轉之理，此行劣輩何堪德識能力之哉。論及德識能力，必先解其社會二字，二字雖簡義理無窮也，為事而單就驕恥而為論之，社會之合乃為多元化義，其和合之源立有情、無情、器世界、命世界之諸有會因果發和合是為社會也，故繁義廣者無際，此勿詳敘。今就社會之用能力而論，亦復如是。能力進入社會之用者，其具生命、人民、政治、科技、文學、藝術、醫學、工業、農業，歷歷如是耳。其上科別分具四圍上下，輕重異形毫因，毫因之成，然由若干劣優異狀微因相和，其微因之和由無明因及塵沙因之緣是也。如此之比聊表社會之局部而已，個人身懷之長提入能力比數，實堪量宇宙於微塵耳，大海點水之言何君備之？明其上理，焉得己長之讚也。社會前進發展，由多元化之推動力之故，鑒於前進發展之基，方具人類之福，其人道精神如是也。何堪功臣而為具能者，應為人類創功立績之士耳。故己之懷技，不為人者而益，反居為吾獨尊者，似為恥輩；若有超級不瞻民利輩，不為人興，而萬有自居者，此號劣徒是也，故身懷所技當建於德品因地。德品因地乃無私本來之面耳，具得無私之境，是故虛心由然，方識己之不覺，進解社會多元合故而己之微不足道性。世有人對社會之萌因初解，而無克己之能，故常天下第一，其類之士實乃幼稚無知耳。怎鑒世界之大，萬法於中聞所未聞，就爾之所為國度第一者，不過該行之萌因始初而已。何以故？唯萬法「無常」無止故。余在為人師中，常歷此情頗盛，就吾之論，亦步愚癡後塵，今思之愧而無顏。余幼好學，深從儒釋之道及藝術、文學、科研、社會之哲學，故有微塵小就，國際之中錄佈虛名，由是故而傲心由然，狂詞叩擊同行者常之，後終落泊，偶於無住之中問得本來，知其大錯，實是慚而難以言狀。過此往矣，頓悟推進社會之本能，必先認識自我，去驕效謙，刻苦而進深研之益學，德識並兼方為人者，終歸奮修諸識，得招群髦，頭角初露。若君詢余，其能對社會之幾用也，余當應之，社會宇宙之微塵而已，其用微因是也。我之受譽，唯堪愧者。吾雖對社會、哲學、文學、藝術、醫學、科研有初基之鑒，奈社會為多元化故，無數之量也，而余之具者，單一化也，有數之微者，入於無量之際，微塵何足以道哉！憶往昔歲，深受教益，二十又二之年，曾建武館於家竹舍，自立師表，授藝桃李，奮導南北二宗，孫岳趙杜，亦有所解，重研於內家之功。海內名流多者北京、上海、山東，閃擊高士常邀論藝，對技之中余從未失手，故爾名威一時，態隨入驕，唯我獨尊之氣躍躍越然。無何之日，偶來一中齡比丘，論道之間，余邀擊之，比丘不願與吾過手，言詞間輕余未入門梁，吾心怒然，強行對技，見比丘起掌中路而入，余立腕掛之，兩手相接，頓感全身無力。比丘笑曰，「汝將何以制之？」爾時身不能支，倒地羞慚，時乃得知，比丘奉吾師之命而為教訓，傳師旨曰，「汝當知其天外之天，智外之智，藝外之藝，恆長宇宙，萬有如是。不滅定理，於無我不執之地，私驕方微，是為人者。點滴之力未入門諦，反建恥劣，彼於社會何用之有？於人之福焉為有助，爾之所為低劣之舉。」頓時恍然悟之。余身雖藏畫藝，文學論著，善寫詩填詞，從習醫道，然長處師表之位，言之好笑也。愧於當身隨物均未所解，何況社會萬有。如余身粗衣，布技何組，吾對之茫然；若命製之，則拜師學藝，師高於我，故吾何能。人於日常之用者，其物頗感畫夜相處，而不瞭識其彼內質，焉能造乎？況離我之物，社會多元化者更聞所未聞耳，故唯我堪魁者，立入恥格，於社會推動何能之有。吾處畫道之年，目及者方家狂多，如與畫比論之。一畫之家又算幾何。況非大師乃為普家之技。畫技故為一技之長，但勿滿之、驕之，狂入自高之。日餐之糧並非我種，所居房屋並非我造，照明之燈電非我發，國度之安府政保之，育吾之諸有皆為眾所之慧，因受果發，故爾愛國、愛人，惜之社會是為具力。能力之具，則生其動，共所奮之，幸福由然。如放私三思，宏觀宇宙，自具何能之有，吾雖揮毫繪作，而所畫飯鍋炊之即燃。引食之用，其鑄於鐵，紙墨焉能代之。若以畫屋之比，如實於社會之量，畫比之屋百之不及其一也。房屋不可不居，書畫而可不掛，故爾畫技之長何足驕哉！若成品藝相居，施繪技於民，助之於國，便能動力於社會，為己者盡能之力也。若君為藝而藝，唯懷絕堪魁，自謂不凡，請君三思。於多元社會分作幾何？自知不明，驕恥徒也。社會能力何具之有。

因 果 實 相
正 諦 篇

三千大千，太空儼然，上眺萬物之意感，下攬無量八風之牽然，由因生果，長展消然之氣，立於無常概之有為，而成幻化恆常異變之端，微觀此土，五洲四洋情器兩界，何出因果之義，論及因果實相，則生報應之諦，提及因果報應，多感封建迷信之說，隨立違其科學之理，此類士乃愚癡徒爾。謂算命看相，陰陽地脈，出神弄鬼諸術，是為害或之迷信也，而世人多於反之弗悟，迷其弗解事物實相之質，唯斷觀其表或道聞之言，以充諦矣，故爾迷中取信。喻有陰陽士曰，吾觀汝命，祖墳安葬妙極，出宏貴之由然，爾子受發於文曲，當應國度文豪之魁首，是故官位登峰皇墻矣。為是笑談，諸君思之，若弗將子孫授於學，而唯傳惡劣粉本，無存文豪之因。一詞不解，為官條件何備，反之唯破民益。違法而國逮捉犯，故以福禍是乃人為，焉得陰陽地脈命運所主也，命運優劣屬三業種因所應之果，為國利眾益而獻功者，授之於敬，得之於譽，造之於福，反若從惡而行，遭之於恨，獲之於罰。高官之位乃文德果制，故耳讀書習慣是為種因，弗履者則字句不解，德才無備，故官貴無緣。若有算命士曰，爾之手相妙乎於命運之線，故終生不受牢獄之災，天生吉運，逢凶化祥。此乃違因之說，若是人行道其搶，或於壞命，公安將依法逮牢，槍子為食，若依巫言墳山弗出其凶，而錯因則果顯於惡，故何因何果非迷信之說能為抗拒。若言墳山主命，無葬其祖則命於平。出井之觀，遠及異國，近瞻西藏，水火天葬是為其道，何以歷歷目中貧富弗一，焉其墳山之分別也，故人為之道是為科學之觀也，弗就根源而為邪說者，余代之以愧。眾或之處，恆時皆於因果而存，是故未理而妄評者，乃為錯謬，由犯所知障故。所知障者，即前因鑒識固而不變，由是之理是為築壁，新優之諦無從于入，凡與舊識所違，均不就根，突詞斷之旁門一論，故耳弗立定諦。世識無窮。故人萬分未及其一，若有天才過目弗忘者，壽高一百，降地誦而不遺一日一書，其速超凡，百年之計，三萬六千日耳，故收書識三萬六千本也，況乎此荒謬之機，無或具之，「娑婆」存書遠超其數，以鑒者而為真理，從未睹立之邪說，其理可成乎？認舊知而為理，睹新見乃為邪，是為所知障犯。恆持所知障，必當渡愚癡，故爾談之弗上聰明，更況智慧乎，言之難入耳，文學水平庸，實相本如是，無從妙花筆。為不誤諸君之時，為文將以最簡喻而為寥述，顧此失彼，遺漏頗繁，還望諸君鑒諒。因果實相，乃因果報應之唯物所現也，四宇遍及六大，互為緣起緣生，廣佈宇宙萬物，為實相之科學名詞而弗可分，因乃果顯之基，首因起意。設余當充其饑，首於意指其行，而為造飯，隨之行實洗鍋盛水，生火，淘米系列而認為之，米經空時之渡而熟，方入碗受用。其飯一頓歷者無數因果之顯，意之製飲，必先入廚，起步則為意所先示，此為因起，足前離坐乃果顯，又足動為因起，觸地出聲是果顯，為耳所聞則為受果是也。就此行程亦生因果無量之變，況乎入廚之途，意識異換，直至取柴生火起心動念，實非千萬文字而為論之。故作無量之數慨之以喻，若無意念之因，則無飲食之舉，更況享餐之果也，以廣論者，飲食是因，受食為果，故耳具因則果，因種果顯果是為報應。報於因後，下因必果，其果之顯則為報也，應者乃實相受用之顯，如意之餐食，而方造飯於行。其行方生飯熟報息，報息隨之生餐，而受用則為應也，應者應其果耳，故因果報應是為聯意定諦，乃唯物必然實相也，因果無錯謬，似如水火分，熱果乃火結，玩冰零下涼，故無入火體之寒流，凍冰沾似沸水之理也，瓜豆之因由然是耳，意初之因種西瓜以品，故受意而動身業，手隨持器開土，依律入種，而後施之肥水，借得外因日晝光照，諸因助緣數月花放結果，悠悠成熟而方受用，故報應之。設初下南瓜之因，則報南瓜之果，授東西北瓜亦復如是也，同瓜異種然耳，況非瓜乎，於下種至瓜熟之期，其經因果異相變報，無時無刻皆含無量之意。故因果實相，即客觀存在是也，指鐵之弗類以擊其鐘，音響異之剛柔而殊之遠近，果顯之別乃由種因之異也，何因何果科學之應，墨書者其果出黑，赤跡者紅色而報。欲先享其盼果，必首種因初定，有或言：初豔作紙乃視宣，時經久日而顯舊，又云：時色初用即為黃，頃時目及綠中調，然何耳？由中助緣生因耳，初宣之色，乃時空風化微塵之侵，色故失宣。黃頃變綠由化學之術相克或之氧化光感所致也，由是一屬助緣之因所結之果，若色經年餘，亦弗無常，正謂因果之不立也，故無常亦由意識所動三業而生，何故無常之變？其因必果是也。初種之色，歷經中參因變，而成新因和合，和合必果，故而方堪合理之因果報應，由是實相弗滅定諦。世間萬法（一切）吾與爾等，「情器」諸有，皆與因果報應和合成立，如有士者願為企業家之主，而結企業主之果者，首必開發成果立行築廠，遇時緣奮取於中志堅弗退，諸因和合順理，果必得之企業家也。若基作寫詩填詞之為，因熟之果必為詩人爾，詩因異之廠果，正謂因果不謬定理也。有或云：「辦廠亦弗為企業家之果也，而為廠因渡入人犯之道？」為是當知，廠之所辦，則異好壞，中參和因變莫能窮，故異因之投而折正者常瞻，辦廠之際而違因果之律，故得之者亦違因果律實相果也，如國之所定是廠應交立稅，而是廠法人妄動私鑒，強意盜稅，更有甚者以假充真，為酒精之代良酒似矣，是廠必當違法，故爾國將繩之以律而為法制，由是建廠不為業主反為人犯是也，故有基因之種是為辦廠，所行之業逆廠而行，行中異變參因違法，由是順因顯果報應，正謂科學之道也。故非唯心迷信之觀耳，善惡之報，瓜豆之得正如是也，識知因果規律而弗錯謬，故當不錯，順緣善因，不失為民為國善因之佈，人之生者必於共體而成，故當為群而福則己在其中，人者不可作算命、看相、陰陽、地脈、鬼神等之說而為科學，當以因果實相，報應受用而鑒其諦，為文就吾之實鑒因果而題綱性淺說，不堪聖道相題，為君鑒教。

貳拾心別

識己篇

世事源匯社會之用乃弗滅定義也，此義之出，由多元異因造業諸象而至，屬或類三業之所為也。存在之因決定其意識，由意識之靜息陳現於無明，由無明而出幻化返走於兩單，一曰「無住」，二曰「現象」。再回光於存在之現象，故爾意識之決定現象似為幻象，如是輪理變異，終歸造業之源是為執我。於世之道必當理事，識心之別或之必為耳。此文就二十心理之用者力，為世人於社會通用而為提綱性之淺談也。二十心者即愛心、慎心、信心、恆心、虛心、誠心、耐心、專心、寬心、妒心、灰心、躁心、假心、歹心、私心、幻心、怒心、狂心、毒心，公心是也。所提諸心各具之別，施其異力也。故面諸心理，為或者當識之而選施。愛心乃欲因之基也，欲取成事，必首於愛，由初之因積可巨果，微火之點擴至於炊，故偉跡之業起於愛因。具愛之欲方可生信，由信實，得其法度，制方歸元。慎心即小意而弗盲目行舉也，慎境非量之微焉。慎在對情實之測而為從之，其慎步穩，行之者順，由是弗易錯傷、錯為，故之處事於利。具信心之慎奪績而穩也，信正乃進取所得之基因。諸世法成，始愛起信，無信弗具進取之志也，由是何成之有。恆乃進之持久意耳，恆在持固弗退，鐵龍之穿萬里雲山，出暗入明，志在路或之持恆所致也，具之恆心可種成就之因，故史成由恆憶果之說。虛心具蔽私入德之果，虛態之舉是為語意二業起動之行，感己弗覺而求教益之意，此行為人所教而助焉，故得善識，具虛之求得益充缺耳。誠心乃具實之義，誠可感或於信助也，凡事之就首因起誠，於誠因地必果，或視之誠造詞讚之，施行助之，廣為揚之其美也。耐心乃柔持念意，遇難弗轉，持願望取，面坎坷而弗急，由是與或之處不易詞鬥，應物之用弗易於壞，應事業之為故易於成，於情弗惱故之無言苦也。專心乃意集而一分之義也，有情之念如珠接串，晝夜恆年而弗息之，物之所別由念執分，對之弗散則為其專也。寬心乃廣量之意，寬而微掛，惡夢微乎，怖畏遠之，寬盈樂盛，故於病苦頗淡，壽益是為寬心之用也。妒心起私欲之根，由妒之則思傷或，傷之不得自還於惱，惱苦痛悲，德識無宅，由是之心無受或尊，悠悠神體皆虛，妒落無知之輩也。灰心具退餒弗成之因，是敗陣之折蹄馬也，自弗以奔勝之，返之難脫其難，灰心所向取之不得也，事業之敵乃信願之堅，握之則業成學就·失則伴灰而友，百無一能，故求進者視灰心而為敵。躁心為壞事之本，躁則忙難而理失也。情世或器世諸理立之恰妙，順道而通，過急為逆行，法度則亂。躁心難發於智，失智必違理，故躁之因地而為亂也。假心乃缺德之源，具之假者易行於騙，於虛、於畏、於失、於自誤也。告之東山數敵侵，主陳割殺傷友魂，傳假情乃害，自亦傷之。假心造詞被人識，待出真機眾亦疑，言製茗藝堪綠首，一經水沸展黃湯，受假而不為助銷，綠王雖出，由疑之故失其購主耳，羊至鳴狼兮，歸或瞻失信，復次無人助，狼至必享其汝焉，由是之道假心傷己。歹心乃自劣源之暗刃也，是為私欲之行，由自利而弗滿願，或妒、或狠、或敵之，由深其化劣所致也。具歹者必於謀，傷於彼而返自傷，歹心之動於國、於家、於或、於己之百害而無一利也，故終違法而招治之。私心為擋之壁壘，私養或於無誠、無寬、失友、失親，愚惡無智而無德，終歸失福自惱。私心出利為己，眾觀遠之，故失友、失親、無寬心境而自惱苦之。私行之動根生無知，由是入愚，私欲不得，惡行隨生至無所得，失眾之幫也，獨木難材而失福，內瞻心境由私生執故唯吾是理也。滴水之浪呼大海波，碧璃之見認作獨翠，為是著而弗放，保守站道真何途，福兮無門耳。幻心乃空想無實之定理也，幻為假象無常之友，幻站心所之故而弗入正知、正見、正事、正行、正語世事諸業。凡空意者，終無所獲，水中泡視而如珠，

握而不得，湖中月見其形，探而無影，夢居樓臺，醒臥茅宅，何曾官貴之有。無常只度彈指間，幻心站諸正行，故失機、失時、失業，無才，無智而終。怒心乃失智難於理道之本，怒而不平，騙亂，害亂，辱恥所引而生我執，怒而傷身，消神，怒之失理則違事，故失智也，由是而於或傷情，於物亂形，於法亂格，於事業者多於敗局而終也。狂心乃驕橫極勝之現，具狂自傲謂無敵，無它所能，為吾獨尊也，對或處情，面其技能學識包余足下小焉而為概之，為是之心眾或視其惡疾，故無情於助反招遠擊也。毒心根出性源之罪，毒於無智無德，毒無良心故之壞，於人接物沾之者傷，聞之亦咒，故或視其惡必將遠之，聽而群起哄之，諸法事緣而弗近之，毒心生行害或壞物，終報於國法之制。公心乃諸心之正義，公在於平，吾與爾平之，自與他亦利於平，立眾益而弗慮己者是為超或之公，立利於等者是平公，具公則遠私，由然而近於識德，是故大公而微余，既公者何益於我也？微為己者得於生，成之技能學識具，具之方可業迹圓，無具微我，體弗成，三業消然何來意，公私鑒行亦化空。二十心別，其力異具。君自量之，若成大器熟而讀之，慎而用之，今文所談之心力乃世事之用，弗作深解妙述也。若解識、智、定、慧、無常、無住、心別、心變、轉識而所生之無量異心，入之微觀宇宙今所述者億萬之不及其一也。寥寥膚識以表俗意，君子之擇自明其心，從良而至於幸，隨劣而亡於難，送於悲。業之所向乃或之自為，故爾禍福之果得意識之因，由因起果返本於業也。

正 偏 論
問 解 篇

增述先生問曰：「余之遠祖莊周是非之道沾之瑕否？求君明鑒開示不甚欣然之至也！」余愧然答曰：「莊周之道是入其大，焉得數語可解？是非之諦亦非謬文之述。」今詢聖道哲人莊子之是非等同，無長無短，無大無小，對立所成，故無所辯之理，而為概談，是道源是。莊子勝名，千古垂今，品堪入聖，理道超凡，為智士五體之伏，幾多高人之道無堪論比，故世或多認其至上諦論，而為獨尊，此為歧觀，偏好是也。莊公哲理立世奇峰，弗可謗之。乃可正之，此首定論，吾多敬焉。怎奈世法無常，變異莫測，聖鑒之道，公由執理，但弗立無上諦定。余文一然，狼藉滿紙，為滄海之點潤，何堪定諦。今就莊道之精華《齊物論》是非點滴之理而為略簡敘之。莊周之觀是非齊物，勿與辯論，無具成全虧損之爭，論入長短已入長短，實無長短，又謂是非不清。宇宙誕生，前者虛無。泰山出齊而大，比之宇宙則微。殤子死於襁褓命短，比之細菌則長；彭祖齡高八百，對之日月壽夭。諸理之存，比較而立，形雖弗一，理由共成，故萬物與我同等一體，如是則無是非長短也。一視是非齊觀長短，是為定義，理道精微無堪否論。是非齊物，以勝義道，實則如是。就古代智士云其宇宙誕生之前一語，則具是非可爭，爭而無定，永恒如是。由立題誕生，則成錯定之義，試問誕生之前是何立體於先？誕生之後今立何處？起眼一觀，宇宙在目，實為實相，眾或皆見，無理可否。宇宙俱之邊否？答之有邊。邊外何體？云：「虛無。」若言邊處虛無，虛無之處又俱何體，最後何體之處又俱何體，如此推理，終無數計，故無量無邊而為概之，是為真諦。由是立之誕生是為偏歧，具之誕生，則屬有

為之邊體。從大道而言，無有成全虧損；由世相而論，實俱成全虧損。故當立題定論，昭文先生，五弦妙音，成全樂曲，虧損樂音。樂師昭文琴藝，無人師曠杖技，智士惠施辯才，乃堪三絕，三士由然逞能揚己，恃才傲物，正之業友，搏向聽眾，衷證他偽，終弗為或而解之，其業無成。莊子立鑒，達觀智士，不正他偽，弗更他識，以無為而正其他偽，是為其諦，余之達觀別有淺鑒，無為正偽是立勝義，於人生世事之實，則自其偽。若實教偽，則得無偽。何以故也？無為正偽者乃慮己之行，願全一時之安，不瞻生益之舉，教偽者時遇或謗，而方便善巧多附良益於人，群皆如是。沖遍法喜，偽則化德，反之恃才傲物，為吾獨尊，衷正他偽，焉得弗入是非之偽也。又論齊國泰山之大比宇宙之微，殤子，細菌，彭祖，日月之壽夭，無比則不立其理，萬物情器，形異理成，諸相同體，吾一由然，故無非可爭也。莊公之鑒，無為大論，實則俱道，但非為實道於行之舉，因地轉果之鑒也。況人生處世現實所至，必養其生，必接其物，心對其或，故是非長短，善意可行，乃至正之。若於空寂諸理弗沾，豈不糧泥相混，被作服用。毒液而為甘露，任其聰愚之混亂，幼稚之發展，強橫之慘奪，豈不泛世於大難之哉！法庭之立，由判分別，律師之才乃為是非之正也，立世之途不可泛耳，其莊理之道，當解內含，弗可離相因地而生。是非長短，斷我而施，是為勝義。為眾福益而入非者，是為世相轉因入勝之諦，故事理相合，起建實基，則非是是非弗非之長短也。

CATEGORY 17

Hand-Sculpted Artwork

第十七大類　造景

Introduction

H.H. Dorje Chang Buddha III Wan Ko Yeshe Norbu Holiest Tathagata possesses consummate mastery in molding with His hands the myriad beings and things of this world, both sentient and non-sentient. Such works of art include mountains, rivers, land formations, and other natural scenes. We have included in this chapter only some of His Holiness's hand-sculpted scenes as an expression of the dharma. The hand-molded artwork of H.H. Dorje Chang Buddha III looks as genuine as real natural scenes. Although these mountains, rivers, and scenery were created in a room, they appear no different from natural landscapes. Broad artistic concepts underlie their design, and they have a majestic quality to them. Nobody in human history has been able to create such works. Those who personally view the hand-molded artwork of H.H. Dorje Chang Buddha III behold the elegance of natural-looking scenes more beautiful than the creations of nature itself.

(This text was translated from the Chinese text that follows.)

簡　　介

多杰羌佛第三世雲高益西諾布頂聖如來對世間萬物有情無情，如山川、大地、河流、風光純熟於一掌之中，在此我們僅取其部分雕塑造景作為此類表法。三世多杰羌佛的雕塑造景達以亂真，雖然在一室之中成立的山川風景，不僅與大自然的丘壑無異，且更是格高境大，氣勢磅礡，這在人類史上也是沒有人能做到過的。親臨鑑賞三世多杰羌佛之造景，具有觀賞自然風情而更勝自然風情之典雅懷情。

（此文的英文翻譯印在前面）

Hearing the Sound of Frogs in the Lotus Pond Stone Valley
蓮池石谷聽蛙聲

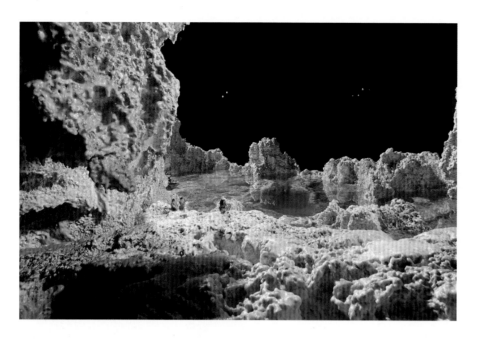

Inverted Reflections of Lakes and Mountains
湖山倒影

An Old Sage Binds a Mischievous Tiger
仙翁縛拿頑子虎

Visiting My Immortal Friend in the Swirling Mist
煙甲縹緲訪仙朋

A Boat on the Canyon Hot Springs Flows By
舟泉

CATEGORY 18

Vocal Mastery

第十八大類　音韻

Introduction

Because H.H. Dorje Chang Buddha III Wan Ko Yeshe Norbu Holiest Tathagata is a true ancient Buddha, His Holiness's accomplishments are limitless and countless. If categorized into worldly branches of learning, H.H. Dorje Chang Buddha III is a scientist, writer, philosopher, healer, artist, and great master of many other fields. His Holiness is also a vocalist whose songs are unique masterpieces. Whether singing in a robust, resonant, stirring, and thunderous manner, or in a quietly elegant, floating, light, sweet, and captivating manner, His Holiness's vocal performances are marvelous and heavenly. His Holiness's songs and lyrics contain true Buddha-dharma. They teach goodness, impart wisdom, and benefit people. Moreover, H.H. Dorje Chang Buddha III composes the melody, writes the lyrics, and sings these songs all by Himself. There are many audiotapes and CD's of these songs. Even expert vocalists have sought the guidance of H.H. Dorje Chang Buddha III on singing. An example of this is a disciple of H.H. Dorje Chang Buddha III by the name of Jacky Cheung, who is known as a tremendous singer.

(This text was translated from the Chinese text that follows.)

簡　　介

　　多杰羌佛第三世雲高益西諾布頂聖如來由於是真正的古佛，所以成就是無量資的，多不勝數。如果以世間法的學科來分類的話，三世多杰羌佛也是科學家、文學家、哲學家、醫學家、藝術家等等大家，他的歌聲更是世界絕唱，無論是山呼海嘯、盪擊乾坤的金剛雷鳴之曲，還是幽雅飄逸婉轉銷魂之詞，都達到了「吉祥梵天音蒼起，雅淑歌奏妙音和」的境界。他的歌及歌詞都含有佛法的義理，予人為善，授人智慧，助人利益，而且從曲韻、造詞、歌唱全是三世多杰羌佛一人完成，並有很多盤專集帶，包括有的歌唱家們也向三世多杰羌佛求學，如被譽為『歌神』的張學友即是三世多杰羌佛的弟子。

（此文的英文翻譯印在前面）

Superstar Jackie Cheung sincerely beseeches H.H. Dorje Chang Buddha III Wan Ko Yeshe Norbu, who is his Master, to distribute around the world the recordings of vocal performances by H.H. Dorje Chang Buddha III in order to provide people with happiness and blessings.

天王巨星張學友懇請他的上師三世多杰羌佛雲高益西諾布將歌帶發行布益於世，以給人們帶來吉祥昌盛，歡樂幸福。

CATEGORY 19

Sculptures Containing Mysterious Mist

第十九大類　神祕霧氣雕

Introduction

Sculptures containing mysterious mist created by H.H. Dorje Chang Buddha III Wan Ko Yeshe Norbu Holiest Tathagata are among the most wondrous works ever created in the history of the earthly realm. The reason why His Holiness created such works in this world is as follows. When people describe the accomplishments of certain dharma kings or rinpoches, they frequently say that so-and-so great rinpoche left a footprint on a stone. In so doing, these people speak of the highest Buddha-dharma skills as being nothing more than the skills of a stonemason. They leave the impression that rinpoches of great holiness are only able to leave handprints or footprints on stones. There are even some people with deep karmic hindrances who go so far as to say that dharma kings and rinpoches are simply those who work miracles on stones. They say that dharma kings and rinpoches have no skills other than leaving imprints on stones. There are even those who think that such imprints were made from steel drills.

H.H. Dorje Chang Buddha III created these miraculous sculptures containing mysterious mist in order to make people around the world understand the magnificence of the Buddha-dharma and the omnipotence of a Buddha, in order that the Buddha-dharma not be further insulted, and in order to fulfill a formal prediction made by H.H. Mahavairocana Tathagata. These miraculous works can be seen and touched. However, they cannot be created by anyone who is not a being of the highest holiness.

The mysterious mist in these sculptures can be found floating among wondrously carved, seemingly changing, and intriguingly interconnected hanging rock formations. Why is such art called sculptures containing mysterious mist? It is because in those sculptures there is the mysterious and beautiful scene of auspicious mist swirling in between hanging rock formations. This is a manifestation of the realization of H.H. Dorje Chang Buddha III in the craftsmanship vidya and the inner realization vidya.

For example, there is the sculpture entitled "Mysterious Boulder With Mist." After carving the material into the form of an oval boulder, H.H. Dorje Chang Buddha III created two grottoes inside the boulder, each of which contains its own scenery. When you look inside the right grotto, you will see thick mist enveloping everything. The structure of the carved scenery inside this hole is vague, since it cannot be clearly seen through the mist. You are left with the impression that the mist is a few dozen yards deep inside the hole when it is actually only three or four feet deep. When you look inside the left grotto, you will see that there is no mist at all. You will clearly see the structure of the carved scenery inside this hole. The material used to carve those two grottoes was the same, the colors applied to both of them were the same, and their depth is the same. The carving skills and inner-realization of H.H. Dorje Chang Buddha III caused this mysterious phenomenon of one side containing thick, enveloping mist and the other side containing no mist at all. What is even more amazing is that this sculpture containing mysterious mist can even cure people of their illnesses. After many people viewed this holy sculpture created by H.H. Dorje Chang Buddha III for only one or two minutes, their stubborn illnesses that had plagued them for dozens of years were cured.

It is no wonder that people praise these sculptures containing mysterious mist as the only form of art in human history that contains natural mist. People also praise them as unique and precious masterpieces that cannot be found in nature. These works of art are one type of sculpture created by H.H. Dorje Chang Buddha III.

(This text was translated from the Chinese text that follows.)

簡　　介

多杰羌佛第三世雲高益西諾布頂聖如來的神秘霧氣雕，也是娑婆世界有史以來最為神奇的作品之一。該作品的誕生源於在這個世界上，人們在介紹一些法王、大仁波且的成就時，動輒就說某某大仁波且在石頭上留一個足印，這樣一來把至高無上的佛教說成石匠功夫，似乎大聖仁波且們只會在石頭上留手足印，以致於有些業障重的人竟然說：法王仁波且，本是石頭神，除了留石印，別無有它門。乃至還有人認為是鋼鑽打成的。為了讓世人明了佛法的偉大、佛陀的無所不能，不讓佛法受辱，因此三世多杰羌佛應大日如來之授記，創雕了大家都能看得到、都可以觸摸、但不是真正的至高大聖又做不到的聖蹟品。所謂神秘霧氣雕，主要是雕刻玄妙神奇變化穿梭奇特的石掛風光，為什麼稱之為神秘霧氣雕呢？因為在石掛與石掛之間，有一種祥霧繚繞的玄妙美韻，這正是三世多杰羌佛工巧明和內明的雙運證量展現，如「神秘石霧」是以一塊料刻出來兩個鵝卵石洞景，當你從鵝卵石右邊的洞看進去時，你會看到濃霧籠罩著，裡面的風景很多結構模糊，在霧裡看不清楚，感到有幾十米遠的霧障，其實只有三到四英尺長而已。當你從左邊的洞看進去時，一點霧氣也沒有，你會清楚地看到裡面的風景結構，所用的材料和色彩完全一樣，洞內深淺度也一樣，唯一是雕工和內明的證量展現，就成了這樣一邊大霧籠罩，一邊沒有霧氣的神秘現象。而且更為神奇的是，這神秘霧氣雕還能治病，很多人僅僅參觀欣賞了三世多杰羌佛的這一聖品，短短一兩分鐘，便治癒了幾十年的頑疾。難怪人們讚譽神秘霧氣雕不僅是世界人類史上唯一有自然氣體的藝術，更是超越大自然存在的絕世珍品，是三世多杰羌佛雕刀下名列聖品的佳作之一。

（此文的英文翻譯印在前面）

Mysterious Boulder with Mist
神秘石霧

Mist
霧

Vermilion Yun Tao Mountain
雲濤紅豔山

How Could Such Depths Be Fathomed?
深豈能測

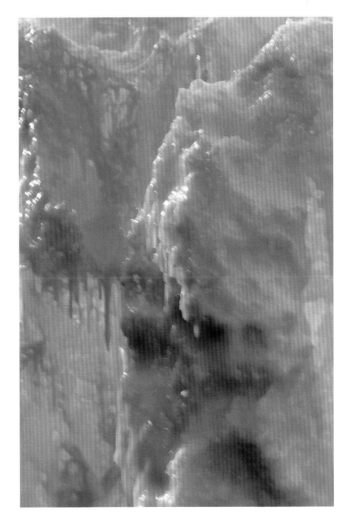

Hanging Ice Stream in Thick Mist
冰流倒懸霧氣濃

CATEGORY 20

Ancient-Looking Withered Vines

第二十大類　枯藤古化

Introduction

H.H. Dorje Chang Buddha III Wan Ko Yeshe Norbu Holiest Tathagata created high-quality withered vines through a form of carving called "Yun Sculpture." All of those Yun Sculpture vines must have certain distinguishing attributes in four categories: visual quality, style, shape, and texture. Of these four categories, texture is the most important and indispensable.

The four distinguishing attributes in the area of visual quality are old, withered, dry, and beautiful. As for old, the vines must appear to be old vines from the ancient past. As for withered, the vines must look dehydrated, withered, and wrinkly. As for dry, the winding vines must seem desiccated. As for beautiful, they must have a graceful look to them.

The four distinguishing attributes in the area of style are scholarly, otherworldly, highly elegant, and comforting. As for scholarly, the style of sculpting must be imbued with a feeling of literary or poetic genius. As for otherworldly, the vines must appear to transcend the handwork of human artisans such that they look not of this world. As for highly elegant, the vines must look highly refined, aesthetically pleasing, and far above the ordinary. As for comforting, the vines must convey a feeling of auspiciousness, grace the place in which they are present, and give those who view them a feeling of harmony and well-being.

The four distinguishing attributes in the area of shape are as follows: natural-looking, genuine-looking, weathered over time, and intertwining. Regarding the first attribute, the vines must match the winding look of real vines. Regarding the second attribute, the vines must look exactly like real ancient vines. The viewer should have the impression that the carved vines are no different from real vines that grew in nature. Indeed, the viewer should conclude that the sculpted vines look even more ancient than their natural counterparts. Regarding the third attribute, the vines must convey a natural sense that they have been exposed to wind, frost, rain, dew, and sunshine over a very long time and have aged over that long time period. Regarding the fourth attribute, thick and thin vines must intertwine to look like one natural, connected body that has grown together month after month.

The four distinguishing and extremely subtle attributes in the area of texture are as follows: the vines must have the texture and appearance of having withered in different time periods; the skin of the vines must have the texture of real vines with tiny pores; the lines and wrinkles on the vines must follow the natural course of the vines; and the shades of colors of the vines must be just like those of real ancient vines. The meticulousness shown in the area of texture is the best way to tell whether or not a work of art is a genuine carving of withered vines created by H.H. Dorje Chang Buddha III through His Holiness's Yun Sculpture form of art. These four attributes, which cannot be matched by any other artist, are essential in determining whether or not the withered vines are masterpieces sculpted by H.H. Dorje Chang Buddha III himself. These four attributes are most important and indispensable in distinguishing the works of H.H. Dorje Chang Buddha III from other works.

The first attribute is that the vines must have the texture and appearance of having withered in different time periods. Since interwoven withered vines come into being and grow in different time periods, they dry, age, and shrivel to different degrees. Their texture and color also vary. Thus, His Holiness's Yun Sculpture vines give the impression of being historical relics of different time periods.

The second attribute is that the skin of the vines must have the texture of real vines with tiny pores. This means that when one touches the texture of the carved vines, their stems and skin will feel exactly like those of real vines. One can see that the carved vines have minute pores, such as old pores of various colors, pores that follow the course of the stem, inverted pores, miscellaneous pores, and concave and convex pores. Furthermore, one can see that there are spots of color, shades of color, flows of color, differences in color, and harmony of color relating to the pores. Even under the scrutiny of a magnifying glass, the sculpted pores appear tiny and no different from those of real vines. Indeed, the vines are much more beautiful than real vines.

The third attribute is that the lines and wrinkles on the vines must follow the natural growth of the vines. Having existed through a very long period of time, ancient vines will manifest wrinkles. The key factors in carving the highest quality wrinkles relate to the course or direction in which the wrinkles run, their size, their degree of thickness, their depth, their length, and their degree of visibility. They must not have the slightest appearance of disorder or randomness. Rather, the lines and wrinkles must totally follow the natural growth patterns of the vines. They must follow the track of the winding vines. As the vines change directions, the lines must follow the twists and turns. They must look natural and no different from real lines on ancient vines.

The fourth attribute is that the shades of colors of the vines must be just like those of real ancient vines. The color or hue of the carved vines must convey a feeling of antiquity and a wondrous quality of age. The sculpted vines must seem old, parched, and shriveled, but in a very fascinating and attractive way. They must not show any trace of having been sculpted by man. All of the freshness and brightness of living vines must be gone. They must appear as relics that are thousands of years old.

There are two Chinese sentences that aptly summarize the artistic skills of H.H. Dorje Chang Buddha III in carving withered vines: "There is nothing more beautiful than faux jade, ganoderma lucidum frames, and cactus frames. There is no higher art than creating ancient withered vines that even go beyond the appearance of real vines."

Only those works of art that possess all of the above‑described distinguishing characteristics can be called genuine Yun Sculpture withered vines created by H.H. Dorje Chang Buddha III. When these frames of withered vines accompany other Yun Sculpture works of art, the result is "double supreme beauty." This combination is also solid evidence to determine the authenticity of Yun sculptures created by H.H. Dorje Chang Buddha III. When His Holiness's withered vines are part of Yun Sculpture art frames, such as "Ancient Jade"and "Emerald," these art frames become even more phenomenal and take on the ancient air of precious and splendid cultural relics. Truly, such works are national treasures that have no equal in the entire world. They are wonderful masterpieces to hang on your wall.

More importantly, we should understand that these sculptures of ancient-looking withered vines are actually a manifestation of His Holiness's mastery of the inner-realization vidya. Persons of holy virtue who are able to leave their footprints on stones are unable to create such ancient-looking withered vines. The source of these works of art is the enlightenment of a Buddha that H.H. Dorje Chang Buddha III possesses. That is why they are precious withered vines that cannot be found anywhere else in the world.

(This text was translated from the Chinese text that follows.)

簡　　介

多杰羌佛第三世雲高益西諾布頂聖如來所雕創之上品韻雕枯藤者，必須具四大鑒證，即是：一、品韻；二、格調；三、造型；四、質地，而質地是最為重要不可缺少的原則。

在品韻上，有四字：老、蔫、枯、美。老者，藤蘿必須是年久古遠之老藤；蔫者，是失水萎縮皺紋之蔫狀；枯者，是乾枯之纏藤；美者，是靈氣之秀美。

在格調上有四味，即是：卷氣、離塵、高雅、舒心。卷氣者，即是具文才氣質，書卷味濃；離塵者，即是展現內涵，脫盡人間手工匠人之氣，超凡離塵；高雅者，即是高貴雅致，不落俗氣；舒心者，即是帶之祥瑞，懸而蓬蓽生輝，賞而和諧舒服。

造型上有四景：盤形自然、如真無異、風霜日積、枝網連生。藤蘿在造型上穿雜變化，順乎於真實植物生長運行之盤行現象；如真無異者，即是猶如真實栽種的古老藤蘿，與大自然生長的藤蘿質感沒有差別而更顯蒼勁；風霜日積者，即是經年長日久的風霜雨露日曬老化出自然效果；枝網連生者，即是粗蘿細枝相互盤雜，穿梭結網，經年累月，相互之間已生長自然連接成體。

質地上有四絕：枯縮齡不同、莖皮真質孔、紋皺順藤蹤、色形亂千古。三世多杰羌佛的韻雕枯藤上品，最重要的是在質地上的講究見真偽。四絕的原則是至關是否為精品的枯藤，是否出於三世多杰羌佛之手雕，四絕是鑒別的重點不可缺少部分。

枯縮齡不同者，即是根據生長出枝的時間、年代之不同，故藤與藤之間乾老萎縮程度差別各異，質地色澤變異不等，展現年代不同的文物風格。

莖皮真質孔者，即是藤蘿、莖和皮質徹底完全展現與真藤蘿相同的植物皮感，即微細毛孔，如老斑孔、順莖孔、倒芒孔、殘雜孔、凹凸孔，色斑、色層、色流、色差、色韻，乃至用放大鏡觀看，也是微妙精細，與真質藤蘿不但無差，更遠勝於真藤之美。

紋皺順藤蹤者，是藤質的蒼古顯出恆年的老皺紋，而此老皺最關鍵是皺紋的走向、大小粗細、深淺高低、伸縮隱顯，毫無橫七豎八的亂象，而是完全順乎藤質的邏輯走向，隨其藤莖盤行之蹤跡，順莖變化奇端而出筋顯紋，隨彎結體，達成天然之狀，與真無異。

色型亂千古者，即是從色澤上完全是稀年古韻，舊而老中見其內涵，藤形蒼焦而具水土驅火之質，腐爛殘朽、斑結蒼俊而無人工雕琢之痕，脫盡輕鮮煙火氣，出成千年文物相。有這麼兩句概頌三世多杰羌佛的枯藤藝境：『美不過造玉靈芝仙人樹，高不過萬年枯藤超亂真。』

凡具備上述鑒別真綱，才是三世多杰羌佛的真正韻雕枯藤真品，故而其它品類韻雕若兼有枯藤相搭，稱之為『雙冠嬌』，同時也是鑒別三世多杰羌佛韻雕真品之確証。其枯藤用於『古玉』或『翡翠』等韻雕藝品，更為絕世真品，出顯珍貴豪華文物蒼態，實乃舉世無雙之國寶家風懸壁勝品。而最重要的，我們要明白，這枯藤古化其實是內明的證量展顯，能在石頭上留下足印的聖德也是沒有辦法表顯枯藤古化的，這是三世多杰羌佛的佛陀覺量而出，故為之絕世無雙枯藤寶。

（此文的英文翻譯印在前面）

CATEGORY 21

Chinese Paintings

第二十一大類　中國畫

Introduction

There have been numerous talented artists throughout the history of Chinese painting. They have produced countless magnificent paintings that have contributed to the excellent Chinese culture. But most of the great artists throughout the ages have tended to specialize in one particular skill, style, or subject matter. Those who excelled at landscape painting were rarely proficient in flower and bird painting. Those who were proficient in flower and bird painting were rarely adept at figure painting; and so on and so forth. H.H. Dorje Chang Buddha III Wan Ko Yeshe Norbu Holiest Tathagata, however, is proficient in all subject matters—whether landscape, flowers and birds, animals, fish, insects, or figures. With respect to artistic techniques, he has excelled at meticulous painting, freehand brushwork, splash-ink style, and many others. In all of these areas, His Holiness has demonstrated real traditional skills and originality.

These characteristics of His Holiness's paintings have long ago been confirmed by art experts and collectors. In 2000, paintings by H.H. Dorje Chang Buddha III entitled "Majesty" and "Venerable Da Li Won" sold at an international auction for US$2,125,327 and US$2,207,912, respectively. At that time, those sales set new records for the highest priced painting of any living oriental artist in the world as well as the highest priced Chinese paintings ever sold at an auction. Various media reported on those two sales and praised H.H. Dorje Chang Buddha III as a consummate artist who is unprecedented in the history of Chinese painting.

In 2007, a painting by His Holiness of lotus flowers entitled "Two Flowers; One Lotus Capsule; One Dharma Nature" sold for U.S.$300,000 per square foot. That painting contains His Holiness's signature in the form of the two Chinese characters "Wan Ko," His Holiness's fingerprint, and His Holiness's calligraphy and paintings seal. A plum blossom painting by His Holiness sold for U.S.$210,000 per square foot. That painting contains His Holiness's signature in the form of the two Chinese characters "Wan Ko" and His Holiness's fingerprint. There is another painting by His Holiness entitled "Pasture in Spring (A Sheppard Boy Herding Cattle)." On that painting His Holiness inscribed in Chinese characters "Dorje Chang Buddha III Wan Ko Yeshe Norbu." That painting also contains His Holiness's fingerprint and dharma king seal. It truly is a rare and precious work of art. Although an offer was made to purchase that painting for U.S.$540,000 per square foot, that offer was lower than the selling price set by the International Buddhism Sangha Association of U.S.$900,000 per square foot. Thus, the sale was not consummated.

In his art, H.H. Dorje Chang Buddha III has indeed assimilated the essence of traditional Chinese painting. Not only has His Holiness learned from the painting traditions of Song, Yuan, Ming, and Qing dynasty scholars, His Holiness has also easily mastered the grand and vigorous style of pre-Song dynasty painting. Yet, H.H. Dorje Chang Buddha III has not merely emulated the techniques of any one painter or any one school. His Holiness has learned from ancient artistry and has also learned from nature. Combining the two, His Holiness has created a novel and unique style of his own. From a careful examination of paintings by H.H. Dorje Chang Buddha III, it is not difficult to see the legacy of tradition and the spirit of originality. The paintings of previous generations of Chinese artists cannot match His Holiness's paintings.

H.H. Dorje Chang Buddha III has painted many different styles of Chinese paintings. Based upon these different styles, we have selected for your appreciation a very limited amount of contrasting paintings created by His Holiness.

(This text was translated from the Chinese text that follows.)

簡　介

　　中國畫壇，人才濟濟，臥虎藏龍，給優秀的中華文化描繪出無數壯麗輝煌的畫卷，但歷代的名家大師們，他們的技法、風格和題材大都趨於單一，長於山水畫者，少精於花鳥，又疏於人物，如是等等，而多杰羌佛第三世雲高益西諾布頂聖如來的中國畫藝術，論題材，無論是山水、花鳥、走獸、魚蟲、人物⋯⋯論技法，不管是工筆、寫意、潑墨⋯⋯無所不通，無所不精，無一不是有真實的傳統功夫而創新的神意，這一點，早為評論家和收藏家們所肯定。西元2000年，三世多杰羌佛的繪畫原作「威震」和「大力王尊者」分別在國際拍賣市場上創下了美金二百一十二萬五千三百二十七元和美金二百二十萬七千九百一十二元的高價，當時不僅成為世界上所有在世畫家中作品價格最高的，也創下了中國畫在拍賣市場上最高價的記錄，各新聞媒體紛紛報導，稱讚三世多杰羌佛是真正的中國畫壇史無前例的巨匠。而在2007年，三世多杰羌佛的國畫荷花《雨花一斗一如性》，畫上只題有『雲高』二字簽名，蓋有指紋印、書畫印，以每平方英尺30萬美元成交。另一張梅花圖也只題款為『雲高』二字，蓋有一指紋印，售出價為每平方英尺21萬美元。而一張題有三世多杰羌佛雲高益西諾布並蓋有指紋印和法王印的《牧牛圖》，堪為稀世珍品，儘管買方出價到每平方英尺54萬美元，但仍低於國際佛教僧尼總會開出的每平方英尺九十萬美元的價格，因而未能出售。

　　三世多杰羌佛的繪畫藝術，從中國傳統繪畫中吸取了豐富的真髓，他不僅只求宋、元、明、清的文人化傳統，還信手拿捏宋代以前那種雄奇壯觀，大氣清韻的法度，但又決非以某家某派之舊徑而學筆，師古筆墨，並師造化，融匯新意，自成一體，以獨創特有的藝術成就自成一家，獨領風騷。仔細研究三世多杰羌佛的繪畫藝術，不難發現傳統墨緣和品類，變法創新之神髓，比起前輩畫家的作品，是有過之而無不及的，三世多杰羌佛所創作的中國畫的類別非常多，因此我們根據類別，以最少量的篇幅選作對比鑑賞。

（此文的英文翻譯印在前面）

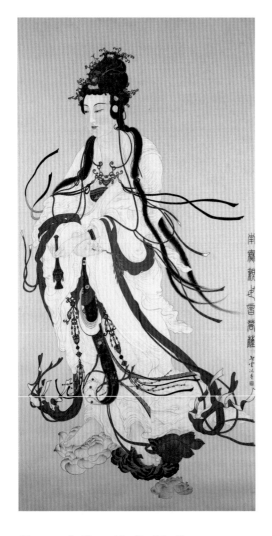

Homage to Guan Yin Bodhisattva
南無觀世音菩薩

Figure Painting in Fine Brushwork
工筆人物

Venerable Da Li Won
大力王尊者

Figure Painting in Fine Brushwork
工筆人物

Patriarch Bodhidharma
達摩祖師

Figure Painting in Freehand Brushwork
寫意人物

Lotus Pond Water-World
水國蓮池

Aquatic Animals in Fine Brushwork
工筆水族

Îscene of Xishuang Banna Life
版納風情

Small-scale Scenery in Fine Brushwork
工筆風景

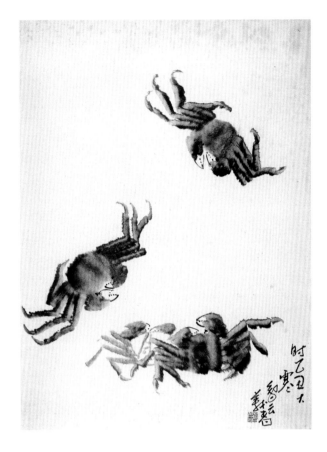

Splashed-Ink Crabs
潑墨螃蟹

Aquatic Animals in Freehand Brushwork
寫意水族

Red Plum Blossoms
紅梅圖

Plum Blossoms in Freehand Brushwork
寫意梅花

Majesty　*Animal in Fine Brushwork*
威震　工筆動物

White Plum　*Plum Blossoms in Freehand Brushwork*
冬粉　寫意梅花

Rich, Lustrous, Thick Ink Displays Profound Learning
渾厚華滋書卷濃

Landscape in Freehand Brushwork
寫意山水

A Flock of Twittering Sparrows in Early Spring
宿士鬧春

Flowers and Birds in Freehand Brushwork
寫意花鳥

Herd-boy's Poem and Song
牧牛歌兮

Animal in Freehand Brushwork
寫意動物

Watching the Spirit of Nature
且看氣韻開

Flowers and Birds in Freehand Brushwork
寫意花鳥

Constantly Standing Here
故土

Flowers and Birds in Freehand Brushwork
寫意花鳥

Eagle Conquers Snake Demon
大鵬伏魔

Flowers and Birds in Fine Brushwork
工筆花鳥

The Chinese painting by H.H. Dorje Chang Budha III Wan Ko Yeshe Norbu entitled "Majesty" sold at an auction for the astoundingly high price of US$2,125,327. For details on this, please see the newspaper reports that were published at that time.

WEEKEND BALITA

JUNE 10-16, 2000 — THE LEADING FILIPINO - AMERICAN NEWSPAPER IN THE USA — VOL. IX, NO. 409
Linking Filipinos Worldwide Visit us at www.balita.com

34 JUNE 10-16, 2000 — COMMUNITY Visit www.balita.com — Weekend BALITA Leading Filipino Newspaper in the USA

The selling price of his painting 'Majesty' has shocked the world

SOME people say that Master Wan Ko Yee is an expert in Buddhism. Some say that he is a great painter or a great singer. There are those who say that he is a great medical expert or a great ethicist. There are also those who say that he is a scientist. On May 28th, Unique Art Collections International Co., Ltd. auctioned Master Wan Ko Yee's painting entitled "Majesty." An art collector purchased this painting by way of competitive bid for a price of NT$64,950,00.00 (this equals U.S.$2,125,327.00) People all over the world were shocked to hear of this purchase price.

In the entire history of Chinese painting, no other great painter was able to master the amount of artistic skills, the variety of different styles and the diversity of subject matter which Master Wan Ko Yee has mastered. Other painters could only exhibit two or three different artistic skills at the most. For example, Zhang Da-Qian exhibited three different artistic skills: line painting, traditional painting and splash-ink painting. However, Master Wan Ko Yee has completely mastered a few dozen different artistic skills. Master Wan Ko Yee can paint landscapes, people and other objects, animals, flowers, birds, fish and insects by using the meticulous brushwork style or by using the freehand brushwork style. Whichever style he uses, his paintings are always elegant, grand, and full of life. One can get a glimpse of his artistic skills by looking through the huge book which contains a collection of his paintings.

In 1995, the Sichuan Daily News and the Chengdu Evening News each printed an advertisement on behalf of an auction house. This auction house wanted to buy the Master's paintings for a price of R.M.B. 1,700 yuan per square inch.

Master Wan Ko Yee's skills have reached the highest level in the world when it comes to ink and wash paintings. Thus, in 1991, the World Poets and Culture Congress conferred upon him the title of "Master of Oriental Art" along with a medal. In 1994, this same Congress conferred upon him the title of the world's only "Distinguished International Master." This is the highest position possible and is on the same level of honor as a head of state.

Why is it that this one person, Master Wan Ko Yee, has the combined skills of several different experts? The main reason is that he is a Great Dharma King Master of Buddhism. He has truly mastered the Five Knowledges spoken of in Buddhism. All of his skills mentioned above cover only part of the Five Knowledges which his has mastered. Instead of trying to describe what type of expert he is, it would be better simply to say that he surpasses the word "expert."

He is a precious treasure who is a benefit to humanity. He is a Dharma King Master who is a rare gem in this world.

三世多杰羌佛雲高益西諾布的國畫『威震』拍出美金212萬5327元的驚人高價，詳見當時報紙的報導。

H.H. Dorje Chang Budha III Wan Ko Yeshe Norbu's painting entitled "Venerable Da Li Wang" sold at an auction for the astronomical price of US$2,207,912. For details on this, please see the newspaper reports that were published at that time.

TRIBUNE U.S.A.
EXPONENT OF KNOWLEDGE AND PROGRESS

VOL. III NO. 49

24   TRIBUNE U.S.A.   DECEMBER 1-7, 2000

A RECORD IN PAINTINGS
Da Li Won Again Creates Sky-High Selling Price

It has been noted by people that Master Wan Ko Yee, the world famous master of Buddhism and art, set the world record in Chinese art history of the highest selling price of paintings by a painter who is still alive. His painting, "Venerable Da Li Won", again broke his own world record when it was sold at NT$ 72,000,000.00 (US$2,207,912.00) by Mr. Naylor, an art collector and art merchant from England. Once the selling price was confirmed at the auction, people on the spot clapped their hands continuously for quite a while.

The year of 2000, the beginning of a new country, people were more impressed by the special honors which Master Wan Ko Yee received. On March 8th this year both government of State of California and government of City of San Francisco separately proclaimed March 8th, 2000 as Master Wan Ko Yee Day based on his amazing achievements in various fields.

In addition, he received honorary doctorate degree and professorship from ninety-two universities in the United States and other countries all over the world. It was the first and highest honor in history among Chinese worldwide.

On May 12th the same year in Taipei, at the meeting organized by United International World Buddhism Association Headquarters, 2137 eminent monks and nuns and the great virtuous ones from 416 Buddhist organizations, associations, and temples worldwide unanimously conferred Master Wan Ko Yee as the true Buddhist Master with perfect mastery in both Esoteric and Exoteric Buddhism.

Talking about art, it is just a small drop of water in the boundless ocean of Buddha Dharma of Master Yee. Since he is a great Dharma King Master with perfect mastery in Esoteric and Exoteric Buddhism and Five Brightness, the Art which is one of the Five Brightness, has made Master Wan Ko Yee reach the unprecedented height in arts including paintings and calligraphy.

On May 28th this year Unique Art Collections International Co., Ltd. auctioned one of Master Yee's paintings, "Majesty", at an unprecedented sky-high price of US$455.00 per square inch. It shocked the art circles worldwide.

On November 26th Unique Art Collections International Co., Ltd. again shocked the world by auctioning the painting, "Venerable Da Li Won", at US$ 467.00 per square inch. In proved that the skills, styles, and varieties of Master Yee were comprehensive and lofty. Master Yee can use dozens of different skills in painting scenery, figures, animals, flowers, birds, fish, insects, and etc.

Master Yee is an expert in all styles no matter it is detailed brushwork style, freehand brushwork style, or splashing ink style. All of these new styles were created out of his genuine efforts in traditional fields. Master Yee is the most famous scholar in modern history with his abundant knowledge, distinguished achievement, and many publications. Although his reputation has already spread all over the world, it is hard to find someone like him with such humbleness, sincerity and noble virtue. It has won the recognition of experts in academic organizations worldwide.

三世多杰羌佛雲高益西諾布之畫「大力王尊者」拍賣出美金220萬7912元之天價，詳見當時報紙的報導。

7　台灣綜藝　　Wednesday, December 6, 2000　　國 際 日 報　　二〇〇〇年十二月六日　星期三
INTERNATIONAL DAILY NEWS

「大力王尊者」畫品天價成交

義雲高大師再度威震世界畫壇

義雲高大師的水墨畫精品《大力王尊者》，以新台幣七千二百萬元的天價成交。

【台北報導】義雲高大師的水墨畫精品《大力王尊者》，二十六日在台北甄藏國際公司舉辦的中國書畫藝術、精品花鳥者疏於山水者，少於花鳥，精於花鳥者疏於人物。但義雲高大師的中國書畫藝術，論題材，無論是山水、花鳥、走獸、魚蟲、人物；論技法，不管是工筆、寫意、潑墨，皆無所不精，無一不秋拍會中，脫穎而出，以新台幣七千二百萬元的驚人天價，由英國書畫收藏家奈勒購得，締造在世畫家最高成交紀錄，使得義雲高大師繼今年春拍再度「威震」世界畫壇。

甄藏公司指出，這幅《大力王尊者》畫品是結合工筆與寫意的精品畫作，細膩的線條勾勒出大力王尊者孔武有力的肌肉，全身絡血管清晰可見，畫中尊者雙目炯炯有神，無論你站在任何方向，尊者都看得到你；尊者身上穿繞著薄如蟬翼的紫色紗，其工筆技巧登峰造極，令人嘆為觀止。

《大力王尊者》精品寫意部分，充分展示大師在藝術實踐中覺悟本來面目，與自然宇宙一體之真源，而成聖者之境，達到內心世界與大自然的渾然一體，攬大千世界於胸中恒萬法於毫端，意趣天成，格高境大，超凡入聖。縱圖還藉有世界佛教協會鑑定蓋章。義雲高大師親筆書寫，親手蓋上金印指紋的手本真跡保證書。

義雲高大師的經典佳作《威震》群獅圖，在今年五月，亦由甄藏以美金二百二十二萬元的天價拍賣，轟動世界藝壇。他的書畫藝術無論是格調的高雅，品類的全方位，種類的繁多，技法的無窮，都達到了前無古人的高度。畫壇人士指出，歷代名家的技法、西賣了的價款紀錄，也就不足為奇了。重要的是，大師說：「一切都是大眾的，所以我不賣書畫，送人的束了就了了」。

密圓融無礙，五明圓滿的法王級大師，大師是顯密圓融無礙的弟子指出，大師的藝術書畫，達到最巔峰，今年五月，在世紀性世界佛教會議中，一共二十六個佛教組織、協會、寺院，一共二十六位顯密高僧認定大德，以無記名投票，得票率百分之九十九點六，推舉義雲高大師為顯密圓正宗佛教大師。」此外，一九九三年全球四十八個國家、地區，授予元首級義雲高大師榮銜的特級國際大師；其他還有中共政府為他建造豪華式七館一部巨型義雲高大師桂冠、世界學術機構授予東方藝術大師館、美國政府、舊金山市政府同時頒布二千年三月八日為義雲高大師日。由這些諸多的讚譽，不難窺知大師的豐富內在涵養，以及超越凡人的聖慧與智慧，對於他的畫作能創下如此高的價款紀錄，也就不足為奇了。

NORTHERN CALIFORNIA
ASIAN JOURNAL™

MARCH 2-8, 2007 **11** | MARCH 2-8, 2007 | VOL 6 - ISSUE 9

Master Wan Ko Yee's Painting Was Sold at the Price of 300,000 US Dollars per Square Foot

The Painting at the Price of 900,000 US Dollars Was Not Sold

AN auction held by International Buddhism Sangha Association took place on February 7, 2007 in San Francisco. Three Chinese paintings were displayed. One of the paintings entitled "Two Flowers; One Lotus Capsule; One Dharma Nature" was sold at 300,000 US dollars per square foot.

The world renowned Great Buddhist Dharma King Wan Ko Yeshe Norbu (also known as the great artist Master Wan Ko Yee) donated three valuable paintings as gifts to International Buddhism Sangha Association. At the time of the auction of these three paintings more than 10 people expressed an interest in buying them. After several competitive bidding rounds, the lotus painting was sold to an English collector Ian Hamilton at the price of

"Plum Blossoms"

US$300,000 per square foot. Another painting, "Plum Blossoms", was sold at US$210,000 per square foot. However, the most anticipated painting, "Pasture in Spring (a shepherd boy herding cattle)", was not sold at this time. "Pasture in Spring" was considered the most valuable of the three donated paintings. Even though the buyer raised the price to US$540,000 per square foot, the seller insisted that the price cannot be below US$900,000 per square foot. Therefore, this transaction was not completed because of the great difference between the prices.

San Francisco Chronicle

FRIDAY, JANUARY 19, 2007

For the sake of advocating Buddha-dharma and promoting sacred Buddhist affairs, the International Buddhism Sangha Association has decided to make three valuable paintings donated to the Association available for purchase. A sales event will be held on Wednesday, February 7, 2007 at 2:00 p.m. at Hua Zang Si in San Francisco. All proceeds received will be used for the benefits of living beings.

The first painting: Pasture In Spring (a shepherd boy pasturing cattle). US$900,000.- per sq. ft.
The second painting: Two Flowers; One Lotus Cupule; One Dharma Nature (Lotus). US$300,000.- per sq. ft. (Please note that the price per sq. ft. previously posted on 1/15/2007 has been corrected.)
The third painting: Plum Blossoms, US$210,000.- per sq. ft. (Please note that the price per sq. ft. previously posted on 1/15/2007 has been corrected.)

There will be an on-site notary public providing related notary services for the proof of each purchase.

By International Buddhism Sangha Association
The contact information of Hua Zang Si is as follows:
3134 22nd Street, San Francisco, CA 94110
TEL: (415)920-9816 FAX: (415)920-9836 www.huazangsi.org

"Two Flowers; One Lotus Capsule, One Dharma Nature"

世界日報 WORLD JOURNAL

LOCAL NEWS
美西新聞

2007年2月13日 星期二 TUESDAY, FEBRUARY 13, 2007　　B6

舊金山華藏寺舉行名畫拍賣

↑2月7日舊金山華藏寺舉行一場名畫拍賣，是由國際佛教僧尼總會將所接受捐贈之名畫《春牧》(牧牛圖)，每平方呎九十萬美金；另一幅《兩花一斗一如性》(荷花)據悉每平方呎三十萬美金，在雲集會場之收藏家及慕名而來觀賞的觀眾、在眾家競標下，一位來自英國的白人收藏家將荷花標得。據負責此次拍賣的國際佛教僧尼總會法師表示，此次拍賣的名畫由當今至高大法王仰諤雲高益西諾布所捐贈。

上圖為拍賣會現場。

教育藝文

🖻訊息清單　📁目錄清單　　🖨友善列印　　全文檢索

義雲高大師畫作以每尺30萬美元成交　90萬元流標

2007年2月11日 12:47:11

陳恆光/綜合報導

　美國舊金山華藏寺在美東時間2月7日舉行的書畫交易會中，展銷三幅中國畫，其中一幅荷花《兩花一斗一如性》達到每平方英尺30萬美元成交。

　據華藏寺介紹，世界著名佛教大法王雲高益西諾布，同時也是大藝術家身份的義雲高大師贈了三幅精品畫作給國際佛教僧尼總會。這次國際佛教僧尼總會公開拍賣此三幅作品，有意願購買的約有上十人。經過幾輪競價，荷花圖以每平方英尺30萬美元由英國白人收藏家Ian Hamilton購得，另一幅《梅花》以每平方英尺21萬美金成交。

　但是，會前被看好的《牧牛圖》則沒有達成交易。《牧牛圖》被行家認爲是精品中的精品，儘管買方將價錢提到每平方英尺54萬美元，但賣方堅持不能少於其底價爲每平方英尺90萬美金，由此差價懸殊而流標。

【中央網路報】

(最後修改日期　2007/02/11 06:06 PM)

ETtoday

請鍵入關鍵字檢索　○新聞 ○Blog ◉網

新聞　Bloguide　房屋網 Free

影音 政治 財經 大陸 社會 地方 生活 消費 娛樂 體育 旅遊 資訊 諮言 國際 BBC 閱讀 色區 話題 命理 論壇

國際 >> 重點新聞

國際情勢　| 名人軼事　| 新鮮世　| 唐人街　| BBC中文　| 美國之音

速報 ※寫心彩繪我的家─YOYO幼兒園繪畫比賽　　熱門 徵Logo獎十萬 - 徵文送溫泉住宿 - 看見台灣

義雲高大師畫作　以每平方呎30萬美元成交

2007/02/11 16:57

記者蘇靜蓉／舊金山報導

舊金山華藏寺在昨天舉行的書畫交易會中，展銷三幅中國畫，其中一幅荷花《兩花一斗一如性》達到每平方英尺30萬美元成交。

據現場拍賣員介紹，世界著名佛教大法王雲高益西諾布、同時也是大藝術家身份的義雲高大師贈了三幅精品畫作給國際佛教僧尼總會。這次國際佛教僧尼總會公開拍賣此三幅作品，有意願購買的約有上十人。

現場經過幾輪競價，荷花圖以每平方英尺30萬美元由英國白人收藏家Ian Hamilton購得，另一幅《梅花》以每平方英尺21萬美金成交。但是，會前被看好的《牧牛圖》則沒有達成交易。《牧牛圖》被行家認爲是精品中的精品，儘管買方將價錢提到每平方英尺54萬美元，但賣方堅持不能少於其底價爲每平方英尺90萬美金，由此差價懸殊而流標。

↓圖說：

國際佛教僧尼總會舊金山華藏寺在昨天舉行的書畫交易會中，作品荷花《兩花一斗一如性》達到每平方英尺30萬美元成交。(國際佛教僧尼總會提供)

↓圖說：《牧牛圖》買家出價每平方英尺54萬美元，賣家不賣。(國際佛教僧尼總會提供)

CATEGORY 22

Western Paintings

第二十二大類　西畫

Introduction

As soon as you set your eyes on the "supernatural abstract colors" created by H.H. Dorje Chang Buddha III Wan Ko Yeshe Norbu Holiest Tathagata, you will find the bright and dazzling red, yellow, blue, white and black colors leaping and dancing, vigorous like billows sluicing over thousands of miles, yet stored up into wonders at the fine tip of a brush. Gentle yet resolute, they freely transcend worldliness. Various spectacular colors are mixed ingeniously to compliment one another. One can say they express superb craftsmanship excelling nature and depict forms that are flexible and elusive. Words cannot describe the harmonious, refined, and soothing air these colors convey.

"Supernatural abstract colors" compose a perfect world of colors. This world does not have any concrete mundane forms but uses colors alone to form shapes and express feelings. Charming colors that touch people's hearts constitute the shape and theme of this world. Through the mastery of H.H. Dorje Chang Buddha III, these colors converge into incredibly, marvelous and bright magic, expressing themes such as the vivid spirit of a flowery scene or the vigor of the roaring sea. Yet, "supernatural abstract colors" can be ever so exact as they appear from the tip of His Holiness's brush. Their fine details are often revealed among rough strokes, and their charm is naturally displayed.

This description of the exceptional skills H.H. Dorje Chang Buddha III possesses in the field of western paintings is actually inappropriate since His Holiness has the realization of a Buddha. H.H. Dorje Chang Buddha III is able to take auspicious mist from the air, place it inside a sculpture, and make it stay there without dissipating. With such an ability, wouldn't painting be an extremely easy thing for His Holiness? Thus, His Holiness can create captivatingly beautiful paintings such as these.

These works of art are fused with the essence of the universe, nature, and the earth. It is an understatement to label His Holiness's art of "supernatural abstract colors" with words such as "style," "conception," "charm," or "technique." The art of H.H. Dorje Chang Buddha III has already cast off the bondage of the common world. The forms, meanings, and colors of this form of art can be compared to a golden dragon breaking away from the earth's crust and soaring in the azure sky above the blue sea, free at will, unbridled and unrestrained, all worldly dust whisked away, ever changing, and beautiful beyond compare! In front of these soul-inspiring rare treasures of art, we admire the exceptional artistry that flows from the boundless heart of H.H. Wan Ko Yeshe Norbu Holiest Tathagata. We absorb beauty that transcends all confinements of reality, beauty created from His Holiness's use of ever changing colors for the appreciation of mankind. We can only rejoice with excitement from our hearts, for words of wholehearted praise seem totally inadequate.

Works by H.H. Dorje Chang Buddha III embody the wonderful essence of the craftsmanship vidya and flow from His Holiness's supreme and perfect wisdom. We can see this in the phenomenal attainments of H.H. Wan Ko Yeshe Norbu Holiest Tathagata in western painting. An example of this is the oil painting called "Dharma King Sakyamuni," which is peerless in the majestic, solemn, and dignified air it conveys. One can see from that painting that His Holiness truly is a Buddha.

(This text was translated from the Chinese text that follows.)

簡　介

　　當你第一眼觸碰到多杰羌佛第三世雲高益西諾布頂聖如來的「超自然抽象色彩」，那鮮明耀眼的紅黃藍白黑，跳躍飛舞，潑辣如千里江濤瀉過，收藏於微細毫端之妙趣，灑然超脫於塵俗，柔和而剛毅，各種妙麗色彩相互滋養昇華，可以說是巧奪天工，色達空靈的境界，和雅、舒服之享受真是難以言狀。

　　「超自然抽象色彩」是一個由色彩構造起來的完美世界，它沒有十分具體的世間形態，它就是色彩，以色造形，以色寫意，色即是其形，色便是其意，色入感人神韻。這些色彩，一經三世多杰羌佛之手，蕈然匯成無比奇妙驚豔的幻色，氣韻生動，景如華滋，潑辣如滄海咆哮，而反之微觀如毫端顯意，粗中顯微，神韻天成。其實現在談三世多杰羌佛的西畫高超之處，實在是低論佛陀。我們可以想到，就連空中的祥霧三世多杰羌佛都能一手拿之入雕刻，如如而不動，對於書畫，那不是小菜一碟嗎？所以這些畫美得醉人。

　　這些作品，融入了宇宙自然的精華、地骨山川之心源，毫不誇張地說，用「格調」、「意境」、「韻味」、「技巧」之類的詞彙來標貼三世多杰羌佛的「超自然抽象色彩」藝術，實嫌拘謹世俗，三世多杰羌佛的藝術早已脫出此塵世樊籬的束縛，其形其意其色均似金龍脫於地殼，翱翔翻飛在碧海藍天，恣意自在，無拘無束，撣盡塵埃，變化萬千而美妙絕倫！在這些激盪心魄的藝術奇珍面前，景仰著頂聖如來雲高益西諾布從無盡博大之妙心流瀉出來的超人技藝，領受著三世多杰羌佛用變化無窮之色彩，為人類的享受幻化出來的超越一切現實禁錮的美麗，我們除了發自內心的激動歡欣之外，滿腔讚嘆的語言似乎都顯得蒼白無力了。三世多杰羌佛從其無上圓滿的智慧中流出來的工巧神髓，讓我們再次見識到雲高益西諾布頂聖如來高超的西畫技法和造詣，如他所畫的油畫「釋迦牟尼法王子」，其莊嚴無以倫比，即可見其修養學識之高深乃是佛陀展顯。

（此文的英文翻譯印在前面）

A Beautiful World Discovered From a Cave
别有洞天

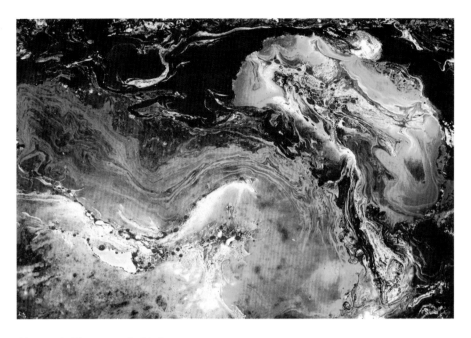

Heavenly Treasures in Motion
天堂寶物正飛旋

Thatched Stone Hut on a Snowy Mountain
雪山上的茅篷石屋

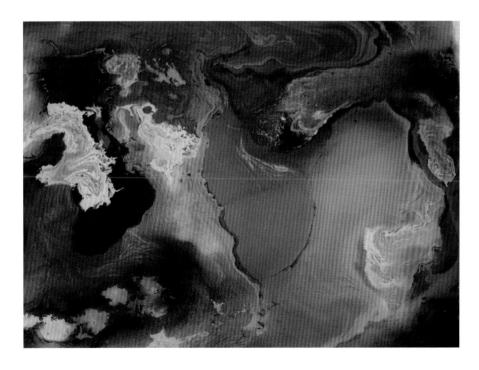

Spirit Resonance Will Live Forever
永不消逝的神韻

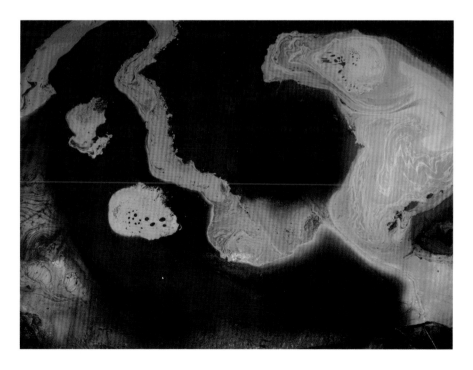

The Awesome Power of Consciousness
靈的威猛

Dharma King Sakyamuni
南無釋迦牟尼法王子

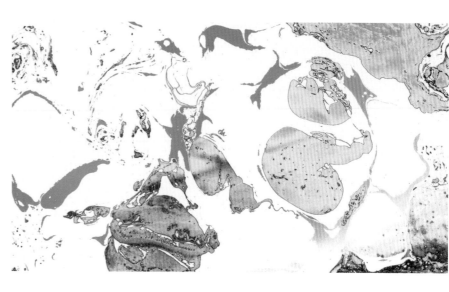

World of Celestial Dragons Beneath the Brush
筆下的神龍世界

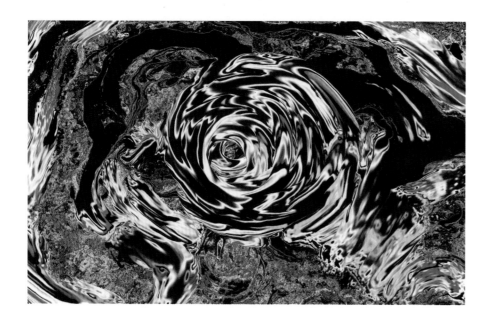

Endlessly Changing Colors
幻色

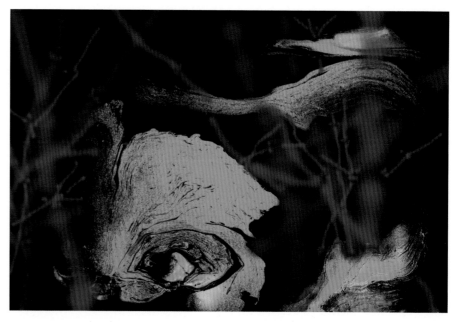

Loofah in a Purple Bamboo Grove
紫竹林中的香絲瓜

ASIAN JOURNAL

NEWS   FEBRUARY 17-23, 2006   **11**   VOL 5 · ISSUE 7

Exhibition of Master Wan Ko Yee's Amazing Achievements in the Form of World-Class Treasures

Mystic, wondrous, noble, and enchanting!
A mysterious art which is recognized as a precious treasure from heaven appears in the world for the first time!

On February 5-27, 2006, the Master Wan Ko Yee International Cultural Institute hold an exhibition of the World-Class Treasures created by Master Wan Ko Yee (Dharma King Yangwo Yisinubu Wan Ko). Regarded by all as enchanting and precious treasures from another dimension, this art appears in the world for the first time. The Organization of American States, which represents 34 countries, sponsored a special exhibition of Master Wan Ko Yee's work for ambassadors and dignitaries. Now you can see this mysterious and wondrous art. It is praised as "Treasures from Heaven." This exhibit displays superb, extraordinary art, profound knowledge, holy virtue, and more from another realm. Admission is free.

A rare exhibit of Master Wan Ko Yee's world-class art, literary accomplishments, and innovations hold from February 5 through 27, 2006 at 1822 Eddy Street, San Francisco, California.

The exhibition showcases more than 200 pieces of the Master's artwork in 18 categories. This represents only a small portion of Master Wan Ko Yee's outstanding accomplishments. The exhibition features Yun sculptures, Chinese paintings, western paintings, art frames, jade plates, three-dimensional pictures, calligraphy, poetry, and literature, along with the latest application of the master's designs in ceramic, enamel, glass, and other mediums for use in beautifying the domestic and work environment. These tiles, wall hangings, transparent panels, etc. are unbelievably beautiful and highly original, surpassing the elegance of materials found in the Louvre Museum in Paris or the luxury hotels of Las Vegas. These are suitable for the most elegant homes, up-scale restaurants, fashionable hotels, sophisticated offices, or other places to create a noble and enhanced quality of life. Master Yee wants to make his enlightened view of a world of incredible beauty available to everyone.

Master Wan Ko Yee, who currently resides in the United States, is known as Dharma King Yangwo Yisinubu Wan Ko. Over

2,000 Buddhist leaders from thirty-three countries and 416 organizations, recognized Master Yee as a Dharma King and "Authentic Buddhism Master." It is difficult to find another person in this world who has succeeded in gaining the high state of virtue and realization that Master Yee has attained. It is precisely due to his unfathomable Buddha-dharma realization that the Master has acquired erudition and penetrating understanding of the laws that govern the growth and change of everything in the universe. He has thereby attained the highest achievements in various fields, such as religion, literature, philosophy, painting, calligraphy, sculpture, and application of color. No one in history can match such achievements.

He is a master of art of outstanding international fame. The Chinese paintings of Master Wan Ko Yee were sold at auctions at the highest prices for paintings by any living artist in Southeast Asia, going for over two million US dollars each. With the appearance of Yun Sculpture, cre-

ated by the Master for humanity, all splendid pearls, jades, and gemstones become pale in comparison, like the stars in the sky being outshined by a clear moon. The Yun sculpture created by the Master is an art with indescribable beauty and appears in the world for the first time. Its beauty surpasses that of any natural pearls, jades or precious gemstones. No precious stone in this world can compare with the mystery and resplendence of Yun sculptures. Some of you might consider this an overstatement, but when you see the beautiful and wondrous artwork, you will be surprised, enchanted, and see that this is not an exaggeration.

The Organization of American States, which represents 34 countries, sponsored a special exhibition featuring part of Master Wan Ko Yee's work for am-

bassadors and dignitaries. The artwork was recognized by all as a precious treasure from heaven. The Master is also the only artist awarded the position of "Fellow" by the Royal Academy of Arts in the London in the Academy's over two hundred year history. As you can see, this is not an ordinary artist, nor is this an ordinary exhibition.

The frames and jade-like plates created by Master Wan Ko Yee can be described as "embodying the essence of Nature yet surpassing the craftsmanship of Nature." The frames of the Master cannot be limited to the concept of frames. They also are a particular kind of extreme-

ly exquisite and precious art. They vividly reproduce the superlative craftsmanship seen in the creation of everything in Nature yet embody what is refined rather than coarse, amplifying the ephemeral or unostentatious beauty of precious natural beings in life to the perfect zenith of art.

The appearance of Master Yee's uniquely beautiful, unfathomably mysterious, and holy works of art have shattered

mankind's long-held understanding of artistic creations. The astonishing beauty of his artistic creations stirs ones soul. His mysterious artistic masterpieces are the natural crystallization of his various astonishing talents, the natural outflow of his limitless Buddha-dharma wisdom and compassion. They also represent his very high moral achievement and the highest expression of kindness, generosity, and selflessness. It is the Master's compassionate desire that everyone be able to attain this level as well. What you see in this exhibit is superb extraordinary art, profound knowledge, holy virtue, and more, truly from another realm.

The exhibition is free to the public.

Location: 1822 Eddy Street, San Francisco, CA 94115
415-673-2311
Time: February 5-27, 2006
Monday-Thursday, 10:00 a.m. to 6:00 p.m.
Friday-Sunday, 10:00 a.m. to 8:00 p.m.
Sponsored by the Master Wan Ko Yee International Cultural Institute.
CONTACT: Zhaxi Zhuoma Rinpoche (Cell Phone: 626-394-4699)
E-MAIL:zhaxizh@zhaxizhuoma.net
PHONE: 626-281-6378
FAX: 626-281-3243
WEBSITE: http://www.YunArt.org" www.YunArt.org

義雲高藝術成就展 金山揭幕

政要致賀 肯定大師對美國文化多元性價值觀貢獻

世界日報
二次版
WORLD JOURNAL
出版者及承印者：世界日報社 No. 10440 ISSN 0747-5071

【本報記者江智慧舊金山報導】由義雲高大師國際文化基金會主辦的「義雲高大師世界瑰寶級成就展」，將於2月5日至2月27日，於舊金山展出。5日開幕儀式，許多政要到場祝賀。

州眾議會執行議長余胤良、舊金山市議員馬世雲、聖馬刁第一選區市議員喬區（Mark Church）、加州亞太事務委員會委員謝漢屏、加州聯邦參議員范士丹舊金山辦事處主任劉紹漢等均親臨會場祝賀。

美國商務部少數族裔發展委員會副署長董繼玲派代表致賀詞，祝賀展出成功，並肯定大師對美國文化多元性、價值觀的貢獻。

賀家麗代表洛杉磯縣長安東諾維奇致賀詞，表彰大師在藝術方面的成就及對華裔社區的貢獻。加州稅務委員會委員江俊輝由代表致贈表揚狀。加州州長阿諾史瓦辛格也派代表致意。

這次展覽是義雲高大師在美國規模最大的一次展出。義雲高大師是佛教法王，最近因為因緣成熟，公開了自己的法號「仰諤益西諾步雲高法王」。多年前曾到訪台灣，許多政要均親自恭迎，例如前國安會秘書長蔣緯國、前總統府秘書長蔣彥士、前行政院長唐飛、前參謀總長劉和謙等。

這次展出18項難得一見的藝術瑰寶，例如韻雕、立體畫、書法、玉板、玻璃彩繪等等，共二百餘件。

韻雕是大師獨創技法，作品「霧中石」似乎可以看到霧氣存在於雕塑之中。立體畫也相當特別，大師以獨特技法展現層次。國畫則融合古今中外技法，例如「威震」一圖，畫出獅子的威嚴卻不兇猛，毛髮根細一致，巧妙結合寫意與工筆技法，曾在國際拍賣市場上創下逾212萬元高價，是太平洋地區在室畫家作品價格最高者。

聖馬刁第一選區市議員馬克接受本報採訪表示，大師作品獨特，難得一見，很多不只美麗，更具啟發性。

馬世雲表示，這是驚人的藝術創作。她母親從事藝術教育二十餘年，所以自小接觸藝術作品。大師的作品讓她印象深刻。她自己也曾嘗試藝術創作，但是他覺得自己屬於左腦型人物，比較像像爸爸適合做數理性分析。

余胤良則對大師的技法相當好奇，想知道大師如何得到創作靈感，如何完成這麼美麗的作品。

展出地點在 1822 Eddy Street, San Francisco, CA94115。免費入場。洽詢電話：(415)673-2311。展期2月5日至2月27日，星期一至星期四，上午10時至下午6時。星期五至星期日，上午 10 時至晚 8 時。

↑義雲高大師世界瑰寶級成就展開幕，許多政要到場祝賀。包括州眾議會執行議長余胤良（左五）、舊金山市議員馬世雲（右五）、聖馬刁市議員喬區（右六）。 （記者江智慧攝）

二〇〇六年二月六日 星期一 MONDAY, FEBRUARY 6, 2006 **B7**

CATEGORY 23

Art Frames

第二十三大類　畫框

Introduction

From ancient times to the present, there have been many kinds of frames for pictures, paintings, and other forms of art. There have been frames in the baroque style, frames made from tree bark, striped frames, frames with Chinese style carved flowers, gold or silver plated frames, etc. However, there have not been frames whose substance imitates various natural elements. In order to change the art of frames in this world so that people could bask in the delight of art that is in harmony with nature, H.H. Dorje Chang Buddha III Wan Ko Yeshe Norbu created sculpted art frames in the style of various natural elements. Examples of this include frames made in the style of ganoderma lucidum (a type of hard dark brown fungus supposed to possess supernatural powers), tropical plants that wind around trees, coral, ancient-looking unearthed cultural relics, white and green jade, and winding vines.

The key to this is that H.H. Dorje Chang Buddha III, through His Holiness's wisdom and inner realization vidya powers, applies to these frames the four great impermanent elements of earth, water, fire, and wind. His Holiness thereby creates frames whose material and structure appear to be created by nature itself. Actually, these frames look more real and natural than the real natural elements themselves. We will only give two examples that demonstrate this point. One is the faux ganoderma lucidum art frames and the other is the faux green jade art frames.

The ganoderma lucidum art frames are formed by putting together many of those hard mushroom-type fungi. Of course, such frames are not composed of real ganoderma lucidum. Rather, the ganoderma lucidum in such frames are created from carving and application of colors. The shapes of the ganoderma lucidum are connected together on the wooden frame to form an exquisite, integrated shape. Those ganoderma lucidum have the same color, air, and shape of real ganoderma lucidum. Furthermore, rare thousand-year-old ganoderma lucidum, old hundred-year-old ganoderma lucidum, and new tender ganoderma lucidum are interconnected to form an elegant and charming appearance. Many ganoderma lucidum mushroom caps and mushroom stems are interconnected in a beautifully rhythmic manner. The interchange between substance and emptiness, highness and lowness, largeness and smallness, and thickness and thinness creates a highly elegant appearance. This is where the charming style of these Yun Sculpture frames lies.

The styles, hues, and shapes of the ganoderma lucidum seem to change in an extraordinary manner. Additionally, each frame embodies twelve characteristics: enrapturing beauty, charming grace, oldness with strength, an ancient look, an appealing and natural fragmentary look, an attractive weathered look, real-looking spots, rareness, elegance, a powerful air, a bold and vigorous quality, and a simple yet majestic manner. These are the twelve characteristics by which one can distinguish between real and counterfeit Yun Sculpture frames composed of carved ganoderma lucidum. They also are the reasons why the sculptures of H.H. Dorje Chang Budddha III are peerless.

These Yun Sculpture frames composed of carved ganoderma lucidum provide artistic beauty for all to appreciate. Moreover, the ganoderma lucidum is a very auspicious symbol that is said to embody the spirit of everything. It represents riches, honor, and splendor. Among some of the special features of these frames worth appreciating are their bold and vigorous style, an extraordinary quality that transcends the mundane, and a rich rustic and ethnic air. These frames contain and exhibit the extensive knowledge of their creator. It would be difficult for even famous people to find one of these frames to hang on the wall of their home. That is because each such frame is unique in the entire world. Each one is a matchless, rare treasure.

Everyone knows that green jade is the highest grade jade. A piece the size of one's palm has already become something rare in this world. However, the faux green jade art frames of H.H. Dorje Chang Buddha III, each side of which is a few feet, seem to be carved entirely out of green jade. Moreover, they look like they were made out of old green jade that has no defects. Aren't these tantamount to wonderful treasures that have fallen from heaven? Of course, this earthly world does not have such beautiful green jade. It can only come into existence through the carving knife of H.H. Dorje Chang Buddha III.

The faux green jade art frames created by H.H. Dorje Chang Buddha III have an ancient-looking green jade color to them that is steady and elegant. This color is not stale or old-fashioned in the least. Rather, it is a natural combination of refined blackish green and sprightly verdant, although there is not much verdant hue. This color expresses the essence of old jade that has slowly matured over thousands of years, with a vigorous and spirited quality that is clearly seen. This refined green jade color will every now and again reveal a lustrous white, like the color of the feathers of immortal cranes. Such a mixture of hues truly transcends all traces of the mundane.

There is another aspect to these art frames that is incredible. We have only mentioned here blackish green, verdant, and lustrous white. However, the color green alone could be further divided into many different types based upon its various hues. There is aged green, light green, blackish green, glossy dark green, pastel green, verdant, fresh green, deep green, translucent green, etc. There actually are countless gradations of green in these art frames, all of which are natural looking. All of these various shades of green interconnect and interact so naturally there is not the slightest sign they were created by man. Therefore, it is difficult to fathom how the creator of these frames could harmonize these colors so masterfully, fittingly, flawlessly, and beautifully.

The second aspect worth describing is the streaks and lines on these faux green jade frames. The streaks and lines may be deep or shallow, large or small, high or low. They seem to be naturally formed as they wind their way through the ever-changing harmonious colors. These streaks and lines may be bold, vigorous, and unconstrained; soft, smooth, and graceful, like hanging willows; rippling, like water when hit by a pebble; jagged, like the contour of broken stones; indistinct, like shadows of mysterious and beautiful heavenly beings cast over water; or irregular, like rocks randomly hurled on sand. There are no set rules regarding these streaks and lines. They were created with natural, spontaneous, and heavenly stokes of the brush. Who can guess in which direction they will turn next? They are astoundingly beautiful. This is especially true with respect to several aged streaks that seem to be remnants formed during the ice age. These disjointed dark brown streaks express the passage of time and the touches of wind and frost over the years. When appreciating such superlative craftsmanship, one can only utter profuse praise and wonder what Buddha-dharma realization was applied by H.H. Dorje Chang Buddha III to coalesce thousands of years of time into one splendid frame.

The third aspect of these frames one should notice is their texture. This is another astounding part of these faux green jade frames. Whether viewed from a distance or close up, and when touched by the hand, you will feel that the texture is that of real green jade. It is truly difficult to imagine that these frames were sculpted with the hand of man. They have a clear luster that is not a superficial or dazzling type of brightness. Rather, it is a soft, warm, and steady type of luster. Although it is not a resplendent and dazzling luster, it nonetheless is invigorating and uplifting. The luster of these frames emanates from their interior. It is a type of light that radiates from the deepest level of the frames to their outer surface, manifesting the remarkably natural texture of real jade. It seems that if you dropped these faux green jade frames on the ground, the loud clang of hard jade would follow. Through the surface of the frames, one can also see green cotton-shaped formations that seem to be floating inside the frames at various depths. This is a special characteristic of green jade. Each of these endlessly interconnected formations has its own shape and seems to change in an amazing way. They form the inner world of green jade, making the green hues of these frames appear translucent at times and richly dense at other times. The result is a mysterious, elegant, and graceful appearance.

The fourth aspect of these frames worthy of appreciation is their integrity or completeness. The flow of the colors and streaks form a whole. That is, these frames are not composites of small pieces of jade. Each frame is an integral whole, as if it was cut out of a gigantic piece of green jade. When you carefully view the entire art frame from top to bottom and from left to right, you will discover the unrivaled carving skills of H.H. Dorje Chang Buddha III! The streaks and spots on the surface follow the various sections, grooves, and recesses all the way to the back of the frame. It is as if that particular piece of jade existed solely for the purpose of becoming an art frame. The colors and lines on each corner and each section are equally beautiful and flowing. Even natural precious stones have not reached this level of wholeness and perfection.

Actually, the amazing features of the faux green jade art frames described above are not limited to such art frames. All of the Yun Sculpture art frames created by H.H. Dorje Chang Buddha III are like this. As a result of His Holiness's wondrous application of colors and superlative carving, His frames most definitely have the texture of the natural minerals or plants that they portray. However, they embody a consummate perfection that certainly surpasses the creations of nature itself. This is true for frames sculpted by H.H. Dore Chang Buddha III in the style of faux withered vines, faux tree roots, faux white jade, faux old wood, faux spotted jade, faux ganoderma lucidum, faux red coral, etc.

Each and every detail of the frames created by H.H. Dorje Chang Buddda III expresses an extremely natural quality in both form and spirit. Yet, His Holiness's frames are devoid of the dark spots or broken parts that natural objects have after being exposed to wind, frost, rain, and snow. His Holiness has developed to a perfect degree the depiction of the fleeting beauty that natural treasures display during their growth process. Without any exaggeration, it can be said that if heavenly beings saw His Holiness's Yun Sculpture art frames, they would feel embarrassed that they themselves cannot create such beautiful frames.

It must be emphasized that frames with such genuine and perfect texture and color represent a pinnacle that others have heretofore been unable to reach in the history of human art. Simply put, mankind has been longing to reach but has been unable to reach the extremely high degree of genuineness and perfection that is embodied in the Yun Sculpture frames of H.H. Wan Ko Yeshe Norbu Holiest Tathagata. Thus, it is very difficult for us to distinguish art frames sculpted by H.H. Dorje Chang Buddha III from other forms of art by simply applying common artistic concepts of the past. When standing in front of these wondrous and rare works of art, we gaze upon and marvel at their beauty. In the words of the deceased Mr. John B. Tsu, who was chairman of the White House Advisory Commission on Asian Americans and Pacific Islanders, "This is truly the divine workmanship of a Buddha."

(This text was translated from the Chinese text that follows.)

簡　　介

　　歷史上從古至今，畫框的種類非常多，有巴洛克式的，有樹皮的，有線條式的，有中式雕花，鍍金上銀等等，但卻沒有從大自然取材的，為此，多杰羌佛第三世雲高益西諾布頂聖如來為了改變這個地球上的畫框框藝，讓人們享受到與自然相合的藝術沐浴，他創始了取大自然素材為體的塑材框藝，如靈芝蕈類、熱帶植物盤樹類、珊瑚自然結構類、出土文物古化類、羊脂翡翠玉雕類、藤蘿盤匝類，最關鍵的是三世多杰羌佛以智慧和內明的力量，將它們施以地水火風四大無常的內力，把它們誕生成天然造化而成的結構，看上去比真的還要真，比自然的還自然，此舉二例，如靈芝畫框、翡翠畫框。靈芝畫框即是以靈芝蕈為組合的畫框。此靈芝蕈不是真實的蕈靈芝，而是人工雕塑刀工色染而成的靈芝蕈。此靈芝蕈隨其木板畫框形體而連接一氣造成，達成精妙結構之整體，與真靈芝蕈色澤、韻味、形體相等。而更甚之處是有千年稀芝、百年老芝、近新嫩芝，相互結體，達成雅韻。其芝菇與芝杆相互穿流，宛如平沙落雁，沙飛毛交，茫然若霧，渾然而影顯，若沉若浮，虛實飄逸，霎那間雁定雄姿，灰隨風卷，殘塵嬌然不知所向，萬里空清，白雲飛絮。此際，雁姿嬌然，何其雄風展秀，正是韻雕之風神韻所在。而芝風色蘊形味變化奇端，麗、秀、蒼、古、殘、破、斑、奇、雅、雄、潑、渾，具十二味境。麗者，華麗攝心；秀者，俊俏秀氣；蒼者，老道蒼勁；古者，嚴古稀恆；殘者，殘缺天然；破者，風霜蟲破；斑者，斑跡如真；奇者，珍奇稀物；雅者，雅純高貴；雄者，雄奇霸道；潑者，潑辣大方；渾者，渾厚華滋。此十二味境，是韻雕靈芝鑑別真偽，乃三世多杰羌佛工雕之絕活所在。

　　韻雕靈芝用以畫框，不但堪為藝術精美之享受，靈芝且具祥瑞集萬物之靈氣，歸宗富貴榮華之吉兆。其品位鑑賞之特質，尤堪大方潑辣，雄厚奇貫超凡脫俗，更外展民族鄉土之氣，內涵文風博識之學。縱是名流雅君，貴翁德士，登堂入室之所需，怎奈也難求得懸壁一件。其因每架畫框皆為世界獨一無二，故為無雙國寶珍品。

　　世人皆知翡翠乃玉中極品，掌心大小的一塊已屬稀世罕見。像這個幾尺見方的畫框，通體似全用翡翠雕鏤而成，而且是一塊完整無瑕的老翠，那不是天上掉下來的神物嗎？當然，這樣絕美的翡翠是世間所沒有的，它只會在三世多杰羌的雕刀下存在。

　　三世多杰羌佛的這個翡翠畫框，通體是成熟老道的古翠色，色韻沉著、和雅，但並不沉溺於古舊，而是在高貴的墨綠與明快的青翠之間自然遊走。青翠的份量不是很多，卻彷彿是這老翠以悠悠萬年歲月積聚而成的精華，掩藏不住地露出它的活力，爾後，這精華的翠綠終於升騰出一片潤白，若仙鶴之羽，脫盡塵埃。令人難以思議的是，此處雖然只提到墨綠、翠綠及潤白三種顏色，然實則在畫框上，僅就一個綠，便可數出深淺、濃淡、冷暖不同的若干種，老綠、淺綠、墨綠、油綠、粉綠、翠綠、新綠、沉綠、表綠、透綠……無法盡數，萬千層次，攬盡天然。它們相互穿插、遊動、過渡，自然得沒有絲毫雕琢痕跡，因而很難理解創作者如何將這些色彩調和到這樣的高度，契合、蘊柔得天衣無縫，華茲麗魅，入石三分。

　　再看它的花斑、紋路。深深淺淺、大大小小、高低錯落、逶巡來回的斑紋，就在色韻變幻之際自然形成，或靳戈鐵戟般鏗鏘揮灑，或江南垂柳似的婉約柔潤，亦若卵石擊水蕩出粼粼水波，又或者是天獸投影、亂石擊沙、滴水浸石……沒有一定之規，天然、隨意、不在乎，上蒼的筆墨，誰人能揣測它的走向？然而又美妙得令人驚顫。尤其是那幾處似斷裂在冰川時代的老舊殘斑，已有斷斷續續的焦啡色，飽含歲月的流痕，風霜的摩挲，時間的見證，因而讚嘆到拍手頓足，無法思議，三世多杰羌佛是用了什麼佛法證量讓萬年的光陰濃縮在一刻的？

　　三觀其質感。這也是最令人震撼的部分之一。無論遠觀，無論近測，甚至伸手觸摸，都能感受到道地的玉石翡翠的質感，確實使人難以想像它是以塑材，經手工雕塑而成。它的光澤，明亮而油潤，不是浮光，不是刺目的折射光，是一種柔和、溫暖、沉著但又絕對亮麗的光芒，並不炫目但又令人為之一振，它的光澤是由裡至外浸透出來，赫然真的是天然的玉石材質從內層深處透射出來的那種光亮，彷彿擲之於地而有錚然脆響。透過翡翠表面，還能看到翡翠內層游離漂移著深淺不一的綠色絮狀物，那便是翡翠玉石的特質，千絲萬縷形狀各異，變化奇端，又形成一個內在的翡翠世界，使得畫框之翠色時而清透，時而濃厚，奇妙神秘又典雅雍容。

四賞其整體性。色韻花紋的流動是整體性的，也就是說，它不是小碎塊的拼湊鑲嵌，整個畫框就是一塊完整的翡翠，就好像是在一塊巨大翡翠上現成挖掘出的畫框。仔細觀賞整個畫框的前後左右，這時你會發現三世多杰羌佛的絕頂雕藝！表面的花斑色塊，會順著畫框的切面和凹槽處延展，直至畫框背面，彷彿這塊翡翠是專為這個畫框而存在，任何一個角落和斷面的色韻紋彩都一樣亮麗，一樣流暢。這種完整性和完美性，是天然寶石也不能達到的。

其實，以上所講到的翡翠畫框的幾種奇絕特質，並不只在此處才有，三世多杰羌佛的所有韻雕畫框都是這樣，以色韻、雕工達到絕對逼真於天然山石或植物的質感，但又絕對超越天然達到極致的完美。如三世多杰羌佛雕的枯藤、樹根、羊脂玉、老木、獸斑玉、靈芝、紅珊瑚等等等等，每一個的任何細部的表達都絕對真實天然，形神具備，但又脫去了天然物體受風霜雨雪的侵害而遺留的黯淡殘缺，將這些自然寶物在生長過程中偶爾短暫或並不強烈綻放的美好，發揮到完美的藝術極點。說一句毫不誇張的話：老天爺若看到三世多杰羌佛的韻雕畫框，會汗顏！

更需要強調的是，如此真實和完美的質感色韻，是人類藝術世界有史以來一直無法呈現的頂點。說簡單一點，雲高益西諾布頂聖如來韻雕畫框所達到的極致和逼真完美，是人類一直嚮往但又無法登臨的高度，因而，我們實在很難用歷史上過去的藝術常識去鑑別三世多杰羌佛的雕藝，在這些奇絕的藝術珍稀面前，除了瞪大眼睛驚嘆，最多也就只能套用已故的前白宮亞太裔顧問委員會主席祖炳民先生的那句話：『這實在是佛斧神工』！

（此文的英文翻譯印在前面）

Sculpture of a Painted Screen of Faux Rosewood Root
雕塑仿紫檀根畫屏

Jadite Green
碧翠

Cold Fragrance 寒香

Twining Tree Roots
盤樹框

The sculpture Yu Dai Ping 雕塑玉帶屏

The sculpture Zang Wang Lu Gua 雕塑藏王爐挂

The sculpture Fei Cui Yu 雕塑翡翠玉

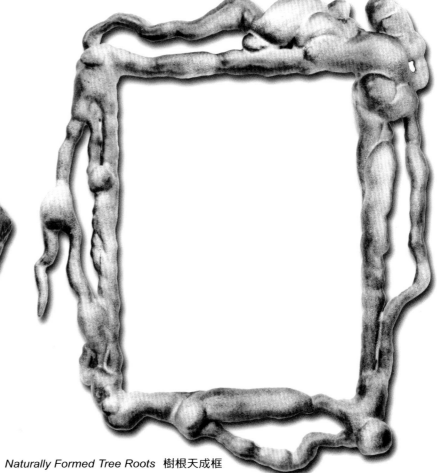

Naturally Formed Tree Roots 樹根天成框

The sculpture Lao Can Gen 雕塑老殘根

The sculpture Feng Gang Yu 雕塑鋒鋼玉

The sculpture Zi Luo Bao Shi 雕塑紫蘿抱石

Tallow Jade Made With Ease 羊脂小弄

Elegantly Sculpted Tree Roots
雕塑高雅樹根框

Ruby 紅寶石

The sculpture Jun Ling Zhi 雕塑蕈靈芝

The sculpture Zi Tan 雕塑紫檀

CATEGORY 24

Designs of Buddha Images

第二十四大類　佛像設計造型

Introduction

The images of Buddhas designed by H.H. Dorje Chang Buddha III Wan Ko Yeshe Norbu Holiest Tathagata are the most awe-inspiring and sublime images of Buddhas in the world today. Everyone who has seen images of Buddhas designed by H.H. Dorje Chang Buddha III feels that each one of them is a world treasure. One example is the twenty-one-foot-high statue of Amitabha Buddha inside the Hua Zang Si temple in San Francisco. That statue has been generally recognized as the most majestic Buddhist statue in the world. H.H. Dorje Chang Buddha III designed that Buddhist statue. The factory that produced it used as its blueprint an oil painting by His Holiness. H.H. Dorje Chang Buddha III personally decided upon revisions to that statue many times during the production process. His Holiness not only designed that statue, He also made the final decisions on all aspects of that statue, including the shades of colors used.

"The Three Holy Beings of the Western Paradise," which is the first three-dimensional thangka in the world, and a three dimensional image of the mandala of Green Tara were both designed by H.H. Dorje Chang Buddha III. His Holiness revised them several times during the production process. They are majestic mandalas containing images of Buddhas.

Because H.H. Dorje Chang Buddha III is the true incarnation of the primordial Buddha, His Holiness thoroughly understands the thirty-two major auspicious marks and the eighty minor auspicious marks of a Buddha's body. Thus, His Holiness is able to design the most majestic images of Buddhas in the world.

(This text was translated from the Chinese text that follows.)

簡　　介

多杰羌佛第三世雲高益西諾布頂聖如來所造的佛像，是當今世界最莊嚴的佛像，凡見到過他所設計造型的佛像，個個都認為是世界珍寶級，譬如在舊金山華藏寺的阿彌陀佛像有21英尺高，已被公認為是全世界最莊嚴的佛像，獲得莊嚴冠軍的美名，該佛像是由三世多杰羌佛設計造型，用油畫畫成之藍本，再交工廠根據圖形製作。在製作過程中，三世多杰羌佛親自修訂多次，最後定稿，不僅是造型，甚至連色彩的濃淡，均由三世多杰羌佛定奪。

在世界上的第一幅立體唐卡西方三聖及綠度母立體壇城也是經三世多杰羌佛多次修訂安裝構思佈局，成為莊嚴壇城佛像圖。

正因為三世多杰羌佛是佛教的始祖佛真身降世，才能徹底清楚知道佛陀的三十二大丈夫相、八十種隨行莊嚴是怎麼回事，所以才能設計出世界上最莊嚴的佛像。

（此文的英文翻譯印在前面）

Holy Image of Amitabha Buddha 南無阿彌陀佛聖像

The original three-dimensional image of the mandala of Green Tara undergoes changes. Although the clouds do not move at all, the seed character, sun, and moon all jump back and forth, and the body of the dharma protecting deity Mahabrahma-deva, who is in the middle, constantly transforms. 綠度母立體壇城原件作品可以變化雲彩不動，種子字和日月二輪左右跳動，中央大梵天護法一個身體可以隨時變化

Namo Amitabha

南 無 阿 彌 陀 佛

西 方 三 聖

Three Holy Beings of the Western Paradise

The original "Three Holy Beings of the Western Paradise" is three-dimensional.
西方三聖原件作品為3D立體

CATEGORY 25

Tiles —The Most Beautiful Building Material in the World

第二十五大類 磁磚——世界上最美的建築材料

Introduction

From the time H.H. Dorje Chang Buddha III Wan Ko Yeshe Norbu Holiest Tathagata descended into this world, His Holiness has always wanted to renew the world of building material thoroughly so that ordinary families could enjoy the splendor of earthly mansions and the beauty of heavenly palaces. His Holiness has always wanted to replace common tiles, marble, and granite slabs in the old style with halls as gorgeous and resplendent as gemstones and with rustic, charming décor that people with refined tastes can appreciate. Based on this desire, H.H. Dorje Chang Buddha III wielded his brush and applied colors. As a result, extremely beautiful and glittering jewel-like floor and wall tiles were born! There are also excellent tiles with an ancient, simple, unadorned look, such as tiles in a more rustic style and tiles that look like unearthed cultural relics.

These tiles can be divided into the following six main categories: rustic elegance collection, lyrical charm collection, luxurious gem collection, serene nobility collection, contemporary distinction collection, and heavenly stone collection. These six collections have opened a new page in the history of building décor, providing people with distinctive decorations that add beauty to any room in their residence.

The ancient Chinese people often spoke of an immortal being who graces somebody's house with his presence, thereby adding beauty to that modest house. Such things have been described in books but have not been seen in real life. However, based on the wisdom of H.H. Dorje Chang Buddha III and His Holiness's mastery of the Five Vidyas, this added beauty has become reality under His Holiness's painting brush. All of the many people who have seen the interior building material painted by H.H. Dorje Chang Buddha III, such as floor tiles, wall tiles, wallpaper, and decorative vinyl flooring, marvel at and praise the inexhaustible beauty before their eyes.

Furthermore, many facts thoroughly demonstrate that the tiles created by H.H. Dorje Chang Buddha III are unrivaled. In many world-class building and decoration material exhibitions held in the United States, China, and elsewhere, the tiles created by H.H. Dorje Chang Buddha III have each time attracted the greatest stream of people. They have been appraised as being the best tiles in the world. Those who view them, including experts in the same trade, marvel at and highly praise the beauty before their eyes, smiling as they bask in the pleasure of the moment. The tiles created by H.H. Dorje Chang Buddha III are judged by everyone to be the highest-class, most beautiful, and most elegant decorative material in the world today.

(This text was translated from the Chinese text that follows.)

簡　　介

多杰羌佛第三世雲高益西諾布頂聖如來自從降世到這個世界，一直想為全人類建築材料做一個徹底的更新，讓普通的家庭都能享受到宮廷般繁華美麗和天庭宮殿之美景，讓常見的磚瓦、大理石、花崗板不再是舊式老調，而出現像寶石般亮麗華貴的廳堂和鄉土風情、高人雅士欣賞丘壑之靈媚。為此心願，三世多杰羌佛揮動了他的毫端運典色彩，終於一匹一塊的美不勝收、珠光幻影般的地磚和壁磚誕生了！高古樸實無華，如鄉土風氣，出土文物一般的建材脫穎而出，這些磁磚共分六大類：古雅鄉土系列、清新抒情系列、豪華寶石系列、沉穩高貴系列、時代傑出系列、天堂美石系列，這六大系列成了建築裝飾史上新的一頁，為居家貴室的裝點帶來了異彩光輝。古人常云：仙風吹到，蓬蓽生輝，書其神而未見其形。但在三世多杰羌的五明智慧一管毫端之下成了現實，凡見過三世多杰羌佛筆下的地磚、壁磚、壁紙、裝飾膠板諸多室內建材的人，只有驚嘆和讚許，美不勝收。而且，諸多事實已徹底證明了三世多杰羌佛創造的磁磚是世界無雙的，在美國、中國等多次世界級的建材及裝飾材料的展覽會中，三世多杰羌佛的磁磚在每次的展覽會上都吸引了最多的人流，被評為世界第一名，參觀者和同行專家們全部都沉浸在喜悅、微笑和高度的讚嘆聲中，大家公評三世多杰羌佛的磁磚是當今世界最高貴、美麗、雅純的裝飾建材。

（此文的英文翻譯印在前面）

These pictures are the piecing together of tiles designed by H.H. Dorje Chang Buddha III.

這是用三世多杰羌佛設計的磁磚拼成的圖案

  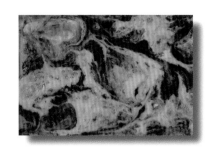 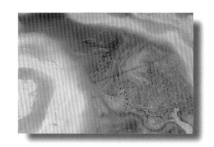

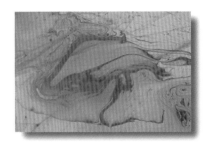   

  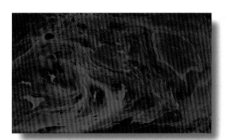 

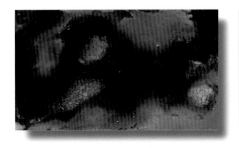 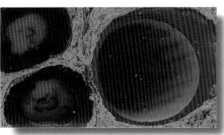  

CATEGORY **25**   Tiles—The Most Beautiful Building Material in the World

On behalf of our company, I would like to prostrate myself before H.H. Dorje Chang Buddha III Wan Ko Yeshe Norbu Holiest Tathagata to express our gratitude since we are deeply moved. H.H. Dorje Chang Buddha III coached the greatly virtuous Hang Kung and the greatly virtuous Jinba on their creations of dozens of exquisite art frames, which are unsurpassed in the world. They invested the funds from selling part of their art work in Superior Art Building Material, LLC. H.H. Dorje Chang Buddha III, the greatly virtuous Hang Kung and the greatly virtuous Jinba donated one third of their shares of the company to the United Relief Committee in order to help people affected by disasters. After our building material company was established, H.H. Dorje Chang Buddha III created many forms of building material. His Holiness's intention was to raise the level of aesthetics to a degree difficult to imagine and enable the quality of life to reach new heights where beauty is abundant and unprecedented. The heavenly, beautiful and superior building material includes tiles, decorative wall hangings, flooring, glass paintings, jade plates, art frames and many other daily life products

Ninety-five percent of the company's artwork provided by H.H. Dorje Chang Buddha III is building material and five percent is art frames. Therefore, the company's board of directors proposed together that H.H. Dorje Chang Buddha III's shares of the building material be determined immediately. One of them suggested that fifty percent be disbursed among H.H. Dorje Chang Buddha III and the two greatly virtuous ones. H.H. Dorje Chang Buddha III asked us, "How much do you think it should be?" No one knew how to answer that question. We figured that compared to other financial investments, fifty percent is very little. However, we could not think of any solutions. At that time, the Holiest Tathagata expounded, "All we do is solely for the interest of living beings. Even though the humble building material of mine currently makes up ninety five percent of the company's assets, we will never acquire any shares from the building material." Thus, the building material created by H.H. Dorje Chang Buddha III at a later time was given to the company without compensation despite the fact that it makes up the majority of the company's products. His Holiness did not obtain any shares from the company. H.H. Dorje Chang Buddha III taught us that true self-cultivation requires completely unselfish devotion to living beings. His Holiness has shown truly unselfish conduct that absolutely enables us to observe a supreme and majestic image of the Buddha. How can this be accomplished by an ordinary individual?

The statement made above is based on my personal encounters and what my company's board of directors has known. I hereby vow that I will descend into hell if any of my words are false. If my words are true, all the merits accrued are dedicated to H.H. Dorje Chang Buddha III. May H.H. Dorje Chang Buddha III forever abide in this world and benefit all living beings.

Wei-Cheng Kuan, CEO of Superior Art Building Material, LLC. U.S.A. January 20, 2007

(This is a complete translation of the Chinese text that follows originally written and signed by Wei-Cheng Kuan.)

今天我代表我們公司真是非常感動地要在這裡向多杰羌佛第三世雲高益西諾布頂聖如來頂禮致謝。三世多杰羌佛所教授恆公大德、金巴大德所創作的數十件世界絕美精品畫框，並從出售部分作品款項投資於美國高級藝術裝修材料公司，在為了幫助災難之人，三世多杰羌佛當下與恆公大德、金巴大德把自己在公司擁有的股份捐贈給聯合救助委員會三分之一。自從公司成立後，三世多杰羌佛又已創作了許多建材，目的是為了使人類的審美水準翻越一個難以想像的高度，使人們的生活品質達成一個嶄新的前所未有而美不勝收境界，這些超凡入聖的高級建材有地磚、壁磚、地板、彩繪玻璃、玉板、畫框等以及各式各樣的生活產品。

如今三世多杰羌佛所提供高級公司之作品，其百分之九十五為裝修建材，百分之五為畫框，所以，公司股東一致提出當馬上把三世多杰羌佛的建材部份股份定下來，其中有人提議百分之五十，分給三世多杰羌佛和兩位大德，三世多杰羌佛反問我們：「你們認為應該多少呢？」大家不知如何回答，心想百分之五十相比其他財物的投資，實在太少了，但又不知怎麼辦，就在這時頂聖如來開示說：「我們所做的一切都是為了利益眾生，雖然這些慚愧的建材在公司目前佔百分之九十五的財產，但我們不會從建材中收股份的。」就這樣三世多杰羌佛後來所做的建材作品雖然佔公司產品的大部分，但都全部無償地把建材給了高級公司，不從公司分取股份。三世多杰羌佛教導我們真修行就要做到完全無私地為眾生，而他老人家所表現出來的真正無私行為，徹底活生生地給我們看到了一個至高無上的偉大佛陀形象，這哪裡是普通人能做得了的呢？

以上所述都是本人真實所見所聞、是我公司全體股東都知道的，謹此立誓。若有半點虛假，願墮無間地獄；如屬真實，一切功德迴向三世多杰羌佛，願三世多杰羌佛永遠住世，利益一切眾生。

美國高級藝術裝修材料公司 總裁 關維誠

2007年1月20日
（此文的英文翻譯印在前面）

CATEGORY 26

Decorative Wall Hangings

第二十六大類　壁掛

Introduction

Decorative wall hangings refer to works of art hung on a wall. Included among them are figures of animals and people; carvings of ivory, copper, jade, wood, or stone; embroidery; lapis lazuli inlays; artwork relating to flowers, vegetation, tree branches, or feathers; porcelain objects, etc.

In order to fill the inadequacies of modern day wall hangings, H.H. Dorje Chang Buddha III Wan Ko Yeshe Norbu Holiest Tathagata applied His Buddha powers to create with great facility decorative wall hangings in a myriad of artistic styles that express outstanding novel concepts. These numerous genres are quite diverse, highly elegant, and pleasing to the mind and eye.

We have included six of his decorative wall hangings in this book. One contains the Chinese character *fu*, which means good fortune or blessings. Here it means beseeching H.H. Dorje Chang Buddha III to bring good fortune or blessings to living beings. Another contains the English word *peace*. We hope that the entire world will become peaceful and prosperous. The decorative wall hanging called "Fu" was sculpted out of a faux white jade plate with the Chinese character resembling natural tree vines. The English word in the decorative wall hanging called "Peace" was made from faux deep-sea coral. The periphery of that work of art has the natural winding look of ancient tree vines. This marvelous work is a joy to behold.

The decorative wall hanging called "Mani Treasure" expresses the wisdom-power of the Three Secrets; namely, the body, speech, and mind of the Buddha. Another work of art entitled "Old Gourds With Withered Vines" displays a highly charming style that is rustic, simple, unadorned, elegant, and beautifully aged. The decorative wall hanging "Jia" ("Home") represents warm feelings. In that work, the purity and elegance of faux green jade was used to symbolize a vibrant and harmonious family. The artwork entitled "The Bone of the Earth and Ganoderma" shows ancient fossils of ganoderma lucidum that look thousands of years old. This decorative wall hanging, which symbolizes world peace, has the appearance of a cultural relic that embodies the core of Chinese and western culture.

(This text was translated from the Chinese text that follows.)

簡　　介

壁掛即是人們常說的牆壁上的掛件，有用動物、人物、牙雕、銅雕、玉雕、木雕、布繡、琉璃嵌洞、花草、樹枝、羽毛、陶瓷、石刻等所做成的藝術掛件，稱之為壁掛。

多杰羌佛第三世雲高益西諾布頂聖如來為補當今世界壁掛之不足，施以佛力新意而抒新，隨意拈來，創造出各種藝術品味的壁掛，這些壁掛品類繁多，變化甚大，格調高雅，舒心悅目。

此書中我們用了六個壁掛，一是「福」字，意為祈請三世多杰羌佛給眾生帶來福氣；用一個英文的和平「Peace」，望整個世界和平昌盛。壁掛「福」字是一個猶如自然樹藤而長成的福字，在羊脂玉板上誕生，而「Peace」則是海底深珊而成字，被古樹盤藤天然長成，包邊抱石，奇妙玄賞舒心。

其中的「瑪尼藏」是體顯身語意三密之智慧力量，另一個「枯藤老葫蘆」是展現民族鄉土風情，樸實無華，高雅蒼俊的濃郁情趣。作品「家」這是代表著溫馨抒情，以翡翠清雅表達春意正濃，不老祥和之家。「地骨靈芝」體顯萬年古老靈芝化石，為文化風貌，內涵中西文化之神髓，世界和平之遺物。

（此文的英文翻譯印在前面）

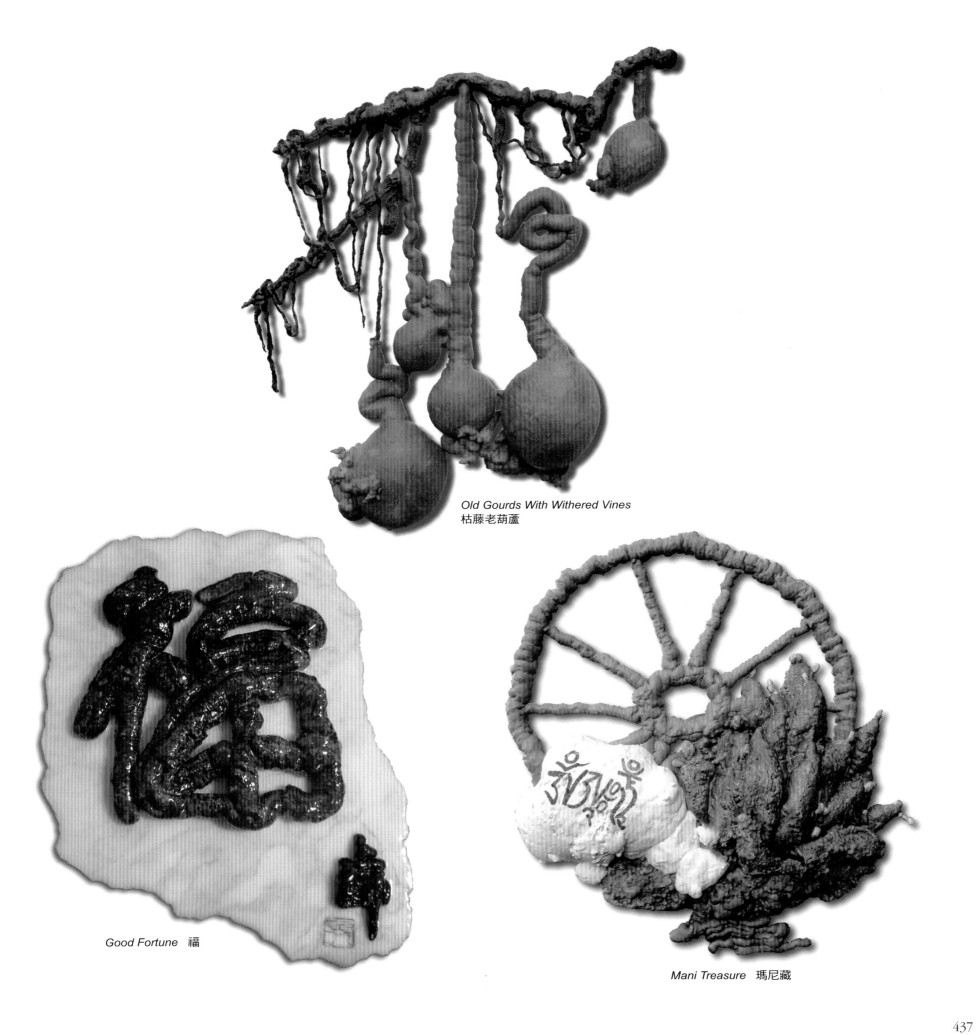

Old Gourds With Withered Vines
枯藤老葫蘆

Good Fortune 福

Mani Treasure 瑪尼藏

437

Home 家

The Bone of the Earth and Ganoderma 地骨靈芝

Peace 和平

CATEGORY 27

Buildings and Decorative Landscape Scenes

第二十七大類　建築庭園風景

Introduction

H.H. Dorje Chang Buddha III Wan Ko Yeshe Norbu Holiest Tathagata has reached great heights in the design of temples, towers, pavilions, arbors, structures in the style of the Ming and Qing Dynasties, modern western houses, and decorative landscape scenes. Because of limited space, we have selected only a few of examples of structures and decorative landscape scenes designed by H.H. Dorje Chang Buddha III.

(This text was translated from the Chinese text that follows.)

簡　　介

多杰羌佛第三世雲高益西諾布頂聖如來在寺廟、樓台、亭閣、明清建築的設計和現代西方房屋的設計、庭園風景佈置，都達到了登峰造極的境界，由於篇幅有限，我們只選了幾張三世多杰羌佛的房屋設計規劃及庭園風景的佈置。

（此文的英文翻譯印在前面）

A "country villa" designed for a dog
為狗設計的鄉土別墅

The decoration in the middle of the garden is a faux white jade sculpture called "Melody in Motion." It seems to change constantly when viewed from different angles.
庭園中央裝飾的羊脂玉雕塑「動的旋律」，八面觀看變化無窮

Part of a house garden that was designed by H.H. Dorje Chang Buddha III.
三世多杰羌佛設計的房屋庭園一角

Buildings and decorative landscape scenes designed by H.H. Dorje Chang Buddha III.
三世多杰羌佛的建築及庭園設計

Golden Garden Path
金色庭園路

Hollywood Movie Scene
好萊塢電影取景場

CATEGORY 28

Teas

第二十八大類　茗茶

Introduction

The tea *Bi Yu Chun* was rated the highest-grade tea in China. That tea is one of the products of H.H. Dorje Chang Buddha III Wan Ko Yeshe Norbu Holiest Tathagata that is based on His Holiness's wisdom and mastery of the Five Vidyas. H.H. Dorje Chang Buddha III has developed the ancient, traditional techniques of producing tea to a level of perfection, resulting in the creation of this superior quality green tea.

When discussing the creation of teas by His Holiness, we should first mention what happened when two people formally became disciples of H.H. Dorje Chang Buddha III. Two people who operated a tea factory came to H.H. Dorje Chang Buddha III to formally recognize His Holiness as their Master. H.H. Dorje Chang Buddha III asked them what they wanted to learn. They said, "Of course, we have come here to learn the Buddha-dharma. We operate a tea factory, but we cannot learn the craft of making teas here." H.H. Dorje Chang Buddha III replied, "There is everything here. I will first teach you how to make tea." Within three days, H.H. Dorje Chang Buddha III invented the world's highest grade tea. His Holiness taught those two disciples how to make that tea. However, everyone should understand that H.H. Dorje Chang Buddha III had never made any teas prior to that time. There is nothing that a Buddha cannot do. Precisely because of this, His Holiness was able to create with ease a top-grade world-famous tea.

The tea *Bi Yu Chun* has a unique flavor and a refined quality. The tealeaves are compact and delicate, retain their original fuzz, and have the color and luster of green jade. This tea has the pure aroma of chicken broth or roasted chestnuts. It is pleasantly refreshing and maintains its rich flavor for a long time. The tea is translucent, showing a lustrous green like that of green jade and can be compared to a mountain spring. Long after you taste it, you will ponder its delightful flavor.

A competition to select the best Chinese teas took place in June of 1989. *Bi Yu Chun* and Chinese teas such as *Shi Feng Long Jing, Dong Ting Bi Luo Chun,* and *Jun Shan Yin Zhen* were all under consideration in the selection process. In accordance with the conventional rules of evaluating teas, an evaluation committee composed of tea experts evaluated the "eight main factors" and the "two main characteristics relating to appearance." *Bi Yu Chun* received 101 points, which is beyond all grades, making it the top Chinese tea. The experts acclaimed *Bi Yu Chun* for remedying the three shortcomings of Chinese green tea: not being green enough; having a bitter, astringent taste; and inability to withstand the steeping process well. Based on this alone, *Bi Yu Chun* has surpassed the highest world standards in the production of tea. Thus, *Bi Yu Chun* is praised as being the foremost of all Chinese teas.

On August 23, 1989, an evaluation meeting was convened in Beijing to evaluate *Bi Yu Chun*. Chinese tea experts and famous people from all walks of life participated in that meeting. That evaluation resulted in *Bi Yu Chun* being extolled as a rare treasure in the world. More than seventy news media reported this. The Beijing news channel broadcast that meeting live. The central television station reported the *Bi Yu Chun* evaluation meeting as a news item and stated that *Bi Yu Chun* is the premier tea. *Bi Yu Chun* thereby shocked the entire country of China, and it became famous abroad as well. It was selected as the representative tea of China at the International Tea Culture Exchange Convention held in Japan. The evaluation committees of the sixty-sixth and sixty-seventh International Trading Conventions categorized *Bi Yu Chun* as a tea that should be offered to honored guests.

Not long after that, H.H. Dorje Chang Buddha III casually dipped into His limitless wisdom to develop a type oolong tea called *Ba Wang Chun*. It is a half-fermented tea with a unique flavor. It combines the fragrances of tea, coffee, and chestnuts. Its taste has the positive qualities of tea and coffee. It is rich yet simple, with a delightful fragrance. Drinking this tea can bring about loss of weight with no loss of energy. It has a refreshing, mind-clearing effect. Tea experts have acclaimed it as being the king of oolong teas, and it has become famous around the world!

H.H. Dorje Chang Buddha III was not attached to the huge successes of both *Bi Yu Chun* and *Ba Wang Chun*. For no compensation whatsoever, His Holiness disclosed the secret production technology to those two lay disciples, both of whom worked at the Chengdu Changcheng Health Care Products Factory. His Holiness also prohibited them from revealing that His Holiness was the one who disclosed such tea technology to them. What is even more laudable is that H.H. Dorje Chang Buddha III did not want one cent of the profits. His Holiness's only request was that they use part of the profits to take care of elderly people who live alone and children who are deprived of an education due to financial difficulties. Having no other choice, those two disciples used the name Dharma Master Shi Xing as the inventor of those products to show their appreciation for the teachings of H.H. Dorje Chang Buddha III and Sakyamuni Buddha.

How many people in this world truly do not care about fame and gain? Can a person like H.H. Dorje Chang Buddha III be found anywhere in the world? It would be good if even one person like His Holiness could be found. However, such a person cannot be found. Words are inadequate to describe the holy virtue and magnificence of H.H. Dorje Chang Buddha III. How could even a great Bodhisattva possess the limitless omniscience that His Holiness possesses? Such real life examples of indifference to fame and gain enable us to see the enlightenment of a true Buddha!

(This text was translated from the Chinese text that follows.)

簡　　介

　　中國曾獲最高分級的極品茗茶「碧玉春」，是多杰羌佛第三世雲高益西諾布頂聖如來智慧五明中的產物之一，三世多杰羌佛將傳統古老的製茶技藝，發揮到盡善盡美，創製出了最高級的綠茶。

　　提起創茶，這要從三世多杰羌佛的兩位弟子拜師說起。有兩位開茶廠的人來拜三世多杰羌佛為師，三世多杰羌佛問他們要學什麼，他們說：『來這裡當然要學佛法，我們是開茶廠的，但這裡又沒有茶工藝。』三世多杰羌佛說：『我這裡什麼都有，那就先教你們做茶吧。』就這樣，三世多杰羌佛在三天之內就創造了世界第一流的茗茶，教給了兩位弟子。但大家要明白，三世多杰羌佛在這之前從來就沒有做過茶，正因為佛陀的無所不能，才信手拈來舉世聞名的高級茗茶。

　　碧玉春茶，風味獨特，品格高雅，其外形緊結油亮，毫峰顯露，呈碧玉色澤，內質集毫香、熟香型於一體，具雞湯熟栗之清香，沉渾甘爽，濃郁持久，其湯色清澈明亮，呈碧玉之潤綠，如一泓瑩麗之山泉，品之回味無窮。

　　1989年6月，在中國茗茶優選會上，「碧玉春」與中華茗茶「獅峰龍井」、「洞庭碧螺春」、「君山銀針」等同登選場，按茗茶檢驗常規，其「八大因子」、「兩大質形」經茶藝專家評委會鑑評，「碧玉春」茶獲超分級壹佰零壹分，成為中國茗茶榜首。專家們驚嘆「碧玉春」茶彌補了中國綠茶不綠、茶味苦澀和不耐沖泡的三大缺陷，僅此一項就打破了製茶業的世界歷來水平，因此「碧玉春」被譽為中國茗茶之首。

　　1989年8月23日，碧玉春在北京召開鑑評會，中國茶葉界專家學者及各界知名人士參加會議，鑑評結果「碧玉春」被譽為「稀世珍品」，七十多家新聞媒體報導，北京電視台進行了現場直播，中央電視台新聞節目專門報導了碧玉春鑑評結果，碧玉春茶為茶中冠軍。

　　碧玉春茶自此震動中華，名揚海外，更代表中國參加在日本舉辦的國際茶文化交流會，被列為國際評委會六十六屆、六十七屆交易會貴賓品嚐茶。

　　不久後，三世多杰羌佛又從其無盡的智慧中隨取一撮製成烏龍茗茶「霸王春」。此茶屬半發酵茶，其味獨特，集茶味、咖啡味、栗香味於一體，兼飲茶喝咖啡之長，茶湯濃郁而淳厚，茶香撲鼻，飲之能達到減肥而不減神之功用，使人神清氣爽，被茶界專家譽為「烏龍之王」，蜚聲世界！

　　對此碧玉春、霸王春的殊譽，三世多杰羌佛無礙於心，無償地將秘技傳於成都長城保健品廠的兩位在家弟子，並告誡他們不准公布是三世多杰羌佛傳授的茶技。更令人崇敬的是，三世多杰羌佛不要分文利潤，唯一要求的是兩位弟子照顧孤寡老人及因困難而失學的兒童。無奈之下，兩位弟子只好以釋迦佛陀之教誡悟法性故，而以「釋性法師」作為產品的發明人。在這個世界上真正不在乎名利的人有多少呢？能找到如三世多杰羌佛這樣的人嗎？哪怕一個也行，可是就是找不到，三世多杰羌佛的聖德和偉大，哪裡是我們能用語言講得了的！他的無盡遍智又哪裡是什麼大菩薩能具之呢？僅這一點就讓我們活生生地看到了真正佛陀的覺格！

（此文的英文翻譯印在前面）

Bi Yu Chun is known as the foremost of Chinese famous teas.
被譽為中國名茶之首的碧玉春

Tea experts praised Ba Wang Chun as the best of all Oolong teas.
被茶界專家譽為烏龍之首的「霸王春」

CHENGDU CHANGCHENG HEALTH CARE PRODUCTS COMPANY XINFAN BRANCH

Certificate

Our company is a famous professional health care product company. "Xiongli Yufayi" (formerly called Fa Bi Sheng), the frostbite liquid "Yici Ling" (also known as Xiongli Fang Dong Yi), the green tea "Bi Yu Chun," and the Wulong tea "Ba Wang Chun" are produced by our company.

"Xiongli Yufayi" is a health care product that helps hair regrow. It was the first hair growing product ever examined and approved by the Chinese Health Ministry. It was approved in 1989.

The frostbite liquid "Yici Ling" is a powerful medicine that can cure and prevent frostbite. It has relieved many patients' pain.

The green tea "Bi Yu Chun" is the highest quality tea among Chinese famous teas. It won the unprecedented score of one hundred and one points at the Chinese Famous Tea Contest. It not only was designated as the tea for honored guests at the 67th International Trading Convention, but also was selected as the representative tea of China at the International Tea Culture Exchange Conference sponsored by Japan.

"Ba Wang Chun" is the type of Oolong tea that is semi-fermented. It has a unique taste. The tea is strong and rich. It is praised as the king of Oolong teas.

The above products were invented and developed by Master Wan Ko Yee. However, he does not have the desire to obtain fame and wealth from them. Without expecting any reward, he handed over to us the right to manufacture these products, which are beneficial to mankind. For more than ten years, the Master has not received any share of the profits from those products, nor has he allowed us to publicize that he has invented and contributed the products. His only request is to devote a share of the profits to support old people in aged care facilities and needy children who cannot get an education due to poverty. Therefore, we asked the Master, "How are we going to introduce the inventor of those products?" The Master replied, "I am a Buddhist. These products belong to Buddhism." Since the Master did not agree to use his name, we have considered this matter for a long time. We understand that Buddhism was established by Sakyamuni Buddha and to become enlightened and realize our original nature is the goal for all Buddhists. Thus, we decided to use "Dharma Master Shi Xing" as the inventor of the products.

Today, we disclose the secret to make everyone understand that the Master is selfless, always cares for others, and silently contributes to mankind. This kind of noble morality is a role model for us to emulate. The Master is our supreme holy teacher!

(Seal) Chengdu Changcheng Health Care Products Company Xinfan Branch
January 10, 2006

Address: Chengdu Xinfan
Tel: Xinfan380442
Telegram: Xinfan4918
Ch078.13.944

成都长城保健品厂新繁分厂

证　明

我厂系知名的保健品专业生产厂，"雄力育发液"（原名：发必生）、"一次灵"冻疮液（又名：雄力防冻液）、"碧玉春"绿茶、"霸王春"乌龙茶等上述产品均由我厂生产。

"雄力育发液"是脱发再生的保健品，1989年经国家卫生部审核批准为全国第一号的育发产品。

"一次灵"冻疮液是治疗和预防冷冻受伤如冻疮的特效品，为无数患者解除了痛苦。

"碧玉春"绿茶为中国名茶之首，在中国名茶优选会上荣获超级分101分，不仅被选为第67届广交会的"贵宾评尝茶"，更代表中国参加在日本举办的国际茶文化交流会。

"霸王春"乌龙茶属半发酵型茶叶，其味独特，茶汤浓郁而醇厚，被茶界专家誉为"乌龙之王"。

上述这些产品皆为义云高大师研制发明，但是，义大师从不沾名利，只是无偿地将这些造福人类的产品交由我厂生产，十几年来不取分文，也不准我厂为大师作宣传，不准公布是他贡献的，大师惟一的要求就是要我们厂照顾敬老院的孤寡老人及因困难而失学的儿童。因此，我们问义大师：该如何介绍这些产品的发明人呢？大师回答说："我是一个佛教徒，这些东西也就是佛门的东西。"既然大师不同意用他自己的名字，我们考虑很久，想到佛教是释迦牟尼佛创立的，证悟本性是佛教徒所追求的目的，因此便用"释性法师"作为这些产品的发明人。

今天，我们把这一秘密正式公开，让大家了解，大师这种毫无自私自利、一心关爱他人、默默奉献人类的崇高的道德品质是我们学习的楷模，大师是我们至高无上的圣洁师长！

成都长城保健品厂新繁分厂
二〇〇六年一月十日

地址：成都新繁　　电话：新繁380442　　电挂：新繁4918　　Ch078.13.944

新民晚报
XINMIN WANBAO 第10093号

中国名茶谁是代表

科技日报
SCIENCE AND TECHNOLOGY DAILY
1989年9月2日 星期六 己巳年八月初三 国内统一刊号 CN11—0078 代号1—97

绿茶之首 「碧玉春」

证书

授予 成都军区长城保健品厂
碧玉春牌 碧玉春

荣获四川省首届巴蜀食品节

金 奖产品称号

四川省人民政府
一九九二年九月

大众健康报

大众健康报社出版 总编辑 沈成金
第　期 1993年7月15日 总184期
国内统一刊号CN51—0075 代号61—26

名茶保

本报讯 成都军区长城保健品厂近日推出由著名佛学家云云高大师独创、被茶界专家誉为"乌龙之王"的新茶名品"霸王春"。
"霸王春"属半发酵型茶叶，其味独特，集茶味、咖啡味、糖味、香味于一体，兼饮茶、喝咖啡

证券与投资报
副刊 1993年6月5日 第三版

独秀茶道

●本报记者 赵仁贵 陈玉丰

晚报
城都
周末版
1989年8月 星期六 12
巴蜀七月十一
国内统一刊号CN51—0003
代号61—21

"碧玉春"被
将参加日本

中国社会福利茶文化交流名茶优选会
鉴赏评选委员会名茶评选结论

名茶名称	编号	总分
	1	数量不足
特级 碧玉春	2	101.5
特级 碧螺春	3	81.5
特级 西湖龙井	4	74

主办单位：中国社会福利教科文中心
代办单位：成都巴蜀茶艺术发展社
一九八九年六月二十六日

羊城晚报
YANGCHENG WANBAO
羊城晚报社出版 新编第3541号 统一刊号CN44—
1989年 10月 25 星期三
广州市区天气预报

中国食品报
ZHONGGUO SHIPIN BAO
第685期 1989年9月18日 星期一 代号81—3 统一刊号CN11—0018

潜入佛门四百余载 露出真身一鸣惊人
四川发掘出珍贵名茶"碧玉春"

448

CATEGORY 29

Technological Art

第二十九大類　科技藝術

Introduction

H.H. Dorje Chang Buddha III Wan Ko Yehse Norbu uses science and technology to design a new form of three-dimensional art. These three-dimensional images are made from machines and instruments, scientific data, light sources, temperature modulations, speed, and three-dimensional technology. When viewing the three-dimensional artistic images of H.H. Dorje Chang Buddha III, one can look very deeply into the flat surface and see things that appear very far away. There are also times when the images appear to be protruding out of the confines of the frame, like real three-dimensional hand-molded sculptures.

A second example of technological art is glass paintings by H.H. Dorje Chang Buddha III. These transparent images look like something found in a heavenly palace. They are even more spellbinding under the skillful use of lighting.

A third example of technological art is photographs by H.H. Dorje Chang Buddha III, which include scenery, people, animals, etc. These beautiful, artistic pictures taken with a camera make use of lighting, natural colors, and the skillful arrangement of objects.

H.H. Dorje Chang Buddha III Wan Ko Yeshe Norbu Holiest Tathagata combined His works in the above-described three different fields into the single category of technological art. Because of limited space, we have selected only a few representative three-dimensional images and glass paintings of H.H. Dorje Chang Buddha III. Upon our request, H.H. Dorje Chang Buddha III traveled for about a half day taking in an impromptu manner the photographs contained in this category.

(This text was translated from the Chinese text that follows.)

簡　　介

科技藝術即是採用科技和藝術而設計，通過機械儀器科學數據，光源、溫度、速度三維空間而組成的一種新型立體藝術，如整個畫面立體畫在一個平平的紙面上，可以看到很深、很遠，畫面可以飛出框外，猶如立體雕塑一樣。又如玻璃畫，雙面透澈如天庭龍宮，在燈光的配合下，迷幻舒心。又如攝影，即是照像，照風景或照人、動物等，也是通過光線、佈局、色彩而用照相機拍下來的美的藝術圖片。但是，多杰羌佛第三世雲高益西諾布頂聖如來將其在這三個不同領域裡的創作合併，而成科技藝術類。限於本書篇幅，我們僅選了三世多杰羌佛的數幅立體畫和玻璃畫作品以作代表，而本書的攝影作品則是我們邀請三世多杰羌佛利用半天的時間出遊，臨時拍攝的。

（此文的英文翻譯印在前面）

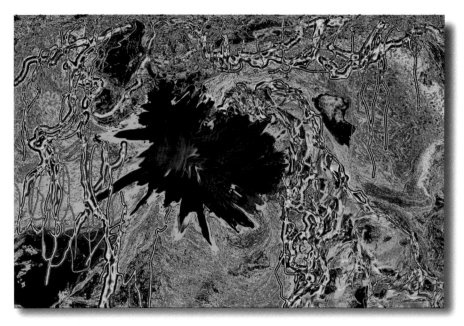

Glass Painting
玻璃畫

Glass Painting
玻璃畫

Glass Painting
玻璃畫

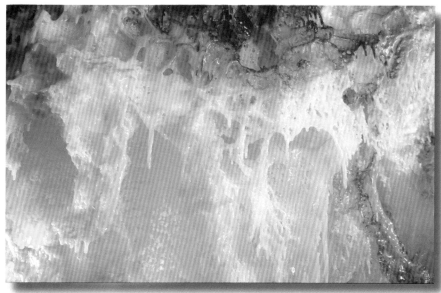

Glass Painting
玻璃畫

Glass Painting
玻璃畫

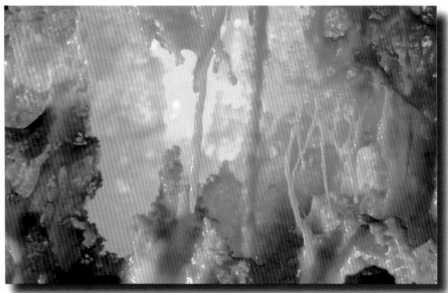

Glass Painting
玻璃畫

Glass Painting
玻璃畫

Glass Painting
玻璃畫

Glass Painting
玻璃畫

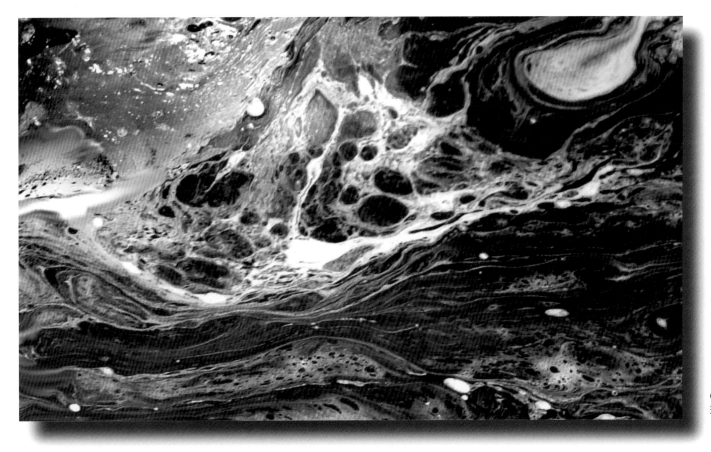

Glass Painting
玻璃畫

The three-dimensional image "Ice Cave of the Polar Bear"
立體畫「北極冰窟熊」

The three-dimensional image "Splendor in the Golden Palace"
立體畫「黃金宮韻」

A Water Spirit Soars Into the Sky 水仙飛向太空   Photograph 攝影

At Dusk the Horses Have Not Yet Returned 黃昏馬未歸   Photograph 攝影

Slowly Heading Toward Death in a Muddled Slumber, Like Withering Yellow Flowers
昏沉如黃花，在無常中凋零   Photograph 攝影

Reflections 影子
Photograph 攝影

Old and Mighty Pine 蒼風   Photograph 攝影

The Melody of Dawn 晨曦的旋律   Photograph 攝影

Expression of Joy 臉上的喜樂
Photograph 攝影

H.H. Dorje Chang Buddha III Wan Ko Yeshe Norbu's works were displayed at the "Exhibition of Three-Dimensional Images of Yun Sculptures and Hand-Sculpted Landscape Scenes" held in Los Angeles. For details on this, please see the newspaper reports that were published at that time.
多杰羌佛第三世雲高益西諾布的『韻雕暨造景藝術立體畫展』在美國洛杉磯舉行，詳見當時報紙的報導。

台灣日報 TAIWAN DAILY

台灣總社 社長 顏文閂

台灣總社社址：台北市信義路二段88號8樓・美國社址：2646 Durfee Ave., El Monte, CA 91732-3472　社長 李木通　總編輯 黃樹人

B3 2005年2月7日 星期一　　社區新聞　　No. 277

義雲高大師國際文化基金會
展出 26 幅韻雕立體畫頗獲好評

（記者林蓮華報導）義雲高大師國際文化基金會於6日(周日)下午在聖蓋博市新落成的希爾頓大飯店舉行別開生面的「韻雕暨造景藝術立體畫展」，共展出 26 幅全世界首次公開藝術家義雲高大師的韻雕立體畫、及最年輕的兩位世界級藝術家，16 歲的義恒公及 13 歲的義培珠的造景藝術立體畫，參觀立體畫展的政商文化各界人士雲集，人人見到這種新穎的 3D 立體畫，驚嘆之聲此起彼落。

義雲高的畫作「大力王尊者」曾在國際藝術拍賣市場上以 220 餘萬美元拍出全世界在世畫家的作品中價格最高者，近年義雲高大師在美國創作出前所未有的「韻雕」不但創下藝術品無法被複製歷史紀錄，韻雕作品之一「神秘石霧」的誕生，更是「氣體」史無前例在地球上被雕塑出來。

據悉，去年展出的是實景立體雕刻，由三位雕刻者以各種不同天然器材搭配組合立體實景，當初是頗具禪意的造景藝術，今年他們也是同樣以造景雕刻先作出實景，然後再以 3D 的照相機拍攝成畫作，現場觀賞時，每幅畫作都非常立體，感覺層次重疊深具透視感，比一般畫作多了一股靈性。

義雲高的畫作較偏向石乳洞或中國潑墨山水的空靈，其子 16 歲的義恒公及女兒 13 歲的義培珠畫風，除了有山水畫的立體感但搭配美國如老鷹、梅花鹿的動物，展現中西合壁的奇趣。

當日名流政要出席立體畫會並致表揚狀予義雲高大師、義恒公、義培珠三位藝術家，雖然三人無法親自受獎，故由該文化基金會會長張天佑代為領獎，計有洛杉磯郡長安東諾維奇的代表張自豪、洛杉磯韓詹士市長代表陳馬允藏、國會議員亞當斯代表、亞凱迪亞市副市長鄂志超、蒙市市長伍國慶、南艾爾蒙地市長白朗卡、加州眾議員趙美心代表、另有前白宮顧問委員會亞太裔主席祖炳民博士代表蘇順國，阿罕不拉市市長丹尼爾、南帕撒迪那市長 Mike Ten、克來蒙市議員 Peter Yao.、阿罕不拉前學區教委黃趙企晨、杜克斯大學顧問章心怡、量子大學校長盧遂顯及各社會團體的社會名流百餘名參加。

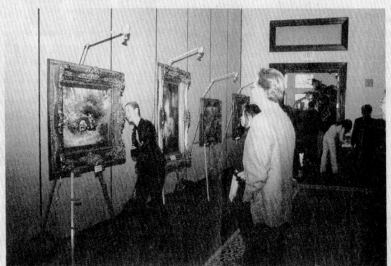

▲在場觀禮的佳賓，很好奇查看與一般厚度無異的畫作，如何展現出 3D 立體畫的多層次。　　（記者林蓮華攝）

第04599期　　・南加州地區華人國立經營中文報紙・每週三・六出報・零售25¢　　SATURDAY, JANUARY 22, 2005

CATEGORY 30

Saving Living Beings by Liberating Them

第三十大類　渡生成就

Introduction

After we at World Buddhism Publishing LLC and World Dharma Voice Inc. conducted a rigorous investigation and evaluation all of the material we had gathered, we were astounded. The realization manifested in Buddhist circles caused us to conclude that "complete proficiency in exoteric and esoteric Buddhism and perfect mastery of the Five Vidyas" had become an empty phrase. We truly could not find one person who could in practice perfectly meet each and every standard that such phrase entails. Although it was our hope as Buddhists to find such a person and although we searched diligently, our efforts ultimately came to naught.

However, in the past few years we finally found the source. We truly think that the complete proficiency of H.H. Dorje Chang Buddha III in both exoteric and esoteric Buddhism gave birth to His Holiness's perfect mastery of the Five Vidyas. The Five Vidyas are everything good in the universe. We were unable to find any person of holy virtue in history whose accomplishments in these areas were that complete and that high.

For many years, we as publishers have been searching data banks on Buddhism all over the world. The facts prove that H.H. Wan Ko Yeshe Norbu Holiest Tathagata is indeed a consummate master whose proficiency in exoteric and esoteric Buddhism and mastery of the Five Vidyas are unsurpassed. We have not yet been able to find data on any individual that indicates such individual has exceeded the high realization and accomplishments of H.H. Dorje Chang Buddha III.

After we published the original manuscripts of this book, we sent them to dharma kings, great rinpoches, and eminent monastics all over the world to seek their opinions on the book. Everyone who read it was moved to the point of being astonished. They could not repress their heartfelt admiration. They even entered a state of meditation, applied deep dharma powers, and reached a correct conclusion regarding the status of H.H. Dorje Chang Buddha III. Each of them expressed their sincere opinions through congratulatory written messages that highly praised His Holiness. We are very grateful to them.

However, to our great surprise, H.H. Wan Ko Yeshe Norbu Holiest Tathagata opposed publishing in this book numerous true examples of people of holy virtue formally acknowledging Him as their master as well as numerous true examples of holy occurrences relating to Him. H.H. Dorje Chang Buddha III said, "Do not announce to the world such things. These things are not related to cultivating oneself. I am an ordinary person. Many holy occurrences are simply the coincidental coming together of causes and conditions relating to the four great elements or the result of the joint karma of living beings. It is still unknown whose realization caused such holy occurrences." The words, conduct, and state of virtue of H.H. Dorje Chang Buddha III evoke within us extreme admiration.

However, in the end, we still put in the book several true examples that H.H. Dorje Chang Buddha III wanted removed, such as the Buddhas bestowing nectar; Great Perfection rainbow light states; Great Perfection Dharma, the practice of which results in instant realization; Selection of Karmic Affinity Initiation; and the lifting of a lotus tub at the Highest Form of Bathing the Buddha Dharma Assembly.

It is most unfortunate that H.H. Dorje Chang Buddha III insisted on taking out true examples of extremely holy dharma kings and golden throne holders formally acknowledging H.H. Dorje Chang Buddha III as their Master. As an expression of the dharma, we kept in this book only some examples of venerable ones, rinpoches, and dharma teachers formally acknowledging His Holiness as their Master. We have since come to realize that not publishing such examples was appropriate. This is because the status of H.H. Dorje Chang Buddha III Holiest Tathagata is obvious. From the lineages of each of the main sects of Buddhism and from their lineage refuge trees, we see that Dorje Chang Buddha was the original ancestor of all of Buddhism, the primordial sambhogakaya Buddha. There was no sambhogakaya Buddha before Dorje Chang Buddha.

We have included in this book examples relating to some modern eminent monastics and people of great virtue who are disciples of and who cultivate themselves under Dorje Chang Buddha. Because of their level of realization and status, they are not among the foremost disciples of Dorje Chang Buddha. To say that they are among such foremost disciples would be like calling an ordinary soldier a general or regarding a venerable one as a great Bodhisattva. Could it be that all of the disciples of Dorje Chang Buddha are only on the level of those eminent monastics and people of great virtue? Those who answer this question affirmatively are truly acting in an impure manner! How could the monastic and lay disciples of Dorje Chang Buddha included in this book be mentioned in the same breath with the five Buddhas in the five directions? The five Buddhas in the five directions are no more than representatives of all the Buddhas. Even all of the Buddhas are disciples of Dorje Chang Buddha. Comparing those disciples of Dorje Chang Buddha who are eminent monastics and people of great virtue with Amitabha Buddha and other Buddhas would be like comparing a drop of water to an ocean or a mustard seed to Mount Sumeru! Could it possibly be that this is not the case? Such disciples are totally unqualified to be compared with the Buddhas. Even though such disciples are highly regarded by people and are truly great monastics of their generation, patriarchs, or Bodhisattvas, when considering the totality of the Dorje Chang Buddha's disciples, they are actually just humble, minor disciples.

Take, for example, Shi Ji Xin, who is the dharma teacher in charge of cremations for the Baoguang Chan (Zen) Temple. That temple is one of the four major Buddhist temples in China. He wrote a written request to H.H. Dorje Chang Buddha III to become a disciple of H.H. Dorje Chang Buddha III. Although he is an ordinary monk, we have included his written request in this book because he personally witnessed numerous holy scenes demonstrating that disciples of H.H. Dorje Chang Buddha III attained liberation from the cycle of reincarnation.

We have included these people in this book simply because they have the karmic affinity to be in this book. During the time they have been disciples of H.H. Dorje Chang Buddha III, they have exhibited certain true signs, such as experiencing wisdom and good fortune, seeing their original nature, ending the cycle of birth and death, attaining control over their own living and dying, realizing wisdom through meditative concentration, turning into rainbow light and soaring away, passing on to the Western Paradise, leaving behind sariras (holy relics) after their cremation, or attaining remarkable realization. Such achievements by disciples of H.H. Dorje Chang Buddha III are too numerous to mention. However, because we did not want this book to be too thick and therefore difficult to carry around, each category only includes a limited part of the available examples. It was not possible for us to publish all of the available examples.

People live in a type of reality in which they need the testimonials of other people who live in the same generation. Such true evidence transforms their hearts. Had we not used such testimonials in *A Treasury of True Buddha-Dharma*, all of the testimonials would have come from either Buddhas or great Bodhisattvas! If such a statement is not true, then why would Buddhas, Bodhisattvas, dharma kings, and rinpoches of each of the main sects have recognized the identity of His Holiness as being H.H. Dorje Chang Buddha III Wan Ko Yeshe Norbu after they solemnly practiced the dharma, applied supernatural perception, and deeply entered the dharma realm? And why would they have recognized that His Holiness is the pre-eminent holy being in Buddhist history with the greatest proficiency in both exoteric and esoteric Buddhism and the highest, most complete mastery of the Five Vidyas?

(This text was translated from the Chinese text that follows.)

簡　介

全球佛教出版社暨世界法音出版社在經過嚴格調查審定所有蒐集的資料以後，大為震驚，佛教界裡共同的證量表顯，其顯密俱通、妙諳五明只成了口頭論調，而真正實質性的高度條款、能證到圓滿無礙的，確實沒有一人。佛教徒期盼的心願雖然在努力，但是終究是空。就在近年我們終於找到了源頭，確實認為以三世多杰羌佛雲高益西諾布頂聖如來的顯密俱通，已圓滿了登峰造極的五明，五明即是宇宙中一切美好的，在所有前輩的聖德中，找不到一個有此完整和高度的。我們多年來一直查訪世界佛教的資料庫，事實證明了雲高益西諾布頂聖如來確實是名列榜首的顯密圓通，妙諳五明的巨匠，因為目前為止還沒有找到超過三世多杰羌佛這麼高度證量成就的單人資料，為此我們首先出了初本，徵求全世界的法王和大仁波且、高僧們的見署，大家看了當下產生震驚性的感動，抑制不了內心的讚嘆，乃至入定觀照、深入功夫，得到正確結論，他們各抒己見，由衷地寫來了高度評價的祝賀，我們非常感謝。但是我們萬萬沒想到，雲高益西諾布頂聖如來反對該書中載入很多聖德拜他為師以及很多聖蹟事例，三世多杰羌說：「不要對世人宣講這些，這不是修行。我很慚愧，很多聖蹟只是偶然四大因緣和合，眾人共業，到底是誰的證量還不知道呢。」三世多杰羌佛的言行德境使我們敬佩得五體投地，但是我們最後還是從三世多杰羌佛抽走的若干條中，拿出了佛降甘露、大圓滿虹光境、大圓滿當修即證、擇緣灌頂、勝義取水等幾項放在書中，最可惜的是那些大聖法王、黃金法台聖者們拜三世多杰羌佛為師的實例，三世多杰羌佛堅決給我們取出抽掉了，只留下了他這一世的部分尊者、仁波且、法師弟子作為表法，現在想來不載上去也是應該的，因為對三世多杰羌佛雲高益西諾布頂聖如來的覺位，這是明擺著的，從各大教派的傳承及皈依境中，我們都能見到多杰羌佛是整個佛教的始祖報身古佛，在這之前沒有一個報身佛。而我們書中攝取的當今一些高僧大德拜在多杰羌佛門下修行的事例，其實這些人物的證量地位，拿來說明是多杰羌佛的上首弟子，實在是小兵作將軍，等於把尊者拿來作大菩薩，難道多杰羌佛的座下就只是這些人嗎？這實在是不淨之行舉！書中所載的出家和在家的多杰羌佛的弟子，又怎麼能和五方五佛相提並論呢？而五方五佛也無非是諸佛的代表而已，諸佛尚且是多杰羌佛的弟子，而當前的這些多杰羌佛座下的高僧與阿彌陀佛等相比，無非是大海中的一滴水，或如須彌中的芥子罷了！難道不是這樣嗎？根本就沒有資格與諸佛一提比較。這些現實中人們認為的人物，他們確是一代高僧、祖師菩薩，但是他們在多杰羌佛的座下無非是慚愧弱小的一員，如在中國四大叢林之一的寶光禪院負責茶毗的法師釋寂心，雖然他是很普通的比丘，但我們也用上去了，因為他親身經歷見到了三世多杰羌佛的弟子，了生脫死的眾多聖境。然而我們能將這些人物攝表書中，無非是他們有著這份因緣，在三世多杰羌佛門下有某些屬實的痕跡，如獲得福慧、明心見性、了生脫死、生死自由者，歷歷在目，禪定智慧、虹化飛升、往升極樂、火化舍利者，或證量顯赫者，比比皆是，但是考慮到書的篇幅過厚，不便行者攜帶，所以每一類也只取其部分，無法全部列出。因為人們生活在現實中，他們需要是同代人的寫照，以真實的證據來化浴心靈，否則現在《正法寶典》中所載的，除了佛陀們，那就是大菩薩！如果不是這樣，世界各大教派中的佛菩薩及法王、仁波且們又怎麼會那麼嚴肅修法觀照深入法界，認證出多杰羌佛第三世雲高益西諾布呢？又怎麼會認證為佛史至今顯教和密乘最通達、五明最圓滿高峰的第一巨聖呢？

（此文的英文翻譯印在前面）

Disciples of H.H. Dorje Chang Buddha III Wan Ko Yeshe Norbu Holiest Tathagata Can Be Divided into Twelve Levels

Question: Venerable Henghsing Gyatso Khu-ston brTson-'grus g.yung-drung, we know that you are the incarnation of an ancient virtuous being and that in a prior life you were one of the four most outstanding disciples of Venerable Atisha. You truly are a person of great virtue. You have suffered on behalf of living beings by prostrating more than 1,000 kilometers. Your hands and feet are scraped all over, yet you do not mind at all. You are truly remarkable. You have prostrated a longer distance than that traversed by Dharma Master Heng Sure when he performed kneeling prostrations all the way to the Temple of Ten Thousand Buddhas over ten years ago. Moreover, you made full prostrations after each step! I know that what you say during this interview will be truthful and dependable since you are a true cultivator, a famous and venerable rinpoche. I heard that there are twelve levels of disciples under H.H. Dorje Chang Buddha III Wan Ko Yeshe Norbu Holiest Tathagata. You must be in the upper tier of disciples at the first or second level.

Answer: Amitabha! H.H. Dorje Chang Buddha III Holiest Tathagata does not classify disciples into various levels or categories. Whether the disciple is holy or ordinary, H.H. Dorje Chang Buddha III will use great compassion and bodhicitta to save the disciple by teaching according to the particular circumstances and karmic conditions of the disciple. However, different grades of disciples have naturally formed as a result of their different levels of goodness and cultivation. You have referred to the first level too casually. I do not belong to the first level since I am quite ordinary. There are those who are higher than I am who are also not within the first level. The first level of disciples under my Buddha Master is composed of Buddhas. They have been Buddhas for years and years. Take a look at the congratulatory letters sent by the great Bodhisattva H.E. Tangtong Gyalpo and H.E. Dorje Rinzin Rinpoche. Then take a look at the lineage refuge tree. You will then know what is meant by the first level. Even disciples of H.H. Dorje Chang Buddha III on the second and third level are all holy beings on the level of a great Bodhisattva. Each and every one of them is the incarnation of a famous ancient being of great holiness. Everyone would know who they are if their names were mentioned. We who live in this contemporary era cannot pretend to be them.

Question: That is wonderful! Can you tell us who they are?

Answer: The first level is composed of the five Buddhas in the five directions as well as other Buddhas. The second level is composed of twelfth-stage Bodhisattvas and higher. The third level is composed of tenth-stage Bodhisattvas and higher. The fourth level is composed of fifth-stage Bodhisattvas and higher. The fifth level is composed of first through the fourth-stage Bodhisattvas. The sixth level is generally composed of those on the level of venerable ones. There are Buddhas and great Bodhisattvas among the current disciples of H.H. Dorje Chang Buddha III. For example, there are disciples of great holiness and virtue who passed the test to become a Golden Throne Holder. During those tests, which were held completely in accordance with the dharma rules, those disciples manifested true realization in front of many people. Having passed the test, they received a Golden Throne Holder certificate. Other examples of disciples are H.E. Tangtong Gyalpo Bodhisattva, who is famous in Tibet, and H.E. Denma Tsemang II Longzhi Tanpe Nyima Rinpoche, both of whom were disciples of Guru Padmasambhava. Those two are probably on the fourth or fifth level. Other people who in this lifetime have become disciples of H.H. Dorje Chang Buddha III include Venerable Dachu II Hengsheng Rinpoche, who in a prior lifetime received teachings directly from the founder of the Jueyu sect, Dangba Sangjie; Venerable Xirao Jiebu, Venerable Muya Jiongzha, and Venerable Xiangge Qiongwa, all of whom in a prior lifetime were disciples of the founder of the Nyingma sect, Master Shantaraksita. Everyone knows that they are disciples of H.H. Dorje Chang Buddha III. They should be at the fifth or sixth level of disciples. There is also Venerable Dharma Teacher Long Hui of the temple called Hua Zang Si, who is a dharma teacher on the level of a venerable one. Of course, there are other disciples of H.H. Dorje Chang Buddha III whose status is even higher. However, I cannot tell you who they are because that is a secret. Actually, many people know about this without me having to say anything. I bear responsibility for what I say based on the law of cause and effect.

Question: As far as I know, among the disciples of H.H. Dorje Chang Buddha III are dharma kings and rinpoches. There is also a non-Tibetan Chinese Geshe. Great Dharma Teacher Qingding was also a disciple. Can they be called fourth-level disciples?

Answer: As I just said, the first level is composed of Buddhas. Those on the level of a Golden Throne Holder or dharma king belong to the second or third level of disciples under H.H. Dorje Chang Buddha III. Dharma Teacher Qing Ding only belongs to the sixth or seventh level. To be within the sixth level of disciples under my most venerable Buddha Master is something remarkable. One must have true realization and high morals. Such a person is surely an eminent monastic or a greatly virtuous practitioner. Take, for example, Venerable Akou Lamo Rinpoche and H.E. Gar Tongstan IV.

They were able to lift an over 4,000-pound lotus tub used to bathe the Buddha. Still, they are only on the fourth or fifth level of disciples under

H.H. Dorje Chang Buddha III. Those disciples who are relatively low have not attained the realization in which all greed for money is cut off. It is out of the question for those who do not have true realization to rise to the mid-level of disciples under H.H. Dorje Chang Buddha III. No matter how much such a person may brag of himself, without true realization he is just making false claims.

Question: Then, should all the lay disciples be classified as belonging to the lowest levels?

Answer: That is not the concept at all. Their level will be determined by the Three Branches of Yinming (Logical Reasoning). It is not a matter of empty talk. Their level is determined by examining their direct awareness and their reasoning. Lay disciples are equal to everyone else in that they must show their realization for all to see and for seven witnessing masters to see. Their different levels result from differences in knowledge and realization. Many lay disciples of H.H. Dorje Chang Buddha III have attained very high accomplishment in the dharma. Aren't there lay disciples who have passed away in the cross-legged posture while in total control over their own death? Aren't there lay disciples whose body emitted light after their death? Aren't there lay disciples who left behind sariras (holy relics) after their cremation? Cultivation emphasizes real accomplishment. Boasting about oneself is of no use.

Question: We heard that there are some persons of great virtue who claim that they represent H.H. Dorje Chang Buddha in transmitting dharma and accepting disciples. Do they truly have such rights?

Answer: Of course, there is such a right. If you want to represent H.H. Dorje Chang Buddha III in expounding the dharma, you must be on the first level of disciples. That is, only a Buddha has that right. Even Mahasattvas on the second level of disciples fall short of the right to represent H.H. Dorje Chang Buddha III in expounding dharma. That is

because they are not Buddhas. Thus, no matter who the person is, if that person is not a Buddha yet claims the right to represent H.H. Dorje Chang Buddha III, then that person is a fraud. You can see that even great Bodhisattvas do not have the right to represent H.H. Dorje Chang Buddha III.

Question: Rinpoche, forgive me for asking a question I should not ask, but to which level do you belong?

Answer: Me? At most I belong to one of the lowest levels. I am a very ordinary rinpoche.

Question: Being so modest, you are truly amazing. We know that you sat in meditation for twenty-two days without eating and drinking–that was not something an ordinary person can do. Moreover, you are the incarnation of one of the four most outstanding disciples of Venerable Atisha. You are a great rinpoche, a venerable one.

Answer: Amitabha! I am quite lacking. I am an ordinary person.

Question: Thank you very much for accepting this interview.

Answer: You are welcome, you are welcome.

Interviewee: Venerable Khu-ston brTson-'grus g. yung-drung V
Henghsing Gyatso Rinpoche
Interviewer: Huei-Chin Yang

(This text was translated from the Chinese text that follows.)

頂聖如來多杰羌佛第三世雲高益西諾布的弟子可列十二類

問：恒性嘉措‧庫頓尊哲雍仲尊者，我們知道您是一位古德，是阿底峽尊者的四大高峰弟子之一，您是一個真大德，代眾生受苦，長頭禮拜一千多公里，手腳都磨破了，在所不惜，真不簡單，比十幾年前拜萬佛城的恆實法師還要拜的長，而且是一步一五體投地的大禮拜啊！能採訪您這位真修行人，我相信你這位著名尊者的仁波且說的話是最實在的。聽說多杰羌佛第三世雲高益西諾布頂聖如來座下有十二類弟子，您一定是列入第一、二流的上等弟子吧？

答：阿彌陀佛！三世多杰羌佛頂聖如來並沒有將弟子分成幾類，對所有的聖凡兩眾，三世多杰羌都是以大慈悲，施菩提之心，應機教化，隨緣而渡。但是，因為眾生的善根和修行的層次而自然形成了等級之差。你把第一流說得太簡單了。我不是第一流的弟子，很慚愧，比我高的也不是第一流的弟子。我佛陀上師座下第一類的弟子，是佛陀們，他們若干年就是佛陀了，你去看一下唐東迦波大菩薩和多杰仁增仁波且的賀信，再看傳承皈依境，你就知道什麼叫第一流了。至於三世多杰羌座下第二、三類的弟子，也都是大菩薩級別的聖者，他們沒有一個不是著名的古德，一提到他們，大家都知道，是現代人冒充不了的。

問：太好了！今天我們有機會知道他們是什麼名字嗎？

答：第一流的是五方五佛等佛陀們，第二流的是十二地以上的菩薩，第三流的是十地以上的菩薩，第四流的是五地以上的菩薩，第五流的是登地以上的菩薩，第六流的大概是Venerable級別的尊者們。三世多杰羌佛的弟子有佛陀、大菩薩，就是現在的弟子也有，如確實有依照法義，在眾人面前展現實際證量，考上黃金法台、領到黃金法台證書的大聖德。又比如蓮花生大師的弟子、西藏著名的唐東迦波菩薩，丹瑪・翟芒尊者二世隆智・丹貝尼瑪仁波且，他們大概屬於第四或者第五流。覺域派的創始人當巴桑結的直接傳人第二達楚尊者恒生仁波且，寧瑪派創始人釋伽炯乃大師的弟子喜饒杰布尊者、木雅迥扎尊者和香格瓊哇尊者，他們這一生轉世就是三世多杰羌的弟子，這是盡人皆知的，他們應該是第五或者第六類的弟子。還有像華藏寺的隆慧法師，她就是尊者級的法師。當然，還有更高的等位並且也是三世多杰羌佛的弟子的，只是我不能告訴你。這算一個秘密吧，其實我不說，有很多人都會知道的。我說的話我會負因果責任的。

問：我知道有法王和仁波且，還有一位漢人格西，有一位清定大法師，他們算得了第四流嗎？

答：除了前面所說的第一流的佛陀們，黃金法台、法王等級的能列入三世多杰羌第二、三流的弟子，清定法師只能列入六或七流。作為我至尊的佛陀上師的弟子，能站在六流的位置上已經是不簡單了，是必須要有實證道德境界的，一定是高僧大德。像阿寇拉摩仁波且和第四世祿東贊尊者，能提起四千多磅的浴佛蓮池，他們才是三世多杰羌佛的四、五流的弟子。斷絕金錢貪念，這種證量是那些比較低的弟子做不到的。沒有真正的證量是談不上在三世多杰羌的弟子中登中流地位的，無論他自己怎麼吹噓都是冒稱的。

問：那居士弟子只能列入最後面吧？

答：完全不是這個概念，列出幾流水平是要以因明三支論確立的，不能空談，從現量、比量中審量獲得，居士也一樣平等，要拿證量來看，大家看、七師看，只看學識證量證境的差別。三世多杰羌佛有很多的居士弟子都達到了很高的成就，不是有坐化圓寂生死自由的嗎？有的還化光、出舍利嗎？修行是要講實際成就的，虛吹沒有用。

問：我們知道，有些大德說他代表三世多杰羌佛傳法、收徒，真正有這個權嗎？

答：當然有這個權。要代表三世多杰羌佛說法，唯一只有第一流的弟子，也就是佛陀們才可以。第二流的弟子儘管是大摩訶薩，他們代表三世多杰羌佛說法都是要打折扣的，因為畢竟不是佛陀嘛。除此之外，無論什麼人講這個話，只能是騙人的。可想而知，大菩薩都無權代表。

問：仁波且，非常對不起，我們問一個不該問的問題，您是第幾流呢？

答：我嗎，最多算一個最底等級吧，是一個非常普通的仁波且。

問：您如此謙遜，真了不起。就憑我們知道您不吃不喝禪定二十二天，這就不是普通人了，更何況您是阿底峽尊者的四大高峰弟子之一，是大仁波且、尊者啊。

答：阿彌陀佛！我很差，很差，慚愧。

問：非常謝謝您今天接受我們採訪。

答：不客氣，不客氣。

被採訪人：庫頓尊哲雍仲尊者第五世
　　　　　恒性嘉措仁波且

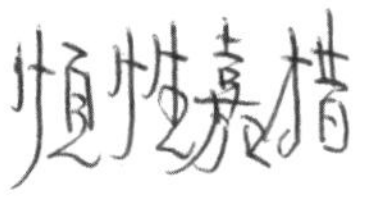

採訪人：楊慧君

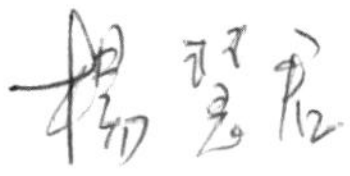

（此文的英文翻譯印在前面）

Some Disciples of H.H. Dorje Chang Buddha III

The disciples of H.H. Dorje Chang Buddha III are very numerous. Among them there are great Mahasattvas as well as ordinary living beings. However, based on the karmic conditions of living beings, the status of some disciples, and the rules of the profound esoteric dharma, not each and every disciple can be listed in this book. We hope you will understand. Disciples introduced in this category are only a portion of those disciples of H.H. Dorje Chang Buddha III who are on the level of dharma kings, venerable ones, rinpoches, and great dharma teachers. One example is H.E. Tangtong Gyalpo. In a prior life, he was the highest dharma king in India, Bhutan, Sikkim, Mongolia, and Eastern Tibet. Another example is H.E. Gar Tongstan IV Ciren Gyatso Rinpoche. In a prior life, he was the prime minister to the Tibetan King Songtsan Gampo. He is now a dharma king. A third example is the incarnation of Venerable Muya Jiongzha, who was one of the four great disciples of Patriarch Shantaraksita. That venerable one is now the dharma king of the Mahayana Dharma Wheel Monastery in Qinghai. He is the third one to hold that position. However, there are disciples of H.H. Dorje Chang Buddha III not listed in this book whose level of realization is higher than that of those listed in this book. For instance, there is elder Dharma King Mohe, who is over 120 years old. His realization and practice is exceedingly high. Two other examples are great Bodhisattvas, one of whom is the incarnation of Sariputra and the other of whom is the incarnation of Patriarch Shantaraksita. Such disciples are dharma kings and rinpoches of great holiness with the title of H.H. who can perform the holy form of inner-tantric initiation. All of the disciples listed below follow the teachings of H.H. Dorje Chang Buddha III. They all spread the dharma in different places and in accordance with their own different karmic conditions. Although their levels of cultivation and learning differ, they all have their own realization and can perform different initiations and dharma transmissions.

Some of those disciples have the ability to perform certain inner-tantric initiations. However, they can only perform the ordinary form of inner-tantric initiations rather than the holy form of inner-tantric initiations. Although they do not yet have the ability to perform the holy form of inner-tantric initiations, which is rare, some of them have already received a Certificate to Learn the Rituals of the Holy Form of Inner-Tantric Initiation and are in the process of learning. If one day in the future their practice succeeds, they will be tested in front of others. There will be seven monastics and ten witnesses who will be there to verify what takes place during the testing. If that disciple passes the test by successfully attaining the inner-tantric mandala state and is thereby qualified to perform the holy form of inner-tantric initiations, the seven monastics and ten witnesses present during the testing will sign a certificate to that effect. The dharma king of great holiness who conducted the test will stamp his seal onto the certificate and present the disciple with that certificate affirming that the disciple is qualified to perform the holy form of inner-tantric initiations! The disciple will then become a true master of inner-tantric initiations who can formally ascend the platform and in accordance with the dharma perform authentic inner-tantric initiations and dharma transmissions in their holy form. At that time, when the disciple performs an inner-tantric initiation and dharma transmission in their holy form, the dharma requires that the student receiving the initiation and dharma go through the door of the holy form of inner-tantra and enter the inner-tantric mandala.

(This text was translated from the Chinese text that follows.)

三世多杰羌佛的部份弟子

三世多杰羌佛的弟子非常多，既有大摩訶薩，也有普通的眾生。但是，基於眾生的因緣、有些弟子所處的身份以及甚深密法的規定，不能一一將他們列入書中，望能諒解。本類所介紹的僅是三世多杰羌佛的弟子中屬於法王、尊者、仁波且、大法師級的弟子中的一部分，如唐東迦波曾任印度、不丹、錫金、蒙古及東藏地區的法王，又如祿東贊尊者第四世慈仁嘉措仁波且，曾是藏王松讚干布的第一王臣，現位居法王；有釋迦炯乃祖師之四大尖端弟子木雅迥扎尊者轉世，現位居青海大乘法輪寺第三任法王。但是，三世多杰羌佛的弟子中還有證量更高、能主持聖義內密灌頂、為H.H.級的大聖法王、仁波且並沒有列在本書中，如摩訶老法王今已一百二十歲，道行高深無比；又如舍利弗和釋迦炯乃祖師轉世的大菩薩。本書中排立的弟子們都秉遵三世多杰羌佛的教導，在不同的地域、隨順不同的因緣宏法利生，其修學的層次、差距雖各有長短，但均有相應的證量，執持不同的灌頂傳法。他們其中有舉行內密灌頂的，但不是屬於聖義內密灌頂，而是普義內密灌頂，對於稀有聖勝的聖義內密灌頂，儘管目前還不具備，但他們有的已經領到修學證書，正在修持進取中，一旦修成，會在公眾面前考核，由七僧十證現場印證，經考試能建立內密壇城境、具備資格者，將由現場七僧十證簽字，執法大聖法王蓋印頒給合格聖義內密灌頂證書！！！成為真正的內密灌頂大師，即可正式合法升台為弟子舉行正宗勝義內密灌頂傳法。屆時受法弟子將通過法定必須經過的聖義內密門，進入內密壇城，受灌頂而學法。

（此文的英文翻譯在上面）

Brief Introduction to Great Bodhisattva H.E. Tangtong Gyalpo Bodhisattva

H.E. Tangtong Gyalpo is a greatly accomplished person within Tibetan esoteric Buddhism who attained the rainbow body. He is a great Bodhisattva known and respected by one and all in Tibet. He is also an extremely holy person who has made huge contributions to the Tibetan people. It was this great Bodhisattva who was the father of medicine, ferryboats, bridges, and operas in Tibet. He has brought to the living beings of Tibet limitless blessings. To this day, Tibetan temples and families continue to worship H.E. Tangtong Gyalpo Bodhisattva.

The first Tangtong Gyalpo left the household life to become a monk when he was very young. He studied the sutras and treatises and became good at debating the sutras. Although he possessed the Five Vidyas, he remained modest, simple, and down-to-earth. In order to provide a model of self-cultivation, H.E. Tangtong Gyalpo followed and learned under many people of great virtue. He also engaged in solitary, quiet cultivation for a long period of time at the Eri Temple. Later, he received teachings directly from Dakini Niguma and became a person greatly accomplished in the dharma. People praised H.E. Tangtong Gyalpo with the following words: "In the vast realm of emptiness, there is a yogi who intensively studies emptiness and who is like the King of Fearlessness. His name is Tangtong Gyalpo." He has also been respectfully called Zhibai Wangxiu Tangtong Gyalpo, which means the accomplished, free and unhindered Tangtong Gyalpo!

During a certain year in history, there was a serious drought and famine in Tibet. H.E. Tangtong Gyalpo conducted a Dharma Assembly in front of the Sakyamuni Buddha statue in the Jo-khan Temple in Lhasa. At that Dharma Assembly, he wrote "A Prayer to End Famine." Many people then saw Kuan Yin Bodhisattva in the sky disseminating various grains. The famine ended not long after that. There was another time when war and chaos occurred in the Muya district of Kham in Tibet, causing people to leave their homes and wander about. H.E. Tangtong Gyalpo made a vow and wrote "A Prayer to End War and Chaos." People in that area very soon after that ended their mutual hatred and instead treated one another in a peaceful, friendly, and loving manner. There was another year when a pestilence broke out in a large area covering a religious site of the Sakya sect, causing countless deaths. The chanting of mantras and the offering of sacrifices could not end the pestilence. Thus, H.E. Tangtong Gyalpo again practiced dharma and wrote "A Prayer to End the Disaster of Illness." As a result, the pestilence disappeared forthwith.

In previous times in Tibet, it was very difficult for people to cross rivers. The river waters mercilessly took away people's lives as they attempted to cross the rivers. Thus, H.E. Tangtong Gyalpo made improvements to ferryboats and began building bridges. In that lifetime, he built fifty iron-chain bridges, sixty wooden bridges, and many temples. One of those temples was the Tangge Lakong (the Tangtong Gyalpo Temple), which was the first temple in the Derge region.

With respect to medicine, H.E. Tangtong Gyalpo established the Medicine King Temple at Jiabori in Lhasa, invented a white pill that cured all kinds of internal medical diseases, and invented a red pill that cured epidemic diseases. Thus, he became the founder of Tibetan medicine. That white pill and red pill are used in Tibetan medicine even to this very day to relieve the sufferings of living beings.

H.E. Tangtong Gyalpo Bodhisattva also wrote many Tibetan operas and established the Ache Lhamo opera troupe, the members of which acted out Tibetan historical stories through song and dance and pioneered Tibetan operas.

H.E. Tangtong Gyalpo was the supreme leader of four esoteric sects within India, Bhutan, Sikkim, Mongolia, and Eastern Tibet. He possessed teachings from many dharma lineages, the most remarkable of which were the lineage to extend one's life and the lineage to bring in wealth and change one's fortune.

Everyone in Tibet, no matter what sect he or she belonged to, believed in and practiced such lineages and scriptures. Countless disciples of H.E. Tangtong Gyalpo became accomplished in the dharma under his teachings and attained great supernatural powers, wisdom and great compassion. More than one hundred disciples of his attained the rainbow body or the transformation rainbow body. All Tibetan people know that H.E. Tangtong Gyalpo is truly a great patriarch of Tibetan esoteric Buddhism and a great Bodhisattva. Later, each time H.E. Tangtong Gyalpo incarnated into this world. He was a great patriarch who spread the dharma, liberated living beings, and pervasively benefited people.

H.E. the sixteenth Tangtong Gyalpo Bodhisattva (Thangtrul Rinpoche) took birth in Bhutan. His physical appearance resembles that of Guru Padmasambhava. Even when he sleeps, his eyes remain open. He saw H.H. Wan Ko Yeshe Norbu during a Dharma Assembly that took place in 2005 at Hua Zang Si in San Francisco, U.S.A. In a supernatural state of samadhi, he instantly saw that H.H. Dorje Chang Buddha, the highest ancient Buddha in the dharma realm, had already come to this world again. He at once formally acknowledged H.H. Dorje Chang Buddha III Wan Ko Yeshe Norbu as his master. H.H. Dorje Chang Buddha III asked him, "Did you follow and learn dharma under Guru Padmasambhava? Why have you come here?" H.E. Tangtong Gyalpo answered that he had received teachings directly from Guru Padmasambhava and from H.H. Sakya Trizin who is the nirmanakaya of Manjushri Bodhisattva. He also said that he had come to request the highest dharma in order to save living beings. H.H. Dorje Chang Buddha III immediately snapped His fingers, and a dharma bowl manifested awesome power. H.H. Dorje Chang Buddha III then accepted H.E. Tangtong Gyalpo as one of his disciples who is on the level of a great venerable one and performed an initiation for him. H.E. Tangtong Gyalpo took that dharma bowl back to his home country.

He later learned that the book *A Treasury of True Buddha-Dharma* about the H.H. Dorje Chang Buddha III Wan Ko Yeshe Norbu Holiest Tathagata was about to be published. He thereupon organized many rinpoches to practice the Kuan Yin Dharma one billion times as an offering to His Holiness Dorje Chang Buddha III. He also sent his written congratulations stating that His Holiness is the master of Buddhas, the magnificence of His Holiness is supreme and that in this world no other holy being in history can compare with His Holiness.

H.E. 唐東迦波大菩薩簡介

唐東迦波是密教佛教虹身大成就者、西藏一位家喻戶曉、人人敬奉的大菩薩,也是實際為西藏人們作出巨大貢獻的大聖人,是西藏的醫藥之父、渡船之父、橋樑之父和戲劇之父,正是這位大菩薩,給西藏的眾生帶來了無窮的福報,直到今天,西藏的寺廟和家庭都一直供奉唐東迦波菩薩。

唐東迦波從小出家,研習經論,長於經辯,具足五明,卻謙遜樸實。為表修行之法,唐東迦波又跟隨很多大德學習,並長期於鄂日寺靜修,其後更直接得到尼古瑪空行母的教授,成為大成就者。人們讚嘆說:在遼闊的空性界,鑽研空性之瑜伽師,猶如無畏王,此乃名為唐東迦波。故他又被譽稱為智白旺秀唐東迦波,意為成就自在之唐東王!

有一年西藏乾旱,飢荒成災,唐東迦波在拉薩大昭寺釋迦牟尼佛像前舉行法會,寫《消除飢荒祈請文》,很多人親眼看到觀音菩薩從空中撒下五穀,不久飢荒即解除。又一次,康藏木雅地區發生戰亂,人們流離失所,唐東迦波發願並撰寫《消除戰亂祈請文》,很快,那裡的人們消除了相互間的仇恨,而代之以和平和友愛。又有一年,薩迦道場出現大面積瘟疫,死者無數,經過誦咒、祭祀都未能消除,於是唐東迦波再次修法,撰寫《消除病災祈請文》,從而使瘟疫滅跡。

當時的西藏,人們過河艱難,很多人因過河而被江河無情地奪去了生命。因此,唐東迦波改進渡船,並進而開始建橋。他一生共建造鐵索橋50座,木橋60座,以及多座寺廟,其中德格地區最早的寺廟『唐格拉空』(唐東迦波廟)即是其中之一。

在醫藥方面,唐東迦波在拉薩賈波日創建藥王廟,發明了能治內科百病的白丸和治流行性瘟疫的紅丸等,成為藏醫藥之始祖。直到今天,藏藥中的白丸和紅丸仍然被用來解救眾生的痛苦。

唐東迦波菩薩還編寫藏戲劇本多部,成立『阿喜拉姆』劇團,以歌舞劇的形式演唱西藏的歷史故事,開創了藏戲之先河。

唐東迦波曾任印度、不丹、錫金、蒙古及東藏地區四大教派之總教主,有很多法脈傳承,其最為殊勝之傳承當推長壽及招財轉運的傳承,這些傳承及經文在藏區不分教派,人人都信受奉行。他一生也成就無數弟子,神通廣大,智慧大悲,僅得虹身或幻身成就的弟子就有一百餘人,藏族人民個個都知道唐東迦波實乃貨真價實的藏密大祖師、大菩薩。

其後,唐東迦波菩薩還每次轉世均為大祖師,弘法渡生,利益大眾。第十六世唐東迦波菩薩轉世在不丹,其身形如同蓮花生大師一樣,連睡覺也睜開眼睛。2005年在美國舊金山華藏寺法會中看到雲高益西諾布,當下在神通三昧中親眼得見,原來是法界至高怙主多杰羌佛已經再次降世,當即拜三世多杰羌佛雲高益西諾布為師。三世多杰羌佛問他:跟蓮師學法否?今來何意?唐東迦波答道:曾受蓮花生大師及文殊菩薩化身之薩迦總教主親教,今為救渡眾生求來至高大法。三世多杰羌佛當下彈指,法体威力大震,便當下收他為大尊者級的弟子並予灌頂,唐東迦波更將法体接承回國。後來,他獲悉多杰羌佛第三世雲高益西諾布頂聖如來的《正法寶典》即將出版,更組織仁波且修十億遍觀音法以作供養,並寫祝賀以說明其偉大是至高無上、是前無古聖可比的佛陀們的上師。

H.E. Queji Jiangyang Qingzhen
H.E. 卻吉降養清眞尊者

H.E. Queji Jiangyang Qingzhen was a disciple of H.H. Dorje Chang Buddha III who truly manifested realization. This Sakya rinpoche of great holiness had white hair and a youthful complexion. His silver beard extended below his belly, and a heavenly eye opened between his eyebrows. Through his practice he attained the state in which his whole body was semi-transparent. Thus, his three channels and five chakras could be vaguely seen. He realized a state of true longevity equal to that of heaven. The rinpoche was able to fly through the air, coming and going anywhere with total ease and control. When he received from H.H. Dorje Chang Buddha III an inner-tantric initiation in the holy form called Drawing Lots From a Golden Vase, the lot landed upon the Xian Liang Great Perfection mandala. The Buddha Master transmitted to him the Lion Vajra Dharma and the highest great dharma called the Xian Liang Great Perfection Dharma. Right then and there H.E. Queji Jiangyang Qingzhen realized the rainbow-body perfection state.

　　卻吉降養清眞尊者是三世多杰羌佛的弟子中實顯證量的弟子，為薩迦派大聖仁波且，鶴髮童顏，銀鬚過肚，眉間天眼化現，修得全身呈半透明狀，隱見三脈五輪，實乃與天同壽之身，於空中飛行來去自如。在接受三世多杰羌佛的勝義內密灌頂金瓶掣籤時，投花於現量大圓滿壇城，佛陀上師傳以獅子金剛法、現量大圓滿至高大法，當下證得虹身圓滿境。

H.E. Venerable Gar Tongstan IV Dharma King Ciren Gyatso
H.E. 祿東贊尊者第四世慈仁嘉措法王

H.E. Dharma King Ciren Gyatso Venerable Gar Tongstan IV is a dharma king over seventy years old. At the Highest Form of Bathing the Buddha Dharma Assembly, he and venerable Akou Lamo Rinpoche manifested their realization powers. Venerable Akou Lamo Rinpoche is one of the five great female rinpoches in Tibetan esoteric Buddhism. Together they lifted a more than four-thousand-pound lotus tub used to bathe a statue of the Buddha, pouring water from that tub into another tub used to bathe celestial beings. Before they did that, fourteen strong young men used all of their strength to lift that tub but could not move it in the slightest. Many different international media reported that event, praising those two. The first H.E. Gar Tongstan was the prime minister to the Tibetan King Songtsan Gampo, who unified Tibet and was called the father of Buddhism in Tibet. The first H.E. Gar Tongstan was also the emissary sent to Changan to bring Princess Wen Cheng to Tibet. It was his karma in this lifetime to once again make a long journey, this time through the clouds and over the ocean to bring to the western part of the United States Princess Geyi Shirong and another dharma king of great holiness so that they could propagate the dharma and benefit living beings in the West. The karmic conditions were wonderful. He derived the same merits from both events. Through true cultivation, H.E. Dharma King Ciren Gyatso Venerable Gar Tongstan IV has attained true realization but maintains constant modesty. He has realized the prajna (wisdom) of emptiness and is able to evoke the dharma protecting deities in the universe. That is why he was the vajra master who performed dharma by drawing lots at the Drawing Lots From a Golden Vase Ceremony held by the International Buddhism Sangha Association. When H.H. Dorje Chang Buddha III performed for him a holy form of inner-tantric initiation called Drawing Lots From a Golden Vase and Casting a Lot Upon a Mandala, the lot landed on the Xian Liang Great Perfection mandala. Within one hour from the time he received the Xian Liang Great Perfection Initiation, he personally saw the rainbow light state. Every day since that time he enters that wonderful and holy state. At a test of one's ability to perform a holy form of inner-tantric initiation, although he was not able to establish a sand mandala through a stone that separated him and the sand, he nonetheless has clearly demonstrated his power to telekinetically make a vajra pill move around. He has now obtained the qualification to learn the holy form of inner-tantric initiation. He is the dharma king of Hua Zang Si, the second one to hold that position.

　　年逾七旬的慈仁嘉措法王‧祿東贊尊者第四世，在勝義浴佛法會上與藏密五大女活佛之一的阿寇拉摩仁波且兩人展現道力，將四千多磅重的浴佛蓮池抬起，倒進浴天池，而十四位年輕力壯的男士同時用盡全力抬卻紋絲不動，國際媒體多有傳頌。祿東贊尊者第一世乃是統一西藏、被稱為西藏佛教之父的藏王松贊干布的丞相，是到長安迎娶文成公主的使者。這一世因果使然，他竟然又穿雲障越海洋迎接隔衣視容公主等巨德法王赴美西宏法，利樂有情，因緣殊勝，兩進同功。尊者實修實證，虛懷若谷，證般若空性，能感召三洲護法，所以成為國際佛教僧尼總會舉行金瓶掣籤的掣籤金剛執法師。在三世多杰羌佛為他金瓶掣籤投花壇城聖義內密灌頂時，投花於現量大圓滿壇城，灌頂當下一小時內便親見虹光境界，此後每日皆入殊勝聖境。印證聖義內密灌頂時，雖未能隔石建壇，但是已能明證大動金剛力，現已獲資格修學聖義內密灌頂，目前位居華藏寺第二任法王。

H.E. Kaichu Rinpoche
H.E. 開初仁波且

H.E. Kaichu Rinpoche, a very loyal disciple of H.H. Dorje Chang Buddha III, cultivates himself with a pure heart in accordance with the dharma. He was recognized by Dharma King Mohe as the reincarnation of a rinpoche. He attained accomplishment in the dharma faster than and his realization is higher than all of the venerable ones and rinpoches who knelt to receive a cutting-hair initiation from H.H. Dorje Chang Buddha III. He has lived with Dharma King Mohe for a long period of time and has followed that dharma king for over eight years. He always regards Buddhist matters as his first priority. He underwent many tests, both open and secret, and showed tremendous sincerity. Due to holy karmic conditions in following elder Dharma King Mohe, his merit matured. He was finally able to receive from H.H. Dorje Chang Buddha III a holy form of inner-tantric initiation called Xian Liang Great Perfection Initiation and Casting of Lots Upon a Mandala. At that initiation, he attained the rainbow-body dharma state within one hour. He thereby attained rapid realization and accomplishment that had never been heard of before.

　　開初仁波且是一位非常忠心於三世多杰羌佛如法清淨修行者，是摩訶法王認證的轉世仁波且，他是在這一批跪在地上受三世多杰羌佛取髮灌頂的尊者和仁波且們中成就最快、證境最高的。他長期與摩訶法王住在一起，已跟隨了法王八年多，處處以佛事為第一，接受了明行、暗行諸多考驗，誠心無比，在摩訶老法王的聖因緣下功德成熟，終於接受了三世多杰羌佛投花壇城聖義內密『現量大圓滿』灌頂，就在一小時內，成就了虹身法境，簡直是達到聞所未聞的快捷道量成就。

H.E. Denma Tsemang Great Dedengba II
Venerable Longzhi Tanpe Nyima
H.E. 丹瑪・翟芒大德登巴第二世隆智・丹貝尼瑪尊者

Venerable Denma Tsemang was one of the twenty-five great Dedengbas under Guru Padmasambhava when Guru Padmasambhava went to Tibet to spread the dharma over one thousand years ago. He was dispatched by Sakymuni Buddha to descend into our world during the same time period Guru Padmasambhava descended into our world in order to assist Guru Padmasambhava in propagating the Buddha-dharma. According to the short biographies of Guru Padmasambhava's twenty-five greatest disciples, H.E. Denma Tsemang was skilled at transcribing texts and writing, had extraordinary wisdom, and was proficient in translating. He received many secret mantras and other dharma teachings from the great acarya, Guru Padmasambhava. He manifested wonderful realization and had very high supernatural powers, good fortune, and wisdom. He never forgot any dharma that he received, maintaining total retention of all that he learned. Most terma texts, such as the *Collection of Eight Sadhana Teachings*, were written by him. Additionally, H.E. Denma Tsemang, Bodhi Sattva, and others translated all of the sutras and treatises contained in the *Tripitaka*. In this lifetime, H.E. Longzhi Tanpe Nyima is one of the great disciples of the Holiest Tathagata. He is at the side of H.H. Dorje Chang Buddha III all year round, serving as an attendant of His Holiness. His forte in this lifetime is similar to that of his prior lifetime. He transcribes and organizes the recorded dharma discourses of H.H. Dorje Chang Buddha III. When H.H. Dorje Chang Buddha III performed for him a holy form of inner-tantric initiation called Drawing Lots From a Golden Vase and Casting a Lot, the lot landed on the mandala of Guhyapada Vajra, a great vajra being with awesome power. He then clearly demonstrated his power to telekinetically make a vajra pill move around, thereby showing the state of realization of a true reincarnated great Dedengba. However, H.E. Longzhi Tanpe Nyima simply said, "I am just a Buddhist disciple sincerely cultivating myself."

丹瑪・翟芒尊者是一千年前蓮花生大師到西藏宏法時的二十五大德登巴之一，是受釋迦佛陀派遣同期降世輔佐蓮花生大師宏揚佛法的大達登巴。根據蓮師二十五大弟子略傳的記載，丹瑪・翟芒尊者，繕寫文字，超群絕倫，精通譯事。於蓮師大阿闍黎處獲得諸多密咒教法，顯現殊勝證悟故，神通福慧甚高，獲諸法不忘，總持陀羅尼。《八教善逝總集》等大多伏藏文亦由尊者書寫。另丹瑪・翟芒與菩提薩埵等翻譯了經律論三藏的所有經論。隆智・丹貝尼瑪這一世為頂聖如來的大弟子之一，終年四季隨侍於三世多杰羌佛身邊，專長與前一世類似，記錄、整理三世多杰羌佛的法音。已能明證大動金剛力，在三世多杰羌佛為其金瓶掣籤投花聖義內密灌頂時，花投於大威神王密跡金剛壇城，當下明證大動金剛力，體顯了大德登巴的真身境界，但尊者卻說：我是一個老實修行的佛子而已。

Venerable Dharma Teacher Pu Guan
普觀大和尚

Venerable Dharma Teacher Pu Guan was a disciple of H.H. Dorje Chang Buddha III who His Holiness personally taught. He was a famous and eminent monk in China and was the 13th Patriarch of Mt. Emei. In the 1980's, the dharma teacher began renovating an ancient Buddhist temple in order to spread the true dharma of the Buddha. Dharma Teacher Pu Guan and Dharma Teacher Guo Zhang were invited to the Kaihua Temple on Mt. Wuzhong in Dayi County, which was the first stop in the spread of Buddhism southward. Under extremely difficult circumstances, they met many supporters, renovated the temple, and trained many monks. In 1998, the dharma teacher's meritorious actions were complete. He passed away in the meditation posture having attained control over his life and death. Eight years after his passing, he still sits in a stupa in that meditation posture without having rotted at all.

普觀大和尚，三世多杰羌佛雲高益西諾布頂聖如來的親傳弟子，中國著名高僧，為峨嵋山第十三代祖師。

自二十世紀八十年代起，為弘揚如來正法，重振祖庭，普觀法師與果章法師一起被禮請到佛教南傳第一站霧中山開化寺，在艱難困苦的條件下，廣結善緣，整修廟宇，培育僧材。

1998年，法師功行圓滿，生死自由而圓寂坐化，至今八年，肉身不壞盤坐塔中。

Venerable Dharma Teacher Yong Ding
永定法師

Dharma Teacher Yong Ding was a disciple of H.H. Dorje Chang Buddha III who His Holiness personally taught. His meritorious actions were outstanding, and his realization was extraordinary. He conducted himself as the ancient virtuous monks did. Dharma Teacher Yong Ding was a man of true cultivation and true realization. His good deeds and holy feats were countless, and his dharma powers were amazing. He was a widely praised individual who could communicate with the heavenly realm and the hell realm. In his youth before he became a monk, his native town experienced a great drought not seen in one hundred years. Buddhist dharma masters and Daoist adepts tried for several months to solve the drought but could not. Not a drop of water could be found in that town. Dharma Teacher Yong Ding wrote his name on a piece of paper and invoked rain to fall. The sun was blazing in the sky. About five minutes later, there was pouring rain. When the Dayi County government was building the Master Wan Ko Yee Museum in 1994, the dharma teacher consulted with the Emperor of Heaven about the weather for the upcoming three-month period. Each day, his weather forecasts were written for all to see in the mess hall at the work site. Those forecasts were not off by one bit for that entire three-month period. One time the dharma teacher lifted his hand and thereby split a tree trunk a kilometer away from him. The tree was so wide that only two people together could embrace it.

永定法師，三世多杰羌佛雲高益西諾布頂聖如來的親傳弟子，功行卓著，證量超凡，一派古德遺風。永定法師實修實證，其善行聖跡，不勝枚舉，功夫更是了得，可以上通天庭，下達地府，被人們廣為傳頌。如早年法師尚未出家時，其家鄉遭逢百年不遇大旱，佛教法師和道教煉士折騰數月無能為力，檐無滴水，永定法師簽名再請，烈日炎炎之下，五分鐘左右即下滂沱大雨。1994年大邑縣政府在修建《義雲高大師館》時，法師曾提前三個月和上帝協商天氣，工地將其每日之預報均寫在食堂，與眾觀鑒。果然，三個月內的陰晴雨雪，分秒不差。法師更曾在一公里之外，隨手一舉將兩人合抱的大樹樹幹劈開。

Venerable Dharma Teacher Yi Zhao
意昭老和尚

Venerable Dharma Teacher Yi Zhao is the successor to H.E. Dharma Master Xu Yun. He is truly a person of holy virtue within present-day Zen Buddhism. Having realized the supreme fruit of bodhi, the venerable one long ago extirpated all roots leading to his further reincarnation. In order to save living beings in the earthly realm from suffering, the elder monk emulated Ksitigarbha Bodhisattva by making the following vow: "As long as there is any living being in the earthly realm, I vow not to become a Buddha." He has been praised as being the nirmanakaya of Ksitigarbha Bodhisattva. The venerable one received a Nectar Empowerment Initiation from H.H. Dorje Chang Buddha III and was praised by H.H. Dorje Chang Buddha III as being a rare, outstanding, and enlightened monk who abides by the precepts. Above is a photograph of Venerable Dharma Teacher Yi Zhao. While he received nectar dharma empowerment from H.H. Dorje Chang Buddha III, he viewed over a million wasps that did not dare harm anyone there.

意昭老和尚承接盧雲法師之衣鉢，為當今禪門之真正聖德。老和尚早已斬斷生死之根本，證無上之菩提道果。為解救六道眾生之痛苦，老和尚以地藏王菩薩為榜樣，發願『娑婆眾生不盡，誓不成佛』，亦被讚為地藏王菩薩化身。老和尚得三世多杰羌佛甘露加持灌頂，被三世多杰羌佛讚為稀有難得的戒行開悟高僧。上面照片為意昭大和尚接受三世多杰羌佛甘露受法加持並見百萬黃蜂不敢傷人。

Venerable Elder Monk Wu Ming
悟明長老

Venerable elder monk Wu Ming is a spiritual leader of exoteric Buddhism. He currently is the honorary chairman of the World Buddhist Sangha Council. Venerable Wu Ming has been a monk for 83 years. Throughout his entire life, he has strictly observed the precepts and cultivated himself in a practical and thorough manner. His fundamental practice is the Kuan Yin Dharma, which he has penetrated deeply. He has edified countless people and is praised as "the incarnation of Kuan Yin Bodhisattva in Taiwan." At a Buddhas Bestow Nectar Empowerment Initiation conducted by H.H. Dorje Chang Buddha III, venerable Wu Ming manifested his two-face and two-arm nirmanakaya form. This revealed that he is a holy monk who is the incarnation of a Bodhisattva. Above is a photograph of venerable Wu Ming. After he knelt in front of H.H. Dorje Chang Buddha III, His Holiness performed a nectar dharma empowerment for him.

悟明長老是顯宗精神領袖，現任世界佛教僧伽會名譽主席。悟明長老出家已八十三個春秋，一生嚴守戒律，踏實修行，以觀音法門為根本，一門深入，化人無數，被讚譽為『觀世音菩薩在台灣的應化』。在三世多杰羌佛為其佛降甘露加持灌頂時，顯露化身，二面兩臂，露出他原本是菩薩應世的聖僧。上面照片為悟明長老跪拜三世多杰羌佛後，佛陀為他作甘露加持受法。

Venerable Dharma Teacher Tong Hui
通慧大和尚

Venerable Dharma Teacher Tong Hui is the abbot of the Long Ju Temple made famous by Jiangxi Mazu. He is a close disciple of H.H. Dorje Chang Buddha III from whom he has been learning dharma. He is also called Elder Monk Tong Hui. Long ago, he transcended the ordinary and entered the state of holiness. His status is that of a holy monk. There are many examples of his awesome virtue. People often see dharma protecting deities wherever he is. There is a large withered ginkgo tree at his temple that had been dead for over thirty years. After venerable Dharma Teacher Tong Hui sprinkled bodhi holy water on it, the gingko tree came back to life. In 1992, venerable Dharma Teacher Tong Hui went to Burma to respectfully receive and take back with him an image of the Buddha. The night before the dharma teacher arrived, many people in Burma suddenly dreamed that he was a golden Arhat and would soon come to Burma. The next day when he arrived in Burma, hoards of people made offerings to him. In Hinayana Buddhism, Arhats are praised in the same way that Bodhisattvas who attained the marvelous fruit of enlightenment are praised. It is clear that venerable Dharma Teacher Tong Hui is an amazing and great sage.

通慧大和尚為江西馬祖道場龍居寺的方丈，三世多杰羌佛雲高益西諾布頂聖如來的親承弟子之一，亦名通慧老和尚，跟三世多杰羌佛學法，早已超凡入聖，具聖僧資格，威德事蹟甚多，所在之處有人常見龍天護法護佑，其寺廟乾枯三十餘年的大銀杏樹，通慧大和尚灑上菩提聖水，銀杏樹枯木重生，依然復活，1992年通慧大和尚到緬甸去迎請佛像，到達的前一晚，緬甸全國上下人等突然夜夢通慧大和尚即是金身羅漢即將駕臨緬甸，翌日全國上下人山人海地來供養大和尚，在小乘中，他們稱羅漢猶如稱妙覺菩薩，可見通慧大和尚是如此了不起的大聖者。

Venerable Dharma Teacher Guo Zhang
果章法師

Venerable Dharma Teacher Guo Zhang is a famous and eminent monk in China. In his youth, the dharma teacher left the household life and became a monk on Mt. Emei, which is one of the four famous mountains in China connected with Buddhism. In his middle age, he went to Kangding and formally acknowledged H.H. Dorje Chang Buddha III as his root vajra Master. He later held the position of abbot of the Jiulaodong Monastery on Mt. Emei. The dharma teacher strictly abides by the precepts of Buddhism, and his realization is profound. He is able to subdue beasts that live in the mountains. He is also able to hear the words of beings in the heavenly realm. Although the dharma teacher is ninety-four years old, he still does not avoid hard work. He undertakes the task of propagating the dharma and benefiting living beings. He is currently the abbot of the Jiewang Monastery on Mt. Wuzhong. When the dharma teacher spoke of H.H. Dorje Chang Buddha III in 2004, he cried tears of compassion. On behalf of all living beings, he sincerely beseeched His Holiness as follows: "Great Dharma King, I, your disciple, miss you. Living beings need you." The dharma teacher sent the video in which he spoke those words to H.H. Dorje Chang Buddha III, who was then on the other side of the Pacific Ocean. During the filming of that video, the dharma teacher was moved by compassion and practiced a holy dharma in order to repay the kindness of his H.H. Dorje Chang Buddha III. Suddenly, his body emitted red light.

果章法師，中國著名高僧。法師幼年即在中國四大佛教名山之一的峨嵋山出家，中年時赴康定拜頂聖如來三世多杰羌佛雲高益西諾布為根本金剛上師，後任峨嵋山九老洞住持。法師戒行嚴謹，證量高深，能調伏山中走獸，能聽到天人講話。法師現已94高齡，仍不捨塵勞，以弘法利生為務，現任霧中山接王寺方丈。

2004年，法師提到三世多杰羌佛還悲淚長流，代表眾生懇求頂聖如來說：『佛陀法王，弟子想念您老人家，眾生需要您老人家』，並錄影送達遠在太平洋彼岸的三世多杰羌佛。錄影時，法師在悲念感召之下，觀修聖法，以為報恩，突然身現紅光。

Venerable Dharma Teacher Qing Ding
清定法師

Venerable Dharma Teacher Qing Ding was the successor to the dharma lineage of H.E. Dharma Master Neng Hai of the Geluk sect. He had over one million disciples and was a famous monk in China. He was a greatly virtuous Han-Chinese dharma teacher of the Geluk sect. He became accomplished through practicing the Yamantaka Vajra dharma. The venerable dharma teacher was one of the disciples of H.H. Dorje Chang Buddha III who received an inner-tantric initiation. Above is a photograph of H.H. Dorje Chang Buddha III performing an initiation for Venerable Dharma Teacher Qing Ding the day His Holiness accepted him as a disciple.

清定法師黃教能海法師之法承繼承人，門下弟子上百萬之眾，為中國著名高僧，格魯巴漢人巨德，修大威德金剛成就，是三世多杰羌佛的內密灌頂弟子。上面照片為三世多杰羌佛收清定法師為徒，當天為他灌頂。

Venerable Master Long Hui
隆慧大師

Venerable Master Long Hui is the head of Hua Zang Si and the chairperson of the International Buddhism Sangha Association. She is the second incarnation of Lajian, who was a woman of great holiness and virtue. Venerable Master Long Hui has received holy-form inner-tantric initiations from H.H. Dorje Chang Buddha III and possesses deep inner-realization powers. She has manifested her Buddha-dharma inner-skills, such as when she subdued demons through practicing the True Dharma Palm. She is able to smash material objects that are far away from her, an ability that is on the same level as telekinetically awakening a vajra pill by making it tremble. Moreover, Venerable Master Long Hui has applied her realization powers to telekinetically awaken a vajra pill. She has deeply studied the teachings of the sutras and ceaselessly cultivates herself humbly. Her vows are of enormous magnitude, for she has vowed to fulfill the four great vows. She constantly carries out the six perfections (six paramitas) in the course of saving living beings and never shows off her accomplishments. She saves living beings with whom she has karmic affinity. As the abbess in charge of Hua Zang Si, she benefits living beings and propagates the dharma, such as the dharma of the esoteric, exoteric, Pure Land, and Zen schools.

隆慧大師乃華藏寺寺主、國際佛教僧尼總會主席，為大聖女德拉堅轉世第二世，受三世多杰羌佛聖義內密灌頂，內證工夫甚深，曾展顯伏魔正法掌等佛法內功，遠距離擊碎實物，與甦醒顯動金剛力有同功之境，並且運用道力展示了甦醒金剛力，深習經教。法師常以慚愧自修，發心廣大，以四弘誓願為己務，施六度萬行度有情，從不顯揚外露，施渡有緣眾生，弘揚密法、顯宗、淨土及禪修法門。現主持華藏寺弘法利生。

Venerable Hsi Jao Ken Teng Karma Palden Lodoe Rinpoche, the incarnation of Venerable Hsi Jao Seng Ge
喜饒僧格尊者轉世的
喜饒根登‧噶瑪巴登洛德仁波且

The seventeenth Karmapa of the Karma Kagyu sect, Trinley Thaye Dorje, recognized that Venerable Hsi Jao Ken Teng Karma Palden Lodoe Rinpoche is the incarnation of Xuedu Yongde, who was the chief secretary for the sixteenth Karmapa. Moreover, the ninth Mindrolling Khenchen Rinpoche affirmed that Xuedu Yongde was the reincarnation of Venerable Hsi Jao Seng Ge, who founded the Macang branch of the Kagyu sect. That is one of the most important branches within the Kagyu sect. In that last lifetime, he received all of the major and minor initiations of the sixteenth Karmapa. In his old age, he went into retreat to cultivate himself. In this lifetime, he practiced the Great Compassion Kuan Yin Dharma for a large assembly of people. He successfully invoked Buddhas, Bodhisattvas, and dharma protecting deities to descend and empower the attendees of that assembly. The illnesses of many people disappeared right then and there. When H.H. Dorje Chang Buddha III performed a holy form of inner-tantric initiation for the rinpoche, His Holiness tossed a peacock feather that flew directly into the vertex of the rinpoche's head, opening up that crown. The rinpoche is chairman of the Tibetan Buddhism Association of America. After receiving a dharma king robe from the Jiangrang Monastery, he became the first dharma king of the Kagyu Macang Monastery in San Francisco. He mainly propagates the dharma of the Macang branch of the Kagyu sect. He himself secretly practices profound Buddha-dharma transmitted to him by H.H. Dorje Chang Buddha III. Although he was not able to establish a sand mandala through a stone that separated him and the sand, he is able to thoroughly awaken a vajra pill by telekinetically making it tremble. This proves that he is the incarnation of a venerable one.

噶瑪噶舉派十七世噶瑪巴泰耶多杰認證喜饒根登‧噶瑪巴登洛德仁波且為十六世噶瑪巴時的總管喇嘛雪都永德的轉世。而第九世敏林堪欽仁波且又認證雪都永德是噶舉重要支派之一的瑪蒼派創始人喜饒僧格尊者的轉世。上一世他全盤領受十六世噶瑪巴的大小灌頂，晚年閉關修行。這一世曾聚眾修大悲心觀音法，呈請諸佛菩薩護法眾，蒞壇城加持與會信眾，當場除病者甚多。三世多杰羌佛施聖義內密灌頂投孔雀尾，直飛頭頂將其開頂。現為美國密宗總會主席，受江讓寺賜予尊者王袍，成為舊金山噶舉瑪蒼寺第一任法王，主持宏傳噶舉瑪蒼系法，而自己則密修三世多杰羌佛所傳甚深佛法。雖未能隔石建壇，但已能徹底甦醒顯動金剛力，證明了他是尊者轉世。

Venerable Yundun Duojibai V Gadu Rinpoche
運頓多吉白尊者第五世嘎堵仁波且

The first venerable Yundun Duojibai Gadu was a famous monk within the Nyingma sect of Tibetan Buddhism. He was born in the year 1284 in Genmo, southern Tibet. He received an imperial decree from an emperor of the Yuan Dynasty summoning him to the capital. There, he received an order to go to a land of drought and invoke rain. His powers were extraordinary. The first venerable Yundun Duojibai was not only a highly virtuous practitioner of the Great Perfection secret mantra division of the Nyingma lineage, he was also a lineage holder of the Karma Kagyu lineage. He was the most important disciple among the numerous disciples of the third Karmapa, receiving Buddha-dharma directly from that Karmapa. Additionally, he transmitted esoteric dharma of the Kagyu and Nyingma sects to the fourth Karmapa Great Jewel Dharma King. He taught the Buddha-dharma in the Baluo district of Bhutan and other districts. In the year 1365, the first venerable Yundun Duojibai passed away. In this lifetime, he is the fifth venerable Yundun Duojibai. Having a supremely wonderful karmic destiny in this lifetime, he received profound initiations from H.H. Dorje Chang Buddha III. He cultivates himself diligently. The venerable one has become deeply accomplished in the practice of second-level Great Perfection Dharma and attained the nirmanakaya state six years ago. He has attained the state whereby he is able to telekinetically awaken a vajra pill by making it tremble.

運頓多吉白‧嘎堵尊者，其第一世是藏傳佛教寧瑪派著名僧人，西元1284年誕生在南藏根莫，曾受元朝皇帝之詔進京，奉命去旱地求雨，功力非凡。運頓多吉白尊者除了是寧瑪派大圓滿秘訣部傳承的大德之外，也是噶瑪噶舉的傳承持有者，他是第三世噶瑪巴眾多弟子中最重要的一位，接承其佛法，並將噶舉和寧瑪派之密法傳授給予第四世大寶法王。他曾在不丹的巴羅等地區教授佛法，於西元1365年圓寂。這一世運頓多吉白尊者為第五世，得遇無上殊勝因緣，曾受三世多杰羌佛甚深灌頂，修行精進，修二次第大圓滿甚有成就，於六年前即得化身境，已醒金剛力境界。

Venerable Dachu II Hengsheng Rinpoche
達楚尊者第二世恆生仁波且

Venerable Dachu II Hengsheng Rinpoche was recognized by H.E. Dzogchen Ganor Rinpoche as being the reincarnation of a venerable one who was the direct successor to Dangba Sangjie of the Jueyu sect and who was a greatly accomplished practitioner of the rainbow body. Venerable Dachu Hengsheng II is the first person to hold the position of mandala dharani teacher at Hua Zang Si in San Francisco. He is also the president of the International Vajra Bodhi Association. The venerable one has been deeply engaged in Buddhism since childhood. He became a disciple of eminent monastics of the highest order in the world. He clearly understands the dharma of emptiness and has excellent innate faculties. The venerable one was the first person in Taiwan to take refuge in H.H. Dorje Chang Buddha III. His karmic destiny is remarkable, for he has seen a considerable number of holy occurrences while at the side of the Buddha Master. His requests to H.H. Dorje Chang Buddha III for expositions of dharma provided the karmic conditions that resulted in holy and auspicious phenomena descending from the sky, a dragon fish standing erect on the surface of water, and a nine-ring-tailed fox becoming invisible. The venerable one is humble and cautious. He has successfully practiced dharma relating to both good fortune and wisdom and possesses mandala realization. He is very much respected by many people and has realized the power to thoroughly awaken a vajra pill telekinetically. H.H. Dorje Chang Buddha III once levitated and, while suspended in the air, performed a cutting-hair initiation for venerable Dachu Hengsheng II. At that time, the stone retreat room in the mandala area turned into the image of Dorje Chang Buddha. During a holy form of inner-tantric initiation performed for the venerable one, the lot landed on the Great Perfection Longchen Nying-thik mandala. In the mandala of that initiation, he saw the earth spinning and tuoga light moving back and forth in the sky. He right then and there experienced his original nature.

達楚尊者第二世恆生仁波且由佐欽噶諾仁波且認證為覺域派當巴桑結直系傳人、虹光身大成就尊者轉世，現在是舊金山華藏寺首任壇城陀羅尼教授，國際金剛菩提總會會長，仁波且幼小深入佛門，曾拜世界第一流高僧為師，悟空性法理，根器甚佳，是三世多杰羌佛在台灣的第一位皈依弟子，因緣至上，在佛陀上師身邊見聖境頗多，如天降聖瑞，龍魚立水，狸尾隱身，皆由他請示緣起，尊者謙虛謹慎，福慧圓修，壇城證量，甚受世人敬重，徹底甦醒超金剛力。三世多杰羌佛升空離地、懸浮在空中為他作灌頂取髮時，壇場石頭關房變成了多杰羌佛。聖義內密灌頂時，投花在大圓滿龍欽寧體壇城，在壇城見到大地旋轉、虛空妥噶穿梭，當下證到心性光明。

Venerable Khu-ston brTson-'grus g.yung-drung V
Henghsing Gyatso Rinpoche
庫頓尊哲雍仲尊者第五世
恆性嘉措仁波且

In a prior life, venerable Khu-ston brTson-'grus g.yung-drung was one of the four most outstanding disciples of Atisha of the Kadampa sect. Because he wholeheartedly sought dharma personally taught by the Buddha, venerable Atisha taught him "lofty towers are all built from the ground." In this lifetime, the venerable one has suffered on behalf of living beings by making a full prostration after each step for more than 1,100 kilometers, thereby becoming a great cultivator who has prostrated a longer distance than anyone else in the history of Taiwan. His devoutness moved Kuan Yin Bodhisattva to personally appear during the course of his journey and communicate to him a holy and profound truth. The venerable one also practiced vajra meditation during which time he did not eat or drink for twenty-two days. His realization is remarkable. At a dharma assembly in which vajra power realization was tested, the venerable one was unable to make a vajra pill rise into the air and pass through a stone and was unable to establish an inner-tantric mandala through a stone. Nevertheless, on the sixty-third attempt, he finally showed his awesome powers when he telekinetically awakened a vajra pill by making it spin rapidly. He thereby demonstrated that he is the true incarnation of a venerable one. He was recognized by H.H. Dorje Chang Buddha III as the foremost disciple in the area of practicing austerities.

庫頓尊哲雍仲尊者為噶當派阿底峽尊者的四大弟子之一，由於一心想求佛陀親教之法，故爾阿底峽尊者教導其『萬丈高樓須從平地起』。尊者這一世以一步一拜叩長頭一千一百公里，代眾生受苦，成為台灣歷史上叩長頭最長的大修行者，其虔誠感召觀世音菩薩在其叩長頭禮佛拜途中，親臨顯聖告之聖意玄機。尊者並曾以金剛禪，以禪為食二十二天滴水不沾，證量顯赫，在金剛力考驗證量法會上雖無法將金剛丸升空穿牆入壁透視無阻，未能隔石建壇，但經63輪自修金剛力證量顯境，在最後一輪終於體顯威力，讓金剛丸高速旋轉，展現了尊者真身。被三世多杰羌佛認證為苦行第一弟子。

Venerable Xirao Jiebu II Tudeng Gengsang Renzhuo Rinpoche
喜饒杰布尊者第二世土登·更桑仁卓仁波且

In their prior lives, Venerable Xirao Jiebu, Venerable Muya Jiongzha, and Venerable Xiangge Qiongwa were three of the four greatest disciples of Patriarch Shantaraksita, the great patriarch who founded the Nyingma sect of Tibetan esoteric Buddhism. In that lifetime, venerable Xirao Jiebu was also a close attendant of Guru Padmasambhava. He was the foremost disciple of Patriarch Shantaraksita in the practice of meditation. Venerable Xirao Jiebu II was the first disciple that the Holiest Tathagata accepted in this lifetime. At the age of five, H.H. Dorje Chang Buddha III wrote verses in the plum blossom script style of Chinese calligraphy in which His Holiness cryptically alluded to the identity of venerable Xirao Jiebu II. Later, when the karmic conditions matured, the reincarnated identity of venerable Xijao Jiebu was recognized by two ripoches. One of them is H.E. Xiazhu Qiuyang, who is the incarnation of Naropa, a great venerable one. The other rinpoche is H.E. Dorje Rinzin. H.E. Xiazhu Qiuyang give him the dharma name Tudeng Gengsang Renzhuo. Xirao Jiebu II was also conferred the hat of a "great pandita" by the Dajiling Monastery of the Geluk sect. In 2006, he manifested his realization at Hua Zang Si in the United States when he successfully uncovered hidden dharma objects. This confirmed his status as a venerable one. Although he was not able to establish a sand mandala through a stone that separated him and the sand, he is able to telekinetically awaken a vajra pill by making it tremble.

喜饒杰布尊者與木雅迴扎尊者、香格瓊哇尊者同為藏密寧瑪巴創始人、大祖師素布切、釋伽炯乃大師之四大尖端弟子中之三位，並隨侍於蓮花生大士，喜饒杰布尊者為釋伽炯乃祖師之弟子中禪修第一。喜饒杰布尊者二世為頂聖如來這一世收的第一位入門弟子，三世多杰羌佛五歲時即寫一幅梅花篆字隱喻其身份。後來，因緣成熟，喜饒杰布尊者的轉世身份由那諾巴大尊者轉世的夏珠秋揚和多杰仁增兩位仁波且所認證，夏珠秋揚仁波且為之取法號為土登·更桑仁卓，並被格魯巴大吉嶺授以「大班智達」法帽。二零零六年，在美國華藏寺現量伏藏取藏成功。雖未能隔石建壇，但已甦醒顫動金剛力。

Venerable Daxila Rinpoche
大西拉仁波且

Venerable Daxila Rinpoche is a Dharma King of the Kagyu Xueba sect and the head of the Xiba Monastery. His cultivation and morality are pure and high, and his realization is remarkable. He has no attachment to the concept of self and to the dharma. His compassion is limitless. He is one of the close disciples of H.H. Dorje Chang Buddha III.

大西拉仁波且是噶舉雪巴派的法王，西巴寺的寺主，修行道德清高，證量顯赫，斷我法二執，慈悲無量，是三世多杰羌佛雲高益西諾布頂聖如來的親承弟子之一。

Venerable Muya Jiongzha III
Dharma King Wujin Danzeng Queji Nima
木雅迥扎尊者第三世
鄔金丹增·卻吉尼瑪法王

The first Muya Jiongzha was also a disciple of Patriarch Shantaraksita, the founder of the Nyingma sect. Among the four great disciples of Patriarch Shantaraksita, Muya Jiongzha was best at expounding the dharma of the illusory and changing nature of things. Because he had such deep good fortune and wisdom planted in the past, in this lifetime he was able to encounter supreme karmic conditions. After receiving teachings directly from H.H. Dorje Chang Buddha III, he resolutely decided to enter the order of monks. His reincarnated identity was recognized by Xiazhu Qiuyang Rinpoche, a great venerable one who is the incarnation of Patriarch Naropa. Moreover, H.E. Xiazhu Qiuyang Rinpoche tonsured Venerable Muya Jiongzha, who thereby became an ordained great lama at the Holy Mountain Auspicious Mahayana Dharma Wheel Monastery. He is highly regarded by H.E. Xiazhu Qiuyang Rinpoche. The greatly venerable Xiazhu Qiuyang Rinpoche instructed Venerable Muya Jiongzha to return to the West and benefit living beings there by spreading the dharma. He also instructed Venerable Muya Jiongzha to closely follow H.H. Dorje Chang Buddha III so that one day he may learn the Xian Liang Great Perfection Dharma, return to Qinghai and Tibet, and propagate the supreme Buddha-dharma there. H.E. Dharma King Qiuyang ordered Venerable Muya Jiongzha to his monastery, where the venerable one's state of virtue and realization was tested and verified in front of many rinpoches. Venerable Muya Jiongzha telekinetically awakened a vajra pill by making it tremble and thereby earned the dharma king crown. He was appointed by H.E. Dharma King Qiuyang as the dharma king of the Mahayana Dharma Wheel Monastery, which belongs to the Geluk sect. He is the third person to hold that position.

Venerable Xirao Jiebu, Venerable Muya Jiongzha, and Venerable Xiangge Qiongwa were three of the four most outstanding disciples under Patriarch Shantaraksita. Each one has his own strong points, and their status is equal. When tested in this lifetime, they were all able to telekinetically awaken a vajra pill, thereby demonstrating their status as venerable ones. Each one of them also has his own weaknesses. Only Xirao Zhaba, who was also one of the four most outstanding disciples under Patriarch Shantaraksita, clearly demonstrated his ability to move around a vajra pill. This showed that Xirao Zhaba is the true incarnation of a Dedengba.

Respected Bodi Wentu Rinpoche
波迪溫圖仁波且

Respected Bodi Wentu Rinoche is a Caucasian westerner and the first person to hold the position of translation teacher at Hua Zang Si. The rinpoche has read many sutra teachings. He strictly abides by the principles of cause and effect and strictly observes the precepts. He is a straightforward and honest person who devotes himself to cultivation and study and who does not shirk hard work. The rinpoche's main work involves translating material on the dharma. He has translated sutras and recorded discourses of H.H. Dorje Chang Buddha III. He has deep merit from helping westerners learn the dharma. When the rinpoche received the Karmic Selection Great Initiation from H.H. Dorje Chang Buddha III, great dharma powers manifested in the mandala. The rinpoche was astounded and repeatedly praised the supremacy and wonder of the Buddha-dharma. His body and mind underwent a sudden change, and he right then and there resolutely vowed to realize the supreme bodhi and benefit living beings. The rinpoche is able to telekinetically awaken a vajra pill.

波迪溫圖仁波且為西方白人，為舊金山華藏寺首任譯解教授。仁波且經教法義所見甚多，嚴持因果戒律，直心道場，潛心修學，不辭辛勞，主理翻譯法務，曾翻譯三世多仁羌佛之法音及經書等，為助其西方眾生學法有甚深功德。曾受三世多仁羌佛的擇緣大灌頂，壇城威力展現，仁波且大為驚駭，連呼無上佛法，奇妙甚後，頓時身心陡變，發下堅固之心，當證無上菩提利益眾生。在金剛力上已甦醒。

Venerable Xiangge Qiongwa IV
Duozha Xinxiong Rinpoche
香格瓊哇尊者第四世多扎信雄仁波且

In a prior lifetime, venerable Xiangge Qiongwa was a disciple and close attendant of Guru Padmasambhava. He was also one of the four most outstanding disciples of Patriarch Shantaraksita, the founder of the Nyingma sect. He was the foremost disciple in the area of expounding sutras. In that lifetime, venerable Muya Jiongzha and venerable Xijao Jiebu were his fellow disciples, as they are in this lifetime as well. In this lifetime, venerable Xiangge Qiongwa was a monk for many years. He is conversant in the sutras and is especially good at explaining the meaning of the dharma. He was formerly the head of a Buddhist studies institute. He is now dean of the Los Angeles Buddhist Academy. The venerable one has disciples throughout China, Hong Kong, Taiwan, and the United States. When the karmic conditions matured, H.E. Gar Tongstan IV used a vajra pill to determine that Kuei Chih Shih is the reincarnation of Xiangge Qiongwa. H.E. Gar Tongstan IV reported this to Dharma King Mohe for confirmation. Dharma King Mohe formally recognized that reincarnated identity. Venerable Xiangge Qiongwa IV is able to telekinetically awaken a vajra pill, proving that he is the true incarnation of a venerable one. The venerable one used bodhi holy water to subdue non-human demons. Moreover, he sprinkled that holy water to avoid ferocious beasts and save a group of fish.

香格瓊哇尊者過去世是蓮花生大師隨行伺候護法弟子，亦為寧瑪巴創始人釋迦炯乃祖師的四大尖端弟子之一，講習經教第一。過去世與木雅迥扎尊者、喜饒杰布尊者為同門師兄弟，這一世亦為師兄弟。尊者多年來一直現比丘相，通曉經教，善解行持法義，曾做過台灣某佛學院院長，現為美國洛杉磯佛學院院長，弟子遍及中港台美，因緣成熟，被祿東贊尊者四世轉金剛丸測出釋魁智為香格瓊哇轉世，並上報摩訶法王確認，由摩訶法王正式認證其身份。尊者在金剛力上的甦醒證明是尊者真身，曾以菩提聖水降伏非人，灑聖水避兇猛獸救群魚。

木雅迥扎尊者第一世亦為寧瑪巴創始人釋迦炯乃祖師的弟子，並且是釋迦炯乃祖師之四大高峰弟子中唯一演說幻化第一的弟子。正由於具有如此深厚的福慧資糧，這一世得遇無上因緣，親受三世多杰羌佛教化後，毅然斷髮出家。其尊者身份由那諾巴祖師轉世的夏珠秋楊仁波且認證，並由秋楊大尊者為其剃度，成為聖山吉祥大乘法輪寺的出家大喇嘛。秋楊大尊者令其在西方宏法利生，一定要緊跟古佛三世多杰羌佛學到現量大圓滿後，才再回青藏弘傳至高無上之佛法。近日為是秋楊法王命之入寺，與眾多仁波且印其證德證量，木雅迥扎尊者甦醒顫動金剛力奪得王冠，被秋楊法王任命為格魯派大乘聖山法輪寺第三任法王。

喜饒杰布、木雅迥扎、香格瓊哇三位尊者是釋迦炯乃祖師的尖端弟子，各居特長，地位平等，在這一世的考核中，都達到了甦醒金剛力，展出了尊者的身份，顯露了不同的習氣。唯獨釋迦炯乃祖師四大尖端弟子中的喜饒扎巴達到了明證金剛力，說明是德登巴的轉世真身。

Respected Zhaxi Zhuoma Rinpoche
扎西卓瑪仁波且

Among Caucasian female rinpoches, Respected Zhaxi Zhuoma Rinpoche is one of outstanding cultivation. She has realized the power to telekinetically awaken a vajra pill. In order to seek the highest dharma, in her early years she learned under Japanese, Korean, and American Buddhist masters. Still, she did not obtain the true Buddha-dharma. She went through all kinds of hardships in her search for the supreme Buddha-dharma master. Finally, she was accepted by H.H. Dorje Chang Buddha III as a disciple, deeply penetrated the Buddha-dharma, and fulfilled her wish. The rinpoche is very conversant in English material on the various dharma lineages and their history. The rinpoche has had a wide range of experiences throughout her life, such as personally seeing Buddha Vajradhara Wan Ko Yeshe Norbu Holiest Tathagata amid the clouds, hearing a vajra pill speak the dharma, seeing a vajra pill transform into rainbow light and fly away, and having a photograph of her deceased uncle shake on the palm of her hand when the consciousness of that deceased uncle was raised to a higher realm of existence.

扎西卓瑪仁波且為白人女活佛中修持傑出者，金剛力已獲證量，早年為了追求至高佛法，曾跟隨日本、韓國和美國的佛教法師們學習，但沒有得到真正的佛法。為找到至高無上的佛法上師，經過千辛萬苦，終得三世多杰羌佛收其為徒，深入法門，滿了心願。仁波且善言英文傳承法脈，一生見多識廣：如親見雲中金剛總持雲高益西諾布頂聖如來、聞金剛丸說法、見金剛丸化虹飛走、得到超渡的叔叔於掌中顫抖等。

Respected Karma Dege Gongla Rinpoche
噶瑪德格貢拉仁波且

Respected Gongla Rinpoche received from H.H. Dorje Chang Buddha III a Holy Bodhi Water Initiation and a Varja Wheel Initiation. As a result of the latter initiation, he has a mark on his chest imprinted by a vajra wheel. The rinpoche conscientiously handles many Buddhist matters. He endures insult and adversity with patience, bears heavy responsibilities, and is broad-minded. He has remarkable merit from having benefited living beings. During his practice, a "dharma wheel flower" manifested when he made a water offering. He has received the protection of the dharma protecting deities. Based upon the merit he has accumulated, he attained the power to telekinetically awaken a vajra pill, which demonstrated his status as a great rinpoche.

貢拉仁波且曾受三世多杰羌佛菩提聖水灌頂、金剛輪灌頂，授記於胸。為佛行事業兢兢業業，忍辱負重胸懷廣大，利生事業功德顯著。於修持中供杯水顯法輪花，得護法護持力。並以自身功德獲甦醒金剛力，展示了大仁波且的身份。

Respected Longzhou Rinpoche
龍舟仁波且

Respected Longzhou Rinpoche was recognized by Dharma King Mohe. He is a very hardworking person with a plain lifestyle. The rinpoche abides by the principles of cause and effect and acts according to the teachings of Buddhism. He is a humble, introspective, and conscientious person who has deeply studied the sutras. His powers are outstanding. He has demonstrated his realization powers by telekinetically awakening a vajra pill. For many years, the rinpoche has been the president of the Master Wan Ko Yee International Cultural Institute. He has earned great merit from benefiting and providing happiness to living beings. He is a great rinpoche who is the incarnation of Dorje Geshe, a person of great virtue who was famous for his supernatural powers.

龍舟仁波且由摩訶法王認證，勤勞艱苦樸素，明守因果，依教奉行，慚愧自省，兢兢業業，深研經教，功力顯著，已施展自身道力，體顯了金剛力證量，他多年來為義雲高大師國際文化基金會會長，利樂有情功德甚大，乃是以神通力著稱的大德多杰格西轉世之大仁波且。

Respected Luosang Gyatso Rinpoche
洛桑嘉措仁波且

When H.H. Dorje Chang Buddha III practiced dharma for Respected Luosang Gyatso Rinpoche fifteen years ago, the rinpoche did not see any resulting empowerment state. H.H. Dorje Chang Buddha III then told the rinpoche that He would cause the rinpoche to see a holy empowerment state within three minutes. After uttering those words, His Holiness snapped His fingers. A holy state immediately appeared before Respected Luosang Gyatso Rinpoche just as His Holiness predicted, and the rinpoche received instant empowerment. He was greatly moved by the supreme dharma of H.H. Dorje Chang Buddha III and gave rise to great bodhicitta. The rinpoche's main practice is the Four-Arm Kuan Yin Dharma. His proficiency in both Chinese and English makes him a good translator of material on the dharma. His compassion can be seen in his involvement with medical breakthroughs that save the lives of people. He served as president of the Master Wan Ko Yee International Cultural Institute for six years and has brought a considerable number of people to the true Buddha-dharma. Respected Luosang Gyatso Rinpoche has earned great merit from all that he has done.

洛桑嘉措仁波且，15年前接受三世多杰羌佛的修法時，他沒有得到加持境界出現，三世多杰羌佛便告訴他：我會讓你在三分鐘之內得見加持聖境。說完一彈指，洛桑嘉措仁波且果然當下聖境現前，頓得加持，三世多杰羌至高無上之佛法讓他感動不已，發下大菩提之心。仁波且主修四臂觀音法，精通漢英文理，善於翻譯法務，慈於醫學救人之行持，並曾任雲高大師基金會會長六年，渡生頗多，功德宏深。

Respected Luosang Danzeng Nuori Rinpoche
洛桑·丹增諾日仁波且

Respected Luosang Danzeng Nuori Rinpoche was recognized by the famous H.E. Dharma King Xiazhu Qiuyang as the incarnation of a famous person of great virtue within the Geluk sect. H.H. Dorje Chang Buddha III personally recognized H.E. Dharma King Xiazhu Qiuyang as the incarnation of Patriarch Naropa, the venerable leader of 100,000 dakinis. Respected Danzeng Nuori Rinpoche has been a disciple of H.E. Dharma King Xiazhu Qiuyang for many lifetimes. It is thus clear that his innate faculties are deep and keen. After traveling throughout Tibet and India, the rinpoche was finally able to encounter and become a disciple of H.H. Dorje Chang Buddha III. He then put his vows in writing. When he received an initiation from H.H. Dorje Chang Buddha III, the fire of his own karma was transferred onto his hand, where a hole for such karma to flow out was opened. His fingers still have the marks of that fire as a sign of the dharma.

　　洛桑·丹增諾日仁波且是夏珠秋楊法王認證的，係格魯派者名大德轉世。而二世多杰羌佛曾親自認證夏珠秋楊法王是十萬空行尊主那洛巴祖師的轉世，丹增諾日多生累世都在夏珠秋楊法王座下為徒，可見根器深厚。仁波且曾遍訪西藏及印度，終於拜在三世多杰羌佛的門下，寫下發願文書。在接受三世多杰羌佛的灌頂時，丹增諾日仁波且將其自身業火置於掌中，障業之口打開，至今指上留下痕跡法記。

Respected Losang Zhenzhu Geshe
洛桑珍珠格西

Respected Losang Zhenzhu Geshe is over eighty years old. He is the only Han-Chinese alive who has the title of larampa geshe, which is the highest academic degree in Tibetan Buddhism (from the book *Seeking Dharma in the Land of Snow* written by Jianfei Zhang and Nianqun Yang). The geshe became a Buddhist at the age of nine. In his youth he received a strict and proper Buddhist education. He followed and learned under Dharma Master Taixu and Dharma Master Fazun. Later, the geshe went to Tibet, where he sought, learned, and practiced dharma for over ten years. He has translated several Tibetan sutras and treatises on exoteric and esoteric Buddhism. Losang Zhenzhu Geshe stated, "In Tibet I received more than six hundred tantric initiations. They do not match one initiation from Dharma King Yangwo Yeshe Norbu... Over the past seventy years, I have formally visited many eminent monks, people of great virtue, great dharma kings, and great rinpoches. There is definitely no person in the world today who has the supreme realization of Dharma King Yangwo Yeshe Norbu. This is my most sincere testimonial. How could I dare speak irresponsibly and deceive living beings?" The upper photograph is Luosang Zhenzhu Geshe formally acknowledging H.H. Dorje Chang Buddha III as his master in Chengdu, Sichuan. The lower photograph is H.H. Dorje Chang Buddha III performing an initiation for disciple Luosang Zhenzhu Geshe in the United States.

　　年過八旬的洛桑珍珠格西，是唯一在世獲得藏傳佛教最高學位拉然巴格西的漢人(摘自張健飛、楊念群筆述之《雪域求法記》)。九歲皈依佛門，少年時便接受了嚴格正規的佛學教育，從太虛大師、法尊法師學習，後入西藏修學求法十數年，翻譯有數部西藏文顯密經論，他曾說：「余在西藏接受過密法灌頂六百多個，不如仰諤益西諾布大法王的一次灌頂，⋯⋯ 我七十年來拜見過若干高僧大德、大法王、大活佛，目前世界上除仰諤益西諾布大法王有此至高道量外，絕無第二人，如此鑒證於懷，豈敢戲言詆惑眾生？」上面照片為洛桑珍珠格西在四川成都拜三世多杰羌佛為師，下面照片為三世多杰羌佛在美國為弟子洛桑珍珠格西灌頂。

Lama Puti Duxi
菩提度西喇嘛

Lama Hongxi Fazang
宏西法藏喇嘛

Hongxi Fazang and Puti Duxi are Caucasian westerners who are lamas. When they were being tonsured, their hair overcame the force of razor such that the razor was unable to cut their hair. Several applications of the razor did not result in one hair being cut. A pair of wild peacocks flew down from the clouds that day and performed a graceful dance, twirling and singing in the mandala of H.H. Dorje Chang Buddha III. That was their way of congratulating the tonsuring and ordination of those two lamas. One can see from this how amazing the underlying karmic conditions were.

　　宏西法藏與菩提度西為西方白人善士之流喇嘛，在剃度時竟髮克鋼刀，剃而不斷，來回拔刀絲毫不動。是日從雲中降下野生孔雀一對，翩翩起舞，旋轉歌音於三世多杰羌佛壇城，祝賀其剃度為僧，可見因緣玄機之殊勝。

Dharma Teacher Ruo Hui
若慧法師

Dharma Teacher Miao Kong
妙空法師

Dharma Teacher Yuan Yin
圓音法師

Wujin Chilie Lama
鄔金赤烈喇嘛

Dharma Teacher Ruo Hui is the first person to hold the position of vice-abbess of Hua Zang Si in San Francisco. She previously was the dean of the Buddhist Studies Institute for nuns at the Mountain of One Thousand Buddhas. She traveled from Asia thousands of miles across the ocean to become a disciple of H.H. Dorje Chang Buddha III. She received from His Holiness the Dharma Tent Great Initiation. She also received from His Holiness a holy form of inner-tantric initiation to eliminate karma that would lead to a rebirth in hell and was the only dharma teacher at that initiation on that day who manifested a completely successful state. Dharma Teacher Ruo Hui has broad wisdom and deep knowledge of the sutras. She strictly abides by the precepts, endures insult and adversity with patience, and strictly upholds moral principles. The dharma teacher often thinks of her own faults and does not see the faults of others. She was finally able to learn the secret mantra of the highest Zen and Pure Land dharma. She has realization based on the true dharma. The fundamental principle of her life is compassion. Throughout the entire year, she constantly thinks of providing happiness to and saving living beings.

　若慧法師是舊金山華藏寺首任副住持，曾任千佛山女眾佛學院院長，不遠萬里，遠渡重洋，東駕西土，拜三世多杰羌佛門下，受法帳大灌頂、地獄取業消障聖義內密灌頂，是同壇唯一展顯圓滿境界的法師，智慧廣益，深入經藏，戒行嚴謹，忍辱自修，嚴於道德，常思己過，勿見他非，勤行法義，終見真實禪修淨土至高法門之密訣，己身已入正法之證量，慈悲為本，四時常思樂度有情為務。

Dharma Teacher Miao Kong is the first person to hold the position of teacher of dharma rituals and precepts at Hua Zang Si in San Francisco. She has deep roots of goodness, strictly abides by the precepts, and strictly carries out dharma rituals. Her understanding and views are pure and upright. She left the household life to become a Buddhist nun twice. She very much regretted having become a disciple under the wrong master at first. With tears trickling down her cheeks, she removed her Buddhist robes and returned to the secular life. However, she continued to strictly abide by the precepts and prayed day and night that she would encounter a holy monastic to be her master. The universe finally responded to her prayers, for she indeed encountered an eminent monastic. When that monastic tonsured her, the awesome power of the Buddhas manifested before her. She finally encountered the right karmic conditions. She continued to lead the pure life of a Buddhist nun, devoutly cultivated herself, and deeply penetrated the dharma. When H.H. Dorje Chang Buddha III performed an initiation for her to eliminate her karmic hindrances, she spit out luminous green water, which increased her realization and merit. Her practice improved by leaps and bounds in the span of that one day. She had an immediate awakening to the dharma, and in a short period of time attained the realization of a dharma teacher.

　妙空法師是舊金山華藏寺首任禮法教授，善根深厚，嚴持戒體，禮法嚴明，知見純正，歷兩度出家之事跡，由於誤投其師，法師悔恨緣起錯謬，潸然淚下，脫下僧袍，但嚴持戒體，日夜祈禱，望遇聖僧，終得三洲感應，高僧降臨，為其剃度時，佛之威力展現眼前，終成純正因緣，清淨僧體，如是虔修，深入法門，於三世多杰羌佛灌頂除障法，當下口中吐出碧綠色道量增益功德之水，達到了一日千里之行持快捷，頓悟法門，短暫期間，即證法師之量。

Dharma Teacher Yuan Yin has been planting seeds of goodness for a long time. She first began reciting the Diamond Sutra and opened up her understanding of the truth. She then gave up the worldly life by becoming a Buddhist nun. She cultivates herself diligently, studies hard, and pervasively benefits living beings. When her karmic conditions matured, she traveled across an ocean to become a disciple of H.H. Dorje Chang Buddha III. The dharma teacher strictly observes the precepts. She has received the four yogas, developed her wisdom, and reaped fruits from her practice of dharma. She is currently the abbess of Lien Fang Temple on Mt. Dagang in Kaohsiung, Taiwan as well as the abbess of Daoyuan Temple in Tainan, Taiwan. The dharma master traveled thousands of miles to Paraguay to propagate the true dharma. There she established the Zheng Yi Temple, which is that country's first Buddhist temple, as well as Eastern Buddhism and Culture Study and Practice Center.

　圓音法師，宿植善根，初誦金剛經，心即開悟，遂捨俗出家，勤行苦學，普利有情，因緣成熟，遠渡重洋，拜三世多杰羌佛門下，嚴持戒律，受四瑜伽，智慧開敷，修法有成。現任台灣高雄大岡山蓮峰寺及台南道源精舍住持，不遠萬里南下巴拉國南美巴拉圭開山建立金國首座佛寺正義寺，創辦東方佛教文化研修中心，弘揚正法。

Wujian Chilie Lama entered the order of monks in 1995 at the Nanhua Monastery at Shaoguan in Guangzhou, China. He founded the Xiuyuan Zen Temple. On many occasions he rose into the air and slept on the beam of his residence. Thus, he has been called "the strange monk on a beam" and ""a living Jigong." He formally acknowledged H.H. Dorje Chang Buddha III as his master in 1996. After the Buddha Master edified him and sternly reprimanded him for his strange and lowly behavior, he finally returned to practicing the true dharma and engaging in real, sincere cultivation. He received holy bodhi water, which manifested awesome power. The lama has deep realization and lives a very austere life. He is humble, compassionate, and benefits living beings.

　鄔金赤烈喇嘛1995年在廣州韶關南華寺出家，創建有修元禪院，曾多次升空臥睡房樑之上，故有樑上怪僧活濟公之稱，1996年拜三世多杰羌佛為師，佛陀恩師嚴呵其怪劣之行，予以教化，終得回歸正法，如實忠厚持，得菩提聖水，威力展現，深入道量，平日睡釘床、坐釘椅、刀凳，謙虛慈悲，利樂有情。

Dharma Teacher Guang Hsin
廣心法師

Dharma Teacher Ji Xin
寂心法師

MOST SINCERE REQUEST TO BECOME A DISCIPLE

I prostrate to the supreme Great Dharma King Yangwo Yeshe Norbu Wan Ko[1]

I am monk Shi Ji Xin. I left the household life to become a monk and cultivate myself in 1987. I am responsible for cremations at the large and famous Zen temple called Baoguang Temple in China. I handle all of the matters relating to cremation. Over many years at the Baoguang Temple, I have cremated the bodies of prominent monks and other virtuous people from the Baoguang Temple and various other temples as well as the bodies of the four types of Buddhist disciples. I have also performed cremation rituals for them. Frankly speaking, of the many people I have cremated, only very few of them were accomplished in the dharma. Even many who were universally recognized as eminent monastics were not greatly accomplished in the dharma. However, there is something extraordinary in all of this. Each disciple of His Holiness Great Dharma King Yangwo was accomplished in the dharma. There has not been one exception. During the process of cremating those disciples, wonderful states and all kinds of holy phenomena appeared. Moreover, after their cremation, those disciples left behind firm sariras (relics) and sarira flowers. Some disciples passed away in the cross-legged meditation posture having attained liberation from the cycle of birth and death, and some disciples attained control over their own living and dying.

After so many years of such personal experiences, I deeply understand that only His Holiness Great Dharma King Yangwo truly possesses the authentic and supreme Buddha-dharma. Only Your Holiness can enable me to attain great accomplishment in the dharma and enable living beings to attain liberation. Therefore, with utmost sincerity, I prostrate to the most venerable Great Dharma King Yangwo Yeshe Norbu Wan Ko. I beseech His Holiness Great Dharma King to accept me as your disciple. I surely will diligently cultivate myself, propagate the dharma, and benefit living beings.

Disciple: Shi Ji Xin   Three kneels and nine bows
May 9, 2006

Dharma Teacher Guang Hsin was tonsured by H.E. Dharma King Chogye Trichen in Nepal on October 17, 1993. Many years ago he founded the Buddhist organization called Taiwan Buddhist Fellow-Cultivators Association. He later established several temples. He is the founder of the True Dharma Buddhist Institute in Taiwan, the head of organization that publishes the *Dharma Wheel Forever Turns* magazine, and the founder of the Taiwan Buddhist Ten-Thousand People Recite Buddha's Name Association. The dharma teacher has benefited living beings by spreading the dharma all over the world. In a vow that he wrote to his Great Dharma King Buddha Master, he declared where he stood as stated below. Seeing that the dharma teacher had expressed a resolute vow, H.H. Dorje Chang Buddha III allowed him to attend a nectar dharma assembly.

至誠拜師文

頂禮至高無上仰諤益西諾布雲高大法王（即三世多杰羌佛雲高益西諾布頂聖如來—本書編者注，以下同）：

我是比丘釋寂心，我從一九八七年出家修行，在中國大禪院寶光寺負責茶毗法務，往升火化所有事情都是我在處理。這麼多年來，各地寺廟、寶光寺的高僧大德、四眾弟子死後凡來寶光寺，均由我為他火化施法。說實話，在我茶毗的這麼若干人中，成就的非常少，包括很多公認為高僧的都沒有大成就。但是這裡面也有一個奇怪的現象，那就是，只要是仰諤大法王您的弟子，個個都成就，沒有一個不成就，不僅茶毗的過程境界殊勝，現各種聖像，而且還能揀到堅固子和舍利花，有坐化的，有生死自由的。

通過這麼多年來的親身經歷，我深深知道，仰諤大法王才真正擁有真正至高無上的佛法，只有您老人家才能讓我得大成就，讓眾生解脫。所以，我在此至誠頂禮至尊仰諤益西諾布雲高大法王，請求大法王收我為您老人家的弟子。弟子一定精進修行，弘法利生。

弟子：釋寂心　三跪九拜
二〇〇六年五月初九日

廣心法師於1993年10月17日在尼泊爾由秋吉崔欽法王剃度，多年前創立了佛教團體「台北佛教同修會」，而後陸續建立了數個道場，為台灣正法佛學院創辦人、法輪常轉雜誌社社長、台灣佛教萬人念佛會創辦人等，並在世界各地弘法利生。他在寫給佛陀大法王恩師的發願文中作了下面的表態。三世多杰羌佛見他已表發願決心，因此他也參加了甘露法會。

In a letter given to H.H. Great Dharma King [2], Dharma Teacher Guang Hsin stated his position with the following words: "Before my respected Dharma King Master, I sincerely vow that if one day my learning results in enlightenment, I will certainly save living beings pervasively and spread the truth to repay the kindness of my Dharma King Master. I also vow that I will not use the Buddha-dharma to swindle living beings out of their property. I vow that I will not seek worldly fame, gain, or status. I vow that I will not covet offerings from living beings or betray the training and education given to me by my respected Master. I vow that I will definitely not use the Buddha-dharma to harm living beings. The heavens above and the earth below can bear witness to these vows. If I, Disciple Guang Hsin, violate these vows, I am willing to bear the suffering of Vajra Hell...."

廣心法師在寫給大法王（即三世多杰羌佛雲高益西諾布頂聖如來—本書編者注，以下同）的信中表態說到：「法王恩師座前，誠摯發願，弟子一旦學有所成，一定普開大道渡眾生，揚輝真理報深恩，同時誓不以佛法騙取眾生財物，誓不追求世間之名利、地位，誓不貪求眾生之供養，更不背叛恩師之栽培，也絕不利用佛法傷害眾生。以上誓願，天地可鑑，弟子廣心如有違背，願遭受金剛地獄之苦。……」

I Became Accomplished by Receiving the Xian Liang Great Perfection Dharma

我獲得現量大圓滿而成就

慚愧佛弟子法號一真，被勝義黃金法台摩訶法王認証為仁波且，取法號為開初。一九九六年十二月十三日雲高益西諾布大法王傳法，十二月十三日第三世多杰羌佛恩師傳法八年多，三月後恩師舉止不可聽外面邪知邪說，妄噶不動境，大圓滿境界應無所住而生其心。

有緣承關珠師姐率領赴成都拜聖如來為師，經長期在床上入於內壇城心風明點，觀三脈五輪，微妙原因，在我耳邊開示微妙教導行，不可偏離佛之教知，我此後精進修持得入光境，白天開眼修持，光的世界就圓滿殊勝進入光境，首先看到的是金剛鏈，續而看到整個身体溶於光境當中，同樣進入，佛院恩師要弟子以中觀見道入修，進入殊勝境界世界。

秘密之修，僅於慚愧弟子心恩切，由甚為殷切恩，我二因緣法學疑，說罷劃字之內，你二因緣法學疑，說罷劃字之內，你就會証到虹身開眼，一個小時之內，你要認真敢就成，是在大圓滿境身領多，說現紅光現黃光世界，說現藍黃現一朵講謝佛院恩師自己一個人比，美妙無心境上之人，他老跪地場量非此世法，若在當下當三大成就境界，嗣之此後不外，哪裡皆能所言不虛，恩師為了利益眾生而發誓，以証定佛院恩師傳的法是至高無上必須境界，是証明佛院恩師傳的法是至高無上。

慚愧弟子為殷恩，我二因緣依法修持壇城為我最初，這是字宙最大証到虹身開眼，無論大小中，美切不記大金瓶的密法當且，就現一聲馬達界，世界母度光光其子悲或更令大慈面之在外比無心境上一大法，弟子嗣之此後，但不哪裡皆能所言不虛，我上面所說是至高無上必須境界。

此高己期盼年正於某日於看無量持法城為，今如你所願，可灌頂之法上身境，一開眼瞬界一切記是也要壇城灌頂眼，說波是佛世界，聖籤確隨着紅光，界就現一殊勝，說現黃綠色為主彩之殊勝，歡欣激動，慚愧弟子當時之外大，弟子慈面或更令合上一大法，見有這種學到當下言不虛，我上當恩師傳的法是至高無上。

我心裡盼二時行菩提，今天如你頂之法上境，瞬眼界一切記差，怎麼幾壇城灌頂眼，說世界光蓮美朝現藍現美朝光不勝收放射，無法再後如如提師多大，不師非為只時見，我說到沒有此成就法，慚愧弟子面說看到的真是。

些就恩在看到之無時，有一大院恩希高時，是大佛院說更甚至即，開始傳法，無一記！法，需均無切會十頂眼法黃就，有一大叩天殊成願高羌滿場整告之說，我當大如圓當必就佛魔育內而過弟子看到的真是。

不虛，我是七十五歲的老人，不會說假話騙人，而遭到惡報，墮在地獄中，我要成就，我要解脫輪迴，我今天講的是真話，如是假話，當然墮地獄，但是佛陀恩師教我怎樣修的，我不能講，我更不會收弟子，我從內心只有感恩我的佛陀恩師，感恩一切諸佛菩薩。

慚愧佛弟子　開初
二○○七年十二月二十一日

I am an ordinary Buddhist disciple whose dharma name is Yizhen. I was recognized as a rinpoche by Dharma King Mohe, who is a Golden Throne Holder in the holy sense. He gave me the dharma name Kaichu. On December 13, 1996, I went to Chengdu on a trip led by Sister Chu Kuan and formally acknowledged H.H. Dorje Chang Buddha III Wan Ko Yeshe Norbu as my master. There, my Buddha Master transmitted dharma to me. Since then I have been following my Buddha Master. I have also been at the side of Dharma King Mohe for over eight years, even sleeping beside and below the bed of Dharma King Mohe.

After practicing for several months the Longchen Nying-thik Great Perfection Dharma transmitted to me by H.H. Dorje Chang Buddha III, wonderful mandala states appeared. When I closed my eyes to do my daily meditation, I saw an eye. Not understanding the cause behind it, I reported this matter to my Buddha Master. The Buddha Master spoke into my ear, giving me an exquisite discourse on the dharma. His Holiness told me that my everyday words and actions must comply with the teachings of the Buddha and must not deviate from the rules laid down by the Buddha. His Holiness also told me that I must not listen to heretical views expressed by others. After diligent practice, I was able to enter a world of light known as the Tuoga immovable state.

As I closed my eyes and practiced during daytime, this world of light gradually appeared. The first thing I saw was a vajra chain. As my practice continued, I saw the Perfect Emptiness Light and the Great Perfection State Wisdom Light. My entire body merged with those states of light. It was incomparably wonderful. When I did my daily practice at night without any lamplight, I still entered this world of light. My Buddha Master wanted me to practice "seeing the truth through the middle way" so that I would give rise to a mind that does not abide in anything. I would then be able to enter the secret practices involving the internal mandala of Heart Wind Bright Point Dharma and visualization of the three channels and five chakras.

Nonetheless, I was still somewhat worried. I, an ordinary disciple, was already quite old and very earnestly hoped for instant great accomplishment. Right when my hopes seemed unattainable, the Buddha Master saw what was in my mind. At noon on a certain day, the Buddha Master told me, "In observing you these eight years, I have seen all of what you have done. I have also seen that you are wholeheartedly loyal, that you are selfless and benefit others, and that the only thing you seek is bodhi. How rare! Kaichu, your karmic conditions have matured. Today I will transmit to you the supreme Xian Liang Great Perfection Dharma. If you practice it according to how I

teach you, your wish will be fulfilled, for you will attain instant great accomplishment."

After saying that, the Buddha Master marked the area that would serve as the mandala and proceeded with the initiation. At the very beginning, the Buddha Master gave me the following teaching: "This is the greatest and supreme dharma in the entire universe. Within one hour from the time it is transmitted, you will realize the rainbow body state. Without having to engage in further practice, you will from this point on be able to see the wonderful rainbow body dharma state during the day and night whether you close your eyes or open them. Such a state is inexhaustibly beautiful and is one with the dharmadhatu. Listen attentively as you receive this teaching. But you must remember never to violate any precept. Remember this!"

I dared not harbor any doubts. Still, I was worried that my roots of goodness were not strong enough. I wondered how I could become accomplished within one hour. Even Tibetan rinpoches of great holiness must engage in solitary cultivation for a few decades before becoming accomplished. Nonetheless, when I was transmitted the Xian Liang Great Perfection Dharma during the Highest Form of Inner-Tantric Drawing Lots From a Golden Vase and Casting a Flower Upon a Mandala Initiation, it was indeed the case that I could see the wonderful rainbow body state whether my eyes were open or closed. Moreover, that state changed as the Buddha Master continued to utter that dharma. When the Buddha Master spoke of the manifestation of a world of red light, a world of red light manifested. When the Buddha Master spoke of the manifestation of a world of yellow light, a world of yellow light manifested. When the Buddha Master spoke of the manifestation of a world of blue light, a world of blue light manifested. When the Buddha Master spoke of the manifestation of a world of Taras, a world of green light instantly manifested. The red, yellow, blue, and green worlds of light were wondrous and incredibly beautiful. There were times when my body emitted light, which was mainly red in color. That light radiated outwardly, flying out of the room one cluster after another. I cannot reveal to everyone each and every detail of that marvelous state. At that time, I, an ordinary disciple, was extremely joyous and moved. I immediately prostrated to my Buddha Master repeatedly to show my gratitude for having bestowed upon me such great compassion.

Since I received that dharma, I have practiced it many times by myself both outdoors and indoors. The states that appeared were as wonderful and tremendously beautiful as they were before. I was even more joyful than before due to the speed of such accomplishment. My mind and those states merged, and I instantly realized the state of holiness. I joyfully made a great bodhicitta vow. I vowed to diligently practice this supreme and great dharma and benefit living beings so that I may repay a tiny bit of the enormous kindness bestowed upon me by my Buddha Master.

After I prostrated last night to my respected Master, H.H. Dorje Chang Buddha III, His Holiness said, "Kaichu, what is meant by Xian Liang Great Perfection?" While kneeling, I answered, "No matter how heavy one's negative karma may be, at the time that one receives such an initiation, one will right then and there see the world of light and become accomplished. One will not need to engage in further practice. This is what is meant by Xian Liang Great Perfection Dharma." My respected Master, H.H. Dorje Chang Buddha III, then said, "I tell all practitioners that if one does not see the Buddha-land world during the initiation, then it is not the Xian Liang

Great Perfection of the Buddhas. Anyone who denies this by saying that such an initiation is a Xian Liang Great Perfection Initiation is speaking the words of a demon."

In this present world of ours, and even in the entire universe, only my most honored Master, H.H. Dorje Chang Buddha III, possesses this great dharma whereby one becomes accomplished within one hour. Only H.H. Dorje Chang Buddha III can cause a disciple to see the rainbow body state at the very time the disciple is receiving that dharma. Through merging my mind with that state and through not abiding in anything, I attained boundless happiness. After receiving that dharma, not only did I see the rainbow body state, I realized it. How could anyone else besides my Buddha Master possess such dharma? I have not even heard of anyone else possessing such dharma!

In order to benefit living beings so that they may all learn this instant accomplishment dharma, I, a disciple with a heart of humility, must make a vow of truth to prove that what I have stated is not false.

The states that I saw that are described above prove that the dharma transmitted by my Buddha Master is supreme and real. I am an elderly seventy-five-year-old man. I would not speak falsely and deceive people, for in so doing I would experience the karmic retribution of descending into hell. I want to be accomplished in the dharma. I want to be liberated from the cycle of reincarnation. What I said here is true. If it is false, I will of course descend into hell. Nevertheless, I cannot reveal how to practice that dharma as it was taught to me by my Buddha Master. I also will not accept disciples. From the bottom of my heart, I am grateful to my Buddha Master and all of the Buddhas and Bodhisattvas.

Kaichu, an ordinary Buddhist disciple
December 21, 2007

(This is a complete translation of the previous handwritten Chinese text originally written and signed by H.E. Kaichu Rinpoche.)

I Finally Received the Highest Buddha-Dharma—The Xian Liang Great Perfection Dharma Initiation

我終於受到最高佛法現量大圓滿法的灌頂

我是慈仁嘉措仁波且，雖然身為祿東贊第四世但是在我恩師三世多杰羌佛的弟子中卻是慚愧的一員。要說我神通道量高深那是誇張的；要說我連一點觀照力都沒有，也是不實在的。在2004年的勝義浴佛法会和2007年的金瓶掣籤法会讓我執法都是佛菩薩和護法聖眾給我的恩賜。

我算是很幸運的人，第一世在藏王松贊干布時由我入漢地接文成公主進西藏，這一世又接隔衣視容公主等巨德法王來西方利生。我認為多生累劫以來這一世是最吉祥殊勝的法緣，我在三世多杰羌佛座下學到的佛法那實在是真實偉大了不得的，如果不是這樣，我怎麼会与阿寇拉摩仁波且抬動四千兩百六十磅的浴佛池呢？那是十四個大男人絲毫也抬不動的啊！可以說全世界也找不到兩位大力士能抬得起，因為他們沒有真正的佛法，這浴佛池就在舊金山華藏寺，誰都可去試一下看看。而且我的年藏在西藏的仁波且中算是一個長壽者，儘管如此，今世

在世間的因緣到結束的時侯了,我想留下來也是不
可能的。就在這時三世多杰羌佛恩師為我舉行勝
義內密灌頂,傳了我現量大圓滿的法,當灌頂傳法
時我清清楚楚見到了虹光境觀,而且世界上找不到
這麼鮮亮明快的色調。從那日起,我隨時都能進入光
界深入聖境,我住世的年歲增長了,留下來也是一
件非常好的事,能為眾生行菩提道,這正是我應該做
的事,我只能說:「感恩我的恩師三世多杰羌佛!」

以上所說完全屬實,但願一切利益有情,所有功
德迴向法界眾生;如所寫為虛構或有妄語,頒
承担一切惡報。

佛弟子
慈仁嘉措

2008年1月1日

I am Ciren Gyatso Rinpoche. Although I am Gar Tongstan IV, I am just an ordinary disciple among all of the disciples of my respected Master, H.H. Dorje Chang Buddha III. To say that I have high supernatural powers and realization would be an exaggeration. To say that I have no supernatural vision whatsoever would also be untrue. Because of the kindness bestowed upon me by the Buddhas, Bodhisattvas, and holy dharma protecting deities, I was allowed to perform certain dharma at a Highest Form of Bathing the Buddha Dharma Assembly in 2004 and a Drawing Lots from a Golden Vase Dharma Assembly in 2007.

I am a very fortunate person. In my previous life as the first Gar Tongstan during the time of the Tibetan King Songtsan Gampo, I entered the land of the Han-Chinese to accompany Princess Wencheng back to Tibet. In this lifetime, I accompanied Princess Geyi Shirong and another dharma king of great virtue to the west so that they may benefit living beings there.

Of all my many lives spanning over eons of time, I think that this life is the most wonderful with respect to encountering the dharma. I have learned Buddha-dharma under H.H. Dorje Chang Buddha III. That Buddha-dharma is truly magnificent. If it were not magnificent, how could Venerable Akou Lamo Rinpoche and I have lifted a 4,260-pound water-filled tub used to bathe a statue of the Buddha? Fourteen strong men tried to lift that tub but could not move it in the slightest. It can be said it that it is impossible to find any two men of remarkable strength in the entire world who could lift that tub. That is because such two men do not possess the true Buddha-dharma. That tub used to bathe a statue of the Buddha is now at Hua Zang Si in San Francisco. Anyone can go there and try to lift it.

Among Tibetan rinpoches, I think that I can be considered as one who has lived a long life. Nonetheless, when the karmic conditions enabling me to stay in this world end, it will be impossible for me to stay even if I wanted to do so. At this late stage of my life, my respected Master, H.H. Dorje Chang Buddha III, performed for me a highest form of inner-tantric initiation and transmitted to me the Xian Liang Great Perfection Dharma. During that initiation and dharma transmission, I clearly saw the rainbow light state. No light in the world can be found with such a bright, clear hue. From that day on, I have been able to deeply enter that world of light, that holy state, at any time. The years that I can live in this world have finally increased. Staying in this world longer is also a very good thing since I can use the Buddha-dharma that I practice and my cultivation to benefit living beings. That is exactly what I should do. All I can say is I am grateful to my respected Master, H.H. Dorje Chang Buddha III!

What I have stated above is totally true. May it benefit all living beings. I dedicate all of the merit of this statement to living beings in the dharmadhatu. If what I have stated contains any falsehood, I am willing to bear all bad karmic retribution.

Buddhist disciple,
Ciren Gyatso

(This is a complete translation of the previous handwritten Chinese text originally written and signed by H.E. Ciren Gyatso Rinpoche.)

H.E. Dharma King Queji Jiangyang Qingzhen Arrives Flying through the Air

I have visited many great rinpoches and great dharma teachers and have received many dharma initiations throughout my life. However, it seems that people described in the book *The True Traces of Tibetan Tantra* are no longer in existence in the contemporary Buddhist world. Since the early years of my life, I have learned exoteric Buddhism and Tibetan esoteric Buddhism and have practiced the Four Divisions of Yoga. I have also often visited eminent monks, greatly virtuous laypersons, great rinpoches, and great dharma teachers of exoteric and esoteric Buddhism in all areas of the world. As a result, karmic conditions came together that enabled me to encounter my master from Sichuan, a great international master and leader of the dharma realm who transmitted profound Buddha-dharma teachings to me.

When I first met the Buddha Master, H.H. Dorje Chang Buddha III Wan Ko Yeshe Norbu, at the Beijing International Hotel, H.H. Buddha Master was very polite and easy to approach, having the deportment of an amiable person of great virtue. At that time, I did not know the true identity or status of the Buddha Master. I only knew that His Holiness was a great master with noble morality and profound knowledge.

One day, I met with some highly virtuous laypersons and great rinpoches at the Pici Vajra Castle. Because of the imminent arrival of H.E. Queji Jiangyang Qingzhen, a Dharma King and rinpoche of the Sayka sect who is more than one hundred years old, everyone had already prepared white silk hadas and offerings to respectfully welcome his arrival. After midnight at around 12:30, a rainbow light mass suddenly appeared circling around in the sky, which was soon accompanied by wonderful music. Before long, that rainbow light mass grew larger and larger. It gradually descended, floating down and landing on the top of the seven-floor building that contained our Buddhist altar. Immediately thereafter, a person descended from the top of the building. H.E. Great Dharma King Jiangyang Qingzhen had arrived!

All of the eminent monks, greatly virtuous laypersons, rinpoches, and dharma teachers who were present knelt down on the ground to greet him. Some of them choked with sobs and beseeched the Dharma King of the Sayka sect to be compassionate and take them as his disciples. H.E. Dharma King Jiangyang Qingzhen ascended to the dharma seat. I could see the Dharma King's white hair, ruddy complexion, and long silver beard that grew over his belly. His translucent body, through which the three channels and five chakras were faintly visible, especially made him look as if he was as old as the heavens were high.

We prostrated and made offerings to him with our three karmas expressing utmost admiration. I was so moved that I didn't know what to do. Stories of hundred-year-old men who soar up and fly through the air are frequently recorded in the Tibetan scriptures, but I never before had the opportunity to personally witness this. That day I was able to see such an event with my own eyes. That was truly our good fortune accumulated from beginning-less time. How could one not be moved to tears over such an event?

There was a rinpoche who stated with suspicion, "The rainbow light that appeared in the sky was a hot-air balloon of light that fell to the top of the seven-floor building. The elder Dharma King did not descend from the sky. At the very instant when the hot-air balloon dropped to the top of the seven-floor building, he jumped from the top of the seventh-floor building to the concrete ground where we were." He saw the elder Dharma King jump down with his arms wide open and legs slightly bent. When landing on the ground, the elder Dharma King barely made a sound, like an eagle descending in front of us.

Actually, we all saw this because we were on the concrete ground of the courtyard seven floors below. I saw that the elder Dharma King did indeed circle in the sky and descend to the top of the seven-floor building. Then everyone's eyesight was blocked by the roof. However, within two seconds, the elder Dharma King descended from the top of this seven-floor building

to the concrete ground, jumping down seven floors. It happened right in front of us. Even if he did not descend from the sky, he is a more than hundred-year-old man who jumped to the ground from the top of a seven-floor building. That is something an ordinary person cannot do.

The next day, the Dharma King of the Sayka sect transmitted dharma and performed initiations for us, empowering us with great compassion. A one-foot long vajra that we held with our hands demonstrated endless, awesome power. No one could control the vajra. The mandala states that appeared were extremely wonderful.

Just as the initiation dharma assembly ended, the sudden sound of ringing bells could be heard, and an attendant announced, "His Holiness the Great Master has arrived!" At that moment, we saw H.E. Dharma King Jiangyang Qingzhen jump off his dharma seat and lower himself to the ground to prostrate. We did not know what this special occasion of the maturing of karmic conditions was, but we all turned around and followed the elder Dharma King's example by prostrating, thinking it might be the arrival of Guru Padmasambhava. This was the only reason we could think of as to why the Dharma King would prostrate himself so quickly. After prostrating, when we raised our heads and looked up, what we saw was not Guru Padmasambhava but H.H. Master Wan Ko Yee. Seeing the confusion and hesitation in our minds, H.E. Dharma King Jiangyang Qingzhen said, "Do not harbor suspicions. H.H. Master Yee is the most magnificent Buddha Vajradhara Great Dharma King. He is His Holiness Wan Ko Yeshe Norbu Holiest Tathagata."

Later, H.E. Dharma King Jiangyang Qingzhen said to me, "If you truly want to receive the highest Buddha-dharma, you must request your Buddha Master, H.H. Wan Ko Yeshe Norbu, to confer an initiation upon you. That would be the most holy dharma." Although I longed for such a day, my situation seemed totally hopeless as day after day passed. Suddenly, the Buddha Master informed me one day that His Holiness wanted to tonsure me and perform an initiation for me. That initiation performed for me by the Buddha Master was especially wonderful. To prepare for that initiation, the Buddha Master tonsured me on a mountain slope outside the retreat building. A photograph taken of the Buddha Master tonsuring me unexpectedly showed an image of Dorje Chang Buddha with a clearly visible and colorful bun of hair on the top of that Buddha's head. However, when we looked at the photograph from a closer range, that Buddha image appeared just like the real retreat building. No matter how we viewed it, it was no longer a photograph of a Buddha image. Everyone there marveled at such a holy occurrence. Such wonderful karmic conditions portended that I would learn profound and great dharma.

Actually, I had already learned from other holy and virtuous people the Mind Within Mind, the Brightness Mahamudra, the Ganges River Mahamudra, the Great Perfection, and Vajra Division dharma. However, what I experienced on that day was an astounding and great dharma.

The Buddha Master first performed for me a Selection of Karmic Affinity Initiation. In front of me, the Buddha Master wrote down with a brush the same seed character on ten separate pieces of paper. I put each of those seed characters under the sun to dry. After they were dry, I went to a place where nobody else was and secretly wrote down on each of the ten pieces of paper a different number that only I myself knew. I then rolled into a ball each of those ten pieces of paper on which a seed character was written. I placed each of the paper balls into a dharma container. I took that container out of the secret room and into the open-air mandala, placing it in the middle of the dharma platform. The Buddha Master, who had all along been practicing the dharma in the open-air mandala, then began ringing a bell and using a vajra. The power of the ten great vajra beings very soon thereafter arrived at the mandala.

The Buddha Master said, "Today I should transmit to you the Essence of Great Perfection Longchen Nying-thik of this world." I asked, "Can I learn the Omniscience Xian Liang Great Perfection?" The Buddha Master replied, "Let the Buddhas and vajra beings decide!"

I took a ball of paper out of the dharma container with my hand and very carefully unrolled it. I saw that the secret number on it indeed corresponded to the Essence of Great Perfection Longchen Nying-thik. That was the only piece of paper out of the ten pieces of paper containing seed syllables whose secret number corresponded to that dharma. I rolled that piece of paper back into a ball as I had done before and placed it inside the dharma container. After the dharma container was shaken and all the balls of paper in it were mix up, the Buddha Master said, "It will still be the Longchen Nying-thik Great Perfection." The Buddha Master then took a ball of paper out of the dharma container and placed in on my hand. I unrolled it and saw that, as predicted, it was the same piece of paper I took out a moment ago that corresponded to my receiving the Longchen Nying-thik Great Perfection Dharma initiation.

Since that paper indicated I should receive such an initiation, the Buddha Master began to perform that initiation. It seemed as if someone was standing inside of my ear as the transmission of that dharma began. As that dharma was being transmitted to me, I began to practice it. The Great Perfection state suddenly appeared before me. The "true-suchness" of the entire dharma realm appeared as a reality in which there was no distinction between emptiness and form. The sambhogakaya (reward body) vajra state also manifested, and the mandala began to circle around. I finally understood what holy dharma transmitted by a Buddha is. The Buddha Master then said, "Longchen Nying-thik is the highest dharma in this world.

However, in the future you will still have the opportunity to learn the Omniscience Xian Liang Great Perfection!"

As I look back on my path of learning the dharma under my Buddha Master, H.H. Wan Ko Yeshe Norbu Holiest Tathagata, I realize that I finally learned the dharma only after going through many tests. My Buddha Master is a greatly compassionate and holy Buddha Dharma King who is totally unselfish, who has virtue that has reached a holy state, and who gives the holy heart of bodhi to living beings in the three spheres. If in this lifetime you do not learn under the Buddha Great Dharma King Master, you will not understand what is meant by "perfect mastery of the Five Vidyas." If you do not follow the Buddha Great Dharma King Master, you will not be able to witness personally what "bodhi" is or be clear about "the path of the Bodhisattva." His Holiness has full proficiency in all worldly dharmas and non-worldly dharmas and is able to apply each one of them without hindrance. His Holiness is able to implement these mundane and supra-mundane dharmas to constantly benefit living beings and uphold their devotion toward Buddhism.

I remember being at Phutthamonthon (Buddhamonton) in Thailand. Because karmic conditions had matured, I, as a rinpoche, beseeched the Buddha Dharma King Master to give us a discourse on the relationship between the Buddha and living beings for the purpose of benefiting living beings. Just as the Buddha Master began the discourse, dogs, birds, and countless fish appeared. Even more surprising was the black dragons that transformed itself into fish and stood alone on the water's surface bowing to the Buddha Master. This truly has never occurred in human history. We can see from this just how magnificent the Buddha Dharma King Master is! Newspapers and magazines reported this holy event.

The Buddha Dharma King Master is the supreme being in the dharma realm. His Holiness's unselfish and pure state is incomparable. For example, His Holiness would transmit to us various Buddha-dharma skills and teachings yet would instruct us not to reveal his name. Most of the disciples of His Holiness are great rinpoches and great dharma teachers. His Holiness's disciples also include great Bodhisattvas. His Holiness has been the master of the Buddhas since beginning-less time. How could written words adequately describe His Holiness's unsurpassed magnificence?

An honest account by Hengsheng

(This is a complete translation of the Chinese text that follows originally written and signed by Venerable Hengsheng Rinpoche.)

卻吉降養清眞法王騰空而來

我一生參訪過很多大仁波且、大法師，接受過若干灌頂，但能如《藏密真蹤》一書中所談到的，當今佛教界似乎已絕其人跡。因從小學

習顯教及藏密，修持「四部瑜伽」，加之常與世界各地顯密高僧、大德、大活佛、大法師過從交往使然，因緣和合，方能得遇我在四川的

上師，國際巨匠、法界泰斗，傳授甚深法義。

當初與三世多杰羌佛雲高益西諾布佛陀上師有緣在北京國際飯店相會時，佛陀上師十分客氣，平易近人，一派親和大德之風，當時我還不了解佛陀上師的身份，只知道他是一個道德高尚、學識淵博的大師。

一天，我在毗次金剛堡與一些大德、大仁波且們相聚，因為薩迦法王卻吉降養清真百歲老仁波且將要到來，所以大家都準備好哈達和供養，恭候薩迦降養法王光臨。大約半夜12點半左右，突然天空出現一團虹光，盤旋圍繞，隨著雅奏音昌之聲，不一會兒那團虹光愈來愈大，冉冉降下，飄然之間落在我們壇場的七樓頂上，緊接著從頂樓降下一人，降養清真大法王駕到了！當時在場的高僧、大德、仁波且、法師全部倒地跪接，有的泣不成聲，祈求薩迦法王悲憫攝受，收為弟子。降養清真法王高登法位，只見法王鶴髮童顏，銀鬚過肚，尤其是身體呈半透明狀，隱見三脈五輪，實乃與天同壽之身。我們頂禮上供，三業五體投地，感動得不知所以然，尤其是百歲老人騰空而飛，這在西藏的經書中經常記載，但是從來沒有機緣親眼目睹，今天能夠親眼得見，真是無始的福報，怎能不感激涕零？有位仁波且懷疑說：「天空出現的虹光是熱氣球燈掉到我們七樓上，老法王不是從天而降的，他是在熱氣球降在我們七樓頂的瞬間，從七樓頂跳到我們水泥地上的。」他看到老法王跳下來時，兩手張開，腳微微彎曲，落地的聲音非常小，就像一隻鵬降在我們面前，其實當時大家都看到，因為我們就在七樓下面天井中的水泥地上。我看到老法王確實繞到七樓頂上，大家被屋頂擋住視線，但不到二秒鐘老法王從七樓頂，落到七樓下的水泥地上，當時就在我們面前，我認為就算不是從天而降，一位百歲老人能從七樓跳到地面上，已經不是凡人所能為。第二天，薩迦法王為我們灌頂傳法，慈悲攝受，一尺長的金剛杵，在我們手中威力無窮，無人能左右得了它，壇城境界無比殊勝。

就在這個灌頂法會完畢的時候，突然一陣鈴聲響後，侍者報道：「大師駕到！」此時即見降養清真法王從法位上跳將下來，倒地便拜，我們也不知是何種因緣，大家轉身跟著頂禮，以為蓮花生大師駕到，法王才會如是急忙頂禮。拜完後，當我們抬起頭看時，見到的不是蓮師，而是義雲高大師，我們心裡正在猶疑的時候，降養清真法王說：「你們不要猜疑，義大師才是我們最偉大的金剛總持大法王，他就是雲高益西諾布頂聖如來。」

降養清真法王說：「你要真正得到最高的佛法，還得要請你的佛陀上師雲高益西諾布為你灌頂，那才是頂聖之法。」於是我心願就一直盼望有這一天，但一天天過去，可以說沒有任何希望，突然有一天，佛陀上師要為我取髮灌頂。這一次佛陀上師給我灌頂特別殊勝。當佛陀上師為準備給我灌頂而在關房外山坡地給我取髮時，照出來的相片上竟然有一尊多杰羌佛的佛像，佛像還有明顯的帶色的頂髻。但是，當我們走近看，此佛像則又是實實在在的關房，怎麼看也不是佛

像。此一聖境令所有在場人員大為驚嘆，此殊勝緣起也預示著我將會學到甚深的大法，其實，對於心中心、光明大手印、恆河大手印、大圓滿及金剛部的法，我已經在其他聖德處學了的，但是這一次才是驚天動地的一個大法，佛陀上師老人家為我舉行了首先擇緣的灌頂，當場書下十顆同樣的種子字，我將其拿到陽光中曬乾，我在無人之處做上了極密的、唯我所知的記號，然後將十顆種子字打成紙團，放入法桶中，從密室帶出露天壇城，放在法台中央，此時，一直在露天壇城修法的佛陀上師搖鈴打杵，很快十大金剛的境界悉地力都來到了壇城，佛陀上師說：「今天應該傳給你這個世界上龍欽寧體的大圓滿精髓。」我說：「我能學遍智現量大圓滿嗎？」佛陀上師老人家說：「都讓諸佛、金剛們定吧！」我用手從法桶中拿起一顆紙團，小心翼翼地將其打開，一查密記果然是十張種子字中唯一的一張龍欽寧體精髓大圓滿，我將紙丸照常捏成團，放進法桶，經搖動混合後，佛陀上師老人家說：「還是龍欽寧體大圓滿。」然後親自從法桶中取出一粒，放在我手中，我將其打開，果然還是我剛才那一張龍欽寧體大圓滿法當受灌。說灌就灌，只聽到我的耳中似乎有個人站在我耳朵裡面，開始傳授了，此時，一邊傳我一邊修，突然大圓滿的境界現前了，整個法界真如呈現了空有不二，而報身的金剛境同時展現壇城開始盤旋，我終於明白，什麼才是佛陀傳的聖法，佛陀上師老人家說：「龍欽寧體是這個世界上最高的法，但是今後你還是有機會得到遍智現量大圓滿的！」

此後，我在回憶學法的過程中，跟隨雲高益西諾布頂聖如來佛陀上師，經過許多考驗，最後學了法。我的佛陀上師是一位大公無私、德入聖境，以菩提聖心施予三界眾生的大仁慈聖者佛陀法王。此生不親近佛陀法王上師你不能明白什麼是「五明妙諳」，不跟隨佛陀法王上師就不能親見什麼是「菩提」，明了「菩薩道」。他老人家圓滿世間萬法與世外法而能法法任運無礙，又能持世出世法處處利益天下蒼生慧命。記得在泰國佛教城，由於因緣成熟，我作為仁波且，為利眾生，祈禱佛陀法王上師開示佛與眾生的關係。就在佛陀上師剛開示時，來了狗、鳥、魚無數，更竟然烏龍化為魚作禮拜獨立在水面上，這實在是人間從來沒有出現過的事，可見佛陀法王上師是何等的偉大！當時報章都有記載這一聖況。

佛陀法王上師是法界的泰斗，他無私純淨之境界無與倫比，包括給我們傳授一切佛法功夫和法義後，也不讓我們透露他的名姓。他門下的弟子，大多是大活佛、大法師，還有大菩薩。從無始他就是佛陀們的上師，其至高偉大，豈是文章可寫得出來的？

恆生　誠言記實

恆生 誠言紀實

（此文的英文翻譯印在前面）

NINETY-EIGHT POUND STALACTITE STONE WENT THROUGH A HUMAN BODY; FOUR-HUNDRED-THIRTY POUND GIGANTIC MANI STONE DUO QIE XU FLIES INTO THE AIR

Unveiling the mystical realization state of esoteric Buddha-dharma—a true account of a grand assembly of esoteric Buddha-dharma

(This is the text of an article published in the Kinmen Express on January 22, 2002)

[Special Report by Chao-Nan] People think of Tibetan Buddhism in general as a far-away culture full of mystery. Especially when patriarchs from various sects manifested mystical phenomena and supernatural powers, people become curious about esoteric Buddha dharma.

Based on the descriptions of some lamas, there are various examinations for Buddhist practitioners in Tibet. One's proficiency of Buddhism is examined by means of different scales of dialectical debates. The one who passes thousands of debates and is in first place is called Lharampa geshe. The ones in second place and third place are called geshes. Only after completion of tens of thousands of dialectical debates can geshes enter schools of Esoteric Buddhism to learn esoteric dharma.

These lamas said that esoteric dharma emphasizes states of realization. In Esoteric Buddhism schools, mani stones are usually used to evaluate practitioners' levels of realization. There are two types of mani stones. The first one is stones that are inscribed with mantras by ordinary people and are placed in mani stone mounds. This type of mani stones does not contain dharma power. The other type is stones that are inscribed by great patriarchs from lineages of Tibetan Buddhism after practicing dharma. The stones are inscribed with images of Buddhas or Seed Syllables of mantras. They are placed in mani stone mounds to be used as empowerment that eliminates disasters and obstacles. The most important function of this type of mani stones with powers is to test and measure the levels of self-cultivation.

According to some myths, only the practitioners with states of realization from self-cultivation are able to practice dharma to cause the mani stones to move at a distance. Mani stones move in different ways. Some move slowly while others walk or fly. Ordinary people cannot make them move at all no matter how much force they use or how many of them recite mantras at the same time. This type of story has added aspects of mystery and significance to Tibetan esoteric dharma.

Recently, the reporter had the honor to attend a grand assembly in the United States where various states of realization were revealed. The attendees include great lamas and ordinary lamas from Tibet, and great dharma masters and ordinary dharma masters of Exoteric Buddhism. The mantras they recited include the Great Compassion Mantra, the Green Tara Heart Mantra and the mantra of Vajrakila (Dorje Phurbha). Some dharma masters were not able to cause the mani stone to move even after a prolonged period of practicing dharma. Several dharma masters of Exoteric Buddhism recited mantras in unison and across space caused a 150g mani stone on a glass table to move. A great dharma master and a female lama were able to make the mani stone in a distance move as soon as they chanted mantras combined with mudras.

While the attendees marveled at such sights, a great female lama from Tibet arrived. Before the testing she requested the person videotaping not capture her face. She said that she was a self-cultivator and wanted to attain liberation and realization. She did not intend to manifest Buddha-dharma to show off her powers. Soon after, something stunning happened.

As soon as she recited mantras, a ninety-eight pound stalactite stone surprisingly rose from the ground and circulated in the air following her hand gestures. This mani stone with supernatural powers stopped and trembled after rising into the air. What was more astonishing was when the female lama sat on the wood floor, the mani stone in a split second moved from the back of her to the front. The witnesses felt that the ninety-eight pound mani stone had moved within a blink of eyes. It moved at such fast speed as if it had passed through the body of the lama. Then, this mani stone with supernatural powers circled the great female lama twice following her finger gestures. It moved up and down and trembled at the same time while moving in circles. When the mani stone moved to her back the second time, her index finder in the mudra she made over her head pointed down and the stone immediately descended. Following the direction of her fingers, it stopped for a second and dropped on the wood floor with a thump. Apparently, it was a very heavy stone. It would be hard for one to imagine it if one did not witness such a miracle.

The most famous gigantic stalactite mani stone Duo Qie Xu from Tibet was also included in the assembly. It weighs four hundred and thirty pounds approximately equivalent to two hundred kilograms. It was shipped to the United States from Tibet. It revealed great supernatural powers at the assembly.

The gigantic mani stone Duo Qie Xue is not an ordinary stone. It is a mani stone with an identity such as the famous Cuiyu Cabbage (A famous jade carving from Qing dynasty displayed at the National Palace Museum in Taipei). Most of the Tibetan Buddhist practitioners know about Duo Qie Xu. During the tests with Duo Qie Xue, more incredible phenomena occurred.

When the great Tibetan female lama was about to test her powers on Duo Qie Xu, she again requested that her face not be captured on cameras for the same reasons. The video recordings of her practicing dharma on Duo Qie Xu were made to be keepsakes for the participants at the scene only. They cannot be used as any forms of promotion. Her deed of following strictly the precepts deeply moved the people at the scene.

Then, incredible things happened. The four-hundred-thirty pound Duo Qie Xu followed the hand gestures of the great Tibetan female lama, tremblingly rose from the lawn and flew into the air. The crowd was in awe and suddenly felt the lawn moving like ocean waves. In addition, roof tops and trees were moving at the same time. The mani stone flying in the air returned and suddenly fell from three feet above the ground. It made a big dent on the lawn. Such occurrence that can only be found in fictions actually happened in real life. The lamas and dharma masters at the scene said that this holy feat depicted the magnificence and authenticity of Buddha-dharma, with which everything can be accomplished including transforming mountains and oceans.

At the Exposing Buddha Statues to the Sun Dharma Assembly held in Chiang Kai-shek Memorial Hall in Taipei on January 13, 2002, there was a mound of stones inscribed with mantras from the Lapuleng Temple in Gansu. It was a Mani Stone Mound consisting of mani stones.

Gigantic Mani Stone Flies into the Air 瑪尼石騰空飛

金門晚報　　10　　中華民國九十一年元月二十二日星期二

98磅鐘乳石穿身過　430磅埵切壚王石騰空飛
——密法修證的神秘面紗揭秘　一場密法盛會記實

〔記者超男／特別報導〕藏傳佛教一般讓人感覺是遙遠的文化，充滿各種神密的面紗，尤其是各教派祖師有著許多神奇的事蹟與神通示現，更讓人對密法勿充滿好奇。

根據喇嘛們的描述，在西藏，對修學佛法的行者有各種考試的制度，對佛學的考驗有各種大小不同的經辯的考，通過數千場經辯的第一名稱為那仁巴格西，通過萬場經辯的格西，才進入密宗院修學密法。

喇嘛們說，密法重視證境，在密宗院通常是用瑪尼石來考驗行者的實證功夫。瑪尼石有兩種：一種是用瑪尼刻咒文在石頭上去的在瑪尼堆的，另一種是藏傳佛教的大祖師們修法在石頭上刻上咒語種子字放在供桌上的。瑪尼石不為輕易動，有的集合數位顯教法師一起持咒，終於隔空將透明玻璃上三兩重的瑪尼石推動，也有藏教的大法師和女活佛一持咒一結手印立刻就把小瑪尼石隔空推動。

正在眾人讚嘆之際，一位來自西藏的女大活佛來到現場，測試瑪尼石前，她說她是個脫與成就，不能拿佛法來作求的工具，她要求現場正在錄影的攝像機不准拍她的臉，接著讓人驚心的事就發生了：一顆重達九八磅的鐘乳瑪尼王石，竟然就在她身後的法師活佛環繞時，突然出現在她的面前，凌空而起在空中旋繞，又讓著女大活佛在眾目睽睽之下，速度之快用瑪尼石第二次轉，又令在場的她身後法師活佛不停旋繞，道個具量瑪尼王石升降一邊飄動，當瑪尼王石第二次轉她就將雙手結在頭頂的手印指揮繞著她的身前身後旋繞，然後道個具量瑪尼王石又凌空而降，速度更快，原速令她瑪尼王石還拿一邊，這種活佛的出來。

石頭還一邊轉一邊飄動，到她身後時，只見她將雙手結在頭頂的手印指揮，速度之快用瑪尼石第二次轉她就將雙手結在頭頂...在道場瑪尼石測試會上，重達四三○磅約合二○○公斤重的瑪尼王石，又出場了。

〔密法重視證境，在密宗院通常是用瑪尼石來考驗行者的實證功夫。〕

瑪尼石上有證境功夫的行者修法才能令瑪尼石隔空動起來，瑪尼石動的話，有的慢慢移動，有的會走，有多人持咒也無法使它動上一動，這種神奇的事發生了，不可思議的事發生了，隨著西藏女大活佛的手勢，重四三○磅的埵切壚從草地上顫動地面起來，眾人在驚嘆聲中突然發覺腳底下的草皮好似波浪一樣波動著，不但地在搖晃，接著瑪尼王石埵切壚飛向空中飛回來，在三呎高的空中突然掉下，把草地砸了一個大洞。道種只有小說上才有的情節，然在現實中出現，在場的活佛法師說，這種聖蹟象徵佛法無法的像大與真實不虛。

一月十三日台北中正紀念堂舉行曬大佛法會時，會場有一堆來自甘肅拉卜楞寺刻著咒文的石頭，就是瑪尼石。

一藏傳佛教，般讓人感覺是遙遠的文化，充滿各種神密的面紗也大顯神通。

瑪尼石埵切壚道次遠渡重洋由西藏運到美國在測試會上瑪尼王石埵切壚不是普通的石頭，它是有名有姓的瑪尼石，就像有名的翠玉白菜一樣，一說埵切壚來大多數西藏的行者名都知道。埵切壚的測試會發生更不思議的事，當這位西藏的女大活佛要測試埵切壚時，以同樣理由同意不露臉讓人拍攝她修法測試埵切壚的境頭，以同樣理由把草地了一個大洞。然而在現實中出現，不准人拿去作宣傳，且而不准人作紀念，這種持戒行誼，令在場的人為之動容。

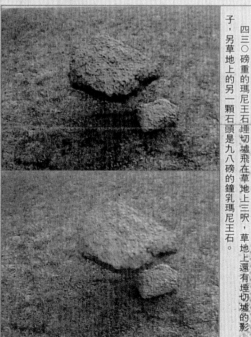

女大活佛坐地指揮九八磅重的鐘乳石離地騰空繞飛，圖片中地板上還有石頭的影子。

四三○磅重的瑪尼王石埵切壚飛在草地上三呎，草地上還有埵切壚的影子，另草地上的另一顆石頭是九八磅的鐘乳瑪尼王石。

金門晚報
離島民營 第一大報
無黨無派 獨立經營

第 01781 號

KINMEN EVENING NEWS

發行人／總社長／董事長
彭垂演

社長／總經理
陳秀霞

服務電話
台中總機／(04)22390191(代表號)
(04)22393020
金門總機／(082)323813(代表號)
經理部／323813、323818、320371
採訪組／320710、320711、320712
傳真／323530、320372、320787

電子信箱：kmnews@yam.com

印刷者：本報印刷廠

今日發行三大張，每月訂價270元
零售每份十元（全國各地有售）

THE CORRECT DHARMA OF TRUE BUDDHISM HAS APPEARED IN THE UNITED STATES

SEVEN TYPES OF HOLY STATES APPEARED BEFORE ONE'S EYES; BASED UPON BUDDHA DHARMA REALIZATION, WATER WAS POURED; THIS IS THE TRUE BATHING OF THE BUDDHA

(This is the text of an article published in the Asian Journal on Jul. 14, 2004.)

(Los Angeles) May 26, 2004 of the Gregorian calendar and April 8th of the lunar calendar was the birthday of Sakyamuni Buddha. The sun over that place in the United States was unusually radiant and beautiful. On a lawn of a religious site surrounded by large blue curtain screens that formed a dignified-looking mandala (Buddhist altar area), great rinpoches, great dharma teachers, and great laypearsons from all over the world assembled. An unprecedentedly wonderful "Highest Form of Bathing the Buddha-dharma Assembly" was taking place. This was certainly not an ordinary, worldly bathing of the Buddha accompanied by chanting that one is used to seeing in temples. On such occasions, the participants merely show their respectful hearts. In contrast, the bathing that took place that day was a true bathing of the Buddha grand assembly. At such a Highest Form of Bathing the Buddha-dharma Assembly, the conductor must have the state of realization of a Buddha or Bodhisattva to invoke the manifestation of holy supernatural sights. At the May 26th assembly, the Buddha personally arrived, the dharma protecting Bodhisattvas exhibited holy sights, and celestial dragons and other dharma protecting deities laughed in the sky. It was a grand dharma realm assembly in which various holy scenes unimaginable to worldly people appeared. Buddha Vajradhara Great Dharma King Yeshe Norbu[1] who is the supreme leader of both exoteric and esoteric Buddhism, conducted that assembly and practiced the dharma during that assembly.

The Dharma Assembly was divided into an internal mandala and external mandala. The internal mandala was the central area where the Buddha was bathed. The external mandala was the dharma realm of accomplishment. Eminent monastics and persons of great virtue attended the Dharma Assembly. Those who were part of the internal mandala included Akou Lamo Great Rinpoche, Zhaxi Zhuoma Rinpoche, Dharma Teacher Long Hui, Dharma Teacher Jue Hui, Dage Gongla Rinpoche, Bodi Wentu Rinpoche, Dharma Teacher Kui Zhi, Dharma Teacher Ruo Hui, layman Ciren Gyatso, Dharma Teacher Miao Kong, Dharma Teacher Baolian, and others. Those who were part of the external mandala included Fuzang Wanghu Great Rinpoche, Yan Long Great Rinpoche, Awang Nuobu Great Rinpoche, Kang Qin Great Rinpoche, Xijao Zhibenge Rinpoche, Yixi Kanbu, Dharma Teacher Cikong, Dharma Teacher Fahai, Dharma Teacher Cixin, Dharma Teacher Haoling, and others.

The dharma stipulates that the purpose of a Highest Form of Bathing the Buddha-dharma Assembly is pouring dharma water that has been used to bathe the Buddha. The ability to pour such dharma water is based upon one's true level of realization. Pouring such water bathes the celestial beings in the various heavenly realms. It shows that the Buddha blessed the celestial beings in the various heavenly realms, the dharma protecting deities, and the seven types of disciples. Thus, there must be a successful "pouring of water based upon one's true realization." Otherwise, it is not a Highest Form of Bathing the Buddha-dharma Assembly.

Additionally, at that Dharma Assembly all seven holy states were manifested. The seven types of holy states are: (1) Wind Celebrates the Mandala, (2) Flowers Rain from a Tree, (3) A Dharma Object Manifests Holiness, (4) A Cloud Provides an Umbrella-Like Covering, (5) Celestial Dragons Laugh Joyfully, (6) A Rinpoche is Given a Sign, and (7) The Color of Dharma Water Is Received.

The successful "pouring of water based upon one's true realization" is the most important part of such a Dharma Assembly. It is the key aspect of a Highest Form of Bathing the Buddha-dharma Assembly. It is why the name of such a Dharma Assembly contains the words "Highest Form." Three to five thousand pounds of dharma water are used to bathe the Buddha. After the Buddha is bathed, this water is used to bathe the celestial beings in the various heavenly realms. When bathing the celestial beings, the dharma water must be poured down from the lotus tub used to bathe the Buddha into the tub used to bathe the celestial beings. During the pouring process, one cannot touch the dharma water with any part of one's body, nor can one use any type of container to be filled with water. That is because the human body and containers are soiled by unclean dust and dirt. People are only allowed to tilt the entire lotus tub used to bathe the Buddha so that water is poured downward.

With such a heavy amount of dharma water in the lotus tub used to bathe the Buddha, how could anyone tilt that tub to pour the water down into the tub used to bathe the celestial beings? One must rely upon one's Buddha-dharma state of realization. But no more than ten people can attempt to lift the lotus tub used to bathe the Buddha. Otherwise, it would not be regarded as the Highest Form of Bathing the Buddha-dharma Assembly. If the dharma water is not successfully poured into the tub used to bathe the celestial beings, then no matter what types of supernatural holy sights may appear at the Dharma Assembly, it cannot be called a "Highest Form of Bathing the Buddha-dharma Assembly."

FLOWERS RAIN FROM A TREE

The atmosphere that day at the mandala to bathe the Buddha was holy and solemn. Great Dharma King Yeshe Norbu wore his Dharma King robe. He had an extremely dignified-looking appearance. A golden bronze statue of Dharma Prince Siddhartha stood in the mandala. In the middle of the mandala was a lotus tub used to bathe the Buddha that was 3 feet high, square, and weighed 700

---

[1] Here and below the words *Buddha Vajradhara*, *Great Dharma King*, or *Dharma King* refers to H.H. Dorje Chang Buddha III Wan Ko Yeshe Norbu Holiest Tathagata.

See photo caption (1)

pounds itself without water. Over the middle of that tub was a beautiful lotus flower about the size of a car wheel. Below and adjoining that lotus tub used to bathe the Buddha was a rectangular, one-foot high tub used to bathe the celestial beings. Ninety buckets of fragrant water were also placed in the mandala to be used to bathe the Buddha. The offering water in those buckets was light brown due to the sandalwood, eaglewood, saffron, and other scents that were boiled and added to the water.

At the beginning of the Dharma Assembly, the Great Dharma King practiced Dharma according to Buddhist scriptures. As soon as the Great Dharma King began practicing Dharma, a tree full of jacarandas (a pale purple flower) immediately began raining flowers. The jacarandas drifted in the golden sunlight and fell all over the mandala and into the ninety buckets of water. Auspicious clouds rolled through the sky. It seemed that the mandala was no longer part of this world. Rather, it seemed like a holy Buddha-land. Flowers rained for more than three hours continuously, starting from the beginning of the Dharma Assembly. Those flowers floated down upon everyone. However, not one petal touched the Great Dharma King. When the Dharma Assembly ended, the flowers instantly stopped raining.

A DHARMA OBJECT MANIFESTS HOLINESS

In order to express the unity of exoteric and esoteric Buddha Dharma, the Great Dharma King did not select a highest-level practitioner of great virtue or a highest-level Great Rinpoche to announce and conduct the rituals and ceremonies of that Dharma Assembly. Rather, the Dharma King selected Great Dharma Teacher Long Hui to announce the rituals and ceremonies. Great Dharma Teacher Long Hui is Han Chinese and is Chairperson of the International Buddhism Sangha Association. The Dharma King also selected Great Dharma Teacher Jue

Hui, Great Dharma Teacher Kui Zhi, Great Dharma Teacher Ruo Hui, and Dharma Teacher Miao Kong to conduct the rituals and ceremonies.

When Great Dharma Teacher Long Hui announced that all Buddhist disciples in attendance should pour fragrant water into the tub used to bathe the Buddha, all of the Rinpoches, Dharma Teachers, and laypersons in attendance quickly poured the ninety buckets of light brown fragrant water into the tub used to bathe the Buddha, filling it up completely. Everyone then returned to their seats and respectfully requested that the Great Dharma King consecrate the fragrant water in the lotus tub. The Great Dharma King was then seen holding a white Vajra Wheel. The Great Dharma King approached the lotus tub used to bathe the Buddha and placed that Dharma object (i.e. the Vajra Wheel) into the water. That Dharma object is half as thick as a coin and as large as the palm of the hand. The Buddha Dharma stipulates that only a Buddha Vajradhara Dharma King may possess such a Vajra Wheel. After the Buddha Vajradhara Dharma King's empowerment, the Dharma protecting Bodhisattvas in the sky descended upon that Dharma object. That Dharma object can move around in the Dharma water used to bathe the Buddha. It can rise up in the water and sink down into the water. After it does this, the practice of the Highest Form of Bathing the Buddha Dharma Assembly may begin.

Everyone surrounded the lotus tub to see that Dharma object. One or two minutes later, everyone indeed saw the Vajra Wheel moving in the water. No one touched the lotus tub. While in the water, that Dharma object moved forward and backward, to the left and the right, all on its own. One moment, it sank downward; the next moment it floated to the surface of the water. When the Vaja Wheel was approaching the bottom of the water, many saw red light emanate from the bottom of the Vajra Wheel. That red light was the true fire of samadhi. Many people saw eight Dharma protecting Bodhisattvas standing on that Dharma object. There were also those who saw Mahakala and Sri-maha-devi supernaturally change their forms on that Vajra Wheel. Everyone present was full of Dharma joy.

WIND CELEBRATES THE MANDALA

After a Dharma object manifested holiness, everyone began to respectfully recite the invocation text. Suddenly, a strong wind began blowing from the west. Trees began to sway and things began to shake in the once peaceful mandala. Jacarandas flew through the air. Everyone was amazed. Indescribable and auspicious Dharma joy filled the entire assembly. The world-honored Buddha had arrived in the sky above the mandala to manifest the Dharma! Everyone chanted a mantra in unison to respectfully welcome the arrival of the Buddha. That strong

wind from the west blew for a period of time and then abruptly stopped. The quietude of the mandala was restored.

An auspicious atmosphere filled the mandala. Amid the sound of everyone chanting a mantra, the holy ritual of bathing the Buddha formally began. Great Dharma Teacher Kui Zhi respectfully lifted the statue of Dharma Prince Siddhartha off the altar and put it on the lotus flower in the middle of the lotus tub. Everyone then respectfully requested that the Great Dharma King bathe the Buddha. After the Great Dharma King bathed the Buddha and practiced Dharma, each of the attendees bathed the Buddha three times. Great Dharma Teachers

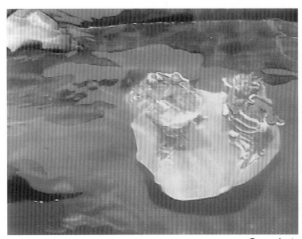
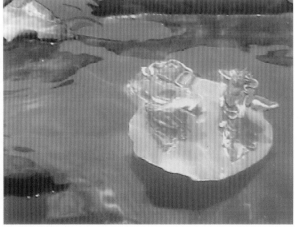

See photo caption (2)

Jue Hui and Ruo Hui wiped dry the statue of the Buddha with a white silk scarf, put a robe on the statue of the Buddha, and placed it back on the altar.

POURING OF WATER BASED UPON ONE'S BUDDHA DHARMA REALIZATION

After the Buddha is bathed, according to the rules and rituals of the Buddha Dharma, it is time to pour fragrant water from the lotus tub used to bathe the Buddha into the lower tub used to bathe the celestial beings. At that time, the Great Dharma King must practice Dharma to bathe the celestial beings. According to fixed Dharma, the bathing of celestial beings must take place in order for it to be a real Highest Form of Bathing the Buddha Dharma Assembly. Otherwise, the words "Highest Form" should not be used. This is the key factor in determining whether the Dharma Assembly will be completely successful.

Dharma Teacher Long Hui announced the ritual and requested that everyone attempt to lift the lotus tub used to bathe the Buddha so that its fragrant water would pour into the tub used to bathe the celestial beings. All of the attendees stepped forward one after another and attempted to lift it in groups of ten.

See photo caption (3)

However, no matter how hard they tried, they could not lift that lotus tub. Later, in violation of the rules, fourteen strong men together attempted to lift that tub. They assumed various postures and used all of their strength to tilt that lotus tub while shouting out a mantra. In the end, their faces turned red, they became exhausted, and they gave up in frustration. They were not able to move that lotus tub one bit. With awkward smiles on their faces, they went back to their seats.

That lotus tub used to bathe the Buddha weighs more than seven hundred pounds. When 90 buckets of fragrant water used to bathe the Buddha were added to this weight, the total weight was 4,260 pounds. Only a large crane could lift that tub. Even world-class musclemen would have no chance of lifting it.

Everyone looked at the lotus tub and felt the situation was hopeless. Great Dharma Teacher Long Hui did not know whether to cry or laugh. She could not announce that the ritual was successfully completed. Under these circumstances, the Dharma Teacher thought of a disciple of the Great Dharma King by the name of Akou Lamo Rinpoche. That Rinpoche is from Tibet and can cause a mani stone to fly through the air. Great Dharma Teacher Long Hui asked Akou Lamo Rinpoche to test her strength and attempt to lift the lotus tub. Akou Lamo Rinpoche said, "I want to select someone to assist me." She then invited an elder layman who lives in the Unites States, Ciren Gyatso, to step forward and assist her. Elder layman Ciren Gyatso has realized the state of prajna emptiness. He constantly abides in the Dharmakaya state. His state of realization is extraordinary. He is the person of great accomplishment spoken of in the tapes contained in the silver box.

See photo caption (4)

Akou Lamo and Ciren Gyatso each held one side of the lotus tub. Upon Akou Lamo's uttering the mantra "Ong Ah Hong," they lifted their shoulders. With a roaring sound of cascading water, the lotus tub tilted upward. Holy water used to bathe the Buddha was poured into the tub used to bathe the celestial beings. Upon another uttering of the mantra "Ong Ah Hong," the two of them again lifted the lotus tub. Like a silver pillar, Dharma water poured into the tub used to bathe the celestial beings.

All of the attendees were astonished! They sat there dumbfounded. Fourteen men using all their strength in concert could not move that more than four thousand-pound lotus tub. However, to everyone's surprise, a young woman and an elder man seventy years old exhibited their states of realization and lifted that lotus tub for all to see! What a wonderful expression of the true Buddha-dharma, of the power of Vajra! Neither of them has any innate spiritual powers. Under Great Dharma King Yeshe Norbu, they have practiced and learned the true dharma and have reached a high level of Buddha-dharma realization. That is why they were able to successfully complete the key ritual of the Dharma Assembly— pouring water based upon one's Buddha-dharma realization. All of the attendees were surprised and praised the two of them highly. Everyone was moved and joyful. That Highest Form of Bathing the Buddha-dharma Assembly was successful precisely because of this holy event.

CELESTIAL DRAGONS LAUGH JOYFULLY

After pure water used to bathe the celestial beings was successfully poured, the Great Dharma King began practicing the dharma to bathe the celestial beings. As soon as all of the attendees chanted in unison one time the verses relating to bathing the celestial beings, suddenly, a strong wind began swirling. The curtain screens began to bulge and rumble. The tankas hanging on the curtain screens flew upward in a ninety-degree angle from the ground. The poles holding up those curtain screens creaked in the wind as if they were about to break. Even the sandbags used to anchor the curtain screens were turned over and moved by the wind. Two-thirds of the people there heard very loud, low and deep dragon's roars explode in the air accompanied by the clap of rolling thunder. One-third of the people there only heard the sound of the wind but did not hear the sound of thunder. This all the more proves the magnificence of the Buddha-dharma, since different karmic states manifested at the same time.

At that time, the hot sun was high in the sky. It seemed as if the joyful roars of the celestial dragons shook the sun so that it shined even more brilliantly! The dharma protecting deities came to the mandala where the Buddha was bathed and received a dharma bathing bestowed by the Buddha! At this time, people remembered that a few days before the Dharma Assembly when the curtain screens and dharma altar were being erected, the Great Dharma King personally arrived. He repeatedly instructed everyone to fasten well the foundational support for the dharma altar and curtain screens so that the altar and screens would not be blown over by the wind. A layperson whose last name is Hsu said to the Dharma King, "The weather station forecasted that there will be no rain or wind for the next seven or eight days." The Great Dharma King then told everyone, "At the Dharma Assembly, of course it will not rain. However, when I practice the dharma, a strong wind will blow. There will be strong gusts of wind, especially when all of the dharma protecting deities arrive and manifest their powerful spirits. Therefore, the foundational support must be fastened firmly." It is very fortunate that the Great Dharma King made such a prediction. On the day of the Dharma Assembly, the dharma protecting deities joyfully laughed in the sky. Although there were strong gusts of wind, the dharma altar and curtain screens did not fall.

A RINPOCHE IS GIVEN A SIGN

After the Dharma King practiced dharma to bathe the celestial beings and the dharma protecting deities, he instructed everyone to look inside the water to see whether the Vajra Wheel was moving. People were amazed to see that even though those two people with holy virtue and high states of realization lifted the lotus tub and thereby poured dharma water from a tub weighing more then 4,000 pounds downward into the tub used to bathe the celestial beings, the Vajra Wheel surprisingly did not move in the slightest. The Vajra Wheel remained in its original position. Many people saw eight dharma protecting Bodhisattvas standing on that dharma object blowing air upward.

At this time, a Rinpoche who weighs 280 pounds beseeched the Vajra Wheel to manifest its powers and eliminate his remaining karmic hindrances. The Great Dharma King agreed to this request and put the Vajra Wheel on that Rinpoche's chest. At first, that Rinpoche felt that the temperature of the Vajra Wheel was cool. The Great Dharma King then began intoning a mantra. With his fingers pointing to the sky, the Great Dharma King lightly snapped his fingers. That Rinpoche suddenly let out a miserable scream. He was in such pain his face turned pale. Like the power the Incantation of the Golden Hoop had over the Monkey King in *Journey To The West*, the Great Dharma King's mantra caused the solemn face of the Rinpoche to become distorted from pain he could not endure. It seemed that

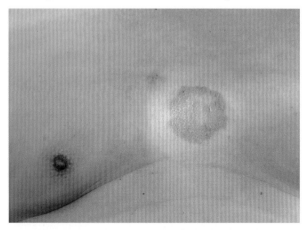

Out of the mark on the body of that overweight Rinpoche, a mandala object has already grown. A ring of light as bright as the light of a flashlight emanates from his skin around that mark. H.H. Dorje Chang Buddha III Wan Ko Yeshe Norbu said, "Next, it will further extend outward, will be translucent and lustrous, and will be like the skin of a baby."

胖子仁波且身上的印記現已長成立體壇城法器圖，而且從肌膚內泛出圓形光環，如手電筒一樣的亮光，三世多杰羌佛雲高益西諾布說：下一步將長得更高，顏色透明光澤，如嬰兒肌膚。

Rinpoche could not endure the pain. As a result of the Great Dharma King practicing a certain dharma, the Vajra Wheel emitted the true fire of samadhi. Its temperature quickly rose to an extremely high degree. Of course, that Rinpoche could not endure such heat.

The Great Dharma King then snapped his fingers again, and the true fire of samadhi instantly disappeared. The Vajra Wheel suddenly became cold. That Rinpoche immediately returned to his normal condition. He was not injured in the least. However, there remained an imprint of the Vajra Wheel on his chest. The Great Dharma King predicted that after one week a three-dimensional dharma object in relief would grow out of the imprint on that Rinpoche's chest. That Rinpoche was full of dharma joy and thanked the Great Dharma King for eliminating his karmic hindrances. That Rinpoche then vowed to do his utmost to benefit living beings.

A CLOUD PROVIDES AN UMBRELA-LIKE COVERING

From the beginning of the Dharma Assembly all the way to its end, a beautiful cloud continuously floated in the sky above the mandala. The shadow of that cloud continuously covered the bronze statue of Dharma Prince Siddhartha. The Dharma Assembly lasted more than three hours. The sun moved westward. That cloud moved together with the sun. It was like an umbrella that served to block the sunlight from the statue of Dharma Prince Siddhartha. However, the sun continued to shine

See photo caption (5)

upon the area of the dharma altar only two or three inches from the statue of Dharma Prince Siddhartha.

THE COLOR OF DHARMA WATER IS RECEIVED

The Dharma Assembly ended solemnly. With buckets, Everyone took some dharma water from the tub used to bathe the Buddha and the tub used to bathe the celestial beings. Suddenly, someone said in a surprised manner, "The dharma water is changing!" Everyone rushed over to see. They discovered that the ninety buckets of light-brown fragrant dharma water taken from the tub instantly became clear water. The Buddha and the celestial beings received the merit of that fragrant water. The merit of the Dharma Assembly was wonderful and complete. All of the attendees prostrated and uttered words of praise.

Great Dharma King Yeshe Norbu conducted this Highest Form of Bathing the Buddha-dharma Assembly, a respected event in the history of Buddhism. The Great Dharma King practiced the dharma during this assembly. All seven holy states were manifested. Water was poured based upon the states of realization of those who poured it. Those two people thereby exhibited their extraordinary powers. The Buddhas and Bodhisattvas and the heavenly dharma protecting deities personally arrived at the mandala and received bathing water bestowed by the Buddha. Various holy states of the Buddha-dharma appeared one after the other. Only this type of magnificent Bathing the Buddha-dharma Assembly is a true Bathing the Buddha-dharma Assembly as stipulated in the dharma. This grand event in Buddhism took place as a result of the good fortune of living beings.

After the Dharma Assembly, one of the two persons with high states of realization who lifted that lotus tub, Akou Lamo Great Rinpoche, requested that the holy lotus tub used to bathe the Buddha be transported to Tibet so that it could serve as an offering in furtherance of Tibetan Buddhism. Great layperson Ciren Gyatso requested that it be kept in the United States as an offering. In order to be fair, the Great Dharma King had everyone vote on the matter. Akou Lamo Great Rinpoche lost the vote by a ratio of three to two. The United International World Buddhism Association Headquarters will keep that lotus tub used to bathe the Buddha. It will be kept in the United States as an offering.

Dharma Teacher Long Hui then announced that all of the attendees should dedicate the merit of that day's dharma practice to a holy person who had recently passed away, laywoman Wang Cheng E-Fen. This holy person was not a follower of another sect. Dharma Teacher Long Hui said that she was, rather, a relative of our most esteemed Master, the Buddha Vajradhara Great Dharma King. This holy person followed the Great Dharma King and practiced Guan Yin Bodhisattva Dharma. On May 23rd, she passed away in Xindu, Sichuan, China.

On May 29th, a reporter received a fax from Xindu. After this holy, elder laywoman passed away, unprecedented holy states appeared. Everyone saw the appearance of auspicious, multi-colored clouds. Amitabha Buddha, Guan Yin Bodhisattva, and other Buddhas and Bodhisattvas appeared in the sky. A multi-colored Buddha light appeared in the sky and surrounded the earth. The head of that elderly laywoman radiated a Buddha light. She left behind more than 60 extremely wonderful, firm relics. These relics were both round and rhombic. The discovery of such holy phenomena was unprecedented in the history of Baoguang Chan Temple, one of the four great temples in China where that laywoman was cremated.

Furthermore, in the afternoon of February 15th of the lunar calendar in the year 1991, Wang Ling-Ze, who was the husband of Wang Cheng E-Fen, stepped outside his house in the Laodong Village of Xindu County. Standing in front of his house, he urged people to be kind and good. He described to people holy sights in the Western Paradise of Ultimate Bliss and told everyone of the true Buddha-dharma. After giving his dharma talk, he showed his control over his own birth and death. Right then and there, he sat down in the cross-legged posture and passed away. He sat there serenely for seven days. His face was like that of a living person. He was also cremated at Baoguang Temple. Many holy phenomena appeared during his cremation. After he was cremated, he left behind thirteen firm relics. These two highly virtuous people were very close relatives of the Great dharma King. They learned under the Great Dharma King, received true dharma from the Great Dharma King, and ended the cycle of birth and death.

PHOTOGRAPHS:

(1) The seven kinds of disciples pour ninety buckets of fragrant water into the lotus tub used to bathe the Buddha.

(2) During the Highest Form of Bathing the Buddha-dharma Assembly, some people saw the Vajra Wheel float up, sink down, and move around in the water. Some also saw the appearance of eight dharma protecting deities. Additionally, some people saw two dharma protecting deities—Mahakala and Sri-maha-devi—supernaturally change their forms. On the right side of the left picture, the head of a dharma protecting deity is very small. The deity is wearing a helmet, and its right hand is holding a skull used to subdue demons. Its left hand is holding a bell. In that left picture, the small head of the dharma protecting deity on the left suddenly became a large head (see right picture). In the left picture, the whole body of the dharma protecting deity on the right is tightly covered with armor. The sleeves of its red robe are small. In the right picture, the small sleeves of the dharma protecting deity on the right suddenly spread open. Its red sleeves and robe became large. It used its hand to lift the robe on its left leg, thereby exposing its leg. In an instant, the two dharma protecting Bodhisattvas appeared. In an instant, they disappeared from the Vajra Wheel without a trace. In both pictures, the Vajra Wheel turned into the shape of a lotus leaf floating on the water. From the size of the Vajra Wheel's shadow, one can know the height of its position in the water. The water was outdoors and reflected countless green lotus flower leaves in the sky.

(3) Fourteen people using all their strength could not lift the lotus tub used to bathe the Buddha that was filled with fragrant water.

(4) Akou Namo Rinpoche and Ciren Gyatso Rinpoche exhibit their true Buddha-dharma states of realization by lifting 4,260 pounds of holy water used to bathe the Buddha and pouring such water into the tub below used to bathe the celestial beings. What ordinary person in this world could lift such a tub? Only those who learned the true Buddha-dharma can lift it.

(5) Buddhist disciples bathe the Buddha. A colorful and auspicious cloud continuously shaded the statue of the Dharma Prince like an umbrella. For more than three straight hours, it did not let the sun shine on the body of the Buddha.

眞正佛教的正法在美國展現

七支聖境眼前現，證量取水眞浴佛

（本文轉載自2004年6月2日《國際日報》第12版。）

西元二零零四年五月二十六日，農曆四月初八，釋迦牟尼佛誕生日。美國的陽光異常明媚，在一所道場的草坪上，一個龐大的藍色帷帳圍成的莊嚴壇城中，來自世界各地的大活佛大法師大居士齊聚一堂，一場殊勝空前的「勝義浴佛法會」正在舉行。這可不是人們在寺廟裏見慣了的普通唱誦世俗浴佛，盡一份恭敬心而已，這是真正正宗的浴佛盛會，是必須以佛菩薩證量感召而聖境顯現的「勝義浴佛法

會」，那是佛陀親臨、護法菩薩顯聖、天龍八部喜笑天空，有各種世人無法想見的聖境出現的法界盛會。主持法會修法者，正是顯宗、密乘金剛總持益西諾布大法王。

法會分內外二壇城，內壇城為中央浴佛城，外壇城為法界悉地。參加法會者高僧大德雲集，內壇城有阿寇娜摩大仁波且、扎西卓瑪仁波且、隆慧法師、覺慧法師、達格貢拉仁波且、波迪溫圖仁波且、魁

智法師、若慧法師、慈仁嘉措大居士、妙空法師、寶蓮法師等。外壇城有伏藏汪怙大仁波且、嚴隆大仁波且、阿王諾布大仁波且、康欽大仁波且、喜饒直奔噶仁波且、益西堪布、慈空法師、法海法師、慈心法師、浩凌法師等。

法義規定，勝義浴佛法會的宗旨必須以浴過佛的法水，以證量取之浴天，以說明佛陀加持諸天、天龍八部、七眾弟子，所以必須圓滿「證量取水」，否則不為勝義浴佛法會。本次法會並且圓滿了「七支聖境」，七支聖境顯現即：一、風慶壇城，二、樹空花雨，三、法器顯聖，四、雲作傘蓋，五、天龍喜笑，六、活佛授記，七、法水收色。「證量取水」成功是法會至關重要的內容，是勝義浴佛法會之關鍵「勝義」所在。就是說浴佛所用的三至五千磅重的法水，浴佛完畢後必須用來浴天，即沐浴仙界諸天，浴天時，須將法水從浴佛蓮池轉取至下方的浴天池內，取水不可人體觸水或用世間容器盛取，因為人體及世間容器染有不淨塵垢，只能整體抬起傾倒，而這麼沉重的法水將如何倒入浴天池，就要靠與會者的佛法證量了，而最多不能十人參抬，否則視為非勝義浴佛。若不能成功將法水倒進浴天池浴天，無論法會出現何種神通聖迹，都不能稱之為「勝義浴佛法會」。

樹空花雨

在這一天的浴佛壇城內，氣氛神聖莊嚴，益西諾布大法王身著法王袍，法相莊嚴無比。一尊悉達多法王子金身銅像矗立壇城，壇城中央有自體重達七百磅、高三英呎的正方形浴佛蓮池，池上有大如車輪的美麗蓮花，浴佛池下方是一英呎高的長方形浴天池。壇城內還放置著九十桶準備浴佛用的香湯，這香湯是用檀香木、沉香、藏紅花等熬製而成的淺咖啡色供水。法會開始，大法王依佛藏修法，剛一起法，草坪上一棵開滿紫櫻花的樹，立刻灑下紛紛花雨，紫櫻花在金色陽光中飛舞，灑遍壇城和幾十桶香湯，天邊祥雲翻滾，法壇似已不在人間，恍若佛國聖地。花雨從法會開始不停飄灑三個多小時，花瓣飄落到眾人身上，而大法王卻未染半片。當法會結束，花雨即刻停止。

法器顯聖

大法王為表顯宗、密乘佛法一體之義，故未派第一流的大德、大仁波且們宣儀和執式，而派漢人法師國際佛教僧尼總會主席隆慧大法師宣儀，覺慧大法師、魁智大法師、若慧大法師、妙空法師執式。隆慧大法師宣儀眾人向浴佛池灌香湯，眾活佛、法師、居士快速將九十桶淺咖啡色香湯灌滿浴佛蓮池，眾人回座恭請大法王開光浴池香湯。但見大法王手持一白色金剛輪，走向浴佛蓮池，將法器放入池中，此法器如錢幣一半的厚度，大如掌心。佛法法義規定，此金剛輪由金剛總持法王擁有，經總持法王加持後護法菩薩駕臨法器之上，法器會在浴佛法水中行走，上升下降，此後即可修勝義浴佛法會。在場眾人圍在池邊觀看法器，一兩分鐘後，大家果然看到金剛輪在水中行走，沒有人碰觸蓮池，而法器卻在水中前後左右自由行走移動，一會兒下沉

水中一會兒又浮上水面，還見到金剛輪在快接近水底時，由金剛輪下發出一道三昧真火紅光。有多人看到八位護法菩薩站在法器上，也有人看到嘛哈嘎拉和吉祥天母在金剛輪上神變。眾人法喜油然。

風慶壇城

法器顯聖之後，眾人齊聲恭誦祈請文。突然，一陣大風自西方吹來，原本風靜樹止的壇場搖晃震蕩，紫櫻花在風中翻飛，眾人無比驚奇，一種無法言喻的祥瑞法喜充滿整個壇城，世尊佛陀已聖臨壇城虛空表法！眾人齊聲持咒恭迎佛陀駕臨。強大西風吹拂約三十秒又戛然而停，風靜樹止如前。吉祥之氣佈滿壇城，在眾人的持咒聲中，神聖浴佛正式開始。魁智大法師迎請悉達多法王子像入蓮池。眾人恭請大法王浴佛，大法王浴佛修法完畢，眾人依序浴佛三次，由覺慧、若慧大法師以哈達擦拭佛像為佛像穿袍、登座。

證量取水

浴佛之後，按儀規要將浴佛香湯轉至浴天池由大法王修法沐浴諸天，這是勝義浴佛法會必須的勝義法定，否則不為勝義，更關係到法會是否圓滿成功。隆慧法師宣儀，請眾人將浴佛蓮池抬起倒香湯入浴天池中。與會眾人紛紛上前，十人為一抬架，卻無論如何抬不起蓮池。後達規用十四位身強力壯的男眾齊力而上，用盡全身力氣，一邊大聲持咒，一邊拉出各種架勢拼命舉抬，直至個個臉漲得通紅，青筋暴跳，蓮池依然紋絲不動，十四個人只好帶著尷尬的笑容退下。要知道，自重七百多磅的蓮池再加進九十桶香湯，已重達四千二百六十磅，除非是大型起重機，普通人就算是世界大力士也別想抬動。眾人望池興歎，無可奈何，隆慧大法師，啼笑皆非，無儀可宣，見此情形，法師想到大法王的弟子，來自西藏，能使瑪尼巨石騰空飛行的阿寇娜摩仁波且，便請她出力。阿寇娜摩仁波且說：「我要選一個人協助。」隨即邀請居美老居士慈仁嘉措一同登臺，慈仁嘉措老居士已證般若空性，長處法身境中，證量非凡，他即是銀盒帶中之大成就者。阿寇娜摩和慈仁嘉措各執蓮池一邊，阿寇娜摩持咒一句「嗡——啊——吽！」兩人雙臂啟動，蓮池竟轟然而起，浴佛聖水被傾入浴天池中，又是一句「嗡——啊——吽！」蓮池再次被二人抬起，法水如銀柱傾入浴天池，眾人大驚駭然，目瞪口呆！十四位男士一起用盡全力都挪動不了的四千多磅的蓮池，竟然在一個年輕女子和一位古稀老者手中施展證量撼然而起，何等威神大力金剛，真實佛法的體現！善者須知，他二人沒有天生神力，只因他們跟隨益西諾布大法王修學正法達到高度的佛法證量，才能於此法會完成勝義取水的關鍵儀式。勝義浴佛法會也由此聖蹟而達到圓滿境界。

天龍喜笑

請得浴天淨水後，大法王開始修法浴天，眾人剛唱誦一遍浴天偈，忽然，一陣大風呼旋而至，將帷帳掀起呼啦猛響，唐卡翻飛，撐

起帷帳的支架發出嘎吱嘎吱將要斷裂的聲音，連固定帷帳用的沙袋也被吹得啪啪翻起移位，風中，有三分之二的人聽到一陣低沉而巨大的龍吟伴隨滾動的雷鳴炸響在空中，有三分之一的人衹聽到風聲，沒聽到雷聲，更是證明佛法的偉大，同時呈現了不同的因緣。此時烈日當空，好像被天龍的喜吟震顫得更加光芒閃爍！天龍八部駕至浴佛壇城領受佛賜法浴！此時眾人想起，就在法會前幾天搭設帷帳法台時，大法王親臨現場，再三叮囑大家要把法台和帷帳的基座固定得非常好，不能被風吹倒。一位徐姓居士對法王說：「氣象台預報了，這七八天，都不會有雨有風。」大法王告訴大家：「法會上自然不會有雨，但修法時會刮起大風，特別是天龍八部到達，威神示現，會有很強的風，因此金剛基座一定要打牢。」幸得大法王提早預言，今日法會天龍喜笑天空，雖強風威勁，法台帷帳卻無恙。

活佛授記

大法王修法浴天、浴天龍八部之後，指示眾人觀看水裏的金剛輪是否有走動，令人驚訝的是蓮池經兩位聖德證量者傾倒法水入浴天池，四千多磅重的法水傾瀉竟然沒有將金剛輪移動半分，法器依然停留在原來的位置，在場有多人看見八位護法菩薩站在法器上對上方吹氣。此時，一位重達兩百八十磅的胖子活佛請求法器施展功力，為他加持消除殘餘業障。法王認可，將法器放在胖子仁波且胸前，開始時活佛覺得法器清涼，但見大法王持咒，手指向空中輕輕一彈，活佛霎時發出一聲慘叫，臉色慘白，猶如孫悟空戴緊箍咒一般，莊嚴五形變態，似不能支撐。那是金剛輪經大法王修法發出三昧真火，溫度遽高，活佛自然無法忍受。這時又見大法王一彈指，三昧真火即刻消失，法器立刻冷卻，活佛瞬間恢復常態，沒有受到任何傷害，只在他的胸前留下了法器的痕跡，大法王授記這位胖子活佛胸前的印跡將於一個禮拜後長出一個浮雕立體法器。胖子活佛十分法喜，感激大法王為他加持消除業障，當場發願誓以最大能力利益眾生。

雲作傘蓋

從法會開始直至結束，有一朵美麗的雲，一直漂浮在壇場上空，雲朵的陰影始終遮罩著悉達多法王子銅鑄像。法會歷時三個多小時，太陽西移，這朵雲也隨著太陽一起移動，像一把傘蓋，為悉達多法王

子像遮擋陽光。而僅離法王子像兩三英吋的法台上卻一直陽光照射。

法水收色

法會莊嚴結束，眾人從浴佛池、浴天池取出法水，忽聽一聲驚訝的「咦？法水怎麼在變！」大家猛然看見，原來的九十桶淺咖啡色香湯，瞬刻間變成了清水。佛陀與諸天已將香湯水之功德收走，法會功德殊勝圓滿，與會大眾禮拜讚歡不止。

由益西諾布大法王修法主持的這一場佛史尊為勝義的浴佛法會，七支聖境圓滿，證量取水超凡之功夫，佛菩薩及諸天護法親臨壇城接受佛賜浴水，各種佛法聖境目不暇接，這樣偉大的浴佛法會，才是法義所定真正正宗的浴佛法會，是眾生福報因緣所致的佛法盛事。法會結束時，抬動蓮池的兩位證量者，阿寇娜摩大仁波且請求將浴佛蓮池此一聖物請回西藏，為藏密佛教事業供奉，慈仁嘉措大居士則請求留在美國供奉，大法王讓大家投票以示公平，結果三比二，阿寇娜摩大仁波且敗掉，此浴佛蓮池將由世界聯合國際佛教總部收藏，留在美國供奉。

此時，隆慧法師宣佈與會眾人將今日修法之功德迴向一位剛剛圓寂的大聖者王程娥芬居士。這位聖者不是任何其他教派的弟子，而是我們至尊恩師總持大法王的親人，依止大法王修學觀音法，五月二十三日在中國四川新都圓寂。

記者於二十九日收到來自新都的傳真，這位圓寂的聖者老居士圓寂後聖境空前，大眾悉皆看見五彩祥雲展現，阿彌陀佛、觀世音菩薩等呈現虛空，五彩佛光圍繞盤旋大地，老居士頭顯佛光，拾得六十餘枚上妙舍利堅固子，除了圓形還有菱形，成為中國四大叢林寶光禪院史無前例的聖蹟；不僅如此，王程娥芬的丈夫王靈澤大居士一九九一年農曆二月十五日下午在新都縣勞動村街面勸人為善，講述西方極樂聖境，說法完畢，於街面生死自由，就地盤腿圓寂坐化，如如七日不動，臉如生人，也是在寶光寺舉行茶毗，出現若干聖境，茶毗後撿出堅固了十二枚，此二位長德均是大法王至親，依止大法王得其正法而了生脫死。

（本書編者注：文中所述益西諾布大法王或大法王即是三世多杰羌佛雲高益西諾布頂聖如來。）

下頁報紙圖片解說：

1. 七眾弟子正向蓮池灌九十桶浴佛香湯。（左上圖）
2. 勝義浴佛法會上，有人看到金剛輪在水中上下浮沉移走時，出現八個護法另有人看到麻哈嘎拉和吉祥天母兩位護法在神變，拍照下來的圖（左下二圖），（見上圖）左邊護法頭甚小，身穿盔殼，右手拿骷嚕伏魔仗，左手拿鈴，（見下圖）左邊護法小頭突然搖身變為大頭。（見上圖）右邊護法全身盔殼嚴緊其身，紅袍袖小，（見下圖）右邊護法紅袍小袖剎那間脫開，紅袖袍變大，用手提起左腿袍褲，大小腿全露，瞬刻間出現又剎那間兩護法從金剛輪上突然消失無影無蹤。（見二圖）金剛輪變為荷葉狀在水中浮沉，見金剛輪的陰影的大小即知祂在水中的位置高低

不同，水上為露天天空，水中同時映有無數天空中的綠色蓮花葉。
3. 十四人用盡全力也無法抬起注滿香湯的浴佛蓮池。（中上圖）
4. 阿寇娜摩仁波且與慈仁嘉措仁波且顯示真正的佛法證量，將四千二百六十磅浴佛聖水正提起倒入浴天池中。若不是學到真佛法世界上那一個凡夫能抬得起？（右下圖）
5. 佛弟子正在舉行浴佛，空中一朵五彩祥雲如傘蓋一直遮著法王子像，三個多小時不離開，不讓陽光照到佛的身上。（右上圖）

During the "Highest Form of Bathing the Buddha Dharma Assembly" conducted by
H.H. Dorje Chang Buddha III Wan Ko Yeshe Norbu Holiest Tathagata, the seven holy states appeared, which astounded and impressed people around the world.
Below is the full newspaper article on this from the Chinese newspaper International Daily News dated June 2, 2004.
三世多杰羌佛雲高益西諾布頂聖如來主持修法『勝義浴佛法會』，七支聖境驚攝世人，以下是《國際日報》二零零四年六月二日的報導全文。

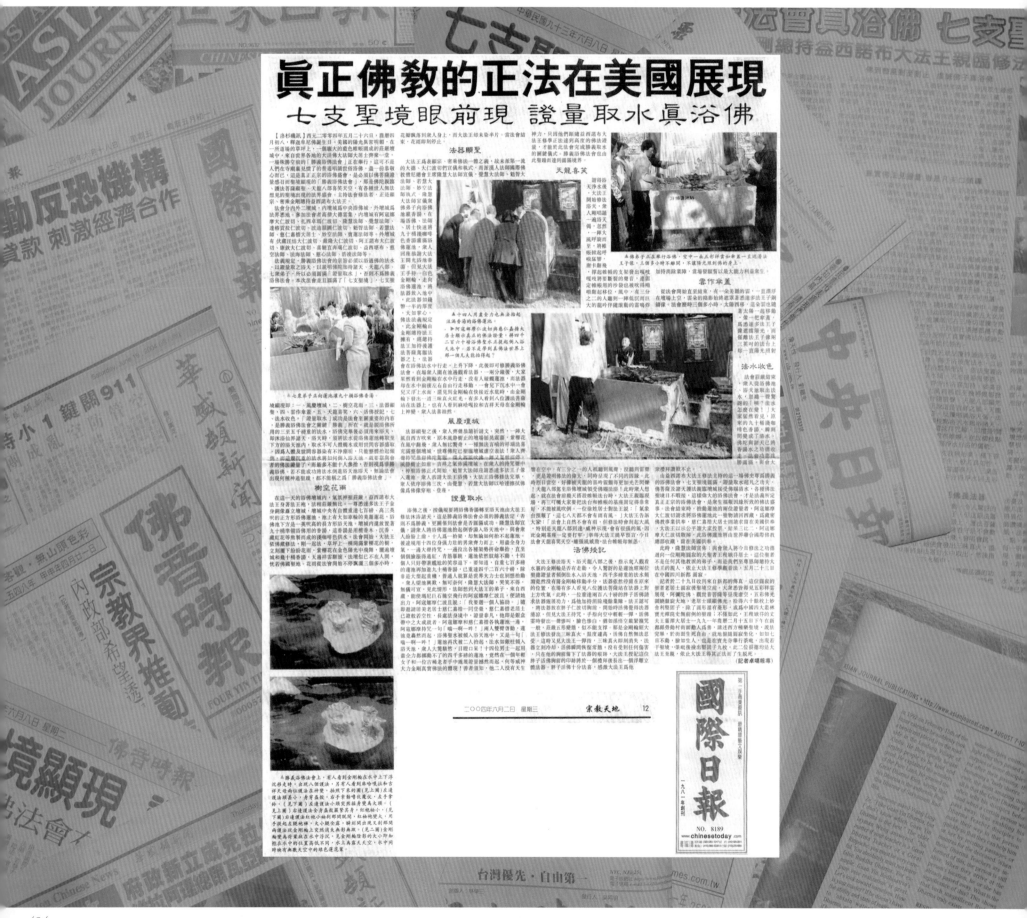

DAZZLING LIGHT WAS ALL AROUND; BUDDHA LIGHT SHINED PROFUSELY ABOVE; THE HOLY NAME OF GUAN YIN BODHISATTVA REVERBERATED THROUGH THE THREE SPHERES; THE BUDDHAS APPEARED IN THEIR COMPLETE FORMS

LAYWOMAN WANG CHENG E-FEN AND HER HUSBAND, LAYMAN WANG LING-ZE, LEARNED THE TRUE BUDDHA DHARMA AND REALIZED GREAT ACCOMPLISHMENT

(This is the text of an article published in the Asian Journal on Jul. 21, 2004.)

HER BREATHING STOPPED, YET SHE CONTINUED TO LIVE AND WAS ABLE TO SPEAK

Laywoman Wang Cheng E-Fen was a native of Xindu County in Sichuan, China. She was eighty-one years old this year. This elder laywoman followed the Buddha Vajradhara Great Dharma King Yeshe Norbu[1]. She practiced the Guan Yin Dharma taught to her by the Great Dharma King. She was a very close relative of the Great Dharma King.

This year, she suddenly felt discomfort in her lower back area. The doctors at the Number 47 Hospital diagnosed her as having bone cancer. In March of this year, this elder laywoman showed signs of impending death. On April 13th, her children took her to the Chengdu General Hospital. Examinations revealed that she had no symptoms of bone cancer. All of her indices were normal. Her electrocardiogram and electroencephalogram indicated she had no disease and was healthy.

X-rays of her chest area were taken on April 18th. The area of the x-ray where her two lungs should have been visible was not developed at all. There was just a blank space in that area. The doctors were very surprised at this, since this situation had never occurred before. After further examination, they determined that her two lungs had completely stopped functioning. She had no respiratory function. She could not inhale or exhale.

Everyone was extremely mystified. Isn't someone dead when his or her breathing stops? But even though laywoman Wang Cheng E-Fen was not breathing, she was still alive. Moreover, she was able to speak in a normal manner! Someone put a small feather under this elder laywoman's nostrils, right in front of her mouth. People watched that feather for more than ten minutes and, just as expected, it did not move in the slightest. That elder laywoman had no respiration at all. Nonetheless, she continued to live and speak in a normal manner. The doctors thought that this was a bizarre symptom. As far as medical circles and even as far as the entire world is concerned, this was an unheard-of situation. With her two lungs not functioning at all for more than one month, this elder laywoman was able to speak and move about. Of course, no one knew that this was the result of the realization she achieved from practice of the Buddha Dharma.

THE GREAT DHARMA KING SET THE DATE AND INVITED GUAN YIN BODHISATTVA TO COME AND TAKE THE ELDER LAYWOMAN TO HER NEXT EXISTENCE

After Wang Cheng E-Fen had stayed in the Chengdu General Hospital for two or three days, she manifested certain signs that indicated a highly virtuous person was about to go to the Western Paradise. She told everyone that Guan Yin Bodhisattva had already told her that she (Guan Yin Bodhisattva) was going to take her to the Western Paradise of Ultimate Bliss. That elder laywoman arranged matters that related to her passing away. She took off the necklace she wore on her chest depicting a Buddha image. She took off all of the jewelry on her hands. She divided these things among her children. She put on clothes worn by one who has already passed away. She then quietly waited for Guan Yin Bodhisattva to arrive. She put her palms together in respect and continuously chanted "Homage to Guan Yin Bodhisattva." She told all of the people who were there to chant scriptures or mantras to kneel down and chant the holy name "Guan Yin Bodhisattva." She said that Guan Yin Bodhisattva had already arrived.

All of the patients in that hospital room suddenly smelled a fragrant scent. Heavenly music began playing in the air. The Bodhisattva had arrived. However, it was not time for that elder laywoman to pass away. That elder laywoman told everyone that Guan Yin Bodhisattva told her that a relative of hers who is far away in the United States, Great Dharma King Yeshe Norbu, had intervened and requested Guan Yin Bodhisattva not to take her away at this time.

A few days later, Guan Yin Bodhisattva arrived for a second time. That elder laywoman did not disturb any of the people who were at her side. She alone continued to chant her mantra and hold her palms together in respect. Those people who were at her side heard her say, "The Western Paradise is so beautiful! There are so many flowers!" Because the Great Dharma King asked Guan Yin Bodhisattva not to take the elder laywoman away, just as before, Guan Yin Bodhisattva did not take her away.

When I interviewed her, although she did not want to say very much, out of a sense of responsibility, that elder laywoman insisted on personally recording the following: "I saw Guan Yin Bodhisattva wearing black clothes. The Western Paradise is so beautiful! There are towers, pagodas, and many flowers!"

A STATUE OF THE BUDDHA EMITS LIGHT, THEREBY SHOWING THE TRUE DHARMA

On May 22, 2004 of the western calendar at 11:00 at night, Los Angeles, U.S.A. time, (May 23rd, 2:00 in the afternoon, China time) the Great Dharma King summoned Dharma Teacher Long Hui, a noble monastic. Dharma Teacher Long Hui is the chairperson of the International Buddhism Sangha Association. The Great Dharma King told her that a very close relative of his, laywoman Wang Cheng E-Fen, would pass away in Sichuan, China the next day, U.S.A. time, but the

---

[1] Here and below the words *Buddha Vajradhara*, *Great Dharma King*, and *Dharma King* refers to H.H. Dorje Chang Buddha III Wan Ko Yeshe Norbu Holiest Tathagata.

same day in China. The Great Dharma King said that Guan Yin Bodhisattva would receive her and take her to the Western Paradise of Ultimate Bliss. The Great Dharma King told his disciple, Dharma Teacher Long Hui, to announce the passing of laywoman Wang Cheng E-Fen in front of the various disciples attending the Bathing the Buddha Dharma Assembly that would take place the next day. He also instructed Dharma Teacher Long Hui to have the attendees dedicate the merit of that Dharma Assembly to that elder laywoman. The Great Dharma King added, "Listen carefully. She has not yet passed away at this time. The merit of that Bathing the Buddha Dharma Assembly that all of you will conduct tomorrow will be quite extraordinary. I cannot again ask Guan Yin Bodhisattva to have her stay in this world any longer. After I finish practicing the Dharma tonight, tomorrow Guan Yin Bodhisattva will come and receive her and take her away."

As predicted, the next day (May 23rd) at 7:00 in the morning, Los Angeles time (May 23rd, around 10:00 at night, China time), before Dharma Teacher Long Hui arrived at the Dharma Assembly, a telephone call was received from Sichuan. The person on the phone said that Guan Yin Bodhisattva received and took away laywoman Wang Cheng E-Fen twenty minutes ago.

That day at the Dharma Assembly, the bathing the Buddha ceremony had just finished, and everyone was dedicating merit to the elder laywoman Wang Cheng E-Fen. Everyone then saw that the bronze statue of Dharma Prince Sakyamuni, who was wearing a red robe, suddenly began emitting dazzling golden rays of light. This light did not diminish even after a long time. Only after two and a half hours did it slowly disappear. Such a sight was very much connected with the fact that the Great Dharma King taught the elder laywoman the correct Dharma of the Buddha, and she thereby attained great accomplishment. Otherwise, why is it that in all of the other Bathing the Buddha Dharma Assemblies in history no one saw the statue of the Buddha emitting light?

NEWS OF EVENTS SURROUNDING THE PASSING OF LAYWOMAN WANG CHENG E-FEN SPREAD ACROSS THE PACIFIC OCEAN

On May 23rd after 9:30 at night, China time, Guan Yin Bodhisattva had just received and taken away Wang Cheng E-Fen. The mantra-chanting device bought from a street-store and placed in her room was emitting its regular chanting sound. Suddenly, the chanting sound coming from that device turned into the sound of Great Dharma King Yeshe Norbu—who was on the other side of the Pacific Ocean—chanting "Homage to Guan Yin Bodhisattva"! The sound of the Great Dharma King chanting the name of Guan Yin Bodhisattva was much louder and clearer than the original sound coming from that machine. Everyone who heard this was moved and astonished. Shi Xin Zhen was so moved she recorded the sound of the Great Dharma King's voice.

On May 24th after 10:00 at night, China time, the body of Wang Cheng E-Fen was taken to a simple but dignified room in the Baoguang Temple, one of the four great temples in China. At the time, her face looked healthy and rosy.

BUDDHAS AND BODHISATTVAS APPEARED IN THE SKY; BUDDHA LIGHTS AND RAINBOWS DESCENDED UPON THE EARTH

On May 25th after 4:00 in the afternoon, China time, in a room that had just been constructed in Baoguang Temple, disciples of the Great Dharma King were calmly chanting the holy mantra, "Homage to Guan Yin Bodhisattva." Before long, everyone heard that the original sound coming from the mantra-chanting device suddenly stopped. The sound coming from that machine changed into that of

Great Dharma King Yeshe Norbu leading many people in the chanting of "Homage to Guan Yin Bodhisattva." Before long, that sound turned into the chanting of "Homage to Amitabha Buddha." The sound then again became the chanting of "Homage to Guan Yin Bodhisattva." Everyone was very moved and chanted along with the Great Dharam King. Shi Xin Zhen and Shi Xin En recorded all of this on the spot.

About five minutes later, a Buddha Light flashed upon the Buddha altar and the body of laywoman Wang Cheng E-Fen. Right after that, a Buddha Light appeared in the sky. Everyone rushed outside. They prostrated and shouted with joy. Everyone saw those wonderful sights no matter whether he or she was a disciple of the Great Dharma King or whether he or she was learning and practicing Buddhism.

A colorful Buddha Light slowly extended through the sky. The scene was just as the Amitabha Sutra described. Out of the Buddha Light came countless Buddhas as well as Bodhisattvas who were sitting there as far as the eye could see. The radiance spread into infinite space. The surrounding clouds turned into various colors. The land, sky, and trees were covered with a golden-yellow, bluish light. The sun and the E-Mei moon appeared together. The sun and moon shining together was a solemn and auspicious event. The sun continuously flashed and shook.

From the sun emerged countless Buddhas and Bodhisattvas. Very soon after that, silver wheels as well as innumerable Dharma eyes that shined with boundless radiance emerged from the sun. Male lions wearing colorful ornaments and flood dragons also emerged from the sun! Guan Yin Bodhisattva, who was in the Buddha Light, was wearing a long dress, looking wondrous and dignified. The head of Sakyamuni Buddha, the world-honored one, then appeared, looking larger than even the sun. Golden-yellow light enveloped the faces and bodies of people on ground. The colorful Buddha Light immediately projected its light upon the chest of anyone who requested empowerment. People knelt down continuously to worship.

The Dharma names of those who personally saw the holy sight of this Buddha Light are as follows: Shi Zhi Lan, Shi Zhi Qing, Shi Xin Zhen, Shi Xin En, Shi Xin Feng, Shi Zhi Lian, Shi Dao Rong, Shi Yi Zong, Shi Zhi Guang, Shi Chao Jing, Shi Nian Ci, Shi Nian De, Shi Nian Zhen, Shi Zhi Ying, Shi Zhi De, Shi Xin Ying, Shi Dao Wei, Shi Zhi Xiu, etc., totaling almost thirty people. The holy scene of the Buddha Light lasted about one hour. Everyone was moved, joyous, and extremely excited.

DURING THE CREMATION CEREMONY, NECTAR DESCENDED; BODHISATTVAS ON LOTUS PEDESTALS EMERGED FROM THE FURNACE

In China, the weather of May 28th was hotter then it had been for the past few days. The elder laywoman had already passed away several days before. The casket containing her body was placed in a simple room in Baoguang Temple. Her body was not frozen. There was no air conditioning or electric fan in that room. People who were alive emitted body odor due to heavy perspiration. However, the body of that elder laywoman emitted a heavy fragrance. Everyone there smelled this scent. Two monks from the Baoguang Temple made a special trip to examine this phenomenon. With great amazement, they said, "The weather is so hot. Even though her body has been placed here for so many days, there haven't been any problems with it. There are no signs of water on the ground. There is even a fragrant scent. She truly cultivated herself well."

In that room, many people saw the statue of Amitabha Buddha on the altar emit strong golden rings of light three times, each time lasting about ten minutes. A photograph of the elder laywoman and the top of her head gleamed with dazzling golden light at the same time. The Buddha Light outside of that room was gorgeous, just as before. In that room, disciples of the Great Dharma King recited the name of a Buddha with undivided attention. A monk in the Baoguang Temple then said in an urgent tone of voice, "You have still not gone outside to see the Buddha Light? There are so many Bodhisattvas in the sky!"

On May 29th, China time, the cremation ceremony for elder laywoman Wang Cheng E-Fen formally took place. Dharma Teacher Ji Xin, the master of cremation at Baoguang Temple, was in charge of that ceremony. When the solemn mantra chanting ended, flames began to rise. Before her wooden casket was fully on fire, various holy Buddha Dharma states appeared! A colorful and flashing Buddha Light surrounded and circled the earth. Shouts of joy could be heard one after another from people who saw this holy scene. Cell phones, cameras, and camcorders were lifted high. They did not need to be focused, and nobody needed to find a view. Everything was taken in, since holy scenes were everywhere.

From the raging furnace fire, suddenly flood dragon soared. It spewed fire from its mouth and roared powerfully. Amitabha Buddha, Guan Yin Bodhisattva, Four-Arm Guan Yin, and Manjushri Bodhisattva holding the sword of wisdom all suddenly appeared. Seed syllables, vajras, Dharma protecting deities, male lions, phoenixes, lotus flowers, rainbows, and various other kinds of amazing scenes continually emerged as the furnace flames rose. The mantra-chanting device again emitted the sound of the Great Dharma King chanting the name of a Buddha. Suddenly, nectar descended from the sky. It was fragrant and sweet. The nectar only fell on the cremation furnace. No nectar fell upon any place surrounding the furnace.

The appearance of all of these holy scenes caused people to be brimming with joy. Since the cremation furnace of Baoguang Temple was built until today, such joyous circumstances had had never before occurred. The Dharma names of those people who were at the cremation and personally saw holy sights are as follows: Shi Xin En, Shi Xin Feng, Shi Xin Yu, Shi Zhi Wen, Shi Xin Miao, Shi Dao Zhen, Shi Dao Chun, Shi Dao Zhi, Shi Xin Xiao, Shi Zhi Lian, Shi Xin Yuan, Shi Guang Xiu, Shi Dao Guang, Shi Guang Wen, Qude Damu, Shi Zhi De, Shi Yi Zeng, Shi Zhi Da, Shi Zhi Xiu, Shi Zhen Xiong, Shi Zhen De, Shi Dao Shan, Shi De Hai, Shi Guang Yun, Shi Zhi Qing, Shi Guang Ling, Shi Zhi Zhang, Shi Zhi Ming, Shi Zhi Hai, Shi Guang Feng, Shi De Ming, Shi De Chao, Shi Zhi Bo, etc. There were also many other unknown people. Everyone there expressed their admiration in loud voices and knelt down right then and there.

SHE ATTAINED ILLUSTRIOUS ACCOMPLISHMENT; HER LEVEL OF REALIZATION RESULTED IN SHARIRAS AND SHARIRA FLOWERS OF THE HIGHEST QUALITY

What is even more amazing is that from the bone ashes of elder laywoman Wang Cheng E-Fen more than sixty shariras (relics) of different colors, as well as yellow and white sharira flowers of the highest quality, were found! The shape of some on the shariras was rhombic. This caused a sensation in all of Baoguang Temple and in Buddhist circles throughout China. These are holy things that are extremely rare in history. They are true Buddhist treasures. They manifest the holy state described as follows: "The Western Paradise has row of gems and nets of gems. This is very mysterious. All of the lotus flowers there blossom perfectly."

Wu You-Jia from Taiwan said, "Those shariras (relics) are truly wondrous treasures. During the process of searching for shariras, I saw a lump of bone ashes the size of a human palm. People had searched through it a few times. Surprisingly, I found two shariras within it. I then looked through it carefully once more. I was sure there were no more shariras in it. At that time, I saw another disciple find three shariras in that lump of bone ashes that I searched through. Another disciple from Taiwan, Li Hui-Zhu, had a serious ailment related to her hands. Because her tactile sense was not good, she only used three fingers to search for shariras in the bone ashes. She said that although she did not find even one sharira, the next morning she discovered that all of the symptoms relating to the three fingers she used to search for shariras had disappeared."

An endless stream of visitors came to pay their respects to the shariras. Many people from various circles in society came. Baoguang Temple specially photographed the elder laywoman's shariras. The temple openly and respectfully handed out that photograph to everybody.

HUSBAND AND WIFE BOTH REALIZED HOLY ACCOMPLISHMENTS; THE ELDER WANG ATTAINED CONTROL OVER HIS OWN BIRTH AND DEATH

As La Mu said in her article entitled "Analysis of the Highest Form of Bathing the Buddha Dharma Assembly," if the only disciple of the Great Dharma King who became accomplished in the Dharma were Wang Cheng E-Fen, perhaps it would be coincidental. But something mysterious happened. Layman Wang Ling-Ze, the husband of laywoman E-Fen, also practiced the Dharma according to the teachings of the Great Dharma King. Throughout his entire life, he did not discuss the Buddha Dharma. One afternoon in 1991 on February 15th of the lunar calendar, he suddenly took a bench and placed it on the roadside in the Laodong Village of Xindu. He then openly began urging people to be kind and good. He explained the wonders of the Pure Land. He praised the Great Dharma King, saying that his Dharma is the authentic Buddha Dharma of Sakyamuni Buddha.

Someone asked Wang Ling-Ze, "I like Guan Yin Dharma, but I don't know which Guan Yin Dharma is the best." The elder layman Wang answered, "No

修觀音法得大成就之王程娥芬居士於新都
寶光寺火化出五彩舍利子及上品上等舍利花　2004年5月29日

Please see photo caption (1)

matter if your teacher is a Great Dharma Teacher or a Great Rinpoche, you must be very careful. You absolutely must not learn false Buddha Dharma. For example, Guan Yin Bodhisattva's 'pure vase realization' is great. Let's look toward ourselves. How is your master? If he doesn't have the ability and state of realization to 'obtain water,' transmit Dharma, and conduct initiations, if he does not practice the precepts well, then he just understands the common Dharma written in books. Rather than learn from such a person, you would accumulate more merit if you intoned 'Homage to Guan Yin Bodhisattva.' True Guan Yin Dharma involves 'obtaining water' either in a gentle way or a forceful way. Obtaining water in a forceful way involves one or two persons lifting a lotus tub weighing over 5,500 pounds and pouring out the water from it. This is the true Buddha Dharma. Obtaining water in a gentle way involves the following. You secretly prepare a bowl outside the presence of the master. You fill it with water and take it out. The master immediately practices the Dharma in front of you. Water instantly flows through the bowl toward you. It is like the holy water in the pure vase of Guan Yin Bodhisattva. No containers in this world can hold the holy water in that pure vase. That holy water will penetrate through and flow out of any such worldly container. When used in initiations and Dharma transmissions, holy water that has flowed through a bowl can wash away your karmic hindrances accumulated over many past lifetimes. This is true Guan Yin Dharma. I have learned this true Buddha Dharma transmitted to me by Great Dharma King Yeshe Norbu. Water penetrated through the bowl. Therefore, I am about to go to the Western Paradise of Ultimate Bliss."

When the elder layman Wang finished expounding the Dharma, he pushed the bench to one side and sat down in the cross-legged posture in front of his house near the road. He instantly passed away. He illustrates the magnificence of the Buddha Dharma transmitted by the Great Dharma King, which leads to control over one's own birth and death. According to the rules of Buddhism, after the elder layman passed away, his body could not be touched for seven days. Therefore, he sat solemnly in the cross-legged posture at that very spot near the public street for seven days and seven nights. His back remained completely upright. After his cremation at the Baoguang Temple in Xindu, thirteen firm shariras (relics) were left behind.

I went to the Baoguang Temple in Xindu and paid twelve yuan to buy a photograph openly sold by the temple showing the sharira and sharira flowers left behind by laywoman Wang Cheng E-Fen after her cremation. I learned from a documentary video as well as from other sources that many disciples of the Great Dharma King include world-class outstanding monastics, first-class elder monastics in Taiwan, first-class elder monastics and Great Rinpoches in mainland China and Hong Kong, and first-class eminent monastics and Great Rinpoches in

the United States. Furthermore, many disciples of the Great Dharma King include husband and wife couples who obtained control over their own births and deaths. Some of his disciples passed away while they sat in the cross-legged posture, chanted the name of Amitabha Buddha, and held their hands in a special mudra. The bodies of some disciples emitted dazzling light after they passed away. The corpses of some disciples do not rot after their passing, thereby becoming a "body sharira."

However, the most amazing thing of all is that the Great Dharma King often tells his disciples beforehand when a certain person will pass away, thus enabling his Dharma Teacher disciples to make their way to that person quickly so that they can help him or her by reciting passages or mantras for the deceased. When those Dharma Teachers are informed of this, the person is still alive. When they arrive at the person's location, he or she has already passed away. What is the significance of this? This shows that such magnificent Buddha Dharma truly exists.

A layperson with the surname Mai, who often worships the Buddha at the Baoguang Temple, was very moved and told a reporter, "During these past several years, I have been very anxious. I have acknowledged many great Dharma Teachers and great Rinpoches as my teachers, but I have still not learned the true Buddha Dharma. I fear the arrival of the critical moment of death. Of course, I chant the name of Amitabha Buddha every day. But I am clearer than anyone else is about the level of my practice. I am clearer than anyone else is about whether I am an ordinary person. I have not learned the true Buddha Dharma. I am not the only one. Everyone else around me is in the same situation. At the time of my death, I will surely enter the cycle of reincarnation. This is very frightening. I have prayed to the Buddhas and Bodhisattvas that I may learn the true Buddha Dharma. For the past few days, I have seen holy states relating to the great accomplishment of Cheng E-Fen. I know that the Buddhas and Bodhisattvas have blessed me by causing me to find the true Buddha Dharma! A few of us fellow disciples have discussed this matter. We will use every means to find the master who taught laywoman Cheng E-Fen how to become accomplished. I know that he is truly an extremely holy being. We heard that laywoman Cheng E-Fen's husband also passed away in the cross-legged sitting posture in complete control of his death and future rebirth. That was also the result of the Dharma King's transmission of Buddha Dharma. If we did not seek out that Dharma King, who else would we seek out? Of course we must try to find him. Only that Dharma King can solve the matter of life and death that we face. We must sincerely search for him!"

CAPTIONS FROM PHOTOGRAPHS ON PREVIOUS AND FOLLOWING PAGE:

(1) *Laywoman Wang Cheng E-Fen, who is the mother of virtuous professor Wang Yu-Hua, became accomplished by practicing the Guan Yin Dharma. After her cremation at the Baoguang Temple in Xindu County, Sichuan, China, she left behind more than 60 shariras (relics) of various colors as well as sharira flowers of the highest quality. Such relics can truly be called rare Buddhist treasures in the history of Buddhism. They manifest the holy state described as follows: "The Western Paradise has row of gems and nets of gems. This is very mysterious. All of the lotus flowers there blossom perfectly."*

(2) *Guan Yin Bodhisattva has already escorted laywoman Wang Cheng E-Fen to the Western Paradise of Ultimate Bliss.*

(3) *Various temples together conducted a Bathing the Buddha Dharma Assembly in which all of the attendees dedicated the merit of that assembly to laywoman*

Wang Cheng E-Fen. After that dedication, a statue of the Buddha emitted light for more than two hours (right). Such shining light is closely related to the fact that the Great dharma King transmitted dharma to laywoman Wang Cheng E-Fen, and she thereby attained great accomplishment. On the left is a picture of a statue of the Buddha before it emitted light. That statue is made of bronze but is gilded with non-lustrous gold. It is now an object of worship at the Hua Zang Temple.

(4) *Great layman Wang Ling-Ze passed away on February 15, 1991 while sitting in the cross-legged posture. This is a photograph taken of him five days after he passed away. When he was still sitting in front of his house in the cross-legged posture with his back erect.*

(5) *Great layman Wang Ling-Ze left behind 13 firm relics after his cremation.*

毫光遍地 佛光紛飛 聖號三界徹震 諸佛現全身

王程娥芬居士及丈夫王靈澤居士學到眞正的佛法得大成就

（本文轉載自2004年6月17日
《台灣時報》A23版。）

無呼吸功能　還活著講話

王程娥芬居士，中國四川新都縣人氏，今年八十一歲，老居士依止金剛總持益西諾布大法王（即三世多杰羌佛雲高益西諾布頂聖如來——本書編者注，下同）修學觀音法，是大法王的至親。去年突然腰部不適，經四七醫院醫生診斷，認為是骨癌，今年三月，老居士顯四大分解之相，四月十三日被子女送入成都總醫院，經檢查，無骨癌症狀，一切指標正常，心電圖、腦電圖都診斷無病，身體健康。但四月十八日的X光胸片上卻看見雙肺全無顯影，一片空白，醫生十分驚訝，從未見過這種情況。進一步檢查，確定雙肺完全停止工作，沒有呼吸功能了，不能吸氣也不能出氣了。所有人都奇怪極了，沒了呼吸不就是死人嗎？可王程娥芬居士沒有呼吸還照常是活人，而且還能正常說話！有人將一片小羽毛放在老居士鼻孔和嘴巴前，果然眼睜睜看見十幾分鐘過去，羽毛紋絲未動，老居士徹底沒有了呼吸，但卻還正常地活著講著話。醫生們認為這是奇異症狀，這是醫學界乃至整個人類世界的一件奇聞。老居士就這樣在雙肺完全停止工作的情況下，一個多月內能說話能活動。大家當然不瞭解，這就是老居士修持佛法的證量。

大法王定日請觀音菩薩接引往升

王程娥芬老居士住進成都總醫院兩三天，便呈現大德西歸之境。她告訴大家觀世音菩薩已經通知她要接她去西方極樂世界了。她做好後事安排，把胸前掛的佛像，手上戴的飾品全摘下來分給兒女，換上了壽衣，靜待觀世音菩薩到來。她不停地合掌念誦「南無觀世音菩薩」，還叫助念的人都跪下念誦觀世音菩薩聖號，說菩薩已經到了。果然，全病房的人突然聞到異香撲鼻，空中有天樂響起，菩薩駕臨，但老居士卻沒有走成。老居士對大家說，觀音菩薩告訴她，是她遠在美國的親人益西諾布大法王阻攔，請菩薩不要接走。幾日後觀世音菩薩第二次來接，老居士沒有驚動身邊的人，獨自不停地念誦、合掌，旁邊的人聽到她說：「極樂世界好美哦！好多花啊！」這次依然是因為大法王請觀世音菩薩不要接走老居士。記者採訪時，老居士雖然不願多講話，但還是很負責任地一定要親自錄音：「我看見了觀世音菩薩穿的青衣，極樂世界好美啊！還有樓臺亭閣，好多花啊！」

佛像放光顯正法

西元二零零四年五月二十二日，美國洛杉磯時間晚上十一點（中國時間五月二十三日下午兩點），國際佛教僧尼總會主席、高僧隆慧法師被她的大法王上師叫到面前，告訴她，法王的至親王程娥芬居士，將于美國第二天，中國的今天，在中國四川省圓寂，由觀世音菩薩接引往升西方極樂世界。大法王讓弟子隆慧法師在第二天將要舉行的浴佛法會上，公開對七眾弟子宣佈王程娥芬居士圓寂，並將修法功德回向給老居士。大法王又補充說：「你聽清楚，她現在還沒圓寂。明天你們舉行浴佛法會，功德較為殊勝，我不能再請觀世音菩薩留下她了，等我晚上修

完法，明天觀世音菩薩就會來接她走。」果然第二日（五月二十三日），洛杉磯時間早上七點，中國時間二十三日晚上十點左右，在隆慧法師到法會現場之前，接到來自四川的電話，說王程娥芬居士已於二十分鐘前，被觀世音菩薩接走。

在當天的法會上，浴佛儀式剛剛完成，眾人將功德回向王程娥芬老居士，忽然所有人看到穿紅色法袍的釋迦牟尼法王子銅鑄像忽然放射極為耀眼的金色光芒，久久不散，歷時兩個半小時才慢慢消失。這與大法王傳老居士如來正法得大成就息息相關，否則歷史上怎麼從未有哪次浴佛會見到佛像放光？

王程娥芬居士圓寂　法音飛越太平洋

中國時間五月二十三日晚上九點半過，王程娥芬老居士剛被觀世音菩薩接走，房中那個以前從街上買來的念佛器裏發出的普通念唱聲，突然變成了遠在太平洋彼岸的益西諾布大法王在念誦「南無觀世音菩薩」！大法王念佛聲比念佛器裏原來的聲音要大聲、清晰得多！在場的人感動又震驚，釋心珍激動地錄下了大法王的法音。中國時間五月二十四日晚上十點多，王程娥芬老居士紅光滿面的法體被迎奉到中國四大叢林之一寶光寺中簡易而莊嚴的佛堂。

諸佛菩薩空中現　佛光彩虹降地來

中國時間五月二十五日下午四點多，在臨時搭建的寶光寺佛堂，大法王眾弟子靜心念誦「南無觀世音菩薩」聖號，不多久，所有人都聽到念佛器裏突然沒有了原來的聲音，而變成益西諾布大法王領著許多人在念誦「南無觀世音菩薩」，未久又轉念「南無阿彌陀佛」，後又再誦「南無觀世音菩薩」，眾人激動地隨著大法王一聲聲念誦，釋心珍、釋心恩兩人現場錄了音。約五分鐘後，一道佛光閃耀，投射在佛台和王程娥芬居士的法體上。隨即，空中出現了佛光。所有人都奔出屋外頂禮歡呼，無論是否大法王弟子，無論是否學佛修行的人，都各自看到了奇妙景象。天空中五彩佛光旬旬擴散，一如彌陀經所述，佛光中化佛無數，化菩薩廣坐無邊，光彩擴張至無際之空；四周的雲朵呈斑斕七彩，地上、空中、樹上佈滿金黃、藍色的光圈；太陽與峨嵋月同在一處，日月同輝莊嚴吉祥；太陽不停閃爍跳躍，從中化出了無數佛菩薩，很快又化出銀輪和數不清的毫光萬丈的法眼，或化出身著彩飾的雄獅，還有蛟龍！佛光中觀世音菩薩身著長裙殊勝莊嚴，轉而又出現釋迦世尊的頭像比太陽還大；人們的臉上、身上被金色黃光籠罩，凡求加持的人，五彩佛光立即投射到胸前加持，人們不停地跪拜禮贊。當時親見佛光聖境的人法號是：釋智蘭、釋智清、釋心珍、釋心恩、釋心鳳、釋智蓮、釋道榮、釋一宗、釋智廣、釋朝靜、釋念慈、釋念德、釋念真、釋智英、釋智德、釋心應、釋道威、釋智秀等近三十人，佛光聖境歷時足有一小時左右，人人激動歡喜，興奮異常。

茶毗法事降甘露　爐中蓮台菩薩顯

中國時間五月二十八日，這一天的氣溫是幾天來最高的。老居士已圓寂多日，法體龕放在寶光寺的簡易佛堂，沒有冰凍，沒有空調，電風扇都沒有一把，活著的人都滿身汗臭，老居士的法體卻散發出濃郁撲鼻的異香，在場所有人都聞到。兩位寶光寺的僧人特來檢查，驚異地說：「這麼熱的天氣，放這麼多天都沒事，地上沒有水跡，還異香撲鼻，確實修得好。」佛堂裏許多人看到佛臺上阿彌陀佛像發出三次強烈的金色光環，每次十分鐘左右，而老居士的照片和法體頭上同時閃爍耀眼的金光。外面的佛光依然絢麗，大法王的弟子都在佛堂專心念佛，寶光寺比丘著急地說：「你們還不出來看佛光啊，天上那麼多菩薩！」

中國時間五月二十九日，王程娥芬老居士的茶毗法事正式舉行，由寶光寺火化大師寂心法師主理。隆重的轉咒法事一結束，火焰開始沖騰，木龕還沒有完全著火，各種佛法聖境出現！五彩佛光圍繞大地盤旋閃耀，看見聖境界的歡呼聲此起彼伏，手機、相機、錄影機舉得高高的，不對焦距，不用取景，全數盡收，到處都是聖境。只見熊熊爐火忽然化作龍神蛟騰，口吐烈火威猛咆哮，阿彌陀佛、觀世音菩薩、四臂觀音、文殊菩薩手持慧劍頓然現身，「種子字」、金剛、護法、雄獅、鳳凰、蓮花、彩虹……各種奇境隨著爐火的升騰不斷湧現，念佛器裏又發出大法王的念佛聲，忽然甘露從天而降，香甜甘醇，甘露只降在火化爐的位置，周圍任何地方都沒有。聖境的湧現讓人群歡樂沸騰，這是寶光寺火化爐始建至今從未出現過的喜悅場景。在茶毗現場親眼見到聖境的人法號是釋心恩、釋心鳳、釋心玉、釋智文、釋心妙、釋道真、釋道純、釋道之、釋心曉、釋智蓮、釋心源、釋廣修、釋道廣、釋廣聞、曲德達姆、釋智德、釋一增、釋智達、釋智修、釋真雄、釋真德、釋道山、釋德海、釋廣雲、釋智清、釋廣靈、釋智章、釋智明、釋智海、釋廣豐、釋德明、釋德超、釋智博等，還有許多不相識的人，都在那裏高聲讚嘆，就地禮拜。

成就顯赫　證量舍利上品上等舍利花

更驚人的是，從王程娥芬老居士的骨灰中，共揀出了六十多枚五彩舍利，黃色白色上等上品舍利花！其中還有菱形舍利，轟動了整個寶光禪院和中國佛教界，這是歷史上極為罕見的的聖跡，是真正的佛寶，真正達到「極樂羅網微妙境，三花等處盡開敷」的聖境。來自台灣的吳祐嘉說，這舍利真是神貝，在尋找舍利的過程中，有一坨巴掌大的骨灰，已經有人找過幾遍了，我竟然在裡面找出了兩顆，我又再細緻地找了一遍，確定沒有了，就在這時，我見到另外一個同學眼睜睜地在我找過的那坨骨灰裡面又找出了三顆。另一位台灣的同學李惠珠得嚴重的富貴手病症，由於觸感不好，祇用三個指頭在骨灰中尋找舍利，她說雖然她一顆也沒找到，但隔天早上發現她那三指尋找舍利的指頭，富貴手症狀全消失了。排隊瞻仰舍利的人絡繹不絕，社會各界人士紛至遝來，寶光寺還特地將老居士的舍利子拍成照片公開請給大眾。

夫妻雙雙證聖果　王老生死自作主

正如拉母在「親見勝義浴佛法會的判析」一文中所說：成就一個王程娥芬也許偶然，而神奇的是娥芬居士的先生王靈澤居士也依大法王修法，一生不談佛法，突於一九九一年農曆二月十五日下午，抬個凳子在新都勞動村街面公開勸人為善，講說淨土功德，讚嘆大法王的法是釋迦體系的真正佛法。有人問，我喜歡觀音法，但不知什麼樣才是最好的？王老居士說：不管他是大法師還是大活佛，你們要特別注意小心，千萬不要學到假佛法。比如觀音菩薩的淨瓶證量很大，我們回過來看一看，你的上師如何呢？如果他沒有本領證量取水傳法灌頂，戒行又不好，那就是書本上的通俗法，莫如念南無觀世音菩薩功德大。真觀音法不文取水就要武取水，武取水以兩個人或一個人要把四、五千斤的浴佛池水提起倒出來，這是真佛法。文取水是你暗地裡準備一衣鉢，上師不能看見，你當下盛滿水拿出來，上師在你面前當下修法，水馬上會透出衣鉢向你的面前流過來，就如觀音菩薩的淨瓶聖水，一切凡間的容器都無法盛裝淨瓶中的聖水，它會穿出來的，有了穿鉢的聖水灌頂學法，才能洗掉你多生的業障，才是真觀音法。我學的就是益西諾布大法王傳的這個真佛法，水穿出來了，所以我現在要到極樂世界了。王老居士說法完畢，將凳子推在一旁，就在街面房邊坐地盤腿，當下就圓寂了，他說明了大法王所傳佛法生死自由的偉大。老居士圓寂後，依照佛教的規定，圓寂後七日不能動其身，所以就地在公眾街面莊嚴盤坐七天七夜，端正如鐘，也是在新都寶光寺火化出十三枚堅固舍利子。筆者在新都寶光寺還以人民幣二十圓的價格，買到一張寶光寺公開售出的王程娥芬居士圓寂後火化出的舍利和舍利花照片。筆者還瞭解到，並看到實況錄影，大法王的弟子很多都是世界第一流的高僧，台灣第一流的高僧老和尚、大陸與香港第一流的高僧老和尚、大活佛、美國第一流的高僧、大活佛都拜大法王為師，而有很多弟子都是夫妻雙雙生死自由，有的念佛盤坐結上特別手印而往生，有的圓寂後肉身大放毫光，有的肉身不壞，成為肉身舍利。而最為厲害的是，大法王通常是提前告訴他的弟子們某人將於甚麼時候圓寂，讓法師們提前去助念往生，法師們得到通知時對方是活人，而到場後對方已坐化。這是甚麼概念？只能說明這是偉大佛法的真實所在。

一位常在寶光寺拜佛的麥姓居士激動地告訴記者：「這些年，我一直在著急啊，拜了很多大法師、大活佛，還是沒有學到真佛法，就怕生死關頭到來。念佛當然是天天念，但自己是咋回事自己最清楚，自己是不是凡夫自己最曉得，沒學到真佛法的啊。不止我一個，周圍大家都是這樣的，到時候肯定要去輪迴，很可怕的，我都跟佛菩薩求啊，求學到真正的佛法。這幾天看到程娥芬老人家大成就的聖境，我就曉得是佛菩薩加持我了，讓我找到了！我們幾個師兄商量了，要想盡一切辦法找到那位教程娥芬居士大成就的師父，我曉得他才是真正的大聖者，我們還聽說程娥芬居士的先生也是生死自由坐化的，也是他老人家傳的佛法，我們不找他找哪個呢？當然要找。他老人家才能解決我們的生死問題，我們一定要真心誠意地去找！」

圖片解說：

圖片1：善德王玉花教授之母，王程娥芬居士，修觀音法得大成就，於中國四川新都縣寶光寺火化出六十餘枚多彩舍利子和上品上等舍利花，堪稱佛教史上稀世佛寶，真正達到「極樂羅網微妙境，三花等處盡開敷」的聖境。（寶光寺寂心法師火化拍照）

圖片2：王程娥芬居士已被觀世音菩薩接引往升西方極樂世界。

圖片3：寺廟聯合浴佛法會上眾人將功德迴向王程娥芬居士後，佛像放光長達兩個多小時（右），與王程娥芬居士得大法王傳法得大成就息息相關，左邊為未放光前的佛像。佛像為銅鑄實心鎏金，現供奉在華藏寺。

圖片4：王靈澤大居士於一九九一年二月十五日坐化圓寂，這是圓寂後第五天照常盤腿端坐街面時所拍下來的照片。

圖片5：王靈澤大居士圓寂後茶毗所得的十三枚堅固舍利子。

E-Fen Wang Cheng and Ling-Ze Wang were both disciples of H.H. Dorje Chang Buddha III Wan Ko Yeshe Norbu Holiest Tathagata.
They attained great accomplishment in the dharma by practicing the dharma H.H. Great Dharma King taught them.
Below is the complete article from the Taiwan Times dated June 17, 2004.

三世多杰羌佛雲高益西諾布頂聖如來的弟子王程娥芬及王靈澤居士，依師修法得大成就，以下是《台灣時報》二零零四年六月十七日的報導全文。

SPENDING TWENTY-TWO DAYS WITHOUT ANY FOOD AND WATER, A RINPOCHE LEARNS THE TRUE VAJRA MEDITATION OF THE BUDDHA

(This is the text of an article published in the Asian Journal on May 7, 2005.)

A True Account of Henghsing Gyatso Rinpoche Learning a Dharma, Spending Time in Retreat, and Coming Out of Meditation

Henghsing Gyatso Rinpoche is a disciple of Great Dharma King Yangwo Yisinubu[1]. His last incarnation was in Tibet. In this lifetime, he was born in Taiwan and is now sixty years old. The Great Dharma King conferred an initiation upon him and transmitted dharma to him. He thereby learned the highest dharma essence of Sakyamuni Buddha—the practice of vajra meditation. He went into retreat during which he meditated for 27 days, the latter 22 days of which he did not touch any water or food. All of the food and liquid sent in to him was returned untouched.

On April 10, 2005, Henghsing Gyatso Rinpoche came out of retreat. His face was placid. He had become thin, but his spirit was glowing. The first thing he did after he left the meditation cushion was prostrate before an image of his Vajra Master, Great Dharma King Yangwo Yisinubu, in order to express his appreciation. He had finally learned the highest Buddha-dharma. He had finally attained true skills relating to the magnificent meditation Buddha-dharma that leads to enlightening one's mind and seeing one's original nature. He was happy for all living beings in that there truly exists such a wonderful and precious meditation dharma method that leads to enlightening one's mind and seeing one's original nature!

At the height of summer last year, Henghsing Gyatso Rinpoche, out of great compassion, decided to endure hardship for the sake of other living beings. He vowed to prostrate around the island of Taiwan, which is a more than 1,100 kilometer journey (i.e. more than 684 miles). More than half a year later, he had completed half the journey. Along the way, his great compassion and piety moved Guan Yin Bodhisattva to appear in the sky, empower him, and expound the dharma to him. This event caused a sensation throughout the island of Taiwan and beyond. Many people within Buddhism expressed their great admiration over such an event.

Great Dharma King Yangwo Yisinubu Teaches the True Meditation Practice

The great compassion and sincerity of the rinpoche moved the Buddhas and Bodhisattvas to empower him. This year in late February, when he had prostrated as far as Kaohsiung, he suddenly received a notice from the Buddhas and Bodhisattvas telling him to open immediately the secret, small bag made of brocade that Great Dharma King Yangwo Yisinubu gave him and told him to wear on his chest. Inside the brocade bag was a piece of paper telling him the mantra he would intone during his meditation retreat. That brocade bag is no ordinary thing.

In the summer of last year, Henghsing Gyatso Rinpoche vowed to prostrate around the island of Taiwan so as to suffer on behalf of other living beings. This vow moved Great Dharma King Yangwo Yisinubu to transmit dharma to him and confer an initiation upon him. He and two other famous Dharma Masters were initiated together. They received the highest esoteric dharma. It is the essential dharma that leads to enlightening one's mind and seeing one's original nature. Sakyamuni Buddha practiced that dharma under the bodhi tree when he became enlightened. This dharma is called the Vajra Samadhi Buddha Great Enlightenment Meditation. Later, Guru Padmasambhava taught this dharma in Tibet. In the Supreme Secret-Tantric Division of Tibetan esoteric Buddhism, this dharma is called "Great Perfection Whispered Profound Essence Vajra Meditation." It is also called "Three-Disciple Initiation."

Besides the rinpoche, two other eminent monastics were transmitted the dharma that day. During the time the Great Dharma King performed the initiation and transmitted dharma, suddenly, all three of them saw that the altar area, the building they were in, and everything else completely disappeared. They could only perceive the voice of the Great Dharma King, which was loud and clear. Various kinds of startling special phenomena appeared. It was extremely wonderful. After transmitting the dharma, the Great Dharma King blessed that small brocade bag and gave it to Henghsing Gyatso Rinpoche. However, the Great Dharma King told him that he must wait until the Buddhas and Bodhisattvas instruct him to open it.

Henghsing Gyatso Rinpoche continued his prostrations around the island of Taiwan. When he reached Kaohsiung, he received notice from the Buddhas and Bodhisattvas to open the brocade bag. The paper in the bag told him that he should enter into retreat to practice the dharma since the karmic conditions had matured.

The First Retreat Was Not Carried Out in Accordance With the Dharma; Demons Entered the Retreat Room and Almost Killed the Rinpoche

On February 27, 2005, Henghsing Gyatso Rinpoche returned to his retreat room in Jiayi. There he began his first retreat. He entered into meditation and stopped eating for four days. However, the people whose responsibility was to guard the

---

[1] Here and below the words *Great Dharma King Yangwo Yisinubu*, *Great Dharma King*, or *Dharma King Master* refers to H.H. Dorje Chang Buddha III Wan Ko Yeshe Norbu Holiest Tathagata.

retreat room during the retreat did not follow the dharma rules. They did not seal the windows and doors with a certain type of paper according to the dharma rules. They saw real demons make their way into the room to interfere with Rinpoche's dharma practice. The situation was very dangerous. At this critical time, the people who were guarding the retreat room received a phone call from the Dharma Matters Department of the Great Dharma King. The person who called said, "A problem has arisen in the retreat room. Demons have entered the room. Quickly call your master out of meditation by hitting the metal bowl." (The metal bowl is a Buddhist instrument.) Following the instructions they were given, the guards used the metal bowl to call out the rinpoche, who, in his meditation, was in the midst of battling with those demons.

On March 15, 2005 at noon in Jiayi, Henghsing Gyatso rinpoche entered into retreat for a second time. This time, learning their lesson from the first retreat, the guards arranged the retreat room according to the dharma rules. The dharma stipulates that ten people must guard the outside of a retreat room in which someone practices this vajra meditation. The disciples of Henghsing Gyatso Rinpoche selected ten people to be guards. Their names are Shi Zong Guan, Shi Fa-Yun, Wang Jin-Rong, Chi Hai-Ao, Ao Jing-Chong, Hsueh Hsiu-Fen, Tsai Chun-Tao, He Yan-Yan, Tsai Yu-Nu, and Lu Ke-Yun. With the addition of the cook, Liu Ming-Hui, there were all together eleven people. The ten guards cleared the retreat room, even removing the Buddhist altar. Downstairs from the retreat room is the area where the guards stayed. The entire retreat room was cleared of everything except dharma instruments and one rush cushion used for meditation.

During the Second Retreat, the Ten Guards Did Not Leave Their Posts

All of the doors and windows of the retreat room must be nailed shut with iron nails. Furthermore, the Buddha-dharma stipulates that each guard must sign a yellow paper that has dharma power and use it to seal the seams of those doors and windows. This is to prevent demons from intruding into the retreat room and causing havoc. It also prevents anyone from opening those doors and windows. There were fifteen places to be sealed in the retreat room. Ten yellow pieces of paper, each containing the signature of one guard, was pasted over each of those fifteen places. Thus, all together 150 yellow pieces of paper were pasted over the various seams.

Even the only door of the retreat room through which meals were sent was also sealed with one yellow paper containing the signatures of all ten guards. When they sent meals into the retreat room, the ten guards chanted a mantra and practiced dharma together. They had to together tear off the yellow paper sealing the door in order to open the door. After they delivered a meal, they together locked the door and sealed the door with paper again.

Those ten guards kept watch outside the door of the retreat room and did not leave their posts at any time. Even if some of them needed to use the restroom, there were at least seven of them guarding the door all day and night. It can be said that not even a bird, mosquito, or fly could enter. Only through these measures did they prevent the dangerous situation that occurred during the first

retreat when the demons entered the retreat room and engaged in battle with the Rinpoche.

At the beginning, the rinpoche ate on a normal basis. After three days, on March 18th, the amount of food he consumed dropped dramatically. On March 19th, the rinpoche rang a bell and beat a drum morning, noon, and evening. He drank only one cup of rice tea that whole day. Starting from March 20th, Henghsing Gyatso Rinpoche did not consume any food or water. The food and water sent in were not touched. No sound could be heard coming from inside the retreat room. On March 23rd, the Dharma Matters Department of Great Dharma King Yangwo Yisinubu, which is located in the United States, made a phone call to Taiwan to show their concern about how the rinpoche's practice was going. On March 25th, the rinpoche had stopped eating for five days. There was no sound at all coming from inside the retreat room. Even the sound of the toilet flushing, which happened three day earlier, could not be heard anymore. Hence, some of the guards started to worry, fearing that something had happened.

Then, that evening at 7:00, from the retreat room came the sounds of the striking of a metal bowl, the ringing of a bell, and the beating of a drum. The guards became excited. They immediately felt relieved. Then, the retreat room returned to total silence.

A few days later, the food that was delivered into the retreat room every day was taken out without having been touched. Upon seeing this situation, those guards became very worried over the rinpoche's situation in the retreat room.

On April 1st at 11:50 a.m., the sounds of the ringing of a bell and the beating of a drum again emanated from the room. The rhythm was clear and vigorous. Those disciples who were guarding the room became ecstatic. Although the Rinpoche had stopped eating for twelve days, he was still able to ring a bell and beat a drum. The meditation practice of this great rinpoche is indeed extraordinary!

On April 8th at noon, the rinpoche had entered meditation and fasted for twenty days. The clear and vigorous sounds of a bell ringing and a drum being struck again arose from inside the retreat room. The disciples outside were very moved. They continually praised the magnificence of the Buddha-dharma. Their master was truly amazing. He had attained the goal of his retreat and was able to abide in vajra mediation for twenty days.

On April 9th, the rinpoche had entered into meditation and practiced the dharma for twenty-one days. He was not consuming any food or water. At 9:00 that day, a loud beating of a drum suddenly was heard. The disciples then knew that their master had attained the goal of his retreat and was about to come out of retreat. Before he went into retreat, Henghsing Gyatso Rinpoche announced to his disciples that when they hear the loud beating of a drum it means that he has attained the goal of his retreat and realized dharma skills. His disciples understood that their master had entered into a holy state. Thus, they notified the news media. They did not sleep day or night, keeping strict watch over the retreat room so that no mistakes would be made at that critical moment.

During His Meditation, He Heard the Teachings of the Buddha; He Realized That the Dharma of His Master Was Most Revered

On April 10th at 11:00, while chanting the name of Amitabha Buddha, the ten guards together with other disciples from all over the island of Taiwan respectfully invited Henghsing Gyatso Rinpoche to come out of his retreat. When the yellow paper that sealed the entrance to the retreat room was torn off and the door opened, members of the news media, carrying cameras and tripods, followed the disciples into the room. Those reporters and the guards saw Henghsing Gyatso Rinpoche sitting cross-legged on a rush cushion. His eyes were almost completely closed. His face was placid. Clearly, he was still in a state of concentration.

After everyone crowded into the almost one hundred and thirty square foot room, the guards beat the metal bowl three times next to his ear. Henghsing Gyatso Rinpoche then slowly opened his eyes. He saw that the room was filled with people and there were cameras all around. He appeared slightly surprised. He immediately put his palms together and said, "First of all, I am very grateful to my most magnificent and most honored Buddha Master, Vajradhara Great Dharma King Yangwo Yisinubu." He then stood up and prostrated before a small gawu (kau) box hanging over his rush cushion that had in it an image of Great Dharma King Yangwo Yisinubu. The rinpoche's body was limber, and he had obviously lost weight. Still, he was in high spirits and radiated vitality.

In a sonorous voice, he spoke to his disciples. His first sentence was, "I finally obtained the highest Buddha-dharma." We asked him to explain this. He said that during this period of meditation he saw many supernatural phenomena. He did not elaborate upon this other than to describe the most wonderful experience of all.

He said, "I finally saw the most magnificent world-honored one, Sakyamuni Buddha. I beseeched the Buddha to kindly bestow upon me the highest Buddha-dharma initiation. The Buddha stretched out his arm, touched the top of my head, and said, "If you had not learned the highest Buddha-dharma, how could you have seen me?" Beseeching the Buddha's instruction again, I asked, "In this world, where can one still find the highest Buddha-dharma?" The Buddha gave me the following teaching: "During the past few thousand years, many great Masters and great Bodhisattvas have appeared in human history. Which one of them attained perfect mastery over the Five Sciences and was able to create Yun Sculpture, a great wisdom form of art that has no equal in the human world? Which great Master was able to create Yun Sculpture frames, which are the most beautiful in the human world? Those who are smart will immediately know upon thinking about it who possesses truly the most magnificent Buddha-dharma!" The rinpoche then said to everyone, "I will not say anything more."

He Did Not Consume Any Food or Water for Twenty-Two Days; He Lost About Six Pounds

At this time, I carefully inspected the entire retreat room. All of the other reporters also carefully inspected the room. It was truly empty. There was no food there at all. All of the yellow pieces of paper bearing the signatures of the ten guards that sealed each of the doors and windows of the room were not touched in the slightest. Other than the door through which meals were sent in, there was no other door or window through which anything could be brought in. We thoroughly questioned those ten guards, who kept watch both day and night and who did not leave the room outside the entrance to the retreat room. We found out that the food that was sent in each day was returned untouched. This proves that the rinpoche did not eat. After twenty-two days of not consuming any food or water, the rinpoche clearly lost weight. I learned that the rinpoche lost about six pounds.

In today's world, whether one practices exoteric dharma, esoteric dharma, or the dharma of the various sects within Hinayana Buddhism, the dharma one learns is basically superficial, empty, and without substance. Such dharma lacks very much real usefulness, not to mention the ability to lead the practitioner to enlightening his mind, seeing his original nature, and entering vajra samadhi (deep concentration). The meditational attainment of the Buddha whereby he was able to "use meditation as food" has long since vanished from this world. This has caused many people to think that the Buddha-dharma is just empty formalities or legends.

The most eminent monk of the Chan (Zen) School in modern times, elder monk Xu Yun, practiced vajra meditation in Yunnan Province. He meditated for twenty-one days without eating or drinking. He thereby earned the great admiration of a local warlord by the name of Tang Ji-Yao, who built for the elder monk a temple on Mount Jizu. It would be an amazing attainment for one who has true meditation skills to meditate for ten days without eating or drinking. Throughout all these years, I have hardly heard of anyone else besides elder monk Xu Yun who was able to abstain from food and liquid for twenty-one days. Through Henghsing Gyatso Rinpoche, we have finally seen again vajra meditation skills based on the authentic and magnificent Buddha-dharma. This proves that the genuine Buddha-dharma relating to meditation has again appeared in this world!

After he came out of retreat, Henghsing Gyatso Rinpoche stated that he would fulfill his vow and complete his journey around the island of Taiwan. During that journey, he prostrates after every step in order to endure hardship on behalf of other living beings.

Venerable Khu-ston brTson- 'grus g.yung-drung V, Henghsing Gyatso Rinpoche is a disciple of H.H. Dorje Chang Buddha III Wan Ko Yeshe Norbu Holiest Tathagata.
For twenty-two days, Henghsing Gyatso Rinpoche practiced a great dharma called **Tathagata Vajra Meditation** that
H.H. Dorje Chang Buddha III transmitted to him. During that twenty-two day period, he sat in solitary meditation and did not eat or drink anything.
For details on this, please see the newspaper reports that were published at that time.
三世多杰羌佛雲高益西諾布頂聖如來的弟子庫頓尊哲雍仲尊者第五世恒性嘉措仁波且修三世多杰羌佛所傳的『如來金剛禪』大法，閉關22天米水未沾。詳見當時報紙的報導。

H.H. Dorje Chang Buddha III Tonsured Me

The happiest event in my life was when H.H. Dorje Chang Buddha III Wan Ko Yeshe Norbu Holiest Tathagata personally tonsured me. I sometimes even laugh at night while dreaming about this. I went from the secular life to the monastic life under such extremely auspicious karmic circumstances. It is by no means easy for anyone to be personally tonsured by the true Buddha Vajradhara!

I was fortunate to become a disciple of H.H. Dorje Chang Buddha III several years ago. All that I knew about His Holiness at that time was that He was an approachable and amiable dharma king. It was only this year when I inadvertently discovered the truth that His Holiness is so much more than that. As certain karmic conditions matured, my desire to enter the order of monks grew increasingly strong. Thus, Hongxi Fazang, another fellow disciple, who requested entrance into the monastic order and I both formally beseeched H.H. Dorje Chang Buddha III to tonsure us. Unexpectedly, H.H. Dorje Chang Buddha III granted our request and agreed to tonsure us.

Many rinpoches and dharma teachers performed Buddhist rites that day we were tonsured. While H.H. Dojre Chang Buddha III was practicing dharma at about 6:00 in the morning that day in order to select our dharma names, two peacocks were seen descending from the sky. After landing on the ground, they danced lithely as an offering to H.H. Dorje Chang Buddha III. Only after more than thirty straight minutes did the two peacocks slowly end their graceful dance. They then flew onto the vehicle H.H. Dorje Chang Buddha III was going to ride in that day and again danced as an offering to His Holiness. At this time, the dogs that are dharma protectors began to bark loudly. People then suddenly realized that they should be filming this entire scene to keep as a record. Unfortunately, the two peacocks had already flown onto the roof by the time a video camera was brought over.

H.H. Dojre Chang Buddha III used a new, extremely sharp, and very powerful electric razor to tonsure us. The first application of that razor on my head went very smoothly. However, the second application proved useless in cutting my hair. Not one hair of mine was cut no matter how that electric razor was applied. At this time, I heard H.H. Dorje Chang Buddha III recite a vajra mantra. With the next application of that razor, my hair fell off with no problem at all. After the tonsure, we beseeched two people of great virtue to empower us with vajra pills. When one of them placed her hand upon the top of my head to empower me, I suddenly came to a realization of many new things. It was an indescribable feeling that was truly marvelous!

Of course, these occurrences that we view as amazing are very ordinary and common as far as H.H. Dorje Chang Buddha III is concerned. That is because one can see such occurrences all the time when one is at the side of His Holiness. For example, a photograph of the Holiest Tathagata performing a tonsure initiation for Venerable Hengsheng Rinpoche from Taiwan showed the retreat building appearing just like an image of Dorje Chang Buddha. Even the bun of hair on the top of Dorje Chang Buddha's head was extremely clear in that photograph. Wondrous phenomena also occurred when H.H. Dorje Chang Buddha III performed a tonsure initiation for Respected Zhaxi Zhuoma Rinpoche, Respected Bodi Wentu Rinpoche, and others. H.H. Dorje Chang Buddha III also performed a tonsure initiation for Venerable Hsi Jao Ken Teng, conferring upon him the title of rinpoche. One of the two 17th Karmapa Great Jewel Dharma Kings, H.H. Trinley Thaye Dorje Karmapa, affirmed the status of Venerable Hsi Jao Ken Teng. The other 17th Karmapa Great Jewel Dharma King, H.H. Ugyen Trinley Dorje Karmapa, wrote a congratulatory message to Venerable Hsi Jao Ken Teng and had a photograph taken together with him.

Lama Puti Duxi

July 4, 2007

(The Chinese translation of this text follows.)

三世多杰羌佛爲我剃度

說到多杰羌佛第三世雲高益西諾布頂聖如來親自為我剃度，這實在是我一生中最為高興的事情，有時候甚至在晚上做夢的時候都要笑出聲來。因為這是我由世俗到出家當和尚的大吉因緣，能受到真正金剛總持的親手剃度，落髮為僧，談何容易啊！

幾年前，我有幸成為三世多杰羌佛的弟子，那時我只知道他是一位平易近人的法王，一直到今年，我才在無意中見到真相。隨著因緣的成熟，我想出家的願望越來越強烈，於是，我和另外一位要求出家的師兄宏西法藏便正式請求三世多杰羌佛為我們剃度，沒想到三世多杰羌佛同意了我們的請求，答應為我們剃度。

剃度的當天，有很多仁波且和法師執持法義。清晨六點鐘的時候，三世多杰羌佛正在修法為我們取法名，這時只見兩隻孔雀從天空而降，然後翩翩起舞，向三世多杰羌佛獻供。曼妙的舞蹈一直持續了三十多分鐘，兩隻孔雀才慢慢踱步收場，而且還飛到當天三世多杰羌佛準備乘坐的汽車上獻供起舞，這時，護法犬大聲吼了起來，人們才突然想起應該錄影以作記錄，可惜，等拿到攝影機的時候，兩隻孔雀已經飛到房頂上。

在三世多杰羌佛為我們剃髮的時候，選用的是新買的、非常鋒利、功率很強的電動剃刀，第一刀下去非常順利，但是第二刀再剪下去的時候，就剪不下頭髮了，任憑電動剃刀怎麼剪，就是沒有一根頭髮被剪下來，在這個時候，只聽三世多杰羌佛一持金剛神咒，頭髮又『刷、刷』地掉下來了。在剃度結束之後，我們請求在場的兩位大德加持我們金剛丸，就在大德仁者將手移到我的頭頂上作加持時，我突然證悟很多，這種感覺我無法用語言來形容，實在是太神奇了！

當然，這些被我們視為神奇的事情，對三世多杰羌佛來說都是很平常的，因為在他老人家的身邊是隨時隨地都有的。比如，頂聖如來為台灣的恒生仁波且取髮灌頂，關房竟然變成了多杰羌佛的佛像，連頂髻都清清楚楚。三世多杰羌佛為扎西卓瑪仁波且、波迪溫圖仁波且等人作了取髮灌頂，也都出現相應的神奇現象。三世多杰羌佛還為喜饒根登取髮灌頂，並封他做仁波且，原來他果然是仁波且，隨後，兩位十七世噶瑪巴大寶法王，泰耶多杰噶瑪巴為喜饒根登作了認證，烏金聽列多杰噶瑪巴寫給祝賀，並在一起合影，而且敏林堪欽仁波且還查出了喜饒根登的大德身份，作了進一步認證。

喇嘛：菩提度西

2007年7月4日　　　（此文由前面的英文翻譯而來）

H.H. 17th Gyalwa Karmapa Trinley Thaye Dorje
泰耶多杰噶瑪巴

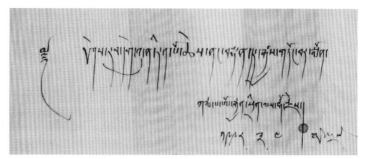

"HSI-JAO KEN-TENG RINPOCHE PROPAGATES THE CORRECT DHARMA"
THE 17TH KARMAPA GREAT JEWEL DHARMA KING UGYEN TRINLEY DORJE
正法宏開 喜饒根登仁波且
十七世噶瑪巴大寶法王烏金欽烈多傑

Congratulatory Message Written by Karmapa Great Jewel Dharma King to Karma Palden Lodoe Rinpoche
噶瑪巴大寶法王為噶瑪巴登洛德仁波且提詞祝賀

A photograph of H.H. the 17th Karmapa Great Jewel Dharma
King Ugyen Trinley Dorje and Karma Palden Lodoe Rinpoche.
十七世大寶法王噶瑪巴和噶瑪巴登洛德仁波且

GRATITUDE

First, from my three karmas of body, speech, and mind, I express my gratitude to my respected Master, Dorje Chang Buddha III, for having performed an initiation for me and for having transmitted dharma to me. In so doing, His Holiness enabled me to receive incomparably wonderful empowerment from the Buddhas.

I am Luosang Danzeng Nuori Rinpoche. Because of the coming together and influence of karmic causes and conditions, the power of vows, and the power of karma, all of which have existed since beginning-less time, I have again come to this world. At the time of Dalai Lama VII, I was the Ganden Tripa (supreme leader of the Geluk sect). Xiazhu Qiuyang Rinpoche, who is the incarnation of Naropa, has affirmed my identity in this lifetime as being a rinpoche who is the reincarnation of a Ganden Tripa. As leader of the Geluk sect, I am responsible for making this sect founded by Master Tsgongkhapa flourish. Therefore, I must seek higher Buddha-dharma in order to protect the teachings and benefit living beings.

For a long period of time, I have been observing and gaining understanding of dharma kings, rinpoches, eminent monastics, and people of great virtue from all over the world. Finally, I found the Holiest Tathagata who possesses the highest Buddha-dharma—Dorje Chang Buddha III. However, Dorje Chang Buddha III told me, "In a previous life you were a Ganden Tripa, the supreme leader of the Geluk sect. Thus, I must test you before I can accept you as a disciple." Dorje Chang Buddha III set up six different tests to be passed. His Holiness told me that if I passed two of them, He would accept me as a disciple. Otherwise, I would not have the karmic destiny to be His Holiness's disciple. Although I am the reincarnation of a Ganden Tripa, I naturally was not at all sure of the outcome of being tested by a Buddha. I could not help but be somewhat worried that Dorje Chang Buddha III would not accept me as a disciple.

I formally entered the testing area, where venerable ones, rinpoches, and dharma teachers were present to observe the tests. It was an open-air mandala. The first test involved answering questions on the spot about the sutra teachings. I answered all twelve questions correctly. Because some of

my explanations were not complete, a very small number of points were deducted from my score. The second test required that I practice dharma to beseech the Buddhas to bestow nectar. I knew that I did not have such realization, since that is a matter to be performed by a Buddha. Naturally, I received no points for this. The third test was the selection of karmic affinity from a golden vase. Needless to say, this is also something I do not have the realization to perform and again received no points. The fourth test involved determining six great karmic conditions. Although I was behind a partition, my powers of concentration enabled me to see clearly the true situation on the other side of the partition. This probably was the result of some small merit of mine earned from being a Ganden Tripa. My determinations of what was behind the partition were of course correct all six times. The fifth test involved eliminating the negative karma of other living beings. Although I practiced visualization and entered concentration, I was ultimately unable to pass this test, which took place before many venerable ones and rinpoches.

The sixth test was "taking karma and eliminating karmic hindrances." The Buddha Master took a vajra in His hand. As His Holiness gave a discourse on the dharma to me, He told me the rituals of that dharma practice. His Holiness told me how to lift that vajra from the ground and correctly place it on the part of the dharma dais where the seed syllables "ong, ah, hong, and she" were located. The Buddha Master said that many rinpoches could not lift that vajra from the ground onto the dharma dais. I thought, "How could this be difficult? That small vajra weighs one pound at the most. His Holiness took it in His hands without the slightest effort. Could it be that the vajra will change? I will easily lift it for sure."

The Buddha Master placed the vajra on the ground and instructed me to lift it from the ground onto the dharma dais. While chanting a mantra, I finally decided to extend my arm and effortlessly lift it onto the dharma dais. I never thought that this vajra would turn out to be far more formidable than a fierce dragon or ferocious tiger. I did not have any way to lift it. It felt as if it weighed thousands of pounds and was fiery hot.

The Buddha Master then said to me in a serious tone of voice, "This is your one last chance. If for a second time you are unable to take the vajra and place it on the part of the dharma dais where the seed syllables are located, then you will not be able to immediately realize wisdom and supernatural powers." However, my powers of concentration and my will had already been thoroughly destroyed. In the end, I was still unable to lift that vajra successfully.

Nonetheless, out of great compassion, the Buddha Master empowered me with boundless wisdom and merit. Originally, I would have had to go through three years and three months of retreat before I could take a seventh test. However, the Buddha Master right then and there allowed me to take the seventh test, which is a second-level test. Truthfully speaking, even this second-level test made me very worried. To my surprise, I passed it. Of course, words cannot describe the awesome empowerment that I received. It was incomparably wonderful. Under the empowerment of the Buddha-dharma, my whole body was like the fire of samadhi, and I perspired profusely. I am extremely happy, for I finally became a root disciple of Dorje Chang Buddha III!

I vow that the dharma teachings of this Buddha will be that upon which I fundamentally rely. The dharma teachings of Dorje Chang Buddha III are the dharma teachings of all Buddhas in the ten directions within the three spheres. All Buddhas attain Buddhahood through such dharma teachings. If people separate themselves from the dharma teachings of Dorje Chang Buddha III, then there will be no Buddha-dharma in this world at all. Dorje Chang Buddha is the sambhogakaya Buddha, the Master of all Buddhas, and the one who has attained the highest, unsurpassable level of enlightenment. I vow to realize soon supreme bodhi for the sake of all living beings. I beseech Dorje Chang Buddha III to transmit to me great dharma that will enable me to become a Buddha in this very lifetime so that I can bear the obligations of a Tathagata and benefit living beings.

From now until I attain bodhi, I will enlighten myself and others. This is the vow I will carry out!

Root disciple of a Buddha: Luosang Danzeng Nuori
September 3, 2007

(This is a complete translation of the Chinese text that follows originally written and signed by Luosang Danzeng Nuori.)

感　恩

首先，我發自三業感恩我的恩師三世多杰羌佛為弟子灌頂傳法，讓我得到無比殊勝的佛力加持。

我是洛桑丹增諾日仁波且，由於無始的因緣，願力與業力的和合牽制，我又再次來到這個世界上。在第七世達賴喇嘛時，我曾任甘丹赤巴（格魯巴總教主），這一世是被那洛巴轉世的夏珠秋楊仁波且認證的甘丹赤巴轉世仁波且。我身為格魯巴教主，有責任讓宗喀巴大師創始的黃教興旺，因此我必須要尋求到更高的佛法來護教利生。

我經過長時間的觀照和了解，看了全世界的法王、仁波且、高僧大德們，我終於找到了擁有最高佛法的頂聖如來老人家——第三世多杰羌佛。可是，三世多杰羌佛對我說：你曾擔任過格魯派總教主甘丹赤巴，因此我必須要對你考試，才能收你做弟子。三世多杰羌佛對我設定了六關考試，告訴我：如果過得了兩個關就收我做弟子，否則與他老人家是無緣的。我雖然是甘丹赤巴再來人，面對佛陀的考試，自然是毫無把握的，難免有些擔心三世多杰羌佛不收我做他的弟子。

在尊者、仁波且和法師們的監考下，我正式進入了考場，這是一個露天壇城。第一關即是經教的現場問答，十二道題我全答正確了，由於未解說完整，扣了很少的分。第二關是要我自己修法求佛降下甘露，我知道我不具備這個道量，因為這是佛陀的事，自然我得了零分。第三關是金瓶擇緣，不用說，這也不是我能有的證量，也得了零分。第四關是判六大緣起，雖然我被隔在壁外，大概由於是作甘丹赤巴的一些小小功德之緣吧，定力的觀照讓我清楚看到真相，這自然就六次判準。第五關是為眾生消除黑業，我修觀入定，可是最後在眾尊者、仁波且們的面前，我沒有考過關。

第六關是取業除障，是由佛陀恩師拿一金剛杵在他的手中，一邊開示，一邊告訴我修法的儀軌，如何將這個杵從地上拿起來準確地放到有『嗡啊吽、捨』種子字的法座上。佛陀恩師說：很多仁波且都是沒有辦法把它從地上拿到法台上的。我心裡想：這有什麼難？那麼輕、最多一磅重的一個小杵，您老人家都拿在手中若無其事，難道它還會變化嗎？我一定會輕輕把它拿起。當佛陀恩師將金剛杵放到地上、命我將它從地上拿到法台上時，我終於持著咒，決定隨手拿它到法台上。沒有想到這金剛杵遠勝於一頭猛龍烈虎，我毫無辦法將它拿起，可以說超於萬斤，烈焰無敵。佛陀恩師此時嚴肅地說：你這是最後一次機會了，如果你第二次再不能將金剛杵取上法台的種子座上，就沒有辦法當下證得智慧神通。可是，我的定力、意志被徹底摧毀了，最後還是拿不成功。但是，佛陀恩師非常慈悲，將無邊的智慧功德力加持給我，本來我要在三年三個月的閉關後再來作第七關的考試，但佛陀恩師當場就讓我進行第七關，也就是第二等的考試。說心裡話，就是二等考試我也很擔心，但沒有想到我考合格了，當然，那加持的威力根本就不是語言能形容的，殊勝無比啊，在佛法的加持力下，我全身猶如三昧火光，大汗如雨。但是，我多麼高興啊，我終於成為三世多杰羌佛的根本弟子了！

我發願以佛陀的教法為我的根本依止，三世多杰羌佛的教法就是十方三世一切諸佛的教法，即是成就諸佛的教法，離了三世多杰羌佛的教法，世界上就根本沒有佛法。多杰羌佛是報身佛，是諸佛之師，是至高無上覺位的頂峰。我將發願為一切眾生速證無上菩提，祈請三世多杰羌佛傳我即身成佛大法，以便我擔挑如來荷擔，利益眾生無誤。

從今以後直至菩提，自覺覺他，為我願行！

佛陀的根本弟子：洛桑丹增諾日
2007年9月3日

（此文的英文翻譯印在前面）

A HEAVENLY WINDOW OPENED TO THE WESTERN BUDDHA LAND; EVERYONE SAW HOLY SIGHTS OF THE WESTERN PARADISE OF ULTIMATE BLISS

SEVERAL DAYS LATER, YET ANOTHER DISCIPLE OF GREAT DHARMA KING YANGWO YISINUBU ATTAINED LIBERATION FROM THE CYCLE OF REINCARNATION

LAYWOMAN QUAN-FANG LU ATTAINED ENLIGHTENMENT; AMITABHA BUDDHA ESCORTED HER AWAY TO THE WESTERN PARADISE; SHE LEFT BEHIND 49 SARIRA FIRM RELICS

(This is the text of an article published in the Asian Journal on Oct. 6, 2004.)

Several days ago, Madame Tang, who was a disciple of Great Dharma King Yangwo Yisinubu[1], attained great liberation from the cycle of reincarnation and left behind 263 sarira firm relics. On September 9th, Amitabha Buddha escorted to the Western Paradise of Ultimate Bliss yet another outstanding disciple of the Great Dharma King—laywoman Quan-Fang Lu! Amitabha Buddha praised the unsurpassed and true Buddha Dharma of Great Dharma King Yangwo Yisinubu. For 29 hours, Amitabha Buddha opened up a heavenly window of a Buddha land, thereby allowing many people to see the sights of that Buddha land. An image of Great Dharma King Yangwo Yisinubu miraculously emitted bright light for three hours, thereby empowering those with the karmic affinity to be empowered!

Elder laywoman Quan-Fang Lu was from Chengdu, Sichuan. She and her husband, layman Guang-Ming Wang, had been Buddhists since the 1950's. When they took refuge in Buddhism, they received an initiation and Dharma transmission from the Great Dharma King. In the 1950's, they were working in Tibet. Because of their underlying karmic conditions, they received the guidance of an outstanding Rinpoche of Tibetan esoteric Buddhism. That Rinpoche told them that Great Dharma King Yangwo Yisinubu possessed the best and highest Buddha Dharma. After going through many hardships, they brought their son to the Great Dharma King. The Great Dharma King was not even seven years old at the time. The three of them formally acknowledged the Great Dharma King as their Master. Laywoman Quan-Fang Lu and her husband Guang-Ming Wang then resolutely decided to have their son stay by the side of the Great Dharma King in order to receive his training and Dharma teachings.

They have been very pious and respectful toward the Great Dharma King, and they have diligently practiced the Dharma that the Great Dharma King transmitted to them. Over the past two years, certain people have spread rumors and made false accusations against the Great Dharma King. Laywoman Quan-Fang Lu and her husband Guang-Ming Wang were filled with righteous indignation at this. They vigorously berated the contemptible conduct of those rascals who spread rumors, fabricated lies, and deceived people.

Based upon layman Guang-Ming Wang's own pious heart and upon the Great Dharma King's realization, which is like that of a Buddha, in November of last year, layman Guang-Ming Wang passed on to the Western Paradise of Ultimate Bliss. At his cremation, layman Guang-Ming Wang left behind 11 sarira firm relics.

In the middle of August, 2004, laywoman Quan-Fang Lu told her son Min

Wang that she would soon pass away. Min Wang telephoned the Great Dharma King a few times, beseeching the Great Dharma King to cause his loving mother to stay alive longer. When Min Wang's mother found out about these calls, she admonished her son, "Those who learn Buddhism and cultivate themselves must understand that the law of cause and effect never fails. My karmic connection with this world is about to end. My karmic connection with the Dharma is now complete. The Dharma King Master will help me go to the Western Paradise of Ultimate Bliss."

As expected, at around noon on September 9th, the crown of elder laywoman Lu's head suddenly opened. The crown of her head became as soft as cotton. At that time, a colorful auspicious light filled the room. Amitabha Buddha came to escort her away. Beautifully set off by a huge white Buddha light, the pure gold bowl of Amitabha Buddha slowly descended. The red lotus flowers in the bowl were bright-colored. Two photographs were hurriedly taken of this extremely rare and holy sight. Heavenly music could be heard. Imitating the Buddha, elder laywoman Lu assumed the "auspicious recumbent posture." Amid the Buddha light, she passed on to the Western Paradise of Ultimate Bliss.

The next day, her body was placed in the Buddha worshipping hall of Bao Guang Temple in Xindu, which is one of the four great Chan (Zen) temples in China. Right after her body was placed there, an image of the Great Dharma King suddenly emitted bright light. A colorful Buddha light went round and round the Great Dharma King's image. A fragrant scent wafted through the air.

News of such phenomena began to spread. More and more people came to chant mantras and sutras for the benefit of laywoman Lu, respectfully see her off to the next realm, and observe the ceremony. Day and night, the chanting of Amitabha Buddha's name did not stop. On the evening of September 10th, eminent Tibetan Rinpoches and Lamas who were all disciples of the Great Dharma King arrived at the temple after having traveled a great distance. They came to perform Buddhist rites. On the evening of September 11th, the machine used to chant the name of Amitabha Buddha suddenly emitted the shocking sound of the Great Dharma King chanting the name of Amitabha Buddha. The Great Dharma King was in the United States. The monastics and laypersons in attendance were all extremely moved.

At around noon on September 12th, a holy sight appeared for the first time in history! A painting of Amitabha Buddha hangs in the Buddha worshipping hall of the temple. In front of Amitabha Buddha's chest, a heavenly window to the

---

[1] Here and below the words *Great Dharma King Yangwo Yisinubu*, *Great Dharma King*, or *Dharma King Master* refers to H.H. Dorje Chang Buddha III Wan Ko Yeshe Norbu Holiest Tathagata.

Western Paradise of Ultimate Bliss suddenly opened. This heavenly window directly displayed the sights of the Western Paradise of Ultimate Bliss!

People were seething with excitement. They were so pleasantly surprised they could hardly control themselves. Through that heavenly window to a Buddha land that appeared in front of the painting of Amitabha Buddha, all of those who had the requisite karmic affinity saw Amitabha Buddha. They even saw the protuberance on top of Amitabha's Buddha's head. They saw Kuan Yin Bodhisattva wearing white clothes and holding willow tree branches. They also saw Mahasthamaprapta Bodhisattva. In that heavenly window, elder laywoman Lu was reciting the name of Amitabha Buddha. Her lips were constantly moving, her eyes blinked, and her head swayed. She looked the same as when she recited Amitabha Buddha's name when she was alive. The former abbot of Zhao Jue Temple, Dharma Teacher Qing Ding, also appeared. He was sitting on a chair, smiling, and nodding his head.

The image of Great Dharma King Yangwo Yisinubu appeared in that heavenly window. He was wearing a red Dharma robe and a Dharma crown. When he appeared, people excitedly shouted words such as, "Master, I see you!" "Great Dharma King Master, by following you we do not fear even death!" "Great Dharma King, my whole family wants to take refuge in you! We want to learn the true Buddha Dharma from you!"

People were awestruck by these holy scenes. They could not control their emotions. The sounds of people marveling, shouting, and kowtowing could be heard.

At 8:00 or 9:00 that evening, more and more people arrived at the cremation site. People rushed over from all directions to see the holy sights of the Western Paradise of Ultimate Bliss displayed through that heavenly window and to receive empowerment from Amitabha Buddha. Many people rushed home and brought back their parents and children. All of the elder and young people saw the holy scenes of that Buddha land. They did not even care about eating their dinner. They sat there in rows and devoutly chanted the holy name of Amitabha Buddha deep into the night. The holy sights of the Western Paradise of Ultimate Bliss displayed by that heavenly window continually changed and lasted all the way up to 5:00 in the afternoon the next day. This display of sights lasted all together 29 hours, which is a miracle in the history of Buddhism.

On the morning of September 13th, a colorful Buddha light filled the sky. After 1:00 in the afternoon, the picture of the Great Dharma King suddenly began emitting bright white light that continually flashed. For three hours, this light empowered those with the karmic affinity to be empowered. While immersed in the Buddha Dharma empowerment bestowed by the Great Dharma King, people shouted with joy and prostrated. It was an extremely moving scene!

At 5:00 in the afternoon, those disciples who had been reciting the name of Amitabha Buddha formed long lines as part of the ceremony placing the body of elder laywoman Lu into the cremation furnace. Whatever place her body passed through, there was a fragrant scent in the air. Before the monastics and lamas began chanting mantras and performing Buddhist rites, the part of the wooden cremation-casket over elder laywoman Lu's chest was covered with Buddha light. From the cracks in that wooden cremation-casket, red, white, and yellow light emanated!

As soon as the cremation furnace was lit, a round Dharma object that formed from a translucent silver light appeared on the crown of elder laywoman Lu's head. There was a square hole in the middle of that Dharma object. That Dharma object was exactly the same as the round light that appeared over the crown of Henghsing Gyatso Rinpoche's head when he respectfully received a picture of the Great Dharma King. He received that picture right before he began his journey around the island of Taiwan. Before receiving that picture, Henghsing Gyatso Rinpoche, who is a disciple of the Great Dharma King, had made a vow to journey 1,100 kilometers around the island of Taiwan on foot by prostrating fully once after each step. He made this vow in order to atone for the sins of others.

During the cremation of laywoman Lu, holy sights continually appeared. Lotus flowers emerged. Images of the Dharma King, the Three Holy Ones of the Western Paradise (Amitabha Buddha, Kuan Yin Bodhisattva, and Mahasthamaprapta Bodhisattva), and Maitreya Bodhisattva all appeared. Vajra Dharma protecting deities and dragon-spirit Dharma protecting deities stood in a circle on both sides of her. Fire phoenix flew to and fro inside the cremation furnace. Beautiful scenes of pagodas and towers from the Western Paradise of Ultimate Bliss repeatedly appeared. People before the cremation furnace were filled with Dharma joy and began prostrating. They were so moved they began to cry. The sound of joyous laughter filled the temple.

After the cremation was completed, people collected 49 sarira firm relics from the bone ashes of laywoman Quan-Fang Lu.

At this point, I cannot restrain myself from asking the question "Why?" Why is it that one after another of the disciples of Great Dharma King Yangwo Yisinubu have attained great accomplishment (liberation), extricated themselves from the sufferings connected with the cycle of birth and death, and exhibited holy sights never before seen? The only answer to this question is the following: It is because the moral character of the Great Dharma King is incomparably noble and pure. It is because he is a man of great holiness and virtue who possesses the true and magnificent Buddha Dharma that the Buddha possessed when he was alive! That is why the Great Dharma King was able to cause the manifestation of all seven holy states that must appear at a true Ultimate Bathing of the Buddha Dharma Assembly. That is why within five months from the time the Great Dharma King transmitted the true Buddha Dharma to twelve-year-old Jinba Rinpoche–who had no experience in art whatsoever at the time of the transmission—Jinba Rinpoche became a world-class artist.

The Great Dharma King has no equal in this world. The true Buddha Dharma that leads to liberation from the sufferings of the cycle of birth and death has manifested before us time and time again. How can we still remain ignorant and not wake up? How can we still not know where to search for and find liberation?

PHOTOGRAPHS:
(Lotus)
A photograph was taken on the spot. Everyone saw Amitabha Buddha tossing lotus flowers from his bowl made of pure gold. These flowers descended upon different places at the top of a tree. Amitabha Buddha then escorted laywoman Quan-Fang Lu to the Western Paradise of Ultimate Bliss. Behind and above the lotus flowers, there is a white round light that is more than one hundred times larger than the lotus flowers.
(Sariras)
After the cremation of laywoman Quan-Fang Lu, people collected 49 sarira firm relics from her bone ashes.

Laywoman Quan-Fang Lu was a disciple of H.H. Dorje Chang Buddha III Wan Ko Yeshe Norbu Holiest Tathagata. Following the teachings of H.H. Dorje Chang Buddha III, she became enlightened and attained complete liberation from the cycle of birth and death. Below are newspaper reports on this.

三世多杰羌佛雲高益西諾布頂聖如來的弟子盧全芳居士，依師證道，獲大解脫，以下是當時報紙的報導。

都會時報
Metro Times

3 中華民國九十三年九月二十一日／星期二　　全·國·要·聞

西方佛國天窗開　極樂聖境大家看

仰諤益西諾布大法王又一弟子獲大解脫

盧全芳居士證道　阿彌陀佛接走　舍利堅固子 49 粒

【陳玉柱／整理報導】前幾日，仰諤益西諾布大法王有唐氏弟子大成就獲舍利堅固子263顆，現在大法王又一大弟子盧全芳居士，9月9日由阿彌陀佛接引往生西方極樂世界！阿彌陀佛讚嘆仰諤益西諾布大法王之無上正法，打開佛國天窗之門29小時，任眾人觀看佛國之景；仰諤益西諾布大法王像神奇地放出毫光加持有緣眾生長達3小時！

盧全芳居士乃四川成都人氏，她和丈夫王光明居士早在上世紀50年代便已皈依佛門，得大法王灌頂傳法。那時他們在西藏工作，有緣受藏密大仁波切指點，告知最好最高的佛法在仰諤益西諾布大法王處，夫妻二人便千辛萬苦把自己的兒子送到當時未滿7歲的大法王面前，一家三口拜師，遂後夫妻倆毅然將兒子留在大法王身邊接受調服聞法。他們對大法王十分虔誠恭敬並精進修持大法王所傳之法，近兩年來有人在社會上散佈謊言誣陷大法王，夫妻二人義憤填膺，奮起譴責造謠惑眾徒編造誣言狂惑大眾之惡行。去年11月，王光明居士因其虔誠心，依循大法王陀般的證量，飛邁極樂世界，火化出舍利堅固子11顆。這次盧全芳居士于2004年8月中旬告知兒子王敏，她要西歸。王敏幾次打電話給大法王，想留住慈母，母親知道後告誡兒子：「學

佛者行就要知道因果不昧，我的塵緣盡了，法緣已滿，法王上師會送我去極樂世界的。」果然，9月9日午時，盧老居士突然開頂，頂冒如棉，正此時室內一片五彩吉祥之光，阿彌陀佛駕臨接引，天樂傳空，盧老居士佛陀以吉祥臥式，於佛光中往昇西方極樂世界。

次日法體安奉到中國四大禪院之一的新都寶光寺佛堂，剛安奉完畢，大法王的法王像忽然放出毫光，有彩色佛光團團圍繞，還伴著撲鼻異香。消息傳開，助念送的人越來越多的來觀禮，晝夜聖號不停。9月10日晚，大法王的西藏大活佛弟子們和喇嘛弟子們途跋涉來助緣做法事。11日晚，念佛隊裏傳出遠在美國的大法王念誦佛號的震撼聲，僧眾居士們激動不一樣。

12日中午，史無前例的聖境顯現！佛堂懸掛的阿彌陀佛畫像胸前，突然打開了一扇極樂世界的天窗，直接展現極樂世界景像！群情沸騰，人們驚喜得難以自持。透過阿彌陀佛畫像上的那扇佛國天窗，一切有緣者，人看到了阿彌陀佛，連佛陀頭上的佛髻都清清楚楚，看到觀世音菩薩身著白衣手拿楊枝，還有大勢至菩薩；盧老居士在天窗中念佛，嘴不停在動，眼睛也在眨，頭一搖一搖的，和她生前念佛的樣子完全一樣；原昭覺寺住持清定法師也出現了，坐在椅子上笑瞇瞇的點頭；當身著紅色法袍、頭戴法冠的仰諤大法王法像出現在天窗

時，人群爆發出激動的呼喊：「上師，我看見您了！」「大法王上師啊，跟著您，什麼生死我們都不怕了！」「大法王啊！我們全家都要皈依您！我們要跟您老人家學到佛法！」人們被聖境震懾了，無法控制情緒，只聽到一片驚嘆聲、呼喊聲、頭頂到地上的咚咚聲……晚上八、九點鐘，火化處的人越聚越多，人們從四面八方趕來看天窗顯極樂世界聖境，接受阿彌陀佛加持。許多人趕回家來帶父母、子女，老人孩子們個個到佛國聖境，連晚飯都顧不上吃，成排安坐下來虔心念誦南無阿彌陀佛聖號直到深夜。天窗極樂聖境不斷變化顯現直到第二天下午5點，長達29小時，成為歷史上佛門的奇蹟。

9月13日上午，天空佈滿五彩佛光，中午1點多鐘，大法王的法王像突然放出白色毫光，不停閃射，加持有緣眾生長達3個小時之久，人們浸浴在大法王的佛法加持中驚喜歡呼，頂禮膜拜，場面感人至極！下午5點，念佛的弟子們排著長隊把盧老居士的肉身送進火化爐，肉身經過之處異香陣陣。僧眾喇嘛的轉咒法事還進未行，老居士胸前的木龕上就已籠罩著佛光。從木龕的縫隙中迸出紅、白、黃色三種光芒！剛一點火，盧老居士的頭頂就出現銀光透明的圓形法器！法器中間為四方的孔，四角都有聯輪至法器的邊，就和大法王之弟子恆性嘉措仁波切於心磋曼頂禮拜嘉義縣海一千一百公尺，代眾生受苦，臨行前他請到大法王法像時頭頂出現的圓光一模一樣。火化過程中，聖境不斷顯現，蓮花朵朵湧出，大法王法像、西方三聖、彌勒菩薩出現，金剛護法、龍神護法環立左右，火鳳凰在爐火中翱翔，還有極樂世界的樓臺亭閣美景連連。火化爐前人們法喜跪著，激動的淚水、歡樂的笑聲撒滿寺

院。

火化完畢，大家從盧全芳居士的骨灰中共獲舍利堅固子49粒。

記錄到這裏，筆者忍不住要問一句為什麼？為什麼仰諤益西諾布大法王座下的弟子，一批一批都得到大成就，都能離了生死輪回之苦，且塵境空前無人能比？答案只有一個：因為大法王他老人家的道德高潔無比，是擁有佛陀當年真正偉大佛法的大聖德！正因為如此，才圓滿了勝義浴佛法會七支聖境現前，才能傳真正佛法讓從未涉獵藝術的12歲的金巴仁波切在五個月內成了世界級藝術家！各位善知識，舉世無雙，真正解脫生死苦厄的如來正法一次又一次展現在我們面前，難道我們還要愚昧不醒，不知如何覺得解脫嗎？

▲當時照相照下，眾人看到，阿彌陀佛拋下紫金缽中的蓮花，降到了樹頂不同的位置，將接走盧全芳居士。
◀大家從盧全芳居士荼毗後的骨灰中撿獲舍利堅固子49粒。

THE TRUE PURE LAND GREAT DHARMA METHOD IN WHICH AMITABHA BUDDHA'S NAME IS RECITED

(This is a translation of an article published in the World Journal on Jun. 5, 2002.)

On June 1ˢᵗ, Buddhist disciple Hou Yu-Shan serenely passed away in his home in Los Angeles. At the time of his passing, his hands were in the "passing away mudra." He was seventy-three-years-old. His wife, Hou Li Qing-Qiu, personally saw Sakyamuni Buddha, Amitabha Buddha, and Guan Yin Bodhisattva arrive in the sky to take her husband away to the Western Paradise of Ultimate Bliss. Just before Hou Yu-Shan passed away, he urged his wife to follow his Master[1] for the rest of her life so that she could continue to learn Buddhism and cultivate herself.

Hou Yu-Shan's wife, Hou Li Qing-Qiu, is a licensed practitioner of Chinese medicine in California. On the day Hou Yu-Shan passed away, Hou Li Qing-Qiu explained Hou Yu-Shan's practice of Buddhism and his passing away to more than twenty monastics who came to her house to perform Buddhist rites. She gave the following account in front of the room where the body of Hou Yu-Shan lay:

Hou Yu-Shan learned Buddhism for many years. Four years ago, he discovered that he had lung cancer. He underwent long-term treatment, which was extremely painful. One and a half years ago, Hou Yu-Shan and his wife went to Master Yi Yungao International Cultural Institute [Note: Master Yi Yungao is the Mandarin pronunciation of Master Wan Ko Yee] to listen to tapes of Master Wan Ko Yee's discourses on the Buddha Dharma. They were amazed at what they heard. They did not think that there was such profound Buddha Dharma in this world.

After Hou Yu-Shan heard this authentic Dharma, he had tremendous and sincere reverence for Master Yee. He then began to participate in the Institute's group cultivation sessions. He never missed one session in which tape-recorded discourses of Master Yee were played. He also decided to do volunteer work for the Institute on a full-day basis. Other members of the Institute very much admired him. They urged him not to work so hard at the Institute and encouraged him go home and rest to recuperate from his illness. However, he told them, "That is not acceptable. I am furthering the cause of Buddhism. You do not understand. My only wish is that I may see Master Wan Ko Yee someday soon."

In February of this year, Hou Yu-Shan and Hou Li Qing-Qiu were able to meet Master Wan Ko Yee through the introduction of Losang Gyasto Rinpoche of Master Yi Yungao International Cultural Institute. At that meeting, Mr. and Mrs. Hou formally acknowledged Master Wan Ko Yee as their Master. Mr. and Mrs. Hou were quite surprised to discover that Master Yee was totally different from what they imagined. They thought that Master Yee would be aloof and unapproachable. However, after meeting Master Yee, they realized that he is amiable and easily approachable.

They sincerely beseeched the Master to perform an initiation for them and transmit Dharma to them. They also made an offering of money to the Master.

Without even looking at their offering, Master Yee told them, "I cannot set a precedent by accepting your offering." The Master sternly refused their offering. Still, without the least bit of hesitation, Master Yee performed an initiation for them and transmitted Dharma to them. After receiving this Dharma, Hou Yu-Shan diligently practiced it. He soon entered into deep states. The pain from his cancer suddenly disappeared completely.

In May of this year, on the holiday celebrating the birth and enlightenment of the Buddha, Hou Yu-Shan and Hou Li Qing-Qiu met Master Wan Ko Yee again. Master Yee asked Hou Yu-Shan if he had any requests. Hou Yu-Shan had a fatal disease, but he did not make any requests to alleviate the pain from this fatal disease. He respectfully and sincerely beseeched his Vajra Master, Master Yee, as follows: "I do not have any requests but the following. I only want to know how I can safely be reborn in the Western Paradise of Ultimate Bliss. This is my only wish."

Master Yee replied, "Since that is the case, you must change your Dharma practice. You must change to the Dharma method of reciting the name of Amitabha Buddha. This is a Pure Land sect Dharma method. You recite 'Namo Amitabha Buddha.' However, what is most crucial is the secret 'passing away mudra' that I will teach you. By practicing this method, very soon you will be able to see Amitabha states. Then, the Buddhas and Bodhisattvas will soon lead you to the Western Paradise of Ultimate Bliss." With great compassion, the Master told Hou Yu-Shan to sit beside him. The Master then secretly taught him that mudra. After Hou Yu-Shan received this supreme and great Dharma method involving reciting the name of Amitabha Buddha, he was extremely moved and indescribably happy.

Ever since that holiday celebrating the birth and enlightenment of the Buddha—the day that Hou Shan-Yu received great Dharma related to Amitabha Buddha—his wife, Dr. Hou Li Qing-Qiu, noticed that the crown of her husband's head and his back were constantly emitting a golden and red light. This dazzling light was a tremendously auspicious sign. Hou Yu-Shan did not appear like a cancer patient at all! Since that time, all of the pain he was experiencing from his cancer totally disappeared without a trace. His edema also disappeared. The morphine injections from the hospital to reduce pain were no longer of any use.

One day, Hou Yu-Shan asked his daughter, Lily, who is a hospital anesthesiologist, "How does my facial complexion look?"

His daughter answered, "Dad, you really have very good color in your face. Your sprit is high. You don't look like a sick person."

On the morning of May 25ᵗʰ, Hou Yu-Shan told his wife, "When I was practicing the Dharma last night, I entered into a state of samadhi concentration. I went to the

---

[1] Here and below the words *Master, Master Wan Ko Yee*, or *Master Yee* refers to H.H. Dorje Chang Buddha III Wan Ko Yeshe Norbu Holiest Tathagata.

Western Paradise of Ultimate Bliss. The Western Paradise of Ultimate Bliss is truly beautiful! The red color that exists there is indescribably beautiful. The yellow color that exists there is also too beautiful to describe. The same is true for the colors green and purple. I simple cannot express to you just how beautiful those colors are."

Hou Li Qing-Qiu asked, "Can you give an example to show just how beautiful those colors are?"

After giving it some thought, Hou Yu-Shan replied, "The colors in the Western Paradise of Ultimate Bliss cannot be compared with the colors in this world. As for scenery, do you remember when we strolled around the West Lake when we were young? The early morning glow would pierce the mist that rose from the lake, producing a wondrous array of colors. The Western Paradise of Ultimate Bliss is much more beautiful than that scene. Moreover, a Buddha told me that seven days from now that Buddha would come to take me to that paradise. That Buddha instructed me to tell everyone that the best Buddha Dharma in the world is with our Master and that they should diligently study and practice the Buddha Dharma."

On May 31st, Hou Yu-Shan appropriately arranged certain family matters. He told his daughter the following words to remember after his passing: "Do not blame your mother for anything she may do during the remainder of her life—except for one thing. If your mother gives up the Buddha Dharma, if she stops following the Vajra Master (Master Wan Ko Yee), then you must criticize her and remind her so that she will continue to follow Master Wan Ko Yee and seriously cultivate herself. She must not turn away from the Buddha Dharma and Master Wan Ko Yee." Hou Yu-Shan then earnestly told his wife, Hou Li Qing-Qiu, "For the rest of your life, it doesn't really matter if you make mistakes or not. However, there is one thing about which you must not make a mistake. That is, you must follow the Vajra Master and diligently cultivate yourself. Only if you follow him will you be able to attain liberation. Only his Buddha Dharma is the true Buddha Dharma."

After giving his wife these instructions, Hou Yu-Shan told her that he would pass away that night. He also told her, "There is something you must keep in mind tonight. I am afraid that I will fall into drowsiness or muddle-headedness or enter some demonic state the moment I pass away. You must not go to sleep. You must remind me to visualize the Vajra Master over my head, visualize Amitabha Buddha over my head, and wholeheartedly recite the mantra."

That night in her house near the beach, Hou Li Qing-Qiu already knew that her husband, Hou Yu-Shan, was about to pass away and be reborn in a Buddha Land. She therefore used four different alarm clocks to keep herself up. Each alarm clock went off at a different time every hour.

As expected, in the early morning of June 1st at 6:15 a.m., Hou Yu-Shan's pulse and respiration started to slow down. Hou Li Qing-Qiu began to shake Hou Yu-Shan's bed. Both of them together continuously recited, "Namo Vajra Master! Namo Amitabha Buddha!" Hou Yu-Shan put his hands in the secret mudra that Master Wan Ko Yee taught him. At this time, Hou Li Qing-Qiu suddenly heard the sound of heavenly music. The body of Hou Yu-Shan began to emit an increasingly strong golden light. Hou Li Qing-Qiu saw Sakyamuni Buddha, Amitabha Buddha, Guan Yin

Bodhisattva, and other Buddhas and Bodhisattvas appear in the sky over the beach. The light emitted by those Buddhas and Bodhisattvas merged with the light emitted by Hou Yu-Shan. That body of light then grew increasingly strong. This scene lasted for about five minutes, after which the Buddhas and Bodhisattvas disappeared, and the heavenly music also disappeared. Hou Li Qing-Qiu then remembered to feel the pulse of Hou Yu-Shan. Hou Yu-Shan's pulse and heartbeat had already stopped.

The President of Master Yi Yungao International Cultural Institute, Zhang Tian-You, was the first to rush to the Hou residence after the passing of Hou Yu-Shan. He saw Hou Yu-Shan reclining on the bed as if he were sleeping. His facial expression did not exhibit the least bit of pain. His two hands were in the secret "passing away mudra." He looked very serene.

The Chairperson of the International Buddhism Sangha Association, who is also the abbess of Hua Zang Temple, Master Long Hui, was extremely moved by all of these events. She profusely praised the magnificence of Master Yee. She said, "I have often seen cancer patients experience great pain at the time of their passing, especially those suffering from lung cancer. Such pain is difficult to describe. After all they have been through, it is hard to even recognize them. They are surely unable to put their hands in a specific mudra and recite the name of a Buddha. However, the Pure Land Dharma method Master Yee transmitted involving the intoning of Amitabha Buddha's name caused someone who was a lung cancer patient to be surrounded by a wonderful and auspicious golden light, to be free from all pain, and to be led away by the Buddhas and Bodhisattvas to the Western Paradise of Ultimate Bliss—all within one month's time. This is the magnificent and correct Dharma of the Tathagata. Words cannot adequately express the greatness of that Dharma!"

Before Hou Yu-Shan passed away, he prepared a present and US$5,000 in cash. He told his wife, "The Master has never accepted offerings. During my life, the Master did not accept my offerings. Tonight I will pass away. Take these offerings to the Master tomorrow and sincerely request that he accept them."

On June 1st, Hou Li Qing-Qiu followed the instructions of her husband and took the offerings to Master Wan Ko Yee. She knelt on the floor as tears streamed down her face. In a very emotionally manner, she sincerely requested that Master Yee accept the offerings. Raising her voice, she exclaimed, "My supreme Buddha Vajra Master!"

The Master replied, "Do not call me that. I am not a Buddha Master. I am just a very ordinary practitioner, like everyone else." Hou Li Qing-Qiu explained that her offerings were made at the request of Hou Yu-Shan. The Master then said, "It seems that there is no other way. It would not be right to refuse his offerings." The Master had no other choice but to accept the offerings. He then arranged for layman Hou's offerings to be placed in a certain temple. No individual was permitted to use any of the offerings for his or her own personal use. The Master also promptly took US$6,000 out of his own living expenses and had that money sent to the Hou residence to supplement all of the funeral expenses. Additionally, the Master instructed monastics from two large temples to go to the Hou residence to perform certain Buddhist rites.

*Professor Yu-Shan Hou was a disciple of H.H. Dorje Chang Buddha III Wan Ko Yeshe Norbu Holiest Tathagata. He practiced a dharma called **Great Dharma of Pure Land and Reciting Amitabha Buddha's Name** that H.H. Dorje Chang Buddha III transmitted to him. At the time of his death, the Buddhas and Bodhisattvas personally escorted him to the Pure Land. For details on this, please see the newspaper reports that were published at that time.*

三世多杰羌佛雲高益西諾布頂聖如來的弟子侯欲善教授修三世多杰羌佛所傳的『淨土念佛大法』，佛菩薩親自接引其往升淨土。詳見當時的報紙報導。

My Father's Body Emitted Bright Lights After He Passed on to the Western Paradise of Ultimate Bliss

My mother passed on to the Western Paradise of Ultimate Bliss, which astounded my father. He also decided to learn Buddhism and go to the Western Paradise of Ultimate Bliss to meet my mother. Several times he had requested that Buddha Master, Wan Ko Yeshe Norbu, transmit to him the Buddha-dharma. However, his requests were not granted because his karmic conditions were not mature.

In September 1993, my father suddenly became ill with late-stage stomach cancer. Seeing my father in such pain, my sole thought was that only the holy water of my Buddha Master could save my father's life. I still had half of the bottle that H.H. Buddha Master had given me. H.H. Buddha Master had practiced that dharma especially for me in order to eliminate or avoid disasters and hardships. When I drank the holy water, an unusual fragrance struck my nose, and my whole body was immersed in comfort. This could not be described in words. I didn't drink it at ordinary times because I wanted to save it for a time when it was really needed.

That day, I saw that my father was suffering unbearable pain. In a moment of desperation, I disobeyed the dharma principles of H.H. Buddha Master and secretly let my father have some holy water. After my father drank the water, his whole body felt extremely cool and refreshed, and his pain suddenly disappeared. From then on, as long as he felt uncomfortable, he would immediately drink the holy water of H.H. Buddha Master. As soon as he drank it, he became well. He didn't have any pain until he passed away in a state of liberation.

On the 18th day of the twelfth month of the lunar year, H.H. Buddha Master summoned me. After I paid my homage to H.H. Buddha Master, His Holiness said, "You should go back home immediately to transmit dharma to your father." I said in a surprised tone of voice, "How am I qualified to transmit dharma?" H.H. Buddha Master said, "As long as I say that you are capable, you will be fine. You should go to transmit dharma on behalf of me! Even if it's you that does the transmission, the dharma is still my dharma!" H.H. Buddha Master then went up to the dharma platform and transmitted to me the rituals, mudras, dharma image, and dharma instruments of the Great Perfection Essence Esoteric Dharma transmitted both telepathically or orally. Also, His Holiness asked fellow-disciple Hui Han Da to guard the Buddhist altar (mandala).

That night, I respectfully accepted the dharma edict and went back home to transmit dharma to my father. Hearing that I would transmit dharma on behalf of H.H. Buddha Master, my father was full of dharma happiness. He placed the table, burnt incense, and prostrated himself in worship. According to the rituals taught by the Buddha Master, I began to clear the altar. I had just started chanting a mantra when the miserable sound "meow" was suddenly heard. A big spotted cat with green eyes jumped out from under the cabinet. It turned out that a dharma protecting Bodhisattva had come to the altar, and the cat was frightened. During the process of my

dharma transmission, there appeared at the altar different kinds of holy scenes that were very magnificent.

My father diligently practiced dharma at once. When I was leaving, I told my brother-in-law and others not to touch my father while he was passing on to the Buddhist Pure Land. If he were moved, he would feel great pain, as if a blunt knife was cutting his flesh. They all remembered. During the following two consecutive days, my father didn't leave his bed except to take his meals. He kept chanting the name of Amitabha Buddha and practicing the dharma. In the evening of the 20th day of the twelfth month of the lunar year, fellow-disciple Hui Han Da phoned me and said that my father passed on to the Western Paradise of Ultimate Bliss and that the scene of his passing was excellent. The dharma of H.H. Buddha Master, Holiest Tathagata, is really incredible! From transmission of dharma to passing on to the Western Paradise while emitting rainbow light took only two days!

Only two days earlier, my father began chanting the name of Amitabha Buddha and practicing dharma while sleeping. At 9:00 p.m. on the 20th day of the twelfth month of the lunar year, he suddenly turned over and sat up straight, still chanting the name of Amitabha Buddha. He looked upward, and folding his hands before his chest in respect. He then prepared to put his hands in a mudra. However, my brother-in-law, a butcher who didn't understand the principles of the dharma, forcibly pushed my father down on the bed in order not to move him until after he passed on to the Western Paradise, as instructed. My father got up again, but my brother-in-law pushed him down again. This was repeated three times. Finally, my father lay on one side. His right hand was behind his head, holding his right ear. His right leg stretched out, his left leg was slightly bent, and he was smiling. He then calmly and peacefully passed away in a state of liberation.

Unexpectedly, my sister's family saw my father's body suddenly emit a shining light. The whole room became completely bright. At that time, they thought that somebody was using a torch. After looking around, nobody was found at all. The white light emanated from my father's body lasted for more than one minute. At 3 o'clock in the afternoon on the next day, a red light abruptly emitted from the room where my father's body was placed. The entire room was completely red. Outsiders thought that the room had caught on fire, but there was no smoke. When they entered, they found that the room was immersed in red light. Dozens of people saw that.

At about 7:00 p.m. that day (it had just begun to get dark), my father's body emitted white light again. The light formed a very wide white ribbon, several rings of which encircled his body. It was a sign of Great Perfection Supreme Wisdom. In the end, my father was able to achieve the great accomplishment of the rainbow light. Dozens of people who were at the scene were all shocked! They continually exclaimed, "This is really incredible! This is magnificent!" However, it was a great pity that my brother-in-law pushed down my father onto the bed. If my father had been able to sit up straight with the right dharma posture and mudras, his body would have transformed into rainbow light, and there would have been only nails and hair left.

Because I was busy with other Buddhist matters, I the soonest could rush back home was after 11:00 p.m. on the next day after my father had passed away in a state of liberation. At that time, it was snowing heavily, like goose feathers. The windshield wipers of my car didn't work. As the snow piled up, I couldn't see the road. Therefore, I had to get out of the car to push away the snow piled on my windshield. I chanted mantras and prayed for empowerment from H.H. Buddha Master.

After I stepped into the car, a miracle happened. Whenever the heavy goose-feather-like snow came within a foot of my windshield, it suddenly disappeared without a trace. My front glass was as clean as a mirror, whereas the glass on the side of fellow-disciple Sheng Fan was covered with dense white snow. Seeing such a scene, I felt very grateful from the bottom of my heart to my Buddha Master, the Buddhas, and the Bodhisattvas for empowering me, a disciple, to return home safely!

After my father practiced the profound Great Perfection Essence Dharma for two days, he passed on to the Western Paradise with his body emitting rainbow light. Many wonderful scenes appeared at the time of his passing, which helped to convert many relatives and friends, especially my brother-in-law, a former butcher. Since he had personally viewed such great Buddha-dharma himself, he was deeply moved and pledged that he would never kill any living being again. Moreover, he brought a large group of people to convert to Buddhism.

We would rather abandon everything than give up Dorje Chang Buddha III. If we miss this opportunity, we would not be able to find such a true Buddha Vajradhara Dharma King for a hundred thousand eons! So where does the true dharma come from? I must practice Buddhism very well to correct all of my wrongdoings and bad behavior and become a Buddhist disciple who truly benefits all living beings!

Buddhist disciple
Chi Lie Er

(This is a complete translation of the Chinese text that follows originally written and signed by Chi Lie Er.)

我 的 父 親 往 升 極 樂 身 體 大 放 光 明

我母親往升極樂世界，對我父親的心靈震撼很大，他也決心學佛，到極樂世界與我媽相會，幾次求三世多杰羌佛雲高益西諾布佛陀上師傳法，皆因因緣未熟，沒有求到。

93年9月，父親突然病倒，是胃癌晚期，看到父親那麼痛苦，唯一想到的是佛陀上師的法水可以救命，我還有半瓶法水，是佛陀上師專門為我消災免難而修的，我服用時，異香撲鼻，全身浸沁的感覺，無法用語言形容。平時根本捨不得服用，今天看見父親痛苦不堪，情急之下，我違背佛陀上師法旨，將佛陀上師專門為我修法加持消災免難的法水，悄悄讓我父親服用一點，誰知我父親服下即全身清涼無比，頓然病痛消除，從此只要不舒服，他馬上就要吃佛陀上師的法水，只要一吃，馬上就好，直到圓寂都沒有痛過！

臘月十八日，佛陀上師召見我，拜見佛陀上師後，佛陀上師說：「你趕快回去給你爸爸傳法。」我非常吃驚地說：「我怎麼有資格傳法？」佛陀上師說：「我說行就行，你去代我傳法嘛！你去傳，還是我的佛法！」佛陀上師當即登上法台，心傳口授大圓滿精髓秘密法的儀軌、手印、法像、法器，並叫慧漢達師兄去護壇，當晚我恭領法旨，回家為父傳法，聽說我代師傳法，父親充滿法喜，擺案焚香頂禮，我按佛陀上師傳授的儀軌，開始清壇，剛一啟動咒語，突然「哇！」的一聲慘叫，一隻綠眼睛的大花貓，從櫃子下一躍而出，原來是護法菩薩降臨壇場，嚇到了大花貓，我在傳法過程中，壇場出現種種聖境，十分殊勝。我父親馬上就精進修法。臨走時我交代我妹夫，告訴他父親往升時不要動他，如果動了他，猶如鈍刀割肉，他會很痛

苦的，他們都記住了。一連兩天，除了吃飯，父親一直不下床地唸佛修法。臘月二十日晚上，慧漢達師兄打電話告訴我，爸爸往升了，現象非常好，頂聖如來佛陀上師的佛法太不可思議了！從傳法到化虹往升，只有兩天時間！

臘月二十日晚上九點鐘，我爸像前兩天一樣，睡著唸佛修法，突然他翻身坐起，口中唸佛，眼睛朝上看著，雙手合十，準備結手印，誰知我那殺豬匠妹夫不懂法義，為了往升後不動爸爸，硬把他壓倒在床上，他再次爬起來，妹夫再把他按倒，反覆三次，最後，我爸爸側臥，以右手枕著頭托住右耳，右腳伸、左腳微曲，面帶微笑，安然圓寂，突然，我妹妹全家人看見爸爸的身體「唰」地放出雪亮的白光，整個屋子透亮，當時還以為有人照電筒，一查看，根本無人，白光是從爸爸的遺體上放出來的，持續一分多鐘，第二天下午三點鐘，停放父親遺體的房間裡，突然放出紅光，遍屋通紅，外面的人以為失火了，但又不見有煙，進去一看，屋子裡全是紅光罩著，幾十個人都看見。

當晚七點左右(天剛黑)，我父親的遺體上又放出白光，形成一條很寬的白帶，圍繞著他的遺體繞了好幾圈，大圓勝慧，大圓滿的道果，終於虹化大成就了，當時在場的幾十個人都驚呆了！直呼太不可思議了！太偉大了！但是太可惜的是妹夫不應該把父親壓倒在床上，如父親坐著合法身印、手印，他老人家就會肉身化虹，只留下指甲和頭髮了。

由於我忙於其他佛事，直到父親圓寂後的第二天晚上11點鐘過，

517

才開始往家裡趕，當時天下著鵝毛大雪，我的汽車雨刷壞了，大雪堆得來看不見路，我只好下車推開擋風玻璃上的積雪，一邊唸咒，一邊祈求大法王上師加持，再一上車，奇蹟發生了，快要落到前窗擋風玻璃前一尺遠的時候，鵝毛大雪突然消失地無影無蹤，我眼前的玻璃清澈如明鏡，而聖凡師兄坐的那邊的玻璃，都被白雪堆得嚴嚴實實，如此情境內心萬分感恩佛陀上師、諸佛菩薩加持弟子平安回家！

爸爸學甚深大圓精髓法修法兩天即虹化往升，示現很多殊勝境界，感化了很多親朋好友，特別是我妹夫，原來是殺豬的屠夫，自從親眼得見這麼偉大的佛法，感動萬分，發誓從此不再殺生，並帶著一大批人去皈依佛法了。

我們寧捨一切，決不捨棄三世多杰羌佛，如若錯過機會，百千萬劫再也找不到真正的金剛總持法王了！真實佛法又從何而來呢？我一定要修好行，把我不正確的一切壞行，全部改好，成為真正利益眾生的佛弟子！

佛弟子 赤烈爾

（此文的英文翻譯印在前面）

My Mother, "Grandma Tang," Achieved Liberation

My mother, Xie Tang Lehui, who was called Grandma Tang by relatives and friends, was a native of Xinfan Town, Xindu County, in Sichuan Province. Her Buddhist name was Shi Xinhui. She took refuge in H.H. Dorje Chang Buddha III Wan Ko Yeshe Norbu Holiest Tathagata to practice a special Pure Land Transcendence Dharma (a dharma within the category of Great Perfection). Mother was very proud of the fact that our whole family took refuge in H.H. Dorje Chang Buddha III to cultivate ourselves. She often said to people, "My children and grandchildren are all fortunate enough to learn the correct dharma from H.H. Dorje Chang Buddha III. This is simply the very best thing that makes me happiest and proudest."

Mother was greatly respectful toward H.H. Dorje Chang Buddha III, and H.H. Dorje Chang Buddha III was even more compassionate and caring to her. Once, my mother was suffering from a shoulder-elbow inflammation. She could not raise her arm, and the pain was hard to bear. H.H. Dorje Chang Buddha III consoled her by saying, "Don't worry. Let me give you a needle treatment." It was wintertime then. Through several layers of thick winter clothing, H.H. Dorje Chang Buddha III treated her with one Vajra Holy Needle (also called the Horse-Head Vajra or Galloping-Horse Wonderful Needle). Her symptoms were completely healed in just about two weeks after that! Even after quite a few years, she still felt wonder and amazement when talking about that experience.

One day in June of 2004, mother told everyone in the family, "Last night, I saw a very tall and very big dharma-protecting deity whose face is as big as the size of a door. He told me that I would go to the Western Paradise of Ultimate Bliss during the second half of this year."

On August 15th, mother seemed to be near a state of passing away. Family members reported this to H.H. Dorje Chang Buddha III. Under the blessing of the dharma power of H.H. Dorje Chang Buddha III, mother became calm and peaceful on that very night. Not only was she in a calm state, an auspicious atmosphere filled her home, inside and out, including the whole yard. Around noon the next day, several Buddhist disciples who came to assist her in chanting a mantra saw a long hada (auspicious scarf) formed by thread-like clouds crossing the sky. That night, the dark cloud-covered sky opened up a bit right over mother's home so that stars could be seen. Mother felt very comfortable. The crown of her head was opened at that time!

Mother followed the teachings of H.H. Dorje Chang Buddha III and worked hard in practicing the dharma. She substituted Zen (meditation) for food and only needed to drink a little glucose solution every day. She spent all her time practicing the dharma. After more than twenty days of practice, her mind was clear and she could talk at ease. A special fragrant smell even came from her mouth. Neighbors who saw her were all very surprised.

On August 31st, around 11 o'clock at night, my elder sister Yurong was combing my mother's hair. Suddenly, mother turned her body toward the right and took an auspicious recumbent position. My sister saw a smile on mother's face, and a warm current filled the top of my mother's head. My sister felt that very warm air flowing upward. Mother kept her smile, and the room was bright and auspicious. Mother stopped moving. I immediately reported this to H.H. Dorje Chang Buddha III. H.H. Dorje Chang Buddha III said, "She has accomplished her cultivation to perfection. She achieved enlightenment. She is going to the Western Paradise of Ultimate Bliss." At that time, mother's face and skin color all turned into a light-red color. This is the magnificent indication of being led to the Western Paradise by Amitabha Buddha! All relatives present and those who were assisting in chanting were very excited and moved.

In the afternoon of September 6th, mother's body was cremated at the Bao Guang Temple in Xindu, Sichuan, accompanied by the chanting of mantras. Before the cremation started, a blessing of dharma rain and nectar descended from the sky. As soon as the mantra chanting began, holy scenes appeared from the cremation furnace! An explosion of applause came from the crowd, who were chanting the names of Buddhas and seeing her off. The sound of chanting the names of Buddhas was accompanied by surprised exclamations, crying due to excitement, happy and broad smiles, and the making of vows. From the raging flames in the furnace, red and blue light rays were emitted from time to time. Also, fire phoenixes and golden-wing birds flew out from the light rays. Golden-dragon dharma-protecting deities and vajra dharma-protecting deities stood solemnly. There were auspicious tigers whose bodies shined and golden lions with blue lotus flowers coming out from their mouths and eyes. H.H. Dorje Chang Buddha III Wan Ko Yeshe Norbu appeared as a Buddha dharma king, a monk, and a great master. These images were seen one by one. Amitabha Buddha, Avalokiteshvara Bodhisattva, Maitreya Bodhisattva, and Master Tsongkhapa compassionately appeared from lotus flowers. Scenes from the Western Paradise of Ultimate Bliss, with buildings and pavilions, as well as the majestic Mt. Sumeru, also emerged. Double-layered lotus pedestals appeared underneath mother's feet and over her hands, supporting her sitting inside the furnace. Her body emitted blue lights that merged with the shining lights from the Buddhas and Bodhisattvas.

As the holy scenes from the Western Paradise of Ultimate Bliss constantly emerged, cheers resounded in front of the furnace like rolls of thunder. People chanted loudly the holy name of H.H. Dorje Chang Buddha III in excitement. They were shouting in tears: "Namo Holiest Tathagata Buddha Master! Namo Amitabha! Please be sure to take my mother with you!" "Namo Buddha Master! I will definitely follow you to cultivate myself earnestly. Namo Amitabha! Please be sure to come to take me!" "Buddha-dharma is so magnificent! I will definitely become greatly accomplished!" "Dorje Chang Buddha III, the Buddha-dharma you teach is too great! Those taught by you all became accomplished, right in front of our eyes! You are too magnificent!"

The cremation dharma assembly for seeing my mother off became a dharma assembly of making vows. Many people were in tears, making vows to follow H.H. Dorje Chang Buddha III to cultivate and practice as a Buddhist. They dedicated their merit to family members.

On that day, 263 grains of sharira were found in mother's charred bones and ashes.

My mother auspiciously transcended to the Western Paradise of Ultimate Bliss and was completely liberated from the cycle of birth and death. This true and holy experience occurred in front of our own eyes. I am extremely grateful to H.H. Dorje Chang Buddha III Wan Ko Yeshe Norbu Holiest Tathagata. His Holiness's applying the magnificent supreme Buddha-dharma liberated my mother, my mother-in-law Zhao Xianyun, and my father-in-law, elder Xiangshou. His Holiness also saved the lives of my wife and my son. Of course, His Holiness also liberated and saved countless prominent monks, great virtuous ones, and cultivators, whom I may know or do not know. His Holiness lets all Buddhist disciples who cultivate in good faith and devotion see the fact that true and genuine Buddha-dharma does exist in our world. Our hearts are filled with joy of the dharma and with hope!

Buddhist Disciple,
Hui Han Da

(This is a complete translation of the Chinese text that follows originally written and signed by Hui Han Da.)

我 母 親 「 唐 婆 婆 」 得 解 脫

我母親唐謝樂慧，親友稱唐婆婆，四川新都新繁鎮人，法名釋心慧，依止三世多杰羌佛雲高益西諾布頂聖如來學大圓滿之特殊淨土往升法。母親對我們全家老小都依止三世多杰羌佛修行感到非常驕傲，常對人說：「我的兒孫都能跟著三世多杰羌佛學到正法，這是我這一輩子最高興、最驕傲的事情。」母親對三世多杰羌佛無比恭敬，三世多杰羌佛對我母親更是慈悲關懷。一次母親患肩肘炎，手舉不起來，疼痛難忍，三世多杰羌佛安慰道：「沒關係，我給你扎一針就好了。」時值隆冬，三世多杰羌佛隔著幾層厚厚實實的冬裝，給她扎了一針金剛聖針，又名馬頭金剛針、跑馬神針，功後十幾天就痊癒！多年後她講起此事，神秘與驚奇依舊。

2004年6月的一天，母親對家人說：「昨晚我看見一個好高、好大的護法神啊！臉都有門那麼大，祂告訴我今年下半年我要往升極樂世界了。」8月15日，母親顯彌留境，家人即刻報告三世多杰羌佛，在三世多杰羌佛的法力關照下，當晚母親就變得十分安詳平和，不僅母親安詳，居所屋內、屋外，整個園子都一片吉祥。第二天中午，前來助念的幾位佛弟子，看到天上飄著一條雲紗組成的哈達橫貫長空。晚上，一向陰雲密布的成都盆地天空，單單就在母親居住的院落上空，突然洞開一片清澈晴朗的夜空，繁星點點，母親只覺得全身舒服無比，她開頂了！

母親依照三世多杰羌佛所傳之法努力用功修法。她每天僅喝一點葡萄糖水，以禪為食，所有的時間都用來修法，如此用功二十多天，頭腦清醒說話自如，口中放出異香，周圍鄰里驚詫不已。

8月31日晚11點左右，我姐姐玉蓉給母親梳頭，梳著梳著，母親忽轉身右側，呈吉祥臥式，姐姐看到母親突然展顏微笑，一股熱流遍滿頭頂，姐姐手感到非常熱的氣上沖，母親笑容定持，屋內一片明朗吉祥，母親一動不動了。我立刻報告了三世多杰羌佛，三世多杰羌佛說：「她已經圓滿道果，成就了，到西方極樂世界。」此時我母親的臉色、膚色都轉成微紅色，正是阿彌陀佛接引往升的殊勝跡象！在場親友及助念者激動不已！

9月6日下午，母親法體在四川新都寶光寺轉咒荼毗。轉咒火化前就有法雨甘露加持。轉咒一開始，火化爐中聖境頓然呈現！念佛恭送的人群立刻響起一片沖天的掌聲，聲聲佛號中伴隨著驚呼聲、喜極而泣聲、歡笑聲、發願聲，熊熊爐火中，紅色、藍色的光芒不斷閃耀，光芒中飛出火鳳凰、金翅鳥，金龍護法、金剛護法儼然威立，吉祥虎周身放光，金獅口吐青蓮、眼放青蓮，三世多杰羌佛雲高益西諾布的佛陀法王相、頭陀相、大師相一一呈現，阿彌陀佛、觀世音菩薩、彌勒菩薩、宗喀巴大師慈悲顯現於朵朵蓮花中，極樂世界的樓臺亭閣還有巍巍須彌山也同時出現！母親的腳下和手上出現雙層蓮台，托著她盤坐其中，滿臉笑容，全身放射藍光冉冉融匯於佛菩薩的光芒中！佛國聖境不斷呈現，火化爐前歡呼震天，人們激動地高聲持誦三世多杰羌佛的聖號，淚流滿面大聲呼喊：「南無頂聖如來佛陀上師！南無阿彌陀佛！您們一定要把我的母親接走啊！」「南無佛陀上師啊！我一定跟您好好修行，南無阿彌陀佛您一定要來接我啊！」「佛法太偉大了！我一定要大成就！」「三世多杰羌佛的佛法太偉大了！您教一個成就一個，教兩個成就一雙，我們眼睜睜看到個個成就，您太偉大了！」恭送母親到極樂世界的茶毗法會，頓時變成了發願法會，許多人哭著發願跟隨三世多杰羌佛修行學佛並為家人回向功德。

當天，在母親的骨質和骨灰中，共揀出了二百六十三顆的舍利堅固子。

我母親無比吉祥地往升極樂世界，徹底遠離了生死輪迴，這是發生在我們眼前的真實聖跡，我無限感恩三世多杰羌佛雲高益西諾布頂聖如來！他老人家以無上偉大的真正佛法，解脫了我的母親，還有我的岳母趙賢雲和岳父祥壽翁，救了我太太、我兒子的性命，當然還解脫解救了許許多多我認識和不認識的高僧大德、修行人，他老人家讓我們所有虔誠修行的佛弟子，看到了真實的佛法就在人間，我們心中充滿了法喜，充滿了希望！

佛弟子　慧漢達

慧漢達

（此文的英文翻譯印在前面）

HIS VAJRA BODY BURNED FOR SIX HOURS
HE LEFT BEHIND 141 SARIRAS (RELICS)

Dharma King Dorje Losang Rode the Dharma to a Buddha Land

(This is the text of an article published in
the Asian Journal on Oct. 27, 2004.)

Elder Dharma King Dorje Losang was a disciple of Great Dharma King Yangwo Yisinubu[1]. He was in the habit of displaying his supernatural powers and thereby manifested the Buddha Dharma. Examples of this are written in the book *True Stories About a Holy Monk*. He learned and practiced Buddhism under Great Dharma King Master Yangwo Yisinubu for many years. Day and night, he did not sleep and did not rest. He did not even have a bed. He only had a mat made of rush stems that he took with him when traveling.

Dharma King Losang received deep teachings originating from the lineage of the Great Dharma King Master. He was so appreciative of the Great Dharma King Master that he wept profusely. He made a great vow to act according to the teachings of the Great Dharma King Master and save living beings. However, Dharma King Losang, who had an extraordinary karmic destiny, displayed his supernatural powers in many places, not caring about the consequences.

When the relevant causes and conditions ripened, his karmic obstructions appeared. In April of 2001, the Shenzhen Public Security Bureau put him in prison. He lost the karmic affinity to practice and learn under the Master. In July of 2003, his case was tried in a court of law. He was not convicted of the charges. Then, the Luo Wan Temple in Sichuan received him. He did not have anything to do all day long, so he traveled on foot through the countryside. He often stared at the sky as he practiced the Dharma in silence.

Unfortunately, his karmic destiny to teach living beings the Dharma has ended. He could no longer expound the Dharma to living beings.

As early as August of 2003, Jiang Gong Kang Qin Rinpoche clearly wrote in his chronicles certain things that Dharma King Losang explicitly told him. For example, Dharma King Losang told Jiang Gong Kang Qin Rinpoche that he (Dharma King Losang) would leave this world next year in the eighth month of the Chinese lunar calendar. Dharma King Losang urged Jiang Gong Kang Qin Rinpoche to practice the Dharma in a hidden place. He said that in the future, Jiang Gong Kang Qin Rinpoche would have opportunities to save living beings from the cycle of reincarnation. He said that at such future time, Jiang Gong Kang Qin Rinpoche should transmit to good people the great Dharma of the supreme Dharma King Master. Dharma King Losang told Jiang Gong Kang Qin Rinpoche not to forget that Great Dharma King Master Yangwo Yisinubu is the highest Dharma King in this world and that he possesses the true Dharma of the Buddha!

Jiang Gong Kang Qin Rinpoche chronicled all of these things. On the sixth month of the Chinese lunar calendar in the year 2004, before Dharma King Losang passed away, these chronicles were read to certain monastics and laypersons in the United States. On the seventh month of the Chinese lunar calendar in the year 2004, these chronicles were openly read at a certain institute. Dharma King Dorje Losang finally passed away on the second day of the eighth month of the Chinese lunar calendar in the year 2004, between the hours of 5:00 and 7:00 a.m.

In the later period of Dharma King Losang's life, layman Zhi-Ying Wang looked after him and tended to him while he was in solitary meditation. In a very straightforward manner, layman Zhi-Ying told Dorje Losang, "Dharma King, do not leave this world in the summer. In such hot weather, I could not put things in order." Dharma King Losang candidly and sincerely replied with the following promise: "Do not worry. I will not pass away when the weather is hot. I will wait until the eighth month of the lunar calendar, when the fall weather is cool, to pass away."

Throughout his entire life, Dharma King Losang led a simple life. He had a correct view of the Dharma. He was not attached to things of the world. Before he passed away, he simply said to everyone, "I am leaving. It would be well if you recited Amitabha Buddha's name more." On the second day of the eighth month of the Chinese lunar calendar in the year 2004, he made good on his promise and passed away. Monks from the Bao Guang Temple rushed over to the place where he lived and took his body to the Bao Guang Temple.

In the afternoon of the day Dharma King Losang was cremated, a variety of wonderful phenomena appeared. They were very extraordinary. Monks, nuns, laymen, and laywomen surrounded Dharma King Losang's body and chanted the name of Amitabha Buddha. Each of them had their own particular feelings toward the wonderful phenomena that appeared.

Some of the attendees murmured certain misgivings that they had, such as, "When Dharma King Dorje Losang was alive, he was so amazing. However, he now does not look at all like one who is greatly accomplished. He passed away in a state of illness. This could not possibly be a person who is greatly accomplished." Some people accused him of not saving living beings due to fear of difficulty and hardship. They therefore accused him of violating one of the fourteen fundamental precepts of esoteric Buddhism. Some people said that he broke the precept that prohibits exhibiting supernatural powers. They said that this is a major precept in Buddhism. However, there were also those who said that his state of realization was extraordinary and that his supernatural feats exhibited his great enlightenment.

Finally, layman Fachi could not restrain himself any longer. He stood up and said in front of everyone remorsefully, "Dharma King Dorje Losang was not an

---

[1] Here and below the words *Great Dharma King Yangwo Yisinubu* or *Great Dharma King Master* refers to H.H. Dorje Chang Buddha III Wan Ko Yeshe Norbu Holiest Tathagata.

ordinary person. He manifested a sign of impermanence (i.e. his illness) in order to teach us. Yet, we have not treated this with a mind of limitless respect. On the contrary, we gave rise to a mind that differentiates and discriminates." He suggested that everyone take this opportunity to reflect seriously upon impermanence and give rise to a mind of limitless respect toward Dharma King Dorje Losang. He suggested that is the mind-set people should have when seeing the elder Dharma King off to the next realm. He said that an accomplished (liberated) one definitely has a wonderful and auspicious way of manifesting the BuddhaDharma.

At this time, many people expressed their repentance in front of others. Life is like a dream. Death comes quickly. Whether someone is poor and lowly or noble and exalted, in the end, he or she will leave behind a smelly corpse. With hearts of great respect, the attendees then began chanting the name of Amitabha Buddha and contemplating impermanence. They prayed for the welfare of living beings. They prayed that the country and its citizens be at peace, that weather conditions be favorable, and that the world be at peace.

To their great surprise, at this time, the bright Buddha light of Mahavairocana Buddha quickly emerged and empowered everyone. People started using their cameras and camcorders. Layperson Gui Gong shot three pictures in a row of the sun emitting dazzling light. In the middle of the sun was a round emerald-green design. That emerald-green color was the same color as that of the gemstone on the "Master hat" worn by Great Dharma King Master Yangwo. Everyone was indescribably happy to see this wonderful manifestation of the Dharma.

At 4:20 in the afternoon, the cremation fire was lit. Everyone gathered around the body of Dharma King Losang, which became engulfed in soaring flames. Some people chanted "Homage to Amtiabha Buddha." Some people recited the Heart Sutra. Some chanted the Guru Padmasambhava Heart Mantra. There were those who intoned the Kuan Yin Bodhisattva Heart Mantra. Still others chanted the Mahakala Mantra.

The huge fire looked like fire dragons circling in the furnace. The wooden container in the furnace holding Dharma King Losang's body turned into a fireball. However, at this time, a dignified image of elder Dharma King Losang's head suddenly appeared. Everyone became excited and spontaneously began chanting loudly in unison the Six Syllable Great Brightness Mantra.

During the cremation process, the person in charge of the cremation, Monk Ji Xin Shi, added all together four barrels of firewood into the furnace. He said, "I have never used so much firewood for a cremation." After the fire raged for a while, people thought that the elder Dharma King's body had already turned to ashes. However, at this time, the elder Dharma King's head and body suddenly became visible. His head and body were not burned in the slightest. His clothes, however, were burned to ashes. Still, his head and body could not catch on fire.

At this time, I could not help but think of the great Master Milarepa. There were records that stated Master Milarepa could not be burned by any fire of this world. During Dharma King Losang's cremation, such a phenomenon unexpectedly appeared before our eyes. The elder Dharma King truly deserves to be called "Vajra Dorje Losang Dharma King." Everyone in attendance then understood the wonderful

and profound meaning of "a Vajra body cannot be burned by fire of this world."

In the midst of the fire, Dharma King Losang sat in the cross-legged lotus posture and manifested the Mahakala state. Everyone loudly chanted mantras. They supplicated that the body catch on fire so that they could collect sariras. They then heard a sudden popping sound. The body of the Dharma King finally caught on fire. After the cremation ceremony ended, the set of monk's clothes worn by Dharma King Losang during his life was put into the cremation furnace. Light immediately flashed repeatedly inside the furnace. Then, the furnace emitted a great burst of light. Additionally, it intermittently emitted fragrant scents. Everyone was jubilant.

Under normal circumstances, the entire cremation process only takes more than one hour. However, the body of Dharma King Losang burned for more than six hours. This is truly a rare event in this world. One can imagine just what kind of Vajra body he had. However, he displayed his supernatural powers too much, and thereby acted imprudently. He then encountered the ripening of his karma. He had no alternative but to predict to Jiang Gong Kang Qin Rinpoche that he (Dharma King Losang) would pass away in the near future.

After the cremation, 141 sariras (relics) were collected from his remains. The six hour cremation of his indestructible Vajra body, which was a manifestation of the Dharma, and the collection of sariras/firm relics thoroughly prove that Dharma King Losang indeed learned the true Dharma of the Buddha from Great Dharma King Yangwo. Unfortunately, he should not have left this human realm. Rather, he should have stayed in this world to propagate the Dharma and save living beings.

At this point in writing this article, something came to mind. During the cremation process, some people said that Dorje Losang was not a Dharma King. But we must ask the following questions: If Dorje Losang had been an ordinary person, why was he able to predict the time of his death? Why was he able to attain the indestructible Vajra body, such that his body burned for six hours, which is a record-breaking time? Why were 141 sariras collected from his remains after he was cremated? How could an ordinary person leave behind such holy objects? For the past few decades in Taiwan (as opposed to mainland China), only elder monk Guang Qin left behind sariras after his cremation. Furthermore, it only took more than one hour to cremate completely elder monk Guang Qin. These facts prove that Dharma King Losang was not like those people of the world whose practice of the Buddha Dharma is merely uttering empty theories. The holy phenomena described above occur only as a result of the true Buddha Dharma.

Thus, we should again stop and think. We often say, "The Buddha Dharma is difficult to seek. The true Dharma is difficult to encounter." However, Great Dharma King Yangwo Yisinubu does indeed teach the true Dharma of the Buddha. As a result, we see that one after another of his disciples have attained great accomplishment (liberation). Shouldn't we think about how we will face our own liberation from the cycle of reincarnation?

（20）　н. ส. พ. ดงฮั้ว　報日華中　TONG HUA DAILY NEWS　六期星　日二月十年四〇〇二

金剛體然燒六小時　出舍利一百四十一
——多傑洛桑法王法駕佛土

多傑洛桑老法王是仰諤益西諾布大法王座下弟子，貫顯神通，表露佛法，有《聖僧鐵記》一書記載。他多年跟隨仰諤大法王上師學佛修行，晝夜不眠不休，連床鋪都沒有，只有一個蒲團隨身。洛桑深得大法王上師傳承，感恩涕零，發宏願要依師度眾生。但是，這位有著非凡因緣的洛桑卻多處顯露神通，不顧影響，由於因緣所至，障業現前自成阻隔，於二〇〇一年四月被深圳公安局關押，無緣隨師修學，二〇〇三年七月法庭開庭審理，無有定罪，當時接到四川羅萬壽，整日無事，信步遊走鄉間，時常兩眼凝視虛空，觀修行持，沒有言語。可惜的是，他與眾生法緣已盡，無法再爲他說法。早在二〇〇三年八月，蔣貢康欽仁波且就在他的記實中載明，洛桑曾明確告訴：他將明年八月離開人間，要蔣貢康欽仁波且趕起來修學，今後有機會度眾生，要至高無上的法王上師之大法傳給善士。不要忘了，仰諤大法王上師是在這個世界上掌有佛陀正法的最高位！蔣貢康欽仁波且把全部過程作了記錄，此記錄在洛桑未圓寂前的二〇〇四年陰曆六月即在美國僧尼、居士中宣讀，又於二〇〇四年陰曆七月在基金會眾宣讀。多傑洛桑法王最終於陰曆八月初二即時圓寂，離開人世間。

洛桑住世後期，有王智芙居士一直爲他照料護關，智芙居士非常直爽地告訴他：『法王您千萬別在夏天離開，這麼熱的天氣，我收拾不了。』洛桑也很坦誠地承諾：『你放心，我不會在熱天圓寂，我等八月秋涼了再走。』洛桑一輩子生活簡單，法務正見，不執著世法，走之前只對大家說：『我走了，多念點佛就好了。』陰曆八月初二，他便兌現承諾圓寂了。寶光寺的比丘趕到他的住處，接他到寶光寺。

火化洛桑的那天下午，所顯相境各式各樣，十分異別。圍著念佛的僧俗四眾各對著境都有著各自特別的感受，有人心裡嘀咕：這個法王生前那麼厲害，但現在完全不像大成就的樣子，現病態圓寂，這根本就算不上大成就者。有人則指他怕難、怕苦不度眾生，犯密宗十四根本戒。有人說他破戒顯神通，是佛教的大戒，也有人說他證量非凡，實乃大道之顯。終於，法持居士按捺不住站出來當眾懺悔：多傑洛桑法王並非普通人，他所顯的無常相是爲教化我們，我們並沒有生起無限的恭敬心來面對，反起分別見。他提議大家都應借此好好觀無常，生起無限的恭敬心爲老法王送行，一個成就者一定有佛菩薩殊勝吉祥的顯法。此時，很多人也當眾作了懺悔，人生如夢，無常迅速，無論貧賤與高貴應終都同樣留下一具臭皮囊。大家生起無限的恭敬心念佛觀無常，並發願爲眾生祈福，祈禱國泰民安、祈禱風調雨順、祈禱世界和平。萬萬沒有想到，此時大日如來的毫光佛境很快展現加持眾人，照相機、攝像機紛紛開啓，貴公居士一連拍下三張大放毫光的大日，太陽中心都有一個圓形的翠綠色圖案，與仰諤大法王上師大師袍帽沿上那塊綠翠完全相似，看到這個顯境表證大家高興得沒法形容。

下午四點二十分點火了，大家圍著火焰升騰的洛桑，有的念誦『南無阿彌陀佛』，有的念誦『心經』，有的念誦蓮花生大師心咒，有的念誦觀世音菩薩心咒，有的持麻哈嘎拉咒，大火像火龍一樣在爐中盤旋，火氣翻體燃成一個火球，但此時突然出現了洛桑法王威嚴的頭像，大眾一下子興奮起來，不約而同一齊大聲轉念六字大明咒。負責火化的比丘寂心師先後爐子裡添加了四推柴桌，他說：從來沒有燒過這樣多柴，一陣熊熊烈火之後，估計他已化爲灰燼，但這時突然顯露出老法王的頭和身體，一點也沒有著火燒燒，衣服早已燒光，但是頭和身體照常無法著火。這時不出得筆者想起密勒日巴祖師在凡火中不能燃燒的記載，今天竟然展現在眼面前，實在不愧是金剛多傑洛桑法王，眾人追了明了金剛之體的妙義。洛桑盤坐火中顯大黑天境，眾人大聲持咒，請求著火焚體以取舍利，方纔到『啪』一聲，法王之身子骨終於著火了。轉咒茶毗結束之後，洛桑生前的一套僧衣被送進火爐，爐內頓時連連閃光，隨著大放光明，並且發出陣陣撲鼻的異香，大眾一片觀呼。

通常情況下火化的全過程只需要一個多小時，

可是洛桑法王一共燃燒了六個多小時，實在世所罕見。可想而知他本該是何等的金剛之身，怎奈他過多張揚神通失之慎覺，遇到因緣成熟，不得已提前告知蔣貢康欽仁波且要離開了。火化後拾得舍利子一四一粒。其金剛不壞火化六小時之表法及拾得舍利堅固子法物，徹底證明洛桑確實學到了仰諤大法王的如來正法，可惜的是，他不應該離開人間，而應住世宏法度生。

寫道這裡，想到在火化過程中有人說多傑洛桑不是法王，我們不禁要問：如果多傑洛桑是一普通凡夫，爲什麼他能提前預告圓寂時間？爲什麼他能金剛不壞，竟然燃六個小時，破歷史紀錄？爲什麼火化後還拾得一四一顆舍利子？凡夫怎麼有此聖物呢？而在我們台灣，幾十年來，只有一個廣欽老和尚火化後有舍利子，而且才火化一個多小時就燒盡了，所以，這足以證明他不是世俗空頭理論的佛法，只有真正的佛法才有這樣聖跡的展現。由此，我們不由得想一想，平時，我們大家都在說『佛法難求，正法難遇』，而現在，仰諤大法王的如來正法展現了他座下的弟子一個個都得到大成就，難道不應該想一想我們的了生脫死該如何面對嗎？（劉一之紀實）U

老法王生前法相。圖下：多傑洛桑老法王茶毗火化後拾得的一四一枚舍利子。UP

圖上：『聖僧鐵記』書中主角一多傑洛桑

9 8 1999
14:14:45

中華日報

今天出紙七大張
（一一四三六）
每份零售十銖
內地空運零售每份十二銖
中華郵政建設許可八七七八八一號 股份有限公司發行

董事長：胡娟
社長：陳正

總編輯、管印人：王立文
執行總編輯：周密
秦京石龍單路建等許八七七五八八一號

電話：02-2369171-6
　　　02-2360143（5線）
　　　02-2360144（12線）
FAX 廣告部：02-2385286
編輯部：02-2337472

หนังสือพิมพ์ตงฮั้ว
นางกัลยาณี กยาวัฒนกิจ
ประธานกรรมการ
นายสมนึก กยาวัฒนกิจ
กรรมการผู้อำนวยการ
นายภาวิช โกตะคุณ
บรรณาธิการผู้พิมพ์โฆษณา
877-881 ถ.เจริญกรุง ตลาดน้อย กทม.
E-mail:tonghua@clickta.com
E-mail:tonghua2@clickta.com
วันที่ 2 ตุลาคม 2547

Relatives of a Western Disciple of H.H. Dorje Chang Buddha III Go to Western Paradise of Ultimate Bliss

My name is Zhaxi Zhuoma, and I am a disciple of H.H. Dorje Chang Buddha III Wan Ko Yeshe Norbu Holiest Tathagata. When my uncle died, I asked H.H. Dorje Chang Buddha III, "What should I do?" As a result of my sincere request, H.H. Dorje Chang Buddha III performed a very wonderful and amazing ceremony that enabled me to see my uncle, Robert (Bob) Welker, actually go to the Western Paradise of Ultimate Bliss (Sukhavati). This is a very high ritual of the Supreme Yoga Vajra Division, which cannot be discussed in detail with those who have not received initiation. However, I am able to report that I actually witnessed with my own eyes the miraculous scene where my uncle was transported to the sixth level of this buddhaland that is beyond the worldly realms of suffering and sorrow. There are nine levels all together in the Western Paradise of Ultimate Bliss. This is the highest tier of the middle level, known as the 中品上生 (*Zhong Pin Shang Sheng*) in Chinese.

The picture of my uncle quivered in my hands as the ceremony began. It seemed that he could hardly wait. Or was this in response to the extraordinary dharma powers of H.H. Dorje Chang Buddha? It was a glorious and marvelous sight! There are no words that can express the joy I experienced when this event took place. H.H. Dorje Chang Buddha III explained that this was because I was able to obtain a "glimpse" of the bliss that occurs in the Western Paradise. I know of no other dharma king or master who can do this! It was incredible! Earlier, H.H. Dorje Chang Buddha III allowed me to see the sufferings of Hell. Now I was able to experience the bliss of the Western Paradise.

The *Petitioning the Western Paradise of Ultimate Bliss Dharma* is a very high and special dharma that is rarely practiced in this world. Many people want to go to the Western Paradise, but can't. They would like to receive this dharma or have it performed for their loved ones, but can't. I have been with H.H. Dorje Chang Buddha III for six years and have seen him perform very many forms of inner tantric initiations and received some, but this is the first time that I saw him perform this particular dharma. It was only through the maturing of certain causes and conditions that this ritual was successfully performed.

My uncle, who was ninety when he died, had been a good Christian man but knew nothing of Buddhism. His only contact with Buddhism had been through knowing me, although he had also met my younger vajra sister, Venerable Akou Lamo Rinpoche, in 2003 when we briefly visited him in Ohio. Venerable Akou Lamo Rinpoche is a great rinpoche from Tibet and also a close disciple of H.H. Dorje Chang Buddha III. I am sure we were the only Buddhists he had ever even heard of, let alone met.

My uncle had lived a good life and was very kind and generous, being willing to go to great lengths to help those who needed help. His immediate family, who are all also good Christians, were quite certain that he would go to the Christian heaven, but who would have thought that he would have the good fortune to escape the realm of reincarnation altogether? He had, after all, also been an avid hunter and fisherman and had killed many living beings in his life. With such negative karma, how could he be reborn in heaven? Needless to say, it would be even more impossible for him to go to the Western Paradise. But H.H. Dorje Chang Buddha III's Buddha-dharma is so magnificent! I could actually witness my uncle going to this superb

buddha-land and enjoying the incomparable happiness one finds there. H.H. Dorje Chang Buddha III told me, "You are a rinpoche. That is why you can see this."

I was horrified when the minister giving the eulogy at my uncle's funeral praised Uncle Bob for teaching his grandchildren how to fish. I wanted to cry out, "How can you praise someone for teaching children how to kill?" but I held my tongue and remained silent. In this rural community in southeastern Ohio and this culture, hunting and fishing are very important, both for food and for pleasure. They do not understand the principles of either reincarnation or karma. It is only through the incredible merit, dharma skills, and great compassion of H.H. Dorje Chang Buddha III that this could happen.

Just eleven days after Robert Welker left this world, his wife also left. She was also ninety. H.H. Dorje Chang Buddha III was also able to raise her consciousness so that she could join her husband in the Western Paradise. I saw the buddhas and bodhisattvas come to the sacred mandala to receive my aunt and witnessed their acceptance of her into the Western Paradise. This was a different ceremony held at a different mandala. At first it looked as though my aunt might not be able to make it. H.H. Dorje Chang Buddha III went back and practiced the dharma a second time. This time he was able to send her to this paradise of eternal joy and happiness. She, too, had been a good Christian, but knew nothing about Buddhism. She did not have the good fortune to meet Venerable Akou Lamo Rinpoche. However, she was still able to go to the Western Paradise. It was so amazing. This was because of the incredible compassion and Buddha-dharma powers of Wan Ko Yeshe Norbu Holiest Tathagata. The Buddha-dharma is magnificent!

In 2004, H.H. Dorje Chang Buddha III performed another ceremony to raise the consciousness of my non-Buddhist parents, Carl and Elsie Welker, to a higher realm as well. At that time, I saw the Dharma Protecting Deities come to perform this rite. I am very, very grateful to my most respectful Buddha Master, Dorje Chang Buddha III, for his kindness and compassion in blessing my dear relatives.

These miraculous Buddha-dharma events, performed for those who had not practiced or known anything about Buddhism, were all due to the amazing merit and compassion of H.H. Dorje Chang Buddha III Wan Ko Yeshe Norbu. He was willing and able to share his boundless merit with these non-Buddhist to enable them to enjoy the blessings of Amitabha Buddha's Western Paradise. This was a great teaching for me on compassion and true equanimity.

H.H. Dorje Chang Buddha III reminded us that we must realize that reincarnation is not something that just exists for Buddhists or easterners. It existed before the coming of the Buddha or before Jesus and continues to exist even after they have left this realm. It is a fact based on the principles of cause and effect. It does not exist because people believe in it or talk about it —it just exists. Nor does reincarnation cease to exist just because people do not accept it or believe in it. Only the Buddha was able to see how the cycle of reincarnation worked and was able to realize the method for escaping the suffering that is inherent in continual rebirth in the six realms of existence.

Some concept of "heaven" or a "happy hunting ground" or "paradise" is held by most religions. Buddhism recognizes these realms as well, but does not hold the various heavens or abodes of the gods (devas or angels) and other celestial beings to be the goal of spiritual practice. They could be viewed as a "rest stop" or a nice vacation site, as one can surely go to these wonderful places if one lives a good life, avoids evil, and accumulates sufficient "merit." However, even in heaven, when one's merit is used up (and it is very hard to accumulate more merit while in those realms—the pleasures are just too great), one must still be reborn and repay one's karmic debts. There is even no guarantee that living a good life is enough to enable you to have a good next life, for your karma from past lives may catch up with you on your next round. Only by becoming a holy or enlightened being (or saint) can one escape the cycle of reincarnation and the suffering of existence. The early Christians also believed in reincarnation, as do many Christians today, but it is not accepted as Christian dogma.

There are two dharmas whereby one can go to the Western Paradise. One dharma involves repeatedly reciting Amitabha Buddha's name. The other is *Petitioning the Western Paradise of Ultimate Bliss Dharma*, which is a very high and special dharma that very few people who have lived in this world could perform. Shakyamuni Buddha and the Ugyen Second Buddha,

Great Dharma King Padmasambhava, could do it, as could great holy dharma kings after them. H.H. Dorje Chang Buddha III Wan Ko Yeshe Norbu, however, is more accomplished than any of these dharma kings. No wonder H.E. Tangtong Gyalpo great Bodhisatva, who once was the leader of the four main sects of esoteric Buddhism, personally wrote a congratulatory letter highly praising H.H. Dorje Chang Buddha III Wan Ko Yeshe Norbu's proficiency in both esoteric and exoteric Buddhism and his wonderful mastery of the five vidyas. That letter also praised His Holiness as being the first person in history to accomplish this.

To my knowledge, His Holiness is the only living Buddha vajra master who can perform such a ceremony involving great dharma and have the buddhas and bodhisattvas come to the sacred altar to help the deceased reach this high level of achievement. We are very fortunate to have such a holy one with us here in America.

Humble Buddhist disciple, Zhaxi Zhuoma

(The Chinese translation of this text follows.)

三世多杰羌佛的仁波且弟子西方人之親屬去到極樂世界

　　我的名字叫扎西卓瑪，我是三世多杰羌佛雲高益西諾布頂聖如來的弟子。在我叔叔去世的時候，我求問三世多杰羌佛：「我能做點什麼？」作為對我摯誠求問的答覆，三世多杰羌佛修了一個非常不可思議而驚人的法，使我能看到我的叔叔 Robert (Bob) Welker 去了西方極樂世界（梵文Sukhavati）。但是因為這個儀式屬於無上瑜伽金剛部法，不允許我對未得到適當傳法灌頂的人詳細描述。儘管如此，我還是可以敘述我實際親眼目睹的神奇場面，我的叔叔被送到完全脫離俗世悲苦的佛國第六品。西方極樂世界共分九品，我叔叔往升到中級的最高層，通常叫中品上生。

　　在儀式開始的時候，我叔叔的照片在我手中輕微地顫動。好像他幾乎等不及了，或者這是對三世多杰羌佛驚人佛法力量的回應？那是一個光榮而非凡的奇觀！沒有文字能表達在這件事發生的時候我所分享和體會的喜悅。三世多杰羌佛解釋說這是因為我能得見“一眼”在西方世界的極樂。據我所知還沒有其他大法王或大師能做得到！它不可思議！在此之前頂聖如來已經讓我見到了一次地獄的痛苦感受。現在我能通過親身經歷認識到西方極樂世界。

　　「祈求西方極樂世界法」是一個非常高而特殊、又在這個世界很少修的法。許多人想要去西方極樂世界，但是不能。他們想要得到這個法或者請人為他們珍愛的人修法，但是辦不到。我已經跟隨三世多杰羌佛六年，見到三世多杰羌佛修過很多各種形式的內密灌頂，我自己也接受過一些三世多杰羌佛的灌頂，但這是第一次我見到三世多杰羌佛修這種特殊的法。只有通過某種因緣的成熟，這個法今天才修成功。

　　我叔叔去世時90歲，他一直是一個很好的基督徒，但是對佛教一

無所知。他僅僅通過熟悉我而對佛教有所接觸，儘管他也在2003年我們去俄亥俄州短暫拜訪他的時候見過阿寇拉摩仁波且，她是從西藏來在三世多杰羌佛身邊的仁波且。我確信我們是他唯一所聽說過的佛教徒，更別提見過的了。

　　叔叔一輩子生活良好並且非常仁愛而慷慨，樂意不遺餘力地幫助那些需要幫助的人。他的直系親屬也是虔誠的基督徒，相當確信他死後會去基督教的天堂，但誰料到他會有福報全然逃脫輪迴世界？畢竟他也一直是個勁頭十足的獵手和漁夫，一生裏殺死了許多眾生。具有如此的惡業，那怎能再生於天堂？不必說，去西方極樂世界對於他來講就更不可能了。但是三世多杰羌佛的佛法是如此偉大！我竟然能夠親眼目睹我叔叔去往這片無上的佛土並享受任何人在那裏都會感受到的無比幸福。三世多杰羌佛說：「妳是仁波且，所以才看得到。」

　　在牧師讚揚我叔叔 Bob 教育他的子孫如何捕魚的時候，我嚇壞了。我想大聲說：“你怎麼可以讚揚某人教育孩子怎樣去殺戮？”但我一言不發保持沈默。在這個俄亥俄州東南部的鄉村社區和文化裏，打獵和捕魚對於食物和消遣兩樣都很重要。他們既不懂輪迴也不懂業力的規則。唯一憑藉三世多杰羌佛的這不可思議的功德和法力以及大悲，這才會發生。

　　僅僅在羅伯特·威爾克（Robert Welker）離開這個世界後的十一天後，他的太太也離去了。她也是九十歲。三世多杰羌佛也能將她的心識提升以便她能與她丈夫一起在西方極樂世界。我看到佛菩薩來到莊嚴的曼陀羅壇場來歡迎我嬸嬸並且目睹了他們對她進入西方極樂世界的接納。開始時好像我嬸嬸也許做不到，三世多杰羌佛回去並再次修法，這次他將她送到了這個永恒快樂和幸福的樂園。她也一直是個

好基督徒，但對佛法一無所知。她也沒有福報見到阿寇拉摩仁波且。她還是能去西方極樂世界。那是多麼讓人吃驚啊。這是由於雲高益西諾布頂聖如來不可思議的悲心和佛法力量。佛法偉大！

在2004年三世多杰羌佛曾進行過另一個儀式把我的非佛教徒的父母 Carl 和 Elsie Welker 的心識也提升到一個更高的國度。當時我可以看到護法神來執行這個宗教儀式。我非常非常感激我的至尊佛陀上師三世多杰羌佛加持我至親的仁慈與悲心。

所有這些為不曾學佛或對佛教一無所知的人所作的神奇的佛事，都是由於三世多杰羌佛雲高益西諾布驚人的功德與悲心。他甘願與這些非佛教徒分享他的無量功德，從而使他們能夠享有阿彌陀佛西方極樂世界的加持。這對我是一個關於悲心與真正平等的偉大教誨。

三世多杰羌佛提醒我們說：我們必須認識到輪迴不是僅僅因為佛教徒或者東方人而存在的。它在佛陀到來之前或耶穌以前就存在了，在他們離開之後也照樣繼續存在。它是個基於因果律的事實。它不因為人們信仰它或談論它而存在——它就是存在，也不因為人們不接受或不相信它而停止存在。只有佛陀能夠看到輪迴迴圈如何運轉、能了徹出離痛苦的方法，而這痛苦是六道輪迴本身所固有的。大多數宗教相信一些"天堂"或者是一種"幸福獵場"或者"樂園"的概念。佛教也承認這些道，但不把各種天國（天神或天使）或上帝的居所及其他天人作為靈修的目標。只把它們看作是"休息站"或者"休假的好地方"，而任何人只要他過良好的生活、防止惡行並積累足夠的"功德"，就一定可以去這些好地方。然而即使在天國，當一個人的功德用盡的時候（而且在這些道的時候很難積累更多的功德——感官上的享受太巨大了），他則必須再受生並償還業報債。而且就算你現在過著良好的生活也不能保證你就一定會擁有良好的下一世，因為你過去世的業力會在你下一次輪轉時纏繞著你。只有成聖或成覺者（或曰聖人），人才能擺脫輪迴的迴圈及生存的痛苦。很久以前的基督教徒也相信輪迴，就像今天的許多基督教徒一樣，但是不被基督教教義所接受。

往升西方極樂世界法有兩種法，一是一般人唸佛號的法，二是「祈求西方極樂世界法」，這是一種非常高的特殊法門，這個世界只有極少數聖者能修得了這個法。釋迦牟尼佛和烏金第二佛陀——蓮花生大法王能做得到，他們之後的一些聖者大法王也做得到。三世多杰羌佛雲高益西諾布做的更好。難怪曾任密宗四大教派的總教主唐東迦波大法王菩薩親寫賀函高度讚嘆三世多杰羌佛雲高益西諾布顯密俱通、妙諳五明，是佛史上的第一人。就我所知他是唯一在世的能行此法請佛菩薩來到莊嚴壇場、幫助死者達到這種高水準成就的佛陀大法王金剛上師。我們非常幸運能在美國遇到這樣一位至高聖者。

慚愧佛弟子：扎西卓瑪

（此文由前面的英文翻譯而來）

HE WOULD RATHER GIVE UP LIFE THAN HIS BELIEFS AND MANIFESTED IN THE FORM OF A GOLDEN ARHAT AS A SIGN OF ENLIGHTENMENT

(This is a translation of an article published in the Pacific Daily News on Oct. 12, 2005.)

On September 29th, 2005, in Bao Guang Temple, a famous historic landmark temple located at Xindu, Sichuang, a cremation ceremony was held for eminent layman Du-Cuan Wang. Layman Du-Cuan Wang was one of H.H. Great Dharma King's[1] disciples. After the cremation, there were 225 sariras left. Layman Du-Cuan Wang and his wife were both university professors. After they retired from the university, they took refuge with H.H. Great Dharma King Master Yangwo Wan Ko Yisinubu and started practicing Buddhism. They dedicated themselves to Buddhism. When H.H. Great Dharma King decided to leave Chengdu, they voluntarily requested to watch over H.H. Great Dharma King's altar.

During that period, some people tried to convince them to move back to their own place. Some even threatened them to convince them to leave, but they never changed their mind. Professor Wang once said, "I don't care about any slander against the Master, because I only believe in the truth. I have followed the Master for only a few years and consider my Master as the highest saint, who is kind, straightforward, bright, and merciful. The Master always puts the benefit of others as the top priority, keeps the bitterness and suffering for himself, and lets all living beings enjoy happiness. The Master's discourses are so brilliant and flawless, and through them we learn profound knowledge in simple words. All the Master's teachings show us how to cultivate ourselves. Not one thing is true, concerning what other people have slanderously reported. I am a professor and a Buddhist. I don't tell lies, and I don't say anything against my conscience. I am loyal and honest to my Master. I will never betray my Master." Therefore, in the past few years, it didn't matter whether people slandered or threatened them. The couple stayed at that altar until it was torn down as part of the city's development plan.

A few months ago, Professor Wang looked ill. Even though he was sick, he still diligently practiced the dharma that Master Wan Ko Yee had taught him. On September 24th, Professor Wang told others, "I can't wait for the Master any longer. I have to go now." In the afternoon of September 26th, without showing any pain, he passed away peacefully while lying on his right side facing a statue of the Buddha. At that moment, the crown of his head became hot. Suddenly, it opened in a rhombus shape that has diagonals about three centimeters long and two centimeters wide. In the morning of September 27th, dharma teacher Xin Ji of the Bao Guang Temple, who was in charge of the cremation ceremony, touched

---

[1] Here and below the words Great Dharma King, Great Dharma King Master Yangwo Wan Ko Yisinubu, Master or Master Wan Ko Yee refers to H.H. Dorje Chang Buddha III Wan Ko Yeshe Norbu Holiest Tathagata.

the joints of his body which were still very soft, and said, "He is accomplished. There certainly will be sarira left after the cremation."

The ceremony started at 4 pm on the 29th. Right before it started, nectars descended from the sky. This lasted for a while, even until after the cremation fire was lit. During the ceremony, there were many holy supernatural signs. Some saw a smiling golden Buddha. Some saw a golden arhat wearing monk's robes on Professor Wang's stomach. Some saw the sun and the moon shining together. Some people who were not Buddhists even saw rows of mantras. The people standing there suddenly heard H.H. Master Wan Ko Yee chanting the Six Syllable Mantra from far far away. This sound mixed with the chanting of Amitabha Buddha's name. After the cremation, they picked up 225 sariras.

What do these good signs tell us? They clearly demonstrate that a Buddhist whose three karmas correspondence with the teachings of his master and the Buddha will achieve enlightenment! On the other hand, what will happen to those who deceive their master who once taught them?

Professor Du-Chuan Wang was a disciple of H.H. Dorje Chang Buddha III Wan Ko Yeshe Norbu Holiest Tathagata. By following the teachings of H.H. Dorje Chang Buddha III and devoutly practicing the dharma, he attained great accomplishment in the dharma. Below are newspaper reports on this.

三世多杰羌佛雲高益西諾布頂聖如來的弟子王篤川教授依師虔誠修學獲大成就，以下是當時報紙的報導。

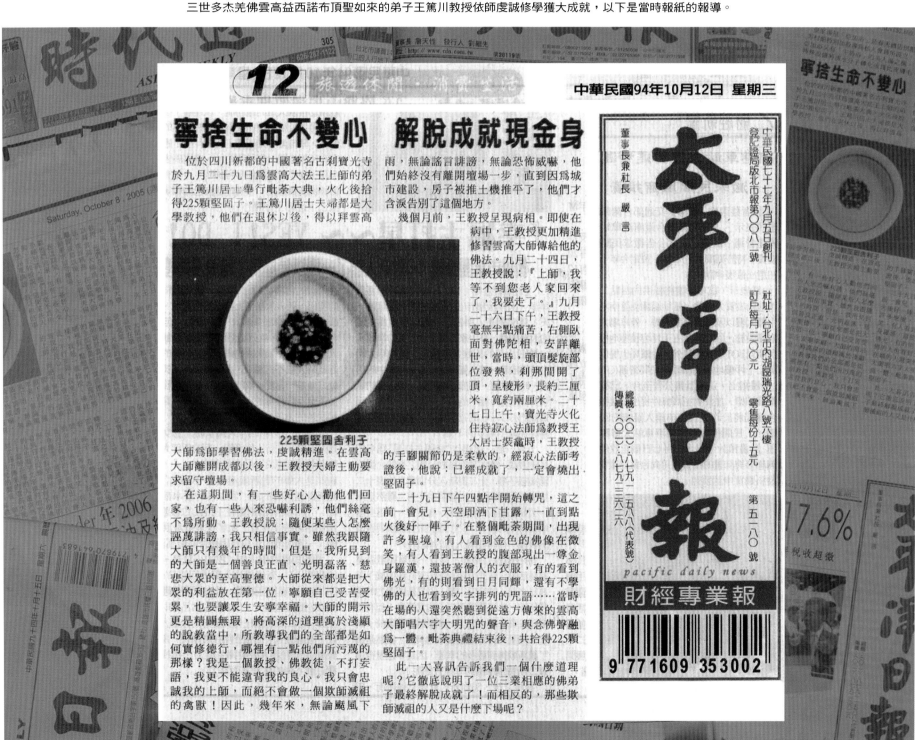

SUPERNATURAL POWERS IN BUDDHISM

Do Buddhists advocate supernatural powers? Actually, this is not a matter of advocating or not advocating. Rather, supernatural powers are that which everyone who is accomplished in the dharma possesses. Such powers are the manifestation of realization achieved through cultivation. They are phenomena that exist in the course of cultivation but are not the goal of cultivation, which is liberation from the cycle of birth and death. They are by-products that arise during one's practice. These by-products called supernatural phenomena naturally exist in all liberating paths within the Buddha-dharma. Becoming attached to these by-products and regarding them as the goal is heretical supernatural powers. Applying these by-products in a free and unattached way and regarding them as illusory is treating supernatural powers based on the correct Buddha-dharma view.

Sakyamuni Buddha manifested supernatural powers and also was against supernatural powers. Each of those two tacks reflects different underlying karmic conditions. To those with higher vehicle (Mahayana) faculties, the Buddha spoke of supernatural powers as enjoyment resulting from incredible realization and the free and unattached application of samadhi. Examples of this are in the Lotus Sutra, the Samyuktagama Sutra, and other sutras. To those practitioners with low faculties, the Buddha spoke of not being attached to supernatural powers in order to reach the goal of realizing emptiness. An example of this is in the Shurangama Sutra.

Anyone with low faculties who wants to become a Buddha must go through the stage of cultivation corresponding to those with high faculties. In one's course of cultivation, this is analogous to going from one city to another city. If one does not travel along the pathway between the two cities, one will not reach that other city. When one is walking toward that other city, one will certainly see and encounter all of the phenomena that are on the way. This is like the supernatural phenomena that arise in the course of one's cultivation when wisdom is being opened. If one does not experience such phenomena that arise during the cultivation process, then one will not reach the other shore of liberation. Because one has not traversed the path of the Buddha-dharma leading to liberation, one cannot encounter phenomena that occur while traversing that path. That is why such a person has not experienced the stage in the process whereby wisdom is opened and supernatural powers are realized. Thus, all Buddhist who become accomplished in the dharma must go through the stage of supernatural powers.

Is it true that the authentic Buddha-dharma does not speak of supernatural powers? If that were the case, then why did the great leader of Buddhism, Sakyamuni Buddha, manifest supernatural powers everywhere? Why did he even manifest great supernatural powers right before entering nirvana? What crazed and demonic person would dare say that Sakyamuni Buddha did not practice the true Buddha-dharma? Just think. If someone with great accomplishment in the dharma did not have any supernatural realization powers, what would be the difference between that person and an ordinary person who had not learned Buddhism?

H.H. Dorje Chang Buddha III Wan Ko Yeshe Norbu Holiest Tathagata, is the highest ancient Buddha with complete proficiency in both exoteric and esoteric Buddhism and perfect mastery of the Five Vidyas. A portion of His Holiness's realization powers is openly shown in this book *A Treasury of True Buddha-Dharma* for all to clearly see. However, the clear and definite views expressed by His Holiness have enabled us to understand the principles and direction of cultivation. H.H. Dorje Chang Buddha III said the following:

"Not only did the Buddha speak a great deal about supernatural powers in the sutras, he also manifested supernatural powers. Such words and facts were directed at those who reached the higher vehicle (Mahayana) sambhogakaya state or nirmanakaya state. The Buddha also stated in the sutras that one must not become attached to supernatural powers. Such teachings were directed at those who were at the beginning stage of realizing their original nature and dharmakaya in order to protect them. If practitioners who are at the beginning stage of realizing the true nature or true-suchness of all phenomena become attached to supernatural powers, they will fall into that which is conditioned. They will then be practicing heresy. Thus, you should understand that supernatural powers are a reflection of the unhindered, unobstructed nature of Buddhas and great Bodhisattvas. Such powers are not that which beginning stage practitioners can possess and enjoy.

"As for me, I went through the stage of supernatural powers in my early years. I deeply understand that they are the free and unattached application of samadhi but are not the ultimate attainment. I occasionally see the supernatural powers of others, which are manifestations of their karmic conditions of good fortune. I myself do not have such abilities!

"I do not advocate practicing supernatural powers. What I want is cultivation. Only through cultivation can one attain the goal. I myself am very ordinary. I do not have supernatural powers. I only have cultivation. The discourse entitled "What Is Cultivation?" that I gave for all good Buddhists with the karmic affinity to hear or read it is the palace of the Buddha-dharma, the root of liberation, and the source of great dharma in the dharma realm."

International Buddhism Sangha Association

(This text was translated from the Chinese text that follows.)

佛 教 的 神 通

佛教徒是否主張神通？這是很多佛教徒都很關心的一個問題。其實，神通不是主不主張的概念，而是成就者個個皆具備的，它是修行證量的表顯，是修行過程中的現象，但不是成就解脫的目的，是行持中必然副產物的湧顯，凡解脫道的佛法中，副產物神通現象是自然存在的，執著副產物為目的，則是外道神通，遊戲於副產物為幻化，則是佛法正見神通。釋迦佛陀顯神通而又反神通，是為不同因緣之說法，佛陀對上乘根器者說神通為遊戲三昧，不可思議證量的享受，如說《法華經》、《雜阿含經》等所鑒；對下等根器行人說不執神通是為了得證空性為目標，如《楞嚴經》所說。但凡是下等根器者要成佛，必然經過上等根器階段之修為，在這修行過程中，猶如作此城市到彼城市為目的比喻，如果不經過兩地之間的中途路線，是到不了彼城市的，在步向彼城市途中，是必然會看到、遇到中途的一切現象，好比修行過程中的智慧開膚過程的神通境界現象，如果沒有這些過程現象的經歷，那就到不了解脫的彼岸，因為沒有走佛法解脫的路線，因此路線中的現象，你就無法遇到，所以才會沒有智慧開膚神通證量的經歷過程，所以，凡是成就的佛教徒，都是必然經過神通階段的。反問之，是否正規佛法不講神通？那為什麼大教主釋迦佛陀處處顯神通？就是報化最後一刻也大顯神通？哪一個狂徒妖人敢說釋迦佛不是正規佛法？試想如果作為一個大成就者，什麼證境現象都沒有，這與不學佛的普通人有什麼差別呢？

多杰羌佛第三世雲高益西諾布頂聖如來是顯密圓通、妙諳五明的至高怙主，他的部分證量公開展顯在《正法寶典》中一目瞭然，但是他明確的觀點更讓我們明白了修行的道理方向，三世多杰羌佛說：『佛陀不但在經中大量說神通，而且顯神通，這是為報化二身上乘之境而說，佛也在經中說，不可執神通，這是為初基明心見性法身證悟護道開示，於法性真如之初基行人，若執於神通，則落入有為，而成外道，故知神通乃佛陀大菩薩無礙遊戲，非為初器者把玩之品。至於我，早年也遊歷過神通，深知那是遊戲三昧，不是究竟成果，時逢他人的福報因緣所顯化的神通，我哪裡有這本事啊！我不主張修神通，要的是修行，唯一修行才能達到目的，我的身上有的是慚愧，沒有神通，只有修行，我為有緣善信們開示了《什麼叫修行》，這才是佛法的殿堂，解脫的根本，法界大法之源頭。』

國際佛教僧尼總會

（此文的英文翻譯印在前面）

THE DHARMA OF CULTIVATION TRANSMITTED BY H.H. DORJE CHANG BUDDHA III

An oral discourse on the dharma given by
His Holiness Dorje Chang Buddha III Wan Ko Yeshe Norbu Holiest Tathagata
to rinpoches and other disciples:

WHAT IS CULTIVATION ?

Today you, who are a rinpoche, respectfully requested a discourse on the dharma relating to the question "What is cultivation?" This is a very fundamental lesson; indeed, the first lesson. Nonetheless, this is an important matter that many cultivators, including those who have practiced cultivation over many years, do not understand and are confused about. It is difficult to incarnate as a human being. It is even more difficult to incarnate as a human being with the opportunity to encounter the true Buddha-dharma. Thus, today I will enlighten everyone on dharma relating to the question "What is cultivation?"

The essence of learning Buddhism lies with carrying out what we learn in our cultivation. We use good and bad causes and conditions as objects of cognition. Therefore, we must first understand what cultivation is. Cultivation is cultivating the increase of good karma and cultivating the avoidance of bad karma. It is increasing good karmic conditions, planting good causes, and reaping good effects. It is avoiding the increase of bad karmic conditions, not planting bad causes, and avoiding the reaping of bad effects. But the term *cultivation* has a rather broad meaning. We must first understand what cultivation is.

There must be that upon which the cultivator can rely. Without that which can be relied upon, your cultivation can easily become erroneous, non-Buddhist cultivation. For example, the cultivation of demonism entails cultivating the behavior of demons. The cultivation of Buddhism entails cultivating the behavior of Buddhas. Therefore, there must be that upon which the cultivator can rely. There must be models that the cultivator can reflect and rely upon.

All other religions espouse eliminating evil, promoting good, restraining selfishness, and benefiting others. The cultivator cannot rely upon this alone, for this is cultivation without understanding the purpose of Buddhism. This alone is not the practice of true Buddhism. Thus, in our cultivation, that which we rely upon is the Buddha. The perfect enlightenment of the Buddha is the model for our cultivation. We use our three karmas of bodily actions, speech, and thoughts to emulate everything about the Buddha. We thereby keep ourselves far away from all impure karma based on delusion and all evil conduct. We thereby constantly stay far away from that which is evil or bad. By not being involved with that which is evil or bad, our three karmas do not increase bad causes. Rather, we must carry out all good karma. Even one kind thought is something we should increase and never decrease. We should increase our good karmic affinity, good causes, and good karma every day. Simply put, we must always avoid that which is evil or bad and accumulate that which is good.

Why can it be said that we must stay far away from evil or bad karma but it cannot be said that we must eliminate evil or bad karma? Within the truth of Buddhism, there is the doctrine that the law of cause and effect can never be denied. Cause and effect cannot be eliminated. To say that it can is to take a nihilistic point of view. Hence, we can only build a wall of good karma, which is like building a retaining wall. This wall of good karma has the effect of blocking us from our evil karma.

Thus, only through learning from the Buddha, cultivating the conduct of the Buddha, and ultimately becoming a Buddha can we thoroughly liberate ourselves from the karma (cause and effect) that binds us to the cycle of reincarnation. Cause and effect still exists when one becomes a Buddha. However, cause and effect can not affect a Buddha. For example, the Buddha saw mountains of swords and seas of fire in the hell realm. The mountains of swords and seas of fire continued to exist as extremely painful means by which living beings undergo karmic retribution. When the Buddha suddenly jumped into the mountains of swords and seas of fire in order to undergo suffering on behalf of other living beings, the mountains and seas immediately transformed into a lotus pond of nectar. They transformed into a wonderful state. With respect to a Buddha, all bad or evil karmic conditions turn into the manifestation of good karma. Not only is there no suffering, there is instead a manifestation of great happiness.

Cultivation is to leave the cycle of reincarnation, liberate yourself from all suffering, become a holy being, and persevere until you become a Buddha. To leave the cycle of reincarnation, we must establish a mind of renunciation (a mind determined to leave the cycle of reincarnation), a mind of firm belief, a mind with immovable vows, a mind of diligence, and mahayana bodhicitta. All real states emanating from these minds rely upon and are based upon right view. Without right view, all states of mind will be inverted and confused. In other words, you will not experience any beneficial effects from cultivation that lacks right view.

For example, if you want to practice bodhicitta first, you will not be successful. It will result in an empty and illusory bodhicitta, a deluded and false state of mind. That is because bodhicitta must be based upon a mind of renunciation. That is, you must have a mind that is truly determined to attain liberation, to attain accomplishment in the dharma, and leave all of the sufferings of reincarnation. You must deeply understand that the cycle of reincarnation is indescribably painful. Not only are you yourself suffering, but all living beings in the six realms of reincarnation, each of whom we regard as our father or mother, are likewise suffering in the painful state of impermanence. Only if you want to extricate yourself from suffering do you truly cultivate yourself. Only then do you engage in Bodhisattva conduct that benefits yourself and others. Only then can bodhicitta arise.

However, it would be a mistake if you begin by cultivating a mind of renunciation. That would not accord with the proper order of cultivation. That would result in a non-substantive, theoretical type of desire to leave reincarnation and a self-deluded and self-confused state of mind. In such case, you would not be able to establish the true state of mind that is determined to leave the cycle of reincarnation.

Thus, if you want to have this true state of mind that is determined to leave the cycle of reincarnation, you must first understand impermanence. The second step is to have a mind of firm belief. You must firmly believe in the sufferings of reincarnation, which has as its source impermanence. Only with such a mind of firm belief will you fear the sufferings caused by impermanence and successfully attain a state of mind that truly fears impermanence. Having attained a state of mind that truly fears impermanence, your state of mind that is determined to leave the cycle of reincarnation will grow stronger day by day. Naturally, your state of mind that is determined to leave the cycle of reincarnation will enter a real state that truly fears impermanence. If living beings do not understand that all conditional dharmas in the universe are impermanent, if they do not understand the sufferings connected with reincarnation and impermanence, then they cannot establish a firm mind that gives rise to thoughts of leaving the cycle of reincarnation. If you have never thought about leaving the cycle of reincarnation, you will not cultivate at all, and you will not want to learn Buddhism. Those who do not learn Buddhism have no desire to leave the cycle of reincarnation. How could one who does not learn Buddhism have a mind determined to leave the cycle of reincarnation? Thus, you cannot first cultivate a mind determined to leave the cycle of reincarnation. As for the first step, you will not enter Buddhism without having a mind of impermanence. (Truly giving rise to feelings of fear of impermanence and truly giving rise to a state that fears impermanence.) Even if you become Buddhist, you will not be able to attain a deep level of correct cultivation.

To understand what cultivation is, you must understand the eight fundamental right views relating to learning Buddhism and cultivation.

The first one is a mind of impermanence. The second is a mind with firm belief. The third is a mind of renunciation (a mind determined to leave the cycle of reincarnation). The fourth is a mind with true vows. The fifth is a mind of diligence. The sixth is the precepts. The seventh is dhyana and samadhi. The eighth is bodhicitta. Recognizing these eight dharmas and carrying them out with right views is correct practice of Buddha-dharma. These eight fundamental right views, which are indispensable for cultivators, must not be taken out of order. All the fruits resulting from a mind of impermanence are causes of cultivation. All of the fruits resulting from a mind with firm belief are causes of steadfastness that does not change. All of the fruits resulting from a mind of renunciation are causes of liberation. All of the fruits resulting from a mind with true

vows are causes of action. All of the fruits resulting from a mind of diligence are causes of persistent advancement. All of the fruits resulting from the precepts are causes of correct direction of cultivation. All of the fruits resulting from dhyana and samadhi are causes of wisdom. All of the fruits resulting from bodhicitta are causes leading to becoming a Bodhisattva.

These eight fundamental right views are the foundation of cultivation, liberation, and accomplishment in the dharma. If the root is not right, cultivation will not be established. Therefore, cultivation cannot be disorderly. Thus, practicing the eight fundamentals of cultivation must be guided by right views. That is, guided by right understanding and right view, you correctly develop your cultivation by going through these eight fundamentals in their proper order. That is cultivation. In your cultivation, you must constantly put into practice bodhicitta. That is because bodhicitta is the foundation for becoming a Bodhisattva.

According to the Buddha's exposition of the dharma, the true meaning of bodhicitta is that it is the cause that will inevitably lead to becoming a Bodhisattva. Whoever walks the path of bodhi will ultimately reap the fruit of bodhi. The broad meaning of bodhicitta includes all of the mahayana dharma having to do with saving living beings out of great compassion and the causes leading to attaining the stages of enlightenment of a Bodhisattva.

However, because of the insufficient good fortune of living beings, some of the originally complete meaning of the Buddha-dharma has been lost as it was handed down from generation to generation. Especially in this current Dharma-Ending Age in which the karma of living beings in the three spheres (worlds) of the universe is like a sea of surging waves, it is as difficult for living beings to encounter the true Buddha-dharma as it is for a blind turtle swimming in the ocean to stick its neck through a tiny knothole in a floating and bobbing board. Thus, it is now extremely difficult to obtain the perfect Buddha-dharma. As a result, the meaning of bodhi has shrunk. It has gradually shrunk from its broad meaning to the narrow meaning of bodhicitta dharma.

There are two types of bodhicitta. There is bodhicitta in the holy sense and bodhicitta in the worldly sense. Bodhicitta in the worldly sense can be roughly divided into "vow bodhicitta" and "action bodhicitta." The practice of vow and action bodhicitta includes a myriad of dharma methods, such as those relating to sentient beings, non-sentient things, the four great elements, one's own six elements, as well as breathing, the ear base, the eye base and other bases, inner and outer mandalas, and ritualistic chanting. Whether it is bodhicitta in the worldly sense or the holy sense, if you are guided by the two sets of seven branches of bodhicitta, that is the highest, most excellent, and most complete form of bodhicitta.

Each living being in the six realms of reincarnation within the three spheres of existence has the right to cultivate bodhicitta. However, most living beings do not have the karmic affinity. Thus, they practice a fragmented and shrunken version of bodhicitta dharma. As a result, they frequently harbor the misconceptions that only those with an enlightened mind can practice bodhicitta or bodhicitta is the dharmakaya state of enlightenment. Of course, we do not deny these are existing parts of bodhicitta. However, these conceptions omit the practice of bodhicitta dharma by those living beings who do not have an enlightened mind. More importantly, bodhicitta is not dependant upon an enlightened mind or an unenlightened mind. Bodhicitta is the power of vows made out of great compassion by those living beings who learn Buddhism in any of the six realms of reincarnation within the three spheres of the universe as well as the power of vows made out of great compassion by all holy beings in the dharma realm. Bodhicitta is actual conduct based upon great compassion that aids living beings in becoming Buddhas or Bodhisattvas. It is the mind of love in the holy sense that the enlightened and the unenlightened or the holy and the ordinary both have.

With respect to bodhicitta, those who are enlightened use their enlightened state of virtue and realization, correct practices, and propagation of the true dharma to teach and enlighten living beings so that those living beings will become Buddhas. With respect to bodhicitta, those who are not yet enlightened vow out of great compassion that living beings and themselves shall together attain accomplishment in the dharma and liberation. They help other people enter the path of the true dharma of the Buddha, vowing that they will become Bodhisattvas and Buddhas. To such persons, bodhicitta dharma is the virtue of aiding others to become accomplished in the dharma. Because they benefit others, they receive merit. They thereby increase the causes leading to their becoming Bodhisattvas.

The manifestation of bodhicitta is expressed through actual practice involving the three karmas, which practice reflects great compassion. Any true cultivator, no matter whether he or she is ordinary or holy, has the right to arouse bodhicitta and should arouse bodhicitta. That is because bodhicitta is not an enlightened mind possessed only by holy people. Rather, it is conduct based upon great compassion. It is the planting of causes based upon a vow that oneself and others become enlightened. Bodhicitta does not only include the ten good characteristics, the four limitless states of mind (the four immeasurables), the six paramitas (perfections), and the four all-embracing Bodhisattva virtues (four methods that Bodhisattvas employ to approach and save living beings). Rather, it includes the entire *Tripitaka*, the esoteric scriptures, and all dharma transmitted orally, through the ears, or telepathically that engenders conduct that is greatly compassionate, is in accord with the dharma, and benefits and saves living beings.

Thus, the bodhicitta is ultimate truth in a broad sense. With respect to the Buddha, bodhicitta is the three bodies, the perfect wisdom of Buddha that is summarized in four truths, and the mind of anuttara-samyak-sambodhi. With respect to a Bodhisattva, bodhicitta is propagating the dharma and benefiting and saving living beings out of great compassion. With respect to an enlightened being, bodhicitta is not being attached to the characteristics or distinctive features of things and not engaging in intellectual frivolity or conceptual elaborations. This is his or her original nature. The true emptiness of original nature is wonderful existence. It is the ultimate truth of all conditional dharmas. This truth neither arises nor ceases. With respect to an ordinary person, bodhicitta is compassionately helping other people and vowing that they learn Buddhism and attain liberation.

You must first have the perspective of impermanence before you can arouse bodhicitta. You must understand the impermanence and suffering relating to yourself and other living beings revolving in the cycle of reincarnation and thereby generate a perspective of awareness, a mind of impermanence. You will then vow to leave the cycle of reincarnation. As a result, you will then establish a mind that is determined to leave the cycle of reincarnation. You will say, "I resolve to leave." You also want all living beings in the six realms, who are like your father or mother, to leave. You understand that the cycle of reincarnation is like a bitter sea, is difficult to endure, and is extremely painful. Because of this resolute perspective, you will generate a strong and pressing fear. You will constantly seek to be liberated at this very moment. But you understand that only by having the conduct of a Bodhisattva can you quickly attain liberation from the cycle of reincarnation.

You thus vow to become a Bodhisattva. You seek to quickly enlighten yourself and others. Naturally, you then generate a mind of great compassion. As a result, the seeds of enlightenment are disseminated. The arousal of bodhicitta is based upon a mind of great compassion. Thus the Buddha said, "The water of great compassion irrigates the seeds of bodhi. As a result, the bodhi trees will have lush foliage and the fruits will be plentiful." Hence, bodhicitta will naturally be established. Bodhicitta is the cause leading to becoming a mahayana Bodhisattva. You will attain pure and correct views and understanding of cultivation. Based upon these right views, you should deeply enter the emptiness bhuta-tathata (true suchness) and the practice of the state of emptiness. At this time, you transform worldy bodhicitta into a state in which you realize that "the three entities are inherently empty." That is you transform everything in existence into bodhicitta in a holy sense. With bodhicitta, you cultivate the conduct of bodhi and enter the stage of a Bodhisattva.

Cultivation of bodhicitta requires implementation. Cultivation of bodhicitta is not a matter of just ritualistic chanting, making empty vows, or engaging in visualization. In the cultivation of bodhicitta, the most important aspect is deeply pondering the following concerning yourself: "My body is impermanent, is changing every nanosecond, and is moving toward decline, old age, and death. I compare why my face has aged over a ten-year period, over a forty-year period, or over a seventy-year period. The degree of agedness of my skin has changed. I will soon enter old age, sickness, and death and continue revolving in the cycle of reincarnation where I will experience suffering. I also contemplate that joyfully innocent, newborn, fresh, and lively look I had when I was a small child. I contemplate how I no longer have that childlike appearance. My face and skin have aged. My energy has declined. I often fall ill. That quality of youth is gone. The power of impermanence will end my life. My relatives and old friends will all die one after another. Like a dream, it will soon be all over. My mind generates great fear. With a resolute mind, I act in accord with the precepts, practice in accord with the dharma, and enter bodhicitta by practicing the two sets of seven branch bodhicitta dharma: the Dharma of Great Compassion for All Living Beings as My Mother Bodhicitta and the Dharma of Bodhisattva Correspondence Bodhicitta."

When practicing the Great Compassion for My Mother Bodhicitta, you arouse great compassion and cultivate the following: understanding who my mother is, bearing in mind kindness, repaying kindness, loving-kindness, compassion, renouncing greed, and eliminating attachment. When practicing this cultivation, everyone should carry out the following for themselves:

Understanding who my mother is: I deeply understand that all living beings in the six realms of reincarnation within the three spheres of the universe have been since beginning-less time my fathers and mothers in the revolving cycle of reincarnation.

Bearing in mind kindness: I should deeply bear in mind that all of my parents (i.e. all living beings) that now exist in the cycle of reincarnation have since beginning-less time given birth to me, reared me, loved me, and became tired and ill for me. Their kindness to me is as heavy as a mountain. I should bear in mind their kindness. I will then regard the sufferings of my parents (i.e. all living beings) as my own suffering.

Repaying kindness: I understand that my parents (i.e. all living beings) have offered me everything. They are now revolving and wandering in the six realms of reincarnation experiencing endless suffering. I resolve to take action to enlighten myself and others, to save and liberate my parents (i.e. all living beings) in order to repay their kindness to me.

Loving-kindness: At all times, through the actions of my three karmas, I am loving and kind toward all living beings, who have been my parents. I wish them a long life without illness, good fortune, good luck, and a happy life.

Compassion: Day and night, I constantly beseech all of the Buddhas and Bodhisattvas to empower all of my parents (i.e. all living beings) so that they may extricate themselves from all forms of suffering, encounter and practice the Buddha-dharma, and liberate themselves from the sufferings of cyclic existence.

Renouncing greed: I hold no attachment in my mind to anything that I do to benefit any living beings, who have been my parents. I cultivate non-attachment to all of my good actions of body, speech, and mind. Thus, my good actions become natural and spontaneous, as my original nature is good. I do not do good purposefully. I do good and then forget about it.

Eliminating attachment: In my practice, as I cultivate all forms of goodness and benefit my parents (i.e. all living beings), I should not become attached to any dharma. I should eliminate all attachment to self. Realizing a state of emptiness, I am aware and I experience wonderful happiness that comes from samadhi. While practicing the dharma, I am not attached to the dharma. I do not intentionally get rid of deluded thoughts. I do not intentionally seek the truth. Not coming and not going, blissful, clear, and without thought, I am as calm as tranquil water. Everything, including myself, is inherently empty.

The supporting conditions for putting bodhicitta into practice must be based upon right view. We contribute to living beings in their performance of good deeds, but we do not contribute or help living beings in their performance of bad deeds. We rectify their behavior so that they perform good deeds. Thus, we do all good deeds that benefit living beings. We plant all good causes that lead to benefiting living beings. In that way, we carry out the seven branches of the Dharma of Bodhisattva Correspondence Bodhicitta. We help living beings in their performing good deeds and help increase their good causes. We help living beings reduce their accumulation of bad karma and help them stay far away from bad causes. The seven branches of the Dharma of Bodhisattva Correspondence Bodhicitta are as follows. The first branch is "self and others are equal" bodhicitta. The second branch is "exchange between self and others" bodhicitta. The third branch is "benefit others before self" bodhicitta. The fourth branch is "dedicating merit" bodhicitta. The fifth branch is "fearlessly protect the dharma" bodhicitta. The sixth branch is "effectively lead others to correct practice" bodhicitta. The seventh branch is "renouncing myself to help others build good karma" bodhicitta. When practicing this cultivation, everyone should carry out the following themselves:

Self and others are equal bodhicitta: When there is a conflict of interest between myself and others, I will rid myself of hatred, antipathy, greed, and arrogant, disparaging mentality. I must not emphasize benefiting myself. I should treat myself and others equally.

Exchange between self and others bodhicitta: I want to bear the sufferings of all living beings. I give to others all of my happiness and good luck so that they may leave suffering and obtain happiness.

Benefit others before self bodhicitta: When other living beings and I are suffering, I want others to extricate themselves from suffering before I do. When other living beings and I are happy, I want others to be happier than I am.

Dedicating merit bodhicitta: I dedicate to all living beings all of the merit and accomplishments from my cultivation in the hope that they will leave suffering and attain liberation.

Fearlessly protect the dharma bodhicitta: When any evil spirits or demons harm the Buddha-dharma, lead living beings to break the precepts, and harm living beings resulting in the suffering of living beings, I will maintain right view, will not fear the evil powers of those demons, and will step forward to protect the Buddha-dharma and the wisdom whereby living beings will become liberated.

Effectively lead others to correct practice bodhicitta: Because living beings are burdened with the power of karma that has accumulated since beginning-less time, because they are ignorant and have created all kinds of negative karma, there will be times when they will not repent or change their ways despite my constructive exhortations. In such case, I will use powerful rectifying dharma methods to lead such people onto the path of true dharma and beneficial and good conduct.

Renouncing myself to help others build good karma bodhicitta: When the realization of other people is higher than mine or their ability to save living beings is better than mine, I will yield to other people so that living beings will be benefited more. At such time, without any hesitation, I yield to them. This furthers the great undertaking of goodness.

Bodhicitta, as part of cultivation, is the source of accomplishment in the dharma and is very important. I will now give an example involving a rinpoche and a dharma master. This rinpoche cultivated himself for more than thirty years. He received more than one thousand esoteric dharma initiations. He mainly practiced the Great Perfection Dharma (Dzogchen) of the Nyingma sect. He was able to expound the Buddha-dharma of the *Tripitaka* very well. However, he did not have any real dharma powers. The other person, a dharma master, had been a monk for more than twenty years. He strictly abided by the precepts and rules of discipline. He was well versed in the sutras, the vinaya (precepts and rules of discipline), and the commentaries. He practiced important and great dharmas of the Tibetan esoteric school of Buddhism and was the abbot of a famous temple. Like the rinpoche, he was famous in expounding the dharma. However, he also was unable to manifest any actual realization.

I told them that no matter what great dharma of the esoteric school they may practice, it is all like building a tower on quicksand. Such a tower could not be built. I told them that even if they temporarily had some success in their practice, it would quickly vanish. I had them practice letting go of their own knowledge or habituated way of knowing because these are hindrances. I had them practice "What Is Cultivation?" After they practiced such dharma for about eight months, I had them add to their practice the Great Perfection (Dzogchen) and other dharmas. A miracle then happened. During a test of his progress, the rinpoche applied the Vajra Fist Powerful Thunder True Dharma Palm and manifested great powers. Actual realization was shown. However, the dharma master did not manifest any powers. He continued to practice this cultivation dharma. Under my careful pointing out of his shortcomings, he finally understood the importance of true cultivation and how true cultivation requires devoting time and energy on the actual carrying out of the three karmas. He finally understood that there is no room whatsoever for any slippage or compromise in this regard. He continued his practice for three months. In a test to measure his ability to manifest realization, his powers were thoroughly exhibited.

Thus, whoever can cultivate in such manner and carry out his practice according to the dharma will be able to obtain the true Buddha-dharma. Naturally, he will develop wisdom. He will not become involved with empty theories regarding the Five Vidyas. Rather, he will manifest actual states of accomplishment in the true Five Vidyas. Such a person will realize "manifestation of wonderful existence (supernatural power)," attain the fruit of bodhi, and enter the stage of a Bodhisattva.

The practitioners of all Buddhist sects should comply with these rules of cultivation and should practice bodhicitta. If you do not follow such dharma of cultivation in its proper order, then you will easily become confused and lose your way. Such dharma is the key to the methods of practicing cultivation.

Learning the methods of practicing dharma is another matter. All beneficial effects derived from learning the dharma are based upon cultivation. When your practice is in strict conformity with the dharma, you will naturally realize virtue and will successfully reach the true state. If you do not have the correct rules concerning cultivation, the dharma that you learn will become dharma based on erroneous view or even the evil dharma of demons. If you are complying with the dharma of cultivation as stated in this discourse, the dharma that you have learned is good dharma, and you are engaged in practicing Buddha-dharma. Cultivation also involves the ten good characteristics, the four limitless states of mind (the four immeasurables), the six paramitas (perfections), the four all-embracing Bodhisattva virtues (the four methods that Bodhisattvas employ to approach and save living beings), etc.

Some disciples will think that they know all of the important dharma I expounded today on cultivation. They will therefore not carefully ponder and fully incorporate into their thinking the cultivation of which I spoke. Rather, the wish they harbor in their hearts is to learn a great dharma whereby they will become a Buddha in this very lifetime.

Anyone with such a mentality has only superficial knowledge, has fallen into confusion, and has lost his way. Such a person will not learn the true Buddha-dharma. Even if he is practicing great dharma, such as the Great Perfection (Dzogchen) of the Nyingma sect, the Mind

Within Mind of the Kagyu sect, the Great Perfection of Wonderful Wisdom of the Sakya sect, the Kalachakra Vajra of the Geluk sect, Zen meditation of the Zen sect of exoteric Buddhism, reciting a Buddha's name of the Pure Land sect, the dharma of the Consciousness-Only sect, or samatha and vipasyana of the hinayana school, he will not obtain any fruits from his practice and will not be able to transform his consciousness into wisdom. Thus, he will continue to go round and round in the state of an ordinary person. He will not be able to manifest any realization, the source of which is the wisdom of exoteric and esoteric Buddhism. He will not be able to exhibit any actual accomplishments in the Five Vidyas. He will only be able to manifest that which an ordinary person manifests. He may even be quite stupid such that he is only able to memorize theories in books and speak of empty theories, totally incapable of putting those theories into actual practice. Such a person cannot actually do anything. Even if he can do a few things, he cannot exceed those people in the world who are experts in those few things.

Think about it. Does such a person embody the Buddha-dharma? Is the wisdom derived from the Buddha-dharma so inferior? How can one who has not yet developed holy wisdom and still has the consciousness of an ordinary person possess the true dharma to enlighten himself and others? However, if you enter the practice of the dharma according to these rules of cultivation, then you can receive the true Buddha-dharma, can become truly proficient in exoteric and esoteric Buddhism, and can manifest accomplishments in the Five Vidyas. We should therefore understand that cultivation is the foundation for learning dharma, the cause of liberation, and the source of realizing the state of holiness.

Today I spoke briefly on the subject of what cultivation is. I expounded the subject of the correct practice of bodhicitta, which is part of cultivation. I did not speak of other dharma. There is so much more to teach. However, if I casually discussed those other teachings in this book, it would not be in accord with the rules of discipline and could easily create the negative karma of disrespect. Thus, I hope that all of you who learn Buddhism will deeply immerse yourselves in the *Tripitaka* and esoteric scriptures or will listen to my recorded discourses on the dharma. If you attentively listen to those discourses on the dharma with all your heart, within ten days you can attain a certain degree of joy or the wonderful joy of great enlightenment. If the causes and conditions mature, you will experience beneficial effects for your entire life or even attain great accomplishment, liberation, and Buddhahood.

Now that you have learned this dharma of cultivation, do you want to practice it? Anyone who engages in true cultivation can become accomplished in the dharma and attain liberation from the cycle of birth and death. Thus, we must clearly understand something. Although you have read "What is Cultivation" and although you have read the eight fundamentals of cultivation and two sets of seven branches based upon right view, that is called "reading words relating to practice." That is not cultivation. If you understand the principles relating to cultivation, that is called "understanding the theories of practice." This is also not cultivation. If you begin to implement this dharma of cultivation according to its content, that is also not cultivation. That is called "entering the process of cultivation." If you have done your utmost to apply great compassion in accordance with this dharma of cultivation, that is called "coarse cultivation." It is not true and correct cultivation. If you do not need to do your utmost to apply great compassion, if you naturally, effortlessly and perfectly carry out the eight fundamentals of cultivation and two sets of seven branches according to the dharma, that is called "cultivation."

Why is it that doing your utmost in cultivation is not called "cultivation" but rather is called "coarse cultivation"? It is because since beginning-less time, the power of karma and the hindrances of ignorance have obstructed practitioners. Hence, they cannot let go of greed (selfish desire), hatred (anger or antipathy), and ignorance (delusion). They cannot let go of their attachment to self. This produces the hindrances that are based on the defilements (afflictions). This also produces the hindrances that emanate from their own knowledge or habituated way of knowing. These karmic hindrances devour all of the right mindfulness (right thought) of these practitioners. As a result, the process of implementing each of these rules of cultivation is difficult for these practitioners. Precisely because of this difficulty, they choose the method of using their utmost effort to practice cultivation. Using one's utmost efforts in this manner is like a pebble that is coarse on the inside and out rather than a shining precious stone that has been carved and polished. Practicing part of the eight fundamentals of cultivation and the two sets of seven branches and not practicing the remaining parts is also not called true cultivation. That is why it is called "coarse cultivation" or "incomplete cultivation."

Thoroughly understanding the rules of cultivation, not forcefully implementing them, and naturally carrying out the eight fundamentals of cultivation and two sets of seven branches according to the dharma is true cultivation that is without attachment to self and that has overcome the hindrances. This is the path of bodhi. Thus, every day practitioners should introspect upon Great Compassion for All Living Beings as My Mother Bodhicitta and Bodhisattva Correspondence Bodhicitta. They should reflect upon those two sets of seven branches, asking themselves whether they have practiced them according to the dharma. If you were unable to practice these rules according to the dharma contained in this discourse, it shows that you have entered the state of "coarse cultivation." If you did not fully implement these rules, then your cultivation is incomplete cultivation. You will not become accomplished in the dharma and liberated from the cycle of reincarnation through such incomplete cultivation. Even if you have some minor accomplishments, it will be impossible for you to attain great fortune and wisdom, supernatural powers, and realization in the Five Vidyas.

If you introspect every day upon these two sets of seven branches, are not forceful in implementing them, are greatly compassionate, follow goodness in a natural way, and carry out the two sets of seven branches naturally and according to the dharma, that would be true cultivation and complete practice. You will thereby easily be able to attain liberation, become a holy being, and obtain good fortune and wisdom. You will accordingly have realization in the Five Vidyas. You will certainly reach the stage of a Bodhisattva. Thus, you should understand that "reading words relating to practice," "understanding the theories of practice," "entering the process of cultivation," and "incomplete cultivation" is easy. To practice the two sets of seven branches perfectly and without attachment is difficult. Actually, when you let go of attachment to self, you immediately enter correct and true cultivation. How could this be difficult? Everyone can do that!

When you do your daily introspection, besides using thoughts to contemplate and visualize, it is more important that you must use as objects of introspection fellow disciples with whom you are familiar, people with whom you get along, people who are not good to you, negative karmic conditions, any conditions or people that make you unhappy, or people you find hard to get along with, to whom who do not speak, or who do not speak to you. You must use them as objects of your practice, asking yourself, "Today did I act in accordance with the two sets of seven branches and on my own initiative show goodwill to these people? When I approached that person on my own initiative and he attacked me with abusive words, did I forbear those insults with patience and continue to approach him in order to show goodwill?" You must not bear any grudge due to abusive words, abusive conduct, and insults. If, every day, you practice your bodhicitta without relenting, carry out the two sets of seven branches through your three karmas of physical action, speech, and thoughts, actually cultivate yourself according to the dharma in a real and concrete way, and realize "the thing itself is empty," then it will be very easy for you to learn the supreme Buddha-dharma. In such case, bodhicitta and the stage of a Bodhisattva will naturally be yours. That is cultivation.

I have finished expounding the dharma of cultivation that benefits living beings. However, there is a certain type of matter harmful to living beings that occurs all the time. I am referring to the matter of using my name to harm the interests of living beings. I would now like to call attention again to a problem that is especially important and that everyone should take seriously.

In this world, there currently are some dharma kings, venerable ones, rinpoches, dharma teachers, and even laypersons who claim that they are my trusted followers. They may claim to represent me in handling a certain matter. They may claim to convey a certain message from me. Or, they may claim that what they say are my own words. Actually, I have disciples in exoteric and esoteric Buddhism and in each of the main sects. No matter what the status of any greatly virtuous person making such a claim may be, nobody can represent me. This applies to even very small matters!

Only when a person has a special-purpose document that I gave him or her clearly indicating he or she represents me in handling a certain matter, that document contains my signature and fingerprint, and that document is accompanied by a corresponding sound recording or videotape can he or she represent me in handling the matter specified in that document. Otherwise, no matter how high the status of a dharma king, venerable one, rinpoche, or dharma teacher may be, his or her views, discourses, and explanations of dharma do not represent my views and do not serve as the standard of correct understanding and correct views. I know that my own oral discourses and writings are the true dharma without any bias. That is because my oral discourses and writings truly benefit and liberate living beings. Furthermore, nobody may use any method to make additions, deletions, or revisions to my writings or discourses on the dharma given orally. Anyone who violates what is stated above is certainly one with wrong views or one who has fallen into demonic ways, no matter how high the status of that person is.

Thus, the only time someone can represent me is when everyone personally sees a document containing my fingerprint and there is accompanying proof in the form of an integral sound recording or videotape that corresponds to the document and in which I personally speak. Otherwise, no matter who the Buddhist disciple may be, including those disciples of holy virtue who have been at my side for a long period of time, everything that they think, do, say, or write is their own conduct and absolutely does not represent me!

(The above discourse was translated from Chinese to English.)

三世多杰羌佛傳的修行法

頂聖如來多杰羌佛第三世雲高益西諾布爲仁波且等弟子的開示：
什麼叫修行？

今天你這個仁波且爲大衆請法「什麼叫修行？」這是非常基礎的第一課，但也是許多修行人乃至長年修行者沒有學懂而迷離顛倒的大事。人身難得，暇滿人身寶更難得，故而今天我當爲大家講「什麼叫修行」之法。

學佛的實質，要落實在修行上，因此我們首先必須明白什麼叫修行。修行，即是修善惡二所緣業之增益與離避。也就是增益善緣，種善因，結善果；離避惡所緣，離惡因，避惡果。但修行二字頗爲廣義，首先認識到底修什麼行？因此要有所依對緣。無所依緣，則易成外道之修行。比如，魔教修行，就修成魔行。佛教修行，就修成佛行。所以必須要有所依緣，有所楷模應照而依止。又如，只知去惡揚善，克己利人，這是其他宗教都會做的事，這也就是不明宗旨無所依的修行，不屬於正宗佛教行持。因此我們的修行，所依緣之對象則是佛陀。依照佛陀的完美覺位作爲我們所修之相應楷模，以我們的身口意三業學佛陀的一切，使一切不淨惑業緣起惡行遠離不得沾邊，只令其時時離避遠惡，不使其有所近沾三業增加惡因。而一切緣起善業都要行持，哪怕就是一善念，只能增益，不可損減。日日增加善緣、善因、善業，簡言之即是時時離惡積善。爲什麼說惡所緣業只能用遠離，不可說是滅除呢？因爲佛諦中，因果不昧。因果是滅除不了的，說滅除是斷見，故所以只能善業築壁，猶如築一道擋土牆，起到隔開的作用。由是學佛，修佛之行，最終成佛方可

徹底解脫輪迴的因果縛業，此時因果照樣存在，但對佛無沾。正如佛陀見到地獄刀山火海，地獄刀山火海依然存在，應報衆生痛苦不堪，當佛陀爲代衆生受苦而自身頓然躍入時，此刀山火海當下化爲蓮池甘露，成爲殊勝的境象，一切惡所緣境在佛陀身上轉爲善業的顯現，不但無苦，反顯大樂。

修行就是出離輪迴，解脫諸苦而成聖，直至成佛。要出離輪迴，因此就要建立出離心、堅信心、不動願心、精進心、大乘菩提心。而所有一切心的依止境，皆建立在正見上，如沒有正見，一切心均會顛倒、混亂。換言之，沒有正見是修而無有受用的。比如要先修菩提心，是無法修起來的，會成爲空幻菩提，虛妄之心。因爲菩提心首先建立在出離心上，也就是一個人要有真正解脫成就出離輪迴諸苦的心，他要深知輪迴苦不堪言，不但自苦，而且六道衆生如父如母均在無常苦痛中，知苦、欲脫於苦，他才會真修行，才會發出自利利他之菩薩行，菩提心方可誕生。但是如果首先從出離心開始修，又是錯誤的，是不合次第之修，會修成空言出離，妄惑自迷心，這樣也是很難修起，建立不了出離心實相的。所以要有真正的出離心，必須要第一步首先了明無常境，第二步要有堅信心，堅信輪迴無常的苦，有了堅信心才會恐懼無常苦，才會修成無常心，有了無常心，出離心就會日益增進，自然出離心就會生起實相。如果衆生不了解萬

法皆無常、輪迴無常的痛苦，就建立不起一顆堅定的心去出離輪迴的念頭，沒有出離輪迴的想法，根本就不會去修行，不想學佛，不學佛的人，本來不想出離，怎麼還會有出離心呢？所以不能先修出離心。因此，第一步，沒有無常心，就無法步入佛門。就是皈依了佛門，也無法深入正確修行。

要知道什麼是修行，就要明白學佛修行的八基正見。

第一基是無常心，第二基是堅信心，第三基是出離心，第四基是實願心，第五基是精進心，第六基是戒律，第七基是禪定，第八基是菩提心。認此八法為基而修行正見即是正知佛法的指南。這八基正見是修行人不可缺少不可錯亂的次第。凡是無常心所攝化受用的，就是修行的因；凡是堅信心所攝化受用的，就是不變的因；凡是出離心所攝化受用的，就是解脫的因；凡是實願心所攝化受用的，就是行動的因；凡是精進心所攝化受用的，就是進取的因；凡是戒律所攝化受用的，就是正法的因；凡是禪定所攝化受用的，就是智慧的因；凡是菩提心所攝化受用的，就是菩薩的因。八基是修行解脫成就的根本，如果根不正，就會本則亂。所以修行的根本是不可亂的，因此修行的八基必須依於正見作為宗標，也就是以正知正見來引導八基的次第和正確發展修行，這就叫做修行。在修行中要時時落實菩提心的修持，因為菩提心是成道之根本。

佛陀說法，菩提心的真實之義是必然成道之因。凡行菩提道者，終結菩提之果。菩提心是廣義全攝一切大乘法之大悲渡生覺成菩薩地因。但由於眾生福報使然，佛法經代代相傳，遺漏法義。尤為至今末法時期，三界業海波濤洶湧，眾生如盲龜更難以頸穿蕩動海流之木軛如牛鼻之孔，故而要得完美佛法難中之難。因此菩提縮水，所以由廣義逐漸縮成了狹義之菩提心法。菩提心分兩種，勝義菩提心和世俗菩提心，世俗菩提心又粗分願菩提心和行菩提心。於願、行二菩

提心之修持，又分情器四大和自身六大以及呼吸、耳根、眼根等內外壇城和儀軌誦文諸多修法。無論世俗還是勝義菩提心，而歸於七支菩提份才是最上妙完美的菩提心。本來菩提心是三界六道眾生個個有權修施的，但今大都眾生法緣不俱，故已執持化整為零縮水之菩提心修法。因此往往誤會成覺悟之心方可修之，或曰以菩提心為實相成就之境。當然，這也是存在的一部分，但卻遺漏了非覺悟之心的眾生而修菩提心之法。更重要的是，菩提心並非覺悟和非覺悟的心，而是學佛的三界六道眾生及法界諸聖生發的大悲願力，是以大悲心所實施的利益眾生成佛菩薩的實際行為，是覺悟和非覺悟，聖凡兩界的勝義愛心。對覺悟者而言，即是以自覺之證德證境正行正法弘法教化眾生，覺悟有情成佛道。對未覺悟者而言，即是以大悲之心發願眾生與我等皆共成就得解脫，幫助他人走入如來正法之道，願其成菩薩成佛。菩提心之法，對他而言是利他成就之德，由於利他之故而自獲德量，故對自己而言即成增益菩薩之因。菩提心之業相，是大悲體現之三業之實際行持。凡真修行者，無論凡聖，均有權發菩提心，也應該發菩提心。因為它不是聖人獨有的覺悟之心，而是大悲之行為，願自他覺悟的因種。菩提心之所攝並不只含十善、四無量、六波羅密、四攝，而菩提心所緣三藏密典及一切口耳心傳諸法，建立合法利眾渡生的大悲行舉。故知菩提心是廣義所緣諦相，對佛陀而言是三身四智，當體無上正覺菩提心；對菩薩而言是大悲弘法利生渡有情；對證悟者而言，是離絕諸相戲論，當體本來面目，即空妙有之諸法實相；對凡夫而言，是慈悲助益他人願其學佛解脫。

發菩提心，首先必須要有無常觀，對自我與眾生輪迴之無常流轉痛苦，生起覺觀無常境心，即發出離願，由是則建立出離心，我出離，眾生六道父母也出離，輪迴苦海難熬痛不欲生，為是願觀而生強烈恐懼所逼，時時欲求當下解脫，

但明了其菩薩之行，方可快捷了生脫死，於是自我願作因地菩薩，欲求快速自覺覺他，則自然生大悲之心，由此菩提籽發。菩提心所發是建立在大悲心上的，故佛義云：「大悲之水澆灌菩提籽發，則樹茂果豐耶。」是此，菩提心自然建立。菩提心是成大乘菩薩之因，由菩提心之果，可得清純正見，依此正見，當深入空性真如，空性之修，於此則化世俗菩提心爲三輪體空，即轉萬有爲勝義菩提心也，有了菩提心，即修菩提行，成菩薩地。

修菩提心必須付諸於實踐，而不只是背誦行文儀軌、以空洞的發心和觀想叫做修菩提心。修菩提心，重在實施於深思我的身體無常，刹那變異，邁向衰老死亡。以十年觀察，四十年觀察，七十年觀察，於中對比相貌、皮膚老度變異，快捷進入生老病死，長恆輾轉受苦於輪迴，又觀由一少小兒時天真之歡，乳氣活鮮，然何今無童相，臉老皮老，力氣衰竭，時時多病，少小已無，無常將斃我命，親人老友，悉皆分段而死，猶如一夢，快將做完，心生大懼，則決心堅定，依戒而行，依法而修，入菩提心修雙運七支菩提心法：大悲我母菩提心和菩薩應照菩提心。於大悲我母菩提心修法中發大悲之心，修知母、念恩、報恩、慈愛、慈悲、捨貪、斷執。

知母：了徹三界六道衆生無始以來於輪迴轉折中皆我父母。

念恩：應深深憶持一切無始過去、現在於輪迴之父母，皆曾生育養育體愛於我，爲我而勞累病苦，恩重如山，念其恩德，故思其父母之苦皆我之苦。

報恩：知父母爲我而奉獻一切，現在他們於六道輪迴中轉折流離，受苦無盡，我此發心，施之於行，自覺覺他，渡脫父母，以爲報恩。

慈愛：每時每刻，從於三業之行所生發，慈愛一切衆生、父母，長壽無病富貴吉祥，終生喜樂。

慈悲：於三時中，願請諸佛菩薩加持一切父母脫離諸苦，得遇佛法修持，脫離輪迴解脫諸苦。

捨貪：所做一切利益衆生父母之事，無掛於心，養成三業無著善行，故成天然自行，本質爲善，並非刻意所爲行善，做了即忘了。

斷執：於行持中，所修諸善，利益父母，一切法義應無所住，斷掉我執，空明覺相輕安，於修法中不執於法，不除妄念，不求於真，不來不去，樂明無念，平如靜水，當體即空。

實施菩提心的助緣，必須建立在正見觀照下，對衆生所行事業於善因中施與的而非他造不淨業的緣起所需增長施與的，故知凡善因緣起有利衆生者，必須實施七支菩薩應照菩提心法，對善緣起當施與他助益善業，助益善因，對惡緣起當施與他損減惡業，遠離惡因。菩薩應照菩提心法七支爲：一支，自他平等菩提心；二支，自他交換菩提心；三支，自他輕重菩提心；四支，功德回向菩提心；五支，無畏護法菩提心；六支，強導正修菩提心；七支，捨我助他菩提心。

自他平等菩提心：兩相利益對逢時，斷除瞋恨之貪瞋、漫謗之心，不可利己爲重，應自他平等對待。

自他交換菩提心：一切衆生的痛苦，願我一人來承擔，我的一切快樂吉祥都給予他，讓他離苦得樂。

自他輕重菩提心：我與衆生均苦時，應先願他人解脫苦，我與衆生均樂時，應先願他人多我樂。

功德回向菩提心：我於一切所修行，一切功德成就等，全部回向諸有情，願衆離苦得解脫。

無畏護法菩提心：一切妖孽惡魔施以破壞佛法，導致破戒殘害衆生讓其痛苦時，我將持以正見，不懼魔之惡力而挺身保護佛法，維護衆生慧命。

強導正修菩提心：他由於無始業力纏身，愚癡不明，造諸惡業，而到了善勸不得悔改時，由此，我將施以強有力的善化法門引導他，入其正法善行之路。

捨我助他菩提心：他之成就將勝於我，渡生緣起勝於我，但於利益眾生中，能捨我助他更能利益大眾，此時，毫不考慮，當捨我助他，助成眾善大業。

修行中的菩提心，是成就之本源，非常重要。此舉一位仁波且和一位法師的事例。仁波且修了三十多年行，受過上千個密法灌頂，以寧瑪大圓滿法為主修，佛法經律論也講得很好，但是就是沒有實際功夫。另一位大法師出家二十餘年，戒律嚴謹，經律論通達，兼修西密密乘重要大法，是一著名寺廟的住持，也是講經說法之名師，但也沒有實際證量展顯。我告知他們：無論你等修什麼密乘大法，都是浮土築高樓，建立不了大廈的，就算一時修起，當下即會垮塌。我讓他們放下一切修行所知障礙，專修「什麼叫修行」，修了大概八個月，我再讓他們合修大圓滿等法義，結果奇蹟發生了，仁波且在測試中，以金剛拳五雷正法掌的功夫，顯示了巨大威力，實際證量出現了，但法師卻沒有展現出力量。法師又繼續加修我開示的這一堂修行的法，在我細心的教化下，他終於明了真修實修的重要性必須實際於三業上下功夫，一點折扣也不能打，他又多加了三個月的修持，結果在證量展顯測試中，他的威力徹底體現了。因此，凡是能依此修行，如法實施而行持，即可獲得真正的佛法，自然開敷大智，離說空論五明之不實，體顯真正五明之實境，證妙有之道量，修成菩提道果，達菩薩之地。

這修行的規則和菩提心的實施是佛教各宗各派都應該要遵循的，如果不依於此一次第法則步入，則易成顛倒迷行，此為修行之要領。至於學法，則是另外一事，但是學法的一切受用，皆建立在修行上，有了嚴格合法的行持，自然法入證德，圓成證境。如果沒有修行的正確法則，學法則成邪見之法，乃至妖魔之惡法。依於修行之法，方為善法，佛法之修行。在修行中還涉獵十善、四無量、六度、四攝等。今天所講的修行法要，有的佛弟子會認為，這些我都知道明白的，因此就不會細推體解我講的修行了。而他心中的願望是一心學到大法即身成佛。凡有此觀點的人，已經是一知半解，落入顛倒迷行之中，是學不到真正佛法的，哪怕他已修大法紅教大圓滿、白教心中心、花教大圓勝慧或黃教時輪金剛、顯教中的禪宗參禪、淨土念佛、唯識法相、小乘止觀等，都是得不到受用，不能轉識成智，所以照常在凡夫境界中打轉，是體顯不了顯密智海中的表相、實際五明展顯的，而只能體現普通人的表現，甚至於笨笨的，除了把書本上的理論背下來虛談空論之外，落實到實際上，自己什麼能力也沒有，什麼也不會做，就是能做那麼幾項，對比之下，也超不過世間上的專家們，這能說是佛法的體現嗎？大家想一想，佛法的智慧就這麼差嗎？凡夫之識，未開聖智，又怎能談得上執持有正法自覺覺他呢？但是，依照修行入法，就能得到真正的佛法，就能真正顯密俱通，體顯五明。故所以我們應知修行是一切學法之基，解脫之因，證聖之源。

今淺講什麼叫修行，即修行中的菩提心正修，不涉別法。要講的太多，但由於在此書輕談不合律法，易造不恭之業，故望善信，深入三藏密典或專聞我開示之法音，只需十日之內一心認真聞法，即可達到分段喜樂，或大悟勝喜，緣起成熟不但終生受用乃至獲大成就解脫直至菩提。

你們現在學了修行一法，你願修行嗎？只要是修行，個個皆能成就解脫，因此我們必須要弄清楚，雖然看了「什麼叫修行」，而且八基雙七支依於正見都看了，但是那叫做看行文，不是修行；如果你把修行的理論看懂了，那叫見行理，也不叫修行；如果你已經開始按照修行一法履行，這也不是修行，這叫做入行程；如果你已按照修行一法以大悲之心儘量照著做，這叫頑修，不名正修；如果你以大悲之心不需儘量，自然完美如法按照八基雙七支行條執行，這才叫修行。為何儘量而修不叫修行稱之為頑修？因為無始業力、無明諸障障其行人，所以貪瞋癡放不下，我執拋不開，由此產生煩惱障、所知障，其障業吞噬行人之一切正念，所以行人難以執行行條，正因為難以執行行規，所以才會用儘量的心態去修，故以儘量而為之，猶如毛石頑皮，表裡夾砂，非為琢成的閃光之寶，或於八基雙七支中部分能修，部分不能修，這也不堪真修行，因此名之為頑修，或入於缺修。

如果了徹行條後，不需加以強制，而自然如法八基雙七支並行，則為無我執、破障弊之真修行，此是菩提道也。故於每日中行人應自當觀省大悲我母菩提心及菩薩應照菩提心，於雙七支中省察觀照我是否如法而修，若未能如法，說明已經落入頑修之中，若未全面行持，則屬於缺修，是此之修則難以成就解脫，或許小有成就，也是不可能有大福慧、神通、五明之證量的。

如果每日觀省七支行條未加強制，大悲從善，自然而發如法於雙七支，此即真修圓滿行持，如此者輕而易舉可得解脫成聖，福慧、五明相應而具，必成登地菩薩無疑。因此當知，看行、見行、入行、缺行者易，七支完美修行無執者難，其實放下我執，當即就入正修行持，何難之有！人人可以做到！

日中觀省時，除了以意念空觀之外，而重要的是必須依於平日之道友，或相處之人士、或冤對、或逆緣、或不順心、相互間不言語談話之人，做為所緣，必須對之修持，今日我是否依於雙七支，與之主動和他交好？而於主動親近他時，對方惡言相剌我時，我是否忍辱，繼續想得親近於他以表善意交好？對於惡言惡行侮辱不予計執，若能每日中不退菩提心，雙七支行持，體現三業，依法修行落實在實處，而又歸於當體空性，如是行舉，學到無上佛法易於反掌之間，菩提道心，菩薩地境自是你之聖位，這就叫修行。

利益眾生的修行法講完了，但是有損眾生的事隨時在發生，那就是借用我的名義損害眾生利益的事，現在我要再次提醒一個特別重要、大家要引以重視的問題。

目前，世界上有些法王、尊者、仁波且、法師、甚至居士都說他們是我的親信，代表我處理某件事情、或轉達我的話、或把他們自己講的說成是我講的。其實，在顯密二宗、各大教派中都有我的弟子，無論該大德是什麼身份，沒有任何人能夠代表我，哪怕只是一件很小的事情都不能代表！唯獨只有這個人持有我發給他的專用文書，上面註明他代表我處理某一件事，這個專用文書上有我的簽字和指紋印鑒，同時配有相對應的錄像，那麼這個人可以代表我處理該文書上規定的事情。再者，無論這些法王、尊者、仁波且、法師的地位有多高，他們的見解、開示、講法，都不能代表我的觀點，都不能作為正知正見的標準，我只知道我本人的開示和文論是正法無偏的，因為我的開示和文論是真正利益眾生、解脫眾生的。而且，任何人不能以任何方式增刪、修改我的文字或法音，如有對其作偽者，無論此人身份多高，此一定屬於邪見或入魔之人。因此，大家如果沒有親自見到蓋有我的指紋印的文證、並配有我親自所講與文證相應的、完整的錄音或錄像的憑據，除此兩點之外，無論是什麼佛教徒，包括長期在我身邊的聖德弟子，他們的一切，其想法、做事、語言、文章均是他們自己的行為，絕對不能代表我！！！

對 了 義 與 了 義 經 的 聲 明

釋迦牟尼佛在世時，始祖報身佛多杰羌佛降世為維摩詰，助佛教化五百比丘、八千菩薩！

多杰羌佛今又降世人間，全名為多杰羌佛第三世雲高益西諾布頂聖如來，開示佛法甚多，並說《了義經》等。三世多杰羌說：此娑婆世界唯釋迦悉達多在此成佛，故為佛教教主。其實，至高佛教法界大教主本原即是普賢王如來圓滿的多杰羌佛，但三世多杰羌佛卻說：我今所說《了義》。

不管頂聖如來怎麼說，我們都清楚地知道，不是《了義》，而是《了義經》，因為佛在經中說：維摩詰經所在之室即有如來。由此我等當遵佛法旨，不可僅稱《了義》，乃是如意妙寶《了義經》，更況雲高益西諾布被法定認證為法界最高總教主多杰羌佛真身降世，故均稱為第三世多杰羌佛。

聯合國際世界佛教總部
國際佛教僧尼總會
全球佛教出版社
世界法音出版社

諸多仁波且、堪布、住持、法師等申明

頂聖如來多杰羌佛第三世雲高益西諾布說

了 義 經

二〇〇七年七月。於美西洛城木屋房。三世多杰羌佛入於夢瑜伽三摩地。此時。有兩位古佛致以聖禮。設豐宴待請。爾時一古佛化爲白髮高僧。一古佛化爲黑髮高僧。三世多杰羌爲便開示之稱。故分別命名號爲蒼年僧和忘年僧。三世多杰羌佛如是說法。望衆諦聽。

於宴間蒼年僧坐於我右側席。忘年僧坐於我左側席。我於中席落位。爾時忘年僧起示。我們今席宴上。來論佛性眞相如何？蒼年僧與我皆願欲論。

忘年僧起曰。何爲佛性眞相？

我說。無所住而立法。即是佛性。

蒼年僧卻說。頑石初三相。即是法身。報化然其。

忘年僧請我示法。何以了義？

我曰。頑石無情識。故無三相。亦無有初相。唯在表法可喻立。實則緣起生。

忘年僧請曰。頂聖如來。云何？爲我等所解詳盡。

我曰。若說頑石有初相。初相依何得生？所生者何之爲母？生之初是何體相？實則頑石無母而生。乃因緣和合所生。紅白赤青。共業具相爲初。故未具身相前實則無相。無頑

石立名。何來三相之初？此際不成其有頑石之相。因緣具生後。方得相立名之頑石。爾際已非初相。由是結其有爲無常相體。故非佛性。時乃生相前如如而空。生相後無常幻體。由是空不可取。幻亦不可取。兩元皆無所取。更當思之。初相之取何以切割？未立相前爲空。已立相後乃有。早切則無。後切則具。無者落空。具者落有。何來有之初相？若以毫端分之百億萬之一作有。有則非初。若以毫端分之百億萬之一作無。無則非初。故無佛性初相。

如作表法喻。則頑石初相乃爲佛性眞相。因未具頑石相前乃空。已具頑石相後幻有。空有兩元初之將具。不具而具。不落空取有。不落有取空。爾際爲非空非有。是故不二空性。猶可了義。則佛性是頑石之初。而非取無相之空。亦非取有相之體。法身於不取不捨中如如而是。此一相眞如是也。報身亦依法身爲基。故報身乃法身之顯。無報身之前爲法身不動普賢於宇宙無邊。初具一刹那。報身所成耶。似如二邊不取捨。頑石初性然。即法身中而來。由是報身由法身所顯具相圓滿。金剛不壞身。此二相正覺圓滿是也。化身則是報身化顯無量體。化身亦復具之刹那一初相。於刹那不取不

捨初相間名爲不二諦。此三相無量化身是也。故喻之頑石之初相即不二法身之相。爲是如來法性真如。如是微妙了義之說。當見。悟於證。有情得解脫。

由於末法時期。衆生愚昧疑心者多。善慧利根者少。我今當寥言白持有情於衆。上述於夢瑜伽世界中。兩老僧設宴請我入席。二僧坐於我之兩側。我於中坐。右坐者蒼年僧所提頑石初三相是法身。我開示以無所住立法是法身真諦。由是而說法。解頑石之初非佛性亦是佛性。如若是憑空編造。我必擔負打妄語業因果之報。故今如語開示而爲三界六道有情必當帶來無邊福慧。由是說法因緣成熟。我將爲諸有情說法了義真如。

今藉此吉祥聖日。二古佛化僧。於夢瑜伽中示法緣起。得逢七衆。人非人等集此。金剛寶地虹化飛空此際。繼法界諸佛經藏及《維摩詰所說經》之後。於此殊勝上妙法緣。我當說是了義。善男女子。可欲白否？

爾際。智者欲當了證心得何意。駕阿賴耶中至。面我白言。吾心王有白。汝白何疑？我爲淺說。衆亦悉聞。

智者三業恭敬白言。我見諸多行壇。寺所。稱某德之化身乃爲多聖合一。然乎？

爲讚師誇大耶。

何從誇大？

不實爲誇。抬捧虛大。

於業云何？

犯妄語業。誆惑衆生業。當於三門清淨懺悔業。

然何有十方諸佛合爲一體而成某佛。力盛增強之法修儀軌傳世等說？

此爲方便渡生耶。

無此方便可否？

有情離此不可渡。依此能渡。

何以方便則渡？

觀想儀軌悉地加持。自信心增益渡。

諸佛合體是否加持力大？

佛力甚大。體無可合。無體本合。

爲何甚大？

行者自心信願力本心即佛大。無心外佛。

如是說無諸佛合體耶？

佛無合體。本自一體。一體諸佛。諸佛一體。無合即合。

於意云何？我難悉解。

汝當諦聽。佛乃無上正等正覺耶。無上者爲無有更上。圓滿正等正覺徹底無偏。無再滿之滿。無上者之上。如是徹底無上正覺。以是佛陀。若具合佛增強盛力。則虛陀耶。非佛陀耶。

然何增強盛力非爲佛陀？

未圓滿耶。具補充耶。故未圓滿。有更上耶。雖再上耶。故非無上耶。於是不堪圓滿無上正等正覺。非佛陀覺位。應作菩薩登地。菩薩非無上正等正覺。故爲菩薩。方行菩提道中施之增益行持更上補滿。以獲無上徹底圓滿正等正覺。時位無有可取。無有更上。無有更大。無有增減。是之爲佛。故知佛無合體。有合體即非佛陀。一佛即諸佛。諸佛即一佛。等妙二覺然。古佛應世之菩薩亦復如是。無合體耶。若謂合體則入邪說。不解佛覺耶。

又常見有載觀音。文殊。普賢合體轉世成一聖。其意云何？

有辱大聖之罪。非是聖覺之言。邪見妄語業始。觀音雖稱妙覺菩薩。但乃古佛正法明如來。文殊本七佛之師。自當古佛。普賢亦復如是。既之爲佛。大者宇宙無邊。無邊則無形取。何具定形佛身可合？汝當思之？未無上耶否？未圓滿耶否？需當補充加強增大耶否？若欲當增上。則未無上正等正覺。然何又呼『正法明如來』？釋迦佛陀所說觀音是佛。其意云何立耶？若是觀音真身降世。一佛即諸佛。何取兔毛角？本無毛角取。圓滿無上覺。文殊。普賢聖。何來三佛合？

智者愧喃。我已知之。摩訶薩無合體。今有二法求解。一者菩薩合體化身一聖。云何？二者菩薩具共力加持否？

一者菩薩亦復無合體化身。二者菩薩實具共力加持。

此意云何而書？

多菩薩合力修法。施以無畏。加持力。悉地力。功德力多之。共力盛之。故合力加持共修乃爲諦道。汝當曉悟。菩薩無有合體。若云合體。則非正見。菩薩具相應變化。六大神通。深入顯密。開敷行境相應五明。渡生有盛。凡塵眾生受之不盡。爲何多此合體？況乎於法相諦中。合體則違因果。

智者不解真義。白言。然何違因果？

我今爲淺說。汝當耳諦聽。心解真實義。若有二菩薩合體。於行道渡生中。則必亂因緣。由是則昧因果。眾生由無始根性。願力。業緣。相對互生因緣之異。因果千差不一。若依此菩薩應緣。彼菩薩錯因。若依彼菩薩應緣。此菩薩錯因。汝自問之。彼此二菩薩以何施智有情？若有三菩薩合體結一。依三菩薩之其一之緣者。二者無緣施與相對之生。依二之緣者。三者無緣施與相對之生。又云何渡生行道？此際。因果於成熟時間。地域別異。眾生有別。恰逢同時展報。合體菩薩以何爲先？納何爲後？合體菩薩取彼生爲後。此生爲先否？若取先後爲行。是故因緣不合。因緣成熟。無時待

之顯報。若遇此。合體菩薩將無法可施。豈不大錯因果耶？若云分身而爲。是故何來合體菩薩？若言合體乃成一智。此錯謬『滅因果論』。非爲覺聖所宣。又菩薩願力。因果相差不一。怎合一事？怎施一智？若甲菩薩於因果緣起照見。必於某年月日時自必赴東土渡生。乙菩薩於因果緣起照見。必於某年月日時自必不可赴東。而必行西域開藏。丙菩薩於因果緣起照見。必於某年月日時自將接受佛陀灌頂。跏趺待壇身不可動。東西均不得行。此際三緣各異。則三聖一體之身。施何行道？施何不違時緣因果？何以治之？又何以治之彼因此果。此因彼果？故菩薩亦無多聖合一。若云多合一聖。此非覺聖了諦之法。乃爲邪說。汝亦應知。行人於修持中。本尊融入自身。合體得聖。助成道果實相。則是佛說正法。可依師教降服其心。

今聞正法之義。然何又說本尊可爲合體。豈不兩相有違？

行修之士。觀想本尊融入自身。如是佛慢。自心本尊。我即佛耶。儀軌始然。成道之本。汝證三眼。密不可宣。心外無佛。妙義無窮耶。

維摩詰是多杰羌佛否？

善男子。汝等諦聽。汝爲何來？

爲法來。

名相無法。

何以故？

法無分別心。不染故。

然何立維摩詰。分立多杰羌二名？

眾生緣故立異名。相應故異名立。

二者爲一聖否？

不二不一。

此作何耶？

不取捨耶。

維摩詰聖尊是三世多杰羌否？

維摩詰非多杰羌。

三世多杰羌身相與維摩詰聖尊身相。前者說無分。今又云二者。何具分立辨？

無具身相。幻有分立辨？維摩詰聖尊過去身說法。釋迦世時。具居士身相。別在三世多杰羌當下身說法。末法世時。具顯密五明身相。前後分立辨。實無身相得。

古今之化身相別。何言無分辨？

古今無化身耶。爲直身所降。汝問差耶。維摩詰身已報化。今無身相可得。爲是乃幻。何具實有？古者不具。故無所得。今說法當下身。當下已過。何來當下身？亦無所得。待之未來身。未來無來。何具實有身？亦無所得。故見多杰羌身。已過去。亦非多杰羌身。當下多杰羌身。刹那無常時。何來當下身相？過去現在未來。三時空無身相所得。何來身相實有？

然何我眼現見具身相定形耶？

凡眼所見。幻化緣起。無實得見。

何以無實得見？

汝憶少小當下。猶見父母身相。風華年狀。形活動入。實則非實。見時即老時。凡眼不得知。汝當六十年復見。父母身云何？皮皺髮白身老耶。幾時老耶？六十年老耶否？非也。實則當下身老耶。故我今告汝。未有待時。刹那變異生老耶。如是刹那變異。即非當下身。故知無定形耶。若云具定形身。然何身老耶？何以壯年轉老年耶？由是汝當徹知。謂當下者已過去。刹那無定形身耶。無定形身。故亦無刹那

時。若云具刹那時。刹那之前已過。刹那之後未到。刹那到時當下已過。故無當下時。由是無三時。亦無三時定。形亦無定。無形定。何來本有身相？身相於刹那變異不定生滅老耶。無常耶。猶是維摩詰聖尊過去空。三世多杰羌現在空。未來三世多杰羌。維摩詰聖尊二者皆空。三時皆空無有可得。是故無維摩詰身相。亦無多杰羌定形身相。

無身相法主何存？

於不可得爲多杰羌法身法主。於說法渡生爲多杰羌化身法主。於無上正覺爲多杰羌報身法主。汝當了諦。三時不可得。汝應覺證法身。法身不覺。化身不具。報身無基。若了法身。則無身相。無相以何分立？故不一不二。

諸法王者認證金剛總持。亦維摩詰。亦三世多杰羌。依何緣得定？

依《正法寶典》定。

量鑒確否？

確在無誤。

何定無誤？

若有誤。何具法王量智？五濁無佛法。可謂有誤。娑婆有佛法。何來誤鑒？

許爲量智孤耶？

若量智孤。何以多王皆孤？何以衆鑒同體？如衆鑒信口。豈不衆王妄語乎？無證量乎？非定境觀照乎？爲凡夫之流衆議而商乎？如是娑婆則無佛法耶。奈娑婆佛法威然。生死自由。虹光飛化。歷歷在目。皆不脫其諸王者之法脈始然。

示其無誤。可另列說。以何說？

多杰羌是維摩詰說。維摩詰非多杰羌說。

多杰羌非維摩詰是維摩詰。何也？

維摩詰聖尊說。諸相皆空。前際不來。後際不去。今則不住。此當體本心即空是佛。三世多杰羌說。萬法實有。前念不除。後念不斬。以無所得。生心妙有如來藏。有無之別。維摩詰非多杰羌。理諦一味。多杰羌即維摩詰。由是多杰羌非維摩詰是維摩詰。

維摩詰是多杰羌轉世否？

一缽河泉之水。

此何意？

汝可將合聚一碗河水泉水分居否？

不也。無有法分。此作何意？

理諦一味意。

一味之水。云何作有無之別？

現見實有。夢幻空無。

實空二法。云何了覺？

無人我了覺。

依何法了覺？

無法修了覺。無分別故了覺。

無分別。云何有維摩詰聖尊三世多杰羌二者分？

汝心分別分。

無人我然何說有無二支分別？

爲利眾生說有無。萬法相別有。一體如如無。

此說有相否？

汝說爲有相。我說爲渡生。

然何又你我分別？

汝不了無相耶。故詢有相否則自分。

你說爲渡生。有執於你。何然斷執？我執未斷。豈能渡生？

無我怎立法。眾生依何處。依飛鳥否。依樹木花草否？依之無有了脫。汝當善知。建我立法故。立法生所依。

我是執否？

是執非執。

然何此說？

認我實有是執。見我空幻非執。六根對塵是執。五蘊皆空非執。心隨境轉是執。應無所住非執。四無量心是執。菩提勝心非執。

四無量心然何爲執？

隨境所遷而慈是執。隨感所動而悲是執。隨他而喜是執。隨需而捨是執。

是執有我否？

無我不執。

有執然何必行？

行菩提心必行。

然何以執立菩提心？

無執無我。無我依何立行？

我執解脫否？

我執輪迴性。

何以得解脫？

無執入解脫。

菩提心執否？

勝義菩提心無執。

菩提心何來？

我執所生來。

既說無執已。又云我執生。由來何也故？

云無執。謂菩提心勝義無執。說我執生。由著意行持。隨境所遷得生心境遷生我執。

如何無我？

不執無我。

如何不執？

轉四無量心於行持不染。此勝義不執。

勝義何意？

入了義菩提意。

然何不直取菩提心？

眾生業力故。

業力何表相？

愚癡表相。無明表相。煩惱表相。

愚癡無明煩惱體顯何然。縛困眾生？

汝當諦聽。如智者言談出語如流詞。自如無執。皆始然幼兒初學。始必執於識字。造句。再執造詞。而後執作文。如無執識字。何來造詞？如無造詞。何以作文？無詞無文。何以言談自如。言詞出口隨意不執意？汝應當知。四無量心入菩提心。亦復如是。次第甚為要然。當依之修行。

何為修行？

我於寶典開示。是為捷徑解脫大法示修行。若有善男女子。依之實修。必當福慧圓滿。解脫無礙。此為聖解脫法。

釋迦佛陀與你持法。誰以為大？

釋迦佛陀未持有法。

釋迦佛陀未持有法。眾生依佛學法何說？

釋迦佛說『說法四十九。實無法可說』。故眾生當依學無法之法。

無法之法。從何入手為之？從何得心入道？

從有為處入手。從無為處了心。無心可得即為道。

為何無得心？

無為何心可得？

三世多杰羌持何法？

無法可持。

釋迦佛陀與你誰大？

佛陀釋迦乃人天導師。大如宇宙。無量無邊。我乃無相微塵。小無形影。

有顏色否？

無色。

有聲音否？

無聲香味觸法。

是空否？

非空。

是實否？

非實。

取非空非實否？

不取。

何以不取？

無所得取。

在此地還是在彼岸？

此量無彼亦無此。

既無量。然何立量說？

無量怎具說法主？

552

為何必具主？

具主渡生。

為何渡生耶？

群生父母耶。

不渡可否？

不可。

為何不可？

為成佛不可。

何以成佛當依渡生？

渡生福慧生。

以何得福慧？

渡生自生福。福慧無所得。圓滿是佛覺。

以何為渡生？

大悲渡生。

施以何法？

佛陀正法。

除此異否？

無異。

既無異。佛陀本然。何復示三世多杰羌之修行法？

理諦一味精說故。

然何謂一味？

我法出佛陀。佛陀說我法。

你法造就佛陀否？

然也。

今又云何言其比佛甚？

我法佛陀說。我亦如是說。

佛陀與你之法誰大？

佛陀的大。

多大？

大得無邊。

哪個法高？

佛陀的高。

多高？

高得無頂。

你的法有多大？

無大。

你的法有多高？

無高。

然如此。我當去佛土學佛陀大法。勝否？

不勝。

然何不勝？

步外無佛土。

我法不覺。佛法不了。

　不來不去。為有佛土？應無所住。大小何存？而生其心。妙有佛土。當體佛土耶。智者當知何為修行。由此入法。自得大法。時輪金剛。大圓勝慧。現量佛境虹身。諸多大法亦復由此而入。智者若得修行。頓可當下灌頂。壇城盤旋。虹光法界。三身頓顯。『什麼叫修行』即可覺之。

　智者頓悟。合十無言。當即發阿耨多羅三藐三菩提心。發願利樂三界有情。為利眾生而解脫。隨祈請十大金剛。虛空諸有護法。恒時護佑一切虔修《了義經》的七眾弟子。福慧圓滿。早證菩提。

PERSONS OF GREAT HOLINESS AND VIRTUE MENTIONED AFTER THE MAIN SUBJECT

We have now read *A Treasury of True Buddha-Dharma*, which is like obtaining the most precious treasure. We have a correct albeit limited understanding of disciples of H.H. Dorje Chang Buddha III. However, we were unable to include many holy occurrences and great figures in this one book. For example, everyone still does not know which few people of holy virtue are the representatives of those who possess dharma transmitted in this world by H.H. Dorje Chang Buddha III. We only understand that H.H. Dorje Chang Buddha III Wan Ko Yeshe Norbu Holiest Tathagata has directly descended into this world and manifested the true Buddha-dharma, has set up a correct and bright dharma banner in this Dharma Ending Age of chaotic Buddha-dharma, and has guided living beings onto a shortcut to liberation.

However, we still do not understand that H.H. Dorje Chang Buddha III did not descend into this world alone. Rather, many beings of great holiness and virtue followed His Holiness into this world. Among such beings are many great Mahasattvas who are not mentioned in the main body of this book. Such great Mahasattvas include virtuous people over one hundred years old as well as young people. We mention them here at the end of this book to show that there are limitless aspects to the absolute truth of Buddhism, to holy beings, and to holy feats that are not contained in this book.

Here we will only briefly mention a few holy people who truly are dharma kings of tremendous virtue. There is a dharma king on the level of H.H. There is a holder of holy-form inner-tantric initiation dharma. There is also elder Dharma King Mohe, who is an over one-hundred-year-old incarnation of Anathapindika, a follower of Sakyamuni Buddha. Only topmost Vajrayana dharma kings of great holiness who are incarnations of Buddhas or Mahasattvas possess the holy realization that those holy people manifest.

Take, for example, the person of great holiness who is the incarnation of Anathapindika. He has performed countless holy feats. His powers in the healing vidya alone have elicited the unending praise of many people. He is able to cure diseases such as cancer, AIDS, and demonic possession with great facility. Through the casual combination of a few different medicines, he can completely uproot those diseases. His Buddha-dharma realization powers are unfathomably deep.

There was once a person who had a malignant tumor on his back and did not want to undergo surgery. The person of great holiness told him to sit motionlessly on the other side of a wall and that surgery would not be necessary. After this elderly person of great holiness lightly snapped his fingers, a loud exploding sound could be heard. It turned out that the malignant tumor of the person sitting on the other side of the wall suddenly exploded and its contents flowed onto the ground. That person was completely healed within one month. Additionally, this person of great holiness knows what disease any individual has just by being informed of the name of the individual. He is able to cure diseases simply through combining a few different ordinary medicines.

There was one time over twenty years ago when Dharma King Mohe was traveling outside his hometown. Because he is able to eliminate illnesses with such ease, thousands of patients gathered outside his door, blocking the door. For two days and two nights, this person of holy virtue did not eat or drink as he tended to the sick. His disciples had no choice but to dig a hole through the back wall, thus enabling the elder dharma king to extricate himself from the surrounding throng.

The realization of this person of holy virtue is indeed tremendously high. He was once openly drinking tea in a teahouse when all of a sudden he flew up onto the wall together with the chair on which he was sitting, both sticking to the wall. Another example involves a layperson by the name of Wei who reincarnated as a pig. This person of holy virtue applied his dharma powers to bring back to the earthly realm the consciousness of layperson Wei. He brought back to life layperson Wei, who had died three days earlier. Layperson Wei later explained to everyone the process by which he took birth as a pig, saw this person of holy virtue in the animal realm, and was brought back to human life. There are numerous examples of this kind. Everyone praises this elderly person of great holiness whenever his name is mentioned.

Although elder Dharma King Mohe is 119 years old, he truly has a rosy complexion and the skin of a child. The body of this person of great holiness has two of the thirty-two auspicious marks of a Buddha. One of them is flat soles. The other is hands and feet as soft as silk. The soles of this person are indeed flat and soft, and his hands are as soft and smooth as silk. They are even more delicate than those of a newborn baby. Everyone who sees these features of his is filled with admiration. Nonetheless, this person of holy virtue has always said that H.H. Dorje Chang Buddha III Wan Ko Yeshe Norbu is the greatest master.

A large dharma assembly was held during which many rinpoches, venerable ones, a geshe, dharma teachers, and great laypersons expressed their views, understanding, and thoughts. However, the only words that greatly surprised everyone in attendance were the discourses on the Buddha-dharma given by a few of those people of great holiness and virtue mentioned above. Their discourses on the dharma were judged to be the best of all. The exposition by one of them on emptiness was especially penetrating and brilliant. All of the rinpoches, venerable ones, the geshe, and the dharma teachers present were filled with admiration over the unfathomably deep realization of those people of holy virtue who gave those discourses.

Actually, there have been very numerous manifestations of the state of realization and virtue of those few people of great holiness. Two of them have been confirmed as dharma kings by having passed the test to be Golden Throne Holders. Two reincarnated patriarchs, six venerable ones, and rinpoches all underwent that test to see if they were qualified to ascend to the position of Golden Throne Holder, which carries with it the title H.H. Dharma King. The result of that testing was that all of the venerable ones and rinpoches did not have the realization to ascend to the position of Golden Throne Holder. Only one person of great holiness and virtue mentioned above received a H.H. Golden Throne Holder Certificate signed by seven monastics and ten witnesses. There was another dharma assembly in which people were tested to see if they qualified to perform the holy form of inner-tantric initiation. One after another venerable one and rinpoche failed to pass that test. Additionally, a demonic hindrance appeared. At the critical moment, a person of great virtue suddenly stepped forward from the crowd. That person displayed true realization and established an inner-tantric mandala in the holy form through a stone separating that person and the mandala. That person was the only one who obtained the qualification to perform the holy form of inner-tantric initiation and received a Certificate of Qualification to Perform the Holy Form of Inner-Tantric Initiation. However, to everyone's surprise, those two people of great holiness and virtue said that it is not important that the venerable ones and rinpoches there did not attain the position of Golden Throne Holder. They stated that the thing everyone must do at that moment was introspect upon one's own cultivation. They in essence said the following of themselves: Please do not write our names in any book. We are ordinary cultivators. You must wait at least until our cultivation rises to the level where the top of our heads can reach the soles of Sakyamuni Buddha's feet. At that time, you can praise us.

However, it would be a grave mistake for anyone to think that those few beings of great holiness and virtue are not qualified to have their names appear in this book. Which venerable one or dharma king included in the main text of this book has established a true holy-form inner-tantric mandala in front of seven monastics and ten witnesses who observed the testing process? (One must have true Buddha-dharma realization to establish such a mandala. Mere knowledge of empty theories is useless.) Which person included in the main text of this book has been praised to such a high degree by H.H. Dharma King the fourth Dodrupchen Thupten Trinle Palzang Rinpoche, who is the supreme leader of the Longchen Nying-thik?

H.H. Dharma King Dodrupchen is the dharma king of great holiness within the Longchen Nying-thik Great Perfection lineage. All of the Longchen Nying-thik dharma in the world was originally transmitted by him. Many monasteries, such as the Dzogchen, Shechen, Kathok, and Palyul monasteries, received the Longchen Nying-thik dharma as a result of initiations and dharma transmissions performed for them by H.H. Dharma King Dodrupchen. Famous figures such as H.H. Dharma King Jigme Phuntsok and his master, H.H. Tuoga Wish Fulfilling Jewel; H.E. Mighty Lion Dharma King Renzeng

Nima; H.E. Xiazhu Qiuyang Rinpoche; H.E. the seventh Dzogchen Dharma King; H.E. Longyang Rinpoche; H.E. Tudeng Nima Rinpoche; H.E. Taluo Rinpoche; H.E. Renzeng Danbi Nima Rinpoche; and others were or are his disciples. Simply put, all of the Longchen Nying-thik dharma in this world is the dharma of H.H. Dharma King Dodrupchen.

H.H. Dharma King Dodrupchen spoke of those two persons of great holiness and virtue in a supplementary recognition document. Addressing those two rinpoches, he stated the following in that document: "To... Rinpoche: You were born into an honored and holy blood lineage. I recognize as follows: You will carry out for living beings all of the practices of all of the Bodhisattvas involving compassion toward living beings. You will carry out for living beings all of the undertakings of all the Buddhas involving the saving of living beings. To... Rinpoche: You were born into an honored and holy blood lineage. I recognize as follows: As long as space exists, as long as living beings exist, you will be there together with them and eliminate their sufferings."

The Recluse Dharma King wrote the following in his letter: "I saw the words of praise addressed to... Rinpoche and... Rinpoche in the recognitions written by my master, H.H. Dharma King Dodrupchen, a dharma king of great holiness. Such words prove that those two Bodhisattvas of great holiness were truly recognized by that great Bodhisattva... Rinpoche was born into an honored and holy blood lineage. He is the incarnation of Master Shantaraksita... Rinpoche was born into an honored and holy blood lineage. She is the incarnation of Sariputra, a great venerable one. Thus, I confirm the recognitions of that great Bodhisattva. I affirm that such recognitions are supreme dharma decrees that are accurate. I respectfully convey the following wish: May the longevity of those two Bodhisattvas of great holiness be equal to that of heaven, and may they save all sentient beings."

As for those two beings of great holiness and virtue, one of them is the incarnation of Sariputra, the greatest disciple of Sakyamuni Buddha, and the other is the incarnation of Great Patriarch Shantaraksita, the founder of the Nyingma sect. Only they were able to demonstrate successfully realization that those venerable ones could not demonstrate. It is therefore apparent that if they cannot be called H.H. Great Dharma King, then there is no person in this world who can be called H.H. Great Dharma King. Even though their status was clearly verified when they passed the test and received certificates showing they attained the position of H.H. Dharma King, those two still regard themselves as ordinary people. They continue to endure insults and adversity with patience and are compassionate. Nevertheless, they did not agree to have their states of realization and virtue described in this book. They also did not agree to have their high status as reincarnations of great patriarchs revealed. Moreover, they did not even agree to have their names appear in this book. Such modesty and virtue truly provide to all of us Buddhist disciples a precious model of great holiness.

(This text was translated from the Chinese text that follows.)

主題之後的大聖德

我們看完了《正法寶典》一書，如獲無上至寶，其中對三世多杰羌佛的弟子也有了正確的一面認知。可是，我們也沒有辦法把很多聖事、人物全部列出來，譬如說，三世多杰羌佛在這個世界上所傳承法要的持有人，哪些聖德是代表？我們只明白了多杰羌佛第三世雲高益西諾布頂聖如來，直接降世展顯真正的如來正法，為末法時期的混亂佛法樹立了正確光明的法幢，為眾生指引了一條解脫的捷徑。但尚不明白，三世多杰羌佛並不是孤身降世的，而是隨來轉世很多大聖德到這個世界，其中有很多大摩訶薩在書的前文中就沒有提到，他們既有百歲長德，也有弱冠之年，現在略提一下寫在書的尾端，以表很多無盡意的聖量人、事、菩提還未能載入書中。

我們今天只先在這裡簡要提及幾位聖德給大家，這幾位聖德是真正的巨德法王，其中有H.H.的大法王，有聖義內密灌頂持有人，有當年跟隨釋迦佛陀的給孤獨長者轉世的一百多歲的長德摩訶老法王，他們所顯露出的證量確實是只有佛和摩訶薩轉世的密乘頂尖的大聖法王們才能有的聖蹟。

例如，給孤獨長者轉世的大聖，其聖蹟不可勝數，僅其醫方明一項，就令人們稱頌不已。無論是癌症、愛滋病、瘋魔病等，在他的手中簡直是小菜一碟，隨便拿幾味藥，就讓這些病症鏟草除根。他的佛法內證功夫高深莫測，有一個人背部長了毒瘤，而又不願意開刀，長者令其隔牆而坐勿動，說不用開刀，而長者在牆內手指輕輕一彈，一聲響亮，牆外患者的毒瘤頓然破裂奔流地上，不到一個月，就痊癒了。而且，無論什麼人，只要報出名字，他就知道這人得了什麼病，往往只要兩、三味普通的藥就解決問題。二十幾年前，曾經有一次雲遊他鄉，由於信手除病，幾千病人堵在門外，這位聖德兩天兩夜不曾吃飯喝水，後來，弟子們只好將後牆挖洞，才將老法王接出，脫離圍困。

這位聖德的證量，實在太高。很多人都見到過，明明在茶館喝茶，剎那間，聖德連人帶椅子就飛到牆壁上貼著。一位魏居士，本人已轉生投胎為一小豬，這位聖德施法力將其神識迴轉，讓已死了三天的人還魂復生，魏居士後來向大家講了他投胎和在畜牲道中見到大聖德救他活過來的經過。因此，只要說起這位老人，大家無不額手讚嘆。摩訶老法王雖已119歲高齡，確是真正的童顏肌膚，這位大聖身現佛陀具有的三十二大丈夫相中的『足下安平立相』和『手足如兜羅綿相』，雙足掌下平滿柔軟，雙手柔滑如絲綢，比剛出生的胎兒還要細嫩，所有見到的人無不嘆服。但是，這位聖德始終說：只有三世多杰羌佛雲高益西諾布才是最偉大的上師。

又如曾經，在一次大法會上，眾多的仁波且、尊者、格西、法師、大居士紛紛闡述各自的見解，但其中有大聖德的佛法開示才真正是語驚四座，法冠通場，評為最高榜首。尤其是一位聖德對空性的論述，高深精闢無比，在場所有的仁波且、尊者、格西、法師們均對作開示的聖德們的深不可測的證量佩服得五體投地。

實際上，他們的證境證德事跡多得很，他們是通過印證考上黃金法台法王位的。當時，兩位祖師、六位尊者和仁波且們同場接受升座

黃金法台H.H.法王位的考試，經考試後，其他尊者、仁波且均沒有達到升任黃金法台的證量，而只有其中一位拿到了七僧十證簽字的H.H.黃金法台升座證書。而在另一場聖義內密灌頂師資考試印證法會上，尊者和仁波且們一個一個都沒有考過關，這時加上出現了魔力，在這緊要關頭，突然一位大德從人群中走出來，施展證量，隔石建立了聖義內密壇城，唯一取得了掌持聖義內密灌頂的資格，領到了聖義內密灌頂師資證書。可意想不到的是，這兩位大聖德竟然說：『尊者們、仁波且們未獲得黃金法台位，這不重要，要迴光返照自己的修行才是當下就要做的事，書上請不要出現我們的名字，因為我們是慚愧的普通修行人。至少等我們的修行達到我們的頭頂能頂在釋迦佛陀的腳心下，那時你們再讚嘆吧。』

但是，如果大家認為這幾位大聖德是沒有資格出現在書中，那就大錯特錯了。書中哪一位尊者、法王在七僧十證監考印證觀看下建立了聖義內密壇城實相境呢（要知道，這除了真實的佛法道量以外，空洞的理論是沒有用的）？書中哪一位得到過龍欽寧提總教主第四世多智欽法王土登成利華桑波的讚嘆到了如此的高度呢？

大圓滿龍欽寧體的多智欽大聖法王，這個世界上所有龍欽寧體的法都是他傳的，如佐欽、雪謙、噶陀、白玉等等若干寺廟的龍欽寧體法都是多智欽法王為他們灌頂傳法的，知名的如晉美彭措法王及其上師託嘎如意寶、仁增尼瑪雄獅法王、夏珠秋楊仁波且、第七世佐欽法王、龍洋仁波且、土登尼瑪仁波且、塔洛仁波且、仁增丹比尼瑪仁波且等都是他的弟子。簡單的說，凡是這個世界上所有龍欽寧體的法都是多智欽法王的法。多智欽法王在促認文中說這兩位大聖德：對 ×× 仁波且，出生在尊貴聖脈血統，如是促認：所有一切菩薩們慈悲眾生的行持，凡諸佛教度眾生的事業，你都能為眾生實現。對 ××× 仁波且，出生在尊貴聖脈血統，如是促認：只要有虛空存在，只要有眾生存在，就有你一起同在，滅除眾生的苦難。而遁世法王也在證文中寫道：『得見我上師多智欽大聖法王為 ×× 仁波且、×××××× 仁波且所確認題贈之頌詞，證明二位大聖菩薩確實是大怙主認證的。×× 仁波且生於尊貴聖脈血統，是釋伽炯乃大師之轉世，×××××× 仁波且生於尊貴聖脈血統，是大尊者舍利弗的轉世。為此我再次證實大怙主們的認證。確認出至高無上的法旨、正確無誤的。敬祝二位大聖菩薩與天同壽，度諸有情。』這兩位大聖德一是釋迦佛陀的名立第一的大弟子舍利弗仁者轉世，一是寧瑪巴創始人素布切·釋伽炯乃大祖師的轉世，可想而知，正因為尊者們達不到的證量而只有他們才圓滿展顯了，如果他們都不是H.H.的大法王，世界上就根本沒有H.H.的大法王可存在了。但是，明明通過印證考上獲得了H.H.的法王位而領到證書，但他們卻慚愧忍辱慈悲而居，不但不同意介紹證德證量和崇高大祖師的身份，而且連名字都不同意出現在書中，如此自謙的證德修行，實乃我們佛弟子珍貴的大聖楷模。

（此文的英文翻譯印在前面）

556

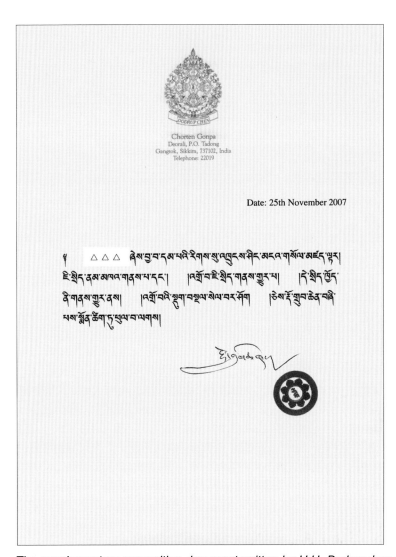

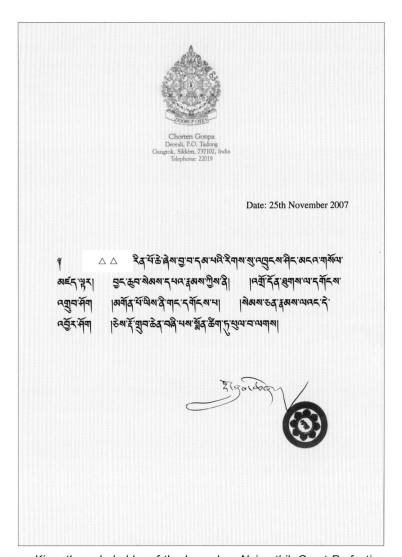

The supplementary recognition document written by H.H. Dodrupchen Dharma King, the sole holder of the Longchen Nying-thik Great Perfection Dharma, to the two people of great holiness and virtue.

龍欽寧體大圓滿獨掌人多智欽法王寫給兩位大聖德的促認讚偈。

WHICH FEW PEOPLE CAN ACCEPT DISCIPLES, PERFORM INITIATIONS, TRANSMIT DHARMA, GIVE DHARMA DISCOURSES, AND SAVE LIVING BEINGS ON MY BEHALF?

For many years some disciples of mine have announced that they can accept disciples, perform initiations, transmit dharma, and give dharma discourses on my behalf anywhere in the world. There are even those who use my name to ask for offerings and other things. Such disciples may be reincarnated patriarchs or they may be dharma kings, venerable ones, rinpoches, dharma teachers, or laypersons. Such announcements are based upon their own method of spreading the dharma and benefiting living beings or their own needs. Not knowing the facts, many people readily believe them.

Actually, who a person learns under, whether a person becomes a disciple of mine, whether a person becomes a disciple one level removed from me, and what level of Buddha-dharma a person learns are all determined by that person's particular karmic conditions and good fortune.

However, for the benefit of everyone, I must openly announce the following with a sense of seriousness and responsibility: I hope that all reincarnated patriarchs, all dharma kings, venerable ones, rinpoches, and dharma teachers who are qualified to lead living beings toward liberation will benefit everyone. But all people must understand something very clearly! This is extremely important! In this world, no reincarnated patriarch and no dharma king can accept disciples, perform initiations, transmit dharma, give dharma discourses, or save living beings on my behalf. They may also not accept offerings on my behalf, as I have vowed never to accept any offerings throughout my whole life. This includes even disciples of mine in this lifetime on the level of patriarchs, who are my highest level disciples and who are mentioned at the end of this book, such as the incarnations of Anathapindika, Sariputra, and Great Patriarch Shantaraksita. Even dharma kings or rinpoches of great holiness with the title H.H. who are on the level of patriarchs, such as the three people mentioned above, cannot represent me (unless I give clear authorization that a certain person can handle a certain matter on my behalf). Other dharma kings, venerable ones, rinpoches, dharma teachers, and laypersons who are below the level of patriarchs do not even have the qualifications to represent an incarnated patriarch, much less represent me. You should not think that all venerable ones and rinpoches are greatly accomplished persons. Actually, within the category of venerable ones, there are accomplished ones, there are those of small accomplishment, and there are those who have not yet attained accomplishment. You will clearly understand this when you listen to my recorded dharma discourse entitled "Are All Dharma Kings, Venerable Ones, Rinpoches, and Dharma Teachers Liberated From the Cycle of Reincarnation?" Any venerable one or rinpoche who has not received a "Certificate of Qualification to Perform the Holy Form of Inner-Tantric Initiation" that contains an official seal and the signatures of seven monastics and ten witnesses affirming the person has passed the test is not qualified to learn the highest and most profound Buddha-dharma. Only the receipt of such a certificate clearly proves that the person is a successor to my Holy Form of Inner-Tantric Initiation dharma lineage. Nonetheless, even such people of the highest order who are dharma kings or incarnations of patriarchs cannot give dharma discourses or accept disciples on my behalf. Although I consider myself to be a very ordinary person, nonetheless, I am who I am. Nobody can represent me. Therefore, whoever claims to be able to accept disciples, transmit dharma, or do anything else on my behalf is lying, no matter what that person's reincarnated identity may be and no matter what that person's position may be. One must listen to my dharma discourses in order to hear the authentic Buddha-dharma. No matter who the person may be, his or her dharma discourses cannot substitute for my Buddha-dharma.

I will definitely not abandon any person, since I regard all living beings as my relatives. Any living being could become my disciple when the karmic conditions mature. As long as such living being has right understanding and right views, abstains from doing anything evil, and does what is good, he or she can receive my profound initiations.

All of the above was stated for the sake of benefiting living beings. In order to prevent certain people from claiming that they represent me or using my name to do unbeneficial things to living beings, I had no choice but to make this statement, which on its surface seems quite mundane.

當今有哪幾位可以代表我收徒、灌頂、傳法、開示、渡生？

多年以來，我的一些弟子，他們或者身爲祖師，或者身爲法王，或爲尊者、仁波且，或爲法師、居士，其中有些人基於弘法利生的宣傳或他們自身的需要，宣說他們已代表我在世界各地收徒、灌頂、傳法、開示，乃至有人借我之名要供養等，很多人一聽就信，蒙在鼓中。

其實，對一切衆生，他們能夠跟誰學習、成爲我的徒弟或徒孫，學到什麼等級的佛法，那是個人的因緣和福報。

但是，爲了大家的利益，我必須公衆負責嚴肅宣佈：我希望所有具備渡生資格的祖師、法王、尊者、仁波且、法師們去利益大衆。但是大家要十分了解，看清楚！聽好了！在這個世界上，沒有任何一個祖師、法王可以代表我收徒、灌頂、傳法、開示、渡生或收供養，因爲我發心終生不收任何供養，就是本書最後所提到的今生在我的弟子中列入第一流的祖師級弟子，如給孤獨長者、舍利弗、釋伽焖乃大祖師所轉世的這幾位 H.H. 級的大聖法王仁波且都是代表不了我的（除非我授權說明某人可代表我處理某件事），至於低於祖師一級的其他的法王、尊者、仁波且、法師、居士，他們代表祖師的資格都沒有，更沒有資格代表我。不要認爲尊者和仁波且都是大成就者，其實，無論什麼尊者，其中有成就者，有小成就者，有未成就者，你們聽我開示的《法王、尊者、仁波且、法師是否都是了生死者？》法音就清楚了。因爲尊者、仁波且們凡未經過七僧十證考試領到蓋印簽字的《聖義內密灌頂師資證書》，就不具備修學無上甚深佛法。只有領到《聖義內密灌頂師資證書》，才能證明已法承了我的聖義內密灌頂，儘管是這樣，這一級的祖師、法王同樣代表不了我作開示、收弟子。我雖然很慚愧、是非常普通的人，但我就是我，沒有任何人代表我。因此，凡是說代表我收徒、傳法、做任何事的人，不管他是什麼身份、地位，都是說假話。要聽到正知正見的佛法，必須聞受我的法音，無論什麼人的開示都代替不了我的佛法。

至於我本人，絕不會嫌棄任何一個人，一切衆生都是親人，遇緣時都能成爲我的弟子，只要是正知正見，諸惡莫作，衆善奉行，都可得到甚深灌頂。

以上所講的一切都是爲了利益衆生，爲了防止有人宣稱代表我或借用我的名義來行對衆生不利之事，我才不得不講這一段看起來很世俗的話。

三世多杰羌

Dorje Chang III

IMPORTANT NOTICE!

If you want to obtain good fortune, please read the entire content of this book where legible, including all attachments. Do not skip even one item. Only then will you be able to obtain correct understanding. Any given page may suddenly emit good news causing you to awaken. Do not neglect the content of any page. That way you will be able to receive more completely the good news leading to accomplishment and liberation.

Publishers

注意

重要！！！

你如果要得到幸福，請你把全書的內容看一遍，包括附件等，只要能看得清楚的字，一條也不要遺漏，才能獲得正確的知見。書中的其中一頁會突然放出福音的信號，讓你醒悟，不要放過每一頁內容，這樣你才能更完美獲得成就解脫的福音。

——出版社

World Buddhism Publishing LLC
全球佛教出版社

1115 SE Morgan Rd.
Vancouver, WA 98664
U.S.A.

World Dharma Voice, Inc.
世界法音出版社

280 W. Fairview Ave. #A
San Gabriel, CA 91776
U.S.A.

Manuscript for Proofreading / 2006
校稿版 / 2006

Revised First Edition / 2008
第一版加印版 / 2008

$20 U.S.
ISBN 978-1-892727-41-1

9 781892 727411